D0088801

## 11th Edition
# 2002 North American
# Coins & Prices

### A GUIDE TO U.S., CANADIAN AND MEXICAN COINS

Edited by David C. Harper, editor of *Numismatic News,*
*World Coin News* and *Bank Note Reporter*

Published by

 **krause
publications**

700 E. State Street • Iola, WI  54990-0001
Telephone: 715/445-2214

Please call or write for our free catalog of numismatic publications.
Our toll-free number to place an order or obtain a free catalog is 800-258-0929
or please use our regular business telephone 715-445-2214
for editorial comment and further information.

Library of Congress Catalog Number: 91-76402
ISBN: 0-87349-297-8

Printed in the United States of America

# Contents

# Preface

Providing coin collectors with accurate, independently produced pricing information on collectible coins has become a trademark of Krause Publications in its 50 years of publishing. Visit our Web site at www.krause.com, or www.coincollecting.net for more information about us. We employ a full-time staff of market analysts who monitor auction results, trading on electronic networks connecting dealers across the United States and trading at major shows.

This information is compiled by our analysts and they determine what price most accurately reflects the trading that has occurred for each date and mintmark in each grade listed in *North American Coins & Prices*. By studying this information and referring back to it repeatedly, a collector can arm himself with the necessary knowledge to go out in the market and make wise purchasing decisions.

U.S. coins are the most popularly collected issues in the world. This is attributable in part to the popularity of coin collecting in the United States, but collectors in many other countries also covet collectible U.S. coins. After collecting U.S. coins for a while, many collectors in the United States branch out into issues of Canada and Mexico. These coins also enjoy a popular following in their countries of origin.

Thus, *North American Coins & Prices* brings together pricing information on all three of these countries. But this book also takes the price-guide concept a step further by providing information on the nuts and bolts of collecting coins: acquiring coins, grading them, organizing them into a collection, storing them properly and much more. Novice collectors can gain the necessary knowledge to collect coins enjoyably; veterans can pick up some pointers to add to their knowledge.

# 1

# "A small beginning"

## *The U.S. Mint grew from a modest start*

### By Robert R. Van Ryzin

It was a "small beginning" but a significant one. In July 1792, a site for the new U.S. Mint not yet having been secured, 1,500 silver half dismes were struck on a small screw press nestled in the cellar of a Philadelphia building owned by sawmaker John Harper. Though some have since categorized these early emissions of the fledgling U.S. Mint as patterns, it is clear that first President George Washington — who is said to have deposited the silver from which the coins were struck — considered this small batch of half dismes the first official U.S. coins.

It is true that this limited coinage, the first since passage of the act establishing the Mint on April 2, 1792, pales by comparison to modern U.S. Mint presses. Today's machines can churn out up to 750 coins a minute, striking as many as four coins at a time and boasting yearly mintages in the billions. But it is also true that these first small pieces — struck from silver and stamped with a plump Liberty on the obverse and a scrawny eagle in flight on the reverse — have tremendous historical importance.

For within what Washington would declare in his 1792 address to Congress as a "small beginning" were the seeds of a monetary system that has lasted more than 200 years and has become the study and admiration of many.

## Before the U.S. Mint

Collectors today can trace much of the nation's development and learn of its struggles and growth through its coinage: from a cumbersome system first proposed by Robert Morris, a Revolutionary War financier and first superintendent of finance, to the refinements tendered by Thomas Jefferson and Alexander Hamilton, which firmly placed the nation on an easily understood decimal system of coinage.

At first there was little coinage in circulation, except for foreign coins that arrived through trade or in the purses of the first settlers. Despite a dire need for coinage in the Colonies, Great Britain considered it a royal right and granted franchises sparingly. Much of the Colonial economy, therefore, revolved around barter, with food staples, crops, and goods serving as currency. Indian waupum or bead money also was used, first in the fur trade and later as a form of money for Colonial use.

Copper pieces were produced around 1616 for Sommer Islands (now Bermuda), but coinage within the American Colonies apparently didn't begin until 1652, when John Hull struck silver threepence, sixpence and shillings under authority of the General Court of Massachusetts. This coinage continued, with design changes (willow, oak and pine trees), through 1682. Most of the coins were dated 1652, apparently to avoid problems with England.

In 1658 Cecil Calvert, second Lord Baltimore, commissioned coins to be struck in England for use in Maryland. Other authorized and unauthorized coinages — including those of Mark Newby, John Holt, William Wood, and Dr. Samuel Higley — all became part of the landscape of circulating coins. In the 1780s this hodgepodge of coinage was augmented by influxes of counterfeit British halfpence and various state coinages.

In terms of the latter, the Articles of Confederation had granted individual states the right to produce copper coins. Many states found this to be appealing, and merchants in the mid-1780s traded copper coins of Vermont, Connecticut, Massachusetts, New Jersey, and New York. Not all were legal issues; various entrepreneurs used this as an invitation to strike imitation state coppers and British halfpence. Mutilated and worn foreign coins also circulated in abundance. Included among these were coins of Portugal, Great Britain and France, with the large majority of the silver arriving from Spain.

The accounting system used by the states was derived from the British system of pounds, shillings and pence. Each state was allowed to set its own rates at which foreign gold and silver coins would trade in relation to the British pound.

In 1782 Robert Morris, newly named superintendent of finance, was appointed to head a committee to determine the values and weights of the gold and silver coins in circulation. Asked simply to draw up a table of values, Morris took the opportunity to propose the establishment of a federal mint. In his Jan. 15, 1782, report (largely prepared by his assistant, Gouverneur Morris), Morris noted that the exchange rates between the states were complicated.

He observed that a farmer in New Hampshire would be hard-pressed if asked to determine the value of a bushel of wheat in South Carolina. Morris recorded that an amount of wheat worth four shillings in his home state of New Hampshire would be worth 21 shillings and eightpence under the

Robert Morris devised a complicated plan for a national coinage based on a common denominator of 1,440.

accounting system used in South Carolina.

Morris claimed these difficulties plagued not only farmers, but that "they are perplexing to most Men and troublesome to all." Morris further pressed for the adoption of an American coin to solve the problems of the need for small change and debased foreign coinages in circulation.

In essence, what he was advocating was a monometallic system based on silver. He said that gold and silver had fluctuated throughout history. Because these fluctuations resulted in the more valuable metal leaving the country, any nation that adopted a bimetallic coinage was doomed to have its gold or silver coins disappear from circulation.

Gouverneur Morris calculated the rate at which the Spanish dollar traded to the British pound in the various states. Leaving out South Carolina, because it threw off his calculations, Gouverneur Morris arrived at a common denominator of 1,440. Robert Morris, therefore, recommended a unit of value of 1/1,440, equivalent to a quarter grain of silver. He suggested the striking of a silver 100-unit coin, or cent; a silver 500-unit coin, or quint; a silver 1,000-unit coin, or mark; and two copper coins, one of eight units and the other of five units.

On Feb. 21, 1782, the Grand Committee of Congress approved the proposal and directed Morris to press forward and report with a plan to establish a mint. Morris had already done so. Apparently feeling confident that Congress would like his coinage ideas, Morris (as shown by his diary) began efforts at the physical establishment prior to his January 1782 report. He had already engaged Benjamin Dudley to acquire necessary equipment for the mint and hoped to have sample coins available to submit with his original report to Congress.

Things went awry, however.

By Dec. 12, 1782, 10 months after Congress had approved his plan, Morris still could not show any samples of his coins. He was forced, ironically, to suggest that Congress draw up a table of rates for foreign coins to be used until his report was ready. It was not until April 2, 1783, that Morris was able to note in his diary that the first of his pattern coins were being struck.

"I sent for Mr. Dudley who delivered me a piece of Silver Coin," he wrote, "being the first that has been struck as an American Coin."

He also recorded that he had urged Dudley to go ahead with production of the silver patterns.

It wasn't until April 23, 1783, that Morris was able to send his Nova Constellatio patterns to Congress and suggest that he was ready to report on establishing a mint. Apparently nothing came of Morris' efforts. Several committees looked into the matter, but nothing was accomplished. Dudley was eventually discharged as Morris' hopes dimmed.

Thomas Jefferson was the next to offer a major plan. Jefferson liked the idea of a decimal system of coinage, but disliked Morris' basic unit of value. As chairman of the Currency Committee, Jefferson reviewed Morris' plan and formulated his own ideas.

To test public reaction, Jefferson gave his "Notes on Coinage" to *The Providence Gazette, and Country Journal*, which published his plan in its July 24, 1784, issue. Jefferson disagreed with Morris' suggestion for a 1/1,440 unit of value and instead proposed a decimal coinage based on the dollar, with the lowest unit of account being the mil, or 1/1,000.

"The most easy ratio of multiplication and division is that by ten," Jefferson wrote. "Every one knows the facility of Decimal Arithmetic."

Jefferson argued that although Morris' unit would have eliminated the unwanted fraction that occurred when merchants converted British farthings to dollars, this was of little significance. After all, the original idea of establishing a mint was to get rid of foreign currencies.

Morris' unit, Jefferson said, was too cumbersome for use in normal business transactions. According to Jefferson, under Morris' plan a horse valued at 80 Spanish dollars would require a notation of six figures and would be shown as 115,200 units.

Jefferson's coinage plan suggested the striking of a dollar, or unit; half dollar, or five-tenths; a double tenth, or fifth of a dollar, equivalent to a pistereen; a tenth, equivalent to a Spanish bit; and a one-fifth copper coin, relating to the British farthing. He also wanted a gold coin of $10, corresponding to the British double guinea; and a copper one-hundredth coin, relating to the British halfpence.

In reference to his coinage denominations, Jefferson said, it was important that the coins "coincide in value with some of the known coins so nearly, that the people may by quick reference in the mind, estimate their value."

Thomas Jefferson proposed that the United States adopt a decimal system of coinage.

More than a year, however, passed without any further action on his plan or that proposed by Morris. In a letter to William Grayson, a member of the Continental Congress, Washington expressed concern for the establishment of a national coinage system, terming it "indispensibly necessary." Washington also complained of the coinage in circulation: "A man must travel with a pair of scales in his pocket, or run the risk of receiving gold at one-fourth less than it counts."

## A plan at last

On May 13, 1785, the 13-member Grand Committee, to whom Jefferson's plan had been submitted, filed its report, generally favoring Jefferson's coinage system. The committee did, however, make slight alterations, including the elimination of the gold $10 coin, the addition of a gold $5 coin, and the dropping of Jefferson's double tenth, which it replaced with a quarter dollar. The committee also added a coin equal to 1/200 of a dollar (half cent). On July 6, 1785, Congress unanimously approved the Grand Committee's plan. It failed, however, to set a standard weight for the silver dollar or to order plans drawn up for a mint. These two factors led to new proposals.

On April 8, 1786, the Board of Treasury, which had been reinstated after Morris' resignation as superintendent of finance two years prior, tendered three distinct coinage proposals based on varying weights and bimetallic ratios for the silver dollar. The first of these three plans (the one passed by Congress on Aug. 8, 1786) required the silver dollar to contain 375.64 grains of pure silver. The board's proposal varied from earlier coinage plans in that it advocated a higher bimetallic ratio of 15.256-to-1 and differing charges to depositors for coining of gold and silver. It called for minting of gold $5 and $10 coins, and silver denominations of the dime, double dime, half dollar, and dollar. In copper were a cent and half cent. The proposal came during the peak of state coinages and influxes of debased coppers, which, as the board reported, were being "Imported into or manufactured in the Several States."

Concerned over the need to control state coinages and foreign coppers, the board suggested that, within nine months of passage of its proposal, the legal-tender status of all foreign coppers be repealed and that values be set at which the state coppers would circulate. The board obviously expected immediate action and ordered a supply of copper that was being stored in Boston to be brought to New York in the hope that it might soon be coined. Their hopes, however, rested on the positive and quick action of Congress, something that hadn't occurred with the other proposals and would not occur this time.

Opposition to the mint was beginning to surface. Several members of Congress expressed their belief that the supply of foreign gold and silver coins in circulation was sufficient to preclude any need for a mint. They also argued that the problem with debased coppers could be solved by contracting with private individuals to strike the nation's cents and half cents.

Several proposals were offered for a contract coinage. On April 21, 1787, the board accepted a proposal by James Jarvis to strike 300 tons of copper coin at the federal standard. Jarvis, however, delivered slightly less than 9,000 pounds of his contract. The contract was voided the following year for his failure to meet scheduled delivery times, but helped to delay further action on a mint. Concerted action on a coinage system and a mint would wait until the formation of the new government.

Alexander Hamilton, named in September 1789 to head the new Treasury, offered three different methods by which the new nation could achieve economic stability, including the funding of the national debt, establishment of the Bank of North America, and the founding of the U.S. Mint. On Jan. 21, 1791, Hamilton submitted to Congress a "Report on the Establishment of a Mint." It was compiled through his study of European economic theories and the earlier works of Morris and Jefferson, along with the 1786 report of the Board of Treasury.

Hamilton agreed with Jefferson that the dollar seemed to be best suited to serve as the basic unit, but believed it necessary to establish a proper weight and fineness for the new coin. To do so, Hamilton had several Spanish coins assayed to determine the fine weight of the Spanish dollar. He also watched the rate at which Spanish dollars traded for fine gold (24 3/4 grains per dollar) on the world market.

From his assays and observations he determined that the Spanish dollar contained 371 grains of silver. He then multiplied 24 3/4 by 15 (the gold value of silver times his suggested bimetallic ratio) and arrived at 371 1/4 as the proper fine silver weight for the new silver dollar.

In regard to his findings, Hamilton admitted that Morris had made similar assays and had arrived at a weight of 373 grains for the Spanish dollar. Hamilton attributed the discrepancy to the differing equipment used in making the assays. He failed, however, to observe that silver coins were traded in the world market at actual weight rather than the weight at time of issue. The Spanish dollar contained 376 grains of pure silver when new, 4 3/4 grains more than Hamilton's proposed silver dollar.

Hamilton also wanted a bimetallic ratio of 15-to-1, in contrast to the Board of Treasury's 15.6-to-1 ratio. Hamilton said his ratio was closer to Great Britain's, which would be important for trade, and Holland's, which would be important for repaying loans from that country.

His report suggested the striking of a gold $10; gold dollar; silver dollar; silver tenth, or disme; and copper one-hundredth and half-hundredth. Hamilton felt the last of these, the half cent, was necessary because it would enable merchants to lower their prices, which would help the poor.

Congress passed the act establishing the U.S. Mint in April 1792. It reinstated several coin denominations left out by Hamilton and dropped his gold dollar. In gold, the act authorized a $10 coin, or "eagle"; a $5 coin, or "half eagle"; and a $2.50 coin, or "quarter eagle". In silver were to be a dollar, half dollar, quarter dollar, disme, and half disme, and in copper a cent and half cent.

Though it established a sound system of U.S. coinage, the act failed to address the problem of foreign coins in circulation. It was amended in February 1793 to cancel their legal-tender status within three years of the Mint's opening.

## Coinage begins

Coinage totals at the first mint were understandably low. Skilled coiners, assayers and others who could handle the mint's daily operations were in short supply in the United States. Also in want were adequate equipment and supplies of metal for coinage. Much of the former had to be built or imported. Much of the latter was also imported or salvaged from various domestic sources, including previously struck tokens and coins, and scrap metal.

Coinage began in earnest in 1793 with the striking of half cents and cents at the new mint located at Seventh Street between Market and Arch streets in Philadelphia. Silver coinage followed in 1794, with half dimes, half dollars and dollars. Gold coinage did not begin until 1795 with the minting of the first $5 and $10 coins. Silver dimes and quarters and gold $2.50

Production at the first U.S. mint, in Philadelphia, was minuscule by today's standards.

coins did not appear until 1796.

Under the bimetallic system of coinage by which gold and silver served as equal representations of the unit of value, much of the success and failure of the nation's coinage to enter and remain in circulation revolved around the supply and valuation of precious metals. One need only to gain a cursory knowledge of such movements to understand what role precious metals played in development of U.S. coinage. That role, to a large extent, determined why some coins today are rare and why some passed down from generation to generation are still plentiful and of lower value to collectors.

From the Mint's beginning, slight miscalculations in the proper weight for the silver dollar and a proper bimetallic ratio led gold and silver to disappear from circulation. The U.S. silver dollar traded at par with Spanish and Mexican dollars, but because the U.S. coin was lighter, it was doomed to export.

A depositor at the first mint could make a profit at the mint's expense by sending the coins to the West Indies. There they could be traded at par for the heavier Spanish or Mexican eight reales, which were then shipped back to the United States for recoinage. As a result, few early silver dollars entered domestic circulation; most failed to escape the melting pots.

Gold fared no better. Calculations of the bimetallic ratio by which silver traded for gold on the world market were also askew at first and were always subject to fluctuations. Gold coins either disappeared quickly after minting or never entered circulation, languishing in bank vaults. These problems led President Jefferson to halt coinage of the gold $10 and silver dollar.

The gold $10 reappeared in 1838 at a new, lower-weight standard. The silver dollar, not coined for circulation since 1803, returned in 1836 with a limited mintage. Full-scale coinage waited until 1840.

Nor was the coining of copper an easy matter for the first mint. Severe shortages of the metal led the Mint to explore various avenues of obtaining sufficient supplies for striking cents and half cents.

Witness, for example, the half-cent issues of 1795 and 1797 struck over privately issued tokens of the New York firm of Talbot, Allum & Lee because of a shortage of copper for the federal issue. Rising copper prices and continued shortages forced the Mint to lower the cent's weight from 208 grains to 168 grains in 1795.

By that same year Congress had begun to investigate the Mint. Complaints about high costs and low production had been raised. Suggestions that a contract coinage might be more suitable for the new nation surfaced again, despite bad experiences with previous attempts.

The Mint survived this and another investigation, but the problems of fluctuating metal supplies continued to plague the nation. In 1798, because of the coinage shortage, the legal-tender status of foreign coins was restored. Several more extensions were given during the 1800s, ending with the withdrawal of legal-tender status for Spanish coins in 1857.

In the 1830s great influxes of silver from foreign mints raised the value of gold in relation to silver, which made it necessary for the Mint to lower the standard weight of all gold coins in 1834. It also led to the melting of great numbers of gold coins of the old specifications.

By the 1850s discovery of gold in California had again made silver the dearer metal. All silver quickly disappeared from circulation. Congress reacted in 1853 by lowering the weight of the silver half dime, dime, quarter, and half dollar, hoping to keep silver in circulation. A new gold coin of $20 value was introduced to absorb a great amount of the gold from Western mines.

Not long after, silver was discovered in Nevada. By the mid-1870s the various mines that made up what was known as the Comstock Lode (after its colorful early proprietor, Henry P. Comstock) had hit the mother lode. Large supplies of silver from the Comstock, combined with European demonetization, caused a severe drop in its value, which continued through the close of the 19th century.

It was believed that the introduction of a heavier, 420-grain silver dollar in 1873, known as the Trade dollar, would create a market for much of the Comstock silver, bolster its price, and at the same time wrest control from Great Britain of lucrative trade with the Orient. It didn't. Large numbers of Trade dollars eventually flooded back into the United States, where they were, ironically, accepted only at a discount to the lesser-weight Morgan dollars.

The latter had been introduced in 1878 as a panacea to the severe economic problems following the Civil War. Those who proudly carried the banner of free silver contended that by taking the rich output of the Comstock mines and turning it into silver dollars, a cheaper, more plentiful form of money would become available. In its wake, they believed, would be a much needed economic recovery.

The Free Silver Movement gained its greatest support during the late 19th century when William Jennings Bryan attempted to gain the White House on a plank largely based on restoration of the free and unlimited coinage of the standard 412.5-grain silver dollar. He failed. Silver failed. Shortly thereafter the United States officially adopted a gold standard.

Silver continued to be a primary coinage metal until 1964, when rising prices led the Mint to remove it from the dime and quarter. Mintage of the silver dollar had ended in 1935. The half dollar continued to be coined through 1969 with a 40-percent-silver composition. It, too, was then debased.

Gold coinage ended in 1933 and exists today only in commemorative issues and American Eagle bullion coins with fictive face values. A clad composition of copper and nickel is now the primary coinage metal. Even the cent is no longer all copper; a copper-coated zinc composition has been used since 1982.

Precious-metal supplies were also linked to the opening of additional mints, which served the parent facility in Philadelphia. The impact of gold discoveries in the 1820s in the southern Appalachian Mountains was directly tied to the construction of branch mints in Dahlonega, Ga., and Charlotte, N.C., in 1838. These new mints struck only gold coins. New Orleans also became the site of a branch mint in the same year as Dahlonega and Charlotte. It took in some of the outflow of gold from Southern mines, but also struck silver coins.

Discovery of gold in California in the late 1840s created a gold rush, and from it sprang a great western migration. Private issues of gold coinage, often of debased quality, were prevalent, and the cost of shipping the metal eastward for coinage at Philadelphia was high. A call for an official branch mint was soon heard and heeded in 1852 with the authorization of the San Francisco Mint, which began taking deposits in 1854.

The discovery of silver in the Comstock Lode led to yet another mint. Located only a short distance via Virginia & Truckee Railroad from the fabulous Comstock Lode, the Carson City Mint began receiving bullion in early 1870. It struck only silver coins during its tenure.

Denver, also located in a mineral-rich region, became the site of an assay office in 1863 when the government purchased the Clark, Gruber & Co. private mint. It became a U.S. branch mint in 1906. In addition to the Denver and Philadelphia mints, San Francisco and a newly upgraded facility in West Point, N.Y., continue to serve as U.S. mints, but the others have left behind a rich legacy.

The collector taking a more extended journey into the history of U.S. coinage can find plenty of interesting tales — some as tall as the day is long and others factually based — all of which are part of the rich and ever-changing panoply of U.S. coinage history. There are stories of denominations that failed, great discoveries, great rarities, great collectors, and, for those with an artistic bent, a rich field of pattern coins to be explored and a wealth of much-heralded designs by famous sculptors such as Augustus Saint-Gaudens, Adolph Weinman, James Earle Fraser, and others.

For those who are drawn to the hobby by the allure of age-old relics of days gone by, or by coins handed down through the family, or even by dreams of great wealth, coin collecting has much to offer. The history of the U.S. Mint, with its small but ever so important beginning, is the starting point.

# 2

# Making money
## How coins are manufactured

**By Alan Herbert**

Just as printing is the process by which paper money is made, so is minting the method of manufacturing coins. The two are often confused by the public, but they are completely different.

The history of minting goes back several centuries before the birth of Christ. The Lydians are credited with making the first crude coins in the Middle East about 700 B.C., although the Chinese and Koreans trace their coinage back even further.

Some early coins were cast. That process continued in China into the 1900s, but only for low-value pieces. Here again the average person often assumes that all coins are cast, but as you will see, only a tiny fraction of a percent are — or were — actually made that way.

The methods developed by the Greeks and Romans centered on making dies that could be hammered by hand into the surface of a lump of metal, flattening it and impressing a design. Hammered coinage continued until after the end of the Middle Ages, about 1500. After that the first machines that could strike coins were invented. Today their successors can pound out 750 or more coins a minute.

From the early days when the fixed die was driven into a stump or a hole drilled in a rock, through fixing it in an anvil (the fixed die is still called the anvil die), to today's modern coin presses, the process is much the same. Force is applied to devices that impress or apply a design to a piece of material, which is transformed into a coin.

Early dies were made of wood. Then came copper, bronze, and finally iron as technology advanced. Today dies are made from exotic steels with special qualities that make them ideal for striking coins.

The history of coinage is fascinating. Interwoven into it are several familiar names: Leonardo da Vinci is credited with inventing one of the first coin presses. James Watt, English inventor of the steam engine, was the first to incorporate steam power to drive the coin presses that earlier had depended on horses or human arms.

Whether the power comes from a hand holding a hammer or a mechanical ram, and whether it comes from above, below, or the side, the process is called "striking" a coin. Modern coin presses use a variety of methods in applying brute force to a piece of metal to turn it into a coin.

Another fable that traces to casting coins is the common belief that coins are made from liquid metal or at the least are red hot when they are struck. Neither is true. A coin's design is formed by the pressure that causes the metal to cold-flow into the pattern that you see on the coins in your pocket.

There are three basic parts of the minting process: (1) the making of the planchet, which is divided into the selection and processing of the metal and the preparation of the planchets, (2) the making of the dies, and (3) the use of the dies to strike the planchets. To help you remember these three parts, think of "P", "D" and "S" for planchet, die and striking.

# Choosing a metal

Many different metals have and are being used for coins. The most popular coinage metals are those commonly found and relatively cheap, so they can be used for striking low-value coins. Precious metals — like silver, gold and platinum — are still used for commemorative coins.

A good coinage metal requires certain properties. The metal must be soft enough to be easily worked yet hard enough to withstand the wear and tear of a thousand pockets, a hundred thousand transactions. Few metals have all the right properties, so coin metals usually are an alloy, or mixture of two or more metals.

Copper is a favorite coin metal, either by itself or in an alloy. Zinc, nickel, iron, and aluminum are also found in coins struck by the United States and other countries. Silver and gold have to be alloyed with some metal, usually copper, to be hard enough to withstand commercial life. The so-called "pure" coins of silver or gold are known as "bullion coins," bought and sold primarily for their precious-metal content.

The metals chosen for a coin are melted and mixed together, and either poured into ingots or blocks, or extruded from furnaces that continuously cast a long strip of the metal. The ingots are passed several times between the big rolls in a rolling mill to reduce the ingot to the thickness of the blanks needed.

Once the strip is rolled to the correct thickness, it is sent to a blanking press. A gang of blunt-end punches are driven through the sheet, producing a dozen or more blanks with each stroke. The rough blanks are then ready to be processed.

Strips of coin metal stand ready to be cut into "blanks."

A binful of blanks are ready for the coin press.

# Making the "blanks"

The piece of metal (occasionally some other material, so it isn't always metal) that becomes a coin is known as a "blank." This is a usually round, flat piece that usually has been punched or cut from a sheet or strip of coin metal.

Before a blank can become a coin it has to be processed, cleaned, softened, and given what is known as an "upset edge" — a raised ridge or rim around both sides. The blank then becomes a "planchet" and is ready to be struck into a coin by the dies.

First they go through what looks like a monstrous cement mixer. A huge cylinder revolves slowly as the planchets are fed in at one end and spiral their way through. This is an annealing oven, which heats the planchets to soften them. When they come out the end, they fall into a bath where they are cleaned with a diluted acid or soap solution.

As the final step, they go through the upsetting mill, the machine that puts the raised rim on the blank and turns it into a planchet, ready to be struck. In a different department the process of making the dies used to strike the coins has already begun.

# Preparing the dies

For those who haven't studied metallurgy, the concept of hard metal flowing about is pretty hard to swallow, but this is actually what happens. It is basically the same process as the one used in an auto plant to turn a flat sheet of steel into a fender with multiple curves and sharp bends. The cold metal is moved about by the pressure applied.

To make the metal move into the desired design, there has to be a die. Actually there has to be two dies, because one of the laws of physics is that for every action there has to be an equal and opposite reaction. You cannot hold a piece of metal in midair and strike one side of it. Instead you make two dies, fix one, and drive the other one against it — with a piece of metal in between to accept the design from each die.

A die is a piece of hard metal, like steel, with a design on its face that helps to form a mirror image on the struck coin. Early dies were made by hand. Engravers used hand tools to laboriously cut each letter, each digit, and each owl or eagle or whatever design was being used into the face of the die. Notice that this is "into" the surface of the die. Each part of the die design is a hole or cavity of varying shape and depth.

This is because we want a mirror image on the coin, but we want it raised, or in "relief." To make a relief image on a coin, the image on the die has to be into the face of the die, or "incuse." Of course, if we want an incuse image on the coin, such as the gold $2.50 and $5 coins of 1908-1929, the design on the die face would have to be in relief.

To fully understand this, take a coin from your pocket and a piece of aluminum foil. Press the foil down over the coin design and rub it with an

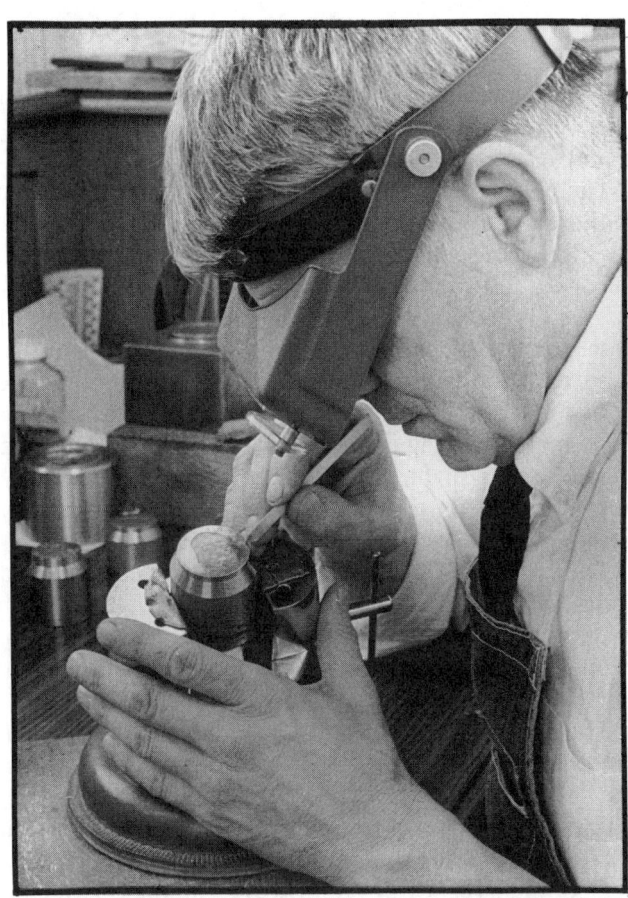

An engraver at the U.S. Mint puts the finishing touches on a die.

eraser. When you take the foil off and look at the side that was in contact with the coin, you have a perfect copy of a die. Everywhere there is a relief design on the coin there is an incuse design on your foil "die."

A galvano goes on the reducing lathe.

# From sketchbook to coin

The design process begins with an artist's sketch. This is translated into a three-dimensional relief design that is hand-carved from plaster or, in recent years, from a form of plastic.

The plaster or plastic design is then transformed into a "galvano," which is an exact copy of the design that has been plated with a thin layer of copper. This is used as a template or pattern in a reducing lathe, which cuts the design into a die blank.

This die becomes the master die, from which all of the following steps descend. The process can be reversed so that the design will be cut in relief, forming a tool called a "hub," which is simply a piece of steel with the design in relief, exactly the same as the relief design on the intended coin.

To make working dies, pieces of special steel are prepared, with one end shaped with a slight cone. The die blank is softened by heating it. Then the hub is forced into the face of the die, forming the incuse, mirror-image design in the face of the die.

The process usually has to be repeated because the die metal will harden from the pressure. The die is removed, softened, and returned to the hubbing press for a second impression from the hub. As you can imagine, it takes several hundred tons per square inch to force the hub into the die. Logically, this process is called "hubbing" a die.

The advantage of hubbing a die is that thousands of working dies can be made from a single hub, each one for all practical purposes as identical as the proverbial peas in a pod. This enables, for example, U.S. mints to strike billions of one-cent coins each year, each with the identical design.

Die making has come a long way from the early days when it took a skilled engraver a full day to carve a single letter into a die. The use of punches with the digits, letters or even parts of the design on the end reduced the amount of time required for the process. Today, thanks to the use of hubs, a complete die can be finished in a matter of hours.

# Striking the coin

Yesterday's die might strike only a few hundred coins. Today it is not unusual for a die to strike well over a million coins.

The coin press used to strike modern coins is a complicated piece of equipment that consists basically of a feed system to place the planchets in position for the stroke of the hammer die to form a coin. This process takes only a fraction of a second, so the press has to operate precisely to spew out the hundreds of coins that are struck every minute.

The end of the early hammered coinage came with the introduction of the collar, which often is called the "third" die. The collar is nothing more than a steel plate with a hole in it. This hole is the exact diameter of the intended coin and often is lined with carbide to prolong its life. It surrounds the lower, or fixed, die. Its sole purpose is to contain the coin metal

Rows of modern coin presses at the Philadelphia Mint turn out billions of coins a year.

A hopper is full of shiny new one-cent coins ready for shipment.

to keep it from spreading sideways under the force of the strike.

If the intended coin has serrations, or "reeds," on the edge, then the collar has the matching design. The strike forces the coin metal against the serrations in the collar, forming the reeded edge at the same time that the two dies form the front and back, or obverse and reverse, of the coin.

Lettered-edge coins are produced usually by running the planchets through an edge-lettering die, or by using a segmented collar that is forced against the edge of the planchet during the strike by hydraulic pressure.

Several hundred tons were required to drive a hub into a die. Not as much but still significant amounts of force are needed to strike coins. A cent, for example, requires about 30 tons per square inch. One of the silver dollars took 150 tons. The other denominations fall in between.

Modern coin presses apply pressure in a variety of ways. A ram, carrying the moving or "hammer" die, is forced against the planchet. Most commonly this is with the mechanical advantage of a "knuckle" or connected pieces to which pressure is applied from the side. When the joint straightens — like straightening your finger — the ram at the end of the piece is driven into the planchet.

Once the strike is complete, at the final impact of the die pair, the coin has been produced. It is officially a coin now, and it's complete and ready to be spent.

# The making of proof coins

While the high-speed coining presses are turning out billions of coins for commerce, there are other presses working at much slower speeds to produce collector coins, such as "proof" coins.

Proof coins started out as special presentation pieces. They were and still are struck on specially prepared planchets with specially prepared dies. Today the definition of a proof coin also requires that it be struck two or more times.

To make a proof coin, the planchets go through much the same process, but with some special care and some extra steps. Currently all proof versions of circulating U.S. coins are struck at the San Francisco Mint, but some of the proof commemorative coins have been struck at the other mints, including West Point.

After the proof blanks are punched from the strip, they go through the annealing oven, but on a conveyor belt rather than being tumbled in the revolving drum. After cleaning and upsetting they go into a huge vibrating machine where they are mixed with steel pellets that look like tiny footballs. The movement of the steel pellets against the planchets burnishes, or smooths, the surface so any scratches and gouges the planchets pick up during processing are smoothed over.

Proof dies get an extra polishing before the hubbing process. Like all other dies, they are made at Philadelphia and shipped to the branch mints.

When the proof dies arrive at San Francisco, they are worked on by a team of specialists who use diamond dust and other polishing agents to turn the fields of the proof dies into mirrorlike surfaces. The incuse design is sandblasted to make the surface rough, producing what is known as a "frosted" design.

Because collectors like the frosted proofs, the design is periodically swabbed with acid to keep the surface rough and increase the number of frosted proofs from each die. This is a relatively recent improvement, so frosted examples of earlier proofs are considerably scarcer.

The presses that strike proof coins usually are hand-operated rather than automatic. Some of the newer presses use equipment such as vacuum suction devices to pick up the planchets, place them in the coining chamber, and then remove the struck coins. This avoids handling the pieces any more than necessary.

On a hand-operated press, the operator takes a freshly washed and dried planchet and, using tongs, places it in the collar. The ram with the die descends two or more times before the finished coin is removed from the collar and carefully stored in a box for transport to storage or the packaging line. After each strike the operator wipes the dies to make sure that lint or other particles don't stick to the dies and damage the coins as they are struck.

Proof dies are used for only a short time before being discarded. Maximum die life is usually less than 10,000 coins, varying with the size of the coin and the alloy being struck.

# Keeping up with demand

The minting process has come a long way from the first metal pellets that are barely recognizable as coins. Companies that manufacture equipment used in the world's mints are constantly researching to develop new methods of producing coins.

The purpose is to strike coins at as low a cost as possible and still retain the desired beauty in the design. Modern machines and new methods help the mints keep up with demand for coins.

The important point to remember is that the coins in your pocket are made no differently from the coins in the pocket of an English schoolchild or a Spanish police officer or an Italian opera singer. Mints around the world use the same methods, same equipment, and same common coin metals, with few if any variations from the basic methods. The minting process was shrouded in secrecy for centuries, but now has become common knowledge.

For the collector, knowing exactly how coins are minted can be some of the most valuable knowledge that can be learned. It often will make the difference between accepting a coin as a valuable addition to a collection or spotting it as a fake, counterfeit, or altered coin.

Because of the improvements in the making of coins, collecting the rare misstrikes and defective coins that escape quality control has become an important segment of the numismatic hobby. For a detailed description of over 400 categories of minting varieties, see the "U.S. Minting Varieties and Errors" section in this book.

# 3

# The thrill of the hunt

## *How to acquire coins for your collection*

### By Al Doyle

Among the many pleasures coin collecting offers is the satisfaction of acquiring that long-sought piece that fills an important hole in a set or completes a collection. Many collectors say half the fun of pursuing the hobby is the thrill of the hunt — trying to find that needed coin in the condition desired and for a good price. Following are the main sources from which collectors acquire coins.

## Circulation finds

Once the most popular method of building a collection, hunting through pocket change has declined substantially since 1965, when silver dimes and quarters were replaced by clad (base-metal) coinage.

Most collectors from 1935 into the 1960s got started in numismatics by searching through circulating coinage. It was worth the effort, as scarce and interesting coins such as the 1909-S "VDB" and 1914-D Lincoln cents, Liberty and Buffalo nickels, 1916-D and 1921 Mercury dimes, and Barber and Standing Liberty quarters were often found. Hobbyists who searched bank rolls and bags obtained at face value had no downside risk, and entire date collections of Lincoln cents were obtained in this manner.

Other denominations were also pursued in the treasure hunt. One Midwestern dealer found dozens of 1939-D Jefferson nickels (worth $1 to $30 each at the time, depending on condition) by searching through change obtained from parking meters of a nearby city. Another well-known numismatist put together a complete date and mintmark set of Walking Liberty half dollars in one afternoon by searching through coins obtained at his bank. Needless to say, those days are gone forever.

What is available to pocket-change searchers today? Even the pre-1959

It's still possible to find collectible coins by searching large quantities of change, such as rolls.

cents, with the wheat-ears reverse, are rare sights, but some interesting coins remain undiscovered.

Jefferson nickels can provide plenty of collecting enjoyment for virtually no financial commitment. A recent sampling of five rolls (200 coins, or $10) turned up 58 different date and mintmark combinations. Some of the highlights were a 1938-S (mintage 4.1 million) in grade fine, a 1947 in very fine, and a 1953-S. Looking through Jeffersons on a regular basis should lead to building the better part of a date and mintmark set.

Half dollars are the other relatively untapped area in modern coinage. The 40-percent-silver pieces of 1965 to 1969 can sometimes be found in bank rolls. Half dollars seldom circulate, which means that older coins may be gathering dust in your local bank vault at this very moment.

Collecting Lincoln cents with the memorial reverse, from 1959 to date, makes an excellent starter set. Many of the dates can be found in circulation.

What else might turn up in pocket change? Modern proofs enter circulation from time to time, and foreign coins are found occasionally. Canadian and U.S. coins frequently cross their respective borders.

Collectors of error coins sometimes find unusual pieces in circulation. What may be scorned as a reject by the average person is a valuable item to the error and variety specialist.

Start examining your pocket change. It's an inexpensive and pleasant way to get involved in the coin hobby.


## Coin shops

Most medium-sized or larger cities and suburbs have at least one coin shop within driving distance, and a surprising number of small towns also boast of having a store that caters to local numismatists. Living in or near a metropolitan area is an advantage for the coin-shop enthusiast. For example, more than 15 dealers live in or near Cincinnati, and southern California and the New York area are home to hundreds of numismatic firms.

In some ways, a coin shop is similar to a small museum. All kinds of items from early coppers to gold coinage and other collectibles such as paper currency, stock certificates, and historic curiosities can be seen. A visit to a well-stocked shop is a visual treat.

It is likely that some of those coins in the display cases will appeal to you, and that means some comparison shopping and determining the value of your favorite coin are desirable. Prices do fluctuate, although collector-oriented coins tend to maintain steadier values than coins sought by investors.

If you are a casual collector, consider a subscription to *Coins* magazine. A monthly publication, *Coins* offers articles on a wide range of topics as well as a Coin Value Guide of retail prices for U.S. coins in most grades.

Serious collectors and others who want more frequent information will find *Numismatic News* to be a timely source of knowledge. Published weekly, the *News* includes coverage of recent market trends and reports from major coin conventions. *World Coin News* is published every other week and covers non-U.S. issues. All three publications also carry display advertisements from dozens of coin dealers.

Prices are determined by supply and demand as well as the grade, or state of preservation. Grading is often described as a subjective art rather than an exact science, and it does take some study and experience to become a competent grader (see Chapter 4).

Numismatic education is a never-ending process. Getting to know an experienced dealer who is enthusiastic about his product will certainly increase your knowledge of coins. Most shops carry a wide assortment of items, but dealers (like anyone else) have their personal favorites. If you find a dealer who is especially knowledgeable about a certain series, it could be to your advantage to do business with him or her if that also happens to be your favorite area too.

Strangely enough, doing business with a dealer who does not share your particular interest could work in your favor. Learning about collectible coins is a massive undertaking, and no one knows everything. Collectors of large cents and Bust half dollars are willing to pay substantial premiums for coins that have minor differences from other specimens struck during the same year, and specialists in those areas frequently "cherrypick" rare varieties that are offered at common-date prices.

Never be embarrassed to ask questions about coins or the dealer's experience in the hobby. As the old saying goes, "There is no such thing as a dumb question." A question asked at the right time could save you plenty of grief and money.

## Mail order

This is one area that generates a fair amount of emotion among collectors. Many hobbyists swear by the convenience of shopping at home; others

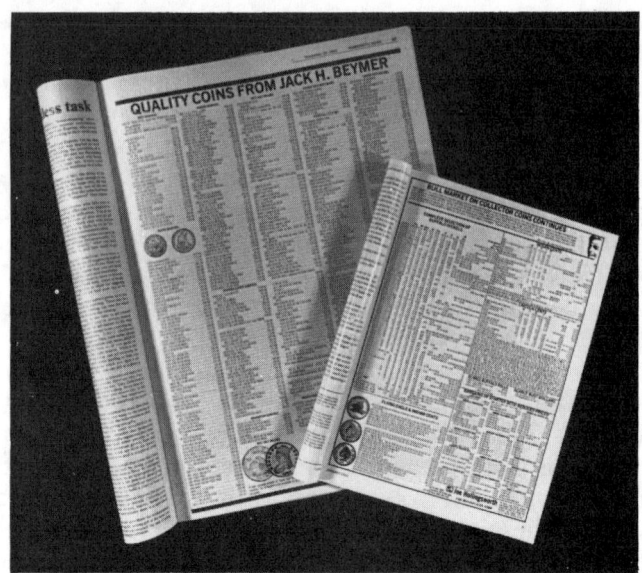

Advertisements in numismatic publications provide the convenience of shopping at home.

swear at mail-order firms that send overgraded and overpriced coins. Common sense and the same guidelines that apply to shopping for any other item should be used in selecting a mail-order coin dealer.

Look for someone who has a fair amount of experience in coins as well as enthusiasm for the hobby. Reputable dealers are willing to answer questions about their numismatic backgrounds and business practices. Word of mouth is often said to be one of the most effective forms of advertising, and it pays to ask other collectors about their favorite mail-order companies.

If several people agree that a firm provides accurately graded coins at fair prices, chances are excellent that you will also be a satisfied customer. How do you avoid being cheated? Collectors can be their own worst enemies and are often victimized by their own greed.

Take a coin that has a retail value in the $100 range in a particular grade. If that same coin is advertised at the same grade for $49.95, the savvy collector should immediately become suspicious. When a coin is offered at a price far under the going rate, remember these two sayings: "If it sounds too good to be true, it usually is," and "there is no Santa Claus in numismatics."

A dealer will generally pay $70 to $80 to acquire a popular coin with a retail value of $100. With that in mind, how can someone offer the same coin in the same grade at far less than wholesale cost? Wouldn't it be much easier to sell those coins to other dealers at a higher price and save on advertising expenses?

Obviously, the "underpriced" coins are not the same quality as their properly graded counterparts. It pays to keep up with current prices and grading standards. It is possible to find good deals at less than full retail cost, but don't expect to purchase decent coins for half price.

Does that mean all coins sold at real market prices are properly graded? Don't get complacent; overgraded coins are sometimes sold at full retail. But not everyone who sells an overgraded coin is intentionally fraudulent.

Grading standards are not carved in stone, which means that one person's MS-63 can be someone else's MS-64. Even though most dealers are extremely knowledgeable about coins, they can be fooled at times. The altered coin that a dealer bought as problem-free may be passed on to a collector in good faith, with no intention of deceit.

There is one important means of protection for consumers who buy through the mail: the return policy. Reputable firms allow buyers to return any unsatisfactory item for a full refund. The time allowed for returns varies widely from three working days to a month, but seven to ten days seems to be the most popular policy among mail-order dealers.

Most dealers list "terms of sale" in their ads. Always look for them and read them before placing your order.

If you don't like coins received through the mail for any reason, send them back within the alloted time for a full refund. Companies might extend the deadline by a day or two if you call and ask for extra time.

What happens if you don't receive a refund or cannot satisfactorily resolve a problem with a mail-order dealer? There are several options:

The first step is to file a written complaint with the advertising department of any publication in which the dealer advertises. Include copies of invoices and other documentation. The publication cannot act on verbal complaints.

Written complaints can also be filed with a local or state chapter of the Better Business Bureau as well as any hobby-related organizations (the American Numismatic Association, Professional Numismatists Guild, and so on) in which the dealer holds membership. If you do business with a reputable dealer, it is unlikely that you will ever have to endure such a drawn-out complaint process, but be ready to take the proper steps if necessary.

For those who live in rural areas or prefer to shop at home, buying coins through the mail can be a rewarding experience and a convenient way to build a collection.

# Coin shows

Dozens of shows are held every weekend across the nation. These events range from simple one-day shows with 10 to 20 tables to nationally known events such as the annual American Numismatic Association convention, Florida United Numismatists convention, the three-times-a-year shows held in Long Beach, Calif., and the Central States Numismatic Society convention.

Admission to club-sponsored shows is usually free. Commercially sponsored shows oftentimes charge a small admission fee.

Shows big and small
are held across the
nation every weekend.

Somewhere between the show at the local VFW hall and Long Beach are state and regional conventions. Often sponsored by a club, these shows will have 40 to 150 dealer tables as compared to the 400 to 600 tables at a major convention. Tables at local and some regional conventions are often manned by part-time, or "vest pocket," dealers. Smaller shows tend to feature less expensive items; the larger shows will have a greater variety of scarce and expensive coins in addition to the more affordable pieces.

Major conventions will have a stunning array of merchandise ranging from coins of ancient Greece to major U.S. rarities. Even if you can't afford the expensive items, it doesn't cost anything to stroll the aisles and see some historic coins.

The big-ticket items are just part of the action at regional and major shows. A large assortment of affordable coins are available, and prices are often lower than at coin shops.

Dealers buy and sell thousands of coins among themselves at shows, and new purchases can often be had for a small markup. Good buys can sometimes be found later in the show when dealers are preparing to return home. A reasonable offer will often result in a new addition to your collection.

Speaking of offers, negotiating and dickering are as much a part of coin shows as silver dollars, but be reasonable. Tossing out an offer of $50 on a $200 coin is not shrewd; it's insulting.

If you make an offer on a coin and it is accepted, the coin is yours. Backing out of a deal is considered bad form. The coin business tends to be informal, and verbal offers carry serious weight. Your word is your bond on the bourse floor.

Purchases at a coin show do not carry a return policy. Unlike a mail-order transaction, you have ample opportunity to carefully examine the coin firsthand before making a financial commitment.

Why attend a show when you can acquire coins through the mail or from a local shop? There are many reasons to give the show circuit a try:

Conventions are an educational experience. Touring the bourse floor and talking to dealers and other collectors will increase your knowledge of numismatics, but there are other learning opportunities as well.

Many shows offer educational forums featuring speakers and presentations on various topics. These seminars cover everything from little-known specialties to advice on obtaining the best buys in a particular area of numismatics.

Exhibits will also add to your knowledge. Most medium-sized and major shows reserve a section of the bourse for collectors to display some of their holdings and compete for awards based on the educational value of their exhibit. The exhibit section offers an excellent opportunity to view something new and different.

You might be motivated to put together an exhibit yourself after a visit to a show. Keep in mind that it does not require a major collection to create a decent exhibit. Some of the most interesting displays incorporate low-priced coins and other collectibles.

Shows are excellent places to search for key-date coins and other material that may not be in stock at your local shop. Dealers do much of their shopping at shows, which should tell you something about the opportunities at a good-sized convention.

Want to introduce a friend or relative to coin collecting? Take them to a show and let them look around. Chances are excellent that the newcomer will become a fellow collector.

Looking for something different to collect? Paper money, world coins, tokens, medals, and medieval coins are often found at shows. You could find a new area of interest, and shows provide collectors with a chance to meet dealers and well-known hobbyists from across the country.

Have a game plan when you attend a show. Decide beforehand what you want to buy and how much money you plan to spend. Buying whatever looks nice will soon deplete your funds.

Coin shows offer something for everyone, so consider bringing the family. Jewelry (usually for much less than jewelry-store prices), baseball cards, antiques, and arts and crafts are also sometimes found at bourse tables.

It's OK to bargain with a dealer at a show or shop, but collectors should be reasonable with their offers.

One final note on coin-show etiquette: If you don't agree with a dealer's prices or grading, do not tell him that you can buy the same coin for less at another table or call him a crook. Just move on to the next table, and enjoy the rest of the show.

Information on upcoming shows in your area can be found in *Coins* and *Numismatic News*. Shows that feature a significant number of world coins are also listed in *World Coin News*. Coin-show advertising sometimes appears in local newspapers during the week prior to a show or in the paper's free listings of community events.

# Auctions

As in other collectible fields, auctions play an important role in the coin business. Prices realized at major auctions can indicate where the coin market is headed, as price fluctuations are a fact of life in numismatics. Important collections with major rarities are usually sold at auction.

However, affordable coins are often sold along with the heart-stopping pieces. A typical sale for a major auction firm will contain 1,000 to 4,000 lots, and most of those coins are not of the headline-grabbing variety.

A collector doesn't have to actually attend an auction to participate in it.

The vast number of coins offered at a typical coin auction can work in favor of the collector who has a limited budget. Typical low- to medium-priced coins are often overlooked, as dealers and collectors focus on the trophy items. That may allow you to pick up some coins at reasonable prices.

How can you participate in an auction that is being held thousands of miles from your home? Catalogs are produced by auction companies for each sale, and mail bids are encouraged.

A typical auction catalog is illustrated with black and white as well as color photos of hundreds of coins. Descriptions of each lot give you an idea of the appearance of any coins that might be of interest.

If you are located near an auction site, it pays to examine your potential purchases at the pre-auction viewing session. The process is simple: Just visit the auction location (usually a major hotel or convention center) prior to the sale. The auction company sets up a room where the lots can be viewed. Long rows of tables with good lighting are provided. All you have to do is tell one of the attendants the lot numbers of the coins you want to view.

You can place written bids before you leave the premises, but it might pay to hang around for the auction and bid on coins in person. The action can be fast and furious at a major auction. Bidding increments of thousands of dollars are the rule when an expensive coin is being sold. It's an unforgettable sight to watch five or six serious competitors run up the price on a truly rare coin.

Keep several things in mind before you get involved in buying through auctions:

■ You are legally responsible to honor all winning bids placed, so plan accordingly. It is unlikely that you will win every coin on which you bid, but placing too many bids could be hazardous to your financial health.

■ Return policies vary among the major firms. Generally, floor bidders (those who personally attend the sale) do not have return privileges, as it is assumed that an adequate opportunity was provided to examine coins during the pre-auction viewing session.

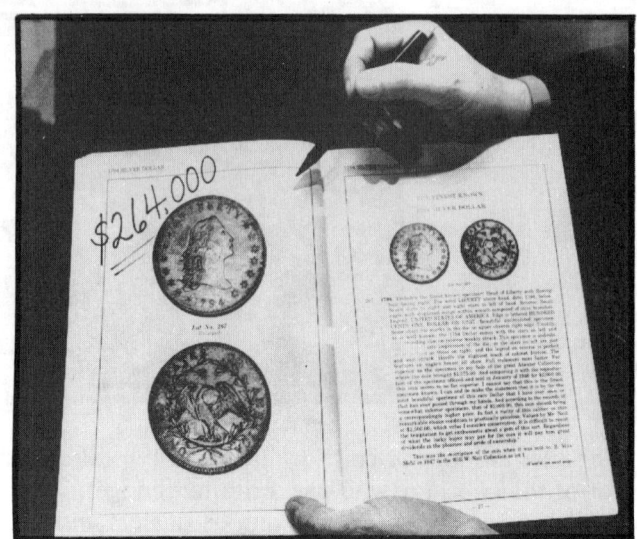

**An auction catalog describes each lot offered.**

One auction house does not allow any returns by mail bidders on certified coins, which are independently graded and encapsulated in a protective holder by an outside grading service. However, return privileges are the rule for all coins graded by the auction company's staff.

■ Winning bids are generally subject to a 10 percent premium, or buyer's fee. If you successfully bid $300 on a coin, your final cost will be $330 plus postage and handling. Consider the buyer's fee when deciding on bids.

Getting started in buying through auctions requires a catalog of an upcoming sale. Typically priced at $10 to $25, auction catalogs can be excellent buys even if you don't participate in the sale, as they provide a wealth of numismatic information.

Following are six major U.S. auction houses:

■ Bowers and Merena Galleries, P.O. Box 1224, Wolfeboro, NH 03894.

■ Ira and Larry Goldberg Coins and Collectibles, Inc., 350 S. Beverly Drive, Suite 350, Beverly Hills, CA 90212.

■ Heritage Numismatic Auctions, Heritage Plaza, 100 Highland Park Village, Second Floor, Dallas, TX 75205-2788.

■ Sotheby's, Inc., 1334 York, Ave., New York, NY 10021.

■ Stack's, 123 W. 57th St., New York, NY 10019.

■ Superior Galleries, 9478 W. Olympic Blvd., Beverly Hills, CA 90212-4246.

Smaller auctions will allow you to test the bidding process before you compete at a major sale. Local firms concentrate on less expensive coins, and a typical sale for these companies ranges from 250 to 1,000 lots. Catalogs are less elaborate, but they are also inexpensive. Prices range from free to $3, and mail bids are accepted.

Among the dozens of local companies that conduct coin auctions are the following:

- Michael Aron, P.O. Box 4388, San Clemente, CA 92674.
- Connecticut Numismatic Auctions, P.O. Box 471, Plantsville, CT 06479.
- Frank D'Atri Auction, 2405 Essington Road, Suite 124, Joliet, IL 60435.
- Sonny Henry's Auction Service, 1510 Illinois Ave., Mendota, IL 61342.

## Where to write for more information

*Coins Magazine:* 700 E. State St, Iola, WI 54990.
*Numismatic News:* 700 E. State St., Iola, WI 54990.
*World Coin News:* 700 E. State St., Iola, WI 54990.
**American Numismatic Association:** 818 N. Cascade Ave., Colorado Springs, CO 80903-3279. Web address is http://www.money.org

## Visit the Krause Publications Web sites
## http://www.krause.com
## http://www.coincollecting.net

# 4

# The grading factor
## How to classify a coin's condition

### By Arlyn G. Sieber

Grading is one of the most important factors in buying and selling coins as collectibles. Unfortunately, it's also one of the most controversial. Since the early days of coin collecting in the United States, buying through the mail has been a convenient way for collectors to acquire coins. As a result, there has always been a need in numismatics for a concise way to classify the amount of wear on a coin and its condition in general.

## A look back

In September 1888, Dr. George Heath, a physician in Monroe, Mich., published a four-page pamphlet titled *The American Numismatist*. Publication of subsequent issues led to the founding of the American Numismatic Association, and *The Numismatist*, as it's known today, is the association's official journal. Heath's first issues were largely devoted to selling world coins from his collection. There were no formal grades listed with the coins and their prices, but the following statement by Heath indicates that condition was a consideration for early collectors:

"The coins are in above average condition," Heath wrote, "and so confident am I that they will give satisfaction, that I agree to refund the money in any unsatisfactory sales on the return of the coins."

As coin collecting became more popular and *The Numismatist* started accepting paid advertising from others, grading became more formal. The February 1892 issue listed seven "classes" for the condition of coins (from worst to best): mutilated, poor, fair, good, fine, uncirculated, and proof. Through the years, the hobby has struggled with developing a grading sys-

The first formal grading guide was Brown and Dunn's *A Guide to the Grading of United States Coins.*

tem that would be accepted by all and could apply to all coins. The hobby's growth was accompanied by a desire for more grades, or classifications, to more precisely define a coin's condition. The desire for more precision, however, was at odds with the basic concept of grading: to provide a *concise* method for classifying a coin's condition.

For example, even the conservatively few classifications of 1892 included fudge factors.

"To give flexibility to this classification," *The Numismatist* said, "such modification of fine, good and fair, as 'extremely,' 'very,' 'almost,' etc. are used to express slight variations from the general condition."

The debate over grading continued for decades in *The Numismatist*. A number of articles and letters prodded the ANA to write grading guidelines and endorse them as the association's official standards. Some submitted specific suggestions for terminology and accompanying standards for each grade. But grading remained a process of "instinct" gained through years of collecting or dealing experience.

A formal grading guide in book form finally appeared in 1958, but it was the work of two individuals rather than the ANA. *A Guide to the Grading of United States Coins* by Martin R. Brown and John W. Dunn was a breakthrough in the great grading debate. Now collectors had a reference that gave them specific guidelines for specific coins and could be studied and restudied at home.

The first editions of Brown and Dunn carried text only, no illustrations. For the fourth edition, in 1964, publication was assumed by Whitman Publishing Co. of Racine, Wis., and line drawings were added to illustrate the text.

The fourth edition listed six principal categories for circulated coins (from worst to best): good, very good, fine, very fine, extremely fine, and about uncirculated. But again, the desire for more precise categories was evidenced. In the book's introduction, Brown and Dunn wrote, "Dealers will sometimes advertise coins that are graded G-VG, VG-F, F-VF, VF-XF. Or the description may be ABT. G. or VG plus, etc. This means that the coin in question more than meets minimum standards for the lower grade but is not quite good enough for the higher grade."

When the fifth edition appeared, in 1969, the "New B & D Grading System" was introduced. The six principal categories for circulated coins were still intact, but variances within those categories were now designated by up to four letters: "A", "B", "C" or "D". For example, an EF-A coin was "almost about uncirculated." An EF-B was "normal extra fine" within the B & D standards. EF-C had a "normal extra fine" obverse, but the reverse was "obviously not as nice as obverse due to poor strike or excessive wear." EF-D had a "normal extra fine" reverse but a problem obverse.

But that wasn't the end. Brown and Dunn further listed 29 problem points that could appear on a coin — from No. 1 for an "edge bump" to No. 29 for "attempted re-engraving outside of the Mint." The number could be followed by the letter "O" or "R" to designate whether the problem appeared on the obverse or reverse and a Roman numeral corresponding to a clock face to designate where the problem appears on the obverse or reverse. For example, a coin described as "VG-B-9-O-X" would grade "VG-B"; the 9 designated a "single rim nick"; the "O" indicated the nick was on the obverse; and the "X" indicated it appeared at the 10 o'clock position, or upper left, of the obverse.

The authors' goal was noble — to create the perfect grading system. They again, however, fell victim to the age-old grading-system problem: Precision comes at the expense of brevity. Dealer Kurt Krueger wrote in the January 1976 issue of *The Numismatist*, ". . . under the new B & D system, the numismatist must contend with a minimum of 43,152 different grading combinations! Accuracy is apparent, but simplicity has been lost." As a result, the "new B & D system" never caught on in the marketplace.

The 1970s saw two important grading guides make their debut. The first was *Photograde* by James F. Ruddy. As the title implies, Ruddy uses photographs instead of line drawings to show how coins look in the various circulated grades. Simplicity is also a virtue of Ruddy's book. Only seven

*Photograde* was the first widely accepted grading guide to use photos to illustrate the amount of wear on circulated coins.

circulated grades are listed (about good, good, very good, fine, very fine, extremely fine, and about uncirculated), and the designations stop there.

In 1977 the longtime call for the ANA to issue grading standards was met with the release of *Official A.N.A. Grading Standards for United States Coins*. Like Brown and Dunn, the first editions of the ANA guide used line drawings to illustrate coins in various states of wear. But instead of using adjectival descriptions, the ANA guide adopted a numerical system for designating grades.

The numerical designations were based on a system used by Dr. William H. Sheldon in his book *Early American Cents*, first published in 1949. He used a scale of 1 to 70 to designate the grades of large cents.

"On this scale," Sheldon wrote, "1 means that the coin is identifiable and not mutilated — no more than that. A 70-coin is one in flawless Mint State, exactly as it left the dies, with perfect mint color and without a blemish or nick."

(Sheldon's scale also had its pragmatic side. At the time, a No. 2 large cent was worth about twice a No. 1 coin; a No. 4 was worth about twice a

*Official A.N.A. Grading Standards for United States Coins* is now in its fourth edition.

No. 2, and so on up the scale.)

With the first edition of its grading guide, the ANA adopted the 70-point scale for grading all U.S. coins. It designated 10 categories of circulated grades: AG-3, G-4, VG-8, F-12, VF-20, VF-30, EF-40, EF-45, AU-50, and AU-55. The third edition, released in 1987, replaced the line drawings with photographs, and another circulated grade was added: AU-58. A fourth edition was released in 1991.

## Grading circulated U.S. coins

Dealers today generally use either the ANA guide or *Photograde* when grading circulated coins for their inventories. (Brown and Dunn is now out of print.) Many local coin shops sell both books. Advertisers in *Numismatic News*, *Coins*, and *Coin Prices* must indicate which standards they are using in grading their coins. If the standards are not listed, they must conform to ANA standards.

Following are some general guidelines, accompanied by photos, for grading circulated U.S. coins. Grading even circulated pieces can be subjective, particularly when attempting to draw the fine line between, for example, AU-55 and AU-58. Two longtime collectors or dealers can disagree in such a case.

But by studying some combination of the following guidelines, the ANA guide, and *Photograde*, and by looking at a lot of coins at shops and shows, collectors can gain enough grading knowledge to buy circulated coins confidently from dealers and other collectors. The more you study, the more knowledge and confidence you will gain. When you decide which series of coins you want to collect, focus on the guidelines for that particular series. Read them, reread them, and then refer back to them again and again.

# AU-50

Indian cent

Lincoln cent

Buffalo nickel

Jefferson nickel

Mercury dime

Standing Liberty quarter

Washington quarter

Walking Liberty half dollar

Morgan dollar

Barber coins

**AU-50 (about uncirculated):** Just a slight trace of wear, the result of brief exposure to circulation or light rubbing from mishandling, may be evident on the elevated design areas. These imperfections may appear as scratches or dull spots, along with bag marks or edge nicks. At least half of the original mint luster generally is still evident.

# XF-40

**Indian cent**

**Lincoln cent**

**Buffalo nickel**

**Jefferson nickel**

**Mercury dime**

**Standing Liberty quarter**

Washington quarter                    Walking Liberty half dollar

Morgan dollar                         Barber coins

**XF-40 (extremely fine):** The coin must show only slight evidence of wear on the highest points of the design, particularly in the hair lines of the portrait on the obverse. The same may be said for the eagle's feathers and wreath leaves on the reverse of most U.S. coins. A trace of mint luster may still show in protected areas of the coin's surface.

# VF-20

**Indian cent**

**Lincoln cent**

**Buffalo nickel**

**Jefferson nickel**

**Mercury dime**

**Standing Liberty quarter**

**Washington quarter**

**Walking Liberty half dollar**

**Morgan dollar**

**Barber coins**

**VF-20 (very fine):** The coin will show light wear at the fine points in the design, though they may remain sharp overall. Although the details may be slightly smoothed, all lettering and major features must remain sharp.

Indian cent: All letters in "Liberty" are complete but worn. Headdress shows considerable flatness, with flat spots on the tips of the feathers.

Lincoln cent: Hair, cheek, jaw, and bow-tie details will be worn but clearly separated, and wheat stalks on the reverse will be full with no weak spots.

Buffalo nickel: High spots on hair braid and cheek will be flat but show some detail, and a full horn will remain on the buffalo.

Jefferson nickel: Well over half of the major hair detail will remain, and the pillars on Monticello will remain well defined, with the triangular roof partially visible.

Mercury dime: Hair braid will show some detail, and three-quarters of the detail will remain in the feathers. The two diagonal bands on the fasces will show completely but will be worn smooth at the middle, with the vertical lines sharp.

Standing Liberty quarter: Rounded contour of Liberty's right leg will be flattened, as will the high point of the shield.

Washington quarter: There will be considerable wear on the hair curls, with feathers on the right and left of the eagle's breast showing clearly.

Walking Liberty half dollar: All lines of the skirt will show but will be worn on the high points. Over half the feathers on the eagle will show.

Morgan dollar: Two-thirds of the hairlines from the forehead to the ear must show. Ear should be well defined. Feathers on the eagle's breast may be worn smooth.

Barber coins: All seven letters of "Liberty" on the headband must stand out sharply. Head wreath will be well outlined from top to bottom.

# F-12

Indian cent

Lincoln cent

Buffalo nickel

Jefferson nickel

Mercury dime

Standing Liberty quarter

Washington quarter

Walking Liberty half dollar

Morgan dollar

Barber coins

**F-12 (fine):** Coins show evidence of moderate to considerable but generally even wear on all high points, though all elements of the design and lettering remain bold. Where the word "Liberty" appears in a headband, it must be fully visible. On 20th century coins, the rim must be fully raised and sharp.

# VG-8

Indian cent

Lincoln cent

Buffalo nickel

Jefferson nickel

Mercury dime

Standing Liberty quarter

**Washington quarter**

**Walking Liberty half dollar**

**Morgan dollar**

**Barber coins**

**VG-8 (very good):** The coin will show considerable wear, with most detail points worn nearly smooth. Where the word "Liberty" appears in a head-band, at least three letters must show. On 20th century coins, the rim will start to merge with the lettering.

# G-4

**Indian cent**

**Lincoln cent**

**Buffalo nickel**

**Jefferson nickel**

**Mercury dime**

**Standing Liberty quarter**

Washington quarter                    Walking Liberty half dollar

Morgan dollar                    Barber coins

**G-4 (good):** Only the basic design remains distinguishable in outline form, with all points of detail worn smooth. The word "Liberty" has disappeared, and the rims are almost merging with the lettering.

**About good or fair:** The coin will be identifiable by date and mint but otherwise badly worn, with only parts of the lettering showing. Such coins are of value only as fillers in a collection until a better example of the date and mintmark can be obtained. The only exceptions would be rare coins.

# Grading uncirculated U.S. coins

The subjectivity of grading and the trend toward more classifications becomes more acute when venturing into uncirculated, or mint-state, coins. A minute difference between one or two grade points can mean a difference in value of hundreds or even thousands of dollars. In addition, the standards are more difficult to articulate in writing and illustrate through drawings or photographs. Thus, the possibilities for differences of opinion on one or two grade points increase in uncirculated coins.

Coins graded and encapsulated by a third-party grading service are nicknamed "slabs." The Professional Coin Grading Service graded this Saint-Gaudens gold $20 coin.

Back in Dr. George Heath's day and continuing through the 1960s, a coin was either uncirculated or it wasn't. Little distinction was made between uncirculated coins of varying condition, largely because there was little if any difference in value. When *Numismatic News* introduced its value guide in 1962 (the forerunner of today's Coin Market section in the *News*), it listed only one grade of uncirculated for Morgan dollars.

But as collectible coins increased in value and buyers of uncirculated coins became more picky, distinctions within grade uncirculated started to surface. In 1975 *Numismatic News* still listed only one uncirculated grade in Coin Market, but added this note: "Uncirculated and proof specimens in especially choice condition will also command proportionately higher premiums than these listed."

The first edition of the ANA guide listed two grades of uncirculated, MS-60 and MS-65, in addition to the theoretical but non-existent MS-70 (a flawless coin). MS-60 was described as "typical uncirculated" and MS-65 as "choice uncirculated." *Numismatic News* adopted both designations for Coin Market. In 1981, when the second edition of the ANA grading guide was released, MS-67 and MS-63 were added. In 1985 *Numismatic News* started listing six grades of uncirculated for Morgan dollars: MS-60, MS-63, MS-65, MS-65+, and MS-63 prooflike.

Then in 1986, a new entity appeared that has changed the nature of grading and trading uncirculated coins ever since. A group of dealers led by David Hall of Newport Beach, Calif., formed the Professional Coin Grading Service. For a fee, collectors could submit a coin through an authorized PCGS dealer and receive back a professional opinion of its grade.

The concept was not new; the ANA had operated an authentication service since 1972 and a grading service since 1979. A collector or dealer could submit a coin directly to the service and receive a certificate giving the service's opinion on authenticity and grade. The grading service was the source of near constant debate among dealers and ANA officials. Dealers charged that ANA graders were too young and inexperienced, and

The Numismatic Guaranty Corp. is another major grading service.

that their grading was inconsistent.

Grading stability was a problem throughout the coin business in the early 1980s, not just with the ANA service. Standards among uncirculated grades would tighten during a bear market and loosen during a bull market. As a result, a coin graded MS-65 in a bull market may have commanded only MS-63 during a bear market.

PCGS created several innovations in the grading business in response to these problems:

1. Coins could be submitted through PCGS-authorized dealers only.

2. Each coin would be graded by at least three members of a panel of "top graders," all prominent dealers in the business. (Since then, however, PCGS does not allow its graders to also deal in coins.)

3. After grading, the coin would be encapsulated in an inert, hard-plastic holder with a serial number and the grade indicated on the holder.

4. PCGS-member dealers pledged to make a market in PCGS-graded coins and honor the grades assigned.

5. In one of the most far-reaching moves, PCGS said it would use all 11 increments of uncirculated on the 70-point numerical scale: MS-60, MS-61, MS-62, MS-63, MS-64, MS-65, MS-66, MS-67, MS-68, MS-69, and MS-70.

The evolution of more uncirculated grades had reached another milestone.

Purists bemoaned the entombment of classic coins in the plastic holders and denounced the 11 uncirculated grades as implausible. Nevertheless, PCGS was an immediate commercial success. The plastic holders were nicknamed "slabs," and dealers couldn't get coins through the system fast enough.

In subsequent years, a number of similar services have appeared. Among them, one of the original PCGS "top graders," John Albanese, left PCGS to found the Numismatic Guaranty Corp. The ANA grading service succumbed to "slab mania" and introduced its own encapsulated product.

Although there are still several other reputable grading services, PCGS

**Slabbing has become an important part of the hobby and the placement of coins in their holders is aided by specialized equipment as shown above.**

and NGC dominate market share. In 1990 the ANA sold its grading service to a private company. The association continues to authenticate coins.

How should a collector approach the buying and grading of uncirculated coins? Collecting uncirculated coins worth thousands of dollars implies a higher level of numismatic expertise by the buyer. Those buyers without that level of expertise should cut their teeth on more inexpensive coins, just as today's experienced collectors did. Inexperienced collectors can start toward that level by studying the guidelines for mint-state coins in the ANA grading guide and looking at lots of coins at shows and shops.

Study the condition and eye appeal of a coin and compare it to other coins of the same series. Then compare prices. Do the more expensive coins look better? If so, why? Start to make your own judgments concerning relationships between condition and value.

According to numismatic legend, a collector walked up to a crusty old dealer at a show one time and asked the dealer to grade a coin the collector had with him. The dealer looked at the coin and said, "I grade it a hundred dollars." Such is the bottom line to coin grading.

# Grading U.S. proof coins

Because proof coins are struck by a special process (see Chapter 2), they receive their own grading designation. A coin does not start out being a proof and then become mint state if it becomes worn. Once a proof coin, always a proof coin.

In the ANA system, proof grades use the same numbers as circulated and uncirculated grades, and the amount of wear on the coin corresponds to those grades. But the number is preceded by the word "proof." For example, Proof-65, Proof-55, Proof-45, and so on. In addition, the ANA says a proof coin with many marks, scratches or other defects should be called an "impaired proof."

# Grading world coins

The state of grading non-U.S. issues is similar to U.S. coin grading before Brown and Dunn. There is no detailed, illustrated guide that covers the enormous scope and variety of world coins; collectors and dealers rely on their experience in the field and knowledge of the marketplace.

The *Standard Catalog of World Coins* gives the following guidelines for grading world coins, which apply to the Canadian and Mexican value listings in this book:

In grading world coins, there are two elements to look for: (1) overall wear and (2) loss of design details, such as strands of hair, feathers on eagles, designs on coats of arms, and so on. Grade each coin by the weaker of the two sides. Age, rarity or type of coin should not be considered in grading.

Grade by the amount of overall wear and loss of detail evident in the main design on each side. On coins with a moderately small design element that is prone to early wear, grade by that design alone.

In the marketplace, adjectival grades are still used for Mexican coins. The numerical system for Canadian coins is now commonplace:

**Uncirculated, MS-60:** No visible signs of wear or handling, even under a 30X microscope. Bag marks may be present.

**Almost uncirculated, AU-50:** All detail will be visible. There will be wear on only the highest point of the coin. There will often be half or more of the original mint luster present.

**Extremely fine, XF-40:** About 95 percent of the original detail will be visible. Or, on a coin with a design that has no inner detail to wear down, there will be light wear over nearly the entire coin. If a small design is used as the grading area, about 90 percent of the original detail will be visible. This latter rule stems from the logic that a smaller amount of detail needs to be present because a small area is being used to grade the whole coin.

**Very fine, VF-20:** About 75 percent of the original detail will be visible. Or, on a coin with no inner detail, there will be moderate wear over the entire coin. Corners of letters and numbers may be weak. A small grading area will have about 60 percent of the original detail.

**Fine, F-12:** About 50 percent of the original detail will be visible. Or, on a coin with no inner detail, there will be fairly heavy wear over the entire coin. Sides of letters will be weak. A typically uncleaned coin will often appear dirty or dull. A small grading area will have just under 50 percent of the original detail.

**Very good, VG-8:** About 25 percent of the original detail will be visible. There will be heavy wear on the entire coin.

**Good, G-4:** Design will be clearly outlined but with substantial wear. Some of the larger detail may be visible. The rim may have a few weak spots of wear.

**About good, AG-3:** Typically only a silhouette of a large design will be visible. The rim will be worn down into the letters, if any.

## Where to write for more information

**American Numismatic Association Authentication Bureau:** 818 N. Cascade Ave., Colorado Springs, CO 80903-3279.

**Independent Coin Grading Co.:** 7901 E. Belleview Ave., Suite 50, Englewood, CO 80111.

**Numismatic Guaranty Corp:** P.O. Box 1776, Parsippany, NJ 07054.

*Official A.N.A. Grading Standards for United States Coins:* Whitman Coin Products, 10101 Science Drive, Sturtevant, WI 53177.

**Photo Certified Coin Institute**, Inc., P.O. Box 8609, Chattanooga, TN 37414.

*Photograde:* Bowers and Merena Galleries, Inc., Books Dept., Box 1224, Wolfeboro, NH 03894.

**Professional Coin Grading Service:** P.O. Box 9458, Newport Beach, CA 92658.

**Sovereign Entities Grading Service:** Suite 2103401, 401 Chestnut St., Chattanooga, TN 37402-4924

See Chapter 13 for Web addresses.

## Visit the Krause Publications Web sites
## http://www.krause.com
## http://www.coincollecting.net

# 5

# Get a map

## *How to organize a collection*

### By David C. Harper

Do you have a jar full of old coins? Did a favorite relative give you a few silver dollars over the years? Or did you just come across something unusual that you set aside?

All three circumstances make good beginnings for collecting coins. It may surprise you, but this is how just about everybody starts in the hobby. It is a rare collector who decides to start down the hobby road without first having come into a few coins one way or another.

What these random groupings lack is organization. It is organization that makes a collection. But think about it another way: Organization is the map that tells you where you can go in coin collecting and how you can get there.

Have you ever been at a large fair or a huge office building and seen the maps that say "you are here"? Did you ever consider that, over time, thousands of other people have stood on the same spot? This is true in numismatics also. Figuratively, you are standing on the same spot on which the writers of this book stood at some point in their lives.

At a fair, the map helps you consider various ways of seeing all the sights. In coin collecting, too, there are different ways to organize a collection. The method you choose helps you see the hobby sights you want to see.

It should be something that suits you. Remember, do what you want to do. See what you want to see. But don't be afraid to make a mistake; there aren't any. Just as one can easily retrace steps at a fair, one can turn around and head in another direction in the coin-collecting hobby. Besides, when you start off for any given point, often you see something along the way that was unplanned but more interesting. That's numismatics.

There are two major ways to organize a collection: by type, and by date and mintmark. These approaches work in basically the same fashion for coins of the United States, Canada and Mexico. Naturally, there are differences. But to establish the concepts, let's focus first on U.S. coins.

# United States

Let's take collecting by type first. Look at your jar of coins, or take the change out of your pocket. You find Abraham Lincoln and the Lincoln Memorial on current cents. You find Thomas Jefferson and his home, Monticello, on the nickel. Franklin D. Roosevelt and a torch share the dime. George Washington and an eagle appear on the quarter. John F. Kennedy and the presidential seal are featured on the half dollar.

Each design is called a "type." If you took one of each and put the five coins in a holder, you would have a type set of the coins that are currently being produced for circulation by the U.S. Mint.

With just these five coins, you can study various metallic compositions. You can evaluate their states of preservation and assign a grade to each. You can learn about the artists who designed the coins, and you can learn of the times in which these designs were created.

As you might have guessed, many different coin types have been used in the United States over the years. You may remember seeing some of them circulating. These designs reflect the hopes and aspirations of people over time. Putting all of them together forms a wonderful numismatic mosaic of American history.

George Washington did not mandate that his image appear on the quarter. Quite the contrary. He would have been horrified. When he was president, he headed off those individuals in Congress who thought the leader of the country should have his image on its coins. Washington said it smacked of monarchy and would have nothing of it.

Almost a century and a half later, during the bicentennial of Washington's birth in 1932, a nation searching for its roots during troubled economic times decided that it needed his portrait on its coins as a reminder of his great accomplishments and as reassurance that this nation was the same place it had been in more prosperous days.

In its broadest definition, collecting coins by type requires that you obtain an example of every design that was struck by the U.S. Mint since it was founded in 1792. That's a tall order. You would be looking for denominations like the half cent, two-cent piece, three-cent piece, and 20-cent piece, which have not been produced in over a century. You would be looking for gold coins ranging in face value from $1 to $50.

But even more important than odd-sounding denominations or high face values is the question of rarity. Some of the pieces in this two-century type set are rare and expensive. That's why type collectors often divide the challenge into more digestible units.

Type collecting can be divided into 18th, 19th and 20th century units. Starting type collectors can focus on 20th century coin designs, which are easily obtainable. The fun and satisfaction of putting the 20th century set together then creates the momentum to continue backward in time.

In the process of putting a 20th century type set together, one is also learning how to grade, learning hobby jargon, and discovering how to obtain coins from dealers, the U.S. Mint, and other collectors. All of this knowledge is then refined as the collector increases the challenge to himself.

This book is designed to help. How many dollar types were struck in the 20th century? Turn to the U.S. price-guide section and check it out. We see the Morgan dollar, Peace dollar, Eisenhower dollar, and Anthony dollar. Hobbyists could also add the Ike dollar with the Bicentennial design of 1976 and the silver American Eagle bullion coin struck since 1986. One can also find out their approximate retail prices from the listings.

The beauty of type collecting is that one can choose the most inexpensive example of each type. There is no need to select a 1903-O Morgan when the 1921 will do just as well. With the 20th century type set, hobbyists can dodge some truly big-league prices.

As a collector's hobby confidence grows, he can tailor goals to fit his desires. He can take the road less traveled if that is what suits him. Type sets can be divided by denomination. You can choose two centuries of one-cent coins. You can take just obsolete denominations or copper, silver or gold denominations.

You can even collect by size. Perhaps you would like to collect all coin types larger than 30 millimeters or all coins smaller than 20 millimeters. Many find this freedom of choice stimulating.

Type collecting has proven itself to be enduringly popular over the years. It provides a maximum amount of design variety while allowing collectors to set their own level of challenge.

The second popular method of collecting is by date and mintmark. What this means, quite simply, is that a collector picks a given type — Jefferson nickels, for example — and then goes after an example of every year, every mintmark, and every type of manufacture that was used with the Jefferson design.

Looking at this method of collecting brings up the subject of mintmarks. The "U.S. Mint" is about as specific as most non-collectors get in describing the government agency that provides everyday coins. Behind that label are the various production facilities that actually do the work.

In two centuries of U.S. coinage, there have been eight such facilities. Four are still in operation. Those eight in alphabetical order are Carson City, Nev., which used a "CC" mintmark to identify its work; Charlotte, N.C. ("C"); Dahlonega, Ga. ("D"); Denver (also uses a "D," but it opened long after the Dahlonega Mint closed, so there was never any confusion); New Orleans ("O"); Philadelphia (because it was the primary mint, it used no mintmark for much of its history, but currently uses a "P"); San Francisco ("S"); and West Point, N.Y. ("W").

A basic type set of 20th century dollar coins would consist of (from top), a Morgan type, Peace type, Eisenhower type, and Anthony type.

A person contemplating the collecting of Jefferson nickels by date and mintmark will find that three mints produced them: San Francisco, Denver and Philadelphia. Because the first two are branch mints serving smaller populations, their output has tended over time to be smaller than that of Philadelphia. This fact, repeated in other series, has helped give mintmarks quite an allure to collectors. It provides one of the major attractions in collecting coins by date and mintmark.

The key date for Jeffersons is the 1950-D when using mintages as a guide. In that year, production was just 2.6 million pieces. Because collectors of the time were aware of the coin's low mintage, many examples were saved. As a result, prices are reasonable.

Jefferson nickels have been produced at the (from top) Philadelphia, Denver and San Francisco mints. Note the Denver and San Francisco mintmarks to the right of Monticello.

The wartime nickels of 1942-45 marked the first time a "P" mintmark, for Philadelphia, was used.

The Depression-era 1939-D comes in as the most valuable regular-issue Jefferson nickel despite a mintage of 3.5 million — almost 1 million more than the 1950-D. The reason: Fewer were saved for later generations of coin collectors.

Date and mintmark collecting teaches hobbyists to use mintage figures as a guide but to take them with a grain of salt. Rarity, after all, is determined by the number of surviving coins, not the number initially created.

The Jefferson series is a good one to collect by date and mintmark, because the mintmarks have moved around, grown in size, and expanded in number.

When the series was first introduced, the Jefferson nickel was produced at the three mints previously mentioned. In 1942, because of a diversion of certain metals to wartime use, the coin's alloy of 75 percent copper and 25 percent nickel was changed. The new alloy was 35 percent silver, 56 percent copper, and 9 percent manganese.

To denote the change, the mintmarks were moved and greatly enlarged. The pre-1942 mintmarks were small and located to the right of Monticello; the wartime mintmarks were enlarged and placed over the dome. What's more, for the first time in American history, the Philadelphia Mint used a mintmark ("P").

The war's end restored the alloy and mintmarks to their previous status. The "P" disappeared. This lasted until the 1960s, when a national coin shortage saw all mintmarks removed for three years (1965-1967) and then returned, but in a different location. Mintmarks were placed on the obverse, to the right of Jefferson's portrait near the date in 1968. In 1980 the "P" came back in a smaller form and is still used.

Another consideration arises with date and mintmark collecting: Should the hobbyist include proof coins in the set? This can be argued both ways. Suffice to say that anyone who has the desire to add proof coins to the set will have a larger one. It is not necessary nor is it discouraged.

Some of the first proof coins to carry mintmarks were Jefferson nickels. When proof coins were made in 1968 after lapsing from 1965 to 1967, production occurred at San Francisco instead of Philadelphia. The "S" mintmark was placed on the proof coins of that year, including the Jefferson nickel, to denote the change. Since that time, mintmarks used on proof

In 1968 mintmarks reappeared on U.S. coins and production of proof coins resumed, this time at the San Francisco Mint. On the nickels, the mintmark moved from the reverse to the obverse below the date.

examples of various denominations have included the "P", "D", "S", and "W".

For all of the mintmark history that is embodied in the Jefferson series, prices are reasonable. For a first attempt at collecting coins by date and mintmark, it provides excellent background for going on to the more expensive and difficult types. After all, if you are ever going to get used to the proper handling of a coin, it is far better to experiment on a low-cost coin than a high-value rarity.

As one progresses in date and mintmark collecting and type collecting, it is important to remember that all of the coins should be of similar states of preservation. Sets look slapdash if one coin is VG and another is MS-65 and still another is VF. Take a look at the prices of all the coins in the series before you get too far, figure out what you can afford, and then stick to that grade or range of grades.

Sure, there is a time-honored practice of filling a spot with any old example until a better one comes along. That is how we got the term "filler." But if you get a few placeholders, don't stop there. By assembling a set of uniform quality, you end up with a more aesthetically pleasing collection.

The date and mintmark method used to be the overwhelmingly dominant form of collecting. It still has many adherents. Give it a try if you think it sounds right for you.

Before we leave the discussion of collecting U.S. coins, it should be pointed out that the two major methods of organizing a collection are simply guidelines. They are no hard-and-fast rules that must be followed without question. Collecting should be satisfying to the hobbyist. It should never be just one more item in the daily grind. Take the elements of these collecting approaches that you like or invent your own.

It should also be pointed out that U.S. coinage history does not start with 1792 nor do all of the coins struck since that time conform precisely to the two major organizational approaches. But these two areas are good places to start.

There are coins and tokens from the American Colonial period (1607-1776) that are just as fascinating and collectible as regular U.S. Mint issues. There are federal issues struck before the Mint was actually established. See the Colonial price-guide section in this book.

There are special coins called commemoratives, which have been struck by the U.S. Mint since 1892 to celebrate some aspect of American history or a contemporary event. They are not intended for circulation. There was a long interruption between 1954 and 1982, but currently numerous commemoratives are being offered for sale directly to collectors by the Mint.

Collecting commemoratives has always been considered something separate from collecting regular U.S. coinage. It is, however, organized the same way. Commemoratives can be collected by date and mintmark or by type.

Current commemoratives can be purchased from the U.S. Mint. To get on its mailing list, write U.S. Mint, Customer Service Center, 10001 Aerospace Drive, Lanham MD 20706. Once on the list, hobbyists will get the various solicitations for not only commemoratives, but regular proof sets and mint sets and American Eagle bullion coinage.

Buying coins from the Mint can be considered a hobby pursuit in its own right. Some collectors let the Mint organize their holdings for them. They buy complete sets and put them away. They never buy anything from anywhere else.

Admittedly, this is a passive form of collecting, but there are individuals around the world who enjoy collecting at this level without ever really going any deeper. They like acquiring every new issue as it comes off the Mint's presses.

Once done, there is a certain knowledge that one has all the examples of the current year. Obviously, too, collectors by date and mintmark of the current types would have to buy the new coins each year, but, of course, they do not stop there.

Varieties and errors make up another area. Under this heading come the coins the Mint did not intend to make. There are all kinds of errors. Many of them are inexpensive. Check out the U.S. Minting Varieties and Errors section in the price guide. If you want to pursue it further, there are specialty books that deal with the topic in more detail.

# Canada

Starting point for the national coinage of Canada is popularly fixed at 1858. In that year a large cent was first produced for use in Upper and Lower Canada (Ontario and Quebec). These pieces were intended to supplant local copper coinage, which in turn had been attempts to give various regions a medium of exchange.

What was circulating in Canada at the time was a hodgepodge of world issues. The large cent predates a unified national government by nine years, but it is considered the beginning of national issues nevertheless.

There are many similarities between the United States and Canada and their respective monetary systems. Both continent-sized nations thought in terms of taming the frontier, new settlements, and growth. Both came to use the dollar as the unit of account because of the pervasiveness of the Spanish milled dollar in trade. For each, the dollar divides into 100 cents.

Canadian coins have depicted (from top) Queen Victoria, King Edward VII, King George V, King George VI, and Queen Elizabeth II.

However, Canada had a far longer colonial history. Many of its residents resisted the tide that carried the United States to independence and worked to preserve their loyalties to the British crown. As a result, Canada was firmly a part of the British Empire. So even today with its constitution (the British North America Act transferred from Westminster to Ottawa in 1982), parliamentary democracy, and a national consciousness perhaps best symbolized by the maple leaf, Canada retains a loyalty to the crown in the person of Queen Elizabeth II of the United Kingdom. Canada is a member of the British Commonwealth of Nations.

The effect of this on coins is obvious. Current issues carry the queen's effigy. How Canada got its coins in the past was also influenced. The fledgling U.S. government set about creating its own mint as one of its earliest goals, despite that better-quality pieces could be purchased abroad at lower cost. Canada found that ties to mints located in England were logical and comfortable.

The Royal Canadian Mint was not established until 1908, when it was called the Ottawa branch of the British Royal Mint, and it was not given its present name until 1931. Both events are within living memory. Canadian coins, therefore, have a unique mixture of qualities. They are tantalizingly familiar to U.S. citizens yet distinctly different.

The coinage of a monarchy brings its own logic to the organization of a collection. Type collecting is delineated by the monarch. United Canada has had six. The first was Queen Victoria, whose image appeared on those large cents of 1858. Her reign began in 1837 and lasted until 1901.

She was followed by Edward VII, 1901-1910; George V, 1910-1936; Edward VIII, 1936; George VI, 1936-1952; and Queen Elizabeth II, 1952-present. All but Edward VIII had coins struck for circulation in Canada. The collectible monarchs, therefore, number five, but the longer reigns inspired changes of portraits over time to show the aging process at work. Legends also changed. When George VI ceased being emperor of India, Canada's coins were modified to recognize the change.

Like U.S. coins, sizes and alloys were altered to meet new demands placed on the coinage. However, the separateness of each nation might best be summed up this way: Though the United States abolished its large cent in 1857, Canada's was just getting under way in 1858. The United States put an end to the silver dollar in 1935, the very year Canada finally got its series going.

And Canada, the nickel-mining giant, used a small-sized silver five-cent coin until 1921, almost 50 years after the half dime was abolished in the United States. But whereas the Civil War was the major cause of the emergence of modern U.S. coinage as specified by the Coinage Act of 1873, World War I influenced the alterations that made Canada's coins what they are today.

It might be assumed that change in the monarch also signaled a change in the reverse designs of the various denominations. A check of the Canadian price guide section shows this is not necessarily the case. Current designs paired with Queen Elizabeth II basically date back to the beginning of her father's reign. The familiar maple-leaf cent, beaver five-cent piece, schooner 10-cent, caribou 25-cent, and coat-of-arms 50-cent have been running for over 50 years. Significant changes were made to the 50-cent coin in 1959, but the reverse design remains the coat of arms.

So where does that leave type collectors? It puts them in a situation similar to categorizing the various eagles on U.S. coins. They can be universalists and accept the broadest definitions of type, or they can narrow the bands to whatever degree suits them best.

By checking the price-guide section, date and mintmark collectors will quickly note that their method of organization more or less turns into collecting by date. Though currently there are three mints in Canada — Hull, Quebec; Ottawa, Ontario; and Winnipeg, Manitoba — they don't use mintmarks. Historically, few mintmarks were employed.

Ottawa used a "C" on gold sovereigns of 1908-1919 and on some exported colonial issues. The private Heaton Mint in Birmingham, England, used an "H" on coins it supplied to Canada from 1871 to 1907.

But the coins supplied to Canada by the British Royal Mint and later by its Ottawa branch did not carry any identifying mark. Collectors who confine their activities to the more recent issues need never think about a mintmark.

It would be easy to slant a presentation on Canadian issues to stress similarities or differences to U.S. issues. One should remember that the monetary structures of each evolved independently, but each was always having an impact on the other.

Common events, such as World War II, had a similar impact. For example, the Canadian five-cent coin changed in much the same way as the U.S. nickel. In Canada, nickel was removed and replaced first by a tombac (brass) alloy and then by chromium-plated steel. Peace brought with it a return to the prewar composition.

To see an example of differences between the United States and Canada, take the Canadian approach to the worldwide trend of removing silver from coinage. Canada made its move in 1968, three years after the United States. Instead of choosing a copper-nickel alloy as a substitute for silver, Canada looked to its own vast natural resources and employed pure nickel.

Canada also seems more comfortable with its coinage than the United States. Whereas the United States often feared confusion and counterfeiting from making the least little changes in its coins, Canada has long embraced coinage to communicate national events, celebrations and culture. Its silver-dollar series actually began as a celebration of George V's 25 years on the throne.

Succeeding years saw additional commemorative $1 designs interspersed with the regular voyageur design. When the centennial of national confederation was observed in 1967, all of the denominations were altered for one year. The United States only reluctantly tried out the idea on three of its denominations for the nation's Bicentennial.

Like the U.S. Mint, the Royal Canadian Mint offers sets of coins in a variety of finishes to the collector market.

Ultimately, Canada began an annual commemorative dollar series in 1971. It issued coins for the 1976 Montreal Olympic Games and again in 1988 for the Calgary Olympic Games. Bullion coins were created to market its gold, silver and platinum output. A commemorative series of gold $100 coins was also undertaken. Canada, too, issues special proof, prooflike and specimen sets, similar to the United States.

Hobbyists who would like to be informed of new issues should write Royal Canadian Mint, P.O. Box 457, Station A, Ontario K1A 8V5, Canada. The mint also maintains special toll-free lines. In the United States, hobbyists may telephone the Royal Canadian Mint at 1-800-268-6468. In Canada, the number is 1-800-267-1871. You can get on the mailing list by using these numbers and you can buy currently available coins.

When collecting Canada, another thing to remember is the importance varieties play in the nation's various series. Certainly, a type collector has no need to dwell on this information, but the date and mintmark collector may puzzle over the many extra identifying abbreviations in the price guide for certain coins. These varieties should not be confused with the U.S. variety-and-error category.

Here the varieties are not mistakes; they are deliberately created and issued variations of the standard design. We see voyageur dollars on which the number of water lines changes. Other dollars count the number of beads.

These differences are minor. Though they were deliberately done to meet varying mint needs, they were not intended to be set apart in the public mind. The hobby, however, likes to look at things under a microscope.

Some varieties were indeed intended to be deliberately and noticeably different. An example of this occurs with 1947-dated issues. A maple leaf was placed on the 1947-dated cent through 50-cent issues. This indicated the coin was struck after George VI lost his title of emperor of India, as proclaimed in the Latin legend, but that the design had not yet been altered to reflect this. All of these varieties are considered integral parts of the Canadian series, and they are listed as such.

Do not construe any of this to mean there is no collecting of varieties and errors of the type common in the United States. There is. Collecting Royal Canadian Mint mistakes is just as active, just as interesting, and just as rewarding. After all, mint errors are universal. The methods of manufacture are the same. So the mistakes can be classified in the same manner.

Canada's numismatic listings also include items from various provinces issued before they were part of the confederation. The largest portion of this section is devoted to Newfoundland, because it retained a separate status far longer than the other provinces — until 1949 in fact.

Advice given to collectors of U.S. coins also applies to collectors of Canadian coins: Do what interests you. Do what you can afford. Create sets of uniform grade.

The rules of rarity transcend national boundaries. The only thing to keep in mind is the relative size of the collecting population. Because Canada has only a tenth of the U.S. population, it stands to reason that the number of collectors in that nation is but a fraction of the U.S. number. A mintage that seems to indicate scarcity for a U.S. coin, therefore, could indicate something quite common in Canada.

Don't forget that mintage is just a guide. The same factors that caused loss of available specimens or preserved unusually large quantities were at work in Canada, too.


# Mexico

Coinage produced in Mexico dates to the establishment of a mint in Mexico City in 1536, over 250 years before a federal mint was set up in the United States and more than 300 years before Canada circulated its own coins. The output of those extra centuries alone would make organizing a Mexican coin collection more challenging than a collection of U.S. or Canadian coins. But there are numerous other factors involved.

You say you like the kings and queens on Canada's coins? Mexico has kings, too — nearly 300 years' worth, plus a couple of emperors. You say the ideals of liberty embodied by the great men and women on U.S. coins is more your cup of tea? Mexico's coins also feature men and women committed to liberty.

In addition, Mexico is the crossroads of civilizations and empires. The great pyramid-building society of southern Mexico and Central America met its end at the hands of the Spanish conquistadors led initially by Hernando Cortez. The great Aztec empire was looted and overturned in 1519-1521 in the name of Spain.

The great natural resources of the area then supported successive Spanish kings in their grand dreams of dominating Europe. Through the doors

**One thousand of these equaled one new peso as 1993 began.**

of the Mexico City Mint and later facilities scattered about the country passed legendary quantities of silver. Even today the country ranks at the top of the list of silver producers.

But while Spain could dominate Mexico for a long time, the basic ideals of liberty and human dignity eventually motivated the people to throw off the foreign yoke. Unfortunately, victory was often neither complete nor wisely led. And in more recent years, the scourge of inflation has exacted a high toll on the currency itself. The numismatic consequences of a long history punctuated by periods of turmoil are an abundance of denominations, metals and types.

It is tempting for a would-be collector of Mexican coins to forget about anything that happened in the country prior to its monetary reform of 1905. By starting at that point, a hobbyist can happily overlook anything other than a decimal monetary system in which 100 centavos equal 1 peso. That system is as modern as any. The coins' striking quality is high. Legends are easy to read and understand, and the variety of issues is wide but not overwhelming.

There always is a certain logic to begin the collecting of any country with recent issues. The costs of learning are minimized, and as one becomes comfortable, a level of confidence can be built up sufficient to prompt diving further into the past.

The issues of 1905 to date also more easily fit into the mold of type collecting and collecting by date and mintmark. To take type collecting, for example, let's look at the peso. In 1905 it was a silver-dollar-sized coin with a silver-dollar-sized quantity of bullion in it, 0.786 ounces. In 1918 it was reduced to 0.4663 ounces; in 1920, 0.3856 ounces; in 1947, 0.2250 ounces; 1950, 0.1285 ounces; 1957, 0.0514 ounces; and in 1970 silver was eliminated completely in favor of a copper-nickel alloy.

At almost every one of those steps, the design changed, too. After sinking to 3,300 to the U.S. dollar, monetary reform dropped three zeroes in 1993. The new peso, equal to 1,000 old ones, is now 9.1 to the U.S. dollar.

By beginning with 1905, a date and mintmark collector misses out on issues of the various branch mints that were located around the country. Regular issues were all struck in Mexico City. Yearly output was reasonably regular for the various denominations, so date sets are extensive.

There have been rumblings since the early 1980s that Mexico would

Mexico also strikes
commemorative coins
for the collector market.
They are available
through private firms in
the United States.

abandon the peso because of its greatly reduced value. The government, however, has been working hard to retain it. So far it has succeeded.

One thing the government cannot do, however, is turn the clock back to a time when the fractional denominations of 1, 2, 5, 10, 20, 25, and 50 centavos had sufficient face value to circulate. However, it is stimulating to assemble sets because they offer a range of rarities. They are neither so expensive that it would prevent a collector from acquiring them at some point, but neither are they so common that you can walk into a shop, write a check, and come away with all of the 20th century sets complete. Check out the price guide section and see.

Gold in the post-1905 era is basically so much bullion. There are some scarcer pieces and some strikingly beautiful designs, such as the centenario, a gold 50-peso coin containing 1.2 ounces of bullion. It was first struck in 1921 to mark 100 years of independence. Because Mexico actively restruck its gold coins, however, it is virtually impossible to tell an original issue from the newer version.

The result is a retail price structure based on metallic content. Gold, however, does not conjure up the images that silver does. Silver is the magic word for Mexico. That, of course, means the peso.

The modern Mexico City Mint also strikes commemoratives and collector sets from time to time. These are generally marketed to collectors through private firms, details of which are published in hobby newspapers like *World Coin News*. Mexico, like the United States and Canada, also issues gold and silver bullion coins.

These also are marketed through arrangements with private firms. Interestingly, Mexico's many gold-coin restrikes were the bullion coins of their day. They had the advantage of ready identification, and they were legally tradable according to gold-coin regulations that existed in the United States from 1933 through 1974.

It is appropriate that we conclude discussion of the modern period on the concept of bullion, because bullion is at the root of Mexico's numismatic history. That is a period to which we now turn.

When Cortez toppled the Aztec Empire, for a time the wealth returning to Spain was merely that taken by the victors from the vanquished. But the business of permanently administering a vast area in the name of the Spanish king, exploiting its natural resources, and funneling the proceeds to Spain quite soon involved the establishment of a mint in Mexico City. This was undertaken in 1536, just 15 years after the end of Aztec dominion.

At first, the authorized coins were low denominations: silver quarter, half, 1, 2, 3, and 4 reales, and copper 2 and 4 maravedis. To understand their face values and how they related to each other, let's take the common reference point of a silver dollar. The silver dollar is 8 reales, and you might recognize the nickname for the denomination of "piece of eight" from pirate lore. The eighth part, the silver real, was divided into 34 copper maravedis. That means the 8 reales was worth 272 copper maravedis.

The copper coinage was hated and soon abolished, not to reappear until 1814. The silver coins were fine as far as they went. When the mines of Mexico began producing undreamed of quantities of metal, however, it was the 8 reales that took center stage. This occurred after 1572. The piece of eight became the standard form for shipping silver back to Spain.

Mexico City's output was prodigious. Minting standards were crude. All denominations produced are called "cobs," because they are basically little more than irregular-looking lumps of metal on which bits and pieces of design can be seen. The only constant was weight, fineness, and the appearance of assayer's initials (which guaranteed the weight and fineness). Not showing those initials was cause for severe punishment.

Designs showed the arms of the monarch on one side, a cross on the other, appropriate legends, and an indication of denomination. The period of cob issues lasted until 1732. Rulers of the period start with Charles and Johanna, 1516-1556; Philip II, 1556-1598; Philip III, 1598-1621; Philip IV, 1621-1665; Charles II, 1665-1700; Philip V, 1700-1724 and 1724-1746; and Luis I, 1724.

Modern mint machinery began turning out coins in 1732. Quality was similar to today. The arms design was continued. It was not until 1772 that the monarch's portrait began appearing. The honor of this numismatic debut belongs to Charles III. Kings of this period are Ferdinand VI, 1746-1759; Charles III, 1760-1788; Charles IV, 1788-1808; and Ferdinand VII, 1808-1821. The *Standard Catalog of Mexican Coins* by Colin R. Bruce II and Dr. George W. Vogt is recommended to those who want to study this period in greater depth.

The revolutionary period begins in 1810, when a parish priest, Miguel Hidalgo y Costilla, issued the call for independence. The first attempts to achieve this were violently suppressed. Hidalgo was executed, but independence did come in 1821.

With revolt against central authority came a dispersal of the right to strike coins. Mexico City continued as the major facility, but other operations began. The list of these over the next century is lengthy. Mintmarks and assayer initials proliferated.

The old colonial coinage standard survived the period. The 8 reales and its parts carried on. A slight reduction in bullion content had been ordered by the king in 1760, but otherwise things continued as they were. Gold was coined during the colonial period beginning in 1679 based on an 8-escudo piece, which divided into eighths just like the 8 reales. Gold, however, was not as important as silver.

Mexico's first emperor came shortly after independence. He was a leader in the struggle that set Mexico free from Spain. Augustin de Iturbide, originally an officer in the service of Spain, was proclaimed emperor in 1822. He abdicated in 1823 and was executed in 1824.

The second emperor had a reign almost as short as the first. Maximilian I, emperor only because he had a French army to secure the throne, reigned from 1863 to 1867. He was shot by a firing squad when the French left.

He is remembered numismatically because he decided to decimalize the coinage. The centavo and peso were born. Soon afterward, the republic was re-established. Further monetary changes were minor thereafter until 1905.

Collectors focusing on Mexico can devote much time to the study of the quasi-official issues of rebels during the periods of instability. They can look at hacienda tokens, which were issued by large farms or ranches that employed hundreds or thousands of people. Or they can pick whichever period in Mexico's history that fascinates them most. Whatever collectors of Mexico eventually settle on, they will find it rewarding.

# Where to write for more information

*World Coin News:* 700 E. State St., Iola, WI 54990.

# Better than map
## *Three mints have Web sites*

### By David C. Kranz

Here's a handy electronic means of finding North American coinage.

The U.S. Mint's Web site, www.usmint.gov, has been most active, making several limited, exclusively online offers. These have involved small bags of the nation's 50 states quarter issues as well as numismatic-philatelic covers and Sacagawea dollars. The U.S. Mint also sells its traditional annual products such as mint sets and proof sets on the Web, along with commemorative coins and other Mint sales catalog items.

In 2000, the U.S. Mint was waiving shipping charges on orders placed on its Web site, making ordering any other way a more costly alternative.

Canadian gold and silver, annual sets and commemoratives are available for purchase on the Royal Canadian Mint's site, www.mint.ca. Both French and English language versions of the RCM site are available. The site is set up for online orders (placed from Canada and the United States only), and the mint accepts Visa, Mastercard and American Express.

At the site of the Mexican Mint, www.cmonedam.com.mx/cmm, you can learn that it was the first mint in America, and that it has served without interruption since its inception by Spanish decree. The Mexican Mint site has Spanish and English language versions, with coinage history, current news, sales and promotions Web pages as well as technical information about the circulating coinage of Mexico. Telephone, fax, mail and e-mail information is provided for placing orders.

The fourth component of the North American continent, Greenland, has no mint within its borders and uses coins of Denmark in commerce. For more on these coins, see the *Standard Catalog of World Coins*, published by Krause Publications (www.krause.com).

For a quick introduction to these countries' latest coinage, their Web sites can't be beat.

# 7

# Caring for coins

## *How to store and preserve your collection*

**By Alan Herbert**

From the day you acquire your first collectible coin, you have to consider where and how to store your collection. Often a shoebox or a small cardboard or plastic box of some kind will be the principal storage point as you start to gather coins, even before they can be considered a collection. Sooner or later you will outgrow that first box and need to think seriously about what to do with your coins to protect and preserve them.

All too often security takes precedence over preservation. We're more worried that the kids will dip into the coins for candy or ice cream or that burglars will somehow learn about your "valuable" collection and pay a visit. It often isn't until years later when you suddenly notice that your once beautiful coins are now dingy and dull, with spots and fingerprints all over them, that preservation becomes a primary consideration.

Learning good storage habits should be one of the first things to do right along with acquiring those first coins. There are a multitude of storage products on the market that are intended for more or less specific situations, so learning which to use and how to use them is vital to the health of your collection. Most if not all of the products mentioned here should be available at your nearest coin shop or hobby store.

## Safe storage methods

The common impulse is to use what's available around the house; never allow that impulse to control your collecting. Plastic wrap, aluminum foil, cardboard, stationery envelopes, and other common household products are not designed for coin storage and never should be used for your collec-

Two-by-two cardboard holders are a common form of short-term, inexpensive coin storage.

Many dealers sell coins in 2-by-2 plastic "flips," but they should not be used for long-term storage.

tion. The same goes for soaps and cleansers found around the home.

There are specific products that have been designed, tested and found safe to use for coins. These are the media your collection deserves. The slight added expense will pay a thousand dividends years from now when you sell your collection or pass it on to your heirs.

The most common storage media are 2-inch by 2-inch cardboard holders with Mylar windows, 2-by-2 plastic "flips," coin tubes, hard-plastic holders, coin boards, and coin albums.

The 2-by-2 cardboard holders are the cheapest and most commonly used storage method. They are usually folded and stapled around the coin. They are intended for short-term general storage. They are not airtight or watertight, and staples driven too close to the coin can ruin it.

The 2-by-2 plastic flips come in good and bad varieties. The old, usually soft flips are made of plastics that contain polyvinylchloride, a chemical found in many plastics. Over time it breaks down into substances that put a green slime on your coins, which attacks the surface and ruins them.

The good flips are made of Mylar, but they are brittle and prone to splitting. So they should not be used to mail coins or when the coins are moved about frequently. Mylar flips, too, are for short-term general storage.

Coin tubes are often used for bulk storage, but there is a proper technique to placing the coins in the tube.

Often you will find coins in PVC holders when you buy them from a dealer. Remove them immediately and put them in some better storage medium.

Coin tubes come in clear and cloudy, or translucent, plastic. These are made of an inert plastic that will not harm your coins. Tubes are intended for bulk, medium- to long-term storage, with one caution: Use care when inserting the coins. Merely dropping one coin onto another in a tube can damage both coins. The best technique is to make a stack or pile of the coins, then slide the pile carefully into the tube while holding it at an angle.

Hard-plastic holders are the elite items for storing your collection. There are a number of varieties, some of which come in three parts that are screwed together. Some come in two pieces that fit together. Some of these are airtight and watertight. They are more expensive, but they deserve to be used for any really valuable coins in your collection.

Coins processed by the third-party grading services come in hard-plastic holders, most of which are at least semiairtight. The hard-plastic holders used by the U.S. Mint for proof sets since 1968 are not airtight, so coins should be watched carefully for signs of problems. In recent years these holders have been improved, but you should check your proof sets periodically.

Any stored coins should be checked regularly, at least twice a year. Check coins for signs of spotting or discoloration. Check the storage media for any signs of deterioration, rust, mildew, or other problems.

The older mint sets and proof sets — issued from 1955 to 1964 — come in soft-plastic envelopes that are not intended for long-term storage. Coins

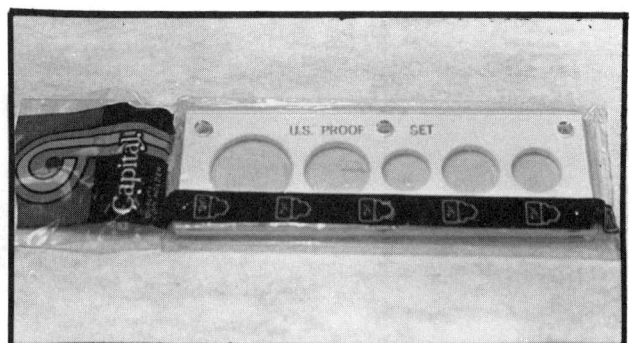

Hard-plastic holders
are the top of the line
in coin storage.

Coin folders are a low-
cost and attractive way
to store inexpensive cir-
culated coins.

in these envelopes should be put in better storage media for the long term. In recent years the Mint has switched to an inert, stiffer plastic for the mint sets. This plastic is safe.

A coin folder is frequently the first piece of equipment the beginning collector buys. It is simply a piece of cardboard with holes to hold the coins. The holder folds up for storage. It is intended for inexpensive circulated coins only.

They give no protection from contamination or fingerprints. Worn coins will often fall out of the holes, which leads some novice collectors to tape the coins in the album. This is another example of misuse of a household

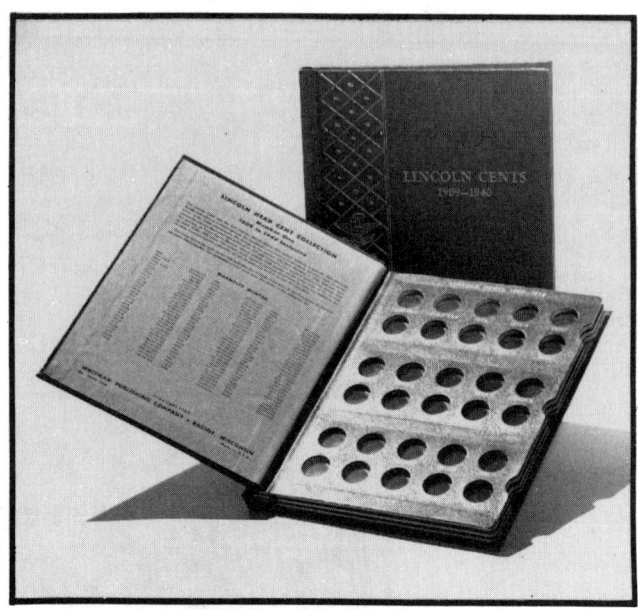

**Coin albums also provide attractive storage for inexpensive circulated coins.**

product; tape can permanently damage a coin's surface.

Pride of ownership and the desire to show off a collection are the moving forces behind the sale of thousands of coin albums. They should also be used for inexpensive circulated coins only, with a couple of exceptions.

Some albums are merely coin boards mounted between covers. Others have pages with sliding plastic strips on both sides of the page so both sides of the coin can be seen.

The open-face albums are subject to fingerprints and contamination. Sneezing on your coins can do as much damage as gouging them with a knife. The slides will rub on your coins, damaging the high points of the design over time. These two types of albums should never be used for expensive uncirculated or proof coins, although they are fine for circulated coins that you want to display.

Fairly new on the market are albums designed for coins in inert, airtight holders. This allows you to display your coins and still keep them safe from handling and contact with the atmosphere.

One more storage medium that deserves mention is the clear-plastic notebook page that has pockets for 2-by-2 holders or flips. Here again there are good and bad. Most old pocket sheets contain PVC, so they cannot be used to hold coins in non-airtight holders because the gases will migrate into the holders and damage the coins. The newer Mylar pages are brittle but will not generate damaging gases or liquids.

When buying storage media, make sure the dealer guarantees that his products are safe for coins. Many of the old albums, flips and pocket pages are still around, especially at flea markets. If you are in doubt, don't buy.

There are also thin, two-piece, inert plastic holders that many collectors use to protect coins put in flips or 2-by-2 cardboard holders, especially to protect them from moving about against the holder and getting scratched. They are virtually airtight, so they do offer some protection.

Coins need to be protected from burglars. A box under the bed or in the closet offers no protection. If you must keep coins at home, a good, fireproof safe is a must. Otherwise, rent a safe-deposit box at a bank, but read the fine print on your box contract to make sure a coin collection is covered.

Most homeowner's insurance policies will not cover a coin collection or will cover only a fraction of its value. Special riders are expensive, but if you keep most of your coins at the bank, this will cut costs. For details, consult your insurance agent. The American Numismatic Association also offers collection insurance.

Where to store coins is often a problem. The commonest solution is to put them in the attic or basement. Those are the two worst places for your collection. Attics are notoriously hot. Heat can damage almost any storage media, and if there is the slightest hint of PVC, you've got trouble.

Basements are equally bad. They can flood, and humidity is high. Mildew can attack holders and other material stored with your coins.

So what's left? Ideally coins should be treated like a family member. They should be stored in some part of the house where temperature and humidity are relatively constant year round. If it's comfortable for you, it's probably much more comfortable for your coins than the basement or attic.

Protecting coins from humidity is always a good idea, even in areas where it is not a major health problem. For your coins, too much dampness can become a serious problem, often before you realize it. A good solution is to get several good-sized packets of silica gel and store them with your coins in your safe or a container of some kind that will isolate them from the general climate in the home.

## To clean or not to clean

Before you store your coins, you should be aware that coins are like dishes: They should never be put away dirty. Ah, but you've probably already heard or read that you should never clean a coin. If you haven't, I'll say it now: Never clean a coin.

OK, so there are exceptions, but be careful of those exceptions and for good reason. Ignoring the exceptions can be excruciatingly and embarassingly expensive.

Coins get dirty, just like anything else. The impulse is to shine them up — polish them to a brilliance that will dazzle the viewer. If you've already succumbed to the temptation to clean even a single coin, stand up, kick yourself, then sit back down and read on. The one exception is loose dirt, grease, oil, or something similar, and there are even exceptions to that rule.

Use a neutral solvent to dissolve the grease and oils that usually coat uncirculated coins as they come from the mint. Follow the instructions on the container exactly, and if the directions say to use the product outdoors, they mean it.

For circulated coins, lighter fluid will often dissolve the accumulated "gunk" that sticks to them, but I don't recommend it for uncirculated coins, especially copper alloy coins. Air dry the coins; don't rub or wipe them. Even the softest cloth or paper towel can pick up sharp-edged particles that will ruin a coin's surface. Proof coins are clean when they are packaged, so this should not be necessary and should be done only as a last resort if they have somehow picked up oil in handling.

Using dips, household cleansers, metal polish, and even soap can permanently damage a coin. Avoid acid-based cleaners at all costs. They work by eating away the coin's surface to remove the embedded dirt or discoloration. Cleaning a coin with any of these products will sharply reduce its collectible value. To put it simply, collectors do not want cleaned coins, so they are heavily discounted.

One of the reasons for this is that once a coin has been cleaned, it will discolor much more quickly, requiring fresh cleaning. Each time it is cleaned, the surface is further dulled, reducing the coin's appeal and reducing its value.

Obviously this advice applies especially to uncirculated and proof coins, but it applies to any coin that is or has the potential to become valuable. But if you clean it, its career ends right there.

There are products specifically designed for removing the green PVC slime from coins. They do not contain acid, so they are safe. They will stop but cannot reverse the damage that the PVC has already done to the coin. Read the label, and use exactly as directed.

I frequently am asked about ultrasonic cleaners. They fall under the same heading as the various cleaning products I've described. In other words, the apparatus should not be used for uncirculated, proof, or other valuable coins. If you do use one, do one coin at a time so there is no chance for the vibration to rub two coins together. Change or filter the cleaning solution frequently to keep abrasive particles from coming in contact with the vibrating coin.

Like anything else, cleaning can be carried to an extreme, so I'll give you one horror story of just such a mistake: Years ago I had a collector fly several hundred miles to bring his collection for me to sell for him. When he laid out the coins on the table, I was shocked to discover that the hundreds of coins had all been harshly cleaned.

When I questioned him he calmly recounted that he had decided that the coins needed cleaning, so he dumped them all into a rock tumbler and left it on for several hours. It ruined all his coins, reducing them to face value. With his passion for cleanliness he had destroyed several thousand dollars worth of collectible value, plus air fare, a rental car, and a motel bill.

The key to a long-term collection that might appreciate in value is to learn what not to do to your coins and what care they need to survive years of waiting in the wings. Learning to protect your coins with the best available storage methods and media is a key first step toward enjoying your collection for years to come.

## Where to write for more information

**American Numismatic Association:** 818 N. Cascade Ave., Colorado Springs, CO 80903-3279. Web address is http://www.money.org

# 8

# Join the club

## *Coin collecting has lots of organizations*

**By David C. Harper**

More than 150 years ago, Alexis de Tocqueville noted in his *Democracy in America* the penchant of people in the United States to create and voluntarily join public groups for a multitude of purposes. This urge to join carries over into coin collecting.

Whether it be a national organization or local coin club, groups have been organized in the United States, Canada and Mexico to help collectors enhance their hobby knowledge and enjoyment. They serve as clearinghouses for new information, maintain libraries, and bring collectors together in meetings to share their hobby experiences with each other. Clubs are so well defined that collectors can find one to serve any activity level and any degree of personal interaction with other collectors.

At the extreme, you can join a national organization by mail, spend a hobby lifetime utilizing its services, and yet never leave the privacy and comfort of home. At the other end, some areas offer such a multitude of clubs that you can find a meeting to attend on many nights of the week.

There are many ways to find a club. Some hobbyists inquire at the local coin shop to identify the organization nearest them. *Numismatic News* publishes news about clubs. Also, watch your local newspaper for listings of community events.

How does a collector match his needs with an appropriate club? The closest thing to a one-stop shopping place for an answer is the American Numismatic Association.

It is the United States' national coin-collecting organization and was granted a perpetual charter by Congress with a mission of education. It can be reached at 818 N. Cascade Ave., Colorado Springs, CO 80903-3279. It offers a wide array of personal hobby services, and its benefits cross national boundaries. In fact, when it was founded in 1891, it was expected that Canadians and Mexicans would be just as likely to join as U.S. citizens.

The most obvious benefit to an ANA member is a subscription to *The Numismatist*, the association's monthly magazine. In it you find news, historical features, membership information, and advertisements placed by dealers who are ready to fill every collector's want list.

More than 30,000 titles are available in the ANA library, and you don't have to walk into the ANA building to check them out. Any member anywhere can do that by mail. The ANA has called upon renowned numismatic authorities to create a correspondence course, which distills into 29 separate readings information that has taken many people a lifetime to learn. There are ANA educational seminars held in Colorado Springs and other sites across the United States.

The ANA sponsors two conventions annually. The early spring convention is usually held in March at locations across the country, selected and announced well in advance. The summer convention, which is so huge that it's billed as the "World's Fair of Money," is a tradition that dates back almost to the organization's founding.

Members also are offered a variety of optional services, ranging from coin-collection insurance to credit cards and car rental discounts. And if you do go to Colorado Springs, the ANA maintains its Money Museum at its headquarters. In it are some of the rarest and most famous coins in history.

Joining the ANA is easy. The membership fee is $39 the first year and $33 thereafter. Members over 65 years old get a $4 discount, and junior members (those under 18) are charged $15.

Beyond simply belonging to the ANA, though, are the doors that open to members. If you want to find a regional, state or local club, you can get help from the ANA. The important thing to remember is that you set your own level of involvement. If your profession is so hectic that you don't need another meeting to go to, the ANA is the place for you. If your hours are so regular that joining in the fun and camaraderie of a local club is just what you are looking for, the ANA can help you find that, too.

And just because the American Numismatic Association has "American" in its name, it doesn't mean that members are focused only on U.S. coins. Far from it. It is more accurate to say that if a coin was struck at any time anywhere in the world in the last 2,600 years, there are ANA members who collect it.

The ANA, if it connotes any exclusivity at all, is basically a regional designation based on where its members live. The farther one gets from the United States, the longer correspondence takes and the greater the possibility of a language barrier between the ANA staff and a potential member. It is therefore not surprising to find that 27,000 members are predominantly located in the United States.

The Canadian Numismatic Association dates to 1950. It publishes *The Canadian Numismatic Journal*, published 11 times a year, and it also spon-

sors an annual convention. Membership is considerably smaller than the
ANA's, in line with the population difference between the United States
and Canada. Membership fee is $33 a year. The mailing address is Exec-
utive Secretary, Canadian Numismatic Association, P.O. Box 226, Barric,
Ontario L4M 4T2, Canada.

The Sociedad Numismatica de Mexico A.C. was established in 1952.
Basically, it oversees an annual convention in Mexico City. It may be
contacted through its U.S. representative at 102 E. Main St., Homer, MI
49245. A related group at the same address is the U.S. Mexican Numismatic Society.

That covers the national hobby umbrella groups. There are many more
organizations of a national character that have somewhat narrower
poses. Among these is the American Numismatic Society in New York
City. It is older than the ANA, having been established in 1858. It also
maintains a superb museum of U.S. and world coins, and a world-class
library. Emphasis in the ANS is on scholarly research.

Numismatics would be nothing if it were not for its research pioneers. If
that is what appeals to you, you can write the ANS at Broadway and 155th
St., New York, NY 10032, for information regarding its structure and various classes of membership.

Other national organizations focus on specific collectible areas, such as
Seated Liberty coinage or tokens and medals. These are popular and active.
Many are member organizations of the ANA and hold meetings in con-
junction with the ANA's conventions.

Coin dealers have organizations of their own. The Professional Numismatists Guild Inc. maintains high standards of membership qualification and
conduct. Members are a who's who of the commercial sector of the hobby.
All are ready to serve you in furthering your collecting goals. For a membership roster, contact Robert Brueggeman, Executive Director, 3950 Concor-
dia Lane, Fallbrook, CA 92028.

This brief review merely puts you on the threshold of the organized
numismatic world. It is up to you to open that door or walk away. Over the
years, many collectors have found membership to be the most rewarding
aspect of the hobby. They have benefited from working with others with a
common interest to further their own knowledge and advance their collecting goals in an environment of mutual support and friendship.

# 9

# Bag quarter limit
## *State program draws nation into hunt*

### By David C. Kranz

As the U.S. Mint's 50-state quarter program enters its fourth year in 2002, Americans in great numbers continue to amass hoards of the different states' circulating representatives. They collect them in boards. They collect them in books. In bags. In pre-packaged plastic sets. A lot of people are buying the quarters they want from the Mint or from coin dealers, and many more are getting them right out of their pocket change. Are you one of them?

Even a disinterested appraisal must recognize the utter success of the state quarter program to date – look at how everybody you talk to knows about the program and which images represent each state. Even the most cynical have taken a second look at their change. The more enthusiastic have mounds of quarters resting on their dresser tops.

Not all state quarters are distributed equally, however. East Coast collectors find far more Philadelphia strikes than Denvers, and vice versa out West. The Mint produces coins to meet the demand anticipated by the Federal Reserve. Each quarter is in production for 10 weeks. Where the coins go after that depends on what areas of the country need them for commerce. No attempts are made to spread each state's quarter evenly over the nation.

That's why collectors turn to dealers for assistance. Dealers seek out quantities of each state design and mintmark, then offer them to collectors who might not encounter the coins otherwise. Naturally, dealers charge fees for the service, basing their fees on the supply of and demand for specific pieces. These do vary.

While at this point no one considers any of the circulating state quarters rare – it's hard to say that anything produced in quantities of 300 million and higher is rare – some do have scarcity value. And, as time passes the chances of finding high-quality examples of earlier issues in

## State quarter mintages:

### 1999:

| | |
|---|---|
| **Delaware-P:** | 373,400,000 |
| **Delaware-D:** | 401,424,000 |
| **Pennsylvania-P:** | 349,000,000 |
| **Pennsylvania-D:** | 358,332,000 |
| **New Jersey-P:** | 363,200,000 |
| **New Jersey-D:** | 299,028,000 |
| **Georgia-P:** | 451,188,000 |
| **Georgia-D:** | 488,744,000 |
| **Connecticut-P:** | 688,744,000 |
| **Connecticut-D:** | 657,880,000 |

### 2000:

| | |
|---|---|
| **Massachusetts-P:** | 628,600,000 |
| **Massachusetts-D:** | 535,184,000 |
| **Maryland-P:** | 678,200,000 |
| **Maryland-D:** | 556,532,000 |
| **South Carolina-P:** | 742,756,000 |
| **South Carolina-D:** | 566,208,000 |
| **New Hampshire-P:** | 673,040,000 |
| **New Hampshire-D:** | 495,976,000 |
| **Virginia-P:** | 943,000,000 |
| **Virginia-D:** | 651,616,000 |

### 2001:

| | |
|---|---|
| **New York-P:** | 655,400,000 |
| **New York-D:** | 619,640,000 |

At the time this was written, mintage figures for additional state quarters were unavailable from the U.S. Mint.

circulation decrease. These facts contribute to the price premiums charged by dealers for certain of the quarters.

Immediately heading to the top of the profit potential list are the first three issues of the program: Delaware, Pennsylvania and New Jersey. These caught many established collectors off guard, as few expected them to realize price gains. By the time realization hit, the program had moved on.

Dealers offering the most common quarters at about 50 cents apiece were charging about $2 for a single Pennsylvania quarter as this was written. Delawares came in at $1.75, while the New Jerseys were valued differently based on mintmark, the "P" at $1.25 and the "D" at $1.50. When offered by the 40-coin roll with $10 face value, the Pennsylvania was garnering nearly $60, Delaware $53, New Jersey "P" $22 and "D" $42. By the 4,000-coin bag, with $1,000 face value, Pennsylvania was over $5,000, Delaware over $4,000, New Jersey "P" about $2,000 and "D" about $3,750.

Even the fourth and fifth quarters of the program were beginning to rate premiums, but not as high as the first three. Excluding the first three, the retail prices appear to be determined by the passage-of-time factor and the raw mintages, which have thus far been increasing. By number four, Georgia, issued in August 1999, circulation mintages were well over 400 million for each mint. The mintage norm since then has been closer to 600 million.

As single coins, all of the 2000-dated quarters – Massachusetts, Maryland, South Carolina, New Hampshire and Virginia – have been available from dealers at minimal mark-up over face value. Though all of the 2001s had not been issued at the time of writing, the expectation was that they,

**The Commission of Fine Arts favored these state designs for the five 2002 quarters: in order of introduction, Tennessee, Ohio, Louisiana, Indiana and Mississippi. Final design selections may differ.**

too, would be available at similar low mark-ups. Collectors will be watching these as well as the 1999s that have already seen increases for any surprises as the program continues. Time will tell.

It must be noted that quarters are available in packaged forms, too. Annual proof sets and mint sets are available, and the Mint has been offering 100-coin and 1,000-coin bags through online-only, limited-time sales at its Web site, www.usmint.gov.

During 2002, five new state quarters are scheduled for issue: Tennessee, Ohio, Louisiana, Indiana, Mississippi, issued in the order the states joined the Union. In 2003, look forward to five more as the 10-year program reaches its halfway point: Illinois, Alabama, Maine, Missouri and Arkansas.

If your state's quarter is a ways off yet, you can still have some fun with it. Get involved in the design selection process through your governor's office. Find out whether an individual or a committee will select designs. Will it involve a contest? Suggest what you think should represent your state on a national scale. Will this look good on a coin? Try your hand at a design or two. If your state's quarter is one of the final 25 in the sequence, don't be surprised if little has been decided at this point.

Many questions remain. When the program ends, how will people look at the 50-state quarters? The end will come six years from now, unless additional quarters are appended to honor Washington, D.C., and some U.S. possessions. How will the quarters be collected? What will people say about them in 50 years? 100? How will they be valued?

Whether quarter hunters bag all 50 states' examples or simply watch them pass through circulation, we can all learn as we have fun.

# 10

# Hot buys for 2002
## *Plan ahead to reap the benefits*

**By David C. Harper**

Buying a coin that will be a sure-fire winner that jumps in value after the purchase is every collector's dream. On a few occasions, that dream is fulfilled spectacularly. On others, it isn't. That makes every coin purchased a little bit like a lottery ticket that never expires and never becomes completely worthless.

Unlike a lottery, hobbyists can increase the favorable odds by focusing on a few fundamental rules.

1. Collectors do better than speculators. Over many years, collectors who put sets together have done much better financially than individuals who try to buy hot coins when everybody else wants them. So improve your own odds by collecting a set of what you like, whether it be Seated Liberty dimes or Barber quarters. The keys here are logical organization and selling the result as a set or as a lifetime collection.

2. Buy coins in the best condition you can afford. This doesn't mean you have to own the finest-known example of every piece or you can't make money, but the hobby does tend to reward coins in top grades with much better price increases over time.

3. Hold for the long term. Unless you are a professional dealer, or at least a recognized vest-pocket dealer on the bourse floor, the odds are you will pay retail prices for coins. That mark-up between wholesale and retail prices has to be made up somehow. If you buy a coin today and sell it next week, the odds are you can't overcome that handicap. Holding coins over the long term helps.

4. Buy a proven rarity. Collectors can get into arguments about what is rare or just scarce, but what they agree on are the keys to various series.

**Whether the 1909-S VDB cent will rise dramatically in the future cannot be accurately forecast. What can be predicted is that it will remain the key to the Lincoln cent series. Always buy the keys first.**

The 1909-S VDB is the key Lincoln cent. The 1932-D and 1932-S quarters are the keys to the Washington set. Use this knowledge of key dates and buy them first. When certain series enter the popularity spotlight, the keys tend to rise the most. With the centennial of the Lincoln cent coming up in 2009, it is reasonable to assume that this series will enjoy an increase in popularity. Buy before this occurs. Washington quarters have been enjoying increased values since the state quarter program began in 1999. Because the state quarter program runs at least 10 years and possibly 11, it might be reasonable to expect further gains.

Even by following these rules, you can still miss the mark. Take the 1950-D nickel. It is the key coin of the Jefferson series. Unfortunately, the whole series has lost popularity and its price has dropped from its 1964 peak of about $25, to a current $6.50 in MS-60 or $9 in MS-65. Someday Jeffersons might be in vogue, but holders have had a very long wait. The same thing might happen with the 1909-S VDB, the 1932-D and 1932-S quarters, or the coin you pick by using the rules. Collectors, however, are nothing if not hopeful, so get out there and collect. Perhaps you will fulfill the dream to buy a big winner.

**Washington quarters have been in the spotlight since the beginning of the state quarter series in 1999. Prices of better dates have risen as a consequence. Here, left to right, are the keys, the 1932-D (obverse and reverse) and 1932-S (reverse).**

# 11

# Sac's second year
## *Don't miss a 'golden' opportunity*
### By Joe Shead

Did you ever notice how when the home team is winning, everyone's a fan? It's not hard to jump on the bandwagon, but throw in a couple losses, or a few bad seasons and the excitement, along with the number of fans, wanes. Should the team find itself at the bottom of the league standings, the fair-weather fans are gone, and all but the most ardent supporters remain.

The same holds true in coin collecting. Remember the Eisenhower dollar? Seemingly everyone wanted an example of this coin when it first came out in 1971, especially a silver proof. As a result, 4,265,234 silver proofs were struck at the San Francisco Mint that year. But after the dazzle of a new coin – in fact, the first U.S. dollar coin issued in 36 years – wore off, people lost interest. That fact is reflected in a reduced second-year silver proof mintage of 1,811,631 pieces. The third year of issue saw another decrease to 1,005,617 silver proofs.  What that means is there are an awful lot of collectors out there wishing they had stuck with the silver Ike after the glory faded, as the current Proof-65 price of the 1971-S Eisenhower $1 silver proof is $7, below its issue price of $10, as is the 1972-S, but the 1973-S silver proof has jumped to $30.

Though the price jump hasn't been as extreme, the same thing happened to the Susan B. Anthony dollar. The initial Philadelphia mintage in 1979 was 360,222,000 pieces. That number plunged to 27,610,000 dollars in 1980 and dropped still further to 3 million pieces in 1981. Both the Denver and San Francisco mints followed the same pattern.

Look at the mintage figures of many other denominations and types through the years, and you'll see that this pattern is nothing new. And that brings us to the Sacagawea dollar.

The U.S. Mint spent a whopping $40 million promoting the Sacagawea dollar in 2000. After the SBA dollar got the cold shoulder from the Ameri-

# Unique luster
*Mint errors can bring big money*

**By Ray Sidman**

Just in case numismatics was growing too predictable or mundane, what with the U.S. Mint's 50-state quarter program and the revamped modern commemorative coin program providing winds of change in recent years, there appears to be another new arena for collectors: error coins. Rather, perhaps this is not a "new" arena, but instead one that has rapidly changed since mid-2000, making for a hive of new possibilities and new collectors.

In all seriousness, the modern commemorative programs – assisted by the Citizens Commemorative Coin Advisory Committee – and particularly the state quarter program, which statistics say has brought new blood into numismatics by the millions, have become a serious source of growth for the hobby. But a lot of attention has likewise gone to a hot topic over the last two years or so: mint errors.

Mint errors do happen on a regular basis. Every year at least a few minor ones slip past the Mint's watching eye. Considering the Mint produced more than 28 billion coins in 2000 – the most it ever has produced in a single calendar year – no one should be surprised at the heightened error quantity. Teamed with the introduction of the Saca-gawea dollar, the resulting hype has kept the hobby abuzz.

However, the number of new error types along with the number of those new types surfacing has raised issues still unanswered. The arrest and sentencing of a Philadelphia Mint employee in late 2000, along with illicit Denver Mint employee activities has the collecting public ponder-ing which coins are legitimate errors and which are clandestine creations for cast.

**Early mintage figures indicate that production of the 2001 Sacagawea dolla be much lower than the 2000 mintage. This will benefit collectors who conti acquire each date after the initial excitement of the new dollar coin wears**

can public a generation ago, the Mint hoped that the Sac dollar wo accepted. Collectors scarfed up coins and even non-collectors tucked a few just to have the first type in the latest dollar-coin series. I 1,286,056,000 golden dollars were produced in 2000. A mintage large, coupled with the fact that a large number of people saved coins, and it doesn't appear that the 2000 Sacagawea dollar will b coin to have in 20 years.

But could the 2001 Sacagawea dollar be it?

Through March 2001, the total production of 2001-dated Sacag dollars was 96,969,500 coins. Projecting that number for the rest o year, the Mint is on pace to produce fewer than 400 million coins – cry from the nearly 1.3 billion produced in 2000.

And the plot thickens. Shh! Do you hear that? Whereas in 2000 e one was talking about the new dollar, now there is silence. This well for collectors. Non-collectors took their coins. Saving the first ye a type coin makes sense if you're a non-collector, as it's the start o series. But non-collectors don't know about the trend of reduced min in a coin's succeeding years of issue. Silver proof Ike dollar colle reaped the benefits in that coin's third year of issue. Many non-colle won't bother to save the 2001 or 2002 golden dollars or proof examp those coins because there's seemingly nothing special about them. some coin collectors will lose interest in the Sac dollar's sophomore For the die-hard collector, the combination of declining interest lower mintage becomes a "golden" opportunity.

Experienced collectors won't mind one bit if people forget to sa succeeding dates in the Sacagawea-dollar series. Instead, they'll q continue to pull each date while they assemble their collections.

There's no guarantee that the 2001 Sacagawea dollar will be t date in the series, but so far there's every indication that it wil better date than the 2000 golden dollars. Will the mintage conti drop, and what will the real key dates be? We'll just have to wait an

**The strike heard round the hobby: the first Sacagawea dollar/Washington quarter mule discovered by Frank Wallis of Mountain Home, Ark., and certified by Numismatic Guaranty Corporation was the advent of a flurry of error-related activity.**

The mother of all 2000 coin errors, as they could be called, is the Sacagawea dollar/Washington quarter mule. A mule is a coin made with two dies never meant to be paired with each other. In this case, it is a quarter obverse die paired with a dollar reverse die.

To date, seven have been found.

Frank Wallis, a Mountain Home, Ark., resident, reported the first of them in June 2000. A few weeks later, a second turned up. Another week passed before the third one appeared. The seventh hit headlines in January 2001.

This begs the question: What are these – and other error varieties – worth? The answer is a classic "good news/bad news" dichotomy.

What makes the Sacagawea/Washington mules so amazing is that they are a double-denomination error. Theoretically, this means that someone placed mismatched dies together and struck them. Given today's Mint security measures, this should be impossible. But it happened.

Many individuals believe the mules and other "error" coins were intentionally made. This does not mean the Mint is directly responsible. The blame has been pointed at a few rogue employees out for self gain.

When the mule coins hit the market, the result was electrifying. Various grading services graded one as Mint State-64, two as MS-67 and four as MS-66. Moreover, three die pairings have been identified to date, pointing out that it was more than a simple one-time mix-up.

This 1999 cent muled with a dime surfaced in late August 2000, one of several pieces adding to the error frenzy.

The first one to sell – which was the second found – went for $41,395 in July 2000. The top seller was the sixth mule, which brought $50,000. The seventh realized close to that at $48,000. Oddly enough, the first mule found was sold for a much lower amount, $29,900.

These are nice sums, given that at least one was found in circulation, thus costing the original owner merely face value.

Here's the flip side to the "how much is it worth?" excitement: mint errors produced unofficially might end up being worth nothing.

The Mint and the U.S. Secret Service, the guardians against counterfeits and false error coins, could determine that an error piece was intentionally made. That coin is thus illegal, and they have the right to confiscate it without compensation. Losing a five-figure investment is a kick in the gut for almost anyone.

The ex-Philadelphia Mint employee was charged with removing and selling error coins from that location from December 1998 until March 2000. Besides the approximately $80,000 he made (and consequently had confiscated) from sales of the errors, he received an $80,000 fine and six months jail time followed by the same length of home detention.

Fortunately for the mule buyers, though a Mint employee was fired, his handiwork was allowed to pass into hobby hands and headlines. They will not be confiscated.

Other types of errors include a virtual plethora of state quarters struck oddly. Some have been reported struck on other state quarters (prompting another cry of "that's not theoretically possible" from knowledgeable numismatists) and on Sacagawea blanks. A Maryland quarter struck on a Sacagawea planchet amassed a final bid of $23,100 on eBay in late August 2000.

Furthermore, quarters and dollars were not alone in the rush. Other denomination errors surfaced as well. In August 2000, a 1999 cent that had been muled with a dime made headlines. This, of course, added to the buzz surrounding error coinage.

One of the more bizarre and talked about pieces was the one-of-a-kind 1999-W George Washington $5 commemorative struck on a dime planchet.

Errors have rarely had so much publicity. Strong auction results show that collectors have noticed and are excited by them, and that's good news for anyone seeking to spread out their numismatic interests.

# 13

# Web spreads

## *Internet growth energizes buying, selling*

### By Ray Sidman

The Internet has taken the world to a whole new level. In turn, many retailers have taken to the so-called 'Net. This includes numismatic dealers who have found a new world to savor in e-business.

Not only are existing organizations repositioning themselves for online purposes, new businesses, clubs, and groups are forming solely online for the specific purpose of capitalizing on Web exposure. What was once innovation is now an institution.

Experienced collectors can practice their art on the Web while bringing new faces into the hobby. Budding numismatists can buy, learn and grow. On the following pages are some numismatic business sites.

A-Mark Precious Metals
*www.amark.com*
Abbott's Corporation
*www.abbottscorp.com*
Advantage Associates
*www.advantagecoin.com*
Albanese Rare Coins
*www.coinace.com*
American Gold Exchange
*www.amergold.com*
American Heritage Mint
*www.americanheritageonline.com*
ANACS
*www.anacs.com*
Andale
*www.andale.com*
Joel Anderson
*www.joelscoins.com*
Antique Carta
*www.antiquecarta.com*
Aspen Coins
*www.aspencoins.com*

Aspen Park Rare Coins
*www.aprci.com*
ATSnotes.com
*www.atsnotes.com*
Austin Rare Coins
*www.austincoins.com*
Lois & Don Bailey Numismatic
   Services
*www.donbailey-mexico.com*
BankNote1 Currency
*www.banknote1.com*
Alexander Basok
*www.rustypennies.com*
Tim Bauer Rare Coins
*www.timbauer.com*
Harlan J. Berk, Ltd.
*www.harlanjberk.com*
Allen G. Berman
*www.bermania.com*
BidXS.com
*www.bidxs.com*
Blanchard and Company
*www.blanchardonline.com*

Bowers and Merena Galleries
*www.bowersandmerena.com*
Brooklyn Gallery Coins & Stamps
*www.brooklyngallery.com*
BuyCoin.com
*www.buycoin.com*
Byers Numismatic Corporation
*www.byersnc.com*
C & D Gale
*www.dol.net / ~cdgale*
California Numismatic Investments
*www.golddealer.com*
Camco Coins
*www.camcocoin.com*
Cameo CC
*www.cameocc.com*
Canadian Coinoisseur
*www.coinoisseur.com*
Capital Collectors Plastics
*www.capitalplastics.com / nnn*
Carlisle Development
*www.carlisledevelopment.com*
Carolina Gold & Silver
*www.carolinacoin.com*
CDA Bullion
*www.cdabullion.com*
Tom Cederlind
*www.tomcederlind.com*
Cellar Coin & Jewelry
*www.cellarcoin.com*
Centerville Coin & Jewelry
*www.centercoin.com*
Certified Coin Auction
*www.cce-auction.com*
CH Coins
*www.chcoins.com*
Cheap Slab Store
*www.cheapslabs.com*
Chicago Coin Company
*www.chicagocoin.com*
Chicago Numismatic Foundation
*www.us-rarecoins.com*
Chinese Cash Coins
*www.cashcoin.homepage.com*
Civil War Tokens
*www.civilwartokens.com*
Classical Numismatic Group
*www.historicalcoins.com*
Cline's Rare Coins
*www.slqs.com*
Coast to Coast Coins
*www.coastcoin.com*
Coincraft
*www.coincraft.com*
CoinCrazy.com
*www.coincrazy.com*
Coin Dealer Newsletter
*www.greysheet.com*
CoinFacts.com
*www.coinfacts.com*

Coin Gallery Online
*www.coin-gallery.com*
CoinIndex.com
*www.CoinIndex.com*
Coin Shop
*www.coin-shop.com*
Coins International
*www.coinsinternational.com*
Coins, Jewelry & Collectibles
*www.monexclub.com*
CoinsOfTheUSA.com
*www.coinsoftheusa.com*
CoinsWanted.com
*www.coinswanted.com*
Coin Webstore
*www.coinwebstore.com*
Coinwire.com
*www.coinwire.com*
CoinZone.com
*www.coinzone.com*
Collector Online
*www.collectoronline.com*
Collectors Universe
*www.collectorsuniverse.com*
Compu-Quote
*www.compu-quote.net*
Continental Coin Corporation
*www.continentalcorp.com*
Corrosion Free Coin Supply, LLC
*www.coinshield.com*
Cybercoins
*www.cybercoins.net*
Chuck D'Ambra Coins
*www.telesphere.com / ts / coins*
Dallas Gold & Silver Exchange
*www.dgse.com*
David Hall's Rare Coins
*www.davidhall.com*
Denly's of Boston
*www.denlys.com*
Dibit.com
*www.dibit.com*
Michael Dixon Rare Coins
*www.geocities.com / michaeldixon*
Gary Duskie Rare Coins
*www.coinmall.com / duskie*
E-Bid
*www.ebid.com.au*
Eagle Coin Holders
*www.eaglecoinholders.com*
Eagle Eye Rare Coins
*www.indiancent.com*
Eagle Numismatics
*www.coinmaven.com*
Early American History Auctions
*www.earlyamerican.com*
Ellesmere Numismatics
*www.ellesmerecoin.com*
Jean Elsen s.a.
*www.elsen.be*

Elusive Spondulix
*www.rarecoin.com*
Steve Estes, P.N., Inc.
*www.steveestes.com*
Euro Coins International
*www.eurocollections.com*
eWanted
*www.ewanted.com*
Steve Eyer
*www.eyersworld.com*
Florida Coin & Jewelry
*www.floridacoin.com*
The Franklin Mint
*www.franklinmint.com*
Quentin Freres
*www.quentinfreres.com*
Gaithersburg Coin Exchange, Inc.
*www.gaithersburgcoin.com*
Gallery Mint Museum
*www.coin-gallery.com / gmm*
Gatewest Coin Ltd.
*www.gatewestcoin.com*
Ronald J. Gillio
*www.gillio.com*
Ira & Larry Goldberg Coins &
    Collectibles
*www.goldbergcoins.com*
Great Lakes Coin Company
*www.greatlakescoin.com*
Ken Hallenbeck Coin Gallery
*www.hallenbeck-coins.com*
Hancock & Harwell
*www.raregold.com*
H.E. Harris & Co.
*www.heharris.com*
Heritage Numismatic Auctions
*www.heritagecoin.com*
*www.currencyauction.com*
Hans W. Hercher Muenzen GmbH
*www.herchercoins.com*
Jeffrey Hoare Auction
*www.jeffreyhoare.on.ca*
Hobby Coin Exchange
*www.hobbycoinexchange.com*
Richard Hokanson Rare Coin Invest-
    ments
*www.hokanson-coins.com*
Fred Holabird Americana
*www.holabird.org*
House of Coins
*www.dsuper.net / ~houscoin*
Hudson Rare Coins, Inc.
*www.hudsonrarecoins.com*
Independent Coin Grading Company
*www.icgcoin.com*
International Coins & Currency
*www.iccoin.com*
iWant.com
*www.iwant.com*
J & J Coins
*www.jjcoins.com*

J & M Coin
*www.jandm.com*
Eric Jackson
*www.ericjackson.com*
Jake's Marketplace
*www.jakesmp.com*
Jamestown Stamp Company
*www.jamestownstamp.com*
Jefferson Coin & Bullion
*www.jeffinc.com*
Peter Jencius
*www.vaticancoins.com*
Glen Johnson Rare U.S. Currency
*www.uspapermoney.com*
Peter Johnson Currency
*www.pjcurrency.com*
Kagin's
*www.kagins.com*
The Kanawha Coin Shop
*www.kanawhacoin.com*
Kelgory Coin and Currency
*www.kelgory.com*
Don C. Kelly
*www.donckelly.com*
Jeff Kierstead Rare Coins
*www.jkrarecoin.com*
King of Carson City
*www.carsoncityking.com*
Kitco
*www.kitco.com*
Knight Coin
*www.knightcoin.com*
Lyn Knight Currency Auctions
*www.lynknight.com*
George Frederick Kolbe
*www.numislit.com*
Bill Kracov
*www.choiceworldbanknotes.com*
Krause Publications
*www.krause.com*
Tim Kyzivat
*www.kyzivatcurrency.com*
George LaBarre Galleries
*www.glabarre.com*
Harry Laibstain Rare Coins
*www.hlrc.com*
David Lawrence Rare Coins
*www.davidlawrence.com*
Legend Numismatics
*www.legendcoin.com*
Julian M. Leidman
*www.juliancoin.com*
Bret Leifer Numismatics
*www.coinguy.com*
Liberty Mint
*www.libertymint.com*
Limited Editions Inc.
*www.limitededitionsinc.org*
Littleton Coin Company
*www.littletoncoin.com*

Lone Star Coins & Collectibles
*www.lonestarcoins.com*
Long Beach Coin & Stamp Expo
*www.longbeachshow.com*
Louisiana Gold & Gems
*www.louisianagold.com*
L.S.C.O.A. Barry Ciociola
*www.iwannagetitnow.com*
Malter Galleries
*www.maltergalleries.com*
Marc One Numismatics
*www.marconenumismatics.com*
Greg Manning Auctions
*www.gregmanning.com*
Mayer's Mint GmbH Germany
*www.mayermint.com*
McKinn's Coins
*www.mckinn.com*
McQueeney Coins
*www.mcqueeneycoins.com*
Mietens & Partner
*www.mietens.de*
Minneapolis Gold, Silver and Numismatic Services, Inc.
*www.coinmarket.com*
Mintmark Numismatics
*www.mintmark.com*
Money-Changers
*www.home.earthlink.net / ~money-changer / index.html*
Colin Narbeth & Son
*www.colin-narbeth.com*
National Gold Exchange
*www.ngegold.com*
New World Rarities
*www.nwrarities.com*
North American Trading
*www.natcoin.com*
Northeast Numismatics
*www.northeastcoin.com*
*www.foreigncoin.com*
Numismatic Assets
*www.numismaticassets.com*
Numismatic Guaranty Corporation of America
*www.ngccoin.com*
Numismatic Wholesalers
*www.numismaticwholesalers.com*
NumisMedia
*www.numismedia.com*
Numis-Phil Pte. Ltd.
*www.worldcurrency.com*
Old Coin Shop
*www.oldcoinshop.com*
Original Weather Company
*www.weathercoin.com*
Pacific Atlantic Coin Company
*www.pacoin.com*
Pandaamerica
*www.pandaamerica.com*

Paradise Coin & Gift
*www.paradisecoin.com*
Park Avenue Numismatics
*www.parkavenumis.com*
Jay Parrino's The Mint LLC
*www.jp-themint.com*
PCI Coin Grading Services
*www.chattanooga.net / pci*
Penny Farmer
*www.pennyfarmer.com*
Perth Numismatics
*www.perthmoney.com*
Pinnacle Rarities
*www.pinnaclerarities.com*
Tony Pisciotta
*www.banknotesoftheworld.com*
Pobjoy Mint
*www.pobjoy.com*
Ponterio & Associates
*www.ponterio.com*
Ken Potter
*koinpro.tripod.com*
PQ Rarities
*www.pqgold.com*
Professional Coin Grading Service
*www.pcgs.com*
Tim Prusmack
*www.money-art.com*
Puro's Coins and Jewelry
*www.vtcoins.com*
R & I Coins
*www.ricoins.com*
Rarcoa
*www.coinsthatmatter.com*
Rare Coin Investments
*www.csmonline.com / rci*
RareCurrency.com
*www.rarecurrency.com*
Hans & Beate Rauch
*www.APCPaperCollect.com*
Richard J. Reed World Paper Money
*www.misterbanknote.com*
Robert Reed
*www.frontier.net / ~reedcoin*
James J. Reeves
*www.jamesjreeves.com*
Regency Coins
*www.rgncycoin.com*
Bob Reis' Anything Anywhere
*www.anythinganywhere.com*
Joel D. Rettew
*www.fastcoin.com*
Roy Reynolds Coins
*www.geocities.com / rodeo-drive / 7533 / royhomepage.html*
Frank S. Robinson
*www.albany.net / ~fr / index.html*
Roxbury's Auction House
*www.roxburys.com*
San Joaquin Valley Rare Coins
*goldcoin.dds-tech.net*

Rich Schemmer
*www.richerrors.com*
Reinhard Schimmer GmbH
*www.schimmer.de*
Scotsman Coin & Jewelry
*www.scoins.com*
Daniel Frank Sedwick
*www.home.att.net / ~danielsedwick*
David Seelye
*www.thempcman.net*
Shawnee Coin Company
*www.shawneecoin.com*
Sigma Ancient Coins
*www.sigmacoins.com*
Silver State Coin & Bullion
*www.silverstatecoin.com*
SilverTowne
*www.silvertowne.com*
Sam Sloat Coins
*sloat.coinnet.com*
R.M. Smythe & Company
*www.smytheonline.com*
*www.rm-smythe.com*
SOS Silver
*www.sossilver.com*
Sotheby's
*www.sothebys.com*
Southern Coin Investments
*www.southerncoin.com*
Southern Coins and Precious Metals
*www.scpm.com*
Sovereign Entities Grading Service
*www.www.segsgrading.com*
Spink &. Son Ltd.
*www.spink-online.com*
Stack's
*www.stacks.com*
Stanton Books & Supplies
*www.stantonbooks.com*
Steinberg's
*www.steinbergs.com*
Sunshine Rarities
*www.sunshinerarities.com*
Superior Galleries
*www.superiorgalleries.com*
Surpluzz.com
*www.surpluzz.com*
Swiatek – Minerva Coins and
  Jewelry Ltd.
*www.anthonyjswiatek.com*
Tangible Asset Galleries
*www.tangibleassets.com*
Teletrade
*www.teletrade.com*
M. Louis Teller
*www.tellercoins.com*
Tias.Com
*www.tias.com*
G.R. Tiso Numismatics
*www.ezy.net / ~tiso*

Tiitus Syngraphics
*www.syngraphics.net / imbl*
Token Publishing
*www.medal-news.com*
Scott Travers Rare Coin Galleries
*www.inch.com / ~travers / travers3.htm*
Trove Software
*www.trovesoftware.com*
The Tulving Company
*www.tulving.com*
USA Rare
*www.usarare.com*
USCents.com
*www.uscents.com*
U.S. Coins
*www.papermoneyonline.com*
USMintQuarters.com
*www.usmintquarters.com*
U.S. State Quarters.com
*www.usstatequarters.com / online-
  store / scstore*
Valley View Coins & Collectibles
*www.valleyviewcoins.com*
Vidiforms Company
*www.showgard.com*
Edward J. Waddell
*www.coin.com*
Wall Street Rarities
*www.wsrarities.com*
Washington Mint
*www.washingtonmint.com*
Washington Square Coin Exchange
*www.wscoin.com*
Fred Weinberg & Co
*www.fredweinberg.com*
Pam West British Bank Notes
*www.west-banknotes.co.uk*
Whyte's
*www.whytes.ie*
Scott J. Winslow Associates
*www.scottwinslow.com*
*www.buffalobid.com*
Douglas Winter Numismatics
*www.raregoldcoins.com*
Charles Woodruff Rare Coins &
  Currency
*www.cwwoodruff.com*
The Working Man's Rare Coins
*members.spree.com / sip / working-
  man / rarecoins*
World Exonumia
*www.exonumia.com*
WVW Classics
*www.wvwclassics.com*
William Youngerman
*www.williamyoungerman.com*
Jeffrey S. Zarit
*www.klippes.com*

# Glossary of coin terms

**Adjustment marks:** Marks made by use of a file to correct the weight of overweight coinage planchets prior to striking. Adjusting the weight of planchets was a common practice at the first U.S. mint in Philadelphia and was often carried out by women hired to weigh planchets and do any necessary filing.

**Altered coin:** A coin that has been changed after it left the mint. Such changes are often to the date or mintmark of a common coin in an attempt to increase its value by passing to an unsuspecting buyer as a rare date or mint.

**Alloy:** A metal or mixture of metals added to the primary metal in the coinage composition, often as a means of facilitating hardness during striking. For example, most U.S. silver coins contain an alloy of 10-percent copper.

**Anneal:** To heat in order to soften. In the minting process planchets are annealed prior to striking.

**Authentication:** The act of determining whether a coin, medal, token or other related item is a genuine product of the issuing authority.

**Bag marks:** Scrapes and impairments to a coin's surface obtained after minting by contact with other coins. The term originates from the storage of coins in bags, but such marks can occur as coins leave the presses and enter hoppers. A larger coin is more susceptible to marks, which affect its grade and, therefore, its value.

**Base metal:** A metal with low intrinsic value.

**Beading:** A form of design around the edge of a coin. Beading once served a functional purpose of deterring clipping or shaving parts of the metal by those looking to make a profit and then return the debased coin to circulation.

**Blank:** Often used in reference to the coinage planchet or disc of metal from which the actual coin is struck. Planchets or blanks are punched out of a sheet of metal by what is known as a blanking press.

**Business strike:** A coin produced for circulation.

Beading

**Cast copy:** A copy of a coin or medal made by a casting process in which molds are used to produce the finished product. Casting imparts a different surface texture to the finished product than striking and often leaves traces of a seam where the molds came together.

**Center dot:** A raised dot at the center of a coin caused by use of a compass to aid the engraver in the circular positioning of die devices, such as stars, letters and dates. Center dots are prevalent on early U.S. coinage.

Chop mark

**Chop mark:** A mark used by Oriental merchants as a means of guaranteeing the silver content of coins paid out. The merchants' chop marks, or stamped insignia, often obliterated the original design of the host coin. U.S. Trade dollars, struck from 1873 through 1878 and intended for use in trade with China, are sometimes found bearing multiple marks.

**Clash marks**: Marks impressed in the coinage dies when they come together without a planchet between them. Such marks will affect coins struck subsequently by causing portions of the obverse design to appear in raised form on the reverse, and vice versa.

**Clipping**: The practice of shaving or cutting small pieces of metal from a coin in circulation. Clipping was prevalent in Colonial times as a means of surreptitiously extracting precious metal from a coin before placing it back into circulation. The introduction of beading and a raised border helped to alleviate the problem.

**Coin alignment**: U.S. coins are normally struck with an alignment by which, when a coin is held by the top and bottom edge and rotated from side-to-side, the reverse will appear upside down.

**Collar**: A ring-shaped die between which the obverse and reverse coinage dies are held during striking. The collar contains the outward flow during striking and can be used to produce edge reeding.

**Commemorative**: A coin issued to honor a special event or person. U.S. commemoratives are generally produced for sale to collectors and are not placed in circulation.

**Copy**: A replica of an original issue. Copies often vary in quality and metallic composition to the original. Since passage of the Hobby Protection Act (Public Law 93-167) of Nov. 29, 1973, it has been illegal to produce or import copies of coins or other numismatic items that are not clearly and permanently marked with the word "Copy."

**Counterfeit**: A coin or medal or other numismatic item made fraudulently, either for entry into circulation or sale to collectors.

**Denticles**: The toothlike pattern found around a coin's obverse or reverse border.

**Die**: A cylindrical piece of metal containing an incuse image that imparts a raised image when stamped into a planchet.

**Die crack**: A crack that develops in a coinage die after extensive usage, or if the die is defective or is used to strike harder metals. Die cracks, which often run through border lettering, appear as raised lines on the finished coin.

**Device**: The principal design element.

**Double eagle**: Name adopted by the Act of March 3, 1849, for the gold coin valued at 20 units or $20.

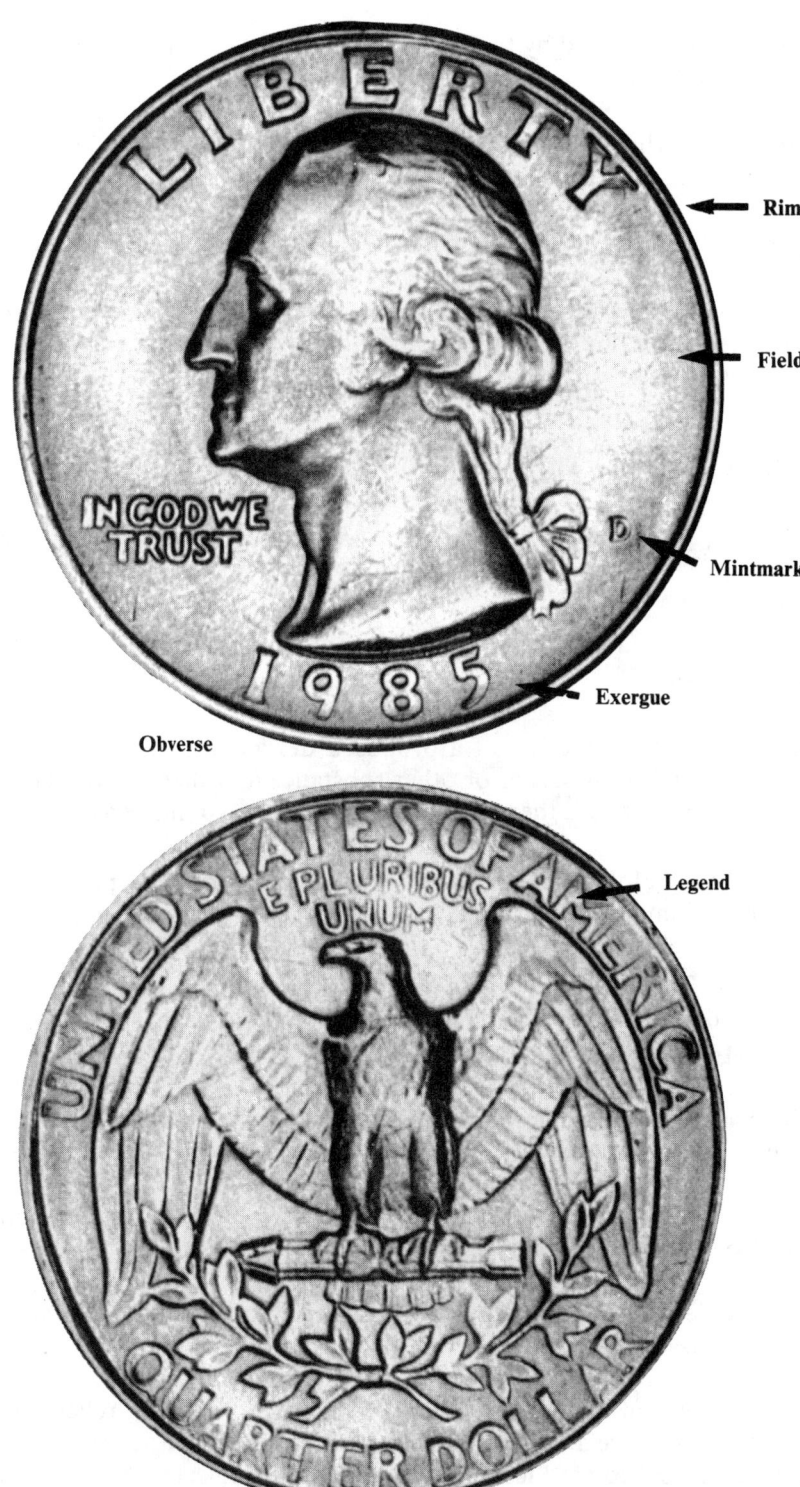

Rim

Field

Mintmark

Exergue

Obverse

Legend

Reverse

**Eagle:** Name adopted by the Coinage Act of 1792 for a gold coin valued at 10 units or $10.

**Edge:** The cylindrical surface of a coin between the two sides. The edge can be plain, reeded, ornamented, or lettered.

**Electrotype:** A copy of a coin, medal or token made by electroplating.

**Exergue:** The lower segment of a coin, below the main design, generally separated by a line and often containing the date, designer initials and mintmark.

**Face value:** The nominal legal-tender value assigned to a given coin by the governing authority.

**Fasces:** A Roman symbol of authority consisting of a bound bundle of rods and an ax.

**Field:** The flat area of a coin's obverse or reverse, devoid of devices or inscriptions.

**Galvano:** A reproduction of a proposed design from an artist's original model produced in plaster or other substance and then electroplated with metal. The galvano is then used in a reducing lathe to make a die or hub.

**Glory:** A heraldic term for stars, rays or other devices placed as if in the sky or luminous.

**Grading:** The largely subjective practice of providing a numerical or adjectival ranking of the condition of a coin, token or medal. The grade is often a major determinant of value.

**Gresham's law:** The name for the observation made by Sir Thomas Gresham, 16th century English financier, that when two coins with the same face value but different intrinsic values are in circulation at the same time, the one with the lesser intrinsic value will remain in circulation while the other is hoarded.

**Half eagle:** Name adopted by the Coinage Act of 1792 for a gold coin valued at five units or $5.

**Hub:** A piece of die steel showing the coinage devices in relief. The hub is used to produce a die that, in contrast, has the relief details incuse. The die is then used to produce the final coin, which looks much the same as the hub. Hubs may be reused to make new dies.

These Canadian Olympic commemoratives have lettered edges.

**Legend:** A coin's principal lettering, generally shown along its outer perimeter.

**Lettered edge:** Incuse or raised lettering on a coin's edge.

**Matte proof:** A proof coin on which the surface is granular or dull. On U.S. coins this type of surface was used on proofs of the early 20th century. The process has since been abandoned.

**Magician's coin:** A term sometimes used to describe a coin with two heads or two tails. Such a coin is impossible in normal production, and all are products made outside the Mint as novelty pieces.

**Medal:** Made to commemorate an event or person. Medals differ from coins in that a medal is not legal tender and, in general, is not produced with the intent of circulating as money.

A medal usually commemorates an event but has no monetary value. It can be issued by a private entity or a government.

**Medal alignment:** Medals are generally struck with the coinage dies facing the same direction during striking. When held by the top and bottom edge and rotated from side-to-side, a piece struck in this manner will show both the obverse and reverse right side up.

**Mintage:** The total number of coins struck during a given time frame, generally one year.

**Mintmark:** A letter or other marking on a coin's surface to identify the mint at which the coin was struck.

**Mule:** The combination of two coinage dies not intended for use together.

**Numismatics:** The science, study or collecting of coins, tokens, medals, paper money, and related items.

**Obverse:** The front or "heads" side of a coin, medal or token.

**Overdate:** Variety produced when one or more digits of the date are re-engraved over an old date on a die at the Mint, generally to save on dies or correct an error. Portions of the old date can still be seen under the new one.

**Overmintmark:** Variety created at the Mint when a different mintmark is punched over an already existing mintmark, generally done to make a coinage die already punched for one mint usable at another. Portions of the old mintmark can still be seen under the new one.

**Overstrike:** A coin, token or medal struck over another coin, token or medal.

**Pattern:** A trial strike of a proposed coin design, issued by the Mint or authorized agent of a governing authority. Patterns can be in a variety of metals, thicknesses and sizes.

**This U.S. Trade dollar
has a reeded edge.**

**Phrygian cap:** A close-fitting, egg-shell-shaped hat placed on the head of a freed slave when Rome was in its ascendancy. Hung from a pole, it was a popular symbol of freedom during the French Revolution and in 18th century United States.

**Planchet:** A disc of metal or other material on which the image of the dies are impressed, resulting in a finished coin. Also sometimes called a blank.

**Proof:** A coin struck twice or more from specially polished dies and polished planchets. Modern proofs are prepared with a mirror finish. Early 20th century proofs were prepared with a matte surface.

**Prooflike:** A prooflike coin exhibits some of the characteristics of a proof despite having been struck by regular production processes. Many Morgan dollars are found with prooflike surfaces. The field will have a mirror background similar to that of a proof, and design details are frosted like some proofs.

**Quarter eagle:** Name adopted by the Coinage Act of 1792 for a gold coin valued at 2.5 units or $2.50.

**Reeding:** Serrated (toothlike) ornamentation applied to the coin's edge during striking.

**Relief:** The portion of a design raised above the surface of a coin, medal or token.

A token is issued by a private entity and can be redeemed for its face value in trade or service.

**Restrike:** A coin, medal or token produced from original dies at a later date, often with the purpose of sale to collectors.

**Reverse:** The backside or "tails" side of a coin, medal or token, opposite from the principal figure of the design or obverse.

**Rim:** The raised area bordering the edge and surrounding the field.

**Series:** The complete group of coins of the same denomination and design and representing all issuing mints.

**Token:** A privately issued piece, generally in metal, with a represented value in trade or offer of service. Tokens are also produced for advertising purposes.

**Type coin:** A coin from a given series representing the basic design. A type coin is collected as an example of a particular design rather than for its date and mintmark.

**Variety:** Any coin noticeably different in dies from another of the same design, date and mint. Overdates and overmintmarks are examples of varieties.

**Wire edge:** Created when coinage metal flows between the coinage die and collar, producing a thin flange of coin metal at the outside edge or edges of a coin.

# PRICING SECTION

# Introduction to pricing

The following value guide is divided into six sections:
1. Colonial coins, issued prior to the establishment of the United States.
2. U.S. issues of 1792.
3. U.S. issues of 1793-present.
4. U.S. minting varieties and errors.
5. Canadian coins.
6. Mexican coins.

### Value listings

Values listed in the following price guide are average retail prices. These are the approximate prices collectors can expect to pay when purchasing coins from dealers. They are not offers to buy or sell. The pricing section should be considered a guide only; actual selling prices will vary.

The values were compiled by Krause Publications' independent staff of market analysts. They derived the values listed by monitoring auction results, business on electronic dealer trading networks, and business at major shows, and in consultation with a panel of dealers. For rare coins, when only a few specimens of a particular date and mintmark are known, a confirmed transaction may occur only once every several years. In those instances, the most recent auction result is listed.

### Grading

Values are listed for coins in various states of preservation, or grades. Standards used in determining grades for U.S. coins are those set by the American Numismatic Association. See Chapter 4 for more on grading.

### Dates and mintmarks

The dates listed are the individual dates that appear on each coin. The letter that follows the date is the mintmark and indicates where the coin was struck: "C" — Charlotte, N.C. (1838-1861); "CC" — Carson City, Nev. (1870-1893); "D" — Dahlonega, Ga. (1838-1861), and Denver (1906-present); "O" — New Orleans (1838-1909); "P" — Philadelphia (1793-present); "S" — San Francisco (1854-present); and "W" — West Point, N.Y. (1984-present). Coins without mintmarks were struck at Philadelphia.

A slash mark in a date indicates an overdate. This means a new date was engraved on a die over an old date. For example, if the date is listed as "1899/8," an 1898 die had a 9 engraved over the last 8 in the date. Portions of the old numeral are still visible on the coin.

A slash mark in a mintmark listing indicates an overmintmark (example: "1922-P/D"). The same process as above occurred, but this time a new mintmark was engraved over an old.

See the "U.S. Minting Varieties and Errors" section for more information on overdates and overmintmarks.

## Price charts
Pricing data for the selected charts in the U.S. section were taken from the January issues of "Coin Prices" for the years indicated.

## Mexican coin mintages
Quantities minted of each date are indicated when that information is available, generally stated in millions and rounded off to the nearest 10,000 pieces. The following mintage conversion formulas are used:

10,000,000 — 10,000.
1,000,000 — 1.000.
100,000 — .100.
10,000 — .010.
9,999 — 9,999.
1,000 — 1,000.
842 — 842 pcs. (pieces).
27 — 27 pcs.

## Precious-metal content
Throughout this book precious-metal content is indicated in troy ounces. One troy ounce equals 480 grains, or 31.103 grams.

## Abbreviations
**AGW.** Actual gold weight.

**APW.** Actual platinum weight.

**ASW.** Actual silver weight.

**BV.** Bullion value. This indicates the coin's current value is based on the amount of its precious-metal content and the current price for that metal.

**Est.** Indicates the exact mintage is not known and the figure listed is an estimate.

**G.** Grams.

**Inc. Abv.** Indicates the mintage for the date and mintmark listed is included in the previous listing.

**KM#.** In the Canadian and Mexican price sections, indicates "Krause-Mishler number." This sequential cataloging numbering system originated with the "Standard Catalog of World Coins" by Chester L. Krause and Clifford Mishler, and provides collectors with a means for identifying world issues.

**Leg.** Legend.

**Mkt value.** Market value.

**MM.** Millimeters.

**Obv.** Obverse.

**P/L.** Indicates "prooflike," a type of finish used on some Canadian coins.

**Rev.** Reverse.

**Spec.** Indicates "specimen," a type of finish used on some Canadian coins.

# U.S. minting varieties and errors

## Introduction
### By Alan Herbert

The P.D.S. cataloging system used here to list minting varieties was originally compiled by the author in 1971. PDS stands for the three main divisions of the minting process, "planchet," "die" and "striking." Two more divisions cover collectible modifications after the strike, as well as non-collectible alterations, counterfeits and damaged coins.

This listing includes 445 classes, each a distinct part of the minting process or from a specific non-mint change in the coin. Classes from like causes are grouped together. The PDS system applies to coins of the world, but is based on U.S. coinage with added classes for certain foreign minting practices.

Price ranges are based on a U.S. coin in MS-60 grade (uncirculated.) The ranges may be applied in general to foreign coins of similar size or value although collector values are not usually as high as for U.S. coins. Prices are only a guide as the ultimate price is determined by a willing buyer and seller.

To define minting varieties, "A coin which exhibits a variation of any kind from the normal, as a result of any portion of the minting process, whether at the planchet stage, as a result of a change or modification of the die, or during the striking process. It includes those classes considered to be intentional changes, as well as those caused by normal wear and tear on the dies or other minting equipment and classes deemed to be "errors."

The three causes are represented as follows:
1. (I) = Intentional Changes
2. (W) = Wear and Tear
3. (E) = Errors
Note: A class may show more than one cause and could be listed as (IWE).

## Rarity level

The rarity ratings are based on the following scale:
1 - Very Common. Ranges from every coin struck down to 1,000,000.
2 - Common. From 1,000,000 down to 100,000.
3 - Scarce. From 100,000 down to 10,000.
4 - Very Scarce. From 10,000 down to 1,000.
5 - Rare. From 1,000 down to 100.
6 - Very Rare. From 100 down to 10.
7 - Extremely Rare. From 10 down to 1.
Unknown: If I don't have a confirmed report of a piece fitting a particular class, it is listed as Unknown and I would appreciate reports from readers in order to update future presentations.

An Unknown does not mean that your piece automatically is very valuable. Even a Rarity 7 piece, extremely rare, even unique, may have a very low collector value because of a lack of demand or interest in that particular class.

Classes, definitions and price ranges are based on material previously offered in my book, *The Official Price Guide to Minting Varieties and Errors*, 5th edition, and in *Coin Prices* Magazine.

Pricing information has also been provided by John A. Wexler and Ken Potter, with special pricing and technical advice from Del Romines.

Also recommended is the *Cherrypicker's Guide to Rare Die Varieties* 3rd edition, by Bill Fivaz and J.T. Stanton, available from Stanton at P.O. Box 932, Savannah, GA 31402.

For help with your coin questions, to report significant new finds and for authentication of your minting varieties, include a loose first class stamp and write to Alan Herbert, Dept.

NA-8, NAC&P, 700 E. State St., Iola, WI 54990-0001. Don't include any numismatic material until you have received specific mailing instructions from me.

# Quick check index

If you have a coin and are not sure where to look for the possible variety:

If your coin shows doubling, first check V-B-I.

Then try II-A, II-B, II-C, II-I (4 & 5), III-J, III-L, or IV-C.

If part of the coin is missing, check III-B, III-C, or III-D.

If there is a raised line of coin metal, check II-D, II-G.

If there is a raised area of coin metal, check II-E, II-F, or III-F.

If the coin is out of round, and too thin, check III-G.

If coin appears to be the wrong metal, check III-A, III-E, III-F-3 and III-G.

If the die appears to have been damaged, check II-E, II-G. (Damage to the coin itself usually is not a minting variety.)

If the coin shows incomplete or missing design, check II-A, II-E, III-B-3, III-B-5 or III-D.

If only part of the planchet was struck, check III-M.

If something was struck into the coin, check III-J and III-K.

If something has happened to the edge of the coin, check II-D-6, II-E-10, III-I, III-M and III-O.

If your coin shows other than the normal design, check II-A or II-C.

If a layer of the coin metal is missing, or a clad layer is missing, check III-B and III-D.

If you have an unstruck blank, or planchet, check I-G.

If your coin may be a restrike, check IV-C.

If your coin has a counterstamp, countermark, additional engraving or apparent official modifications, check IV-B and V-A-8.

Do not depend on the naked eye to examine your coins. Use a magnifying lens whenever possible, as circulation damage, wear and alterations frequently can be mistaken for legitimate minting varieties.

# Division I: planchet varieties

The first division of the PDS System includes those minting varieties that occur in the manufacture of the planchet upon which the coins will ultimately be struck and includes classes resulting from faulty metallurgy, mechanical damage, faulty processing, or equipment or human malfunction prior to the actual coin striking.

## Planchet alloy mix (I-A)

This section includes those classes pertaining to mixing and processing the various metals which will be used to make a coin alloy.

I-A-1 Improper Alloy Mix (WE), Rarity Level: 3-4, Values: $5 to $10.

I-A-2 Slag Inclusion Planchet (WE), Rarity Level: 5-6, Values: $25 up.

## Damaged and defective planchets (I-B)

To be a class in this section the blank, or planchet, must for some reason not meet the normal standards or must have been damaged in processing. The classes cover the areas of defects in the melting, rolling, punching and processing of the planchets up to the point where they are sent to the coin presses to be struck.

I-B-1 Defective Planchet (WE), Rarity Level: 6, Values: $25 up.

I-B-2 Mechanically Damaged Planchet (WE), Rarity Level: –, Values: No Value. (See values for the coin struck on a mechanically damaged planchet.)

I-B-3 Rolled Thin Planchet (WE), Rarity Level: 6 - (Less rare on half cents of 1795, 1797 and restrikes of 1831-52.) Values: $10 up.

I-B-4 Rolled Thick Planchet (WE), Rarity Level: 7 - (Less rare in Colonial copper coins. Notable examples occur on the restrike half cents of 1840-52.) Values: $125 up.

I-B-5 Tapered Planchet (WE), Rarity Level: 7, Values: $25 up.

I-B-6 Partially Unplated Planchet (WE), Rarity Level: 6, Values: $15 up.

I-B-7 Unplated Planchet (WE), Rarity Level: 6-7, Values: $50 up.

I-B-8 Bubbled Plating Planchet (WE), Rarity Level: 1, Values: No Value.

I-B-9 Included Gas Bubble Planchet (WE), Rarity Level: 6-7, Values: $50 up.

I-B-10 Partially Unclad Planchet (WE), Rarity Level: 6, Values: $20 up.

I-B-11 Unclad Planchet (WE), Rarity Level: 6-7, Values: $50 up.

I-B-12 Undersize Planchet (WE), Rarity Level: 7, Values: $250 up.

I-B-13 Oversize Planchet (WE), Rarity Level: 7, Values: $250 up.

I-B-14 Improperly Prepared Proof Planchet (WE), Rarity Level: 7, Values: $100 up.

I-B-15 Improperly Annealed Planchet (WE), Rarity Level: - , Values: No Value.

I-B-16 Faulty Upset Edge Planchet (WE), Rarity Level: 5-6, Values: $10 up.

I-B-17 Rolled-In Metal Planchet (WE), Rarity Level: 6-7, Values: $50 up.

I-B-18 Weld Area Planchet (WE), Rarity Level: Unknown, Values: No Value Established. (See values for the coins struck on weld area planchets.)

I-B-19 Strike Clip Planchet (WE), Rarity Level: 7, Values: $150 up.

I-B-20 Unpunched Center-Hole Planchet (WE), Rarity Level: 5-7, Values: $5 and up.

I-B-21 Incompletely Punched Center-Hole Planchet (WE), Rarity Level: 6-7, Values: $15 up.

I-B-22 Uncentered Center-Hole Planchet (WE), Rarity Level: 6-7, Values: $10 up.

I-B-23 Multiple Punched Center-Hole Planchet (WE), Rarity Level: 7, Values: $35 up.

I-B-24 Unintended Center-Hole Planchet (WE), Rarity Level: Unknown, Values: -.

I-B-25 Wrong Size or Shape Center-Hole Planchet (IWE), Rarity Level: 5-7, Values: $10 up.

## Clipped planchets (I-C)

Clipped blanks, or planchets, occur when the strip of coin metal fails to move forward between successive strokes of the gang punch to clear the previously punched holes, in the same manner as a cookie cutter overlapping a previously cut hole in the dough. The size of the clip is a function of the amount of overlap of the next punch.

The overlapping round punches produce a missing arc with curve matching the outside circumference of the blanking punch. Straight clips occur when the punch overlaps the beginning or end of a strip which has had the end sheared or sawed off. Ragged clips occur in the same manner when the ends of the strip have been left as they were rolled out.

The term "clip" as used here should not be confused with the practice of clipping or shaving small pieces of metal from a bullion coin after it is in circulation.

I-C-1 Disc Clip Planchet (WE), Rarity Level: 3-5, Values: $5 up.

I-C-2 Curved Clip Planchet - (To 5%) (WE), Rarity Level: 5-6, Values: $5 up.

I-C-3 Curved Clip Planchet - (6 to 10%) (WE), Rarity Level: 6, Values: $10 up.

I-C-4 Curved Clip Planchet - (11 to 25%) (WE), Rarity Level: 5-6, Values: $15 up.

I-C-5 Curved Clip Planchet - (26 to 60%) (WE), Rarity Level: 6-7, Values: $25 up.

I-C-6 Double Curved Clip Planchet (WE), Rarity Level: 6, Values: $10 up.

I-C-7 Triple Curved Clip Planchet (WE), Rarity Level: 5-6, Values: $25 up.

I-C-8 Multiple Curved Clip Planchet (WE), Rarity Level: 6-7, Values: $35 up.

I-C-9 Overlapping Curved Clipped Planchet (WE), Rarity Level: 6-7, Values: $50 up.

I-C-10 Incompletely Punched Curved Clip Planchet (WE), Rarity Level: 6, Values: $35 up.

I-C-11 Oval Curved Clip Planchet (WE), Rarity Level: 6-7, Values: $50 up.

I-C-12 Crescent Clip Planchet - (61% or more) (WE), Rarity Level: 7, Values: $200 up.

I-C-13 Straight Clip Planchet (WE), Rarity Level: 6, Values: $30 up.

I-C-14 Incompletely Sheared Straight Clip Planchet (WE), Rarity Level: 6, Values: $50 up.

I-C-15 Ragged Clip Planchet (WE), Rarity Level: 6-7, Values: $35 up.

I-C-16 Outside Corner Clip Planchet (E), Rarity Level: -, Values: No Value.

I-C-17 Inside Corner Clip Planchet (E), Rarity Level: -, Values: No Value.

I-C-18 Irregularly Clipped Planchet (E) Rarity Level: -, Values: Value not established.

I-C-19 Incompletely Punched Scalloped or Multi-Sided Planchet (E), Rarity Level: 7, Values: $25 up.

## Laminated, split, or broken planchet (I-D)

For a variety of reasons the coin metal may split into thin layers (delaminate) and either split completely off the coin, or be retained. Common causes are included gas or alloy mix problems. Lamination cracks usually enter the surface of the planchet at a very shallow angle or are at right angles to the edge. The resulting layers differ from slag in that they appear as normal metal.

Lamination cracks and missing metal of any size below a split planchet are too common in the 35 percent silver 1942-1945 nickels to be collectible or have any significant value.

I-D-1 Small Lamination Crack Planchet (W), Rarity Level: 4-5, Values: $1 up.

I-D-2 Large Lamination Crack Planchet (W), Rarity Level: 3-4, Values: $5 up.

I-D-3 Split Planchet (W), Rarity Level: 5-6, Values: $15 up.

I-D-4 Hinged Split Planchet (W), Rarity Level: 6-7, Values: $75 up.

I-D-5 Clad Planchet With a Clad Layer Missing (W), Rarity Level: 5-6, Values: $35 up.

I-D-6 Clad Planchet With Both Clad Layers Missing (W), Rarity Level: 6-7, Values: $75 up.

I-D-7 Separated Clad Layer (W), Rarity Level: 5, Values: $25 up.

I-D-8 Broken Planchet (WE), Rarity Level: 3-4, Values: $5 up.

## Wrong stock planchet (I-E)

The following classes cover those cases where the wrong coin metal stock was run through the blanking press, making blanks of the correct diameter, but of the wrong thickness, alloy or metal or a combination of the wrong thickness and the wrong metal.

I-E-1 Half Cent Stock Planchet (IE), Rarity Level: Unknown, Values: No Value Established.

I-E-2 Cent Stock Planchet (IE), Rarity Level: Unknown, Values: No Value Established.

I-E-3 Two Cent Stock Planchet (E), Rarity Level: Unknown, Values: No Value Established.

I-E-4 Three Cent Silver Stock Planchet (E), Rarity Level: Unknown, Values: No Value Established.

I-E-5 Three Cent Nickel Stock Planchet (E), Rarity Level: Unknown, Values: No Value Established.

I-E-6 Half Dime Stock Planchet (E), Rarity Level: Unknown, Values: No Value Established.

I-E-7 Dime Stock Planchet (E), Rarity Level: 7, Values: $200 up.

I-E-8 Twenty Cent Stock Planchet (E), Rarity Level: Unknown, Values: No Value Established.

I-E-9 Quarter Stock Planchet (E), Rarity Level: Unknown, Values: No Value Established.

I-E-10 Half Dollar Stock Planchet (E), Rarity Level: Unknown, Values: No Value Established.

I-E-11 Dollar Stock Planchet (E), Rarity Level: 7, Values: $300 up.

I-E-12 Token or Medal Stock Planchet (E), Rarity Level: Unknown, Values: No Value Established.

I-E-13 Wrong Thickness Spoiled Planchet (IWE), Rarity Level: Unknown, Values: No Value Established.

I-E-14 Correct Thickness Spoiled Planchet (IWE), Rarity Level: Unknown, Values: No Value Established.

I-E-15 Cut Down Struck Token Planchet (IWE), Rarity Level: Unknown, Values: No Value Established.

I-E-16 Experimental or Pattern Stock Planchet (IE), Rarity Level: Unknown, Values: No Value Established.

I-E-17 Proof Stock Planchet (IE), Rarity Level: Unknown, Values: No Value Established.

I-E-18 Adjusted Specification Stock Planchet (IE), Rarity Level: 7, Values: $25 up.

I-E-19 Trial Strike Stock Planchet (IE), Rarity Level: Unknown, Values: No Value Established.

I-E-20 U.S. Punched Foreign Stock Planchet (E), Rarity Level: 7, Values: $75 up.

I-E-21 Foreign Punched Foreign Stock Planchet (E), Rarity Level: 7, Values: $75 up.

I-E-22 Non-Standard Coin Alloy Planchet (IE), Rarity Level: 7, Values: Unknown.

## Extra metal on a blank, or planchet (I-F)

True extra metal is only added to the blank during the blanking operation. This occurs as metal is scraped off the sides of the blanks as they are driven down through the thimble, or lower die in the blanking press. The metal is eventually picked up by a blank passing through, welded to it by the heat of friction.

A second form of extra metal has been moved to this section, the sintered coating planchet, the metal deposited on the planchet in the form of dust during the annealing operation.

I-F-1 Extra Metal on a Type 1 Blank (W), Rarity Level: 7, Values: $50 up.
I-F-2 Extra Metal on a Type 2 Planchet (W), Rarity Level: 6-7, Values: $75 up.
I-F-3 Sintered Coating Planchet (W), Rarity Level: 7, Values: $75 up.

## Normal or abnormal planchets (I-G )

This section consists of the two principal forms – the blank as it comes from the blanking press – and in the form of a planchet after it has passed through the upsetting mill. It also includes a class for purchased planchets and one for planchets produced by the mint.

I-G-1 Type I Blank (IWE), Rarity Level: 3-5, Values: $2 up.
I-G-2 Type II Planchet (IWE), Rarity Level: 3-4, Values: 50 up.
I-G-3 Purchased Planchet (I), Rarity Level: 1, Values: No Value.
I-G-4 Mint Made Planchet (I), Rarity Level: 1, Values: No Value.
I-G-5 Adjustment-Marked Planchet (I), Rarity Level: Unknown, Values: No Value.
I-G-6 Hardness Test-Marked Planchet (I), Rarity Level: -, Values: No Value Established.
Note: There are no classes between I-G-6 and I-G-23
I-G-23 Proof Planchet (IE), Rarity Level: 6-7, Values: $1 up.

## Coin metal strip (I-H)

When the coin metal strip passes through the blanking press it goes directly to a chopper. This cuts the remaining web into small pieces to be sent back to the melting furnace. Pieces of the web or the chopped up web may escape into the hands of collectors.

I-H-1 Punched Coin Metal Strip (IWE), Rarity Level: 4-6, Values: $5 up, depending on size, denomination and number of holes showing.
I-H-2 Chopped Coin Metal Strip (IE), Rarity Level: 3-5, Values: $5 up.

# The die varieties
## Division II

Die varieties may be unique to a given die, but will repeat for the full life of the die unless a further change occurs. Anything that happens to the die will affect the appearance of the struck coin. This includes all the steps of the die making:

● Cutting a die blank from a tool steel bar.
● Making the design.
● Transferring it to a model.
● Transferring it to the master die or hub.
● The hubbing process of making the die.
● Punching in the mintmark.
● Heat treating of the die.

The completed dies are also subject to damage in numerous forms, plus wear and tear during the striking process and repair work done with abrasives. All of these factors can affect how the struck coin looks.

## Engraving varieties (II-A)

In all cases in this section where a master die, or master hub is affected by the class, the class will affect all the working hubs and all working dies descending from it.

Identification as being on a master die or hub depends on it being traced to two or more of the working hubs descended from the same master tools.

II-A-1 Overdate (IE), Rarity Level: 1-7, Values: $1 up.
II-A-2 Doubled Date (IE), Rarity Level: 1-7, Values: $1 up.
II-A-3 Small Date (IE), Rarity Level: 2-5, Values: $1 up.
II-A-4 Large Date (IE), Rarity Level: 2-5, Values: $1 up.
II-A-5 Small Over Large Date (IE), Rarity Level: 4-6, Values: $15 up.
II-A-6 Large Over Small Date (IE), Rarity Level: 3-5, Values: $10 up.
II-A-7 Blundered Date (E), Rarity Level: 6-7, Values: $50 up.
II-A-8 Corrected Blundered Date (IE), Rarity Level: 3-5, Values: $5 up.

II-A-9 Wrong Font Date Digit (IE), Rarity Level: 5-6, Values: Minimal.

II-A-10 Worn, Broken or Damaged Punch (IWE), Rarity Level: 5-6, Values: $5 up.

II-A-11 Expedient Punch (IWE), Rarity Level: 5-6, Values: $10 up.

II-A-12 Blundered Digit (E), Rarity Level: 4-5, Values: $50 up.

II-A-13 Corrected Blundered Digit (IE), Rarity Level: 3-6, Values: $10 up.

II-A-14 Doubled Digit (IWE), Rarity Level: 2-6, Values: $2 up.

II-A-15 Wrong Style or Font Letter or Digit (IE), Rarity Level: 3-5, Values: Minimal.

II-A-16 One Style or Font Over Another (IE), Rarity Level: 4-6, Values: $10 up.

II-A-17 Letter Over Digit (E), Rarity Level: 6-7, Values: $25 up.

II-A-18 Digit Over Letter (E), Rarity Level: 6-7, Values: $25 up.

II-A-19 Omitted Letter or Digit (IWE), Rarity Level: 4-6, Values: $5 up.

II-A-20 Blundered Letter (E), Rarity Level: 6-7, Values: $50 up.

II-A-21 Corrected Blundered Letter (IE), Rarity Level: 1-3, Values: $10 up.

II-A-22 Doubled Letter (IWE), Rarity Level: 2-6, Values: $2 up.

II-A-23 Blundered Design Element (IE), Rarity Level: 6-7, Values: $50 up.

II-A-24 Corrected Blundered Design Element (IE), Rarity Level: 3-5, Values: $10 up.

II-A-25 Large Over Small Design Element (IE), Rarity Level: 4-6, Values: $2 up.

II-A-26 Omitted Design Element (IWE), Rarity Level: 5-7, Values: $10 up.

II-A-27 Doubled Design Element (IWE), Rarity Level: 2-6, Values: $2 up.

II-A-28 One Design Element Over Another (IE), Rarity Level: 3-6, Values: $5 up.

II-A-29 Reducing Lathe Doubling (WE), Rarity Level: 6-7, Values: $50 up.

II-A-30 Extra Design Element (IE), Rarity Level: 3-5, Values: $10 up.

II-A-31 Modified Design (IWE), Rarity Level: 1-5, Values: No Value up.

II-A-32 Normal Design (I), Rarity Level: 1, Values: No Value.

II-A-33 Design Mistake (IE), Rarity Level: 2-6, Values: $1 up.

II-A-34 Defective Die Design (IWE), Rarity Level: 1, Values: No Value.

II-A-35 Pattern (I), Rarity Level: 6-7, Values: $100 up.

II-A-36 Trial Design (I), Rarity Level: 5-7, Values: $100 up.

II-A-37 Omitted Designer's Initial (IWE), Rarity Level: 3-7, Values: $1 up.

II-A-38 Layout Mark (IE), Rarity Level: 5-7, Values: Minimal.

II-A-39 Abnormal Reeding (IWE), Rarity Level: 2-5, Values: $1 up.

II-A-40 Modified Die or Hub (IWE), Rarity Level: 1-5, Values: No Value up.

II-A-41 Numbered Die (I), Rarity Level: 3-5, Values: $5 up.

II-A-42 Plugged Die (IW), Rarity Level: 5-6, Values: Minimal.

II-A-43 Cancelled Die (IE), Rarity Level: 3-6, Values: No Value up.

II-A-44 Hardness Test Marked Die (IE), Rarity Level: 7, Values: $100 up.

II-A-45 Coin Simulation (IE), Rarity Level: 6-7, Values: $100 up, but may be illegal to own.

II-A-46 Punching Mistake (IE), Rarity Level: 2-6, Values: $1 up.

II-A-47 Small Over Large Design (IE), Rarity Level: 4-6, Values: $5 up.

II-A-48 Doubled Punch (IE), Rarity Level: 5-7, Values: $5 up.

II-A-49 Mint Display Sample (I) Rarity Level: 7, Values not established.

II-A-50 Center Dot, Stud or Circle (IE) Rarity Level: 7, much more common on early cents, Values not established

## Hub doubling varieties (II-B)

This section includes eight classes of hub doubling. Each class is from a different cause, described by the title of the class. At the latest count over 2,500 doubled dies have been reported in the U.S. coinage, the most famous being examples of the 1955, 1969-S and 1972 cent dies.

Rotated hub doubling

Hub break

II-B-I Rotated Hub Doubling (WE), Rarity Level: 3-6, Values: $1 up
II-B-II Distorted Hub Doubling (WE), Rarity Level: 3-6, Values: $1 up.
II-B-III Design Hub Doubling (IWE), Rarity Level: 3-6, Values: $1 up to five figure amounts.
II-B-IV Offset Hub Doubling (WE), Rarity Level: 4-6, Values: $15 up.
II-B-V Pivoted Hub Doubling (WE), Rarity Level: 3-6, Values: $10 up.
II-B-VI Distended Hub Doubling (WE), Rarity Level: 2-5, Values: $1 up.
II-B-VII Modified Hub Doubling (IWE), Rarity Level: 2-5, Values: $1 up.
II-B-VIII Tilted Hub Doubling (WE), Rarity Level: 4-6, Values: $5 up.

## Mintmark varieties (II-C)

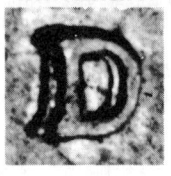 

**Double**                **Triple**

Mintmarks are punched into U.S. coin dies by hand (Up to 1985 for proof coins, to 1990 for cents and nickels and 1991 for other denominations). Variations resulting from mistakes in the punching are listed in this section. Unless exceptionally mispunched, values are usually estimated at 150 percent of numismatic value. Slightly tilted or displaced mintmarks have no value.

II-C-1 Doubled Mintmark (IE), Rarity Level: 2-6, Values: 50 cents up.
II-C-2 Separated Doubled Mintmark (IE), Rarity Level: 5-6, Values: $15 up.
II-C-3 Over Mintmark (IE), Rarity Level: 3-6, Values: $2 up.
II-C-4 Tripled Mintmark (IE), Rarity Level: 3-5, Values: 50 up.
II-C-5 Quadrupled Mintmark (IE), Rarity Level: 4-6, Values: $1 up.
II-C-6 Small Mintmark (IE), Rarity Level: 2-5, Values: No Extra Value up.
II-C-7 Large Mintmark (IE), Rarity Level: 2-5, Values: No Extra Value up.
II-C-8 Large Over Small Mintmark (IE), Rarity Level: 2-5, Values: $2 up.
II-C-9 Small Over Large Mintmark (IE), Rarity Level: 3-6, Values: $5 up.
II-C-10 Broken Mintmark Punch (W), Rarity Level: 5-6, Values: $5 up.
II-C-11 Omitted Mintmark (IWE), Rarity Level: 4-7, Values: $125 up.
II-C-12 Tilted Mintmark (IE), Rarity Level: 5-7, Values: $5 up.
II-C-13 Blundered Mintmark (E), Rarity Level: 4-6, Values: $5 up.
II-C-14 Corrected Horizontal Mintmark (IE), Rarity Level: 4-6, Values: $5 up.
II-C-15 Corrected Upside Down Mintmark (IE), Rarity Level: 4-6, Values: $5 up.
II-C-16 Displaced Mintmark (IE), Rarity Level: 4-6, Values: $5 to $10.
II-C-17 Modified Mintmark (IWE), Rarity Level: 1-4, Values: No Extra Value up.
II-C-18 Normal Mintmark (I), Rarity Level: 1, Values: No Extra Value.
II-C-19 Doubled Mintmark Punch (I), Rarity Level: 6-7, Values: No Extra Value up.
II-C-20 Upside Down Mintmark (E) Rarity Level 6-7, Values: $5 up.
II-C-21 Horizontal Mintmark (E) Rarity Level 6-7, Values: $5 up.
II-C-22 Wrong Mintmark (E) Rarity Level 6-7, Values $15 up. (Example has a D mintmark in the date, but was used at Philadelphia.)

## Die, collar and hub cracks (II-D)

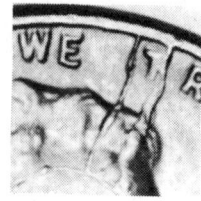

**Die cracks**

Cracks in the surface of the die allow coin metal to be forced into the crack during the strike, resulting in raised irregular lines of coin metal above the normal surface of the coin. These are one of the commonest forms of die damage and wear, making them easily collectible.

Collar cracks and hub cracks are added to this section because the causes and effects are similar or closely associated.

Die cracks, collar cracks and hub cracks are the result of wear and tear on the tools, with intentional use assumed for all classes.

II-D-1 Die Crack (W), Rarity Level: 1-3, Values: 10 to $1, $25 up on a proof coin with a rarity level of 6-7.

II-D-2 Multiple Die Cracks (W), Rarity Level: 1-3, Values: 25 cents to $2.

II-D-3 Head-To-Rim Die Crack (Lincoln Cent) (W), Rarity Level: 2-6, Values: 25 to $10 for multiple die cracks.

II-D-4 Split Die (W), Rarity Level: 5-6, Values: $10 up.

II-D-5 Rim-To-Rim Die Crack (W), Rarity Level: 2-5, Values: $1 up.

II-D-6 Collar Crack (W), Rarity Level: 4-6, Values: $10 up.

II-D-7 Hub Crack (W), Rarity Level: 3-5, Values: $1-$2.

# Die breaks (II-E)

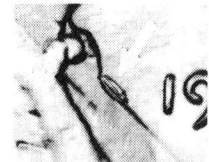

Small die break II-E-2

Clogged letter II-E-1

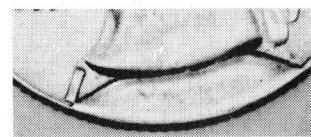

Major die break II-E-5

Rim die break II-E-4

Breaks in the surface of the die allow coin metal to squeeze into the resulting holes, causing raised irregular areas above the normal surface of the coin. Die chips and small die breaks are nearly as common as the die cracks, but major die breaks, which extend in from the edge of the coin, are quite rare on the larger coins.

If the broken piece of the die is retained, the resulting design will be above or below the level of the rest of the surface.

II-E-1 Die Chip (W), Rarity Level: 1-2, Values: 10 to $1.

II-E-2 Small Die Break (W), Rarity Level: 1-3, Values: 10 to $2.

II-E-3 Large Die Break (W), Rarity Level: 3-5, Values: $1 to $50 and up.

II-E-4 Rim Die Break (W), Rarity Level: 2-3, Values: 25 cents to $5.

II-E-5 Major Die Break (WE), Rarity Level: 3-6, Values: $5 to $100 and up.

II-E-6 Retained Broken Die (W), Rarity Level: 3-5, Values: $1 to $10 and up.

II-E-7 Retained Broken Center of the Die (W), Rarity Level: 6-7, Values: $100 up.

II-E-8 Laminated Die (W), Rarity Level: 3-5, Values: 10 cents to $5.

II-E-9 Chipped Chrome Plating (W), Rarity Level: 4-5, Values: $10 to $25 on proofs.

II-E-10 Collar Break (W), Rarity Level: 4-6, Values: $5 to $25 and up.

II-E-11 Broken Letter or Digit on an Edge Die (W), Rarity Level: 4-6, Values: Minimal.

II-E-12 "Bar" Die Break (W), Rarity Level: 3-5, Values: 25 to $20.

II-E-13 Hub Break (W), Rarity Level: 4-6, Values: 50 to $10 and up.

# "BIE" varieties (II-F)

A series of small die breaks or die chips in the letters of "LIBERTY" mostly on the wheat-reverse Lincoln cent are actively collected. The name results from the resemblance to an "I" between the "B" and "E" on many of the dies, but they are found between all of the letters in different cases. Well over 1,500 dies are known and cataloged. Numerous more recent examples are known.

**BIE variety II-F-4**

II-F-1 ILI Die Variety (W), Rarity Level: 4-5, Values: 25 cents to $10.
II-F-2 LII Die Variety (W), Rarity Level: 3-5, Values: 50 cents to $15.
II-F-3 IIB Die Variety (W), Rarity Level: 3-5, Values: 50 cents to $15.
II-F-4 BIE Die Variety (W), Rarity Level: 3-5, Values: $1 to $20.
II-F-5 EIR Die Variety (W), Rarity Level: 3-5, Values: 50 to $15.
II-F-6 RIT Die Variety (W), Rarity Level: 4-5, Values: $2 to $25.
II-F-7 TIY Die Variety (W), Rarity Level: 4-5, Values: $5 to $30.
II-F-8 TYI Die Variety (W), Rarity Level: 4-5, Values: $2 to $25.

## Worn and damaged dies, collars and hubs (II-G)

**Die clashes and design transfer**

 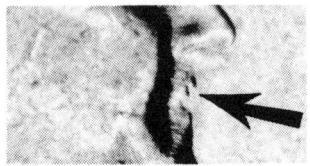

Many dies are continued deliberately in service after they have been damaged, dented, clashed or show design transfer, since none of these classes actually affect anything but the appearance ofthe coin. The root cause is wear, but intent or mistakes may enter the picture.

II-G-1 Dented Die, Collar or Hub (IWE), Rarity Level: 3-5, Values: 25 to $5.
II-G-2 Damaged Die, Collar or Hub (IWE), Rarity Level: 3-5, Values: 25 to $5.
II-G-3 Worn Die, Collar or Hub (IWE), Rarity Level: 2-3, Values: No Extra Value to Minimal Value.
II-G-4 Pitted or Rusted Die, Collar or Hub (IWE), Rarity Level: 3-4, Values:No Extra Value, marker only.
II-G-5 Heavy Die Clash (IWE), Rarity Level: 4-5, Values: $1 to $10 and up.
II-G-6 Heavy Collar Clash (IWE), Rarity Level: 3-4, Values: $1 to $5 and up.
II-G-7 Heavy Design Transfer (IWE), Rarity Level: 3-4, Values: 10 cents to $1.

## Die progressions (II-H)

The progression section consists of three classes. These are useful as cataloging tools for many different die varieties, but especially the die cracks and die breaks which may enlarge, lengthen or increase in number.

II-H-1 Progression (W), Rarity Level: 3-5, Values: $1 up.
II-H-2 Die Substitution (IW), Rarity Level: 2-4, Values: No Extra Value to Minimal Value.
II-H-3 Die Repeat (I), Rarity Level: 2-4, Values: No Extra Value to Minimal Value.

## Die scratches, polished and abraded dies (II-I)

**Die scratches II-I-1**

This section consists of those classes having to do with the use of an abrasive in some form to intentionally polish proof dies, or repair the circulating die surface. Several classes which previously were referred to as "polished" now are listed as "abraded."

II-I-1 Die Scratch (IW), Rarity Level: 1-2, Values: No Extra Value to 10 cents to 25 cents, as a marker.
II-I-2 Polished (proof) Die (IW), Rarity Level: 1, Values: No Extra Value.
II-I-3 Abraded (Circulation) Die (IW), Rarity Level: 1-2, Values: No Extra Value up to $10.

II-I-4 Inside Abraded Die Doubling (IW), Rarity Level: 1-3, Values: No Extra Value to $1.

II-I-5 Outside Abraded Die Doubling (IW), Rarity Level: 1-3, Values: No Extra Value to $1.

II-I-6 Lathe Marks (IW), Rarity Level: 5-7, Values: No Extra Value, marker only.

# Striking varieties
## Division III

Once the dies are made and the planchets have been prepared, they are struck by a pair of dies and become a coin. In this division, we list the misstrikes resulting from human or mechanical malfunction in the striking process. These are one-of-a-kind varieties, but there may be many similar coins that fall in a given class.

Multiples and combinations of classes must be considered on a case by case basis. The first several sections match the planchet sections indicated in the title.

### Struck on defective alloy mix planchets (III-A)

This section includes those classes of coins struck on planchets that were made from a defective alloy.

III-A-1 Struck on an Improper Alloy Mix Planchet (IE), Rarity Level: 2-3, Values: 10 cents to $2.

III-A-2 Struck on a Planchet With Slag Inclusions(IE), Rarity Level: 5-6, Values: $10 up.

## Struck on damaged, defective or abnormal planchet (III-B)

Coins get struck on many strange objects. The more common of course are planchets which have been damaged in some way in the production process. In most of the classes in this section intent is at least presumed, if not specifically listed as a cause.

III-B-1 Struck on a Defective Planchet (IWE), Rarity Level: 4-6, Values: $5 to $10 and up.

III-B-2 Struck on a Mechanically Damaged Planchet (IWE), Rarity Level: 5-6, Values: $10 to $20 and up.

III-B-3 Struck on a Rolled Thin Planchet (IWE), Rarity Level: 5-6, Values: $2 to $5 and up.

III-B-4 Struck on a Rolled Thick Planchet (IWE), Rarity Level: 5-6, Values: $35 to $50 and up.

III-B-5 Struck on a Tapered Planchet (WE), Rarity Level: 4-6, Values: $2 to $5 and up.

III-B-6 Struck on a Partially Unplated Planchet (WE), Rarity Level: 5, Values: $10 up.

III-B-7 Struck on an Unplated Planchet (WE), Rarity Level: 6-7, Values: $100 up.

III-B-8 Struck on a Bubbled Plating Planchet (IWE), Rarity Level: 1, Values: No Value.

III-B-9 Struck on an Included Gas Bubble Planchet (WE), Rarity Level: 5-6, Values: $5 up.

III-B-10 Struck on a Partially Unclad Planchet (WE), Rarity Level: 5-6, Values: $5 up.

III-B-11 Struck on an Unclad Planchet (WE), Rarity Level: 4-5, Values: $5 and up.

III-B-12 Struck on an Undersize Planchet (WE), Rarity Level: 4-6, Values: Minimal.

III-B-13 Struck on an Oversize Planchet (WE), Rarity Level: 6-7, Values: Minimal.

III-B-14 Struck on an Improperly Prepared Proof Planchet (IWE), Rarity Level: 3-5, Values: $5 up.

III-B-15 Struck on an Improperly Annealed Planchet (IWE), Rarity Level: 4-5, Values: $5 up.

III-B-16 Struck on a Faulty Upset Edge Planchet (IWE), Rarity Level: 4-5, Values: $1 to $2.

III-B-17 Struck on a Rolled In Metal Planchet (WE), Rarity Level: 4-6, Values: $2 up.

III-B-18 Struck on a Weld Area Planchet (WE), Rarity Level: 6, Values: $25 to $50.

III-B-19 Struck on a Strike Clip Planchet (W), Rarity Level: 6-7, Values: $25 up.

III-B-20 Struck on an Unpunched Center Hole Planchet (WE), Rarity Level: 4-6, Values: $1 and up.

III-B-21 Struck on an Incompletely Punched Center Hole Planchet (WE), Rarity Level: 6-7, Values: $5 up.

III-B-22 Struck on an Uncentered Center Hole Planchet (WE), Rarity Level: 6-7, Values: $10 up.

III-B-23 Struck on a Multiple Punched Center Hole Planchet (WE), Rarity Level: 7, Values: $25 up.

III-B-24 Struck on an Unintended Center Hole Planchet (WE), Rarity Level: 6-7, Values: $25 and up.

III-B-25 Struck on a Wrong Size or Shape Center Hole Planchet (WE), Rarity Level: 5-7, Values: $5 up.

III-B-26 Struck on Scrap Coin Metal (E), Rarity Level: 4-6, Values: $10 up.

III-B-27 Struck on Junk Non Coin Metal (E), Rarity Level: 4-6, Values: $15 up.

III-B-28 Struck on a False Planchet (E), Rarity Level: 3-5, Values: $35 up.

III-B-29 Struck on Bonded Planchets (E), Rarity Level: 6-7, Values: $50 up.

**Struck on a defective planchet III-B-1**          **Struck on a tapered planchet III-B-5**

## Struck on a clipped planchet (III-C)

Coins struck on clipped blanks, or planchets, exhibit the same missing areas as they did before striking, modified by the metal flow from the strike which rounds the edges and tends to move metal into the missing areas. Values for blanks will run higher than planchets with similar clips.

III-C-1 Struck on a Disc Clip Planchet (WE), Rarity Level: 4-5, Values: $1 on regular coins, $20 and up for clad coins.

III-C-2 Struck on a Curved Clip Planchet - to 5% (WE), Rarity Level: 3-5, Values: 50 cents up.

III-C-3 Struck on a Curved Clip Planchet - (6 to 10%) (WE), Rarity Level: 4-5, Values: $1 up.

III-C-4 Struck on a Curved Clip Planchet - (11 to 25%) (WE), Rarity Level: 4-5, Values: $2 up.

III-C-5 Struck on a Curved Clip Planchet - (26 to 60%) (WE), Rarity Level: 4-6, Values: $10 up.

III-C-6 Struck on a Double Curved Clip Planchet (WE), Rarity Level: 3-4, Values: $2 up.

III-C-7 Struck on a Triple Curved Clip Planchet (WE), Rarity Level: 4-5, Values: $5 up.

III-C-8 Struck on a Multiple Curved Clip Planchet (WE), Rarity Level: 4-6, Values: $5 up.

III-C-9 Struck on an Overlapping Curved Clipped Planchet (WE), Rarity Level: 5-6, Values: $15 up.

III-C-10 Struck on an Incomplete Curved Clip Planchet (WE), Rarity Level: 4-5, Values: $10 up.

III-C-11 Struck on an Oval Clip Planchet (WE), Rarity Level: 5-6, Values: $20 up.

III-C-12 Struck on a Crescent Clip Planchet - (61% or more) (WE), Rarity Level: 6-7, Values: $100 up.

III-C-13 Struck on a Straight Clip Planchet (E), Rarity Level: 4-6, Values: $10 up.

III-C-14 Struck on an Incomplete Straight Clip Planchet (WE), Rarity Level: 5-6, Values: $20 up.

III-C-15 Struck on a Ragged Clip Planchet (E), Rarity Level: 4-6, Values: $15 up.

III-C-16 Struck on an Outside Corner Clip Planchet (E), Rarity Level: 7, Values: $100 up.

III-C-17 Struck on an Inside Corner Clip Planchet (E), Rarity Level: Unknown outside mint., Values: -.

III-C-18 Struck on an Irregularly Clipped Planchet (E), Rarity Level: 6-7, Values: $20 up.

III-C-19 Struck on an Incompletely Punched Scalloped or Multi-Sided Planchet (E), Rarity Level: 7, Values: $20 up.

**Ragged edge clip III-C-15**

**Multiple clip III-C-8**          **Incomplete curved clip III-C-10**

## Struck on a laminated, split or broken planchet (III-D)

This section has to do with the splitting, cracking or breaking of a coin parallel to the faces of the coin, or at least very nearly parallel, or breaks at right angles to the faces of the coin.

Lamination cracks and missing metal of any size below a split planchet are too common in the 35-percent silver 1942-1945 nickels to be collectible or have any significant value.

III-D-1 Struck on a Small Lamination Crack Planchet (W), Rarity Level: 3-4, Values: 10 up.

III-D-2 Struck on a Large Lamination Crack Planchet (W), Rarity Level: 3-6, Values: $1 up.

III-D-3 Struck on a Split Planchet (W), Rarity Level: 4-6, Values: $5 up.

III-D-4 Struck on a Hinged Split Planchet (W), Rarity Level: 5-6, Values: $35 up.

III-D-5 Struck on a Planchet With a Clad Layer Missing (W), Rarity Level: 4-5, Values: $15 up.

III-D-6 Struck on a Planchet With Both Clad Layers Missing (W), Rarity Level: 4-5, Values: $25 up.

III-D-7 Struck on a Separated Clad Layer or Lamination (W), Rarity Level: 6-7, Values: $75 up.

III-D-8 Struck on a Broken Planchet Before the Strike (W), Rarity Level: 3-5, Values: $10 up.

III-D-9 Broken Coin During or After the Strike (W), Rarity Level: 4-6, Values: $20 up.

III-D-10 Struck Coin Fragment Split or Broken During or After the Strike (W), Rarity Level: 3-5, Values: $5 up.

III-D-11 Reedless Coin Broken During or After the Strike (W), Rarity Level: Unknown, Values: -

**Lamination crack III-D-1**      **Split planchet III-D-3**      **Layer peeled off III-D-2**

## Struck on wrong stock planchets (III-E)

These classes cover those cases where the wrong stock was run through the blanking press, making planchets of the correct diameter, but of the wrong thickness, alloy or metal or a combination of incorrect thickness and metal.

III-E-1 Struck on a Half Cent-Stock Planchet (IE), Rarity Level: Unknown, Values: No Value Established.

III-E-2 Struck on a Cent-Stock Planchet (IE), Rarity Level: Unknown, Values: No Value Established.

III-E-3 Struck on a Two-Cent-Stock Planchet (E), Rarity Level: Unknown, Values: -.

III-E-4 Struck on a Three-Cent-Silver Stock Planchet (E), Rarity Level: Unknown, Values: -.

III-E-5 Struck on a Three-Cent-Nickel Stock Planchet (E), Rarity Level: Unknown, Values: -.

III-E-6 Struck on a Half Dime-Stock Planchet (E), Rarity Level: Unknown, Values: -.

III-E-7 Struck on a Dime-Stock Planchet (E), Rarity Level: 5-6, Values: $20 up.

III-E-8 Struck on a Twenty-Cent-Stock Planchet (E), Rarity Level: Unknown, Values: -.

III-E-9 Struck on a Quarter-Stock Planchet (E), Rarity Level: 6, Values: $50 up.

III-E-10 Struck on a Half Dollar-Stock Planchet (E), Rarity Level: 6-7, Values: $100 up.

III-E-11 Struck on a Dollar-Stock Planchet (E), Rarity Level: 6-7, Values: $300 up.

III-E-12 Struck on a Token/Medal-Stock Planchet (E), Rarity Level: 7, Values: No Value Established.

III-E-13 Struck on a Wrong Thickness Spoiled Planchet (IWE), Rarity Level: 7, Values: $50 up.

III-E-14 Struck on a Correct Thickness Spoiled Planchet (IWE), Rarity Level: Unknown, Values: No Value Established.

III-E-15 Struck on a Cut Down Struck Token (IWE), Rarity Level: 6-7, Values: $50 up.

III-E-16 Struck on an Experimental or Pattern-Stock Planchet (IE), Rarity Level: 7, Values: $50 up.

III-E-17 Struck on a Proof-Stock Planchet (IE), Rarity Level: 7, Values: $100 up.

III-E-18 Struck on an Adjusted Specification-Stock Planchet (IE), Rarity Level: 3-7, Values: No Value to $5 and up.

III-E-19 Struck on a Trial Strike-Stock Planchet (IE), Rarity Level: Unknown, Values: No Value Established.

III-E-20 U.S. Coin Struck on a Foreign-Stock Planchet. (E), Rarity Level: 5, Values: $35 up.

III-E-21 Foreign Coin Struck on a Foreign-Stock Planchet (E), Rarity Level: 5-6, Values: $25 up.

III-E-22 Struck on a Non-Standard Coin Alloy (IE), Rarity Level: 4-7, Values: $20 up.

**Quarter on dime stock III-E-7 (lower coin edge)**        **Extra metal on a struck coin (III-F)**

The term "extra metal" for the purpose of this section includes both extra metal added to the blank during the blanking operation and metal powder added to the planchet during the annealing operation.

III-F-1 Struck on a Type 1 Blank With Extra Metal (W), Rarity Level: Unknown, Values:

III-F-2 Struck on a Type 2 Planchet With Extra Metal (W), Rarity Level: 4-5, Values: $10 up.

III-F-3 Struck on a Sintered Coating Planchet (W), Rarity Level: 6-7, Values: $35 up.

**Sintered coating III-F-3**

# Struck on normal or abnormal blanks, or planchets (III-G)

This section includes coins struck on either a blank, as it comes from the blanking press, or as a planchet that has passed through the upsetting mill. Added to this section are those planchets which are normal until they are struck by the wrong dies. These differ from the wrong stock planchets because the wrong stock planchets are already a variety before they are struck.

III-G-1 Struck on a Type 1 Blank (IWE), Rarity Level: 4-6, Values: $10 up.

III-G-2 Struck on a Type 2 Planchet (I), Rarity Level: 1, Values: No Extra Value.

III-G-3 Struck on a Purchased Planchet (I), Rarity Level: 1, Values: No Extra Value.

III-G-4 Struck on a Mint-Made Planchet (I), Rarity Level: 1, Values: No Extra Value.

III-G-5 Struck on an Adjustment-Marked Planchet (I), Rarity Level: 4-7, Values: Minimal, and may reduce value of coin in some cases.

III-G-6 Struck on a Hardness Test-Marked Planchet (I), Rarity Level: 6-7, Values: $10 up.

III-G-7 Wrong Planchet or Metal on a Half Cent Planchet (IE), Rarity Level: 5-7, Values: $100 up.

III-G-8 Wrong Planchet or Metal on a Cent Planchet (IE), Rarity Level: 3-6, Values: $25 up.

III-G-9 Wrong Planchet or Metal on a Nickel Planchet (E), Rarity Level: 4-6, Values: $35 up

III-G-10 Wrong Planchet or Metal on a Dime Planchet (E), Rarity Level: 4-6, Values: $50 up.

III-G-11 Wrong Planchet or Metal on a Quarter Planchet (E), Rarity Level: 4-6. Values: $100 up.

III-G-12 Wrong Planchet or Metal on a Half Dollar Planchet (E), Rarity Level: 6-7, Values: $500 up.

III-G-13 Wrong Planchet or Metal on a Dollar Planchet (E), Rarity Level: 7, Values: $500 up.

III-G-14 Wrong Planchet or Metal on a Gold Planchet (E), Rarity Level: 7, Values: $1000 up.

III-G-15 Struck on a Wrong Series Planchet (IE), Rarity Level: 6-7, Values: $1500 up.

III-G-16 U.S. Coin Struck on a Foreign Planchet (E), Rarity Level: 5-7, Values: $35 up.

III-G-17 Foreign Coin Struck on a U.S. Planchet (E), Rarity Level: 6-7, Values: $50 up.

III-G-18 Foreign Coin Struck on a Wrong Foreign Planchet (E), Rarity Level: 6-7, Values: $50 up.

III-G-19 Struck on a Medal Planchet (E), Rarity Level: 6-7, Values: $100 up.

III-G-20 Medal Struck on a Coin Planchet (IE), Rarity Level: 3-5, Values: $10 up.

III-G-21 Struck on an Official Sample Planchet (IE), Rarity Level: Unknown, Values: No Value Established.

III-G-22 Struck Intentionally on a Wrong Planchet (I), Rarity Level: 6-7, Values: Mainly struck as Presentation Pieces, full numismatic value.

III-G-23 Non-Proof Struck on a Proof Planchet (IE), Rarity Level: 6-7, Values: $500 up.

**Cent on dime planchet III-G-10**

**Half on dime planchet III-G-12**

**Half on quarter planchet III-G-11**

## Struck on coin metal strip (III-H)

Pieces of the coin metal strip do manage at times to escape into the coin press.

III-H-1 (See I-H-1 Punched Coin Metal Strip), Rarity Level: Impossible, Values: -.

III-H-2 Struck on Chopped Coin Metal Strip (E), Rarity Level: 6-7, Values: $25 up.

# Die adjustment strikes (III-I)

As the dies are set up and adjusted in the coin press, variations in the strike occur until the dies are properly set. Test strikes are normally scrapped, but on occasion reach circulation.

III-I-1 Die Adjustment Strike (IE), Rarity Level: 5-6, Values: $35 up.

III-I-2 Edge Strike (E), Rarity Level: 5-6, Values: $10 to $20 and up.

III-I-3 Weak Strike (W), Rarity Level: 1, Values: No Extra Value.

III-I-4 Strong Strike (IWE), Rarity Level: 1, Values: No value except for the premium that might be paid for a well struck coin.

III-I-5 Jam Strike (IE), Rarity Level: 7, Values: $50 up.

III-I-6 Trial Piece Strike (I), Rarity Level: 6-7, Values: $100 up.

III-I-7 Edge-Die Adjustment Strike (I), Rarity Level: 5-7, Values: $5 up.

III-I-8 Uniface Strike (I), Rarity Level 7, Values: $50 up.

# Indented, brockage and counter-brockage strikes (III-J)

Indented and uniface strikes involve an extra unstruck planchet between one of the dies and the planchet being struck. Brockage strikes involve a struck coin between one of the dies and the planchet and a counter-brockage requires a brockage coin between one of the dies and the planchet.

A cap, or capped die strike results when a coin sticks to the die and is squeezed around it in the shape of a bottle cap.

III-J-1 Indented Strike (W), Rarity Level: 3-6, Values: $5 up.

III-J-2 Uniface Strike (W), Rarity Level: 3-5, Values: $15 up.

III-J-3 Indented Strike By a Smaller Planchet (WE), Rarity Level: 5-7, Values: $100 up.

III-J-4 Indented Second Strike (W), Rarity Level: 3-5, Values: $10 up, about the same as a regular double strike of comparable size.

III-J-5 Partial Brockage Strike (W), Rarity Level: 3-6, Values: $15 up.

III-J-6 Full Brockage Strike (W), Rarity Level: 3-6, Values: $5 up.

III-J-7 Brockage Strike of a Smaller Coin (WE), Rarity Level: 6-7, Values: $200 up.

III-J-8 Brockage Strike of a Struck Coin Fragment (WE), Rarity Level: 4-6, Values: $5 up.

III-J-9 Brockage Second Strike (WE), Rarity Level: 3-5, Values: $5 up.

III-J-10 Partial Counter-Brockage Strike (WE), Rarity Level: 3-5, Values: $10 up.

III-J-11 Full Counter-Brockage Strike (WE), Rarity Level: 5-7, Values: $100 up.

III-J-12 Counter-Brockage Second Strike (WE), Rarity Level: 4-6, Values: $10 up.

III-J-13 Full Brockage-Counter-Brockage Strike (WE), Rarity Level: 6-7, Values: $150 up.

III-J-14 Multiple Brockage or Counter-Brockage Strike (WE), Rarity Level: 5-7, Values: $100 up.

III-J-15 Capped Die Strike (WE), Rarity Level: 6-7, Values: $500 up.

III-J-16 Reversed Capped Die Strike (WE), Rarity Level: 7, Values: $1,000 up.

**Indented strike III-J-1**     **Counter-brockage strike III-J-11**     **Capped die strike III-J-15**

# Struck through abnormal objects (III-K)

This section covers most of the objects or materials which might come between the planchet and the die and be struck into the surface of the coin. Unless noted, the materials - even the soft ones - are driven into the surface of the coin.

III-K-1 Struck Through Cloth (IWE), Rarity Level: 3-6, Values: $35 up.

III-K-2 Struck Through Wire (IWE), Rarity Level: 3-6, Values: $5 up.

III-K-3 Struck Through Thread (IWE), Rarity Level: 3-6, Values: $5 up.

III-K-4 Struck Through Dirt-and-Grease-Filled Die (IWE), Rarity Level: 1-4, Values: 10 cents to 25 cents up, but no value on a worn or circulated coin.

III-K-5 Struck Through a Dropped Filling (IWE), Rarity Level: 5-6, Values: $10 up.

III-K-6 Struck Through Wrong Metal Fragments (IWE), Rarity Level: 4-6, Values: $1 up.

III-K-7 Struck Through an Unstruck Planchet Fragment (IWE), Rarity Level: 3-5, Values: $1 up.

III-K-8 Struck Through a Rim Burr (IWE), Rarity Level: 3-5, Values: $1 to $2 and up.

III-K-9 Struck Through plit-Off Reeding (IWE), Rarity Level: 5-6, Values: $25 up.

III-K-10 Struck Through a Feed Finger (IWE), Rarity Level: 5-7, Values: $25 to $50 and up.

III-K-11 Struck Through Miscellaneous Objects (IWE), Rarity Level: 4-6, Values: $1 up.

III-K-12 Struck Through Progression (IWE), Rarity Level: 4-6, Values: $1 up.

**Struck through cloth III-K-1**

**Struck through a filled die III-K-4**

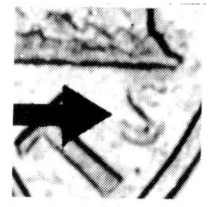

**Struck through dropped filling III-K-5**

Note: Some 1987 through 1994 quarters are found without mintmarks, classed as III-K-4, a Filled Die. Values depend on market conditions. Filled dies have value ONLY on current, uncirculated grade coins.

## Double strikes (III-L)

Only coins which receive two or more strikes by the die pair fall in this section and are identified by the fact that both sides of the coin are affected. Unless some object interferes, an equal area of both sides of the coin will be equally doubled.

The exception is the second strike with a loose die, which will double only one side of a coin, but is a rare form usually occurring only on proofs. A similar effect is flat field doubling from die chatter.

III-L-1 Close Centered Double Strike (WE), Rarity Level: 4-6, Values: $15 up.

III-L-2 Rotated Second Strike Over a Centered First Strike (WE), Rarity Level: 4-6, Values: $15 up.

III-L-3 Off-Center Second Strike Over a Centered First Strike (WE), Rarity Level: 4-6, Values: $15 up.

III-L-4 Off-Center Second Strike Over an Off-Center First Strike (WE), Rarity Level: 4-6, Values: $10 up.

III-L-5 Off-Center Second Strike Over a Broadstrike (WE), Rarity Level: 5-6, Values: $20 up.

III-L-6 Centered Second Strike Over an Off-Center First Strike (WE), Rarity Level: 5-6, Values: $50 up.

III-L-7 Obverse Struck Over Reverse (WE), Rarity Level: 5-6, Values: $25 up.

III-L-8 Nonoverlapping Double Strike (WE), Rarity Level: 5-6 Values: $20 up.

III-L-9 Struck Over a Different Denomination or Series (WE), Rarity Level: 6, Values: $300 and up.

III-L-10 Chain Strike (WE), Rarity Level: 6, Values: $300 up for the pair of coins that were struck together.

III-L-11 Second-Strike Doubling From a Loose Die (W), Rarity Level: 6-7, Values: $200 up.

III-L-12 Second-Strike Doubling From a Loose Screw Press Die (W), Rarity Level: 5-6, Values: $100 up.

III-L-13 Second Strike on an Edge Strike (WE), Rarity Level: 5-6, Values: $20 up.

III-L-14 Folded Planchet Strike (WE), Rarity Level: 5-7, Values: $100 up.

III-L-15 Triple Strike (WE), Rarity Level: 6-7, Values: $100 up.

III-L-16 Multiple Strike (WE), Rarity Level: 6-7, Values: $200 up.

III-L-17 U.S. Coin Struck Over a Struck Foreign Coin (WE), Rarity Level: 6-7, Values: $300 up.

III-L-18 Foreign Coin Struck Over a Struck U.S. Coin (WE), Rarity Level: 6-7, Values: $400 up.

III-L-19 Foreign Coin Struck Over a Struck Foreign Coin (WE), Rarity Level: 7, Values: $500 up.

III-L-20 Double Strike on Scrap or Junk (E), Rarity Level: 6, Values: $50 up.

III-L-21 Struck on a Struck Token or Medal (E), Rarity Level: 5-6, Values: $100 up.

III-L-22 Double-Struck Edge Motto or Design (E), Rarity Level: 6-7, Values: $200 up.

III-L-23 One Edge Motto or Design Struck Over Another (E), Rarity Level: 7, Values: $300 up.

III-L-24 Flat Field Doubling (W), Rarity Level: 2-3, Values: $1 to $5.

III-L-25 Territorial Struck over Struck U.S. Coin: (I) Rarity Level: 6-7, Values: $200 up.

III-L-26 Pattern Struck over Struck U.S. Coin: (I) Rarity Level: 6-7, Values: $200 up.

III-L-27 Pattern Struck over Struck Pattern:(I) Rarity Level 6-7, Values: $200 up.

III-L-28 Pattern Struck Over Foreign Coin:(I) Rarity Level 6-7, Values - $200 up.

 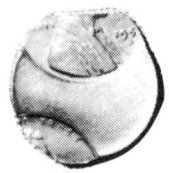 

| Off-center second strike over centered 1st strike III-L-3 | Non-overlapping double strike III-L-8 | Multiple strike III-L-16 |

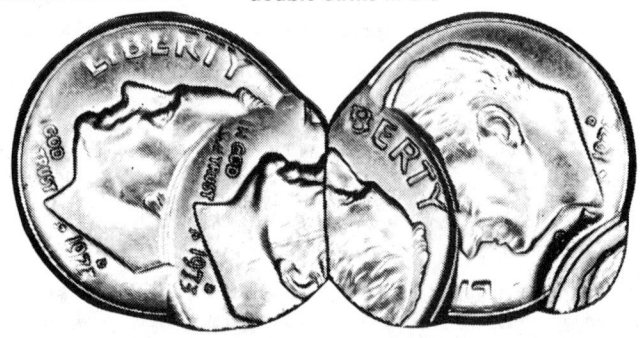

Chain strike III-L-10

## Collar striking varieties (III-M)

The collar is often referred to as the "Third Die," and is involved in a number of forms of misstrikes. The collar normally rises around the planchet, preventing it from squeezing sideways between the dies and at the same time forming the reeding on reeded coins.

If the collar is out of position or tilted, a partial collar strike results; if completely missing, it causes a broadstrike; if the planchet is not entirely between the dies, an off-center strike.

III-M-1 Flanged Partial Collar Strike (WE), Rarity Level: 5-6, Values: $20 up.

III-M-2 Reversed Flanged Partial Collar Strike (WE), Rarity Level: 6-7, Values: $35 up.

III-M-3 Tilted Partial Collar Strike (WE), Rarity Level: 5-6, Values: $20 up.

III-M-4 Centered Broadstrike (WE), Rarity Level: 5-6, Values: $5 up.

III-M-5 Uncentered Broadstrike (WE), Rarity Level: 5, Values: $3 up.

III-M-6 Reversed Broadstrike (WE), Rarity Level: 6, Values: $10 up.

III-M-7 Struck Off-Center 10-30% (W), Rarity Level: 3-6, Values: $3 up.

III-M-8 Struck Off-Center 31-70% (W), Rarity Level: 4-6, Values: $5 up.

III-M-9 Struck Off-Center 71% or More (W), Rarity Level: 3-5, Values: $2 up.

III-M-10 Rotated Multi-sided Planchet Strike (W), Rarity Level: 5-6, Values: $10 up.

III-M-11 Wire Edge Strike (IWE), Rarity Level: 1-2, Values: No Extra Value.

III-M-12 Struck With the Collar Too High (WE), Rarity Level: 6-7, Values: $20 up.

III-M-13 Off-Center Slide Strike (W), Rarity Level:3-6 $4 up.

Flanged partial collar III-M-1

| Struck off center 10 to 30 percent III-M-7 | Struck off center 31 to 70 percent III-M-8 |

**Struck off center 71 percent or more III-M-9**

# Misaligned and rotated (die) strike varieties (III-N)

**Misaligned die III-N-1**

**Normal rotation**            **90 degrees**      **135 degrees**

One (rarely both) of the dies may be Offset Misaligned, off to one side, or may be tilted (Vertically Misaligned). One die may either have been installed so that it is turned in relation to the other die, or may turn in the holder, or the shank may break allowing the die face to rotate in relation to the opposing die.

Vertical misaligned dies are rarely found, and like rotated dies, find only limited collector interest. Ninety and 180 degree rotations are the most popular. Rotations of 14 degrees or less have no value. The 1989-D Congress dollar is found with a nearly 180 degree rotated reverse, currently retailing for around $2,000. Only about 30 have been reported to date.

III-N-1 Offset Die Misalignment Strike (WE), Rarity Level: 3-5, Values: $2 up.

III-N-2 Vertical Die Misalignment Strike (WE), Rarity Level: 4-6, Values: $1 up.

III-N-3 Rotated Die Strike - 15 to 45 Degrees (IWE), Rarity Level: 4-6, Values: $2 up.

III-N-4 Rotated Die Strike - 46 to 135 Degrees (IWE), Rarity Level: 5-6, Values: $10 up.

III-N-5 Rotated Die Strike - 136 to 180 Degrees (IWE), Rarity Level: 5-6, Values: $25 up.

## Lettered and design edge strike varieties (III-O)

Early U.S. coins and a number of foreign coins have either lettered edges, or designs on the edge of the coin. Malfunctions of the application of the motto or design to the edge fall in this section.

III-O-1 Overlapping Edge Motto or Design (WE), Rarity Level: 3-4, Values: $5 to $10 and up.

III-O-2 Wrong Edge Motto or Design (WE), Rarity Level: 5-6-7, Values: $50 up.

III-O-3 Missing Edge Motto, Design or Security Edge (IWE), Rarity Level: 5-6-7, Values: $50 up.

III-O-4 Jammed Edge Die Strike (W), Rarity Level: 6, Values: $10 up.

III-O-5 Misplaced Segment of an Edge Die (E), Rarity Level: 4-7, Values: $25 up.

III-O-6 Reeded Edge Struck Over a Lettered Edge (IE), Rarity Level: 3-6, Values: No Extra Value up.

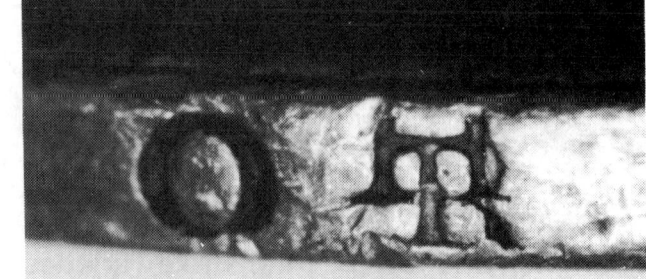

**Overlapping edge letters III-O-1**

## Defective strikes and mismatched dies (III-P)

The final section of the Striking Division covers coins which are not properly struck for reasons other than those in previous classes, such as coins struck with mismatched (muled) dies. The mismatched die varieties must be taken on a case by case basis, while the other classes presently have little collector demand or premium.

III-P-1 Defective Strike (WE), Rarity Level: 1, Values: No Extra Value.

III-P-2 Mismatched Die Strike (E), Rarity Level: 4-7, Values: $25 up.

III-P-3 Single-Strike Proof (WE), Rarity Level: 4-5, Values: Minimal.

III-P-4 Single Die-Proof Strike (IE), Rarity Level: 5-6, Values: $100 up.

III-P-5 Reversed Die Strike (I), Rarity Level: 4-5, Values: No Extra Value to Minimal.

# Official Mint modifications
## Division IV

Several mint produced varieties occur after the coin has been struck, resulting in the addition of the fourth division to my PDS System. Since most of these coins are either unique or are special varieties, each one must be taken on a case by case basis. All classes listed here are by definition intentional.

I have not listed values as the coins falling in these classes which are sold through regular numismatic channels, are cataloged with the regular issues or are covered in specialized catalogs in their particular area.

## Matte proofs (IV-A)

**Matte proof IV-A-1**

Matte proofs as a section include several of the forms of proof coins which have the striking characteristics of a mirror proof but have been treated AFTER striking to give them a grainy, non-reflective surface.

IV-A-1 Matte Proof (I), Rarity Level: 3-5, Values: Normal Numismatic Value.

IV-A-2 Matte Proof on One Side (I), Rarity Level: 7, Values: Normal Numismatic Value.

IV-A-3 Sandblast Proof (I), Rarity Level: 4-6, Values: Normal Numismatic Value.

## Additional engraving (IV-B)

**Counterstamp IV-B-III**

This section includes any added markings which are placed on the struck coin and struck coins which later were cut into pieces for various purposes. The warning is repeated: Anything done to a coin after the strike is extremely difficult to authenticate and is much easier to fake than a die struck coin.

IV-B-1 Counterstamp and Countermark (I), Rarity Level: 3-6, Values: Normal Numismatic Value.

IV-B-2 Perforated and Cut Coins (I), Rarity Level: 4-6, Values: Normal Numismatic Value.

## Restrikes (IV-C)

**Restrike with new dies IV-C-7**

Restrikes cover a complicated mixture of official use of dies from a variety of sources. Whether or not some were officially sanctioned is always a problem for the collector.

IV-C-1) Restrike on the Same Denomination Planchet (I), Rarity Level: 4-6, Values: Normal Numismatic Value.

IV-C-2 Restrike on a Different Denomination or Series Planchet (I), Rarity Level: 4-6, Values: Normal Numismatic Value.

IV-C-3 Restrike on a Foreign Coin (I), Rarity Level: 6-7, Values: Normal Numismatic Value.

IV-C-4 Restrike on a Token or Medal (I), Rarity Level: 5-6, Values: Normal Numismatic Value.

IV-C-5 Restruck With the Original Dies (I), Rarity Level: 4-6, Values: Normal Numismatic Value.

IV-C-6 Restruck With Mismatched Dies (I), Rarity Level: 4-6, Values: Normal Numismatic Value.

IV-C-7 Copy Strike With New Dies (I), Rarity Level: 3-5, Values: Normal Numismatic Value.

IV-C-8 Fantasy Strike (I), Rarity Level: 4-6, Values: Normal Numismatic Value.

# After strike modifications
## Division V

This division includes both modifications that have value to collectors – and those that don't. I needed a couple of divisions to cover other things that happen to coins to aid in cataloging them. This avoids the false conclusion that an unlisted coin is quite rare, when the exact opposite is more likely to be the case.

## Collectible modifications after strike (V-A)

This section includes those classes having to do with deliberate modifications of the coin done with a specific purpose or intent which makes them of some value to collectors. Quite often these pieces were made specifically to sell to collectors, or at least to the public under the guise of being collectible.

V-A-1 Screw Thaler, Rarity Level: 5-6, Values: Normal Numismatic Value.

V-A-2 Love Token, Rarity Level: 3-6, Values: $10 up.

V-A-3 Satirical or Primitive Engraving, Rarity Level: 6-7, Values: $5 up.

V-A-4 Elongated Coin, Rarity Level: 2-7, Values: 50 cents to $1 and up.

V-A-5 Coin Jewelry, Rarity Level: 2-5, Values: $1 up.

V-A-6 Novelty Coin, Rarity Level: 1-3, Values: No Value up to $5 to $10.

V-A-7 Toning, Rarity Level: 3-6, Values: No value up, depending on coloration. Easily faked.

V-A-8 Mint Modification, Rarity Level: 4-7, Values: $5 up. Easily faked.

V-A-9 Mint Packaging Mistake, Rarity Level: 5-7, Values: Nominal $1. Very easily faked.

**Mint modification V-A-8**

## Alterations and damage after the strike(V-B)

This section includes those changes in a coin which have no collector value. In most cases their effect on the coin is to reduce or entirely eliminate any collector value - and in the case of counterfeits they are actually illegal to even own.

V-B-1 Machine Doubling Damage: NOTE: Machine doubling damage is defined as: "Damage to a coin after the strike, due to die bounce or chatter or die displacement, showing on the struck coin as scrapes on the sides of the design elements, with portions of the coin metal in the relief elements either displaced sideways or downward, depending on the direction of movement of the loose die." Machine doubling damage, or MDD, is by far the most common form of doubling found on almost any coin in the world. Rarity Level: 0, Values: Reduces the coin's value.

V-B-2 Accidental or Deliberate Damage, Rarity Level: 0, Values: Reduces the coin's value.

V-B-3 Test Cut or Mark, Rarity Level: 0, Values: Reduces value of coin to face or bullion value.

V-B-4 Alteration, Rarity Level: 0, Values: Reduces value to face or bullion value.

V-B-5 Whizzing, Rarity Level: 0, Values: Reduces value sharply and may reduce it to face or bullion value.

V-B-6 Counterfeit, Copy, Facsimile, Forgery or Fake, Rarity Level: 0, Values: No Value and may be illegal to own.

V-B-7 Planchet Deterioration. Very common on copper-plated zinc cents. Rarity level: 0, Values: No Value

**Machine doubling damage V-B-1**

COLONIAL AMERICA

# COLONY COINAGE
## MARYLAND

### LORD BALTIMORE

### PENNY (DENARIUM)

**Composition:** Copper.

| Date | AG | Good | VG | Fine | VF | XF | Unc |
|------|----|----|----|------|----|----|-----|
| (1659) 4 known | — | — | — | — | — | — | — |

### 4 PENCE (GROAT)

**Composition:** Silver. **Obverse:** Large bust. **Reverse:** Large shield.

| Date | AG | Good | VG | Fine | VF | XF | Unc |
|------|----|----|----|------|----|----|-----|
| (1659) | 750 | 1,250 | 2,500 | 4,500 | 8,500 | 15,000 | — |

**Composition:** Silver. **Obverse:** Small bust. **Reverse:** Small shield.

| Date | AG | Good | VG | Fine | VF | XF | Unc |
|------|----|----|----|------|----|----|-----|
| (1659) unique | — | — | — | — | — | — | — |

**Note:** Norweb $26,400

### 6 PENCE

**Composition:** Silver. **Obverse:** Small bust. **Note:** Known in two other rare small-bust varieties and two rare large-bust varieties.

| Date | AG | Good | VG | Fine | VF | XF | Unc |
|------|----|----|----|------|----|----|-----|
| (1659) | 450 | 950 | 1,750 | 3,500 | 6,750 | 12,500 | — |

### SHILLING

**Composition:** Silver. **Note:** Varieties exist; one is very rare.

| Date | AG | Good | VG | Fine | VF | XF | Unc |
|------|----|----|----|------|----|----|-----|
| (1659) | 500 | 1,000 | 2,000 | 4,000 | 8,000 | 14,500 | — |

# MASSACHUSETTS

## NEW ENGLAND

### 3 PENCE

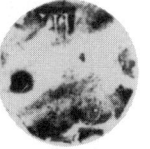

**Composition:** Silver. **Obverse:** NE. **Reverse:** III.

| Date | AG | Good | VG | Fine | VF | XF | Unc |
|------|-----|------|-----|------|-----|-----|-----|
| (1652) 2 known | — | — | — | — | — | — | — |

### 6 PENCE

**Composition:** Silver. **Obverse:** NE. **Reverse:** VI.

| Date | AG | Good | VG | Fine | VF | XF | Unc |
|------|-----|------|-----|------|-----|-----|-----|
| (1652) 8 known | — | — | — | — | — | — | — |

**Note:** Garrett $75,000

### SHILLING

**Composition:** Silver. **Obverse:** NE. **Reverse:** XII.

| Date | AG | Good | VG | Fine | VF | XF | Unc |
|------|-----|------|-----|------|-----|-----|-----|
| (1652) | 2,000 | 4,500 | 7,500 | 15,000 | 35,000 | — | — |

## OAK TREE

### 2 PENCE

| Date | AG | Good | VG | Fine | VF | XF | Unc |
|------|-----|------|-----|------|-----|-----|-----|
| 1662 | 150 | 300 | 550 | 850 | 2,150 | — | — |

### 3 PENCE

**Note:** Two types of legends.

| Date | AG | Good | VG | Fine | VF | XF | Unc |
|------|-----|------|-----|-------|-------|-----|-----|
| 1652 | 200 | 400 | 650 | 1,000 | 2,600 | — | |

## 6 PENCE

**Note:** Three types of legends.

| Date | AG | Good | VG | Fine | VF | XF | Unc |
|------|-----|------|-----|-------|-------|-----|-----|
| 1652 | 250 | 450 | 750 | 1,250 | 3,000 | — | — |

## SHILLING

**Note:** Two types of legends.

| Date | AG | Good | VG | Fine | VF | XF | Unc |
|------|-----|------|-----|-------|-------|-----|-----|
| 1652 | 175 | 300 | 650 | 1,150 | 2,850 | — | — |

# PINE TREE

## 3 PENCE

**Obverse:** Tree without berries.

| Date | AG | Good | VG | Fine | VF | XF | Unc |
|------|-----|------|-----|-------|-------|-----|-----|
| 1652 | 150 | 300 | 450 | 750 | 1,600 | — | — |

**Obverse:** Tree with berries.

| Date | AG | Good | VG | Fine | VF | XF | Unc |
|------|-----|------|-----|-------|-------|-----|-----|
| 1652 | 165 | 325 | 500 | 850 | 1,850 | — | — |

## 6 PENCE

**Obverse:** Tree without berries; "spiney tree".

| Date | AG | Good | VG | Fine | VF | XF | Unc |
|------|-----|------|-----|-------|-------|-----|-----|
| 1652 | 525 | 950 | 1,650 | 2,000 | 3,000 | — | — |

**Obverse:** Tree with berries.

| Date | AG | Good | VG | Fine | VF | XF | Unc |
|------|-----|------|-----|-------|-------|-----|-----|
| 1652 | 150 | 300 | 575 | 1,150 | 2,100 | — | — |

## SHILLING

**Note:** Large planchet. Many varieties exist; some are very rare.

| Date | AG | Good | VG | Fine | VF | XF | Unc |
|------|-----|------|-----|-------|-------|-----|-----|
| 1652 | 200 | 425 | 775 | 1,350 | 2,650 | — | — |

**Note:** Small planchet; large dies. All examples are thought to be contemporary fabrications.

| Date | AG | Good | VG | Fine | VF | XF | Unc |
|------|-----|------|-----|-------|-------|-----|-----|
| 1652 | — | — | — | — | — | — | — |

**Note:** Small planchet; small dies. Many varieties exist; some are very rare.

| Date | AG | Good | VG | Fine | VF | XF | Unc |
|------|-----|------|-----|------|------|-----|-----|
| 1652 | 150 | 300 | 575 | 1,250 | 2,300 | — | — |

# WILLOW TREE

## 3 PENCE

| Date | AG | Good | VG | Fine | VF | XF | Unc |
|------|-----|------|-----|------|------|-----|-----|
| 1652 3 known | — | — | — | — | — | — | — |

## 6 PENCE

| Date | AG | Good | VG | Fine | VF | XF | Unc |
|------|-----|------|-----|------|------|-----|-----|
| 1652 | 3,500 | 7,500 | 10,000 | 18,000 | 35,000 | — | — |

## SHILLING

| Date | AG | Good | VG | Fine | VF | XF | Unc |
|------|-----|------|-----|------|------|-----|-----|
| 1652 | 4,000 | 10,000 | 12,500 | 20,000 | 36,500 | — | — |

# NEW JERSEY

## ST. PATRICK OR MARK NEWBY

### FARTHING

**Composition:** Copper.

| Date | AG | Good | VG | Fine | VF | XF | Unc |
|------|-----|------|-----|------|------|-----|-----|
| (1682) | 20.00 | 40.00 | 80.00 | 200 | 425 | — | — |

**Composition:** Silver.

| Date | AG | Good | VG | Fine | VF | XF | Unc |
|---|---|---|---|---|---|---|---|
| (1682) | 350 | 550 | 1,150 | 1,650 | 2,750 | — | — |

## HALFPENNY

**Composition:** Copper.

| Date | AG | Good | VG | Fine | VF | XF | Unc |
|---|---|---|---|---|---|---|---|
| (1682) | 50.00 | 100.00 | 200 | 400 | 900 | — | — |

# EARLY AMERICAN TOKENS

## AMERICAN PLANTATIONS

### 1/24 REAL

**Composition:** Tin. **Obverse Legend:** ET HIB REX

| Date | AG | Good | VG | Fine | VF | XF | Unc |
|---|---|---|---|---|---|---|---|
| (1688) | 65.00 | 125 | 165 | 210 | 285 | 450 | — |

**Composition:** Tin. **Reverse:** Horizontal 4.

| Date | AG | Good | VG | Fine | VF | XF | Unc |
|---|---|---|---|---|---|---|---|
| (1688) | 175 | 300 | 400 | 500 | 650 | 1,350 | — |

**Composition:** Tin. **Obverse Legend:** ET HIB REX

| Date | AG | Good | VG | Fine | VF | XF | Unc |
|---|---|---|---|---|---|---|---|
| (1688) | — | — | — | — | — | — | 6,000 |

**Composition:** Tin. **Reverse:** Arms of Scotland left, Ireland right.

| Date | AG | Good | VG | Fine | VF | XF | Unc |
|---|---|---|---|---|---|---|---|
| (1688) | 450 | 750 | 1,250 | 2,000 | 2,500 | — | — |

**Obverse:** Rider's head left of "B" in legend. **Note:** Restrikes made in 1828 from two obverse dies.

| Date | AG | Good | VG | Fine | VF | XF | Unc |
|---|---|---|---|---|---|---|---|
| (1828) | 35.00 | 65.00 | 100.00 | 150 | 225 | 325 | — |

## ELEPHANT

**Note:** Thick planchet.

| Date | AG | Good | VG | Fine | VF | XF | Unc |
|---|---|---|---|---|---|---|---|
| (1664) | 65.00 | 100.00 | 150 | 250 | 450 | 850 | — |

**Note:** Thin planchet.

| Date | AG | Good | VG | Fine | VF | XF | Unc |
|------|-----|------|-----|------|-----|------|-----|
| (1664) | 80.00 | 150 | 200 | 350 | 600 | 1,250 | — |

**Reverse:** Diagnols tie shield.

| Date | AG | Good | VG | Fine | VF | XF | Unc |
|------|-----|------|-----|------|-----|------|-----|
| (1664) | 120 | 185 | 225 | 400 | 700 | 1,450 | — |

**Reverse:** Sword right side of shield.

| Date | AG | Good | VG | Fine | VF | XF | Unc |
|------|-----|------|-----|------|-----|------|-----|
| (1664) 3 known | — | — | — | — | — | — | — |

**Note:** Norweb $1,320

**Obverse Legend: LON DON.**

| Date | AG | Good | VG | Fine | VF | XF | Unc |
|------|-----|------|-----|------|-----|------|-----|
| (1684) | 175 | 300 | 500 | 1,000 | 1,850 | 3,750 | — |

**Obverse Legend: NEW ENGLAND.**

| Date | AG | Good | VG | Fine | VF | XF | Unc |
|------|-----|------|-----|------|-----|------|-----|
| 1694 2 known | — | — | — | — | — | — | — |

**Note:** Norweb $25,300

**Obverse Legend: CAROLINA (PROPRIETORS)**

| Date | AG | Good | VG | Fine | VF | XF | Unc |
|------|-----|------|-----|------|-----|------|-----|
| 1694 5 known | — | — | — | — | — | — | — |

**Note:** Norweb $35,200

**Obverse Legend: CAROLINA (PROPRIETORS, O over E)**

| Date | AG | Good | VG | Fine | VF | XF | Unc |
|------|-----|------|-----|------|-----|------|-----|
| 1694 | 700 | 1,100 | 1,700 | 2,750 | 5,750 | 11,000 | — |

**Note:** Norweb $17,600

# GLOUCESTER

| Date | AG | Good | VG | Fine | VF | XF | Unc |
|------|-----|------|-----|------|-----|------|-----|
| (1714) 2 known | — | — | — | — | — | — | — |

**Note:** Garrett $36,000

# HIBERNIA-VOCE POPULI

## FARTHING

**Note:** Large letters

| Date | AG | Good | VG | Fine | VF | XF | Unc |
|---|---|---|---|---|---|---|---|
| 1760 | 90.00 | 150 | 275 | 450 | 750 | 1,550 | — |

**Note:** Small letters

| Date | AG | Good | VG | Fine | VF | XF | Unc |
|---|---|---|---|---|---|---|---|
| 1760 extremely rare | — | — | — | — | — | — | — |

**Note:** Norweb $5,940

## HALFPENNY

| Date | AG | Good | VG | Fine | VF | XF | Unc |
|---|---|---|---|---|---|---|---|
| 1700 date is error, extremely rare | — | — | — | — | — | — | — |

**Note:** ex-Roper $575. Norweb $577.50. Stack's Americana, VF, $2,900

| Date | AG | Good | VG | Fine | VF | XF | Unc |
|---|---|---|---|---|---|---|---|
| 1760 varieties | 10.00 | 30.00 | 50.00 | 100.00 | 185 | 350 | — |
| 1760 legend VOOE POPULI | 20.00 | 35.00 | 60.00 | 110 | 200 | 400 | — |

# HIGLEY OR GRANBY

**Composition:** Copper. **Obverse Legend:** CONNECTICVT. **Note:** THE VALVE OF THREE PENCE.

| Date | AG | Good | VG | Fine | VF | XF | Unc |
|---|---|---|---|---|---|---|---|
| 1737 | — | — | — | — | — | — | — |

**Note:** Garrett $16,000

**Composition:** Copper. **Obverse Legend:** THE VALVE OF THREE PENCE **Reverse Legend:** I AM GOOD COPPER

| Date | AG | Good | VG | Fine | VF | XF | Unc |
|---|---|---|---|---|---|---|---|
| 1737 2 known | — | — | — | — | — | — | — |

**Note:** ex-Norweb $6,875

**Composition:** Copper. **Obverse Legend:** VALUE ME AS YOU PLEASE **Reverse:** I AM GOOD COPPER

| Date | AG | Good | VG | Fine | VF | XF | Unc |
|---|---|---|---|---|---|---|---|
| 1737 | 6,500 | 8,500 | 10,500 | 14,500 | 25,000 | — | — |

**Composition:** Copper. **Obverse Legend:** VALVE ME AS YOU PLEASE **Reverse Legend:** I AM GOOD COP-PER

| Date | AG | Good | VG | Fine | VF | XF | Unc |
|---|---|---|---|---|---|---|---|
| 1737 2 known | — | — | — | — | — | — | — |

**Composition:** Copper. **Reverse:** Broad axe.

| Date | AG | Good | VG | Fine | VF | XF | Unc |
|---|---|---|---|---|---|---|---|
| (1737) | — | — | — | — | — | — | — |

**Note:** Garrett $45,000

| 1739 5 known | — | — | — | — | — | — | — |

**Note:** Eliasberg $12,650. Oechsner $9,900. Steinberg (holed) $4,400

**Obverse Legend:** THE WHEELE GOES ROUND **Reverse:** J CUT MY WAY THROUGH

| Date | AG | Good | VG | Fine | VF | XF | Unc |
|---|---|---|---|---|---|---|---|
| (1737) unique | — | — | — | — | — | — | — |

**Note:** Roper $60,500

# NEW YORKE

**Composition:** Brass. **Note:** The 1700 date is circa.

| Date | AG | Good | VG | Fine | VF | XF | Unc |
|---|---|---|---|---|---|---|---|
| 1700 | 650 | 1,250 | 2,850 | 4,500 | 7,500 | — | — |

**Composition:** White Metal.

| Date | AG | Good | VG | Fine | VF | XF | Unc |
|---|---|---|---|---|---|---|---|
| 1700 4 known | — | — | — | — | — | — | — |

# PITT

## FARTHING

| Date | AG | Good | VG | Fine | VF | XF | Unc |
|---|---|---|---|---|---|---|---|
| 1766 | — | — | — | 1,350 | 2,850 | 6,000 | — |

## HALFPENNY

| Date | AG | Good | VG | Fine | VF | XF | Unc |
|---|---|---|---|---|---|---|---|
| 1766 | 45.00 | 85.00 | 175 | 350 | 700 | 1,500 | — |

# ROYAL PATENT COINAGE

## HIBERNIA

### FARTHING

**Note:** Pattern.

| Date | AG | Good | VG | Fine | VF | XF | Unc |
|---|---|---|---|---|---|---|---|
| 1722 | 25.00 | 50.00 | 125 | 220 | 325 | 700 | — |

**Obverse:** 1722 obverse. **Obverse Legend:** D:G:REX.

| Date | AG | Good | VG | Fine | VF | XF | Unc |
|---|---|---|---|---|---|---|---|
| 1723 | 20.00 | 40.00 | 60.00 | 90.00 | 150 | 350 | — |

**Obverse Legend:** DEI. GRATIA. REX.

| Date | AG | Good | VG | Fine | VF | XF | Unc |
|---|---|---|---|---|---|---|---|
| 1723 | 10.00 | 20.00 | 40.00 | 65.00 | 90.00 | 200 | — |

**Composition:** Silver.

| Date | Good | VG | Fine | VF | XF | Unc | Proof |
|---|---|---|---|---|---|---|---|
| 1723 | — | — | — | 800 | 1,600 | — | 2,700 |

**Composition:** Silver.

| Date | AG | Good | VG | Fine | VF | XF | Unc |
|---|---|---|---|---|---|---|---|
| 1724 | 32.00 | 45.00 | 75.00 | 125 | 250 | 485 | — |

## HALFPENNY

**Reverse:** Harp left, head right.

| Date | AG | Good | VG | Fine | VF | XF | Unc |
|---|---|---|---|---|---|---|---|
| 1722 | 7.00 | 15.00 | 35.00 | 65.00 | 135 | 350 | — |

**Obverse:** Harp left, head right. **Note:** Pattern.

| Date | AG | Good | VG | Fine | VF | XF | Unc |
|---|---|---|---|---|---|---|---|
| 1722 | — | — | — | 1,150 | 1,750 | 3,000 | — |

**Reverse:** Harp right.

| Date | AG | Good | VG | Fine | VF | XF | Unc |
|---|---|---|---|---|---|---|---|
| 1722 | 7.00 | 15.00 | 35.00 | 60.00 | 125 | 250 | — |
| 1723 | 7.00 | 15.00 | 25.00 | 40.00 | 80.00 | 175 | — |
| 1723/22 | 10.00 | 20.00 | 45.00 | 90.00 | 185 | 375 | — |
| 1724 | 7.00 | 15.00 | 35.00 | 60.00 | 125 | 265 | — |

**Obverse:** DEII error in legend.

| Date | AG | Good | VG | Fine | VF | XF | Unc |
|---|---|---|---|---|---|---|---|
| 1722 | 40.00 | 90.00 | 180 | 300 | 500 | 750 | — |

**Reverse:** Large head. **Note:** Rare. Generally mint state only. Probably a pattern.

| Date | AG | Good | VG | Fine | VF | XF | Unc |
|---|---|---|---|---|---|---|---|
| 1723 | — | — | — | — | — | — | — |

**Reverse:** Continuous legend over head.

| Date | AG | Good | VG | Fine | VF | XF | Unc |
|---|---|---|---|---|---|---|---|
| 1724 | 30.00 | 65.00 | 150 | 300 | 475 | 750 | — |

# ROSA AMERICANA

## HALFPENNY

**Obverse Legend:** D.G. REX.

| Date | AG | Good | VG | Fine | VF | XF | Unc |
|---|---|---|---|---|---|---|---|
| 1722 | 20.00 | 40.00 | 60.00 | 100.00 | 220 | 475 | — |

**Obverse:** Uncrowned rose. **Obverse Legend:** DIE GRATIA REX. **Note:** Several varieties exist.

| Date | AG | Good | VG | Fine | VF | XF | Unc |
|---|---|---|---|---|---|---|---|
| 1722 | 18.00 | 35.00 | 55.00 | 100.00 | 200 | 475 | — |
| 1723 | 285 | 525 | 750 | 1,350 | 2,250 | — | — |

**Reverse Legend:** VTILE DVLCI

| Date | AG | Good | VG | Fine | VF | XF | Unc |
|---|---|---|---|---|---|---|---|
| 1722 | 250 | 450 | 650 | 1,100 | — | — | — |

**Reverse:** Crowned rose.

| Date | AG | Good | VG | Fine | VF | XF | Unc |
|---|---|---|---|---|---|---|---|
| 1723 | 10.00 | 35.00 | 55.00 | 100.00 | 200 | 450 | — |

# PENNY

**Reverse Legend:** UTILE DULCI **Note:** Several varieties exist.

| Date | AG | Good | VG | Fine | VF | XF | Unc |
|------|-----|------|-----|------|-----|-----|-----|
| 1722 | 18.00 | 35.00 | 55.00 | 100.00 | 175 | 385 | — |

**Note:** Several varieties exist. Also know in two rare pattern types with long hair ribbons, one with V's for U's on the obverse.

| Date | AG | Good | VG | Fine | VF | XF | Unc |
|------|-----|------|-----|------|-----|-----|-----|
| 1722 | 18.00 | 35.00 | 55.00 | 100.00 | 220 | 475 | — |

**Note:** Several varieties exist.

| Date | AG | Good | VG | Fine | VF | XF | Unc |
|------|-----|------|-----|------|-----|-----|-----|
| 1723 | 18.00 | 35.00 | 55.00 | 100.00 | 200 | 420 | — |

**Note:** Pattern.

| Date | AG | Good | VG | Fine | VF | XF | Unc |
|------|-----|------|-----|------|-----|-----|-----|
| 1724 2 known | — | — | — | — | — | — | — |

| Date | AG | Good | VG | Fine | VF | XF | Unc |
|------|-----|------|-----|------|-----|-----|-----|
| (1724) 5 known | — | — | — | — | — | — | — |

**Note:** Norweb $2,035

**Obverse:** George II. **Note:** Pattern.

| Date | AG | Good | VG | Fine | VF | XF | Unc |
|------|-----|------|-----|------|-----|-----|-----|
| 1727 2 known | — | — | — | — | — | — | — |

# 2 PENCE

**Reverse:** Motto with scroll.

| Date | AG | Good | VG | Fine | VF | XF | Unc |
|---|---|---|---|---|---|---|---|
| (1722) | 35.00 | 60.00 | 110 | 200 | 350 | 700 | — |

**Reverse:** Motto without scroll.

| Date | AG | Good | VG | Fine | VF | XF | Unc |
|---|---|---|---|---|---|---|---|
| (1722) 3 known | — | — | — | — | — | — | — |

**Obverse:** Period after REX. **Reverse:** Dated.

| Date | AG | Good | VG | Fine | VF | XF | Unc |
|---|---|---|---|---|---|---|---|
| 1722 | 22.00 | 40.00 | 70.00 | 125 | 265 | 500 | — |

**Obverse:** Without period after REX.

| Date | AG | Good | VG | Fine | VF | XF | Unc |
|---|---|---|---|---|---|---|---|
| 1722 | 22.00 | 40.00 | 70.00 | 125 | 275 | 525 | — |

**Note:** Several varieties exist.

| Date | AG | Good | VG | Fine | VF | XF | Unc |
|---|---|---|---|---|---|---|---|
| 1723 | 25.00 | 45.00 | 75.00 | 140 | 285 | 550 | — |

**Note:** Patterns. Two types exist; both extremely rare.

| Date | AG | Good | VG | Fine | VF | XF | Unc |
|---|---|---|---|---|---|---|---|
| 1724 | — | — | — | — | — | — | — |

**Note:** ex-Garrett $5,775. Stack's Americana, XF, $10,925

**Note:** Pattern.

| Date | AG | Good | VG | Fine | VF | XF | Unc |
|------|----|----|----|----|----|----|----|
| 1733 4 known | — | — | — | — | — | — | — |

**Note:** Norweb $19,800

# VIRGINIA HALFPENNY

**Composition:** Copper. **Reverse:** Small 7s in date. **Note:** Struck on Irish halfpenny planchets.

| Date | Good | VG | Fine | VF | XF | Unc | Proof |
|------|------|----|----|----|----|----|----|
| 1773 | — | — | — | — | — | — | 3,500 |

**Composition:** Copper. **Obverse:** Period after GEORGIVS. **Reverse:** Varieties with 7 or 8 strings in harp.

| Date | AG | Good | VG | Fine | VF | XF | Unc |
|------|----|----|----|----|----|----|----|
| 1773 | 6.00 | 12.00 | 25.00 | 50.00 | 100.00 | 250 | 465 |

**Composition:** Copper. **Obverse:** Without period after GEORGIVS. **Reverse:** Varieties with 6, 7 or 8 strings in harp.

| Date | AG | Good | VG | Fine | VF | XF | Unc |
|------|----|----|----|----|----|----|----|
| 1773 | 7.00 | 15.00 | 30.00 | 60.00 | 135 | 275 | 525 |

**Composition:** Copper. **Obverse:** Without period after GEORGIVS. **Reverse:** 8 harp strings, dot on cross.

| Date | AG | Good | VG | Fine | VF | XF | Unc |
|------|----|----|----|----|----|----|----|
| 1773 | — | — | — | — | — | — | — |

**Note:** ex-Steinberg $2,600

**Note:** So-called "shilling" silver proofs.

| Date | AG | Good | VG | Fine | VF | XF | Unc |
|------|----|----|----|----|----|----|----|
| 1774 6 known | — | — | — | — | — | — | — |

**Note:** Garrett, $23,000

# REVOLUTIONARY

## CONTINENTAL "DOLLAR".

**Composition:** Pewter. **Obverse Legend:** CURRENCY.

| Date | AG | Good | VG | Fine | VF | XF | Unc |
|---|---|---|---|---|---|---|---|
| 1776 | — | — | 1,850 | 3,000 | 4,750 | 8,750 | 18,500 |

**Composition:** Pewter. **Obverse Legend:** CURRENCY, EG FECIT.

| Date | AG | Good | VG | Fine | VF | XF | Unc |
|---|---|---|---|---|---|---|---|
| 1776 | — | — | 1,750 | 2,850 | 4,250 | 7,750 | 16,000 |

**Composition:** Silver. **Obverse Legend:** CURRENCY, EG FECIT.

| Date | AG | Good | VG | Fine | VF | XF | Unc |
|---|---|---|---|---|---|---|---|
| 1776 2 known | — | — | — | — | — | — | — |

**Composition:** Pewter. **Obverse Legend:** CURRENCY.

| Date | AG | Good | VG | Fine | VF | XF | Unc |
|---|---|---|---|---|---|---|---|
| 1776 extremely rare | — | — | — | — | — | — | — |

**Composition:** Pewter. **Obverse Legend:** CURRENCY. **Reverse:** Floral cross.

| Date | AG | Good | VG | Fine | VF | XF | Unc |
|---|---|---|---|---|---|---|---|
| 1776 3 recorded | — | — | — | — | — | — | — |

**Note:** Norweb $50,600. Johnson $25,300

**Composition:** Pewter. **Obverse Legend:** CURENCY.

| Date | AG | Good | VG | Fine | VF | XF | Unc |
|---|---|---|---|---|---|---|---|
| 1776 | — | — | 1,650 | 2,750 | 4,000 | 8,000 | 16,000 |

**Composition:** Brass. **Obverse Legend:** CURENCY. **Note:** Two varieties exist.

| Date | AG | Good | VG | Fine | VF | XF | Unc |
|---|---|---|---|---|---|---|---|
| 1776 | — | — | — | — | 13,500 | 17,500 | — |

**Composition:** Silver. **Obverse Legend:** CURENCY.

| Date | AG | Good | VG | Fine | VF | XF | Unc |
|---|---|---|---|---|---|---|---|
| 1776 unique | — | — | — | — | — | — | — |

**Note:** Romano $99,000

# STATE COINAGE
## CONNECTICUT

**Obverse:** Bust facing right.

| Date | AG | Good | VG | Fine | VF | XF | Unc |
|------|------|------|------|------|------|------|------|
| 1785 | 20.00 | 30.00 | 50.00 | 85.00 | 190 | 450 | — |

**Obverse:** "African head".

| Date | AG | Good | VG | Fine | VF | XF | Unc |
|------|------|------|------|------|------|------|------|
| 1785 | 25.00 | 45.00 | 85.00 | 200 | 450 | 1,500 | — |

**Obverse:** Bust facing left.

| Date | AG | Good | VG | Fine | VF | XF | Unc |
|------|------|------|------|------|------|------|------|
| 1785 | 60.00 | 100.00 | 150 | 275 | 400 | 750 | — |
| 1786 | 20.00 | 30.00 | 50.00 | 90.00 | 185 | 465 | — |
| 1787 | 22.00 | 35.00 | 60.00 | 110 | 125 | 350 | — |
| 1788 | 20.00 | 30.00 | 50.00 | 100.00 | 220 | 500 | — |

**Obverse:** Small mailed bust facing right. **Reverse Legend:** ETLIB INDE.

| Date | AG | Good | VG | Fine | VF | XF | Unc |
|------|------|------|------|------|------|------|------|
| 1786 | 22.00 | 35.00 | 55.00 | 85.00 | 165 | 400 | — |

**Obverse:** Small mailed bust facing right. **Reverse Legend:** INDE ET LIB.

| Date | AG | Good | VG | Fine | VF | XF | Unc |
|------|------|------|------|------|------|------|------|
| 1786 | 30.00 | 55.00 | 75.00 | 115 | 225 | 475 | — |

**Obverse:** Large mailed bust facing right.

| Date | AG | Good | VG | Fine | VF | XF | Unc |
|------|------|------|------|------|------|------|------|
| 1786 | 30.00 | 50.00 | 90.00 | 165 | 350 | 850 | — |

**Obverse:** "Hercules head."

| Date | AG | Good | VG | Fine | VF | XF | Unc |
|------|------|------|------|------|------|------|------|
| 1786 | 25.00 | 40.00 | 75.00 | 135 | 300 | 700 | — |

**Obverse:** Draped bust.

| Date | AG | Good | VG | Fine | VF | XF | Unc |
|------|------|------|------|------|------|------|------|
| 1786 | 22.00 | 35.00 | 65.00 | 120 | 275 | 600 | — |

**Obverse:** Small head. **Reverse Legend:** ETLIB INDE.

| Date | AG | Good | VG | Fine | VF | XF | Unc |
|------|------|------|------|------|------|------|------|
| 1787 | 25.00 | 40.00 | 90.00 | 150 | 350 | 800 | — |

**Obverse:** Small head. **Reverse Legend:** INDE ET LIB.

| Date | AG | Good | VG | Fine | VF | XF | Unc |
|------|------|------|------|------|------|------|------|
| 1787 | 75.00 | 135 | 175 | 275 | 450 | 950 | — |

**Obverse:** Medium bust. **Note:** Two reverse legend types exist.

| Date | AG | Good | VG | Fine | VF | XF | Unc |
|------|------|------|------|------|------|------|------|
| 1787 | 50.00 | 80.00 | 140 | 200 | 325 | 625 | — |

**Obverse:** "Muttonhead" variety. **Note:** Extremely rare with legend INDE ET LIB.

| Date | AG | Good | VG | Fine | VF | XF | Unc |
|------|------|------|------|------|------|------|------|
| 1787 | 30.00 | 50.00 | 120 | 250 | 650 | 1,500 | — |

**Obverse:** Perfect date. **Reverse Legend:** IN DE ET.

| Date | AG | Good | VG | Fine | VF | XF | Unc |
|------|------|------|------|------|------|------|------|
| 1787 | 35.00 | 65.00 | 85.00 | 135 | 250 | 600 | — |

**Obverse:** "Laughing head".

| Date | AG | Good | VG | Fine | VF | XF | Unc |
|------|-----|------|------|------|-----|-----|-----|
| 1787 | 22.00 | 35.00 | 60.00 | 110 | 250 | 700 | — |

**Obverse:** "Horned head".

| Date | AG | Good | VG | Fine | VF | XF | Unc |
|------|-----|------|------|------|-----|-----|-----|
| 1787 | 15.00 | 25.00 | 40.00 | 70.00 | 175 | 475 | — |

**Reverse Legend:** IND ET LIB.

| Date | AG | Good | VG | Fine | VF | XF | Unc |
|------|-----|------|------|------|-----|-----|-----|
| 1787/8 | 25.00 | 40.00 | 75.00 | 130 | 250 | 650 | — |
| 1787/1887 | 20.00 | 30.00 | 50.00 | 90.00 | 200 | 520 | — |

**Obverse Legend:** CONNECT. **Reverse Legend:** INDE ET LIB. **Note:** Two additional scarce reverse legend types exist.

| Date | AG | Good | VG | Fine | VF | XF | Unc |
|------|-----|------|------|------|-----|-----|-----|
| 1787 | 22.00 | 37.50 | 60.00 | 115 | 220 | 550 | — |

**Obverse:** Draped bust. **Note:** Many varieties exist.

| Date | AG | Good | VG | Fine | VF | XF | Unc |
|------|-----|------|------|------|-----|-----|-----|
| 1787 | 12.00 | 20.00 | 40.00 | 80.00 | 135 | 275 | — |

**Obverse Legend:** AUCIORI.

| Date | AG | Good | VG | Fine | VF | XF | Unc |
|------|-----|------|------|------|-----|-----|-----|
| 1787 | 15.00 | 25.00 | 50.00 | 110 | 250 | 600 | — |

**Obverse Legend:** AUCTOPI.

| Date | AG | Good | VG | Fine | VF | XF | Unc |
|------|-----|------|------|------|-----|-----|-----|
| 1787 | 20.00 | 30.00 | 60.00 | 125 | 265 | 650 | — |

**Obverse Legend:** AUCTOBI.

| Date | AG | Good | VG | Fine | VF | XF | Unc |
|------|-----|------|------|------|-----|-----|-----|
| 1787 | 15.00 | 25.00 | 50.00 | 110 | 225 | 550 | — |

**Obverse Legend:** CONNFC.

| Date | AG | Good | VG | Fine | VF | XF | Unc |
|------|-----|------|------|------|-----|-----|-----|
| 1787 | 12.00 | 20.00 | 40.00 | 85.00 | 200 | 525 | — |

**Obverse Legend:** CONNLC.

| Date | AG | Good | VG | Fine | VF | XF | Unc |
|------|-----|------|------|------|-----|-----|-----|
| 1787 | 20.00 | 30.00 | 60.00 | 125 | 265 | 650 | — |

**Reverse Legend:** FNDE.

| Date | AG | Good | VG | Fine | VF | XF | Unc |
|------|-----|------|------|------|-----|-----|-----|
| 1787 | 15.00 | 25.00 | 45.00 | 90.00 | 210 | 535 | — |

**Reverse Legend:** ETLIR.

| Date | AG | Good | VG | Fine | VF | XF | Unc |
|------|-----|------|------|------|-----|-----|-----|
| 1787 | 15.00 | 25.00 | 45.00 | 90.00 | 210 | 535 | — |

**Reverse Legend:** ETIIB.

| Date | AG | Good | VG | Fine | VF | XF | Unc |
|------|-----|------|------|------|-----|-----|-----|
| 1787 | 20.00 | 30.00 | 50.00 | 100.00 | 225 | 550 | — |

# What they're worth, numismatically speaking . . .

$175.

$85.

$85.

$225.

$90.

$150.

$125.

$12.50

$400.

$300.

$260.

$5.00

$500.

$700.

$225.

$65.

$600.

$485.

$12.50

# PAGEANT'S BIG-MONEY PAGE

INDIAN HEAD
CENT 1877

INDIAN HEAD
CENT 1909-S

LINCOLN CENT
1909-S-VDB

LINCOLN CENT
1914-D

LIBERTY HEAD
NICKEL 1885

BUFFALO
NICKEL 1926-S

BUFFALO
NICKEL 1927-S

JEFFERSON
NICKEL 1939-D

LIBERTY HEAD
DIME 1895-O

LIBERTY HEAD
DIME 1901-S

MERCURY
DIME 1916

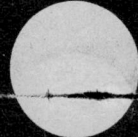

ROOSEVELT
DIME 1949-S

LIBERTY HEAD
QUARTER 1896-S

LIBERTY HEAD
QUARTER 1901-S

STANDING LIBERTY
QUARTER 1916

WASHINGTON
QUARTER 1932-D

LIBERTY HEAD
HALF 1901-S

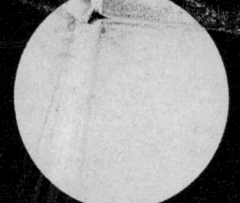

WALKING LIBERTY
HALF 1919-S

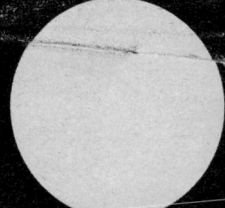

FRANKLIN
HALF 1949

**Obverse:** Mailed bust facing right.

| Date | AG | Good | VG | Fine | VF | XF | Unc |
|------|-----|------|-----|------|-----|-----|-----|
| 1788 | 15.00 | 25.00 | 45.00 | 90.00 | 200 | 425 | — |

**Obverse:** Small mailed bust facing right.

| Date | AG | Good | VG | Fine | VF | XF | Unc |
|------|-----|------|-----|------|-----|-----|-----|
| 1788 | 75.00 | 150 | 285 | 550 | 1,100 | 2,500 | — |

**Obverse Legend:** CONNLC.

| Date | AG | Good | VG | Fine | VF | XF | Unc |
|------|-----|------|-----|------|-----|-----|-----|
| 1788 | 15.00 | 25.00 | 40.00 | 80.00 | 175 | 400 | — |

**Obverse:** Draped bust facing left. **Reverse Legend:** INDE ET LIB.

| Date | AG | Good | VG | Fine | VF | XF | Unc |
|------|-----|------|-----|------|-----|-----|-----|
| 1788 | 12.00 | 20.00 | 35.00 | 55.00 | 135 | 375 | — |

**Reverse Legend:** INDLET LIB.

| Date | AG | Good | VG | Fine | VF | XF | Unc |
|------|-----|------|-----|------|-----|-----|-----|
| 1788 | 20.00 | 30.00 | 55.00 | 90.00 | 185 | 400 | — |

**Obverse Legend:** CONNLC. **Reverse Legend:** INDE ET LIB.

| Date | AG | Good | VG | Fine | VF | XF | Unc |
|------|-----|------|-----|------|-----|-----|-----|
| 1788 | 22.00 | 35.00 | 60.00 | 100.00 | 200 | 425 | — |

**Obverse Legend:** CONNLC. **Reverse Legend:** INDL ET LIB.

| Date | AG | Good | VG | Fine | VF | XF | Unc |
|------|-----|------|-----|------|-----|-----|-----|
| 1788 | 22.00 | 35.00 | 60.00 | 100.00 | 200 | 425 | — |

# MASSACHUSETTS
## HALF CENT

**Note:** Varieties exist; some are rare.

| Date | AG | Good | VG | Fine | VF | XF | Unc |
|------|-----|------|-----|------|-----|-----|-----|
| 1787 | 30.00 | 50.00 | 90.00 | 175 | 350 | 800 | — |
| 1788 | 35.00 | 55.00 | 100.00 | 185 | 375 | 850 | — |

# HALFPENNY

| Date | AG | Good | VG | Fine | VF | XF | Unc |
|------|-----|------|-----|------|-----|-----|-----|
| 1776 unique | — | — | — | — | — | — | — |

**Note:** Garrett $40,000

# CENT

**Reverse:** Arrows in right talon.

| Date | AG | Good | VG | Fine | VF | XF | Unc |
|------|-----|------|-----|------|-----|-----|-----|
| 1787 7 known | — | — | — | — | — | — | |

**Note:** Ex-Bushnell-Brand $8,800. Garrett $5,500

**Reverse:** Arrows in left talon.

| Date | AG | Good | VG | Fine | VF | XF | Unc |
|------|-----|------|-----|------|-----|-----|-----|
| 1787 | 25.00 | 40.00 | 65.00 | 120 | 285 | 785 | — |

**Reverse:** "Horned eagle" die break.

| Date | AG | Good | VG | Fine | VF | XF | Unc |
|------|-----|------|-----|------|-----|-----|-----|
| 1787 | 28.00 | 45.00 | 70.00 | 130 | 300 | 785 | — |

**Reverse:** Without period after Massachusetts.

| Date | AG | Good | VG | Fine | VF | XF | Unc |
|------|-----|------|-----|------|-----|-----|-----|
| 1788 | 28.00 | 45.00 | 70.00 | 135 | 320 | 850 | — |

**Reverse:** Period after Massachusetts, normal S's.

| Date | AG | Good | VG | Fine | VF | XF | Unc |
|------|-----|------|-----|------|-----|-----|-----|
| 1788 | 28.00 | 45.00 | 70.00 | 120 | 275 | 775 | — |

**Reverse:** Period after Massachusetts, S's like 8's.

| Date | AG | Good | VG | Fine | VF | XF | Unc |
|------|-----|------|------|------|-----|-----|-----|
| 1788 | 22.00 | 35.00 | 60.00 | 120 | 275 | 775 | — |

## PENNY

| Date | AG | Good | VG | Fine | VF | XF | Unc |
|------|-----|------|------|------|-----|-----|-----|
| 1776 unique | — | — | — | — | — | — | — |

# NEW HAMPSHIRE

| Date | AG | Good | VG | Fine | VF | XF | Unc |
|------|-----|------|------|------|-----|-----|-----|
| 1776 extremely rare | — | — | — | — | — | — | — |

**Note:** Garrett $13,000

# NEW JERSEY

**Obverse:** Date below draw bar.

| Date | AG | Good | VG | Fine | VF | XF | Unc |
|------|-----|------|------|------|-----|-----|-----|
| 1786 extremely rare | — | — | — | — | — | — | — |

**Note:** Garrett $52,000

**Obverse:** Large horse head, date below plow, no coulter on plow.

| Date | AG | Good | VG | Fine | VF | XF | Unc |
|------|-----|------|-----|------|-------|-------|-----|
| 1786 | 75.00 | 150 | 285 | 550 | 1,450 | 5,500 | — |

**Reverse:** Narrow shield, straight beam.

| Date | AG | Good | VG | Fine | VF | XF | Unc |
|------|-----|------|-----|------|-----|-----|-----|
| 1786 | 25.00 | 40.00 | 65.00 | 150 | 350 | 975 | — |

**Reverse:** Wide shield, curved beam. **Note:** Varieties exist.

| Date | AG | Good | VG | Fine | VF | XF | Unc |
|------|-----|------|-----|------|-----|-------|-----|
| 1786 | 28.00 | 45.00 | 85.00 | 180 | 425 | 1,000 | — |

**Obverse:** Bridle variety (die break). **Note:** Reverse varieties exist.

| Date | AG | Good | VG | Fine | VF | XF | Unc |
|------|-----|------|-----|------|-----|-------|-----|
| 1786 | 30.00 | 50.00 | 90.00 | 185 | 425 | 1,000 | — |

**Reverse:** Plain shield. **Note:** Small planchet. Varieties exist.

| Date | AG | Good | VG | Fine | VF | XF | Unc |
|------|-----|------|-----|------|--------|-----|-----|
| 1787 | 20.00 | 30.00 | 60.00 | 100.00 | 200 | 675 | — |

**Reverse:** Shield heavily outlined. **Note:** Small planchet.

| Date | AG | Good | VG | Fine | VF | XF | Unc |
|------|-----|------|-----|------|-----|-----|-----|
| 1787 | 22.00 | 35.00 | 75.00 | 125 | 285 | 800 | — |

**Obverse:** "Serpent head."

| Date | AG | Good | VG | Fine | VF | XF | Unc |
|------|-----|------|-----|------|-----|------|-----|
| 1787 | 40.00 | 60.00 | 120 | 285 | 700 | 1,275 | — |

**Reverse:** Plain shield. **Note:** Large planchet. Varieties exist.

| Date | AG | Good | VG | Fine | VF | XF | Unc |
|------|-----|------|-----|------|-----|------|-----|
| 1787 | 22.00 | 35.00 | 75.00 | 135 | 300 | 850 | — |

**Reverse Legend:** PLURIBS.

| Date | AG | Good | VG | Fine | VF | XF | Unc |
|------|-----|------|-----|------|-----|------|-----|
| 1787 | 30.00 | 50.00 | 100.00 | 225 | 600 | 1,100 | — |

**Obverse:** Horse's head facing right. **Note:** Varieties exist.

| Date | AG | Good | VG | Fine | VF | XF | Unc |
|------|-----|------|-----|------|-----|------|-----|
| 1788 | 20.00 | 30.00 | 65.00 | 125 | 375 | 750 | — |

**Reverse:** Fox before legend. **Note:** Varieties exist.

| Date | AG | Good | VG | Fine | VF | XF | Unc |
|------|-----|------|-----|------|-----|------|-----|
| 1788 | 35.00 | 55.00 | 110 | 275 | 725 | 1,550 | — |

**Obverse:** Horse's head facing left. **Note:** Varieties exist.

| Date | AG | Good | VG | Fine | VF | XF | Unc |
|------|-----|------|-----|------|-----|------|-----|
| 1788 | 65.00 | 125 | 285 | 575 | 1,150 | 3,000 | — |

# NEW YORK

**Composition:** Copper. **Obverse Legend:** NON VI VIRTUTE VICI.

| Date | AG | Good | VG | Fine | VF | XF | Unc |
|---|---|---|---|---|---|---|---|
| 1786 | 1,200 | 2,200 | 3,750 | 6,000 | 11,500 | — | — |

**Composition:** Copper. **Obverse:** Eagle on globe facing right.

| Date | AG | Good | VG | Fine | VF | XF | Unc |
|---|---|---|---|---|---|---|---|
| 1787 | 375 | 750 | 1,250 | 3,500 | 6,500 | 12,750 | — |

**Composition:** Copper. **Obverse:** Eagle on globe facing left.

| Date | AG | Good | VG | Fine | VF | XF | Unc |
|---|---|---|---|---|---|---|---|
| 1787 | 350 | 700 | 1,200 | 3,250 | 6,000 | 12,000 | — |

**Composition:** Copper. **Reverse:** Large eagle, arrows in right talon.

| Date | AG | Good | VG | Fine | VF | XF | Unc |
|---|---|---|---|---|---|---|---|
| 1787 2 known | — | — | — | — | — | — | — |

**Note:** Norweb $18,700

**Obverse:** George Clinton.

| Date | AG | Good | VG | Fine | VF | XF | Unc |
|---|---|---|---|---|---|---|---|
| 1787 | 2,250 | 4,000 | 5,500 | 9,500 | 20,000 | — | — |

**Obverse:** Indian. **Reverse:** New York arms.

| Date | AG | Good | VG | Fine | VF | XF | Unc |
|------|-----|------|------|------|------|------|-----|
| 1787 | 1,050 | 2,000 | 4,000 | 6,500 | 10,500 | 25,000 | — |

**Obverse:** Indian. **Reverse:** Eagle on globe.

| Date | AG | Good | VG | Fine | VF | XF | Unc |
|------|-----|------|------|------|------|------|-----|
| 1787 | 1,650 | 3,000 | 6,500 | 11,500 | 23,500 | 35,000 | — |

**Obverse:** Indian **Reverse:** George III

| Date | AG | Good | VG | Fine | VF | XF | Unc |
|------|-----|------|------|------|------|------|-----|
| 1787 | 125 | 200 | 350 | 650 | 1,350 | 4,200 | — |

# MACHIN'S MILL

**Composition:** Copper. **Note:** British halfpenny imitation.

| Date | AG | Good | VG | Fine | VF | XF | Unc |
|------|-----|------|------|------|------|------|-----|
| | 25.00 | 45.00 | 75.00 | 150 | 300 | 875 | — |

# NOVA EBORACS

**Obverse Legend:** NOVA EBORAC. **Reverse:** Figure seated right.

| Date | AG | Good | VG | Fine | VF | XF | Unc |
|------|-----|------|------|------|------|------|-----|
| 1787 | 40.00 | 75.00 | 125 | 260 | 525 | 1,100 | — |

**Reverse:** Figure seated left.

| Date | AG | Good | VG | Fine | VF | XF | Unc |
|------|----|------|-----|------|-----|-----|-----|
| 1787 | 35.00 | 55.00 | 110 | 225 | 500 | 1,000 | — |

**Obverse:** Small head, star above. **Obverse Legend:** NOVA EBORAC.

| Date | AG | Good | VG | Fine | VF | XF | Unc |
|------|----|------|-----|------|-----|-----|-----|
| 1787 | 300 | 600 | 1,750 | 3,000 | 4,500 | 6,500 | — |

**Obverse:** Large head, two quatrefoils left. **Obverse Legend:** NOVA EBORAC.

| Date | AG | Good | VG | Fine | VF | XF | Unc |
|------|----|------|-----|------|-----|-----|-----|
| 1787 | 200 | 300 | 400 | 650 | 1,150 | 2,500 | — |

# VERMONT

**Reverse Legend:** IMMUNE COLUMBIA

| Date | AG | Good | VG | Fine | VF | XF | Unc |
|------|----|------|-----|------|-----|-----|-----|
| (1785) | 1,250 | 2,000 | 3,000 | 5,000 | 9,000 | — | — |

**Obverse Legend:** VEMONTIS

| Date | AG | Good | VG | Fine | VF | XF | Unc |
|------|-----|------|-----|------|-----|-----|-----|
| 1785 | 120 | 200 | 300 | 600 | 1,150 | — | — |

**Obverse Legend:** VERMONTS

| Date | AG | Good | VG | Fine | VF | XF | Unc |
|------|-----|------|-----|------|-----|-----|-----|
| 1785 | 85.00 | 150 | 225 | 450 | 900 | 3,200 | — |

**Obverse Legend:** VERMONTENSIUM

| Date | AG | Good | VG | Fine | VF | XF | Unc |
|------|-----|------|-----|------|-----|-----|-----|
| 1786 | 75.00 | 125 | 200 | 450 | 950 | 3,250 | — |

**Obverse:** "Baby head." **Obverse Legend:** AUCTORI: VERMON:

| Date | AG | Good | VG | Fine | VF | XF | Unc |
|------|-----|------|-----|------|-----|-----|-----|
| 1786 | 120 | 200 | 300 | 550 | 1,150 | 4,500 | — |

**Obverse:** Bust facing left. **Obverse Legend:** VERMON: AUCTORI:

| Date | AG | Good | VG | Fine | VF | XF | Unc |
|------|-----|------|-----|------|-----|-----|-----|
| 1786 | 60.00 | 100.00 | 185 | 300 | 750 | 2,250 | — |
| 1787 extremely rare | — | — | — | — | — | — | — |

**Obverse:** Bust facing right. **Note:** Varieties exist.

| Date | AG | Good | VG | Fine | VF | XF | Unc |
|------|-----|------|------|------|-----|------|-----|
| 1787 | 30.00 | 50.00 | 100.00 | 200 | 425 | 1,250 | — |

**Note:** Brittania mule.

| Date | AG | Good | VG | Fine | VF | XF | Unc |
|------|-----|------|------|------|-----|------|-----|
| 1787 | 25.00 | 40.00 | 65.00 | 140 | 285 | 950 | — |

**Reverse Legend:** INDE ET LIB. **Note:** Varieties exist.

| Date | AG | Good | VG | Fine | VF | XF | Unc |
|------|-----|------|------|------|-----|------|-----|
| 1788 | 40.00 | 65.00 | 120 | 220 | 550 | 1,850 | — |

**Obverse:** "C" backward in AUCTORI.

| Date | AG | Good | VG | Fine | VF | XF | Unc |
|------|-----|------|------|------|-----|------|-----|
| 1788 extremely rare | — | — | — | — | — | — | — |

**Note:** Stack's Americana, Fine, $9,775

**Reverse Legend:** ET LIB INDE.

| Date | AG | Good | VG | Fine | VF | XF | Unc |
|------|-----|------|------|------|-----|------|-----|
| 1788 | 75.00 | 125 | 300 | 600 | 1,100 | — | — |

**Note:** George III Rex mule.

| Date | AG | Good | VG | Fine | VF | XF | Unc |
|------|-----|------|------|------|-----|------|-----|
| 1788 | 85.00 | 145 | 325 | 650 | 1,250 | 2,750 | — |

# EARLY AMERICAN TOKENS
## ALBANY CHURCH "PENNY"

**Obverse:** Without "D" above church. **Note:** Uniface.

| Date | AG | Good | VG | Fine | VF | XF | Unc |
|------|-----|------|------|------|-----|------|-----|
| (1790) 5 known | — | — | 3,500 | 7,000 | 14,000 | — | — |

**Obverse:** With "D" above church. **Note:** Uniface.

| Date | AG | Good | VG | Fine | VF | XF | Unc |
|------|-----|------|-----|------|------|-----|-----|
| (1790) rare | — | — | 3,000 | 5,000 | 10,000 | — | — |

# AUCTORI PLEBIS

| Date | AG | Good | VG | Fine | VF | XF | Unc |
|------|-----|------|-----|------|------|-----|-----|
| 1787 | 20.00 | 45.00 | 90.00 | 150 | 300 | 600 | — |

# BAR "CENT"

| Date | AG | Good | VG | Fine | VF | XF | Unc |
|------|-----|------|-----|------|------|-----|-----|
| (1785) | 85.00 | 150 | 275 | 675 | 1,200 | 2,500 | — |

# BRASHER DOUBLOON

**Composition:** Gold. **Reverse:** EB on wing.

| Date | AG | Good | VG | Fine | VF | XF | Unc |
|------|-----|------|-----|------|------|-----|-----|
| 1787 6 known | — | — | — | — | — | — | — |

**Note:** Garrett $725,000

**Composition:** Gold. **Reverse:** EG on breast.

| Date | AG | Good | VG | Fine | VF | XF | Unc |
|------|----|------|----|------|----|----|-----|
| 1787 unique | — | — | — | — | — | — | — |

**Note:** Garrett $625,000

# Castorland "Half Dollar"

**Composition:** Silver. **Edge:** Reeded.

| Date | AG | Good | VG | Fine | VF | XF | Unc |
|------|----|------|----|------|----|----|-----|
| 1796 | — | — | — | — | — | 3,550 | — |

**Composition:** Copper. **Edge:** Reeded.

| Date | AG | Good | VG | Fine | VF | XF | Unc |
|------|----|------|----|------|----|----|-----|
| 1796 3 known | — | — | — | — | — | 1,650 | — |

**Composition:** Brass. **Edge:** Reeded.

| Date | AG | Good | VG | Fine | VF | XF | Unc |
|------|----|------|----|------|----|----|-----|
| 1796 unique | — | — | — | — | — | — | — |

**Composition:** Copper. **Edge:** Plain. **Note:** Thin planchet.

| Date | AG | Good | VG | Fine | VF | XF | Unc |
|------|----|------|----|------|----|----|-----|
| 1796 unique | — | — | — | — | — | — | — |

**Note:** Norweb $467.50

**Composition:** Silver. **Edge:** Reeded. **Note:** Thin planchet. Restrike.

| Date | Good | VG | Fine | VF | XF | Unc | Proof |
|------|------|----|------|----|----|-----|-------|
| 1796 | — | — | — | — | — | — | 325 |

**Composition:** Silver. **Edge:** Lettered. **Edge Lettering:** ARGENT. **Note:** Thin planchet. Restrike.

| Date | Good | VG | Fine | VF | XF | Unc | Proof |
|------|------|----|------|----|----|-----|-------|
| 1796 | — | — | — | — | — | — | 60.00 |

**Composition:** Copper. **Edge:** Reeded. **Note:** Thin planchet. Restrike.

| Date | Good | VG | Fine | VF | XF | Unc | Proof |
|------|------|----|------|----|----|-----|-------|
| 1796 | — | — | — | — | — | — | 285 |

**Composition:** Copper. **Edge:** Lettered. **Edge Lettering:** CUIVRE. **Note:** Thin planchet. Restrike.

| Date | Good | VG | Fine | VF | XF | Unc | Proof |
|------|------|----|------|----|----|-----|-------|
| 1796 | — | — | — | — | — | — | 40.00 |

**Note:** Modern restrikes with large and small lettering on the reverse have been produced in gold, silver, copper and bronze. Original dies distinguished by wavy die breaks about the upper right corner of pot on the reverse.

# Chalmers

## 3 Pence

**Composition:** Silver.

| Date | AG | Good | VG | Fine | VF | XF | Unc |
|------|----|------|----|------|----|----|-----|
| 1783 | 250 | 500 | 1,000 | 1,500 | 2,650 | 5,500 | — |

# 6 PENCE

**Composition:** Silver. **Reverse:** Small date.

| Date | AG | Good | VG | Fine | VF | XF | Unc |
|------|-----|------|------|-------|-------|--------|-----|
| 1783 | 350 | 700 | 1,500 | 2,250 | 5,500 | 12,000 | — |

**Composition:** Silver. **Reverse:** Large date.

| Date | AG | Good | VG | Fine | VF | XF | Unc |
|------|-----|------|------|-------|-------|--------|-----|
| 1783 | 300 | 600 | 1,300 | 2,000 | 4,000 | 10,000 | — |

# SHILLING

**Composition:** Silver. **Reverse:** Birds with long worm.

| Date | AG | Good | VG | Fine | VF | XF | Unc |
|------|-----|------|------|-------|-------|-------|-----|
| 1783 | 180 | 300 | 500 | 1,000 | 2,000 | 4,500 | — |

**Composition:** Silver. **Reverse:** Birds with short worm.

| Date | AG | Good | VG | Fine | VF | XF | Unc |
|------|-----|------|------|-------|-------|-------|-----|
| 1783 | 150 | 250 | 475 | 900 | 1,850 | 4,500 | — |

**Composition:** Silver. **Reverse:** Rings and stars.

| Date | AG | Good | VG | Fine | VF | XF | Unc |
|------|-----|------|------|------|-----|-----|-----|
| 1783 4 known | — | — | — | — | — | — | — |

**Note:** Garrett $75,000

# COPPER COMPANY OF UPPER CANADA

## HALFPENNY

**Composition:** Copper.

| Date | Good | VG | Fine | VF | XF | Unc | Proof |
|------|------|-----|------|-----|-----|-----|-------|
| 1796 | — | — | — | — | — | — | 3,750 |

# FRANKLIN PRESS

**Edge:** Plain.

| Date | AG | Good | VG | Fine | VF | XF | Unc |
|------|------|------|------|------|------|------|------|
| 1794 | 18.00 | 35.00 | 55.00 | 85.00 | 175 | 300 | 600 |

# KENTUCKY TOKEN

**Edge:** Plain. **Note:** 1793 date is circa.

| Date | AG | Good | VG | Fine | VF | XF | Unc |
|------|------|------|------|------|------|------|------|
| 1793 | 12.00 | 25.00 | 40.00 | 60.00 | 100.00 | 265 | 575 |

**Edge:** Engrailed.

| Date | AG | Good | VG | Fine | VF | XF | Unc |
|------|------|------|------|------|------|------|------|
| (1793) | 35.00 | 75.00 | 125 | 200 | 350 | 950 | 1,850 |

**Edge:** Lettered. **Edge Lettering:** PAYABLE AT BEDWORTH.

| Date | AG | Good | VG | Fine | VF | XF | Unc |
|------|------|------|------|------|------|------|------|
| (1793) unique | — | — | — | — | — | 1,980 | — |

**Edge:** Lettered. **Edge Lettering:** PAYABLE AT LANCASTER.

| Date | AG | Good | VG | Fine | VF | XF | Unc |
|------|------|------|------|------|------|------|------|
| (1793) | 14.00 | 28.00 | 45.00 | 65.00 | 110 | 285 | 725 |

**Edge:** Lettered. **Edge Lettering:** PAYABLE AT I.FIELDING.

| Date | AG | Good | VG | Fine | VF | XF | Unc |
|------|------|------|------|------|------|------|------|
| (1793) unique | — | — | — | — | — | — | — |

**Edge:** Lettered. **Edge Lettering:** PAYABLE AT W. PARKERS.

| Date | AG | Good | VG | Fine | VF | XF | Unc |
|------|------|------|------|------|------|------|------|
| (1793) unique | — | — | — | — | 1,800 | — | — |

**Edge:** Ornamented branch with two leaves.

| Date | AG | Good | VG | Fine | VF | XF | Unc |
|------|------|------|------|------|------|------|------|
| (1793) unique | — | — | — | — | — | — | — |

# MOTT TOKEN

**Note:** Thin planchet.

| Date | AG | Good | VG | Fine | VF | XF | Unc |
|------|------|------|------|------|------|------|------|
| 1789 | 30.00 | 60.00 | 120 | 220 | 350 | 825 | — |

**Note:** Thick planchet. Weight generally about 170 grams.

| Date | AG | Good | VG | Fine | VF | XF | Unc |
|------|------|------|------|------|------|------|------|
| 1789 | 25.00 | 50.00 | 100.00 | 175 | 300 | 700 | — |

**Edge:** Fully engrailed. **Note:** Specimens struck with perfect dies are scarcer and generally command higher prices.

| Date | AG | Good | VG | Fine | VF | XF | Unc |
|------|------|------|------|------|------|------|------|
| 1789 | 40.00 | 85.00 | 175 | 350 | 600 | 1,250 | — |

# MYDDELTON TOKEN

**Composition:** Copper.

| Date | Good | VG | Fine | VF | XF | Unc | Proof |
|------|------|------|------|------|------|------|------|
| 1796 | — | — | — | — | — | — | 6,500 |

**Composition:** Silver.

| Date | Good | VG | Fine | VF | XF | Unc | Proof |
|------|------|------|------|------|------|------|------|
| 1796 | — | — | — | — | — | — | 5,500 |

# NEW YORK THEATRE

**Note:** 1796 date is circa.

| Date | AG | Good | VG | Fine | VF | XF | Unc |
|------|------|------|------|------|------|------|------|
| (1796) | — | — | 300 | 900 | 2,000 | 3,250 | 8,000 |

# NORTH AMERICAN
## HALFPENNY

| Date | AG | Good | VG | Fine | VF | XF | Unc |
|------|------|------|------|------|------|------|------|
| 1781 | 6.50 | 12.50 | 25.00 | 75.00 | 135 | 365 | 750 |

# RHODE ISLAND SHIP

**Composition:** Brass. **Obverse:** Without wreath below ship.

| Date | AG | Good | VG | Fine | VF | XF | Unc |
|------|------|------|------|------|------|------|------|
| 1779 | 50.00 | 100 | 175 | 275 | 500 | 1,000 | 2,000 |

**Composition:** Pewter. **Obverse:** Without wreath below ship.

| Date | AG | Good | VG | Fine | VF | XF | Unc |
|------|------|------|------|------|------|------|------|
| 1779 | — | — | — | — | 1,250 | 2,500 | 5,500 |

**Composition:** Brass. **Obverse:** Wreath below ship.

| Date | AG | Good | VG | Fine | VF | XF | Unc |
|------|-----|------|-----|------|-----|------|------|
| 1779 | 60.00 | 120 | 200 | 325 | 600 | 1,150 | 2,200 |

**Composition:** Pewter. **Obverse:** Wreath below ship.

| Date | AG | Good | VG | Fine | VF | XF | Unc |
|------|-----|------|-----|------|-----|------|------|
| 1779 | — | — | — | — | 1,500 | 3,000 | 6,500 |

**Composition:** Brass. **Obverse:** VLUGTENDE below ship.

| Date | AG | Good | VG | Fine | VF | XF | Unc |
|------|-----|------|-----|------|-----|------|------|
| 1779 unique | — | — | — | — | — | — | — |

**Note:** Garrett $16,000

# STANDISH BARRY

## 3 PENCE

**Composition:** Silver.

| Date | AG | Good | VG | Fine | VF | XF | Unc |
|------|-----|------|-----|------|-----|------|------|
| 1790 | 850 | 1,350 | 2,000 | 3,000 | 6,500 | 12,000 | — |

# TALBOT, ALLUM & LEE

## CENT

**Composition:** Copper. **Reverse:** NEW YORK above ship. **Edge:** Lettered. **Edge Lettering:** PAYABLE AT THE STORE OF

| Date | AG | Good | VG | Fine | VF | XF | Unc |
|------|-----|------|-----|------|-----|------|------|
| 1794 | 12.00 | 25.00 | 45.00 | 90.00 | 175 | 300 | 925 |

**Composition:** Copper. **Reverse:** NEW YORK above ship. **Edge:** Plain. **Note:** Size of ampersand varies on obverse and reverse dies.

| Date | AG | Good | VG | Fine | VF | XF | Unc |
|------|-----|------|-----|------|-----|------|------|
| 1794 4 known | — | — | — | — | 2,350 | 3,000 | — |

**Composition:** Copper. **Reverse:** Without NEW YORK above ship. **Edge:** Lettered. **Edge Lettering:** PAYABLE AT THE STORE OF

| Date | AG | Good | VG | Fine | VF | XF | Unc |
|------|-----|------|-----|------|-----|------|------|
| 1794 | 100 | 200 | 350 | 650 | 1,000 | 2,250 | 4,550 |

**Composition:** Copper. **Edge:** Lettered. **Edge Lettering:** WE PROMISE TO PAY THE BEARER ONE CENT.

| Date | AG | Good | VG | Fine | VF | XF | Unc |
|------|------|------|------|------|------|------|------|
| 1795 | 10.00 | 20.00 | 40.00 | 75.00 | 160 | 300 | 725 |

**Composition:** Copper. **Edge:** Lettered. **Edge Lettering:** CURRENT EVERYWHERE.

| Date | AG | Good | VG | Fine | VF | XF | Unc |
|------|------|------|------|------|------|------|------|
| 1795 unique | — | — | — | — | — | — | — |

**Composition:** Copper. **Edge:** Olive leaf.

| Date | AG | Good | VG | Fine | VF | XF | Unc |
|------|------|------|------|------|------|------|------|
| 1795 unique | — | — | — | — | — | — | — |

**Note:** Norweb $4,400

**Composition:** Copper. **Edge:** Plain.

| Date | AG | Good | VG | Fine | VF | XF | Unc |
|------|------|------|------|------|------|------|------|
| 1795 2 known | — | — | — | — | — | — | — |
| 1795 edge: Cambridge Bedford Huntington.X.X., unique | — | — | — | — | — | — | — |

**Note:** Norweb, $3,960

# WASHINGTON PIECES

**Obverse Legend:** GEORGIVS TRIUMPHO

| Date | AG | Good | VG | Fine | VF | XF | Unc |
|------|------|------|------|------|------|------|------|
| 1783 | 25.00 | 40.00 | 65.00 | 150 | 325 | 750 | — |

**Obverse:** Large military bust. **Note:** Varieties exist.

| Date | AG | Good | VG | Fine | VF | XF | Unc |
|------|------|------|------|------|------|------|------|
| 1783 | 8.00 | 15.00 | 25.00 | 50.00 | 110 | 280 | — |

**Obverse:** Small military bust. **Edge:** Plain.

| Date | AG | Good | VG | Fine | VF | XF | Unc |
|------|------|------|------|------|------|------|------|
| 1783 | 10.00 | 20.00 | 35.00 | 65.00 | 125 | 300 | — |

**Note:** One proof example is known. Value: 12,500

**Obverse:** Small military bust. **Edge:** Engrailed.

| Date | AG | Good | VG | Fine | VF | XF | Unc |
|------|------|------|------|------|------|------|------|
| 1783 | 18.00 | 35.00 | 50.00 | 80.00 | 175 | 345 | — |

**Obverse:** Draped bust, no button on drapery, small letter.

| Date | AG | Good | VG | Fine | VF | XF | Unc |
|---|---|---|---|---|---|---|---|
| 1783 | 10.00 | 20.00 | 35.00 | 65.00 | 125 | 285 | — |

**Obverse:** Draped bust, button on drapery, large letter.

| Date | AG | Good | VG | Fine | VF | XF | Unc |
|---|---|---|---|---|---|---|---|
| 1783 | 25.00 | 40.00 | 60.00 | 100.00 | 200 | 350 | — |

**Composition:** Copper. **Obverse:** Large modern lettering. **Edge:** Plain. **Note:** Restrike.

| Date | Good | VG | Fine | VF | XF | Unc | Proof |
|---|---|---|---|---|---|---|---|
| 1783 | — | — | — | — | — | — | 550 |

**Edge:** Engrailed. **Note:** Restrike.

| Date | Good | VG | Fine | VF | XF | Unc | Proof |
|---|---|---|---|---|---|---|---|
| 1783 | — | — | — | — | — | — | 450 |

**Note:** Bronzed. Restrike.

| Date | Good | VG | Fine | VF | XF | Unc | Proof |
|---|---|---|---|---|---|---|---|
| 1783 | — | — | — | — | — | — | 350 |

**Composition:** Silver. **Note:** Restrike.

| Date | Good | VG | Fine | VF | XF | Unc | Proof |
|---|---|---|---|---|---|---|---|
| 1783 | — | — | — | — | — | — | 1,000 |

**Composition:** Gold. **Note:** Restrike.

| Date | AG | Good | VG | Fine | VF | XF | Unc |
|---|---|---|---|---|---|---|---|
| 1783 2 known | — | — | — | — | — | — | — |

**Composition:** Copper. **Obverse Legend:** WASHINGTON PRESIDENT **Edge:** Plain.

| Date | AG | Good | VG | Fine | VF | XF | Unc |
|---|---|---|---|---|---|---|---|
| 1792 | 850 | 1,450 | 3,250 | 5,000 | 7,500 | — | — |

**Note:** Steinberg $12,650. Garrett $15,500

**Composition:** Copper. **Obverse Legend:** WASHINGTON PRESIDENT **Edge:** Lettered. **Edge Lettering:** UNITED STATES OF AMERICA

| Date | AG | Good | VG | Fine | VF | XF | Unc |
|---|---|---|---|---|---|---|---|
| 1792 | 1,350 | 2,250 | 4,500 | 7,500 | 12,500 | — | — |

**Composition:** Copper. **Obverse Legend:** BORN VIRGINIA **Note:** Varieties exist.

| Date | AG | Good | VG | Fine | VF | XF | Unc |
|---|---|---|---|---|---|---|---|
| (1792) | 250 | 500 | 1,000 | 2,200 | 3,750 | 7,500 | — |

**Composition:** Silver. **Edge:** Lettered. **Edge Lettering:** UNITED STATES OF AMERICA

| Date | AG | Good | VG | Fine | VF | XF | Unc |
|---|---|---|---|---|---|---|---|
| (1792) 2 known | — | — | — | — | — | — | — |

**Composition:** Silver. **Edge:** Plain.

| Date | AG | Good | VG | Fine | VF | XF | Unc |
|---|---|---|---|---|---|---|---|
| (1792) 4 known | — | — | — | — | — | — | — |

**Note:** Roper $16,500

**Reverse:** Heraldic eagle. 1792 half dollar. **Note:** Mule.

| Date | AG | Good | VG | Fine | VF | XF | Unc |
|---|---|---|---|---|---|---|---|
| (1792) 3 known | — | — | — | — | — | — | — |

**Obverse Legend:** LIBERTY AND SECURITY. **Edge:** Lettered. **Note:** "Penny."

| Date | AG | Good | VG | Fine | VF | XF | Unc |
|------|-----|------|-----|------|-----|-----|-----|
| (1795) | 25.00 | 40.00 | 75.00 | 135 | 275 | 625 | 2,000 |

**Edge:** Plain. **Note:** "Penny."

| Date | AG | Good | VG | Fine | VF | XF | Unc |
|------|-----|------|-----|------|-----|-----|-----|
| (1795) extremely rare | — | — | — | — | — | — | — |

**Note:** "Penny." Engine-turned borders.

| Date | AG | Good | VG | Fine | VF | XF | Unc |
|------|-----|------|-----|------|-----|-----|-----|
| (1795) 12 known | — | — | — | — | — | — | 3,750 |

**Note:** Similar to "halfpenny" with date on reverse.

| Date | AG | Good | VG | Fine | VF | XF | Unc |
|------|-----|------|-----|------|-----|-----|-----|
| 1795 very rare | — | — | — | — | — | — | — |

**Note:** Roper $6,600

# CENT

**Obverse Legend:** UNITY STATES

| Date | AG | Good | VG | Fine | VF | XF | Unc |
|------|-----|------|-----|------|-----|-----|-----|
| 1783 | 13.00 | 22.00 | 40.00 | 70.00 | 160 | 325 | — |

**Note:** Double head.

| Date | AG | Good | VG | Fine | VF | XF | Unc |
|------|-----|------|-----|------|-----|-----|-----|
| (1783) | 10.00 | 20.00 | 35.00 | 65.00 | 135 | 300 | — |

**Obverse:** "Ugly head." **Note:** 3 known in copper, 1 in white metal.

| Date | AG | Good | VG | Fine | VF | XF | Unc |
|------|-----|------|-----|------|-----|-----|-----|
| 1784 | — | — | — | — | — | — | — |

**Note:** Roper $14,850

**Reverse:** Small eagle.

| Date | AG | Good | VG | Fine | VF | XF | Unc |
|------|-----|-------|-----|------|-----|-----|-----|
| 1791 | 30.00 | 60.00 | 125 | 250 | 335 | 675 | — |

**Reverse:** Large eagle.

| Date | AG | Good | VG | Fine | VF | XF | Unc |
|------|-----|-------|-----|------|-----|-----|-----|
| 1791 | 35.00 | 65.00 | 145 | 275 | 375 | 725 | — |

**Obverse:** "Roman" head.

| Date | Good | VG | Fine | VF | XF | Unc | Proof |
|------|------|-----|------|-----|-----|-----|-------|
| 1792 | — | — | — | — | — | — | 17,600 |

# HALF DOLLAR

**Reverse:** Small eagle. **Edge:** Plain.

| Date | AG | Good | VG | Fine | VF | XF | Unc |
|------|-----|-------|-----|------|-----|-----|-----|
| 1792 | 4,500 | 7,000 | 9,000 | 12,500 | 20,000 | 37,500 | — |

**Edge:** Ornamented, circles and squares.

| Date | AG | Good | VG | Fine | VF | XF | Unc |
|------|-----|-------|-----|------|-----|-----|-----|
| 1792 5 known | — | — | — | — | — | — | — |

**Composition:** Copper. **Edge:** Lettered. **Edge Lettering:** UNITED STATES OF AMERICA

| Date | AG | Good | VG | Fine | VF | XF | Unc |
|------|-----|-------|-----|------|-----|-----|-----|
| 1792 2 known | — | — | — | — | — | — | — |

**Note:** Roper $2,860. Benson, EF, $48,300

**Composition:** Copper. **Edge:** Plain.

| Date | AG | Good | VG | Fine | VF | XF | Unc |
|------|-----|-------|-----|------|-----|-----|-----|
| 1792 3 known | — | — | — | — | — | — | — |

**Composition:** Silver. **Edge:** Lettered. **Edge Lettering:** UNITED STATES OF AMERICA

| Date | AG | Good | VG | Fine | VF | XF | Unc |
|------|-----|-------|-----|------|-----|-----|-----|
| 1792 rare | — | — | — | — | — | — | — |

**Note:** Roper $35,200

**Composition:** Silver. **Edge:** Plain.

| Date | AG | Good | VG | Fine | VF | XF | Unc |
|------|-----|-------|-----|------|-----|-----|-----|
| 1792 rare | — | — | — | — | — | — | — |

**Composition:** Gold. **Edge:** Lettered. **Edge Lettering:** UNITED STATES OF AMERICA

| Date | AG | Good | VG | Fine | VF | XF | Unc |
|------|-----|-------|-----|------|-----|-----|-----|
| 1792 unique | — | — | — | — | — | — | — |

**Composition:** Copper. **Edge:** Plain.

| Date | AG | Good | VG | Fine | VF | XF | Unc |
|---|---|---|---|---|---|---|---|
| 1792 | 750 | 1,500 | 3,500 | 5,750 | 8,500 | — | — |

**Note:** Garrett $32,000

**Composition:** Silver. **Edge:** Two olive leaves.

| Date | AG | Good | VG | Fine | VF | XF | Unc |
|---|---|---|---|---|---|---|---|
| 1792 unique | — | — | — | — | — | — | — |

**Composition:** Silver. **Reverse:** Large heraldic eagle.

| Date | AG | Good | VG | Fine | VF | XF | Unc |
|---|---|---|---|---|---|---|---|
| 1792 unique | — | — | — | — | — | — | — |

**Note:** Garrett $16,500

# HALFPENNY

**Obverse Legend:** LIVERPOOL HALFPENNY

| Date | AG | Good | VG | Fine | VF | XF | Unc |
|---|---|---|---|---|---|---|---|
| 1791 | 300 | 450 | 550 | 850 | 1,650 | 2,350 | — |

**Reverse:** Ship. **Edge:** Lettered.

| Date | AG | Good | VG | Fine | VF | XF | Unc |
|---|---|---|---|---|---|---|---|
| 1793 | 20.00 | 30.00 | 60.00 | 110 | 235 | 500 | — |

**Reverse:** Ship. **Edge:** Plain.

| Date | AG | Good | VG | Fine | VF | XF | Unc |
|---|---|---|---|---|---|---|---|
| 1793 5 known | — | — | — | — | 2,000 | — | — |

**Obverse:** Large coat buttons. **Reverse:** Grate. **Edge:** Reeded.

| Date | AG | Good | VG | Fine | VF | XF | Unc |
|---|---|---|---|---|---|---|---|
| 1795 | 12.00 | 20.00 | 30.00 | 60.00 | 120 | 265 | 575 |

**Reverse:** Grate. **Edge:** Lettered.

| Date | AG | Good | VG | Fine | VF | XF | Unc |
|------|-----|------|-----|------|-----|-----|-----|
| 1795 | 45.00 | 85.00 | 165 | 225 | 300 | 625 | 1,200 |

**Obverse:** Small coat buttons. **Reverse:** Grate. **Edge:** Reeded.

| Date | AG | Good | VG | Fine | VF | XF | Unc |
|------|-----|------|-----|------|-----|-----|-----|
| 1795 | 10.00 | 35.00 | 60.00 | 100.00 | 175 | 375 | 850 |

**Obverse Legend:** LIBERTY AND SECURITY. **Edge:** Plain.

| Date | AG | Good | VG | Fine | VF | XF | Unc |
|------|-----|------|-----|------|-----|-----|-----|
| 1795 | 10.00 | 35.00 | 60.00 | 100.00 | 175 | 435 | 975 |

**Edge:** Lettered. **Edge Lettering:** PAYABLE AT LONDON ...

| Date | AG | Good | VG | Fine | VF | XF | Unc |
|------|-----|------|-----|------|-----|-----|-----|
| 1795 | 12.00 | 20.00 | 30.00 | 60.00 | 125 | 375 | 800 |

**Edge:** Lettered. **Edge Lettering:** BIRMINGHAM ...

| Date | AG | Good | VG | Fine | VF | XF | Unc |
|------|-----|------|-----|------|-----|-----|-----|
| 1795 | 14.00 | 28.00 | 35.00 | 70.00 | 150 | 425 | 950 |

**Edge:** Lettered. **Edge Lettering:** AN ASYLUM ...

| Date | AG | Good | VG | Fine | VF | XF | Unc |
|------|-----|------|-----|------|-----|-----|-----|
| 1795 | 18.00 | 35.00 | 60.00 | 100.00 | 225 | 450 | 1,000 |

**Edge:** Lettered. **Edge Lettering:** PAYABLE AT LIVERPOOL ...

| Date | AG | Good | VG | Fine | VF | XF | Unc |
|------|-----|------|-----|------|-----|-----|-----|
| 1795 unique | — | — | — | — | — | — | — |

**Edge:** Lettered. **Edge Lettering:** PAYABLE AT LONDON-LIVERPOOL.

| Date | AG | Good | VG | Fine | VF | XF | Unc |
|------|-----|------|-----|------|-----|-----|-----|
| 1795 unique | — | — | — | — | — | — | — |

**Obverse Legend:** NORTH WALES. **Edge:** Plain.

| Date | AG | Good | VG | Fine | VF | XF | Unc |
|------|-----|------|-----|------|-----|-----|-----|
| (1795) | 25.00 | 45.00 | 85.00 | 145 | 250 | 550 | 1,450 |

**Obverse Legend:** NORTH WALES. **Edge:** Lettered.

| Date | AG | Good | VG | Fine | VF | XF | Unc |
|------|-----|------|-----|------|-----|-----|-----|
| (1795) | 120 | 250 | 400 | 600 | 950 | 2,000 | 4,500 |

**Obverse Legend:** NORTH WALES. **Reverse:** Four stars at bottom.

| Date | AG | Good | VG | Fine | VF | XF | Unc |
|------|-----|------|-----|------|-----|-----|-----|
| (1795) | 200 | 400 | 700 | 1,500 | 2,850 | 5,500 | — |

# EARLY AMERICAN PATTERNS

**Obverse Legend:** IMMUNIS COLUMBIA. **Reverse:** Eagle.

| Date | AG | Good | VG | Fine | VF | XF | Unc |
|------|-----|------|-----|------|-----|-----|-----|
| 1786 3 known | — | — | — | — | — | — | — |

**Obverse:** Washington

| Date | AG | Good | VG | Fine | VF | XF | Unc |
|------|-----|------|-----|------|-----|-----|-----|
| (1786) 3 known | — | — | — | — | — | — | — |

**Note:** Garrett $50,000. Steinberg $12,650

**Obverse:** Eagle

| Date | AG | Good | VG | Fine | VF | XF | Unc |
|---|---|---|---|---|---|---|---|
| 1786 unique | — | — | — | — | — | — | — |

**Note:** Garrett $37,500

**Obverse:** Washington **Reverse:** Eagle

| Date | AG | Good | VG | Fine | VF | XF | Unc |
|---|---|---|---|---|---|---|---|
| 1786 2 known | — | — | — | — | — | — | — |

**Obverse Legend:** IMMUNIS COLUMBIA

| Date | AG | Good | VG | Fine | VF | XF | Unc |
|---|---|---|---|---|---|---|---|
| 1786 extremely rare | — | — | — | — | — | — | — |

**Note:** Rescigno, AU, $33,000. Steinberg, VF, $11,000

# CONFEDERATIO

**Reverse:** Small circle of stars

| Date | AG | Good | VG | Fine | VF | XF | Unc |
|---|---|---|---|---|---|---|---|
| 1785 | — | — | — | — | 8,800 | 16,500 | — |

**Composition:** Copper. **Reverse:** Large circle of stars **Note:** The Confederatio dies were struck in combination with 13 other dies of the period. All surviving examples of these combinations are extremely rare.

| Date | AG | Good | VG | Fine | VF | XF | Unc |
|---|---|---|---|---|---|---|---|
| 1785 extremely rare | — | — | — | — | — | — | — |

# IMMUNE COLUMBIA

**Obverse:** George III.

| Date | AG | Good | VG | Fine | VF | XF | Unc |
|---|---|---|---|---|---|---|---|
| 1785 | 750 | 1,250 | 1,850 | 2,250 | 5,000 | 9,000 | — |

**Obverse:** Vermon

| Date | AG | Good | VG | Fine | VF | XF | Unc |
|---|---|---|---|---|---|---|---|
| 1785 | 600 | 1,000 | 1,650 | 2,000 | 4,750 | 8,500 | — |

**Composition:** Silver. **Reverse Legend:** CONSTELLATIO.

| Date | AG | Good | VG | Fine | VF | XF | Unc |
|---|---|---|---|---|---|---|---|
| 1785 | — | — | — | — | — | 20,700 | — |

**Composition:** Gold. **Reverse Legend:** CONSTELATIO.

| Date | AG | Good | VG | Fine | VF | XF | Unc |
|---|---|---|---|---|---|---|---|
| 1785 unique | — | — | — | — | — | — | — |

**Composition:** Copper. **Reverse Legend:** CONSTELLATIO

| Date | AG | Good | VG | Fine | VF | XF | Unc |
|---|---|---|---|---|---|---|---|
| 1785 | — | — | — | — | — | 14,375 | — |

**Composition:** Copper. **Obverse Legend:** Extra star in border **Reverse Legend:** CONSTELLATIO

| Date | AG | Good | VG | Fine | VF | XF | Unc |
|---|---|---|---|---|---|---|---|
| 1785 | — | — | — | — | — | — | — |

**Note:** Caldwell $4,675

**Composition:** Copper. **Reverse:** Blunt rays. **Reverse Legend:** CONSTELLATIO

| Date | AG | Good | VG | Fine | VF | XF | Unc |
|---|---|---|---|---|---|---|---|
| 1785 2 known | — | — | — | — | — | — | — |

**Note:** Norweb $22,000

# NOVA CONSTELLATIO

## 5

**Composition:** Copper.

| Date | AG | Good | VG | Fine | VF | XF | Unc |
|---|---|---|---|---|---|---|---|
| 1783 unique | — | — | — | — | — | — | — |

## 100 (Bit)

**Composition:** Silver. **Edge:** Leaf.

| Date | AG | Good | VG | Fine | VF | XF | Unc |
|---|---|---|---|---|---|---|---|
| 1783 2 known | — | — | — | — | — | — | — |

**Note:** Garrett $97,500. Stack's auction, May 1991, $72,500

**Composition:** Silver. **Edge:** Plain.

| Date | AG | Good | VG | Fine | VF | XF | Unc |
|---|---|---|---|---|---|---|---|
| 1783 unique | — | — | — | — | — | — | — |

## 500 (Quint)

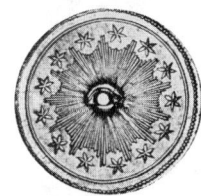 

**Obverse:** Without legend

| Date | AG | Good | VG | Fine | VF | XF | Unc |
|---|---|---|---|---|---|---|---|
| 1783 unique | — | — | — | — | — | — | — |

**Note:** Garrett $55,000

**Composition:** Silver. **Obverse Legend:** NOVA CONSTELLATIO

| Date | AG | Good | VG | Fine | VF | XF | Unc |
|---|---|---|---|---|---|---|---|
| 1783 unique | — | — | — | — | — | — | — |

**Note:** Garrett $165,000

## 1000 (Mark)

**Composition:** Silver.

| Date | AG | Good | VG | Fine | VF | XF | Unc |
|---|---|---|---|---|---|---|---|
| 1783 unique | — | — | — | — | — | — | — |

**Note:** Garrett $190,000

# EARLY FEDERAL COINAGE

## Fugio "Cent"

**Composition:** Copper. **Obverse:** Club rays, round ends.

| Date | AG | Good | VG | Fine | VF | XF | Unc |
|------|-----|------|-----|------|-----|------|-----|
| 1787 | 40.00 | 75.00 | 150 | 375 | 850 | 1,600 | — |

**Composition:** Copper. **Obverse:** Club rays, concave ends.

| Date | AG | Good | VG | Fine | VF | XF | Unc |
|------|-----|------|-----|------|-----|------|-----|
| 1787 | 250 | 700 | 1,800 | 2,750 | 5,000 | — | — |

**Composition:** Copper. **Obverse Legend:** FUCIO.

| Date | AG | Good | VG | Fine | VF | XF | Unc |
|------|-----|------|-----|------|-----|------|-----|
| 1787 | 300 | 750 | 1,850 | 2,850 | 5,500 | — | — |

**Composition:** Copper. **Obverse:** Pointed rays. **Reverse:** UNITED above, STATES below.

| Date | AG | Good | VG | Fine | VF | XF | Unc |
|------|-----|------|-----|------|-----|------|-----|
| 1787 | 100 | 250 | 550 | 1,000 | 1,500 | 3,500 | — |

**Composition:** Copper. **Reverse:** UNITED STATES at sides of ring.

| Date | AG | Good | VG | Fine | VF | XF | Unc |
|------|-----|------|-----|------|-----|------|-----|
| 1787 | 20.00 | 45.00 | 90.00 | 175 | 300 | 650 | — |

**Composition:** Copper. **Reverse:** STATES UNITED at sides of ring.

| Date | AG | Good | VG | Fine | VF | XF | Unc |
|------|-----|------|-----|------|-----|------|-----|
| 1787 | 25.00 | 55.00 | 110 | 220 | 350 | 700 | — |

**Composition:** Copper. **Reverse:** Eight-pointed stars on ring.

| Date | AG | Good | VG | Fine | VF | XF | Unc |
|------|-----|------|-----|------|-----|------|-----|
| 1787 | 30.00 | 65.00 | 120 | 250 | 400 | 800 | — |

**Composition:** Copper. **Reverse:** Raised rims on ring, large lettering in center

| Date | AG | Good | VG | Fine | VF | XF | Unc |
|------|-----|------|-----|------|-----|------|-----|
| 1787 | 35.00 | 75.00 | 135 | 275 | 450 | 950 | — |

**Composition:** Copper. **Obverse:** No cinquefoils, cross after date. **Obverse Legend:** UNITED STATES.

| Date | AG | Good | VG | Fine | VF | XF | Unc |
|------|-----|------|-----|------|-----|------|-----|
| 1787 | 50.00 | 110 | 250 | 425 | 650 | 1,250 | — |

**Composition:** Copper. **Obverse:** No cinquefoils, cross after date. **Obverse Legend:** STATES UNITED.

| Date | AG | Good | VG | Fine | VF | XF | Unc |
|------|-----|------|-----|------|-----|------|-----|
| 1787 | 60.00 | 135 | 285 | 475 | 750 | 1,500 | — |

**Composition:** Copper. **Obverse:** No cinquefoils, cross after date. **Reverse:** Raised rims on ring.

| Date | AG | Good | VG | Fine | VF | XF | Unc |
|------|-----|------|-----|------|-----|------|-----|
| 1787 | — | — | — | — | 2,600 | — | — |

**Composition:** Copper. **Obverse:** No cinquefoils, cross after date. **Reverse:** With rays. **Reverse Legend:** AMERICAN CONGRESS.

| Date | AG | Good | VG | Fine | VF | XF | Unc |
|------|-----|------|-----|------|-----|------|-----|
| 1787 extremely rare | — | — | — | — | — | — | — |

**Note:** Norweb $63,800

**Composition:** Brass. **Note:** New Haven restrike.

| Date | AG | Good | VG | Fine | VF | XF | Unc |
|------|----|------|----|------|----|----|-----|
| (1858) | — | — | — | — | — | — | 500 |

**Composition:** Copper. **Note:** New Haven restrike.

| Date | AG | Good | VG | Fine | VF | XF | Unc |
|------|----|------|----|------|----|----|-----|
| (1858) | — | — | — | — | — | — | 500 |

**Composition:** Silver. **Note:** New Haven restrike.

| Date | AG | Good | VG | Fine | VF | XF | Unc |
|------|----|------|----|------|----|----|-----|
| (1858) | — | — | — | — | — | — | 1,850 |

**Composition:** Gold. **Note:** New Haven restrike.

| Date | AG | Good | VG | Fine | VF | XF | Unc |
|------|----|------|----|------|----|----|-----|
| (1858) 2 known | — | — | — | — | — | — | — |

**Note:** Norweb (holed) $1,430

# NOVA CONSTELLATIO

**Composition:** Copper. **Obverse:** Pointed rays. **Obverse Legend:** CONSTELLATIO. **Reverse:** Small "US".

| Date | AG | Good | VG | Fine | VF | XF | Unc |
|------|----|------|----|------|----|----|-----|
| 1783 | 20.00 | 35.00 | 65.00 | 125 | 255 | 585 | — |

**Composition:** Copper. **Obverse:** Pointed rays. **Obverse Legend:** CONSTELLATIO. **Reverse:** Large "US".

| Date | AG | Good | VG | Fine | VF | XF | Unc |
|------|----|------|----|------|----|----|-----|
| 1783 | 20.00 | 35.00 | 70.00 | 140 | 285 | 650 | — |

**Composition:** Copper. **Obverse:** Blunt rays. **Obverse Legend:** CONSTELATIO.

| Date | AG | Good | VG | Fine | VF | XF | Unc |
|------|----|------|----|------|----|----|-----|
| 1783 | 22.00 | 40.00 | 80.00 | 150 | 350 | 750 | — |

**Composition:** Copper. **Obverse:** Blunt rays. **Obverse Legend:** CONSTELATIO.

| Date | AG | Good | VG | Fine | VF | XF | Unc |
|------|----|------|----|------|----|----|-----|
| 1785 | 22.00 | 40.00 | 80.00 | 160 | 375 | 775 | — |

**Composition:** Copper. **Obverse:** Pointed rays. **Obverse Legend:** CONSTELLATIO.

| Date | AG | Good | VG | Fine | VF | XF | Unc |
|------|-----|------|-----|------|-----|-----|-----|
| 1785 | 20.00 | 35.00 | 70.00 | 140 | 285 | 650 | — |

**Composition:** Copper. **Note:** Contemporary circulating countefeit. Similar to previously listed coin.

| Date | AG | Good | VG | Fine | VF | XF | Unc |
|------|-----|------|-----|------|-----|-----|-----|
| 1786 extremely rare | — | — | — | — | — | — | — |

# ISSUES OF 1792
## CENT

**Composition:** Copper with Silver center.

| Date | AG | Good | VG | Fine | VF | XF | Unc |
|------|-----|------|-----|------|-----|-----|-----|
| 1792 12 known | — | — | — | — | — | — | — |

**Note:** Norweb, MS-60, $143,000

**Composition:** Copper. **Note:** No silver center.

| Date | AG | Good | VG | Fine | VF | XF | Unc |
|------|-----|------|-----|------|-----|-----|-----|
| 1792 8 known | — | — | — | — | — | — | — |

**Note:** Norweb, EF-40, $35,200; Benson, VG-10, $57,500

**Composition:** Copper. **Edge:** Plain **Note:** Commonly called "Birch cent."

| Date | AG | Good | VG | Fine | VF | XF | Unc |
|------|-----|------|-----|------|-----|-----|-----|
| 1792 unique | — | — | — | — | — | — | — |

**Obverse:** One star in edge legend **Note:** Commonly called "Birch cent."

| Date | AG | Good | VG | Fine | VF | XF | Unc |
|------|-----|------|-----|------|-----|-----|-----|
| 1792 2 known | — | — | — | — | — | — | — |

**Note:** Norweb, EF-40, $59,400

**Obverse:** Two stars in edge legend **Note:** Commonly called "Birch cent."

| Date | AG | Good | VG | Fine | VF | XF | Unc |
|------|-----|------|-----|------|-----|-----|-----|
| 1792 6 known | — | — | — | — | — | — | — |

**Note:** Hawn, strong VF, $57,750

**Composition:** White Metal. **Reverse:** "G.W.Pt." below wreath tie **Note:** Commonly called "Birch cent."

| Date | AG | Good | VG | Fine | VF | XF | Unc |
|------|----|----|----|----|----|----|----|
| 1792 unique | — | — | — | — | — | — | — |

**Note:** Garrett, $90,000

# HALF DISME

**Composition:** Silver.

| Date | AG | Good | VG | Fine | VF | XF | Unc |
|------|----|----|----|----|----|----|----|
| 1792 | 1,250 | 2,000 | 3,500 | 6,500 | 8,500 | 16,500 | — |

**Composition:** Copper.

| Date | AG | Good | VG | Fine | VF | XF | Unc |
|------|----|----|----|----|----|----|----|
| 1792 unique | — | — | — | — | — | — | — |

# DISME

**Composition:** Silver.

| Date | AG | Good | VG | Fine | VF | XF | Unc |
|------|----|----|----|----|----|----|----|
| 1792 3 known | — | — | — | — | — | — | — |

**Note:** Norweb, EF-40, $28,600

**Composition:** Copper. **Edge:** Reeded

| Date | AG | Good | VG | Fine | VF | XF | Unc |
|------|----|----|----|----|----|----|----|
| 1792 14 known | — | — | — | — | — | — | — |

**Note:** Hawn, VF, $30,800; Benson, EF-45, $109,250

**Composition:** Copper. **Edge:** Plain

| Date | AG | Good | VG | Fine | VF | XF | Unc |
|------|----|----|----|----|----|----|----|
| 1792 2 known | — | — | — | — | — | — | — |

**Note:** Garrett, $45,000

# QUARTER

**Composition:** Copper. **Edge:** Reeded **Note:** Commonly called "Wright quarter."

| Date | AG | Good | VG | Fine | VF | XF | Unc |
|------|----|----|----|----|----|----|----|
| 1792 2 known | — | — | — | — | — | — | — |

**Composition:** White Metal. **Edge:** Plain **Note:** Commonly called "Wright quarter."

| Date | AG | Good | VG | Fine | VF | XF | Unc |
|------|----|----|----|----|----|----|----|
| 1792 2 known | — | — | — | — | — | — | — |

**Note:** Norweb, VF-30 to EF-40, $28,600

**Composition:** White Metal. **Note:** Commonly called "Wright quarter."

| Date | AG | Good | VG | Fine | VF | XF | Unc |
|------|----|----|----|----|----|----|----|
| 1792 die trial | — | — | — | — | — | — | — |

**Note:** Garrett, $12,000

# CIRCULATION COINAGE

## HALF CENT

### Liberty cap. Head facing left.

**Designer:** Adam Eckfeldt. **Diameter:** 22 mm. **Weight:** 6.7400 g. **Composition:** Copper.

| Date | Mintage | G-4 | VG-8 | F-12 | VF-20 | XF-40 | MS-60 |
|------|---------|-----|------|------|-------|-------|-------|
| 1793 | 35,334 | 1,400 | 2,000 | 3,000 | 5,000 | 11,000 | 35,000 |

### Liberty cap. Head facing right.

**Designer:** Robert Scot (1794) and John Smith Gardner (1795). **Diameter:** 23.5 mm. **Composition:** Copper. **Weight:** 6.74 g. (1794-95) and 5.44 g. (1795-97) **Notes:** The "lettered edge" varieties have "Two Hundred for a Dollar" inscribed around the edge. The "pole" varieties have a pole upon which the cap is hanging, resting on Liberty's shoulder. The "punctuated date" varieties have a comma after the 1 in the date. The 1797 "1 above 1" variety has a second 1 above the 1 in the date.

| Date | Mintage | G-4 | VG-8 | F-12 | VF-20 | XF-40 | MS-60 |
|------|---------|-----|------|------|-------|-------|-------|
| 1794 | 81,600 | 265 | 500 | 750 | 1,500 | 3,250 | 18,000 |
| 1795 lettered edge, pole | 25,600 | 245 | 450 | 700 | 1,250 | 3,500 | 15,000 |
| 1795 plain edge, no pole | 109,000 | 175 | 325 | 525 | 1,100 | 3,000 | 15,000 |
| 1795 lettered edge, punctuated date | Inc. above | 350 | 500 | 750 | 1,200 | 3,500 | 18,500 |
| 1795 plain edge, punctuated date | Inc. above | 210 | 335 | 625 | 1,100 | 2,500 | 25,000 |
| 1796 pole | 5,090 | 6,300 | 9,000 | 13,000 | 19,000 | 27,500 | — |
| 1796 no pole | 1,390 | 20,000 | 30,000 | 45,000 | 85,000 | — | — |
| 1797 plain edge | 119,215 | 265 | 425 | 750 | 1,700 | 4,500 | 25,000 |
| 1797 lettered edge | Inc. above | 900 | 1,300 | 2,750 | 6,000 | 20,000 | — |
| 1797 1 above 1 | Inc. above | 160 | 300 | 450 | 975 | 3,000 | 15,000 |
| 1797 gripped edge | Inc. above | 9,000 | 15,000 | — | — | — | — |

### Draped bust.

**Designer:** Robert Scot. **Diameter:** 23.5 mm. **Weight:** 5.4400 g. **Composition:** Copper. **Notes:** The wreath on the reverse was redesigned slightly in 1802, resulting in "reverse of 1800" and "reverse of 1802" varieties. The "stems" varieties have stems extending from the wreath above and on both sides of the fraction on the reverse. On the 1804 "crosslet 4" variety, a serif appears at the far right of the crossbar on the 4 in the date. The "spiked chin" variety appears to have a spike extending from Liberty's chin, the result of a damaged die. Varieties of the 1805 strikes are distinguished by the size of the 5 in the date. Varieties of the 1806 strikes are distinguished by the size of the 6 in the date.

| Date | Mintage | G-4 | VG-8 | F-12 | VF-20 | XF-40 | MS-60 |
|------|---------|-----|------|------|-------|-------|-------|
| 1800 | 211,530 | 40.00 | 60.00 | 85.00 | 150 | 450 | 1,800 |
| 1802/0 rev. 1800 | 14,366 | 12,000 | 19,500 | 27,500 | — | — | — |
| 1802/0 rev. 1802 | Inc. above | 600 | 975 | 2,000 | 4,750 | 9,800 | — |
| 1803 | 97,900 | 33.00 | 48.00 | 100.00 | 225 | 800 | 6,500 |

## 1825 Half Cent
### Grade F-12

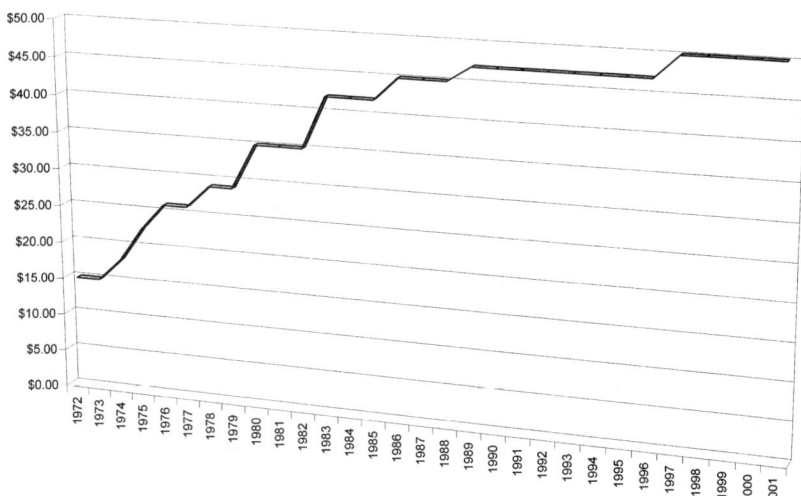

Retail Price

| Date | Mintage | G-4 | VG-8 | F-12 | VF-20 | XF-40 | MS-60 |
|------|---------|-----|------|------|-------|-------|-------|
| 1804 plain 4, stemless wreath | 1,055,312 | 30.00 | 38.00 | 50.00 | 80.00 | 250 | 1,200 |
| 1804 plain 4, stems | Inc. above | 40.00 | 75.00 | 140 | 250 | 1,500 | 12,000 |
| 1804 crosslet 4, stemless | Inc. above | 30.00 | 45.00 | 75.00 | 110 | 350 | 1,250 |
| 1804 crosslet 4, stems | Inc. above | 30.00 | 40.00 | 65.00 | 100.00 | 325 | 1,100 |
| 1804 spiked chin | Inc. above | 30.00 | 45.00 | 70.00 | 100.00 | 300 | 1,050 |
| 1805 small 5, stemless | 814,464 | 30.00 | 42.00 | 65.00 | 105 | 350 | 2,750 |
| 1805 small 5, stems | 700 | 1,250 | 2,250 | 4,250 | 12,500 | — |
| 1805 large 5, stems | Inc. above | 30.00 | 49.00 | 70.00 | 110 | 350 | 2,500 |
| 1806 small 6, stems | 356,000 | 150 | 300 | 450 | 900 | 2,500 | — |
| 1806 small 6, stemless | Inc. above | 29.00 | 40.00 | 50.00 | 70.00 | 195 | 1,250 |
| 1806 large 6, stems | Inc. above | 28.00 | 40.00 | 50.00 | 70.00 | 225 | 1,050 |
| 1807 | 476,000 | 28.00 | 45.00 | 65.00 | 110 | 400 | 3,000 |
| 1808/7 | 400,000 | 150 | 275 | 550 | 1,000 | 5,000 | 25,000 |
| 1808 | Inc. above | 29.00 | 40.00 | 60.00 | 150 | 750 | 4,500 |

## Classic head.

**Designer:** John Reich. **Diameter:** 23.5 mm. **Weight:** 5.4400 g. **Composition:** Copper. **Notes:** Restrikes listed were produced privately in the mid-1800s. The 1831 restrikes have two varieties with different-size berries in the wreath on the reverse. The 1828 strikes have either 12 or 13 stars on the obverse.

| Date | Mintage | G-4 | VG-8 | F-12 | VF-20 | XF-40 | MS-60 |
|------|---------|-----|------|------|-------|-------|-------|
| 1809/6 | 1,154,572 | 28.00 | 40.00 | 45.00 | 60.00 | 175 | 850 |
| 1809 | Inc. above | 28.00 | 40.00 | 50.00 | 75.00 | 200 | 750 |
| 1809 circle in 0 | — | 32.00 | 45.00 | 65.00 | 100.00 | 350 | 2,000 |
| 1810 | 215,000 | 36.00 | 48.00 | 100.00 | 140 | 600 | 3,000 |
| 1811 | 63,140 | 150 | 200 | 500 | 1,250 | 3,500 | — |
| 1811 restrike, reverse of 1802, uncirculated | — | — | — | — | — | — | 25,000 |
| 1825 | 63,000 | 29.00 | 37.00 | 50.00 | 75.00 | 200 | 850 |
| 1826 | 234,000 | 27.00 | 35.00 | 40.00 | 60.00 | 125 | 600 |
| 1828 13 stars | 606,000 | 27.00 | 30.00 | 35.00 | 50.00 | 85.00 | 300 |
| 1828 12 stars | Inc. above | 30.00 | 33.00 | 40.00 | 60.00 | 180 | 600 |
| 1829 | 487,000 | 27.00 | 30.00 | 35.00 | 50.00 | 125 | 475 |
| 1831 original | 2,200 | — | — | 4,900 | 5,600 | 7,700 | — |

| Date | Mintage | G-4 | VG-8 | F-12 | VF-20 | XF-40 | MS-60 |
|---|---|---|---|---|---|---|---|
| 1831 1st restrike, lg. berries, reverse of 1836 | — | — | — | — | — | — | 6,000 |
| 1831 2nd restrike, sm. berries, reverse of 1840, proof | — | — | — | — | — | — | 20,000 |
| 1832 | 154,000 | 27.00 | 30.00 | 35.00 | 55.00 | 90.00 | 300 |
| 1833 | 120,000 | 27.00 | 30.00 | 35.00 | 45.00 | 80.00 | 250 |
| 1834 | 141,000 | 27.00 | 30.00 | 35.00 | 45.00 | 80.00 | 250 |
| 1835 | 398,000 | 27.00 | 30.00 | 35.00 | 45.00 | 80.00 | 250 |
| 1836 original, proof only | — | — | — | — | — | — | 5,000 |
| 1836 restrike, reverse of 1840, proof only | — | — | — | — | — | — | 18,000 |

## Braided hair.

**Designer:** Christian Gobrecht. **Diameter:** 23 mm. **Weight:** 5.4400 g. **Composition:** Copper. **Notes:** 1840-1849 and 1852 strikes, both originals and restrikes, are known in proof only; mintages are unknown. The small-date varieties of 1849, both originals and restrikes are known in proof only. The Restrikes were produced clandestinely by Philadelphia Mint personnel in the mid-1800s.

| Date | Mintage | G-4 | VG-8 | F-12 | VF-20 | XF-40 | MS-60 | Prf-60 |
|---|---|---|---|---|---|---|---|---|
| 1840 original | — | — | — | — | — | — | — | 3,800 |
| 1840 1st restrike | — | — | — | — | — | — | — | 3,500 |
| 1840 2nd restrike | — | — | — | — | — | — | — | 3,200 |
| 1841 original | — | — | — | — | — | — | — | 3,800 |
| 1841 1st restrike | — | — | — | — | — | — | — | 3,500 |
| 1841 2nd restrike | — | — | — | — | — | — | — | 3,000 |
| 1842 original | — | — | — | — | — | — | — | 3,800 |
| 1842 1st restrike | — | — | — | — | — | — | — | 3,500 |
| 1842 2nd restrike | — | — | — | — | — | — | — | 3,200 |
| 1843 original | — | — | — | — | — | — | — | 3,800 |
| 1843 1st restrike | — | — | — | — | — | — | — | 3,500 |
| 1843 2nd restrike | — | — | — | — | — | — | — | 3,200 |
| 1844 original | — | — | — | — | — | — | — | 3,800 |
| 1844 1st restrike | — | — | — | — | — | — | — | 3,500 |
| 1844 2nd restrike | — | — | — | — | — | — | — | 3,200 |
| 1845 original | — | — | — | — | — | — | — | 3,800 |
| 1845 1st restrike | — | — | — | — | — | — | — | 3,500 |
| 1845 2nd restrike | — | — | — | — | — | — | — | 3,200 |
| 1846 original | — | — | — | — | — | — | — | 3,800 |
| 1846 1st restrike | — | — | — | — | — | — | — | 3,500 |
| 1846 2nd restrike | — | — | — | — | — | — | — | 3,200 |
| 1847 original | — | — | — | — | — | — | — | 3,800 |
| 1847 1st restrike | — | — | — | — | — | — | — | 10,000 |
| 1847 2nd restrike | — | — | — | — | — | — | — | 3,200 |
| 1848 original | — | — | — | — | — | — | — | 3,800 |
| 1848 1st restrike | — | — | — | — | — | — | — | 3,500 |
| 1848 2nd restrike | — | — | — | — | — | — | — | 3,200 |
| 1849 original, small date | — | — | — | — | — | — | — | 3,800 |
| 1849 1st restrike small date | — | — | — | — | — | — | — | 3,200 |
| 1849 large date | 39,864 | 30.00 | 38.00 | 42.00 | 55.00 | 90.00 | 600 | — |
| 1850 | 39,812 | 36.00 | 45.00 | 55.00 | 75.00 | 100.00 | 750 | — |
| 1851 | 147,672 | 23.00 | 28.00 | 35.00 | 50.00 | 70.00 | 200 | — |
| 1852 original | — | — | — | — | — | — | — | 35,000 |
| 1852 1st restrike | — | — | — | — | — | — | — | 3,500 |
| 1852 2nd restrike | — | — | — | — | — | — | — | 5,000 |
| 1853 | 129,694 | 24.00 | 29.00 | 35.00 | 45.00 | 65.00 | 195 | — |
| 1854 | 55,358 | 25.00 | 32.00 | 35.00 | 45.00 | 65.00 | 195 | — |
| 1855 | 56,500 | 25.00 | 32.00 | 35.00 | 45.00 | 65.00 | 195 | — |
| 1856 | 40,430 | 30.00 | 38.00 | 44.00 | 52.00 | 90.00 | 275 | — |
| 1857 | 35,180 | 50.00 | 60.00 | 70.00 | 90.00 | 140 | 350 | — |

# CENT

### Flowing hair. Chain.

**Designer:** Henry Voigt. **Diameter:** 26-27 mm. **Weight:** 13.4800 g. **Composition:** Copper.

| Date | Mintage | G-4 | VG-8 | F-12 | VF-20 | XF-40 | MS-60 |
|------|---------|-----|------|------|-------|-------|-------|
| 1793 | 36,103 | 2,400 | 3,750 | 5,500 | 11,000 | 17,500 | 63,000 |

### Flowing hair. Wreath.

**Designer:** Adam Eckfeldt. **Diameter:** 26-28 mm. **Weight:** 13.4800 g. **Composition:** Copper.

| Date | Mintage | G-4 | VG-8 | F-12 | VF-20 | XF-40 | MS-60 |
|------|---------|-----|------|------|-------|-------|-------|
| 1793 | 63,353 | 980 | 1,200 | 2,650 | 4,000 | 7,000 | 23,000 |

### Liberty cap.

**Designer:** Joseph Wright (1793-1795) and John Smith Gardner (1795-1796). **Diameter:** 29 mm. **Composition:** Copper. **Weight:** 13.48 g. (1793-95) and 10.89 g. (1795-96) **Notes:** The heavier pieces were struck on a thicker planchet. The Liberty design on the obverse was revised slightly in 1794, but the 1793 design was used on some 1794 strikes. A 1795 "lettered edge" variety has "One Hundred for a Dollar" and a leaf inscribed on the edge.

| Date | Mintage | G-4 | VG-8 | F-12 | VF-20 | XF-40 | MS-60 |
|------|---------|-----|------|------|-------|-------|-------|
| 1793 cap | 11,056 | 4,500 | 6,000 | 9,000 | 20,000 | 30,000 | — |
| 1794 | 918,521 | 165 | 250 | 460 | 850 | 2,450 | — |
| 1794 head '93 | Inc. above | 1,000 | 2,000 | 3,000 | 6,500 | 10,000 | — |
| 1795 | 501,500 | 130 | 240 | 375 | 630 | 1,750 | 3,500 |

### Liberty cap.

**Designer:** Joseph Wright (1793-1795) and John Smith Gardner (1795-1796). **Diameter:** 29 mm. **Weight:** 10.8900 g. **Composition:** Copper.

## 1804 Cent
### Grade F-12

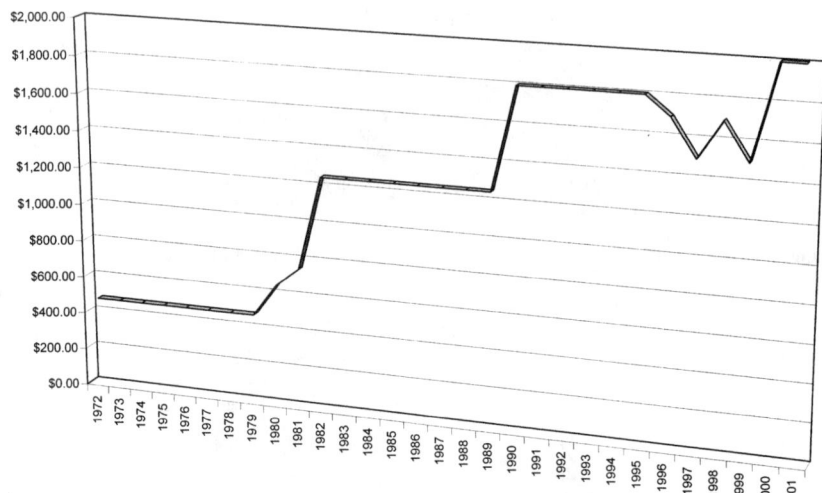

| Date | Mintage | G-4 | VG-8 | F-12 | VF-20 | XF-40 | MS-60 |
|------|---------|-----|------|------|-------|-------|-------|
| 1795 lettered edge, "One Cent" high in wreath | 37,000 | 160 | 310 | 525 | 1,150 | 2,900 | 5,750 |
| 1796 | 109,825 | 145 | 260 | 600 | 1,500 | 3,100 | 6,100 |

## Draped bust.

Stems          Stemless

**Designer:** Robert Scot. **Diameter:** 29 mm. **Weight:** 10.9800 g. **Composition:** Copper. **Notes:** The "stemless" variety does not have stems extending from the wreath above and on both sides of the fraction on the reverse. The 1801 "3 errors" variety has the fraction on the reverse reading "1/000," has only one stem extending from the wreath above and on both sides of the fraction on the reverse, and "United" in "United States of America" appears as "linited."

| Date | Mintage | G-4 | VG-8 | F-12 | VF-20 | XF-40 | MS-60 |
|------|---------|-----|------|------|-------|-------|-------|
| 1796 | 363,375 | 160 | 270 | 650 | 1,400 | 3,100 | — |
| 1797 | 897,510 | 49.00 | 100.00 | 160 | 335 | 1,150 | 3,300 |
| 1797 stemless | Inc. above | 125 | 210 | 385 | 910 | 3,200 | — |
| 1798 | 1,841,745 | 48.00 | 85.00 | 130 | 385 | 975 | 3,100 |
| 1798/7 | Inc. above | 91.00 | 180 | 310 | 1,050 | 3,900 | — |
| 1799 | 42,540 | 2,900 | 4,000 | 5,500 | 15,000 | 27,500 | — |
| 1800 | 2,822,175 | 37.00 | 65.00 | 115 | 350 | 1,250 | — |
| 1801 | 1,362,837 | 36.00 | 65.00 | 125 | 280 | 1,000 | — |
| 1801 3 errors | Inc. above | 85.00 | 175 | 900 | 1,750 | 5,500 | — |
| 1802 | 3,435,100 | 34.00 | 55.00 | 110 | 225 | 775 | 2,250 |
| 1803 | 2,471,353 | 34.00 | 55.00 | 110 | 225 | 775 | 2,250 |
| 1804 | 96,500 | 950 | 1,400 | 2,000 | 2,550 | 7,000 | — |
| 1805 | 941,116 | 35.00 | 55.00 | 125 | 300 | 875 | 2,450 |
| 1806 | 348,000 | 39.00 | 75.00 | 125 | 350 | 1,100 | 4,700 |
| 1807 | 727,221 | 31.00 | 53.00 | 110 | 225 | 775 | 2,250 |
| 1807/6 | — | 34.00 | 55.00 | 125 | 250 | 1,275 | — |

# Classic head.

**Designer:** John Reich. **Diameter:** 29 mm. **Weight:** 10.8900 g. **Composition:** Copper.

| Date | Mintage | G-4 | VG-8 | F-12 | VF-20 | XF-40 | MS-60 |
|------|---------|-----|------|------|-------|-------|-------|
| 1808 | 1,109,000 | 35.00 | 75.00 | 175 | 425 | 1,200 | 3,600 |
| 1809 | 222,867 | 90.00 | 150 | 350 | 1,300 | 2,650 | 6,300 |
| 1810 | 1,458,500 | 36.00 | 75.00 | 210 | 600 | 1,100 | 3,850 |
| 1811 | 218,025 | 75.00 | 150 | 400 | 1,000 | 1,500 | 7,000 |
| 1811/10 | Inc. above | 75.00 | 140 | 360 | 975 | 1,500 | — |
| 1812 | 1,075,500 | 36.00 | 65.00 | 180 | 525 | 975 | 2,800 |
| 1813 | 418,000 | 45.00 | 95.00 | 600 | 1,000 | 1,300 | — |
| 1814 | 357,830 | 36.00 | 65.00 | 180 | 530 | 975 | 2,800 |

# Coronet.

**Designer:** Robert Scot. **Diameter:** 28-29 mm. **Weight:** 10.8900 g. **Composition:** Copper. **Notes:** The 1817 strikes have either 13 or 15 stars on the obverse.

| Date | Mintage | G-4 | VG-8 | F-12 | VF-20 | XF-40 | MS-60 |
|------|---------|-----|------|------|-------|-------|-------|
| 1816 | 2,820,982 | 14.00 | 17.00 | 28.00 | 84.00 | 175 | 420 |
| 1817 13 stars | 3,948,400 | 12.50 | 15.00 | 24.00 | 56.00 | 120 | 275 |
| 1817 15 stars | Inc. above | 16.00 | 25.00 | 45.00 | 125 | 350 | 1,550 |
| 1818 | 3,167,000 | 12.50 | 16.00 | 24.00 | 56.00 | 125 | 250 |
| 1819 | 2,671,000 | 12.50 | 14.00 | 23.00 | 63.00 | 120 | 275 |
| 1820 | 4,407,550 | 12.50 | 17.00 | 23.00 | 63.00 | 120 | 275 |
| 1821 | 389,000 | 25.00 | 38.00 | 110 | 400 | 1,500 | 6,000 |
| 1822 | 2,072,339 | 12.50 | 15.00 | 32.00 | 84.00 | 195 | 575 |
| 1823 Included in 1824 mintage | — | 80.00 | 120 | 310 | 690 | 2,750 | — |
| 1823/22 Included in 1824 mintage | — | 80.00 | 110 | 300 | 675 | 2,450 | — |
| 1823 Restrike | — | 300 | 400 | 450 | 500 | 550 | 700 |
| 1824 | 1,262,000 | 14.00 | 23.00 | 38.00 | 145 | 350 | 625 |
| 1824/22 | Inc. above | 17.00 | 25.00 | 56.00 | 225 | 975 | — |
| 1825 | 1,461,100 | 13.00 | 16.00 | 35.00 | 110 | 300 | 840 |
| 1826 | 1,517,425 | 12.50 | 16.00 | 26.00 | 84.00 | 175 | 700 |
| 1826/25 | Inc. above | 16.00 | 24.00 | 60.00 | 175 | 700 | 1,800 |
| 1827 | 2,357,732 | 12.50 | 15.00 | 23.00 | 75.00 | 135 | 385 |
| 1828 | 2,260,624 | 12.50 | 14.00 | 26.00 | 84.00 | 175 | 425 |
| 1829 | 1,414,500 | 12.50 | 14.00 | 22.00 | 100.00 | 140 | 425 |
| 1830 | 1,711,500 | 12.50 | 14.00 | 22.00 | 70.00 | 135 | 385 |
| 1831 | 3,359,260 | 12.50 | 14.00 | 22.00 | 63.00 | 125 | 315 |
| 1832 | 2,362,000 | 12.50 | 14.00 | 22.00 | 63.00 | 125 | 315 |
| 1833 | 2,739,000 | 12.50 | 14.00 | 22.00 | 56.00 | 120 | 265 |
| 1834 | 1,855,100 | 12.50 | 14.00 | 22.00 | 56.00 | 140 | 250 |
| 1835 | 3,878,400 | 12.50 | 14.00 | 22.00 | 56.00 | 91.00 | 225 |
| 1836 | 2,111,000 | 13.00 | 15.00 | 23.00 | 57.00 | 105 | 250 |
| 1837 | 5,558,300 | 12.50 | 14.00 | 22.00 | 51.00 | 91.00 | 300 |
| 1838 | 6,370,200 | 12.50 | 14.00 | 22.00 | 51.00 | 91.00 | 225 |
| 1839 | 3,128,661 | 12.50 | 14.00 | 22.00 | 51.00 | 105 | 350 |
| 1839/36 | Inc. above | 300 | 450 | 700 | 1,500 | 3,900 | — |

# Braided hair.

**Designer:** Christian Gobrecht. **Diameter:** 27.5 mm. **Weight:** 10.8900 g. **Composition:** Copper. **Notes:** 1840 and 1842 strikes are known with both small and large dates, with little difference in value. 1855 and 1856 strikes are known with both slanting and upright 5s in the date, with little difference in value. A slightly larger Liberty head and larger reverse lettering were used beginning in 1843. One 1843 variety uses the old obverse with the new reverse.

| Date | Mintage | G-4 | VG-8 | F-12 | VF-20 | XF-40 | MS-60 |
|------|---------|-----|------|------|-------|-------|-------|
| 1840 | 2,462,700 | 11.00 | 14.00 | 17.00 | 38.00 | 70.00 | 475 |
| 1841 | 1,597,367 | 14.00 | 16.00 | 19.00 | 40.00 | 75.00 | 440 |
| 1842 | 2,383,390 | 11.00 | 14.00 | 17.00 | 38.00 | 70.00 | 425 |
| 1843 | 2,425,342 | 11.00 | 14.00 | 17.00 | 38.00 | 75.00 | 445 |
| 1843 obverse 1842 with reverse of 1844 | Inc. above | 12.00 | 15.00 | 21.00 | 38.00 | 80.00 | 350 |
| 1844 | 2,398,752 | 9.00 | 14.00 | 14.00 | 22.00 | 54.00 | 215 |
| 1844/81 | Inc. above | 14.00 | 25.00 | 40.00 | 65.00 | 200 | 600 |
| 1845 | 3,894,804 | 9.00 | 12.00 | 14.00 | 19.50 | 44.00 | 225 |
| 1846 | 4,120,800 | 9.00 | 12.00 | 14.00 | 19.50 | 44.00 | 225 |
| 1847 | 6,183,669 | 9.00 | 12.00 | 14.00 | 19.50 | 44.00 | 160 |
| 1848 | 6,415,799 | 9.00 | 12.00 | 14.00 | 19.50 | 44.00 | 160 |
| 1849 | 4,178,500 | 9.00 | 12.00 | 14.00 | 28.00 | 60.00 | 275 |
| 1850 | 4,426,844 | 9.00 | 12.00 | 14.00 | 19.50 | 44.00 | 160 |
| 1851 | 9,889,707 | 9.00 | 12.00 | 14.00 | 19.50 | 41.00 | 160 |
| 1851/81 | Inc. above | 15.00 | 19.00 | 35.00 | 60.00 | 100.00 | 500 |
| 1852 | 5,063,094 | 9.00 | 12.00 | 14.00 | 19.50 | 41.00 | 160 |
| 1853 | 6,641,131 | 9.00 | 12.00 | 14.00 | 19.50 | 41.00 | 160 |
| 1854 | 4,236,156 | 9.00 | 12.00 | 14.00 | 19.50 | 41.00 | 160 |
| 1855 | 1,574,829 | 12.00 | 14.00 | 17.00 | 21.00 | 45.00 | 170 |
| 1856 | 2,690,463 | 11.00 | 13.00 | 15.00 | 16.00 | 40.00 | 160 |
| 1857 | 333,456 | 45.00 | 55.00 | 65.00 | 75.00 | 100.00 | 250 |

## 1857 Cent
### Grade XF-40

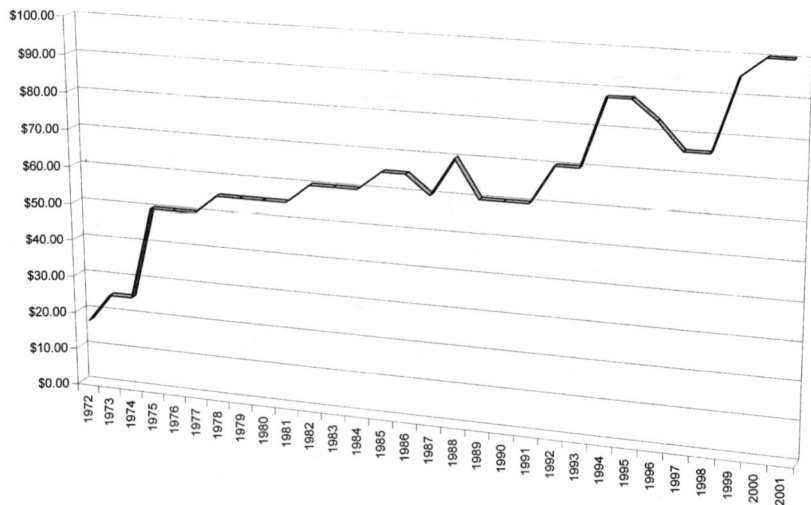

☐ Retail Price

# Flying eagle.

Large Letters

Small Letters

**Designer:** James B. Longacre. **Diameter:** 19 mm. **Weight:** 4.6700 g. **Composition:** Copper-nickel. **Notes:** On the large-letter variety of 1858, the "A" and "M" in "America" are connected at their bases; on the small-letter variety, the two letters are separated.

| Date | Mintage | G-4 | VG-8 | F-12 | VF-20 | XF-40 | AU-50 | MS-60 | MS-65 | Prf-65 |
|------|---------|-----|------|------|-------|-------|-------|-------|-------|--------|
| 1856 | Est. 2,500 | 4,000 | 4,350 | 4,750 | 5,300 | 5,800 | 6,750 | 9,000 | 30,000 | 20,000 |
| 1856 | — | 4,000 | 4,350 | 4,750 | 5,300 | 5,800 | 6,750 | 9,000 | 30,000 | 20,000 |
| 1857 | 17,450,000 | 16.00 | 18.50 | 27.00 | 39.00 | 100.00 | 150 | 240 | 3,500 | 28,000 |
| 1858/7 | — | 90.00 | 110 | 175 | 350 | 800 | 1,500 | 2,800 | — | — |
| 1858 large letters | 24,600,000 | 17.00 | 19.00 | 28.00 | 40.00 | 105 | 165 | 265 | 3,600 | 20,000 |
| 1858 small letters | Inc. above | 16.00 | 18.00 | 27.00 | 40.00 | 105 | 160 | 265 | 3,600 | 25,500 |

# Indian head.

**Designer:** James B. Longacre. **Diameter:** 19 mm. **Weight:** 4.6700 g. **Composition:** Copper-nickel.

| Date | Mintage | G-4 | VG-8 | F-12 | VF-20 | XF-40 | AU-50 | MS-60 | MS-65 | Prf-65 |
|------|---------|-----|------|------|-------|-------|-------|-------|-------|--------|
| 1859 | 36,400,000 | 10.00 | 12.50 | 16.00 | 35.00 | 75.00 | 150 | 200 | 2,600 | 5,000 |

# Indian head. Shield added at top of wreath.

**Designer:** James B. Longacre. **Diameter:** 19 mm. **Weight:** 4.6700 g. **Composition:** Copper-nickel.

| Date | Mintage | G-4 | VG-8 | F-12 | VF-20 | XF-40 | AU-50 | MS-60 | MS-65 | Prf-65 |
|------|---------|-----|------|------|-------|-------|-------|-------|-------|--------|
| 1860 | 20,566,000 | 6.50 | 10.50 | 12.00 | 15.00 | 45.00 | 75.00 | 125 | 900 | 3,700 |
| 1861 | 10,100,000 | 18.00 | 27.00 | 37.00 | 45.00 | 90.00 | 140 | 160 | 950 | 7,000 |
| 1862 | 28,075,000 | 5.00 | 8.00 | 10.00 | 12.00 | 25.00 | 50.00 | 70.00 | 900 | 2,400 |
| 1863 | 49,840,000 | 5.00 | 8.25 | 10.00 | 12.50 | 25.00 | 50.00 | 70.00 | 930 | 3,200 |
| 1864 | 13,740,000 | 12.00 | 14.00 | 28.00 | 37.00 | 57.00 | 80.00 | 125 | 1,150 | 3,400 |

# Indian head.

'L' on Ribbon

**Designer:** James B. Longacre. **Diameter:** 19 mm. **Weight:** 3.1100 g. **Composition:** Bronze. **Notes:** The 1864 "L" variety has the designer's initial in Liberty's hair to the right of her neck.

| Date | Mintage | G-4 | VG-8 | F-12 | VF-20 | XF-40 | AU-50 | MS-60 | MS-65 | Prf-65 |
|------|---------|-----|------|------|-------|-------|-------|-------|-------|--------|
| 1864 | 39,233,714 | 6.00 | 12.50 | 18.00 | 30.00 | 55.00 | 62.00 | 80.00 | 325 | 4,300 |
| 1864 L | Inc. above | 40.00 | 60.00 | 95.00 | 125 | 185 | 235 | 290 | 1,500 | 110,000 |
| 1865 | 35,429,286 | 6.00 | 11.50 | 18.00 | 23.50 | 38.00 | 53.00 | 80.00 | 450 | 1,550 |
| 1866 | 9,826,500 | 36.00 | 45.00 | 59.50 | 80.00 | 160 | 195 | 230 | 1,150 | 950 |
| 1867 | 9,821,000 | 35.00 | 50.00 | 65.00 | 95.00 | 155 | 195 | 240 | 1,140 | 1,050 |
| 1868 | 10,266,500 | 33.00 | 40.00 | 50.00 | 80.00 | 145 | 175 | 225 | 970 | 985 |
| 1869/9 | 6,420,000 | 100.00 | 135 | 235 | 300 | 350 | 400 | 435 | 1,700 | — |
| 1869 | Inc. above | 46.00 | 77.50 | 175 | 235 | 280 | 345 | 385 | 1,450 | 950 |
| 1870 | 5,275,000 | 39.50 | 65.00 | 145 | 215 | 290 | 310 | 400 | 1,500 | 1,075 |
| 1871 | 3,929,500 | 52.00 | 70.00 | 200 | 260 | 325 | 385 | 425 | 2,400 | 1,100 |

## 1864-L Indian Cent
### Grade F-12

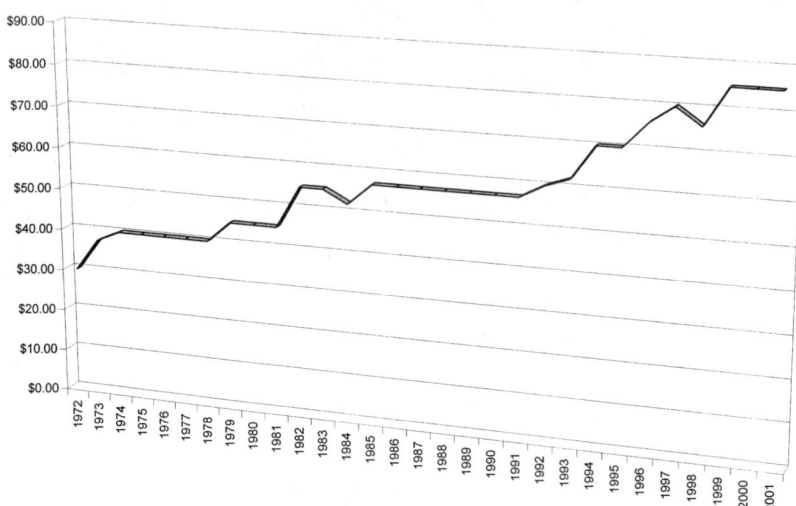

Retail Price

| Date | Mintage | G-4 | VG-8 | F-12 | VF-20 | XF-40 | AU-50 | MS-60 | MS-65 | Prf-65 |
|------|---------|-----|------|------|-------|-------|-------|-------|-------|--------|
| 1872 | 4,042,000 | 59.00 | 80.00 | 250 | 275 | 330 | 390 | 500 | 4,200 | 1,100 |
| 1873 | 11,676,500 | 18.50 | 29.50 | 45.00 | 55.00 | 135 | 150 | 175 | 1,175 | 850 |
| 1874 | 14,187,500 | 13.00 | 21.00 | 32.00 | 45.00 | 90.00 | 125 | 165 | 700 | 800 |
| 1875 | 13,528,000 | 13.00 | 24.00 | 45.00 | 50.00 | 86.00 | 125 | 165 | 850 | 1,500 |
| 1876 | 7,944,000 | 25.50 | 32.50 | 45.00 | 60.00 | 125 | 160 | 190 | 1,150 | 925 |
| 1877 | 852,500 | 450 | 550 | 750 | 935 | 1,200 | 1,900 | 2,250 | 8,000 | 4,900 |
| 1878 | 5,799,800 | 25.50 | 35.00 | 53.00 | 75.00 | 145 | 170 | 195 | 975 | 490 |
| 1879 | 16,231,200 | 6.00 | 11.00 | 17.50 | 32.50 | 65.00 | 73.00 | 80.00 | 350 | 450 |
| 1880 | 38,964,955 | 3.00 | 5.50 | 8.00 | 12.50 | 29.50 | 45.00 | 65.00 | 325 | 435 |
| 1881 | 39,211,575 | 3.00 | 4.50 | 7.00 | 9.00 | 21.00 | 30.00 | 45.00 | 275 | 425 |
| 1882 | 38,581,100 | 3.00 | 4.50 | 6.00 | 10.00 | 20.00 | 30.00 | 45.00 | 300 | 425 |
| 1883 | 45,589,109 | 2.60 | 3.50 | 5.00 | 8.50 | 17.50 | 30.00 | 42.00 | 300 | 425 |
| 1884 | 23,261,742 | 3.00 | 4.00 | 8.00 | 12.00 | 27.50 | 35.00 | 65.00 | 500 | 425 |
| 1885 | 11,765,384 | 5.50 | 9.00 | 18.00 | 35.00 | 52.00 | 65.00 | 95.00 | 700 | 425 |
| 1886 | 17,654,290 | 3.75 | 8.50 | 20.00 | 42.00 | 100.00 | 120 | 135 | 1,150 | 460 |
| 1887 | 45,226,483 | 1.65 | 2.45 | 4.50 | 7.00 | 22.00 | 30.00 | 50.00 | 375 | 475 |
| 1888 | 37,494,414 | 1.65 | 2.45 | 6.00 | 9.00 | 24.50 | 30.00 | 48.00 | 950 | 525 |
| 1889 | 48,869,361 | 1.65 | 2.40 | 4.00 | 7.00 | 13.00 | 29.00 | 45.00 | 370 | 450 |
| 1890 | 57,182,854 | 1.45 | 1.90 | 3.50 | 5.00 | 12.00 | 27.00 | 45.00 | 370 | 500 |
| 1891 | 47,072,350 | 1.60 | 2.50 | 4.00 | 6.00 | 12.00 | 27.00 | 44.00 | 340 | 520 |
| 1892 | 37,649,832 | 1.90 | 2.60 | 4.25 | 6.50 | 17.00 | 27.00 | 44.00 | 320 | 525 |
| 1893 | 46,642,195 | 1.60 | 2.50 | 4.00 | 6.00 | 12.50 | 27.00 | 37.00 | 330 | 540 |
| 1894 | 16,752,132 | 2.75 | 5.00 | 11.00 | 15.00 | 45.00 | 52.50 | 65.00 | 405 | 525 |
| 1895 | 38,343,636 | 1.75 | 2.35 | 4.25 | 5.50 | 13.50 | 28.00 | 35.00 | 215 | 475 |
| 1896 | 39,057,293 | 1.40 | 2.25 | 3.50 | 5.50 | 12.50 | 28.00 | 38.00 | 220 | 425 |
| 1897 | 50,466,330 | 1.40 | 2.00 | 3.00 | 4.00 | 11.50 | 26.00 | 35.00 | 190 | 425 |
| 1898 | 49,823,079 | 1.30 | 2.15 | 3.00 | 4.00 | 11.50 | 26.00 | 33.00 | 180 | 425 |
| 1899 | 53,600,031 | 1.30 | 1.60 | 2.40 | 4.00 | 11.50 | 24.50 | 30.00 | 140 | 415 |
| 1900 | 66,833,764 | 1.30 | 1.75 | 2.50 | 3.50 | 12.50 | 22.00 | 28.00 | 145 | 425 |
| 1901 | 79,611,143 | 1.20 | 1.45 | 2.10 | 3.00 | 8.50 | 18.00 | 26.00 | 145 | 425 |
| 1902 | 87,376,722 | 1.20 | 1.45 | 2.10 | 3.00 | 8.50 | 18.00 | 26.00 | 145 | 425 |
| 1903 | 85,094,493 | 1.20 | 1.45 | 2.10 | 3.00 | 8.50 | 18.00 | 26.00 | 145 | 425 |
| 1904 | 61,328,015 | 1.20 | 1.45 | 2.10 | 3.00 | 8.50 | 18.00 | 26.00 | 145 | 475 |
| 1905 | 80,719,163 | 1.20 | 1.45 | 2.10 | 3.00 | 8.50 | 18.00 | 26.00 | 145 | 475 |
| 1906 | 96,022,255 | 1.15 | 1.40 | 1.95 | 3.00 | 8.00 | 17.00 | 25.00 | 150 | 395 |
| 1907 | 108,138,618 | 1.15 | 1.40 | 1.90 | 3.00 | 8.00 | 17.00 | 25.00 | 150 | 485 |
| 1908 | 32,327,987 | 1.30 | 1.85 | 2.60 | 4.00 | 9.00 | 18.00 | 26.00 | 150 | 395 |
| 1908S | 1,115,000 | 37.00 | 41.00 | 46.00 | 52.50 | 90.00 | 140 | 195 | 650 | — |
| 1909 | 14,370,645 | 2.75 | 3.00 | 4.00 | 5.00 | 17.50 | 26.00 | 35.00 | 155 | 400 |
| 1909S | 309,000 | 240 | 275 | 300 | 345 | 390 | 450 | 485 | 1,400 | — |

# Lincoln. Wheat.

**Designer:** Victor D. Brenner. **Diameter:** 19 mm. **Weight:** 3.1100 g. **Composition:** Bronze. **Notes:** The 1909 "VDB" varieties have the designer's initials inscribed at the 6 o'clock position on the reverse. The initials were removed until 1918, when they were restored on the obverse.

| Date | Mintage | G-4 | VG-8 | F-12 | VF-20 | XF-40 | AU-50 | MS-60 | MS-65 | Prf-65 |
|------|---------|-----|------|------|-------|-------|-------|-------|-------|--------|
| 1909 | 72,702,618 | 1.25 | 1.35 | 1.80 | 2.00 | 3.50 | 8.50 | 14.00 | 75.00 | 520 |
| 1909 VDB | 27,995,000 | 3.30 | 3.40 | 3.55 | 3.85 | 4.85 | 6.50 | 10.00 | 65.00 | 6,000 |
| 1909S | 1,825,000 | 37.00 | 45.00 | 57.00 | 77.00 | 110 | 130 | 150 | 585 | — |
| 1909S VDB | 484,000 | 360 | 420 | 450 | 510 | 570 | 660 | 750 | 3,000 | — |
| 1910 | 146,801,218 | 0.25 | 0.30 | 0.45 | 0.60 | 2.75 | 6.50 | 14.50 | 100.00 | 700 |
| 1910S | 6,045,000 | 7.00 | 8.00 | 9.50 | 12.00 | 26.50 | 54.00 | 60.00 | 365 | — |
| 1911 | 101,177,787 | 0.35 | 0.55 | 1.35 | 1.95 | 4.50 | 8.50 | 18.00 | 175 | 600 |
| 1911D | 12,672,000 | 5.00 | 6.00 | 8.50 | 13.50 | 40.00 | 65.00 | 80.00 | 950 | — |
| 1911S | 4,026,000 | 15.00 | 16.50 | 19.00 | 23.00 | 42.00 | 80.00 | 145 | 1,350 | — |
| 1912 | 68,153,060 | 1.35 | 1.50 | 2.25 | 5.50 | 11.00 | 17.00 | 32.00 | 275 | 950 |
| 1912D | 10,411,000 | 5.75 | 6.25 | 7.50 | 20.00 | 42.00 | 70.00 | 140 | 1,000 | — |
| 1912S | 4,431,000 | 11.00 | 13.00 | 15.00 | 20.00 | 45.00 | 65.00 | 110 | 1,600 | — |
| 1913 | 76,532,352 | 0.65 | 1.00 | 1.75 | 4.00 | 15.00 | 18.50 | 32.00 | 270 | 550 |
| 1913D | 15,804,000 | 2.70 | 3.00 | 3.75 | 8.50 | 28.00 | 55.00 | 85.00 | 1,175 | — |
| 1913S | 6,101,000 | 5.75 | 6.25 | 8.00 | 12.00 | 38.00 | 65.00 | 135 | 2,500 | — |
| 1914 | 75,238,432 | 0.50 | 0.80 | 1.50 | 4.50 | 11.50 | 29.00 | 42.00 | 310 | 600 |
| 1914D | 1,193,000 | 85.00 | 120 | 150 | 235 | 500 | 825 | 1,100 | 8,600 | — |
| 1914S | 4,137,000 | 10.00 | 11.00 | 13.00 | 19.00 | 45.00 | 135 | 235 | 7,500 | — |
| 1915 | 29,092,120 | 1.40 | 1.75 | 4.50 | 12.50 | 48.00 | 68.00 | 80.00 | 575 | 600 |
| 1915D | 22,050,000 | 1.50 | 1.70 | 2.60 | 5.00 | 14.00 | 33.00 | 62.00 | 650 | — |
| 1915S | 4,833,000 | 7.00 | 8.00 | 9.00 | 13.00 | 42.00 | 65.00 | 135 | 3,000 | — |
| 1916 | 131,833,677 | 0.20 | 0.30 | 0.50 | 1.50 | 5.00 | 8.50 | 12.00 | 135 | 1,650 |
| 1916D | 35,956,000 | 0.45 | 0.55 | 1.60 | 3.00 | 10.00 | 20.00 | 52.00 | 1,750 | — |
| 1916S | 22,510,000 | 1.20 | 1.50 | 1.85 | 3.00 | 11.00 | 25.00 | 68.00 | 4,000 | — |
| 1917 | 196,429,785 | 0.20 | 0.30 | 0.45 | 1.60 | 4.00 | 8.00 | 13.00 | 140 | — |
| 1917D | 55,120,000 | 0.30 | 0.40 | 1.00 | 2.50 | 10.00 | 22.00 | 58.00 | 1,275 | — |
| 1917S | 32,620,000 | 0.60 | 0.70 | 1.00 | 2.25 | 8.50 | 19.50 | 58.00 | 4,000 | — |
| 1918 | 288,104,634 | 0.20 | 0.30 | 0.40 | 1.00 | 4.00 | 7.00 | 12.50 | 195 | — |
| 1918D | 47,830,000 | 0.35 | 0.70 | 1.25 | 2.50 | 9.00 | 19.50 | 58.00 | 1,500 | — |
| 1918S | 34,680,000 | 0.40 | 0.75 | 1.00 | 2.25 | 8.00 | 30.00 | 60.00 | 4,600 | — |
| 1919 | 392,021,000 | 0.20 | 0.30 | 0.40 | 0.75 | 2.00 | 5.00 | 9.00 | 120 | — |

## 1914-D Cent
### Grade F-12

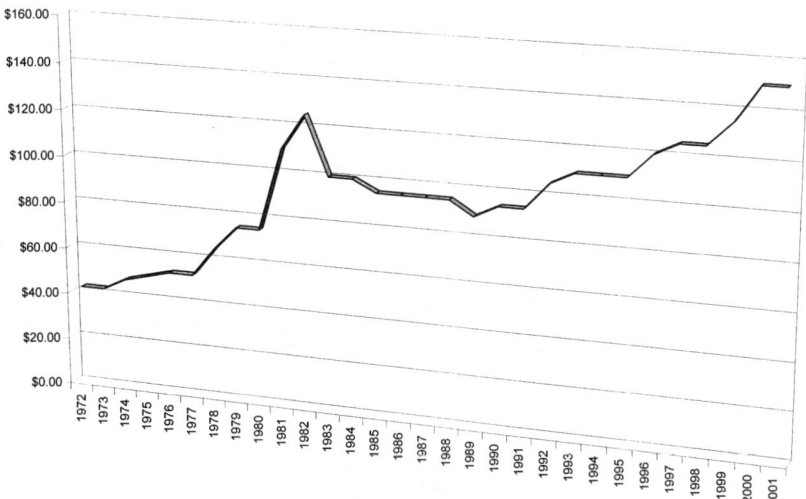

Retail Price

| Date | Mintage | G-4 | VG-8 | F-12 | VF-20 | XF-40 | AU-50 | MS-60 | MS-65 | Prf-65 |
|------|---------|-----|------|------|-------|-------|-------|-------|-------|--------|
| 1919D | 57,154,000 | 0.40 | 0.50 | 0.65 | 2.00 | 7.50 | 29.00 | 50.00 | 1,150 | — |
| 1919S | 139,760,000 | 0.20 | 0.30 | 1.25 | 1.65 | 3.50 | 14.50 | 35.00 | 2,750 | — |
| 1920 | 310,165,000 | 0.20 | 0.25 | 0.40 | 0.75 | 2.50 | 5.50 | 11.00 | 110 | — |
| 1920D | 49,280,000 | 0.30 | 0.45 | 0.95 | 2.50 | 10.00 | 25.00 | 55.00 | 900 | — |
| 1920S | 46,220,000 | 0.25 | 0.35 | 1.25 | 2.00 | 7.00 | 29.00 | 85.00 | 4,400 | — |
| 1921 | 39,157,000 | 0.30 | 0.40 | 0.60 | 1.50 | 5.50 | 17.50 | 35.00 | 195 | — |
| 1921S | 15,274,000 | 1.40 | 1.50 | 2.00 | 4.00 | 17.50 | 65.00 | 85.00 | 4,100 | — |
| 1922D | 7,160,000 | 8.50 | 9.00 | 11.00 | 13.50 | 26.00 | 47.00 | 75.00 | 875 | — |
| 1922 | Inc. above | 310 | 395 | 460 | 600 | 1,350 | 2,650 | 5,200 | 65,000 | — |
| 1923 | 74,723,000 | 0.20 | 0.30 | 0.40 | 1.25 | 4.50 | 8.50 | 12.00 | 240 | — |
| 1923S | 8,700,000 | 1.60 | 2.00 | 3.50 | 6.00 | 25.00 | 75.00 | 185 | 4,100 | — |
| 1924 | 75,178,000 | 0.20 | 0.30 | 0.50 | 1.25 | 5.00 | 10.00 | 20.00 | 145 | — |
| 1924D | 2,520,000 | 10.00 | 12.50 | 14.50 | 30.00 | 80.00 | 145 | 235 | 4,100 | — |
| 1924S | 11,696,000 | 0.85 | 1.10 | 2.00 | 3.00 | 14.50 | 60.00 | 100.00 | 7,000 | — |
| 1925 | 139,949,000 | 0.20 | 0.30 | 0.40 | 1.00 | 3.50 | 7.50 | 10.00 | 80.00 | — |
| 1925D | 22,580,000 | 0.40 | 0.70 | 1.00 | 2.00 | 9.50 | 27.00 | 50.00 | 1,700 | — |
| 1925S | 26,380,000 | 0.30 | 0.40 | 0.80 | 1.25 | 8.00 | 19.50 | 60.00 | 5,950 | — |
| 1926 | 157,088,000 | 0.15 | 0.20 | 0.30 | 0.80 | 2.00 | 5.50 | 8.00 | 60.00 | — |
| 1926D | 28,020,000 | 0.25 | 0.40 | 0.70 | 1.50 | 7.00 | 25.00 | 60.00 | 1,700 | — |
| 1926S | 4,550,000 | 3.00 | 3.75 | 5.50 | 7.00 | 16.00 | 57.00 | 105 | 30,000 | — |
| 1927 | 144,440,000 | 0.15 | 0.20 | 0.30 | 0.80 | 2.00 | 5.00 | 8.00 | 95.00 | — |
| 1927D | 27,170,000 | 0.20 | 0.30 | 0.60 | 1.25 | 4.00 | 13.50 | 55.00 | 1,250 | — |
| 1927S | 14,276,000 | 0.80 | 1.00 | 1.60 | 3.50 | 13.00 | 28.50 | 68.00 | 3,700 | — |
| 1928 | 134,116,000 | 0.15 | 0.20 | 0.30 | 0.80 | 2.00 | 5.00 | 8.50 | 90.00 | — |
| 1928D | 31,170,000 | 0.20 | 0.30 | 0.50 | 1.00 | 4.00 | 10.00 | 28.00 | 510 | — |
| 1928S | 17,266,000 | 0.65 | 0.75 | 1.20 | 1.75 | 5.00 | 13.50 | 67.50 | 1,700 | — |
| 1929 | 185,262,000 | 0.15 | 0.20 | 0.30 | 0.80 | 1.50 | 5.00 | 6.50 | 90.00 | — |
| 1929D | 41,730,000 | 0.15 | 0.20 | 0.50 | 0.90 | 3.50 | 9.00 | 17.50 | 240 | — |
| 1929S | 50,148,000 | 0.15 | 0.20 | 0.35 | 0.75 | 2.75 | 4.75 | 12.00 | 130 | — |
| 1930 | 157,415,000 | 0.15 | 0.20 | 0.30 | 0.50 | 1.75 | 3.00 | 5.50 | 47.00 | — |
| 1930D | 40,100,000 | 0.15 | 0.20 | 0.45 | 0.75 | 2.50 | 5.50 | 12.00 | 95.00 | — |
| 1930S | 24,286,000 | 0.20 | 0.25 | 0.35 | 0.80 | 1.60 | 5.75 | 10.00 | 47.00 | — |
| 1931 | 19,396,000 | 0.50 | 0.60 | 1.00 | 1.40 | 2.00 | 7.00 | 17.50 | 100.00 | — |
| 1931D | 4,480,000 | 3.25 | 3.40 | 3.75 | 4.75 | 8.50 | 35.50 | 49.00 | 560 | — |
| 1931S | 866,000 | 36.50 | 37.50 | 41.00 | 43.00 | 48.00 | 67.00 | 72.00 | 460 | — |
| 1932 | 9,062,000 | 1.50 | 1.80 | 2.35 | 3.00 | 3.60 | 9.50 | 18.50 | 78.00 | — |
| 1932D | 10,500,000 | 1.00 | 1.35 | 1.45 | 1.75 | 2.75 | 8.00 | 14.50 | 80.00 | — |
| 1933 | 14,360,000 | 1.00 | 1.20 | 1.50 | 1.90 | 3.50 | 9.00 | 16.50 | 67.00 | — |
| 1933D | 6,200,000 | 2.00 | 2.25 | 3.00 | 3.50 | 6.00 | 11.50 | 16.50 | 65.00 | — |
| 1934 | 219,080,000 | — | 0.15 | 0.20 | 0.25 | 0.75 | 1.50 | 4.00 | 27.00 | — |
| 1934D | 28,446,000 | 0.15 | 0.20 | 0.25 | 0.45 | 1.50 | 5.00 | 16.50 | 52.00 | — |
| 1935 | 245,338,000 | — | 0.10 | 0.15 | 0.25 | 0.75 | 1.00 | 2.50 | 13.00 | — |
| 1935D | 11,100,000,000 | — | 0.15 | 0.20 | 0.30 | 0.95 | 2.50 | 5.50 | 9.50 | — |
| 1935S | 38,702,000 | 0.10 | 0.20 | 0.30 | 0.40 | 1.00 | 3.00 | 12.00 | 46.00 | — |
| 1936 | 309,637,569 | — | 0.10 | 0.15 | 0.25 | 0.75 | 1.00 | 2.00 | 6.00 | 1,200 |
| 1936D | 40,620,000 | — | 0.10 | 0.15 | 0.25 | 0.75 | 1.50 | 2.75 | 8.50 | — |
| 1936S | 29,130,000 | 0.10 | 0.15 | 0.25 | 0.35 | 0.85 | 1.75 | 2.75 | 8.50 | — |
| 1937 | 309,179,320 | — | 0.10 | 0.15 | 0.20 | 0.70 | 0.90 | 1.75 | 7.00 | 125 |
| 1937D | 50,430,000 | — | 0.10 | 0.15 | 0.25 | 0.70 | 1.00 | 2.50 | 9.50 | — |
| 1937S | 34,500,000 | — | 0.10 | 0.15 | 0.25 | 0.60 | 1.25 | 3.00 | 8.50 | — |
| 1938 | 156,696,734 | — | 0.10 | 0.15 | 0.20 | 0.50 | 1.00 | 2.00 | 5.75 | 85.00 |
| 1938D | 20,010,000 | 0.20 | 0.25 | 0.35 | 0.45 | 0.75 | 1.50 | 2.70 | 8.50 | — |
| 1938S | 15,180,000 | 0.30 | 0.40 | 0.50 | 0.70 | 0.90 | 1.25 | 2.80 | 8.50 | — |
| 1939 | 316,479,520 | — | 0.10 | 0.15 | 0.20 | 0.30 | 0.50 | 1.00 | 5.75 | 78.00 |
| 1939D | 15,160,000 | 0.30 | 0.30 | 0.35 | 0.60 | 0.85 | 1.90 | 2.25 | 8.50 | — |
| 1939S | 52,070,000 | — | 0.15 | 0.20 | 0.25 | 0.45 | 0.90 | 1.35 | 9.50 | — |
| 1940 | 586,825,872 | — | 0.15 | 0.20 | 0.25 | 0.30 | 0.45 | 0.95 | 5.75 | 70.00 |
| 1940D | 81,390,000 | — | 0.15 | 0.20 | 0.25 | 0.35 | 0.50 | 1.00 | 5.75 | — |
| 1940S | 112,940,000 | — | 0.15 | 0.20 | 0.25 | 0.30 | 0.75 | 1.00 | 5.85 | — |
| 1941 | 887,039,100 | — | — | 0.10 | 0.15 | 0.25 | 0.40 | 0.85 | 5.75 | 65.00 |
| 1941D | 128,700,000 | — | — | 0.15 | 0.20 | 0.25 | 1.00 | 2.00 | 8.50 | — |
| 1941S | 92,360,000 | — | — | 0.15 | 0.20 | 0.25 | 1.25 | 2.25 | 11.00 | — |
| 1942 | 657,828,600 | — | — | 0.10 | 0.15 | 0.20 | 0.25 | 0.50 | 4.60 | 78.00 |
| 1942D | 206,698,000 | — | — | 0.10 | 0.15 | 0.20 | 0.30 | 0.50 | 5.75 | — |
| 1942S | 85,590,000 | — | — | 0.10 | 0.20 | 0.30 | 1.50 | 3.50 | 16.00 | — |

**Designer:** Victor D. Brenner. **Diameter:** 19 mm. **Weight:** 2.7000 g. **Composition:** Zinc Coated Steel.

| Date | Mintage | G-4 | VG-8 | F-12 | VF-20 | XF-40 | AU-50 | MS-60 | MS-65 | Prf-65 |
|------|---------|-----|------|------|-------|-------|-------|-------|-------|--------|
| 1943 | 684,628,670 | — | — | 0.25 | 0.30 | 0.50 | 0.70 | 0.85 | 4.60 | — |
| 1943D | 217,660,000 | — | — | 0.25 | 0.35 | 0.60 | 0.65 | 1.00 | 6.50 | — |
| 1943S | 191,550,000 | — | 0.30 | 0.35 | 0.40 | 0.70 | 1.00 | 1.75 | 9.50 | — |

**Designer:** Victor D. Brenner. **Diameter:** 19 mm. **Weight:** 3.1100 g. **Composition:** Copper-zinc. **Notes:** The 1955 "doubled die" has distinct doubling of the date and lettering on the obverse.

| Date | Mintage | XF-40 | MS-65 | Prf-65 |
|------|---------|-------|-------|--------|
| 1944 | 1,435,400,000 | 0.20 | 2.00 | — |
| 1944D | 430,578,000 | 0.20 | 2.00 | — |
| 1944D/S | — | 160 | 1,400 | — |

| Date | Mintage | XF-40 | MS-65 | Prf-65 |
|------|---------|-------|-------|--------|
| 1944S | 282,760,000 | 0.20 | 5.50 | — |
| 1945 | 1,040,515,000 | 0.20 | 2.00 | — |
| 1945D | 226,268,000 | 0.20 | 2.00 | — |
| 1945S | 181,770,000 | 0.20 | 5.50 | — |
| 1946 | 991,655,000 | 0.20 | 2.00 | — |
| 1946D | 315,690,000 | 0.20 | 4.50 | — |
| 1946S | 198,100,000 | 0.20 | 4.60 | — |
| 1947 | 190,555,000 | 0.20 | 2.25 | — |
| 1947D | 194,750,000 | 0.20 | 2.00 | — |
| 1947S | 99,000,000 | 0.20 | 5.50 | — |
| 1948 | 317,570,000 | 0.20 | 2.00 | — |
| 1948D | 172,637,000 | 0.20 | 2.25 | — |
| 1948S | 81,735,000 | 0.20 | 5.50 | — |
| 1949 | 217,775,000 | 0.20 | 3.50 | — |
| 1949D | 153,132,000 | 0.20 | 3.50 | — |
| 1949S | 64,290,000 | 0.25 | 5.75 | — |
| 1950 | 272,686,386 | 0.20 | 1.75 | 40.00 |
| 1950D | 334,950,000 | 0.20 | 1.50 | — |
| 1950S | 118,505,000 | 0.20 | 2.50 | — |
| 1951 | 295,633,500 | 0.20 | 2.00 | 40.00 |
| 1951D | 625,355,000 | 0.10 | 1.65 | — |
| 1951S | 136,010,000 | 0.15 | 3.00 | — |
| 1952 | 186,856,980 | 0.15 | 2.75 | 34.00 |
| 1952D | 746,130,000 | 0.10 | 1.60 | — |
| 1952S | 137,800,004 | 0.15 | 3.00 | — |
| 1953 | 256,883,800 | 0.10 | 1.25 | 28.00 |
| 1953D | 700,515,000 | 0.10 | 1.25 | — |
| 1953S | 181,835,000 | 0.15 | 1.75 | — |
| 1954 | 71,873,350 | 0.15 | 1.25 | 9.00 |
| 1954D | 251,552,500 | 0.10 | 0.50 | — |
| 1954S | 96,190,000 | 0.15 | 0.75 | — |
| 1955 | 330,958,000 | 0.10 | 0.75 | 13.00 |
| 1955 doubled die | — | 570 | 27,000 | — |
| 1955D | 563,257,500 | 0.10 | 0.75 | — |
| 1955S | 44,610,000 | 0.25 | 1.00 | — |
| 1956 | 421,414,384 | — | 0.50 | 3.00 |
| 1956D | 1,098,201,100 | — | 0.50 | — |
| 1957 | 283,787,952 | — | 0.50 | 2.00 |
| 1957D | 1,051,342,000 | — | 0.50 | — |
| 1958 | 253,400,652 | — | 0.50 | 3.00 |
| 1958D | 800,953,300 | — | 0.50 | — |

## Lincoln. Lincoln Memorial.

**Rev. Designer:** Frank Gasparro. **Weight:** 3.1100 g. **Composition:** Copper-zinc. **Notes:** The dates were modified in 1960, 1970 and 1982, resulting in large-date and small-date varieties for those years. The 1972 "doubled die" shows doubling of "In God We Trust." The 1979-S and 1981-S Type II proofs have a clearer mint mark than the Type I proofs of those years. Some 1982 cents have the predominantly copper composition; others have the predominantly zinc composition. They can be distinguished by weight.

| Date | Mintage | XF-40 | MS-65 | Prf-65 |
|------|---------|-------|-------|--------|
| 1959 | 610,864,291 | — | 0.50 | 1.50 |
| 1959D | 1,279,760,000 | — | 0.50 | — |
| 1960 small date | 588,096,602 | 2.10 | 5.00 | 16.00 |
| 1960 large date | Inc. above | — | 0.30 | 1.25 |
| 1960 | — | — | 0.30 | 1.25 |
| 1960D small date | 1,580,884,000 | — | 0.30 | — |
| 1960D large date | Inc. above | — | 0.30 | — |
| 1960D | — | — | 0.30 | — |
| 1961 | 756,373,244 | — | 0.30 | 1.00 |
| 1961D | 1,753,266,700 | — | 0.30 | — |
| 1962 | 609,263,019 | — | 0.30 | 1.00 |
| 1962D | 1,793,148,400 | — | 0.30 | — |
| 1963 | 757,185,645 | — | 0.30 | 1.00 |
| 1963D | 1,774,020,400 | — | 0.30 | — |
| 1964 | 2,652,525,762 | — | 0.30 | 1.00 |
| 1964D | 3,799,071,500 | — | 0.30 | — |
| 1965 | 1,497,224,900 | — | 0.30 | — |
| 1966 | 2,188,147,783 | — | 0.30 | — |
| 1967 | 3,048,667,100 | — | 0.30 | — |
| 1968 | 1,707,880,970 | — | 0.30 | — |
| 1968D | 2,886,269,600 | — | 0.40 | — |
| 1968S | 261,311,510 | — | 0.40 | 1.00 |
| 1969 | 1,136,910,000 | — | 0.60 | — |
| 1969D | 4,002,832,200 | — | 0.40 | — |
| 1969S | 547,309,631 | — | 0.40 | 1.10 |
| 1970 | 1,898,315,000 | — | 0.40 | — |
| 1970D | 2,891,438,900 | — | 0.40 | — |
| 1970S | 693,192,814 | — | 0.40 | 0.90 |
| 1970S small date | — | — | 55.00 | 60.00 |
| 1971 | 1,919,490,000 | — | 0.35 | — |

1955 doubled die

1972 doubled die

1983 doubled die

Small date

Large date

Large date

Small date

Large date

Small date

| Date | Mintage | XF-40 | MS-65 | Prf-65 |
|---|---|---|---|---|
| 1971D | 2,911,045,600 | — | 0.40 | — |
| 1971S | 528,354,192 | — | 0.25 | 1.10 |
| 1972 | 2,933,255,000 | — | 0.25 | — |
| 1972 doubled die | — | 165 | 410 | — |
| 1972D | 2,665,071,400 | — | 0.25 | — |
| 1972S | 380,200,104 | — | 0.25 | 1.15 |
| 1973 | 3,728,245,000 | — | 0.25 | — |
| 1973D | 3,549,576,588 | — | 0.25 | — |
| 1973S | 319,937,634 | — | 0.25 | 0.80 |
| 1974 | 4,232,140,523 | — | 0.25 | — |
| 1974D | 4,235,098,000 | — | 0.25 | — |
| 1974S | 412,039,228 | — | 0.25 | 0.75 |
| 1975 | 5,451,476,142 | — | 0.25 | — |
| 1975D | 4,505,245,300 | — | 0.25 | — |
| 1975S | (2,845,450) | — | — | 5.50 |
| 1976 | 4,674,292,426 | — | 0.25 | — |
| 1976D | 4,221,592,455 | — | 0.25 | — |
| 1976S | (4,149,730) | — | — | 4.50 |
| 1977 | 4,469,930,000 | — | 0.25 | — |
| 1977D | 4,149,062,300 | — | 0.25 | — |
| 1977S | (3,251,152) | — | — | 4.00 |
| 1978 | 5,558,605,000 | — | 0.25 | — |
| 1978D | 4,280,233,400 | — | 0.25 | — |
| 1978S | (3,127,781) | — | — | 3.00 |
| 1979 | 6,018,515,000 | — | 0.25 | — |
| 1979D | 4,139,357,254 | — | 0.25 | — |
| 1979S type I, proof only | (3,677,175) | — | — | 3.00 |
| 1979S type II, proof only | Inc. above | — | — | 4.25 |
| 1980 | 7,414,705,000 | — | 0.25 | — |
| 1980D | 5,140,098,660 | — | 0.25 | — |
| 1980S | (3,554,806) | — | — | 2.25 |
| 1981 | 7,491,750,000 | — | 0.25 | — |
| 1981D | 5,373,235,677 | — | 0.25 | — |
| 1981S type I, proof only | (4,063,083) | — | — | 3.00 |
| 1981S type II, proof only | Inc. above | — | — | 50.00 |
| 1982 large date | 10,712,525,000 | — | 0.25 | — |
| 1982 small date | — | — | 0.25 | — |
| 1982D large date | 6,012,979,368 | — | 0.25 | — |

**Diameter:** 19 mm. **Weight:** 2.5000 g. **Composition:** Copper Plated Zinc.

| Date | Mintage | XF-40 | MS-65 | Prf-65 |
|---|---|---|---|---|
| 1982 large date | — | — | 0.50 | — |
| 1982 small date | — | — | 1.00 | — |
| 1982D large date | — | — | 0.30 | — |
| 1982D small date | — | — | 0.25 | — |

**Diameter:** 19 mm **Composition:** Copper Plated Zinc. **Notes:** The 1983 "doubled die reverse" shows doubling of "United States of America." The 1984 "doubled die" shows doubling of Lincoln's ear on the obverse.

| Date | Mintage | XF-40 | MS-65 | Prf-65 |
|---|---|---|---|---|
| 1982S | (3,857,479) | — | — | 3.00 |
| 1983 | 7,752,355,000 | — | 0.25 | — |
| 1983 doubled die | — | — | 400 | — |
| 1983D | 6,467,199,428 | — | 0.25 | — |
| 1983S | (3,279,126) | — | — | 4.50 |
| 1984 | 8,151,079,000 | — | 0.25 | — |
| 1984 doubled die | — | — | 275 | — |
| 1984D | 5,569,238,906 | — | 0.70 | — |
| 1984S | (3,065,110) | — | — | 4.50 |
| 1985 | 5,648,489,887 | — | 0.25 | — |
| 1985D | 5,287,399,926 | — | 0.25 | — |
| 1985S | (3,362,821) | — | — | 6.00 |
| 1986 | 4,491,395,493 | — | 0.70 | — |
| 1986D | 4,442,866,698 | — | 0.25 | — |
| 1986S | (3,010,497) | — | — | 7.50 |
| 1987 | 4,682,466,931 | — | 0.25 | — |
| 1987D | 4,879,389,514 | — | 0.25 | — |
| 1987S | (4,227,728) | — | — | 5.00 |
| 1988 | 6,092,810,000 | — | 0.25 | — |
| 1988D | 5,253,740,443 | — | 0.25 | — |
| 1988S | (3,262,948) | — | — | 12.00 |
| 1989 | 7,261,535,000 | — | 0.25 | — |
| 1989D | 5,345,467,111 | — | 0.25 | — |
| 1989S | (3,220,194) | — | — | 12.00 |
| 1990 | 6,851,765,000 | — | 0.25 | — |
| 1990D | 4,922,894,533 | — | 0.25 | — |
| 1990S | (3,299,559) | — | — | 5.75 |
| 1990 no S | — | — | — | 2,750 |
| 1991 | 5,165,940,000 | — | 0.25 | — |

| Date | Mintage | XF-40 | MS-65 | Prf-65 |
|---|---|---|---|---|
| 1991D | 4,158,442,076 | — | 0.25 | — |
| 1991S | (2,867,787) | — | — | 26.00 |
| 1992 | 4,648,905,000 | — | 0.25 | — |
| 1992D | 4,448,673,300 | — | 0.25 | — |
| 1992S | (4,176,560) | — | — | 6.50 |
| 1993 | 5,684,705,000 | — | 0.25 | — |
| 1993D | 6,426,650,571 | — | 0.25 | — |
| 1993S | (3,394,792) | — | — | 9.50 |
| 1994 | 6,500,850,000 | — | 0.25 | — |
| 1994D | 7,131,765,000 | — | 0.25 | — |
| 1994S | (3,269,923) | — | — | 8.50 |
| 1995 | 6,411,440,000 | — | 0.25 | — |
| 1995 doubled die | — | — | 27.00 | — |
| 1995D | 7,128,560,000 | — | 0.25 | — |
| 1995S | — | — | — | 9.50 |
| 1996 | 6,612,465,000 | — | 0.25 | — |
| 1996D | 6,510,795,000 | — | 0.25 | — |
| 1996S | — | — | — | 6.50 |
| 1997 | 4,622,800,000 | — | 0.25 | — |
| 1997D | 4,576,555,000 | — | 0.25 | — |
| 1997S | (1,975,000) | — | — | 10.50 |
| 1998 | 5,032,155,000 | — | 0.25 | — |
| 1998D | 5,255,353,500 | — | 0.25 | — |
| 1998S | — | — | — | 9.50 |
| 1999 | 5,237,600,000 | — | 0.25 | — |
| 1999D | 6,360,065,000 | — | 0.25 | — |
| 1999S | — | — | — | 6.00 |
| 2000 | — | — | 0.25 | — |
| 2000D | — | — | 0.25 | — |
| 2000S | — | — | — | 5.00 |
| 2001 | — | — | — | — |
| 2001D | — | — | — | — |
| 2001S | — | — | — | — |

# 2 CENTS

Small letters    Large letters

**Designer:** James B. Longacre. **Diameter:** 23 mm. **Weight:** 6.2200 g. **Composition:** Copper-tin-zinc. **Notes:** The motto "In God We Trust" was modified in 1864, resulting in small-motto and large-motto varieties for that year.

| Date | Mintage | G-4 | VG-8 | F-12 | VF-20 | XF-40 | AU-50 | MS-60 | MS-65 | Prf-65 |
|---|---|---|---|---|---|---|---|---|---|---|
| 1864 small motto | 19,847,500 | 60.00 | 75.00 | 115 | 175 | 290 | 360 | 525 | 1,700 | 45,000 |
| 1864 large motto | Inc. above | 11.00 | 12.00 | 18.00 | 25.00 | 37.00 | 65.00 | 70.00 | 500 | 1,400 |
| 1865 | 13,640,000 | 11.00 | 12.00 | 18.00 | 26.00 | 37.00 | 65.00 | 70.00 | 500 | 850 |
| 1866 | 3,177,000 | 11.00 | 13.50 | 19.00 | 27.50 | 37.00 | 65.00 | 70.00 | 600 | 850 |
| 1867 | 2,938,750 | 12.00 | 14.50 | 20.00 | 27.50 | 38.00 | 67.00 | 95.00 | 500 | 850 |
| 1868 | 2,803,750 | 12.00 | 14.00 | 20.00 | 27.50 | 40.00 | 72.00 | 120 | 560 | 850 |
| 1869 | 1,546,000 | 12.00 | 14.00 | 20.00 | 29.50 | 42.00 | 80.00 | 120 | 575 | 850 |
| 1870 | 861,250 | 12.00 | 14.00 | 22.50 | 37.50 | 65.00 | 95.00 | 185 | 725 | 850 |
| 1871 | 721,250 | 14.00 | 16.00 | 27.00 | 42.00 | 80.00 | 120 | 185 | 700 | 850 |
| 1872 | 65,000 | 110 | 150 | 210 | 275 | 450 | 550 | 800 | 2,300 | 900 |
| 1873 proof only | Est. 1,100 | — | — | 925 | 950 | 975 | 1,000 | — | — | 2,000 |

# SILVER 3 CENTS

## No outlines in star; Type 1.

**Designer:** James B. Longacre. **Diameter:** 14 mm. **Weight:** 0.8000 g. **Composition:** 0.7500 Silver, 0.0193 oz. ASW.

| Date | Mintage | G-4 | VG-8 | F-12 | VF-20 | XF-40 | AU-50 | MS-60 | MS-65 | Prf-65 |
|------|---------|------|-------|-------|--------|--------|--------|--------|--------|--------|
| 1851 | 5,447,400 | 19.50 | 23.00 | 26.00 | 32.00 | 65.00 | 130 | 150 | 900 | — |
| 1851O | 720,000 | 23.00 | 26.00 | 38.00 | 58.00 | 130 | 210 | 290 | 2,200 | — |
| 1852 | 18,663,500 | 19.50 | 23.00 | 26.00 | 32.00 | 65.00 | 130 | 150 | 900 | — |
| 1853 | 11,400,000 | 19.50 | 23.00 | 26.00 | 32.00 | 65.00 | 130 | 150 | 900 | — |

## Three outlines in star; Type 2.

**Designer:** James B. Longacre. **Diameter:** 14 mm. **Weight:** 0.7500 g. **Composition:** 0.9000 Silver, 0.0218 oz. ASW.

| Date | Mintage | G-4 | VG-8 | F-12 | VF-20 | XF-40 | AU-50 | MS-60 | MS-65 | Prf-65 |
|------|---------|------|-------|-------|--------|--------|--------|--------|--------|--------|
| 1854 | 671,000 | 19.50 | 23.50 | 26.00 | 40.00 | 95.00 | 220 | 325 | 3,200 | 33,500 |
| 1855 | 139,000 | 22.00 | 35.00 | 49.00 | 85.00 | 145 | 265 | 460 | 8,400 | 15,000 |
| 1856 | 1,458,000 | 19.50 | 23.00 | 26.00 | 47.00 | 87.00 | 160 | 260 | 4,100 | 15,500 |
| 1857 | 1,042,000 | 19.50 | 23.00 | 27.00 | 45.00 | 87.00 | 230 | 285 | 3,100 | 13,500 |
| 1858 | 1,604,000 | 19.50 | 23.00 | 26.00 | 42.00 | 87.00 | 160 | 240 | 3,200 | 6,400 |

### 1851-O Silver Three-Cent Piece
#### Grade XF-40

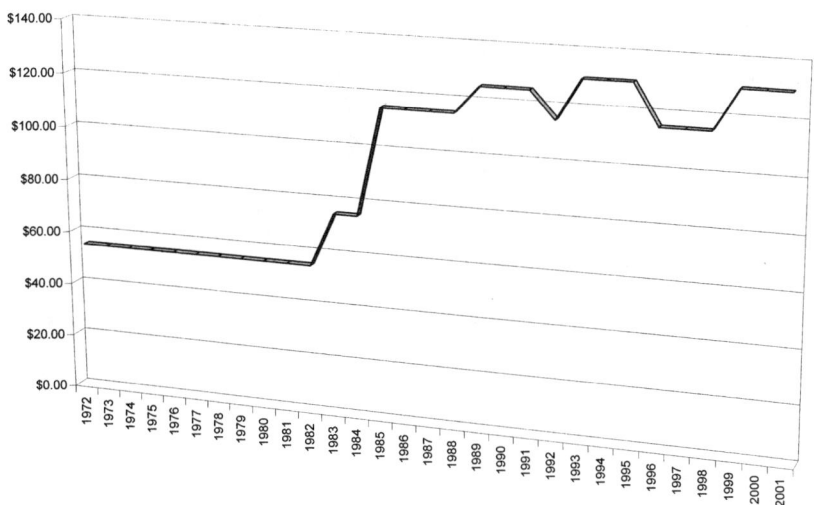

Retail Price

## Two outlines in star; Type 3.

**Designer:** James B. Longacre. **Diameter:** 14 mm. **Weight:** 0.7500 g. **Composition:** 0.9000 Silver, 0.0218 oz. ASW.

| Date | Mintage | G-4 | VG-8 | F-12 | VF-20 | XF-40 | AU-50 | MS-60 | MS-65 | Prf-65 |
|---|---|---|---|---|---|---|---|---|---|---|
| 1859 | 365,000 | 19.00 | 22.50 | 26.00 | 39.00 | 65.00 | 130 | 155 | 940 | 2,150 |
| 1860 | 287,000 | 19.00 | 22.50 | 26.00 | 42.00 | 68.00 | 130 | 155 | 940 | 4,000 |
| 1861 | 498,000 | 19.50 | 23.00 | 26.00 | 35.00 | 65.00 | 130 | 160 | 975 | 1,800 |
| 1862 | 343,550 | 19.50 | 23.00 | 27.00 | 45.00 | 65.00 | 130 | 160 | 975 | 1,400 |
| 1863 | 21,460 | 275 | 300 | 320 | 340 | 370 | 440 | 650 | 1,950 | 1,350 |
| 1864 | 12,470 | 275 | 300 | 320 | 340 | 370 | 450 | 590 | 1,500 | 1,350 |
| 1865 | 8,500 | 350 | 375 | 390 | 415 | 430 | 450 | 620 | 1,450 | 1,350 |
| 1866 | 22,725 | 275 | 325 | 320 | 340 | 375 | 400 | 560 | 1,650 | 1,325 |
| 1867 | 4,625 | 325 | 375 | 390 | 420 | 425 | 450 | 600 | 2,400 | 1,300 |
| 1868 | 4,100 | 325 | 375 | 390 | 420 | 425 | 450 | 600 | 4,900 | 1,400 |
| 1869 | 5,100 | 325 | 375 | 390 | 420 | 425 | 450 | 600 | 1,900 | 1,400 |
| 1870 | 4,000 | 310 | 375 | 350 | 400 | 425 | 450 | 750 | 4,200 | 1,350 |
| 1871 | 4,360 | 325 | 375 | 400 | 420 | 435 | 460 | 625 | 1,450 | 1,450 |
| 1872 | 1,950 | 375 | 400 | 420 | 450 | 460 | 575 | 690 | 4,600 | 1,350 |
| 1873 proof only | 600 | — | — | 625 | 665 | 700 | 750 | — | — | 1,575 |

# NICKEL 3 CENTS

**Designer:** James B. Longacre. **Diameter:** 17.9 mm. **Weight:** 1.9400 g. **Composition:** Copper-nickel.

| Date | Mintage | G-4 | VG-8 | F-12 | VF-20 | XF-40 | AU-50 | MS-60 | MS-65 | Prf-65 |
|---|---|---|---|---|---|---|---|---|---|---|
| 1865 | 11,382,000 | 10.50 | 11.50 | 12.50 | 14.50 | 20.00 | 50.00 | 83.00 | 700 | 6,000 |
| 1866 | 4,801,000 | 10.50 | 11.50 | 12.00 | 14.50 | 20.00 | 50.00 | 83.00 | 700 | 1,550 |
| 1867 | 3,915,000 | 10.50 | 12.00 | 12.50 | 14.50 | 20.00 | 50.00 | 83.00 | 750 | 1,450 |
| 1868 | 3,252,000 | 10.50 | 11.50 | 12.00 | 14.50 | 20.00 | 50.00 | 83.00 | 700 | 1,400 |
| 1869 | 1,604,000 | 10.75 | 12.00 | 12.50 | 14.50 | 20.00 | 56.00 | 100.00 | 750 | 1,050 |
| 1870 | 1,335,000 | 10.75 | 11.50 | 13.00 | 17.50 | 23.00 | 56.00 | 110 | 740 | 1,500 |
| 1871 | 604,000 | 10.75 | 11.50 | 13.00 | 15.50 | 23.00 | 58.00 | 120 | 750 | 1,200 |
| 1872 | 862,000 | 11.00 | 11.50 | 12.50 | 15.00 | 20.00 | 56.00 | 120 | 1,100 | 1,050 |
| 1873 | 1,173,000 | 11.00 | 12.50 | 13.00 | 15.50 | 22.00 | 56.00 | 115 | 1,250 | 1,050 |
| 1874 | 790,000 | 11.00 | 12.00 | 13.00 | 15.50 | 20.00 | 58.00 | 120 | 1,000 | 950 |
| 1875 | 228,000 | 11.00 | 12.00 | 13.00 | 18.00 | 30.00 | 67.00 | 150 | 750 | 1,500 |
| 1876 | 162,000 | 11.75 | 14.50 | 16.00 | 25.00 | 38.00 | 85.00 | 175 | 1,700 | 1,000 |
| 1877 proof only | Est. 900 | — | — | 900 | 950 | 1,000 | 1,050 | — | — | 2,050 |
| 1878 proof only | 2,350 | — | — | 445 | 455 | 475 | 485 | — | — | 700 |
| 1879 | 41,200 | 48.00 | 55.00 | 67.00 | 75.00 | 85.00 | 125 | 250 | 755 | 525 |
| 1880 | 24,955 | 75.00 | 80.00 | 85.00 | 100.00 | 125 | 160 | 280 | 745 | 525 |
| 1881 | 1,080,575 | 10.50 | 11.50 | 12.00 | 14.50 | 20.00 | 50.00 | 85.00 | 750 | 525 |
| 1882 | 25,300 | 72.00 | 75.00 | 84.00 | 95.00 | 115 | 140 | 250 | 1,000 | 565 |
| 1883 | 10,609 | 135 | 145 | 190 | 210 | 250 | 300 | 385 | 3,650 | 560 |
| 1884 | 5,642 | 290 | 310 | 400 | 400 | 420 | 450 | 550 | 4,500 | 550 |
| 1885 | 4,790 | 350 | 370 | 520 | 490 | 520 | 520 | 700 | 2,100 | 590 |
| 1886 proof only | 4,290 | — | — | — | 275 | 300 | 320 | — | — | 525 |
| 1887/6 proof only | 7,961 | — | — | — | 330 | 350 | 360 | — | — | 700 |
| 1887 | Inc. above | 235 | 250 | 270 | 280 | 325 | 355 | 435 | 975 | 1,050 |
| 1888 | 41,083 | 38.00 | 47.00 | 48.00 | 54.00 | 65.00 | 125 | 240 | 750 | 525 |
| 1889 | 21,561 | 65.00 | 78.00 | 90.00 | 100.00 | 120 | 130 | 265 | 775 | 525 |

# HALF DIME

## Flowing hair.

**Designer:** Robert Scot. **Diameter:** 16.5 mm. **Weight:** 1.3500 g. **Composition:** 0.8920 Silver, 0.0388 oz. ASW.

| Date | Mintage | G-4 | VG-8 | F-12 | VF-20 | XF-40 | MS-60 |
|------|---------|-----|------|------|-------|-------|-------|
| 1794 | 86,416 | 750 | 900 | 1,150 | 1,900 | 3,250 | 6,700 |
| 1795 | Inc. above | 540 | 650 | 950 | 1,350 | 2,300 | 4,750 |

## Draped bust. Small eagle.

**Designer:** Robert Scot. **Diameter:** 16.5 mm. **Weight:** 1.3500 g. **Composition:** 0.8920 Silver, 0.0388 oz. ASW. **Notes:** Some 1796 strikes have "Liberty" spelled as "Likerty." The 1797 strikes have either 13, 15 or 16 stars on the obverse.

| Date | Mintage | G-4 | VG-8 | F-12 | VF-20 | XF-40 | MS-60 |
|------|---------|-----|------|------|-------|-------|-------|
| 1796 | 10,230 | 700 | 850 | 1,175 | 1,950 | 3,250 | 6,500 |
| 1796 "Likerty" | Inc. above | 700 | 850 | 1,200 | 1,950 | 3,350 | 6,750 |
| 1796/5 | Inc. above | 800 | 1,100 | 1,500 | 3,250 | 4,500 | 16,000 |
| 1797 13 stars | 44,527 | 650 | 850 | 1,200 | 2,150 | 4,250 | 12,500 |
| 1797 15 stars | Inc. above | 650 | 850 | 1,150 | 1,950 | 3,250 | 6,250 |
| 1797 16 stars | Inc. above | 650 | 850 | 1,200 | 2,000 | 3,400 | 7,000 |

## Draped bust. Heraldic eagle.

**Designer:** Robert Scot. **Diameter:** 16.5 mm. **Weight:** 1.3500 g. **Composition:** 0.8920 Silver, 0.0388 oz. ASW. **Notes:** Some 1800 strikes have "Liberty" spelled as "Libekty."

| Date | Mintage | G-4 | VG-8 | F-12 | VF-20 | XF-40 | MS-60 |
|------|---------|-----|------|------|-------|-------|-------|
| 1800 | 24,000 | 400 | 500 | 725 | 1,150 | 2,100 | 4,650 |
| 1800 "Libekty" | Inc. above | 425 | 550 | 750 | 1,200 | 2,150 | 4,950 |
| 1801 | 33,910 | 525 | 675 | 975 | 1,375 | 2,750 | 7,500 |
| 1802 | 13,010 | 12,500 | 16,500 | 30,000 | 45,000 | 75,000 | — |
| 1803 | 37,850 | 550 | 650 | 850 | 1,200 | 2,600 | 5,050 |
| 1805 | 15,600 | 650 | 825 | 975 | 1,450 | 3,200 | 10,000 |

## Liberty cap.

**Designer:** William Kneass. **Diameter:** 15.5 mm. **Weight:** 1.3500 g. **Composition:** 0.8920 Silver, 0.0388 oz. ASW. **Notes:** Design modifications in 1835, 1836 and 1837 resulted in variety combinations with large and small dates, and large and small "5C." inscriptions on the reverse.

| Date | Mintage | G-4 | VG-8 | F-12 | VF-20 | XF-40 | AU-50 | MS-60 | MS-65 |
|------|---------|-----|------|------|-------|-------|-------|-------|-------|
| 1829 | 1,230,000 | 24.00 | 28.00 | 32.00 | 60.00 | 125 | 210 | 270 | 2,650 |
| 1830 | 1,240,000 | 23.00 | 28.00 | 32.00 | 60.00 | 120 | 205 | 270 | 2,650 |
| 1831 | 1,242,700 | 22.00 | 27.00 | 30.00 | 60.00 | 115 | 205 | 270 | 2,600 |
| 1832 | 965,000 | 21.00 | 26.00 | 30.00 | 60.00 | 115 | 205 | 270 | 2,600 |
| 1833 | 1,370,000 | 21.00 | 26.00 | 30.00 | 60.00 | 115 | 205 | 290 | 2,650 |
| 1834 | 1,480,000 | 20.00 | 25.00 | 29.00 | 58.00 | 110 | 200 | 270 | 2,600 |
| 1835 lg. dt., lg. 5C. | 2,760,000 | 20.00 | 25.00 | 29.00 | 58.00 | 110 | 200 | 270 | 2,600 |
| 1835 lg. dt., sm. 5C. | Inc. above | 20.00 | 25.00 | 29.00 | 58.00 | 110 | 200 | 270 | 2,600 |
| 1835 sm. dt., lg. 5C. | Inc. above | 20.00 | 25.00 | 29.00 | 58.00 | 110 | 200 | 270 | 2,600 |

## 1802 Half Dime
### Grade F-12

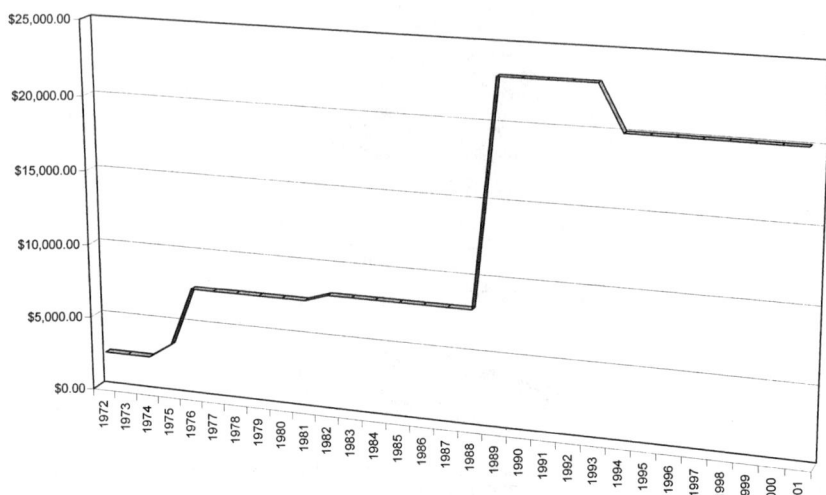

Retail Price

| Date | Mintage | G-4 | VG-8 | F-12 | VF-20 | XF-40 | AU-50 | MS-60 | MS-65 |
|---|---|---|---|---|---|---|---|---|---|
| 1835 sm. dt., sm. 5C | Inc. above | 20.00 | 25.00 | 29.00 | 58.00 | 110 | 200 | 270 | 2,600 |
| 1836 lg. 5C. | 1,900,000 | 20.00 | 25.00 | 29.00 | 58.00 | 110 | 200 | 270 | 2,600 |
| 1836 sm. 5C. | Inc. above | 20.00 | 25.00 | 29.00 | 58.00 | 110 | 200 | 270 | 2,600 |
| 1837 lg. 5C. | 2,276,000 | 22.00 | 28.00 | 33.00 | 60.00 | 115 | 200 | 300 | 3,500 |
| 1837 sm. 5C. | Inc. above | 26.00 | 30.00 | 42.00 | 88.00 | 145 | 350 | 950 | 8,750 |

## Seated Liberty. No stars around rim.

**Designer:** Christian Gobrecht. **Diameter:** 15.5 mm. **Weight:** 1.3400 g. **Composition:** 0.9000 Silver, 0.0388 oz. ASW. **Notes:** A design modification in 1837 resulted in small-date and large-date varieties for that year.

| Date | Mintage | G-4 | VG-8 | F-12 | VF-20 | XF-40 | AU-50 | MS-60 | MS-65 |
|---|---|---|---|---|---|---|---|---|---|
| 1837 small date | Inc. above | 26.00 | 35.00 | 53.00 | 100.00 | 185 | 375 | 600 | 3,400 |
| 1837 large date | Inc. above | 25.00 | 35.00 | 53.00 | 100.00 | 210 | 375 | 600 | 3,250 |
| 1838O | 70,000 | 80.00 | 125 | 225 | 400 | 750 | 1,450 | 2,000 | — |

## Seated Liberty. Stars around rim. No drapery.

**Designer:** Christian Gobrecht. **Diameter:** 15.5 mm. **Weight:** 1.3400 g. **Composition:** 0.9000 Silver, 0.0388 oz. ASW. **Notes:** The two varieties of 1838 are distinguished by the size of the stars on the obverse. The 1839-O with reverse of 1838-O was struck from rusted reverse dies. The result is a bumpy surface on this variety's reverse.

| Date | Mintage | G-4 | VG-8 | F-12 | VF-20 | XF-40 | AU-50 | MS-60 | MS-65 |
|---|---|---|---|---|---|---|---|---|---|
| 1838 large stars | 2,255,000 | 12.00 | 13.50 | 16.00 | 25.00 | 60.00 | 150 | 240 | 2,250 |
| 1838 small stars | Inc. above | 18.00 | 27.50 | 45.00 | 100.00 | 175 | 300 | 650 | 3,850 |
| 1839 | 1,069,150 | 13.50 | 15.00 | 18.00 | 29.00 | 65.00 | 160 | 250 | 2,500 |
| 1839O | 1,034,039 | 14.00 | 16.00 | 19.00 | 31.00 | 70.00 | 170 | 550 | 5,500 |
| 1839O reverse 1838O | — | 375 | 575 | 750 | 1,200 | 2,250 | 3,500 | — | — |
| 1840 | 1,344,085 | 14.00 | 16.00 | 19.00 | 25.00 | 60.00 | 140 | 240 | 2,100 |
| 1840O | 935,000 | 15.00 | 17.00 | 27.00 | 30.00 | 75.00 | 210 | 700 | — |

## 1846 Half Dime Grade XF-40

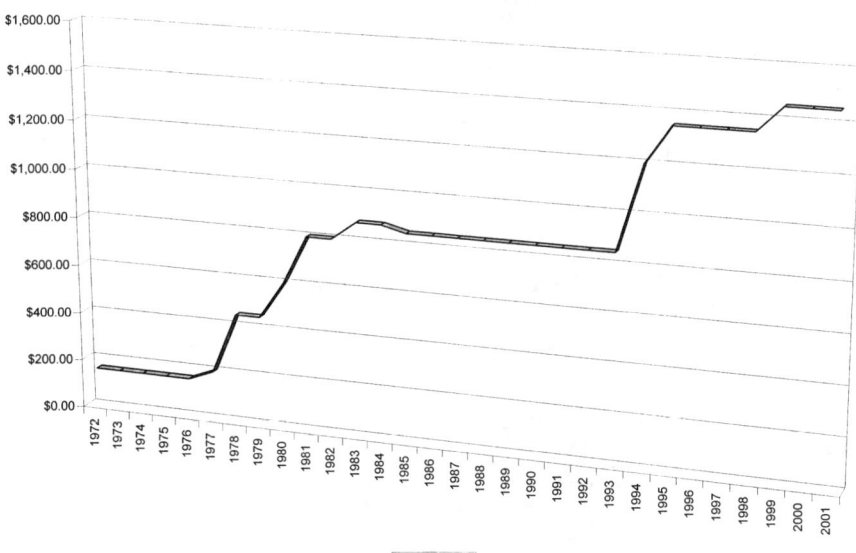

Retail Price

# Seated Liberty. Drapery added to Liberty's left elbow.

**Designer:** Christian Gobrecht. **Diameter:** 15.5 mm. **Weight:** 1.3400 g. **Composition:** 0.9000 Silver, 0.0388 oz. ASW. **Notes:** In 1840 drapery was added to Liberty's left elbow. Varieties for the 1848 Philadelphia strikes are distinguished by the size of the numerals in the date.

| Date | Mintage | G-4 | VG-8 | F-12 | VF-20 | XF-40 | AU-50 | MS-60 | MS-65 |
|------|---------|-----|------|------|-------|-------|-------|-------|-------|
| 1840 | Inc. above | 22.00 | 35.00 | 60.00 | 115 | 200 | 325 | 450 | 300 |
| 1840O | Inc. above | 33.00 | 55.00 | 100.00 | 165 | 400 | 950 | 3,250 | — |
| 1841 | 1,150,000 | 11.00 | 12.00 | 14.00 | 24.00 | 55.00 | 115 | 150 | 1,250 |
| 1841O | 815,000 | 12.50 | 15.00 | 22.50 | 42.00 | 110 | 275 | 650 | 6,500 |
| 1842 | 815,000 | 11.00 | 12.00 | 14.00 | 24.00 | 55.00 | 115 | 150 | 1,750 |
| 1842O | 350,000 | 28.00 | 40.00 | 60.00 | 150 | 425 | 850 | 1,150 | — |
| 1843 | 1,165,000 | 11.00 | 12.00 | 14.00 | 24.00 | 50.00 | 110 | 150 | 1,350 |
| 1844 | 430,000 | 11.00 | 12.00 | 14.00 | 24.00 | 50.00 | 110 | 150 | 1,150 |
| 1844O | 220,000 | 75.00 | 105 | 175 | 450 | 950 | 1,900 | 5,400 | — |
| 1845 | 1,564,000 | 11.00 | 12.00 | 14.00 | 22.00 | 50.00 | 110 | 150 | 1,150 |
| 1845/1845 | Inc. above | 12.00 | 13.00 | 15.00 | 24.00 | 50.00 | 115 | 160 | 1,200 |
| 1846 | 27,000 | 225 | 325 | 500 | 750 | 1,550 | 3,600 | 7,500 | — |
| 1847 | 1,274,000 | 11.00 | 12.00 | 14.00 | 20.00 | 55.00 | 110 | 160 | 1,150 |
| 1848 medium date | 668,000 | 12.00 | 13.00 | 15.00 | 25.00 | 60.00 | 115 | 210 | 2,600 |
| 1848 large date | Inc. above | 15.00 | 20.00 | 30.00 | 50.00 | 110 | 250 | 450 | 4,000 |
| 1848O | 600,000 | 13.00 | 17.50 | 25.00 | 45.00 | 95.00 | 240 | 400 | 1,950 |
| 1849/8 | 1,309,000 | 14.00 | 20.00 | 25.00 | 50.00 | 100.00 | 180 | 375 | 1,800 |
| 1849/6 | Inc. above | 12.00 | 13.00 | 15.00 | 40.00 | 85.00 | 175 | 375 | 1,500 |
| 1849 | Inc. above | 11.00 | 12.00 | 14.00 | 20.00 | 50.00 | 110 | 175 | 1,650 |
| 1849O | 140,000 | 22.00 | 35.00 | 75.00 | 175 | 425 | 650 | 1,950 | 14,000 |
| 1850 | 955,000 | 11.00 | 12.00 | 14.00 | 20.00 | 50.00 | 115 | 150 | 1,400 |
| 1850O | 690,000 | 13.00 | 16.00 | 22.50 | 50.00 | 100.00 | 275 | 675 | 4,000 |
| 1851 | 781,000 | 11.00 | 12.00 | 14.00 | 20.00 | 50.00 | 110 | 150 | 1,500 |
| 1851O | 860,000 | 12.00 | 15.00 | 20.00 | 35.00 | 95.00 | 185 | 500 | 3,750 |
| 1852 | 1,000,500 | 11.00 | 12.00 | 14.00 | 20.00 | 50.00 | 110 | 150 | 1,150 |
| 1852O | 260,000 | 23.00 | 32.00 | 55.00 | 115 | 250 | 475 | 750 | 10,000 |
| 1853 | 135,000 | 28.00 | 36.00 | 56.00 | 100.00 | 185 | 350 | 650 | 3,000 |
| 1853O | 160,000 | 150 | 200 | 295 | 550 | 1,200 | 2,500 | 4,800 | 25,000 |

# Seated Liberty. Arrows at date.

**Designer:** Christian Gobrecht. **Weight:** 1.2400 g. **Composition:** 0.9000 Silver, 0.0362 oz. ASW.

| Date | Mintage | G-4 | VG-8 | F-12 | VF-20 | XF-40 | AU-50 | MS-60 | MS-65 | Prf-65 |
|------|---------|-----|------|------|-------|-------|-------|-------|-------|--------|
| 1853 | 13,210,020 | 11.00 | 12.00 | 14.00 | 17.00 | 50.00 | 120 | 190 | 1,850 | 35,000 |
| 1853O | 2,200,000 | 12.00 | 14.00 | 16.00 | 25.00 | 65.00 | 135 | 275 | 3,500 | — |
| 1854 | 5,740,000 | 10.50 | 12.00 | 14.00 | 17.00 | 45.00 | 110 | 185 | 1,850 | 16,000 |
| 1854O | 1,560,000 | 11.00 | 13.00 | 15.00 | 23.00 | 60.00 | 145 | 250 | 4,250 | — |
| 1855 | 1,750,000 | 11.00 | 13.00 | 15.00 | 18.00 | 47.00 | 115 | 190 | 1,950 | 18,000 |
| 1855O | 600,000 | 15.00 | 20.00 | 28.00 | 55.00 | 125 | 210 | 600 | 4,000 | — |

# Seated Liberty. Arrows at date removed.

**Designer:** Christian Gobrecht. **Weight:** 1.2400 g. **Composition:** 0.9000 Silver, 0.0362 oz. ASW. **Notes:** On the 1858/inverted date variety, the date was engraved into the die upside down and then re-engraved right side up. Another 1858 variety has the date doubled.

| Date | Mintage | G-4 | VG-8 | F-12 | VF-20 | XF-40 | AU-50 | MS-60 | MS-65 | Prf-65 |
|------|---------|-----|------|------|-------|-------|-------|-------|-------|--------|
| 1856 | 4,880,000 | 10.50 | 12.00 | 14.00 | 18.00 | 45.00 | 95.00 | 140 | 1,650 | 15,000 |
| 1856O | 1,100,000 | 11.00 | 13.00 | 15.00 | 38.00 | 80.00 | 250 | 550 | 2,000 | — |
| 1857 | 7,280,000 | 10.00 | 12.00 | 14.00 | 18.00 | 45.00 | 95.00 | 150 | 1,550 | 5,500 |
| 1857O | 1,380,000 | 11.00 | 13.00 | 18.00 | 33.00 | 55.00 | 180 | 325 | 1,800 | — |
| 1858 | 3,500,000 | 10.50 | 12.00 | 14.00 | 18.00 | 55.00 | 175 | 300 | 1,700 | 5,500 |
| 1858 inverted date | Inc. above | 25.00 | 40.00 | 60.00 | 90.00 | 175 | 275 | 650 | 2,600 | — |
| 1858 doubled date | Inc. above | 45.00 | 60.00 | 90.00 | 175 | 285 | 425 | 700 | — | — |
| 1858O | 1,660,000 | 11.00 | 13.00 | 16.00 | 36.00 | 65.00 | 135 | 265 | 1,600 | — |
| 1859 | 340,000 | 11.00 | 13.00 | 20.00 | 34.00 | 70.00 | 135 | 225 | 1,550 | 4,000 |
| 1859O | 560,000 | 12.00 | 14.00 | 23.00 | 38.00 | 110 | 200 | 240 | 1,700 | — |

# Seated Liberty. "United States of America" replaced stars.

**Designer:** Christian Gobrecht. **Weight:** 1.2400 g. **Composition:** 0.9000 Silver, 0.0362 oz. ASW. **Notes:** In 1860 the legend "United States of America" replaced the stars on the obverse.

| Date | Mintage | G-4 | VG-8 | F-12 | VF-20 | XF-40 | AU-50 | MS-60 | MS-65 | Prf-65 |
|------|---------|-----|------|------|-------|-------|-------|-------|-------|--------|
| 1860 | 799,000 | 11.00 | 13.00 | 15.00 | 17.00 | 30.00 | 65.00 | 125 | 1,150 | '1,850 |
| 1860O | 1,060,000 | 12.00 | 14.00 | 16.00 | 18.00 | 36.00 | 75.00 | 175 | 1,450 | — |
| 1861 | 3,361,000 | 11.00 | 13.00 | 15.00 | 17.00 | 30.00 | 65.00 | 125 | 1,175 | 2,500 |
| 1861/0 | Inc. above | 20.00 | 30.00 | 55.00 | 125 | 260 | 360 | 500 | 4,000 | — |
| 1862 | 1,492,550 | 12.00 | 14.00 | 16.00 | 20.00 | 33.00 | 68.00 | 135 | 1,150 | 1,650 |
| 1863 | 18,460 | 150 | 175 | 220 | 270 | 400 | 500 | 650 | 1,650 | 1,700 |
| 1863S | 100,000 | 20.00 | 28.00 | 35.00 | 40.00 | 110 | 260 | 700 | 2,500 | — |
| 1864 | 48,470 | 275 | 350 | 425 | 600 | 750 | 900 | 1,050 | 2,250 | 1,750 |
| 1864S | 90,000 | 38.00 | 45.00 | 85.00 | 115 | 225 | 425 | 650 | 3,750 | — |
| 1865 | 13,500 | 275 | 300 | 375 | 450 | 550 | 625 | 750 | 1,950 | 1,750 |
| 1865S | 120,000 | 22.00 | 28.00 | 37.00 | 55.00 | 135 | 375 | 800 | — | — |
| 1866 | 10,725 | 275 | 300 | 375 | 450 | 525 | 600 | 750 | 2,550 | 1,700 |
| 1866S | 120,000 | 20.00 | 30.00 | 34.00 | 55.00 | 125 | 285 | 450 | 5,000 | — |
| 1867 | 8,625 | 375 | 425 | 500 | 575 | 675 | 800 | 975 | 2,250 | 1,750 |
| 1867S | 120,000 | 20.00 | 27.00 | 32.00 | 60.00 | 120 | 265 | 550 | 3,850 | — |
| 1868 | 89,200 | 45.00 | 60.00 | 95.00 | 150 | 250 | 375 | 570 | 2,400 | 1,750 |
| 1868S | 280,000 | 13.00 | 15.00 | 20.00 | 25.00 | 40.00 | 110 | 300 | 3,250 | — |
| 1869 | 208,600 | 13.00 | 15.00 | 22.00 | 30.00 | 45.00 | 125 | 235 | 1,500 | 1,750 |
| 1869S | 230,000 | 13.00 | 15.00 | 20.00 | 25.00 | 40.00 | 115 | 325 | 4,000 | — |
| 1870 | 536,600 | 9.50 | 10.00 | 12.50 | 17.00 | 35.00 | 125 | 175 | 1,200 | 1,650 |
| 1870S unique | — | — | — | — | — | — | — | — | — | — |
| **Note:** 1870S, Superior Galleries, July 1986, brilliant uncirculated, $253,000. | | | | | | | | | | |
| 1871 | 1,873,960 | 11.00 | 13.00 | 15.00 | 17.00 | 32.00 | 65.00 | 120 | 1,250 | 1,650 |
| 1871S | 161,000 | 14.00 | 22.00 | 30.00 | 45.00 | 65.00 | 165 | 250 | 2,450 | — |
| 1872 | 2,947,950 | 11.00 | 13.00 | 15.00 | 18.00 | 32.00 | 65.00 | 120 | 1,200 | 1,650 |
| 1872S mint mark in wreath | 837,000 | 11.00 | 13.00 | 15.00 | 18.00 | 32.00 | 65.00 | 120 | 1,200 | — |

| Date | Mintage | G-4 | VG-8 | F-12 | VF-20 | XF-40 | AU-50 | MS-60 | MS-65 | Prf-65 |
|---|---|---|---|---|---|---|---|---|---|---|
| 1872S mint mark below wreath | Inc. above | 11.00 | 13.00 | 15.00 | 18.00 | 32.00 | 65.00 | 120 | 1,200 | — |
| 1873 | 712,600 | 11.00 | 13.00 | 15.00 | 20.00 | 35.00 | 70.00 | 125 | 1,300 | 1,750 |
| 1873S | 324,000 | 12.00 | 14.00 | 16.00 | 20.00 | 40.00 | 75.00 | 140 | 1,350 | — |

# 5 CENTS

## Shield. Rays between stars.

**Designer:** James B. Longacre. **Diameter:** 20.5 mm. **Weight:** 5.0000 g. **Composition:** Copper-nickel.

| Date | Mintage | G-4 | VG-8 | F-12 | VF-20 | XF-40 | AU-50 | MS-60 | MS-65 | Prf-65 |
|---|---|---|---|---|---|---|---|---|---|---|
| 1866 | 14,742,500 | 16.00 | 18.00 | 22.00 | 37.50 | 100.00 | 155 | 235 | 2,250 | 3,400 |
| 1867 | 2,019,000 | 18.00 | 21.00 | 27.00 | 42.00 | 125 | 200 | 310 | 3,000 | 75,000 |

## Shield. No rays between stars.

**Weight:** 5.0000 g. **Composition:** Copper-nickel.

| Date | Mintage | G-4 | VG-8 | F-12 | VF-20 | XF-40 | AU-50 | MS-60 | MS-65 | Prf-65 |
|---|---|---|---|---|---|---|---|---|---|---|
| 1867 | 28,890,500 | 11.50 | 12.50 | 16.00 | 18.50 | 34.00 | 60.00 | 90.00 | 675 | 2,750 |
| 1868 | 28,817,000 | 11.50 | 12.50 | 16.00 | 18.50 | 34.00 | 60.00 | 90.00 | 675 | 1,400 |
| 1869 | 16,395,000 | 11.50 | 12.50 | 16.00 | 18.50 | 36.00 | 60.00 | 90.00 | 650 | 1,025 |
| 1870 | 4,806,000 | 11.75 | 13.50 | 17.50 | 21.00 | 38.00 | 62.00 | 100.00 | 850 | 1,275 |
| 1871 | 561,000 | 35.00 | 45.00 | 55.00 | 75.00 | 120 | 165 | 260 | 1,200 | 1,075 |
| 1872 | 6,036,000 | 12.00 | 13.50 | 17.00 | 23.00 | 40.00 | 62.50 | 115 | 850 | 750 |
| 1873 | 4,550,000 | 12.50 | 14.00 | 18.00 | 27.00 | 43.00 | 67.50 | 125 | 950 | 800 |
| 1874 | 3,538,000 | 13.50 | 14.50 | 29.00 | 30.00 | 56.00 | 75.00 | 125 | 870 | 850 |
| 1875 | 2,097,000 | 13.50 | 17.00 | 32.00 | 43.00 | 65.00 | 90.00 | 150 | 1,750 | 1,750 |
| 1876 | 2,530,000 | 13.50 | 14.50 | 29.00 | 36.00 | 62.00 | 80.00 | 125 | 825 | 950 |
| 1877 proof only | Est. 900 | — | — | — | 1,100 | 1,150 | 1,200 | — | — | 2,300 |
| 1878 proof only | 2,350 | — | — | 500 | 525 | 550 | 565 | — | — | 800 |
| 1879 | 29,100 | 250 | 285 | 345 | 400 | 440 | 475 | 600 | 1,500 | 790 |
| 1880 | 19,995 | 350 | 380 | 425 | 460 | 575 | 710 | 875 | 5,100 | 650 |
| 1881 | 72,375 | 165 | 190 | 240 | 290 | 390 | 450 | 600 | 1,200 | 630 |
| 1882 | 11,476,600 | 11.50 | 12.50 | 16.00 | 20.00 | 36.00 | 65.00 | 90.00 | 675 | 600 |
| 1883 | 1,456,919 | 13.00 | 14.00 | 17.00 | 21.00 | 36.00 | 60.00 | 90.00 | 675 | 570 |
| 1883/2 | — | 65.00 | 90.00 | 130 | 175 | 245 | 300 | 415 | 3,000 | — |

## Liberty. Without "Cents" below "V".

**Designer:** Charles E. Barber. **Diameter:** 21.2 mm. **Weight:** 5.0000 g. **Composition:** Copper-nickel.

| Date | Mintage | G-4 | VG-8 | F-12 | VF-20 | XF-40 | AU-50 | MS-60 | MS-65 | Prf-65 |
|---|---|---|---|---|---|---|---|---|---|---|
| 1883 | 5,479,519 | 4.25 | 4.40 | 4.80 | 6.00 | 7.50 | 12.00 | 29.00 | 225 | 1,200 |

## 1884 Nickel Five-Cent
### Grade F-12

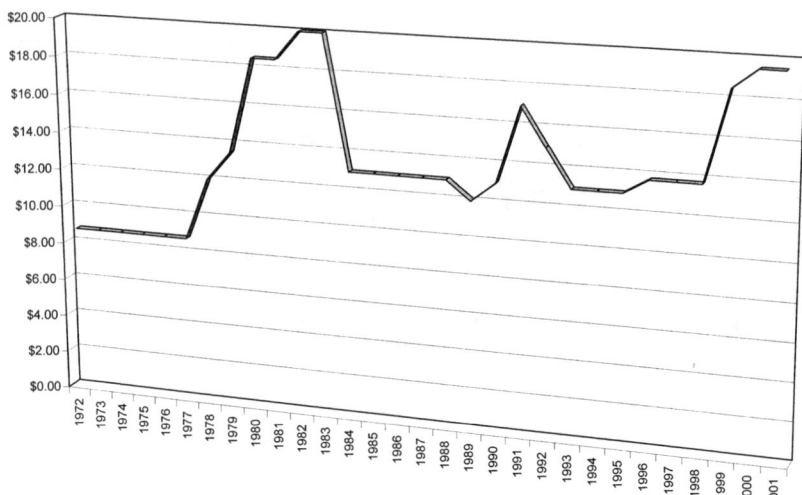

☐ Retail Price

## Liberty. "Cents" below "V".

**Weight:** 5.0000 g. **Composition:** Copper Nickel.

| Date | Mintage | G-4 | VG-8 | F-12 | VF-20 | XF-40 | AU-50 | MS-60 | MS-65 | Prf-65 |
|------|---------|-----|------|------|-------|-------|-------|-------|-------|--------|
| 1883 | 16,032,983 | 7.00 | 11.00 | 16.00 | 25.00 | 45.00 | 65.00 | 90.00 | 500 | 500 |
| 1884 | 11,273,942 | 12.00 | 16.00 | 21.50 | 28.00 | 49.00 | 80.00 | 135 | 950 | 550 |
| 1885 | 1,476,490 | 275 | 300 | 375 | 460 | 600 | 720 | 875 | 2,450 | 950 |
| 1886 | 3,330,290 | 95.00 | 125 | 170 | 235 | 320 | 425 | 535 | 2,550 | 525 |
| 1887 | 15,263,652 | 7.50 | 11.00 | 22.00 | 26.00 | 50.00 | 70.00 | 100.00 | 650 | 520 |
| 1888 | 10,720,483 | 14.50 | 17.50 | 25.00 | 50.00 | 65.00 | 115 | 180 | 925 | 520 |
| 1889 | 15,881,361 | 5.50 | 8.50 | 17.00 | 22.00 | 40.00 | 70.00 | 94.00 | 560 | 520 |
| 1890 | 16,259,272 | 5.50 | 12.00 | 17.00 | 22.00 | 40.00 | 75.00 | 130 | 980 | 600 |
| 1891 | 16,834,350 | 5.50 | 7.50 | 13.00 | 19.00 | 38.00 | 68.00 | 130 | 860 | 520 |
| 1892 | 11,699,642 | 5.00 | 8.00 | 15.00 | 20.00 | 40.00 | 80.00 | 120 | 950 | 520 |
| 1893 | 13,370,195 | 4.50 | 6.50 | 14.00 | 20.00 | 39.00 | 70.00 | 100.00 | 850 | 520 |
| 1894 | 5,413,132 | 8.00 | 15.00 | 55.00 | 85.00 | 150 | 195 | 225 | 800 | 500 |
| 1895 | 9,979,884 | 3.50 | 5.00 | 17.50 | 27.50 | 46.00 | 80.00 | 120 | 1,175 | 600 |
| 1896 | 8,842,920 | 5.50 | 11.00 | 22.00 | 30.00 | 50.00 | 80.00 | 125 | 1,250 | 600 |
| 1897 | 20,428,735 | 2.75 | 4.00 | 9.00 | 13.50 | 29.00 | 55.00 | 90.00 | 800 | 600 |
| 1898 | 12,532,087 | 2.35 | 4.50 | 8.50 | 13.00 | 34.00 | 65.00 | 125 | 860 | 500 |
| 1899 | 26,029,031 | 1.50 | 3.50 | 6.00 | 11.50 | 30.00 | 52.50 | 85.00 | 525 | 500 |
| 1900 | 27,255,995 | 1.60 | 3.00 | 5.75 | 11.00 | 30.00 | 57.00 | 75.00 | 535 | 500 |
| 1901 | 26,480,213 | 1.25 | 3.25 | 6.50 | 11.50 | 27.50 | 48.00 | 60.00 | 500 | 500 |
| 1902 | 31,480,579 | 1.25 | 3.25 | 5.00 | 9.00 | 27.50 | 48.00 | 65.00 | 490 | 500 |
| 1903 | 28,006,725 | 1.25 | 3.25 | 5.00 | 11.50 | 27.50 | 48.00 | 60.00 | 490 | 500 |
| 1904 | 21,404,984 | 1.25 | 3.00 | 5.25 | 11.50 | 28.50 | 48.00 | 60.00 | 490 | 675 |
| 1905 | 29,827,276 | 1.25 | 1.90 | 4.25 | 9.50 | 27.50 | 48.00 | 60.00 | 495 | 520 |
| 1906 | 38,613,725 | 1.25 | 1.90 | 4.00 | 9.00 | 27.50 | 48.00 | 60.00 | 500 | 500 |
| 1907 | 39,214,800 | 1.25 | 1.90 | 4.00 | 8.75 | 27.50 | 48.00 | 60.00 | 700 | 590 |
| 1908 | 22,686,177 | 1.25 | 1.90 | 4.00 | 8.75 | 27.50 | 48.00 | 60.00 | 700 | 500 |
| 1909 | 11,590,526 | 2.50 | 3.00 | 5.00 | 9.00 | 30.00 | 49.00 | 75.00 | 640 | 500 |
| 1910 | 30,169,353 | 1.25 | 1.90 | 4.00 | 8.75 | 25.00 | 45.00 | 60.00 | 590 | 490 |
| 1911 | 39,559,372 | 1.25 | 1.90 | 4.00 | 8.75 | 25.00 | 45.00 | 60.00 | 500 | 490 |
| 1912 | 26,236,714 | 1.25 | 1.90 | 4.00 | 8.75 | 25.00 | 45.00 | 60.00 | 500 | 535 |
| 1912D | 8,474,000 | 1.75 | 2.50 | 6.00 | 22.50 | 55.00 | 135 | 235 | 870 | — |
| 1912S | 238,000 | 48.00 | 63.00 | 95.00 | 250 | 480 | 700 | 850 | 2,500 | — |

| Date | Mintage | G-4 | VG-8 | F-12 | VF-20 | XF-40 | AU-50 | MS-60 | MS-65 | Prf-65 |
|------|---------|-----|------|------|-------|-------|-------|-------|-------|--------|
| 1913 only 5 known | — | — | — | — | — | — | — | — | — | — |

**Note:** 1913, Superior Sale, March 2001, Proof, $1,840,000.

## Indian head. Buffalo standing on a mound.

**Designer:** James Earle Fraser. **Diameter:** 21.2 mm. **Weight:** 5.0000 g. **Composition:** Copper-nickel.

| Date | Mintage | G-4 | VG-8 | F-12 | VF-20 | XF-40 | AU-50 | MS-60 | MS-65 | Prf-65 |
|------|---------|-----|------|------|-------|-------|-------|-------|-------|--------|
| 1913 | 30,993,520 | 5.75 | 6.25 | 6.75 | 9.00 | 14.00 | 21.00 | 32.00 | 110 | 2,350 |
| 1913D | 5,337,000 | 11.00 | 13.00 | 14.50 | 19.00 | 26.00 | 41.50 | 52.00 | 250 | — |
| 1913S | 2,105,000 | 18.00 | 22.00 | 27.50 | 37.00 | 50.00 | 62.00 | 72.00 | 600 | — |

## Indian head. Buffalo standing on a line.

  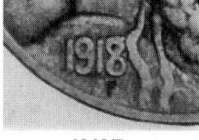 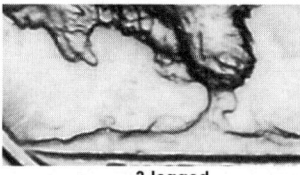

1918/7

3 legged

**Designer:** James Earle Fraser. **Diameter:** 21.2 mm. **Weight:** 5.0000 g. **Composition:** Copper Nickel.
**Notes:** In 1913 the reverse design was modified so the ground under the buffalo was represented as a line rather than a mound. On the 1937D 3-legged variety, the buffalo's right front leg is missing, the result of a damaged die.

| Date | Mintage | G-4 | VG-8 | F-12 | VF-20 | XF-40 | AU-50 | MS-60 | MS-65 | Prf-65 |
|------|---------|-----|------|------|-------|-------|-------|-------|-------|--------|
| 1913 | 29,858,700 | 7.50 | 8.50 | 9.50 | 11.00 | 16.00 | 23.00 | 32.50 | 355 | 1,675 |
| 1913D | 4,156,000 | 49.50 | 57.50 | 75.00 | 85.00 | 95.00 | 120 | 162 | 975 | — |
| 1913S | 1,209,000 | 125 | 165 | 185 | 225 | 245 | 290 | 365 | 2,700 | — |
| 1914 | 20,665,738 | 13.50 | 14.25 | 15.00 | 19.50 | 25.00 | 35.00 | 47.00 | 410 | 1,475 |
| 1914D | 3,912,000 | 47.00 | 60.00 | 75.00 | 85.00 | 135 | 170 | 225 | 1,400 | — |
| 1914S | 3,470,000 | 13.50 | 14.50 | 23.00 | 30.00 | 47.00 | 75.00 | 135 | 1,650 | — |
| 1915 | 20,987,270 | 5.00 | 5.50 | 7.00 | 10.50 | 17.50 | 37.00 | 47.00 | 285 | 1,400 |

### 1921-S Nickel
#### Grade F-12

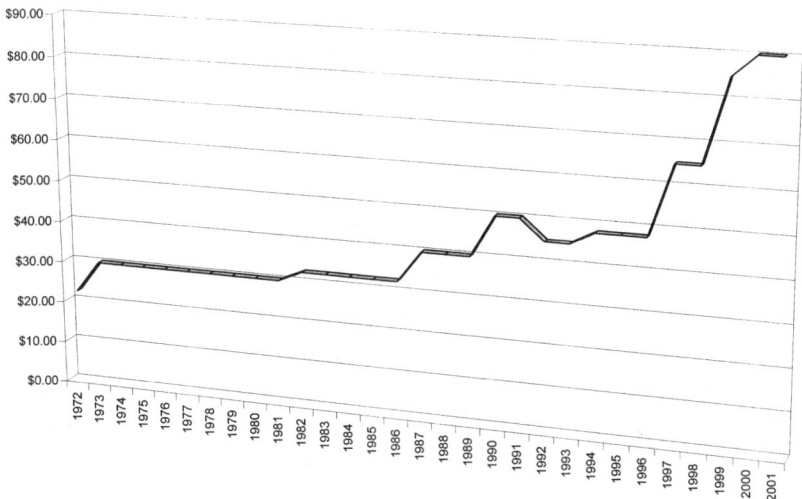

Retail Price

| Date | Mintage | G-4 | VG-8 | F-12 | VF-20 | XF-40 | AU-50 | MS-60 | MS-65 | Prf-65 |
|------|---------|-----|------|------|-------|-------|-------|-------|-------|--------|
| 1915D | 7,569,500 | 14.50 | 16.50 | 29.00 | 40.00 | 75.00 | 100.00 | 190 | 1,750 | — |
| 1915S | 1,505,000 | 22.00 | 33.00 | 65.00 | 90.00 | 160 | 310 | 460 | 2,100 | — |
| 1916 | 63,498,066 | 3.50 | 3.75 | 4.00 | 6.00 | 11.00 | 20.00 | 40.00 | 275 | 2,350 |
| 1916/16 | Inc. above | 1,700 | 3,400 | 6,000 | 8,000 | 11,500 | 21,500 | 33,000 | 240,000 | — |
| 1916D | 13,333,000 | 9.00 | 13.50 | 17.50 | 28.50 | 65.00 | 90.00 | 140 | 1,700 | — |
| 1916S | 11,860,000 | 5.00 | 8.00 | 13.50 | 24.50 | 55.00 | 90.00 | 160 | 1,750 | — |
| 1917 | 51,424,029 | 3.00 | 3.25 | 5.00 | 9.00 | 17.50 | 35.00 | 55.00 | 490 | — |
| 1917D | 9,910,800 | 9.00 | 15.00 | 30.00 | 65.00 | 115 | 170 | 280 | 3,250 | — |
| 1917S | 4,193,000 | 11.00 | 17.00 | 37.50 | 70.00 | 135 | 250 | 330 | 3,100 | — |
| 1918 | 32,086,314 | 2.75 | 3.90 | 6.00 | 12.50 | 30.00 | 45.00 | 85.00 | 1,250 | — |
| 1918/17D | 8,362,314 | 400 | 750 | 1,050 | 2,250 | 5,200 | 8,500 | 13,500 | 250,000 | — |
| 1918D | Inc. above | 8.50 | 16.50 | 33.00 | 85.00 | 175 | 275 | 340 | 3,800 | — |
| 1918S | 4,882,000 | 9.00 | 17.50 | 35.00 | 79.00 | 160 | 250 | 390 | 25,000 | — |
| 1919 | 60,868,000 | 1.25 | 1.50 | 2.50 | 6.50 | 15.00 | 35.00 | 50.00 | 485 | — |
| 1919D | 8,006,000 | 10.00 | 16.50 | 38.00 | 89.00 | 195 | 300 | 475 | 5,200 | — |
| 1919S | 7,521,000 | 5.50 | 15.00 | 32.00 | 80.00 | 195 | 310 | 440 | 10,000 | — |
| 1920 | 63,093,000 | 1.00 | 1.50 | 2.50 | 7.00 | 15.00 | 35.00 | 52.00 | 650 | — |
| 1920D | 9,418,000 | 6.50 | 14.00 | 35.00 | 85.00 | 250 | 325 | 450 | 5,000 | — |
| 1920S | 9,689,000 | 3.50 | 6.50 | 18.50 | 80.00 | 175 | 275 | 375 | 15,750 | — |
| 1921 | 10,663,000 | 2.15 | 3.50 | 5.00 | 17.50 | 45.00 | 60.00 | 110 | 700 | — |
| 1921S | 1,557,000 | 34.00 | 55.00 | 90.00 | 400 | 725 | 1,100 | 1,500 | 5,800 | — |
| 1923 | 35,715,000 | 1.50 | 1.75 | 3.00 | 7.50 | 15.00 | 32.50 | 48.00 | 500 | — |
| 1923S | 6,142,000 | 3.50 | 6.00 | 16.50 | 100.00 | 260 | 325 | 385 | 7,500 | — |
| 1924 | 21,620,000 | 1.25 | 1.90 | 3.00 | 8.00 | 20.00 | 35.00 | 62.00 | 660 | — |
| 1924D | 5,258,000 | 3.50 | 6.00 | 17.50 | 65.00 | 185 | 250 | 335 | 3,350 | — |
| 1924S | 1,437,000 | 8.00 | 17.00 | 70.00 | 400 | 1,100 | 1,500 | 2,000 | 8,500 | — |
| 1925 | 35,565,100 | 2.50 | 2.75 | 3.50 | 8.00 | 15.00 | 36.00 | 42.00 | 525 | — |
| 1925D | 4,450,000 | 7.50 | 16.50 | 40.00 | 80.00 | 165 | 245 | 340 | 3,600 | — |
| 1925S | 6,256,000 | 3.50 | 9.00 | 17.50 | 69.00 | 175 | 260 | 375 | 32,000 | — |
| 1926 | 44,693,000 | 1.00 | 1.15 | 1.50 | 6.00 | 14.50 | 25.00 | 35.00 | 175 | — |
| 1926D | 5,638,000 | 4.50 | 10.00 | 29.00 | 85.00 | 160 | 260 | 275 | 3,650 | — |
| 1926S | 970,000 | 10.00 | 19.00 | 50.00 | 335 | 725 | 1,500 | 2,975 | 38,500 | — |
| 1927 | 37,981,000 | 1.00 | 1.15 | 1.50 | 6.00 | 14.50 | 25.00 | 34.00 | 250 | — |
| 1927D | 5,730,000 | 2.50 | 6.00 | 8.00 | 30.00 | 85.00 | 125 | 160 | 4,800 | — |
| 1927S | 3,430,000 | 2.00 | 3.00 | 5.00 | 29.50 | 85.00 | 165 | 450 | 14,500 | — |
| 1928 | 23,411,000 | 1.10 | 1.25 | 1.60 | 7.00 | 15.00 | 30.00 | 35.00 | 300 | — |
| 1928D | 6,436,000 | 1.50 | 2.50 | 6.00 | 17.50 | 39.00 | 55.00 | 59.00 | 675 | — |
| 1928S | 6,936,000 | 1.50 | 1.75 | 2.75 | 12.50 | 30.00 | 125 | 210 | 3,850 | — |
| 1929 | 36,446,000 | 0.90 | 1.05 | 1.50 | 7.00 | 13.00 | 25.00 | 35.00 | 290 | — |
| 1929D | 8,370,000 | 1.10 | 1.45 | 2.00 | 8.00 | 35.00 | 45.00 | 55.00 | 1,550 | — |
| 1929S | 7,754,000 | 1.00 | 1.15 | 1.45 | 4.00 | 14.00 | 30.00 | 45.00 | 375 | — |
| 1930 | 22,849,000 | 0.95 | 1.00 | 1.50 | 4.00 | 9.00 | 20.00 | 29.00 | 135 | — |
| 1930S | 5,435,000 | 1.00 | 1.10 | 2.00 | 5.00 | 12.50 | 30.00 | 43.00 | 460 | — |
| 1931S | 1,200,000 | 5.50 | 5.75 | 6.25 | 7.50 | 19.50 | 38.00 | 45.00 | 235 | — |
| 1934 | 20,213,003 | 0.85 | 0.95 | 1.40 | 4.00 | 10.00 | 19.00 | 28.00 | 335 | — |
| 1934D | 7,480,000 | 1.00 | 1.15 | 2.00 | 8.00 | 18.50 | 42.00 | 52.00 | 875 | — |
| 1935 | 58,264,000 | 0.85 | 0.95 | 1.15 | 2.75 | 4.50 | 9.50 | 18.00 | 100.00 | — |
| 1935D | 12,092,000 | 0.90 | 1.00 | 2.00 | 6.00 | 17.00 | 38.00 | 46.00 | 390 | — |
| 1935S | 10,300,000 | 0.90 | 1.00 | 1.15 | 2.90 | 5.50 | 15.00 | 35.00 | 150 | — |
| 1936 | 119,001,420 | 0.85 | 0.95 | 1.10 | 1.75 | 3.50 | 8.50 | 14.00 | 90.00 | 1,100 |
| 1936D | 24,814,000 | 0.85 | 0.95 | 1.15 | 2.00 | 5.50 | 12.50 | 25.00 | 115 | — |
| 1936S | 14,930,000 | 0.85 | 0.95 | 1.15 | 2.00 | 3.50 | 12.00 | 24.00 | 100.00 | — |
| 1937 | 79,485,769 | 0.85 | 0.95 | 1.15 | 1.75 | 3.50 | 8.50 | 24.00 | 53.00 | 850 |
| 1937D | 17,826,000 | 0.85 | 0.95 | 1.15 | 1.75 | 3.75 | 9.50 | 15.00 | 57.00 | — |
| 1937D 3-legged | Inc. above | 200 | 260 | 280 | 375 | 435 | 650 | 1,200 | 16,500 | — |
| 1937S | 5,635,000 | 0.95 | 1.05 | 1.20 | 1.90 | 3.90 | 9.00 | 18.50 | 55.00 | — |
| 1938D | 7,020,000 | 1.60 | 1.75 | 2.00 | 3.25 | 4.50 | 9.00 | 13.00 | 38.00 | — |
| 1938D/D | — | 2.25 | 4.25 | 5.75 | 10.00 | 14.00 | 17.00 | 19.00 | 60.00 | — |
| 1938D/S | Inc. above | 6.00 | 8.00 | 11.00 | 15.00 | 19.00 | 32.00 | 45.00 | 190 | — |

# Jefferson.

**Designer:** Felix Schlag. **Diameter:** 21.2 mm. **Weight:** 5.0000 g. **Composition:** Copper-nickel. **Notes:** Some 1939 strikes have doubling of the word "Monticello" on the reverse.

| Date | Mintage | G-4 | VG-8 | F-12 | VF-20 | XF-40 | MS-60 | MS-65 | Prf-65 |
|------|---------|-----|------|------|-------|-------|-------|-------|--------|
| 1938 | 19,515,365 | 0.15 | 0.25 | 0.40 | 0.80 | 1.25 | 4.00 | 8.00 | 70.00 |
| 1938D | 5,376,000 | 0.60 | 0.90 | 1.00 | 1.25 | 1.75 | 4.25 | 8.00 | — |
| 1938S | 4,105,000 | 1.25 | 1.35 | 1.50 | 1.75 | 2.25 | 4.00 | 8.50 | — |
| 1939 | 120,627,535 | — | — | 0.20 | 0.25 | 0.30 | 1.75 | 3.50 | 70.00 |
| 1939 doubled Monticello | — | — | 20.00 | 30.00 | 45.00 | 75.00 | 200 | 550 | — |

| Date | Mintage | G-4 | VG-8 | F-12 | VF-20 | XF-40 | MS-60 | MS-65 | Prf-65 |
|------|---------|-----|------|------|-------|-------|-------|-------|--------|
| 1939D | 3,514,000 | 2.50 | 3.00 | 3.50 | 5.00 | 10.00 | 38.00 | 60.00 | — |
| 1939S | 6,630,000 | 0.40 | 0.45 | 0.60 | 1.50 | 2.75 | 13.00 | 30.00 | — |
| 1940 | 176,499,158 | — | — | — | — | 0.25 | 1.00 | 1.25 | 65.00 |
| 1940D | 43,540,000 | — | — | 0.20 | 0.30 | 0.40 | 2.50 | 2.75 | — |
| 1940S | 39,690,000 | — | — | 0.20 | 0.25 | 0.50 | 2.75 | 5.00 | — |
| 1941 | 203,283,720 | — | — | — | — | 0.20 | 1.00 | 2.00 | 60.00 |
| 1941D | 53,432,000 | — | — | 0.20 | 0.30 | 0.50 | 2.50 | 5.00 | — |
| 1941S | 43,445,000 | — | — | 0.20 | 0.30 | 0.50 | 3.75 | 6.75 | — |
| 1942 | 49,818,600 | — | — | — | — | 0.40 | 5.00 | 8.50 | 55.00 |
| 1942D | 13,938,000 | 0.20 | 0.30 | 0.40 | 0.60 | 2.00 | 27.00 | 39.00 | — |

## Jefferson. Mint mark above Monticello.

**Designer:** Felix Schlag. **Diameter:** 21.2 mm. **Composition:** 0.3500 Copper-silver-manganese, 0.0563 oz. ASW. **Notes:** War-time composition nickels have a large mint mark above Monticello on the reverse.

| Date | Mintage | G-4 | VG-8 | F-12 | VF-20 | XF-40 | MS-60 | MS-65 | Prf-65 |
|------|---------|-----|------|------|-------|-------|-------|-------|--------|
| 1942P | 57,900,600 | 0.40 | 0.65 | 0.85 | 1.00 | 1.75 | 6.00 | 22.50 | 140 |
| 1942S | 32,900,000 | 0.45 | 0.70 | 1.00 | 1.10 | 1.75 | 6.00 | 20.00 | — |
| 1943P | 271,165,000 | 0.35 | 0.50 | 0.85 | 1.00 | 1.50 | 2.75 | 15.00 | — |
| 1943/2P | Inc. above | 10.00 | 15.00 | 20.00 | 30.00 | 40.00 | 125 | 450 | — |
| 1943D | 15,294,000 | 0.75 | 0.90 | 1.20 | 1.50 | 1.75 | 3.00 | 13.00 | — |
| 1943S | 104,060,000 | 0.35 | 0.55 | 0.70 | 1.00 | 1.50 | 3.00 | 13.00 | — |
| 1944P | 119,150,000 | 0.35 | 0.50 | 0.70 | 1.00 | 1.50 | 3.00 | 17.00 | — |
| 1944D | 32,309,000 | 0.40 | 0.60 | 0.80 | 1.00 | 1.75 | 6.00 | 13.00 | — |
| 1944S | 21,640,000 | 0.50 | 0.70 | 1.00 | 1.25 | 2.00 | 3.50 | 13.00 | — |
| 1945P | 119,408,100 | 0.30 | 0.50 | 0.70 | 1.00 | 1.50 | 3.50 | 12.00 | — |
| 1945D | 37,158,000 | 0.40 | 0.55 | 0.75 | 1.00 | 1.50 | 3.50 | 7.00 | — |
| 1945S | 58,939,000 | 0.35 | 0.50 | 0.70 | 0.80 | 0.90 | 2.00 | 6.50 | — |

## Jefferson. Pre-war design resumed.

**Designer:** Felix Schlag. **Diameter:** 21.2 mm. **Weight:** 5.0000 g. **Composition:** Copper-nickel. **Notes:** The 1979-S and 1981-S Type II proofs have clearer mint marks than the Type I proofs of those years.

| Date | Mintage | G-4 | VG-8 | F-12 | VF-20 | XF-40 | MS-60 | MS-65 | Prf-65 |
|------|---------|-----|------|------|-------|-------|-------|-------|--------|
| 1946 | 161,116,000 | — | — | — | 0.20 | 0.25 | 0.50 | 1.00 | — |
| 1946D | 45,292,200 | — | — | — | 0.25 | 0.35 | 0.85 | 1.50 | — |
| 1946S | 13,560,000 | — | — | — | 0.30 | 0.40 | 0.50 | 1.00 | — |
| 1947 | 95,000,000 | — | — | — | 0.20 | 0.25 | 0.75 | 2.00 | — |
| 1947D | 37,822,000 | — | — | — | 0.20 | 0.30 | 0.90 | 2.00 | — |
| 1947S | 24,720,000 | — | — | — | 0.20 | 0.25 | 0.80 | 2.25 | — |
| 1948 | 89,348,000 | — | — | — | 0.20 | 0.25 | 0.50 | 1.50 | — |
| 1948D | 44,734,000 | — | — | — | 0.25 | 0.35 | 1.20 | 2.75 | — |
| 1948S | 11,300,000 | — | — | — | 0.25 | 0.50 | 1.00 | 2.25 | — |
| 1949 | 60,652,000 | — | — | — | 0.25 | 0.30 | 1.25 | 3.50 | — |
| 1949D | 36,498,000 | — | — | — | 0.30 | 0.40 | 1.00 | 2.50 | — |
| 1949D/S | Inc. above | — | — | 35.00 | 40.00 | 65.00 | 170 | 325 | — |
| 1949S | 9,716,000 | — | 0.25 | 0.35 | 0.45 | 0.90 | 1.50 | 3.50 | — |
| 1950 | 9,847,386 | — | 0.20 | 0.30 | 0.35 | 0.75 | 1.50 | 3.50 | 45.00 |
| 1950D | 2,630,030 | — | 5.00 | 5.15 | 5.25 | 5.50 | 6.50 | 9.00 | — |
| 1951 | 28,609,500 | — | — | — | 0.40 | 0.50 | 1.25 | 2.75 | 30.00 |
| 1951D | 20,460,000 | — | 0.25 | 0.30 | 0.40 | 0.50 | 1.45 | 3.00 | — |
| 1951S | 7,776,000 | — | 0.30 | 0.40 | 0.50 | 1.10 | 1.75 | 4.00 | — |
| 1952 | 64,069,980 | — | — | — | 0.20 | 0.25 | 0.85 | 3.00 | 26.00 |
| 1952D | 30,638,000 | — | — | — | 0.30 | 0.45 | 1.50 | 3.50 | — |
| 1952S | 20,572,000 | — | — | — | 0.20 | 0.25 | 0.75 | 3.50 | — |
| 1953 | 46,772,800 | — | — | — | 0.20 | 0.25 | 0.40 | 1.50 | 28.00 |
| 1953D | 59,878,600 | — | — | — | 0.20 | 0.25 | 0.40 | 1.50 | — |
| 1953S | 19,210,900 | — | — | — | 0.20 | 0.25 | 0.50 | 2.50 | — |
| 1954 | 47,917,350 | — | — | — | — | — | 0.35 | 1.50 | 16.00 |
| 1954D | 117,136,560 | — | — | — | — | — | 0.35 | 1.00 | — |
| 1954S | 29,384,000 | — | — | — | — | 0.20 | 0.35 | 2.50 | — |

| Date | Mintage | G-4 | VG-8 | F-12 | VF-20 | XF-40 | MS-60 | MS-65 | Prf-65 |
|---|---|---|---|---|---|---|---|---|---|
| 1954S/D | Inc. above | — | — | 5.00 | 8.00 | 12.00 | 22.00 | 65.00 | — |
| 1955 | 8,266,200 | — | 0.25 | 0.35 | 0.40 | 0.45 | 0.75 | 2.00 | 16.00 |
| 1955D | 74,464,100 | — | — | — | — | — | 0.30 | 1.00 | — |
| 1955D/S | Inc. above | — | — | 5.00 | 8.50 | 13.00 | 33.00 | 75.00 | — |
| 1956 | 35,885,384 | — | — | — | — | — | 0.30 | 0.70 | 2.50 |
| 1956D | 67,222,940 | — | — | — | — | — | 0.25 | 0.60 | — |
| 1957 | 39,655,952 | — | — | — | — | — | 0.25 | 0.60 | 1.50 |
| 1957D | 136,828,900 | — | — | — | — | — | 0.25 | 0.60 | — |
| 1958 | 17,963,652 | — | — | — | 0.15 | 0.20 | 0.30 | 0.65 | 6.00 |
| 1958D | 168,249,120 | — | — | — | — | — | 0.25 | 0.60 | — |

| Date | Mintage | MS-65 | Prf-65 | Date | Mintage | MS-65 | Prf-65 |
|---|---|---|---|---|---|---|---|
| 1959 | 28,397,291 | 0.65 | 1.25 | 1982P | 292,355,000 | 3.50 | — |
| 1959D | 160,738,240 | 0.55 | — | 1982D | 373,726,544 | 3.50 | — |
| 1960 | 57,107,602 | 0.55 | 1.00 | 1982S | — | — | 3.25 |
| 1960D | 192,582,180 | 0.55 | — | 1983P | 561,615,000 | 3.00 | — |
| 1961 | 76,668,244 | 0.55 | 1.00 | 1983D | 536,726,276 | 2.00 | — |
| 1961D | 229,342,760 | 0.55 | — | 1983S | (3,279,126) | — | 4.00 |
| 1962 | 100,602,019 | 0.55 | 1.00 | 1984P | 746,769,000 | 3.00 | — |
| 1962D | 280,195,720 | 0.55 | — | 1984D | 517,675,146 | 0.85 | — |
| 1963 | 178,851,645 | 0.55 | 1.00 | 1984S | (3,065,110) | — | 5.00 |
| 1963D | 276,829,460 | 0.55 | — | 1985P | 647,114,962 | 0.75 | — |
| 1964 | 1,028,622,762 | 0.55 | 1.00 | 1985D | 459,747,446 | 0.75 | — |
| 1964D | 1,787,297,160 | 0.50 | — | 1985S | (3,362,821) | — | 4.00 |
| 1965 | 136,131,380 | 0.50 | — | 1986P | 536,883,483 | 1.00 | — |
| 1966 | 156,208,283 | 0.50 | — | 1986D | 361,819,140 | 2.00 | — |
| 1967 | 107,325,800 | 0.50 | — | 1986S | (3,010,497) | — | 6.50 |
| 1968 none minted | — | — | — | 1987P | 371,499,481 | 0.75 | — |
| 1968D | 91,227,880 | 0.50 | — | 1987D | 410,590,604 | 0.75 | — |
| 1968S | 103,437,510 | 0.50 | 0.75 | 1987S | (4,227,728) | — | 3.50 |
| 1969 none minted | — | — | — | 1988P | 771,360,000 | 0.75 | — |
| 1969D | 202,807,500 | 0.50 | — | 1988S | (3,262,948) | — | 4.50 |
| 1969S | 123,099,631 | 0.50 | 0.75 | 1989P | 898,812,000 | 0.75 | — |
| 1970 none minted | — | — | — | 1989D | 570,842,474 | 0.75 | — |
| 1970D | 515,485,380 | 0.50 | — | 1989S | (3,220,194) | — | 3.25 |
| 1970S | 241,464,814 | 0.50 | 0.75 | 1990P | 661,636,000 | 0.75 | — |
| 1971 | 106,884,000 | 2.00 | — | 1990D | 663,938,503 | 0.75 | — |
| 1971D | 316,144,800 | 0.50 | — | 1990S | — | — | 5.00 |
| 1971S | (3,220,733) | — | 1.60 | 1991P | 614,104,000 | 0.75 | — |
| 1972 | 202,036,000 | 0.50 | — | 1991D | 436,496,678 | 0.75 | — |
| 1972D | 351,694,600 | 0.50 | — | 1991S | (2,867,787) | — | 5.50 |
| 1972S | (3,260,996) | — | 2.00 | 1992P | 399,552,000 | 1.50 | — |
| 1973 | 384,396,000 | 0.50 | — | 1992D | 450,565,113 | 0.75 | — |
| 1973D | 261,405,000 | 0.50 | — | 1992S | (4,176,560) | — | 4.00 |
| 1973S | (2,760,339) | — | 1.75 | 1993P | 412,076,000 | 0.75 | — |
| 1974 | 601,752,000 | 0.50 | — | 1993D | 406,084,135 | 0.75 | — |
| 1974D | 277,373,000 | 0.50 | — | 1993S | (3,394,792) | — | 4.00 |
| 1974S | (2,612,568) | — | 2.50 | 1994P | 722,160,000 | 0.75 | — |
| 1975 | 181,772,000 | 0.75 | — | 1994P matte finish | 167,703 | 75.00 | — |
| 1975D | 401,875,300 | 0.50 | — | 1994D | 715,762,110 | 0.75 | — |
| 1975S | (2,845,450) | — | 2.25 | 1994S | (3,269,923) | — | 3.50 |
| 1976 | 367,124,000 | 0.75 | — | 1995P | 774,156,000 | 0.75 | — |
| 1976D | 563,964,147 | 0.60 | — | 1995D | 888,112,000 | 0.85 | — |
| 1976S | (4,149,730) | — | 2.00 | 1995S | — | — | 7.50 |
| 1977 | 585,376,000 | 0.40 | — | 1996P | 829,332,000 | 0.75 | — |
| 1977D | 297,313,460 | 0.55 | — | 1996D | 817,736,000 | 0.75 | — |
| 1977S | (3,251,152) | — | 2.00 | 1996S | — | — | 3.00 |
| 1978 | 391,308,000 | 0.40 | — | 1997P | 470,972,000 | 0.75 | — |
| 1978D | 313,092,780 | 0.40 | — | 1997P matte finish | 25,000 | 250 | — |
| 1978S | (3,127,781) | — | 1.75 | 1997D | 466,640,000 | 0.80 | — |
| 1979 | 463,188,000 | 0.40 | — | 1997S | (1,975,000) | — | 4.75 |
| 1979D | 325,867,672 | 0.40 | — | 1998P | 688,272,000 | 0.80 | — |
| 1979S type I, proof only | — | — | 1.50 | 1998D | 635,360,000 | 0.80 | — |
| 1979S type II, proof only | — | — | 1.75 | 1998S | — | — | 4.00 |
| 1980P | 593,004,000 | 0.40 | — | 1999P | — | 0.80 | — |
| 1980D | 502,323,448 | 0.40 | — | 1999D | — | 0.80 | — |
| 1980S | (3,554,806) | — | 1.60 | 1999S | — | — | 3.00 |
| 1981P | 657,504,000 | 0.40 | — | 2000P | — | 0.80 | — |
| 1981D | 364,801,843 | 0.40 | — | 2000D | — | 0.80 | — |
| 1981S type I, proof only | — | — | 2.00 | 2000S | — | — | 2.00 |
| 1981S type II, proof only | — | — | 2.00 | | | | |

# DIME

## Draped bust. Small eagle.

**Designer:** Robert Scot. **Diameter:** 19 mm. **Weight:** 2.7000 g. **Composition:** 0.8920 Silver, 0.0775 oz. ASW.
**Notes:** 1797 strikes have either 13 or 16 stars on the obverse.

| Date | Mintage | G-4 | VG-8 | F-12 | VF-20 | XF-40 | MS-60 |
|------|---------|-----|------|------|-------|-------|-------|
| 1796 | 22,135 | 1,000 | 1,650 | 1,800 | 2,750 | 4,250 | 7,500 |
| 1797 13 stars | 25,261 | 1,100 | 1,650 | 2,000 | 2,850 | 5,250 | 8,250 |
| 1797 16 stars | Inc. above | 1,100 | 1,650 | 2,000 | 2,850 | 5,400 | 8,500 |

## Draped bust. Heraldic eagle.

**Designer:** Robert Scot. **Diameter:** 19 mm. **Weight:** 2.7000 g. **Composition:** 0.8920 Silver, 0.0775 oz. ASW.
**Notes:** The 1798 overdates have either 13 or 16 stars on the obverse. Varieties of the regular 1798 strikes are distinguished by the size of the 8 in the date. The 1805 strikes have either 4 or 5 berries on the olive branch held by the eagle.

| Date | Mintage | G-4 | VG-8 | F-12 | VF-20 | XF-40 | MS-60 |
|------|---------|-----|------|------|-------|-------|-------|
| 1798 | 27,550 | 450 | 525 | 750 | 1,050 | 2,000 | 4,000 |
| 1798/97 13 stars | Inc. above | 900 | 1,600 | 2,350 | 3,750 | 5,500 | — |
| 1798/97 16 stars | Inc. above | 475 | 600 | 800 | 1,100 | 2,100 | 4,300 |
| 1798 small 8 | Inc. above | 600 | 850 | 1,350 | 1,950 | 3,000 | 7,500 |
| 1800 | 21,760 | 450 | 560 | 750 | 1,125 | 1,975 | — |
| 1801 | 34,640 | 450 | 560 | 875 | 1,375 | 3,200 | — |
| 1802 | 10,975 | 500 | 850 | 1,200 | 2,200 | 4,200 | — |
| 1803 | 33,040 | 450 | 560 | 750 | 1,125 | 1,975 | — |
| 1804 13 stars | 8,265 | 1,000 | 1,400 | 2,100 | 4,400 | 7,500 | — |
| 1804 14 stars | Inc. above | 1,200 | 1,700 | 2,750 | 4,750 | 8,000 | — |
| 1805 4 berries | 120,780 | 375 | 525 | 725 | 950 | 1,800 | 4,050 |
| 1805 5 berries | Inc. above | 650 | 800 | 1,000 | 1,500 | 2,500 | 4,400 |
| 1807 | 165,000 | 375 | 525 | 725 | 975 | 1,800 | 4,050 |

## Liberty cap.

**Designer:** John Reich. **Diameter:** 18.8 mm. **Weight:** 2.7000 g. **Composition:** 0.8920 Silver, .0775 oz. ASW.
**Notes:** Varieties of the 1814, 1821 and 1828 strikes are distinguished by the size of the numerals in the dates. The 1820 varieties are distinguished by the size of the 0 in the date. The 1823 overdates have either large E's or small E's in "United States of America" on the reverse.

| Date | Mintage | G-4 | VG-8 | F-12 | VF-20 | XF-40 | AU-50 | MS-60 | MS-65 |
|------|---------|-----|------|------|-------|-------|-------|-------|-------|
| 1809 | 51,065 | 100.00 | 200 | 375 | 650 | 925 | 2,500 | 4,200 | 22,500 |
| 1811/9 | 65,180 | 90.00 | 165 | 240 | 425 | 750 | 1,500 | 4,000 | 22,500 |
| 1814 small date | 421,500 | 40.00 | 60.00 | 90.00 | 210 | 450 | 700 | 800 | 8,000 |
| 1814 large date | Inc. above | 17.50 | 26.00 | 44.00 | 115 | 350 | 625 | 800 | 8,000 |
| 1820 large O | 942,587 | 17.00 | 24.00 | 38.00 | 105 | 330 | 625 | 800 | 8,000 |
| 1820 small O | Inc. above | 22.00 | 40.00 | 55.00 | 175 | 425 | 725 | 975 | 8,000 |
| 1821 large date | 1,186,512 | 16.00 | 23.00 | 38.00 | 105 | 330 | 625 | 800 | 8,000 |
| 1821 small date | Inc. above | 18.50 | 25.00 | 45.00 | 125 | 370 | 625 | 800 | 8,000 |
| 1822 | 100,000 | 300 | 450 | 800 | 1,450 | 2,500 | 4,450 | 6,000 | — |
| 1823/22 large E's | 440,000 | 15.00 | 22.00 | 40.00 | 110 | 300 | 625 | 800 | 8,000 |
| 1823/22 small E's | Inc. above | 15.00 | 22.00 | 40.00 | 110 | 300 | 625 | 800 | 8,000 |
| 1824/22 mintage undetermined | — | 30.00 | 48.00 | 90.00 | 325 | 525 | 1,275 | 2,500 | — |
| 1825 | 510,000 | 20.00 | 27.00 | 40.00 | 145 | 375 | 775 | 1,250 | 8,000 |

## 1809 Dime
### Grade F-12

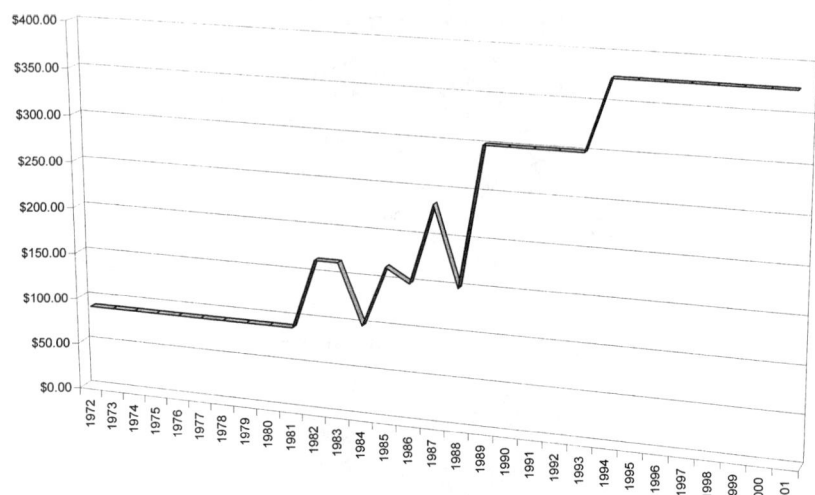

Retail Price

| Date | Mintage | G-4 | VG-8 | F-12 | VF-20 | XF-40 | AU-50 | MS-60 | MS-65 |
|------|---------|-----|------|------|-------|-------|-------|-------|-------|
| 1827 | 1,215,000 | 15.00 | 22.00 | 35.00 | 95.00 | 300 | 775 | 1,000 | 8,000 |
| 1828 large date | 125,000 | 80.00 | 110 | 150 | 265 | 650 | 900 | 2,600 | — |

## Liberty cap.

**Designer:** John Reich. **Diameter:** 18.5 mm. **Composition:** Silver. **Notes:** The three varieties of 1829 strikes and two varieties of 1830 strikes are distinguished by the size of "10C." on the reverse. On the 1833 "high 3" variety, the last 3 in the date is higher than the first 3. The two varieties of the 1834 strikes are distinguished by the size of the 4 in the date.

| Date | Mintage | G-4 | VG-8 | F-12 | VF-20 | XF-40 | AU-50 | MS-60 | MS-65 |
|------|---------|-----|------|------|-------|-------|-------|-------|-------|
| 1828 small date | Inc. above | 30.00 | 45.00 | 75.00 | 195 | 475 | 775 | 1,750 | — |
| 1829 very large 10C. | 770,000 | 35.00 | 45.00 | 85.00 | 150 | 375 | 600 | 1,500 | — |
| 1829 large 10C. | — | 14.00 | 17.00 | 22.00 | 60.00 | 185 | 415 | 675 | 8,000 |
| 1829 medium 10C. | Inc. above | 14.00 | 17.00 | 22.00 | 60.00 | 185 | 415 | 625 | 8,000 |
| 1829 small 10C. | Inc. above | 14.00 | 17.00 | 22.00 | 60.00 | 185 | 415 | 625 | 8,000 |
| 1829 curl base 2 | — | 3,200 | 3,950 | 7,500 | — | — | — | — | — |
| 1830 large 10C. | 510,000 | 14.00 | 17.00 | 22.00 | 60.00 | 185 | 415 | 625 | 8,000 |
| 1830 small 10C. | Inc. above | 15.00 | 19.00 | 25.00 | 63.00 | 200 | 415 | 625 | 8,000 |
| 1830/29 | Inc. above | 20.00 | 25.00 | 35.00 | 90.00 | 260 | 500 | 1,000 | — |
| 1831 | 771,350 | 14.00 | 17.00 | 22.00 | 60.00 | 185 | 350 | 600 | 5,050 |
| 1832 | 522,500 | 14.00 | 17.00 | 22.00 | 60.00 | 185 | 350 | 600 | 5,050 |
| 1833 | 485,000 | 15.00 | 18.00 | 23.00 | 62.00 | 190 | 350 | 600 | 5,050 |
| 1834 | 635,000 | 14.00 | 17.00 | 22.00 | 60.00 | 185 | 350 | 600 | 5,050 |
| 1835 | 1,410,000 | 14.00 | 17.00 | 22.00 | 60.00 | 185 | 350 | 600 | 5,050 |
| 1836 | 1,190,000 | 14.00 | 17.00 | 22.00 | 60.00 | 185 | 350 | 600 | 5,050 |
| 1837 | 1,042,000 | 14.00 | 17.00 | 22.00 | 60.00 | 185 | 350 | 625 | 5,050 |

## Seated Liberty. No stars around rim.

**Designer:** Christian Gobrecht. **Diameter:** 17.9 mm. **Weight:** 2.6700 g. **Composition:** 0.9000 Silver, 0.0773 oz. ASW. **Notes:** The two 1837 varieties are distinguished by the size of the numerals in the date.

| Date | Mintage | G-4 | VG-8 | F-12 | VF-20 | XF-40 | AU-50 | MS-60 | MS-65 |
|------|---------|-----|------|------|-------|-------|-------|-------|-------|
| 1837 small date | Inc. above | 29.00 | 40.00 | 75.00 | 275 | 550 | 750 | 1,100 | 6,500 |
| 1837 large date | Inc. above | 29.00 | 40.00 | 75.00 | 275 | 550 | 750 | 1,100 | 6,500 |
| 1838O | 406,034 | 35.00 | 45.00 | 90.00 | 300 | 725 | 1,250 | 3,500 | 21,000 |

## Seated Liberty. Stars around rim. No drapery.

No drapery

**Obv. Designer:** Christian Gobrecht. **Diameter:** 17.9 mm. **Weight:** 2.6700 g. **Composition:** 0.9000 Silver, 0.0773 oz. ASW. **Notes:** The two 1838 varieties are distinguished by the size of the stars on the obverse. The 1838 "partial drapery" variety has drapery on Liberty's left elbow. The 1839-O with reverse of 1838-O variety was struck from rusted dies. This variety has a bumpy surface on the reverse.

| Date | Mintage | G-4 | VG-8 | F-12 | VF-20 | XF-40 | AU-50 | MS-60 | MS-65 |
|------|---------|-----|------|------|-------|-------|-------|-------|-------|
| 1838 small stars | 1,992,500 | 20.00 | 30.00 | 45.00 | 75.00 | 175 | 300 | 950 | — |
| 1838 large stars | Inc. above | 9.00 | 11.00 | 15.00 | 25.00 | 60.00 | 170 | 575 | 8,500 |
| 1838 partial drapery | Inc. above | 30.00 | 45.00 | 60.00 | 125 | 195 | 325 | 550 | — |
| 1839 | 1,053,115 | 9.00 | 15.00 | 17.50 | 35.00 | 70.00 | 170 | 265 | 2,500 |
| 1839O | 1,323,000 | 8.75 | 12.00 | 20.00 | 40.00 | 85.00 | 300 | 1,250 | — |
| 1839O reverse 1838O | — | 145 | 200 | 350 | 550 | 950 | — | — | — |
| 1840 | 1,358,580 | 9.00 | 15.00 | 20.00 | 30.00 | 60.00 | 170 | 300 | 2,500 |
| 1840O | 1,175,000 | 12.50 | 22.00 | 40.00 | 70.00 | 125 | 295 | 975 | — |

## Seated Liberty. Drapery added to Liberty's left elbow.

with drapery

**Designer:** Christian Gobrecht. **Diameter:** 17.9 mm. **Weight:** 2.6700 g. **Composition:** 0.9000 Silver, 0.0773 oz. ASW.

| Date | Mintage | G-4 | VG-8 | F-12 | VF-20 | XF-40 | AU-50 | MS-60 | MS-65 |
|------|---------|-----|------|------|-------|-------|-------|-------|-------|
| 1840 | Inc. above | 30.00 | 45.00 | 85.00 | 165 | 275 | 1,250 | — | — |
| 1841 | 1,622,500 | 10.00 | 13.00 | 16.00 | 25.00 | 45.00 | 175 | 260 | 2,550 |
| 1841O | 2,007,500 | 9.00 | 11.00 | 15.00 | 28.00 | 60.00 | 250 | 1,500 | — |
| 1841O large O | Inc. above | 600 | 900 | 1,200 | 2,500 | — | — | — | — |
| 1842 | 1,887,500 | 8.75 | 9.50 | 10.00 | 17.00 | 45.00 | 175 | 260 | 2,550 |
| 1842O | 2,020,000 | 10.00 | 18.00 | 30.00 | 75.00 | 225 | 1,350 | 2,900 | — |
| 1843 | 1,370,000 | 8.75 | 9.25 | 10.00 | 17.00 | 45.00 | 175 | 260 | 2,550 |
| 1843/1843 | — | 9.00 | 12.00 | 18.00 | 30.00 | 75.00 | 200 | 295 | — |
| 1843O | 150,000 | 35.00 | 65.00 | 125 | 250 | 700 | 2,000 | — | — |
| 1844 | 72,500 | 275 | 350 | 550 | 800 | 1,450 | 2,200 | 3,000 | — |
| 1845 | 1,755,000 | 8.75 | 9.25 | 10.00 | 19.00 | 45.00 | 120 | 260 | 2,550 |
| 1845/1845 | Inc. above | 12.00 | 15.00 | 35.00 | 55.00 | 100.00 | 175 | — | — |
| 1845O | 230,000 | 19.00 | 35.00 | 60.00 | 165 | 475 | 1,200 | — | — |
| 1846 | 31,300 | 120 | 150 | 200 | 295 | 850 | 2,000 | — | — |
| 1847 | 245,000 | 17.50 | 25.00 | 35.00 | 60.00 | 125 | 350 | 950 | — |
| 1848 | 451,500 | 12.00 | 15.00 | 22.00 | 40.00 | 75.00 | 185 | 750 | 7,050 |
| 1849 | 839,000 | 10.00 | 13.00 | 18.00 | 28.00 | 55.00 | 140 | 500 | 7,050 |
| 1849O | 300,000 | 15.00 | 22.00 | 35.00 | 90.00 | 275 | 950 | — | — |
| 1850 | 1,931,500 | 8.75 | 9.25 | 10.00 | 25.00 | 60.00 | 120 | 260 | 2,550 |
| 1850O | 510,000 | 14.00 | 17.00 | 28.00 | 60.00 | 160 | 400 | 1,250 | — |
| 1851 | 1,026,500 | 8.75 | 9.25 | 10.00 | 19.00 | 60.00 | 120 | 325 | — |
| 1851O | 400,000 | 14.00 | 17.00 | 30.00 | 75.00 | 175 | 450 | 1,500 | — |
| 1852 | 1,535,500 | 8.75 | 9.25 | 10.00 | 15.00 | 50.00 | 120 | 290 | 2,550 |
| 1852O | 430,000 | 16.00 | 22.00 | 39.00 | 100.00 | 195 | 425 | 1,800 | — |
| 1853 | 95,000 | 70.00 | 90.00 | 110 | 180 | 300 | 450 | 800 | — |

## Seated Liberty. Arrows at date.

**Designer:** Christian Gobrecht. **Weight:** 2.4900 g. **Composition:** 0.9000 Silver, 0.0721 oz. ASW.

## 1866-S Dime
### Grade F-12

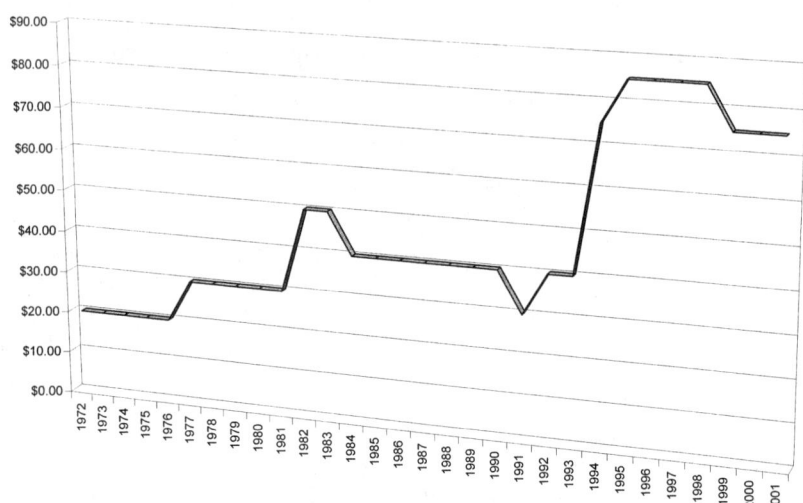

| | Retail Price |

| Date | Mintage | G-4 | VG-8 | F-12 | VF-20 | XF-40 | AU-50 | MS-60 | MS-65 | Prf-65 |
|------|---------|-----|------|------|-------|-------|-------|-------|-------|--------|
| 1853 | 12,078,010 | 8.00 | 9.00 | 10.00 | 14.00 | 45.00 | 125 | 330 | 2,500 | 31,500 |
| 1853O | 1,100,000 | 10.00 | 13.00 | 20.00 | 45.00 | 145 | 400 | 900 | — | — |
| 1854 | 4,470,000 | 8.75 | 9.25 | 10.00 | 14.00 | 45.00 | 125 | 330 | 2,500 | 31,500 |
| 1854O | 1,770,000 | 10.00 | 11.00 | 14.00 | 25.00 | 75.00 | 175 | 600 | — | — |
| 1855 | 2,075,000 | 8.75 | 9.25 | 14.00 | 20.00 | 55.00 | 150 | 350 | 3,800 | 31,500 |

## Seated Liberty. Arrows at date removed.

**Designer:** Christian Gobrecht. **Weight:** 2.4900 g. **Composition:** 0.9000 Silver, 0.0721 oz. ASW. **Notes:** The two 1856 varieties are distinguished by the size of the numerals in the date.

| Date | Mintage | G-4 | VG-8 | F-12 | VF-20 | XF-40 | AU-50 | MS-60 | MS-65 | Prf-65 |
|------|---------|-----|------|------|-------|-------|-------|-------|-------|--------|
| 1856 small date | 5,780,000 | 8.75 | 9.25 | 10.00 | 12.50 | 32.00 | 115 | 250 | 7,050 | 38,000 |
| 1856 large date | Inc. above | 10.00 | 12.00 | 15.00 | 25.00 | 65.00 | 175 | 475 | — | — |
| 1856O | 1,180,000 | 9.00 | 15.00 | 20.00 | 35.00 | 85.00 | 200 | 500 | — | — |
| 1856S | 70,000 | 145 | 170 | 250 | 425 | 900 | 1,750 | — | — | — |
| 1857 | 5,580,000 | 8.75 | 9.25 | 11.25 | 13.00 | 32.00 | 100.00 | 260 | 2,500 | 3,400 |
| 1857O | 1,540,000 | 10.00 | 12.00 | 14.00 | 25.00 | 65.00 | 200 | 350 | — | — |
| 1858 | 1,540,000 | 10.00 | 14.00 | 20.00 | 35.00 | 55.00 | 145 | 260 | 2,500 | 3,400 |
| 1858O | 290,000 | 15.00 | 19.00 | 35.00 | 70.00 | 125 | 275 | 800 | — | — |
| 1858S | 60,000 | 110 | 150 | 200 | 325 | 675 | 1,400 | — | — | — |
| 1859 | 430,000 | 11.00 | 15.00 | 20.00 | 40.00 | 60.00 | 140 | 350 | — | 3,400 |
| 1859O | 480,000 | 11.00 | 14.00 | 21.00 | 35.00 | 70.00 | 225 | 550 | — | — |
| 1859S | 60,000 | 125 | 160 | 250 | 425 | 1,000 | 2,000 | — | — | — |
| 1860S | 140,000 | 28.00 | 36.00 | 48.00 | 100.00 | 275 | 800 | — | — | — |

## Seated Liberty. "United States of America" replaced stars.

**Obv. Designer:** Christian Gobrecht. **Weight:** 2.4900 g. **Composition:** 0.9000 Silver, 0.0721 oz. ASW.
**Notes:** The 1873 "closed-3" and "open-3" varieties are distinguished by the amount of space between the upper left and lower left serifs of the 3 in the date.

| Date | Mintage | G-4 | VG-8 | F-12 | VF-20 | XF-40 | AU-50 | MS-60 | MS-65 | Prf-65 |
|------|---------|-----|------|------|-------|-------|-------|-------|-------|--------|
| 1860 | 607,000 | 15.00 | 22.00 | 29.00 | 31.00 | 55.00 | 125 | 275 | — | 1,400 |
| 1860O | 40,000 | 300 | 425 | 600 | 1,150 | 2,500 | 4,200 | 6,000 | — | — |
| 1861 | 1,884,000 | 8.75 | 10.00 | 13.00 | 18.00 | 35.00 | 65.00 | 125 | — | 1,400 |
| 1861S | 172,500 | 45.00 | 80.00 | 125 | 225 | 375 | 900 | — | — | — |
| 1862 | 847,550 | 10.00 | 13.00 | 19.00 | 25.00 | 45.00 | 65.00 | 150 | — | 1,400 |
| 1862S | 180,750 | 40.00 | 60.00 | 95.00 | 175 | 300 | 775 | — | — | — |
| 1863 | 14,460 | 250 | 375 | 500 | 600 | 750 | 900 | 1,200 | — | 1,400 |
| 1863S | 157,500 | 30.00 | 35.00 | 55.00 | 90.00 | 275 | 550 | 1,200 | — | — |
| 1864 | 11,470 | 250 | 325 | 400 | 500 | 600 | 775 | 1,650 | — | 1,400 |
| 1864S | 230,000 | 24.00 | 30.00 | 40.00 | 80.00 | 225 | 425 | 1,200 | — | — |
| 1865 | 10,500 | 275 | 350 | 450 | 550 | 675 | 1,050 | 1,250 | — | 1,400 |
| 1865S | 175,000 | 35.00 | 45.00 | 60.00 | 100.00 | 250 | 700 | — | — | — |
| 1866 | 8,725 | 300 | 375 | 575 | 675 | 800 | 1,200 | 1,800 | — | 1,750 |
| 1866S | 135,000 | 35.00 | 45.00 | 75.00 | 145 | 325 | 675 | 1,900 | — | — |
| 1867 | 6,625 | 425 | 575 | 800 | 900 | 1,150 | 1,300 | 1,600 | — | 1,750 |
| 1867S | 140,000 | 35.00 | 45.00 | 70.00 | 125 | 275 | 575 | 1,200 | — | — |
| 1868 | 464,000 | 13.00 | 17.00 | 22.00 | 32.00 | 70.00 | 175 | 300 | — | 1,400 |
| 1868S | 260,000 | 20.00 | 25.00 | 35.00 | 70.00 | 145 | 285 | 600 | — | — |
| 1869 | 256,600 | 16.00 | 22.00 | 36.00 | 55.00 | 115 | 220 | 600 | — | 1,400 |
| 1869S | 450,000 | 12.00 | 17.00 | 30.00 | 38.00 | 65.00 | 150 | 400 | — | — |
| 1870 | 471,000 | 13.00 | 17.00 | 21.00 | 32.00 | 70.00 | 135 | 300 | — | 1,400 |
| 1870S | 50,000 | 215 | 280 | 375 | 450 | 575 | 850 | 2,000 | — | — |
| 1871 | 907,710 | 11.00 | 15.00 | 20.00 | 28.00 | 45.00 | 130 | 300 | — | 1,400 |
| 1871CC | 20,100 | 850 | 1,150 | 1,950 | 3,500 | 6,750 | 10,500 | — | — | — |
| 1871S | 320,000 | 35.00 | 55.00 | 75.00 | 115 | 175 | 350 | 900 | — | — |
| 1872 | 2,396,450 | 8.75 | 9.50 | 11.00 | 18.00 | 31.00 | 95.00 | 175 | — | 1,400 |
| 1872CC | 35,480 | 350 | 525 | 850 | 1,750 | 3,000 | 4,750 | — | — | — |
| 1872S | 190,000 | 40.00 | 50.00 | 70.00 | 125 | 215 | 450 | 1,100 | — | — |
| 1873 closed 3 | 1,568,600 | 9.00 | 11.00 | 14.00 | 27.00 | 50.00 | 100.00 | 200 | — | 1,400 |
| 1873 open 3 | Inc. above | 15.00 | 18.00 | 30.00 | 48.00 | 100.00 | 225 | 650 | — | — |
| 1873CC | 12,400 | — | — | — | — | — | — | — | — | — |

**Note:** 1873-CC, Heritage Sale, April 1999, MS-64, $632,500.

## Seated Liberty. Arrows at date.

**Designer:** Christian Gobrecht. **Weight:** 2.5000 g. **Composition:** 0.9000 Silver, 0.0724 oz. ASW.

| Date | Mintage | G-4 | VG-8 | F-12 | VF-20 | XF-40 | AU-50 | MS-60 | MS-65 | Prf-65 |
|------|---------|-----|------|------|-------|-------|-------|-------|-------|--------|
| 1873 | 2,378,500 | 8.75 | 13.00 | 25.00 | 50.00 | 150 | 350 | 500 | 4,500 | 4,500 |
| 1873CC | 18,791 | 750 | 975 | 1,850 | 3,750 | 5,750 | 9,750 | — | — | — |
| 1873S | 455,000 | 15.00 | 20.00 | 28.00 | 60.00 | 180 | 320 | 1,500 | — | — |
| 1874 | 2,940,700 | 8.75 | 13.00 | 17.50 | 50.00 | 150 | 315 | 500 | 4,500 | 4,500 |
| 1874CC | 10,817 | 2,950 | 4,500 | 6,500 | 9,750 | 17,500 | — | — | — | — |
| 1874S | 240,000 | 45.00 | 52.00 | 80.00 | 140 | 250 | 450 | 1,500 | — | — |

## Seated Liberty. Arrows at date removed.

**Designer:** Christian Gobrecht. **Weight:** 2.5000 g. **Composition:** 0.9000 Silver, 0.0724 oz. ASW. **Notes:** On the 1876-CC doubled-obverse variety, doubling appears in the words "of America" in the legend.

| Date | Mintage | G-4 | VG-8 | F-12 | VF-20 | XF-40 | AU-50 | MS-60 | MS-65 | Prf-65 |
|------|---------|-----|------|------|-------|-------|-------|-------|-------|--------|
| 1875 | 10,350,700 | 8.75 | 9.25 | 10.00 | 12.00 | 22.00 | 60.00 | 125 | 2,250 | 4,600 |
| 1875CC mint mark in wreath | 4,645,000 | 8.75 | 9.50 | 11.00 | 18.00 | 37.50 | 90.00 | 160 | 2,700 | — |
| 1875CC mint mark under wreath | Inc. above | 10.00 | 15.00 | 22.50 | 37.50 | 65.00 | 165 | 235 | 3,000 | — |
| 1875S mint mark in wreath | 9,070,000 | 12.00 | 17.50 | 28.00 | 43.00 | 65.00 | 125 | 225 | 3,100 | — |
| 1875S mint mark under wreath | Inc. above | 10.00 | 14.00 | 17.50 | 25.00 | 35.00 | 70.00 | 125 | 1,100 | — |
| 1876 | 11,461,150 | 8.75 | 9.25 | 11.00 | 12.00 | 24.00 | 60.00 | 110 | 1,100 | 1,200 |
| 1876CC | 8,270,000 | 8.75 | 9.25 | 11.00 | 18.00 | 30.00 | 60.00 | 175 | — | — |

## 1901-S Dime
### Grade F-12

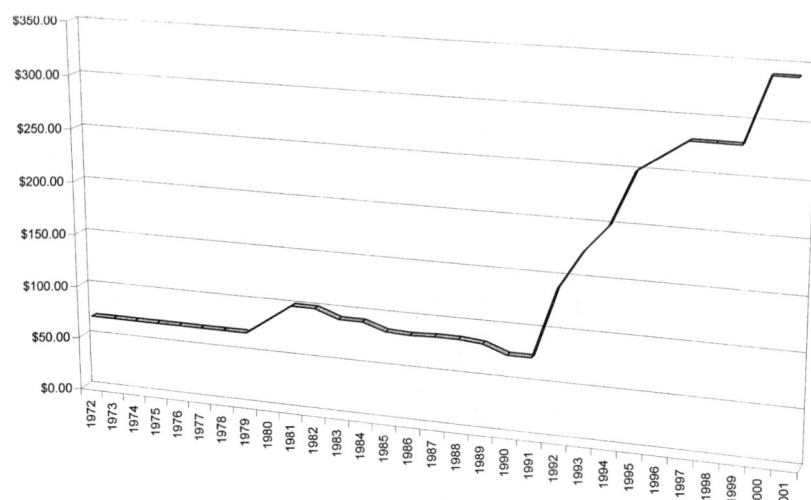

☑ Retail Price

| Date | Mintage | G-4 | VG-8 | F-12 | VF-20 | XF-40 | AU-50 | MS-60 | MS-65 | Prf-65 |
|---|---|---|---|---|---|---|---|---|---|---|
| 1876CC doubled obverse | Inc. above | 12.00 | 20.00 | 25.00 | 75.00 | 110 | 300 | 500 | — | — |
| 1876S | 10,420,000 | 10.00 | 13.00 | 15.00 | 20.00 | 35.00 | 85.00 | 165 | 1,100 | — |
| 1877 | 7,310,510 | 8.75 | 9.25 | 9.75 | 13.00 | 23.00 | 60.00 | 110 | 1,100 | 1,200 |
| 1877CC | 7,700,000 | 8.75 | 9.25 | 10.75 | 18.00 | 35.00 | 75.00 | 175 | — | — |
| 1877S | 2,340,000 | 14.00 | 18.00 | 20.00 | 30.00 | 50.00 | 105 | 225 | — | — |
| 1878 | 1,678,800 | 9.00 | 9.50 | 10.00 | 18.00 | 30.00 | 60.00 | 110 | 1,100 | 1,200 |
| 1878CC | 200,000 | 50.00 | 75.00 | 110 | 165 | 275 | 450 | 775 | 3,900 | — |
| 1879 | 15,100 | 165 | 200 | 250 | 285 | 350 | 475 | 675 | 1,750 | 1,500 |
| 1880 | 37,335 | 130 | 165 | 190 | 220 | 250 | 325 | 450 | 1,750 | 1,500 |
| 1881 | 24,975 | 145 | 175 | 215 | 260 | 325 | 425 | 650 | 2,500 | 1,600 |
| 1882 | 3,911,100 | 8.75 | 9.25 | 11.00 | 15.00 | 27.00 | 60.00 | 110 | 1,100 | 1,200 |
| 1883 | 7,675,712 | 8.75 | 9.25 | 11.00 | 12.00 | 24.00 | 60.00 | 110 | 1,100 | 1,200 |
| 1884 | 3,366,380 | 8.75 | 9.25 | 11.00 | 15.00 | 27.00 | 60.00 | 110 | 1,100 | 1,200 |
| 1884S | 564,969 | 24.00 | 28.00 | 40.00 | 65.00 | 125 | 200 | 500 | — | — |
| 1885 | 2,533,427 | 8.75 | 9.25 | 10.75 | 15.00 | 27.00 | 60.00 | 110 | 1,100 | 1,200 |
| 1885S | 43,690 | 350 | 475 | 725 | 1,450 | 2,200 | 2,950 | 3,750 | — | — |
| 1886 | 6,377,570 | 8.75 | 9.25 | 10.00 | 12.00 | 22.00 | 60.00 | 110 | 1,100 | 1,200 |
| 1886S | 206,524 | 45.00 | 60.00 | 60.00 | 95.00 | 145 | 265 | 600 | — | — |
| 1887 | 11,283,939 | 8.75 | 9.25 | 10.00 | 12.00 | 22.00 | 60.00 | 110 | 1,100 | 1,200 |
| 1887S | 4,454,450 | 9.00 | 12.00 | 16.00 | 22.00 | 38.00 | 80.00 | 110 | 1,100 | — |
| 1888 | 5,496,487 | 8.75 | 9.25 | 10.00 | 12.00 | 22.00 | 60.00 | 110 | 1,100 | 1,200 |
| 1888S | 1,720,000 | 10.00 | 13.00 | 17.00 | 25.00 | 40.00 | 95.00 | 200 | — | — |
| 1889 | 7,380,711 | 8.75 | 9.25 | 10.00 | 12.00 | 22.00 | 60.00 | 110 | 1,100 | 1,200 |
| 1889S | 972,678 | 14.00 | 18.00 | 25.00 | 35.00 | 70.00 | 150 | 475 | 4,500 | — |
| 1890 | 9,911,541 | 8.75 | 9.25 | 10.00 | 12.00 | 22.00 | 60.00 | 110 | 1,100 | 1,200 |
| 1890S | 1,423,076 | 11.00 | 14.00 | 20.00 | 57.50 | 85.00 | 155 | 400 | 4,900 | — |
| 1890S/S | Inc. above | 25.00 | 30.00 | 40.00 | 85.00 | 135 | 250 | — | — | — |
| 1891 | 15,310,600 | 8.75 | 9.25 | 10.00 | 12.00 | 22.00 | 60.00 | 110 | 1,100 | 1,200 |
| 1891O | 4,540,000 | 9.00 | 9.75 | 11.00 | 13.00 | 24.00 | 70.00 | 175 | 1,750 | — |
| 1891O /horizontal O | Inc. above | 65.00 | 95.00 | 125 | 175 | 225 | 400 | — | — | — |
| 1891S | 3,196,116 | 10.00 | 12.00 | 18.00 | 35.00 | 55.00 | 135 | 225 | 1,650 | — |

## Liberty.

**Designer:** Charles E. Barber. **Diameter:** 17.9 mm. **Weight:** 2.5000 g. **Composition:** 0.9000 Silver, 0.0724 oz. ASW. **Notes:** Commonly called "Barber dime."

| Date | Mintage | G-4 | VG-8 | F-12 | VF-20 | XF-40 | AU-50 | MS-60 | MS-65 | Prf-65 |
|------|---------|-----|------|------|-------|-------|-------|-------|-------|--------|
| 1892 | 12,121,245 | 2.50 | 5.00 | 14.00 | 19.50 | 22.00 | 55.00 | 90.00 | 540 | 1,450 |
| 1892O | 3,841,700 | 5.85 | 11.50 | 27.00 | 38.00 | 45.00 | 72.00 | 145 | 1,200 | — |
| 1892S | 990,710 | 38.00 | 65.00 | 145 | 170 | 210 | 230 | 350 | 2,500 | — |
| 1893 | 3,340,792 | 5.50 | 10.50 | 17.50 | 21.00 | 32.00 | 72.00 | 145 | 810 | 1,450 |
| 1893O | 1,760,000 | 15.00 | 30.00 | 90.00 | 110 | 135 | 155 | 260 | 2,900 | — |
| 1893S | 2,491,401 | 7.75 | 19.00 | 25.00 | 30.00 | 49.00 | 110 | 230 | 3,600 | — |
| 1894 | 1,330,972 | 10.00 | 24.00 | 84.00 | 110 | 130 | 155 | 250 | 1,110 | 1,450 |
| 1894O | 720,000 | 39.00 | 78.00 | 160 | 205 | 290 | 600 | 1,100 | 8,400 | — |
| 1894S | 24 | — | — | — | — | — | — | — | — | — |
| Note: 1894S, Eliasberg Sale, May 1996, Prf-64, $451,000. | | | | | | | | | | |
| 1895 | 690,880 | 55.00 | 85.00 | 200 | 400 | 450 | 500 | 600 | 2,400 | 2,000 |
| 1895O | 440,000 | 225 | 300 | 690 | 950 | 1,825 | 2,500 | 2,800 | 10,000 | — |
| 1895S | 1,120,000 | 26.00 | 40.00 | 105 | 145 | 175 | 230 | 440 | 6,300 | — |
| 1896 | 2,000,762 | 8.00 | 19.00 | 44.00 | 58.00 | 74.00 | 100.00 | 145 | 1,320 | 1,450 |
| 1896O | 610,000 | 50.00 | 100.00 | 215 | 285 | 380 | 600 | 755 | 6,000 | — |
| 1896S | 575,056 | 65.00 | 110 | 250 | 275 | 295 | 440 | 695 | 3,500 | — |
| 1897 | 10,869,264 | 2.25 | 2.75 | 5.85 | 8.50 | 23.00 | 68.00 | 110 | 700 | 1,450 |
| 1897O | 666,000 | 40.00 | 74.00 | 225 | 280 | 345 | 505 | 755 | 4,150 | — |
| 1897S | 1,342,844 | 14.00 | 28.00 | 80.00 | 100.00 | 140 | 200 | 390 | 3,500 | — |
| 1898 | 16,320,735 | 1.45 | 1.95 | 6.50 | 9.00 | 20.00 | 50.00 | 91.00 | 540 | 1,450 |
| 1898O | 2,130,000 | 5.50 | 12.00 | 60.00 | 91.00 | 130 | 195 | 425 | 3,500 | — |
| 1898S | 1,702,507 | 4.50 | 8.50 | 22.00 | 31.00 | 52.00 | 110 | 325 | 3,800 | — |
| 1899 | 19,580,846 | 1.45 | 1.75 | 5.85 | 8.50 | 20.00 | 52.00 | 91.00 | 540 | 1,450 |
| 1899O | 2,650,000 | 4.50 | 9.75 | 58.00 | 78.00 | 115 | 200 | 360 | 4,800 | — |
| 1899S | 1,867,493 | 4.75 | 11.00 | 16.50 | 20.00 | 35.00 | 85.00 | 295 | 3,500 | — |
| 1900 | 17,600,912 | 1.50 | 2.10 | 6.00 | 8.50 | 20.00 | 52.00 | 91.00 | 900 | 1,450 |
| 1900O | 2,010,000 | 9.00 | 22.00 | 85.00 | 125 | 190 | 325 | 520 | 6,000 | — |
| 1900S | 5,168,270 | 2.75 | 3.60 | 8.50 | 11.00 | 21.00 | 72.00 | 165 | 1,675 | — |
| 1901 | 18,860,478 | 1.45 | 1.65 | 5.25 | 7.75 | 20.00 | 45.00 | 100.00 | 1,170 | 1,450 |
| 1901O | 5,620,000 | 2.75 | 4.50 | 12.00 | 18.00 | 42.00 | 115 | 360 | 2,900 | — |
| 1901S | 593,022 | 50.00 | 88.00 | 340 | 380 | 450 | 565 | 790 | 5,000 | — |
| 1902 | 21,380,777 | 1.30 | 1.75 | 4.50 | 6.75 | 21.00 | 52.00 | 91.00 | 540 | 1,450 |
| 1902O | 4,500,000 | 2.50 | 6.50 | 13.00 | 20.00 | 41.00 | 105 | 325 | 3,350 | — |
| 1902S | 2,070,000 | 5.50 | 11.00 | 44.00 | 58.00 | 84.00 | 145 | 325 | 3,600 | — |
| 1903 | 19,500,755 | 1.30 | 1.75 | 4.50 | 7.15 | 20.00 | 52.00 | 91.00 | 1,150 | 1,450 |
| 1903O | 8,180,000 | 2.00 | 3.00 | 8.75 | 13.00 | 26.00 | 91.00 | 240 | 5,050 | — |
| 1903S | 613,300 | 44.00 | 85.00 | 320 | 415 | 680 | 855 | 1,050 | 3,800 | — |
| 1904 | 14,601,027 | 1.30 | 1.75 | 5.50 | 9.00 | 20.00 | 52.00 | 105 | 2,100 | 1,450 |
| 1904S | 800,000 | 25.00 | 41.00 | 120 | 155 | 225 | 430 | 565 | 4,700 | — |
| 1905 | 14,552,350 | 1.30 | 1.75 | 4.00 | 6.50 | 19.00 | 52.00 | 91.00 | 540 | 1,450 |
| 1905O | 3,400,000 | 2.50 | 5.75 | 30.00 | 43.00 | 58.00 | 105 | 230 | 2,050 | — |
| 1905S | 6,855,199 | 2.25 | 4.75 | 7.75 | 16.50 | 30.00 | 72.00 | 210 | 725 | — |
| 1906 | 19,958,406 | 1.30 | 1.75 | 3.50 | 6.50 | 21.00 | 52.00 | 91.00 | 540 | 1,450 |
| 1906D | 4,060,000 | 2.25 | 3.75 | 9.00 | 14.00 | 27.00 | 72.00 | 155 | 1,950 | — |
| 1906O | 2,610,000 | 4.00 | 6.00 | 41.00 | 57.00 | 78.00 | 125 | 180 | 1,250 | — |
| 1906S | 3,136,640 | 2.50 | 4.75 | 10.00 | 18.00 | 36.00 | 91.00 | 230 | 1,200 | — |
| 1907 | 22,220,575 | 1.30 | 1.60 | 3.50 | 6.50 | 21.00 | 52.00 | 91.00 | 540 | 1,450 |
| 1907D | 4,080,000 | 2.25 | 4.75 | 9.00 | 15.00 | 32.00 | 91.00 | 260 | 3,550 | — |
| 1907O | 5,058,000 | 1.75 | 3.00 | 25.00 | 37.00 | 52.00 | 72.00 | 200 | 1,100 | — |
| 1907S | 3,178,470 | 2.25 | 5.00 | 9.75 | 18.00 | 41.00 | 100.00 | 325 | 2,300 | — |
| 1908 | 10,600,545 | 1.30 | 1.75 | 3.50 | 6.50 | 18.00 | 52.00 | 91.00 | 540 | 1,450 |
| 1908D | 7,490,000 | 1.75 | 2.25 | 6.50 | 9.50 | 26.00 | 59.00 | 125 | 960 | — |
| 1908O | 1,789,000 | 3.00 | 8.00 | 39.00 | 52.00 | 72.00 | 130 | 260 | 1,860 | — |
| 1908S | 3,220,000 | 2.75 | 4.50 | 9.00 | 14.00 | 32.00 | 145 | 260 | 2,300 | — |
| 1909 | 10,240,650 | 1.75 | 2.25 | 3.50 | 6.50 | 18.00 | 52.00 | 91.00 | 540 | 1,700 |
| 1909D | 954,000 | 3.75 | 11.00 | 58.00 | 85.00 | 105 | 195 | 390 | 2,300 | — |
| 1909O | 2,287,000 | 2.75 | 5.00 | 8.50 | 15.00 | 27.00 | 91.00 | 180 | 1,250 | — |
| 1909S | 1,000,000 | 5.00 | 13.00 | 78.00 | 110 | 145 | 295 | 470 | 3,000 | — |
| 1910 | 11,520,551 | 1.30 | 2.25 | 5.75 | 10.50 | 20.00 | 52.00 | 91.00 | 540 | 1,450 |
| 1910D | 3,490,000 | 2.75 | 4.75 | 7.75 | 15.00 | 34.00 | 91.00 | 195 | 1,800 | — |
| 1910S | 1,240,000 | 4.00 | 9.00 | 45.00 | 62.00 | 88.00 | 150 | 350 | 1,925 | — |
| 1911 | 18,870,543 | 1.30 | 1.75 | 3.00 | 6.50 | 18.00 | 52.00 | 91.00 | 540 | 1,700 |
| 1911D | 11,209,000 | 1.30 | 1.75 | 3.75 | 7.50 | 20.00 | 52.00 | 91.00 | 685 | — |
| 1911S | 3,520,000 | 1.75 | 2.75 | 7.75 | 15.00 | 31.00 | 85.00 | 145 | 725 | — |
| 1912 | 19,350,700 | 1.30 | 1.75 | 2.75 | 6.50 | 20.00 | 52.00 | 91.00 | 540 | 1,700 |
| 1912D | 11,760,000 | 1.30 | 1.75 | 3.75 | 7.50 | 18.00 | 52.00 | 91.00 | 720 | — |
| 1912S | 3,420,000 | 1.75 | 2.75 | 6.50 | 10.00 | 26.00 | 85.00 | 150 | 1,150 | — |
| 1913 | 19,760,622 | 1.50 | 1.75 | 2.75 | 6.50 | 20.00 | 52.00 | 91.00 | 540 | 1,450 |
| 1913S | 510,000 | 9.00 | 14.00 | 67.00 | 100.00 | 175 | 260 | 390 | 1,100 | — |
| 1914 | 17,360,655 | 1.50 | 1.75 | 3.50 | 6.50 | 18.00 | 52.00 | 91.00 | 540 | 1,700 |
| 1914D | 11,908,000 | 1.50 | 1.75 | 3.50 | 6.75 | 18.00 | 52.00 | 91.00 | 540 | — |
| 1914S | 2,100,000 | 2.00 | 2.40 | 6.50 | 10.00 | 31.00 | 72.00 | 145 | 1,250 | — |
| 1915 | 5,620,450 | 1.50 | 1.75 | 3.90 | 7.00 | 20.00 | 52.00 | 91.00 | 540 | 2,000 |
| 1915S | 960,000 | 3.00 | 5.00 | 29.00 | 39.00 | 52.00 | 125 | 235 | 1,775 | — |
| 1916 | 18,490,000 | 1.30 | 1.75 | 3.75 | 6.00 | 18.00 | 50.00 | 91.00 | 540 | — |
| 1916S | 5,820,000 | 1.50 | 2.25 | 4.75 | 6.50 | 20.00 | 52.00 | 91.00 | 780 | — |

# Winged Liberty, commonly called "Mercury".

Mint mark          1942/1 overdate

**Designer:** Adolph A. Weinman. **Diameter:** 17.9 mm. **Weight:** 2.5000 g. **Composition:** 0.9000 Silver, 0.0724 oz. ASW. **Notes:** All specimens listed as -65FSB are for fully struck MS-65 coins with fully split and rounded horizontal bands on the fasces.

| Date | Mintage | G-4 | VG-8 | F-12 | VF-20 | XF-40 | MS-60 | MS-65 | Prf-65 | -65FSB |
|------|---------|-----|------|------|-------|-------|-------|-------|--------|--------|
| 1916 | 22,180,080 | 2.75 | 4.00 | 5.50 | 6.00 | 7.50 | 30.00 | 90.00 | — | 120 |
| 1916D | 264,000 | 595 | 800 | 1,300 | 1,650 | 2,650 | 4,800 | 19,000 | — | 35,000 |
| 1916S | 10,450,000 | 3.50 | 4.00 | 7.00 | 8.00 | 16.50 | 34.00 | 170 | — | 600 |
| 1917 | 55,230,000 | 1.25 | 1.60 | 2.00 | 4.75 | 7.00 | 28.00 | 155 | — | 375 |
| 1917D | 9,402,000 | 3.50 | 4.75 | 9.50 | 20.00 | 38.00 | 120 | 1,100 | — | 6,500 |
| 1917S | 27,330,000 | 1.35 | 2.00 | 3.00 | 5.50 | 9.50 | 62.00 | 475 | — | 1,150 |
| 1918 | 26,680,000 | 1.80 | 2.00 | 5.00 | 10.00 | 24.00 | 70.00 | 450 | — | 1,200 |
| 1918D | 22,674,800 | 2.50 | 3.00 | 4.00 | 9.50 | 20.00 | 105 | 600 | — | 35,000 |
| 1918S | 19,300,000 | 2.00 | 2.20 | 3.00 | 8.00 | 14.00 | 90.00 | 675 | — | 7,000 |
| 1919 | 35,740,000 | 1.35 | 1.75 | 2.50 | 5.00 | 9.50 | 37.00 | 320 | — | 700 |
| 1919D | 9,939,000 | 2.50 | 5.00 | 10.00 | 20.00 | 32.00 | 175 | 1,400 | — | 35,000 |
| 1919S | 8,850,000 | 2.50 | 2.75 | 7.00 | 13.00 | 30.00 | 175 | 1,000 | — | 12,500 |
| 1920 | 59,030,000 | 1.35 | 1.60 | 2.00 | 3.50 | 6.50 | 27.50 | 240 | — | 550 |
| 1920D | 19,171,000 | 1.75 | 2.50 | 3.50 | 6.50 | 16.00 | 110 | 750 | — | 4,200 |
| 1920S | 13,820,000 | 1.75 | 2.50 | 3.50 | 7.00 | 15.00 | 110 | 1,300 | — | 9,000 |
| 1921 | 1,230,000 | 29.00 | 45.00 | 78.00 | 170 | 450 | 1,000 | 3,000 | — | 3,750 |
| 1921D | 1,080,000 | 41.00 | 80.00 | 120 | 235 | 500 | 1,100 | 2,800 | — | 5,200 |
| 1923 | 50,130,000 | 1.20 | 1.60 | 2.00 | 3.50 | 6.00 | 27.50 | 110 | — | 295 |
| 1923S | 6,440,000 | 1.75 | 2.50 | 6.50 | 12.00 | 53.00 | 160 | 1,200 | — | 6,750 |
| 1924 | 24,010,000 | 1.35 | 1.65 | 2.50 | 4.25 | 12.00 | 42.00 | 175 | — | 520 |
| 1924D | 6,810,000 | 2.00 | 3.50 | 5.50 | 13.00 | 42.00 | 160 | 1,000 | — | 1,400 |
| 1924S | 7,120,000 | 1.65 | 2.75 | 3.50 | 8.00 | 42.00 | 170 | 1,100 | — | 14,000 |
| 1925 | 25,610,000 | 1.15 | 1.50 | 2.00 | 4.00 | 7.50 | 28.00 | 195 | — | 1,000 |
| 1925D | 5,117,000 | 3.50 | 4.00 | 11.00 | 36.00 | 100.00 | 350 | 1,700 | — | 3,500 |
| 1925S | 5,850,000 | 1.75 | 2.25 | 5.75 | 11.50 | 58.00 | 175 | 1,400 | — | 5,000 |
| 1926 | 32,160,000 | 1.00 | 1.50 | 1.70 | 2.75 | 4.50 | 25.00 | 240 | — | 600 |
| 1926D | 6,828,000 | 2.25 | 3.50 | 4.25 | 8.00 | 22.50 | 110 | 550 | — | 2,850 |
| 1926S | 1,520,000 | 5.75 | 7.50 | 20.00 | 45.00 | 200 | 870 | 3,000 | — | 6,500 |
| 1927 | 28,080,000 | 1.00 | 1.50 | 1.75 | 3.50 | 4.50 | 26.00 | 130 | — | 400 |
| 1927D | 4,812,000 | 2.00 | 4.50 | 6.00 | 18.00 | 60.00 | 175 | 1,200 | — | 8,500 |
| 1927S | 4,770,000 | 1.35 | 3.50 | 4.25 | 7.75 | 22.00 | 280 | 1,400 | — | 7,000 |

## 1916-D Dime
### Grade F-12

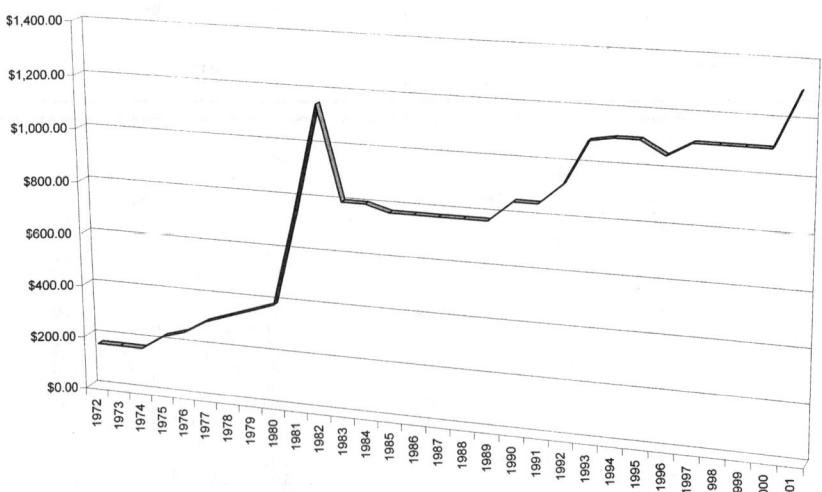

Retail Price

| Date | Mintage | G-4 | VG-8 | F-12 | VF-20 | XF-40 | MS-60 | MS-65 | Prf-65 | -65FSB |
|------|---------|-----|------|------|-------|-------|-------|-------|--------|--------|
| 1928 | 19,480,000 | 1.00 | 1.50 | 1.75 | 3.50 | 4.00 | 27.50 | 110 | — | 350 |
| 1928D | 4,161,000 | 2.75 | 3.25 | 8.00 | 17.00 | 41.00 | 170 | 900 | — | 3,000 |
| 1928S | 7,400,000 | 1.35 | 1.75 | 2.50 | 5.50 | 15.50 | 110 | 425 | — | 2,000 |
| 1929 | 25,970,000 | 1.25 | 1.50 | 2.00 | 2.75 | 4.00 | 20.00 | 60.00 | — | 265 |
| 1929D | 5,034,000 | 1.50 | 3.00 | 3.50 | 6.00 | 14.50 | 25.00 | 70.00 | — | 225 |
| 1929S | 4,730,000 | 1.35 | 1.60 | 2.00 | 4.00 | 7.00 | 32.50 | 120 | — | 600 |
| 1930 | 6,770,000 | 1.35 | 1.50 | 2.00 | 3.50 | 7.00 | 26.00 | 115 | — | 600 |
| 1930S | 1,843,000 | 2.50 | 3.50 | 4.50 | 5.50 | 13.50 | 70.00 | 175 | — | 600 |
| 1931 | 3,150,000 | 2.00 | 2.50 | 3.00 | 4.25 | 8.50 | 35.00 | 135 | — | 900 |
| 1931D | 1,260,000 | 5.00 | 7.00 | 9.00 | 15.00 | 27.50 | 84.00 | 210 | — | 400 |
| 1931S | 1,800,000 | 2.00 | 2.50 | 3.50 | 6.00 | 11.00 | 84.00 | 210 | — | 2,000 |
| 1934 | 24,080,000 | 1.00 | 1.45 | 1.75 | 3.00 | 5.00 | 13.00 | 36.00 | — | 150 |
| 1934D | 6,772,000 | 1.60 | 2.10 | 2.75 | 4.00 | 8.00 | 45.00 | 72.00 | — | 375 |
| 1935 | 58,830,000 | 0.80 | 1.00 | 1.50 | 2.15 | 4.25 | 8.00 | 30.00 | — | 75.00 |
| 1935D | 10,477,000 | 1.25 | 1.75 | 2.50 | 3.75 | 7.50 | 35.00 | 72.00 | — | 600 |
| 1935S | 15,840,000 | 1.25 | 1.50 | 1.75 | 3.00 | 5.50 | 24.00 | 31.50 | — | 550 |
| 1936 | 87,504,130 | 0.80 | 1.00 | 1.50 | 2.25 | 3.50 | 8.00 | 25.00 | — | 90.00 |
| 1936D | 16,132,000 | 1.00 | 1.25 | 1.50 | 3.00 | 6.50 | 26.00 | 42.00 | — | 325 |
| 1936S | 9,210,000 | 1.00 | 1.25 | 1.50 | 2.50 | 3.00 | 20.00 | 28.00 | — | 85.00 |
| 1937 | 56,865,756 | 0.80 | 1.00 | 1.50 | 2.00 | 3.25 | 8.00 | 23.00 | — | 45.00 |
| 1937D | 14,146,000 | 1.00 | 1.25 | 1.50 | 3.00 | 5.50 | 21.00 | 43.00 | — | 120 |
| 1937S | 9,740,000 | 1.00 | 1.25 | 1.50 | 3.00 | 5.50 | 24.00 | 34.00 | — | 195 |
| 1938 | 22,198,728 | 0.80 | 1.00 | 1.50 | 2.25 | 3.50 | 13.00 | 23.00 | — | 80.00 |
| 1938D | 5,537,000 | 1.50 | 1.75 | 2.00 | 3.50 | 6.00 | 16.00 | 26.00 | — | 65.00 |
| 1938S | 8,090,000 | 1.35 | 1.55 | 1.75 | 2.35 | 3.75 | 20.00 | 26.00 | — | 140 |
| 1939 | 67,749,321 | 0.80 | 1.00 | 1.50 | 2.00 | 3.25 | 8.50 | 25.00 | — | 160 |
| 1939D | 24,394,000 | 1.00 | 1.25 | 1.50 | 2.00 | 3.50 | 7.50 | 23.00 | — | 45.00 |
| 1939S | 10,540,000 | 1.25 | 1.50 | 2.00 | 2.50 | 4.25 | 21.00 | 35.00 | — | 750 |
| 1940 | 65,361,827 | 0.60 | 0.70 | 0.90 | 1.10 | 2.50 | 5.00 | 27.00 | — | 55.00 |
| 1940D | 21,198,000 | 0.60 | 0.70 | 0.90 | 1.10 | 1.50 | 7.00 | 30.00 | — | 55.00 |
| 1940S | 21,560,000 | 0.60 | 0.70 | 0.90 | 1.10 | 1.50 | 7.00 | 30.00 | — | 110 |
| 1941 | 175,106,557 | 0.60 | 0.70 | 0.90 | 1.10 | 1.50 | 4.00 | 30.00 | — | 45.00 |
| 1941D | 45,634,000 | 0.60 | 0.70 | 0.90 | 1.10 | 1.50 | 6.00 | 23.00 | — | 40.00 |
| 1941S | 43,090,000 | 0.60 | 0.70 | 0.90 | 1.10 | 1.50 | 7.00 | 30.00 | — | 50.00 |
| 1942 | 205,432,329 | 0.60 | 0.70 | 0.90 | 1.10 | 1.50 | 4.00 | 30.00 | — | 50.00 |
| 1942/41 | Inc. above | 275 | 300 | 360 | 370 | 450 | 1,600 | 7,800 | — | 25,000 |
| 1942D | 60,740,000 | 0.60 | 0.70 | 0.90 | 1.10 | 1.50 | 6.00 | 24.00 | — | 40.00 |
| 1942/41D | Inc. above | 285 | 300 | 375 | 400 | 550 | 1,900 | 5,400 | — | 17,500 |
| 1942S | 49,300,000 | 0.60 | 0.70 | 0.90 | 1.10 | 1.50 | 8.00 | 24.00 | — | 140 |
| 1943 | 191,710,000 | 0.60 | 0.70 | 0.90 | 1.10 | 1.50 | 4.00 | 30.00 | — | 60.00 |
| 1943D | 71,949,000 | 0.60 | 0.70 | 0.90 | 1.10 | 1.50 | 5.50 | 27.50 | — | 40.00 |
| 1943S | 60,400,000 | 0.60 | 0.70 | 0.90 | 1.10 | 1.50 | 7.00 | 25.00 | — | 85.00 |
| 1944 | 231,410,000 | 0.60 | 0.70 | 0.90 | 1.10 | 1.50 | 4.00 | 23.00 | — | 95.00 |
| 1944D | 62,224,000 | 0.60 | 0.70 | 0.90 | 1.10 | 1.50 | 5.50 | 23.00 | — | 43.50 |
| 1944S | 49,490,000 | 0.60 | 0.70 | 0.90 | 1.10 | 1.50 | 6.50 | 30.00 | — | 50.00 |
| 1945 | 159,130,000 | 0.60 | 0.70 | 0.90 | 1.10 | 1.50 | 4.00 | 23.00 | — | 7,000 |
| 1945D | 40,245,000 | 0.60 | 0.70 | 0.90 | 1.10 | 1.50 | 4.50 | 23.00 | — | 45.00 |
| 1945S | 41,920,000 | 0.60 | 0.70 | 0.90 | 1.10 | 1.50 | 6.50 | 29.00 | — | 140 |
| 1945S micro | Inc. above | 1.00 | 1.25 | 1.50 | 3.00 | 4.25 | 23.00 | 84.00 | — | 700 |

## Roosevelt.

Reverse mint mark
1946-64

Obverse mint mark
1968-present

**Designer:** John R. Sinnock. **Diameter:** 17.9 mm. **Weight:** 2.5000 g. **Composition:** 0.9000 Silver, 0.0724 oz. ASW.

| Date | Mintage | G-4 | VG-8 | F-12 | VF-20 | XF-40 | AU-50 | MS-60 | MS-65 | Prf-65 |
|------|---------|-----|------|------|-------|-------|-------|-------|-------|--------|
| 1946 | 225,250,000 | — | — | — | 0.50 | 0.65 | 0.95 | 1.05 | 4.50 | — |
| 1946D | 61,043,500 | — | — | — | 0.50 | 0.65 | 1.10 | 1.25 | 7.00 | — |
| 1946S | 27,900,000 | — | — | — | 0.50 | 0.65 | 0.90 | 1.50 | 10.00 | — |
| 1947 | 121,520,000 | — | — | — | 0.50 | 0.65 | 0.95 | 1.00 | 4.75 | — |
| 1947D | 46,835,000 | — | — | — | 0.50 | 0.95 | 1.50 | 2.25 | 10.00 | — |
| 1947S | 34,840,000 | — | — | — | 0.50 | 0.95 | 1.25 | 1.75 | 12.50 | — |
| 1948 | 74,950,000 | — | — | — | 0.50 | 0.95 | 1.50 | 3.00 | 14.00 | 0.50 |
| 1948D | 52,841,000 | — | — | — | 0.50 | 1.20 | 2.00 | 2.50 | 10.00 | — |
| 1948S | 35,520,000 | — | — | — | 0.50 | 0.95 | 1.10 | 2.00 | 9.00 | — |
| 1949 | 30,940,000 | — | — | — | 1.00 | 1.50 | 4.00 | 9.00 | 25.00 | — |
| 1949D | 26,034,000 | — | — | 0.60 | 0.80 | 1.25 | 2.00 | 3.50 | 15.00 | — |
| 1949S | 13,510,000 | — | 1.00 | 1.25 | 1.50 | 2.75 | 6.00 | 12.00 | 40.00 | — |
| 1950 | 50,181,500 | — | — | — | 0.50 | 0.95 | 1.35 | 2.00 | 10.00 | 37.00 |
| 1950D | 46,803,000 | — | — | — | 0.50 | 0.65 | 1.60 | 2.75 | 8.00 | — |
| 1950S | 20,440,000 | — | 0.85 | 1.00 | 1.10 | 1.25 | 6.00 | 9.00 | 25.00 | — |
| 1951 | 102,937,602 | — | — | — | 0.50 | 0.85 | 1.00 | 1.25 | 3.50 | 26.00 |

| Date | Mintage | G-4 | VG-8 | F-12 | VF-20 | XF-40 | AU-50 | MS-60 | MS-65 | Prf-65 |
|------|---------|-----|------|------|-------|-------|-------|-------|-------|--------|
| 1951D | 56,529,000 | — | — | — | 0.50 | 0.65 | 0.95 | 1.40 | 4.00 | — |
| 1951S | 31,630,000 | — | — | — | 0.75 | 1.05 | 3.25 | 5.00 | 24.00 | — |
| 1952 | 99,122,073 | — | — | — | 0.50 | 0.90 | 1.15 | 1.65 | 4.00 | 29.00 |
| 1952D | 122,100,000 | — | — | — | 0.50 | 0.65 | 0.95 | 1.00 | 4.00 | — |
| 1952S | 44,419,500 | — | — | — | 0.75 | 1.05 | 1.50 | 3.00 | 11.00 | — |
| 1953 | 53,618,920 | — | — | — | 0.50 | 0.65 | 1.00 | 1.10 | 4.00 | 24.00 |
| 1953D | 136,433,000 | — | — | — | 0.50 | 0.65 | 0.95 | 1.00 | 3.50 | — |
| 1953S | 39,180,000 | — | — | — | 0.50 | 0.65 | 0.75 | 1.00 | 3.25 | — |
| 1954 | 114,243,503 | — | — | — | 0.50 | 0.65 | 0.75 | 1.00 | 3.25 | 11.00 |
| 1954D | 106,397,000 | — | — | — | 0.50 | 0.65 | 0.75 | 1.00 | 3.25 | — |
| 1954S | 22,860,000 | — | — | — | 0.50 | 0.65 | 0.80 | 0.90 | 3.25 | — |
| 1955 | 12,828,381 | — | — | — | 0.70 | 0.80 | 0.85 | 0.95 | 5.00 | 15.00 |
| 1955D | 13,959,000 | — | — | — | 0.65 | 0.75 | 0.80 | 0.90 | 3.50 | — |
| 1955S | 18,510,000 | — | — | — | 0.65 | 0.75 | 0.80 | 0.90 | 4.50 | — |
| 1956 | 109,309,384 | — | — | — | 0.50 | 0.50 | 0.60 | 0.90 | 2.50 | 2.50 |
| 1956D | 108,015,100 | — | — | — | 0.50 | 0.50 | 0.60 | 0.90 | 2.50 | — |
| 1957 | 161,407,952 | — | — | — | 0.50 | 0.50 | 0.60 | 0.90 | 2.60 | 2.00 |
| 1957D | 113,354,330 | — | — | — | 0.50 | 0.50 | 0.60 | 0.90 | 3.50 | — |
| 1958 | 32,785,652 | — | — | — | 0.50 | 0.50 | 0.60 | 0.90 | 3.80 | 2.00 |
| 1958D | 136,564,600 | — | — | — | 0.50 | 0.50 | 0.60 | 0.90 | 3.50 | — |
| 1959 | 86,929,291 | — | — | — | 0.50 | 0.50 | 0.60 | 0.90 | 2.50 | 2.00 |
| 1959D | 164,919,790 | — | — | — | 0.50 | 0.50 | 0.60 | 0.90 | 3.00 | — |
| 1960 | 72,081,602 | — | — | — | 0.50 | 0.50 | 0.60 | 0.90 | 2.50 | 2.00 |
| 1960D | 200,160,400 | — | — | — | 0.50 | 0.50 | 0.60 | 0.90 | 2.50 | — |
| 1961 | 96,758,244 | — | — | — | 0.50 | 0.50 | 0.60 | 0.90 | 2.35 | 2.00 |
| 1961D | 209,146,550 | — | — | — | 0.50 | 0.50 | 0.60 | 0.90 | 2.35 | — |
| 1962 | 75,668,019 | — | — | — | 0.50 | 0.50 | 0.60 | 0.90 | 2.35 | 2.00 |
| 1962D | 334,948,380 | — | — | — | 0.50 | 0.50 | 0.60 | 0.90 | 2.75 | — |
| 1963 | 126,725,645 | — | — | — | 0.50 | 0.50 | 0.60 | 0.90 | 2.35 | 2.00 |
| 1963D | 421,476,530 | — | — | — | 0.50 | 0.50 | 0.60 | 0.90 | 2.35 | — |
| 1964 | 933,310,762 | — | — | — | 0.50 | 0.50 | 0.60 | 0.90 | 2.35 | 2.00 |
| 1964D | 1,357,517,180 | — | — | — | 0.50 | 0.50 | 0.60 | 0.90 | 2.35 | — |

## Roosevelt.

No 'P' mint mark

**Designer:** John R. Sinnock. **Diameter:** 17.9 mm. **Weight:** 2.2700 g. **Composition:** Copper-nickel Clad Copper. **Notes:** The 1979-S and 1981-S Type II proofs have clearer mint marks than the Type I proofs of those years. On the 1982 no-mint-mark variety, the mint mark was inadvertently left off.

| Date | Mintage | MS-65 | Prf-65 | Date | Mintage | MS-65 | Prf-65 |
|------|---------|-------|--------|------|---------|-------|--------|
| 1965 | 1,652,140,570 | 0.75 | — | 1977S | (3,251,152) | — | 1.25 |
| 1966 | 1,382,734,540 | 0.65 | — | 1978 | 663,980,000 | 0.50 | — |
| 1967 | 2,244,007,320 | 0.65 | — | 1978D | 282,847,540 | 0.50 | — |
| 1968 | 424,470,000 | 0.60 | — | 1978S | (3,127,781) | — | 1.25 |
| 1968D | 480,748,280 | 0.60 | — | 1979 | 315,440,000 | 0.50 | — |
| 1968S | (3,041,506) | — | 0.65 | 1979D | 390,921,184 | 0.50 | — |
| 1969 | 145,790,000 | 0.75 | — | 1979 type I | — | — | 1.00 |
| 1969D | 563,323,870 | 0.75 | — | 1979S type I | — | — | 1.00 |
| 1969S | (2,934,631) | — | 0.65 | 1979S type II | — | — | 1.25 |
| 1970 | 345,570,000 | 0.60 | — | 1980P | 735,170,000 | 0.50 | — |
| 1970D | 754,942,100 | 0.60 | — | 1980D | 719,354,321 | 0.50 | — |
| 1970S | (2,632,810) | — | 0.65 | 1980S | (3,554,806) | — | 1.00 |
| 1971 | 162,690,000 | 0.75 | — | 1981P | 676,650,000 | 0.50 | — |
| 1971D | 377,914,240 | 0.60 | — | 1981D | 712,284,143 | 0.50 | — |
| 1971S | (3,220,733) | — | 0.80 | 1981S type I | — | — | 1.00 |
| 1972 | 431,540,000 | 0.60 | — | 1981S type II | — | — | 4.00 |
| 1972D | 330,290,000 | 0.60 | — | 1982P | 519,475,000 | 1.50 | — |
| 1972S | (3,260,996) | — | 1.00 | 1982 no mint mark | | 200 | — |
| 1973 | 315,670,000 | 0.60 | — | 1982D | 542,713,584 | 0.60 | — |
| 1973D | 455,032,426 | 0.50 | — | 1982S | (3,857,479) | — | 1.10 |
| 1973S | (2,760,339) | — | 1.00 | 1983P | 647,025,000 | 0.75 | — |
| 1974 | 470,248,000 | 0.50 | — | 1983D | 730,129,224 | 0.70 | — |
| 1974D | 571,083,000 | 0.50 | — | 1983S | (3,279,126) | — | 1.10 |
| 1974S | (2,612,568) | — | 1.50 | 1984P | 856,669,000 | 0.50 | — |
| 1975 | 585,673,900 | 0.60 | — | 1984D | 704,803,976 | 0.60 | — |
| 1975D | 313,705,300 | 0.50 | — | 1984S | (3,065,110) | — | 1.60 |
| 1975S | (2,845,450) | — | 1.25 | 1985P | 705,200,962 | 0.60 | — |
| 1976 | 568,760,000 | 0.60 | — | 1985D | 587,979,970 | 0.55 | — |
| 1976D | 695,222,774 | 0.60 | — | 1985S | (3,362,821) | — | 1.10 |
| 1976S | (4,149,730) | — | 1.00 | 1986P | 682,649,693 | 0.70 | — |
| 1977 | 796,930,000 | 0.50 | — | 1986D | 473,326,970 | 0.75 | — |
| 1977D | 376,607,228 | 0.50 | — | 1986S | (3,010,497) | — | 2.00 |

| Date | Mintage | MS-65 | Prf-65 | Date | Mintage | MS-65 | Prf-65 |
|------|---------|-------|--------|------|---------|-------|--------|
| 1987P | 762,709,481 | 0.50 | — | 1994D | 1,303,268,110 | 0.50 | — |
| 1987D | 653,203,402 | 0.50 | — | 1994S | (2,484,594) | — | 2.60 |
| 1987S | (4,227,728) | — | 1.25 | 1995P | 1,125,500,000 | 0.50 | — |
| 1988P | 1,030,550,000 | 0.50 | — | 1995D | 1,274,890,000 | 0.50 | — |
| 1988D | 962,385,488 | 0.50 | — | 1995S | (2,010,384) | — | 2.60 |
| 1988S | (3,262,948) | — | 1.50 | 1996P | 1,421,163,000 | 0.50 | — |
| 1989P | 1,298,400,000 | 0.50 | — | 1996D | 1,400,300,000 | 0.50 | — |
| 1989D | 896,535,597 | 0.50 | — | 1996W | 1,457,949 | 8.00 | — |
| 1989S | (3,220,194) | — | 1.45 | 1996S | — | — | 2.50 |
| 1990P | 1,034,340,000 | 0.50 | — | 1997P | 991,640,000 | 0.50 | — |
| 1990D | 839,995,824 | 0.50 | — | 1997D | 979,810,000 | 0.50 | — |
| 1990S | (3,299,559) | — | 2.75 | 1997S | (1,975,000) | — | 3.50 |
| 1991P | 927,220,000 | 0.50 | — | 1998P | 1,163,000,000 | 0.50 | — |
| 1991D | 601,241,114 | 0.50 | — | 1998D | 1,172,250,000 | 0.50 | — |
| 1991S | (2,867,787) | — | 3.25 | 1999P | — | 0.50 | — |
| 1992P | 593,500,000 | 0.50 | — | 1999D | — | 0.50 | — |
| 1992D | 616,273,932 | 0.50 | — | 2000P | — | 0.50 | — |
| 1992S | (2,858,981) | — | 3.40 | 2000D | — | 0.50 | — |
| 1993P | 766,180,000 | 0.50 | — | 2000S | — | — | 2.00 |
| 1993D | 750,110,166 | 0.50 | — | 2001P | — | — | — |
| 1993S | (2,633,439) | — | 2.85 | 2001D | — | — | — |
| 1994P | 1,189,000,000 | 0.50 | — | 2001S | — | — | — |

## Roosevelt.

**Composition:** Silver.

| Date | Mintage | MS-65 | Prf-65 | Date | Mintage | MS-65 | Prf-65 |
|------|---------|-------|--------|------|---------|-------|--------|
| 1992S | 1,317,579 | — | 3.25 | 1997S | — | — | 3.50 |
| 1993S | (761,353) | — | 4.00 | 1998S | — | — | 3.50 |
| 1994S | — | — | 3.75 | 1999S | — | — | 3.00 |
| 1995S | — | — | 3.75 | 2000S | — | — | — |
| 1996S | — | — | 3.50 | 2001S | — | — | — |

# 20 CENTS

## Seated Liberty.

**Designer:** William Barber. **Diameter:** 22 mm. **Weight:** 5.0000 g. **Composition:** 0.9000 Silver, 0.1447 oz. ASW.

| Date | Mintage | G-4 | VG-8 | F-12 | VF-20 | XF-40 | AU-50 | MS-60 | MS-65 | Prf-65 |
|------|---------|-----|------|------|-------|-------|-------|-------|-------|--------|
| 1875 | 39,700 | 85.00 | 90.00 | 125 | 160 | 225 | 400 | 575 | 5,500 | 9,000 |
| 1875S | 1,155,000 | 52.00 | 59.00 | 70.00 | 110 | 150 | 245 | 450 | 4,900 | — |
| 1875CC | 133,290 | 90.00 | 100.00 | 140 | 175 | 250 | 475 | 700 | 9,000 | — |
| 1876 | 15,900 | 100.00 | 120 | 160 | 225 | 320 | 440 | 750 | 5,200 | 8,900 |
| 1876CC | 10,000 | — | — | — | — | — | — | — | — | — |
| **Note:** 1876CC, Eliasberg Sale, April 1997, MS-65, $148,500. Heritage 1999 ANA, MS-63, $86,500. |
| 1877 proof only | 510 | — | — | 1,400 | 1,650 | 1,900 | 2,300 | — | — | 9,500 |
| 1878 proof only | 600 | — | — | 1,100 | 1,250 | 1,450 | 1,600 | — | — | 9,000 |

## 1876 20-Cent
### Grade F-12

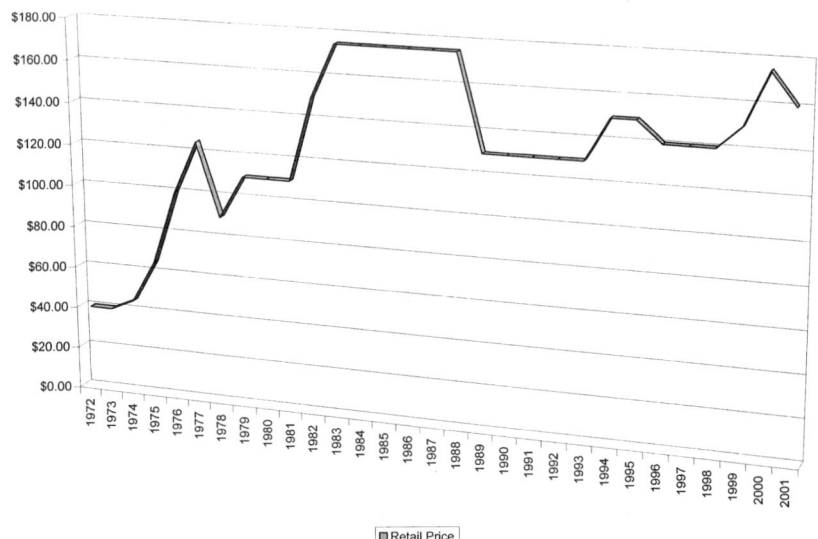

☐ Retail Price

# QUARTER

## Draped bust. Small eagle.

**Designer:** Robert Scot. **Diameter:** 27.5 mm. **Weight:** 6.7400 g. **Composition:** 0.8920 Silver, 0.1935 oz. ASW.

| Date | Mintage | G-4 | VG-8 | F-12 | VF-20 | XF-40 | AU-50 | MS-60 | MS-65 |
|------|---------|-----|------|------|-------|-------|-------|-------|-------|
| 1796 | 6,146 | 3,950 | 5,500 | 8,250 | 11,500 | 14,500 | 18,500 | 26,000 | 125,000 |

## Draped bust. Heraldic eagle.

**Designer:** Robert Scot. **Diameter:** 27.5 mm. **Weight:** 6.7400 g. **Composition:** 0.8920 Silver, .1935 oz. ASW.

| Date | Mintage | G-4 | VG-8 | F-12 | VF-20 | XF-40 | AU-50 | MS-60 | MS-65 |
|------|---------|-----|------|------|-------|-------|-------|-------|-------|
| 1804 | 6,738 | 1,600 | 1,850 | 2,600 | 3,500 | 8,500 | 16,500 | 40,000 | — |
| 1805 | 121,394 | 175 | 250 | 385 | 750 | 1,600 | 2,750 | 4,750 | 55,000 |
| 1806 | 206,124 | 180 | 275 | 375 | 725 | 1,450 | 2,250 | 4,450 | 46,500 |
| 1806/5 | Inc. above | 195 | 315 | 450 | 850 | 2,400 | 3,450 | 5,450 | 60,000 |
| 1807 | 220,643 | 170 | 250 | 385 | 675 | 1,500 | 2,900 | 4,450 | 48,500 |

## 1804 Quarter
### Grade XF-40

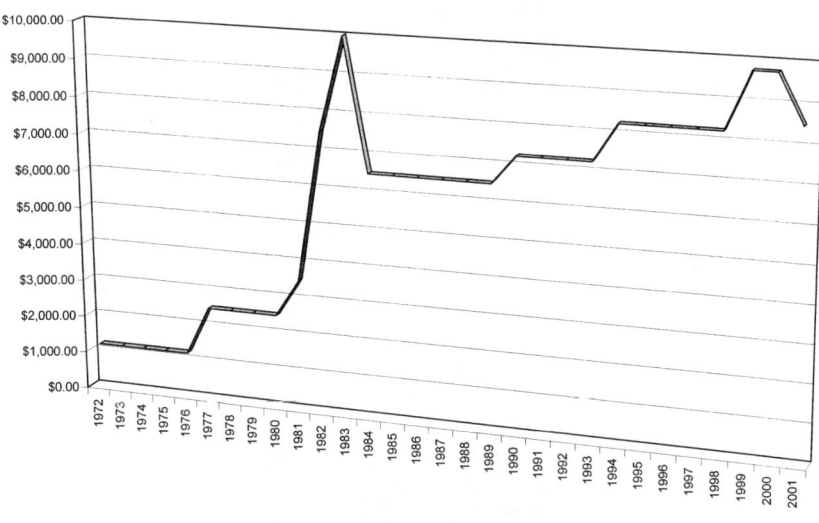

☐ Retail Price

# Liberty cap. "E Pluribus Unum" above eagle.

**Designer:** John Reich. **Diameter:** 27 mm. **Weight:** 6.7400 g. **Composition:** 0.8920 Silver, 0.1935 oz. ASW.
**Notes:** Varieties of the 1819 strikes are distinguished by the size of the 9 in the date. Varieties of the 1820 strikes are distinguished by the size of the 0 in the date. One 1822 variety and one 1828 variety have "25" engraved over "50" in the denomination. The 1827 restrikes were produced privately using dies sold as scrap by the U.S. Mint.

| Date | Mintage | G-4 | VG-8 | F-12 | VF-20 | XF-40 | AU-50 | MS-60 | MS-65 |
|---|---|---|---|---|---|---|---|---|---|
| 1815 | 89,235 | 50.00 | 65.00 | 100.00 | 275 | 700 | 1,200 | 2,000 | 25,000 |
| 1818 | 361,174 | 50.00 | 65.00 | 110 | 285 | 675 | 1,200 | 2,000 | 16,000 |
| 1818/15 | Inc. above | 55.00 | 70.00 | 110 | 350 | 750 | 1,350 | 2,250 | 20,000 |
| 1819 small 9 | 144,000 | 55.00 | 65.00 | 110 | 265 | 650 | 1,200 | 2,000 | 22,000 |
| 1819 large 9 | Inc. above | 55.00 | 65.00 | 110 | 265 | 650 | 1,200 | 2,000 | 22,000 |
| 1820 small O | 127,444 | 60.00 | 75.00 | 110 | 265 | 700 | 1,250 | 3,000 | 28,000 |
| 1820 large O | Inc. above | 50.00 | 65.00 | 100.00 | 235 | 600 | 1,100 | 1,900 | 25,000 |
| 1821 | 216,851 | 50.00 | 60.00 | 100.00 | 275 | 675 | 1,250 | 1,850 | 16,500 |
| 1822 | 64,080 | 65.00 | 90.00 | 140 | 375 | 775 | 1,500 | 2,850 | — |
| 1822 25/50C. | Inc. above | 1,250 | 2,750 | 4,250 | 5,750 | 8,900 | 17,500 | — | — |
| 1823/22 | 17,800 | 7,500 | 10,000 | 17,500 | 27,500 | 36,000 | 50,000 | — | — |
| **Note:** 1823/22, Superior, Aug. 1990, Proof, $62,500. | | | | | | | | | |
| 1824/2 mintage unrecorded | | 80.00 | 130 | 200 | 550 | 1,550 | 2,150 | 5,500 | — |
| 1825/22 | 168,000 | 70.00 | 100.00 | 145 | 350 | 850 | 1,500 | 2,300 | 22,500 |
| 1825/23 | Inc. above | 50.00 | 65.00 | 100.00 | 265 | 650 | 1,200 | 1,850 | 16,500 |
| 1825/24 | Inc. above | 50.00 | 65.00 | 100.00 | 265 | 650 | 1,200 | 1,850 | 16,500 |
| 1827 original | 4,000 | — | — | — | — | — | — | — | — |
| **Note:** Eliasberg, April 1997, VF-20, $39,600. | | | | | | | | | |
| 1827 restrike | Inc. above | — | — | — | — | — | — | — | — |
| **Note:** 1827 restrike, Eliasberg, April 1997, Prf-65, $77,000. | | | | | | | | | |
| 1828 | 102,000 | 50.00 | 65.00 | 95.00 | 275 | 650 | 1,400 | 2,500 | 19,500 |
| 1828 25/50C. | Inc. above | 110 | 265 | 385 | 825 | 1,350 | 2,750 | 6,500 | — |

# Liberty cap. "E Pluribus Unum" removed from above eagle.

**Designer:** William Kneass. **Diameter:** 24.3 mm. **Composition:** 0.8920 Silver. **Notes:** Varieties of the 1831 strikes are distinguished by the size of the lettering on the reverse.

| Date | Mintage | G-4 | VG-8 | F-12 | VF-20 | XF-40 | AU-50 | MS-60 | MS-65 |
|---|---|---|---|---|---|---|---|---|---|
| 1831 small letter | 398,000 | 40.00 | 46.00 | 50.00 | 82.00 | 225 | 600 | 800 | 12,500 |
| 1831 large letter | Inc. above | 40.00 | 46.00 | 50.00 | 82.00 | 225 | 600 | 800 | 12,500 |
| 1832 | 320,000 | 40.00 | 46.00 | 50.00 | 82.00 | 225 | 600 | 800 | 16,000 |
| 1833 | 156,000 | 45.00 | 50.00 | 55.00 | 120 | 260 | 725 | 1,275 | 15,000 |
| 1834 | 286,000 | 40.00 | 46.00 | 50.00 | 82.00 | 225 | 600 | 800 | 12,500 |
| 1835 | 1,952,000 | 40.00 | 46.00 | 50.00 | 82.00 | 225 | 600 | 800 | 12,500 |
| 1836 | 472,000 | 40.00 | 46.00 | 50.00 | 82.00 | 225 | 600 | 800 | — |
| 1837 | 252,400 | 45.00 | 50.00 | 60.00 | 90.00 | 240 | 600 | 800 | 12,500 |
| 1838 | 832,000 | 50.00 | 55.00 | 68.00 | 95.00 | 250 | 625 | 850 | 14,000 |

# Seated Liberty. No drapery.

**Designer:** Christian Gobrecht. **Diameter:** 24.3 mm. **Weight:** 6.6800 g. **Composition:** 0.9000 Silver, 0.1934 oz. ASW.

| Date | Mintage | G-4 | VG-8 | F-12 | VF-20 | XF-40 | AU-50 | MS-60 | MS-65 |
|---|---|---|---|---|---|---|---|---|---|
| 1838 | Inc. above | 18.00 | 25.00 | 35.00 | 65.00 | 300 | 550 | 1,250 | 23,000 |
| 1839 | 491,146 | 20.00 | 28.00 | 35.00 | 65.00 | 275 | 550 | 1,250 | 25,000 |
| 1840O | 425,200 | 14.00 | 25.00 | 45.00 | 110 | 375 | 575 | 1,350 | 30,000 |

# Seated Liberty. Drapery added to Liberty's left elbow.

**Designer:** Christian Gobrecht. **Diameter:** 24.3 mm. **Weight:** 6.6800 g. **Composition:** 0.9000 Silver, 0.1934 oz. ASW. **Notes:** Two varieties for 1842 and 1842-O are distinguished by the size of the numerals in the date. 1852 obverse dies were used to strike the 1853 no-arrows variety, with the 2 being recut to form a 3.

| Date | Mintage | G-4 | VG-8 | F-12 | VF-20 | XF-40 | AU-50 | MS-60 | MS-65 |
|---|---|---|---|---|---|---|---|---|---|
| 1840 | 188,127 | 50.00 | 90.00 | 120 | 175 | 250 | 350 | 950 | 12,000 |
| 1840O | Inc. above | 40.00 | 75.00 | 90.00 | 180 | 275 | 450 | 1,000 | — |
| 1841 | 120,000 | 75.00 | 90.00 | 120 | 185 | 300 | 385 | 750 | 11,000 |
| 1841O | 452,000 | 13.00 | 35.00 | 75.00 | 125 | 200 | 350 | 700 | 10,000 |
| 1842 small date | 88,000 | — | — | — | — | — | — | — | — |
| **Note:** 1842 small date, Eliasberg, April 1997, Prf-63, $66,000. | | | | | | | | | |
| 1842 large date | Inc. above | 75.00 | 110 | 140 | 225 | 300 | 500 | 1,250 | — |
| 1842O small date | 769,000 | 275 | 550 | 700 | 1,250 | 2,750 | — | — | — |
| 1842O large date | Inc. above | 14.00 | 18.00 | 30.00 | 45.00 | 125 | 300 | — | 4,000 |
| 1843 | 645,600 | 14.00 | 18.00 | 27.00 | 32.00 | 55.00 | 150 | 400 | 3,500 |
| 1843O | 968,000 | 18.00 | 28.00 | 42.00 | 100.00 | 275 | 750 | 2,000 | 11,000 |
| 1844 | 421,200 | 14.00 | 18.00 | 30.00 | 36.00 | 60.00 | 160 | 450 | 5,000 |
| 1844O | 740,000 | 13.00 | 24.00 | 37.50 | 60.00 | 115 | 275 | 1,000 | 6,000 |
| 1845 | 922,000 | 14.00 | 18.00 | 27.00 | 32.00 | 50.00 | 150 | 450 | 5,000 |
| 1846 | 510,000 | 17.00 | 23.00 | 36.50 | 50.00 | 75.00 | 160 | 475 | 6,000 |
| 1847 | 734,000 | 14.00 | 18.00 | 27.00 | 32.00 | 50.00 | 150 | 425 | 5,000 |
| 1847O | 368,000 | 22.00 | 35.00 | 50.00 | 110 | 185 | 600 | 1,900 | — |
| 1848 | 146,000 | 25.00 | 36.00 | 70.00 | 145 | 175 | 325 | 1,000 | 10,000 |
| 1849 | 340,000 | 16.00 | 22.00 | 36.00 | 65.00 | 125 | 275 | 750 | 9,000 |

| Date | Mintage | G-4 | VG-8 | F-12 | VF-20 | XF-40 | AU-50 | MS-60 | MS-65 |
|------|---------|-----|------|------|-------|-------|-------|-------|-------|
| 1849O mintage unrecorded | — | 390 | 595 | 975 | 1,500 | 2,750 | 5,000 | 7,500 | — |
| 1850 | 190,800 | 28.00 | 37.50 | 60.00 | 80.00 | 125 | 250 | 800 | — |
| 1850O | 412,000 | 20.00 | 30.00 | 45.00 | 90.00 | 135 | 450 | 1,300 | — |
| 1851 | 160,000 | 35.00 | 50.00 | 80.00 | 125 | 185 | 300 | 850 | 8,500 |
| 1851O | 88,000 | 135 | 265 | 375 | 575 | 1,000 | 2,250 | 4,000 | — |
| 1852 | 177,060 | 37.50 | 47.50 | 85.00 | 145 | 185 | 300 | 500 | 4,800 |
| 1852O | 96,000 | 165 | 240 | 335 | 595 | 1,200 | 3,500 | 8,000 | — |
| 1853 recut date | 44,200 | 300 | 375 | 550 | 650 | 950 | 1,350 | 2,600 | 9,000 |

## Seated Liberty. Arrows at date. Rays around eagle.

**Designer:** Christian Gobrecht. **Diameter:** 24.3 mm. **Weight:** 6.6800 g. **Composition:** 0.9000 Silver, 0.1800 oz. ASW.

| Date | Mintage | G-4 | VG-8 | F-12 | VF-20 | XF-40 | AU-50 | MS-60 | MS-65 | Prf-65 |
|------|---------|-----|------|------|-------|-------|-------|-------|-------|--------|
| 1853 | 15,210,020 | 15.00 | 20.00 | 27.50 | 45.00 | 150 | 275 | 950 | 19,000 | 90,000 |
| 1853/4 | Inc. above | 40.00 | 65.00 | 100.00 | 200 | 275 | 750 | 1,750 | — | — |
| 1853O | 1,332,000 | 18.00 | 35.00 | 50.00 | 100.00 | 275 | 1,100 | 2,750 | — | — |

## Seated Liberty. Rays around eagle removed.

**Designer:** Christian Gobrecht. **Diameter:** 24.3 mm. **Weight:** 6.6800 g. **Composition:** 0.9000 Silver, 0.1800 oz. ASW. **Notes:** The 1854-O "huge O" variety has an oversized mint mark.

| Date | Mintage | G-4 | VG-8 | F-12 | VF-20 | XF-40 | AU-50 | MS-60 | MS-65 | Prf-65 |
|------|---------|-----|------|------|-------|-------|-------|-------|-------|--------|
| 1854 | 12,380,000 | 15.00 | 20.00 | 27.50 | 35.00 | 75.00 | 225 | 440 | 7,500 | 17,500 |
| 1854O | 1,484,000 | 17.00 | 24.00 | 35.00 | 60.00 | 125 | 300 | 1,750 | — | — |
| 1854O huge O | Inc. above | 150 | 150 | 225 | 285 | 550 | 1,000 | 3,000 | — | — |
| 1855 | 2,857,000 | 15.00 | 20.00 | 27.50 | 35.00 | 75.00 | 225 | 440 | 8,500 | 18,500 |
| 1855O | 176,000 | 40.00 | 60.00 | 100.00 | 240 | 400 | 950 | 2,750 | — | — |
| 1855S | 396,400 | 40.00 | 60.00 | 80.00 | 225 | 500 | 1,250 | 2,000 | — | — |

## Seated Liberty. Arrows at date removed.

**Designer:** Christian Gobrecht. **Diameter:** 24.3 mm. **Weight:** 6.6800 g. **Composition:** 0.9000 Silver, 0.1800 oz. ASW.

| Date | Mintage | G-4 | VG-8 | F-12 | VF-20 | XF-40 | AU-50 | MS-60 | MS-65 | Prf-65 |
|------|---------|-----|------|------|-------|-------|-------|-------|-------|--------|
| 1856 | 7,264,000 | 15.00 | 20.00 | 27.50 | 35.00 | 60.00 | 145 | 290 | 4,250 | 15,000 |
| 1856O | 968,000 | 17.00 | 24.00 | 30.00 | 50.00 | 90.00 | 250 | 1,000 | 8,500 | — |
| 1856S | 286,000 | 45.00 | 65.00 | 110 | 250 | 375 | 900 | 2,200 | — | — |
| 1856S/S | Inc. above | 60.00 | 80.00 | 175 | 350 | 550 | 1,250 | 2,750 | — | — |
| 1857 | 9,644,000 | 15.00 | 20.00 | 27.50 | 35.00 | 60.00 | 145 | 290 | 4,000 | 9,500 |
| 1857O | 1,180,000 | 15.00 | 20.00 | 29.00 | 40.00 | 80.00 | 275 | 975 | — | — |
| 1857S | 82,000 | 70.00 | 125 | 225 | 375 | 600 | 950 | 2,750 | — | — |
| 1858 | 7,368,000 | 15.00 | 20.00 | 27.50 | 35.00 | 60.00 | 160 | 300 | 4,000 | 6,500 |
| 1858O | 520,000 | 18.00 | 25.00 | 35.00 | 55.00 | 110 | 360 | 1,350 | — | — |
| 1858S | 121,000 | 50.00 | 85.00 | 150 | 250 | 450 | 1,250 | 5,500 | — | — |
| 1859 | 1,344,000 | 17.00 | 24.00 | 30.00 | 40.00 | 75.00 | 175 | 375 | 6,000 | 7,000 |
| 1859O | 260,000 | 22.00 | 28.00 | 40.00 | 65.00 | 200 | 400 | 1,000 | 15,000 | — |
| 1859S | 80,000 | 90.00 | 125 | 195 | 300 | 725 | 2,000 | 4,000 | — | — |

## 1856-S Quarter
### Grade F-12

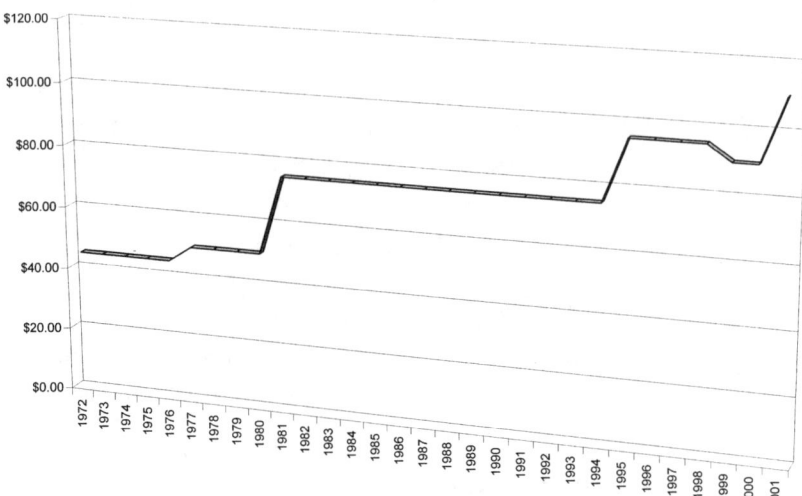

□ Retail Price

| Date | Mintage | G-4 | VG-8 | F-12 | VF-20 | XF-40 | AU-50 | MS-60 | MS-65 | Prf-65 |
|------|---------|-----|------|------|-------|-------|-------|-------|-------|--------|
| 1860 | 805,400 | 18.00 | 22.00 | 28.00 | 33.00 | 60.00 | 160 | 500 | — | 5,250 |
| 1860O | 388,000 | 18.00 | 22.00 | 33.00 | 50.00 | 80.00 | 275 | 1,200 | — | — |
| 1860S | 56,000 | 165 | 285 | 425 | 750 | 1,750 | 5,000 | 10,000 | — | — |
| 1861 | 4,854,600 | 16.00 | 19.00 | 27.00 | 32.00 | 55.00 | 150 | 290 | 4,200 | 5,500 |
| 1861S | 96,000 | 60.00 | 80.00 | 190 | 310 | 950 | 2,750 | 5,250 | — | — |
| 1862 | 932,550 | 18.00 | 22.00 | 33.00 | 40.00 | 65.00 | 165 | 300 | 4,350 | 5,350 |
| 1862S | 67,000 | 80.00 | 125 | 165 | 275 | 500 | 1,600 | 2,750 | — | — |
| 1863 | 192,060 | 30.00 | 45.00 | 60.00 | 110 | 195 | 300 | 650 | 4,350 | 5,500 |
| 1864 | 94,070 | 65.00 | 75.00 | 115 | 150 | 250 | 400 | 650 | 5,000 | 5,500 |
| 1864S | 20,000 | 275 | 450 | 600 | 1,100 | 2,200 | 3,750 | 7,000 | — | — |
| 1865 | 59,300 | 75.00 | 90.00 | 115 | 140 | 250 | 375 | 875 | 9,500 | 5,500 |
| 1865S | 41,000 | 85.00 | 125 | 175 | 325 | 600 | 1,250 | 2,350 | 11,500 | — |
| 1866 unique | — | — | — | — | — | — | — | — | — | — |

# Seated Liberty. "In God We Trust" above eagle.

**Designer:** Christian Gobrecht. **Diameter:** 24.3 mm. **Weight:** 6.6800 g. **Composition:** 0.9000 Silver, 0.1800 oz. ASW. **Notes:** The 1873 closed-3 and open-3 varieties are distinguished by the amount of space between the upper left and lower left serifs in the 3.

| Date | Mintage | G-4 | VG-8 | F-12 | VF-20 | XF-40 | AU-50 | MS-60 | MS-65 | Prf-65 |
|------|---------|-----|------|------|-------|-------|-------|-------|-------|--------|
| 1866 | 17,525 | 400 | 500 | 650 | 850 | 1,200 | 1,500 | 2,250 | 7,500 | 3,000 |
| 1866S | 28,000 | 200 | 290 | 525 | 900 | 1,250 | 2,000 | 3,000 | — | — |
| 1867 | 20,625 | 175 | 260 | 425 | 500 | 675 | 875 | 1,100 | — | 2,450 |
| 1867S | 48,000 | 145 | 250 | 390 | 525 | 600 | 1,250 | 2,350 | — | — |
| 1868 | 30,000 | 130 | 155 | 200 | 275 | 400 | 525 | 900 | 7,000 | 3,450 |
| 1868S | 96,000 | 65.00 | 80.00 | 135 | 245 | 575 | 975 | 2,000 | — | — |
| 1869 | 16,600 | 235 | 300 | 425 | 550 | 675 | 950 | 1,275 | — | 2,500 |
| 1869S | 76,000 | 75.00 | 125 | 180 | 325 | 625 | 1,400 | 2,400 | 16,000 | — |
| 1870 | 87,400 | 45.00 | 70.00 | 110 | 165 | 250 | 350 | 850 | 6,000 | 2,750 |
| 1870CC | 8,340 | 2,000 | 3,250 | 6,000 | 11,000 | 16,000 | 25,000 | 35,000 | — | — |
| 1871 | 119,160 | 40.00 | 60.00 | 70.00 | 125 | 175 | 350 | 650 | 6,000 | 2,500 |
| 1871CC | 10,890 | 1,700 | 2,750 | 4,000 | 8,500 | 14,500 | 25,000 | 40,000 | — | — |
| 1871S | 30,900 | 275 | 400 | 460 | 750 | 1,100 | 1,850 | 3,000 | 10,000 | — |
| 1872 | 182,950 | 30.00 | 40.00 | 80.00 | 110 | 155 | 300 | 600 | 6,500 | 2,500 |

| Date | Mintage | G-4 | VG-8 | F-12 | VF-20 | XF-40 | AU-50 | MS-60 | MS-65 | Prf-65 |
|---|---|---|---|---|---|---|---|---|---|---|
| 1872CC | 22,850 | 500 | 675 | 1,150 | 2,400 | 4,000 | 7,500 | 14,000 | — | — |
| 1872S | 83,000 | 900 | 1,250 | 1,650 | 2,000 | 2,750 | 4,250 | 6,750 | — | — |
| 1873 closed 3 | 212,600 | 125 | 210 | 325 | 525 | 600 | 1,000 | 2,000 | — | 2,600 |
| 1873 open 3 | Inc. above | 30.00 | 42.50 | 70.00 | 110 | 150 | 210 | 450 | 5,000 | — |
| 1873CC | 4,000 | — | — | — | — | — | — | — | — | — |

**Note:** 1873CC, Heritage, April 1999, MS-62, $106,375.

# Seated Liberty. Arrows at date.

**Designer:** Christian Gobrecht. **Diameter:** 24.3 mm. **Weight:** 6.6800 g. **Composition:** 0.9000 Silver, 0.1808 oz. ASW.

| Date | Mintage | G-4 | VG-8 | F-12 | VF-20 | XF-40 | AU-50 | MS-60 | MS-65 | Prf-65 |
|---|---|---|---|---|---|---|---|---|---|---|
| 1873 | 1,271,700 | 16.00 | 23.00 | 30.00 | 60.00 | 200 | 400 | 775 | 4,250 | 8,000 |
| 1873CC | 12,462 | 1,700 | 2,500 | 4,250 | 7,750 | 12,000 | 18,000 | 35,000 | — | — |
| 1873S | 156,000 | 25.00 | 40.00 | 85.00 | 125 | 275 | 550 | 1,200 | 8,000 | — |
| 1874 | 471,900 | 16.00 | 22.00 | 35.00 | 65.00 | 210 | 400 | 850 | 4,000 | 6,750 |
| 1874S | 392,000 | 18.50 | 24.00 | 50.00 | 110 | 210 | 425 | 850 | 4,500 | — |

# Seated Liberty. Arrows at date removed.

**Designer:** Christian Gobrecht. **Diameter:** 24.3 mm. **Weight:** 6.6800 g. **Composition:** 0.9000 Silver, 0.1808 oz. ASW. **Notes:** The 1876-CC fine-reeding variety has a more finely reeded edge.

| Date | Mintage | G-4 | VG-8 | F-12 | VF-20 | XF-40 | AU-50 | MS-60 | MS-65 | Prf-65 |
|---|---|---|---|---|---|---|---|---|---|---|
| 1875 | 4,293,500 | 14.00 | 17.00 | 25.00 | 30.00 | 50.00 | 135 | 225 | 1,600 | 2,300 |
| 1875CC | 140,000 | 60.00 | 90.00 | 160 | 250 | 500 | 775 | 1,600 | 15,000 | — |
| 1875S | 680,000 | 25.00 | 36.00 | 67.00 | 110 | 175 | 275 | 575 | 3,200 | — |
| 1876 | 17,817,150 | 14.00 | 17.00 | 25.00 | 30.00 | 50.00 | 135 | 225 | 1,600 | 2,250 |
| 1876CC | 4,944,000 | 17.00 | 20.00 | 30.00 | 40.00 | 70.00 | 150 | 325 | 3,600 | — |
| 1876CC fine reeding | Inc. above | 17.00 | 20.00 | 30.00 | 40.00 | 70.00 | 150 | 325 | 3,600 | — |
| 1876S | 8,596,000 | 14.00 | 17.00 | 25.00 | 30.00 | 50.00 | 135 | 225 | 2,000 | — |
| 1877 | 10,911,710 | 14.00 | 17.00 | 25.00 | 30.00 | 50.00 | 135 | 225 | 1,600 | 2,250 |
| 1877CC | 4,192,000 | 17.00 | 20.00 | 30.00 | 37.50 | 60.00 | 150 | 325 | 2,000 | — |
| 1877S | 8,996,000 | 14.00 | 17.00 | 25.00 | 30.00 | 50.00 | 135 | 225 | 1,600 | — |
| 1877S /horizontal S | Inc. above | 32.00 | 48.00 | 75.00 | 125 | 225 | 375 | 650 | — | — |
| 1878 | 2,260,800 | 16.00 | 18.00 | 28.00 | 34.00 | 55.00 | 145 | 250 | 2,750 | 2,300 |
| 1878CC | 996,000 | 18.00 | 29.00 | 45.00 | 80.00 | 110 | 150 | 450 | 3,500 | — |
| 1878S | 140,000 | 100.00 | 160 | 260 | 300 | 550 | 750 | 1,450 | — | — |
| 1879 | 14,700 | 130 | 150 | 215 | 250 | 300 | 375 | 475 | 1,700 | 2,250 |
| 1880 | 14,955 | 130 | 150 | 215 | 250 | 300 | 375 | 500 | 1,600 | 2,250 |
| 1881 | 12,975 | 145 | 170 | 250 | 260 | 325 | 385 | 525 | 1,650 | 2,200 |
| 1882 | 16,300 | 150 | 185 | 225 | 275 | 340 | 425 | 550 | 1,850 | 2,200 |
| 1883 | 15,439 | 145 | 175 | 240 | 275 | 330 | 400 | 525 | 2,450 | 2,200 |
| 1884 | 8,875 | 250 | 285 | 375 | 400 | 475 | 550 | 650 | 1,900 | 2,200 |
| 1885 | 14,530 | 130 | 150 | 215 | 275 | 300 | 385 | 525 | 2,600 | 2,200 |
| 1886 | 5,886 | 275 | 350 | 475 | 600 | 700 | 800 | 950 | 2,600 | 2,200 |
| 1887 | 10,710 | 225 | 275 | 345 | 400 | 475 | 550 | 650 | 2,350 | 2,200 |
| 1888 | 10,833 | 185 | 240 | 290 | 380 | 450 | 500 | 600 | 2,000 | 2,350 |
| 1888S | 1,216,000 | 15.00 | 20.00 | 27.50 | 30.00 | 60.00 | 160 | 245 | 2,450 | — |
| 1889 | 12,711 | 135 | 175 | 235 | 285 | 340 | 425 | 550 | 1,750 | 2,350 |
| 1890 | 80,590 | 50.00 | 75.00 | 85.00 | 110 | 185 | 275 | 400 | — | 2,350 |
| 1891 | 3,920,600 | 15.00 | 20.00 | 27.50 | 30.00 | 60.00 | 160 | 245 | 1,750 | 2,350 |
| 1891O | 68,000 | 125 | 175 | 300 | 475 | 875 | 1,100 | 3,000 | 14,500 | — |
| 1891S | 2,216,000 | 15.00 | 20.00 | 27.50 | 35.00 | 52.50 | 185 | 275 | 2,400 | — |

# Liberty.

**Designer:** Charles E. Barber. **Diameter:** 24.3 mm. **Weight:** 6.2500 g. **Composition:** 0.9000 Silver, 0.1809 oz. ASW. **Notes:** Commonly called "Barber quarter."

| Date | Mintage | G-4 | VG-8 | F-12 | VF-20 | XF-40 | AU-50 | MS-60 | MS-65 | Prf-65 |
|------|---------|-----|------|------|-------|-------|-------|-------|-------|--------|
| 1892 | 8,237,245 | 4.50 | 6.75 | 19.50 | 30.00 | 65.00 | 115 | 175 | 1,250 | 2,000 |
| 1892O | 2,640,000 | 5.75 | 9.50 | 27.50 | 38.00 | 72.00 | 135 | 275 | 1,600 | — |
| 1892S | 964,079 | 15.00 | 30.00 | 52.50 | 70.00 | 115 | 265 | 410 | 6,250 | — |
| 1893 | 5,484,838 | 4.50 | 7.00 | 22.50 | 30.00 | 65.00 | 115 | 205 | 1,750 | 2,000 |
| 1893O | 3,396,000 | 5.00 | 7.50 | 25.00 | 40.00 | 72.00 | 145 | 260 | 1,850 | — |
| 1893S | 1,454,535 | 8.00 | 17.00 | 40.00 | 70.00 | 110 | 270 | 475 | 7,500 | — |
| 1894 | 3,432,972 | 4.50 | 7.00 | 24.00 | 35.00 | 77.50 | 135 | 240 | 1,550 | 2,000 |
| 1894O | 2,852,000 | 5.50 | 8.50 | 30.00 | 48.00 | 80.00 | 195 | 330 | 2,200 | — |
| 1894S | 2,648,821 | 6.25 | 8.00 | 27.00 | 45.00 | 80.00 | 175 | 300 | 3,750 | — |
| 1895 | 4,440,880 | 4.75 | 6.25 | 23.00 | 30.00 | 67.50 | 135 | 225 | 1,850 | 2,000 |
| 1895O | 2,816,000 | 5.00 | 10.00 | 35.00 | 45.00 | 90.00 | 210 | 390 | 2,650 | — |
| 1895S | 1,764,681 | 7.75 | 13.50 | 37.50 | 63.00 | 95.00 | 215 | 360 | 3,750 | — |
| 1896 | 3,874,762 | 5.00 | 6.25 | 22.50 | 33.00 | 68.00 | 135 | 235 | 1,650 | 2,000 |
| 1896O | 1,484,000 | 7.00 | 18.00 | 70.00 | 185 | 350 | 650 | 845 | 7,500 | — |
| 1896S | 188,039 | 375 | 550 | 750 | 1,200 | 2,250 | 3,600 | 5,000 | 20,000 | — |
| 1897 | 8,140,731 | 3.75 | 5.50 | 19.50 | 33.00 | 67.00 | 115 | 175 | 1,250 | 2,000 |
| 1897O | 1,414,800 | 8.00 | 19.00 | 70.00 | 175 | 335 | 600 | 825 | 3,850 | — |
| 1897S | 542,229 | 30.00 | 60.00 | 160 | 230 | 350 | 625 | 1,000 | 6,900 | — |
| 1898 | 11,100,735 | 3.75 | 4.50 | 19.50 | 32.00 | 67.00 | 115 | 170 | 1,250 | 2,000 |
| 1898O | 1,868,000 | 6.75 | 15.00 | 60.00 | 125 | 235 | 385 | 675 | 9,500 | — |
| 1898S | 1,020,592 | 5.75 | 12.50 | 40.00 | 48.00 | 75.00 | 175 | 400 | 7,900 | — |
| 1899 | 12,624,846 | 4.00 | 4.75 | 19.00 | 32.00 | 67.00 | 115 | 170 | 1,250 | 2,000 |
| 1899O | 2,644,000 | 5.00 | 12.00 | 28.00 | 44.00 | 88.00 | 250 | 380 | 3,850 | — |
| 1899S | 708,000 | 8.50 | 26.00 | 60.00 | 72.00 | 110 | 225 | 395 | 3,600 | — |
| 1900 | 10,016,912 | 4.75 | 6.50 | 20.00 | 35.00 | 65.00 | 145 | 170 | 1,250 | 2,000 |
| 1900O | 3,416,000 | 7.00 | 17.50 | 50.00 | 83.00 | 120 | 330 | 550 | 3,700 | — |
| 1900S | 1,858,585 | 6.50 | 11.00 | 36.00 | 48.00 | 68.00 | 115 | 360 | 5,500 | — |
| 1901 | 8,892,813 | 5.75 | 6.75 | 18.00 | 30.00 | 65.00 | 115 | 170 | 2,350 | 2,200 |
| 1901O | 1,612,000 | 25.00 | 37.50 | 86.00 | 180 | 350 | 625 | 800 | 5,750 | — |
| 1901S | 72,664 | 2,400 | 3,600 | 5,500 | 7,500 | 9,900 | 11,500 | 16,500 | 45,000 | — |
| 1902 | 12,197,744 | 4.00 | 4.50 | 17.00 | 29.00 | 65.00 | 110 | 170 | 1,250 | 2,100 |
| 1902O | 4,748,000 | 5.25 | 11.50 | 35.00 | 54.00 | 100.00 | 180 | 385 | 5,250 | — |
| 1902S | 1,524,612 | 7.75 | 13.50 | 38.00 | 56.00 | 115 | 190 | 500 | 3,500 | — |
| 1903 | 9,670,064 | 4.00 | 5.50 | 17.00 | 29.00 | 65.00 | 110 | 170 | 2,500 | 2,000 |
| 1903O | 3,500,000 | 5.25 | 7.00 | 33.00 | 46.00 | 86.00 | 235 | 400 | 6,500 | — |
| 1903S | 1,036,000 | 9.00 | 17.50 | 37.50 | 60.00 | 100.00 | 260 | 425 | 2,600 | — |
| 1904 | 9,588,813 | 3.75 | 5.50 | 17.50 | 30.00 | 65.00 | 110 | 170 | 1,650 | 2,000 |
| 1904O | 2,456,000 | 6.50 | 11.00 | 45.00 | 72.00 | 175 | 375 | 775 | 3,100 | — |
| 1905 | 4,968,250 | 4.40 | 6.00 | 24.00 | 32.00 | 65.00 | 110 | 175 | 1,950 | 2,000 |
| 1905O | 1,230,000 | 10.00 | 18.50 | 62.00 | 110 | 195 | 340 | 465 | 6,000 | — |
| 1905S | 1,884,000 | 6.00 | 11.00 | 34.00 | 48.00 | 90.00 | 210 | 340 | 4,100 | — |
| 1906 | 3,656,435 | 3.50 | 5.50 | 16.00 | 30.00 | 67.00 | 110 | 170 | 1,300 | 2,000 |
| 1906D | 3,280,000 | 3.75 | 6.00 | 23.00 | 37.50 | 67.00 | 150 | 210 | 2,500 | — |
| 1906O | 2,056,000 | 3.75 | 7.50 | 30.00 | 42.50 | 86.00 | 185 | 285 | 1,400 | — |
| 1907 | 7,192,575 | 3.25 | 4.25 | 17.00 | 30.00 | 65.00 | 110 | 170 | 1,250 | 2,000 |
| 1907D | 2,484,000 | 3.75 | 6.25 | 25.00 | 40.00 | 80.00 | 175 | 240 | 2,500 | — |
| 1907O | 4,560,000 | 3.75 | 5.75 | 17.00 | 32.00 | 67.00 | 135 | 200 | 2,400 | — |
| 1907S | 1,360,000 | 5.00 | 8.75 | 38.00 | 58.00 | 125 | 270 | 440 | 3,600 | — |
| 1908 | 4,232,545 | 3.75 | 5.50 | 19.00 | 30.00 | 67.00 | 110 | 195 | 1,400 | 2,200 |
| 1908D | 5,788,000 | 3.75 | 4.25 | 17.00 | 29.00 | 67.00 | 115 | 215 | 1,750 | — |
| 1908O | 6,244,000 | 3.75 | 4.25 | 17.00 | 29.00 | 72.00 | 125 | 195 | 1,250 | — |
| 1908S | 784,000 | 12.00 | 20.00 | 65.00 | 110 | 240 | 420 | 700 | 5,800 | — |
| 1909 | 9,268,650 | 3.25 | 4.25 | 17.00 | 29.00 | 65.00 | 110 | 170 | 1,250 | 2,000 |
| 1909D | 5,114,000 | 3.75 | 4.25 | 17.00 | 30.00 | 70.00 | 150 | 190 | 2,100 | — |
| 1909O | 712,000 | 12.00 | 25.00 | 67.00 | 160 | 290 | 460 | 750 | 8,500 | — |
| 1909S | 1,348,000 | 3.75 | 6.25 | 27.00 | 40.00 | 68.00 | 185 | 275 | 2,800 | — |
| 1910 | 2,244,551 | 3.75 | 5.00 | 23.00 | 33.00 | 68.00 | 145 | 190 | 1,425 | 2,000 |
| 1910D | 1,500,000 | 5.50 | 6.50 | 36.50 | 55.00 | 98.00 | 220 | 340 | 2,400 | — |
| 1911 | 3,720,543 | 3.50 | 5.50 | 17.00 | 30.00 | 72.00 | 120 | 180 | 1,250 | 2,000 |
| 1911D | 933,600 | 6.50 | 11.00 | 67.00 | 175 | 300 | 450 | 625 | 5,250 | — |
| 1911S | 988,000 | 5.00 | 7.50 | 45.00 | 60.00 | 135 | 300 | 375 | 1,750 | — |
| 1912 | 4,400,700 | 4.75 | 5.25 | 16.00 | 32.00 | 65.00 | 110 | 170 | 1,250 | 2,000 |
| 1912S | 708,000 | 5.25 | 6.50 | 37.50 | 56.00 | 95.00 | 225 | 375 | 3,200 | — |
| 1913 | 484,613 | 8.50 | 16.00 | 60.00 | 139 | 385 | 495 | 900 | 4,250 | 2,200 |
| 1913D | 1,450,800 | 5.50 | 8.50 | 30.00 | 45.00 | 75.00 | 155 | 265 | 1,375 | — |

## 1913-S Quarter
### Grade XF-40

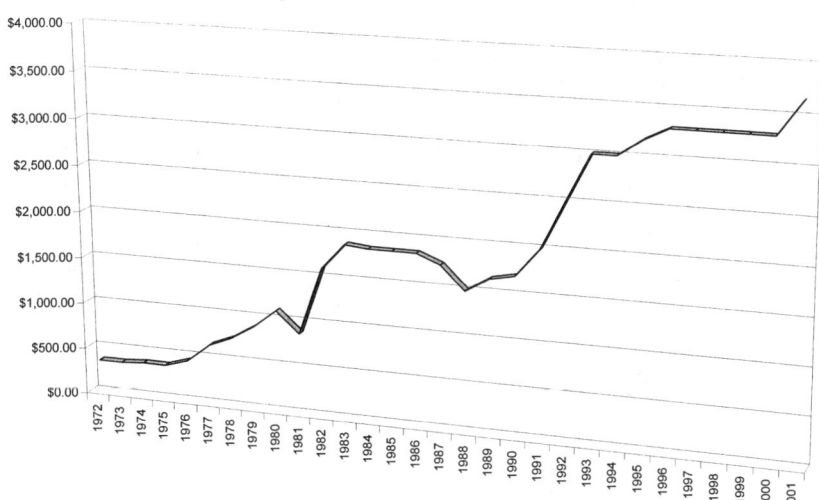

Retail Price

| Date | Mintage | G-4 | VG-8 | F-12 | VF-20 | XF-40 | AU-50 | MS-60 | MS-65 | Prf-65 |
|------|---------|-----|------|------|-------|-------|-------|-------|-------|--------|
| 1913S | 40,000 | 525 | 775 | 2,000 | 3,000 | 3,650 | 4,350 | 4,850 | 13,500 | — |
| 1914 | 6,244,610 | 3.60 | 4.75 | 16.00 | 26.50 | 55.00 | 110 | 170 | 1,250 | 2,200 |
| 1914D | 3,046,000 | 3.60 | 4.25 | 15.00 | 26.50 | 58.00 | 110 | 170 | 1,250 | — |
| 1914S | 264,000 | 55.00 | 75.00 | 145 | 180 | 375 | 575 | 875 | 3,250 | — |
| 1915 | 3,480,450 | 3.60 | 4.25 | 15.00 | 26.50 | 65.00 | 110 | 170 | 1,250 | 2,200 |
| 1915D | 3,694,000 | 3.60 | 4.25 | 15.00 | 26.50 | 65.00 | 110 | 170 | 1,250 | — |
| 1915S | 704,000 | 4.00 | 6.00 | 23.50 | 37.50 | 77.00 | 185 | 225 | 1,400 | — |
| 1916 | 1,788,000 | 3.50 | 4.25 | 16.00 | 30.00 | 70.00 | 115 | 170 | 1,250 | — |
| 1916D | 6,540,800 | 3.50 | 4.25 | 15.00 | 27.50 | 55.00 | 110 | 170 | 1,250 | — |

## Standing Liberty. Right breast exposed; Type 1.

**Designer:** Hermon A. MacNeil. **Diameter:** 24.3 mm. **Weight:** 6.2500 g. **Composition:** 0.9000 Silver, 0.1809 oz. ASW.

| Date | Mintage | G-4 | VG-8 | F-12 | VF-20 | XF-40 | AU-50 | MS-60 | MS-65 | -65FH |
|------|---------|-----|------|------|-------|-------|-------|-------|-------|-------|
| 1916 | 52,000 | 1,450 | 2,100 | 2,750 | 3,250 | 4,150 | 5,500 | 6,000 | 14,500 | 24,000 |
| 1917 | 8,792,000 | 17.50 | 21.00 | 35.00 | 46.00 | 62.00 | 135 | 250 | 750 | 1,450 |
| 1917D | 1,509,200 | 22.50 | 26.00 | 39.00 | 55.00 | 85.00 | 150 | 225 | 850 | 1,900 |
| 1917S | 1,952,000 | 22.50 | 24.00 | 39.00 | 67.00 | 140 | 190 | 250 | 1,600 | 2,675 |

## Standing Liberty. Right breast covered; Type 2.
## Three stars below eagle.

Mint mark

**Designer:** Hermon A. MacNeil. **Diameter:** 24.3 mm. **Weight:** 6.2500 g. **Composition:** 0.9000 Silver, 0.1809 oz. ASW.

| Date | Mintage | G-4 | VG-8 | F-12 | VF-20 | XF-40 | AU-50 | MS-60 | MS-65 | -65FH |
|------|---------|-----|------|------|-------|-------|-------|-------|-------|-------|
| 1917 | 13,880,000 | 14.00 | 20.00 | 23.00 | 27.50 | 48.00 | 75.00 | 135 | 640 | 925 |
| 1917D | 6,224,400 | 28.50 | 35.00 | 65.00 | 68.00 | 94.00 | 125 | 100 | 1,400 | 3,500 |
| 1917S | 5,522,000 | 28.50 | 35.00 | 47.50 | 55.00 | 75.00 | 105 | 195 | 1,150 | 3,300 |
| 1918 | 14,240,000 | 17.50 | 21.00 | 28.50 | 35.00 | 45.00 | 80.00 | 140 | 625 | 1,700 |
| 1918D | 7,380,000 | 27.50 | 35.00 | 44.00 | 65.00 | 87.00 | 135 | 220 | 1,395 | 5,500 |
| 1918S | 11,072,000 | 17.00 | 21.00 | 39.00 | 42.00 | 49.50 | 85.00 | 175 | 1,300 | 18,000 |
| 1918/17S | Inc. above | 1,400 | 1,500 | 2,100 | 2,900 | 4,900 | 8,900 | 14,500 | 85,000 | 300,000 |
| 1919 | 11,324,000 | 30.00 | 37.00 | 44.00 | 50.00 | 65.50 | 95.00 | 150 | 600 | 1,450 |
| 1919D | 1,944,000 | 65.00 | 85.00 | 135 | 189 | 300 | 495 | 650 | 2,500 | 24,500 |
| 1919S | 1,836,000 | 65.00 | 87.00 | 135 | 225 | 395 | 550 | 925 | 3,300 | 31,000 |
| 1920 | 27,860,000 | 15.00 | 17.50 | 28.00 | 33.00 | 39.00 | 69.00 | 130 | 550 | 1,900 |
| 1920D | 3,586,400 | 39.00 | 49.00 | 70.00 | 90.00 | 120 | 180 | 250 | 2,100 | 6,250 |
| 1920S | 6,380,000 | 20.00 | 22.00 | 28.00 | 38.00 | 57.50 | 98.00 | 250 | 2,400 | 30,000 |
| 1921 | 1,916,000 | 85.00 | 110 | 145 | 210 | 295 | 325 | 450 | 1,650 | 3,975 |
| 1923 | 9,716,000 | 14.00 | 18.00 | 27.00 | 32.50 | 39.00 | 67.00 | 125 | 550 | 3,950 |
| 1923S | 1,360,000 | 195 | 250 | 310 | 380 | 475 | 550 | 660 | 1,800 | 3,500 |
| 1924 | 10,920,000 | 15.00 | 16.50 | 20.00 | 24.00 | 32.00 | 64.00 | 120 | 495 | 1,400 |
| 1924D | 3,112,000 | 45.00 | 52.50 | 65.00 | 75.00 | 95.00 | 130 | 155 | 560 | 4,900 |
| 1924S | 2,860,000 | 25.00 | 29.50 | 37.50 | 42.50 | 87.00 | 175 | 360 | 2,000 | 5,250 |
| 1925 | 12,280,000 | 2.50 | 3.25 | 5.50 | 14.00 | 30.00 | 65.00 | 120 | 550 | 950 |
| 1926 | 11,316,000 | 2.25 | 3.00 | 5.00 | 13.00 | 29.00 | 62.00 | 115 | 500 | 2,250 |
| 1926D | 1,716,000 | 6.50 | 10.00 | 15.00 | 34.00 | 65.00 | 95.00 | 135 | 525 | 26,000 |
| 1926S | 2,700,000 | 3.25 | 4.00 | 12.00 | 25.00 | 99.00 | 295 | 350 | 2,100 | 28,000 |
| 1927 | 11,912,000 | 3.25 | 5.00 | 6.00 | 13.00 | 32.00 | 60.00 | 110 | 490 | 950 |
| 1927D | 976,400 | 7.00 | 12.00 | 16.00 | 39.00 | 90.00 | 135 | 175 | 550 | 3,000 |
| 1927S | 396,000 | 10.00 | 12.50 | 55.00 | 165 | 1,000 | 2,750 | 3,500 | 9,700 | 175,000 |
| 1928 | 6,336,000 | 3.25 | 4.00 | 5.00 | 12.00 | 29.00 | 58.50 | 110 | 525 | 1,500 |
| 1928D | 1,627,600 | 4.50 | 7.00 | 9.50 | 22.00 | 36.00 | 75.00 | 140 | 535 | 5,900 |
| 1928S | 2,644,000 | 3.00 | 3.50 | 6.00 | 13.50 | 32.00 | 70.00 | 135 | 540 | 900 |
| 1929 | 11,140,000 | 3.25 | 5.00 | 6.00 | 13.00 | 29.00 | 60.00 | 110 | 475 | 750 |
| 1929D | 1,358,000 | 4.75 | 6.00 | 9.50 | 18.00 | 32.00 | 70.00 | 140 | 525 | 6,250 |
| 1929S | 1,764,000 | 3.25 | 4.75 | 5.50 | 15.00 | 30.00 | 64.00 | 120 | 490 | 750 |
| 1930 | 5,632,000 | 3.25 | 4.00 | 5.00 | 12.00 | 29.00 | 60.00 | 100.00 | 475 | 725 |
| 1930S | 1,556,000 | 3.50 | 4.00 | 6.50 | 15.50 | 35.00 | 70.00 | 130 | 525 | 900 |

# Washington.

Reverse mint mark
1932-64

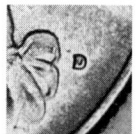

Obverse mint mark
1968-present

**Designer:** John Flanagan. **Diameter:** 24.3 mm. **Weight:** 6.2500 g. **Composition:** 0.9000 Silver, 0.1809 oz. ASW.

| Date | Mintage | G-4 | VG-8 | F-12 | VF-20 | XF-40 | AU-50 | MS-60 | MS-65 | Prf-65 |
|------|---------|-----|------|------|-------|-------|-------|-------|-------|--------|
| 1932 | 5,404,000 | 3.75 | 5.00 | 6.00 | 7.50 | 9.00 | 14.00 | 21.00 | 350 | — |
| 1932D | 436,800 | 48.00 | 65.00 | 75.00 | 88.00 | 160 | 325 | 600 | 9,500 | — |
| 1932S | 408,000 | 52.00 | 65.00 | 70.00 | 80.00 | 95.00 | 150 | 280 | 3,200 | — |
| 1934 | 31,912,052 | 2.00 | 2.25 | 2.50 | 3.00 | 4.00 | 9.00 | 22.00 | 75.00 | — |
| 1934D | 3,527,200 | 3.75 | 5.75 | 7.00 | 10.00 | 17.00 | 80.00 | 195 | 1,350 | — |
| 1935 | 32,484,000 | 1.75 | 2.00 | 2.50 | 2.75 | 4.00 | 8.00 | 21.00 | 70.00 | — |
| 1935D | 5,780,000 | 2.00 | 3.25 | 4.50 | 10.00 | 19.00 | 95.00 | 220 | 700 | — |
| 1935S | 5,660,000 | 2.00 | 2.75 | 5.00 | 6.00 | 12.50 | 30.00 | 70.00 | 300 | — |
| 1936 | 41,303,837 | 1.75 | 2.00 | 2.25 | 2.75 | 3.50 | 8.50 | 21.00 | 70.00 | 1,050 |
| 1936D | 5,374,000 | 3.00 | 3.50 | 4.75 | 15.00 | 44.00 | 200 | 400 | 850 | — |
| 1936S | 3,828,000 | 2.25 | 2.75 | 3.50 | 5.50 | 11.00 | 45.00 | 74.00 | 225 | — |
| 1937 | 19,701,542 | 1.75 | 2.00 | 3.00 | 3.50 | 3.75 | 16.00 | 22.00 | 90.00 | 380 |
| 1937D | 7,189,600 | 1.90 | 2.50 | 3.00 | 4.50 | 12.00 | 28.00 | 52.00 | 135 | — |
| 1937S | 1,652,000 | 3.00 | 4.00 | 4.00 | 11.50 | 19.00 | 85.00 | 110 | 275 | — |
| 1938 | 9,480,045 | 3.00 | 3.75 | 5.00 | 6.00 | 15.00 | 35.00 | 63.00 | 180 | 225 |
| 1938S | 2,832,000 | 3.60 | 4.50 | 5.50 | 7.00 | 15.00 | 38.00 | 65.00 | 185 | — |
| 1939 | 33,548,795 | 1.75 | 2.00 | 2.25 | 2.50 | 3.50 | 7.00 | 14.00 | 70.00 | 150 |
| 1939D | 7,092,000 | 2.00 | 2.25 | 3.25 | 4.00 | 8.00 | 16.00 | 34.00 | 85.00 | — |
| 1939S | 2,628,000 | 3.00 | 3.25 | 3.75 | 6.50 | 14.00 | 44.00 | 72.00 | 175 | — |
| 1940 | 35,715,246 | 1.75 | 2.00 | 2.25 | 2.50 | 3.00 | 6.50 | 12.50 | 65.00 | 150 |
| 1940D | 2,797,600 | 2.00 | 2.50 | 6.00 | 8.50 | 18.00 | 47.00 | 75.00 | 185 | — |
| 1940S | 8,244,000 | 1.75 | 2.25 | 4.75 | 5.00 | 6.50 | 14.00 | 24.00 | 55.00 | — |
| 1941 | 79,047,287 | — | — | 1.65 | 1.75 | 2.50 | 4.00 | 6.00 | 50.00 | 110 |
| 1941D | 16,714,800 | — | — | 1.75 | 2.25 | 3.50 | 7.50 | 20.00 | 70.00 | — |
| 1941S | 16,080,000 | — | — | 1.75 | 2.25 | 3.25 | 6.50 | 20.00 | 80.00 | — |
| 1942 | 102,117,123 | — | — | 1.65 | 1.75 | 2.50 | 3.00 | 4.00 | 45.00 | 110 |
| 1942D | 17,487,200 | — | — | 1.75 | 2.50 | 3.75 | 7.00 | 13.50 | 50.00 | — |
| 1942S | 19,384,000 | — | — | 2.00 | 3.00 | 5.50 | 16.00 | 55.00 | 110 | — |

# 1932-D Quarter
## Grade F-12

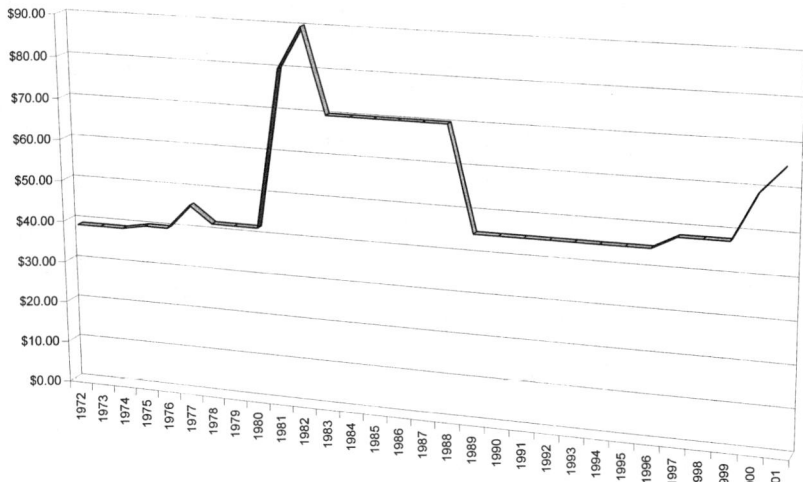

☐ Retail Price

| Date | Mintage | G-4 | VG-8 | F-12 | VF-20 | XF-40 | AU-50 | MS-60 | MS-65 | Prf-65 |
|------|---------|-----|------|------|-------|-------|-------|-------|-------|--------|
| 1943 | 99,700,000 | — | — | 1.50 | 1.75 | 2.10 | 2.75 | 3.50 | 45.00 | — |
| 1943D | 16,095,600 | — | — | 1.75 | 2.25 | 4.00 | 7.00 | 22.00 | 46.00 | — |
| 1943S | 21,700,000 | — | — | 1.75 | 2.25 | 5.50 | 11.00 | 27.00 | 55.00 | — |
| 1944 | 104,956,000 | — | — | 1.50 | 1.75 | 2.10 | 2.85 | 3.75 | 45.00 | — |
| 1944D | 14,600,800 | — | — | 1.75 | 2.50 | 3.75 | 8.00 | 14.00 | 46.00 | — |
| 1944S | 12,560,000 | — | — | 1.85 | 2.75 | 4.00 | 9.00 | 14.00 | 45.00 | — |
| 1945 | 74,372,000 | — | — | 1.50 | 1.75 | 2.10 | 2.85 | 3.75 | 45.00 | — |
| 1945D | 12,341,600 | — | — | 1.75 | 3.00 | 6.00 | 10.50 | 16.00 | 40.00 | — |
| 1945S | 17,004,001 | — | — | 1.65 | 2.50 | 3.75 | 6.00 | 8.00 | 42.00 | — |
| 1946 | 53,436,000 | — | — | 1.50 | 1.85 | 2.25 | 2.75 | 3.75 | 42.00 | — |
| 1946D | 9,072,800 | — | — | 1.50 | 1.85 | 2.25 | 2.75 | 4.00 | 43.00 | — |
| 1946S | 4,204,000 | — | — | 1.65 | 2.00 | 3.00 | 4.00 | 4.00 | 43.00 | — |
| 1947 | 22,556,000 | — | — | 1.65 | 2.25 | 2.75 | 3.50 | 5.00 | 43.00 | — |
| 1947D | 15,338,400 | — | — | 1.65 | 2.25 | 2.50 | 2.75 | 4.50 | 43.00 | — |
| 1947S | 5,532,000 | — | — | 1.65 | 2.25 | 2.75 | 3.00 | 4.00 | 45.00 | — |
| 1948 | 35,196,000 | — | — | 1.65 | 1.85 | 2.25 | 2.75 | 3.50 | 43.00 | — |
| 1948D | 16,766,800 | — | — | 1.65 | 1.85 | 2.25 | 2.75 | 4.00 | 43.00 | — |
| 1948S | 15,960,000 | — | — | 1.75 | 1.95 | 2.50 | 3.00 | 4.50 | 44.00 | — |
| 1949 | 9,312,000 | — | — | 1.65 | 2.50 | 4.50 | 13.00 | 25.00 | 48.00 | — |
| 1949D | 10,068,400 | — | — | 1.60 | 2.25 | 4.00 | 6.00 | 12.00 | 50.00 | — |
| 1950 | 24,971,512 | — | — | 1.50 | 1.65 | 1.75 | 2.10 | 3.00 | 28.00 | 55.00 |
| 1950D | 21,075,600 | — | — | 1.65 | 1.85 | 2.10 | 2.40 | 3.25 | 30.00 | — |
| 1950D/S | Inc. above | 22.00 | 25.00 | 36.00 | 60.00 | 150 | 225 | 275 | 800 | — |
| 1950S | 10,284,004 | — | — | 1.65 | 1.85 | 2.40 | 4.50 | 6.50 | 25.00 | — |
| 1950S/D | Inc. above | 22.00 | 30.00 | 40.00 | 65.00 | 190 | 315 | 400 | 775 | — |
| 1951 | 43,505,602 | — | — | 1.50 | 1.65 | 1.75 | 2.25 | 4.50 | 28.00 | 40.00 |
| 1951D | 35,354,800 | — | — | 1.50 | 1.75 | 2.00 | 2.25 | 3.00 | 35.00 | — |
| 1951S | 9,048,000 | — | — | 1.50 | 1.75 | 3.75 | 7.00 | 17.00 | 50.00 | — |
| 1952 | 38,862,073 | — | — | 1.50 | 1.65 | 1.75 | 2.25 | 3.50 | 28.00 | 37.00 |
| 1952D | 49,795,200 | — | — | 1.50 | 1.65 | 1.75 | 2.25 | 3.25 | 28.00 | — |
| 1952S | 13,707,800 | — | — | 1.50 | 1.75 | 3.25 | 7.00 | 15.00 | 40.00 | — |
| 1953 | 18,664,920 | — | — | 1.50 | 1.65 | 1.75 | 2.10 | 3.25 | 28.00 | 25.00 |
| 1953D | 56,112,400 | — | — | 1.50 | 1.65 | 1.75 | 1.95 | 2.50 | 25.00 | — |
| 1953S | 14,016,000 | — | — | 1.50 | 1.75 | 2.10 | 2.75 | 4.00 | 28.00 | — |
| 1954 | 54,645,503 | — | — | — | 1.50 | 1.65 | 1.75 | 3.00 | 28.00 | 13.00 |
| 1954D | 42,305,500 | — | — | — | 1.50 | 1.65 | 1.75 | 3.00 | 28.00 | — |
| 1954S | 11,834,722 | — | — | — | 1.50 | 1.75 | 2.00 | 2.75 | 25.00 | — |
| 1955 | 18,558,381 | — | — | — | 1.65 | 1.75 | 2.00 | 2.50 | 25.00 | 14.00 |
| 1955D | 3,182,400 | — | — | 1.65 | 2.00 | 2.50 | 2.75 | 3.00 | 25.00 | — |
| 1956 | 44,813,384 | — | — | 1.50 | 1.65 | 1.85 | 2.00 | 2.50 | 20.00 | 4.00 |
| 1956D | 32,334,500 | — | — | — | 1.75 | 1.85 | 2.10 | 2.40 | 24.00 | — |
| 1957 | 47,779,952 | — | — | — | 1.65 | 1.75 | 1.95 | 2.25 | 26.00 | 4.00 |
| 1957D | 77,924,160 | — | — | — | 1.65 | 1.75 | 1.95 | 2.50 | 20.00 | — |
| 1958 | 7,235,652 | — | — | — | 1.65 | 1.75 | 2.00 | 2.75 | 20.00 | 6.00 |

| Date | Mintage | G-4 | VG-8 | F-12 | VF-20 | XF-40 | AU-50 | MS-60 | MS-65 | Prf-65 |
|------|---------|-----|------|------|-------|-------|-------|-------|-------|--------|
| 1958D | 78,124,900 | — | — | — | 1.65 | 1.75 | 1.95 | 2.25 | 20.00 | — |
| 1959 | 25,533,291 | — | — | — | 1.65 | 1.75 | 1.95 | 2.25 | 20.00 | 4.25 |
| 1959D | 62,054,232 | — | — | — | 1.65 | 1.75 | 1.95 | 2.25 | 20.00 | — |
| 1960 | 30,855,602 | — | — | — | 1.65 | 1.75 | 1.95 | 2.25 | 17.00 | 3.75 |
| 1960D | 63,000,324 | — | — | — | 1.65 | 1.75 | 1.95 | 2.25 | 17.00 | — |
| 1961 | 40,064,244 | — | — | — | 1.65 | 1.75 | 1.95 | 2.50 | 18.00 | 3.50 |
| 1961D | 83,656,928 | — | — | — | 1.65 | 1.75 | 1.95 | 2.25 | 16.00 | — |
| 1962 | 39,374,019 | — | — | — | 1.65 | 1.75 | 1.95 | 2.50 | 18.00 | 3.50 |
| 1962D | 127,554,756 | — | — | — | 1.65 | 1.75 | 1.95 | 2.25 | 16.00 | — |
| 1963 | 77,391,645 | — | — | — | 1.50 | 1.60 | 1.75 | 1.95 | 15.00 | 3.50 |
| 1963D | 135,288,184 | — | — | — | 1.50 | 1.60 | 1.75 | 1.95 | 15.00 | — |
| 1964 | 564,341,347 | — | — | — | 1.50 | 1.60 | 1.75 | 1.95 | 15.00 | 3.50 |
| 1964D | 704,135,528 | — | — | — | 1.50 | 1.60 | 1.75 | 1.95 | 15.00 | — |

## Washington.

**Designer:** John Flanagan. **Diameter:** 24.3 mm. **Weight:** 5.6700 g. **Composition:** Copper-nickel Clad Copper.

| Date | Mintage | MS-65 | Prf-65 | Date | Mintage | MS-65 | Prf-65 |
|------|---------|-------|--------|------|---------|-------|--------|
| 1965 | 1,819,717,540 | 2.75 | — | 1971D | 258,634,428 | 2.25 | — |
| 1966 | 821,101,500 | 2.75 | — | 1971S | (3,220,733) | — | 1.05 |
| 1967 | 1,524,031,848 | 2.75 | — | 1972 | 215,048,000 | 2.00 | — |
| 1968 | 220,731,500 | 2.75 | — | 1972D | 311,067,732 | 2.00 | — |
| 1968D | 101,534,000 | 3.00 | — | 1972S | (3,260,996) | — | 1.10 |
| 1968S | (3,041,506) | — | 1.00 | 1973 | 346,924,000 | 2.00 | — |
| 1969 | 176,212,000 | 2.75 | — | 1973D | 232,977,400 | 2.25 | — |
| 1969D | 114,372,000 | 2.50 | — | 1973S | (2,760,339) | — | 0.95 |
| 1969S | (2,934,631) | — | 1.20 | 1974 | 801,456,000 | 2.00 | — |
| 1970 | 136,420,000 | 2.50 | — | 1974D | 353,160,300 | 2.25 | — |
| 1970D | 417,341,364 | 2.25 | — | 1974S | (2,612,568) | — | 1.25 |
| 1970S | (2,632,810) | — | 0.95 | 1975 none minted | — | — | — |
| 1971 | 109,284,000 | 2.25 | — | 1975D none minted | — | — | — |
|  |  |  |  | 1975S none minted | — | — | — |

## Washington. Bicentennial design, drummer boy.

**Rev. Designer:** Jack L. Ahr. **Diameter:** 24.3 mm. **Weight:** 5.6700 g. **Composition:** Copper-nickel Clad Copper.

| Date | Mintage | G-4 | VG-8 | F-12 | VF-20 | XF-40 | MS-60 | MS-65 | Prf-65 |
|------|---------|-----|------|------|-------|-------|-------|-------|--------|
| 1976 | 809,784,016 | — | — | — | — | — | 0.95 | 1.75 | — |
| 1976D | 860,118,839 | — | — | — | — | — | 0.95 | 1.75 | — |
| 1976S | — | — | — | — | — | — | — | — | 0.90 |

## Washington. Bicentennial design, drummer boy.

**Rev. Designer:** Jack L. Ahr. **Diameter:** 24.3 mm. **Weight:** 5.7500 g. **Composition:** Silver Clad, 0.074 oz. ASW.

| Date | Mintage | G-4 | VG-8 | F-12 | VF-20 | XF-40 | MS-60 | MS-65 | Prf-65 |
|------|---------|-----|------|------|-------|-------|-------|-------|--------|
| 1976S | 11,000,000 | — | — | — | — | — | 1.25 | 1.75 | 1.95 |

## Washington. Regular design resumed.

**Diameter:** 24.3 mm. **Weight:** 5.6700 g. **Composition:** Copper-nickel Clad Copper. **Notes:** The 1979-S and 1981 Type II proofs have clearer mint marks than the Type I proofs for those years.

| Date | Mintage | MS-65 | Prf-65 | Date | Mintage | MS-65 | Prf-65 |
|------|---------|-------|--------|------|---------|-------|--------|
| 1977 | 468,556,000 | 1.00 | — | 1981P | 601,716,000 | 1.00 | — |
| 1977D | 256,524,978 | 1.00 | — | 1981D | 575,722,833 | 1.00 | — |
| 1977S | (3,251,152) | — | 1.10 | 1981S T-I | — | — | 1.10 |
| 1978 | 521,452,000 | 1.00 | — | 1981S T-II | — | — | 3.00 |
| 1978D | 287,373,152 | 1.00 | — | 1982P | 500,931,000 | 4.00 | — |
| 1978S | (3,127,781) | — | 1.20 | 1982D | 480,042,788 | 3.00 | — |
| 1979 | 515,708,000 | 1.00 | — | 1982S | (3,857,479) | — | 2.00 |
| 1979D | 489,789,780 | 1.00 | — | 1983P | 673,535,000 | 8.00 | — |
| 1979S T-I | — | — | 0.95 | 1983D | 617,806,446 | 7.50 | — |
| 1979S T-II | — | — | 1.45 | 1983S | (3,279,126) | — | 2.25 |
| 1980P | 635,832,000 | 1.00 | — | 1984P | 676,545,000 | 1.75 | — |
| 1980D | 518,327,487 | 1.00 | — | 1984D | 546,483,064 | 2.50 | — |
| 1980S | (3,554,806) | — | 1.15 | 1984S | (3,065,110) | — | 2.40 |

| Date | Mintage | MS-65 | Prf-65 | Date | Mintage | MS-65 | Prf-65 |
|------|---------|-------|--------|------|---------|-------|--------|
| 1985P | 775,818,962 | 3.50 | — | 1992P | 384,764,000 | 1.00 | — |
| 1985D | 519,962,888 | 5.00 | — | 1992D | 389,777,107 | 1.35 | — |
| 1985S | (3,362,821) | 5.00 | 1.45 | 1992S | (2,858,981) | — | 3.25 |
| 1986P | 551,199,333 | 7.00 | — | 1993P | 639,276,000 | 1.20 | — |
| 1986D | 504,298,660 | 5.50 | — | 1993D | 645,476,128 | 1.50 | — |
| 1986S | (3,010,497) | — | 2.25 | 1993S | (2,633,439) | — | 5.00 |
| 1987P | 582,499,481 | 1.00 | — | 1994P | 825,600,000 | 1.25 | — |
| 1987D | 655,594,696 | 1.00 | — | 1994D | 880,034,110 | 1.25 | — |
| 1987S | (4,227,728) | — | 1.50 | 1994S | (2,484,594) | — | 4.00 |
| 1988P | 562,052,000 | 3.00 | — | 1995P | 1,004,336,000 | 1.20 | — |
| 1988D | 596,810,688 | 1.50 | — | 1995D | 1,103,216,000 | 1.20 | — |
| 1988S | (3,262,948) | — | 2.10 | 1995S | (2,010,384) | — | 24.00 |
| 1989P | 512,868,000 | 1.50 | — | 1996P | 925,040,000 | 1.20 | — |
| 1989D | 896,535,597 | 1.50 | — | 1996D | 906,868,000 | 1.20 | — |
| 1989S | (3,220,194) | — | 2.10 | 1996S | — | — | 4.00 |
| 1990P | 613,792,000 | 1.00 | — | 1997P | 595,740,000 | 1.25 | — |
| 1990D | 927,638,181 | 1.00 | — | 1997D | 599,680,000 | 1.25 | — |
| 1990S | (3,299,559) | — | 4.50 | 1997S | (1,975,000) | — | 8.00 |
| 1991P | 570,968,000 | 1.00 | — | 1998P | 896,268,000 | 1.00 | — |
| 1991D | 630,966,693 | 1.00 | — | 1998D | 821,000,000 | 1.00 | — |
| 1991S | (2,867,787) | — | 3.00 | 1998S | — | — | 9.00 |

**Composition:** Silver.

| Date | Mintage | MS-65 | Prf-65 | Date | Mintage | MS-65 | Prf-65 |
|------|---------|-------|--------|------|---------|-------|--------|
| 1992S | (1,317,579) | — | 7.00 | 1996S | — | — | 7.00 |
| 1993S | (761,353) | — | 8.00 | 1997S | — | — | 7.00 |
| 1994S | (785,329) | — | 8.00 | 1998S | — | — | 7.00 |
| 1995S | — | — | 12.00 | | | | |

# 50 State Quarters

Alphabetically listed within the year of release.

## Connecticut

**Composition:** Copper-nickel Clad Copper.

| Date | Mintage | MS-63 | MS-65 | Prf-65 |
|------|---------|-------|-------|--------|
| 1999P | 688,744,000 | 0.75 | 1.00 | — |
| 1999D | 657,480,000 | 0.75 | 1.00 | — |
| 1999S | — | — | — | — |

**Composition:** 0.9000 Silver.

| Date | Mintage | MS-63 | MS-65 | Prf-65 |
|------|---------|-------|-------|--------|
| 1999S | — | — | — | — |

## Delaware

**Diameter:** 24.3 mm. **Weight:** 5.6700 g. **Composition:** Copper-nickel Clad Copper.

| Date | Mintage | MS-63 | MS-65 | Prf-65 |
|------|---------|-------|-------|--------|
| 1999P | 373,400,000 | 1.25 | 1.50 | — |
| 1999D | 401,424,000 | 1.25 | 1.50 | — |
| 1999S | — | — | — | 6.50 |

**Composition:** 0.9000 Silver.

| Date | Mintage | MS-63 | MS-65 | Prf-65 |
|------|---------|-------|-------|--------|
| 1999S | — | — | — | 13.50 |

# Georgia

**Composition:** Copper-nickel Clad Copper.

| Date | Mintage | MS-63 | MS-65 | Prf-65 |
|---|---|---|---|---|
| 1999P | 451,188,000 | 0.75 | 1.00 | — |
| 1999D | 488,744,000 | 0.75 | 1.00 | — |
| 1999S | — | — | — | — |

**Composition:** 0.9000 Silver.

| Date | Mintage | MS-63 | MS-65 | Prf-65 |
|---|---|---|---|---|
| 1999S | — | — | — | — |

# New Jersey

**Composition:** Copper-nickel Clad Copper.

| Date | Mintage | MS-63 | MS-65 | Prf-65 |
|---|---|---|---|---|
| 1999P | 363,200,000 | 1.00 | 1.75 | — |
| 1999D | 299,028,000 | 1.00 | 1.50 | — |
| 1999S | — | — | — | 6.50 |

**Composition:** 0.9000 Silver.

| Date | Mintage | MS-63 | MS-65 | Prf-65 |
|---|---|---|---|---|
| 1999S | — | — | — | — |

# Pennsylvania

**Diameter:** 24.3 mm. **Weight:** 5.6700 g. **Composition:** Copper-nickel Clad Copper.

| Date | Mintage | MS-63 | MS-65 | Prf-65 |
|---|---|---|---|---|
| 1999P | 349,000,000 | 1.50 | 2.00 | — |
| 1999D | 358,332,000 | 1.25 | 1.50 | — |
| 1999S | — | — | — | 6.50 |

**Composition:** 0.9000 Silver.

| Date | Mintage | MS-63 | MS-65 | Prf-65 |
|---|---|---|---|---|
| 1999S | — | — | — | 13.50 |

# Maryland

**Composition:** Copper-nickel Clad Copper.

| Date | Mintage | MS-63 | MS-65 | Prf-65 |
|---|---|---|---|---|
| 2000P | 678,200,000 | — | — | — |
| 2000D | 556,526,000 | — | — | — |
| 2000S | — | — | — | — |

**Composition:** 0.9000 Silver.

| Date | Mintage | MS-63 | MS-65 | Prf-65 |
|---|---|---|---|---|
| 2000S | — | | | — |

## Massachusetts

**Composition:** Copper-nickel Clad Copper.

| Date | Mintage | MS-63 | MS-65 | Prf-65 |
|---|---|---|---|---|
| 2000P | 629,800,000 | 0.75 | 1.00 | — |
| 2000D | 535,184,000 | 0.75 | 1.00 | — |
| 2000S | — | — | — | — |

**Composition:** 0.9000 Silver.

| Date | Mintage | MS-63 | MS-65 | Prf-65 |
|---|---|---|---|---|
| 2000S | — | — | — | — |

## New Hampshire

**Composition:** Copper-nickel Clad Copper.

| Date | Mintage | MS-63 | MS-65 | Prf-65 |
|---|---|---|---|---|
| 2000P | 673,040,000 | — | — | — |
| 2000D | 495,976,000 | — | — | — |
| 2000S | — | — | — | — |

**Composition:** 0.9000 Silver.

| Date | Mintage | MS-63 | MS-65 | Prf-65 |
|---|---|---|---|---|
| 2000S | — | — | — | — |

## South Carolina

**Composition:** Copper-nickel Clad Copper.

| Date | Mintage | MS-63 | MS-65 | Prf-65 |
|---|---|---|---|---|
| 2000P | 742,756,000 | — | — | — |
| 2000D | 566,208,000 | — | — | — |
| 2000S | — | — | — | — |

**Composition:** 0.9000 Silver.

| Date | Mintage | MS-63 | MS-65 | Prf-65 |
|---|---|---|---|---|
| 2000S | — | — | — | — |

## Virginia

**Composition:** Copper-nickel Clad Copper.

| Date | Mintage | MS-63 | MS-65 | Prf-65 |
|---|---|---|---|---|
| 2000P | 943,000,000 | — | — | — |
| 2000D | 651,616,000 | — | — | — |

| Date | Mintage | MS-63 | MS-65 | Prf-65 |
|------|---------|-------|-------|--------|
| 2000S | — | — | — | — |

**Composition:** 0.9000 Silver.

| Date | Mintage | MS-63 | MS-65 | Prf-65 |
|------|---------|-------|-------|--------|
| 2000S | — | — | — | — |

## Kentucky

**Composition:** Copper-nickel Clad Copper.

| Date | Mintage | MS-63 | MS-65 | Prf-65 |
|------|---------|-------|-------|--------|
| 2001P | — | — | — | — |
| 2001D | — | — | — | — |
| 2001S | — | — | — | — |

**Composition:** Silver.

| Date | Mintage | MS-63 | MS-65 | Prf-65 |
|------|---------|-------|-------|--------|
| 2001S | — | — | — | — |

## New York

**Composition:** Copper-nickel Clad Copper.

| Date | Mintage | MS-63 | MS-65 | Prf-65 |
|------|---------|-------|-------|--------|
| 2001P | — | 0.75 | 1.00 | — |
| 2001D | — | 0.75 | 1.00 | — |
| 2001S | — | — | — | 6.50 |

**Composition:** Silver.

| Date | Mintage | MS-63 | MS-65 | Prf-65 |
|------|---------|-------|-------|--------|
| 2001S | — | — | — | — |

## North Carolina

**Composition:** Copper-nickel Clad Copper.

| Date | Mintage | MS-63 | MS-65 | Prf-65 |
|------|---------|-------|-------|--------|
| 2001P | — | 0.75 | 1.00 | — |
| 2001D | — | 0.75 | 1.00 | — |
| 2001S | — | — | — | 6.50 |

**Composition:** Silver.

| Date | Mintage | MS-63 | MS-65 | Prf-65 |
|------|---------|-------|-------|--------|
| 2001S | — | — | — | — |

## Rhode Island

**Composition:** Copper-nickel Clad Copper.

| Date | Mintage | MS-63 | MS-65 | Prf-65 |
|------|---------|-------|-------|--------|
| 2001P | — | — | — | — |
| 2001D | — | — | — | — |
| 2001S | — | — | — | — |

**Composition:** Silver.

| Date | Mintage | MS-63 | MS-65 | Prf-65 |
|------|---------|-------|-------|--------|
| 2001S | — | — | — | — |

## Vermont

**Composition:** Copper-nickel Clad Copper.

| Date | Mintage | MS-63 | MS-65 | Prf-65 |
|------|---------|-------|-------|--------|
| 2001P | — | — | — | — |
| 2001D | — | — | — | — |
| 2001S | — | — | — | — |

**Composition:** Silver.

| Date | Mintage | MS-63 | MS-65 | Prf-65 |
|------|---------|-------|-------|--------|
| 2001S | — | — | — | — |

# HALF DOLLAR

## Flowing hair.

**Designer:** Robert Scot. **Diameter:** 32.5 mm. **Weight:** 13.4800 g. **Composition:** 0.8920 Silver, 0.3869 oz. ASW. **Notes:** The 1795 "recut date" variety had the date cut into the dies twice, so both sets of numbers are visible on the coin. The 1795 "3 leaves" variety has three leaves under each of the eagle's wings on the reverse.

| Date | Mintage | G-4 | VG-8 | F-12 | VF-20 | XF-40 | MS-60 |
|------|---------|-----|------|------|-------|-------|-------|
| 1794 | 23,464 | 1,200 | 1,875 | 2,800 | 4,500 | 8,000 | 55,000 |
| 1795 | 299,680 | 450 | 625 | 850 | 1,600 | 5,000 | 15,000 |
| 1795 recut date | Inc. above | 550 | 650 | 950 | 2,100 | 5,250 | 18,000 |
| 1795 3 leaves | Inc. above | 800 | 1,450 | 2,000 | 3,750 | 9,500 | — |

## Draped bust. Small eagle.

**Designer:** Robert Scot. **Diameter:** 32.5 mm. **Weight:** 13.4800 g. **Composition:** 0.8920 Silver, 0.3869 oz. ASW. **Notes:** The 1796 strikes have either 15 or 16 stars on the obverse.

| Date | Mintage | G-4 | VG-8 | F-12 | VF-20 | XF-40 | MS-60 |
|------|---------|-----|------|------|-------|-------|-------|
| 1796 15 stars | 3,918 | 9,750 | 11,500 | 15,000 | 25,000 | 37,500 | 95,000 |
| 1796 16 stars | Inc. above | 10,000 | 12,000 | 17,000 | 27,000 | 39,000 | 120,000 |
| 1797 | Inc. above | 9,500 | 11,500 | 15,000 | 24,000 | 37,500 | 95,000 |

## Draped bust. Heraldic eagle.

**Designer:** Robert Scot. **Diameter:** 32.5 mm. **Weight:** 13.4800 g. **Composition:** 0.8920 Silver, 0.3869 oz. ASW. **Notes:** The two varieties of the 1803 strikes are distinguished by the size of the 3 in the date. The several varieties of the 1806 strikes are distinguished by the style of 6 in the date, size of the stars on the obverse, and whether the stem of the olive branch held by the reverse eagle extends through the claw.

| Date | Mintage | G-4 | VG-8 | F-12 | VF-20 | XF-40 | MS-60 |
|------|---------|-----|------|------|-------|-------|-------|
| 1801 | 30,289 | 225 | 275 | 550 | 1,250 | 3,200 | 35,000 |
| 1802 | 29,890 | 225 | 295 | 495 | 850 | 1,950 | 35,000 |
| 1803 small 3 | 188,234 | 150 | 170 | 285 | 450 | 900 | 7,500 |
| 1803 large 3 | Inc. above | 125 | 150 | 200 | 350 | 750 | 6,000 |
| 1805 | 211,722 | 125 | 150 | 200 | 350 | 800 | 6,500 |
| 1805/4 | Inc. above | 175 | 250 | 350 | 650 | 1,700 | 20,000 |
| 1806 round-top 6, large stars | 839,576 | 125 | 150 | 190 | 325 | 675 | 6,000 |

## 1797 Half Dollar
### Grade F-12

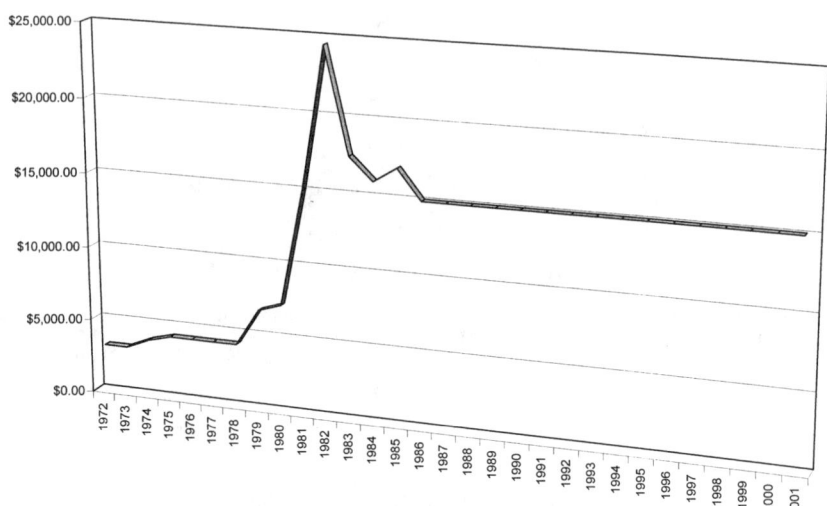

| Date | Mintage | G-4 | VG-8 | F-12 | VF-20 | XF-40 | MS-60 |
|------|---------|-----|------|------|-------|-------|-------|
| 1806 round-top 6, small stars | Inc. above | 125 | 140 | 180 | 320 | 600 | 6,250 |
| 1806 knobbed 6, stem not through claw | — | — | 35,000 | 45,000 | 70,000 | 95,000 | — |
| 1806 pointed-top 6, stem not through claw | Inc. above | 115 | 130 | 160 | 290 | 550 | 5,000 |
| 1806 pointed-top 6, stem through claw | Inc. above | 120 | 150 | 190 | 290 | 600 | 5,750 |
| 1806/5 | Inc. above | 125 | 160 | 210 | 350 | 675 | 6,500 |
| 1806 /inverted 6 | Inc. above | 200 | 250 | 475 | 750 | 1,750 | 10,000 |
| 1807 | 301,076 | 120 | 150 | 190 | 290 | 600 | 5,750 |

## Liberty cap. "50 C." below eagle.

**Designer:** John Reich. **Diameter:** 32.5 mm. **Weight:** 13.4800 g. **Composition:** 0.8920 Silver, 0.3869 oz. ASW. **Notes:** There are three varieties of the 1807 strikes. Two are distinguished by the size of the stars on the obverse. The third was struck from a reverse die that had a 5 cut over a 2 in the "50C" denomination. Two varieties of the 1811 are distinguished by the size of the 8 in the date. A third has a period between the 8 and second 1 in the date. One variety of the 1817 has a period between the 1 and 7 in the date. Two varieties of the 1819/18 overdate are distinguished by the size of the 9 in the date. Two varieties of the 1820 are distinguished by the size of the date. On the 1823 varieties, the "broken 3" appears to be almost separated in the middle of the 3 in the date; the "patched 3" has the error repaired; the "ugly 3" has portions of its detail missing. The 1827 "curled-2" and "square-2" varieties are distinguished by the numeral's base -- either curled or square. Among the 1828 varieties, "knobbed 2" and "no knob" refers to whether the upper left serif of the digit is rounded. The 1830 varieties are distinguished by the size of the 0 in the date. The four 1834 varieties are distinguished by the sizes of the stars, date and letters in the inscriptions. The 1836 "50/00" variety was struck from a reverse die that had "50" recut over "00" in the denomination.

| Date | Mintage | G-4 | VG-8 | F-12 | VF-20 | XF-40 | AU-50 | MS-60 | MS-65 |
|------|---------|-----|------|------|-------|-------|-------|-------|-------|
| 1807 small stars | 750,500 | 65.00 | 90.00 | 175 | 325 | 800 | 3,500 | 5,900 | 35,000 |
| 1807 large stars | Inc. above | 50.00 | 80.00 | 165 | 300 | 750 | 3,500 | 5,500 | — |
| 1807 50/20 C. | Inc. above | 45.00 | 70.00 | 85.00 | 175 | 450 | 1,850 | 4,000 | 30,000 |
| 1807 bearded goddess | — | 300 | 500 | 675 | 1,175 | 2,750 | 7,500 | — | — |

| Date | Mintage | G-4 | VG-8 | F-12 | VF-20 | XF-40 | AU-50 | MS-60 | MS-65 |
|---|---|---|---|---|---|---|---|---|---|
| 1808 | 1,368,600 | 37.50 | 42.50 | 53.00 | 90.00 | 185 | 700 | 1,800 | 12,500 |
| 1808/7 | Inc. above | 40.00 | 50.00 | 60.00 | 125 | 250 | 800 | 1,750 | 15,000 |
| 1809 | 1,405,810 | 36.00 | 42.50 | 55.00 | 85.00 | 185 | 550 | 1,600 | 15,000 |
| 1810 | 1,276,276 | 34.50 | 38.00 | 46.00 | 90.00 | 170 | 550 | 1,750 | 15,000 |
| 1811 small 8 | 1,203,644 | 32.00 | 37.50 | 45.00 | 60.00 | 110 | 450 | 750 | 7,500 |
| 1811 large 8 | Inc. above | 32.50 | 38.00 | 50.00 | 70.00 | 140 | 500 | 900 | 8,500 |
| 1811 18.11 | Inc. above | 40.00 | 47.00 | 72.00 | 135 | 275 | 650 | 1,500 | 12,000 |
| 1812 | 1,628,059 | 32.50 | 37.50 | 45.00 | 60.00 | 105 | 350 | 775 | 7,500 |
| 1812/1 small 8 | Inc. above | 42.50 | 50.00 | 75.00 | 110 | 250 | 800 | 2,000 · | 12,000 |
| 1812/1 large 8 | Inc. above | 1,275 | 1,875 | 2,450 | 4,000 | 6,000 | 17,500 | — | — |
| 1813 | 1,241,903 | 32.50 | 37.50 | 45.00 | 70.00 | 125 | 450 | 1,250 | 11,000 |
| 1813 50/UNI reverse | 1,241,903 | 40.00 | 70.00 | 100.00 | 195 | 325 | 875 | 1,900 | 12,000 |
| 1814 | 1,039,075 | 34.50 | 38.00 | 45.00 | 60.00 | 125 | 500 | 1,350 | 9,000 |
| 1814/3 | Inc. above | 40.00 | 60.00 | 95.00 | 145 | 295 | 800 | 1,800 | 12,000 |
| 1815/2 | 47,150 | 750 | 900 | 1,300 | 1,750 | 2,500 | 4,750 | 11,000 | 50,000 |
| 1817 | 1,215,567 | 31.50 | 33.00 | 40.00 | 60.00 | 100.00 | 350 | 900 | 9,000 |
| 1817/3 | Inc. above | 70.00 | 105 | 165 | 290 | 550 | 1,700 | 3,750 | 25,000 |
| 1817/4 | — | 50,000 | 60,000 | 95,000 | 145,000 | 175,000 | — | — | — |
| 1817 181.7 | Inc. above | 37.00 | 47.00 | 60.00 | 100.00 | 175 | 650 | 1,500 | 10,000 |
| 1818 | 1,960,322 | 31.50 | 33.00 | 40.00 | 60.00 | 100.00 | 350 | 900 | 8,500 |
| 1818/7 | Inc. above | 35.00 | 40.00 | 55.00 | 85.00 | 165 | 600 | 1,400 | 11,000 |
| 1819 | 2,208,000 | 31.50 | 33.00 | 40.00 | 60.00 | 100.00 | 375 | 900 | 8,500 |
| 1819/8 small 9 | Inc. above | 31.50 | 33.00 | 40.00 | 70.00 | 130 | 450 | 1,100 | 9,500 |
| 1819/8 large 9 | Inc. above | 31.50 | 33.00 | 40.00 | 70.00 | 120 | 400 | 1,100 | 9,000 |
| 1820 small date | 751,122 | 40.00 | 55.00 | 80.00 | 145 | 250 | 650 | 1,500 | 10,000 |
| 1820 large date | Inc. above | 37.00 | 50.00 | 68.00 | 120 | 220 | 600 | 1,350 | 10,000 |
| 1820/19 | Inc. above | 40.00 | 53.00 | 75.00 | 130 | 240 | 800 | 1,700 | 12,000 |
| 1821 | 1,305,797 | 33.00 | 35.00 | 40.00 | 70.00 | 95.00 | 500 | 1,200 | 9,750 |
| 1822 | 1,559,573 | 32.00 | 34.00 | 40.00 | 55.00 | 85.00 | 300 | 750 | 7,750 |
| 1822/1 | Inc. above | 40.00 | 49.00 | 60.00 | 125 | 235 | 700 | 1,400 | 11,000 |
| 1823 | 1,694,200 | 31.50 | 33.00 | 40.00 | 50.00 | 85.00 | 290 | 750 | 7,500 |
| 1823 broken 3 | Inc. above | 43.00 | 63.00 | 90.00 | 160 | 300 | 900 | 1,700 | 12,000 |
| 1823 patched 3 | Inc. above | 38.00 | 53.00 | 78.00 | 125 | 200 | 500 | 1,100 | 8,000 |
| 1823 ugly 3 | Inc. above | 40.00 | 58.00 | 83.00 | 145 | 235 | 750 | 1,500 | 11,000 |
| 1824 | 3,504,954 | 31.00 | 33.00 | 40.00 | 47.00 | 80.00 | 225 | 600 | 7,500 |
| 1824/21 | Inc. above | 35.00 | 40.00 | 55.00 | 65.00 | 130 | 380 | 950 | 7,900 |
| 1824 1824/various dates | Inc. above | 35.00 | 45.00 | 70.00 | 145 | 265 | 700 | 1,500 | 12,000 |
| 1825 | 2,943,166 | 31.50 | 33.00 | 40.00 | 50.00 | 77.00 | 210 | 500 | 7,000 |
| 1826 | 4,004,180 | 31.50 | 33.00 | 40.00 | 50.00 | 77.00 | 210 | 500 | 7,000 |
| 1827 curled 2 | 5,493,400 | 33.00 | 45.00 | 58.00 | 85.00 | 165 | 325 | 900 | 7,750 |
| 1827 square 2 | Inc. above | 31.50 | 33.00 | 40.00 | 45.00 | 77.00 | 250 | 650 | 7,500 |
| 1827/6 | Inc. above | 35.00 | 40.00 | 43.00 | 60.00 | 125 | 375 | 975 | 9,000 |
| 1828 curled-base 2, no knob | 3,075,200 | 33.00 | 36.00 | 40.00 | 55.00 | 90.00 | 275 | 650 | 7,000 |
| 1828 curled-base 2, knobbed 2 | Inc. above | 35.00 | 40.00 | 50.00 | 65.00 | 100.00 | 300 | 700 | 7,250 |
| 1828 small 8s, square-base 2, large letters | Inc. above | 27.50 | 33.00 | 36.00 | 43.00 | 80.00 | 210 | 550 | 6,250 |
| 1828 small 8s, square-base 2, small letters | Inc. above | 45.00 | 58.00 | 100.00 | 185 | 275 | 700 | 1,200 | 9,500 |
| 1828 large 8s, square-base 2 | Inc. above | 33.00 | 37.00 | 43.00 | 55.00 | 95.00 | 325 | 750 | 8,000 |
| 1829 | 3,712,156 | 27.50 | 33.00 | 36.00 | 43.00 | 77.00 | 250 | 500 | 9,000 |
| 1829/7 | Inc. above | 35.00 | 40.00 | 60.00 | 85.00 | 165 | 300 | 800 | — |
| 1830 small 0 in date | 4,764,800 | 27.50 | 33.00 | 36.00 | 43.00 | 77.00 | 240 | 500 | 6,500 |
| 1830 large 0 in date | Inc. above | 27.50 | 33.00 | 36.00 | 43.00 | 77.00 | 240 | 500 | 6,500 |
| 1831 | 5,873,660 | 27.50 | 33.00 | 36.00 | 43.00 | 77.00 | 240 | 500 | 6,500 |
| 1832 small letters | 4,797,000 | 27.50 | 33.00 | 36.00 | 43.00 | 77.00 | 240 | 500 | 6,500 |
| 1832 large letters | Inc. above | 30.00 | 45.00 | 58.00 | 85.00 | 145 | 300 | 650 | 7,500 |
| 1833 | 5,206,000 | 27.50 | 33.00 | 36.00 | 43.00 | 77.00 | 240 | 500 | 6,500 |
| 1834 small date, large stars, small letters | 6,412,004 | 27.50 | 33.00 | 36.00 | 43.00 | 77.00 | 240 | 500 | 6,500 |
| 1834 small date, small stars, small letters | Inc. above | 27.50 | 33.00 | 36.00 | 43.00 | 77.00 | 240 | 500 | 6,500 |
| 1834 large date, small letters | Inc. above | 27.50 | 33.00 | 36.00 | 43.00 | 77.00 | 240 | 500 | 6,500 |
| 1834 large date, large letters | Inc. above | 27.50 | 33.00 | 36.00 | 43.00 | 77.00 | 240 | 500 | 6,500 |
| 1835 | 5,352,006 | 27.50 | 33.00 | 36.00 | 43.00 | 77.00 | 275 | 600 | 9,000 |
| 1836 | 6,545,000 | 27.50 | 33.00 | 36.00 | 43.00 | 77.00 | 240 | 500 | 6,500 |
| 1836 50/00 | Inc. above | 55.00 | 80.00 | 105 | 185 | 300 | 800 | 1,750 | 10,000 |

## Liberty cap. "50 Cents" below eagle.

**Designer:** Christian Gobrecht. **Diameter:** 30 mm. **Edge:** Reeded. **Weight:** 13.3600 g. **Composition:** 0.9000 Silver, 0.3867 oz. ASW.

| Date | Mintage | G-4 | VG-8 | F-12 | VF-20 | XF-40 | AU-50 | MS-60 | MS-65 |
|------|---------|-----|------|------|-------|-------|-------|-------|-------|
| 1836 | 1,200 | 600 | 700 | 900 | 1,200 | 1,900 | 3,000 | 5,000 | 22,500 |
| 1837 | 3,629,820 | 32.00 | 38.00 | 43.00 | 60.00 | 115 | 325 | 750 | 12,500 |

## Liberty cap. "Half Dol." below eagle.

**Designer:** Christian Gobrecht. **Diameter:** 30 mm. **Weight:** 13.3600 g. **Composition:** 0.9000 Silver, 0.3867 oz. ASW.

| Date | Mintage | G-4 | VG-8 | F-12 | VF-20 | XF-40 | AU-50 | MS-60 | MS-65 |
|------|---------|-----|------|------|-------|-------|-------|-------|-------|
| 1838 | 3,546,000 | 32.00 | 38.00 | 43.00 | 60.00 | 125 | 475 | 825 | 14,000 |
| 1838O proof only | Est. 20 | — | — | — | — | 45,000 | 75,000 | 90,000 | 200,000 |
| 1839 | 1,392,976 | 32.00 | 38.00 | 41.00 | 60.00 | 125 | 365 | 900 | 16,000 |
| 1839O | 178,976 | 125 | 145 | 195 | 280 | 500 | 1,200 | 2,500 | 17,500 |

## Seated Liberty.

**Designer:** Christian Gobrecht. **Diameter:** 30.6 mm. **Weight:** 13.3600 g. **Composition:** 0.9000 Silver, .3867 oz. ASW. **Notes:** The 1839 varieties are distinguished by whether there's drapery extending from Liberty's left elbow. One variety of the 1840 strikes has smaller lettering; another used the old reverse of 1838. Varieties of 1842 and 1846 are distinguished by the size of the numerals in the date.

| Date | Mintage | G-4 | VG-8 | F-12 | VF-20 | XF-40 | AU-50 | MS-60 | MS-65 |
|------|---------|-----|------|------|-------|-------|-------|-------|-------|
| 1839 no drapery from elbow | Inc. above | 38.00 | 65.00 | 110 | 250 | 725 | 1,500 | 2,350 | 107,000 |
| 1839 drapery | Inc. above | 20.00 | 28.00 | 40.00 | 75.00 | 145 | 265 | 450 | — |
| 1840 small letters | 1,435,008 | 16.50 | 24.00 | 30.00 | 60.00 | 110 | 350 | 575 | 8,250 |
| 1840 reverse 1838 | Inc. above | 115 | 165 | 215 | 325 | 500 | 1,200 | 2,500 | — |
| 1840O | 855,100 | 17.00 | 29.00 | 45.00 | 80.00 | 125 | 300 | 585 | — |
| 1841 | 310,000 | 35.00 | 45.00 | 80.00 | 140 | 265 | 425 | 1,300 | — |
| 1841O | 401,000 | 17.00 | 29.00 | 45.00 | 85.00 | 150 | 240 | 875 | — |
| 1842 small date | 2,012,764 | 27.00 | 37.00 | 55.00 | 95.00 | 165 | 325 | 1,300 | 12,000 |
| 1842 large date | Inc. above | 16.00 | 24.00 | 39.00 | 50.00 | 85.00 | 120 | 1,250 | 12,000 |
| 1842O small date | 957,000 | 575 | 800 | 1,400 | 2,250 | 4,000 | — | — | — |
| 1842O large date | Inc. above | 22.00 | 29.00 | 48.00 | 115 | 225 | 750 | 1,750 | — |
| 1843 | 3,844,000 | 16.00 | 24.00 | 39.00 | 50.00 | 85.00 | 180 | 350 | 4,500 |
| 1843O | 2,268,000 | 16.00 | 24.00 | 39.00 | 55.00 | 90.00 | 250 | 550 | — |
| 1844 | 1,766,000 | 16.00 | 24.00 | 39.00 | 50.00 | 85.00 | 180 | 350 | 4,500 |
| 1844O | 2,005,000 | 16.00 | 24.00 | 39.00 | 55.00 | 80.00 | 195 | 525 | |

| Date | Mintage | G-4 | VG-8 | F-12 | VF-20 | XF-40 | AU-50 | MS-60 | MS-65 |
|------|---------|-----|------|------|-------|-------|-------|-------|-------|
| 1844/1844O | Inc. above | 425 | 650 | 1,000 | 1,375 | 2,300 | 4,900 | — | — |
| 1845 | 589,000 | 30.00 | 40.00 | 50.00 | 90.00 | 170 | 340 | 900 | — |
| 1845O | 2,094,000 | 18.00 | 24.00 | 39.00 | 52.00 | 110 | 240 | 550 | — |
| 1845O no drapery | Inc. above | 25.00 | 35.00 | 65.00 | 115 | 185 | 375 | 750 | — |
| 1846 medium date | 2,210,000 | 18.00 | 24.00 | 39.00 | 50.00 | 70.00 | 175 | 500 | 9,000 |
| 1846 tall date | Inc. above | 22.00 | 30.00 | 60.00 | 85.00 | 145 | 250 | 650 | 12,000 |
| 1846 /horizontal 6 | Inc. above | 140 | 215 | 285 | 375 | 550 | 1,000 | 2,500 | — |
| 1846O medium date | 2,304,000 | 17.00 | 24.00 | 39.00 | 45.00 | 100.00 | 225 | 550 | 12,000 |
| 1846O tall date | Inc. above | 135 | 245 | 325 | 575 | 950 | 2,000 | 3,600 | — |
| 1847/1846 | 1,156,000 | 2,000 | 2,750 | 3,200 | 4,250 | 6,500 | — | — | — |
| 1847 | Inc. above | 20.00 | 30.00 | 45.00 | 60.00 | 90.00 | 190 | 480 | 9,000 |
| 1847O | 2,584,000 | 17.00 | 25.00 | 39.00 | 50.00 | 95.00 | 250 | 640 | 7,000 |
| 1848 | 580,000 | 35.00 | 55.00 | 75.00 | 150 | 240 | 475 | 1,000 | 9,000 |
| 1848O | 3,180,000 | 18.00 | 25.00 | 40.00 | 50.00 | 95.00 | 285 | 750 | 9,000 |
| 1849 | 1,252,000 | 26.00 | 40.00 | 55.00 | 90.00 | 150 | 365 | 1,250 | 9,000 |
| 1849O | 2,310,000 | 16.00 | 25.00 | 40.00 | 60.00 | 115 | 250 | 650 | 9,000 |
| 1850 | 227,000 | 250 | 300 | 340 | 400 | 575 | 875 | 1,500 | — |
| 1850O | 2,456,000 | 16.00 | 25.00 | 45.00 | 65.00 | 125 | 250 | 650 | 9,000 |
| 1851 | 200,750 | 325 | 400 | 550 | 800 | 925 | 1,000 | 1,900 | — |
| 1851O | 402,000 | 37.00 | 45.00 | 75.00 | 105 | 175 | 300 | 675 | 9,000 |
| 1852 | 77,130 | 300 | 375 | 525 | 700 | 875 | 1,100 | 1,450 | — |
| 1852O | 144,000 | 70.00 | 110 | 175 | 350 | 525 | 1,050 | 1,850 | — |
| 1853O mintage unrecorded | — | — | — | — | — | — | — | — | — |

Note: 1853O, Eliasberg Sale, 1997, VG-8, $154,000.

## Seated Liberty. Arrows at date. Rays around eagle.

**Designer:** Christian Gobrecht. **Weight:** 12.4400 g. **Composition:** 0.9000 Silver, 0.3600 oz. ASW.

| Date | Mintage | G-4 | VG-8 | F-12 | VF-20 | XF-40 | AU-50 | MS-60 | MS-65 | Prf-65 |
|------|---------|-----|------|------|-------|-------|-------|-------|-------|--------|
| 1853 | 3,532,708 | 16.50 | 27.00 | 40.00 | 90.00 | 250 | 505 | 1,700 | 21,500 | — |
| 1853O | 1,328,000 | 19.00 | 31.00 | 50.00 | 125 | 290 | 700 | 2,100 | 21,500 | — |

## Seated Liberty. Rays around eagle removed.

**Designer:** Christian Gobrecht. **Weight:** 12.4400 g. **Composition:** 0.9000 Silver, 0.3600 oz. ASW.

| Date | Mintage | G-4 | VG-8 | F-12 | VF-20 | XF-40 | AU-50 | MS-60 | MS-65 | Prf-65 |
|------|---------|-----|------|------|-------|-------|-------|-------|-------|--------|
| 1854 | 2,982,000 | 16.00 | 22.00 | 33.00 | 50.00 | 100.00 | 270 | 675 | 8,000 | — |
| 1854O | 5,240,000 | 16.00 | 22.00 | 33.00 | 50.00 | 100.00 | 265 | 500 | 8,000 | — |
| 1855 | 759,500 | 23.00 | 30.00 | 40.00 | 65.00 | 150 | 325 | 1,200 | 8,000 | 22,500 |
| 1855/4 | Inc. above | 35.00 | 60.00 | 80.00 | 125 | 225 | 400 | 1,500 | — | — |
| 1855O | 3,688,000 | 16.00 | 22.00 | 33.00 | 50.00 | 100.00 | 270 | 650 | 8,000 | — |
| 1855S | 129,950 | 220 | 325 | 600 | 1,300 | 2,650 | 6,000 | — | — | — |

## 1855-S Half Dollar
### Grade XF-40

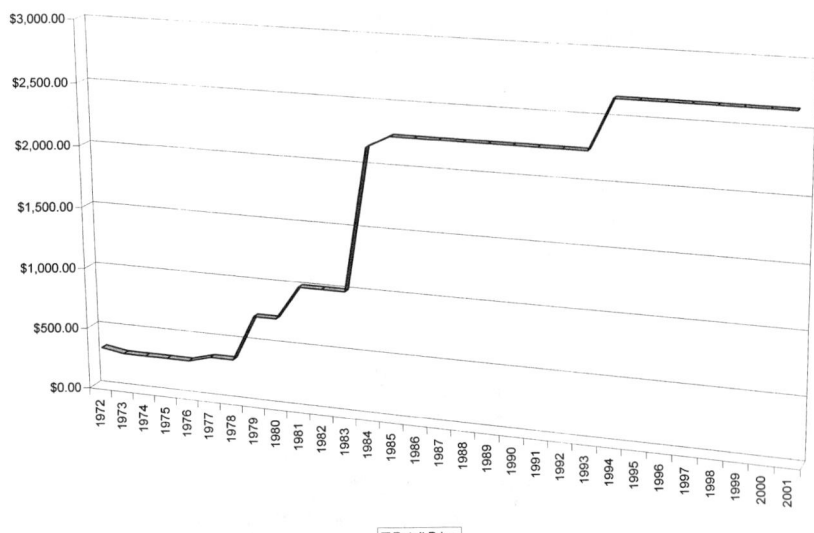

Retail Price

## Seated Liberty. Arrows at date removed.

**Designer:** Christian Gobrecht. **Weight:** 12.4400 g. **Composition:** 0.9000 Silver, 0.3600 oz. ASW.

| Date | Mintage | G-4 | VG-8 | F-12 | VF-20 | XF-40 | AU-50 | MS-60 | MS-65 | Prf-65 |
|------|---------|-----|------|------|-------|-------|-------|-------|-------|--------|
| 1856 | 938,000 | 19.00 | 25.00 | 39.00 | 52.00 | 90.00 | 150 | 350 | 6,500 | 12,500 |
| 1856O | 2,658,000 | 16.00 | 21.00 | 28.00 | 45.00 | 82.00 | 150 | 450 | 12,500 | — |
| 1856S | 211,000 | 70.00 | 80.00 | 130 | 240 | 450 | 1,250 | 2,500 | 19,000 | — |
| 1857 | 1,988,000 | 16.00 | 18.00 | 28.00 | 45.00 | 82.00 | 150 | 350 | 5,150 | 12,500 |
| 1857O | 818,000 | 18.00 | 21.00 | 38.00 | 65.00 | 110 | 250 | 850 | 12,500 | — |
| 1857S | 158,000 | 75.00 | 95.00 | 145 | 285 | 575 | 800 | 2,400 | 19,000 | — |
| 1858 | 4,226,000 | 16.00 | 18.00 | 35.00 | 60.00 | 80.00 | 150 | 350 | 6,500 | 12,500 |
| 1858O | 7,294,000 | 16.00 | 17.00 | 35.00 | 45.00 | 70.00 | 150 | 450 | 12,500 | — |
| 1858S | 476,000 | 20.00 | 30.00 | 48.00 | 90.00 | 175 | 400 | 950 | 12,500 | — |
| 1859 | 748,000 | 16.50 | 27.00 | 42.00 | 55.00 | 90.00 | 200 | 650 | 6,600 | 5,500 |
| 1859O | 2,834,000 | 16.00 | 25.00 | 40.00 | 50.00 | 75.00 | 150 | 450 | 6,500 | — |
| 1859S | 566,000 | 20.00 | 38.00 | 55.00 | 85.00 | 215 | 375 | 750 | 12,500 | — |
| 1860 | 303,700 | 25.00 | 35.00 | 47.50 | 75.00 | 120 | 350 | 1,000 | 6,500 | 5,500 |
| 1860O | 1,290,000 | 16.00 | 20.00 | 35.00 | 45.00 | 76.00 | 160 | 450 | 5,150 | — |
| 1860S | 472,000 | 20.00 | 30.00 | 50.00 | 75.00 | 130 | 245 | 850 | 12,500 | — |
| 1861 | 2,888,400 | 16.00 | 23.00 | 35.00 | 45.00 | 70.00 | 150 | 410 | 5,150 | 5,500 |
| 1861O | 2,532,633 | 16.00 | 25.00 | 40.00 | 60.00 | 85.00 | 150 | 450 | 5,150 | — |
| 1861S | 939,500 | 17.00 | 28.00 | 42.50 | 60.00 | 100.00 | 195 | 975 | 9,500 | — |
| 1862 | 253,550 | 28.00 | 40.00 | 55.00 | 95.00 | 175 | 285 | 750 | 5,150 | 5,500 |
| 1862S | 1,352,000 | 16.00 | 27.00 | 39.00 | 60.00 | 90.00 | 175 | 450 | 9,000 | — |
| 1863 | 503,660 | 20.00 | 32.00 | 42.00 | 75.00 | 130 | 250 | 750 | 5,150 | 5,500 |
| 1863S | 916,000 | 16.00 | 25.00 | 39.00 | 50.00 | 80.00 | 150 | 410 | 9,000 | — |
| 1864 | 379,570 | 24.00 | 32.00 | 55.00 | 85.00 | 160 | 200 | 750 | 5,150 | 5,500 |
| 1864S | 658,000 | 18.00 | 23.00 | 45.00 | 60.00 | 115 | 275 | 675 | 9,000 | — |
| 1865 | 511,900 | 25.00 | 32.00 | 49.00 | 80.00 | 125 | 240 | 750 | 5,150 | 5,500 |
| 1865S | 675,000 | 17.00 | 23.00 | 39.00 | 55.00 | 85.00 | 160 | 450 | 9,000 | — |
| 1866 unique | — | — | — | — | — | — | — | — | — | — |
| 1866S | 60,000 | 80.00 | 120 | 170 | 325 | 795 | 1,500 | 5,000 | — | — |

## Seated Liberty. "In God We Trust" above eagle.

**Designer:** Christian Gobrecht. **Weight:** 12.4400 g. **Composition:** 0.9000 Silver, 0.3600 oz. ASW. **Notes:** In 1866 the motto "In God We Trust" was added to the reverse. The "closed-3" and "open-3" varieties are distinguished by the amount of space between the upper and lower left serifs of the 3.

| Date | Mintage | G-4 | VG-8 | F-12 | VF-20 | XF-40 | AU-50 | MS-60 | MS-65 | Prf-65 |
|------|---------|-----|------|------|-------|-------|-------|-------|-------|--------|
| 1866 | 745,625 | 16.00 | 27.00 | 45.00 | 65.00 | 90.00 | 155 | 350 | 4,800 | 3,750 |
| 1866S | 994,000 | 16.00 | 27.00 | 45.00 | 60.00 | 95.00 | 275 | 650 | 5,000 | — |
| 1867 | 449,925 | 25.00 | 35.00 | 55.00 | 85.00 | 145 | 240 | 350 | 4,800 | 3,750 |
| 1867S | 1,196,000 | 16.00 | 24.00 | 40.00 | 50.00 | 75.00 | 155 | 350 | 7,000 | — |
| 1868 | 418,200 | 35.00 | 49.00 | 80.00 | 135 | 225 | 300 | 525 | 7,100 | 3,750 |
| 1868S | 1,160,000 | 16.00 | 24.00 | 39.00 | 50.00 | 105 | 165 | 350 | 7,000 | — |
| 1869 | 795,900 | 18.00 | 24.00 | 39.00 | 45.00 | 85.00 | 160 | 385 | 4,600 | 3,750 |
| 1869S | 656,000 | 16.00 | 27.00 | 39.00 | 50.00 | 100.00 | 175 | 600 | 7,000 | — |
| 1870 | 634,900 | 18.00 | 27.00 | 39.00 | 65.00 | 100.00 | 160 | 475 | 7,000 | 3,750 |
| 1870CC | 54,617 | 500 | 800 | 1,450 | 2,750 | 10,000 | — | — | — | — |
| 1870S | 1,004,000 | 18.00 | 29.00 | 45.00 | 70.00 | 110 | 275 | 575 | 7,000 | — |
| 1871 | 1,204,560 | 16.00 | 24.00 | 39.00 | 50.00 | 70.00 | 155 | 350 | 7,000 | 3,750 |
| 1871CC | 153,950 | 145 | 225 | 375 | 650 | 1,300 | 2,750 | — | — | — |
| 1871S | 2,178,000 | 16.00 | 24.00 | 39.00 | 50.00 | 69.00 | 155 | 400 | 7,000 | — |
| 1872 | 881,550 | 16.00 | 24.00 | 39.00 | 55.00 | 80.00 | 160 | 430 | 2,850 | 3,750 |
| 1872CC | 272,000 | 60.00 | 95.00 | 190 | 300 | 650 | 1,700 | 2,500 | 8,800 | — |
| 1872S | 580,000 | 23.00 | 28.00 | 55.00 | 90.00 | 170 | 375 | 975 | 7,000 | — |
| 1873 closed 3 | 801,800 | 19.00 | 24.00 | 38.00 | 90.00 | 125 | 235 | 500 | 4,500 | 3,750 |
| 1873 open 3 | Inc. above | 2,200 | 2,700 | 4,100 | 5,500 | 7,500 | — | — | — | — |
| 1873CC | 122,500 | 150 | 210 | 300 | 625 | 1,350 | 2,500 | 4,100 | 9,000 | 3,750 |

1873S no arrows, 5,000 minted, no specimens known to survive

## Seated Liberty. Arrows at date.

**Designer:** Christian Gobrecht. **Weight:** 12.5000 g. **Composition:** 0.9000 Silver, 0.3618 oz. ASW.

| Date | Mintage | G-4 | VG-8 | F-12 | VF-20 | XF-40 | AU-50 | MS-60 | MS-65 | Prf-65 |
|------|---------|-----|------|------|-------|-------|-------|-------|-------|--------|
| 1873 | 1,815,700 | 16.50 | 25.00 | 36.00 | 85.00 | 225 | 530 | 950 | 15,000 | 9,000 |
| 1873CC | 214,560 | 110 | 160 | 250 | 525 | 1,350 | 2,250 | 4,500 | — | — |
| 1873S | 233,000 | 60.00 | 80.00 | 110 | 225 | 475 | 825 | 1,600 | 15,000 | — |
| 1874 | 2,360,300 | 16.50 | 25.00 | 36.00 | 85.00 | 225 | 530 | 950 | 15,000 | 9,000 |
| 1874CC | 59,000 | 300 | 400 | 525 | 975 | 1,850 | 2,900 | 4,500 | 14,000 | — |
| 1874S | 394,000 | 29.00 | 39.00 | 70.00 | 135 | 275 | 575 | 1,400 | 15,000 | — |

## Seated Liberty. Arrows at date removed.

**Designer:** Christian Gobrecht. **Weight:** 12.5000 g. **Composition:** 0.9000 Silver, 0.3618 oz. ASW.

## 1878-S Half Dollar
### Grade F-12

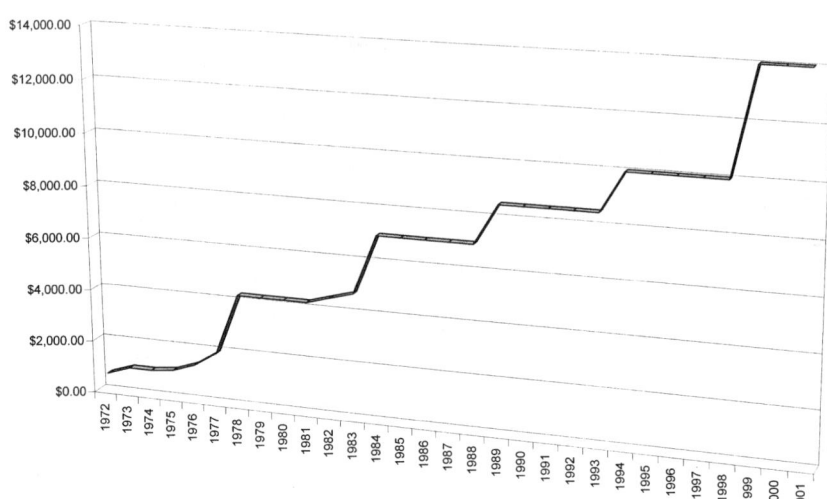

☐ Retail Price

| Date | Mintage | G-4 | VG-8 | F-12 | VF-20 | XF-40 | AU-50 | MS-60 | MS-65 | Prf-65 |
|------|---------|-----|------|------|-------|-------|-------|-------|-------|--------|
| 1875 | 6,027,500 | 15.00 | 24.00 | 29.00 | 43.00 | 60.00 | 120 | 425 | 3,500 | 3,200 |
| 1875CC | 1,008,000 | 18.00 | 34.00 | 53.00 | 95.00 | 185 | 300 | 540 | 5,450 | — |
| 1875S | 3,200,000 | 15.00 | 24.00 | 29.00 | 45.00 | 80.00 | 135 | 340 | 2,700 | — |
| 1876 | 8,419,150 | 15.00 | 24.00 | 32.00 | 43.00 | 60.00 | 135 | 340 | 5,300 | 3,200 |
| 1876CC | 1,956,000 | 17.00 | 30.00 | 48.00 | 85.00 | 175 | 275 | 560 | 4,200 | — |
| 1876S | 4,528,000 | 15.00 | 24.00 | 32.00 | 43.00 | 70.00 | 145 | 340 | 2,700 | — |
| 1877 | 8,304,510 | 15.00 | 24.00 | 29.00 | 43.00 | 65.00 | 145 | 340 | 2,700 | 3,750 |
| 1877CC | 1,420,000 | 17.00 | 33.00 | 43.00 | 75.00 | 145 | 275 | 630 | 3,250 | — |
| 1877S | 5,356,000 | 15.00 | 24.00 | 29.00 | 43.00 | 65.00 | 145 | 340 | 2,700 | — |
| 1878 | 1,378,400 | 20.00 | 28.00 | 36.00 | 55.00 | 115 | 170 | 425 | 3,650 | 3,200 |
| 1878CC | 62,000 | 300 | 385 | 500 | 850 | 1,350 | 2,300 | 4,000 | — | — |
| 1878S | 12,000 | 8,500 | 11,000 | 14,000 | 17,500 | 22,500 | 30,000 | 35,000 | — | — |
| 1879 | 5,900 | 215 | 245 | 290 | 350 | 400 | 475 | 700 | 2,900 | 3,250 |
| 1880 | 9,755 | 190 | 210 | 240 | 310 | 375 | 475 | 700 | 2,900 | 3,250 |
| 1881 | 10,975 | 180 | 195 | 240 | 300 | 365 | 465 | 700 | 2,900 | 3,250 |
| 1882 | 5,500 | 250 | 270 | 310 | 390 | 470 | 550 | 850 | 3,600 | 3,250 |
| 1883 | 9,039 | 200 | 220 | 250 | 290 | 375 | 475 | 750 | 2,900 | 3,250 |
| 1884 | 5,275 | 275 | 300 | 365 | 425 | 475 | 550 | 800 | 2,900 | 3,250 |
| 1885 | 6,130 | 245 | 265 | 300 | 360 | 435 | 525 | 800 | 2,900 | 3,250 |
| 1886 | 5,886 | 295 | 345 | 410 | 450 | 495 | 600 | 850 | 4,800 | 3,250 |
| 1887 | 5,710 | 365 | 420 | 475 | 550 | 650 | 750 | 900 | 2,900 | 3,250 |
| 1888 | 12,833 | 200 | 215 | 260 | 300 | 390 | 450 | 700 | 2,900 | 3,250 |
| 1889 | 12,711 | 185 | 210 | 240 | 310 | 375 | 425 | 700 | 2,900 | 3,250 |
| 1890 | 12,590 | 190 | 210 | 245 | 310 | 385 | 450 | 700 | 3,250 | 3,250 |
| 1891 | 200,600 | 45.00 | 55.00 | 70.00 | 100.00 | 140 | 290 | 500 | 3,250 | 3,250 |

## Liberty.

Mint mark

**Designer:** Charles E. Barber. **Diameter:** 30.6 mm. **Weight:** 12.5000 g. **Composition:** 0.9000 Silver, 0.3618 oz. ASW. **Notes:** Commonly called "Barber half dollar."

| Date | Mintage | G-4 | VG-8 | F-12 | VF-20 | XF-40 | AU-50 | MS-60 | MS-65 | Prf-65 |
|---|---|---|---|---|---|---|---|---|---|---|
| 1892 | 935,245 | 16.00 | 23.00 | 48.00 | 90.00 | 180 | 260 | 390 | 2,600 | 3,300 |
| 1892O | 390,000 | 165 | 190 | 230 | 285 | 405 | 425 | 820 | 5,500 | — |
| 1892 micro o | — | 1,500 | 3,450 | 4,250 | 5,750 | 9,500 | 16,500 | — | 55,000 | — |
| 1892S | 1,029,028 | 170 | 195 | 235 | 295 | 380 | 565 | 855 | 9,900 | — |
| 1893 | 1,826,792 | 13.50 | 20.00 | 49.00 | 87.00 | 150 | 310 | 500 | 4,125 | 3,300 |
| 1893O | 1,389,000 | 20.00 | 34.00 | 70.00 | 125 | 275 | 370 | 520 | 16,500 | — |
| 1893S | 740,000 | 75.00 | 120 | 180 | 330 | 400 | 500 | 1,100 | 12,500 | — |
| 1894 | 1,148,972 | 18.00 | 33.00 | 68.00 | 100.00 | 215 | 350 | 520 | 3,125 | 3,300 |
| 1894O | 2,138,000 | 13.00 | 19.00 | 63.00 | 95.00 | 235 | 340 | 500 | 4,500 | — |
| 1894S | 4,048,690 | 11.00 | 16.00 | 48.00 | 80.00 | 200 | 340 | 440 | 9,600 | — |
| 1895 | 1,835,218 | 9.00 | 15.00 | 50.00 | 85.00 | 165 | 310 | 560 | 3,850 | 3,300 |
| 1895O | 1,766,000 | 12.50 | 22.00 | 55.00 | 100.00 | 230 | 360 | 560 | 6,000 | — |
| 1895S | 1,108,086 | 26.00 | 35.00 | 75.00 | 140 | 260 | 360 | 540 | 7,800 | — |
| 1896 | 950,762 | 14.00 | 21.00 | 55.00 | 90.00 | 200 | 325 | 535 | 5,400 | 3,400 |
| 1896O | 924,000 | 20.00 | 28.00 | 90.00 | 145 | 345 | 620 | 1,150 | 17,600 | — |
| 1896S | 1,140,948 | 60.00 | 80.00 | 125 | 200 | 350 | 540 | 1,100 | 8,800 | — |
| 1897 | 2,480,731 | 8.00 | 10.00 | 30.00 | 75.00 | 130 | 310 | 435 | 4,675 | 3,300 |
| 1897O | 632,000 | 60.00 | 100.00 | 350 | 650 | 850 | 1,150 | 1,450 | 4,950 | — |
| 1897S | 933,900 | 110 | 125 | 260 | 400 | 630 | 945 | 1,250 | 8,000 | — |
| 1898 | 2,956,735 | 6.75 | 8.00 | 28.00 | 71.00 | 135 | 300 | 390 | 2,600 | 3,300 |
| 1898O | 874,000 | 15.00 | 36.00 | 100.00 | 180 | 360 | 495 | 800 | 10,450 | — |
| 1898S | 2,358,550 | 12.00 | 19.00 | 42.00 | 86.00 | 200 | 350 | 800 | 12,000 | — |
| 1899 | 5,538,846 | 6.75 | 8.00 | 26.00 | 71.00 | 135 | 300 | 390 | 5,225 | 3,900 |
| 1899O | 1,724,000 | 8.00 | 13.00 | 45.00 | 90.00 | 210 | 360 | 585 | 6,100 | — |
| 1899S | 1,686,411 | 14.00 | 22.00 | 54.00 | 88.00 | 190 | 340 | 585 | 6,600 | — |
| 1900 | 4,762,912 | 6.00 | 7.75 | 28.00 | 71.00 | 130 | 300 | 390 | 2,600 | 3,300 |
| 1900O | 2,744,000 | 7.00 | 9.00 | 40.00 | 90.00 | 250 | 310 | 750 | 14,500 | — |
| 1900S | 2,560,322 | 8.00 | 12.00 | 42.00 | 95.00 | 190 | 310 | 625 | 9,600 | — |
| 1901 | 4,268,813 | 6.00 | 7.75 | 28.00 | 71.00 | 130 | 300 | 390 | 4,200 | 3,500 |
| 1901O | 1,124,000 | 8.00 | 13.00 | 53.00 | 115 | 285 | 450 | 1,250 | 14,500 | — |
| 1901S | 847,044 | 13.00 | 29.00 | 110 | 240 | 500 | 880 | 1,400 | 12,500 | — |
| 1902 | 4,922,777 | 5.85 | 7.75 | 28.00 | 71.00 | 130 | 260 | 390 | 3,400 | 3,700 |
| 1902O | 2,526,000 | 6.50 | 11.00 | 38.00 | 77.00 | 190 | 350 | 690 | 9,900 | — |
| 1902S | 1,460,670 | 8.00 | 13.00 | 48.00 | 87.00 | 200 | 360 | 585 | 5,500 | — |
| 1903 | 2,278,755 | 7.50 | 10.00 | 37.00 | 78.00 | 165 | 325 | 500 | 8,000 | 3,825 |
| 1903O | 2,100,000 | 7.00 | 12.00 | 43.00 | 75.00 | 180 | 325 | 690 | 9,000 | — |
| 1903S | 1,920,772 | 7.00 | 12.00 | 43.00 | 75.00 | 210 | 365 | 565 | 5,900 | — |
| 1904 | 2,992,670 | 5.85 | 8.00 | 28.00 | 71.00 | 130 | 300 | 390 | 4,200 | 4,100 |
| 1904O | 1,117,600 | 9.00 | 17.00 | 50.00 | 110 | 300 | 500 | 1,000 | 9,600 | — |
| 1904S | 553,038 | 16.00 | 29.00 | 135 | 365 | 750 | 1,250 | 2,250 | 14,000 | — |
| 1905 | 662,727 | 12.00 | 19.00 | 52.00 | 78.00 | 195 | 300 | 540 | 5,400 | 3,900 |
| 1905O | 505,000 | 15.00 | 29.00 | 80.00 | 150 | 240 | 415 | 715 | 6,000 | — |
| 1905S | 2,494,000 | 6.00 | 9.00 | 38.00 | 79.00 | 190 | 345 | 550 | 9,000 | — |
| 1906 | 2,638,675 | 5.50 | 7.50 | 27.00 | 71.00 | 130 | 300 | 390 | 3,400 | 3,300 |
| 1906D | 4,028,000 | 5.50 | 7.50 | 27.00 | 71.00 | 140 | 300 | 390 | 4,100 | — |
| 1906O | 2,446,000 | 5.50 | 7.50 | 35.00 | 74.00 | 165 | 300 | 585 | 5,400 | — |
| 1906S | 1,740,154 | 6.75 | 12.00 | 42.00 | 80.00 | 190 | 300 | 565 | 5,650 | — |
| 1907 | 2,598,575 | 5.50 | 6.75 | 26.00 | 75.00 | 130 | 300 | 400 | 2,600 | 4,000 |
| 1907D | 3,856,000 | 5.50 | 8.25 | 27.00 | 75.00 | 150 | 300 | 390 | 2,600 | — |
| 1907O | 3,946,000 | 5.50 | 8.25 | 27.00 | 71.00 | 150 | 300 | 490 | 3,400 | — |
| 1907S | 1,250,000 | 6.50 | 12.00 | 50.00 | 125 | 300 | 450 | 850 | 10,750 | — |
| 1908 | 1,354,545 | 5.75 | 8.00 | 31.00 | 74.00 | 150 | 300 | 390 | 3,250 | 4,000 |
| 1908D | 3,280,000 | 5.50 | 7.50 | 28.00 | 71.00 | 145 | 300 | 480 | 2,600 | — |
| 1908O | 5,360,000 | 5.50 | 7.50 | 28.00 | 71.00 | 150 | 300 | 480 | 2,600 | — |
| 1908S | 1,644,828 | 6.00 | 12.00 | 42.00 | 82.00 | 190 | 340 | 750 | 5,200 | — |
| 1909 | 2,368,650 | 5.50 | 7.50 | 26.00 | 60.00 | 130 | 260 | 390 | 2,600 | 4,000 |
| 1909O | 925,400 | 7.00 | 10.00 | 45.00 | 84.00 | 260 | 475 | 700 | 4,750 | — |
| 1909S | 1,764,000 | 5.75 | 8.50 | 28.00 | 71.00 | 175 | 330 | 550 | 3,350 | — |
| 1910 | 418,551 | 8.00 | 12.00 | 64.00 | 115 | 260 | 415 | 585 | 3,850 | 4,250 |
| 1910S | 1,948,000 | 5.50 | 8.25 | 28.00 | 71.00 | 175 | 325 | 625 | 4,300 | — |
| 1911 | 1,406,543 | 5.50 | 6.75 | 28.00 | 60.00 | 130 | 300 | 390 | 2,600 | 3,300 |
| 1911D | 695,080 | 6.50 | 11.00 | 39.00 | 82.00 | 180 | 260 | 540 | 2,600 | — |
| 1911S | 1,272,000 | 5.50 | 9.00 | 31.00 | 74.00 | 165 | 320 | 550 | 4,900 | — |
| 1912 | 1,550,700 | 5.50 | 7.50 | 26.00 | 60.00 | 150 | 320 | 390 | 3,700 | 4,000 |
| 1912D | 2,300,800 | 5.50 | 8.25 | 26.00 | 71.00 | 130 | 300 | 425 | 2,600 | — |
| 1912S | 1,370,000 | 5.50 | 9.00 | 29.00 | 71.00 | 165 | 320 | 500 | 5,300 | — |
| 1913 | 188,627 | 20.00 | 25.00 | 100.00 | 175 | 345 | 630 | 880 | 3,800 | 3,800 |
| 1913D | 534,000 | 7.00 | 10.00 | 35.00 | 73.00 | 175 | 285 | 495 | 4,550 | — |
| 1913S | 604,000 | 7.50 | 11.00 | 44.00 | 80.00 | 190 | 350 | 585 | 4,000 | — |
| 1914 | 124,610 | 33.00 | 45.00 | 160 | 295 | 460 | 730 | 915 | 9,200 | 4,300 |
| 1914S | 992,000 | 6.50 | 9.00 | 34.00 | 71.00 | 175 | 345 | 550 | 3,400 | — |
| 1915 | 138,450 | 22.00 | 32.00 | 90.00 | 190 | 350 | 665 | 945 | 4,550 | 4,250 |
| 1915D | 1,170,400 | 5.50 | 7.00 | 27.00 | 71.00 | 135 | 260 | 390 | 2,600 | — |
| 1915S | 1,604,000 | 5.50 | 7.00 | 27.00 | 71.00 | 145 | 270 | 470 | 2,600 | — |

# Walking Liberty.

Obverse mint mark          Reverse mint mark

**Designer:** Adolph A. Weinman. **Diameter:** 30.6 mm. **Weight:** 12.5000 g. **Composition:** 0.9000 Silver, 0.3618 oz. ASW. **Notes:** The mint mark appears on the obverse below the word "Trust" on 1916 and some 1917 issues. Starting with some 1917 issues and continuing through the remainder of the series, the mint mark was changed to the reverse, at about the 8 o'clock position near the rim.

| Date | Mintage | G-4 | VG-8 | F-12 | VF-20 | XF-40 | AU-50 | MS-60 | MS-65 | Prf-65 |
|---|---|---|---|---|---|---|---|---|---|---|
| 1916 | 608,000 | 27.50 | 32.50 | 55.00 | 110 | 150 | 210 | 270 | 1,425 | — |
| 1916D | 1,014,400 | 21.00 | 27.50 | 40.00 | 70.00 | 135 | 185 | 260 | 1,800 | — |
| 1916S | 508,000 | 85.00 | 90.00 | 130 | 310 | 550 | 700 | 950 | 4,800 | — |
| 1917D obverse mint mark | 765,400 | 14.00 | 21.00 | 40.00 | 84.00 | 140 | 215 | 500 | 6,000 | — |
| 1917S obverse mint mark | 952,000 | 17.00 | 29.00 | 50.00 | 250 | 675 | 1,100 | 1,950 | 16,000 | — |
| 1917 | 12,292,000 | 3.50 | 5.00 | 8.00 | 16.00 | 32.50 | 60.00 | 110 | 800 | — |
| 1917D reverse mint mark | 1,940,000 | 9.00 | 14.00 | 24.00 | 80.00 | 195 | 400 | 700 | 16,000 | — |
| 1917S reverse mint mark | 5,554,000 | 4.00 | 6.50 | 12.00 | 27.50 | 50.00 | 125 | 300 | 9,500 | — |
| 1918 | 6,634,000 | 4.00 | 6.00 | 14.00 | 47.50 | 130 | 245 | 500 | 3,500 | — |
| 1918D | 3,853,040 | 5.50 | 7.50 | 27.50 | 51.00 | 150 | 350 | 825 | 21,000 | — |
| 1918S | 10,282,000 | 4.00 | 6.00 | 14.00 | 27.00 | 55.00 | 145 | 400 | 15,500 | — |
| 1919 | 962,000 | 17.00 | 22.00 | 40.00 | 150 | 400 | 600 | 1,000 | 5,000 | — |
| 1919D | 1,165,000 | 12.00 | 16.00 | 47.50 | 150 | 575 | 875 | 2,700 | 100,000 | — |
| 1919S | 1,552,000 | 14.00 | 18.00 | 32.00 | 150 | 700 | 1,500 | 2,100 | 13,200 | — |
| 1920 | 6,372,000 | 4.00 | 5.00 | 10.00 | 25.00 | 60.00 | 95.00 | 300 | 6,000 | — |
| 1920D | 1,551,000 | 9.00 | 11.00 | 27.50 | 130 | 350 | 665 | 1,075 | 9,800 | — |
| 1920S | 4,624,000 | 5.00 | 7.00 | 14.00 | 47.50 | 195 | 385 | 700 | 10,500 | — |
| 1921 | 246,000 | 100.00 | 135 | 200 | 575 | 1,400 | 2,300 | 3,250 | 12,300 | — |
| 1921D | 208,000 | 145 | 180 | 265 | 690 | 2,000 | 2,700 | 3,200 | 13,800 | — |
| 1921S | 548,000 | 24.00 | 27.00 | 100.00 | 630 | 4,200 | 6,700 | 8,700 | 60,000 | — |
| 1923S | 2,178,000 | 8.00 | 10.00 | 20.00 | 55.00 | 210 | 575 | 1,150 | 12,000 | — |
| 1927S | 2,392,000 | 4.00 | 6.00 | 10.00 | 30.00 | 95.00 | 275 | 720 | 8,200 | — |

## 1923-S Half Dollar
Grade XF-40

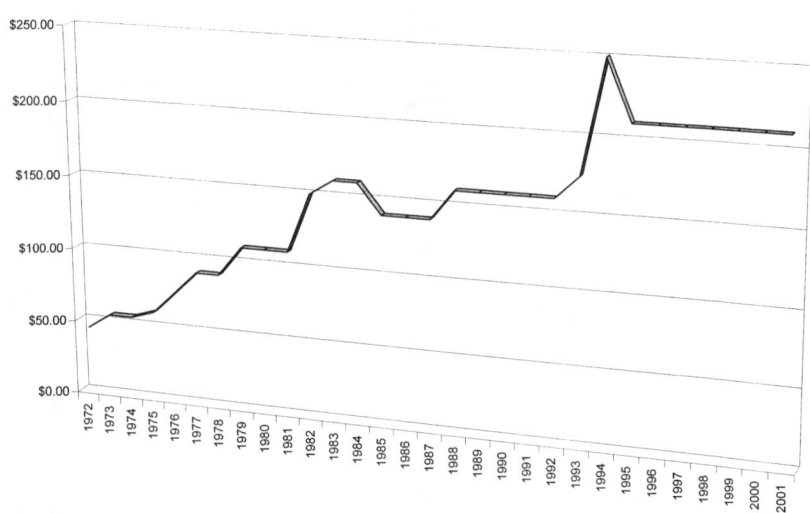

☐ Retail Price

| Date | Mintage | G-4 | VG-8 | F-12 | VF-20 | XF-40 | AU-50 | MS-60 | MS-65 | Prf-65 |
|------|---------|-----|------|------|-------|-------|-------|-------|-------|--------|
| 1928S | 1,940,000 | 4.00 | 6.00 | 11.00 | 35.00 | 100.00 | 300 | 700 | 7,500 | — |
| 1929D | 1,001,200 | 6.00 | 8.00 | 12.00 | 21.00 | 70.00 | 150 | 280 | 2,050 | — |
| 1929S | 1,902,000 | 4.00 | 6.00 | 10.00 | 18.00 | 70.00 | 175 | 325 | 2,200 | — |
| 1933S | 1,786,000 | 5.00 | 7.00 | 9.00 | 11.50 | 45.00 | 215 | 500 | 3,250 | — |
| 1934 | 6,964,000 | 3.25 | 3.50 | 3.75 | 4.00 | 8.00 | 25.00 | 53.00 | 370 | — |
| 1934D | 2,361,400 | 3.50 | 5.00 | 5.50 | 7.50 | 25.00 | 60.00 | 150 | 800 | — |
| 1934S | 3,652,000 | 3.25 | 3.50 | 4.00 | 5.00 | 25.00 | 90.00 | 275 | 3,000 | — |
| 1935 | 9,162,000 | 3.00 | 3.50 | 3.75 | 4.50 | 6.00 | 22.00 | 44.00 | 300 | — |
| 1935D | 3,003,800 | 3.50 | 3.75 | 4.00 | 6.00 | 22.50 | 53.00 | 140 | 1,320 | — |
| 1935S | 3,854,000 | 3.25 | 3.50 | 3.75 | 4.50 | 25.00 | 98.00 | 190 | 2,000 | — |
| 1936 | 12,617,901 | 3.00 | 3.25 | 3.50 | 4.00 | 6.00 | 21.00 | 37.00 | 145 | 3,250 |
| 1936D | 4,252,400 | 3.25 | 3.50 | 4.00 | 4.50 | 16.00 | 42.00 | 76.00 | 350 | — |
| 1936S | 3,884,000 | 3.25 | 3.50 | 4.50 | 5.00 | 19.00 | 60.00 | 125 | 420 | — |
| 1937 | 9,527,728 | 3.00 | 3.25 | 3.50 | 4.50 | 6.00 | 21.00 | 38.00 | 200 | 850 |
| 1937D | 1,676,000 | 5.00 | 6.00 | 8.00 | 11.00 | 28.00 | 80.00 | 150 | 420 | — |
| 1937S | 2,090,000 | 4.00 | 5.00 | 6.00 | 8.00 | 18.00 | 63.00 | 125 | 450 | — |
| 1938 | 4,118,152 | 3.00 | 3.50 | 4.50 | 6.50 | 11.00 | 40.00 | 65.00 | 260 | 580 |
| 1938D | 491,600 | 22.00 | 25.00 | 28.00 | 34.00 | 90.00 | 240 | 400 | 900 | — |
| 1939 | 6,820,808 | 3.00 | 3.25 | 3.50 | 4.50 | 10.00 | 21.00 | 39.00 | 140 | 525 |
| 1939D | 4,267,800 | 3.00 | 3.50 | 4.50 | 5.50 | 10.50 | 22.00 | 39.00 | 160 | — |
| 1939S | 2,552,000 | 4.00 | 5.00 | 6.00 | 9.00 | 13.00 | 49.00 | 100.00 | 210 | — |
| 1940 | 9,167,279 | 3.00 | 3.25 | 3.50 | 5.50 | 9.00 | 11.00 | 29.00 | 125 | 450 |
| 1940S | 4,550,000 | 3.00 | 3.25 | 3.50 | 5.50 | 10.00 | 16.00 | 32.50 | 425 | — |
| 1941 | 24,207,412 | 3.00 | 3.25 | 3.50 | 4.50 | 7.00 | 11.00 | 30.00 | 110 | 375 |
| 1941D | 11,248,400 | 3.00 | 3.25 | 3.50 | 4.50 | 6.00 | 14.00 | 36.00 | 125 | — |
| 1941S | 8,098,000 | 3.00 | 3.25 | 3.50 | 4.75 | 7.00 | 26.00 | 72.00 | 1,150 | — |
| 1942 | 47,839,120 | 3.00 | 3.25 | 3.50 | 4.50 | 5.50 | 11.00 | 30.00 | 105 | 375 |
| 1942D | 10,973,800 | 3.00 | 3.25 | 3.50 | 4.50 | 6.00 | 16.00 | 38.00 | 175 | — |
| 1942S | 12,708,000 | 3.00 | 3.25 | 3.50 | 4.75 | 7.00 | 20.00 | 38.00 | 550 | — |
| 1943 | 53,190,000 | 3.00 | 3.25 | 3.50 | 4.50 | 5.50 | 11.00 | 28.00 | 100.00 | — |
| 1943D | 11,346,000 | 3.00 | 3.25 | 3.50 | 4.50 | 6.00 | 20.00 | 40.00 | 125 | — |
| 1943S | 13,450,000 | 3.00 | 3.25 | 3.50 | 4.75 | 6.00 | 18.00 | 35.00 | 390 | — |
| 1944 | 28,206,000 | 3.00 | 3.25 | 3.50 | 4.50 | 5.50 | 11.00 | 30.00 | 105 | — |
| 1944D | 9,769,000 | 3.00 | 3.25 | 3.50 | 4.50 | 6.00 | 16.00 | 35.00 | 110 | — |
| 1944S | 8,904,000 | 3.00 | 3.25 | 3.50 | 4.75 | 6.25 | 17.00 | 36.00 | 450 | — |
| 1945 | 31,502,000 | 3.00 | 3.25 | 3.50 | 4.50 | 5.50 | 11.00 | 26.00 | 100.00 | — |
| 1945D | 9,966,800 | 3.00 | 3.25 | 3.50 | 4.50 | 6.00 | 14.00 | 32.50 | 95.00 | — |
| 1945S | 10,156,000 | 3.00 | 3.25 | 3.50 | 4.75 | 6.00 | 15.00 | 34.00 | 145 | — |
| 1946 | 12,118,000 | 3.00 | 3.25 | 3.50 | 4.50 | 5.50 | 12.00 | 30.00 | 145 | — |
| 1946D | 2,151,000 | 3.00 | 3.50 | 4.00 | 5.50 | 7.00 | 19.00 | 35.00 | 90.00 | — |
| 1946S | 3,724,000 | 2.65 | 3.00 | 3.25 | 5.00 | 5.50 | 16.00 | 33.00 | 120 | — |
| 1947 | 4,094,000 | 2.65 | 3.00 | 3.25 | 5.00 | 7.00 | 18.00 | 34.00 | 160 | — |
| 1947D | 3,900,600 | 2.65 | 3.00 | 3.25 | 5.00 | 7.00 | 20.00 | 35.00 | 125 | — |

## Franklin.

  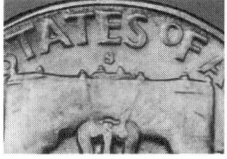

Mint mark

**Designer:** John R. Sinnock. **Diameter:** 30.6 mm. **Weight:** 12.5000 g. **Composition:** 0.9000 Silver, 0.3618 oz. ASW.

| Date | Mintage | G-4 | VG-8 | F-12 | VF-20 | XF-40 | AU-50 | MS-60 | MS-65 | -65FBL | -65CAM |
|------|---------|-----|------|------|-------|-------|-------|-------|-------|--------|--------|
| 1948 | 3,006,814 | — | 3.00 | 4.00 | 4.25 | 4.50 | 6.00 | 13.75 | 90.00 | 315 | — |
| 1948D | 4,028,600 | — | 3.00 | 3.25 | 3.50 | 3.75 | 5.00 | 10.00 | 195 | 325 | — |
| 1949 | 5,614,000 | — | 3.00 | 3.25 | 3.50 | 4.00 | 10.00 | 28.00 | 150 | 290 | — |
| 1949D | 4,120,600 | — | 3.00 | 3.50 | 3.75 | 4.00 | 13.00 | 29.00 | 1,050 | 2,350 | — |
| 1949S | 3,744,000 | — | 3.50 | 4.00 | 6.25 | 8.00 | 21.00 | 48.00 | 210 | 775 | — |
| 1950 | 7,793,509 | — | — | 3.00 | 3.50 | 6.00 | 7.00 | 20.00 | 150 | 350 | 3,700 |
| 1950D | 8,031,600 | — | — | 3.00 | 3.50 | 6.50 | 7.75 | 16.00 | 575 | 1,150 | — |
| 1951 | 16,859,602 | — | — | 3.00 | 3.50 | 4.00 | 4.50 | 9.00 | 95.00 | 375 | 2,200 |
| 1951D | 9,475,200 | — | — | 3.00 | 4.25 | 5.00 | 11.50 | 19.00 | 300 | 550 | — |
| 1951S | 13,696,000 | — | — | 2.75 | 3.00 | 3.50 | 10.00 | 18.00 | 125 | 775 | — |
| 1952 | 21,274,073 | — | — | 2.50 | 2.75 | 3.00 | 4.00 | 7.00 | 90.00 | 325 | 1,100 |
| 1952D | 25,395,600 | — | — | 2.50 | 2.75 | 3.00 | 4.00 | 8.50 | 250 | 450 | — |
| 1952S | 5,526,000 | — | — | 2.50 | 3.25 | 3.75 | 17.00 | 38.00 | 135 | 1,100 | — |
| 1953 | 2,796,920 | 3.00 | 3.00 | 3.25 | 3.50 | 5.00 | 10.00 | 14.00 | 275 | 1,100 | 475 |
| 1953D | 20,900,400 | — | — | 2.25 | 3.50 | 4.00 | 4.25 | 7.00 | 250 | 400 | — |
| 1953S | 4,148,000 | — | — | 2.60 | 4.25 | 4.75 | 8.50 | 17.00 | 70.00 | 9,000 | — |
| 1954 | 13,421,503 | — | — | 2.25 | 3.50 | 3.75 | 4.00 | 5.50 | 85.00 | 275 | 250 |
| 1954D | 25,445,580 | — | — | 2.25 | 3.25 | 3.50 | 4.00 | 5.50 | 165 | 250 | — |

## 1953 Half Dollar
### Grade MS-60

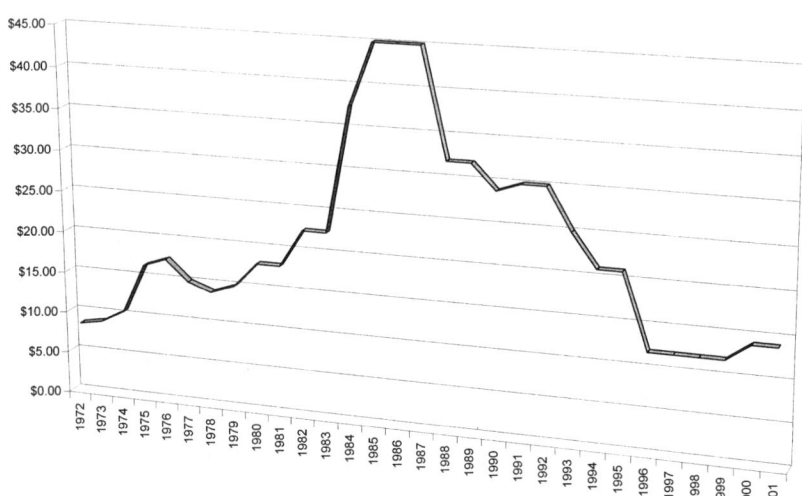

☐ Retail Price

| Date | Mintage | G-4 | VG-8 | F-12 | VF-20 | XF-40 | AU-50 | MS-60 | MS-65 | -65FBL | -65CAM |
|------|---------|-----|------|------|-------|-------|-------|-------|-------|--------|--------|
| 1954S | 4,993,400 | — | — | 2.25 | 3.75 | 4.00 | 4.25 | 8.50 | 60.00 | 425 | — |
| 1955 | 2,876,381 | 5.00 | 5.00 | 5.25 | 5.50 | 5.75 | 6.00 | 7.50 | 75.00 | 160 | 195 |
| 1956 | 4,701,384 | — | — | 2.50 | 3.00 | 3.50 | 4.25 | 5.00 | 50.00 | 120 | 75.00 |
| 1957 | 6,361,952 | — | — | 2.50 | 2.75 | 3.00 | 3.75 | 6.00 | 50.00 | 120 | 135 |
| 1957D | 19,966,850 | — | — | — | 2.10 | 2.25 | 2.50 | 5.00 | 50.00 | 105 | — |
| 1958 | 4,917,652 | — | — | 2.25 | 2.50 | 2.75 | 3.00 | 5.00 | 50.00 | 135 | 250 |
| 1958D | 23,962,412 | — | — | — | 2.25 | 2.50 | 2.75 | 4.25 | 50.00 | 105 | — |
| 1959 | 7,349,291 | — | — | — | 2.25 | 2.50 | 2.75 | 4.50 | 150 | 295 | 475 |
| 1959D | 13,053,750 | — | — | — | 2.25 | 2.50 | 2.75 | 5.00 | 150 | 275 | — |
| 1960 | 7,715,602 | — | — | — | 2.25 | 2.50 | 2.75 | 4.25 | 175 | 400 | 75.00 |
| 1960D | 18,215,812 | — | — | — | 2.25 | 2.50 | 2.75 | 4.50 | 750 | 1,450 | — |
| 1961 | 11,318,244 | — | — | — | 2.25 | 2.50 | 2.75 | 4.25 | 275 | 1,900 | 75.00 |
| 1961D | 20,276,442 | — | — | — | 2.25 | 2.50 | 2.75 | 4.50 | 450 | 1,050 | — |
| 1962 | 12,932,019 | — | — | — | 2.25 | 2.50 | 2.75 | 4.25 | 290 | 2,600 | 50.00 |
| 1962D | 35,473,281 | — | — | — | 2.25 | 2.50 | 2.75 | 4.25 | 400 | 1,000 | — |
| 1963 | 25,239,645 | — | — | — | — | 2.50 | 2.75 | 4.00 | 90.00 | 975 | 50.00 |
| 1963D | 67,069,292 | — | — | — | — | 2.50 | 2.75 | 4.00 | 90.00 | 250 | — |

## Kennedy.

Reverse mint mark
1964

Obverse mint mark
1968-present

**Obv. Designer:** Gilroy Roberts. **Rev. Designer:** Frank Gasparro. **Diameter:** 30.6 mm. **Weight:** 12.5000 g.
**Composition:** 0.9000 Silver, 0.3618 oz. ASW.

| Date | Mintage | G-4 | VG-8 | F-12 | VF-20 | XF-40 | MS-60 | MS-65 | Prf-65 |
|------|---------|-----|------|------|-------|-------|-------|-------|--------|
| 1964 | 277,254,766 | — | — | — | — | — | 3.00 | 9.00 | 10.00 |
| 1964D | 156,205,446 | — | — | — | — | — | 3.50 | 12.00 | — |

**Obv. Designer:** Gilroy Roberts. **Rev. Designer:** Frank Gasparro. **Diameter:** 30.6 mm. **Weight:** 11.5000 g.
**Composition:** 0.4000 Silver, 0.1480 oz. ASW.

| Date | Mintage | G-4 | VG-8 | F-12 | VF-20 | XF-40 | MS-60 | MS-65 | Prf-65 |
|------|---------|-----|------|------|-------|-------|-------|-------|--------|
| 1965 | 65,879,366 | — | — | — | — | — | 1.25 | 9.50 | — |
| 1966 | 108,984,932 | — | — | — | — | — | 1.40 | 11.00 | — |
| 1967 | 295,046,978 | — | — | — | — | — | 1.50 | 9.50 | — |

| Date | Mintage | G-4 | VG-8 | F-12 | VF-20 | XF-40 | MS-60 | MS-65 | Prf-65 |
|------|---------|-----|------|------|-------|-------|-------|-------|--------|
| 1968D | 246,951,930 | — | — | — | — | — | 1.25 | 9.00 | — |
| 1968S | 3,041,506 | — | — | — | — | — | — | — | 5.00 |
| 1969D | 129,881,800 | — | — | — | — | — | 1.25 | 7.50 | — |
| 1969S | 2,934,631 | — | — | — | — | — | — | — | 5.00 |
| 1970D | 2,150,000 | — | — | — | — | — | 9.00 | 32.00 | — |
| 1970S | 2,632,810 | — | — | — | — | — | — | — | 7.50 |

**Obv. Designer:** Gilroy Roberts. **Rev. Designer:** Frank Gasparro. **Diameter:** 30.6 mm. **Weight:** 11.3400 g. **Composition:** Copper-nickel Clad Copper.

| Date | Mintage | G-4 | VG-8 | F-12 | VF-20 | XF-40 | MS-60 | MS-65 | Prf-65 |
|------|---------|-----|------|------|-------|-------|-------|-------|--------|
| 1971 | 155,640,000 | — | — | — | — | — | 1.50 | 12.00 | — |
| 1971D | 302,097,424 | — | — | — | — | — | 1.00 | 5.00 | — |
| 1971S | 3,244,183 | — | — | — | — | — | — | — | 3.00 |
| 1972 | 153,180,000 | — | — | — | — | — | 1.00 | 9.00 | — |
| 1972D | 141,890,000 | — | — | — | — | — | 1.00 | 6.00 | — |
| 1972S | 3,267,667 | — | — | — | — | — | — | — | 2.50 |
| 1973 | 64,964,000 | — | — | — | — | — | 1.00 | 6.00 | — |
| 1973D | 83,171,400 | — | — | — | — | — | — | 5.50 | — |
| 1973S | — | — | — | — | — | — | — | — | 2.50 |
| 1974 | 201,596,000 | — | — | — | — | — | 1.00 | 5.00 | — |
| 1974D | 79,066,300 | — | — | — | — | — | 1.00 | 6.00 | — |
| 1974S | — | — | — | — | — | — | — | — | 3.00 |
| 1975 | — | — | — | — | — | — | — | — | — |
| 1975D none minted | — | — | — | — | — | — | — | — | — |
| 1975S none minted | — | — | — | — | — | — | — | — | — |

## Kennedy. Bicentennial design, Independence Hall.

**Rev. Designer:** Seth Huntington. **Composition:** Copper-nickel Clad Copper.

| Date | Mintage | G-4 | VG-8 | F-12 | VF-20 | XF-40 | MS-60 | MS-65 | Prf-65 |
|------|---------|-----|------|------|-------|-------|-------|-------|--------|
| 1976 | 234,308,000 | — | — | — | — | — | 1.00 | 10.00 | — |
| 1976D | 287,565,248 | — | — | — | — | — | 1.00 | 4.50 | — |
| 1976S | — | — | — | — | — | — | — | — | 1.75 |

## Kennedy. Bicentennial design, Independence Hall.

**Rev. Designer:** Seth Huntington. **Weight:** 11.5000 g. **Composition:** 0.4000 Silver, 0.1480 oz. ASW.

| Date | Mintage | G-4 | VG-8 | F-12 | VF-20 | XF-40 | MS-60 | MS-65 | Prf-65 |
|------|---------|-----|------|------|-------|-------|-------|-------|--------|
| 1976S | 11,000,000 | — | — | — | — | — | — | 6.50 | 5.00 |

## Kennedy. Regular design resumed.

**Diameter:** 30.6 mm. **Weight:** 11.3400 g. **Composition:** Copper-nickel Clad Copper. **Notes:** The 1979-S and 1981-S Type II proofs have clearer mint marks than the Type I proofs of those years.

| Date | Mintage | MS-65 | Prf-65 | Date | Mintage | MS-65 | Prf-65 |
|------|---------|-------|--------|------|---------|-------|--------|
| 1977 | 43,598,000 | 6.50 | — | 1984P | 26,029,000 | 5.00 | — |
| 1977D | 31,449,106 | 6.00 | — | 1984D | 26,262,158 | 5.00 | — |
| 1977S | — | — | 1.75 | 1984S | — | — | 4.00 |
| 1978 | 14,350,000 | 6.50 | — | 1985P | 18,706,962 | 5.00 | — |
| 1978D | 13,765,799 | 6.50 | — | 1985D | 19,814,034 | 5.00 | — |
| 1978S | — | — | 2.50 | 1985S | — | — | 4.50 |
| 1979 | 68,312,000 | 5.50 | — | 1986P | 13,107,633 | 16.00 | — |
| 1979D | 15,815,422 | 6.00 | — | 1986D | 15,336,145 | 7.00 | — |
| 1979S type I, proof only | — | — | 2.50 | 1986S | — | — | 7.50 |
| 1979S type II, proof only | — | — | 18.00 | 1987P | 2,890,758 | 9.00 | — |
| 1980P | 44,134,000 | 5.00 | — | 1987D | 2,890,758 | 9.00 | — |
| 1980D | 33,456,449 | 4.50 | — | 1987S | — | — | 3.50 |
| 1980S | — | — | 2.00 | 1988P | 13,626,000 | 6.00 | — |
| 1981P | 29,544,000 | 4.50 | — | 1988D | 12,000,096 | 6.00 | — |
| 1981D | 27,839,533 | 4.50 | — | 1988S | — | — | 4.00 |
| 1981S type I, proof only | — | — | 2.00 | 1989P | 24,542,000 | 8.00 | — |
| 1981S type II, proof only | — | — | 14.50 | 1989D | 23,000,216 | 8.00 | — |
| 1982P | 10,819,000 | 5.00 | — | 1989S | — | — | 3.50 |
| 1982D | 13,140,102 | 5.00 | — | 1990P | 22,780,000 | 15.00 | — |
| 1982S | — | — | 3.50 | 1990D | 20,096,242 | 15.00 | — |
| 1983P | 34,139,000 | 5.00 | — | 1990S | — | — | 5.00 |
| 1983D | 32,472,244 | 5.00 | — | 1991P | 14,874,000 | 7.00 | — |
| 1983S | — | — | 3.00 | 1991D | 15,054,678 | 7.00 | — |

| Date | Mintage | MS-65 | Prf-65 | Date | Mintage | MS-65 | Prf-65 |
|------|---------|-------|--------|------|---------|-------|--------|
| 1991S | (2,867,787) | — | 8.50 | 1997P | 20,882,000 | 7.00 | — |
| 1992P | 17,628,000 | 7.00 | — | 1997D | 19,876,000 | 6.00 | — |
| 1992D | 17,000,106 | 7.00 | — | 1997S | (1,975,000) | — | — |
| 1992S | (2,858,981) | — | 8.50 | 1997S silver proof | | | 28.00 |
| 1993P | 15,510,000 | 1.50 | — | 1998P | 15,646,000 | 9.00 | — |
| 1993D | 15,000,006 | 7.00 | — | 1998D | 15,064,000 | 8.00 | — |
| 1993S | (2,633,439) | — | 14.00 | 1998S | 62,350 | — | — |
| 1994P | 23,718,000 | 6.00 | — | 1998S matte finish | — | 190 | 400 |
| 1994D | 23,828,110 | 6.00 | — | 1999P | — | 6.00 | — |
| 1994S | (2,484,594) | — | — | 1999D | — | 6.00 | — |
| 1995P | 26,496,000 | 6.00 | — | 1999S | — | — | — |
| 1995D | 26,288,000 | 6.00 | — | 2000P | — | — | — |
| 1995S | — | — | 30.00 | 2000D | — | — | — |
| 1995S | (2,010,384) | — | — | 2000S | — | — | — |
| 1996P | 24,442,000 | 6.00 | — | 2001P | — | — | — |
| 1996D | 24,744,000 | 6.00 | — | 2001D | — | — | — |
| 1996S | — | — | — | 2001S | — | — | — |

**Composition:** Silver.

| Date | Mintage | MS-65 | Prf-65 | Date | Mintage | MS-65 | Prf-65 |
|------|---------|-------|--------|------|---------|-------|--------|
| 1992S | (1,317,579) | — | 12.00 | 1998S | — | — | — |
| 1993S | (761,353) | — | 19.00 | 1999S | — | — | — |
| 1994S | (785,329) | — | 25.00 | 2000S | — | — | — |
| 1996S | — | — | — | 2001S | — | — | — |
| 1997S | — | — | — | | | | |

# DOLLAR

## Flowing hair.

**Designer:** Robert Scot. **Diameter:** 39-40 mm. **Weight:** 26.9600 g. **Composition:** 0.8920 Silver, 0.7737 oz. ASW. **Notes:** The two 1795 varieties have either two or three leaves under each of the eagle's wings on the reverse.

| Date | Mintage | G-4 | VG-8 | F-12 | VF-20 | XF-40 | MS-60 |
|------|---------|-----|------|------|-------|-------|-------|
| 1794 | 1,758 | 10,000 | 13,500 | 18,500 | 27,500 | 42,500 | — |
| 1795 2 leaves | 203,033 | 800 | 900 | 1,500 | 2,200 | 4,400 | 40,000 |
| 1795 3 leaves | Inc. above | 800 | 900 | 1,500 | 2,200 | 4,400 | 40,000 |

## Draped bust. Small eagle.

**Designer:** Robert Scot. **Diameter:** 39-40 mm. **Weight:** 26.9600 g. **Composition:** 0.8920 Silver, 0.7737 oz. ASW. **Notes:** The 1796 varieties are distinguished by the size of the numerals in the date and letters in

## 1794 Silver Dollar
### Grade XF-40

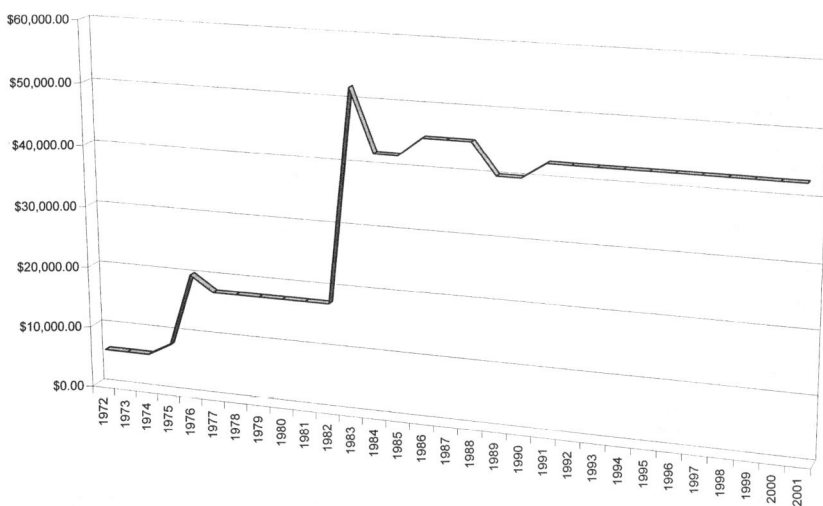

"United States of America." The 1797 varieties are distinguished by the number of stars to the left and right of the word "Liberty" and by the size of the letters in "United States of America." The 1798 varieties have either 13 or 15 stars on the obverse.

| Date | Mintage | G-4 | VG-8 | F-12 | VF-20 | XF-40 | MS-60 |
|------|---------|-----|------|------|-------|-------|-------|
| 1795 | Inc. above | 600 | 800 | 1,070 | 1,825 | 3,750 | 17,000 |
| 1796 small date, small letters | 72,920 | 625 | 825 | 1,150 | 1,950 | 3,650 | 16,000 |
| 1796 small date, large letters | Inc. above | 625 | 825 | 1,100 | 1,600 | 3,500 | 16,000 |
| 1796 large date, small letters | Inc. above | 575 | 765 | 1,050 | 1,400 | 3,300 | 16,000 |
| 1797 9 stars left, 7 stars right, small letters | 7,776 | 1,500 | 2,000 | 2,750 | 4,500 | 8,450 | 22,000 |
| 1797 9 stars left, 7 stars right, large letters | Inc. above | 585 | 775 | 1,050 | 1,400 | 3,300 | 16,000 |
| 1797 10 stars left, 6 stars right | Inc. above | 585 | 775 | 1,050 | 1,400 | 3,300 | 16,000 |
| 1798 13 stars | 327,536 | 900 | 1,150 | 1,450 | 2,400 | 4,500 | 18,000 |
| 1798 15 stars | Inc. above | 1,100 | 1,600 | 2,100 | 3,150 | 6,900 | 18,000 |

## Draped bust. Heraldic eagle.

**Designer:** Robert Scot. **Diameter:** 39-40 mm. **Weight:** 26.9600 g. **Composition:** 0.8920 Silver, 0.7737 oz. ASW. **Notes:** The 1798 "knob 9" variety has a serif on the lower left of the 9 in the date. The 1798 varieties are distinguished by the number of arrows held by the eagle on the reverse and the number of berries on the olive branch. On the 1798 "high-8" variety, the 8 in the date is higher than the other numerals. The 1799 varieties are distinguished by the number and positioning of the stars on the obverse and by the size of the berries in the olive branch on the reverse. On the 1700 "irregular date" variety, the first 9 in the date is smaller than the other numerals. Some varieties of the 1800 strikes had letters in the legend cut twice into the dies; as the dies became worn, the letters were touched up. On the 1800 "very wide date, low 8" variety, the spacing between the numerals in the date are wider than other varieties and the 8 is lower than the other numerals. The 1800 "small berries" variety refers to the size of the berries in the olive branch on the reverse. The 1800 "12 arrows" and "10 arrows" varieties refer to the number of arrows held by the eagle. The 1800 "Americai"

variety appears to have the faint outline of an "I" after "America" in the reverse legend. The "close" and "wide" varieties of 1802 refer to the amount of space between the numerals in the date. The 1800 large-3 and small-3 varieties are distinguished by the size of the 3 in the date.

| Date | Mintage | G-4 | VG-8 | F-12 | VF-20 | XF-40 | MS-60 |
|---|---|---|---|---|---|---|---|
| 1798 knob 9 | Inc. above | 375 | 450 | 575 | 850 | 1,675 | 9,600 |
| 1798 10 arrows | Inc. above | 350 | 440 | 550 | 700 | 1,300 | 9,600 |
| 1798 4 berries | Inc. above | 350 | 440 | 550 | 700 | 1,300 | 9,600 |
| 1798 5 berries, 12 arrows | Inc. above | 350 | 440 | 550 | 700 | 1,300 | 9,600 |
| 1798 high 8 | Inc. above | 350 | 440 | 550 | 700 | 1,300 | 9,600 |
| 1798 13 arrows | Inc. above | 350 | 440 | 550 | 700 | 1,300 | 9,600 |
| 1799/98 13-star reverse | 423,515 | 350 | 440 | 550 | 700 | 1,300 | 15,000 |
| 1799/98 15-star reverse | Inc. above | 400 | 500 | 850 | 1,150 | 2,000 | 15,000 |
| 1799 irregular date, 13-star reverse | Inc. above | 350 | 440 | 550 | 700 | 1,300 | 9,600 |
| 1799 irregular date, 15-star reverse | Inc. above | 350 | 425 | 550 | 700 | 1,300 | 9,600 |
| 1799 perfect date, 7- and 6-star obverse, no berries | Inc. above | 350 | 425 | 550 | 700 | 1,300 | 9,600 |
| 1799 perfect date, 7- and 6-star obverse, small berries | Inc. above | 350 | 425 | 550 | 700 | 1,300 | 9,600 |
| 1799 perfect date, 7- and 6-star obverse, medium large berries | Inc. above | 350 | 425 | 550 | 700 | 1,300 | 9,600 |
| 1799 perfect date, 7- and 6-star obverse, extra large berries | Inc. above | 350 | 440 | 550 | 700 | 1,300 | 9,600 |
| 1799 8 stars left, 5 stars right on obverse | Inc. above | 425 | 500 | 800 | 1,100 | 2,000 | 9,600 |
| 1800 "R" in "Liberty" double cut | 220,920 | 350 | 440 | 550 | 700 | 1,300 | 9,600 |
| 1800 first "T" in "States" double cut | Inc. above | 350 | 440 | 550 | 700 | 1,300 | 9,600 |
| 1800 both letters double cut | Inc. above | 350 | 440 | 550 | 700 | 1,300 | 9,600 |
| 1800 "T" in "United" double cut | Inc. above | 350 | 440 | 550 | 700 | 1,300 | 9,600 |
| 1800 very wide date, low 8 | Inc. above | 350 | 440 | 550 | 700 | 1,300 | 9,600 |
| 1800 small berries | Inc. above | 350 | 440 | 550 | 700 | 1,300 | 9,600 |
| 1800 dot date | Inc. above | 350 | 440 | 550 | 700 | 1,300 | 9,600 |
| 1800 12 arrows | Inc. above | 350 | 440 | 550 | 700 | 1,300 | 9,600 |
| 1800 10 arrows | Inc. above | 350 | 440 | 550 | 700 | 1,300 | 9,600 |
| 1800 "Americai" | Inc. above | 360 | 440 | 550 | 700 | 1,500 | 9,600 |
| 1801 | 54,454 | 400 | 475 | 600 | 850 | 1,900 | 10,000 |
| 1801 proof restrike | — | — | — | — | — | — | — |
| 1802/1 close | Inc. above | 360 | 450 | 550 | 850 | 1,600 | 9,600 |
| 1802/1 wide | Inc. above | 360 | 450 | 550 | 850 | 1,600 | 9,600 |
| 1802 close, perfect date | Inc. above | 375 | 450 | 600 | 875 | 1,650 | 7,500 |
| 1802 wide, perfect date | Inc. above | 375 | 450 | 600 | 875 | 1,650 | 9,600 |
| 1802 proof restrike, mintage unrecorded | — | — | — | — | — | — | — |
| 1803 large 3 | 85,634 | 360 | 440 | 600 | 850 | 1,575 | 9,600 |
| 1803 small 3 | Inc. above | 395 | 475 | 675 | 975 | 1,850 | 7,500 |
| 1803 proof restrike, mintage unrecorded | — | — | — | — | — | — | — |
| 1804 15 known | — | — | — | — | — | — | — |

**Note:** 1804, Childs Sale, Aug. 1999, Prf-68, $4,140,000.

# Seated Liberty. No motto above eagle.

**Designer:** Christian Gobrecht. **Diameter:** 38.1 mm. **Weight:** 26.7300 g. **Composition:** 0.9000 Silver, 0.7736 oz. ASW.

| Date | Mintage | G-4 | VG-8 | F-12 | VF-20 | XF-40 | AU-50 | MS-60 | MS-65 | Prf-65 |
|---|---|---|---|---|---|---|---|---|---|---|
| 1840 | 61,005 | 160 | 180 | 225 | 300 | 525 | 750 | 1,600 | — | — |
| 1841 | 173,000 | 100.00 | 130 | 180 | 220 | 350 | 575 | 1,300 | 24,000 | — |
| 1842 | 184,618 | 100.00 | 120 | 175 | 220 | 300 | 550 | 1,100 | 24,000 | — |
| 1843 | 165,100 | 100.00 | 120 | 175 | 220 | 300 | 550 | 1,400 | 24,000 | — |
| 1844 | 20,000 | 180 | 245 | 300 | 385 | 500 | 900 | 3,000 | — | — |
| 1845 | 24,500 | 175 | 235 | 250 | 350 | 500 | 800 | 2,000 | — | — |
| 1846 | 110,600 | 100.00 | 120 | 175 | 220 | 275 | 500 | 1,400 | 24,000 | — |
| 1846O | 59,000 | 110 | 140 | 210 | 285 | 475 | 1,400 | 4,000 | — | — |

| Date | Mintage | G-4 | VG-8 | F-12 | VF-20 | XF-40 | AU-50 | MS-60 | MS-65 | Prf-65 |
|------|---------|-----|------|------|-------|-------|-------|-------|-------|--------|
| 1847 | 140,750 | 100.00 | 120 | 175 | 220 | 300 | 650 | 950 | 15,000 | — |
| 1848 | 15,000 | 250 | 290 | 400 | 525 | 700 | 1,400 | 2,050 | — | — |
| 1849 | 62,600 | 110 | 140 | 190 | 240 | 350 | 700 | 1,600 | — | — |
| 1850 | 7,500 | 600 | 700 | 800 | 900 | 1,100 | 1,975 | 3,500 | — | — |
| 1850O | 40,000 | 220 | 260 | 350 | 650 | 1,400 | 3,200 | 5,000 | — | — |
| 1851 | 1,300 | — | — | 8,000 | 9,500 | 13,500 | 21,500 | — | — | — |
| 1852 | 1,100 | — | — | 6,500 | 7,500 | 11,500 | 21,500 | — | — | — |
| 1853 | 46,110 | 175 | 225 | 270 | 375 | 575 | 800 | 1,300 | — | — |
| 1854 | 33,140 | 1,000 | 1,200 | 1,500 | 2,250 | 3,900 | 4,850 | 7,000 | — | — |
| 1855 | 26,000 | 800 | 1,000 | 1,300 | 1,900 | 2,650 | 4,500 | 9,000 | — | — |
| 1856 | 63,500 | 400 | 500 | 600 | 750 | 975 | 1,650 | 2,250 | — | — |
| 1857 | 94,000 | 375 | 475 | 550 | 900 | 1,500 | 1,900 | 3,000 | — | — |
| 1858 proof only | Est. 200 | — | — | — | 4,200 | 5,500 | 6,250 | 9,000 | — | — |
| 1859 | 256,500 | 180 | 220 | 300 | 450 | 700 | 1,000 | 2,500 | 15,000 | 13,500 |
| 1859O | 360,000 | 100.00 | 110 | 175 | 210 | 265 | 500 | 950 | 15,000 | — |
| 1859S | 20,000 | 225 | 275 | 400 | 600 | 1,350 | 3,000 | — | — | — |
| 1860 | 218,930 | 140 | 180 | 230 | 300 | 475 | 600 | 1,300 | 15,000 | 13,500 |
| 1860O | 515,000 | 100.00 | 110 | 175 | 210 | 265 | 500 | 900 | 15,000 | — |
| 1861 | 78,500 | 440 | 500 | 600 | 800 | 1,250 | 1,400 | 3,000 | — | 13,500 |
| 1862 | 12,090 | 450 | 525 | 625 | 850 | 1,300 | 1,750 | 3,200 | — | 13,500 |
| 1863 | 27,660 | 325 | 375 | 475 | 600 | 900 | 1,500 | 2,750 | — | 13,500 |
| 1864 | 31,170 | 220 | 265 | 315 | 425 | 675 | 1,300 | 2,900 | — | 13,500 |
| 1865 | 47,000 | 195 | 245 | 290 | 400 | 625 | 1,250 | 2,750 | — | 13,500 |
| 1866 2 known without motto | — | — | — | — | — | — | — | — | — | — |

# Seated Liberty. "In God We Trust" above eagle.

**Designer:** Christian Gobrecht. **Diameter:** 38.1 mm. **Weight:** 26.7300 g. **Composition:** 0.9000 Silver, 0.7736 oz. ASW. **Notes:** In 1866 the motto "In God We Trust" was added to the reverse above the eagle.

| Date | Mintage | G-4 | VG-8 | F-12 | VF-20 | XF-40 | AU-50 | MS-60 | MS-65 | Prf-65 |
|------|---------|-----|------|------|-------|-------|-------|-------|-------|--------|
| 1866 | 49,625 | 150 | 200 | 250 | 350 | 550 | 900 | 1,600 | 28,500 | 7,000 |
| 1867 | 47,525 | 170 | 250 | 300 | 415 | 600 | 1,000 | 1,800 | 28,500 | 7,000 |
| 1868 | 162,700 | 140 | 190 | 225 | 350 | 525 | 900 | 1,700 | 28,500 | 7,000 |
| 1869 | 424,300 | 115 | 150 | 200 | 245 | 415 | 800 | 2,000 | 28,500 | 7,000 |
| 1870 | 416,000 | 100.00 | 120 | 175 | 225 | 325 | 600 | 1,500 | 28,500 | 7,000 |
| 1870CC | 12,462 | 200 | 245 | 325 | 500 | 1,250 | 3,000 | 9,000 | 38,500 | — |
| 1870S mintage unrecorded | — | — | — | — | — | — | — | — | — | — |
| Note: 1870S, Eliasberg Sale, April 1997, EF-45 to AU-50, $264,000. | | | | | | | | | | |
| 1871 | 1,074,760 | 90.00 | 95.00 | 165 | 210 | 315 | 550 | 900 | 24,000 | 7,000 |
| 1871CC | 1,376 | 2,000 | 2,500 | 3,750 | 5,750 | 8,950 | 18,500 | — | — | — |
| 1872 | 1,106,450 | 90.00 | 95.00 | 165 | 210 | 315 | 550 | 1,250 | 24,000 | 7,000 |
| 1872CC | 3,150 | 900 | 1,250 | 1,600 | 2,575 | 4,250 | 8,500 | 15,000 | — | — |
| 1872S | 9,000 | 175 | 225 | 400 | 575 | 1,100 | 3,000 | 10,000 | — | — |
| 1873 | 293,600 | 130 | 150 | 200 | 250 | 350 | 600 | 1,350 | 28,500 | 7,000 |
| 1873CC | 2,300 | 3,250 | 4,750 | 6,500 | 9,500 | 17,500 | 35,000 | 47,500 | — | — |
| 1873S none known to exist | 700 | — | — | — | — | — | — | — | — | — |

# "Trade Dollar".

**Designer:** William Barber. **Diameter:** 38.1 mm. **Weight:** 27.2200 g. **Composition:** 0.9000 Silver, 0.7878 oz. ASW.

| Date | Mintage | G-4 | VG-8 | F-12 | VF-20 | XF-40 | AU-50 | MS-60 | MS-65 | Prf-65 |
|------|---------|-----|------|------|-------|-------|-------|-------|-------|--------|
| 1873 | 397,500 | 100.00 | 110 | 125 | 165 | 250 | 325 | 1,000 | 12,000 | 12,000 |
| 1873CC | 124,500 | 150 | 175 | 225 | 450 | 700 | 1,200 | 2,100 | 80,000 | — |
| 1873S | 703,000 | 130 | 145 | 160 | 180 | 260 | 375 | 1,200 | 25,000 | — |
| 1874 | 987,800 | 120 | 130 | 150 | 185 | 240 | 340 | 700 | 15,000 | 12,000 |
| 1874CC | 1,373,200 | 80.00 | 90.00 | 105 | 165 | 240 | 350 | 1,000 | 40,000 | — |
| 1874S | 2,549,000 | 70.00 | 80.00 | 95.00 | 120 | 165 | 250 | 675 | 30,000 | — |
| 1875 | 218,900 | 260 | 350 | 425 | 525 | 675 | 800 | 1,850 | 13,000 | 6,500 |
| 1875CC | 1,573,700 | 80.00 | 90.00 | 105 | 130 | 200 | 375 | 900 | 40,000 | — |
| 1875S | 4,487,000 | 60.00 | 70.00 | 85.00 | 100.00 | 120 | 210 | 500 | 7,000 | — |
| 1875S/CC | Inc. above | 275 | 325 | 400 | 525 | 695 | 1,100 | 1,900 | — | — |
| 1876 | 456,150 | 70.00 | 80.00 | 100.00 | 125 | 165 | 400 | 675 | 7,500 | 6,500 |
| 1876CC | 509,000 | 125 | 145 | 180 | 220 | 325 | 450 | 2,100 | 75,000 | — |
| 1876S | 5,227,000 | 60.00 | 70.00 | 85.00 | 100.00 | 120 | 210 | 475 | 10,000 | — |
| 1877 | 3,039,710 | 60.00 | 70.00 | 85.00 | 105 | 130 | 210 | 525 | 16,000 | 19,000 |
| 1877CC | 534,000 | 130 | 150 | 190 | 260 | 370 | 600 | 1,275 | 70,000 | — |
| 1877S | 9,519,000 | 60.00 | 70.00 | 85.00 | 100.00 | 120 | 210 | 475 | 8,000 | — |
| 1878 proof only | 900 | — | — | — | 1,100 | 1,250 | 1,500 | — | — | 22,000 |
| 1878CC | 97,000 | 425 | 525 | 675 | 850 | 1,750 | 2,100 | 5,500 | 67,500 | — |
| 1878S | 4,162,000 | 60.00 | 70.00 | 85.00 | 100.00 | 120 | 210 | 475 | 7,000 | — |
| 1879 proof only | 1,541 | — | — | — | 900 | 950 | 1,100 | — | — | 22,000 |
| 1880 proof only | 1,987 | — | — | — | 900 | 950 | 1,100 | — | — | 19,500 |
| 1881 proof only | 960 | — | — | — | 950 | 1,000 | 1,250 | — | — | 20,000 |
| 1882 proof only | 1,097 | — | — | — | 950 | 1,000 | 1,250 | — | — | 20,000 |
| 1883 proof only | 979 | — | — | — | 1,100 | 1,200 | 1,400 | — | — | 20,000 |

## 1875 Trade Dollar
### Grade F-12

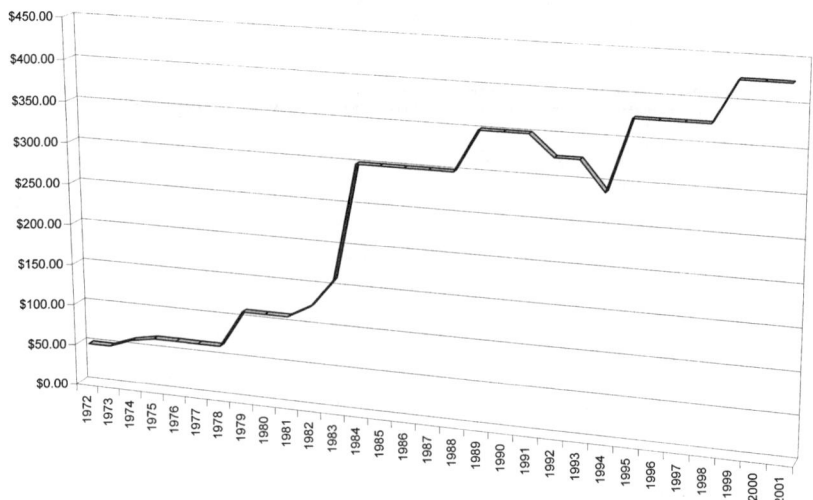

Retail Price

| Date | Mintage | G-4 | VG-8 | F-12 | VF-20 | XF-40 | AU-50 | MS-60 | MS-65 | Prf-65 |
|---|---|---|---|---|---|---|---|---|---|---|
| 1884 proof only | 10 | — | — | — | — | — | — | — | — | — |
| **Note:** 1884, Eliasberg Sale, April 1997, Prf-66, $396,000. | | | | | | | | | | |
| 1885 proof only | 5 | — | — | — | — | — | — | — | — | — |
| **Note:** 1885, Eliasberg Sale, April 1997, Prf-65, $907,500. | | | | | | | | | | |

# Liberty, commonly called "Morgan dollars".

7 tail feathers

8 tail feathers

7/8 tail feathers

**Designer:** George T. Morgan. **Diameter:** 38.1 mm. **Weight:** 26.7300 g. **Composition:** 0.9000 Silver, 0.7736 oz. ASW. **Notes:** "65DMPL" values are for coins grading MS-65 deep-mirror prooflike. The 1878 "8 tail feathers" and "7 tail feathers" varieties are distinguished by the number of feathers in the eagle's tail. On the "reverse of 1878" varieties, the top of the top feather in the arrows held by the eagle is straight across and the eagle's breast is concave. On the "reverse of 1879 varieties," the top feather in the arrows held by the eagle is slanted and the eagle's breast is convex. The 1890-CC "tail-bar variety has a bar extending from the arrow feathers to the wreath on the reverse, the result of a die gouge.

| Date | Mintage | VG-8 | F-12 | VF-20 | XF-40 | AU-50 | MS-60 | MS-63 | MS-64 | MS-65 | 65DMPL | Prf-65 |
|---|---|---|---|---|---|---|---|---|---|---|---|---|
| 1878 8 tail feathers | 750,000 | 15.00 | 17.00 | 20.00 | 25.00 | 39.00 | 88.00 | 135 | 300 | 1,450 | 6,300 | 6,250 |
| 1878 7 tail feathers, reverse of 1878 | Inc. above | 12.50 | 13.00 | 15.00 | 20.00 | 25.00 | 45.00 | 76.00 | 300 | 1,500 | 6,300 | 5,350 |
| 1878 7 tail feathers, reverse of 1879 | Inc. above | 12.50 | 13.00 | 15.00 | 20.00 | 25.00 | 40.00 | 135 | 315 | 2,600 | 8,800 | 55,000 |
| 1878 7 over 8 tail feathers | 9,759,550 | 13.00 | 15.00 | 22.00 | 30.00 | 48.00 | 115 | 145 | 330 | 2,650 | 14,500 | — |
| 1878CC | 2,212,000 | 38.00 | 42.00 | 44.00 | 48.00 | 80.00 | 150 | 180 | 300 | 1,250 | 3,150 | — |
| 1878S | 9,744,000 | 12.50 | 13.50 | 16.00 | 18.00 | 22.00 | 38.00 | 49.00 | 70.00 | 225 | 2,250 | — |
| 1879 | 14,807,100 | 12.00 | 12.50 | 13.00 | 14.00 | 18.00 | 28.00 | 58.00 | 140 | 1,000 | 6,950 | 5,500 |
| 1879CC | 756,000 | 48.00 | 78.00 | 145 | 400 | 790 | 1,600 | 3,550 | 5,350 | 17,500 | 50,000 | — |
| 1879O | 2,887,000 | 12.00 | 12.50 | 13.00 | 17.00 | 21.00 | 63.00 | 130 | 320 | 3,300 | 16,500 | — |
| 1879S reverse of 1878 | 9,110,000 | 12.00 | 13.50 | 15.00 | 20.00 | 33.00 | 90.00 | 360 | 1,500 | 7,250 | 22,000 | — |
| 1879S reverse of 1879 | 9,110,000 | 12.00 | 12.50 | 13.50 | 14.00 | 19.00 | 28.00 | 35.00 | 51.00 | 105 | 450 | — |
| 1880 | 12,601,335 | 12.00 | 12.50 | 13.50 | 14.00 | 18.00 | 24.00 | 50.00 | 100.00 | 900 | 3,450 | 5,500 |
| 1880CC reverse of 1878 | 591,000 | 53.00 | 63.00 | 76.00 | 110 | 190 | 300 | 325 | 700 | 2,250 | 11,000 | — |
| 1880CC reverse of 1879 | 591,000 | 53.00 | 63.00 | 76.00 | 110 | 190 | 270 | 300 | 375 | 900 | 3,150 | — |
| 1880O | 5,305,000 | 12.00 | 12.50 | 13.00 | 17.00 | 20.00 | 43.00 | 285 | 1,500 | 14,500 | 70,000 | — |
| 1880S | 8,900,000 | 12.00 | 12.50 | 13.50 | 15.00 | 18.00 | 26.00 | 35.00 | 51.00 | 105 | 410 | — |
| 1881 | 9,163,975 | 12.00 | 12.50 | 13.00 | 13.50 | 19.00 | 27.00 | 46.00 | 100.00 | 900 | 13,750 | 5,500 |
| 1881CC | 296,000 | 110 | 120 | 130 | 140 | 190 | 265 | 295 | 325 | 650 | 1,450 | — |
| 1881O | 5,708,000 | 12.00 | 12.50 | 13.00 | 13.50 | 18.00 | 24.00 | 40.00 | 125 | 1,950 | 15,000 | — |
| 1881S | 12,760,000 | 12.00 | 14.00 | 15.00 | 16.00 | 18.00 | 26.00 | 35.00 | 51.00 | 105 | 460 | — |
| 1882 | 11,101,100 | 12.00 | 12.50 | 13.00 | 13.50 | 18.00 | 24.00 | 39.00 | 55.00 | 480 | 4,100 | 5,500 |
| 1882CC | 1,133,000 | 38.00 | 39.00 | 41.00 | 52.00 | 53.00 | 95.00 | 120 | 150 | 410 | 825 | — |
| 1882O | 6,090,000 | 12.00 | 12.50 | 13.00 | 13.50 | 18.00 | 24.00 | 32.00 | 65.00 | 850 | 4,200 | — |
| 1882S | 9,250,000 | 12.00 | 12.50 | 13.00 | 14.00 | 18.00 | 26.00 | 35.00 | 51.00 | 105 | 1,100 | — |
| 1883 | 12,291,039 | 12.00 | 12.50 | 13.00 | 14.00 | 18.00 | 26.00 | 32.00 | 55.00 | 140 | 760 | 5,500 |
| 1883CC | 1,204,000 | 38.00 | 41.00 | 44.00 | 47.00 | 50.00 | 95.00 | 120 | 135 | 340 | 690 | — |

## 1889-O Silver Dollar
### Grade F-12

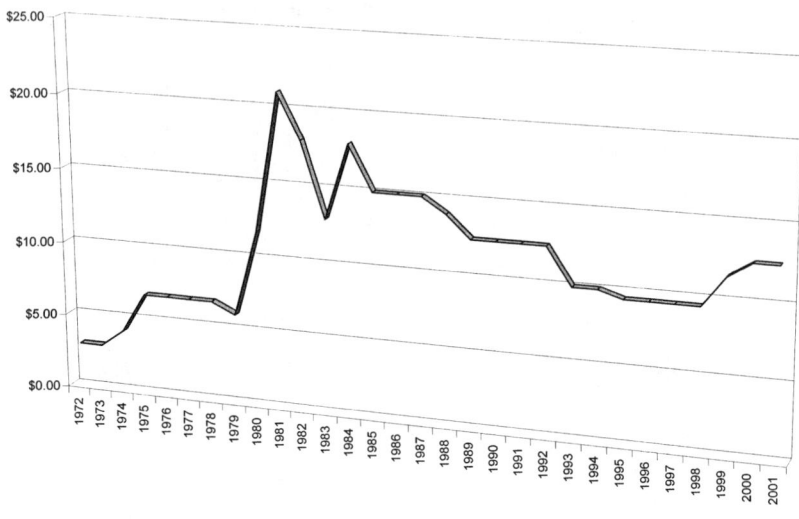

Retail Price

## 1897-O Dollar
### Grade MS-60

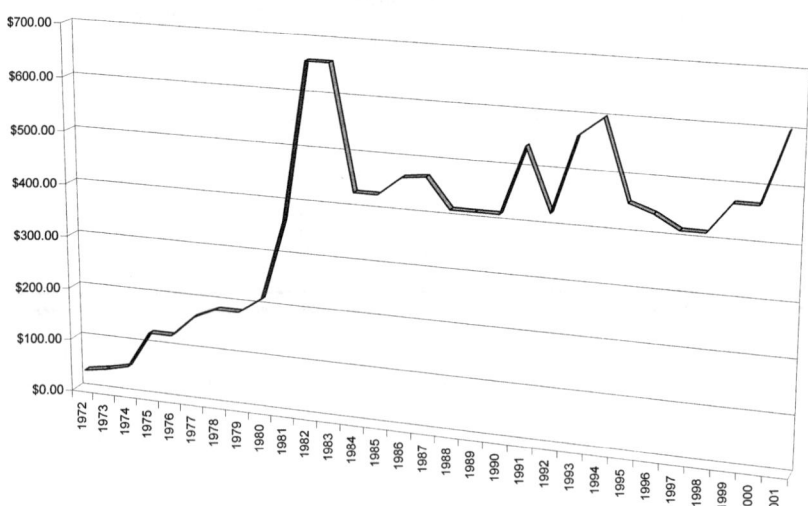

Retail Price

| Date | Mintage | VG-8 | F-12 | VF-20 | XF-40 | AU-50 | MS-60 | MS-63 | MS-64 | MS-65 | 65DMPL | Prf-65 |
|---|---|---|---|---|---|---|---|---|---|---|---|---|
| 1883O | 8,725,000 | 12.00 | 12.50 | 13.00 | 13.50 | 18.00 | 24.00 | 35.00 | 51.00 | 105 | 575 | — |
| 1883S | 6,250,000 | 12.00 | 13.50 | 18.00 | 26.00 | 150 | 425 | 1,600 | 5,000 | 26,500 | 94,500 | — |
| 1884 | 14,070,875 | 12.00 | 12.50 | 13.00 | 13.50 | 18.00 | 24.00 | 35.00 | 55.00 | 270 | 2,200 | 5,500 |
| 1884CC | 1,136,000 | 47.00 | 50.00 | 55.00 | 63.00 | 68.00 | 95.00 | 120 | 135 | 340 | 760 | — |
| 1884O | 9,730,000 | 12.00 | 12.50 | 13.00 | 13.50 | 18.00 | 24.00 | 35.00 | 51.00 | 105 | 670 | — |
| 1884S | 3,200,000 | 12.00 | 14.00 | 19.00 | 36.00 | 220 | 3,800 | 30,000 | 90,000 | 150,000 | 220,000 | — |
| 1885 | 17,787,767 | 12.00 | 12.50 | 13.00 | 13.50 | 18.00 | 24.00 | 35.00 | 51.00 | 115 | 570 | 5,500 |
| 1885CC | 228,000 | 170 | 190 | 200 | 210 | 225 | 275 | 310 | 340 | 800 | 1,600 | — |
| 1885O | 9,185,000 | 12.00 | 12.50 | 13.00 | 13.50 | 18.00 | 24.00 | 35.00 | 51.00 | 105 | 490 | — |
| 1885S | 1,497,000 | 12.00 | 13.50 | 17.00 | 21.00 | 46.00 | 115 | 200 | 400 | 2,500 | 16,500 | — |
| 1886 | 19,963,886 | 12.00 | 12.50 | 13.00 | 13.50 | 18.00 | 24.00 | 35.00 | 51.00 | 105 | 575 | 5,500 |
| 1886O | 10,710,000 | 12.00 | 12.50 | 15.00 | 18.00 | 76.00 | 325 | 3,000 | 10,000 | 235,000 | 283,500 | — |
| 1886S | 750,000 | 22.00 | 26.00 | 37.00 | 47.00 | 70.00 | 170 | 240 | 550 | 3,650 | 16,500 | — |
| 1887 | 20,290,710 | 12.00 | 12.50 | 13.00 | 13.50 | 18.00 | 24.00 | 35.00 | 51.00 | 115 | 530 | 5,500 |
| 1887O | 11,550,000 | 12.00 | 12.50 | 13.00 | 17.00 | 24.00 | 41.00 | 95.00 | 330 | 5,500 | 8,500 | — |
| 1887S | 1,771,000 | 12.00 | 13.50 | 15.00 | 20.00 | 37.00 | 70.00 | 150 | 500 | 3,800 | 27,000 | — |
| 1888 | 19,183,833 | 12.00 | 12.50 | 13.00 | 13.50 | 18.00 | 24.00 | 35.00 | 53.00 | 190 | 2,350 | 5,500 |
| 1888O | 12,150,000 | 12.00 | 12.50 | 13.00 | 13.50 | 22.00 | 26.00 | 39.00 | 75.00 | 550 | 1,600 | — |
| 1888S | 657,000 | 26.00 | 32.00 | 35.00 | 41.00 | 85.00 | 165 | 235 | 550 | 4,400 | 10,500 | — |
| 1889 | 21,726,811 | 12.00 | 12.50 | 13.00 | 13.50 | 18.00 | 24.00 | 35.00 | 51.00 | 350 | 2,950 | 5,500 |
| 1889CC | 350,000 | 225 | 290 | 500 | 1,200 | 2,900 | 7,000 | 19,000 | 35,000 | 280,000 | 296,500 | — |
| 1889O | 11,875,000 | 12.00 | 12.50 | 13.00 | 18.00 | 31.00 | 100.00 | 265 | 625 | 5,650 | 14,500 | — |
| 1889S | 700,000 | 21.00 | 26.00 | 31.00 | 39.00 | 65.00 | 135 | 195 | 375 | 2,000 | 7,550 | — |
| 1890 | 16,802,590 | 12.00 | 12.50 | 13.00 | 13.50 | 18.00 | 24.00 | 35.00 | 140 | 3,400 | 12,500 | 5,500 |
| 1890CC | 2,309,041 | 38.00 | 39.00 | 44.00 | 55.00 | 110 | 295 | 355 | 875 | 7,900 | 9,750 | — |
| 1890CC tail bar | Inc. above | 43.00 | 50.00 | 60.00 | 90.00 | 150 | 390 | 475 | 1,200 | 8,050 | 9,750 | — |
| 1890O | 10,701,000 | 12.00 | 12.50 | 13.00 | 18.00 | 23.00 | 37.00 | 85.00 | 200 | 2,450 | 7,550 | — |
| 1890S | 8,230,373 | 12.00 | 13.50 | 14.00 | 17.00 | 21.00 | 42.00 | 91.00 | 200 | 900 | 8,200 | — |
| 1891 | 8,694,206 | 12.00 | 12.50 | 13.00 | 18.00 | 23.00 | 40.00 | 135 | 590 | 8,200 | 25,000 | 5,500 |
| 1891CC | 1,618,000 | 38.00 | 40.00 | 46.00 | 58.00 | 120 | 295 | 350 | 700 | 3,150 | 20,000 | — |
| 1891O | 7,954,529 | 12.00 | 12.50 | 13.00 | 17.00 | 33.00 | 89.00 | 220 | 650 | 7,000 | 21,500 | — |
| 1891S | 5,296,000 | 12.00 | 13.50 | 15.00 | 17.00 | 24.00 | 42.00 | 100.00 | 250 | 1,700 | 7,250 | — |
| 1892 | 1,037,245 | 12.00 | 12.50 | 19.00 | 26.00 | 66.00 | 150 | 325 | 660 | 3,800 | 15,750 | 5,500 |
| 1892CC | 1,352,000 | 46.00 | 56.00 | 80.00 | 125 | 225 | 450 | 850 | 1,400 | 8,200 | 19,000 | — |
| 1892O | 2,744,000 | 12.00 | 12.50 | 20.00 | 23.00 | 66.00 | 110 | 225 | 625 | 7,300 | 27,000 | — |
| 1892S | 1,200,000 | 18.00 | 20.00 | 43.00 | 170 | 2,150 | 18,000 | 51,500 | 85,000 | 94,500 | 157,500 | — |
| 1893 | 378,792 | 69.00 | 79.00 | 89.00 | 160 | 215 | 400 | 825 | 1,400 | 7,600 | 38,000 | 5,500 |
| 1893CC | 677,000 | 100.00 | 120 | 230 | 550 | 750 | 1,400 | 4,650 | 7,950 | 53,500 | 88,000 | — |
| 1893O | 300,000 | 77.00 | 120 | 150 | 220 | 600 | 1,400 | 650 | 14,500 | 195,000 | 201,500 | — |
| 1893S | 100,000 | 1,100 | 1,300 | 2,200 | 5,000 | 13,500 | 47,000 | 90,000 | 155,000 | 285,000 | 315,000 | — |
| 1894 | 110,972 | 300 | 350 | 400 | 450 | 600 | 900 | 4,300 | 5,650 | 18,500 | 44,000 | 5,500 |
| 1894O | 1,723,000 | 22.00 | 25.00 | 35.00 | 50.00 | 160 | 550 | 3,800 | 7,500 | 45,500 | 56,500 | — |
| 1894S | 1,260,000 | 30.00 | 42.00 | 63.00 | 110 | 250 | 450 | 800 | 1,600 | 5,850 | 19,000 | — |
| 1895 proof only | 12,880 | — | 11,250 | 13,750 | 16,500 | 18,500 | — | — | — | — | — | 32,000 |
| 1895O | 450,000 | 105 | 140 | 190 | 275 | 800 | 10,750 | 36,500 | 80,000 | 215,000 | — | — |
| 1895S | 400,000 | 160 | 200 | 230 | 460 | 825 | 1,600 | 3,800 | 6,500 | 17,500 | 40,500 | — |
| 1896 | 9,967,762 | 12.00 | 12.50 | 13.00 | 13.50 | 18.00 | 24.00 | 35.00 | 53.00 | 160 | 975 | 5,500 |
| 1896O | 4,900,000 | 12.00 | 12.50 | 17.00 | 20.00 | 120 | 800 | 7,700 | 41,000 | 138,500 | 170,000 | — |
| 1896S | 5,000,000 | 13.00 | 24.00 | 45.00 | 165 | 410 | 725 | 1,600 | 2,950 | 11,000 | 25,000 | — |
| 1897 | 2,822,731 | 12.00 | 12.50 | 13.00 | 13.50 | 18.00 | 27.00 | 35.00 | 53.00 | 250 | 2,900 | 5,500 |
| 1897O | 4,004,000 | 12.00 | 12.50 | 14.00 | 22.00 | 105 | 600 | 4,900 | 19,500 | 49,000 | 56,500 | — |
| 1897S | 5,825,000 | 12.00 | 12.50 | 14.00 | 18.00 | 22.00 | 42.00 | 81.00 | 125 | 630 | 1,700 | — |
| 1898 | 5,884,735 | 12.00 | 12.50 | 14.00 | 15.00 | 18.00 | 24.00 | 35.00 | 53.00 | 220 | 1,075 | 5,500 |
| 1898O | 4,440,000 | 13.50 | 14.00 | 14.50 | 15.00 | 27.00 | 29.00 | 35.00 | 51.00 | 110 | 510 | — |
| 1898S | 4,102,000 | 13.00 | 14.00 | 15.00 | 28.00 | 65.00 | 175 | 250 | 500 | 2,400 | 11,250 | — |
| 1899 | 330,846 | 25.00 | 30.00 | 44.00 | 48.00 | 77.00 | 100.00 | 135 | 200 | 650 | 2,250 | 5,500 |
| 1899O | 12,290,000 | 12.00 | 12.50 | 13.00 | 13.50 | 27.00 | 31.00 | 37.00 | 53.00 | 120 | 825 | — |
| 1899S | 2,562,000 | 12.00 | 18.00 | 22.00 | 30.00 | 90.00 | 190 | 200 | 500 | 2,100 | 8,600 | — |
| 1900 | 8,880,938 | 12.00 | 12.50 | 13.00 | 13.50 | 18.00 | 30.00 | 36.00 | 55.00 | 160 | 11,000 | 5,500 |
| 1900O | 12,590,000 | 12.00 | 13.00 | 14.00 | 15.00 | 29.00 | 40.00 | 40.00 | 60.00 | 130 | 3,000 | — |
| 1900O/CC | Inc. above | 22.00 | 27.00 | 38.00 | 49.00 | 120 | 200 | 340 | 550 | 1,640 | 19,000 | — |
| 1900S | 3,540,000 | 14.00 | 19.00 | 21.00 | 35.00 | 77.00 | 180 | 220 | 350 | 925 | 9,450 | — |
| 1901 | 6,962,813 | 15.00 | 22.00 | 33.00 | 60.00 | 230 | 1,500 | 18,000 | 61,000 | 189,000 | 220,000 | 8,100 |
| 1901O | 13,320,000 | 12.00 | 12.50 | 13.00 | 13.50 | 27.00 | 30.00 | 35.00 | 53.00 | 170 | 3,800 | — |
| 1901S | 2,284,000 | 15.00 | 18.00 | 27.00 | 50.00 | 165 | 265 | 525 | 850 | 5,350 | 12,500 | — |
| 1902 | 7,994,777 | 12.00 | 12.50 | 13.00 | 19.00 | 22.00 | 34.00 | 90.00 | 135 | 460 | 15,750 | 5,750 |
| 1902O | 8,636,000 | 12.00 | 12.50 | 13.00 | 13.50 | 23.00 | 25.00 | 35.00 | 51.00 | 140 | 3,600 | — |
| 1902S | 1,530,000 | 27.00 | 37.00 | 80.00 | 125 | 130 | 210 | 310 | 625 | 3,700 | 15,000 | — |
| 1903 | 4,652,755 | 12.50 | 14.00 | 15.00 | 21.00 | 24.00 | 34.00 | 57.00 | 65.00 | 180 | 9,150 | 5,500 |
| 1903O | 4,450,000 | 125 | 150 | 170 | 180 | 200 | 240 | 275 | 275 | 460 | 4,650 | — |
| 1903S | 1,241,000 | 22.00 | 27.00 | 77.00 | 250 | 1,100 | 2,900 | 4,500 | 5,250 | 7,450 | 35,000 | — |
| 1904 | 2,788,650 | 12.00 | 12.50 | 13.00 | 18.00 | 31.00 | 60.00 | 170 | 560 | 4,400 | 38,000 | 5,500 |
| 1904O | 3,720,000 | 12.00 | 12.50 | 13.00 | 14.00 | 21.00 | 24.00 | 35.00 | 51.00 | 105 | 550 | — |
| 1904S | 2,304,000 | 16.00 | 25.00 | 42.00 | 185 | 520 | 950 | 2,100 | 2,750 | 6,550 | 19,000 | — |
| 1921 | 44,690,000 | 11.00 | 11.50 | 12.00 | 13.00 | 14.00 | 18.00 | 23.00 | 35.00 | 150 | 8,800 | — |
| 1921D | 20,345,000 | 11.00 | 11.50 | 12.00 | 13.00 | 15.00 | 32.00 | 37.00 | 70.00 | 300 | 15,000 | — |
| 1921S | 21,695,000 | 11.00 | 11.50 | 12.00 | 13.00 | 16.00 | 26.00 | 53.00 | 150 | 1,850 | 22,000 | — |

## 1903-O Dollar
### Grade MS-60

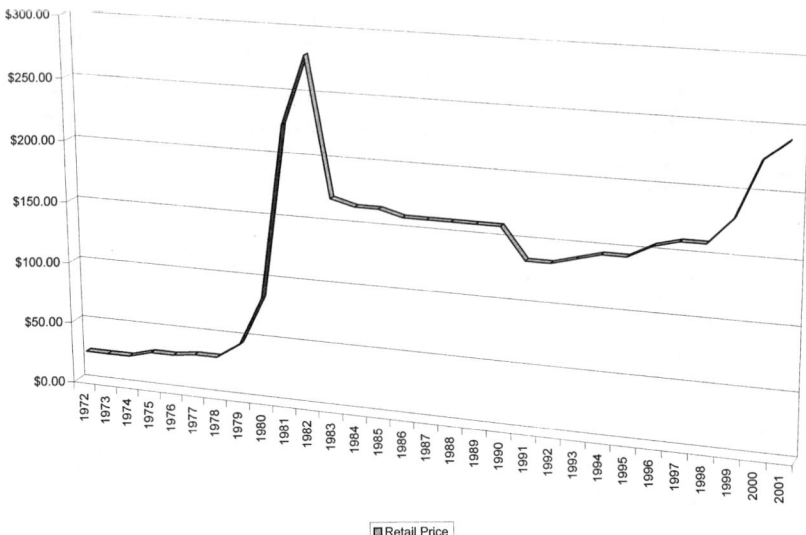

## 1921 Silver Dollar
### Grade MS-60

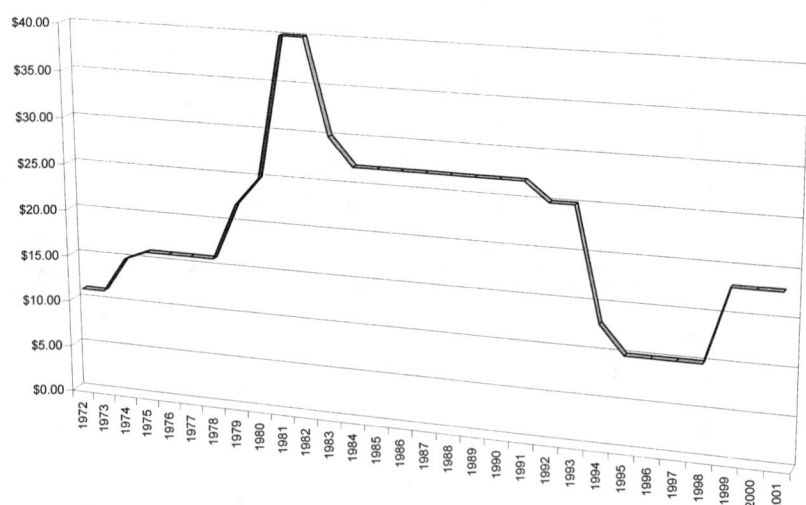

# Eagle with "Peace" below it.

Mint mark

**Designer:** Anthony DeFrancisci. **Diameter:** 38.1 mm. **Weight:** 26.7300 g. **Composition:** 0.9000 Silver, 0.7736 oz. ASW. **Notes:** Commonly called Peace dollars.

| Date | Mintage | G-4 | VG-8 | F-12 | VF-20 | XF-40 | AU-50 | MS-60 | MS-63 | MS-64 | MS-65 |
|---|---|---|---|---|---|---|---|---|---|---|---|
| 1921 | 1,006,473 | 29.00 | 35.00 | 38.00 | 44.00 | 53.00 | 105 | 145 | 220 | 540 | 2,650 |
| 1922 | 51,737,000 | 8.00 | 8.25 | 8.50 | 9.00 | 11.00 | 14.00 | 17.00 | 31.00 | 46.00 | 110 |
| 1922D | 15,063,000 | 8.00 | 8.25 | 8.50 | 9.00 | 11.00 | 14.00 | 20.00 | 40.00 | 80.00 | 365 |
| 1922S | 17,475,000 | 8.00 | 8.25 | 8.50 | 9.00 | 11.00 | 14.00 | 20.00 | 60.00 | 230 | 2,150 |
| 1923 | 30,800,000 | 8.00 | 8.25 | 8.50 | 9.00 | 11.00 | 14.00 | 17.00 | 31.00 | 46.00 | 110 |
| 1923D | 6,811,000 | 8.00 | 8.25 | 8.50 | 9.00 | 14.00 | 17.00 | 42.00 | 100.00 | 210 | 1,050 |
| 1923S | 19,020,000 | 8.00 | 8.25 | 8.50 | 9.00 | 12.00 | 16.00 | 20.00 | 60.00 | 210 | 7,000 |
| 1924 | 11,811,000 | 8.00 | 8.25 | 8.50 | 9.00 | 11.00 | 14.00 | 17.00 | 33.00 | 51.00 | 110 |
| 1924S | 1,728,000 | 9.00 | 13.00 | 14.00 | 15.00 | 21.00 | 50.00 | 180 | 350 | 1,300 | 8,500 |
| 1925 | 10,198,000 | 8.00 | 8.25 | 8.50 | 9.00 | 11.00 | 14.00 | 17.00 | 33.00 | 51.00 | 110 |
| 1925S | 1,610,000 | 9.00 | 11.00 | 12.00 | 14.00 | 17.00 | 30.00 | 65.00 | 120 | 600 | 21,000 |
| 1926 | 1,939,000 | 8.00 | 10.00 | 11.00 | 13.00 | 17.00 | 19.00 | 22.00 | 45.00 | 80.00 | 300 |
| 1926D | 2,348,700 | 8.00 | 10.00 | 14.00 | 15.00 | 18.00 | 25.00 | 50.00 | 110 | 240 | 550 |
| 1926S | 6,980,000 | 8.00 | 8.25 | 8.50 | 9.00 | 16.00 | 18.00 | 32.00 | 79.00 | 135 | 850 |
| 1927 | 848,000 | 13.00 | 17.00 | 19.00 | 22.00 | 28.00 | 44.00 | 58.00 | 120 | 250 | 2,350 |
| 1927D | 1,268,900 | 10.00 | 13.00 | 15.00 | 18.00 | 26.00 | 71.00 | 130 | 210 | 580 | 4,900 |
| 1927S | 866,000 | 10.00 | 13.00 | 15.00 | 18.00 | 24.00 | 64.00 | 115 | 270 | 630 | 9,950 |
| 1928 | 360,649 | 100.00 | 125 | 140 | 150 | 165 | 205 | 245 | 320 | 675 | 3,150 |
| 1928S | 1,632,000 | 10.00 | 15.00 | 16.00 | 19.00 | 24.00 | 42.00 | 105 | 285 | 1,050 | 22,000 |
| 1934 | 954,057 | 10.00 | 15.00 | 16.00 | 19.00 | 22.00 | 33.00 | 72.00 | 120 | 265 | 1,150 |
| 1934D | 1,569,500 | 10.00 | 13.00 | 15.00 | 17.00 | 20.00 | 36.00 | 78.00 | 200 | 475 | 2,000 |
| 1934S | 1,011,000 | 13.00 | 16.00 | 21.00 | 55.00 | 135 | 475 | 1,000 | 2,700 | 4,050 | 6,500 |
| 1935 | 1,576,000 | 10.00 | 12.00 | 14.00 | 16.00 | 18.00 | 30.00 | 52.00 | 77.00 | 140 | 600 |
| 1935S | 1,964,000 | 10.00 | 12.00 | 14.00 | 16.00 | 22.00 | 77.00 | 140 | 260 | 450 | 1,050 |

## 1927-S Dollar
### Grade MS-60

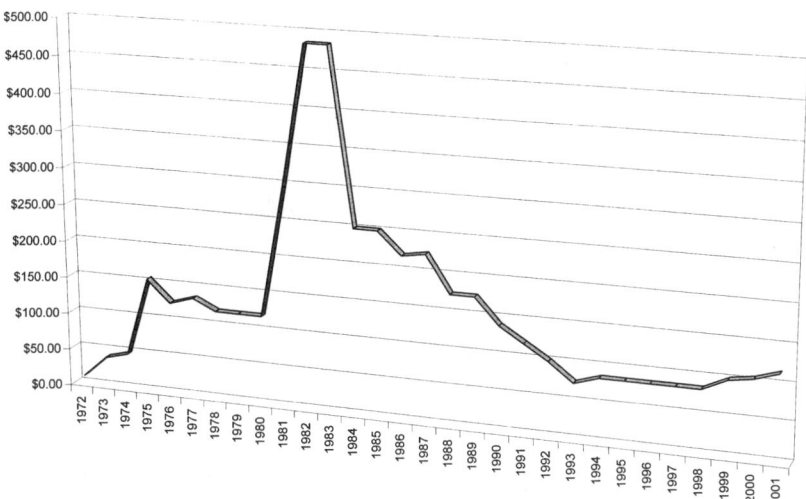

Retail Price

# Eisenhower.

**Designer:** Frank Gasparro. **Diameter:** 38.1 mm. **Weight:** 22.6800 g. **Composition:** Copper-nickel Clad Copper.

| Date | Mintage | (Proof) | MS-63 | Prf-65 |
|---|---|---|---|---|
| 1971 | 47,799,000 | — | 3.75 | — |
| 1971D | 68,587,424 | — | 3.00 | — |
| 1972 | 75,890,000 | — | 2.75 | — |
| 1972D | 92,548,511 | — | 2.50 | — |
| 1973 | 2,000,056 | — | 7.00 | 7.50 |
| 1973D | 2,000,000 | — | 6.50 | 7.50 |
| 1973S | 2,769,624 | — | — | 8.00 |
| 1974 | 27,366,000 | — | 3.00 | — |
| 1974D | 35,466,000 | — | 3.00 | — |
| 1974S | (2,617,350) | — | — | 7.00 |

# Eisenhower.

**Designer:** Frank Gasparro. **Diameter:** 38.1 **Weight:** 24.5900 g. **Composition:** Silver.

| Date | Mintage | (Proof) | MS-63 | Prf-65 |
|---|---|---|---|---|
| 1971S | (4,265,234) | — | 7.00 | 7.00 |
| 1971S | 6,868,530 | — | 7.00 | 7.00 |
| 1972S | (1,811,631) | — | 7.50 | 7.00 |
| 1972S | 2,193,056 | — | 7.50 | 7.00 |
| 1973S | (1,005,617) | — | 8.00 | 30.00 |
| 1973S | 1,833,140 | — | 8.00 | 30.00 |
| 1974S | (1,306,579) | — | 7.50 | 8.50 |
| 1974S | 1,720,000 | — | 7.50 | 8.50 |

# Eisenhower. Bicentennial design, moon behind Liberty Bell.

Type I Bicentennial reverse                        Type II Bicentennial reverse

**Rev. Designer:** Dennis R. Williams. **Diameter:** 38.1mm **Weight:** 22.6800 g. **Composition:** Copper-nickel Clad Copper. **Notes:** In 1976 the lettering on the reverse on the reverse was changed to thinner letters, resulting in Type I and Type II varieties for that year.

| Date | Mintage | (Proof) | MS-63 | Prf-65 |
|---|---|---|---|---|
| 1976 type I | 117,337,000 | — | 4.00 | — |
| 1976 type II | Inc. above | — | 2.00 | — |

| Date | Mintage | (Proof) | MS-63 | Prf-65 |
|------|---------|---------|-------|--------|
| 1976D type I | 103,228,274 | — | 3.25 | — |
| 1976D type II | Inc. above | — | 2.00 | — |
| 1976S type I | (2,909,369) | — | — | 5.75 |
| 1976S type II | (4,149,730) | — | — | 5.75 |
| 1976S type II | — | — | — | 5.75 |

## Eisenhower. Bicentennial design, moon behind Liberty Bell.

**Rev. Designer:** Dennis R. Williams. **Weight:** 24.5900 g. **Composition:** 0.4000 Silver, 0.3162 oz. ASW.

| Date | Mintage | (Proof) | MS-63 | Prf-65 |
|------|---------|---------|-------|--------|
| 1976S | (4,000,000) | — | 9.50 | 12.00 |
| 1976S | 11,000,000 | — | 9.50 | 12.00 |

## Eisenhower. Regular design resumed.

**Diameter:** 38.1 mm. **Composition:** Copper-nickel Clad Copper.

| Date | Mintage | (Proof) | MS-63 | Prf-65 |
|------|---------|---------|-------|--------|
| 1977 | 12,596,000 | — | 4.50 | — |
| 1977D | 32,983,006 | — | 2.75 | — |
| 1977S | (3,251,152) | — | — | 7.00 |
| 1978 | 25,702,000 | — | 2.75 | — |
| 1978D | 33,012,890 | — | 3.30 | — |
| 1978S | (3,127,788) | — | — | 8.00 |

## Susan B. Anthony.

**Designer:** Frank Gasparro. **Diameter:** 26.5 mm. **Weight:** 8.1000 g. **Composition:** Copper-nickel Clad Copper. **Notes:** The 1979-S and 1981-S Type II coins have a clearer mint mark than the Type I varieties for those years.

| Date | Mintage | MS-63 | Date | Mintage | MS-63 |
|------|---------|-------|------|---------|-------|
| 1979P | 360,222,000 | 2.00 | 1980S | 3,547,030 | — |
| 1979P near date | Inc. above | 15.00 | 1981P | 3,000,000 | 6.00 |
| 1979D | 288,015,744 | 1.75 | 1981D | 3,250,000 | 6.00 |
| 1979S | 109,576,000 | 2.00 | 1981S | 3,492,000 | 6.00 |
| 1979S type I | 3,677,175 | — | 1981S type I | 4,063,083 | — |
| 1979S type II | — | — | 1981S type II | — | — |
| 1980P | 27,610,000 | 1.75 | 1999P | — | 2.75 |
| 1980D | 41,628,708 | 2.00 | 1999D | — | 2.25 |
| 1980S | 20,422,000 | 2.00 | 1999P | — | — |

## Sacagawea.

**Diameter:** 26.4 mm. **Weight:** 8.0700 g. **Composition:** Copper-zinc-manganese-nickel Clad Copper.

| Date | Mintage | MS-63 | Date | Mintage | MS-63 |
|------|---------|-------|------|---------|-------|
| 2000P | — | 1.50 | 2001P | — | — |
| 2000D | — | 1.50 | 2001D | — | — |
| 2000S | — | — | 2001S | — | — |

# Liberty.

**Designer:** James B. Longacre. **Diameter:** 13 mm. **Weight:** 1.6720 g. **Composition:** 0.9000 Gold, 0.0484 oz. AGW. **Notes:** On the "closed wreath" varieties of 1849, the wreath on the reverse extends closer to the numeral 1.

| Date | Mintage | F-12 | VF-20 | XF-40 | AU-50 | MS-60 |
|---|---|---|---|---|---|---|
| 1849 open wreath | 688,567 | 110 | 125 | 165 | 190 | 450 |
| 1849 closed wreath | Inc. above | 110 | 125 | 165 | 180 | 365 |
| 1849C closed wreath | 11,634 | 275 | 425 | 875 | 1,600 | 7,500 |
| 1849C open wreath | Inc. above | — | — | — | — | — |
| 1849D open wreath | 21,588 | 285 | 400 | 800 | 1,100 | 2,900 |
| 1849O open wreath | 215,000 | 135 | 165 | 210 | 325 | 700 |
| 1850 | 481,953 | 120 | 135 | 170 | 190 | 380 |
| 1850C | 6,966 | 390 | 585 | 950 | 2,200 | 6,000 |
| 1850D | 8,382 | 350 | 575 | 1,200 | 2,000 | 6,100 |
| 1850O | 14,000 | 195 | 260 | 370 | 650 | 2,750 |
| 1851 | 3,317,671 | 120 | 135 | 165 | 175 | 275 |
| 1851C | 41,267 | 275 | 410 | 650 | 950 | 2,300 |
| 1851D | 9,882 | 275 | 400 | 750 | 1,600 | 3,200 |
| 1851O | 290,000 | 150 | 175 | 195 | 250 | 690 |
| 1852 | 2,045,351 | 100.00 | 120 | 165 | 190 | 255 |
| 1852C | 9,434 | 275 | 450 | 750 | 1,200 | 3,400 |
| 1852D | 6,360 | 315 | 600 | 1,150 | 1,600 | 4,600 |
| 1852O | 140,000 | 120 | 150 | 210 | 295 | 1,100 |
| 1853 | 4,076,051 | 115 | 130 | 165 | 190 | 255 |
| 1853C | 11,515 | 240 | 475 | 1,150 | 1,650 | 5,000 |
| 1853D | 6,583 | 325 | 675 | 925 | 1,700 | 5,750 |
| 1853O | 290,000 | 140 | 160 | 195 | 220 | 575 |
| 1854 | 736,709 | 115 | 150 | 170 | 195 | 265 |
| 1854D | 2,935 | 530 | 840 | 1,750 | 4,800 | 12,500 |
| 1854S | 14,632 | 260 | 300 | 440 | 650 | 1,800 |

# Small Indian head.

**Designer:** James B. Longacre. **Diameter:** 15 mm. **Weight:** 1.6720 g. **Composition:** 0.9000 Gold, 0.0484 oz. AGW.

| Date | Mintage | F-12 | VF-20 | XF-40 | AU-50 | MS-60 |
|---|---|---|---|---|---|---|
| 1854 | 902,736 | 210 | 265 | 340 | 520 | 2,700 |
| 1855 | 758,269 | 210 | 265 | 340 | 520 | 2,700 |
| 1855C | 9,803 | 625 | 985 | 2,500 | 5,750 | 17,000 |
| 1855D | 1,811 | 1,300 | 2,100 | 4,500 | 8,500 | 27,500 |
| 1855O | 55,000 | 315 | 425 | 595 | 975 | 5,200 |
| 1856S | 24,600 | 390 | 650 | 1,100 | 1,700 | 6,900 |

# Large Indian head.

**Designer:** James B. Longacre. **Diameter:** 15 mm. **Weight:** 1.6720 g. **Composition:** 0.9000 Gold, 0.0484 oz. AGW. **Notes:** The 1856 varieties are distinguished by whether the 5 in the date is slanted or upright. The 1873 varieties are distinguished by the amount of space between the upper left and lower left serifs in the 3.

| Date | Mintage | F-12 | VF-20 | XF-40 | AU-50 | MS-60 | Prf-65 |
|---|---|---|---|---|---|---|---|
| 1856 upright 5 | 1,762,936 | 130 | 155 | 195 | 315 | 475 | — |
| 1856 slanted 5 | Inc. above | 120 | 140 | 170 | 190 | 300 | — |
| 1856D | 1,460 | 2,100 | 3,250 | 5,150 | 8,000 | 27,000 | — |
| 1857 | 774,789 | 120 | 140 | 170 | 190 | 300 | — |
| 1857C | 13,280 | 350 | 500 | 1,200 | 2,900 | 9,700 | — |
| 1857D | 3,533 | 275 | 825 | 1,650 | 3,000 | 10,000 | — |
| 1857S | 10,000 | 260 | 500 | 600 | 1,000 | 5,650 | — |
| 1858 | 117,995 | 120 | 140 | 170 | 190 | 300 | 20,000 |
| 1858D | 3,477 | 375 | 775 | 1,300 | 1,900 | 9,000 | — |
| 1858S | 10,000 | 280 | 375 | 500 | 1,200 | 5,600 | — |
| 1859 | 168,244 | 120 | 140 | 160 | 190 | 300 | 13,000 |
| 1859C | 5,235 | 300 | 500 | 1,250 | 2,650 | 11,500 | — |
| 1859D | 4,952 | 475 | 750 | 1,100 | 1,950 | 7,800 | — |
| 1859S | 15,000 | 225 | 250 | 480 | 1,000 | 5,500 | — |
| 1860 | 36,668 | 120 | 140 | 170 | 190 | 360 | 13,500 |

| Date | Mintage | F-12 | VF-20 | XF-40 | AU-50 | MS-60 | Prf-65 |
|---|---|---|---|---|---|---|---|
| 1860D | 1,566 | 1,700 | 2,500 | 3,800 | 5,750 | 25,000 | — |
| 1860S | 13,000 | 200 | 325 | 475 | 700 | 2,500 | — |
| 1861 | 527,499 | 120 | 140 | 160 | 190 | 3,000 | 15,000 |
| 1861D mintage unrecorded | — | 4,300 | 6,000 | 8,500 | 15,000 | 32,500 | — |
| 1862 | 1,361,390 | 110 | 120 | 150 | 175 | 280 | 18,000 |
| 1863 | 6,250 | 360 | 450 | 875 | 1,700 | 4,000 | 16,500 |
| 1864 | 5,950 | 285 | 370 | 475 | 750 | 900 | 23,000 |
| 1865 | 3,725 | 285 | 370 | 585 | 750 | 1,600 | 16,500 |
| 1866 | 7,130 | 290 | 380 | 450 | 700 | 1,000 | 16,500 |
| 1867 | 5,250 | 345 | 440 | 550 | 750 | 1,200 | 18,000 |
| 1868 | 10,525 | 260 | 295 | 400 | 585 | 1,100 | 16,000 |
| 1869 | 5,925 | 325 | 360 | 520 | 800 | 1,100 | 14,000 |
| 1870 | 6,335 | 260 | 285 | 500 | 775 | 1,050 | 15,000 |
| 1870S | 3,000 | 350 | 475 | 800 | 1,400 | 2,300 | — |
| 1871 | 3,930 | 260 | 285 | 440 | 480 | 700 | — |
| 1872 | 3,530 | 285 | 315 | 480 | 575 | 900 | 16,750 |
| 1873 closed 3 | 125,125 | 325 | 425 | 700 | 1,000 | 2,000 | — |
| 1873 open 3 | Inc. above | 110 | 120 | 150 | 190 | 280 | — |
| 1874 | 198,820 | 110 | 120 | 155 | 190 | 280 | — |
| 1875 | 420 | 1,800 | 2,500 | 3,600 | 4,500 | 5,700 | 38,000 |
| 1876 | 3,245 | 220 | 250 | 360 | 475 | 690 | 17,500 |
| 1877 | 3,920 | 150 | 175 | 335 | 480 | 700 | 18,500 |
| 1878 | 3,020 | 180 | 215 | 365 | 470 | 650 | 16,000 |
| 1879 | 3,030 | 165 | 190 | 300 | 330 | 500 | 12,500 |
| 1880 | 1,636 | 145 | 160 | 200 | 235 | 400 | 17,500 |
| 1881 | 7,707 | 145 | 160 | 200 | 235 | 380 | 13,500 |
| 1882 | 5,125 | 160 | 175 | 210 | 235 | 380 | 9,750 |
| 1883 | 11,007 | 145 | 165 | 200 | 235 | 380 | 9,750 |
| 1884 | 6,236 | 140 | 160 | 190 | 230 | 370 | 9,750 |
| 1885 | 12,261 | 145 | 160 | 200 | 235 | 370 | 9,750 |
| 1886 | 6,016 | 145 | 165 | 200 | 235 | 370 | 9,750 |
| 1887 | 8,543 | 145 | 165 | 200 | 235 | 360 | 9,750 |
| 1888 | 16,580 | 145 | 165 | 200 | 235 | 350 | 9,750 |
| 1889 | 30,729 | 145 | 165 | 200 | 235 | 330 | 9,750 |

# $2.50 (QUARTER EAGLE)

## Liberty cap.

No stars    Stars

**Designer:** Robert Scot. **Diameter:** 20 mm. **Weight:** 4.3700 g. **Composition:** 0.9160 Gold, 0.1289 oz. AGW.
**Notes:** The 1796 "no stars" variety does not have stars on the obverse. The 1804 varieties are distinguished by the number of stars on the obverse.

| Date | Mintage | F-12 | VF-20 | XF-40 | MS-60 |
|---|---|---|---|---|---|
| 1796 no stars | 963 | 9,500 | 19,500 | 36,000 | 148,000 |
| 1796 stars | 432 | 8,500 | 12,000 | 19,000 | 105,000 |
| 1797 | 427 | 8,500 | 10,000 | 13,750 | 85,000 |
| 1798 | 1,094 | 3,500 | 4,100 | 4,750 | 48,000 |
| 1802/1 | 3,035 | 3,000 | 4,100 | 4,600 | 17,500 |
| 1804 13-star reverse | 3,327 | 16,000 | 29,000 | 62,000 | 155,000 |
| 1804 13-star reverse | 3,327 | 16,000 | 29,000 | 62,000 | 155,000 |
| 1804 14-star reverse | Inc. above | 3,250 | 4,100 | 4,950 | 21,000 |
| 1804 14-star reverse | Inc. above | 3,250 | 4,100 | 4,950 | 21,000 |
| 1805 | 1,781 | 3,000 | 4,200 | 4,850 | 19,500 |
| 1806/4 | 1,616 | 3,000 | 4,200 | 5,000 | 20,000 |
| 1806/5 | Inc. above | 5,750 | 8,000 | 11,500 | 65,000 |
| 1807 | 6,812 | 3,000 | 4,000 | 5,000 | 16,000 |

## Turban head.

**Designer:** John Reich. **Diameter:** 20 mm. **Weight:** 4.3700 g. **Composition:** 0.9160 Gold, 0.1289 oz. AGW.

| Date | Mintage | F-12 | VF-20 | XF-40 | MS-60 |
|------|---------|------|-------|-------|-------|
| 1808 | 2,710 | 9,000 | 13,500 | 20,000 | 45,000 |

## Turban head

**Designer:** John Reich. **Diameter:** 18.5 mm. **Weight:** 4.3700 g. **Composition:** 0.9160 Gold, 0.1289 oz. AGW.

| Date | Mintage | F-12 | VF-20 | XF-40 | MS-60 |
|------|---------|------|-------|-------|-------|
| 1821 | 6,448 | 3,250 | 3,600 | 4,500 | 16,250 |
| 1824/21 | 2,600 | 3,450 | 3,900 | 4,200 | 12,000 |
| 1825 | 4,434 | 2,850 | 3,600 | 4,200 | 11,000 |
| 1826/25 | 760 | 3,450 | 4,250 | 5,000 | 28,500 |
| 1827 | 2,800 | 3,600 | 4,700 | 6,350 | 15,500 |

## Turban head

**Designer:** John Reich. **Diameter:** 18.2 mm. **Weight:** 4.3700 g. **Composition:** 0.9160 Gold, 0.1289 oz. AGW.

| Date | Mintage | F-12 | VF-20 | XF-40 | MS-60 |
|------|---------|------|-------|-------|-------|
| 1829 | 3,403 | 3,000 | 3,250 | 4,000 | 9,250 |
| 1830 | 4,540 | 3,000 | 3,250 | 4,000 | 9,250 |
| 1831 | 4,520 | 3,000 | 3,250 | 4,000 | 9,250 |
| 1832 | 4,400 | 3,000 | 3,250 | 4,000 | 9,250 |
| 1833 | 4,160 | 3,000 | 3,500 | 4,150 | 9,750 |
| 1834 | 4,000 | 6,750 | 9,800 | 16,000 | 32,000 |

## Classic head.

**Designer:** William Kneass. **Diameter:** 18.2 mm. **Weight:** 4.1800 g. **Composition:** 0.8990 Gold, 0.1209 oz. AGW.

| Date | Mintage | VF-20 | XF-40 | AU-50 | MS-60 | MS-65 |
|------|---------|-------|-------|-------|-------|-------|
| 1834 | 112,234 | 300 | 440 | 700 | 1,750 | 25,000 |
| 1835 | 131,402 | 265 | 420 | 700 | 1,750 | 25,000 |
| 1836 | 547,986 | 255 | 420 | 565 | 1,750 | 25,000 |
| 1837 | 45,080 | 265 | 420 | 700 | 2,450 | 25,000 |
| 1838 | 47,030 | 265 | 420 | 700 | 1,750 | 25,000 |
| 1838C | 7,880 | 950 | 2,100 | 5,750 | 22,000 | 45,000 |
| 1839 | 27,021 | 300 | 600 | 1,600 | 3,800 | — |
| 1839C | 18,140 | 775 | 1,800 | 3,500 | 19,500 | — |
| 1839D | 13,674 | 940 | 2,500 | 5,750 | 21,000 | — |
| 1839O | 17,781 | 455 | 875 | 1,250 | 5,150 | — |

## Coronet head.

1848 "Cal."

**Designer:** Christian Gobrecht. **Diameter:** 18 mm. **Weight:** 4.1800 g. **Composition:** 0.9000 Gold, 0.121 oz. AGW. **Notes:** Varieties for 1843 are distinguished by the size of the numerals in the date. One 1848 variety has "Cal." inscribed on the reverse, indicating it was made from California gold. The 1873 "closed-3" and "open-3" varieties are distinguished by the amount of space between the upper left and lower left serifs in the 3 in the date.

| Date | Mintage | F-12 | VF-20 | XF-40 | AU-50 | MS-60 | Prf-65 |
|------|---------|------|-------|-------|-------|-------|--------|
| 1840 | 18,859 | 180 | 200 | 800 | 2,800 | 5,900 | — |
| 1840C | 12,822 | 325 | 575 | 1,150 | 4,700 | 13,000 | — |
| 1840D | 3,532 | 600 | 2,200 | 6,750 | 15,500 | 32,000 | — |
| 1840O | 33,580 | 225 | 250 | 800 | 1,700 | 10,000 | — |
| 1841 | — | — | — | 27,500 | 50,000 | — | — |
| 1841C | 10,281 | 275 | 550 | 1,100 | 3,250 | 18,500 | — |
| 1841D | 4,164 | 600 | 1,300 | 3,150 | 9,000 | 22,500 | — |
| 1842 | 2,823 | 350 | 800 | 2,700 | 6,000 | 17,000 | — |
| 1842C | 6,729 | 525 | 1,050 | 2,800 | 6,500 | 24,000 | — |
| 1842D | 4,643 | 660 | 1,375 | 2,700 | 11,750 | 33,000 | — |
| 1842O | 19,800 | 220 | 360 | 1,100 | 1,575 | 12,000 | — |
| 1843 | 100,546 | 160 | 180 | 205 | 285 | 1,250 | — |
| 1843C small date | 26,064 | 900 | 2,100 | 4,800 | 8,250 | 23,000 | — |
| 1843C large date | Inc. above | 440 | 575 | 930 | 2,850 | 7,700 | — |
| 1843D small date | 36,209 | 370 | 600 | 1,050 | 2,200 | 8,700 | — |
| 1843O small date | 288,002 | 150 | 190 | 250 | 335 | 1,400 | — |
| 1843O large date | 76,000 | 200 | 250 | 400 | 1,250 | 3,450 | — |
| 1844 | 6,784 | 190 | 350 | 750 | 1,950 | 6,400 | — |
| 1844C | 11,622 | 365 | 600 | 1,600 | 6,250 | 16,500 | — |
| 1844D | 17,332 | 315 | 590 | 1,150 | 2,200 | 6,200 | — |
| 1845 | 91,051 | 160 | 240 | 280 | 340 | 1,075 | — |
| 1845D | 19,460 | 325 | 585 | 1,100 | 2,300 | 10,500 | — |
| 1845O | 4,000 | 600 | 875 | 1,800 | 5,500 | 14,000 | — |
| 1846 | 21,598 | 225 | 275 | 450 | 975 | 4,950 | — |
| 1846C | 4,808 | 450 | 975 | 1,950 | 8,000 | 18,750 | — |
| 1846D | 19,303 | 345 | 715 | 975 | 2,100 | 10,500 | — |
| 1846O | 66,000 | 170 | 270 | 475 | 1,100 | 4,750 | — |
| 1847 | 29,814 | 170 | 225 | 350 | 675 | 3,250 | — |
| 1847C | 23,226 | 270 | 515 | 975 | 1,850 | 5,500 | — |
| 1847D | 15,784 | 270 | 550 | 1,050 | 1,950 | 7,400 | — |
| 1847O | 124,000 | 185 | 240 | 425 | 1,150 | 3,000 | — |
| 1848 | 7,497 | 315 | 490 | 900 | 1,675 | 7,900 | — |
| 1848 "Cal." | 1,389 | 6,000 | 8,500 | 13,000 | 21,000 | 34,000 | — |
| 1848C | 16,788 | 360 | 575 | 1,300 | 2,400 | 14,000 | — |
| 1848D | 13,771 | 350 | 550 | 1,175 | 2,100 | 10,000 | — |
| 1849 | 23,294 | 160 | 250 | 450 | 800 | 2,100 | — |
| 1849C | 10,220 | 350 | 675 | 1,350 | 4,500 | 20,500 | — |
| 1849D | 10,945 | 390 | 750 | 1,250 | 3,100 | 19,000 | — |
| 1850 | 252,923 | 135 | 160 | 200 | 300 | 975 | — |
| 1850C | 9,148 | 260 | 550 | 1,200 | 2,650 | 17,500 | — |
| 1850D | 12,148 | 330 | 675 | 1,175 | 2,500 | 14,000 | — |
| 1850O | 84,000 | 170 | 225 | 450 | 1,375 | 4,500 | — |
| 1851 | 1,372,748 | 115 | 155 | 170 | 190 | 300 | — |
| 1851C | 14,923 | 330 | 575 | 1,275 | 4,800 | 13,500 | — |
| 1851D | 11,264 | 290 | 640 | 1,200 | 3,100 | 12,250 | — |
| 1851O | 148,000 | 140 | 200 | 240 | 900 | 4,700 | — |
| 1852 | 1,159,681 | 115 | 160 | 170 | 225 | 325 | — |
| 1852C | 9,772 | 300 | 575 | 1,450 | 3,700 | 16,500 | — |
| 1852D | 4,078 | 400 | 925 | 2,250 | 6,250 | 22,000 | — |
| 1852O | 140,000 | 150 | 200 | 270 | 950 | 5,000 | — |
| 1853 | 1,404,668 | 115 | 165 | 175 | 225 | 350 | — |
| 1853D | 3,178 | 500 | 1,400 | 2,500 | 4,250 | 18,500 | — |
| 1854 | 596,258 | 135 | 160 | 190 | 215 | 330 | — |
| 1854C | 7,295 | 250 | 625 | 1,700 | 4,400 | 15,500 | — |
| 1854D | 1,760 | 1,300 | 2,400 | 4,700 | 10,000 | 25,000 | — |
| 1854O | 153,000 | 140 | 170 | 190 | 450 | 1,500 | — |
| 1854S | 246 | 11,500 | 17,500 | 35,000 | 58,000 | 145,000 | — |
| 1855 | 235,480 | 135 | 160 | 180 | 215 | 330 | — |
| 1855C | 3,677 | 475 | 1,150 | 2,550 | 5,250 | 25,000 | — |
| 1855D | 1,123 | 1,500 | 3,250 | 7,500 | 18,500 | 36,000 | — |
| 1856 | 384,240 | 115 | 155 | 175 | 200 | 330 | — |
| 1856C | 7,913 | 385 | 880 | 1,975 | 4,400 | 15,500 | — |
| 1856D | 874 | 3,150 | 5,700 | 9,750 | 23,000 | 45,000 | — |
| 1856O | 21,100 | 150 | 215 | 715 | 1,500 | 7,000 | — |
| 1856S | 71,120 | 120 | 180 | 350 | 850 | 4,400 | — |
| 1857 | 214,130 | 135 | 165 | 175 | 215 | 360 | — |
| 1857D | 2,364 | 450 | 850 | 2,000 | 3,700 | 13,500 | — |
| 1857O | 34,000 | 140 | 165 | 335 | 950 | 4,400 | — |
| 1857S | 69,200 | 140 | 165 | 350 | 900 | 6,000 | — |
| 1858 | 47,377 | 130 | 160 | 230 | 330 | 1,200 | — |
| 1858C | 9,056 | 325 | 600 | 1,100 | 2,350 | 9,000 | — |
| 1859 | 39,444 | 130 | 170 | 230 | 350 | 1,150 | — |
| 1859D | 2,244 | 570 | 1,400 | 2,600 | 4,700 | 24,000 | — |
| 1859S | 15,200 | 170 | 345 | 950 | 2,500 | 7,750 | — |
| 1860 | 22,675 | 130 | 160 | 250 | 450 | 1,100 | 19,000 |
| 1860C | 7,469 | 350 | 775 | 1,450 | 3,850 | 20,000 | — |
| 1860S | 35,600 | 150 | 200 | 675 | 1,150 | 4,400 | — |
| 1861 | 1,283,878 | 120 | 160 | 180 | 215 | 325 | 20,000 |
| 1861S | 24,000 | 150 | 325 | 950 | 2,750 | 6,750 | — |

| Date | Mintage | F-12 | VF-20 | XF-40 | AU-50 | MS-60 | Prf-65 |
|------|---------|------|-------|-------|-------|-------|--------|
| 1862 | 98,543 | 150 | 200 | 300 | 500 | 1,200 | 20,000 |
| 1862/1 | Inc. above | 450 | 900 | 1,900 | 3,300 | 8,750 | — |
| 1862S | 8,000 | 400 | 825 | 2,000 | 4,500 | 15,500 | — |
| 1863 | 30 | — | — | — | — | — | 75,000 |
| 1863S | 10,800 | 300 | 500 | 1,375 | 3,100 | 12,750 | — |
| 1864 | 2,874 | 2,400 | 5,400 | 11,000 | 24,000 | 37,500 | 22,500 |
| 1865 | 1,545 | 2,000 | 4,250 | 8,500 | 16,000 | 32,000 | 32,000 |
| 1865S | 23,376 | 140 | 200 | 575 | 1,350 | 4,200 | — |
| 1866 | 3,110 | 550 | 1,200 | 3,900 | 8,500 | 16,000 | 24,000 |
| 1866S | 38,960 | 170 | 300 | 750 | 1,550 | 8,000 | — |
| 1867 | 3,250 | 165 | 300 | 775 | 1,100 | 4,300 | 25,000 |
| 1867S | 28,000 | 150 | 230 | 600 | 1,600 | 5,000 | — |
| 1868 | 3,625 | 150 | 230 | 400 | 650 | 2,100 | 28,000 |
| 1868S | 34,000 | 125 | 190 | 350 | 1,150 | 4,500 | — |
| 1869 | 4,345 | 135 | 235 | 425 | 600 | 2,300 | 24,500 |
| 1869S | 29,500 | 135 | 215 | 480 | 775 | 4,300 | — |
| 1870 | 4,555 | 140 | 240 | 400 | 750 | 3,700 | 30,000 |
| 1870S | 16,000 | 135 | 200 | 355 | 875 | 4,800 | — |
| 1871 | 5,350 | 150 | 230 | 285 | 700 | 2,350 | 30,000 |
| 1871S | 22,000 | 130 | 190 | 290 | 575 | 2,450 | — |
| 1872 | 3,030 | 200 | 360 | 775 | 1,100 | 4,500 | 28,000 |
| 1872S | 18,000 | 120 | 190 | 400 | 975 | 4,300 | — |
| 1873 closed 3 | 178,025 | 110 | 175 | 190 | 240 | 500 | 24,000 |
| 1873 open 3 | Inc. above | 110 | 160 | 180 | 230 | 285 | — |
| 1873S | 27,000 | 120 | 225 | 425 | 880 | 2,450 | — |
| 1874 | 3,940 | 140 | 235 | 425 | 800 | 2,300 | 28,000 |
| 1875 | 420 | 1,500 | 3,600 | 5,250 | 8,000 | 16,000 | — |
| 1875S | 11,600 | 120 | 180 | 400 | 850 | 2,700 | — |
| 1876 | 4,221 | 160 | 260 | 600 | 875 | 3,300 | 25,000 |
| 1876S | 5,000 | 150 | 220 | 500 | 880 | 3,500 | — |
| 1877 | 1,652 | 200 | 380 | 750 | 1,000 | 3,250 | 32,500 |
| 1877S | 35,400 | 115 | 160 | 185 | 210 | 650 | — |
| 1878 | 286,260 | 115 | 150 | 175 | 210 | 300 | 34,000 |
| 1878S | 178,000 | 115 | 150 | 175 | 210 | 300 | — |
| 1879 | 88,990 | 115 | 150 | 175 | 210 | 265 | 24,500 |
| 1879S | 43,500 | 125 | 160 | 260 | 470 | 1,400 | — |
| 1880 | 2,996 | 160 | 180 | 335 | 550 | 1,300 | 26,000 |
| 1881 | 691 | 750 | 1,800 | 2,750 | 4,500 | 8,400 | 27,500 |
| 1882 | 4,067 | 125 | 210 | 280 | 360 | 600 | 15,000 |
| 1883 | 2,002 | 125 | 210 | 400 | 850 | 2,000 | 15,000 |
| 1884 | 2,023 | 125 | 210 | 400 | 600 | 1,500 | 17,000 |
| 1885 | 887 | 400 | 600 | 1,650 | 2,350 | 3,900 | 16,000 |
| 1886 | 4,088 | 125 | 175 | 260 | 425 | 1,150 | 17,000 |
| 1887 | 6,282 | 125 | 170 | 235 | 325 | 650 | 15,000 |
| 1888 | 16,098 | 125 | 175 | 225 | 160 | 210 | 6,250 |
| 1889 | 17,648 | 125 | 180 | 235 | 165 | 210 | 5,500 |
| 1890 | 8,813 | 125 | 175 | 210 | 165 | 215 | 7,750 |
| 1891 | 11,040 | 125 | 175 | 250 | 160 | 200 | 6,700 |
| 1892 | 2,545 | 135 | 195 | 225 | 185 | 200 | 8,000 |
| 1893 | 30,106 | 125 | 150 | 180 | 215 | 275 | 14,000 |
| 1894 | 4,122 | 125 | 160 | 210 | 260 | 725 | 14,000 |
| 1895 | 6,199 | 125 | 160 | 210 | 260 | 725 | 14,000 |
| 1896 | 19,202 | 125 | 140 | 170 | 185 | 250 | 14,000 |
| 1897 | 29,904 | 120 | 140 | 170 | 185 | 250 | 14,000 |
| 1898 | 24,165 | 120 | 140 | 170 | 185 | 250 | 14,000 |
| 1899 | 27,350 | 110 | 150 | 170 | 185 | 250 | 13,000 |
| 1900 | 67,205 | 130 | 160 | 250 | 315 | 450 | 13,000 |
| 1901 | 91,322 | 110 | 145 | 170 | 180 | 240 | 13,000 |
| 1902 | 133,733 | 110 | 145 | 170 | 180 | 240 | 13,000 |
| 1903 | 201,257 | 110 | 145 | 170 | 180 | 240 | 13,000 |
| 1904 | 160,960 | 110 | 145 | 170 | 180 | 240 | 13,000 |
| 1905 | 217,944 | 110 | 145 | 170 | 180 | 240 | 13,000 |
| 1906 | 176,490 | 110 | 145 | 170 | 180 | 240 | 13,000 |
| 1907 | 336,448 | 110 | 145 | 170 | 180 | 240 | 13,000 |

## Indian head.

**Designer:** Bela Lyon Pratt. **Diameter:** 18 mm. **Weight:** 4.1800 g. **Composition:** 0.9000 Gold, 0.121 oz. AGW.

| Date | Mintage | VF-20 | XF-40 | AU-50 | MS-60 | MS-63 | MS-65 | Prf-65 |
|------|---------|-------|-------|-------|-------|-------|-------|--------|
| 1908 | 565,057 | 135 | 175 | 185 | 230 | 550 | 2,500 | 15,000 |
| 1909 | 441,899 | 135 | 175 | 185 | 240 | 725 | 3,000 | 29,000 |

## 1911-D $2.50 Gold
### Grade MS-60

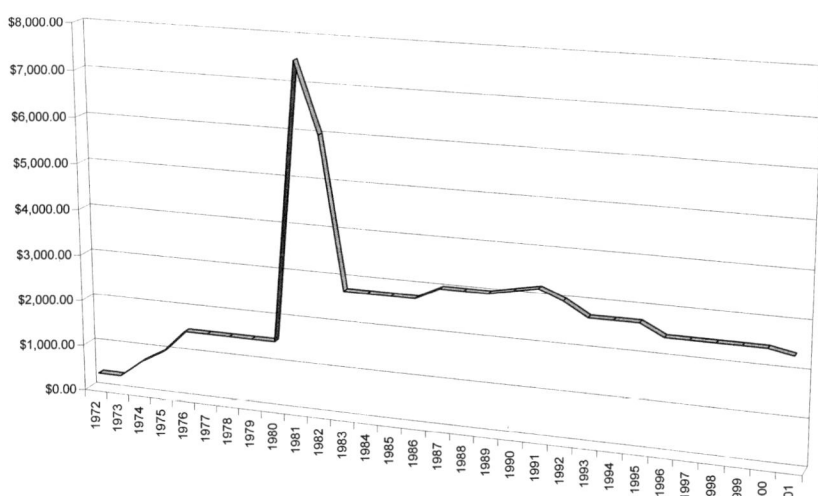

☐ Retail Price

| Date | Mintage | VF-20 | XF-40 | AU-50 | MS-60 | MS-63 | MS-65 | Prf-65 |
|------|---------|-------|-------|-------|-------|-------|-------|--------|
| 1910 | 492,682 | 135 | 175 | 185 | 240 | 735 | 5,200 | 16,000 |
| 1911 | 704,191 | 135 | 175 | 185 | 250 | 625 | 3,000 | 15,000 |
| 1911D | 55,680 | 700 | 1,000 | 1,200 | 2,350 | 7,800 | 40,000 | — |
| 1912 | 616,197 | 135 | 175 | 185 | 250 | 900 | 5,200 | 15,500 |
| 1913 | 722,165 | 135 | 175 | 185 | 250 | 600 | 3,300 | 15,800 |
| 1914 | 240,117 | 135 | 175 | 200 | 370 | 2,750 | 10,000 | 16,500 |
| 1914D | 448,000 | 135 | 175 | 185 | 250 | 1,000 | 8,000 | — |
| 1915 | 606,100 | 135 | 175 | 185 | 240 | 560 | 3,200 | 15,250 |
| 1925D | 578,000 | 135 | 175 | 185 | 230 | 500 | 2,000 | — |
| 1926 | 446,000 | 135 | 175 | 185 | 230 | 500 | 2,000 | — |
| 1927 | 388,000 | 135 | 175 | 185 | 230 | 500 | 2,000 | — |
| 1928 | 416,000 | 135 | 175 | 185 | 230 | 500 | 2,000 | — |
| 1929 | 532,000 | 135 | 175 | 185 | 230 | 500 | 3,000 | — |

# $3

**Designer:** James B. Longacre. **Diameter:** 20.5 mm. **Weight:** 5.0150 g. **Composition:** 0.9000 Gold, 0.1452 oz. AGW. **Notes:** The 1873 "closed-3" and "open-3" varieties are distinguished by the amount of space between the upper left and lower left serifs of the 3 in the date.

| Date | Mintage | VF-20 | XF-40 | AU-50 | MS-60 | MS-65 | Prf-65 |
|------|---------|-------|-------|-------|-------|-------|--------|
| 1854 | 138,618 | 550 | 650 | 875 | 1,550 | 13,500 | 35,000 |
| 1854D | 1,120 | 7,250 | 10,500 | 23,500 | 75,000 | — | — |
| 1854O | 24,000 | 750 | 1,300 | 2,500 | 14,000 | 55,000 | — |
| 1855 | 50,555 | 490 | 675 | 895 | 1,700 | 21,000 | — |
| 1855S | 6,600 | 900 | 1,700 | 4,750 | 20,000 | — | — |
| 1856 | 26,010 | 615 | 700 | 900 | 2,250 | 24,000 | — |
| 1856S | 34,500 | 650 | 915 | 1,900 | 8,250 | 45,000 | — |
| 1857 | 20,891 | 600 | 650 | 900 | 2,700 | 27,500 | 40,000 |
| 1857S | 14,000 | 810 | 1,700 | 4,000 | 13,000 | — | — |
| 1858 | 2,133 | 775 | 1,175 | 2,300 | 6,500 | 35,000 | 35,000 |
| 1859 | 15,638 | 500 | 675 | 880 | 2,200 | 23,000 | 35,000 |
| 1860 | 7,155 | 600 | 900 | 1,000 | 2,400 | 18,000 | 35,000 |
| 1860S | 7,000 | 700 | 1,400 | 5,000 | 12,000 | — | — |

| Date | Mintage | VF-20 | XF-40 | AU-50 | MS-60 | MS-65 | Prf-65 |
|------|---------|-------|-------|-------|-------|-------|--------|
| 1861 | 6,072 | 670 | 850 | 1,350 | 2,700 | 22,500 | 35,000 |
| 1862 | 5,785 | 670 | 800 | 1,400 | 2,700 | 25,000 | 34,000 |
| 1863 | 5,039 | 680 | 770 | 1,375 | 2,700 | 20,000 | 32,000 |
| 1864 | 2,680 | 700 | 1,150 | 1,375 | 2,500 | 24,000 | 33,000 |
| 1865 | 1,165 | 1,000 | 1,700 | 3,800 | 7,000 | 36,000 | 35,000 |
| 1866 | 4,030 | 700 | 950 | 1,500 | 2,500 | 23,500 | 35,000 |
| 1867 | 2,650 | 700 | 950 | 1,275 | 2,400 | 25,000 | 27,000 |
| 1868 | 4,875 | 700 | 850 | 1,275 | 2,500 | 22,500 | 31,000 |
| 1869 | 2,525 | 750 | 900 | 1,275 | 3,500 | 26,000 | 35,000 |
| 1870 | 3,535 | 625 | 850 | 1,350 | 3,200 | 32,500 | 35,000 |
| 1870S unique | — | — | — | — | — | — | — |
| Note: 1870S, private sale, 1992, XF-40, $1,500,000. | | | | | | | |
| 1871 | 1,330 | 750 | 1,000 | 1,450 | 3,400 | 24,000 | 35,000 |
| 1872 | 2,030 | 700 | 800 | 1,300 | 2,900 | 26,000 | 35,000 |
| 1873 open 3, proof only | 25 | — | — | — | — | — | — |
| 1873 closed 3, mintage unknown | — | 3,500 | 4,500 | 7,750 | 23,000 | — | — |
| 1874 | 41,820 | 550 | 625 | 750 | 1,700 | 9,800 | 28,000 |
| 1875 proof only | 20 | — | — | 40,000 | — | — | 200,000 |
| 1876 | 45 | — | 9,000 | 12,000 | — | — | 50,000 |
| 1877 | 1,488 | 1,100 | 2,450 | 4,400 | 10,000 | 58,000 | 37,000 |
| 1878 | 82,324 | 550 | 625 | 875 | 2,300 | 9,500 | 40,000 |
| 1879 | 3,030 | 600 | 700 | 1,250 | 2,250 | 13,000 | 27,000 |
| 1880 | 1,036 | 650 | 1,250 | 1,800 | 2,250 | 14,000 | 26,000 |
| 1881 | 554 | 1,100 | 1,850 | 3,300 | 4,250 | 3,300 | 30,000 |
| 1882 | 1,576 | 700 | 900 | 1,400 | 2,300 | 17,000 | 24,000 |
| 1883 | 989 | 700 | 1,100 | 1,750 | 2,300 | 15,000 | 24,000 |
| 1884 | 1,106 | 1,000 | 1,400 | 2,000 | 2,800 | 20,000 | 24,000 |
| 1885 | 910 | 950 | 1,500 | 2,000 | 2,900 | 21,000 | 25,000 |
| 1886 | 1,142 | 975 | 1,200 | 1,800 | 2,900 | — | 21,000 |
| 1887 | 6,160 | 625 | 700 | 1,300 | 1,500 | 13,000 | 24,000 |
| 1888 | 5,291 | 625 | 800 | 1,150 | 1,750 | 11,000 | 21,000 |
| 1889 | 2,429 | 625 | 800 | 1,050 | 1,750 | 12,000 | 24,000 |

# $5 (HALF EAGLE)

## Liberty cap.

Small eagle          Large eagle

**Designer:** Robert Scot. **Diameter:** 25 mm. **Weight:** 8.7500 g. **Composition:** 0.9160 Gold, 0.258 oz. AGW.
**Notes:** From 1795 through 1798, varieties exist with either a "small eagle" or a "large (heraldic) eagle" on the reverse. After 1798, only the heraldic eagle was used. Two 1797 varieties are distinguished by the size of the 8 in the date. 1806 varieties are distinguished by whether the top of the 6 has a serif.

| Date | Mintage | F-12 | VF-20 | XF-40 | MS-60 |
|------|---------|------|-------|-------|-------|
| 1795 small eagle | 8,707 | 5,250 | 7,250 | 10,000 | 37,500 |
| 1795 large eagle | Inc. above | 7,000 | 11,000 | 16,500 | 74,000 |
| 1796/95 small eagle | 6,196 | 6,000 | 8,500 | 14,000 | — |
| 1797/95 large eagle | 3,609 | 7,500 | 10,500 | 17,500 | 130,000 |
| 1797 15 stars, small eagle | Inc. above | 8,500 | 10,500 | 25,000 | 98,000 |
| 1797 16 stars, small eagle | Inc. above | 7,250 | 9,250 | 21,750 | 99,000 |
| 1798 small eagle | — | 75,000 | 125,000 | 200,000 | — |
| 1798 large eagle, small 8 | 824,867 | 1,500 | 1,950 | 2,950 | 18,500 |
| 1798 large eagle, large 8, 13-star reverse | Inc. above | 1,300 | 2,200 | 2,950 | 17,500 |
| 1798 large eagle, large 8, 14-star reverse | Inc. above | 1,750 | 2,750 | 5,250 | 25,000 |
| 1799 | 7,451 | 1,550 | 1,950 | 3,300 | 13,000 |
| 1800 | 37,628 | 1,300 | 1,600 | 2,300 | 5,900 |
| 1802/1 | 53,176 | 1,300 | 1,600 | 2,300 | 5,900 |
| 1803/2 | 33,506 | 1,300 | 1,600 | 2,300 | 5,900 |
| 1804 small 8 | 30,475 | 1,375 | 1,650 | 2,500 | 6,250 |
| 1804 large 8 | Inc. above | 1,375 | 1,600 | 2,300 | 6,600 |
| 1805 | 33,183 | 1,375 | 1,600 | 2,300 | 5,950 |
| 1806 pointed 6 | 64,093 | 1,375 | 1,625 | 2,350 | 7,500 |
| 1806 round 6 | Inc. above | 1,375 | 1,600 | 2,300 | 5,800 |
| 1807 | 32,488 | 1,400 | 1,650 | 2,450 | 5,750 |

# Turban head, capped draped bust.

**Designer:** John Reich. **Diameter:** 25 mm. **Weight:** 8.7500 g. **Composition:** 0.9160 Gold, 0.258 oz. AGW.
**Notes:** The 1810 varieties are distinguished by the size of the numerals in the date and the size of the 5 in the "5D." on the reverse. The 1811 varieties are distinguished by the size of the 5 in the "5D." on the reverse.

| Date | Mintage | F-12 | VF-20 | XF-40 | MS-60 |
|---|---|---|---|---|---|
| 1807 | 51,605 | 1,350 | 1,650 | 2,150 | 5,100 |
| 1808 | 55,578 | 1,350 | 1,650 | 2,150 | 5,100 |
| 1808/7 | Inc. above | 1,400 | 1,775 | 2,350 | 5,600 |
| 1809/8 | 33,875 | 1,250 | 1,650 | 2,150 | 5,250 |
| 1810 small date, small 5 | 100,287 | 7,500 | 18,500 | 31,000 | 84,000 |
| 1810 small date, large 5 | Inc. above | 1,300 | 1,650 | 2,210 | 5,750 |
| 1810 large date, small 5 | Inc. above | 12,000 | 24,000 | 39,500 | 100,000 |
| 1810 large date, large 5 | Inc. above | 1,350 | 1,600 | 2,100 | 5,250 |
| 1811 small 5 | 99,581 | 1,350 | 1,600 | 2,100 | 5,200 |
| 1811 large 5 | Inc. above | 1,250 | 1,500 | 2,000 | 5,100 |
| 1812 | 58,087 | 1,550 | 1,650 | 2,200 | 5,150 |

# Turban head, capped head.

**Designer:** John Reich. **Diameter:** 25 mm. **Weight:** 8.7500 g. **Composition:** 0.9160 Gold, 0.258 oz. AGW.
**Notes:** 1820 varieties are distinguished by whether the 2 in the date has a curved base or square base and by the size of the letters in the reverse inscriptions. 1832 varieties are distinguished by whether the 2 in the date has a curved base or square base and by the number of stars on the reverse. 1834 varieties are distinguished by whether the 4 has a serif at its far right.

| Date | Mintage | F-12 | VF-20 | XF-40 | MS-60 |
|---|---|---|---|---|---|
| 1813 | 95,428 | 1,550 | 1,875 | 2,400 | 5,600 |
| 1814/13 | 15,454 | 1,650 | 2,200 | 2,800 | 8,000 |
| 1815 | 635 | — | — | — | — |
| **Note:** 1815, private sale, Jan. 1994, MS-61, $150,000 | | | | | |
| 1818 | 48,588 | 1,700 | 2,100 | 2,800 | 7,250 |
| 1819 | 51,723 | 7,750 | 13,500 | 23,000 | 36,500 |
| 1820 curved-base 2, small letters | 263,806 | 1,700 | 2,200 | 2,850 | 8,500 |
| 1820 curved-base 2, large letters | Inc. above | 1,700 | 2,200 | 2,850 | 20,000 |
| 1820 square-base 2 | Inc. above | 1,750 | 2,200 | 2,850 | 8,500 |
| 1821 | 34,641 | 3,000 | 8,500 | 13,500 | 31,000 |
| 1822 3 known | — | — | — | — | — |
| **Note:** 1822, private sale, 1993, VF-30, $1,000,000. | | | | | |
| 1823 | 14,485 | 1,750 | 2,750 | 3,700 | 14,500 |
| 1824 | 17,340 | 4,500 | 8,000 | 12,000 | 26,000 |
| 1825/21 | 29,060 | 4,500 | 6,750 | 9,000 | 26,500 |
| 1825/24 | Inc. above | — | — | — | — |
| **Note:** 1825/4, Bowers & Merena, March 1989, XF, $148,500. | | | | | |
| 1826 | 18,069 | 3,500 | 6,000 | 7,100 | 20,000 |
| 1827 | 24,913 | 4,500 | 6,750 | 9,000 | 27,000 |
| 1828/7 | 28,029 | — | — | — | — |
| **Note:** 1828/7, Bowers & Merena, June 1989, XF, $20,900. | | | | | |
| 1828 | Inc. above | 4,000 | 6,250 | 14,000 | 44,000 |
| 1829 large planchet | 57,442 | — | — | — | — |
| **Note:** 1829 large planchet, Superior, July 1985, MS-65, $104,500. | | | | | |
| 1829 small planchet | Inc. above | — | — | — | — |
| **Note:** 1829 small planchet, private sale, 1992 (XF-45), $89,000. | | | | | |
| 1830 small "5D." | 126,351 | 3,500 | 4,500 | 5,850 | 12,200 |
| 1830 large "5D." | Inc. above | 3,500 | 4,400 | 6,000 | 12,500 |
| 1831 | 140,594 | 3,500 | 4,600 | 6,500 | 15,500 |
| 1832 curved-base 2, 12 stars | 157,487 | 35,000 | 50,000 | 75,000 | — |
| 1832 square-base 2, 13 stars | Inc. above | 2,400 | 4,500 | 6,000 | 15,000 |
| 1833 | 193,630 | 3,300 | 4,100 | 5,250 | 11,000 |
| 1834 plain 4 | 50,141 | 3,600 | 4,500 | 7,500 | 17,500 |

| Date | Mintage | F-12 | VF-20 | XF-40 | MS-60 |
|---|---|---|---|---|---|
| 1834 crosslet 4 | Inc. above | 3,800 | 4,500 | 7,000 | 19,000 |

## Classic head.

**Designer:** William Kneass. **Diameter:** 22.5 mm. **Weight:** 8.3600 g. **Composition:** 0.8990 Gold, 0.2418 oz. AGW. **Notes:** 1834 varieties are distinguished by whether the 4 has a serif at its far right.

| Date | Mintage | VF-20 | XF-40 | AU-50 | MS-60 | MS-65 |
|---|---|---|---|---|---|---|
| 1834 plain 4 | 658,028 | 250 | 400 | 650 | 2,000 | 46,000 |
| 1834 crosslet 4 | Inc. above | 1,300 | 2,300 | 4,600 | 14,000 | — |
| 1835 | 371,534 | 245 | 400 | 750 | 2,650 | 55,000 |
| 1836 | 553,147 | 250 | 400 | 650 | 2,000 | 55,000 |
| 1837 | 207,121 | 250 | 410 | 925 | 3,000 | 57,000 |
| 1838 | 286,588 | 250 | 400 | 900 | 3,000 | 58,000 |
| 1838C | 17,179 | 1,550 | 3,700 | 13,000 | 31,000 | — |
| 1838D | 20,583 | 1,450 | 3,300 | 5,500 | 19,000 | — |

## Coronet head. No motto above eagle.

**Designer:** Christian Gobrecht. **Diameter:** 21.6 mm. **Weight:** 8.3590 g. **Composition:** 0.9000 Gold, 0.242 oz. AGW. **Notes:** Varieties for the 1842 Philadelphia strikes are distinguished by the size of the letters in the reverse inscriptions. Varieties for the 1842-C and -D strikes are distinguished by the size of the numerals in the date. Varieties for the 1843-O strikes are distinguished by the size of the letters in the reverse inscriptions.

| Date | Mintage | F-12 | VF-20 | XF-40 | MS-60 | Prf-65 |
|---|---|---|---|---|---|---|
| 1839 | 118,143 | 220 | 250 | 400 | 3,300 | — |
| 1839/8 curved date | Inc. above | 200 | 300 | 600 | 1,750 | — |
| 1839C | 17,205 | 400 | 800 | 2,000 | 24,000 | — |
| 1839D | 18,939 | 400 | ·775 | 1,800 | 16,500 | — |

### 1852-C $5 Gold
#### Grade MS-60

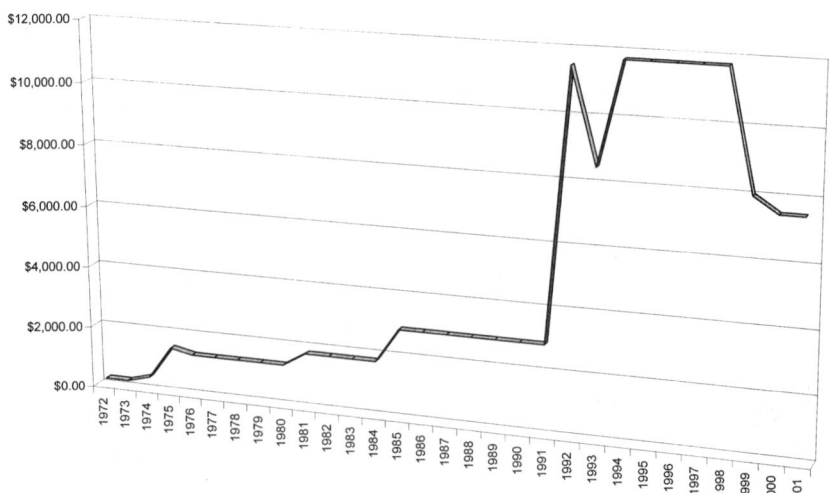

□ Retail Price

| Date | Mintage | F-12 | VF-20 | XF-40 | MS-60 | Prf-65 |
|------|---------|------|-------|-------|-------|--------|
| 1840 | 137,382 | 180 | 200 | 275 | 3,400 | — |
| 1840C | 18,992 | 400 | 700 | 2,400 | 21,500 | — |
| 1840D | 22,896 | 400 | 700 | 1,400 | 13,500 | — |
| 1840O | 40,120 | 160 | 250 | 725 | 9,500 | — |
| 1841 | 15,833 | 200 | 330 | 800 | 5,200 | — |
| 1841C | 21,467 | 300 | 675 | 1,300 | 14,500 | — |
| 1841D | 30,495 | 325 | 700 | 1,000 | 12,000 | — |
| 1841O 2 known | 50 | — | — | — | — | — |
| 1842 small letters | 27,578 | 125 | 280 | 1,000 | 12,000 | — |
| 1842 large letters | Inc. above | 250 | 700 | 1,800 | 13,500 | — |
| 1842C small date | 28,184 | 2,500 | 7,000 | 23,000 | 115,000 | — |
| 1842C large date | Inc. above | 300 | 750 | 1,350 | 14,000 | — |
| 1842D small date | 59,608 | 350 | 650 | 1,200 | 13,500 | — |
| 1842D large date | Inc. above | 900 | 1,950 | 5,000 | 37,500 | — |
| 1842O | 16,400 | 350 | 900 | 2,500 | 19,500 | — |
| 1843 | 611,205 | 125 | 200 | 215 | 1,600 | — |
| 1843C | 44,201 | 275 | 625 | 1,250 | 12,000 | — |
| 1843D | 98,452 | 250 | 550 | 1,000 | 9,500 | — |
| 1843O small letters | 19,075 | 225 | 450 | 1,200 | 19,000 | — |
| 1843O large letters | 82,000 | 175 | 225 | 900 | 10,500 | — |
| 1844 | 340,330 | 125 | 190 | 225 | 2,000 | — |
| 1844C | 23,631 | 300 | 725 | 2,600 | 18,500 | — |
| 1844D | 88,982 | 300 | 600 | 950 | 10,000 | — |
| 1844O | 364,600 | 170 | 225 | 350 | 4,000 | — |
| 1845 | 417,099 | 150 | 200 | 215 | 1,850 | — |
| 1845D | 90,629 | 335 | 650 | 1,150 | 10,500 | — |
| 1845O | 41,000 | 170 | 350 | 675 | 8,500 | — |
| 1846 | 395,942 | 150 | 200 | 215 | 2,700 | — |
| 1846C | 12,995 | 400 | 800 | 2,500 | 19,500 | — |
| 1846D | 80,294 | 300 | 550 | 1,100 | 11,000 | — |
| 1846O | 58,000 | 170 | 325 | 900 | 12,000 | — |
| 1847 | 915,981 | 135 | 190 | 215 | 1,250 | — |
| 1847C | 84,151 | 275 | 575 | 1,150 | 12,800 | — |
| 1847D | 64,405 | 300 | 500 | 1,050 | 7,500 | — |
| 1847O | 12,000 | 475 | 1,700 | 7,000 | 22,000 | — |
| 1848 | 260,775 | 150 | 200 | 230 | 1,300 | — |
| 1848C | 64,472 | 275 | 625 | 1,100 | 17,000 | — |
| 1848D | 47,465 | 275 | 550 | 1,250 | 12,000 | — |
| 1849 | 133,070 | 140 | 190 | 235 | 2,500 | — |
| 1849C | 64,823 | 275 | 500 | 1,000 | 13,000 | — |
| 1849D | 39,036 | 275 | 700 | 1,000 | 12,500 | — |
| 1850 | 64,491 | 165 | 250 | 525 | 3,200 | — |
| 1850C | 63,591 | 250 | 500 | 1,000 | 13,000 | — |
| 1850D | 43,984 | 250 | 525 | 1,300 | 24,500 | — |
| 1851 | 377,505 | 150 | 200 | 215 | 2,700 | — |
| 1851C | 49,176 | 250 | 550 | 950 | 14,000 | — |
| 1851D | 62,710 | 250 | 525 | 1,400 | 12,500 | — |
| 1851O | 41,000 | 250 | 500 | 1,200 | 10,500 | — |
| 1852 | 573,901 | 150 | 200 | 215 | 1,250 | — |
| 1852C | 72,574 | 250 | 550 | 900 | 7,500 | — |
| 1852D | 91,584 | 250 | 500 | 1,000 | 10,750 | — |
| 1853 | 305,770 | 150 | 215 | 215 | 1,600 | — |
| 1853C | 65,571 | 250 | 525 | 1,000 | 8,000 | — |
| 1853D | 89,678 | 265 | 500 | 850 | 6,500 | — |
| 1854 | 160,675 | 160 | 200 | 225 | 2,200 | — |
| 1854C | 39,283 | 250 | 475 | 1,350 | 12,000 | — |
| 1854D | 56,413 | 235 | 500 | 1,000 | 8,500 | — |
| 1854O | 46,000 | 175 | 275 | 450 | 6,750 | — |
| 1854S | — | — | — | — | — | — |
| **Note:** 1854S, Bowers & Merena, Oct. 1982, AU-55, $170,000. | | | | | | |
| 1855 | 117,098 | 140 | 185 | 225 | 1,500 | — |
| 1855C | 39,788 | 325 | 650 | 1,600 | 15,000 | — |
| 1855D | 22,432 | 350 | 625 | 1,250 | 17,000 | — |
| 1855O | 11,100 | 200 | 600 | 1,950 | 20,000 | — |
| 1855S | 61,000 | 185 | 350 | 950 | 13,500 | — |
| 1856 | 197,990 | 150 | 200 | 240 | 2,100 | — |
| 1856C | 28,457 | 200 | 525 | 1,000 | 18,000 | — |
| 1856D | 19,786 | 250 | 600 | 1,150 | 8,700 | — |
| 1856O | 10,000 | 250 | 600 | 1,150 | 15,750 | — |
| 1856S | 105,100 | 150 | 275 | 600 | 5,900 | — |
| 1857 | 98,188 | 135 | 190 | 225 | 2,000 | — |
| 1857C | 31,360 | 250 | 500 | 1,000 | 8,750 | — |
| 1857D | 17,046 | 250 | 525 | 950 | 12,750 | — |
| 1857O | 13,000 | 275 | 600 | 1,275 | 18,000 | — |
| 1857S | 87,000 | 165 | 300 | 500 | 7,250 | — |
| 1858 | 15,136 | 150 | 235 | 550 | 3,600 | 70,000 |
| 1858C | 38,856 | 290 | 600 | 1,150 | 11,000 | — |
| 1858D | 15,362 | 280 | 600 | 1,350 | 13,500 | — |
| 1858S | 18,600 | 300 | 650 | 2,150 | 20,000 | — |

| Date | Mintage | F-12 | VF-20 | XF-40 | MS-60 | Prf-65 |
|------|---------|------|-------|-------|-------|--------|
| 1859 | 16,814 | 160 | 275 | 600 | 6,500 | — |
| 1859C | 31,847 | 250 | 525 | 1,400 | 15,000 | — |
| 1859D | 10,366 | 300 | 650 | 1,750 | 13,000 | — |
| 1859S | 13,220 | 400 | 1,250 | 3,750 | 28,000 | — |
| 1860 | 19,825 | 150 | 265 | 550 | 3,400 | — |
| 1860C | 14,813 | 300 | 800 | 1,850 | 13,500 | — |
| 1860D | 14,635 | 300 | 800 | 2,000 | 14,500 | — |
| 1860S | 21,200 | 400 | 1,100 | 2,000 | 22,000 | — |
| 1861 | 688,150 | 150 | 200 | 225 | 1,100 | — |
| 1861C | 6,879 | 600 | 1,600 | 3,400 | 29,500 | — |
| 1861D | 1,597 | 1,800 | 4,000 | 7,000 | 45,000 | — |
| 1861S | 18,000 | 400 | 1,000 | 4,500 | 30,000 | — |
| 1862 | 4,465 | 300 | 700 | 1,650 | 19,000 | — |
| 1862S | 9,500 | 1,200 | 3,500 | 5,350 | 52,000 | — |
| 1863 | 2,472 | 400 | 1,150 | 3,450 | 22,000 | — |
| 1863S | 17,000 | 425 | 1,200 | 3,900 | 32,000 | — |
| 1864 | 4,220 | 275 | 600 | 1,800 | 13,500 | — |
| 1864S | 3,888 | 2,000 | 4,600 | 12,500 | 47,500 | — |
| 1865 | 1,295 | 500 | 1,150 | 3,750 | 22,000 | — |
| 1865S | 27,612 | 425 | 1,200 | 2,900 | 15,000 | — |
| 1866S | 9,000 | 600 | 1,600 | 4,000 | 30,000 | — |

## Coronet head. "In God We Trust" above eagle.

**Designer:** Christian Gobrecht. **Diameter:** 21.6 mm. **Weight:** 8.3590 g. **Composition:** 0.9000 Gold, 0.242 oz. AGW. **Notes:** The 1873 "closed-3" and "open-3" varieties are known and are distinguished by the amount of space between the upper left and lower left serifs of the 3 in the date.

| Date | Mintage | VF-20 | XF-40 | AU-50 | MS-60 | MS-65 | Prf-65 |
|------|---------|-------|-------|-------|-------|-------|--------|
| 1866 | 6,730 | 725 | 1,500 | 3,500 | 14,000 | — | 80,000 |
| 1866S | 34,920 | 1,000 | 2,600 | 8,000 | 21,000 | — | — |
| 1867 | 6,920 | 485 | 1,600 | 3,500 | 8,000 | — | 70,000 |
| 1867S | 29,000 | 1,250 | 2,700 | 8,500 | 23,000 | — | — |
| 1868 | 5,725 | 600 | 950 | 3,300 | 9,000 | — | 70,000 |
| 1868S | 52,000 | 450 | 1,600 | 3,900 | 19,000 | — | — |
| 1869 | 1,785 | 850 | 2,300 | 3,600 | 19,500 | — | 70,000 |
| 1869S | 31,000 | 500 | 1,700 | 5,000 | 23,500 | — | — |
| 1870 | 4,035 | 700 | 1,900 | 2,650 | 20,000 | — | 70,000 |
| 1870CC | 7,675 | 4,400 | 10,000 | 25,000 | 90,000 | — | — |
| 1870S | 17,000 | 950 | 2,300 | 7,500 | 25,000 | — | — |
| 1871 | 3,230 | 875 | 1,750 | 4,500 | 17,000 | — | 70,000 |
| 1871CC | 20,770 | 975 | 3,000 | 12,500 | 54,500 | — | — |
| 1871S | 25,000 | 500 | 1,000 | 3,250 | 12,500 | — | — |
| 1872 | 1,690 | 750 | 2,000 | 3,500 | 13,000 | — | 60,000 |
| 1872CC | 16,980 | 1,100 | 4,000 | 15,000 | 55,000 | — | — |
| 1872S | 36,400 | 425 | 900 | 3,300 | 10,000 | — | — |
| 1873 closed 3 | 49,305 | 200 | 225 | 375 | 1,150 | — | 70,000 |
| 1873 open 3 | 63,200 | 200 | 215 | 350 | 800 | — | — |
| 1873CC | 7,416 | 2,000 | 8,000 | 24,000 | 47,500 | — | — |
| 1873S | 31,000 | 500 | 1,250 | 4,700 | 19,500 | — | — |
| 1874 | 3,508 | 625 | 1,600 | 2,750 | 16,500 | — | 66,000 |
| 1874CC | 21,198 | 750 | 1,550 | 9,000 | 33,000 | — | — |
| 1874S | 16,000 | 600 | 2,200 | 7,000 | 20,000 | — | — |
| 1875 | 220 | 40,000 | 55,000 | 72,500 | 165,000 | — | 185,000 |
| 1875CC | 11,828 | 1,400 | 4,500 | 10,500 | 42,500 | — | — |
| 1875S | 9,000 | 625 | 2,800 | 5,750 | 21,000 | — | — |
| 1876 | 1,477 | 1,100 | 2,600 | 4,200 | 11,000 | 47,000 | 60,000 |
| 1876CC | 6,887 | 1,250 | 5,000 | 13,000 | 33,500 | — | — |
| 1876S | 4,000 | 1,700 | 3,750 | 9,500 | 25,000 | — | — |
| 1877 | 1,152 | 800 | 2,600 | 4,250 | 11,500 | — | 75,000 |
| 1877CC | 8,680 | 1,000 | 3,300 | 9,500 | 33,500 | — | — |
| 1877S | 26,700 | 340 | 675 | 2,500 | 8,300 | — | — |
| 1878 | 131,740 | 175 | 210 | 250 | 375 | — | 50,000 |
| 1878CC | 9,054 | 3,200 | 7,000 | 16,000 | 49,000 | — | — |
| 1878S | 144,700 | 165 | 190 | 260 | 575 | — | — |
| 1879 | 301,950 | 165 | 185 | 195 | 330 | 11,000 | 55,000 |
| 1879CC | 17,281 | 450 | 1,200 | 3,000 | 17,500 | — | — |
| 1879S | 426,200 | 165 | 180 | 285 | 900 | — | — |
| 1880 | 3,166,436 | 150 | 170 | 190 | 225 | — | 54,000 |
| 1880CC | 51,017 | 350 | 700 | 1,700 | 9,000 | — | — |
| 1880S | 1,348,900 | 160 | 170 | 180 | 225 | — | — |

| Date | Mintage | VF-20 | XF-40 | AU-50 | MS-60 | MS-65 | Prf-65 |
|------|---------|-------|-------|-------|-------|-------|--------|
| 1881 | 5,708,802 | 150 | 165 | 185 | 225 | 6,600 | 54,000 |
| 1881/80 | Inc. above | 275 | 600 | 750 | 1,400 | — | — |
| 1881CC | 13,886 | 450 | 1,250 | 6,000 | 19,000 | — | — |
| 1881S | 969,000 | 160 | 165 | 185 | 225 | — | — |
| 1882 | 2,514,568 | 150 | 160 | 180 | 220 | 7,700 | 54,000 |
| 1882CC | 82,817 | 300 | 475 | 625 | 5,100 | — | — |
| 1882S | 969,000 | 135 | 195 | 215 | 240 | — | — |
| 1883 | 233,461 | 135 | 195 | 225 | 350 | — | 40,000 |
| 1883CC | 12,958 | 375 | 900 | 2,800 | 17,000 | — | — |
| 1883S | 83,200 | 165 | 220 | 250 | 1,050 | — | — |
| 1884 | 191,078 | 135 | 155 | 190 | 600 | — | 35,000 |
| 1884CC | 16,402 | 450 | 850 | 2,500 | 16,000 | — | — |
| 1884S | 177,000 | 135 | 160 | 175 | 1,700 | — | — |
| 1885 | 601,506 | 135 | 160 | 170 | 225 | — | 35,000 |
| 1885S | 1,211,500 | 135 | 155 | 170 | 240 | 5,000 | — |
| 1886 | 388,432 | 135 | 160 | 170 | 250 | — | 44,000 |
| 1886S | 3,268,000 | 130 | 150 | 165 | 240 | — | — |
| 1887 | 87 | — | — | 12,000 | — | — | 130,000 |
| 1887S | 1,912,000 | 130 | 150 | 165 | 225 | — | — |
| 1888 | 18,296 | 140 | 160 | 170 | 225 | — | 28,000 |
| 1888S | 293,900 | 140 | 225 | 300 | 1,150 | — | — |
| 1889 | 7,565 | 260 | 440 | 515 | 1,100 | — | 29,000 |
| 1890 | 4,328 | 385 | 625 | 815 | 2,000 | — | 27,000 |
| 1890CC | 53,800 | 290 | 340 | 500 | 1,100 | — | — |
| 1891 | 61,413 | 140 | 180 | 175 | 450 | 5,400 | 28,000 |
| 1891CC | 208,000 | 250 | 350 | 475 | 750 | 29,000 | — |
| 1892 | 753,572 | 135 | 160 | 170 | 225 | — | 30,000 |
| 1892CC | 82,968 | 285 | 400 | 585 | 1,400 | — | — |
| 1892O | 10,000 | 450 | 900 | 1,350 | 3,100 | — | — |
| 1892S | 298,400 | 160 | 190 | 200 | 675 | — | — |
| 1893 | 1,528,197 | 160 | 170 | 180 | 235 | 5,200 | 34,000 |
| 1893CC | 60,000 | 250 | 415 | 700 | 1,400 | — | — |
| 1893O | 110,000 | 215 | 300 | 475 | 975 | — | — |
| 1893S | 224,000 | 160 | 210 | 180 | 260 | 12,500 | — |
| 1894 | 957,955 | 150 | 190 | 185 | 250 | — | 35,000 |
| 1894O | 16,600 | 180 | 350 | 475 | 1,125 | — | — |
| 1894S | 55,900 | 230 | 325 | 600 | 2,800 | — | — |
| 1895 | 1,345,936 | 150 | 160 | 180 | 220 | 5,800 | 29,000 |
| 1895S | 112,000 | 175 | 260 | 400 | 2,800 | 21,000 | — |
| 1896 | 59,063 | 155 | 160 | 225 | 280 | — | 30,000 |
| 1896S | 155,400 | 190 | 215 | 330 | 1,150 | — | — |
| 1897 | 867,883 | 150 | 160 | 175 | 230 | 4,500 | 35,000 |
| 1897S | 354,000 | 155 | 165 | 250 | 940 | — | — |
| 1898 | 633,495 | 150 | 160 | 175 | 250 | 9,000 | 30,000 |
| 1898S | 1,397,400 | 150 | 160 | 170 | 230 | — | — |
| 1899 | 1,710,729 | 150 | 160 | 170 | 230 | 4,200 | 30,000 |
| 1899S | 1,545,000 | 155 | 160 | 170 | 230 | 7,800 | — |
| 1900 | 1,405,730 | 150 | 160 | 170 | 235 | 4,400 | 30,000 |
| 1900S | 329,000 | 160 | 175 | 185 | 250 | 11,500 | — |
| 1901 | 616,040 | 155 | 165 | 180 | 230 | 3,850 | 12,500 |
| 1901S | 3,648,000 | 150 | 160 | 170 | 230 | 2,900 | — |
| 1902 | 172,562 | 150 | 165 | 180 | 225 | 4,400 | 22,000 |
| 1902S | 939,000 | 150 | 155 | 180 | 215 | 3,100 | — |
| 1903 | 227,024 | 150 | 155 | 180 | 220 | 4,800 | 22,000 |
| 1903S | 1,855,000 | 150 | 155 | 180 | 210 | 3,800 | — |
| 1904 | 392,136 | 150 | 165 | 180 | 215 | 3,900 | 25,000 |
| 1904S | 97,000 | 160 | 170 | 265 | 850 | 16,000 | — |
| 1905 | 302,308 | 150 | 160 | 180 | 215 | 4,500 | 25,000 |
| 1905S | 880,700 | 150 | 160 | 185 | 485 | 11,500 | — |
| 1906 | 348,820 | 150 | 155 | 180 | 220 | 3,800 | 22,000 |
| 1906D | 320,000 | 150 | 160 | 180 | 220 | 4,700 | — |
| 1906S | 598,000 | 150 | 160 | 180 | 220 | 5,750 | — |
| 1907 | 626,192 | 150 | 155 | 175 | 215 | 3,900 | 23,000 |
| 1907D | 888,000 | 150 | 155 | 180 | 215 | 3,200 | — |
| 1908 | 421,874 | 150 | 155 | 180 | 215 | 3,200 | — |

## Indian head.

**Designer:** Bela Lyon Pratt. **Diameter:** 21.6 mm. **Weight:** 8.3590 g. **Composition:** 0.9000 Gold, .2420 oz. AGW.

| Date | Mintage | VF-20 | XF-40 | AU-50 | MS-60 | MS-63 | MS-65 | Prf-65 |
|------|---------|-------|-------|-------|-------|-------|-------|--------|
| 1908 | 578,012 | 180 | 215 | 225 | 325 | 1,000 | 11,000 | 16,000 |
| 1908D | 148,000 | 180 | 215 | 225 | 325 | 950 | 18,000 | — |
| 1908S | 82,000 | 195 | 415 | 450 | 1,150 | 2,500 | 16,000 | — |
| 1909 | 627,138 | 180 | 215 | 225 | 325 | 1,200 | 14,000 | 29,000 |
| 1909D | 3,423,560 | 175 | 200 | 220 | 310 | 1,150 | 10,000 | — |
| 1909O | 34,200 | 600 | 1,100 | 1,450 | 5,400 | 40,000 | 160,000 | — |
| 1909S | 297,200 | 185 | 240 | 250 | 1,300 | 6,600 | 39,000 | — |
| 1910 | 604,250 | 175 | 200 | 240 | 300 | 1,350 | 14,000 | 32,000 |
| 1910D | 193,600 | 175 | 200 | 240 | 350 | 1,750 | 34,500 | — |
| 1910S | 770,200 | 175 | 220 | 260 | 900 | 5,500 | 36,000 | — |
| 1911 | 915,139 | 175 | 200 | 240 | 300 | 1,200 | 13,000 | 26,000 |
| 1911D | 72,500 | 350 | 440 | 500 | 2,900 | 16,500 | 140,000 | — |
| 1911S | 1,416,000 | 180 | 215 | 250 | 500 | 2,700 | 37,000 | — |
| 1912 | 790,144 | 180 | 210 | 240 | 300 | 1,200 | 14,500 | 26,000 |
| 1912S | 392,000 | 195 | 230 | 270 | 1,450 | 7,500 | 70,000 | — |
| 1913 | 916,099 | 180 | 210 | 230 | 290 | 1,150 | 11,000 | 26,000 |
| 1913S | 408,000 | 200 | 220 | 270 | 1,250 | 9,800 | 100,000 | — |
| 1914 | 247,125 | 180 | 225 | 240 | 335 | 1,400 | 11,500 | 26,000 |
| 1914D | 247,000 | 185 | 225 | 240 | 315 | 2,300 | 29,000 | — |
| 1914S | 263,000 | 200 | 235 | 255 | 1,100 | 8,000 | 72,000 | — |
| 1915 | 588,075 | 190 | 225 | 240 | 300 | 1,200 | 15,000 | 33,000 |
| 1915S | 164,000 | 260 | 300 | 350 | 1,650 | 8,000 | 80,000 | — |
| 1916S | 240,000 | 190 | 250 | 280 | 525 | 2,300 | 18,500 | — |
| 1929 | 662,000 | 2,400 | 4,600 | 4,800 | 5,400 | 7,500 | 23,500 | — |

# $10 (EAGLE)

## Liberty cap. Small eagle.

**Designer:** Robert Scot. **Diameter:** 33 mm. **Weight:** 17.5000 g. **Composition:** 0.9160 Gold, 0.5159 oz. AGW.

| Date | Mintage | F-12 | VF-20 | XF-40 | MS-60 |
|------|---------|------|-------|-------|-------|
| 1795 13 leaves | 5,583 | 6,000 | 8,500 | 16,000 | 47,000 |
| 1795 9 leaves | Inc. above | 17,000 | 30,000 | 47,000 | — |
| 1796 | 4,146 | 6,700 | 9,500 | 16,500 | 56,000 |
| 1797 small eagle | 3,615 | 8,000 | 12,500 | 22,500 | — |

## Liberty cap. Heraldic eagle.

**Designer:** Robert Scot. **Diameter:** 33 mm. **Weight:** 17.5000 g. **Composition:** 0.9160 Gold, 0.5159 oz. AGW. **Notes:** The 1798/97 varieties are distinguished by the positioning of the stars on the obverse.

| Date | Mintage | F-12 | VF-20 | XF-40 | MS-60 |
|------|---------|------|-------|-------|-------|
| 1797 large eagle | 10,940 | 2,500 | 3,500 | 5,500 | 21,000 |
| 1798/97, 9 stars left, 4 right | 900 | 5,500 | 9,500 | 19,500 | 70,000 |
| 1798/97, 7 stars left, 6 right | 842 | 12,000 | 19,500 | 47,000 | — |
| 1799 | 37,449 | 2,300 | 3,300 | 5,400 | 10,000 |
| 1800 | 5,999 | 2,400 | 3,450 | 5,500 | 16,000 |
| 1801 | 44,344 | 2,300 | 3,250 | 5,250 | 10,000 |
| 1803 | 15,017 | 2,300 | 3,500 | 5,600 | 12,500 |
| 1804 | 3,757 | 3,400 | 4,000 | 6,200 | 23,500 |

# Coronet head, old style. No motto above eagle.

**Designer:** Christian Gobrecht. **Diameter:** 27 mm. **Weight:** 16.7180 g. **Composition:** 0.9000 Gold, 0.4839 oz. AGW.

| Date | Mintage | F-12 | VF-20 | XF-40 | MS-60 | Prf-65 |
|------|---------|------|-------|-------|-------|--------|
| 1838 | 7,200 | 750 | 1,000 | 2,825 | 27,000 | — |
| 1839 large letters | 38,248 | 650 | 950 | 1,750 | 23,000 | — |

# Coronet head, new style. No motto above eagle.

**Designer:** Christian Gobrecht. **Diameter:** 27 mm. **Weight:** 16.7180 g. **Composition:** 0.9000 Gold, 0.4839 oz. AGW. **Notes:** The 1842 varieties are distinguished by the size of the numerals in the date.

| Date | Mintage | F-12 | VF-20 | XF-40 | MS-60 | Prf-65 |
|------|---------|------|-------|-------|-------|--------|
| 1839 small letters | Inc. above | 800 | 1,500 | 3,500 | 25,000 | — |
| 1840 | 47,338 | 300 | 360 | 600 | 9,250 | — |
| 1841 | 63,131 | 300 | 360 | 600 | 9,500 | — |
| 1841O | 2,500 | 750 | 2,100 | 4,500 | 29,500 | — |
| 1842 small date | 81,507 | 300 | 350 | 500 | 25,000 | — |
| 1842 large date | Inc. above | 300 | 325 | 450 | 10,000 | — |
| 1842O | 27,400 | 250 | 325 | 450 | 15,500 | — |
| 1843 | 75,462 | 250 | 325 | 450 | 15,000 | — |
| 1843O | 175,162 | 250 | 325 | 400 | 10,000 | — |
| 1844 | 6,361 | 700 | 1,200 | 2,700 | 16,500 | — |
| 1844O | 118,700 | 250 | 325 | 425 | 13,500 | — |
| 1845 | 26,153 | 260 | 600 | 700 | 15,500 | — |
| 1845O | 47,500 | 250 | 380 | 650 | 13,000 | — |
| 1846 | 20,095 | 370 | 550 | 850 | 20,000 | — |
| 1846O | 81,780 | 250 | 425 | 800 | 14,750 | — |
| 1847 | 862,258 | 240 | 310 | 350 | 3,000 | — |
| 1847O | 571,500 | 250 | 325 | 375 | 5,200 | — |
| 1848 | 145,484 | 260 | 340 | 375 | 4,200 | — |
| 1848O | 38,850 | 325 | 525 | 1,050 | 14,000 | — |
| 1849 | 653,618 | 240 | 310 | 350 | 3,400 | — |
| 1849O | 23,900 | 250 | 350 | 2,000 | 20,500 | — |
| 1850 | 291,451 | 240 | 300 | 340 | 3,600 | — |
| 1850O | 57,500 | 285 | 380 | 650 | 650 | — |
| 1851 | 176,328 | 240 | 315 | 400 | 5,700 | — |
| 1851O | 263,000 | 250 | 330 | 370 | 5,600 | — |
| 1852 | 263,106 | 240 | 300 | 350 | 4,200 | — |
| 1852O | 18,000 | 350 | 515 | 1,000 | 22,000 | — |
| 1853 | 201,253 | 240 | 300 | 385 | 3,500 | — |
| 1853O | 51,000 | 300 | 325 | 400 | 12,500 | — |
| 1854 | 54,250 | 300 | 324 | 425 | 6,000 | — |
| 1854O small date | 52,500 | 270 | 350 | 650 | 10,500 | — |
| 1854O large date | Inc. above | 300 | 400 | 900 | — | — |
| 1854S | 123,826 | 310 | 365 | 500 | 10,000 | — |
| 1855 | 121,701 | 250 | 325 | 350 | 3,400 | — |
| 1855O | 18,000 | 400 | 575 | 1,150 | 20,000 | — |
| 1855S | 9,000 | 800 | 1,300 | 2,100 | 29,500 | — |
| 1856 | 60,490 | 250 | 315 | 350 | 3,400 | — |
| 1856O | 14,500 | 325 | 650 | 1,450 | 14,750 | — |
| 1856S | 68,000 | 250 | 320 | 500 | 8,750 | — |
| 1857 | 16,606 | 275 | 365 | 850 | 12,000 | — |
| 1857O | 5,500 | 575 | 875 | 1,750 | 18,000 | — |
| 1857S | 26,000 | 300 | 375 | 800 | 10,000 | — |
| 1858 | 2,521 | 2,500 | 4,600 | 6,500 | 32,000 | — |
| 1858O | 20,000 | 400 | 475 | 750 | 9,000 | — |

## 1853 $10 Gold
### Grade XF-40

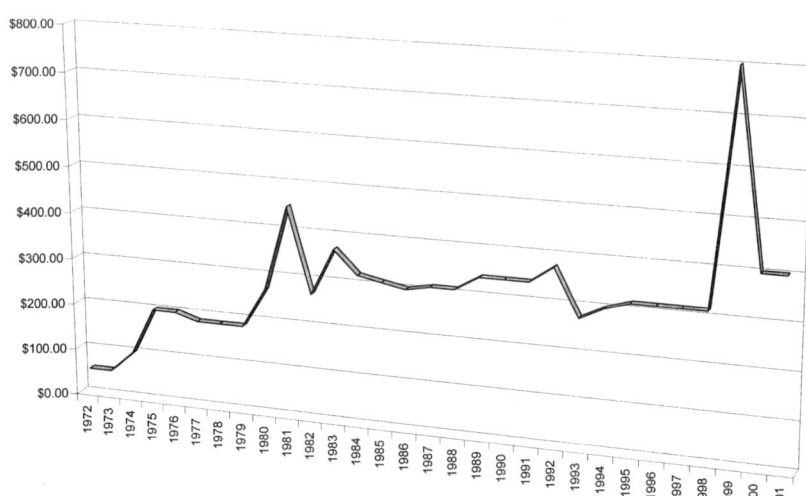

☐ Retail Price

| Date | Mintage | F-12 | VF-20 | XF-40 | MS-60 | Prf-65 |
|------|---------|------|-------|-------|-------|--------|
| 1858S | 11,800 | 800 | 1,400 | 3,100 | 30,000 | — |
| 1859 | 16,093 | 300 | 350 | 750 | 10,500 | — |
| 1859O | 2,300 | 1,900 | 3,700 | 6,500 | 47,500 | — |
| 1859S | 7,000 | 900 | 1,950 | 4,500 | 40,000 | — |
| 1860 | 15,105 | 300 | 385 | 775 | 8,000 | — |
| 1860O | 11,100 | 410 | 550 | 1,100 | 13,500 | — |
| 1860S | 5,000 | 1,000 | 2,400 | 5,800 | 40,500 | — |
| 1861 | 113,233 | 250 | 325 | 350 | 2,900 | — |
| 1861S | 15,500 | 725 | 1,400 | 2,800 | 32,500 | — |
| 1862 | 10,995 | 400 | 475 | 1,000 | 13,500 | — |
| 1862S | 12,500 | 800 | 1,700 | 3,200 | 37,000 | — |
| 1863 | 1,248 | 2,400 | 3,650 | 8,500 | 49,500 | — |
| 1863S | 10,000 | 600 | 1,350 | 3,200 | 24,000 | — |
| 1864 | 3,580 | 975 | 1,900 | 3,900 | 16,500 | — |
| 1864S | 2,500 | 2,200 | 4,800 | 12,500 | 50,000 | — |
| 1865 | 4,005 | 1,200 | 1,850 | 3,400 | 31,500 | — |
| 1865S | 16,700 | 1,600 | 4,000 | 9,400 | 45,000 | — |
| 1865S /inverted 186 | — | 1,300 | 3,500 | 6,100 | 47,000 | — |
| 1866S | 8,500 | 900 | 2,300 | 3,200 | 44,000 | — |

## Coronet head, new style. "In God We Trust" above eagle.

**Designer:** Christian Gobrecht. **Diameter:** 27 mm. **Weight:** 16.7180 g. **Composition:** 0.9000 Gold, 0.4839 oz. AGW. **Notes:** The 1873 "closed-3" and "open-3" varieties are distinguished by the amount of space between the upper left and lower left serifs of the 3 in the date.

| Date | Mintage | VF-20 | XF-40 | AU-50 | MS-60 | MS-65 | Prf-65 |
|------|---------|-------|-------|-------|-------|-------|--------|
| 1866 | 3,780 | 550 | 1,650 | 3,500 | 15,500 | — | 75,000 |
| 1866S | 11,500 | 1,550 | 3,400 | 6,000 | 23,000 | — | — |
| 1867 | 3,140 | 1,500 | 2,600 | 4,800 | 26,000 | — | 75,000 |
| 1867S | 9,000 | 2,450 | 5,600 | 8,000 | 40,000 | — | — |
| 1868 | 10,655 | 525 | 750 | 1,600 | 13,750 | — | 60,000 |
| 1868S | 13,500 | 1,250 | 2,100 | 3,500 | 24,000 | — | — |
| 1869 | 1,855 | 1,400 | 2,800 | 4,400 | 32,500 | — | — |

| Date | Mintage | VF-20 | XF-40 | AU-50 | MS-60 | MS-65 | Prf-65 |
|------|--------|------|------|------|------|------|------|
| 1869S | 6,430 | 1,350 | 2,500 | 5,250 | 24,000 | — | — |
| 1870 | 4,025 | 800 | 1,175 | 2,150 | 17,000 | — | 60,000 |
| 1870CC | 5,908 | 9,000 | 22,000 | 42,000 | 90,000 | — | — |
| 1870S | 8,000 | 950 | 2,500 | 5,750 | 32,000 | — | — |
| 1871 | 1,820 | 1,450 | 2,650 | 4,000 | 18,000 | — | 75,000 |
| 1871CC | 8,085 | 2,150 | 4,950 | 14,500 | 53,500 | — | — |
| 1871S | 16,500 | 1,075 | 1,500 | 5,700 | 26,000 | — | — |
| 1872 | 1,650 | 2,400 | 3,600 | 9,500 | 16,500 | — | 60,000 |
| 1872CC | 4,600 | 2,100 | 7,750 | 20,000 | 55,000 | — | — |
| 1872S | 17,300 | 550 | 850 | 1,800 | 22,000 | — | — |
| 1873 closed 3 | 825 | 4,500 | 9,500 | 27,500 | 58,000 | — | 60,000 |
| 1873CC | 4,543 | 3,300 | 8,750 | 26,000 | 57,500 | — | — |
| 1873S | 12,000 | 950 | 1,700 | 4,750 | 26,000 | — | — |
| 1874 | 53,160 | 220 | 240 | 275 | 2,100 | — | 60,000 |
| 1874CC | 16,767 | 850 | 2,500 | 7,500 | 40,000 | — | — |
| 1874S | 10,000 | 1,150 | 3,250 | 5,800 | 39,500 | — | — |
| 1875 | 120 | 38,000 | 47,500 | 68,000 | 72,500 | — | 185,000 |

Note: 1875, Akers, Aug. 1990, Proof, $115,000.

| Date | Mintage | VF-20 | XF-40 | AU-50 | MS-60 | MS-65 | Prf-65 |
|------|--------|------|------|------|------|------|------|
| 1875CC | 7,715 | 3,500 | 8,250 | 25,000 | 65,000 | — | — |
| 1876 | 732 | 3,000 | 6,750 | 12,500 | 55,000 | — | 60,000 |
| 1876CC | 4,696 | 3,200 | 6,500 | 20,500 | 50,000 | — | — |
| 1876S | 5,000 | 1,250 | 2,000 | 5,500 | 38,000 | — | — |
| 1877 | 817 | 2,300 | 5,200 | 8,200 | 40,000 | — | — |
| 1877CC | 3,332 | 2,300 | 4,750 | 14,000 | 47,000 | — | — |
| 1877S | 17,000 | 500 | 700 | 2,200 | 22,500 | — | — |
| 1878 | 73,800 | 190 | 220 | 250 | 800 | — | 60,000 |
| 1878CC | 3,244 | 2,300 | 4,750 | 140,000 | 47,000 | — | — |
| 1878S | 26,100 | 500 | 525 | 1,500 | 18,000 | — | — |
| 1879 | 384,770 | 190 | 220 | 250 | 500 | — | 50,000 |
| 1879CC | 1,762 | 5,200 | 9,800 | 21,750 | 60,000 | — | — |
| 1879O | 1,500 | 1,850 | 3,750 | 10,000 | 28,750 | — | — |
| 1879S | 224,000 | 190 | 220 | 250 | 1,100 | — | — |
| 1880 | 1,644,876 | 185 | 210 | 225 | 290 | — | 45,000 |
| 1880CC | 11,190 | 490 | 700 | 1,450 | 12,500 | — | — |
| 1880O | 9,200 | 425 | 700 | 1,450 | 12,750 | — | — |
| 1880S | 506,250 | 185 | 210 | 225 | 290 | — | — |
| 1881 | 3,877,260 | 185 | 210 | 220 | 290 | — | 45,000 |
| 1881CC | 24,015 | 395 | 550 | 950 | 6,500 | — | — |
| 1881O | 8,350 | 360 | 650 | 1,100 | 6,250 | — | — |
| 1881S | 970,000 | 185 | 210 | 220 | 250 | — | — |
| 1882 | 2,324,480 | 185 | 210 | 220 | 250 | — | 41,500 |
| 1882CC | 6,764 | 900 | 1,400 | 3,000 | 12,500 | — | — |
| 1882O | 10,820 | 350 | 575 | 1,300 | 4,950 | — | — |
| 1882S | 132,000 | 185 | 210 | 220 | 250 | — | — |
| 1883 | 208,740 | 185 | 210 | 220 | 250 | — | 41,500 |
| 1883CC | 12,000 | 440 | 700 | 2,350 | 12,500 | — | — |
| 1883O | 800 | 2,400 | 6,750 | 9,500 | 33,500 | — | — |
| 1883S | 38,000 | 190 | 215 | 295 | 975 | — | — |
| 1884 | 76,905 | 185 | 215 | 225 | 750 | — | 46,000 |
| 1884CC | 9,925 | 625 | 950 | 2,250 | 10,750 | — | — |
| 1884S | 124,250 | 185 | 210 | 220 | 475 | — | — |
| 1885 | 253,527 | 185 | 210 | 220 | 375 | — | 43,000 |
| 1885S | 228,000 | 190 | 215 | 230 | 375 | 6,500 | — |
| 1886 | 236,160 | 185 | 210 | 220 | 375 | — | 42,500 |
| 1886S | 826,000 | 185 | 210 | 220 | 350 | — | — |
| 1887 | 53,680 | 190 | 220 | 230 | 650 | — | 37,000 |
| 1887S | 817,000 | 185 | 210 | 220 | 315 | — | — |
| 1888 | 132,996 | 185 | 210 | 275 | 585 | — | 38,500 |
| 1888O | 21,335 | 195 | 210 | 275 | 515 | — | — |
| 1888S | 648,700 | 185 | 210 | 220 | 300 | — | — |
| 1889 | 4,485 | 675 | 750 | 1,100 | 2,350 | — | 43,000 |
| 1889S | 425,400 | 185 | 200 | 225 | 350 | 4,200 | — |
| 1890 | 58,043 | 190 | 200 | 265 | 650 | 7,750 | 37,500 |
| 1890CC | 17,500 | 400 | 440 | 590 | 1,850 | — | — |
| 1891 | 91,868 | 185 | 210 | 240 | 325 | — | 32,500 |
| 1891CC | 103,732 | 370 | 395 | 530 | 715 | — | — |
| 1892 | 797,552 | 185 | 200 | 225 | 285 | 12,000 | 37,500 |
| 1892CC | 40,000 | 385 | 450 | 600 | 3,100 | — | — |
| 1892O | 28,688 | 200 | 225 | 270 | 375 | — | — |
| 1892S | 115,500 | 170 | 200 | 235 | 360 | — | — |
| 1893 | 1,840,895 | 170 | 200 | 215 | 265 | — | 34,500 |
| 1893CC | 14,000 | 425 | 625 | 1,450 | 6,200 | — | — |
| 1893O | 17,000 | 290 | 315 | 350 | 625 | — | — |
| 1893S | 141,350 | 175 | 200 | 250 | 350 | — | — |
| 1894 | 2,470,778 | 175 | 200 | 250 | 265 | 11,500 | 35,000 |
| 1894O | 107,500 | 225 | 260 | 285 | 900 | — | — |
| 1894S | 25,000 | 225 | 365 | 875 | 3,500 | — | — |
| 1895 | 567,826 | 175 | 200 | 250 | 265 | 8,800 | 33,000 |
| 1895O | 98,000 | 200 | 230 | 300 | 480 | — | — |

| Date | Mintage | VF-20 | XF-40 | AU-50 | MS-60 | MS-65 | Prf-65 |
|------|---------|-------|-------|-------|-------|-------|--------|
| 1895S | 49,000 | 200 | 230 | 550 | 2,250 | — | — |
| 1896 | 76,348 | 175 | 200 | 260 | 295 | — | 31,500 |
| 1896S | 123,750 | 180 | 235 | 450 | 2,500 | — | — |
| 1897 | 1,000,159 | 175 | 200 | 225 | 285 | 6,500 | 35,000 |
| 1897O | 42,500 | 200 | 250 | 290 | 000 | — | |
| 1897S | 234,750 | 200 | 225 | 275 | 870 | — | — |
| 1898 | 812,197 | 200 | 215 | 235 | 270 | 3,800 | 35,000 |
| 1898S | 473,600 | 200 | 210 | 235 | 265 | — | — |
| 1899 | 1,262,305 | 200 | 215 | 230 | 250 | 2,800 | 31,000 |
| 1899O | 37,047 | 230 | 275 | 335 | 550 | — | — |
| 1899S | 841,000 | 200 | 215 | 265 | 320 | — | — |
| 1900 | 293,960 | 200 | 215 | 230 | 250 | 7,750 | 30,500 |
| 1900S | 81,000 | 210 | 275 | 350 | 775 | — | — |
| 1901 | 1,718,825 | 200 | 210 | 220 | 250 | 2,800 | 30,500 |
| 1901O | 72,041 | 225 | 250 | 300 | 375 | — | — |
| 1901S | 2,812,750 | 200 | 210 | 220 | 250 | 2,500 | — |
| 1902 | 82,513 | 230 | 260 | 295 | 340 | — | 30,500 |
| 1902S | 469,500 | 200 | 210 | 220 | 275 | 2,700 | — |
| 1903 | 125,926 | 210 | 250 | 290 | 315 | — | 30,000 |
| 1903O | 112,771 | 230 | 250 | 290 | 350 | — | — |
| 1903S | 538,000 | 200 | 215 | 230 | 290 | 2,650 | — |
| 1904 | 162,038 | 200 | 215 | 230 | 280 | — | 31,500 |
| 1904O | 108,950 | 230 | 250 | 285 | 340 | — | — |
| 1905 | 201,078 | 200 | 215 | 225 | 265 | 4,800 | 30,000 |
| 1905S | 369,250 | 210 | 230 | 260 | 1,100 | — | — |
| 1906 | 165,497 | 210 | 220 | 230 | 275 | 7,750 | 30,000 |
| 1906D | 981,000 | 230 | 245 | 275 | 325 | 3,850 | — |
| 1906O | 86,895 | 210 | 250 | 310 | 375 | — | — |
| 1906S | 457,000 | 220 | 250 | 300 | 475 | 12,500 | — |
| 1907 | 1,203,973 | 190 | 200 | 220 | 250 | — | 30,000 |
| 1907D | 1,030,000 | 190 | 200 | 240 | 275 | — | — |
| 1907S | 210,500 | 240 | 260 | 300 | 575 | — | — |

## Indian head. No motto next to eagle.

**Designer:** Augustus Saint-Gaudens. **Diameter:** 27 mm. **Weight:** 16.7180 g. **Composition:** 0.9000 Gold, 0.4839 oz. AGW. **Notes:** 1907 varieties are distinguished by whether the edge is rolled or wired, and whether the legend "E Pluribus Unum" has periods between each word.

| Date | Mintage | VF-20 | XF-40 | AU-50 | MS-60 | MS-63 | MS-65 | Prf-65 |
|------|---------|-------|-------|-------|-------|-------|-------|--------|
| 1907 wire edge, periods before and after legend | 500 | — | 4,500 | 6,000 | 9,500 | 15,500 | 42,000 | — |
| 1907 same, without stars on edge, unique | — | — | — | — | — | — | — | — |
| 1907 rolled edge, periods | 42 | 13,000 | 19,000 | — | 22,000 | 32,500 | 90,000 | — |
| 1907 without periods | 239,406 | 350 | 375 | 400 | 475 | 1,700 | 5,500 | — |
| 1908 without motto | 33,500 | 350 | 375 | 400 | 475 | 1,700 | 5,500 | — |
| 1908D without motto | 210,000 | 320 | 375 | 400 | 675 | 4,500 | 34,000 | — |

## Indian head. "In God We Trust" left of eagle.

**Designer:** Augustus Saint-Gaudens. **Diameter:** 27 mm. **Weight:** 16.7180 g. **Composition:** 0.9000 Gold, 0.4839 oz. AGW.

| Date | Mintage | VF-20 | XF-40 | AU-50 | MS-60 | MS-63 | MS-65 | Prf-65 |
|------|---------|-------|-------|-------|-------|-------|-------|--------|
| 1908 | 341,486 | 315 | 350 | 365 | 440 | 1,200 | 5,000 | 29,500 |
| 1908D | 836,500 | 320 | 360 | 370 | 625 | 2,950 | 17,500 | — |
| 1908S | 59,850 | 315 | 360 | 400 | 1,400 | 4,900 | 17,000 | — |
| 1909 | 184,863 | 310 | 340 | 360 | 470 | 1,500 | 8,000 | 31,500 |
| 1909D | 121,540 | 310 | 340 | 360 | 515 | 2,150 | 36,000 | — |

## 1933 $10 Gold
### Grade MS-60

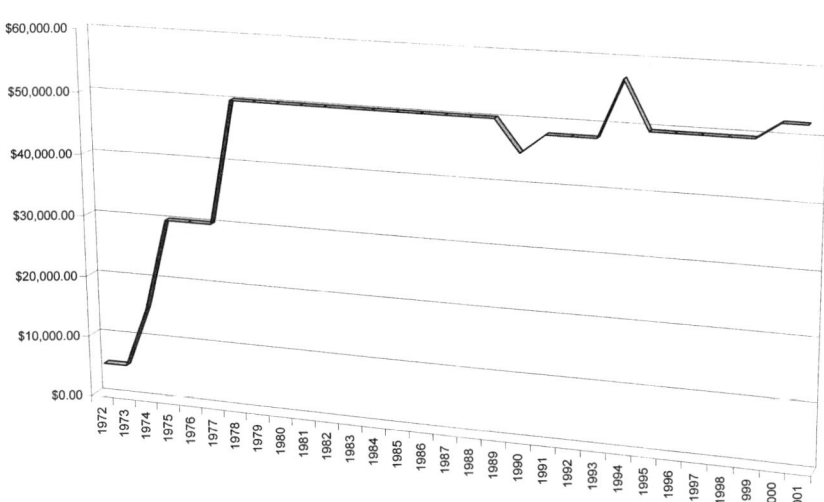

□ Retail Price

| Date | Mintage | VF-20 | XF-40 | AU-50 | MS-60 | MS-63 | MS-65 | Prf-65 |
|------|---------|-------|-------|-------|-------|-------|-------|--------|
| 1909S | 292,350 | 315 | 345 | 370 | 570 | 2,450 | 10,000 | — |
| 1910 | 318,704 | 300 | 325 | 350 | 450 | 850 | 4,500 | 37,000 |
| 1910D | 2,356,640 | 300 | 325 | 350 | 465 | 875 | 5,150 | — |
| 1910S | 811,000 | 300 | 325 | 350 | 685 | 3,100 | 49,000 | — |
| 1911 | 505,595 | 300 | 325 | 350 | 480 | 850 | 5,150 | 32,000 |
| 1911D | 30,100 | 350 | 750 | 800 | 3,500 | 11,000 | 85,000 | — |
| 1911S | 51,000 | 350 | 600 | 675 | 950 | 3,900 | 8,600 | — |
| 1912 | 405,083 | 300 | 325 | 350 | 480 | 750 | 5,900 | 32,000 |
| 1912S | 300,000 | 320 | 340 | 360 | 650 | 2,950 | 43,000 | — |
| 1913 | 442,071 | 300 | 330 | 350 | 440 | 900 | 4,500 | 32,000 |
| 1913S | 66,000 | 350 | 615 | 775 | 3,150 | 9,500 | 85,000 | — |
| 1914 | 151,050 | 300 | 335 | 385 | 525 | 1,350 | 5,850 | 32,000 |
| 1914D | 343,500 | 300 | 335 | 375 | 515 | 1,250 | 100,000 | — |
| 1914S | 208,000 | 290 | 330 | 360 | 650 | 3,500 | 32,500 | — |
| 1915 | 351,075 | 300 | 340 | 370 | 530 | 1,150 | 5,100 | 40,000 |
| 1915S | 59,000 | 350 | 675 | 735 | 2,600 | 7,800 | 52,500 | — |
| 1916S | 138,500 | 310 | 330 | 350 | 660 | 2,200 | 14,500 | — |
| 1920S | 126,500 | 4,700 | 6,000 | 7,500 | 14,500 | 32,000 | 150,000 | — |
| 1926 | 1,014,000 | 275 | 295 | 315 | 415 | 650 | 3,250 | — |
| 1930S | 96,000 | 3,300 | 6,000 | 7,700 | 8,200 | 110,000 | 24,000 | — |
| 1932 | 4,463,000 | 275 | 295 | 315 | 415 | 640 | 2,950 | — |
| 1933 | 312,500 | 22,500 | 29,000 | 35,000 | 49,000 | 85,000 | 300,000 | — |

# $20 (DOUBLE EAGLE)

## Coronet head. "Twenty D." below eagle. No motto above eagle.

**Designer:** James B. Longacre. **Diameter:** 34 mm. **Weight:** 33.4360 g. **Composition:** 0.9000 Gold, 0.9677 oz. AGW.

| Date | Mintage | VF-20 | XF-40 | AU-50 | MS-60 | MS-65 | Prf-65 |
|------|--------:|------:|------:|------:|------:|------:|-------:|
| 1849 unique, in Smithsonian collection | 1 | — | — | — | — | — | — |
| 1850 | 1,170,261 | 450 | 675 | 2,100 | 5,250 | 225,000 | — |
| 1850O | 141,000 | 675 | 1,200 | 5,200 | 28,000 | — | — |
| 1851 | 2,087,155 | 550 | 625 | 825 | 2,700 | — | — |
| 1851O | 315,000 | 625 | 725 | 1,500 | 14,000 | — | — |
| 1852 | 2,053,026 | 600 | 625 | 880 | 3,800 | — | — |
| 1852O | 190,000 | 625 | 700 | 1,800 | 13,000 | — | — |
| 1853 | 1,261,326 | 580 | 610 | 1,000 | 4,400 | — | — |
| 1853O | 71,000 | 615 | 975 | 2,800 | 32,000 | — | — |
| 1854 | 757,899 | 565 | 615 | 800 | 6,500 | — | — |
| 1854O | 3,250 | 24,000 | 50,000 | 82,500 | 170,000 | — | — |
| 1854S | 141,468 | 600 | 700 | 1,200 | 3,100 | 35,000 | — |
| 1855 | 364,666 | 625 | 675 | 1,100 | 7,500 | — | — |
| 1855O | 8,000 | 2,200 | 5,500 | 16,000 | 80,000 | — | — |
| 1855S | 879,675 | 575 | 625 | 1,050 | 6,750 | — | — |
| 1856 | 329,878 | 575 | 625 | 2,000 | 10,000 | — | — |
| 1856O | 2,250 | 36,000 | 65,000 | 97,500 | 185,000 | — | — |
| 1856S | 1,189,750 | 575 | 625 | 1,000 | 5,650 | — | — |
| 1857 | 439,375 | 575 | 625 | 850 | 3,600 | — | — |
| 1857O | 30,000 | 950 | 1,600 | 4,000 | 21,500 | — | — |
| 1857S | 970,500 | 575 | 625 | 850 | 3,700 | — | — |
| 1858 | 211,714 | 650 | 925 | 1,450 | 10,000 | — | — |
| 1858O | 35,250 | 1,200 | 1,850 | 4,500 | 23,000 | — | — |
| 1858S | 846,710 | 565 | 625 | 1,000 | 12,000 | — | — |
| 1859 | 43,597 | 875 | 2,000 | 4,400 | 35,000 | — | — |
| 1859O | 9,100 | 3,150 | 6,500 | 13,500 | 65,000 | — | — |
| 1859S | 636,445 | 575 | 625 | 1,900 | 4,350 | — | — |
| 1860 | 577,670 | 575 | 625 | 800 | 5,000 | — | — |
| 1860O | 6,600 | 3,200 | 5,500 | 14,500 | 75,000 | — | — |
| 1860S | 544,950 | 575 | 625 | 2,000 | 5,100 | — | — |
| 1861 | 2,976,453 | 575 | 600 | 800 | 4,000 | — | — |
| 1861O | 17,741 | 1,600 | 3,000 | 7,500 | 40,000 | — | — |
| 1861S | 768,000 | 600 | 625 | 1,100 | 12,000 | — | — |

## Coronet head. Paquet design.

**Weight:** 33.4360 g. **Composition:** 0.9000 Gold, 0.9677 oz. AGW. **Notes:** In 1861 the reverse was redesigned by Anthony C. Paquet, but it was withdrawn soon after its release. The letters in the inscriptions on the Paquet-reverse variety are taller than on the regular reverse.

| Date | Mintage | VF-20 | XF-40 | AU-50 | MS-60 | MS-65 | Prf-65 |
|------|--------:|------:|------:|------:|------:|------:|-------:|
| 1861S | Inc. above | 5,950 | 13,500 | 23,000 | 200,000 | — | — |

**Note:** 1861S Paquet reverse, Bowers & Merena, Nov. 1988, MS-67, $660,000.

## Coronet head. Longacre design resumed.

**Weight:** 33.4360 g. **Composition:** 0.9000 Gold, 0.9677 oz. AGW.

| Date | Mintage | VF-20 | XF-40 | AU-50 | MS-60 | MS-65 | Prf-65 |
|------|--------:|------:|------:|------:|------:|------:|-------:|
| 1862 | 92,133 | 825 | 1,400 | 2,500 | 25,000 | — | — |
| 1862S | 854,173 | 575 | 625 | 1,500 | 12,000 | — | — |
| 1863 | 142,790 | 575 | 625 | 1,800 | 13,000 | — | — |
| 1863S | 966,570 | 575 | 615 | 1,350 | 6,800 | — | — |
| 1864 | 204,285 | 690 | 810 | 1,600 | 16,000 | — | — |
| 1864S | 793,660 | 585 | 650 | 1,750 | 7,150 | — | — |
| 1865 | 351,200 | 580 | 630 | 975 | 7,000 | — | — |
| 1865S | 1,042,500 | 545 | 630 | 1,300 | 3,950 | 25,000 | — |
| 1866S | — | 1,500 | 2,700 | 8,850 | 150,000 | — | — |

# Coronet head. "Twenty D." below eagle.
# "In God We Trust" above eagle.

**Designer:** James B. Longacre. **Diameter:** 34 mm. **Weight:** 33.4360 g. **Composition:** 0.9000 Gold, 0.9677 oz. AGW. **Notes:** The 1873 "closed-3" and "open-3" varieties are known and are distinguished by the amount of space between the upper left and lower left serif in the 3 in the date.

| Date | Mintage | VF-20 | XF-40 | AU-50 | MS-60 | MS-65 | Prf-65 |
|------|---------|-------|-------|-------|-------|-------|--------|
| 1866 | 698,775 | 600 | 700 | 1,050 | 9,000 | — | — |
| 1866S | 842,250 | 540 | 650 | 3,100 | 18,000 | — | — |
| 1867 | 251,065 | 540 | 575 | 775 | 2,150 | — | — |
| 1867S | 920,750 | 540 | 575 | 1,750 | 15,500 | — | — |
| 1868 | 98,600 | 750 | 1,100 | 1,700 | 7,850 | — | — |
| 1868S | 837,500 | 540 | 635 | 1,600 | 7,450 | — | — |
| 1869 | 175,155 | 525 | 775 | 1,000 | 5,000 | — | — |
| 1869S | 686,750 | 525 | 560 | 950 | 4,900 | — | — |
| 1870 | 155,185 | 650 | 775 | 3,150 | 7,250 | — | — |
| 1870CC | 3,789 | 27,000 | 69,000 | 125,000 | 200,000 | — | — |
| 1870S | 982,000 | 550 | 600 | 1,000 | 8,000 | — | — |
| 1871 | 80,150 | 675 | 950 | 1,450 | 8,000 | — | — |
| 1871CC | 17,387 | 3,000 | 4,700 | 12,500 | 50,000 | — | — |
| 1871S | 928,000 | 525 | 570 | 825 | 5,200 | — | — |
| 1872 | 251,880 | 525 | 550 | 800 | 2,500 | — | — |
| 1872CC | 26,900 | 1,000 | 1,450 | 4,600 | 21,500 | — | — |
| 1872S | 780,000 | 500 | 525 | 625 | 5,000 | — | — |
| 1873 closed 3 | Est. 208,925 | 540 | 600 | 900 | 2,250 | — | — |
| 1873 open 3 | Est. 1,500,900 | 525 | 560 | 580 | 850 | — | — |
| 1873CC | 22,410 | 775 | 1,650 | 3,900 | 28,000 | — | — |
| 1873S | 1,040,600 | 500 | 525 | 560 | 1,650 | — | — |
| 1874 | 366,800 | 500 | 525 | 570 | 1,100 | — | — |
| 1874CC | 115,085 | 685 | 750 | 1,700 | 12,000 | — | — |
| 1874S | 1,214,000 | 525 | 550 | 565 | 1,500 | — | — |
| 1875 | 295,740 | 525 | 540 | 550 | 900 | — | — |
| 1875CC | 111,151 | 630 | 750 | 1,150 | 2,200 | — | — |
| 1875S | 1,230,000 | 490 | 510 | 535 | 850 | — | — |
| 1876 | 583,905 | 420 | 450 | 500 | 800 | — | — |
| 1876CC | 138,441 | 650 | 725 | 1,100 | 3,400 | — | — |
| 1876S | 1,597,000 | 465 | 485 | 515 | 785 | — | — |

# Coronet head. "Twenty Dollars" below eagle.

**Weight:** 33.4360 g. **Composition:** 0.9000 Gold, 0.9677 oz. AGW.

| Date | Mintage | VF-20 | XF-40 | AU-50 | MS-60 | MS-65 | Prf-65 |
|------|---------|-------|-------|-------|-------|-------|--------|
| 1877 | 397,670 | 415 | 475 | 440 | 585 | — | — |
| 1877CC | 42,565 | 750 | 875 | 1,300 | 14,500 | — | — |
| 1877S | 1,735,000 | 385 | 415 | 440 | 575 | — | — |
| 1878 | 543,645 | 400 | 450 | 480 | 590 | — | — |
| 1878CC | 13,180 | 875 | 1,400 | 3,400 | 20,000 | — | — |
| 1878S | 1,739,000 | 390 | 400 | 425 | 675 | — | — |
| 1879 | 207,630 | 440 | 450 | 485 | 1,100 | — | — |
| 1879CC | 10,708 | 1,100 | 1,650 | 4,500 | 23,000 | — | — |
| 1879O | 2,325 | 3,000 | 4,750 | 10,750 | 28,000 | — | — |

## 1907-S $20 Gold
### Grade VF-20

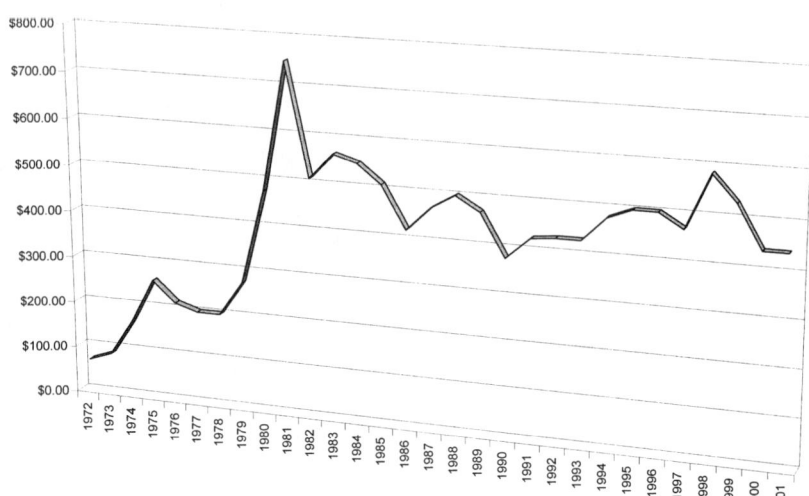

Retail Price

| Date | Mintage | VF-20 | XF-40 | AU-50 | MS-60 | MS-65 | Prf-65 |
|------|---------|-------|-------|-------|-------|-------|--------|
| 1879S | 1,223,800 | 360 | 380 | 400 | 1,450 | — | — |
| 1880 | 51,456 | 360 | 380 | 485 | 4,000 | — | — |
| 1880S | 836,000 | 375 | 385 | 440 | 1,100 | — | — |
| 1881 | 2,260 | 3,700 | 6,300 | 12,500 | 38,000 | — | 105,000 |
| 1881S | 727,000 | 375 | 385 | 440 | 1,150 | — | — |
| 1882 | 630 | 6,800 | 13,750 | 24,000 | 52,500 | — | 90,000 |
| 1882CC | 39,140 | 715 | 750 | 1,150 | 6,000 | — | — |
| 1882S | 1,125,000 | 375 | 385 | 500 | 700 | — | — |
| 1883 proof only | 92 | — | — | — | — | — | — |
| 1883CC | 59,962 | 715 | 735 | 1,100 | 4,000 | — | — |
| 1883S | 1,189,000 | 350 | 400 | 425 | 525 | — | — |
| 1884 proof only | 71 | — | — | — | — | — | 150,000 |
| 1884CC | 81,139 | 650 | 735 | 900 | 2,600 | — | — |
| 1884S | 916,000 | 350 | 400 | 435 | 525 | — | — |
| 1885 | 828 | 6,250 | 7,750 | 10,500 | 29,000 | — | — |
| 1885CC | 9,450 | 1,050 | 1,600 | 3,600 | 10,750 | — | — |
| 1885S | 683,500 | 360 | 415 | 450 | 550 | — | — |
| 1886 | 1,106 | 8,000 | 10,500 | 18,750 | 36,500 | — | 67,000 |
| 1887 | 121 | — | — | — | — | — | 85,000 |
| 1887S | 283,000 | 350 | 385 | 430 | 550 | — | — |
| 1888 | 226,266 | 350 | 385 | 430 | 500 | — | — |
| 1888S | 859,600 | 440 | 450 | 485 | 625 | — | — |
| 1889 | 44,111 | 365 | 390 | 515 | 615 | — | 57,500 |
| 1889CC | 30,945 | 750 | 850 | 1,300 | 3,500 | — | — |
| 1889S | 774,700 | 350 | 400 | 415 | 525 | — | — |
| 1890 | 75,995 | 355 | 410 | 425 | 525 | — | 27,000 |
| 1890CC | 91,209 | 675 | 725 | 1,050 | 2,600 | — | — |
| 1890S | 802,750 | 350 | 380 | 425 | 550 | — | — |
| 1891 | 1,442 | 3,300 | 4,900 | 8,000 | 26,000 | — | 62,500 |
| 1891CC | 5,000 | 1,750 | 2,750 | 5,250 | 13,000 | — | — |
| 1891S | 1,288,125 | 350 | 385 | 425 | 450 | — | — |
| 1892 | 4,523 | 1,250 | 1,525 | 2,750 | 5,500 | — | 55,000 |
| 1892CC | 27,265 | 625 | 825 | 1,250 | 3,100 | — | — |
| 1892S | 930,150 | 345 | 365 | 380 | 425 | — | — |
| 1893 | 344,339 | 345 | 365 | 380 | 440 | — | 60,000 |
| 1893CC | 18,402 | 725 | 770 | 1,150 | 2,450 | — | — |
| 1893S | 996,175 | 345 | 365 | 380 | 440 | — | — |
| 1894 | 1,368,990 | 345 | 365 | 380 | 425 | — | 55,000 |
| 1894S | 1,048,550 | 345 | 365 | 380 | 430 | — | — |
| 1895 | 1,114,656 | 345 | 365 | 380 | 430 | — | 54,000 |
| 1895S | 1,143,500 | 345 | 365 | 380 | 440 | 13,500 | — |
| 1896 | 792,663 | 345 | 365 | 380 | 450 | — | 49,000 |
| 1896S | 1,403,925 | 345 | 365 | 380 | 450 | — | — |
| 1897 | 1,383,261 | 345 | 365 | 380 | 450 | — | 55,000 |
| 1897S | 1,470,250 | 345 | 365 | 380 | 450 | — | — |
| 1898 | 170,470 | 350 | 375 | 390 | 525 | — | 49,000 |

| Date | Mintage | VF-20 | XF-40 | AU-50 | MS-60 | MS-65 | Prf-65 |
|------|---------|-------|-------|-------|-------|-------|--------|
| 1898S | 2,575,175 | 345 | 365 | 380 | 425 | 10,000 | — |
| 1899 | 1,669,384 | 345 | 365 | 380 | 425 | 10,000 | 49,000 |
| 1899S | 2,010,300 | 345 | 365 | 380 | 425 | 10,500 | — |
| 1900 | 1,874,584 | 345 | 365 | 380 | 425 | 5,250 | 49,000 |
| 1900S | 2,459,500 | 345 | 365 | 380 | 425 | 4,900 | — |
| 1901 | 111,526 | 345 | 375 | 400 | 500 | 3,200 | — |
| 1901S | 1,596,000 | 345 | 365 | 380 | 425 | — | — |
| 1902 | 31,254 | 360 | 380 | 415 | 815 | — | — |
| 1902S | 1,753,625 | 345 | 365 | 380 | 425 | — | — |
| 1903 | 287,428 | 340 | 350 | 385 | 450 | 4,250 | 51,500 |
| 1903S | 954,000 | 345 | 365 | 380 | 425 | 10,500 | — |
| 1904 | 6,256,797 | 345 | 365 | 380 | 425 | 2,400 | 50,000 |
| 1904S | 5,134,175 | 345 | 365 | 380 | 425 | 4,700 | — |
| 1905 | 59,011 | 350 | 395 | 475 | 875 | — | — |
| 1905S | 1,813,000 | 345 | 365 | 425 | 550 | — | — |
| 1906 | 69,690 | 345 | 385 | 425 | 515 | 13,500 | 52,500 |
| 1906D | 620,250 | 345 | 365 | 400 | 450 | — | — |
| 1906S | 2,065,750 | 345 | 365 | 400 | 450 | — | — |
| 1907 | 1,451,864 | 340 | 360 | 375 | 415 | 5,800 | — |
| 1907D | 842,250 | 345 | 365 | 395 | 440 | 4,750 | — |
| 1907S | 2,165,800 | 340 | 360 | 375 | 440 | — | — |

## Liberty. No motto below eagle.

**Designer:** Augustus Saint-Gaudens. **Diameter:** 34 mm. **Edge:** Plain. **Weight:** 33.4360 g. **Composition:** 0.9000 Gold, 0.9677 oz. AGW. **Notes:** The "Roman numerals" varieties for 1907 use Roman numerals for the date instead of Arabic numerals. The lettered-edge varieties have "E Pluribus Unum" on the edge, with stars between the words.

| Date | Mintage | VF-20 | XF-40 | AU-50 | MS-60 | MS-63 | MS-65 | Prf-65 |
|------|---------|-------|-------|-------|-------|-------|-------|--------|
| 1907 extremely high relief, unique | — | — | — | — | — | — | — | — |
| 1907 extremely high relief, lettered edge | — | — | — | — | — | — | — | — |

**Note:** 1907 extremely high relief, lettered edge, Prf-68, private sale, 1990, $1,500,000.

## Liberty. Roman numerals in date. No motto below eagle.

**Designer:** Augustus Saint-Gaudens. **Diameter:** 34 mm. **Edge:** Plain. **Weight:** 33.4360 g. **Composition:** 0.9000 Gold, 0.9677 oz. AGW.

| Date | Mintage | VF-20 | XF-40 | AU-50 | MS-60 | MS-63 | MS-65 | Prf-65 |
|------|---------|-------|-------|-------|-------|-------|-------|--------|
| 1907 high relief, unique, AU-55, $150,000 | — | — | — | — | — | — | — | — |
| 1907 high relief, wire rim | 11,250 | 3,000 | 4,750 | 5,300 | 8,250 | 12,750 | 28,500 | — |
| 1907 high relief, flat rim | Inc. above | 3,000 | 4,800 | 5,400 | 8,350 | 12,750 | 29,500 | — |

## Liberty. Arabic numerals in date. No motto below eagle.

**Designer:** Augustus Saint-Gaudens. **Diameter:** 34 mm. **Edge:** Lettered; large letters. **Weight:** 33.4360 g. **Composition:** 0.9000 Gold, 0.9677 oz. AGW.

| Date | Mintage | VF-20 | XF-40 | AU-50 | MS-60 | MS-63 | MS-65 | Prf-65 |
|------|---------|-------|-------|-------|-------|-------|-------|--------|
| 1907 large letters on edge, unique | — | — | — | — | — | — | — | — |
| 1907 small letters on edge | 361,667 | 430 | 450 | 480 | 500 | 675 | 2,600 | — |
| 1908 | 4,271,551 | 415 | 435 | 465 | 475 | 650 | 900 | — |
| 1908D | 663,750 | 425 | 440 | 460 | 515 | 750 | 10,500 | — |

## 1908-D $20 Gold
### Grade MS-60

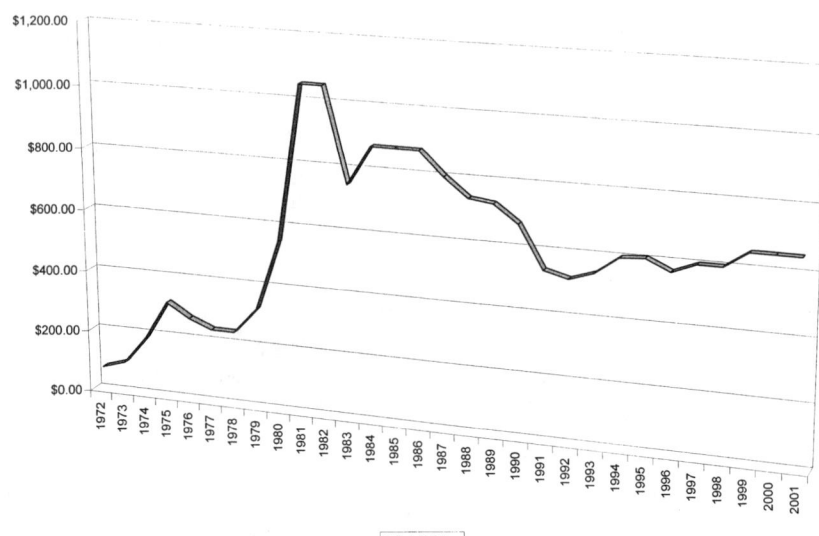

☐ Retail Price

## Liberty. "In God We Trust" below eagle.

**Designer:** Augustus Saint-Gaudens. **Diameter:** 34 mm. **Weight:** 33.4360 g. **Composition:** 0.9000 Gold, 0.9677 oz. AGW.

| Date | Mintage | VF-20 | XF-40 | AU-50 | MS-60 | MS-63 | MS-65 | Prf-65 |
|---|---|---|---|---|---|---|---|---|
| 1908 | 156,359 | 375 | 400 | 415 | 430 | 485 | 950 | 38,000 |
| 1908D | 349,500 | 375 | 400 | 415 | 500 | 750 | 4,750 | — |
| 1908S | 22,000 | 650 | 1,100 | 1,400 | 3,900 | 10,000 | 35,000 | — |
| 1909/8 | 161,282 | 525 | 580 | 625 | 1,200 | 4,900 | 24,000 | — |
| 1909 | Inc. above | 450 | 560 | 600 | 700 | 2,700 | 42,000 | 49,000 |
| 1909D | 52,500 | 500 | 690 | 735 | 1,250 | 3,250 | 33,500 | — |
| 1909S | 2,774,925 | 360 | 385 | 400 | 460 | 550 | 4,800 | — |
| 1910 | 482,167 | 365 | 390 | 400 | 440 | 535 | 6,250 | 49,000 |
| 1910D | 429,000 | 365 | 390 | 400 | 440 | 530 | 2,750 | — |
| 1910S | 2,128,250 | 365 | 400 | 425 | 625 | 850 | 7,850 | — |
| 1911 | 197,350 | 365 | 390 | 400 | 490 | 1,475 | 10,500 | 39,500 |
| 1911D | 846,500 | 365 | 385 | 400 | 460 | 495 | 1,350 | — |
| 1911S | 775,750 | 365 | 385 | 400 | 470 | 485 | 4,700 | — |
| 1912 | 149,824 | 385 | 415 | 515 | 560 | 950 | 14,500 | 40,000 |
| 1913 | 168,838 | 365 | 385 | 415 | 465 | 1,675 | 28,000 | 40,000 |
| 1913D | 393,500 | 365 | 385 | 415 | 440 | 675 | 4,500 | — |
| 1913S | 34,000 | 550 | 775 | 750 | 1,150 | 2,900 | 38,000 | — |
| 1914 | 95,320 | 400 | 500 | 520 | 550 | 1,175 | 13,750 | 41,500 |
| 1914D | 453,000 | 360 | 380 | 410 | 450 | 490 | 2,500 | — |
| 1914S | 1,498,000 | 360 | 380 | 400 | 430 | 480 | 1,950 | — |
| 1915 | 152,050 | 390 | 450 | 525 | 600 | 1,450 | 14,000 | 47,500 |
| 1915S | 567,500 | 360 | 380 | 400 | 435 | 550 | 1,950 | — |
| 1916S | 796,000 | 360 | 380 | 410 | 540 | 600 | 1,950 | — |
| 1920 | 228,250 | 365 | 385 | 400 | 450 | 675 | 24,500 | — |
| 1920S | 558,000 | 4,300 | 8,000 | 10,500 | 25,000 | 52,000 | 150,000 | — |
| 1921 | 528,500 | 8,000 | 13,000 | 18,750 | 33,500 | 77,000 | 200,000 | — |

| Date | Mintage | VF-20 | XF-40 | AU-50 | MS-60 | MS-63 | MS-65 | Prf-65 |
|------|---------|-------|-------|-------|-------|-------|-------|--------|
| 1922 | 1,375,500 | 365 | 380 | 400 | 420 | 460 | 3,600 | — |
| 1922S | 2,658,000 | 445 | 650 | 715 | 825 | 1,650 | 36,000 | — |
| 1923 | 566,000 | 360 | 380 | 410 | 440 | 465 | 6,000 | — |
| 1923D | 1,702,250 | 360 | 380 | 400 | 440 | 490 | 1,100 | — |
| 1924 | 4,323,500 | 360 | 375 | 400 | 420 | 460 | 825 | — |
| 1924D | 3,049,500 | 775 | 1,150 | 1,350 | 1,800 | 4,950 | 50,000 | — |
| 1924S | 2,927,500 | 650 | 1,075 | 1,175 | 2,200 | 5,350 | 40,000 | — |
| 1925 | 2,831,750 | 360 | 375 | 400 | 420 | 460 | 825 | — |
| 1925D | 2,938,500 | 1,200 | 1,675 | 1,875 | 3,200 | 7,750 | 50,000 | — |
| 1925S | 3,776,500 | 900 | 1,300 | 1,600 | 5,500 | 18,000 | 72,000 | — |
| 1926 | 816,750 | 365 | 380 | 400 | 425 | 480 | 825 | — |
| 1926D | 481,000 | 1,100 | 2,850 | 3,200 | 7,500 | 19,500 | 85,000 | — |
| 1926S | 2,041,500 | 700 | 1,200 | 1,300 | 1,800 | 2,750 | 32,000 | — |
| 1927 | 2,946,750 | 350 | 375 | 390 | 415 | 475 | 900 | — |
| 1927D | 180,000 | — | — | 150,000 | 265,000 | — | 600,000 | — |
| 1927S | 3,107,000 | 2,000 | 3,900 | 4,550 | 12,500 | 24,000 | 90,000 | — |
| 1928 | 8,816,000 | 350 | 375 | 390 | 415 | 460 | 900 | — |
| 1929 | 1,779,750 | 4,750 | 6,900 | 7,750 | 9,000 | 12,500 | 32,000 | — |
| 1930S | 74,000 | 6,000 | 8,250 | 9,000 | 17,000 | 34,000 | 75,000 | — |
| 1931 | 2,938,250 | 4,250 | 8,000 | 9,250 | 13,500 | 20,000 | 59,000 | — |
| 1931D | 106,500 | 5,500 | 7,750 | 9,000 | 15,000 | 21,000 | 52,000 | — |
| 1932 | 1,101,750 | 7,000 | 10,000 | 11,750 | 16,000 | 22,500 | 33,500 | — |
| 1933 none placed in circulation | 445,500 | — | — | — | — | — | — | — |

# UNCIRCULATED ROLLS

Listings are for rolls containing uncirculated coins. Large date and small date varieties for 1960 and 1970 apply to the one cent coins.

| Date | Cents | Nickels | Dimes | Quarters | Halves |
|---|---|---|---|---|---|
| 1938 | 180 | 200 | 1,000 | 3,200 | 1,850 |
| 1938D | 330 | 170 | 900 | — | — |
| 1938S | 215 | 180 | 1,250 | 3,200 | — |
| 1939 | 49.00 | 65.00 | 600 | 825 | 1,200 |
| 1939D | 175 | 2,200 | 500 | 1,700 | 1,550 |
| 1939S | 115 | 820 | 1,250 | 3,200 | 2,350 |
| 1940 | 59.00 | 32.00 | 350 | 1,150 | 1,000 |
| 1940D | 93.00 | 66.00 | 620 | 4,400 | — |
| 1940S | 115 | 120 | 500 | 1,200 | 1,150 |
| 1941 | 58.00 | 35.00 | 300 | 630 | 750 |
| 1941D | 148 | 110 | 600 | 2,400 | 1,150 |
| 1941S | 175 | 130 | 400 | 1,600 | 3,100 |
| 1942 | 29.00 | 210 | 265 | 250 | 750 |
| 1942P | — | 240 | — | — | — |
| 1942D | 19.00 | 1,450 | 550 | 840 | 1,320 |
| 1942S | 415 | 275 | 700 | 3,600 | 1,400 |
| 1943 | 50.00 | 175 | 265 | 340 | 750 |
| 1943D | 85.00 | 200 | 475 | 1,320 | 1,750 |
| 1943S | 300 | 125 | 550 | 1,750 | 1,350 |
| 1944 | 5.75 | 260 | 270 | 300 | 800 |
| 1944D | 14.00 | 290 | 375 | 600 | 1,200 |
| 1944S | 15.50 | 150 | 390 | 720 | 1,250 |
| 1945 | 28.00 | 160 | 265 | 220 | 700 |
| 1945D | 22.00 | 140 | 265 | 1,100 | 1,000 |
| 1945S | 12.00 | 100.00 | 300 | 400 | 900 |
| 1946 | 16.00 | 21.50 | 50.00 | 250 | 1,000 |
| 1946D | 11.00 | 42.00 | 55.00 | 200 | 850 |
| 1946S | 19.00 | 10.00 | 100.00 | 300 | 850 |
| 1947 | 50.00 | 29.00 | 65.00 | 420 | 900 |
| 1947D | 13.00 | 28.00 | 140 | 380 | 800 |
| 1947S | 20.00 | 20.00 | 125 | 500 | — |
| 1948 | 29.00 | 13.00 | 145 | 190 | 300 |
| 1948D | 17.75 | 30.00 | 125 | 370 | 260 |
| 1948S | 21.00 | 18.50 | 130 | 280 | — |
| 1949 | 55.00 | 90.00 | 930 | 1,500 | 960 |
| 1949D | 28.50 | 26.00 | 330 | 865 | 1,000 |
| 1949S | 58.00 | 37.00 | 1,200 | — | 1,450 |
| 1950 | 29.00 | 42.00 | 145 | 200 | 660 |
| 1950D | 28.00 | 280 | 145 | 190 | 690 |
| 1950S | 34.00 | — | 660 | 400 | — |
| 1951 | 33.00 | 32.00 | 45.00 | 275 | 320 |
| 1951D | 8.00 | 80.00 | 60.00 | 150 | 600 |
| 1951S | 27.00 | 53.00 | 340 | 1,150 | 500 |
| 1952 | 34.00 | 73.00 | 58.00 | 180 | 270 |
| 1952D | 9.00 | 54.00 | 50.00 | 180 | 220 |
| 1952S | 77.00 | 20.00 | 185 | 1,100 | 850 |
| 1953 | 6.00 | 5.50 | 45.00 | 300 | 300 |
| 1953D | 5.10 | 7.20 | 47.00 | 160 | 125 |
| 1953S | 15.00 | 12.50 | 36.00 | 230 | 400 |
| 1954 | 6.50 | 13.00 | 38.00 | 190 | 130 |
| 1954D | 5.00 | 5.75 | 34.00 | 185 | 100.00 |
| 1954S | 9.50 | 5.00 | 47.00 | 155 | 160 |
| 1955 | 8.50 | 6.50 | 35.00 | 140 | 145 |
| 1955D | 5.50 | 5.00 | 31.00 | 140 | — |
| 1955S | 23.50 | — | 42.00 | — | — |
| 1956 | 6.50 | 7.20 | 36.00 | 135 | 100.00 |
| 1956D | 8.25 | 6.00 | 34.00 | 160 | — |
| 1957 | 5.50 | 5.50 | 38.00 | 145 | 135 |
| 1957D | 6.50 | 3.20 | 45.00 | 135 | 92.00 |
| 1958 | 5.00 | 5.50 | 30.00 | 80.00 | 96.00 |
| 1958D | 4.75 | 3.30 | 30.00 | 85.00 | 88.00 |
| 1959 | 1.30 | 3.70 | 26.00 | 88.00 | 92.00 |
| 1959D | 1.35 | 3.85 | 31.50 | 100.00 | 110 |
| 1960 large date | 1.10 | 3.30 | 26.00 | 90.00 | 90.00 |
| 1960 small date | 105 | — | — | — | — |
| 1960D large date | 1.40 | 3.50 | 26.00 | 80.00 | 100.00 |
| 1960D small date | 1.65 | — | — | — | — |
| 1961 | 1.20 | 3.30 | 26.00 | 110 | 100.00 |
| 1961D | 1.15 | 4.20 | 26.00 | 85.00 | 100.00 |
| 1962 | 1.60 | 3.50 | 26.00 | 110 | 88.00 |
| 1962D | 1.60 | 3.50 | 26.00 | 85.00 | 85.00 |
| 1963 | 1.10 | 2.85 | 26.00 | 55.00 | 85.00 |
| 1963D | 1.10 | 3.50 | 26.00 | 55.00 | 85.00 |
| 1964 | 1.20 | 3.00 | 25.00 | 50.00 | 55.00 |

| Date | Cents | Nickels | Dimes | Quarters | Halves |
|---|---|---|---|---|---|
| 1964D | 1.40 | 3.50 | 25.00 | 55.00 | 55.00 |
| 1965 | 2.25 | 3.50 | 9.50 | 17.00 | 20.00 |
| 1966 | 3.50 | 3.50 | 9.00 | 21.50 | 24.00 |
| 1967 | 5.00 | 3.30 | 8.00 | 21.00 | 19.50 |
| 1968 | 2.30 | — | 11.00 | 28.00 | — |
| 1968D | 1.60 | 3.60 | 9.00 | 30.00 | 19.50 |
| 1968S | 1.30 | 3.50 | — | — | — |
| 1969 | 5.25 | — | 34.00 | 50.00 | — |
| 1969D | 2.00 | 4.50 | 12.00 | 48.00 | 20.00 |
| 1969S | 2.75 | 3.50 | — | — | — |
| 1970 | 3.50 | — | 9.50 | 16.00 | — |
| 1970D | 1.95 | 3.30 | 8.50 | 15.00 | 220 |
| 1970S | 2.50 | 2.85 | — | — | — |
| 1970S small date | 1,285 | — | — | — | — |
| 1971 | 5.25 | 24.00 | 12.50 | 19.00 | 20.00 |
| 1971D | 3.00 | 4.80 | 9.00 | 18.00 | 18.00 |
| 1971S | 3.75 | — | — | — | — |
| 1972 | 2.10 | 4.80 | 8.00 | 14.00 | 24.00 |
| 1972D | 2.50 | 3.15 | 8.80 | 15.00 | 20.00 |
| 1972S | 2.30 | — | — | — | — |
| 1973 | 1.40 | 4.00 | 7.00 | 15.00 | 25.00 |
| 1973D | 1.40 | 3.50 | 9.00 | 15.00 | 23.00 |
| 1973S | 2.75 | — | — | — | — |
| 1974 | 1.00 | 2.80 | 8.00 | 14.00 | 21.00 |
| 1974D | 1.00 | 5.65 | 7.00 | 17.00 | 21.00 |
| 1974S | 2.75 | — | — | — | — |
| 1975 | 1.60 | 10.00 | 9.50 | — | — |
| 1975D | 1.80 | 4.50 | 9.50 | — | — |
| 1976 | 1.25 | 11.50 | 12.50 | 14.00 | 20.00 |
| 1976D | 2.50 | 8.50 | 14.50 | 18.00 | 18.50 |
| 1977 | 1.85 | 3.15 | 7.50 | 15.00 | 26.00 |
| 1977D | 1.65 | 6.00 | 8.00 | 16.00 | 25.00 |
| 1978 | 2.00 | 3.20 | 7.50 | 14.50 | 27.50 |
| 1978D | 1.80 | 4.00 | 8.00 | 14.50 | 30.00 |
| 1979 | 1.50 | 3.50 | 8.00 | 15.00 | 24.00 |
| 1979D | 1.25 | 4.20 | 7.50 | 18.00 | 22.00 |
| 1980 | 1.60 | 3.90 | 7.50 | 16.00 | 18.00 |
| 1980D | 1.50 | 3.30 | 7.00 | 14.00 | 22.00 |
| 1981 | 1.25 | 3.30 | 7.50 | 14.00 | 27.50 |
| 1981D | 1.10 | 3.30 | 7.50 | 14.00 | 22.00 |
| 1982 | 1.25 | 55.00 | 135 | 130 | 27.50 |
| 1982D | 1.25 | 42.00 | 50.00 | 32.50 | 32.00 |
| 1983 | 1.90 | 45.00 | 75.00 | 320 | 50.00 |
| 1983D | 2.50 | 20.00 | 30.00 | 120 | 45.00 |
| 1984 | 3.50 | 26.50 | 9.00 | 19.00 | 34.00 |
| 1984D | 16.00 | 5.00 | 14.50 | 26.00 | 34.00 |
| 1985 | 4.25 | 5.50 | 10.00 | 30.00 | 30.00 |
| 1985D | 3.75 | 5.00 | 10.00 | 25.00 | 27.50 |
| 1986 | 18.50 | 7.25 | 26.00 | 100.00 | 110 |
| 1986D | 10.50 | 25.00 | 25.00 | 90.00 | 70.00 |
| 1987 | 2.95 | 4.40 | 7.00 | 14.50 | 75.00 |
| 1987D | 3.25 | 4.00 | 7.00 | 15.00 | 72.00 |
| 1988 | 5.00 | 3.30 | 8.50 | 27.50 | 42.00 |
| 1988D | 5.25 | 5.40 | 8.00 | 21.00 | 50.00 |
| 1989 | 1.95 | 3.85 | 8.50 | 17.00 | 30.00 |
| 1989D | 1.40 | 4.50 | 7.30 | 18.00 | 30.00 |
| 1990 | 1.60 | 3.30 | 8.50 | 25.00 | 27.50 |
| 1990D | 1.75 | 4.00 | 7.00 | 23.00 | 52.00 |
| 1991 | 1.65 | 8.00 | 10.00 | 20.00 | 27.50 |
| 1991D | 1.80 | 8.00 | 13.00 | 29.00 | 52.00 |
| 1992 | 2.40 | 17.00 | 7.00 | 20.00 | 19.00 |
| 1992D | 2.00 | 5.00 | 8.50 | 32.50 | 52.00 |
| 1993 | 2.40 | 4.80 | 8.50 | 26.00 | 21.00 |
| 1993D | 2.00 | 5.50 | 8.00 | 29.00 | 21.00 |
| 1994 | 1.75 | 4.00 | 8.00 | 18.50 | 13.50 |
| 1994D | 1.75 | 4.00 | 7.50 | 20.00 | 20.00 |
| 1995 | 1.10 | 3.50 | 7.50 | 21.00 | 14.50 |
| 1995D | 1.85 | 9.00 | 13.00 | 22.00 | 14.00 |
| 1996 | 1.75 | 3.75 | 7.50 | 14.50 | 14.50 |
| 1996D | 1.65 | 3.75 | 7.50 | 17.50 | 15.00 |
| 1997 | 1.60 | 4.00 | 7.50 | 20.00 | 14.50 |
| 1997D | 1.70 | 5.00 | 7.50 | 20.00 | 16.00 |
| 1998 | 1.60 | 4.20 | 7.50 | 14.00 | 15.50 |
| 1998D | 1.70 | 4.20 | 7.50 | 14.00 | 16.00 |
| 1999P | 1.60 | 3.30 | 8.00 | — | 16.00 |
| 1999D | 1.40 | 3.30 | 7.50 | — | 16.00 |
| 2000P | 1.25 | 3.30 | 7.50 | — | — |
| 2000P | 1.25 | 3.30 | 7.50 | — | — |
| 2000D | 1.10 | 3.30 | 7.50 | — | — |

# COMMEMORATIVES 1892-1954

All commemorative half dollars of 1892-1954 have the following specifications: diameter -- 24.3 millimeters; weight -- 6.2500 grams; composition -- 0.9000 silver, 0.1808 ounces actual silver weight. Values for "PDS sets" contain one example each from the Philadelphia, Denver and San Francisco mints. "Type coin" prices are the most inexpensive single coin available from the date and mint-mark combinations listed.

## QUARTER

**COLUMBIAN EXPOSITION.**    **Obverse:** Queen Isabella. **Diameter:** 24.3 mm. **Weight:** 6.2500 g. **Composition:** 0.9000 Silver, 0.1808 oz. ASW.

| Date | Mintage | AU-50 | MS-60 | MS-63 | MS-64 | MS-65 |
|------|---------|-------|-------|-------|-------|-------|
| 1893 | 24,214 | 450 | 650 | 750 | 1,100 | 3,150 |

## HALF DOLLAR

**COLUMBIAN EXPO.**    **Obv. Designer:** Charles E. Barber **Rev. Designer:** George T. Morgan

| Date | Mintage | AU-50 | MS-60 | MS-63 | MS-64 | MS-65 |
|------|---------|-------|-------|-------|-------|-------|
| 1892 | 950,000 | 14.00 | 26.00 | 80.00 | 200 | 750 |

### 1892 Columbian Expo Half
#### Grade MS-60

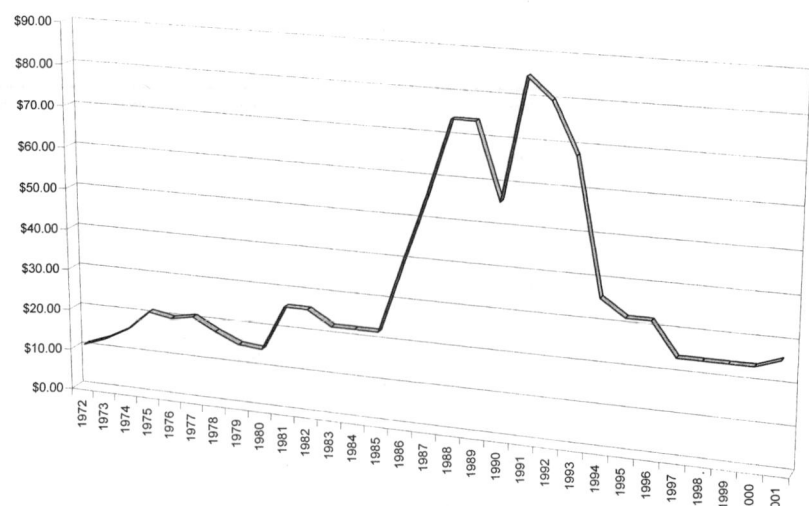

Retail Price

| Date | Mintage | AU-50 | MS-60 | MS-63 | MS-64 | MS-65 |
|------|---------|-------|-------|-------|-------|-------|
| 1893 | 1,550,405 | 14.00 | 26.00 | 80.00 | 200 | 930 |

**PANAMA-PACIFIC EXPOSITION.** **Designer:** Charles E. Barber.

| Date | Mintage | AU-50 | MS-60 | MS-63 | MS-64 | MS-65 |
|------|---------|-------|-------|-------|-------|-------|
| 1915S | 27,134 | 220 | 335 | 680 | 1,250 | 2,700 |

**LINCOLN-ILLINOIS.** **Obv. Designer:** George T. Morgan **Rev. Designer:** John R. Sinnock

| Date | Mintage | AU-50 | MS-60 | MS-63 | MS-64 | MS-65 |
|------|---------|-------|-------|-------|-------|-------|
| 1918 | 100,058 | 80.00 | 105 | 115 | 185 | 520 |

**MAINE CENTENNIAL.** **Designer:** Anthony de Francisci.

| Date | Mintage | AU-50 | MS-60 | MS-63 | MS-64 | MS-65 |
|------|---------|-------|-------|-------|-------|-------|
| 1920 | 50,028 | 95.00 | 115 | 150 | 260 | 630 |

**PILGRIM TERCENTENARY.** **Designer:** Cyrus E. Dallin.

| Date | Mintage | AU-50 | MS-60 | MS-63 | MS-64 | MS-65 |
|------|---------|-------|-------|-------|-------|-------|
| 1920 | 152,112 | 59.00 | 70.00 | 85.00 | 145 | 550 |

  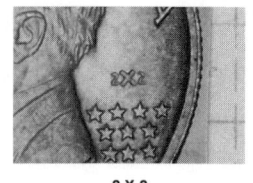

2 X 2

**ALABAMA CENTENNIAL.**  **Designer:** Laura G. Fraser.  **Obverse:** "2x2" at right above stars.

| Date | Mintage | AU-50 | MS-60 | MS-63 | MS-64 | MS-65 |
|------|---------|-------|-------|-------|-------|-------|
| 1921 | 6,006 | 200 | 300 | 525 | 850 | 2,650 |

**ALABAMA CENTENNIAL.**  **Obv. Designer:** Laura G. Fraser

| Date | Mintage | AU-50 | MS-60 | MS-63 | MS-64 | MS-65 |
|------|---------|-------|-------|-------|-------|-------|
| 1921 | 59,038 | 115 | 210 | 450 | 800 | 2,600 |

**MISSOURI CENTENNIAL.**  **Designer:** Robert Aitken.

| Date | Mintage | AU-50 | MS-60 | MS-63 | MS-64 | MS-65 |
|------|---------|-------|-------|-------|-------|-------|
| 1921 | 15,428 | 235 | 430 | 800 | 1,375 | 5,650 |

2 ☆ 4

**MISSOURI CENTENNIAL.**  **Designer:** Robert Aitken.  **Obverse:** 2 star 4 in field at left.

| Date | Mintage | AU-50 | MS-60 | MS-63 | MS-64 | MS-65 |
|------|---------|-------|-------|-------|-------|-------|
| 1921 | 5,000 | 420 | 500 | 950 | 1,800 | 5,600 |

**PILGRIM TERCENTENARY.**  **Designer:** Cyrus E. Dallin.  **Obverse:** 1921 date next to Pilgrim.

| Date | Mintage | AU-50 | MS-60 | MS-63 | MS-64 | MS-65 |
|------|---------|-------|-------|-------|-------|-------|
| 1921 | 20,053 | 110 | 125 | 160 | 240 | 725 |

**GRANT MEMORIAL. Designer:** Laura G. Fraser.

| Date | Mintage | AU-50 | MS-60 | MS-63 | MS-64 | MS-65 |
|------|---------|-------|-------|-------|-------|-------|
| 1922 | 67,405 | 80.00 | 85.00 | 160 | 295 | 975 |

**GRANT MEMORIAL. Designer:** Laura G. Fraser. **Obverse:** Star above the word "Grant".

| Date | Mintage | AU-50 | MS-60 | MS-63 | MS-64 | MS-65 |
|------|---------|-------|-------|-------|-------|-------|
| 1922 | 4,256 | 690 | 980 | 1,550 | 2,350 | 7,800 |

**MONROE DOCTRINE CENTENNIAL. Designer:** Chester Beach.

| Date | Mintage | AU-50 | MS-60 | MS-63 | MS-64 | MS-65 |
|------|---------|-------|-------|-------|-------|-------|
| 1923S | 274,077 | 29.00 | 41.00 | 162 | 400 | 2,550 |

**HUGUENOT-WALLOON TERCENTENARY. Designer:** George T. Morgan.

| Date | Mintage | AU-50 | MS-60 | MS-63 | MS-64 | MS-65 |
|------|---------|-------|-------|-------|-------|-------|
| 1924 | 142,080 | 95.00 | 110 | 130 | 220 | 530 |

**CALIFORNIA DIAMOND JUBILEE.**   **Designer:** Jo Mora.

| Date | Mintage | AU-50 | MS-60 | MS-63 | MS-64 | MS-65 |
|------|---------|-------|-------|-------|-------|-------|
| 1925S | 86,594 | 110 | 120 | 170 | 275 | 1,050 |

**FORT VANCOUVER CENTENNIAL.**   **Designer:** Laura G. Fraser.

| Date | Mintage | AU-50 | MS-60 | MS-63 | MS-64 | MS-65 |
|------|---------|-------|-------|-------|-------|-------|
| 1925 | 14,994 | 240 | 300 | 360 | 600 | 1,500 |

**LEXINGTON-CONCORD SESQUICENTENNIAL.**   **Designer:** Chester Beach.

| Date | Mintage | AU-50 | MS-60 | MS-63 | MS-64 | MS-65 |
|------|---------|-------|-------|-------|-------|-------|
| 1925 | 162,013 | 65.00 | 70.00 | 105 | 185 | 660 |

**STONE MOUNTAIN MEMORIAL.**   **Designer:** Gutzon Borglum.

| Date | Mintage | AU-50 | MS-60 | MS-63 | MS-64 | MS-65 |
|------|---------|-------|-------|-------|-------|-------|
| 1925 | 1,314,709 | 35.00 | 40.00 | 66.00 | 90.00 | 210 |

## 1926 Oregon Trail Half
### Grade MS-60

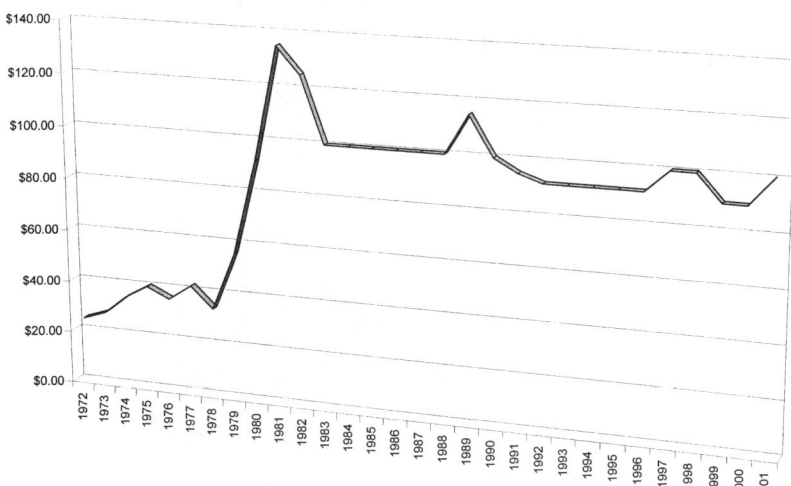

☐ Retail Price

**OREGON TRAIL MEMORIAL.  Designer:** James E. and Laura G. Fraser.

| Date | Mintage | AU-50 | MS-60 | MS-63 | MS-64 | MS-65 |
|------|---------|-------|-------|-------|-------|-------|
| 1926 | 47,955 | 95.00 | 100.00 | 110 | 145 | 230 |
| 1926S | 83,055 | 95.00 | 100.00 | 115 | 140 | 200 |
| Type coin | — | 95.00 | 100.00 | 110 | 140 | 200 |
| 1928 | 6,028 | 150 | 160 | 170 | 180 | 275 |
| 1933D | 5,008 | 230 | 245 | 270 | 295 | 465 |
| 1934D | 7,006 | 145 | 150 | 160 | 190 | 295 |
| 1936 | 10,006 | 105 | 115 | 125 | 145 | 220 |
| 1936S | 5,006 | 125 | 135 | 170 | 200 | 280 |
| 1937D | 12,008 | 125 | 140 | 150 | 180 | 200 |
| 1938 PDS set | 6,005 | 490 | 540 | 630 | 660 | 670 |
| 1939 PDS Set | 3,004 | 1,170 | 1,200 | 1,350 | 1,450 | 1,750 |

**U.S. SESQUICENTENNIAL.  Designer:** John R. Sinnock.

| Date | Mintage | AU-50 | MS-60 | MS-63 | MS-64 | MS-65 |
|------|---------|-------|-------|-------|-------|-------|
| 1926 | 141,120 | 60.00 | 72.00 | 155 | 600 | 5,800 |

**VERMONT SESQUICENTENNIAL.** **Obv. Designer:** Charles Keck

| Date | Mintage | AU-50 | MS-60 | MS-63 | MS-64 | MS-65 |
|------|---------|-------|-------|-------|-------|-------|
| 1927 | 28,142 | 155 | 165 | 190 | 300 | 1,000 |

**HAWAIIAN SESQUICENTENNIAL.** **Designer:** Juliette M. Fraser.

| Date | Mintage | AU-50 | MS-60 | MS-63 | MS-64 | MS-65 |
|------|---------|-------|-------|-------|-------|-------|
| 1928 | 10,008 | 1,100 | 1,300 | 1,850 | 2,600 | 5,400 |

**DANIEL BOONE BICENTENNIAL.** **Designer:** Augustus Lukeman.

| Date | Mintage | AU-50 | MS-60 | MS-63 | MS-64 | MS-65 |
|------|---------|-------|-------|-------|-------|-------|
| 1934 | 10,007 | 65.00 | 72.00 | 85.00 | 110 | 180 |
| 1935 PDS set | 2,003 | 210 | 225 | 300 | 325 | 565 |

**DANIEL BOONE BICENTENNIAL.** **Designer:** Augustus Lukeman. **Reverse:** "1934" added above the word "Pioneer."

| Date | Mintage | AU-50 | MS-60 | MS-63 | MS-64 | MS-65 |
|------|---------|-------|-------|-------|-------|-------|
| Type coin | — | 65.00 | 72.00 | 78.00 | 95.00 | 185 |
| 1935 PDS set | 5,005 | 580 | 660 | 820 | 1,100 | 1,850 |
| 1936 PDS set | 5,005 | 210 | 225 | 280 | 325 | 550 |
| 1937 PDS set | 2,506 | 540 | 630 | 660 | 810 | 1,100 |
| 1938 PDS set | 2,100 | 750 | 820 | 1,000 | 1,150 | 1,500 |

**MARYLAND TERCENTENARY.** **Designer:** Hans Schuler.

| Date | Mintage | AU-50 | MS-60 | MS-63 | MS-64 | MS-65 |
|------|---------|-------|-------|-------|-------|-------|
| 1934 | 25,015 | 110 | 125 | 160 | 190 | 350 |

**TEXAS CENTENNIAL.**   **Designer:** Pompeo Coppini.

| Date | Mintage | AU-50 | MS-60 | MS-63 | MS-64 | MS-65 |
|------|---------|-------|-------|-------|-------|-------|
| 1934 | 61,463 | 90.00 | 95.00 | 105 | 110 | 160 |
| Type coin | — | 90.00 | 95.00 | 100.00 | 110 | 160 |
| 1935 PDS set | 9,994 | 270 | 300 | 320 | 340 | 530 |
| 1936 PDS set | 8,911 | 270 | 300 | 310 | 330 | 520 |
| 1937 PDS set | 6,571 | 280 | 300 | 310 | 330 | 510 |
| 1938 PDS set | 3,775 | 550 | 650 | 750 | 810 | 1,150 |

**ARKANSAS CENTENNIAL.**   **Designer:** Edward E. Burr.

| Date | Mintage | AU-50 | MS-60 | MS-63 | MS-64 | MS-65 |
|------|---------|-------|-------|-------|-------|-------|
| Type coin | — | 62.00 | 70.00 | 78.00 | 90.00 | 230 |
| 1935 PDS set | 5,505 | 200 | 215 | 235 | 320 | 780 |
| 1936 PDS set | 9,600 | 200 | 215 | 235 | 300 | 840 |
| 1937 PDS set | 5,505 | 210 | 225 | 250 | 325 | 1,050 |
| 1938 PDS set | 3,155 | 270 | 360 | 420 | 500 | 1,900 |
| 1939 PDS set | — | 550 | 625 | 900 | 1,100 | 3,200 |

**CONNECTICUT TERCENTENARY.**   **Designer:** Henry Kreiss.

| Date | Mintage | AU-50 | MS-60 | MS-63 | MS-64 | MS-65 |
|------|---------|-------|-------|-------|-------|-------|
| 1935 | 25,018 | 175 | 190 | 210 | 290 | 560 |

**HUDSON, N.Y., SESQUICENTENNIAL.**   **Designer:** Chester Beach.

| Date | Mintage | AU-50 | MS-60 | MS-63 | MS-64 | MS-65 |
|------|---------|-------|-------|-------|-------|-------|
| 1935 | 10,008 | 445 | 485 | 530 | 730 | 1,500 |

**OLD SPANISH TRAIL.**   **Designer:** L.W. Hoffecker.

| Date | Mintage | AU-50 | MS-60 | MS-63 | MS-64 | MS-65 |
|------|---------|-------|-------|-------|-------|-------|
| 1935 | 10,008 | 800 | 850 | 875 | 1,000 | 1,150 |

**SAN DIEGO-CALIFORNIA-PACIFIC EXPOSITION.**   **Designer:** Robert Aitken.

| Date | Mintage | AU-50 | MS-60 | MS-63 | MS-64 | MS-65 |
|------|---------|-------|-------|-------|-------|-------|
| 1935S | 70,132 | 53.00 | 60.00 | 64.00 | 75.00 | 115 |
| 1936D | 30,092 | 58.00 | 62.00 | 66.00 | 80.00 | 120 |

**ALBANY, N.Y., CHARTER ANNIVERSARY.**   **Designer:** Gertrude K. Lathrop.

| Date | Mintage | AU-50 | MS-60 | MS-63 | MS-64 | MS-65 |
|------|---------|-------|-------|-------|-------|-------|
| 1936 | 17,671 | 200 | 210 | 220 | 235 | 340 |

**ARKANSAS CENTENNIAL.**   **Obv. Designer:** Henry Kreiss **Rev. Designer:** Edward E. Burr **Obverse:** Sen. Joseph T. Robinson

| Date | Mintage | AU-50 | MS-60 | MS-63 | MS-64 | MS-65 |
|------|---------|-------|-------|-------|-------|-------|
| 1936 | 25,265 | 100.00 | 110 | 120 | 130 | 350 |

**BATTLE OF GETTYSBURG 75TH ANNIVERSARY.** **Designer:** Frank Vittor.

| Date | Mintage | AU-50 | MS-60 | MS-63 | MS-64 | MS-65 |
|------|---------|-------|-------|-------|-------|-------|
| 1936 | 26,928 | 270 | 280 | 300 | 385 | 640 |

**BRIDGEPORT, CONN., CENTENNIAL.** **Designer:** Henry Kreiss.

| Date | Mintage | AU-50 | MS-60 | MS-63 | MS-64 | MS-65 |
|------|---------|-------|-------|-------|-------|-------|
| 1936 | 25,015 | 110 | 125 | 130 | 140 | 250 |

**CINCINNATI MUSIC CENTER.** **Designer:** Constance Ortmayer.

| Date | Mintage | AU-50 | MS-60 | MS-63 | MS-64 | MS-65 |
|------|---------|-------|-------|-------|-------|-------|
| Type coin | — | 200 | 215 | 225 | 300 | 650 |

**CLEVELAND-GREAT LAKES EXPOSITION.** **Designer:** Brenda Putnam.

| Date | Mintage | AU-50 | MS-60 | MS-63 | MS-64 | MS-65 |
|------|---------|-------|-------|-------|-------|-------|
| 1936 | 50,030 | 60.00 | 65.00 | 72.00 | 92.50 | 240 |

**COLUMBIA, S.C., SESQUICENTENNIAL.    Designer:** A. Wolfe Davidson.

| Date | Mintage | AU-50 | MS-60 | MS-63 | MS-64 | MS-65 |
|------|---------|-------|-------|-------|-------|-------|
| 1936 PDS set | 9,007 | 500 | 540 | 550 | 610 | 740 |
| Type coin | — | 165 | 180 | 190 | 200 | 210 |

**DELAWARE TERCENTENARY.    Designer:** Carl L. Schmitz.

| Date | Mintage | AU-50 | MS-60 | MS-63 | MS-64 | MS-65 |
|------|---------|-------|-------|-------|-------|-------|
| 1936 | 20,993 | 215 | 225 | 235 | 240 | 355 |

**ELGIN, ILL., CENTENNIAL.    Designer:** Trygve Rovelstad.

| Date | Mintage | AU-50 | MS-60 | MS-63 | MS-64 | MS-65 |
|------|---------|-------|-------|-------|-------|-------|
| 1936 | 20,015 | 160 | 175 | 185 | 210 | 275 |

**LONG ISLAND TERCENTENARY.    Designer:** Howard K. Weinman.

| Date | Mintage | AU-50 | MS-60 | MS-63 | MS-64 | MS-65 |
|------|---------|-------|-------|-------|-------|-------|
| 1936 | 81,826 | 60.00 | 65.00 | 75.00 | 120 | 440 |

**LYNCHBURG, VA., SESQUICENTENNIAL.** **Designer:** Charles Keck.

| Date | Mintage | AU-50 | MS-60 | MS-63 | MS-64 | MS-65 |
|---|---|---|---|---|---|---|
| 1936 | 20,013 | 145 | 155 | 170 | 215 | 300 |

**NORFOLK, VA., BICENTENNIAL.** **Designer:** William M. and Marjorie E. Simpson.

| Date | Mintage | AU-50 | MS-60 | MS-63 | MS-64 | MS-65 |
|---|---|---|---|---|---|---|
| 1936 | 16,936 | 395 | 400 | 420 | 440 | 500 |

**RHODE ISLAND TERCENTENARY.** **Designer:** Arthur G. Carey and John H. Benson.

| Date | Mintage | AU-50 | MS-60 | MS-63 | MS-64 | MS-65 |
|---|---|---|---|---|---|---|
| 1936 PDS set | 15,010 | 200 | 215 | 250 | 330 | 700 |
| Type coin | — | 65.00 | 70.00 | 75.00 | 115 | 230 |

**SAN FRANCISCO-OAKLAND BAY BRIDGE.** **Designer:** Jacques Schnier.

| Date | Mintage | AU-50 | MS-60 | MS-63 | MS-64 | MS-65 |
|---|---|---|---|---|---|---|
| 1936 | 71,424 | 100.00 | 110 | 120 | 160 | 270 |

**WISCONSIN TERRITORIAL CENTENNIAL.**    **Designer:** David Parsons.

| Date | Mintage | AU-50 | MS-60 | MS-63 | MS-64 | MS-65 |
|------|---------|-------|-------|-------|-------|-------|
| 1936 | 25,015 | 155 | 170 | 180 | 210 | 245 |

**YORK COUNTY, MAINE, TERCENTENARY.**    **Designer:** Walter H. Rich.

| Date | Mintage | AU-50 | MS-60 | MS-63 | MS-64 | MS-65 |
|------|---------|-------|-------|-------|-------|-------|
| 1936 | 25,015 | 155 | 160 | 170 | 180 | 190 |

**BATTLE OF ANTIETAM 75TH ANNIVERSARY.**    **Designer:** William M. Simpson.

| Date | Mintage | AU-50 | MS-60 | MS-63 | MS-64 | MS-65 |
|------|---------|-------|-------|-------|-------|-------|
| 1937 | 18,028 | 425 | 450 | 460 | 550 | 750 |

**ROANOKE ISLAND, N.C.**    **Designer:** William M. Simpson.

| Date | Mintage | AU-50 | MS-60 | MS-63 | MS-64 | MS-65 |
|------|---------|-------|-------|-------|-------|-------|
| 1937 | 29,030 | 150 | 230 | 240 | 250 | 260 |

**NEW ROCHELLE, N.Y.**   **Designer:** Gertrude K. Lathrop.

| Date | Mintage | AU-50 | MS-60 | MS-63 | MS-64 | MS-65 |
|------|---------|-------|-------|-------|-------|-------|
| 1938 | 15,266 | 265 | 280 | 295 | 320 | 430 |

**BOOKER T. WASHINGTON.**   **Designer:** Isaac S. Hathaway.

| Date | Mintage | AU-50 | MS-60 | MS-63 | MS-64 | MS-65 |
|------|---------|-------|-------|-------|-------|-------|
| 1946 PDS set | 200,113 | — | 43.00 | 54.00 | 67.00 | 120 |
| Type coin | — | 13.00 | 14.50 | 17.00 | 18.00 | 38.50 |
| 1947 PDS set | 100,017 | — | 72.00 | 80.00 | 110 | 250 |
| 1948 PDS set | 8,005 | — | 85.00 | 140 | 160 | 185 |
| 1949 PDS set | 6,004 | — | 215 | 235 | 240 | 320 |
| 1950 PDS set | 6,004 | — | 110 | 115 | 120 | 175 |
| 1951 PDS set | 7,004 | — | 110 | 130 | 140 | 175 |

**IOWA STATEHOOD CENTENNIAL.**   **Designer:** Adam Pietz.

| Date | Mintage | AU-50 | MS-60 | MS-63 | MS-64 | MS-65 |
|------|---------|-------|-------|-------|-------|-------|
| 1946 | 100,057 | 63.00 | 68.00 | 72.00 | 80.00 | 115 |

**BOOKER T. WASHINGTON AND GEORGE WASHINGTON CARVER.**   **Designer:** Isaac S. Hathaway.

| Date | Mintage | AU-50 | MS-60 | MS-63 | MS-64 | MS-65 |
|------|---------|-------|-------|-------|-------|-------|
| 1951 PDS set | 10,004 | — | 85.00 | 100.00 | 120 | 565 |
| Type coin | — | 13.00 | 14.50 | 16.50 | 17.00 | 45.00 |
| 1952 PDS set | 8,006 | — | 80.00 | 110 | 125 | 360 |
| 1953 PDS set | 8,003 | — | 80.00 | 110 | 130 | 540 |
| 1954 PDS set | 12,006 | — | 78.00 | 90.00 | 110 | 390 |

# DOLLAR

**LAFAYETTE. Designer:** Charles E. Barber. **Diameter:** 38.1 mm. **Weight:** 26.7300 g. **Composition:** 0.9000 Silver, 0.7736 oz. ASW.

| Date | Mintage | AU-50 | MS-60 | MS-63 | MS-64 | MS-65 |
|------|---------|-------|-------|-------|-------|-------|
| 1900 | 36,026 | 320 | 565 | 1,400 | 2,600 | 9,900 |

**LOUISIANA PURCHASE EXPOSITION. Designer:** Charles E. Barber. **Obverse:** Jefferson **Diameter:** 15 mm. **Weight:** 1.6720 g. **Composition:** 0.9000 Gold, 0.0484 oz. AGW.

| Date | Mintage | AU-50 | MS-60 | MS-63 | MS-64 | MS-65 |
|------|---------|-------|-------|-------|-------|-------|
| 1903 | 17,500 | 350 | 445 | 700 | 1,225 | 2,600 |

**LOUISIANA PURCHASE EXPOSITION. Obv. Designer:** Charles E. Barber **Obverse:** McKinley. **Diameter:** 15 mm. **Weight:** 1.6720 g. **Composition:** 0.9000 Gold, 0.0484 oz. AGW.

| Date | Mintage | AU-50 | MS-60 | MS-63 | MS-64 | MS-65 |
|------|---------|-------|-------|-------|-------|-------|
| 1903 | 17,500 | 320 | 395 | 670 | 1,250 | 2,800 |

**LEWIS AND CLARK EXPO. Obv. Designer:** Charles E. Barber **Diameter:** 15 mm. **Weight:** 1.6720 g. **Composition:** 0.9000 Gold, 0.7736 oz. AGW.

| Date | Mintage | AU-50 | MS-60 | MS-63 | MS-64 | MS-65 |
|------|---------|-------|-------|-------|-------|-------|
| 1904 | 10,025 | 550 | 800 | 1,900 | 3,850 | 8,500 |
| 1905 | 10,041 | 535 | 930 | 2,400 | 5,600 | 17,000 |

**PANAMA-PACIFIC EXPO. Obv. Designer:** Charles Keck **Diameter:** 15 mm. **Weight:** 1.6720 g. **Composition:** 0.9000 Gold, 0.0484 oz. AGW.

| Date | Mintage | AU-50 | MS-60 | MS-63 | MS-64 | MS-65 |
|------|---------|-------|-------|-------|-------|-------|
| 1915S | 15,000 | 330 | 380 | 500 | 1,000 | 2,600 |

**MCKINLEY MEMORIAL. Obv. Designer:** Charles E. Barber **Rev. Designer:** George T. Morgan **Diameter:** 15 mm. **Weight:** 1.6720 g. **Composition:** 0.9000 Gold, 0.0484 oz. AGW.

| Date | Mintage | AU-50 | MS-60 | MS-63 | MS-64 | MS-65 |
|------|---------|-------|-------|-------|-------|-------|
| 1916 | 9,977 | 275 | 370 | 510 | 920 | 2,600 |
| 1917 | 10,000 | 360 | 530 | 950 | 1,900 | 3,300 |

**GRANT MEMORIAL.** **Obv. Designer:** Laura G. Fraser **Obverse:** Without a star above the word "Grant". **Diameter:** 15 mm. **Weight:** 1.6720 g. **Composition:** 0.9000 Gold, 0.0484 oz. AGW. **Notes:** The Grant gold-dollar varieties are distinguished by whether a star appears on the obverse above the word 'Grant.'

| Date | Mintage | AU-50 | MS-60 | MS-63 | MS-64 | MS-65 |
|------|---------|-------|-------|-------|-------|-------|
| 1922 | 5,016 | 1,100 | 1,200 | 1,550 | 2,500 | 3,250 |

Grant

**GRANT MEMORIAL.** **Obv. Designer:** Laura G. Fraser **Obverse:** With a star above the word "Grant". **Diameter:** 15 mm. **Weight:** 1.6720 g. **Composition:** 0.9000 Gold, 0.0484 oz. AGW.

| Date | Mintage | AU-50 | MS-60 | MS-63 | MS-64 | MS-65 |
|------|---------|-------|-------|-------|-------|-------|
| 1922 | 5,000 | 1,200 | 1,400 | 1,850 | 2,650 | 3,200 |

# $2.50 (QUARTER EAGLE)

**PANAMA PACIFIC EXPO.** **Obv. Designer:** Charles E. Barber **Rev. Designer:** George T. Morgan **Diameter:** 18 mm. **Weight:** 4.1800 g. **Composition:** 0.9000 Gold, 0.121 oz. AGW.

| Date | Mintage | AU-50 | MS-60 | MS-63 | MS-64 | MS-65 |
|------|---------|-------|-------|-------|-------|-------|
| 1915S | 6,749 | 1,225 | 1,450 | 2,950 | 4,250 | 5,500 |

**PHILADELPHIA SESQUICENTENNIAL.** **Obv. Designer:** John R. Sinnock **Diameter:** 18 mm. **Weight:** 4.1800 g. **Composition:** 0.9000 Gold, 0.121 oz. AGW.

| Date | Mintage | AU-50 | MS-60 | MS-63 | MS-64 | MS-65 |
|------|---------|-------|-------|-------|-------|-------|
| 1926 | 46,019 | 280 | 320 | 510 | 860 | 3,675 |

# $50

**PANAMA PACIFIC EXPO. Obv. Designer:** Robert Aitken **Diameter:** 44 mm. **Weight:** 83.5900 g. **Composition:** 0.9000 Gold, 2.419 oz. AGW.

| Date | Mintage | AU-50 | MS-60 | MS-63 | MS-64 | MS-65 |
|------|---------|-------|-------|-------|-------|-------|
| 1915S | 483 | 25,000 | 28,000 | 41,000 | 51,000 | 129,000 |

**PANAMA PACIFIC EXPO. Obv. Designer:** Robert Aitken **Diameter:** 44 mm. **Weight:** 83.5900 g. **Composition:** 0.9000 Gold, 2.419 oz. AGW.

| Date | Mintage | AU-50 | MS-60 | MS-63 | MS-64 | MS-65 |
|------|---------|-------|-------|-------|-------|-------|
| 1915S | 645 | 22,500 | 26,500 | 37,000 | 51,000 | 110,000 |

**Note:** In 1982, after a hiatus of nearly 20 years, coinage of commemorative half dollars resumed. Those designated with a 'W' were struck at the West Point Mint. Some issues were struck in copper-nickel. Those struck in silver have the same size, weight and composition

# COMMEMORATIVES 1982-PRESENT

All commemorative silver dollar coins of 1982-present have the following specifications: diameter -- 38.1 millimeters; weight -- 26.7300 grams; composition -- 0.9000 silver, 0.7736 ounces actual silver weight. All commemorative $5 coins of 1982-present have the following specificiations: diameter -- 21.6 millimeters; weight -- 8.3590 grams; composition: 0.9000 gold, 0.242 ounces actual gold weight.

## HALF DOLLAR

**250TH ANNIVERSARY OF GEORGE WASHINGTON'S BIRTH. Obv. Designer:** Elizabeth Jones **Diameter:** 30.6 **Weight:** 12.5000 g. **Composition:** 0.9000 Silver, 0.3618 oz. ASW.

| Date | Mintage | (Proof) | MS-65 | Prf-65 |
|------|---------|---------|-------|--------|
| 1982D | 2,210,458 | — | 5.00 | — |
| 1982S | — | (4,894,044) | — | 5.25 |

**STATUE OF LIBERTY CENTENNIAL.** **Weight:** 11.3400 g. **Composition:** Copper-nickel Clad Copper

| Date | Mintage | (Proof) | MS-65 | Prf-65 |
|------|---------|---------|-------|--------|
| 1986D | 928,008 | — | 4.50 | — |
| 1986S | — | (6,925,627) | — | 5.00 |

**BICENTENNIAL OF THE CONGRESS.** **Weight:** 11.3400 g. **Composition:** Copper-nickel Clad Copper

| Date | Mintage | (Proof) | MS-65 | Prf-65 |
|------|---------|---------|-------|--------|
| 1989D | 163,753 | — | 8.00 | — |
| 1989S | — | — | — | 5.25 |

**MOUNT RUSHMORE GOLDEN ANNIVERSARY.** **Weight:** 11.3400 g. **Composition:** Copper-nickel Clad Copper

| Date | Mintage | (Proof) | MS-65 | Prf-65 |
|------|---------|---------|-------|--------|
| 1991D | 172,754 | — | 10.00 | — |
| 1991S | — | — | — | 9.00 |

**500TH ANNIVERSARY OF COLUMBUS DISCOVERY.** **Weight:** 11.3400 g. **Composition:** Copper-nickel Clad Copper

| Date | Mintage | (Proof) | MS-65 | Prf-65 |
|------|---------|---------|-------|--------|
| 1992D | 135,702 | — | 10.00 | — |
| 1992S | — | (390,154) | — | 11.00 |

**OLYMPICS.** **Weight:** 11.3400 g. **Composition:** Copper-nickel Clad Copper

| Date | Mintage | (Proof) | MS-65 | Prf-65 |
|------|---------|---------|-------|--------|
| 1992P | 161,607 | — | 5.25 | — |
| 1992S | — | (519,645) | — | 8.00 |

**JAMES MADISON AND BILL OF RIGHTS.**    **Weight:** 12.5000 g. **Composition:** 0.9000 Silver, 0.3618 oz. ASW.

| Date | Mintage | (Proof) | MS-65 | Prf-65 |
|---|---|---|---|---|
| 1993W | 173,224 | — | 14.00 | — |
| 1993S | — | (559,758) | — | 13.00 |

**WORLD WAR II 50TH ANNIVERSARY.**    **Weight:** 11.3400 g. **Composition:** Copper-nickel Clad Copper

| Date | Mintage | (Proof) | MS-65 | Prf-65 |
|---|---|---|---|---|
| 1993P | 192,968 | (290,343) | 10.00 | 12.00 |

**1994 WORLD CUP SOCCER.**    **Weight:** 11.3400 g. **Composition:** Copper-nickel Clad Copper

| Date | Mintage | (Proof) | MS-65 | Prf-65 |
|---|---|---|---|---|
| 1994D | 168,208 | — | 9.00 | — |
| 1994P | 122,412 | (609,354) | — | 10.00 |

**ATLANTA OLYMPICS.**    **Obverse:** Basketball. **Weight:** 11.3400 g. **Composition:** Copper-nickel Clad Copper

| Date | Mintage | (Proof) | MS-65 | Prf-65 |
|---|---|---|---|---|
| 1995S | 171,001 | (169,655) | 23.00 | 16.00 |

**ATLANTA OLYMPICS.**    **Obverse:** Baseball **Weight:** 11.3400 g. **Composition:** Copper-nickel Clad Copper

| Date | Mintage | (Proof) | MS-65 | Prf-65 |
|------|---------|---------|-------|--------|
| 1995S | 164,605 | (118,087) | 23.00 | 14.00 |

**CIVIL WAR.**    **Weight:** 11.3400 g. **Composition:** Copper-nickel Clad Copper

| Date | Mintage | (Proof) | MS-65 | Prf-65 |
|------|---------|---------|-------|--------|
| 1995S | 119,510 | (330,099) | 17.00 | 17.00 |

**ATLANTA OLYMPICS.**    **Obverse:** Soccer. **Weight:** 11.3400 g. **Composition:** Copper-nickel Clad Copper

| Date | Mintage | (Proof) | MS-65 | Prf-65 |
|------|---------|---------|-------|--------|
| 1996S | 52,836 | (122,412) | 31.00 | 66.00 |

**ATLANTA OLYMPICS.**    **Obverse:** Swimming. **Weight:** 11.3400 g. **Composition:** Copper-nickel Clad Copper

| Date | Mintage | (Proof) | MS-65 | Prf-65 |
|------|---------|---------|-------|--------|
| 1996S | 49,533 | (114,315) | 42.00 | 12.00 |

# DOLLAR

**LOS ANGELES XXIII OLYMPIAD.** **Obv. Designer:** Elizabeth Jones **Diameter:** 38.1 mm. **Weight:** 26.7300 g. **Composition:** 0.9000 Silver, 0.7736 oz. ASW.

| Date | Mintage | (Proof) | MS-65 | Prf-65 |
|------|---------|---------|-------|--------|
| 1983P | 294,543 | — | 11.00 | — |
| 1983D | 174,014 | — | 11.00 | — |
| 1983S | 174,014 | (1,577,025) | — | 11.00 |

**LOS ANGELES XXIII OLYMPIAD.** **Obv. Designer:** Robert Graham **Diameter:** 38.1 mm. **Weight:** 26.7300 g. **Composition:** 0.9000 Silver, 0.7736 oz. ASW.

| Date | Mintage | (Proof) | MS-65 | Prf-65 |
|------|---------|---------|-------|--------|
| 1984P | 217,954 | — | 14.00 | — |
| 1984D | 116,675 | — | 20.00 | — |
| 1984S | 116,675 | (1,801,210) | 20.00 | 11.00 |

**STATUE OF LIBERTY CENTENNIAL.** **Obv. Designer:** John Mercanti **Diameter:** 38.1 mm. **Weight:** 26.7300 g. **Composition:** 0.9000 Silver, 0.7736 oz. ASW.

| Date | Mintage | (Proof) | MS-65 | Prf-65 |
|------|---------|---------|-------|--------|
| 1986P | 723,635 | — | 11.00 | — |
| 1986S | — | (6,414,638) | — | 13.00 |

**CONSTITUTION BICENTENNIAL.** **Obv. Designer:** Patricia Lewis Verani **Diameter:** 38.1 mm. **Weight:** 26.7300 g. **Composition:** 0.9000 Silver, 0.7736 oz. ASW.

| Date | Mintage | (Proof) | MS-65 | Prf-65 |
|------|---------|---------|-------|--------|
| 1987P | 451,629 | — | 10.00 | — |
| 1987S | — | (2,747,116) | — | 12.00 |

**OLYMPICS.** **Obv. Designer:** Patricia Lewis Verani **Rev. Designer:** Sherl Joseph Winter **Diameter:** 38.1 mm. **Weight:** 26.7300 g. **Composition:** 0.9000 Silver, 0.7736 oz. ASW.

| Date | Mintage | (Proof) | MS-65 | Prf-65 |
|------|---------|---------|-------|--------|
| 1988D | 191,368 | — | 11.00 | — |
| 1988S | — | (1,359,366) | — | 11.00 |

**BICENTENNIAL OF THE CONGRESS.** **Obv. Designer:** William Woodward **Diameter:** 38.1 mm. **Weight:** 26.7300 g. **Composition:** 0.9000 Silver, 0.7736 oz. ASW.

| Date | Mintage | (Proof) | MS-65 | Prf-65 |
|------|---------|---------|-------|--------|
| 1989D | 135,203 | — | 16.00 | — |
| 1989S | — | (762,198) | — | 14.00 |

**EISENHOWER CENTENNIAL.    Obv. Designer:** John Mercanti **Rev. Designer:** Marcel Jovine **Diameter:** 38.1 mm. **Weight:** 26.7300 g. **Composition:** 0.9000 Silver, 0.7736 oz. ASW.

| Date | Mintage | (Proof) | MS-65 | Prf-65 |
|------|---------|---------|-------|--------|
| 1990W | 241,669 | — | 15.00 | — |
| 1990P | — | (638,335) | — | 14.00 |

**KOREAN WAR.    Obv. Designer:** John Mercanti **Rev. Designer:** James Ferrell **Diameter:** 38.1 mm. **Weight:** 26.7300 g. **Composition:** 0.9000 Silver, 0.7736 oz. ASW.

| Date | Mintage | (Proof) | MS-65 | Prf-65 |
|------|---------|---------|-------|--------|
| 1991D | 213,049 | — | 14.50 | — |
| 1991P | — | (618,488) | — | 14.00 |

**MOUNT RUSHMORE GOLDEN ANNIVERSARY.    Obv. Designer:** Marika Somogyi **Rev. Designer:** Frank Gasparro **Diameter:** 38.1 mm. **Weight:** 26.7300 g. **Composition:** 0.9000 Silver, 0.7736 oz. ASW. **Notes:** I

| Date | Mintage | (Proof) | MS-65 | Prf-65 |
|------|---------|---------|-------|--------|
| 1991P | 133,139 | — | 28.00 | — |
| 1991S | — | (738,419) | — | 28.00 |

**USO 50TH ANNIVERSARY.** **Obv. Designer:** Robert Lamb **Rev. Designer:** John Mercanti **Diameter:** 38.1 mm. **Weight:** 26.7300 g. **Composition:** 0.9000 Silver, 0.7736 oz. ASW.

| Date | Mintage | (Proof) | MS-65 | Prf-65 |
|------|---------|---------|-------|--------|
| 1991D | 124,958 | — | 14.50 | — |
| 1991S | — | (321,275) | — | 14.00 |

**COLUMBUS QUINCENTENARY.** **Diameter:** 38.1 mm. **Weight:** 26.7300 g. **Composition:** 0.9000 Silver, 0.7736 oz. ASW.

| Date | Mintage | (Proof) | MS-65 | Prf-65 |
|------|---------|---------|-------|--------|
| 1992D | 106,949 | — | 26.00 | — |
| 1992P | — | (385,241) | — | 30.00 |

**OLYMPICS.** **Obv. Designer:** John R. Deecken **Rev. Designer:** Marcel Jovine **Diameter:** 38.1 mm. **Weight:** 26.7300 g. **Composition:** 0.9000 Silver, 0.7736 oz. ASW.

| Date | Mintage | (Proof) | MS-65 | Prf-65 |
|------|---------|---------|-------|--------|
| 1992D | 187,552 | — | 18.00 | — |
| 1992S | — | (504,505) | — | 23.00 |

**WHITE HOUSE BICENTENNIAL.** **Diameter:** 38.1 mm. **Weight:** 26.7300 g. **Composition:** 0.9000 Silver, 0.7736 oz. ASW.

| Date | Mintage | (Proof) | MS-65 | Prf-65 |
|------|---------|---------|-------|--------|
| 1992D | 123,803 | — | 25.00 | — |
| 1992W | — | (375,851) | — | 24.00 |

**JAMES MADISON AND BILL OF RIGHTS.** **Diameter:** 38.1 mm. **Weight:** 26.7300 g. **Composition:** 0.9000 Silver, 0.7736 oz. ASW.

| Date | Mintage | (Proof) | MS-65 | Prf-65 |
|------|---------|---------|-------|--------|
| 1993D | 98,383 | — | 18.00 | — |
| 1993S | — | (534,001) | — | 20.00 |

**THOMAS JEFFERSON 250TH ANNIVERSARY OF BIRTH.** **Diameter:** 38.1 mm. **Weight:** 26.7300 g. **Composition:** 0.9000 Silver, 0.7736 oz. ASW.

| Date | Mintage | (Proof) | MS-65 | Prf-65 |
|------|---------|---------|-------|--------|
| 1993P | 266,927 | — | 25.00 | — |
| 1993S | — | (332,891) | — | 27.00 |

**WORLD WAR II 50TH ANNIVERSARY.** Diameter: 38.1 mm. **Weight:** 26.7300 g. **Composition:** 0.9000 Silver, 0.7736 oz. ASW.

| Date | Mintage | (Proof) | MS-65 | Prf-65 |
|------|---------|---------|-------|--------|
| 1993D | 94,708 | — | 23.00 | — |
| 1993W | — | (322,422) | — | 29.00 |

**NATIONAL PRISONER OF WAR MUSEUM.** Diameter: 38.1 mm. **Weight:** 26.7300 g. **Composition:** 0.9000 Silver, 0.7736 oz. ASW.

| Date | Mintage | (Proof) | MS-65 | Prf-65 |
|------|---------|---------|-------|--------|
| 1994W | 54,790 | — | 34.00 | — |
| 1994P | — | (220,100) | — | 30.00 |

**U.S. CAPITOL BICENTENNIAL.** Diameter: 38.1 mm. **Weight:** 26.7300 g. **Composition:** 0.9000 Silver, 0.7736 oz. ASW.

| Date | Mintage | (Proof) | MS-65 | Prf-65 |
|------|---------|---------|-------|--------|
| 1994D | 68,352 | — | 19.00 | — |
| 1994S | — | (279,416) | — | 20.00 |

**VIETNAM VETERANS MEMORIAL.**    **Diameter:** 38.1 mm. **Weight:** 26.7300 g. **Composition:** 0.9000 Silver, 0.7736 oz. ASW.

| Date | Mintage | (Proof) | MS-65 | Prf-65 |
|---|---|---|---|---|
| 1994W | 57,317 | — | 42.00 | — |
| 1994P | — | (226,262) | — | 41.00 |

**WOMEN IN MILITARY SERVICE MEMORIAL.**    **Diameter:** 38.1 mm. **Weight:** 26.7300 g. **Composition:** 0.9000 Silver, 0.7736 oz. ASW.

| Date | Mintage | (Proof) | MS-65 | Prf-65 |
|---|---|---|---|---|
| 1994W | 53,054 | — | 22.00 | — |
| 1994P | — | (213,201) | — | 22.00 |

**WORLD CUP SOCCER.**    **Diameter:** 38.1 mm. **Weight:** 26.7300 g. **Composition:** 0.9000 Silver, 0.7736 oz. ASW.

| Date | Mintage | (Proof) | MS-65 | Prf-65 |
|---|---|---|---|---|
| 1994D | 81,698 | — | 27.00 | — |
| 1994S | — | (576,978) | — | 28.00 |

 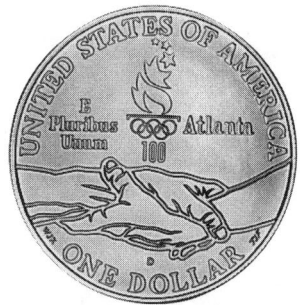

**ATLANTA OLYMPICS.** **Obverse:** Gymnastics. **Diameter:** 38.1 mm. **Weight:** 26.7300 g. **Composition:** 0.9000 Silver, 0.7736 oz. ASW.

| Date | Mintage | (Proof) | MS-65 | Prf-65 |
|------|---------|---------|-------|--------|
| 1995D | 42,497 | — | 60.00 | — |
| 1995P | — | (182,676) | — | 29.00 |

**ATLANTA OLYMPICS.** **Obverse:** Track and field. **Diameter:** 38.1 mm. **Weight:** 26.7300 g. **Composition:** 0.9000 Silver, 0.7736 oz. ASW.

| Date | Mintage | (Proof) | MS-65 | Prf-65 |
|------|---------|---------|-------|--------|
| 1995D | 24,796 | — | 55.00 | — |
| 1995P | — | (136,935) | — | 26.50 |

**ATLANTA OLYMPICS.** **Obverse:** Cycling. **Diameter:** 38.1 mm. **Weight:** 26.7300 g. **Composition:** 0.9000 Silver, 0.7736 oz. ASW.

| Date | Mintage | (Proof) | MS-65 | Prf-65 |
|------|---------|---------|-------|--------|
| 1995D | 19,662 | — | 80.00 | — |
| 1995P | — | (118,795) | — | 32.50 |

**ATLANTA OLYMPICS, PARALYMPICS.**    **Obverse:** Blind runner. **Diameter:** 38.1 mm. **Weight:** 26.7300 g. **Composition:** 0.9000 Silver, 0.7736 oz. ASW.

| Date | Mintage | (Proof) | MS-65 | Prf-65 |
|---|---|---|---|---|
| 1995D | 28,649 | — | 80.00 | — |
| 1995P | — | (138,337) | — | 32.50 |

**CIVIL WAR.**   **Diameter:** 38.1 mm. **Weight:** 26.7300 g. **Composition:** 0.9000 Silver, 0.7736 oz. ASW.

| Date | Mintage | (Proof) | MS-65 | Prf-65 |
|---|---|---|---|---|
| 1995P | 45,866 | — | 28.00 | — |
| 1995S | — | (55,246) | — | 36.00 |

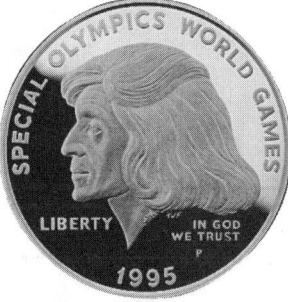

**SPECIAL OLYMPICS WORLD GAMES.**    **Diameter:** 38.1 mm. **Weight:** 26.7300 g. **Composition:** 0.9000 Silver, 0.7736 oz. ASW.

| Date | Mintage | (Proof) | MS-65 | Prf-65 |
|---|---|---|---|---|
| 1995W | 89,301 | — | 22.00 | — |
| 1995P | — | (351,764) | — | 27.00 |

**ATLANTA OLYMPICS.** **Obverse:** Tennis. **Diameter:** 38.1 mm. **Weight:** 26.7300 g. **Composition:** 0.9000 Silver, 0.7736 oz. ASW.

| Date | Mintage | (Proof) | MS-65 | Prf-65 |
|------|---------|---------|-------|--------|
| 1996D | 15,983 | — | 135 | — |
| 1996P | — | (92,016) | — | 50.00 |

**ATLANTA OLYMPICS.** **Obverse:** Rowing. **Diameter:** 38.1 mm. **Weight:** 26.7300 g. **Composition:** 0.9000 Silver, 0.7736 oz. ASW.

| Date | Mintage | (Proof) | MS-65 | Prf-65 |
|------|---------|---------|-------|--------|
| 1996D | 16,258 | — | 200 | — |
| 1996P | — | (151,890) | — | 40.00 |

**ATLANTA OLYMPICS.** **Obverse:** High jumper **Weight:** 26.7300 g. **Composition:** 0.9000 Silver, .7736 oz. ASW.

| Date | Mintage | (Proof) | MS-65 | Prf-65 |
|------|---------|---------|-------|--------|
| 1996D | 15,697 | — | 200 | — |
| 1996P | — | (124,502) | — | 32.00 |

**ATLANTA OLYMPICS, PARALYMPICS.    Obverse:** Wheelchair racer. **Diameter:** 38.1 mm. **Weight:** 26.7300 g. **Composition:** 0.9000 Silver, 0.7736 oz. ASW.

| Date | Mintage | (Proof) | MS-65 | Prf-65 |
|------|---------|---------|-------|--------|
| 1996D | 14,497 | — | 190 | — |
| 1996P | — | (84,280) | — | 48.00 |

**NATIONAL COMMUNITY SERVICE.    Diameter:** 38.1 mm. **Weight:** 26.7300 g. **Composition:** 0.9000 Silver, 0.7736 oz. ASW.

| Date | Mintage | (Proof) | MS-65 | Prf-65 |
|------|---------|---------|-------|--------|
| 1996S | 23,500 | — | 240 | — |
| 1996S | — | (101,543) | — | 30.00 |

**SMITHSONIAN 150TH ANNIVERSARY.    Diameter:** 38.1 mm. **Weight:** 26.7300 g. **Composition:** 0.9000 Silver, 0.7736 oz. ASW.

| Date | Mintage | (Proof) | MS-65 | Prf-65 |
|------|---------|---------|-------|--------|
| 1996D | 31,230 | — | 85.00 | — |
| 1996P | — | (129,152) | — | 32.50 |

**JACKIE ROBINSON 50TH ANNIVERSARY.** **Diameter:** 38.1 mm. **Weight:** 26.7300 g. **Composition:**
0.9000 Silver, 0.7736 oz. ASW.

| Date | Mintage | (Proof) | MS-65 | Prf-65 |
|------|---------|---------|-------|--------|
| 1997S | 30,007 | (110,495) | 50.00 | 30.00 |

**NATIONAL LAW ENFORCEMENT OFFICERS MEMORIAL.** **Diameter:** 38.1 mm. **Weight:** 26.7300 g.
**Composition:** 0.9000 Silver, 0.7736 oz. ASW.

| Date | Mintage | (Proof) | MS-65 | Prf-65 |
|------|---------|---------|-------|--------|
| 1997P | 28,575 | (110,428) | 90.00 | 100.00 |

**U.S. BOTANIC GARDENS 175TH ANNIVERSARY.** **Diameter:** 38.1 mm. **Weight:** 26.7300 g. **Composi-**
**tion:** 0.9000 Silver, 0.7736 oz. ASW.

| Date | Mintage | (Proof) | MS-65 | Prf-65 |
|------|---------|---------|-------|--------|
| 1997P | 57,272 | (264,528) | 45.00 | 37.00 |

**BLACK PATRIOTS.   Obverse:** Crispus Attucks. **Diameter:** 38.1 mm. **Weight:** 26.7300 g. **Composition:** 0.9000 Silver, 0.7736 oz. ASW.

| Date | Mintage | (Proof) | MS-65 | Prf-65 |
|---|---|---|---|---|
| 1998S | 37,210 | (75,070) | 85.00 | 80.00 |

**ROBERT F. KENNEDY.   Diameter:** 38.1 mm. **Weight:** 26.7300 g. **Composition:** 0.9000 Silver, 0.7736 oz. ASW.

| Date | Mintage | (Proof) | MS-65 | Prf-65 |
|---|---|---|---|---|
| 1998S | 106,422 | (99,020) | 30.00 | 40.00 |

**DOLLEY MADISON.   Diameter:** 38.1 mm. **Weight:** 26.7300 g. **Composition:** 0.9000 Silver, 0.7736 oz. ASW.

| Date | Mintage | (Proof) | MS-65 | Prf-65 |
|---|---|---|---|---|
| 1999P | — | — | 38.00 | 41.00 |

**YELLOWSTONE.   Diameter:** 38.1 mm. **Weight:** 26.7300 g. **Composition:** 0.9000 Silver, 0.7736 oz. ASW.

| Date | Mintage | (Proof) | MS-65 | Prf-65 |
|---|---|---|---|---|
| 1999P | — | — | 38.00 | 38.00 |

# $5 (HALF EAGLE)

**STATUE OF LIBERTY CENTENNIAL.   Diameter:** 21.6 mm. **Weight:** 8.3590 g. **Composition:** 0.9000 Gold, 0.242 oz. AGW.

| Date | Mintage | (Proof) | MS-65 | Prf-65 |
|---|---|---|---|---|
| 1986W | 95,248 | (404,013) | 100.00 | 100.00 |

**CONSTITUTION BICENTENNIAL.    Obv. Designer:** Marcel Jovine **Diameter:** 21.6 mm. **Weight:** 8.3590 g. **Composition:** 0.9000 Gold, 0.242 oz. AGW.

| Date | Mintage | (Proof) | MS-65 | Prf-65 |
|------|---------|---------|-------|--------|
| 1987W | 214,225 | (651,659) | 100.00 | 100.00 |

**OLYMPICS.   Obv. Designer:** Elizabeth Jones **Rev. Designer:** Marcel Jovine **Diameter:** 21.6 mm. **Weight:** 8.3590 g. **Composition:** 0.9000 Gold, 0.242 oz. AGW.

| Date | Mintage | (Proof) | MS-65 | Prf-65 |
|------|---------|---------|-------|--------|
| 1988W | 62,913 | (281,456) | 100.00 | 100.00 |

**BICENTENNIAL OF THE CONGRESS.   Obv. Designer:** John Mercanti **Diameter:** 21.6 mm. **Weight:** 8.3590 g. **Composition:** 0.9000 Gold, 0.242 oz. AGW.

| Date | Mintage | (Proof) | MS-65 | Prf-65 |
|------|---------|---------|-------|--------|
| 1989W | 46,899 | (164,690) | 105 | 105 |

**MOUNT RUSHMORE GOLDEN ANNIVERSARY.   Obv. Designer:** John Mercanti **Rev. Designer:** Robert Lamb **Diameter:** 21.6 mm. **Weight:** 8.3590 g. **Composition:** 0.9000 Gold, 0.242 oz. AGW.

| Date | Mintage | (Proof) | MS-65 | Prf-65 |
|------|---------|---------|-------|--------|
| 1991W | 31,959 | (111,991) | 120 | 115 |

**COLUMBUS QUINCENTENARY.    Diameter:** 21.6 mm. **Weight:** 8.3590 g. **Composition:** 0.9000 Gold, 0.242 oz. AGW.

| Date | Mintage | (Proof) | MS-65 | Prf-65 |
|------|---------|---------|-------|--------|
| 1992W | 24,329 | (79,730) | 130 | 130 |

**OLYMPICS.   Obv. Designer:** James C. Sharpe **Rev. Designer:** James M. Peed **Diameter:** 21.6 mm. **Weight:** 8.3590 g. **Composition:** 0.9000 Gold, 0.242 oz. AGW.

| Date | Mintage | (Proof) | MS-65 | Prf-65 |
|------|---------|---------|-------|--------|
| 1992W | 27,732 | (77,313) | 120 | 115 |

**JAMES MADISON AND BILL OF RIGHTS.**    **Diameter:** 21.6 mm. **Weight:** 8.3590 g. **Composition:** 0.9000 Gold, 0.242 oz. AGW.

| Date | Mintage | (Proof) | MS-65 | Prf-65 |
|------|---------|---------|-------|--------|
| 1993W | 22,266 | (78,651) | 135 | 110 |

**WORLD WAR II 50TH ANNIVERSARY.**    **Diameter:** 21.6 mm. **Weight:** 8.3590 g. **Composition:** 0.9000 Gold, 0.242 oz. AGW.

| Date | Mintage | (Proof) | MS-65 | Prf-65 |
|------|---------|---------|-------|--------|
| 1993W | 23,089 | — | 125 | 135 |

**WORLD CUP SOCCER.**    **Diameter:** 21.6 mm. **Weight:** 8.3590 g. **Composition:** 0.9000 Gold, 0.242 oz. AGW.

| Date | Mintage | (Proof) | MS-65 | Prf-65 |
|------|---------|---------|-------|--------|
| 1994W | 22,464 | (89,619) | 130 | 115 |

**CIVIL WAR.**    **Diameter:** 21.6 mm. **Weight:** 8.3590 g. **Composition:** 0.9000 Gold, 0.242 oz. AGW.

| Date | Mintage | (Proof) | MS-65 | Prf-65 |
|------|---------|---------|-------|--------|
| 1995W | 12,735 | (55,246) | 275 | 200 |

**OLYMPICS.**    **Obverse:** Torch runner. **Diameter:** 21.6 mm. **Weight:** 8.3590 g. **Composition:** 0.9000 Gold, 0.242 oz. AGW.

| Date | Mintage | (Proof) | MS-65 | Prf-65 |
|------|---------|---------|-------|--------|
| 1995W | 14,675 | (57,442) | 200 | 140 |

**OLYMPICS.** **Obverse:** Stadium. **Diameter:** 21.6 mm. **Weight:** 8.3590 g. **Composition:** 0.9000 Gold, 0.242 oz. AGW.

| Date | Mintage | (Proof) | MS-65 | Prf-65 |
|------|---------|---------|-------|--------|
| 1995W | 10,579 | (43,124) | 260 | 160 |

**OLYMPICS.** **Obverse:** Flag bearer. **Diameter:** 21.6 mm. **Weight:** 8.3590 g. **Composition:** 0.9000 Gold, 0.242 oz. AGW.

| Date | Mintage | (Proof) | MS-65 | Prf-65 |
|------|---------|---------|-------|--------|
| 1996W | 9,174 | (32,886) | 270 | 235 |

**OLYMPICS.** **Obverse:** Cauldron. **Diameter:** 21.6 mm. **Weight:** 8.3590 g. **Composition:** 0.9000 Gold, 0.242 oz. AGW.

| Date | Mintage | (Proof) | MS-65 | Prf-65 |
|------|---------|---------|-------|--------|
| 1996W | 9,210 | (38,555) | 270 | 235 |

**SMITHSONIAN 150TH ANNIVERSARY.** **Diameter:** 21.6 mm. **Weight:** 8.3590 g. **Composition:** 0.9000 Gold, 0.242 oz. AGW.

| Date | Mintage | (Proof) | MS-65 | Prf-65 |
|------|---------|---------|-------|--------|
| 1996W | 9,068 | (21,772) | 360 | 205 |

**FRANKLIN DELANO ROOSEVELT.** **Diameter:** 21.6 mm. **Weight:** 8.3590 g. **Composition:** 0.9000 Gold, 0.242 oz. AGW.

| Date | Mintage | (Proof) | MS-65 | Prf-65 |
|------|---------|---------|-------|--------|
| 1997W | 11,894 | (29,474) | 225 | 190 |

**JACKIE ROBINSON 50TH ANNIVERSARY.** **Diameter:** 21.6 mm. **Weight:** 8.3590 g. **Composition:** 0.9000 Gold, 0.242 oz. AGW.

| Date | Mintage | (Proof) | MS-65 | Prf-65 |
|------|---------|---------|-------|--------|
| 1997W | 5,202 | (24,546) | 875 | 250 |

**GEORGE WASHINGTON.** **Diameter:** 21.6 mm. **Weight:** 8.3590 g. **Composition:** 0.9000 Gold, 0.242 oz. AGW.

| Date | Mintage | (Proof) | MS-65 | Prf-65 |
|------|---------|---------|-------|--------|
| 1999W | — | — | 235 | 195 |

# $10 (EAGLE)

**LOS ANGELES XXIII OLYMPIAD.** **Diameter:** 27 mm. **Weight:** 16.7180 g. **Composition:** 0.9000 Gold, 0.4839 oz. AGW.

| Date | Mintage | (Proof) | MS-65 | Prf-65 |
|------|---------|---------|-------|--------|
| 1984W | 75,886 | (381,085) | 215 | 215 |
| 1984P | 33,309 | — | — | 275 |
| 1984D | 34,533 | — | — | 260 |
| 1984S | 48,551 | — | — | 220 |

**LIBRARY OF CONGRESS.** **Weight:** 16.2590 g. **Composition:** Platinum-gold-alloy **Notes:** Composition is 48 percent platinum, 48 percent gold, and 4 percent alloy.

| Date | Mintage | (Proof) | MS-65 | Prf-65 |
|------|---------|---------|-------|--------|
| 2000P | 7,200 | — | 405 | — |
| 2000P | — | (27,400) | — | 425 |
| 2000W | — | — | — | — |
| 2000W | — | — | — | — |

# MODERN COMMEMORATIVE COIN SETS (CCS)

## Olympic, 1983-1984

| Date | Price |
|------|-------|
| 1983 collectors set: 1983 PDS uncirculated dollars; KM209. | 30.00 |
| 1983 & 1984 gold and silver uncirculated set: One 1983 and one 1984 uncirculated dollar and one 1984 uncirculated gold $10; KM209,210,211. | 265 |
| 1983 & 1984 gold and silver proof set: One 1983 and one 1984 proof dollar and one 1984 proof gold $10; KM209,210,211. | 265 |
| 1983 & 1984 6 coin set: One 1983 and one 1984 uncirculated and proof dollar, one uncirculated and one proof gold $10; KM209,210,211. | 500 |
| 1983 & 1984 proof dollars | — |
| 1984 collectors set:  1984 PDS uncirculated dollars; KM210. | 50.00 |

## Statue of Liberty

| Date | Price |
|------|-------|
| 1986 2 coin set: uncirculated silver dollar and clad half dollar; KM212,214. | 16.00 |
| 1986 2 coin set: proof silver dollar and clad half dollar; KM212,214. | 16.50 |
| 1986 3 coin set: uncirculated silver dollar, clad half dollar and gold $5; KM212,214,215. | 160 |
| 1986 3 coin set: proof silver dollar, clad half dollar and gold $5; KM212,214,215. | 160 |
| 1986 6 coin set: 1 each of the proof and uncirculated issues; KM212,214,215. | 270 |

## Constitution

| Date | Price |
|------|-------|
| 1987 2 coin set: uncirculated silver dollar and gold $5; KM220,221. | 140 |
| 1987 2 coin set: proof silver dollar and gold $5; KM220,221. | 130 |
| 1987 4 coin set: 1 each of the proof and uncirculated issues; KM220,221. | 275 |

## Olympic, 1988

| Date | Price |
|------|-------|
| 1988 2 coin set: uncirculated silver dollar and gold $5; KM222,223. | 145 |
| 1988 2 coin set: Proof silver dollar and gold $5; KM222,223 . | 135 |
| 1988 4 coin set: 1 each of proof and uncirculated issues; KM222,223. | 290 |

## Congress

| Date | Price |
|------|-------|
| 1989 2 coin set: uncirculated silver dollar and clad half dollar; KM224,225. | 22.00 |
| 1989 2 coin set: proof silver dollar and clad half dollar; KM224,225. | 17.50 |
| 1989 3 coin set: uncirculated silver dollar, clad half and gold $5; KM224,225,226. | 160 |
| 1989 3 coin set: proof silver dollar, clad half and gold $5; KM224, 225, 226. | 160 |
| 1989 6 coin set: 1 each of the proof and uncirculated issues; KM224,225,226. | 310 |

## Mt. Rushmore

| Date | Price |
|------|-------|
| 1991 2 coin set: uncirculated half dollar and silver dollar; KM228,229. | 36.00 |
| 1991 2 coin set: proof half dollar and silver dollar; KM228,229. | 35.00 |
| 1991 3 coin set: uncirculated half dollar, silver dollar and gold $5; KM228,229,230. | 170 |
| 1991 3 coin set: proof half dollar, silver dollar and gold $5; KM228,229,230. | 165 |
| 1991 6 coin set: 1 each of proof and uncirculated issues; KM228,229,230. | 310 |

## Olympic, 1992

| Date | Price |
|------|-------|
| 1992 2 coin set: uncirculated half dollar and silver dollar; KM233,234. | 25.00 |
| 1992 2 coin set: proof half dollar and silver dollar; KM233,234. | 35.00 |
| 1992 3 coin set: uncirculated half dollar, silver dollar and gold $5; KM233,234,235. | 160 |
| 1992 3 coin set: proof half dollar, silver dollar and gold $5; KM233,234,235. | 160 |
| 1992 6 coin set: 1 each of proof and uncirculated issues; KM233,234,235. | 315 |

## Columbus Quincentenary

| Date | Price |
|------|-------|
| 1992 2 coin set: uncirculated half dollar and silver dollar; KM237,238. | 34.00 |
| 1992 2 coin set: proof half dollar and silver dollar; KM237,238. | 36.00 |
| 1992 3 coin set: uncirculated half dollar, silver dollar and gold $5; KM237,238,239. | 180 |
| 1992 3 coin set: proof half dollar, silver dollar and gold $5; KM237,238,239. | 165 |
| 1992 6 coin set: 1 each of proof and uncirculated issues; KM237,238,239. | 360 |

## Jefferson

| Date | Price |
|------|-------|
| 1993 Jefferson: dollar, nickel and $2 note; KM249,192. | 80.00 |

## Madison / Bill of Rights

| Date | Price |
|------|-------|
| 1993 2 coin set: uncirculated half dollar and silver dollar; KM240,241. | 27.50 |
| 1993 2 coin set: proof half dollar and silver dollar; KM240,241. | 27.50 |
| 1993 3 coin set: uncirculated half dollar, silver dollar and gold $5; KM240,241,242. | 180 |
| 1993 3 coin set: proof half dollar, silver dollar and gold $5; KM240,241,242. | 170 |
| 1993 6 coin set: 1 each of proof and uncirculated issues; KM240,241,242. | 340 |

# World War II

| Date | Price |
|---|---|
| 1993 2 coin set: uncirculated half dollar and silver dollar; KM243,244. | 27.50 |
| 1993 2 coin set: proof half dollar and silver dollar; KM243,244. | 31.00 |
| 1993 3 coin set: uncirculated half dollar, silver dollar and gold $5; KM243,244,245. | 180 |
| 1993 3 coin set: proof half dollar, silver dollar and gold $5; KM243,244,245. | 175 |
| 1993 6 coin set: 1 each of proof and uncirculated issues; KM243,244,245. | 325 |

# World Cup

| Date | Price |
|---|---|
| 1994 2 coin set: uncirculated half dollar and silver dollar; KM246,247. | 31.00 |
| 1994 2 coin set: proof half dollar and silver dollar; KM246,247. | 32.50 |
| 1994 3 coin set: uncirculated half dollar, silver dollar and gold $5; KM246,247,248. | 185 |
| 1994 3 coin set: proof half dollar, silver dollar and gold $5; KM246,247,248. | 175 |
| 1994 6 coin set: 1 each of proof and uncirculated issues; KM246,247,248. | 530 |

# U.S. Veterans

| Date | Price |
|---|---|
| 1994 3 coin set: uncirculated POW, Vietnam, Women dollars; KM250,251,252. | 85.00 |
| 1994 3 coin set: proof POW, Vietnam, Women dollars; KM250,251,252. | 70.00 |

# Olympic, 1995-96

| Date | Price |
|---|---|
| 1995 4 coin set: uncirculated basketball half, $1 gymnast & blind runner, $5 torch runner; KM257,259,260,261. | 290 |
| 1995 4 coin set: proof basketball half, $1 gymnast & blind runner, $5 torch runner; KM257,259,260,261. | 200 |
| 1995 2 coin set: proof $1 gymnast & blind runner; KM259,260. | 72.00 |
| 1995 2 coin set: proof $1 track & field, cycling; KM263,264. | 76.00 |
| 1995-96 4 coin set: proof halves, basketball, baseball, swimming, soccer; KM257,262,267,271. | 58.00 |

# Civil War

| Date | Price |
|---|---|
| 1995 2 coin set: uncirculated half and dollar; KM254,255. | 40.00 |
| 1995 2 coin set: proof half and dollar; KM254,255. | 40.00 |
| 1995 3 coin set: uncirculated half, dollar and gold $5; KM254,255,256. | 325 |
| 1995 3 coin set: proof half, dollar and gold $5; KM254,255,256. | 210 |
| 1995 6 coin set: 1 each of proof and uncirculated issues; KM254,255,256. | 530 |

# Smithsonian

| Date | Price |
|---|---|
| 1996 2 coin set: Smithsonian proof dollar and $5 gold; KM276,277. | 230 |
| 1996 4 coin set: proof and B.U. ; KM276,277. | 700 |

# Botanic Garden

| Date | Price |
|---|---|
| 1997 dollar, Jefferson nickel and $1 note; KM278,192. | 180 |

# Jackie Robinson

| Date | Price |
|---|---|
| 1997 2 coin set: proof dollar & $5 gold; KM279,280. | 240 |
| 1997 4 coin set: proof & BU; KM279,280. | 1,100 |
| 1997 legacy set. | 400 |

# Kennedy

| Date | Price |
|---|---|
| 1998 2 coin set: proof; KM287. | 80.00 |
| 1998 2 coin collectors set: matte finished Robert Kennedy dollar and John Kennedy half dollar; KM287,202b. | 235 |

# Dolley Madison

| Date | Price |
|---|---|
| 2000 Proof and uncirculated silver dollars | 80.00 |

# George Washington

| Date | Price |
|---|---|
| 2000 Proof and uncirculated gold $5 | 450.00 |

# Yellowstone National Park

| Date | Price |
|---|---|
| 2000 Proof and uncirculated silver dollars | 90.00 |

# Leif Erickson

| Date | Price |
|---|---|
| 2000 Proof and uncirculated silver dollars | 130.00 |

# MINT SETS (MS)

Mint, or uncirculated, sets contain one uncirculated coin of each denomination from each mint produced for circulation that year. Values listed here are only for those sets sold by the U.S. Mint. Sets were not offered in years not listed. In years when the Mint did not offer the sets, some private companies compiled and marketed uncirculated sets. Mint sets from 1947 through 1958 contained two examples of each coin mounted in cardboard holders, which caused the coins to tarnish. Beginning in 1959, the sets have been packaged in sealed Pliofilm packets and include only one specimen of each coin struck for that year. Listings for 1965, 1966 and 1967 are for "special mint sets," which were of higher quality than regular mint sets and were prooflike. They were packaged in plastic cases. The 1970 large-date and small-date varieties are distinguished by the size of the date on the coin. The 1976 three-piece set contains the quarter, half dollar and dollar with the Bicentennial design. The 1971 and 1972 sets do not include a dollar coin; the 1979 set does not include an S-mint-marked dollar.

| Date | | Sets Sold | Issue Price | Value | Date | | Sets Sold | Issue Price | Value |
|---|---|---|---|---|---|---|---|---|---|
| 1947 | Est. 5,000 | 5,000 | 4.87 | 875 | 1974 | | 1,975,981 | 6.00 | 8.00 |
| 1948 | Est. 6,000 | 6,000 | 4.92 | 400 | 1975 | | 1,921,488 | 6.00 | 9.00 |
| 1949 | Est. 5,200 | 5,200 | 5.45 | 630 | 1976 3 coins | | 4,908,319 | 9.00 | 13.00 |
| 1950 | None issued | — | — | — | 1976 | | 1,892,513 | 6.00 | 9.00 |
| 1951 | | 8,654 | 6.75 | 575 | 1977 | | 2,006,869 | 7.00 | 9.00 |
| 1952 | | 11,499 | 6.14 | 525 | 1978 | | 2,162,609 | 7.00 | 9.00 |
| 1953 | | 15,538 | 6.14 | 385 | 1979 | | 2,526,000 | 8.00 | 8.00 |
| 1954 | | 25,599 | 6.19 | 230 | 1980 | | 2,815,066 | 9.00 | 8.00 |
| 1955 | | 49,656 | 3.57 | 110 | 1981 | | 2,908,145 | 11.00 | 19.00 |
| 1956 | | 45,475 | 3.34 | 100.00 | 1982 & 1983 None | | | | |
| 1957 | | 32,324 | 4.40 | 150 | issued | | — | — | — |
| 1958 | | 50,314 | 4.43 | 115 | 1984 | | 1,832,857 | 7.00 | 7.00 |
| 1959 | | 187,000 | 2.40 | 30.00 | 1985 | | 1,710,571 | 7.00 | 8.00 |
| 1960 | | 260,485 | 2.40 | 21.00 | 1986 | | 1,153,536 | 7.00 | 22.00 |
| 1961 | | 223,704 | 2.40 | 33.00 | 1987 | | 2,890,758 | 7.00 | 8.00 |
| 1962 | | 385,285 | 2.40 | 18.00 | 1988 | | 1,646,204 | 7.00 | 9.00 |
| 1963 | | 606,612 | 2.40 | 15.00 | 1989 | | 1,987,915 | 7.00 | 9.00 |
| 1964 | | 1,008,108 | 2.40 | 12.00 | 1990 | | 1,809,184 | 7.00 | 9.00 |
| 1965 SMS* | | 2,360,000 | 4.00 | 11.00 | 1991 | | 1,352,101 | 7.00 | 8.00 |
| 1966 SMS* | | 2,261,583 | 4.00 | 9.00 | 1992 | | 1,500,143 | 7.00 | 8.00 |
| 1967 SMS* | | 1,863,344 | 4.00 | 10.00 | 1993 | | 1,297,094 | 8.00 | 9.00 |
| 1968 | | 2,105,128 | 2.50 | 4.00 | 1994 | | 1,234,813 | 8.00 | 10.00 |
| 1969 | | 1,817,392 | 2.50 | 6.00 | 1995 | | 1,038,787 | 8.00 | 19.00 |
| 1970 large date | | 2,038,134 | 2.50 | 13.00 | 1996 | | 1,457,949 | 8.00 | 14.00 |
| 1970 small date | | Inc. above | 2.50 | 36.00 | 1997 | | 950,473 | 8.00 | 12.00 |
| 1971 | | 2,193,396 | 3.50 | 4.00 | 1998 | | 1,187,325 | 8.00 | 19.00 |
| 1972 | | 2,750,000 | 3.50 | 4.00 | 1999 | | 1,243,867 | 14.95 | 22.00 |
| 1973 | | 1,767,691 | 6.00 | 21.00 | | | | | |

# PROOF SETS (PS)

Proof coins are produced through a special process involving specially selected, highly polished planchets and dies. They usually receive two strikings from the coin press at increased pressure. The result is a coin with mirrorlike surfaces and, in recent years, a cameo effect on its raised design surfaces. Proof sets have been sold off and on by the U.S. Mint since 1858. Listings here are for sets from what is commonly called the modern era, since 1936. Values for earlier proofs are included in regular date listings. Sets were not offered in years not listed. Since 1968, proof coins have been produced at the San Francisco Mint; before that they were produced at the Philadelphia Mint. In 1942 the five-cent coin was struck in two compositions. Some proof sets for that year contain only one type (five-coin set); others contain both types. Two types of packaging were used in 1955 -- a box and a flat, plastic holder. The 1960 large-date and small-date sets are distinguished by the size of the date on the cent. Some 1968 sets are missing the mint mark on the dime, the result of an error in the preparation of an obverse die. The 1970 large-date and small-date sets are distinguished by the size of the date on the cent. Some 1970 sets are missing the mint mark on the dime, the result of an error in the preparation of an obverse die. Some 1971 sets are missing the mint mark on the five-cent piece, the result of an error in the preparation of an obverse die. The 1976 three-piece set contains the quarter, half dollar and dollar with the Bicentennial designs. The 1979 and 1981 Type II sets have clearer mint marks than the Type I sets for those years. Some 1983 sets are missing the mint mark on the dime, the result of an error in the preparation of an obverse die. Prestige sets contain the five regular-issue coins plus a commemorative silver dollar from that year.

| Date | Sets Sold | Issue Price | Value | Date | Sets Sold | Issue Price | Value |
|---|---|---|---|---|---|---|---|
| 1936 | 3,837 | 1.89 | 5,000 | 1951 | 57,500 | 2.10 | 510 |
| 1937 | 5,542 | 1.89 | 2,200 | 1952 | 81,980 | 2.10 | 265 |
| 1938 | 8,045 | 1.89 | 1,000 | 1953 | 128,800 | 2.10 | 240 |
| 1939 | 8,795 | 1.89 | 1,000 | 1954 | 233,300 | 2.10 | 100.00 |
| 1940 | 11,246 | 1.89 | 800 | 1955 box | 378,200 | 2.10 | 80.00 |
| 1941 | 15,287 | 1.89 | 675 | 1955 flat pack | Inc. above | 2.10 | 85.00 |
| 1942 6 coins | 21,120 | 1.89 | 825 | 1956 | 669,384 | 2.10 | 35.00 |
| 1942 5 coins | Inc. above | 1.89 | 700 | 1957 | 1,247,952 | 2.10 | 18.00 |
| 1950 | 51,386 | 2.10 | 515 | 1958 | 875,652 | 2.10 | 31.00 |

| Date | Sets Sold | Issue Price | Value | Date | Sets Sold | Issue Price | Value |
|---|---|---|---|---|---|---|---|
| 1959 | 1,149,291 | 2.10 | 23.00 | 1988S Prestige set | 231,661 | 45.00 | 37.00 |
| 1960 large date | 1,691,602 | 2.10 | 15.00 | 1989S | 3,009,107 | 11.00 | 17.00 |
| 1960 small date | Inc. above | 2.10 | 25.00 | 1989S Prestige set | 211,087 | 45.00 | 39.00 |
| 1961 | 3,028,244 | 2.10 | 11.00 | 1990S | 2,793,433 | 11.00 | 26.00 |
| 1962 | 3,218,019 | 2.10 | 11.00 | 1990S no S 1¢ | 3,555 | 11.00 | 1,850 |
| 1963 | 3,075,645 | 2.10 | 12.00 | 1990S Prestige set | 506,126 | 45.00 | 26.00 |
| 1964 | 3,950,762 | 2.10 | 9.00 | 1990S Prestige set, | | | |
| 1968S | 3,041,509 | 5.00 | 6.00 | no-mint-mark cent | 506,126 | 45.00 | 1,900 |
| 1968S no-mint-mark | | | | 1991s | 2,610,833 | 11.00 | 41.00 |
| dime | 3,041,509 | 5.00 | 8,200 | 1991s Prestige set | 256,954 | 59.00 | 70.00 |
| 1969S | 2,934,631 | 5.00 | 7.00 | 1992S | 2,675,618 | 12.50 | 15.00 |
| 1970S large date | 2,632,810 | 5.00 | 11.00 | 1992S Prestige set | 183,285 | 59.00 | 48.00 |
| 1970S small date | Inc. above | 5.00 | 55.00 | 1992S Silver | 1,009,585 | 21.00 | 18.00 |
| 1970S no-mint-mark | | | | 1992S Silver premier | 308,055 | 37.00 | 19.00 |
| dime | Inc. above | 5.00 | 440 | 1993S | 2,337,819 | 12.50 | 21.00 |
| 1971S | 3,224,138 | 5.00 | 5.00 | 1993S Prestige set | 224,045 | 57.00 | 37.00 |
| 1971S no-mint-mark | | | | 1993S Silver | 570,213 | 21.00 | 33.00 |
| nickel Est. 1,655 | 1,655 | 5.00 | 660 | 1993S Silver premier | 191,140 | 37.00 | 33.00 |
| 1972S | 3,267,667 | 5.00 | 6.00 | 1994S | 2,308,701 | 13.00 | 14.00 |
| 1973S | 2,769,624 | 7.00 | 12.00 | 1994S Prestige Set | 175,893 | 57.00 | 58.00 |
| 1974S | 2,617,350 | 7.00 | 12.00 | 1994S Silver | 636,009 | 21.00 | 42.00 |
| 1975S | 2,909,369 | 7.00 | 13.00 | 1994S Silver premier | 149,320 | 37.50 | 53.00 |
| 1976S 3 coins | 3,998,621 | 12.00 | 19.00 | 1995S | 2,010,384 | 12.50 | 72.00 |
| 1976S | 4,149,730 | 7.00 | 12.00 | 1995S Silver | 549,878 | 21.00 | 130 |
| 1977S | 3,251,152 | 9.00 | 10.00 | 1995S Prestige Set | 17,112 | 57.00 | 130 |
| 1978S | 3,127,788 | 9.00 | 11.00 | 1995S Silver premier | 130,107 | 37.50 | 150 |
| 1979S Type I | 3,677,175 | 9.00 | 16.00 | 1996S | 2,085,191 | 12.50 | 12.00 |
| 1979S Type II | Inc. above | 9.00 | 130 | 1996S Silver | 623,655 | 21.00 | 65.00 |
| 1980S | 3,547,030 | 10.00 | 17.00 | 1996S Prestige set | 55,000 | 57.00 | 282 |
| 1981S Type I | 4,063,083 | 11.00 | 14.00 | 1996S Silver premier | 151,366 | 37.50 | 70.00 |
| 1981S Type II | 4,063,083 | 11.00 | 300 | 1997S | 1,975,000 | 12.50 | 38.00 |
| 1982S | 3,857,479 | 11.00 | 6.00 | 1997S Silver | 605,473 | 21.00 | 115 |
| 1983S Prestige set | 140,361 | 59.00 | 85.00 | 1997S Prestige set | 80,000 | 57.00 | 250 |
| 1983S | 3,138,765 | 11.00 | 7.00 | 1997S Silver premier | 136,205 | 37.50 | 132 |
| 1983S no-mint-mark | | | | 1998S | 136,205 | 12.50 | 26.00 |
| dime | 3,138,765 | 11.00 | 460 | 1998S Silver | 638,134 | 21.00 | 44.00 |
| 1984S Prestige set | 316,680 | 59.00 | 23.00 | 1998S Silver premier | 240,658 | 37.50 | 44.00 |
| 1984S | 2,748,430 | 11.00 | 8.00 | 1999S | 2,543,401 | 19.95 | 38.00 |
| 1985S | 3,362,821 | 11.00 | 8.00 | 1999S 5 quarter set | 1,169,958 | 13.95 | 29.00 |
| 1986S Prestige set | 599,317 | 48.50 | 40.00 | 1999S Silver | 800,000 | 31.95 | 75.00 |
| 1986S | 2,411,180 | 11.00 | 36.00 | 2000S | — | 19.95 | 24.00 |
| 1987S | 3,972,233 | 11.00 | 6.00 | 2000S 5 quarter set | — | 13.95 | 16.00 |
| 1987S Prestige set | 435,495 | 45.00 | 19.00 | 2000S Silver | — | 31.95 | 35.00 |
| 1988S | 3,031,287 | 11.00 | 18.00 | | | | |

## 1952 Proof Set

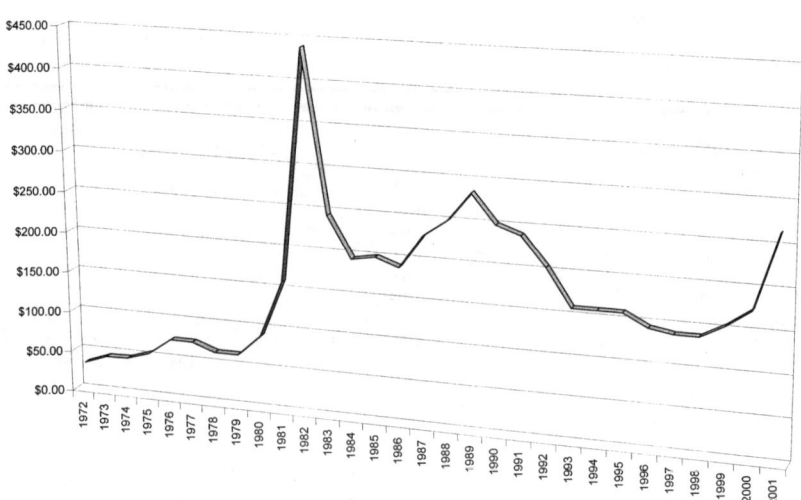

☐ Retail Price

# AMERICAN EAGLE BULLION COINS

## GOLD $5

**Obv. Designer:** Augustus Saint-Gaudens. **Rev. Designer:** Miley Busiek. **Diameter:** 16.5 mm. **Weight:** 3.3930 g. **Composition:** 0.9167 Gold, 0.1 oz. AGW.

| Date | Mintage | Unc | Prf. |
|---|---|---|---|
| MCMLXXXVI (1986) | 912,609 | 45.00 | — |
| MCMLXXXVII (1987) | 580,266 | 45.00 | — |
| MCMLXXXVIII (1988) | 159,500 | 85.00 | — |
| MCMLXXXVIIIP (1988)P | 143,881 | — | 56.00 |
| MCMLXXXIX (1989) | 264,790 | 70.00 | — |
| MCMLXXXIXP (1989)P | 82,924 | — | 56.00 |
| MCMXC (1990) | 210,210 | 75.00 | — |
| MCMXCP (1990)P | 99,349 | — | 56.00 |
| MCMXCI (1991) | 165,200 | 80.00 | — |
| MCMXCIP (1991)P | 70,344 | — | 58.00 |
| 1992 | 209,300 | 48.00 | — |
| 1992P | 64,902 | — | 71.00 |
| 1993 | 210,709 | 48.00 | — |
| 1993P | 58,649 | — | 66.00 |
| 1994 | 206,380 | 65.00 | — |
| 1994W | — | — | 60.00 |
| 1995 | 223,025 | 80.00 | — |
| 1995W | — | — | 56.00 |
| 1996 | — | 42.00 | — |
| 1996W | — | — | 74.00 |
| 1997 | 528,515 | 65.00 | — |
| 1997W | — | — | 91.00 |
| 1998 | 1,344,520 | 42.00 | — |
| 1998W | — | — | 58.00 |
| 1999 | — | 42.00 | — |
| 1999W | — | — | 58.00 |
| 2000 | — | 38.00 | — |
| 2000W | — | — | 59.00 |
| 2001 | — | — | — |
| 2001W | — | — | — |

## GOLD $10

**Obv. Designer:** Augustus Saint-Gaudens. **Rev. Designer:** Miley Busiek. **Diameter:** 22 mm. **Weight:** 8.4830 g. **Composition:** 0.9167 Gold, 0.25 oz. AGW.

| Date | Mintage | Unc | Prf. |
|---|---|---|---|
| MCMLXXXVI (1986) | 726,031 | 110 | — |
| MCMLXXXVII (1987) | 269,255 | 105 | — |
| MCMLXXXVIII (1988) | 49,000 | 110 | — |
| MCMLXXXVIIIP (1988)P | 98,028 | — | 150 |
| MCMLXXXIX (1989) | 81,789 | 110 | — |
| MCMLXXXIX (1989P) | 53,593 | — | 150 |
| MCMXC (1990) | 41,000 | 185 | — |
| MCMXCP (1990)P | 62,674 | — | 150 |
| MCMXCI (1991) | 36,100 | 230 | — |
| MCMXCIP (1991)P | 50,839 | — | 150 |
| 1992 | 59,546 | 115 | — |
| 1992P | 46,290 | — | 150 |
| 1993 | 71,864 | 120 | — |
| 1993P | 46,271 | — | 150 |
| 1994 | 72,650 | 100.00 | — |

| Date | Mintage | Unc | Prf. |
|------|--------:|----:|-----:|
| 1994W | — | — | 150 |
| 1995 | 83,752 | 100.00 | — |
| 1995W | — | — | 150 |
| 1996 | 60,318 | 100.00 | — |
| 1996W | — | — | 150 |
| 1997 | 108,805 | 170 | — |
| 1997W | — | — | 150 |
| 1998 | 309,829 | 100.00 | — |
| 1998W | — | — | 150 |
| 1999 | — | 95.00 | — |
| 1999W | — | — | 150 |
| 2000 | — | 95.00 | — |
| 2000W | — | — | 135 |
| 2001 | — | — | — |
| 2001W | — | — | — |

# GOLD $25

**Obv. Designer:** Augustus Saint-Gaudens. **Rev. Designer:** Miley Busiek. **Diameter:** 27 mm. **Weight:** 16.9660 g. **Composition:** 0.9167 Gold, 0.5 oz. AGW.

| Date | Mintage | Unc | Prf. |
|------|--------:|----:|-----:|
| MCMLXXXVI (1986) | 599,566 | 280 | — |
| MCMLXXXVII (1987) | 131,255 | 300 | — |
| MCMLXXXVIIP (1987)P | 143,398 | — | 295 |
| MCMLXXXVIII (1988) | 45,000 | 350 | — |
| MCMLXXXVIIIP (1988)P | 76,528 | — | 280 |
| MCMLXXXIX (1989) | 44,829 | 500 | — |
| MCMLXXXIXP (1989)P | 44,264 | — | 280 |
| MCMXC (1990) | 31,000 | 510 | — |
| MCMXCP (1990)P | 51,636 | — | 280 |
| MCMXCI (1991) | 24,100 | 525 | — |
| MCMXCIP (1991)P | 53,125 | — | 280 |
| 1992 | 54,404 | 280 | — |
| 1992P | 40,982 | — | 280 |
| 1993 | 73,324 | 240 | — |
| 1993P | 43,319 | — | 280 |
| 1994 | 62,400 | 280 | — |
| 1994W | — | — | 280 |
| 1995 | 53,474 | 300 | — |
| 1995W | — | — | 280 |
| 1996 | 39,287 | 400 | — |
| 1996W | — | — | 280 |
| 1997 | 79,605 | 225 | — |
| 1997W | — | — | 280 |
| 1998 | 169,029 | 180 | — |
| 1998W | — | — | 280 |
| 1999 | — | 180 | — |
| 1999W | — | — | 280 |
| 2000 | — | 180 | — |
| 2000W | — | — | 280 |
| 2001 | — | — | — |
| 2001W | — | — | — |

# GOLD $50

**Obv. Designer:** Augustus Saint-Gaudens. **Rev. Designer:** Miley Busiek. **Diameter:** 32.7 mm. **Weight:** 33.9310 g. **Composition:** 0.9167 Gold, 1 oz. AGW.

| Date | Mintage | Unc | Prf. |
|---|---|---|---|
| MCMLXXXVI (1986) | 1,362,650 | 320 | — |
| MCMLXXXVIW (1986)W | 446,290 | — | 570 |
| MCMLXXXVII (1987) | 1,045,500 | 320 | — |
| MCMLXXXVIIW (1987)W | 147,498 | — | 520 |
| MCMLXXXVIII (1988) | 465,000 | 320 | — |
| MCMLXXXVIIIW (1988)W | 87,133 | — | 570 |
| MCMLXXXIX (1989) | 415,790 | 320 | — |
| MCMLXXXIXW (1989)W | 53,960 | — | 570 |
| MCMXC (1990) | 373,210 | 325 | — |
| MCMXCW (1990)W | 62,401 | — | 570 |
| MCMXCI (1991) | 243,100 | 325 | — |
| MCMXCIW (1991)W | 50,411 | — | 570 |
| 1992 | 275,000 | 325 | — |
| 1992W | 44,835 | — | 570 |
| 1993 | 480,192 | 320 | — |
| 1993W | 34,389 | — | 570 |
| 1994 | 221,633 | 325 | — |
| 1994W | — | — | 570 |
| 1995 | 200,636 | 325 | — |
| 1995W | — | — | 570 |
| 1996 | 189,148 | 330 | — |
| 1996W | — | — | 570 |
| 1997 | 664,508 | 320 | — |
| 1997W | — | — | 570 |
| 1998 | 1,468,530 | 320 | — |
| 1998W | — | — | 570 |
| 1999 | — | 320 | — |
| 1999W | — | — | 570 |
| 2000 | — | 320 | — |
| 2000W | — | — | 570 |
| 2001 | — | — | — |
| 2001W | — | — | — |

# SILVER DOLLAR

**Obv. Designer:** Adolph A. Weinman. **Rev. Designer:** John Mercanti. **Diameter:** 40.6 **Weight:** 31.1010 g. **Composition:** 0.9993 Silver, 1 oz. ASW. **Notes:** Prices based on $5.50 spot silver.

| Date | Mintage | Unc | Prf. |
|---|---|---|---|
| 1986 | 5,393,005 | 16.00 | — |
| 1987 | 11,442,335 | 8.50 | — |

| Date | Mintage | Unc | Prf. |
|------|--------:|----:|-----:|
| 1987S | 904,732 | — | — |
| 1988 | 5,004,646 | 10.00 | — |
| 1988S | 557,370 | — | — |
| 1989 | 5,203,327 | 10.00 | — |
| 1989S | 617,694 | — | — |
| 1990 | 5,840,210 | 10.00 | — |
| 1990S | 695,510 | — | — |
| 1991 | 7,191,066 | 9.00 | — |
| 1991S | 511,924 | — | — |
| 1992 | 5,540,068 | 9.50 | — |
| 1992S | 498,552 | — | — |
| 1993 | 6,763,762 | 9.00 | — |
| 1993P | 403,625 | — | — |
| 1994 | 4,227,319 | 11.00 | — |
| 1994P | 372,168 | — | — |
| 1995 | 4,672,051 | 9.00 | — |
| 1995P | 395,400 | — | — |
| 1995W 10th anniversary | 30,125 | — | — |
| 1996 | 3,603,386 | 17.00 | — |
| 1996P | 473,021 | — | — |
| 1996D | 15,697 | — | — |
| 1996P | — | — | — |
| 1997 | 4,295,004 | 11.00 | — |
| 1997P | 429,682 | — | — |
| 1998 | 4,847,549 | 10.00 | — |
| 1998P | 452,319 | — | — |
| 1999 | — | 12.50 | — |
| 1999P | 549,769 | — | — |
| 2000 | — | 7.50 | — |
| 2000P | — | — | 50.00 |
| 2001 | — | 7.00 | — |
| 2001W | — | — | — |

# PLATINUM $10

**Obv. Designer:** John Mercanti. **Rev. Designer:** Thomas D. Rogers Sr.. **Composition:** 0.9990 Platinum, 0.1 oz.

| Date | Mintage | Unc | Prf. |
|------|--------:|----:|-----:|
| 1997 | 56,000 | 80.00 | — |
| 1997W | — | — | 125 |
| 1998 | 39,525 | 80.00 | — |
| 1998W | — | — | 125 |
| 1999 | — | 85.00 | — |
| 1999W | — | — | 125 |
| 2000 | — | 80.00 | — |
| 2000W | — | — | 125 |
| 2001 | — | — | — |
| 2001W | — | — | — |

# PLATINUM $25

**Obv. Designer:** John Mercanti. **Rev. Designer:** Thomas D. Rogers Sr. **Composition:** 0.9995 Platinum, 0.25 oz.

| Date | Mintage | Unc | Prf. |
|------|--------:|----:|-----:|
| 1997 | 20,500 | 220 | — |
| 1997W | — | — | 210 |
| 1998 | 38,887 | 195 | — |
| 1998W | — | — | 225 |
| 1999 | — | 195 | — |
| 1999W | — | — | 225 |
| 2000 | — | 195 | — |
| 2000W | — | — | 225 |

| Date | Mintage | Unc | Prf. |
|------|---------|-----|------|
| 2001 | — | — | — |
| 2001W | — | — | — |

# PLATINUM $50

**Obv. Designer:** John Mercanti. **Rev. Designer:** Thomas D. Rogers Sr. **Composition:** 0.9995 Platinum, 0.5 oz.

| Date | Mintage | Unc | Prf. |
|------|---------|-----|------|
| 1997 | 27,100 | 430 | — |
| 1997W | — | — | 370 |
| 1998 | 32,415 | 350 | — |
| 1998W | — | — | 410 |
| 1999 | — | 300 | — |
| 1999W | — | — | 410 |
| 2000 | — | 340 | — |
| 2000W | — | — | 415 |
| 2001 | — | — | — |
| 2001W | — | — | — |

# PLATINUM $100

Uncirculated reverse, all dates      1998 proof reverse

2000 proof reverse      2001 proof reverse

**Composition:** 0.9995 Platinum, 1 oz. **Notes:** Prices based on $374.00 spot platinum.

| Date | Mintage | Unc | Prf. |
|------|---------|-----|------|
| 1997 | 70,250 | 630 | — |
| 1997W | — | — | 725 |
| 1998 | 133,002 | 630 | — |
| 1998W | — | — | 715 |
| 1999 | — | 630 | — |
| 1999W | — | — | 715 |
| 2000 | — | 630 | — |
| 2000W | — | — | 715 |
| 2001 | — | — | — |
| 2001W | — | — | — |

# PATTERNS

## HALF DIME

### Seated Liberty.

**Weight:** 1.2400 g. **Composition:** 0.9000 Silver, 0.0362 oz. ASW. **Notes:** These non-circulation pieces were struck as experiments in transferring the legend "United States of America" from the reverse to the obverse.

| Date | Mintage | G-4 | VG-8 | F-12 | VF-20 | XF-40 | AU-50 | MS-60 | MS-65 | Prf-65 |
|------|---------|-----|------|------|-------|-------|-------|-------|-------|--------|
| 1859 obverse 1859, reverse 1860 | — | — | — | — | — | — | — | — | 8,500 | 17,500 |

### Seated Liberty.

**Weight:** 1.2400 g. **Composition:** 0.9000 Silver, 0.0362 oz. ASW. **Notes:** These non-circulation pieces were struck as experiments in transferring the legend "United States of America" from the reverse to the obverse.

| Date | Mintage | G-4 | VG-8 | F-12 | VF-20 | XF-40 | AU-50 | MS-60 | MS-65 | Prf-65 |
|------|---------|-----|------|------|-------|-------|-------|-------|-------|--------|
| 1860 obverse 1859, reverse 1860 | — | — | — | — | — | — | — | 3,250 | 6,500 | — |

## DIME

### Seated Liberty.

**Weight:** 2.4900 g. **Composition:** 0.9000 Silver, 0.0724 oz. ASW. **Notes:** This non-circulation strike was an experiment in transferring the legend "United States of America" from the reverse to the obverse.

| Date | Mintage | G-4 | VG-8 | F-12 | VF-20 | XF-40 | AU-50 | MS-60 | MS-65 | Prf-65 |
|------|---------|-----|------|------|-------|-------|-------|-------|-------|--------|
| 1859 obverse 1859, reverse 1860 | — | — | — | — | — | — | — | — | — | 25,000 |

## DOLLAR

### "C. Gobrecht F." below base. Eagle flying left amid stars.

**Obv. Designer:** Christian Gobrecht. **Diameter:** 38.1 mm. **Edge:** Plain. **Weight:** 26.7300 g. **Composition:** 0.9000 Silver, 0.7736 oz. ASW.

| Date | Mintage | VF-20 | XF-40 | AU-50 | Prf-60 |
|------|---------|-------|-------|-------|--------|
| 1836 | 1,000 | 3,750 | 4,750 | — | 12,500 |

## "C. Gobrecht F." below base. Eagle flying in plain field.

**Obv. Designer:** Christian Gobrecht. **Diameter:** 38.1 mm. **Edge:** Plain. **Weight:** 26.7300 g. **Composition:** 0.9000 Silver, 0.7736 oz. ASW.

| Date | Mintage | VF-20 | XF-40 | AU-50 | Prf-60 |
|---|---|---|---|---|---|
| 1836 Restrike | — | — | — | — | — |

## "C. Gobrecht F." on base.

**Diameter:** 38.1 mm. **Edge:** Plain. **Weight:** 26.7300 g. **Composition:** 0.9000 Silver, 0.7736 oz. ASW.

| Date | Mintage | VF-20 | XF-40 | AU-50 | Prf-60 |
|---|---|---|---|---|---|
| 1836 | 600 | — | — | — | — |

## "C. Gobrecht F." on base. Eagle flying left amid stars.

**Diameter:** 38.1 mm. **Edge:** Reeded. **Weight:** 26.7300 g. **Composition:** 0.9000 Silver, 0.7736 oz. ASW.

| Date | Mintage | VF-20 | XF-40 | AU-50 | Prf-60 |
|---|---|---|---|---|---|
| 1836 Restrike | — | — | — | — | — |

## Similar to 1836 but designer's name omitted. Eagle in plain field.

**Diameter:** 38.1 mm. **Edge:** Reeded. **Weight:** 26.7300 g. **Composition:** 0.9000 Silver, 0.7736 oz. ASW.

| Date | Mintage | VF-20 | XF-40 | AU-50 | Prf-60 |
|---|---|---|---|---|---|
| 1839 | 300 | — | — | — | — |

**Diameter:** 38.1mm **Weight:** 26.7300 g. **Composition:** 0.9000 Silver, .7734 oz. ASW.

| Date | Mintage | VF-20 | XF-40 | AU-50 | Prf-60 |
|---|---|---|---|---|---|
| 1839 Restrike | — | — | — | — | — |

**Note:** All other combinations are restrikes of the late 1850's.

CANADA

# CIRCULATION COINAGE

## CENT

**Weight:** 3.2400 g. **Composition:** Bronze. **Notes:** Struck for 1862 proof sets.

| KM# | Date | Mintage | VG-8 | F-12 | VF-20 | XF-40 | MS-60 | MS-63 | Prf-63 |
|-----|------|---------|------|------|-------|-------|-------|-------|--------|
| 1 | 1858 | 421,000 | 35.00 | 45.00 | 60.00 | 90.00 | 225 | 800 | — |
| | 1859/8 wide 9 | Inc. above | 22.00 | 29.00 | 50.00 | 80.00 | 225 | 275 | — |
| | 1859 narrow 9 | 9,579,000 | 2.25 | 3.00 | 4.00 | 5.00 | 25.00 | 140 | — |
| | 1859 double punched narrow 9 type I | Inc. above | 175 | 250 | 350 | 540 | 1,150 | 2,000 | — |
| | 1859 double punched narrow 9 type II | Inc. above | 35.00 | 60.00 | 85.00 | 100.00 | 250 | 500 | — |

**Weight:** 3.2400 g. **Composition:** Bronze.

| KM# | Date | Mintage | VG-8 | F-12 | VF-20 | XF-40 | MS-60 | MS-63 | Prf-63 |
|-----|------|---------|------|------|-------|-------|-------|-------|--------|
| 7 | 1876H | 4,000,000 | 1.60 | 2.75 | 4.00 | 7.00 | 40.00 | 180 | — |
| | 1881H | 2,000,000 | 2.50 | 3.50 | 5.00 | 10.00 | 50.00 | 200 | — |
| | 1882H | 4,000,000 | 1.60 | 2.75 | 4.00 | 6.00 | 30.00 | 140 | — |
| | 1884 | 2,500,000 | 2.00 | 3.00 | 4.00 | 7.50 | 40.00 | 180 | — |
| | 1886 | 1,500,000 | 3.50 | 4.50 | 9.00 | 15.00 | 75.00 | 250 | — |
| | 1887 | 1,500,000 | 2.50 | 3.25 | 5.00 | 10.00 | 50.00 | 200 | — |
| | 1888 | 4,000,000 | 1.50 | 2.50 | 3.00 | 5.00 | 30.00 | 100.00 | — |
| | 1890H | 1,000,000 | 4.00 | 7.00 | 12.00 | 20.00 | 80.00 | 300 | — |
| | 1891 lg. date | 1,452,000 | 4.50 | 7.00 | 11.00 | 20.00 | 90.00 | 300 | — |
| | 1891 S.D.L.L. | Inc. above | 40.00 | 60.00 | 85.00 | 135 | 500 | 1,500 | — |
| | 1891 S.D.S.L. | Inc. above | 30.00 | 45.00 | 60.00 | 90.00 | 200 | 550 | — |
| | 1892 | 1,200,000 | 3.00 | 4.50 | 6.00 | 10.00 | 40.00 | 130 | — |
| | 1893 | 2,000,000 | 2.00 | 2.50 | 4.00 | 6.00 | 30.00 | 100.00 | — |
| | 1894 | 1,000,000 | 7.00 | 9.00 | 13.00 | 20.00 | 65.00 | 175 | — |
| | 1895 | 1,200,000 | 3.00 | 5.00 | 7.00 | 10.00 | 45.00 | 160 | — |
| | 1896 | 2,000,000 | 1.75 | 2.75 | 3.50 | 5.50 | 30.00 | 100.00 | — |
| | 1897 | 1,500,000 | 2.00 | 2.75 | 4.00 | 6.00 | 30.00 | 110 | — |
| | 1898H | 1,000,000 | 4.00 | 6.00 | 8.00 | 11.00 | 55.00 | 200 | — |
| | 1899 | 2,400,000 | 1.50 | 2.25 | 3.00 | 5.00 | 30.00 | 90.00 | — |
| | 1900 | 1,000,000 | 3.00 | 6.00 | 10.00 | 15.00 | 60.00 | 250 | — |
| | 1900H | 2,600,000 | 2.00 | 2.50 | 4.00 | 5.00 | 22.00 | 60.00 | — |
| | 1901 | 4,100,000 | 1.50 | 2.50 | 3.00 | 5.00 | 22.00 | 60.00 | — |

**Weight:** 3.2400 g. **Composition:** Bronze.

| KM# | Date | Mintage | VG-8 | F-12 | VF-20 | XF-40 | MS-60 | MS-63 | Prf-63 |
|-----|------|---------|------|------|-------|-------|-------|-------|--------|
| 8 | 1902 | 3,000,000 | 1.25 | 1.50 | 2.00 | 5.00 | 13.00 | 45.00 | — |

| KM# | Date | Mintage | VG-8 | F-12 | VF-20 | XF-40 | MS-60 | MS-63 | Prf-63 |
|-----|------|---------|------|------|-------|-------|-------|-------|--------|
|  | 1903 | 4,000,000 | 1.25 | 1.50 | 2.00 | 4.00 | 18.00 | 50.00 | — |
|  | 1904 | 2,500,000 | 1.50 | 2.00 | 3.25 | 5.00 | 25.00 | 75.00 | — |
|  | 1905 | 2,000,000 | 2.50 | 4.00 | 5.00 | 7.00 | 30.00 | 85.00 | — |
|  | 1906 | 4,100,000 | 1.25 | 1.50 | 2.00 | 4.00 | 22.00 | 100.00 | — |
|  | 1907 | 2,400,000 | 1.25 | 2.00 | 3.00 | 5.00 | 25.00 | 90.00 | — |
|  | 1907H | 800,000 | 8.00 | 11.00 | 16.00 | 30.00 | 80.00 | 275 | — |
|  | 1908 | 2,401,506 | 1.25 | 2.00 | 3.00 | 5.00 | 22.00 | 80.00 | — |
|  | 1909 | 3,973,339 | 1.25 | 1.50 | 2.00 | 4.00 | 18.00 | 55.00 | — |
|  | 1910 | 5,146,487 | 1.25 | 1.50 | 2.00 | 3.00 | 13.00 | 55.00 | — |

**Weight:** 3.2400 g. **Composition:** Bronze.

| KM# | Date | Mintage | VG-8 | F-12 | VF-20 | XF-40 | MS-60 | MS-63 | Prf-63 |
|-----|------|---------|------|------|-------|-------|-------|-------|--------|
| 15 | 1911 | 4,663,486 | 0.75 | 1.25 | 1.75 | 3.50 | 15.00 | 55.00 | — |

**Weight:** 3.2400 g. **Composition:** Bronze. **Notes:** Earlier dates (1876-1900) exist for this type.

| KM# | Date | Mintage | VG-8 | F-12 | VF-20 | XF-40 | MS-60 | MS-63 | Prf-63 |
|-----|------|---------|------|------|-------|-------|-------|-------|--------|
| 21 | 1912 | 5,107,642 | 0.75 | 1.00 | 1.50 | 2.50 | 15.00 | 50.00 | — |
|  | 1913 | 5,735,405 | 0.75 | 1.00 | 1.50 | 2.50 | 15.00 | 75.00 | — |
|  | 1914 | 3,405,958 | 0.75 | 1.00 | 1.50 | 2.50 | 25.00 | 90.00 | — |
|  | 1915 | 4,932,134 | 0.75 | 1.00 | 1.50 | 2.50 | 18.00 | 65.00 | — |
|  | 1916 | 11,022,367 | 0.50 | 0.65 | 0.90 | 2.00 | 12.00 | 45.00 | — |
|  | 1917 | 11,899,254 | 0.50 | 0.65 | 0.90 | 1.50 | 8.00 | 40.00 | — |
|  | 1918 | 12,970,798 | 0.50 | 0.65 | 0.90 | 1.50 | 8.00 | 40.00 | — |
|  | 1919 | 11,279,634 | 0.50 | 0.65 | 0.90 | 1.50 | 8.00 | 40.00 | — |
|  | 1920 | 6,762,247 | 0.50 | 0.65 | 0.90 | 1.50 | 10.00 | 50.00 | — |

  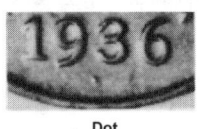

Dot

**Weight:** 3.2400 g. **Composition:** Bronze.

| KM# | Date | Mintage | VG-8 | F-12 | VF-20 | XF-40 | MS-60 | MS-63 | Prf-63 |
|-----|------|---------|------|------|-------|-------|-------|-------|--------|
| 28 | 1920 | 15,483,923 | 0.25 | 0.50 | 1.00 | 2.00 | 7.00 | 30.00 | — |
|  | 1921 | 7,601,627 | 0.50 | 0.75 | 1.75 | 3.00 | 18.00 | 70.00 | — |
|  | 1922 | 1,243,635 | 8.75 | 10.00 | 14.50 | 22.00 | 130 | 300 | — |
|  | 1923 | 1,019,002 | 14.25 | 16.25 | 23.00 | 34.00 | 200 | 600 | — |
|  | 1924 | 1,593,195 | 3.00 | 4.00 | 5.00 | 10.00 | 70.00 | 200 | — |
|  | 1925 | 1,000,622 | 10.00 | 12.00 | 18.75 | 28.00 | 130 | 400 | — |
|  | 1926 | 2,143,372 | 2.25 | 3.00 | 4.50 | 8.75 | 65.00 | 200 | — |
|  | 1927 | 3,553,928 | 0.90 | 1.25 | 2.25 | 4.00 | 30.00 | 95.00 | — |
|  | 1928 | 9,144,860 | 0.15 | 0.30 | 0.65 | 1.50 | 10.00 | 40.00 | — |
|  | 1929 | 12,159,840 | 0.15 | 0.30 | 0.65 | 1.50 | 10.00 | 40.00 | — |
|  | 1930 | 2,538,613 | 1.35 | 1.80 | 3.00 | 5.00 | 30.00 | 90.00 | — |
|  | 1931 | 3,842,776 | 0.65 | 1.00 | 1.75 | 3.50 | 25.00 | 80.00 | — |
|  | 1932 | 21,316,190 | 0.15 | 0.20 | 0.50 | 1.50 | 9.00 | 35.00 | — |
|  | 1933 | 12,079,310 | 0.15 | 0.20 | 0.50 | 1.50 | 9.00 | 35.00 | — |
|  | 1934 | 7,042,358 | 0.20 | 0.30 | 0.75 | 1.50 | 9.00 | 35.00 | — |
|  | 1935 | 7,526,400 | 0.20 | 0.30 | 0.75 | 1.50 | 9.00 | 35.00 | — |
|  | 1936 | 8,768,769 | 0.15 | 0.20 | 0.75 | 1.50 | 9.00 | 35.00 | — |
|  | 1936 dot below date | 678,823 | — | — | — | — | — | — | — |

**Note:** Only one possible business strike is known to exist. No other examples (or possible business strikes) have ever surfaced.

|  | 1936 dot below date, specimen, 3 known | — | — | — | — | — | — | — | — |

**Note:** At the David Akers auction of the John Jay Pittman collection (Part 1, 10-97), a gem specimen realized $121,000. At the David Akers auction of the John Jay Pittman collection (Part 3, 10-99), a near choice specimen realized $115,000.

Maple leaf

**Weight:** 3.2400 g. **Composition:** Bronze.

| KM# | Date | Mintage | VG-8 | F-12 | VF-20 | XF-40 | MS-60 | MS-63 | Prf-63 |
|-----|------|---------|------|------|-------|-------|-------|-------|--------|
| 32 | 1937 | 10,040,231 | 0.10 | 0.25 | 0.50 | 0.75 | 1.50 | 5.50 | — |
| | 1938 | 18,365,608 | 0.10 | 0.15 | 0.25 | 0.50 | 1.50 | 6.00 | — |
| | 1939 | 21,600,319 | 0.10 | 0.15 | 0.25 | 0.50 | 1.50 | 4.50 | — |
| | 1940 | 85,740,532 | 0.10 | 0.15 | 0.25 | 0.50 | 1.50 | 5.50 | — |
| | 1941 | 56,336,011 | 0.10 | 0.15 | 0.25 | 0.50 | 4.00 | 35.00 | — |
| | 1942 | 76,113,708 | 0.10 | 0.15 | 0.25 | 0.50 | 4.00 | 25.00 | — |
| | 1943 | 89,111,969 | 0.10 | 0.15 | 0.25 | 0.50 | 1.50 | 10.00 | — |
| | 1944 | 44,131,216 | 0.10 | 0.15 | 0.25 | 0.50 | 4.00 | 32.00 | — |
| | 1945 | 77,268,591 | 0.10 | 0.15 | 0.20 | 0.30 | 1.00 | 5.00 | — |
| | 1946 | 56,662,071 | 0.10 | 0.15 | 0.20 | 0.30 | 1.00 | 5.00 | — |
| | 1947 | 31,093,901 | 0.10 | 0.15 | 0.20 | 0.30 | 1.00 | 6.00 | — |
| | 1947 ML | 47,855,448 | 0.10 | 0.15 | 0.20 | 0.30 | 1.00 | 5.00 | — |

**Weight:** 3.2400 g. **Composition:** Bronze. **Obverse:** Modified legend.

| KM# | Date | Mintage | VG-8 | F-12 | VF-20 | XF-40 | MS-60 | MS-63 | Prf-63 |
|-----|------|---------|------|------|-------|-------|-------|-------|--------|
| 41 | 1948 | 25,767,779 | — | 0.10 | 0.25 | 0.60 | 2.25 | 8.00 | — |
| | 1949 | 33,128,933 | — | 0.10 | 0.15 | 0.25 | 1.25 | 4.00 | — |
| | 1950 | 60,444,992 | — | 0.10 | 0.15 | 0.25 | 0.85 | 4.00 | — |
| | 1951 | 80,430,379 | — | 0.10 | 0.15 | 0.20 | 0.85 | 4.00 | — |
| | 1952 | 67,631,736 | — | 0.10 | 0.15 | 0.20 | 0.85 | 4.00 | — |

Without strap                With strap

**Weight:** 3.2400 g. **Composition:** Bronze. **Obverse:** Elizabeth II effigy. **Obv. Designer:** Gillick.

| KM# | Date | Mintage | VG-8 | F-12 | VF-20 | XF-40 | MS-60 | MS-63 | Prf-63 |
|-----|------|---------|------|------|-------|-------|-------|-------|--------|
| 49 | 1953 without strap | 67,806,016 | 0.15 | 0.20 | 0.25 | 0.30 | 0.65 | 1.50 | — |
| | 1953 with strap | Inc. above | 0.50 | 1.00 | 1.50 | 2.50 | 10.00 | 35.00 | — |
| | 1954 with strap | 22,181,760 | 0.10 | 0.15 | 0.30 | 0.40 | 1.00 | 4.00 | — |
| | 1954 without strap, proof-like only | Inc. above | — | — | — | — | 150 | 250 | — |
| | 1955 with strap | 56,403,193 | — | 0.15 | 0.20 | 0.25 | 0.35 | 1.00 | — |
| | 1955 without strap | Inc. above | 80.00 | 110 | 150 | 250 | 500 | 950 | — |
| | 1956 | 78,658,535 | — | — | — | 0.10 | 0.50 | 0.90 | — |
| | 1957 | 100,601,792 | — | — | — | 0.10 | 0.30 | 0.70 | — |
| | 1958 | 59,385,679 | — | — | — | 0.10 | 0.30 | 0.70 | — |
| | 1959 | 83,615,343 | — | — | — | 0.10 | 0.25 | 0.50 | — |
| | 1960 | 75,772,775 | — | — | — | 0.10 | 0.25 | 0.50 | — |
| | 1961 | 139,598,404 | — | — | — | — | 0.15 | 0.25 | — |
| | 1962 | 227,244,069 | — | — | — | — | 0.10 | 0.20 | — |
| | 1963 | 279,076,334 | — | — | — | — | 0.10 | 0.20 | — |
| | 1964 | 484,655,322 | — | — | — | — | 0.10 | 0.20 | — |

**Weight:** 3.2400 g. **Composition:** Bronze. **Obverse:** Elizabeth II effigy. **Obv. Designer:** Machin.

| KM# | Date | Mintage | VG-8 | F-12 | VF-20 | XF-40 | MS-60 | MS-63 | Prf-63 |
|-----|------|---------|------|------|-------|-------|-------|-------|--------|
| 59.1 | 1965 sm. beads, pointed 5 | 304,441,082 | — | — | — | 0.45 | 1.00 | 1.50 | — |
| | 1965 sm. beads, blunt 5 | Inc. above | — | — | — | — | 0.20 | 0.40 | — |
| | 1965 lg. beads, pointed 5 | Inc. above | — | — | 3.00 | 5.00 | 12.00 | 30.00 | — |
| | 1965 lg. beads, blunt 5 | Inc. above | — | — | — | 0.10 | 0.35 | 0.70 | — |
| | 1966 | 184,151,087 | — | — | — | — | 0.10 | 0.20 | — |
| | 1968 | 329,695,772 | — | — | — | — | 0.10 | 0.20 | — |
| | 1969 | 335,240,929 | — | — | — | — | 0.10 | 0.20 | — |
| | 1970 | 311,145,010 | — | — | — | — | 0.10 | 0.20 | — |
| | 1971 | 298,228,936 | — | — | — | — | 0.10 | 0.20 | — |
| | 1972 | 451,304,591 | — | — | — | — | 0.10 | 0.20 | — |
| | 1973 | 457,059,852 | — | — | — | — | 0.10 | 0.20 | — |
| | 1974 | 692,058,489 | — | — | — | — | 0.10 | 0.20 | — |
| | 1975 | 642,318,000 | — | — | — | — | 0.10 | 0.20 | — |
| | 1976 | 701,122,890 | — | — | — | — | 0.10 | 0.20 | — |
| | 1977 | 453,762,670 | — | — | — | — | 0.10 | 0.20 | — |
| | 1978 | 911,170,647 | — | — | — | — | 0.10 | 0.20 | — |

**Weight:** 3.2400 g. **Composition:** Bronze. **Obverse:** Elizabeth II effigy. Smaller bust. **Obv. Designer:** Machin.

| KM# | Date | Mintage | VG-8 | F-12 | VF-20 | XF-40 | MS-60 | MS-63 | Prf-63 |
|-----|------|---------|------|------|-------|-------|-------|-------|--------|
| 59.2 | 1979 | 754,394,064 | — | — | — | — | 0.10 | 0.20 | — |

**Weight:** 2.8000 g. **Composition:** Bronze. **Obverse:** Elizabeth II effigy. **Obv. Designer:** Machin. **Notes:** Reduced weight.

| KM# | Date | Mintage | VG-8 | F-12 | VF-20 | XF-40 | MS-60 | MS-63 | Prf-63 |
|-----|------|---------|------|------|-------|-------|-------|-------|--------|
| 127 | 1980 | 912,052,318 | — | — | — | — | 0.10 | 0.15 | — |
| | 1981 | 1,209,468,500 | — | — | — | — | 0.10 | 0.15 | — |
| | 1981 | 199,000 | — | — | — | — | — | — | 1.50 |

**Weight:** 2.5000 g. **Composition:** Bronze. **Obverse:** Elizabeth II effigy. **Obv. Designer:** Machin. **Edge:** Multi-sided. **Notes:** Reduced weight.

| KM# | Date | Mintage | VG-8 | F-12 | VF-20 | XF-40 | MS-60 | MS-63 | Prf-63 |
|-----|------|---------|------|------|-------|-------|-------|-------|--------|
| 132 | 1982 | 911,001,000 | — | — | — | — | 0.10 | 0.15 | — |
| | 1982 | 180,908 | — | — | — | — | — | — | 1.50 |
| | 1983 | 975,510,000 | — | — | — | — | 0.10 | 0.15 | — |
| | 1983 | 168,000 | — | — | — | — | — | — | 1.50 |
| | 1984 | 838,225,000 | — | — | — | — | 0.10 | 0.15 | — |
| | 1984 | 161,602 | — | — | — | — | — | — | 1.50 |
| | 1985 pointed 5 | 771,772,500 | — | — | — | 7.25 | 12.50 | 18.50 | — |
| | 1985 blunt 5 | Inc. above | — | — | — | — | 0.10 | 0.15 | — |
| | 1985 | 157,037 | — | — | — | — | — | — | 1.50 |
| | 1986 | 740,335,000 | — | — | — | — | 0.10 | 0.15 | — |
| | 1986 | 175,745 | — | — | — | — | — | — | 2.25 |
| | 1987 | 774,549,000 | — | — | — | — | 0.10 | 0.15 | — |
| | 1987 | 179,004 | — | — | — | — | — | — | 2.25 |
| | 1988 | 482,676,752 | — | — | — | — | 0.10 | 0.15 | — |
| | 1988 | 175,259 | — | — | — | — | — | — | 2.25 |
| | 1989 | 1,077,347,200 | — | — | — | — | 0.10 | 0.15 | — |
| | 1989 | 170,928 | — | — | — | — | — | — | 2.25 |

**Weight:** 2.5000 g. **Composition:** Bronze. **Obverse:** Elizabeth II effigy. **Obv. Designer:** dePedery-Hunt.

| KM# | Date | Mintage | VG-8 | F-12 | VF-20 | XF-40 | MS-60 | MS-63 | Prf-63 |
|-----|------|---------|------|------|-------|-------|-------|-------|--------|
| 181 | 1990 | 218,035,000 | — | — | — | — | 0.10 | 0.15 | — |
| | 1990 | 140,649 | — | — | — | — | — | — | 2.50 |
| | 1991 | 831,001,000 | — | — | — | — | 0.10 | 0.15 | — |
| | 1991 | 131,888 | — | — | — | — | — | — | 3.50 |
| | 1993 | 752,034,000 | — | — | — | — | 0.10 | 0.15 | — |
| | 1993 | 145,065 | — | — | — | — | — | — | 2.00 |
| | 1994 | 639,516,000 | — | — | — | — | 0.10 | 0.15 | — |
| | 1994 | 146,424 | — | — | — | — | — | — | 2.50 |
| | 1995 | 624,983,000 | — | — | — | — | 0.10 | 0.15 | — |
| | 1995 | — | — | — | — | — | — | — | 2.50 |
| | 1996 | 445,746,000 | — | — | — | — | 0.10 | 0.15 | — |
| | 1996 | — | — | — | — | — | — | — | 2.50 |

**Composition:** Bronze-plated Zinc. **Edge:** Round and plain.

| KM# | Date | Mintage | VG-8 | F-12 | VF-20 | XF-40 | MS-60 | MS-63 | Prf-63 |
|-----|------|---------|------|------|-------|-------|-------|-------|--------|
| 289 | 1997 | 506,928,000 | — | — | — | — | 0.10 | 0.15 | — |
| | 1997 | — | — | — | — | — | — | — | 2.75 |
| | 1998 | — | — | — | — | — | — | 0.10 | 0.15 | — |
| | 1998O in proof sets only | — | — | — | — | — | — | — | 2.00 |
| | 1998W in mint sets only | — | — | — | — | — | — | 1.75 | — |
| | 1999O | — | — | — | — | — | — | 0.10 | 0.15 | — |
| | 1999W | — | — | — | — | — | — | — | — |
| | 2000O | — | — | — | — | — | — | 0.10 | 0.15 | — |
| | 2000W | — | — | — | — | — | — | 1.75 | — |

**Composition:** Copper Plated Steel.

| KM# | Date | Mintage | VG-8 | F-12 | VF-20 | XF-40 | MS-60 | MS-63 | Prf-63 |
|-----|------|---------|------|------|-------|-------|-------|-------|--------|
| 181a | 1996 | 445,746,000 | — | — | — | — | 0.10 | 0.15 | — |

**Composition:** Bronze.

| KM# | Date | Mintage | VG-8 | F-12 | VF-20 | XF-40 | MS-60 | MS-63 | Prf-63 |
|-----|------|---------|------|------|-------|-------|-------|-------|--------|
| 289a | 1998 In Specimen sets only. | — | — | — | — | — | — | 0.75 | — |

# 5 CENTS

Oval 0's                    Round 0's

**Weight:** 1.1620 g. **Composition:** 0.9250 Silver., 0.0346 oz. ASW.

| KM# | Date | Mintage | VG-8 | F-12 | VF-20 | XF-40 | MS-60 | MS-63 | Prf-63 |
|---|---|---|---|---|---|---|---|---|---|
| 2 | 1858 small date | 1,500,000 | 10.00 | 15.00 | 25.00 | 40.00 | 225 | 450 | — |
| | 1858 large date over small date | Inc. above | 90.00 | 150 | 250 | 375 | 1,000 | 2,350 | — |
| | 1870 flat rim | 2,800,000 | 9.00 | 15.00 | 25.00 | 45.00 | 225 | 500 | — |
| | 1870 wire rim | Inc. above | 9.00 | 15.00 | 25.00 | 45.00 | 200 | 450 | — |
| | 1871 | 1,400,000 | 9.00 | 15.00 | 25.00 | 45.00 | 250 | 550 | — |
| | 1872H | 2,000,000 | 6.00 | 12.00 | 25.00 | 40.00 | 225 | 600 | — |
| | 1874H plain 4 | 800,000 | 12.50 | 27.00 | 55.00 | 100.00 | 350 | 875 | — |
| | 1874H crosslet 4 | Inc. above | 10.00 | 20.00 | 40.00 | 65.00 | 350 | 750 | — |
| | 1875H large date | 1,000,000 | 125 | 175 | 325 | 575 | 2,200 | 4,250 | — |
| | 1875H small date | Inc. above | 80.00 | 150 | 250 | 450 | 1,400 | 3,250 | — |
| | 1880H | 3,000,000 | 4.00 | 7.50 | 16.00 | 35.00 | 225 | 550 | — |
| | 1881H | 1,500,000 | 4.50 | 9.00 | 17.50 | 35.00 | 225 | 600 | — |
| | 1882H | 1,000,000 | 5.00 | 10.00 | 20.00 | 40.00 | 250 | 650 | — |
| | 1883H | 600,000 | 13.00 | 25.00 | 60.00 | 125 | 650 | 1,750 | — |
| | 1884 | 200,000 | 75.00 | 125 | 225 | 475 | 2,200 | 6,000 | — |
| | 1885 small 5 | 1,000,000 | 7.50 | 14.00 | 35.00 | 70.00 | 400 | 1,250 | — |
| | 1885 large 5 | Inc. above | 8.25 | 15.50 | 35.00 | 80.00 | 425 | 1,350 | — |
| | 1885 large 5 over small 5 | Inc. above | 35.00 | 75.00 | 150 | 400 | 1,950 | 2,750 | — |
| | 1886 small 6 | 1,700,000 | 4.50 | 9.00 | 17.50 | 35.00 | 250 | 700 | — |
| | 1886 large 6 | Inc. above | 7.00 | 10.00 | 20.00 | 45.00 | 300 | 750 | — |
| | 1887 | 500,000 | 13.00 | 25.00 | 45.00 | 85.00 | 300 | 675 | — |
| | 1888 | 1,000,000 | 3.50 | 6.00 | 14.00 | 25.00 | 140 | 350 | — |
| | 1889 | 1,200,000 | 14.00 | 28.00 | 60.00 | 100.00 | 350 | 1,000 | — |
| | 1890H | 1,000,000 | 4.50 | 8.00 | 18.00 | 35.00 | 165 | 400 | — |
| | 1891 | 1,800,000 | 3.00 | 5.00 | 10.00 | 16.00 | 125 | 285 | — |
| | 1892 | 860,000 | 4.50 | 8.00 | 16.00 | 35.00 | 200 | 550 | — |
| | 1893 | 1,700,000 | 3.00 | 5.00 | 10.00 | 18.00 | 150 | 350 | — |
| | 1894 | 500,000 | 9.50 | 20.00 | 40.00 | 80.00 | 285 | 850 | — |
| | 1896 | 1,500,000 | 3.50 | 7.00 | 12.00 | 25.00 | 150 | 325 | — |
| | 1897 | 1,319,283 | 3.75 | 6.50 | 12.00 | 25.00 | 125 | 285 | — |
| | 1898 | 580,717 | 8.00 | 15.00 | 30.00 | 50.00 | 180 | 500 | — |
| | 1899 | 3,000,000 | 2.75 | 4.00 | 7.50 | 18.00 | 90.00 | 275 | — |
| | 1900 oval 0's | 1,800,000 | 3.00 | 4.50 | 8.00 | 18.00 | 100.00 | 300 | — |
| | 1900 round 0's | Inc. above | 13.00 | 25.00 | 45.00 | 90.00 | 250 | 750 | — |
| | 1901 | 2,000,000 | 2.75 | 4.00 | 8.00 | 18.00 | 100.00 | 325 | — |

**Weight:** 1.1620 g. **Composition:** 0.9250 Silver., 0.0346 oz. ASW.

| KM# | Date | Mintage | VG-8 | F-12 | VF-20 | XF-40 | MS-60 | MS-63 | Prf-63 |
|---|---|---|---|---|---|---|---|---|---|
| 9 | 1902 | 2,120,000 | 1.50 | 2.00 | 3.25 | 7.00 | 30.00 | 50.00 | — |
| | 1902 lg. broad H | 2,200,000 | 1.50 | 2.00 | 3.25 | 7.00 | 30.00 | 50.00 | — |
| | 1902 sm. narrow H | Inc. above | 5.00 | 9.00 | 20.00 | 35.00 | 80.00 | 150 | — |

**Weight:** 1.1620 g. **Composition:** 0.9250 Silver., 0.0346 oz. ASW.

| KM# | Date | Mintage | VG-8 | F-12 | VF-20 | XF-40 | MS-60 | MS-63 | Prf-63 |
|---|---|---|---|---|---|---|---|---|---|
| 13 | 1903 | 1,000,000 | 4.00 | 7.00 | 14.00 | 30.00 | 120 | 280 | — |
| | 1903H | 2,640,000 | 1.75 | 3.00 | 7.00 | 13.00 | 90.00 | 200 | — |
| | 1904 | 2,400,000 | 1.75 | 3.00 | 7.00 | 18.00 | 140 | 400 | — |
| | 1905 | 2,600,000 | 1.75 | 3.00 | 6.00 | 12.00 | 85.00 | 200 | — |
| | 1906 | 3,100,000 | 1.50 | 2.00 | 4.00 | 8.00 | 65.00 | 175 | — |
| | 1907 | 5,200,000 | 1.50 | 2.00 | 4.00 | 7.00 | 45.00 | 125 | — |
| | 1908 | 1,220,524 | 4.00 | 6.50 | 12.00 | 25.00 | 85.00 | 150 | — |
| | 1909 round leaves | 1,983,725 | 2.00 | 2.50 | 7.00 | 15.00 | 125 | 350 | — |
| | 1909 pointed leaves | Inc. above | 6.00 | 11.00 | 25.00 | 50.00 | 300 | 1,000 | — |
| | 1910 pointed leaves | 3,850,325 | 1.50 | 1.75 | 3.25 | 7.00 | 45.00 | 75.00 | — |
| | 1910 round leaves | Inc. above | 8.50 | 13.50 | 28.00 | 70.00 | 320 | 1,000 | — |

**Weight:** 1.1620 g. **Composition:** 0.9250 Silver., 0.0346 oz. ASW.

| KM# | Date | Mintage | VG-8 | F-12 | VF-20 | XF-40 | MS-60 | MS-63 | Prf-63 |
|-----|------|---------|------|------|-------|-------|-------|-------|--------|
| 16 | 1911 | 3,692,350 | 1.25 | 2.00 | 4.00 | 8.00 | 50.00 | 85.00 | — |

**Weight:** 1.1620 g. **Composition:** 0.9250 Silver., 0.0346 oz. ASW.

| KM# | Date | Mintage | VG-8 | F-12 | VF-20 | XF-40 | MS-60 | MS-63 | Prf-63 |
|-----|------|---------|------|------|-------|-------|-------|-------|--------|
| 22 | 1912 | 5,863,170 | 1.25 | 2.00 | 3.00 | 6.00 | 45.00 | 125 | — |
| | 1913 | 5,488,048 | 1.25 | 1.75 | 2.50 | 5.00 | 20.00 | 45.00 | — |
| | 1914 | 4,202,179 | 1.25 | 2.00 | 3.00 | 6.00 | 45.00 | 130 | — |
| | 1915 | 1,172,258 | 5.50 | 10.50 | 20.00 | 40.00 | 175 | 475 | — |
| | 1916 | 2,481,675 | 1.75 | 3.00 | 5.00 | 11.00 | 75.00 | 175 | — |
| | 1917 | 5,521,373 | 1.25 | 1.75 | 2.00 | 4.00 | 30.00 | 70.00 | — |
| | 1918 | 6,052,298 | 1.25 | 1.75 | 2.00 | 4.00 | 25.00 | 55.00 | — |
| | 1919 | 7,835,400 | 1.25 | 1.75 | 2.00 | 4.00 | 25.00 | 55.00 | — |

**Weight:** 1.1664 g. **Composition:** 0.8000 Silver., .0300 oz. ASW.

| KM# | Date | Mintage | VG-8 | F-12 | VF-20 | XF-40 | MS-60 | MS-63 | Prf-63 |
|-----|------|---------|------|------|-------|-------|-------|-------|--------|
| 22a | 1920 | 10,649,851 | 1.25 | 1.75 | 2.00 | 4.00 | 20.00 | 35.00 | — |
| | 1921 | 2,582,495 | 1,450 | 1,850 | 2,400 | 3,150 | 6,500 | 12,500 | — |

**Note:** Approximately 460 known; balance remelted. Stack's A.G. Carter Jr. Sale (12-89) choice BU, finest known, realized $57,200.

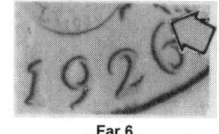

Near 6          Far 6

**Composition:** Nickel.

| KM# | Date | Mintage | VG-8 | F-12 | VF-20 | XF-40 | MS-60 | MS-63 | Prf-63 |
|-----|------|---------|------|------|-------|-------|-------|-------|--------|
| 29 | 1922 | 4,794,119 | 0.25 | 0.75 | 1.75 | 7.00 | 35.00 | 75.00 | — |
| | 1923 | 2,502,279 | 0.40 | 1.25 | 3.50 | 12.00 | 75.00 | 225 | — |
| | 1924 | 3,105,839 | 0.30 | 0.70 | 2.50 | 7.00 | 60.00 | 165 | — |
| | 1925 | 201,921 | 20.00 | 30.00 | 50.00 | 155 | 800 | 2,000 | — |
| | 1926 near 6 | 938,162 | 1.50 | 4.00 | 12.00 | 40.00 | 300 | 1,200 | — |
| | 1926 far 6 | Inc. above | 60.00 | 85.00 | 150 | 275 | 1,000 | 2,750 | — |
| | 1927 | 5,285,627 | 0.25 | 0.65 | 1.75 | 6.50 | 45.00 | 130 | — |
| | 1928 | 4,577,712 | 0.25 | 0.65 | 1.75 | 6.50 | 40.00 | 90.00 | — |
| | 1929 | 5,611,911 | 0.25 | 0.65 | 1.75 | 6.50 | 45.00 | 130 | — |
| | 1930 | 3,704,673 | 0.25 | 0.65 | 1.75 | 6.50 | 70.00 | 150 | — |
| | 1931 | 5,100,830 | 0.25 | 0.65 | 2.00 | 10.25 | 75.00 | 200 | — |
| | 1932 | 3,198,566 | 0.25 | 0.65 | 2.25 | 10.50 | 75.00 | 150 | — |
| | 1933 | 2,597,867 | 0.40 | 1.00 | 4.00 | 13.00 | 150 | 400 | — |
| | 1934 | 3,827,304 | 0.25 | 0.65 | 3.00 | 10.75 | 80.00 | 200 | — |
| | 1935 | 3,900,000 | 0.25 | 0.65 | 1.75 | 6.50 | 70.00 | 160 | — |
| | 1936 | 4,400,450 | 0.25 | 0.65 | 1.75 | 6.50 | 40.00 | 85.00 | — |

**Composition:** Nickel.

| KM# | Date | Mintage | VG-8 | F-12 | VF-20 | XF-40 | MS-60 | MS-63 | Prf-63 |
|-----|------|---------|------|------|-------|-------|-------|-------|--------|
| 33 | 1937 dot | 4,593,263 | 0.20 | 0.35 | 1.25 | 2.50 | 9.00 | 22.00 | — |
| | 1938 | 3,898,974 | 0.20 | 1.00 | 2.00 | 7.00 | 50.00 | 135 | — |
| | 1939 | 5,661,123 | 0.20 | 0.50 | 1.00 | 3.00 | 30.00 | 70.00 | — |
| | 1940 | 13,920,197 | 0.15 | 0.30 | 0.75 | 2.25 | 12.00 | 40.00 | — |
| | 1941 | 8,681,785 | 0.10 | 0.30 | 0.75 | 2.25 | 15.00 | 42.00 | — |
| | 1942 round | 6,847,544 | 0.20 | 0.35 | 0.75 | 1.75 | 12.00 | 40.00 | — |

**Composition:** Tombac. (Brass)

| KM# | Date | Mintage | VG-8 | F-12 | VF-20 | XF-40 | MS-60 | MS-63 | Prf-63 |
|-----|------|---------|------|------|-------|-------|-------|-------|--------|
| 39  | 1942 - 12 sided | 3,396,234 | 0.40 | 0.65 | 1.25 | 1.75 | 3.00 | 9.00 | — |

Dot                                              Maple leaf

**Composition:** Nickel.

| KM# | Date | Mintage | VG-8 | F-12 | VF-20 | XF-40 | MS-60 | MS-63 | Prf-63 |
|-----|------|---------|------|------|-------|-------|-------|-------|--------|
| 39a | 1946 | 6,952,684 | 0.15 | 0.25 | 0.50 | 2.00 | 8.00 | 18.00 | — |
|     | 1947 | 7,603,724 | 0.15 | 0.25 | 0.50 | 1.25 | 6.50 | 12.50 | — |
|     | 1947 dot | Inc. above | 12.00 | 15.00 | 22.00 | 50.00 | 175 | 275 | — |
|     | 1947 maple leaf | 9,595,124 | 0.15 | 0.25 | 0.50 | 1.25 | 6.00 | 12.00 | — |

**Composition:** Nickel. **Obverse:** Modified legend.

| KM# | Date | Mintage | VG-8 | F-12 | VF-20 | XF-40 | MS-60 | MS-63 | Prf-63 |
|-----|------|---------|------|------|-------|-------|-------|-------|--------|
| 42  | 1948 | 1,810,789 | 0.40 | 0.70 | 1.00 | 3.00 | 12.00 | 20.00 | — |
|     | 1949 | 13,037,090 | 0.15 | 0.20 | 0.35 | 0.75 | 4.00 | 7.00 | — |
|     | 1950 | 11,970,521 | 0.15 | 0.20 | 0.35 | 0.75 | 4.00 | 7.00 | — |

**Composition:** Chromium And Nickel-plated Steel. **Notes:** * A in GRATIA points between denticles. * *NOTE: A in GRATIA points to a denticle.

| KM# | Date | Mintage | VG-8 | F-12 | VF-20 | XF-40 | MS-60 | MS-63 | Prf-63 |
|-----|------|---------|------|------|-------|-------|-------|-------|--------|
| 42a | 1951 Low relief. "A" in GRATIA points between denticles. | 4,313,410 | 0.15 | 0.25 | 0.50 | 0.85 | 2.50 | 4.50 | — |
|     | 1951 High relief. "A" in GRATIA points to a denticle. | Inc. above | 325 | 425 | 550 | 950 | 1,400 | 1,850 | — |
|     | 1952 | 10,891,148 | 0.15 | 0.25 | 0.50 | 0.85 | 3.00 | 5.00 | — |

**Composition:** Chromium And Nickel-plated Steel. **Shape:** 12-sided. **Obverse:** Elizabeth II effigy. **Obv. Designer:** Gillick.

| KM# | Date | Mintage | VG-8 | F-12 | VF-20 | XF-40 | MS-60 | MS-63 | Prf-63 |
|-----|------|---------|------|------|-------|-------|-------|-------|--------|
| 50  | 1953 w/o strap | 16,635,552 | 0.15 | 0.25 | 0.40 | 1.00 | 3.00 | 4.50 | — |
|     | 1953 w/strap | Inc. above | 0.15 | 0.25 | 0.45 | 1.00 | 3.50 | 7.00 | — |
|     | 1954 | 6,998,662 | 0.15 | 0.25 | 0.50 | 1.00 | 4.00 | 8.00 | — |

**Composition:** Nickel.

| KM# | Date | Mintage | VG-8 | F-12 | VF-20 | XF-40 | MS-60 | MS-63 | Prf-63 |
|-----|------|---------|------|------|-------|-------|-------|-------|--------|
| 50a | 1955 | 5,355,028 | 0.15 | 0.25 | 0.40 | 0.75 | 2.50 | 4.50 | — |
|     | 1956 | 9,399,854 | — | 0.20 | 0.30 | 0.45 | 1.50 | 3.00 | — |
|     | 1957 | 7,387,703 | — | — | 0.25 | 0.30 | 1.25 | 3.00 | — |
|     | 1958 | 7,607,521 | — | — | 0.25 | 0.30 | 1.25 | 3.00 | — |

| KM# | Date | Mintage | VG-8 | F-12 | VF-20 | XF-40 | MS-60 | MS-63 | Prf-63 |
|-----|------|---------|------|------|-------|-------|-------|-------|--------|
| | 1959 | 11,552,523 | — | — | — | 0.20 | 0.55 | 1.25 | — |
| | 1960 | 37,157,433 | — | — | — | 0.15 | 0.35 | 0.70 | — |
| | 1961 | 47,889,051 | — | — | — | — | 0.20 | 0.40 | — |
| | 1962 | 46,307,305 | — | — | — | — | 0.20 | 0.40 | — |

**Composition:** Nickel. **Shape:** Round.

| KM# | Date | Mintage | VG-8 | F-12 | VF-20 | XF-40 | MS-60 | MS-63 | Prf-63 |
|-----|------|---------|------|------|-------|-------|-------|-------|--------|
| 57 | 1963 | 43,970,320 | — | — | — | — | 0.20 | 0.35 | — |
| | 1964 | 78,075,068 | — | — | — | — | 0.20 | 0.35 | — |
| | 1964 XWL | — | 8.00 | 10.00 | 13.50 | 16.00 | 28.00 | 40.00 | — |

**Composition:** Nickel. **Obverse:** Elizabeth II effigy. **Obv. Designer:** Machin.

| KM# | Date | Mintage | VG-8 | F-12 | VF-20 | XF-40 | MS-60 | MS-63 | Prf-63 |
|-----|------|---------|------|------|-------|-------|-------|-------|--------|
| 60.1 | 1965 | 84,876,018 | — | — | — | — | 0.20 | 0.30 | — |
| | 1966 | 27,976,648 | — | — | — | — | 0.20 | 0.30 | — |
| | 1968 | 101,930,379 | — | — | — | — | 0.20 | 0.30 | — |
| | 1969 | 27,830,229 | — | — | — | — | 0.20 | 0.30 | — |
| | 1970 | 5,726,010 | — | — | — | 0.20 | 0.35 | 0.75 | — |
| | 1971 | 27,312,609 | — | — | — | — | 0.20 | 0.30 | — |
| | 1972 | 62,417,387 | — | — | — | — | 0.20 | 0.30 | — |
| | 1973 | 53,507,435 | — | — | — | — | 0.20 | 0.30 | — |
| | 1974 | 94,704,645 | — | — | — | — | 0.20 | 0.30 | — |
| | 1975 | 138,882,000 | — | — | — | — | 0.20 | 0.30 | — |
| | 1976 | 55,140,213 | — | — | — | — | 0.20 | 0.30 | — |
| | 1977 | 89,120,791 | — | — | — | — | 0.20 | 0.30 | — |
| | 1978 | 137,079,273 | — | — | — | — | 0.20 | 0.30 | — |

**Composition:** Nickel. **Obverse:** Smaller bust.

| KM# | Date | Mintage | VG-8 | F-12 | VF-20 | XF-40 | MS-60 | MS-63 | Prf-63 |
|-----|------|---------|------|------|-------|-------|-------|-------|--------|
| 60.2 | 1979 | 186,295,825 | — | — | — | — | 0.20 | 0.30 | — |
| | 1980 | 134,878,000 | — | — | — | — | 0.20 | 0.30 | — |
| | 1981 | 99,107,900 | — | — | — | — | 0.20 | 0.30 | — |
| | 1981 | 199,000 | — | — | — | — | — | — | 1.00 |

**Composition:** Copper-nickel.

| KM# | Date | Mintage | VG-8 | F-12 | VF-20 | XF-40 | MS-60 | MS-63 | Prf-63 |
|-----|------|---------|------|------|-------|-------|-------|-------|--------|
| 60.2a | 1982 | 64,924,400 | — | — | — | — | 0.20 | 0.30 | — |
| | 1982 | 180,908 | — | — | — | — | — | — | 1.00 |
| | 1983 | 72,596,000 | — | — | — | — | 0.20 | 0.30 | — |
| | 1983 | 168,000 | — | — | — | — | — | — | 1.00 |
| | 1984 | 84,088,000 | — | — | — | — | 0.20 | 0.30 | — |
| | 1984 | 161,602 | — | — | — | — | — | — | 2.00 |
| | 1985 | 126,618,000 | — | — | — | — | 0.20 | 0.30 | — |
| | 1985 | 157,037 | — | — | — | — | — | — | 2.00 |
| | 1986 | 156,104,000 | — | — | — | — | 0.20 | 0.30 | — |
| | 1986 | 175,745 | — | — | — | — | — | — | 2.00 |
| | 1987 | 106,299,000 | — | — | — | — | 0.10 | 0.15 | — |
| | 1987 | 179,004 | — | — | — | — | — | — | 2.00 |
| | 1988 | 75,025,000 | — | — | — | — | 0.10 | 0.15 | — |
| | 1988 | 175,259 | — | — | — | — | — | — | 2.00 |
| | 1989 | 141,570,538 | — | — | — | — | 0.10 | 0.15 | — |
| | 1989 | 170,928 | — | — | — | — | — | — | 2.00 |

**Composition:** Copper-nickel. **Obverse:** Elizabeth II effigy. **Obv. Designer:** dePedery-Hunt.

| KM# | Date | Mintage | VG-8 | F-12 | VF-20 | XF-40 | MS-60 | MS-63 | Prf-63 |
|-----|------|---------|------|------|-------|-------|-------|-------|--------|
| 182 | 1990 | 42,537,000 | — | — | — | — | 0.10 | 0.15 | — |
| | 1990 | 140,649 | — | — | — | — | — | — | 2.50 |
| | 1991 | 10,931,000 | — | — | — | — | 0.20 | 0.70 | — |
| | 1991 | 131,888 | — | — | — | — | — | — | 10.50 |
| | 1993 | 86,877,000 | — | — | — | — | 0.10 | 0.15 | — |
| | 1993 | 143,065 | — | — | — | — | — | — | 2.50 |
| | 1994 | 99,352,000 | — | — | — | — | 0.10 | 0.15 | — |
| | 1994 | 146,424 | — | — | — | — | — | — | 3.00 |
| | 1995 | 78,528,000 | — | — | — | — | 0.10 | 0.15 | — |
| | 1995 | 50,000 | — | — | — | — | — | — | 2.50 |
| | 1996 | 36,686,000 | — | — | — | — | 0.10 | 0.15 | — |
| | 1997 | 26,573,000 | — | — | — | — | 0.10 | 0.15 | — |
| | 1998 | — | — | — | — | — | 0.10 | 0.15 | — |
| | 1998W in unc sets only | — | — | — | — | — | — | 2.75 | — |
| | 1999 | — | — | — | — | — | 0.10 | 0.15 | — |
| | 1999W | — | — | — | — | — | — | — | — |
| | 2000 | — | — | — | — | — | 0.10 | 0.15 | — |
| | 2000W | — | — | — | — | — | — | 2.75 | — |

**Composition: Nickel Plated Steel.**

| KM# | Date | Mintage | VG-8 | F-12 | VF-20 | XF-40 | MS-60 | MS-63 | Prf-63 |
|-----|------|---------|------|------|-------|-------|-------|-------|--------|
| 182a | 1996 | 36,686,000 | — | — | — | — | 0.10 | 0.15 | — |
| | 1997 | 26,573,000 | — | — | — | — | 0.10 | 0.15 | — |
| | 1998 | — | — | — | — | — | 0.10 | 0.15 | — |
| | 1998W In Unc sets only | — | — | — | — | — | — | 2.75 | — |

**Weight: 5.3500 g. Composition: 0.9250 Silver., 0.1591 oz. ASW.**

| KM# | Date | Mintage | VG-8 | F-12 | VF-20 | XF-40 | MS-60 | MS-63 | Prf-63 |
|-----|------|---------|------|------|-------|-------|-------|-------|--------|
| 182b | 1996 | — | — | — | — | — | — | — | 5.50 |
| | 1997 | — | — | — | — | — | — | — | 5.50 |
| | 1998 in proof sets only | — | — | — | — | — | — | — | 4.00 |
| | 1998O in proof sets only | — | — | — | — | — | — | — | 4.00 |

# 10 CENTS

**Weight: 2.3240 g. Composition: 0.9250 Silver., 0.0691 oz. ASW.**

| KM# | Date | Mintage | VG-8 | F-12 | VF-20 | XF-40 | MS-60 | MS-63 | Prf-63 |
|-----|------|---------|------|------|-------|-------|-------|-------|--------|
| 3 | 1858/5 | -2Inc. above | 400 | 600 | 900 | 1,450 | 3,250 | — | — |
| | 1858 | 1,250,000 | 15.00 | 25.00 | 45.00 | 80.00 | 275 | 850 | — |
| | 1870 narrow 0 | 1,600,000 | 13.00 | 27.50 | 60.00 | 100.00 | 300 | 900 | — |
| | 1870 wide 0 | Inc. above | 20.00 | 40.00 | 80.00 | 150 | 375 | 1,000 | — |
| | 1871 | 800,000 | 20.00 | 35.00 | 80.00 | 160 | 400 | 1,550 | — |
| | 1871H | 1,870,000 | 20.00 | 35.00 | 85.00 | 175 | 450 | 1,000 | — |
| | 1872H | 1,000,000 | 80.00 | 125 | 250 | 425 | 1,400 | 2,850 | — |
| | 1874H | 600,000 | 10.00 | 20.00 | 40.00 | 80.00 | 275 | 750 | — |
| | 1875H | 1,000,000 | 175 | 325 | 575 | 1,150 | 4,050 | 7,500 | — |
| | 1880H | 1,500,000 | 10.00 | 20.00 | 35.00 | 60.00 | 250 | 700 | — |
| | 1881H | 950,000 | 12.00 | 25.00 | 45.00 | 90.00 | 325 | 750 | — |
| | 1882H | 1,000,000 | 12.00 | 25.00 | 45.00 | 90.00 | 385 | 1,100 | — |
| | 1883H | 300,000 | 30.00 | 65.00 | 150 | 250 | 600 | 1,500 | — |
| | 1884 | 150,000 | 140 | 300 | 575 | 1,300 | 5,150 | 10,000 | — |
| | 1885 | 400,000 | 25.00 | 50.00 | 125 | 300 | 1,500 | 3,250 | — |
| | 1886 small 6 | 800,000 | 15.00 | 30.00 | 75.00 | 150 | 600 | 1,550 | — |
| | 1886 large 6 | Inc. above | 25.00 | 35.00 | 75.00 | 150 | 575 | 1,350 | — |
| | 1887 | 350,000 | 25.00 | 55.00 | 125 | 300 | 900 | 2,750 | — |
| | 1888 | 500,000 | 6.75 | 18.00 | 40.00 | 75.00 | 275 | 800 | — |
| | 1889 | 600,000 | 400 | 725 | 1,450 | 2,900 | 8,750 | 14,000 | — |
| | 1890H | 450,000 | 11.50 | 25.00 | 50.00 | 125 | 325 | 750 | — |
| | 1891 21 leaves | 800,000 | 12.00 | 25.00 | 60.00 | 125 | 450 | 950 | — |
| | 1891 22 leaves | Inc. above | 12.00 | 25.00 | 65.00 | 125 | 375 | 825 | — |
| | 1892/1 | 520,000 | 110 | 175 | 325 | 525 | 1,750 | 2,550 | — |
| | 1892 | Inc. above | 12.00 | 25.00 | 40.00 | 90.00 | 350 | 800 | — |
| | 1893 flat top 3 | 500,000 | 18.00 | 45.00 | 80.00 | 150 | 475 | 1,450 | — |
| | 1893 round top 3 | Inc. above | 450 | 900 | 1,700 | 2,900 | 6,950 | 13,000 | — |
| | 1894 | 500,000 | 20.00 | 30.00 | 70.00 | 130 | 350 | 1,000 | — |
| | 1896 | 650,000 | 8.00 | 15.00 | 30.00 | 65.00 | 250 | 550 | — |
| | 1898 | 720,000 | 8.00 | 20.00 | 35.00 | 65.00 | 275 | 600 | — |
| | 1899 small 9's | 1,200,000 | 6.75 | 12.00 | 30.00 | 65.00 | 210 | 575 | — |
| | 1899 large 9's | Inc. above | 12.00 | 20.00 | 40.00 | 100.00 | 325 | 850 | — |
| | 1900 | 1,100,000 | 6.75 | 10.50 | 25.00 | 60.00 | 150 | 390 | — |

| KM# | Date | Mintage | VG-8 | F-12 | VF-20 | XF-40 | MS-60 | MS-63 | Prf-63 |
|-----|------|---------|------|------|-------|-------|-------|-------|--------|
|     | 1901 | 1,200,000 | 6.75 | 10.50 | 25.00 | 60.00 | 150 | 390 | — |

**Weight:** 2.3240 g. **Composition:** 0.9250 Silver., 0.0691 oz. ASW.

| KM# | Date | Mintage | VG-8 | F-12 | VF-20 | XF-40 | MS-60 | MS-63 | Prf-63 |
|-----|------|---------|------|------|-------|-------|-------|-------|--------|
| 10 | 1902 | 720,000 | 3.50 | 9.00 | 20.00 | 50.00 | 250 | 650 | — |
|    | 1902H | 1,100,000 | 2.75 | 5.00 | 12.50 | 28.00 | 75.00 | 200 | — |
|    | 1903 | 500,000 | 8.00 | 20.00 | 50.00 | 150 | 800 | 1,900 | — |
|    | 1903H | 1,320,000 | 4.50 | 7.00 | 20.00 | 42.00 | 200 | 450 | — |
|    | 1904 | 1,000,000 | 4.50 | 9.00 | 30.00 | 65.00 | 250 | 450 | — |
|    | 1905 | 1,000,000 | 4.00 | 10.00 | 30.00 | 80.00 | 350 | 800 | — |
|    | 1906 | 1,700,000 | 2.75 | 7.50 | 15.00 | 40.00 | 200 | 400 | — |
|    | 1907 | 2,620,000 | 2.75 | 7.50 | 15.00 | 30.00 | 180 | 350 | — |
|    | 1908 | 776,666 | 5.00 | 10.00 | 27.00 | 65.00 | 180 | 250 | — |
|    | 1909 Victorian leaves, similar to 1902-1908 coinage | 1,697,200 | 3.50 | 9.00 | 25.00 | 60.00 | 285 | 700 | — |
|    | 1909 broad leaves, similar to 1910-1912 coinage | Inc. above | 5.50 | 12.00 | 30.00 | 70.00 | 375 | 800 | — |
|    | 1910 | 4,468,331 | 2.75 | 5.00 | 12.50 | 28.00 | 100.00 | 275 | — |

**Weight:** 2.3240 g. **Composition:** 0.9250 Silver., 0.0691 oz. ASW.

| KM# | Date | Mintage | VG-8 | F-12 | VF-20 | XF-40 | MS-60 | MS-63 | Prf-63 |
|-----|------|---------|------|------|-------|-------|-------|-------|--------|
| 17 | 1911 | 2,737,584 | 3.00 | 7.00 | 12.00 | 30.00 | 80.00 | 200 | — |

**Small leaves**               **Broad Leaves**

**Weight:** 2.3240 g. **Composition:** 0.9250 Silver., 0.0691 oz. ASW.

| KM# | Date | Mintage | VG-8 | F-12 | VF-20 | XF-40 | MS-60 | MS-63 | Prf-63 |
|-----|------|---------|------|------|-------|-------|-------|-------|--------|
| 23 | 1912 | 3,235,557 | 1.75 | 2.50 | 6.00 | 22.00 | 150 | 400 | — |
|    | 1913 sm. leaves | 3,613,937 | 1.50 | 2.25 | 5.00 | 17.50 | 80.00 | 250 | — |
|    | 1913 lg. leaves | Inc. above | 70.00 | 125 | 250 | 650 | 4,000 | 6,800 | — |
|    | 1914 | 2,549,811 | 1.50 | 2.50 | 5.50 | 18.50 | 80.00 | 350 | — |
|    | 1915 | 688,057 | 4.00 | 10.00 | 22.00 | 70.00 | 225 | 500 | — |
|    | 1916 | 4,218,114 | 1.25 | 1.50 | 4.00 | 11.00 | 60.00 | 200 | — |
|    | 1917 | 5,011,988 | 1.25 | 1.50 | 3.00 | 8.75 | 40.00 | 70.00 | — |
|    | 1918 | 5,133,602 | 1.25 | 1.50 | 3.00 | 6.00 | 35.00 | 65.00 | — |
|    | 1919 | 7,877,722 | 1.25 | 1.50 | 3.00 | 6.00 | 35.00 | 65.00 | — |

**Weight:** 2.3328 g. **Composition:** 0.8000 Silver., 0.0600 oz. ASW.

| KM# | Date | Mintage | VG-8 | F-12 | VF-20 | XF-40 | MS-60 | MS-63 | Prf-63 |
|-----|------|---------|------|------|-------|-------|-------|-------|--------|
| 23a | 1920 | 6,305,345 | 1.25 | 1.50 | 3.00 | 8.00 | 40.00 | 75.00 | — |
|     | 1921 | 2,469,562 | 1.25 | 2.00 | 4.00 | 12.50 | 50.00 | 150 | — |
|     | 1928 | 2,458,602 | 1.00 | 1.75 | 4.00 | 8.00 | 40.00 | 100.00 | — |

| KM# | Date | Mintage | VG-8 | F-12 | VF-20 | XF-40 | MS-60 | MS-63 | Prf-63 |
|---|---|---|---|---|---|---|---|---|---|
| | 1929 | 3,253,888 | 1.00 | 2.25 | 3.50 | 8.00 | 40.00 | 90.00 | — |
| | 1930 | 1,831,043 | 1.50 | 2.50 | 4.50 | 9.00 | 40.00 | 90.00 | — |
| | 1931 | 2,067,421 | 1.50 | 1.75 | 4.00 | 8.00 | 40.00 | 90.00 | — |
| | 1932 | 1,154,317 | 1.50 | 2.50 | 6.00 | 15.00 | 60.00 | 150 | — |
| | 1933 | 672,368 | 2.00 | 3.00 | 8.00 | 25.00 | 100.00 | 275 | — |
| | 1934 | 409,067 | 3.00 | 6.00 | 16.00 | 40.00 | 200 | 400 | — |
| | 1935 | 384,056 | 3.50 | 6.00 | 15.00 | 40.00 | 200 | 400 | — |
| | 1936 | 2,460,871 | 0.60 | 1.25 | 3.00 | 6.00 | 30.00 | 70.00 | — |
| | 1936 dot on rev. *Specimen, 4 known | — | — | — | — | — | — | — | — |

**Note:** *At the David Akers sale of the John Jay Pittman collection, Part 1, 10-97, a gem specimen realized $120,000.

**Maple leaf**

**Weight:** 2.3328 g. **Composition:** 0.8000 Silver., 0.0600 oz. ASW.

| KM# | Date | Mintage | VG-8 | F-12 | VF-20 | XF-40 | MS-60 | MS-63 | Prf-63 |
|---|---|---|---|---|---|---|---|---|---|
| 34 | 1937 | 2,500,095 | 1.00 | 1.50 | 2.50 | 3.75 | 8.00 | 12.00 | — |
| | 1938 | 4,197,323 | 1.00 | 2.00 | 3.25 | 6.50 | 40.00 | 60.00 | — |
| | 1939 | 5,501,748 | 0.70 | 1.50 | 2.50 | 5.00 | 30.00 | 40.00 | — |
| | 1940 | 16,526,470 | BV | 0.50 | 2.25 | 3.00 | 10.00 | 20.00 | — |
| | 1941 | 8,716,386 | BV | 1.50 | 2.50 | 6.00 | 25.00 | 60.00 | — |
| | 1942 | 10,214,011 | BV | 0.50 | 1.25 | 4.00 | 20.00 | 30.00 | — |
| | 1943 | 21,143,229 | BV | 0.50 | 1.25 | 4.00 | 11.00 | 20.00 | — |
| | 1944 | 9,383,582 | BV | 0.50 | 1.50 | 4.50 | 15.00 | 25.00 | — |
| | 1945 | 10,979,570 | BV | 0.50 | 1.25 | 4.00 | 11.00 | 15.00 | — |
| | 1946 | 6,300,066 | BV | 1.50 | 2.00 | 4.50 | 20.00 | 35.00 | — |
| | 1947 | 4,431,926 | BV | 1.75 | 2.50 | 6.00 | 20.00 | 30.00 | — |
| | 1947 Maple leaf | 9,638,793 | BV | 0.50 | 1.50 | 3.00 | 8.00 | 12.00 | — |

**Weight:** 2.3328 g. **Composition:** 0.8000 Silver., 0.0600 oz. ASW. **Obverse:** Modified legend.

| KM# | Date | Mintage | VG-8 | F-12 | VF-20 | XF-40 | MS-60 | MS-63 | Prf-63 |
|---|---|---|---|---|---|---|---|---|---|
| 43 | 1948 | 422,741 | 2.00 | 3.50 | 7.50 | 13.00 | 30.00 | 40.00 | — |
| | 1949 | 11,336,172 | — | | 0.85 | 2.00 | 7.00 | 12.00 | — |
| | 1950 | 17,823,075 | — | | 0.65 | 1.50 | 5.00 | 7.00 | — |
| | 1951 | 15,079,265 | — | | 0.50 | 1.50 | 4.00 | 7.00 | — |
| | 1952 | 10,474,455 | — | | 0.50 | 1.50 | 3.00 | 5.00 | — |

**Weight:** 2.3328 g. **Composition:** 0.8000 Silver., 0.0600 oz. ASW. **Obverse:** Elizabeth II effigy. **Obv. Designer:** Gllick.

| KM# | Date | Mintage | VG-8 | F-12 | VF-20 | XF-40 | MS-60 | MS-63 | Prf-63 |
|---|---|---|---|---|---|---|---|---|---|
| 51 | 1953 Without straps | 17,706,395 | — | — | | 1.25 | 3.00 | 6.00 | — |
| | 1953 With straps | Inc. above | — | — | | 1.25 | 3.50 | 6.50 | — |
| | 1954 | 4,493,150 | — | — | 1.00 | 2.25 | 6.00 | 11.00 | — |
| | 1955 | 12,237,294 | — | — | | 0.75 | 3.00 | 5.00 | — |
| | 1956 | 16,732,844 | — | — | | 0.75 | 3.50 | 5.00 | — |
| | 1956 Dot below date | Inc. above | 1.00 | 2.00 | 3.00 | 5.00 | 11.25 | 20.50 | — |
| | 1957 | 16,110,229 | — | — | — | 0.70 | 1.25 | 2.25 | — |
| | 1958 | 10,621,236 | — | — | — | 0.70 | 1.25 | 2.25 | — |
| | 1959 | 19,691,433 | — | — | — | 0.70 | 1.25 | 2.25 | — |
| | 1960 | 45,446,835 | — | — | — | | 0.50 | 1.50 | — |
| | 1961 | 26,850,859 | — | — | — | | 0.50 | 1.50 | — |
| | 1962 | 41,864,335 | — | — | — | | 0.50 | 1.50 | — |
| | 1963 | 41,916,208 | — | — | — | | 0.50 | 1.50 | — |
| | 1964 | 49,518,549 | — | — | — | | 0.50 | 1.50 | — |

**Weight:** 2.3328 g. **Composition:** 0.8000 Silver., 0.0600 oz. ASW. **Obverse:** Elizabeth II effigy **Obv. Designer:** Machin.

| KM# | Date | Mintage | VG-8 | F-12 | VF-20 | XF-40 | MS-60 | MS-63 | Prf-63 |
|---|---|---|---|---|---|---|---|---|---|
| 61 | 1965 | 56,965,392 | — | — | — | | 0.50 | 1.50 | — |

| KM# | Date | Mintage | VG-8 | F-12 | VF-20 | XF-40 | MS-60 | MS-63 | Prf-63 |
|---|---|---|---|---|---|---|---|---|---|
| | 1966 | 34,567,898 | — | — | — | | 0.50 | 1.50 | — |

**Weight:** 2.3328 g. **Composition:** 0.8000 Silver., 0.0600 oz. ASW.

| KM# | Date | Mintage | VG-8 | F-12 | VF-20 | XF-40 | MS-60 | MS-63 | Prf-63 |
|---|---|---|---|---|---|---|---|---|---|
| 72 | 1968 Ottawa reeding | 70,460,000 | — | — | — | | 0.50 | 1.25 | — |

 Ottawa reeding

**Composition:** Nickel.

| KM# | Date | Mintage | VG-8 | F-12 | VF-20 | XF-40 | MS-60 | MS-63 | Prf-63 |
|---|---|---|---|---|---|---|---|---|---|
| 72a | 1968 Ottawa reeding | 87,412,930 | — | — | — | 0.15 | 0.25 | 0.35 | — |

   Philadelphia reeding

**Composition:** Nickel.

| KM# | Date | Mintage | VG-8 | F-12 | VF-20 | XF-40 | MS-60 | MS-63 | Prf-63 |
|---|---|---|---|---|---|---|---|---|---|
| 73 | 1968 Philadelphia reeding | 85,170,000 | — | — | — | 0.15 | 0.25 | 0.35 | — |
| | 1969 lg.date, lg.ship, 4 known | — | — | 4,750 | 6,600 | 10,000 | 14,150 | — | — |

**Composition:** Nickel. **Reverse:** Redesigned smaller ship.

| KM# | Date | Mintage | VG-8 | F-12 | VF-20 | XF-40 | MS-60 | MS-63 | Prf-63 |
|---|---|---|---|---|---|---|---|---|---|
| 77.1 | 1969 | 55,833,929 | — | — | — | 0.15 | 0.25 | 0.35 | — |
| | 1970 | 5,249,296 | — | — | — | 0.25 | 0.65 | 0.95 | — |
| | 1971 | 41,016,968 | — | — | — | 0.15 | 0.25 | 0.35 | — |
| | 1972 | 60,169,387 | — | — | — | 0.15 | 0.25 | 0.35 | — |
| | 1973 | 167,715,435 | — | — | — | 0.15 | 0.25 | 0.35 | — |
| | 1974 | 201,566,565 | — | — | — | 0.15 | 0.25 | 0.35 | — |
| | 1975 | 207,680,000 | — | — | — | 0.15 | 0.25 | 0.35 | — |
| | 1976 | 95,018,533 | — | — | — | 0.15 | 0.25 | 0.35 | — |
| | 1977 | 128,452,206 | — | — | — | 0.15 | 0.25 | 0.35 | — |
| | 1978 | 170,366,431 | — | — | — | 0.15 | 0.25 | 0.35 | — |

**Composition:** Nickel. **Obverse:** Smaller bust.

| KM# | Date | Mintage | VG-8 | F-12 | VF-20 | XF-40 | MS-60 | MS-63 | Prf-63 |
|---|---|---|---|---|---|---|---|---|---|
| 77.2 | 1979 | 237,321,321 | — | — | — | 0.15 | 0.25 | 0.35 | — |
| | 1980 | 170,111,533 | — | — | — | 0.15 | 0.25 | 0.35 | — |
| | 1981 | 123,912,900 | — | — | — | 0.15 | 0.25 | 0.35 | — |
| | 1981 | 199,000 | — | — | — | — | — | — | 1.50 |
| | 1982 | 93,475,000 | — | — | — | 0.15 | 0.25 | 0.35 | — |
| | 1982 | 180,908 | — | — | — | — | — | — | 1.50 |
| | 1983 | 111,065,000 | — | — | — | 0.15 | 0.25 | 0.35 | — |
| | 1983 | 168,000 | — | — | — | — | — | — | 2.00 |
| | 1984 | 121,690,000 | — | — | — | 0.15 | 0.25 | 0.35 | — |
| | 1984 | 161,602 | — | — | — | — | — | — | 2.00 |
| | 1985 | 143,025,000 | — | — | — | 0.15 | 0.25 | 0.35 | — |
| | 1985 | 157,037 | — | — | — | — | — | — | 2.00 |
| | 1986 | 168,620,000 | — | — | — | 0.15 | 0.25 | 0.35 | — |
| | 1986 | 175,745 | — | — | — | — | — | — | 2.00 |
| | 1987 | 147,309,000 | — | — | — | 0.15 | 0.25 | 0.35 | — |
| | 1987 | 179,004 | — | — | — | — | — | — | 2.00 |
| | 1988 | 162,998,558 | — | — | — | 0.15 | 0.25 | 0.35 | — |
| | 1988 | 175,259 | — | — | — | — | — | — | 2.00 |
| | 1989 | 199,104,414 | — | — | — | 0.15 | 0.25 | 0.35 | — |
| | 1989 | 170,528 | — | — | — | — | — | — | 3.00 |

**Composition:** Nickel. **Obverse:** Elizabeth II effigy **Obv. Designer:** dePedery-Hunt.

| KM# | Date | Mintage | VG-8 | F-12 | VF-20 | XF-40 | MS-60 | MS-63 | Prf-63 |
|---|---|---|---|---|---|---|---|---|---|
| 183 | 1990 | 65,023,000 | — | — | — | 0.15 | 0.25 | 0.35 | — |
| | 1990 | 140,649 | — | — | — | — | — | — | 3.00 |

| KM# | Date | Mintage | VG-8 | F-12 | VF-20 | XF-40 | MS-60 | MS-63 | Prf-63 |
|---|---|---|---|---|---|---|---|---|---|
| | 1991 | 50,397,000 | — | — | — | 0.15 | 0.25 | 0.35 | — |
| | 1991 | 131,888 | — | — | — | — | — | — | 6.50 |
| | 1993 | 135,569,000 | — | — | — | 0.15 | 0.25 | 0.35 | — |
| | 1993 | 143,065 | — | — | — | — | — | 3.00 | 3.00 |
| | 1994 | 145,800,000 | — | | — | 0.15 | 0.25 | 0.35 | — |
| | 1994 | 146,424 | — | — | — | — | — | — | 3.00 |
| | 1995 | 145,800,000 | — | — | — | 0.15 | 0.25 | 0.35 | — |
| | 1995 | 50,000 | — | — | — | — | — | — | 3.00 |
| | 1998 | — | — | — | — | 0.15 | 0.25 | 0.35 | — |
| | 1998W in mint sets only | — | — | — | — | — | — | 2.75 | — |
| | 1999 | — | — | — | — | 0.15 | 0.25 | 0.35 | — |
| | 1999W | — | — | — | — | — | — | — | — |
| | 2000 | — | — | — | — | 0.15 | 0.25 | 0.35 | — |
| | 2000W in mint sets only | — | — | — | — | — | — | 2.75 | — |

**Composition:** Nickel Plated Steel.

| KM# | Date | Mintage | VG-8 | F-12 | VF-20 | XF-40 | MS-60 | MS-63 | Prf-63 |
|---|---|---|---|---|---|---|---|---|---|
| 183a | 1996 | 51,814,000 | — | — | — | 0.15 | 0.25 | 0.35 | — |
| | 1997 | 42,882,000 | — | — | — | 0.15 | 0.25 | 0.35 | — |
| | 1998 | — | — | — | — | 0.15 | 0.25 | 0.35 | — |
| | 1998W In Mint sets only | — | — | — | — | — | — | 2.75 | — |

**Weight:** 2.4000 g. **Composition:** 0.9250 Silver., 0.0713 oz. ASW.

| KM# | Date | Mintage | VG-8 | F-12 | VF-20 | XF-40 | MS-60 | MS-63 | Prf-63 |
|---|---|---|---|---|---|---|---|---|---|
| 183b | 1996 | — | — | — | — | — | — | 5.50 | — |
| | 1997 | — | — | — | — | — | — | 5.50 | — |
| | 1998 in proof sets only | — | — | — | — | — | — | 4.00 | — |
| | 1998O in proof sets only | — | — | — | — | — | — | 4.00 | — |

# 20 CENTS

**Weight:** 4.6480 g. **Composition:** 0.9250 Silver., 0.1382 oz. ASW.

| KM# | Date | Mintage | VG-8 | F-12 | VF-20 | XF-40 | MS-60 | MS-63 | Prf-63 |
|---|---|---|---|---|---|---|---|---|---|
| 4 | 1858 | 750,000 | 40.00 | 60.00 | 90.00 | 170 | 725 | 1,950 | — |

# 25 CENTS

**Weight:** 5.8100 g. **Composition:** 0.9250 Silver., 0.1728 oz. ASW.

| KM# | Date | Mintage | VG-8 | F-12 | VF-20 | XF-40 | MS-60 | MS-63 | Prf-63 |
|---|---|---|---|---|---|---|---|---|---|
| 5 | 1870 | 900,000 | 11.00 | 25.00 | 55.00 | 110 | 450 | 1,250 | — |
| | 1871 | 400,000 | 14.00 | 30.00 | 75.00 | 180 | 600 | 1,800 | — |
| | 1871H | 748,000 | 16.00 | 30.00 | 85.00 | 175 | 500 | 1,500 | — |
| | 1872H | 2,240,000 | 7.00 | 15.00 | 35.00 | 75.00 | 365 | 1,000 | — |
| | 1874H | 1,600,000 | 7.00 | 12.00 | 35.00 | 80.00 | 300 | 800 | — |
| | 1875H | 1,000,000 | 225 | 450 | 1,200 | 2,250 | 8,750 | 14,750 | — |
| | 1880H narrow 0 | 400,000 | 30.00 | 60.00 | 165 | 345 | 800 | 2,250 | — |
| | 1880H wide 0 | Inc. above | 75.00 | 165 | 325 | 750 | 2,150 | 4,250 | — |
| | 1880H wide/narrow 0 | Inc. above | 90.00 | 165 | 350 | 650 | — | — | — |
| | 1881H | 820,000 | 15.00 | 35.00 | 65.00 | 175 | 800 | 1,600 | — |
| | 1882H | 600,000 | 15.00 | 35.00 | 65.00 | 175 | 800 | 1,700 | — |
| | 1883H | 960,000 | 12.00 | 25.00 | 50.00 | 120 | 450 | 1,250 | — |
| | 1885 | 192,000 | 75.00 | 150 | 325 | 825 | 3,000 | 6,000 | — |
| | 1886/3 | 540,000 | 15.00 | 35.00 | 75.00 | 215 | 850 | 2,200 | — |
| | 1886 | Inc. above | 12.00 | 25.00 | 65.00 | 200 | 800 | 2,000 | — |
| | 1887 | 100,000 | 75.00 | 175 | 350 | 845 | 3,650 | 7,000 | — |
| | 1888 | 400,000 | 12.00 | 25.00 | 55.00 | 150 | 550 | 1,400 | — |

| KM# | Date | Mintage | VG-8 | F-12 | VF-20 | XF-40 | MS-60 | MS-63 | Prf-63 |
|-----|------|---------|------|------|-------|-------|-------|-------|--------|
| | 1889 | 66,324 | 95.00 | 175 | 350 | 825 | 3,500 | 6,500 | — |
| | 1890H | 200,000 | 15.00 | 35.00 | 75.00 | 200 | 950 | 2,250 | — |
| | 1891 | 120,000 | 50.00 | 90.00 | 210 | 410 | 1,200 | 2,500 | — |
| | 1892 | 510,000 | 9.00 | 16.00 | 45.00 | 130 | 550 | 1,600 | — |
| | 1893 | 100,000 | 75.00 | 145 | 275 | 540 | 1,450 | 3,000 | — |
| | 1894 | 220,000 | 15.00 | 28.00 | 70.00 | 180 | 700 | 1,600 | — |
| | 1899 | 415,580 | 6.00 | 9.75 | 27.00 | 80.00 | 450 | 1,000 | — |
| | 1900 | 1,320,000 | 6.00 | 9.75 | 27.00 | 80.00 | 325 | 975 | — |
| | 1901 | 640,000 | 6.00 | 9.75 | 27.00 | 80.00 | 350 | 975 | — |

**Weight:** 5.8100 g. **Composition:** 0.9250 Silver., 0.1728 oz. ASW.

| KM# | Date | Mintage | VG-8 | F-12 | VF-20 | XF-40 | MS-60 | MS-63 | Prf-63 |
|-----|------|---------|------|------|-------|-------|-------|-------|--------|
| 11 | 1902 | 464,000 | 7.00 | 12.00 | 35.00 | 110 | 500 | 1,450 | — |
| | 1902H | 800,000 | 4.00 | 7.25 | 32.00 | 60.00 | 200 | 375 | — |
| | 1903 | 846,150 | 5.00 | 12.00 | 35.00 | 110 | 400 | 1,250 | — |
| | 1904 | 400,000 | 10.00 | 28.00 | 80.00 | 250 | 1,250 | 4,000 | — |
| | 1905 | 800,000 | 5.50 | 15.00 | 65.00 | 160 | 1,350 | 4,250 | — |
| | 1906 large crown | 1,237,843 | 5.00 | 7.25 | 27.00 | 70.00 | 350 | 1,200 | — |
| | 1906 small crown | Inc. above | — | — | — | — | — | — | — |
| | 1907 | 2,088,000 | 4.00 | 7.25 | 27.00 | 70.00 | 325 | 1,000 | — |
| | 1908 | 495,016 | 6.00 | 12.00 | 45.00 | 125 | 300 | 825 | — |
| | 1909 | 1,335,929 | 5.00 | 9.00 | 40.00 | 150 | 485 | 1,350 | — |

**Weight:** 5.8319 g. **Composition:** 0.9250 Silver., 0.1734 oz. ASW.

| KM# | Date | Mintage | VG-8 | F-12 | VF-20 | XF-40 | MS-60 | MS-63 | Prf-63 |
|-----|------|---------|------|------|-------|-------|-------|-------|--------|
| 11a | 1910 | 3,577,569 | 3.00 | 7.25 | 26.00 | 60.00 | 225 | 500 | — |

**Weight:** 5.8319 g. **Composition:** 0.9250 Silver., 0.1734 oz. ASW.

| KM# | Date | Mintage | VG-8 | F-12 | VF-20 | XF-40 | MS-60 | MS-63 | Prf-63 |
|-----|------|---------|------|------|-------|-------|-------|-------|--------|
| 18 | 1911 | 1,721,341 | 4.00 | 12.00 | 25.00 | 60.00 | 225 | 350 | — |

**Weight:** 5.8319 g. **Composition:** 0.9250 Silver., 0.1734 oz. ASW.

| KM# | Date | Mintage | VG-8 | F-12 | VF-20 | XF-40 | MS-60 | MS-63 | Prf-63 |
|-----|------|---------|------|------|-------|-------|-------|-------|--------|
| 24 | 1912 | 2,544,199 | 2.25 | 3.50 | 10.00 | 30.00 | 250 | 1,000 | — |
| | 1913 | 2,213,595 | 2.25 | 3.50 | 10.00 | 30.00 | 200 | 850 | — |
| | 1914 | 1,215,397 | 2.50 | 4.00 | 15.00 | 40.00 | 400 | 1,500 | — |
| | 1915 | 242,382 | 6.00 | 20.00 | 80.00 | 280 | 1,550 | 4,000 | — |
| | 1916 | 1,462,566 | 2.50 | 3.25 | 10.00 | 25.00 | 150 | 450 | — |
| | 1917 | 3,365,644 | 2.25 | 3.00 | 7.00 | 15.00 | 110 | 200 | — |
| | 1918 | 4,175,649 | 2.25 | 3.00 | 6.00 | 15.00 | 75.00 | 185 | — |
| | 1919 | 5,852,262 | 2.25 | 3.00 | 6.00 | 15.00 | 75.00 | 185 | — |

Dot

**Weight:** 5.8319 g. **Composition:** 0.8000 Silver., 0.1500 oz. ASW.

| KM# | Date | Mintage | VG-8 | F-12 | VF-20 | XF-40 | MS-60 | MS-63 | Prf-63 |
|-----|------|---------|------|------|-------|-------|-------|-------|--------|
| 24a | 1920 | 1,975,278 | 2.25 | 3.00 | 8.00 | 22.00 | 140 | 425 | — |
| | 1921 | 597,337 | 7.00 | 16.00 | 55.00 | 175 | 825 | 2,000 | — |
| | 1927 | 468,096 | 15.00 | 28.00 | 65.00 | 150 | 520 | 1,200 | — |
| | 1928 | 2,114,178 | 2.25 | 3.00 | 8.00 | 22.00 | 110 | 300 | — |
| | 1929 | 2,690,562 | 2.25 | 2.75 | 8.00 | 22.00 | 110 | 350 | — |
| | 1930 | 968,748 | 2.25 | 3.50 | 10.00 | 25.00 | 185 | 525 | — |
| | 1931 | 537,815 | 2.25 | 3.50 | 12.00 | 27.50 | 175 | 400 | — |

| KM# | Date | Mintage | VG-8 | F-12 | VF-20 | XF-40 | MS-60 | MS-63 | Prf-63 |
|-----|------|---------|------|------|-------|-------|-------|-------|--------|
|  | 1932 | 537,994 | 2.50 | 4.00 | 13.00 | 30.00 | 150 | 400 | — |
|  | 1933 | 421,282 | 3.00 | 4.50 | 15.00 | 30.00 | 150 | 250 | — |
|  | 1934 | 384,350 | 3.50 | 6.00 | 22.00 | 45.00 | 150 | 400 | — |
|  | 1935 | 537,772 | 3.50 | 5.00 | 17.50 | 42.00 | 125 | 275 | — |
|  | 1936 | 972,094 | 2.25 | 3.50 | 8.00 | 15.00 | 70.00 | 185 | — |
|  | 1936 dot | 153,322 | 20.00 | 40.00 | 110 | 225 | 600 | — | — |

**Note:** David Akers John Jay Pittman sale Part Three, 10-99, nearly Choice Unc. realized $6,900.

**Maple leaf**

**Weight:** 5.8319 g. **Composition:** 0.8000 Silver., 0.1500 oz. ASW.

| KM# | Date | Mintage | VG-8 | F-12 | VF-20 | XF-40 | MS-60 | MS-63 | Prf-63 |
|-----|------|---------|------|------|-------|-------|-------|-------|--------|
| 35 | 1937 | 2,690,176 | 1.75 | 2.75 | 4.00 | 5.00 | 10.00 | 25.00 | — |
|  | 1938 | 3,149,245 | 1.75 | 2.75 | 4.50 | 6.50 | 40.00 | 85.00 | — |
|  | 1939 | 3,532,495 | 1.50 | 2.25 | 3.00 | 6.50 | 35.00 | 75.00 | — |
|  | 1940 | 9,583,650 | BV | 1.50 | 2.50 | 4.50 | 10.00 | 20.00 | — |
|  | 1941 | 6,654,672 | BV | 1.50 | 2.50 | 4.50 | 10.00 | 20.00 | — |
|  | 1942 | 6,935,871 | BV | 1.50 | 2.50 | 4.50 | 10.00 | 20.00 | — |
|  | 1943 | 13,559,575 | BV | 1.50 | 2.50 | 4.00 | 10.00 | 20.00 | — |
|  | 1944 | 7,216,237 | BV | 1.50 | 2.50 | 4.50 | 15.00 | 25.00 | — |
|  | 1945 | 5,296,495 | BV | 1.50 | 2.50 | 4.00 | 10.00 | 20.00 | — |
|  | 1946 | 2,210,810 | BV | 1.50 | 3.00 | 5.00 | 30.00 | 45.00 | — |
|  | 1947 | 1,524,554 | BV | 1.50 | 4.00 | 8.00 | 30.00 | 55.00 | — |
|  | 1947 Dot after 7 | Inc. above | 25.00 | 30.00 | 50.00 | 85.00 | 175 | 450 | — |
|  | 1947 Maple leaf | 4,393,938 | BV | 1.50 | 2.75 | 4.00 | 12.00 | 25.00 | — |

**Weight:** 5.8319 g. **Composition:** 0.8000 Silver., 0.1500 oz. ASW. **Obverse:** Modified legend.

| KM# | Date | Mintage | VG-8 | F-12 | VF-20 | XF-40 | MS-60 | MS-63 | Prf-63 |
|-----|------|---------|------|------|-------|-------|-------|-------|--------|
| 44 | 1948 | 2,564,424 | BV | 1.50 | 3.00 | 5.00 | 40.00 | 90.00 | — |
|  | 1949 | 7,988,830 | — | | 2.25 | 2.50 | 6.00 | 13.00 | — |
|  | 1950 | 9,673,335 | — | | 2.25 | 2.50 | 5.00 | 10.00 | — |
|  | 1951 | 8,290,719 | — | | 2.25 | 2.50 | 4.00 | 9.00 | — |
|  | 1952 | 8,859,642 | — | | 2.25 | 2.50 | 4.00 | 9.00 | — |

**Weight:** 5.8319 g. **Composition:** 0.8000 Silver., 0.1500 oz. ASW. **Obverse:** Elizabeth II effigy. **Obv. Designer:** Gillick.

| KM# | Date | Mintage | VG-8 | F-12 | VF-20 | XF-40 | MS-60 | MS-63 | Prf-63 |
|-----|------|---------|------|------|-------|-------|-------|-------|--------|
| 52 | 1953 NSS | 10,546,769 | — | | 2.25 | 2.50 | 4.00 | 7.00 | — |
|  | 1953 SS | Inc. above | — | | 2.25 | 3.00 | 6.00 | 12.00 | — |
|  | 1954 | 2,318,891 | BV | 2.25 | 3.00 | 6.00 | 15.00 | 25.00 | — |
|  | 1955 | 9,552,505 | — | — | | 2.25 | 3.50 | 6.00 | — |
|  | 1956 | 11,269,353 | — | — | | 2.25 | 3.00 | 5.00 | — |
|  | 1957 | 12,770,190 | — | — | | 1.50 | 2.00 | 4.00 | — |
|  | 1958 | 9,336,910 | — | — | | 1.50 | 2.00 | 4.00 | — |
|  | 1959 | 13,503,461 | — | — | — | | 2.25 | 2.50 | — |
|  | 1960 | 22,835,327 | — | — | — | | 1.50 | 2.50 | — |
|  | 1961 | 18,164,368 | — | — | — | | 1.50 | 2.50 | — |
|  | 1962 | 29,559,266 | — | — | — | | 1.50 | 2.25 | — |
|  | 1963 | 21,180,652 | — | — | — | | 1.25 | 1.75 | — |
|  | 1964 | 36,479,343 | — | — | — | | 1.25 | 1.75 | — |

**Weight:** 5.8319 g. **Composition:** 0.8000 Silver., 0.1500 oz. ASW. **Obverse:** Elizabeth II effigy. **Obv. Designer:** Machin.

| KM# | Date | Mintage | VG-8 | F-12 | VF-20 | XF-40 | MS-60 | MS-63 | Prf-63 |
|-----|------|---------|------|------|-------|-------|-------|-------|--------|
| 62 | 1965 | 44,708,869 | — | — | — | | 1.25 | 1.75 | — |
| | 1966 | 25,626,315 | — | — | — | | 1.25 | 1.75 | — |

**Weight:** 5.8319 g. **Composition:** 0.5000 Silver., 0.0937 oz. ASW. **Obverse:** Elizabeth II effigy. **Obv. Designer:** Machin.

| KM# | Date | Mintage | VG-8 | F-12 | VF-20 | XF-40 | MS-60 | MS-63 | Prf-63 |
|-----|------|---------|------|------|-------|-------|-------|-------|--------|
| 62a | 1968 | 71,464,000 | — | — | — | | 0.75 | 1.75 | — |

**Composition:** Nickel. **Obverse:** Elizabeth II effigy. **Obv. Designer:** Machin. **Previous Catalog#:** 74.1

| KM# | Date | Mintage | VG-8 | F-12 | VF-20 | XF-40 | MS-60 | MS-63 | Prf-63 |
|-----|------|---------|------|------|-------|-------|-------|-------|--------|
| 62b | 1968 | 88,686,931 | — | — | — | 0.30 | 0.50 | 0.75 | — |
| | 1969 | 133,037,929 | — | — | — | 0.30 | 0.50 | 0.75 | — |
| | 1970 | 10,302,010 | — | — | — | 0.30 | 1.25 | 2.25 | — |
| | 1971 | 48,170,428 | — | — | — | 0.30 | 0.50 | 0.75 | — |
| | 1972 | 43,743,387 | — | — | — | 0.30 | 0.50 | 0.75 | — |
| | 1974 | 192,360,598 | — | — | — | 0.30 | 0.50 | 0.75 | — |
| | 1975 | 141,148,000 | — | — | — | 0.30 | 0.50 | 0.75 | — |
| | 1976 | 86,898,261 | — | — | — | 0.30 | 0.50 | 0.75 | — |
| | 1977 | 99,634,555 | — | — | — | 0.30 | 0.50 | 0.75 | — |
| | 1978 | 176,475,408 | — | — | — | 0.30 | 0.50 | 0.75 | — |

**Composition:** Nickel. **Obverse:** Elizabeth II effigy, smaller bust. **Obv. Designer:** Machin.

| KM# | Date | Mintage | VG-8 | F-12 | VF-20 | XF-40 | MS-60 | MS-63 | Prf-63 |
|-----|------|---------|------|------|-------|-------|-------|-------|--------|
| 74 | 1979 | 131,042,905 | — | — | — | 0.30 | 0.50 | 0.75 | — |
| | 1980 | 76,178,000 | — | — | — | 0.30 | 0.50 | 0.75 | — |
| | 1981 | 131,580,272 | — | — | — | 0.30 | 0.50 | 0.75 | — |
| | 1981 | 199,000 | — | — | — | — | — | — | 2.00 |
| | 1982 | 171,926,000 | — | — | — | 0.30 | 0.50 | 0.75 | — |
| | 1982 | 180,908 | — | — | — | — | — | — | 2.00 |
| | 1983 | 13,162,000 | — | — | — | 0.30 | 0.75 | 1.50 | — |
| | 1983 | 168,000 | — | — | — | — | — | — | 3.00 |
| | 1984 | 121,668,000 | — | — | — | 0.30 | 0.50 | 0.75 | — |
| | 1984 | 161,602 | — | — | — | — | — | — | 2.00 |
| | 1985 | 158,734,000 | — | — | — | 0.30 | 0.50 | 0.75 | — |
| | 1985 | 157,037 | — | — | — | — | — | — | 2.00 |
| | 1986 | 132,220,000 | — | — | — | 0.30 | 0.50 | 0.75 | — |
| | 1986 | 175,745 | — | — | — | — | — | — | 3.00 |
| | 1987 | 53,408,000 | — | — | — | 0.30 | 0.65 | 1.25 | — |
| | 1987 | 179,004 | — | — | — | — | — | — | 3.00 |
| | 1988 | 80,368,473 | — | — | — | 0.30 | 0.65 | 1.25 | — |
| | 1988 | 175,259 | — | — | — | — | — | — | 3.50 |
| | 1989 | 119,796,307 | — | — | — | 0.30 | 0.50 | 0.75 | — |
| | 1989 | 170,928 | — | — | — | — | — | — | 3.50 |

**Composition:** Nickel. **Obverse:** Elizabeth II effigy. **Obv. Designer:** dePedery-Hunt.

| KM# | Date | Mintage | VG-8 | F-12 | VF-20 | XF-40 | MS-60 | MS-63 | Prf-63 |
|-----|------|---------|------|------|-------|-------|-------|-------|--------|
| 184 | 1990 | 31,258,000 | — | — | — | 0.30 | 0.65 | 1.25 | — |
| | 1990 | 140,649 | — | — | — | — | — | — | 3.50 |
| | 1991 | 459,000 | — | — | 2.00 | 4.00 | 8.00 | 12.00 | — |
| | 1991 | 131,888 | — | — | — | — | — | — | 40.00 |
| | 1993 | 73,758,000 | — | — | — | 0.30 | 0.65 | 1.25 | — |
| | 1993 | 143,065 | — | — | — | — | — | — | 3.00 |
| | 1994 | 77,670,000 | — | — | — | 0.30 | 0.65 | 1.25 | — |
| | 1994 | 146,424 | — | — | — | — | — | — | 5.00 |
| | 1995 | 89,210,000 | — | — | — | 0.30 | 0.65 | 1.25 | — |
| | 1995 | 50,000 | — | — | — | — | — | — | 5.00 |
| | 1998 in mint sets only | — | — | — | — | — | — | 1.75 | — |
| | 1998W | — | — | — | — | — | — | 5.00 | — |

| KM# | Date | Mintage | VG-8 | F-12 | VF-20 | XF-40 | MS-60 | MS-63 | Prf-63 |
|-----|------|---------|------|------|-------|-------|-------|-------|--------|
| | 1999 | — | — | — | — | — | — | 1.75 | — |
| | 1999W | — | — | — | — | — | — | — | — |
| | 2000 | — | — | — | — | — | — | 1.75 | — |
| | 2000W | — | — | — | — | — | — | 5.00 | — |

**Composition:** Nickel Plated Steel.

| KM# | Date | Mintage | VG-8 | F-12 | VF-20 | XF-40 | MS-60 | MS-63 | Prf-63 |
|-----|------|---------|------|------|-------|-------|-------|-------|--------|
| 184a | 1996 | 28,106,000 | — | — | — | 0.30 | 0.65 | 1.25 | — |
| | 1997 | — | — | — | — | 0.30 | 0.65 | 1.25 | — |
| | 1998 | — | — | — | — | — | — | 1.75 | — |
| | 1998W In Mint sets only | — | — | — | — | — | — | 5.00 | — |

**Weight:** 5.9000 g. **Composition:** 0.9250 Silver., 0.1754 oz. ASW.

| KM# | Date | Mintage | VG-8 | F-12 | VF-20 | XF-40 | MS-60 | MS-63 | Prf-63 |
|-----|------|---------|------|------|-------|-------|-------|-------|--------|
| 184b | 1996 | — | — | — | — | — | — | — | 6.50 |
| | 1997 | — | — | — | — | — | — | — | 6.50 |
| | 1998 in proof sets only | — | — | — | — | — | — | — | 3.50 |
| | 1998O in proof sets only | — | — | — | — | — | — | — | 3.50 |

# 50 CENTS

**Weight:** 11.6200 g. **Composition:** 0.9250 Silver., .3456 oz. ASW.

| KM# | Date | Mintage | VG-8 | F-12 | VF-20 | XF-40 | MS-60 | MS-63 | Prf-63 |
|-----|------|---------|------|------|-------|-------|-------|-------|--------|
| 6 | 1870 | 450,000 | 475 | 800 | 1,600 | 3,100 | 13,500 | 24,500 | — |
| | 1870 LCW | Inc. above | 40.00 | 70.00 | 160 | 375 | 3,250 | 10,000 | — |
| | 1871 | 200,000 | 45.00 | 100.00 | 220 | 500 | 4,000 | 10,500 | — |
| | 1871H | 45,000 | 80.00 | 175 | 350 | 800 | 6,500 | 11,000 | — |
| | 1872H | 80,000 | 40.00 | 70.00 | 170 | 400 | 3,600 | 10,250 | — |
| | 1872H inverted A for V in Victoria | Inc. above | 95.00 | 200 | 495 | 1,500 | 6,600 | 11,000 | — |
| | 1881H | 150,000 | 40.00 | 80.00 | 175 | 450 | 4,000 | 10,500 | — |
| | 1888 | 60,000 | 150 | 220 | 475 | 950 | 5,400 | 11,000 | — |
| | 1890H | 20,000 | 600 | 1,200 | 1,800 | 3,200 | 11,000 | 20,000 | — |
| | 1892 | 151,000 | 45.00 | 90.00 | 300 | 500 | 6,000 | 10,500 | — |
| | 1894 | 29,036 | 225 | 425 | 920 | 2,000 | 8,100 | 15,000 | — |
| | 1898 | 100,000 | 45.00 | 100.00 | 225 | 450 | 4,500 | 10,500 | — |
| | 1899 | 50,000 | 90.00 | 190 | 425 | 1,100 | 7,100 | 12,000 | — |
| | 1900 | 118,000 | 40.00 | 65.00 | 160 | 365 | 4,000 | 10,500 | — |
| | 1901 | 80,000 | 42.00 | 70.00 | 165 | 400 | 4,200 | 10,500 | — |

Victorian leaves          Edwardian leaves

**Weight:** 11.6200 g. **Composition:** 0.9250 Silver., .3456 oz. ASW.

| KM# | Date | Mintage | VG-8 | F-12 | VF-20 | XF-40 | MS-60 | MS-63 | Prf-63 |
|-----|------|---------|------|------|-------|-------|-------|-------|--------|
| 12 | 1902 | 120,000 | 11.00 | 22.50 | 75.00 | 200 | 1,100 | 3,000 | — |
| | 1903H | 140,000 | 18.00 | 35.00 | 90.00 | 225 | 1,100 | 3,000 | — |
| | 1904 | 60,000 | 75.00 | 150 | 285 | 625 | 2,650 | 7,000 | — |
| | 1905 | 40,000 | 85.00 | 200 | 415 | 1,000 | 4,000 | 10,000 | — |
| | 1906 | 350,000 | 10.00 | 25.00 | 70.00 | 190 | 1,150 | 3,250 | — |
| | 1907 | 300,000 | 8.00 | 25.00 | 70.00 | 200 | 1,150 | 3,850 | — |
| | 1908 | 128,119 | 14.75 | 45.00 | 125 | 275 | 800 | 1,650 | — |
| | 1909 | 302,118 | 13.00 | 40.00 | 150 | 350 | 2,175 | 6,000 | — |
| | 1910 Victorian leaves | 649,521 | 9.00 | 22.00 | 65.00 | 180 | 950 | 3,150 | — |

**Weight:** 11.6638 g. **Composition:** 0.9250 Silver., .3461 oz. ASW.

| KM# | Date | Mintage | VG-8 | F-12 | VF-20 | XF-40 | MS-60 | MS-63 | Prf-63 |
|-----|------|---------|------|------|-------|-------|-------|-------|--------|
| 12a | 1910 Edwardian leaves | Inc. above | 9.00 | 22.00 | 65.00 | 180 | 1,000 | 3,150 | — |

**Weight:** 11.6638 g. **Composition:** 0.9250 Silver., .3461 oz. ASW.

| KM# | Date | Mintage | VG-8 | F-12 | VF-20 | XF-40 | MS-60 | MS-63 | Prf-63 |
|-----|------|---------|------|------|-------|-------|-------|-------|--------|
| 19 | 1911 | 209,972 | 8.00 | 55.00 | 200 | 425 | 1,100 | 2,900 | — |

**Weight:** 11.6638 g. **Composition:** 0.9250 Silver., .3461 oz. ASW. **Obverse:** Modified legend

| KM# | Date | Mintage | VG-8 | F-12 | VF-20 | XF-40 | MS-60 | MS-63 | Prf-63 |
|-----|------|---------|------|------|-------|-------|-------|-------|--------|
| 25 | 1912 | 285,867 | 4.50 | 16.00 | 65.00 | 175 | 850 | 2,200 | — |
| | 1913 | 265,889 | 4.50 | 16.00 | 85.00 | 210 | 1,100 | 4,000 | — |
| | 1914 | 160,128 | 8.00 | 40.00 | 120 | 375 | 2,000 | 6,000 | — |
| | 1916 | 459,070 | 3.00 | 9.00 | 35.00 | 85.00 | 550 | 1,800 | — |
| | 1917 | 752,213 | 3.00 | 7.00 | 25.00 | 70.00 | 350 | 950 | — |
| | 1918 | 754,989 | 3.00 | 6.00 | 20.00 | 60.00 | 300 | 800 | — |
| | 1919 | 1,113,429 | 3.00 | 6.00 | 20.00 | 60.00 | 300 | 1,100 | — |

**Weight:** 11.6638 g. **Composition:** 0.8000 Silver., .3000 oz. ASW.

| KM# | Date | Mintage | VG-8 | F-12 | VF-20 | XF-40 | MS-60 | MS-63 | Prf-63 |
|-----|------|---------|------|------|-------|-------|-------|-------|--------|
| 25a | 1920 | 584,691 | 3.00 | 7.00 | 25.00 | 90.00 | 400 | 950 | — |
| | 1921 75 to 100 known | — | 12,300 | 17,000 | 20,750 | 25,000 | 35,850 | 45,300 | |
| **Note:** David Akers John Jay Pittman sale, Part Three, 10-99, Gem Unc. realized $63,250 | | | | | | | | | |
| | 1929 | 228,328 | 3.00 | 7.00 | 25.00 | 70.00 | 375 | 850 | — |
| | 1931 | 57,581 | 5.00 | 18.00 | 60.00 | 160 | 725 | 1,900 | — |
| | 1932 | 19,213 | 50.00 | 100.00 | 250 | 600 | 2,800 | 6,000 | — |
| | 1934 | 39,539 | 8.00 | 20.00 | 60.00 | 160 | 500 | 1,150 | — |
| | 1936 | 38,550 | 7.00 | 15.00 | 50.00 | 125 | 400 | 900 | — |

**Weight:** 11.6638 g. **Composition:** 0.8000 Silver., .3000 oz. ASW.

| KM# | Date | Mintage | VG-8 | F-12 | VF-20 | XF-40 | MS-60 | MS-63 | Prf-63 |
|-----|------|---------|------|------|-------|-------|-------|-------|--------|
| 36 | 1937 | 192,016 | 2.50 | 3.00 | 5.50 | 7.00 | 20.00 | 45.00 | — |
| | 1938 | 192,018 | 3.00 | 5.00 | 10.00 | 28.00 | 90.00 | 250 | — |
| | 1939 | 287,976 | 3.00 | 4.25 | 7.50 | 16.50 | 60.00 | 160 | — |

| KM# | Date | Mintage | VG-8 | F-12 | VF-20 | XF-40 | MS-60 | MS-63 | Prf-63 |
|---|---|---|---|---|---|---|---|---|---|
|  | 1940 | 1,996,566 | BV | 1.75 | 3.00 | 5.00 | 18.00 | 60.00 | — |
|  | 1941 | 1,714,874 | BV | 1.75 | 3.00 | 5.00 | 18.00 | 60.00 | — |
|  | 1942 | 1,974,164 | BV | 1.75 | 3.00 | 5.00 | 18.00 | 60.00 | — |
|  | 1943 | 3,109,583 | BV | 1.75 | 3.00 | 5.00 | 18.00 | 60.00 | — |
|  | 1944 | 2,460,205 | BV | 1.75 | 3.00 | 5.00 | 18.00 | 60.00 | — |
|  | 1945 | 1,959,528 | BV | 1.75 | 3.00 | 5.00 | 18.00 | 60.00 | — |
|  | 1946 | 950,235 | BV | 2.25 | 4.00 | 8.50 | 55.00 | 110 | — |
|  | 1946 Hoof in 6 | Inc. above | 10.00 | 20.00 | 35.00 | 100.00 | 900 | 1,800 | — |
|  | 1947 Straight 7 | 424,885 | 2.00 | 4.50 | 6.00 | 9.00 | 50.00 | 160 | — |
|  | 1947 Curved 7 | Inc. above | 2.00 | 4.50 | 6.00 | 9.00 | 50.00 | 160 | — |
|  | 1947 Straight 7 | 38,433 | 14.00 | 18.00 | 25.00 | 50.00 | 125 | 215 | — |
|  | 1947 Curved 7 | Inc. above | 800 | 1,000 | 1,450 | 2,000 | 3,000 | 5,000 | — |

**Weight:** 11.6638 g. **Composition:** 0.8000 Silver., .3000 oz. ASW. **Obverse:** Modified legend

| KM# | Date | Mintage | VG-8 | F-12 | VF-20 | XF-40 | MS-60 | MS-63 | Prf-63 |
|---|---|---|---|---|---|---|---|---|---|
| 45 | 1948 | 37,784 | 30.00 | 40.00 | 50.00 | 70.00 | 110 | 150 | — |
|  | 1949 | 858,991 | 2.00 | 3.00 | 5.50 | 9.50 | 25.00 | 100.00 | — |
|  | 1949 Hoof over 9 | Inc. above | 5.00 | 11.50 | 22.00 | 45.00 | 225 | 550 | — |
|  | 1950 | 2,384,179 | 3.00 | 4.50 | 9.00 | 19.00 | 110 | 150 | — |
|  | 1950 Lines in 0 | Inc. above | BV | 2.00 | 3.00 | 4.00 | 8.00 | 20.00 | — |
|  | 1951 | 2,421,730 | BV | 1.50 | 2.50 | 3.50 | 6.00 | 17.00 | — |
|  | 1952 | 2,596,465 | BV | 1.50 | 2.50 | 3.50 | 6.00 | 11.00 | — |

**Weight:** 11.6638 g. **Composition:** 0.8000 Silver., .3000 oz. ASW. **Obverse:** Elizabeth II Effigy **Obv. Designer:** Gillick.

| KM# | Date | Mintage | VG-8 | F-12 | VF-20 | XF-40 | MS-60 | MS-63 | Prf-63 |
|---|---|---|---|---|---|---|---|---|---|
| 53 | 1953 Small date | 1,630,429 | — |  | 2.00 | 2.50 | 5.50 | 12.00 | — |
|  | 1953 Large date, straps | Inc. above | — |  | 3.50 | 5.00 | 12.00 | 22.00 | — |
|  | 1953 Large date without straps | Inc. above | BV | 3.00 | 4.50 | 11.50 | 50.00 | 90.00 | — |
|  | 1954 | 506,305 | BV | 2.50 | 4.75 | 7.00 | 20.00 | 30.00 | — |
|  | 1955 | 753,511 | BV | 2.00 | 3.00 | 5.00 | 12.00 | 22.00 | — |
|  | 1956 | 1,379,499 | — |  | 2.00 | 3.00 | 4.50 | 9.00 | — |
|  | 1957 | 2,171,689 | — |  | — | 1.75 | 3.50 | 6.00 | — |
|  | 1958 | 2,957,266 | — |  | — | 1.75 | 3.00 | 5.50 | — |

**Weight:** 11.6638 g. **Composition:** 0.8000 Silver., .3000 oz. ASW. **Reverse:** New shield

| KM# | Date | Mintage | VG-8 | F-12 | VF-20 | XF-40 | MS-60 | MS-63 | Prf-63 |
|---|---|---|---|---|---|---|---|---|---|
| 56 | 1959 | 3,095,535 | — | — | — | 1.75 | 2.50 | 4.50 | — |
|  | 1960 | 3,488,897 | — | — | — |  | 2.25 | 3.25 | — |
|  | 1961 | 3,584,417 | — | — | — |  | 2.00 | 3.00 | — |
|  | 1962 | 5,208,030 | — | — | — |  | 1.75 | 3.00 | — |
|  | 1963 | 8,348,871 | — | — | — |  | 1.75 | 3.00 | — |
|  | 1964 | 9,377,676 | — | — | — |  | 1.75 | 3.00 | — |

**Weight:** 11.6638 g. **Composition:** 0.8000 Silver., .3000 oz. ASW. **Obverse:** Elizabeth II effigy **Obv. Designer:** Machin.

| KM# | Date | Mintage | VG-8 | F-12 | VF-20 | XF-40 | MS-60 | MS-63 | Prf-63 |
|------|------|---------|------|------|-------|-------|-------|-------|--------|
| 63 | 1965 | 12,629,974 | — | — | — | | 1.75 | 3.00 | — |
| | 1966 | 7,920,496 | — | — | — | | 1.75 | 3.00 | — |

**Composition:** Nickel.

| KM# | Date | Mintage | VG-8 | F-12 | VF-20 | XF-40 | MS-60 | MS-63 | Prf-63 |
|------|------|---------|------|------|-------|-------|-------|-------|--------|
| 75.1 | 1968 | 3,966,932 | — | — | — | 0.50 | 0.65 | 1.00 | — |
| | 1969 | 7,113,929 | — | — | — | 0.50 | 0.65 | 1.00 | — |
| | 1970 | 2,429,526 | — | — | — | 0.50 | 0.65 | 1.00 | — |
| | 1971 | 2,166,444 | — | — | — | 0.50 | 0.65 | 1.00 | — |
| | 1972 | 2,515,632 | — | — | — | 0.50 | 0.65 | 1.00 | — |
| | 1973 | 2,546,096 | — | — | — | 0.50 | 0.65 | 1.00 | — |
| | 1974 | 3,436,650 | — | — | — | 0.50 | 0.65 | 1.00 | — |
| | 1975 | 3,710,000 | — | — | — | 0.50 | 0.65 | 1.00 | — |
| | 1976 | 2,940,719 | — | — | — | 0.50 | 0.65 | 1.00 | — |

**Composition:** Nickel. **Obverse:** Smaller bust

| KM# | Date | Mintage | VG-8 | F-12 | VF-20 | XF-40 | MS-60 | MS-63 | Prf-63 |
|------|------|---------|------|------|-------|-------|-------|-------|--------|
| 75.2 | 1977 | 709,839 | — | — | 0.50 | 0.75 | 1.35 | 2.00 | — |

**Composition:** Nickel. **Reverse:** Redesigned arms

| KM# | Date | Mintage | VG-8 | F-12 | VF-20 | XF-40 | MS-60 | MS-63 | Prf-63 |
|------|------|---------|------|------|-------|-------|-------|-------|--------|
| 75.3 | 1978 square jewels | 3,341,892 | — | — | — | 0.50 | 0.65 | 1.00 | — |
| | 1978 round jewels | Inc. above | — | — | 0.50 | 2.50 | 3.00 | 4.00 | — |
| | 1979 | 3,425,000 | — | — | — | 0.50 | 0.65 | 1.00 | — |
| | 1980 | 1,574,000 | — | — | — | 0.50 | 0.65 | 1.00 | — |
| | 1981 | 2,690,272 | — | — | — | 0.50 | 0.65 | 1.00 | — |
| | 1981 | 199,000 | — | — | — | — | — | — | 3.00 |
| | 1982 small beads (120) | 2,236,674 | — | — | — | 0.50 | 0.65 | 1.00 | — |
| | 1982 small beads (120) | 180,908 | — | — | — | — | — | — | 3.00 |
| | 1982 large beads (118) | Inc. above | — | — | — | 0.50 | 0.65 | 1.00 | — |
| | 1983 | 1,177,000 | — | — | — | 0.50 | 0.65 | 1.00 | — |
| | 1983 | 168,000 | — | — | — | — | — | — | 3.00 |
| | 1984 | 1,502,989 | — | — | — | 0.50 | 0.65 | 1.00 | — |
| | 1984 | 161,602 | — | — | — | — | — | — | 3.00 |
| | 1985 | 2,188,374 | — | — | — | 0.50 | 0.65 | 1.00 | — |
| | 1985 | 157,037 | — | — | — | — | — | — | 3.50 |
| | 1986 | 781,400 | — | — | — | 0.50 | 1.35 | 2.00 | — |
| | 1986 | 175,745 | — | — | — | — | — | — | 3.50 |
| | 1987 | 373,000 | — | — | — | 0.50 | 1.75 | 2.50 | — |
| | 1987 | 179,004 | — | — | — | — | — | — | 4.00 |
| | 1988 | 220,000 | — | — | — | 0.50 | 1.50 | 2.20 | — |

| KM# | Date | Mintage | VG-8 | F-12 | VF-20 | XF-40 | MS-60 | MS-63 | Prf-63 |
|-----|------|---------|------|------|-------|-------|-------|-------|--------|
|     | 1988 | 175,259 | — | — | — | — | — | — | 4.00 |
|     | 1989 | 266,419 | — | — | — | 0.50 | 1.75 | 2.75 | — |
|     | 1989 | 170,928 | — | — | — | — | — | — | 4.50 |

**Composition:** Nickel. **Obverse:** Elizabeth II effigy **Obv. Designer:** dePedery-Hunt.

| KM# | Date | Mintage | VG-8 | F-12 | VF-20 | XF-40 | MS-60 | MS-63 | Prf-63 |
|-----|------|---------|------|------|-------|-------|-------|-------|--------|
| 185 | 1990 | 207,000 | — | — | — | 0.50 | 2.00 | 3.00 | — |
|     | 1990 | 140,649 | — | — | — | — | — | — | 7.50 |
|     | 1991 | 490,000 | — | — | — | 0.50 | 0.85 | 1.50 | — |
|     | 1991 | 131,888 | — | — | — | — | — | — | 10.00 |
|     | 1993 | 393,000 | — | — | — | 0.50 | 0.85 | 1.50 | — |
|     | 1993 | 143,065 | — | — | — | — | — | — | 5.00 |
|     | 1994 | 987,000 | — | — | — | 0.50 | 0.75 | 1.00 | — |
|     | 1994 | 146,424 | — | — | — | — | — | — | 6.00 |
|     | 1995 | 626,000 | — | — | — | 0.50 | 0.75 | 1.00 | — |
|     | 1995 | 50,000 | — | — | — | — | — | — | 6.00 |
|     | 1996 | — | — | — | — | 0.50 | 0.65 | 1.00 | — |

**Composition:** Nickel Plated Steel.

| KM# | Date | Mintage | VG-8 | F-12 | VF-20 | XF-40 | MS-60 | MS-63 | Prf-63 |
|-----|------|---------|------|------|-------|-------|-------|-------|--------|
| 185a | 1996 | 458,000 | — | — | — | 0.50 | 0.65 | 1.00 | — |

**Weight:** 11.6638 g. **Composition:** 0.9250 Silver., .3461 oz. ASW.

| KM# | Date | Mintage | VG-8 | F-12 | VF-20 | XF-40 | MS-60 | MS-63 | Prf-63 |
|-----|------|---------|------|------|-------|-------|-------|-------|--------|
| 185b | 1996 | — | — | — | — | — | — | — | 7.50 |
|      | 1997 | — | — | — | — | — | — | — | 7.50 |

**Composition:** Nickel Plated Steel. **Reverse:** Redesigned arms

| KM# | Date | Mintage | VG-8 | F-12 | VF-20 | XF-40 | MS-60 | MS-63 | Prf-63 |
|-----|------|---------|------|------|-------|-------|-------|-------|--------|
| 290 | 1997 Redesigned Arms | 387,000 | — | — | — | 0.50 | 0.65 | 1.00 | — |
|     | 1998 | — | — | — | — | 0.50 | 0.65 | 1.00 | — |
|     | 1998W In Mint sets only | — | — | — | — | — | — | 5.00 | — |
|     | 1999 | — | — | — | — | 0.50 | 0.65 | 1.00 | — |
|     | 1999W | — | — | — | — | — | — | — | — |
|     | 2000 | — | — | — | — | 0.50 | 0.65 | 1.00 | — |
|     | 2000W | — | — | — | — | — | — | 5.00 | — |

**Weight:** 11.6638 g. **Composition:** 0.9250 Silver., .3461 oz. ASW. **Reverse:** Redesigned Arms

| KM# | Date | Mintage | VG-8 | F-12 | VF-20 | XF-40 | MS-60 | MS-63 | Prf-63 |
|-----|------|---------|------|------|-------|-------|-------|-------|--------|
| 290a | 1997 | — | — | — | — | — | — | — | 7.00 |
|      | 1998O in proof sets only | — | — | — | — | — | — | — | 6.00 |

# DOLLAR

**Weight:** 23.3276 g. **Composition:** 0.8000 Silver., 0.6000 oz. ASW. **Reverse:** Voyageur.

| KM# | Date | Mintage | F-12 | VF-20 | XF-40 | AU-50 | MS-60 | MS-63 |
|-----|------|---------|------|-------|-------|-------|-------|-------|
| 31 | 1936 | 339,600 | 8.50 | 12.50 | 16.50 | 21.50 | 35.00 | 72.00 |

| Pointed 7 | Blunt 7 | Maple leaf |

**Weight:** 23.3276 g. **Composition:** 0.8000 Silver., 0.6000 oz. ASW. **Reverse:** Voyageur.

| KM# | Date | Mintage | F-12 | VF-20 | XF-40 | AU-50 | MS-60 | MS-63 |
|-----|------|---------|------|-------|-------|-------|-------|-------|
| 37 | 1937 | 207,406 | 9.00 | 9.50 | 11.00 | 13.00 | 22.00 | 55.00 |
| | 1937 | 1,295 | — | — | — | — | — | — |
| | 1937 matte proof | Inc. above | — | — | — | — | — | — |
| | 1938 | 90,304 | 23.50 | 32.00 | 40.00 | 50.00 | 60.00 | 175 |
| | 1945 | 38,391 | 65.00 | 90.00 | 110 | 125 | 175 | 350 |
| | 1945 specimen | — | — | — | — | — | — | 1,800 |
| | 1946 | 93,055 | 12.50 | 22.50 | 31.00 | 37.50 | 60.00 | 175 |
| | 1947 pointed 7 | -2Inc. above | 55.00 | 70.00 | 85.00 | 110 | 245 | 800 |
| | 1947 blunt 7 | 65,595 | 35.00 | 50.00 | 70.00 | 90.00 | 110 | 200 |
| | 1947 maple leaf | 21,135 | 100.00 | 130 | 150 | 160 | 200 | 425 |

**Weight:** 23.3276 g. **Composition:** 0.8000 Silver., 0.6000 oz. ASW. **Obverse:** Modified left legend **Reverse:** Voyageur

| KM# | Date | Mintage | F-12 | VF-20 | XF-40 | AU-50 | MS-60 | MS-63 |
|-----|------|---------|------|-------|-------|-------|-------|-------|
| 46 | 1948 | 18,780 | 400 | 450 | 500 | 600 | 700 | 1,000 |
| | 1950 with 4 water lines | 261,002 | 5.00 | 7.00 | 9.00 | 12.00 | 15.00 | 28.00 |
| | 1950 with 4 water lines, 1 known, matte proof | — | — | — | — | — | — | — |
| | 1950 arnprior with 1-1/2 water lines | Inc. above | 6.50 | 8.50 | 12.50 | 16.00 | 30.00 | 80.00 |
| | 1951 with 4 water lines | 416,395 | 4.00 | 5.00 | 6.50 | 7.50 | 9.00 | 22.50 |
| | 1951 with 4 water lines | — | — | — | — | — | — | 375 |
| | 1951 arnprior with 1-1/2 water lines | Inc. above | 15.00 | 23.50 | 35.00 | 45.00 | 70.00 | 250 |
| | 1952 with 4 water lines | 406,148 | 4.00 | 5.00 | 6.50 | 7.50 | 10.00 | 22.50 |
| | 1952 arnprior | Inc. above | 35.00 | 55.00 | 70.00 | 120 | 175 | 375 |
| | 1952 arnprior | — | — | — | — | — | — | — |
| | 1952 without water lines | Inc. above | 5.00 | 6.00 | 8.00 | 10.00 | 16.50 | 30.00 |

**Weight:** 23.3276 g. **Composition:** 0.8000 Silver., 0.6000 oz. ASW. **Obverse:** Elizabeth II effigy **Reverse:** Voyageur **Obv. Designer:** Gillick. **Notes:** All genuine circulation strike 1955 Arnprior dollars have a die break running along the top of TI in the word GRATIA on the obverse.

| KM# | Date | Mintage | F-12 | VF-20 | XF-40 | AU-50 | MS-60 | MS-63 |
|-----|------|---------|------|-------|-------|-------|-------|-------|
| 54 | 1953 Without strap, wire rim | 1,074,578 | | 3.90 | 4.50 | 5.00 | 8.00 | 15.00 |
| | 1953 With strap, flat rim | Inc. above | | 3.90 | 4.50 | 5.00 | 8.00 | 15.00 |
| | 1954 | 246,606 | 4.00 | 7.00 | 10.00 | 12.00 | 16.50 | 31.50 |
| | 1955 With 4 water lines | 268,105 | 4.50 | 7.00 | 10.00 | 12.00 | 16.50 | 31.50 |
| | 1955 Arnprior with 1-1/2 water lines* | Inc. above | 40.00 | 45.00 | 55.00 | 65.00 | 75.00 | 140 |
| | 1956 | 209,092 | 7.00 | 9.00 | 12.50 | 15.50 | 19.00 | 30.00 |
| | 1957 With 4 water lines | 496,389 | — | | 4.75 | 5.50 | 7.50 | 11.00 |
| | 1957 With 1 water line | Inc. above | 4.50 | 5.50 | 7.50 | 8.50 | 10.00 | 20.00 |
| | 1959 | 1,443,502 | — | — | — | BV | 5.00 | 6.50 |
| | 1960 | 1,420,486 | — | — | — | BV | 5.00 | 6.50 |
| | 1961 | 1,262,231 | — | — | — | BV | 5.00 | 6.50 |
| | 1962 | 1,884,789 | — | — | — | BV | 5.00 | 6.50 |
| | 1963 | 4,179,981 | — | — | — | BV | 5.00 | 6.50 |

Large beads          Medium beads          Small beads

**Weight:** 23.3276 g. **Composition:** 0.8000 Silver., 0.6000 oz. ASW. **Obverse:** Elizabeth II effigy **Reverse:** Voyageur **Obv. Designer:** Machin.

| KM# | Date | Mintage | F-12 | VF-20 | XF-40 | AU-50 | MS-60 | MS-63 |
|-----|------|---------|------|-------|-------|-------|-------|-------|
| 64.1 | 1965 Small beads, pointed 5 | 10,768,569 | — | — | — | BV | 4.75 | 6.00 |
| | 1965 Small beads, blunt 5 | Inc. above | — | — | — | BV | 4.75 | 6.00 |
| | 1965 Large beads, blunt 5 | Inc. above | — | — | — | BV | 7.50 | 10.00 |
| | 1965 Large beads, pointed 5 | Inc. above | — | — | — | BV | 4.75 | 9.50 |
| | 1965 Medium beads, pointed 5 | Inc. above | | 5.75 | 8.75 | 10.75 | 14.00 | 27.50 |
| | 1966 Large beads | 9,912,178 | — | — | — | BV | 4.50 | 6.00 |
| | 1966 Small beads | 485 | — | — | 750 | 1,250 | 1,350 | 1,675 |

**Composition:** Nickel. **Diameter:** 32 mm. **Obverse:** Large bust **Reverse:** Voyageur

| KM# | Date | Mintage | MS-63 | P/L | Spec. |
|---|---|---|---|---|---|
| 76.1 | 1968 | 5,579,714 | 1.25 | — | — |
| | 1968 | 1,408,143 | — | 2.50 | — |
| | 1969 | 4,809,313 | 1.25 | — | — |
| | 1969 | 594,258 | — | 2.75 | — |
| | 1972 | 2,676,041 | 1.50 | — | — |
| | 1972 | 405,865 | — | 3.00 | — |

**Weight:** 23.3276 g. **Composition:** 0.5000 Silver., 0.3750 oz. ASW. **Diameter:** 36 mm. **Obverse:** Smaller bust **Reverse:** Voyageur

| KM# | Date | Mintage | F-12 | VF-20 | XF-40 | AU-50 | MS-60 | MS-63 |
|---|---|---|---|---|---|---|---|---|
| 64.2a | 1972 | 341,598 | — | — | — | — | — | — |

**Composition:** Nickel. **Diameter:** 32 mm. **Obverse:** Smaller bust **Reverse:** Voyageur

| KM# | Date | Mintage | MS-63 | P/L | Spec. |
|---|---|---|---|---|---|
| 76.2 | 1975 | 3,256,000 | 1.50 | — | — |
| | 1975 | 322,325 | — | 3.00 | — |
| | 1976 | 2,498,204 | 1.50 | — | — |
| | 1976 | 274,106 | — | 3.00 | — |

**Composition:** Nickel. **Diameter:** 32 mm. **Reverse:** Voyageur **Notes:** Only known in prooflike sets with 1976 obverse slightly modified.

| KM# | Date | Mintage | MS-63 | P/L | Spec. |
|---|---|---|---|---|---|
| 76.3 | 1975 mule w/1976 obv. | Inc. above | — | — | — |
| | 1975 mule w/1976 obv. * | — | — | — | — |

**Composition:** Nickel. **Diameter:** 32 mm. **Reverse:** Voyageur modified

| KM# | Date | Mintage | MS-63 | P/L | Spec. |
|---|---|---|---|---|---|
| 117 | 1977 | 1,393,745 | 2.50 | — | — |
| | 1977 | — | — | 3.25 | — |

**Composition:** Nickel. **Diameter:** 32 mm. **Reverse:** Voyageur

| KM# | Date | Mintage | MS-63 | P/L | Spec. |
|---|---|---|---|---|---|
| 120.1 | 1978 | 2,948,488 | 1.50 | — | — |
| | 1978 | — | — | 2.75 | — |
| | 1979 | 2,954,842 | 1.50 | — | — |
| | 1979 | — | — | 3.25 | — |
| | 1980 | 3,291,221 | 1.50 | — | — |
| | 1980 | — | — | 3.75 | — |
| | 1981 | 2,778,900 | 1.50 | — | — |
| | 1981 | — | — | 4.00 | — |
| | 1982 | 1,098,500 | 1.50 | — | — |
| | 1982 | — | — | 4.00 | — |
| | 1983 | 2,267,525 | 1.50 | — | — |
| | 1983 | — | — | 4.00 | — |
| | 1984 | 1,223,486 | 1.50 | 4.00 | — |
| | 1984 | — | — | — | — |
| | 1984 | 161,602 | — | — | — |
| | 1984 | — | — | — | — |
| | 1985 | 3,104,092 | 1.50 | 4.50 | — |
| | 1985 | — | — | 5.00 | — |
| | 1985 | 157,037 | — | — | — |

| KM# | Date | Mintage | MS-63 | P/L | Spec. |
|-----|------|---------|-------|-----|-------|
| | 1985 | — | — | — | — |
| | 1986 | 3,089,225 | 2.00 | — | — |
| | 1986 | — | — | 6.00 | — |
| | 1986 | 175,259 | — | — | — |
| | 1986 | — | — | — | — |
| | 1987 | 287,330 | 3.50 | — | — |
| | 1987 | — | — | 7.00 | — |
| | 1987 | 179,004 | — | — | — |
| | 1987 | — | — | — | — |

**Composition:** Nickel. **Diameter:** 32 mm. **Reverse:** Voyageur **Notes:** Modified design.

| KM# | Date | Mintage | MS-63 | P/L | Spec. |
|-----|------|---------|-------|-----|-------|
| 120.2 | 1985 mule w/New Zealand 50 cent, KM-37 obverse | — | — | — | — |

**Composition:** Aureate-bronze Plated Nickel. **Obverse:** Elizabeth II effigy **Reverse:** Loon **Obv. Designer:** Machin.

| KM# | Date | Mintage | MS-63 | P/L | (Proof) |
|-----|------|---------|-------|-----|---------|
| 157 | 1987 | 205,405,000 | 2.25 | — | — |
| | 1987 | 178,120 | — | — | 8.00 |
| | 1988 | 138,893,539 | 2.25 | 4.00 | — |
| | 1988 | 175,259 | — | — | 6.75 |
| | 1989 | 184,773,902 | 2.25 | 4.00 | — |
| | 1989 | 170,928 | — | — | 6.75 |

**Composition:** Nickel. **Obverse:** Elizabeth II effigy **Reverse:** Loon **Obv. Designer:** dePedery-Hunt.

| KM# | Date | Mintage | MS-63 | P/L | (Proof) |
|-----|------|---------|-------|-----|---------|
| 186 | 1990 | 68,402,000 | 1.75 | 4.00 | — |
| | 1990 | 140,649 | — | — | 9.00 |
| | 1991 | 23,156,000 | 1.75 | 6.50 | — |
| | 1991 | — | — | — | 18.00 |
| | 1993 | 33,662,000 | 2.00 | 4.25 | — |
| | 1993 | — | — | — | 9.00 |
| | 1994 | 36,237,000 | 2.00 | 4.25 | — |
| | 1994 | — | — | — | 9.00 |
| | 1995 | 41,813,000 | 2.00 | 6.50 | — |
| | 1995 | — | — | — | 9.00 |
| | 1996 | 17,101,000 | 2.00 | 4.00 | — |
| | 1996 | — | — | — | 7.50 |
| | 1997 | — | 2.50 | 6.25 | — |
| | 1998 | — | 2.50 | — | — |
| | 1998O in proof sets only | — | — | — | 10.00 |
| | 1998W in mint sets only | — | — | — | 6.00 |

# 5 DOLLARS

**Weight:** 8.3592 g. **Composition:** 0.9000 Gold., 0.2419 oz. AGW.

| KM# | Date | Mintage | F-12 | VF-20 | XF-40 | AU-50 | MS-60 | MS-63 |
|---|---|---|---|---|---|---|---|---|
| 26 | 1912 | 165,680 | 135 | 150 | 185 | 200 | 300 | 550 |
| | 1913 | 98,832 | 135 | 150 | 185 | 200 | 300 | 550 |
| | 1914 | 31,122 | 150 | 250 | 300 | 400 | 625 | 1,975 |

# 10 DOLLARS

**Weight:** 16.7185 g. **Composition:** 0.9000 Gold., 0.4838 oz. AGW.

| KM# | Date | Mintage | F-12 | VF-20 | XF-40 | AU-50 | MS-60 | MS-63 |
|---|---|---|---|---|---|---|---|---|
| 27 | 1912 | 74,759 | 225 | 275 | 325 | 375 | 500 | 1,650 |
| | 1913 | 149,232 | 225 | 275 | 325 | 375 | 525 | 2,650 |
| | 1914 | 140,068 | 225 | 275 | 350 | 400 | 575 | 2,750 |

# SOVEREIGN

**Weight:** 7.9881 g. **Composition:** 0.9170 Gold., .2354 oz. AGW. **Reverse:** Mint mark below horse's rear hooves

| KM# | Date | Mintage | VG-8 | F-12 | VF-20 | XF-40 | MS-60 | MS-63 | Prf-63 |
|---|---|---|---|---|---|---|---|---|---|
| 14 | 1908C | 636 | — | 1,000 | 1,750 | 2,350 | 3,450 | 4,250 | — |
| | 1909C | 16,273 | — | 150 | 210 | 220 | 450 | 1,350 | — |
| | 1910C | 28,012 | — | 125 | 175 | 220 | 475 | 2,000 | — |

**Weight:** 7.9881 g. **Composition:** 0.9170 Gold., 0.2354 oz. AGW.

| KM# | Date | Mintage | MS-63 | (Proof) |
|---|---|---|---|---|
| 20 | 1911C | 256,946 | 245 | — |
| | 1911C specimen | — | 6,500 | — |
| | 1913C | 3,715 | 2,000 | — |
| | 1914C | 14,871 | 1,000 | — |
| | 1916C about 20 known | — | 31,000 | — |

**Note:** Stacks' A.G. Carter Jr. Sale 12-89 Gem BU realized $82,500.

| | | | | |
|---|---|---|---|---|
| | 1917C | 58,845 | 400 | — |
| | 1919C | 135,889 | 625 | — |

**Weight:** 7.9881 g. **Composition:** 0.9170 Gold., .2354 oz. AGW.

| KM# | Date | Mintage | MS-63 | (Proof) |
|---|---|---|---|---|
| 106,516 | 1918C | — | 400 | — |

**Weight:** 7.9881 g. **Composition:** 0.9170 Gold., 0.2354 oz. AGW.

| KM# | Date | Mintage | VG-8 | F-12 | VF-20 | XF-40 | MS-60 | MS-63 | Prf-63 |
|---|---|---|---|---|---|---|---|---|---|
| 20 | 1918C | 106,514 | — | — | — | 110 | 160 | 700 | — |

# COMMEMORATIVES

## CENT

**Composition:** Bronze.

| KM# | Date | Mintage | VG-8 | F-12 | VF-20 | XF-40 | MS-60 | MS-63 | Prf-63 |
|-----|------|---------|------|------|-------|-------|-------|-------|--------|
| 65 | 1967 Confederation Centennial | 345,140,645 | — | — | — | — | 0.10 | 0.20 | — |

**Composition:** Bronze.

| KM# | Date | Mintage | VG-8 | F-12 | VF-20 | XF-40 | MS-60 | MS-63 | Prf-63 |
|-----|------|---------|------|------|-------|-------|-------|-------|--------|
| 204 | 1992 Confederation 125 | 673,512,000 | — | — | — | — | 0.10 | 0.15 | — |
|  | 1992 Confederation 125 | 147,061 | — | — | — | — | — | — | 2.50 |

**Weight:** 5.6700 g. **Composition:** 0.9250 Copper-plated Silver., 0.1677 oz.

| KM# | Date | Mintage | VG-8 | F-12 | VF-20 | XF-40 | MS-60 | MS-63 | Prf-63 |
|-----|------|---------|------|------|-------|-------|-------|-------|--------|
| 309 | in unc sets only 90th Anniversary Royal Canadian Mint | 25,000 | — | — | — | — | — | 16.50 | — |

**Weight:** 5.6700 g. **Composition:** 0.9250 Silver., .1677 oz. ASW. **Obverse:** With "Canada"

| KM# | Date | Mintage | VG-8 | F-12 | VF-20 | XF-40 | MS-60 | MS-63 | Prf-63 |
|-----|------|---------|------|------|-------|-------|-------|-------|--------|
| 332 | 90th anniversary Royal Canadian Mint | — | — | — | — | — | — | — | — |

## 5 CENTS

**Composition:** Tombac. (Brass)

| KM# | Date | Mintage | VG-8 | F-12 | VF-20 | XF-40 | MS-60 | MS-63 | Prf-63 |
|-----|------|---------|------|------|-------|-------|-------|-------|--------|
| 40 | 1943 Victory | 24,760,256 | 0.20 | 0.30 | 0.40 | 0.85 | 2.00 | 7.00 | — |
|  | 1944 Victory | 8,000 | — | — | — | — | — | — | — |

**Composition:** Chrome Plated Steel.

| KM# | Date | Mintage | VG-8 | F-12 | VF-20 | XF-40 | MS-60 | MS-63 | Prf-63 |
|-----|------|---------|------|------|-------|-------|-------|-------|--------|
| 40a | 1944 | 11,532,784 | 0.15 | 0.25 | 0.45 | 1.00 | 2.00 | 4.50 | — |
|  | 1945 | 18,893,216 | 0.15 | 0.25 | 0.45 | 1.00 | 2.00 | 4.50 | — |

**Composition:** Nickel.

| KM# | Date | Mintage | VG-8 | F-12 | VF-20 | XF-40 | MS-60 | MS-63 | Prf-63 |
|---|---|---|---|---|---|---|---|---|---|
| 48 | 1951 Nickel bicentennial | 9,028,507 | 0.15 | 0.20 | 0.25 | 0.50 | 1.75 | 4.00 | — |

**Composition:** Copper Nickel.

| KM# | Date | Mintage | VG-8 | F-12 | VF-20 | XF-40 | MS-60 | MS-63 | Prf-63 |
|---|---|---|---|---|---|---|---|---|---|
| 66 | 1967 Confederation centennial | 36,876,574 | — | — | — | — | 0.20 | 0.30 | — |

**Composition:** Copper-nickel.

| KM# | Date | Mintage | VG-8 | F-12 | VF-20 | XF-40 | MS-60 | MS-63 | Prf-63 |
|---|---|---|---|---|---|---|---|---|---|
| 205 | 1992 Confederation 125 | 53,732,000 | — | — | — | — | 0.10 | 0.15 | — |
|  | 1992 Confederation 125 | 147,061 | — | — | — | — | — | — | 5.25 |

**Weight:** 1.1670 g. **Composition:** 0.9250 Silver., .0347 oz. ASW.

| KM# | Date | Mintage | VG-8 | F-12 | VF-20 | XF-40 | MS-60 | MS-63 | Prf-63 |
|---|---|---|---|---|---|---|---|---|---|
| 310 | in unc sets only 90th Anniversary Royal Canadian Mint | 25,000 | — | — | — | — | — | 2.75 | — |
|  | in proof sets only 90th Anniversary Royal Canadian Mint | 25,000 | — | — | — | — | — | 2.75 | — |

**Composition:** 0.9250 Silver.

| KM# | Date | Mintage | VG-8 | F-12 | VF-20 | XF-40 | MS-60 | MS-63 | Prf-63 |
|---|---|---|---|---|---|---|---|---|---|
| 400 | 2000 First French-Canadian regiment | — | — | — | — | — | — | — | 11.50 |

# 10 CENTS

**Weight:** 2.3328 g. **Composition:** 0.8000 Silver., 0.0600 oz. ASW.

| KM# | Date | Mintage | VG-8 | F-12 | VF-20 | XF-40 | MS-60 | MS-63 | Prf-63 |
|---|---|---|---|---|---|---|---|---|---|
| 67 | 1967 Confederation Centennial. | 62,998,215 | — | — | — | — | 0.50 | 1.50 | — |

**Weight:** 2.3328 g. **Composition:** 0.5000 Silver., 0.0372 oz. ASW.

| KM# | Date | Mintage | VG-8 | F-12 | VF-20 | XF-40 | MS-60 | MS-63 | Prf-63 |
|---|---|---|---|---|---|---|---|---|---|
| 67a | 1967 Confederation Centennial. | Inc. above | — | — | — | | 0.50 | 1.50 | — |

**Composition: Nickel.**

| KM# | Date | Mintage | VG-8 | F-12 | VF-20 | XF-40 | MS-60 | MS-63 | Prf-63 |
|---|---|---|---|---|---|---|---|---|---|
| 206 | 1992 Confederation 125 | 174,476,000 | — | — | — | 0.15 | 0.25 | 0.35 | — |
| | 1992 Confederation 125 | 147,061 | — | — | — | — | — | — | 3.00 |

**Weight: 2.4000 g. Composition: 0.9250 Silver., .0714 oz. ASW.**

| KM# | Date | Mintage | VG-8 | F-12 | VF-20 | XF-40 | MS-60 | MS-63 | Prf-63 |
|---|---|---|---|---|---|---|---|---|---|
| 299 | John Cabot | 50,000,000 | — | — | — | — | — | — | 16.25 |

**Weight: 2.3200 g. Composition: 0.9250 Silver., .0690 oz. ASW.**

| KM# | Date | Mintage | VG-8 | F-12 | VF-20 | XF-40 | MS-60 | MS-63 | Prf-63 |
|---|---|---|---|---|---|---|---|---|---|
| 311 | in matte sets only 90th Anniversary Royal Canadian Mint | 25,000 | — | — | — | — | — | — | 5.50 |
| | in proof sets only 90th Anniversary Royal Canadian Mint | 25,000 | — | — | — | — | — | — | 5.50 |

| KM# | Date | Mintage | VG-8 | F-12 | VF-20 | XF-40 | MS-60 | MS-63 | Prf-63 |
|---|---|---|---|---|---|---|---|---|---|
| 409 | 2000 Desjardins, founder of first credit union in North America | — | — | — | — | — | — | — | 11.00 |

# 25 CENTS

**Weight: 5.8319 g. Composition: 0.8000 Silver., 0.1500 oz. ASW.**

| KM# | Date | Mintage | VG-8 | F-12 | VF-20 | XF-40 | MS-60 | MS-63 | Prf-63 |
|---|---|---|---|---|---|---|---|---|---|
| 68 | 1967 Confederation Centennial | 48,855,500 | — | — | — | | 1.00 | 1.75 | — |

**Weight: 5.8319 g. Composition: 0.5000 Silver., 0.0937 oz. ASW.**

| KM# | Date | Mintage | VG-8 | F-12 | VF-20 | XF-40 | MS-60 | MS-63 | Prf-63 |
|---|---|---|---|---|---|---|---|---|---|
| 68a | 1967 Confederation Centennial | Inc. above | — | — | — | | 1.00 | 1.75 | — |

**Composition:** Nickel. **Notes:** 120 beads.

| KM# | Date | Mintage | VG-8 | F-12 | VF-20 | XF-40 | MS-60 | MS-63 | Prf-63 |
|-----|------|---------|------|------|-------|-------|-------|-------|--------|
| 81.1 | 1973 RCMP Centennial | 134,958,587 | — | — | — | 0.30 | 0.50 | 0.80 | — |

**Composition:** Nickel. **Notes:** 132 beads.

| KM# | Date | Mintage | VG-8 | F-12 | VF-20 | XF-40 | MS-60 | MS-63 | Prf-63 |
|-----|------|---------|------|------|-------|-------|-------|-------|--------|
| 81.2 | 1973 RCMP Centennial | Inc. above | 30.00 | 50.00 | 60.00 | 70.00 | 85.00 | 110 | — |

**Composition:** Nickel.

| KM# | Date | Mintage | VG-8 | F-12 | VF-20 | XF-40 | MS-60 | MS-63 | Prf-63 |
|-----|------|---------|------|------|-------|-------|-------|-------|--------|
| 207 | 1992 Confederation 125 | 442,986 | — | — | — | — | — | 12.50 | — |
|  | 1992 Confederation 125 | 147,061 | — | — | — | — | — | — | 20.00 |

| KM# | Date | Mintage | VG-8 | F-12 | VF-20 | XF-40 | MS-60 | MS-63 | Prf-63 |
|-----|------|---------|------|------|-------|-------|-------|-------|--------|
| 312 | in matte sets only 90th Anniversary Royal Canadian Mint | 25,000 | — | — | — | — | — | — | 16.50 |
|  | in proof sets only 90th Anniversary Royal Canadian Mint | — | — | — | — | — | — | — | 16.50 |

**Composition:** Nickel. **Reverse:** Ribbon and caduceus

| KM# | Date | Mintage | VG-8 | F-12 | VF-20 | XF-40 | MS-60 | MS-63 | Prf-63 |
|-----|------|---------|------|------|-------|-------|-------|-------|--------|
| 373 | 2000 Health | — | — | — | — | — | 0.50 | 1.00 | — |

**Composition:** 0.9250 Silver. **Reverse:** Ribbon and caduceus

| KM# | Date | Mintage | VG-8 | F-12 | VF-20 | XF-40 | MS-60 | MS-63 | Prf-63 |
|-----|------|---------|------|------|-------|-------|-------|-------|--------|
| 373a | 2000 Health | — | — | — | — | — | — | — | 9.50 |

**Composition:** Nickel. **Reverse:** 2 children and rising sun

| KM# | Date | Mintage | VG-8 | F-12 | VF-20 | XF-40 | MS-60 | MS-63 | Prf-63 |
|-----|------|---------|------|------|-------|-------|-------|-------|--------|
| 374 | 2000 Freedom | — | — | — | — | — | 0.50 | 1.00 | — |

**Composition:** 0.9250 Silver. **Reverse:** 2 children and rising sun

| KM# | Date | Mintage | VG-8 | F-12 | VF-20 | XF-40 | MS-60 | MS-63 | Prf-63 |
|-----|------|---------|------|------|-------|-------|-------|-------|--------|
| 374a | 2000 Freedom | — | — | — | — | — | — | — | 9.50 |

**Composition:** Nickel. **Reverse:** Circular native carvings

| KM# | Date | Mintage | VG-8 | F-12 | VF-20 | XF-40 | MS-60 | MS-63 | Prf-63 |
|-----|------|---------|------|------|-------|-------|-------|-------|--------|
| 375 | 2000 Family | — | — | — | — | — | 0.50 | 1.00 | — |

**Composition:** 0.9250 Silver.

| KM# | Date | Mintage | VG-8 | F-12 | VF-20 | XF-40 | MS-60 | MS-63 | Prf-63 |
|-----|------|---------|------|------|-------|-------|-------|-------|--------|
| 375a | 2000 Family | — | — | — | — | — | — | — | 9.50 |

**Composition:** Nickel. **Reverse:** Map on globe

| KM# | Date | Mintage | VG-8 | F-12 | VF-20 | XF-40 | MS-60 | MS-63 | Prf-63 |
|-----|------|---------|------|------|-------|-------|-------|-------|--------|
| 376 | 2000 Community | — | — | — | — | — | 0.50 | 1.00 | — |

**Composition:** 0.9250 Silver. **Reverse:** Map on globe

| KM# | Date | Mintage | VG-8 | F-12 | VF-20 | XF-40 | MS-60 | MS-63 | Prf-63 |
|-----|------|---------|------|------|-------|-------|-------|-------|--------|
| 376a | 2000 Community | — | — | — | — | — | — | — | 9.50 |

**Composition:** Nickel. **Reverse:** Maple leaf

| KM# | Date | Mintage | VG-8 | F-12 | VF-20 | XF-40 | MS-60 | MS-63 | Prf-63 |
|-----|------|---------|------|------|-------|-------|-------|-------|--------|
| 377 | 2000 Harmony | — | — | — | — | — | 0.50 | 1.00 | — |

**Composition:** 0.9250 Silver. **Obv. Legend:** Maple leaf

| KM# | Date | Mintage | VG-8 | F-12 | VF-20 | XF-40 | MS-60 | MS-63 | Prf-63 |
|---|---|---|---|---|---|---|---|---|---|
| 377a | 2000 Harmony | — | — | — | — | — | — | — | 9.50 |

**Composition:** Nickel. **Reverse:** Man with young child

| KM# | Date | Mintage | VG-8 | F-12 | VF-20 | XF-40 | MS-60 | MS-63 | Prf-63 |
|---|---|---|---|---|---|---|---|---|---|
| 378 | 2000 Wisdom | — | — | — | — | — | 0.50 | 1.00 | — |

**Composition:** 0.9250 Silver. **Obv. Legend:** Man with young child

| KM# | Date | Mintage | VG-8 | F-12 | VF-20 | XF-40 | MS-60 | MS-63 | Prf-63 |
|---|---|---|---|---|---|---|---|---|---|
| 378a | 2000 Wisdom | — | — | — | — | — | — | — | 9.50 |

**Composition:** Nickel. **Reverse:** Canoe full of children

| KM# | Date | Mintage | VG-8 | F-12 | VF-20 | XF-40 | MS-60 | MS-63 | Prf-63 |
|---|---|---|---|---|---|---|---|---|---|
| 379 | 2000 Creativity | — | — | — | — | — | 0.50 | 1.00 | — |

**Composition:** 0.9250 Silver. **Reverse:** Canoe full of children

| KM# | Date | Mintage | VG-8 | F-12 | VF-20 | XF-40 | MS-60 | MS-63 | Prf-63 |
|---|---|---|---|---|---|---|---|---|---|
| 379a | 2000 Creativity | — | — | — | — | — | — | — | 9.50 |

**Composition:** Nickel. **Reverse:** Crescent-shaped city views

| KM# | Date | Mintage | VG-8 | F-12 | VF-20 | XF-40 | MS-60 | MS-63 | Prf-63 |
|---|---|---|---|---|---|---|---|---|---|
| 380 | 2000 Ingenuity | — | — | — | — | — | 0.50 | 1.00 | — |

**Composition:** 0.9250 Silver. **Reverse:** Crescent-shaped city view

| KM# | Date | Mintage | VG-8 | F-12 | VF-20 | XF-40 | MS-60 | MS-63 | Prf-63 |
|---|---|---|---|---|---|---|---|---|---|
| 380a | 2000 Ingenuity | — | — | — | — | — | — | — | 9.50 |

**Composition:** Nickel. **Reverse:** Rocket above jagged design

| KM# | Date | Mintage | VG-8 | F-12 | VF-20 | XF-40 | MS-60 | MS-63 | Prf-63 |
|---|---|---|---|---|---|---|---|---|---|
| 381 | 2000 Achievement | — | — | — | — | — | 0.50 | 1.00 | — |

**Composition:** 0.9250 Silver. **Reverse:** Rocket above jagged design

| KM# | Date | Mintage | VG-8 | F-12 | VF-20 | XF-40 | MS-60 | MS-63 | Prf-63 |
|---|---|---|---|---|---|---|---|---|---|
| 381a | 2000 Achievement | — | — | — | — | — | — | — | 9.50 |

**Composition:** Nickel. **Reverse:** Environmental elements

| KM# | Date | Mintage | VG-8 | F-12 | VF-20 | XF-40 | MS-60 | MS-63 | Prf-63 |
|---|---|---|---|---|---|---|---|---|---|
| 382 | 2000 Natural legacy | — | — | — | — | — | 0.50 | 1.00 | — |

**Composition:** 0.9250 Silver. **Obv. Legend:** Environmental elements

| KM# | Date | Mintage | VG-8 | F-12 | VF-20 | XF-40 | MS-60 | MS-63 | Prf-63 |
|---|---|---|---|---|---|---|---|---|---|
| 382a | 2000 Natural legacy | — | — | — | — | — | — | — | 9.50 |

**Composition:** Nickel. **Reverse:** Fireworks, children behind flag

| KM# | Date | Mintage | VG-8 | F-12 | VF-20 | XF-40 | MS-60 | MS-63 | Prf-63 |
|---|---|---|---|---|---|---|---|---|---|
| 383 | 2000 Celebration | — | — | — | — | — | 0.50 | 1.00 | — |

**Composition:** 0.9250 Silver. **Reverse:** Fireworks, children behind flag

| KM# | Date | Mintage | VG-8 | F-12 | VF-20 | XF-40 | MS-60 | MS-63 | Prf-63 |
|---|---|---|---|---|---|---|---|---|---|
| 383a | 2000 Celebration | — | — | — | — | — | — | — | 9.50 |

**Composition:** Nickel. **Reverse:** Red with 3 small maple leaves on large maple leaf **Notes:** Colorized version.

| KM# | Date | Mintage | VG-8 | F-12 | VF-20 | XF-40 | MS-60 | MS-63 | Prf-63 |
|---|---|---|---|---|---|---|---|---|---|
| 384.1 | 2000 Pride | — | — | — | — | — | — | 6.50 | — |

**Composition:** Nickel. **Reverse:** 2 with three small maple leaves on large maple leaf

| KM# | Date | Mintage | VG-8 | F-12 | VF-20 | XF-40 | MS-60 | MS-63 | Prf-63 |
|---|---|---|---|---|---|---|---|---|---|
| 384.2 | 2000 Pride | — | — | — | — | — | 0.50 | 1.00 | — |

**Composition:** 0.9250 Silver. **Reverse:** 2 with 3 small maple leaves on large maple leaf

| KM# | Date | Mintage | VG-8 | F-12 | VF-20 | XF-40 | MS-60 | MS-63 | Prf-63 |
|---|---|---|---|---|---|---|---|---|---|
| 384.2a | 2000 Pride | — | — | — | — | — | — | — | 9.50 |

# 125th Anniversary of Confederation

## Alberta

**Composition:** Nickel.

| KM# | Date | Mintage | VG-8 | F-12 | VF-20 | XF-40 | MS-60 | MS-63 | Prf-63 |
|---|---|---|---|---|---|---|---|---|---|
| 221 | 1992 Alberta | 12,133,000 | — | — | — | — | 0.35 | 0.75 | — |

**Weight:** 5.8319 g. **Composition:** 0.9250 Silver., 0.1734 oz. ASW.

| KM# | Date | Mintage | VG-8 | F-12 | VF-20 | XF-40 | MS-60 | MS-63 | Prf-63 |
|---|---|---|---|---|---|---|---|---|---|
| 221a | 1992 Alberta | — | — | — | — | — | — | — | 7.50 |

## British Columbia

**Composition:** Nickel.

| KM# | Date | Mintage | VG-8 | F-12 | VF-20 | XF-40 | MS-60 | MS-63 | Prf-63 |
|---|---|---|---|---|---|---|---|---|---|
| 232 | 1992 British Columbia | 14,001,000 | — | — | — | — | 0.35 | 0.75 | — |

**Weight:** 5.8319 g. **Composition:** 0.9250 Silver., 0.1734 oz. ASW.

| KM# | Date | Mintage | VG-8 | F-12 | VF-20 | XF-40 | MS-60 | MS-63 | Prf-63 |
|-----|------|---------|------|------|-------|-------|-------|-------|--------|
| 232a | 1992 British Columbia | 149,579 | — | — | — | — | — | — | 7.50 |

## Manitoba

**Composition:** Nickel.

| KM# | Date | Mintage | VG-8 | F-12 | VF-20 | XF-40 | MS-60 | MS-63 | Prf-63 |
|-----|------|---------|------|------|-------|-------|-------|-------|--------|
| 214 | 1992 Manitoba | 11,349,000 | — | — | — | — | 0.35 | 0.75 | — |

**Weight:** 5.8319 g. **Composition:** 0.9250 Silver., 0.1734 oz. ASW.

| KM# | Date | Mintage | VG-8 | F-12 | VF-20 | XF-40 | MS-60 | MS-63 | Prf-63 |
|-----|------|---------|------|------|-------|-------|-------|-------|--------|
| 214a | 1992 Manitoba | 149,579 | — | — | — | — | — | — | 7.50 |

## New Brunswick

**Composition:** Nickel.

| KM# | Date | Mintage | VG-8 | F-12 | VF-20 | XF-40 | MS-60 | MS-63 | Prf-63 |
|-----|------|---------|------|------|-------|-------|-------|-------|--------|
| 203 | 1992 New Brunswick | 12,174,000 | — | — | — | — | 0.35 | 0.75 | — |

**Weight:** 5.8319 g. **Composition:** 0.9250 Silver., 0.1734 oz. ASW.

| KM# | Date | Mintage | VG-8 | F-12 | VF-20 | XF-40 | MS-60 | MS-63 | Prf-63 |
|-----|------|---------|------|------|-------|-------|-------|-------|--------|
| 203a | 1992 New Brunswick | 149,579 | — | — | — | — | — | — | 7.50 |

## Newfoundland

**Composition:** Nickel.

| KM# | Date | Mintage | VG-8 | F-12 | VF-20 | XF-40 | MS-60 | MS-63 | Prf-63 |
|-----|------|---------|------|------|-------|-------|-------|-------|--------|
| 213 | 1992 Newfoundland | 11,405,000 | — | — | — | — | 0.35 | 0.75 | — |

**Weight:** 5.8319 g. **Composition:** 0.9250 Silver., 0.1734 oz. ASW.

| KM# | Date | Mintage | VG-8 | F-12 | VF-20 | XF-40 | MS-60 | MS-63 | Prf-63 |
|-----|------|---------|------|------|-------|-------|-------|-------|--------|
| 213a | 1992 Newfoundland | 149,579 | — | — | — | — | — | — | 7.50 |

## North West Territories

**Composition:** Nickel.

| KM# | Date | Mintage | VG-8 | F-12 | VF-20 | XF-40 | MS-60 | MS-63 | Prf-63 |
|-----|------|---------|------|------|-------|-------|-------|-------|--------|
| 212 | 1992 North West Territories | 12,582,000 | — | — | — | — | 0.35 | 0.75 | — |

**Weight:** 5.8319 g. **Composition:** 0.9250 Silver., 0.1734 oz. ASW.

| KM# | Date | Mintage | VG-8 | F-12 | VF-20 | XF-40 | MS-60 | MS-63 | Prf-63 |
|-----|------|---------|------|------|-------|-------|-------|-------|--------|
| 212a | 1992 North West Territories | 149,579 | — | — | — | — | — | — | 7.50 |

## Nova Scotia

**Composition:** Nickel.

| KM# | Date | Mintage | VG-8 | F-12 | VF-20 | XF-40 | MS-60 | MS-63 | Prf-63 |
|-----|------|---------|------|------|-------|-------|-------|-------|--------|
| 231 | 1992 Nova Scotia | 13,600,000 | — | — | — | — | 0.35 | 0.75 | — |

**Weight:** 5.8319 g. **Composition:** 0.9250 Silver., 0.1734 oz. ASW.

| KM# | Date | Mintage | VG-8 | F-12 | VF-20 | XF-40 | MS-60 | MS-63 | Prf-63 |
|-----|------|---------|------|------|-------|-------|-------|-------|--------|
| 231a | 1992 Nova Scotia | 149,579 | — | — | — | — | — | — | 7.50 |

## Ontario

**Composition:** Nickel.

| KM# | Date | Mintage | VG-8 | F-12 | VF-20 | XF-40 | MS-60 | MS-63 | Prf-63 |
|-----|------|---------|------|------|-------|-------|-------|-------|--------|
| 223 | 1992 Ontario | 14,263,000 | — | — | — | — | 0.35 | 0.75 | — |

**Weight:** 5.8319 g. **Composition:** 0.9250 Silver., 0.1734 oz. ASW.

| KM# | Date | Mintage | VG-8 | F-12 | VF-20 | XF-40 | MS-60 | MS-63 | Prf-63 |
|-----|------|---------|------|------|-------|-------|-------|-------|--------|
| 223a | 1992 Ontario | 149,579 | — | — | — | — | — | — | 7.50 |

## Prince Edward Island

**Composition:** Nickel.

| KM# | Date | Mintage | VG-8 | F-12 | VF-20 | XF-40 | MS-60 | MS-63 | Prf-63 |
|-----|------|---------|------|------|-------|-------|-------|-------|--------|
| 222 | 1992 Prince Edward Island | 13,001,000 | — | — | — | — | 0.35 | 0.75 | — |

**Weight:** 5.8319 g. **Composition:** 0.9250 Silver., 0.1734 oz. ASW.

| KM# | Date | Mintage | VG-8 | F-12 | VF-20 | XF-40 | MS-60 | MS-63 | Prf-63 |
|-----|------|---------|------|------|-------|-------|-------|-------|--------|
| 222a | 1992 Prince Edward Island | 149,579 | — | — | — | — | — | — | 7.50 |

## Quebec

**Composition:** Nickel.

| KM# | Date | Mintage | VG-8 | F-12 | VF-20 | XF-40 | MS-60 | MS-63 | Prf-63 |
|-----|------|---------|------|------|-------|-------|-------|-------|--------|
| 234 | 1992 Quebec | 13,607,000 | — | — | — | — | 0.35 | 0.75 | — |

**Weight:** 5.8319 g. **Composition:** 0.9250 Silver., 0.1734 oz. ASW.

| KM# | Date | Mintage | VG-8 | F-12 | VF-20 | XF-40 | MS-60 | MS-63 | Prf-63 |
|-----|------|---------|------|------|-------|-------|-------|-------|--------|
| 234a | 1992 Quebec | 149,579 | — | — | — | — | — | — | 7.50 |

## Saskatchewan

**Composition:** Nickel.

| KM# | Date | Mintage | VG-8 | F-12 | VF-20 | XF-40 | MS-60 | MS-63 | Prf-63 |
|-----|------|---------|------|------|-------|-------|-------|-------|--------|
| 233 | 1992 Saskatchewan | 14,165,000 | — | — | — | — | 0.35 | 0.75 | — |

**Weight:** 5.8319 g. **Composition:** 0.9250 Silver., 0.1734 oz. ASW.

| KM# | Date | Mintage | VG-8 | F-12 | VF-20 | XF-40 | MS-60 | MS-63 | Prf-63 |
|-----|------|---------|------|------|-------|-------|-------|-------|--------|
| 233a | 1992 Saskatchewan | 149,579 | — | — | — | — | — | — | 7.50 |

## Yukon

**Composition:** Nickel.

| KM# | Date | Mintage | VG-8 | F-12 | VF-20 | XF-40 | MS-60 | MS-63 | Prf-63 |
|-----|------|---------|------|------|-------|-------|-------|-------|--------|
| 220 | 1992 Yukon | 10,388,000 | — | — | — | — | 0.35 | 0.75 | — |

**Weight:** 5.8319 g. **Composition:** 0.9250 Silver., 0.1734 oz. ASW.

| KM# | Date | Mintage | VG-8 | F-12 | VF-20 | XF-40 | MS-60 | MS-63 | Prf-63 |
|-----|------|---------|------|------|-------|-------|-------|-------|--------|
| 220a | 1992 Yukon | 149,579 | — | — | — | — | — | — | 7.50 |

# Millennium

**Composition:** Nickel. **Reverse:** Totem pole, portraits.

| KM# | Date | Mintage | VG-8 | F-12 | VF-20 | XF-40 | MS-60 | MS-63 | Prf-63 |
|-----|------|---------|------|------|-------|-------|-------|-------|--------|
| 342 | 1999 January | — | — | — | — | — | 0.50 | 1.00 | — |

**Weight:** 5.8319 g. **Composition:** 0.9250 Silver., 0.1734 oz. ASW. **Reverse:** Totem pole, portraits.

| KM# | Date | Mintage | VG-8 | F-12 | VF-20 | XF-40 | MS-60 | MS-63 | Prf-63 |
|-----|------|---------|------|------|-------|-------|-------|-------|--------|
| 342a | 1999 January | — | — | — | — | — | — | — | 9.50 |

**Composition:** Nickel. **Reverse:** Native petroglyphs.

| KM# | Date | Mintage | VG-8 | F-12 | VF-20 | XF-40 | MS-60 | MS-63 | Prf-63 |
|-----|------|---------|------|------|-------|-------|-------|-------|--------|
| 343 | 1999 February | — | — | — | — | — | 0.50 | 1.00 | — |

**Weight:** 5.8319 g. **Composition:** 0.9250 Silver., 0.1734 oz. ASW. **Reverse:** Native petroglyphs.

| KM# | Date | Mintage | VG-8 | F-12 | VF-20 | XF-40 | MS-60 | MS-63 | Prf-63 |
|-----|------|---------|------|------|-------|-------|-------|-------|--------|
| 343a | 1999 February | — | — | — | — | — | — | — | 9.50 |

**Composition:** Nickel. **Reverse:** Lumberjack.

| KM# | Date | Mintage | VG-8 | F-12 | VF-20 | XF-40 | MS-60 | MS-63 | Prf-63 |
|-----|------|---------|------|------|-------|-------|-------|-------|--------|
| 344 | 1999 March | — | — | — | — | — | 0.50 | 1.00 | — |

**Weight:** 5.8319 g. **Composition:** 0.9250 Silver., 0.1734 oz. ASW. **Reverse:** Lumberjack.

| KM# | Date | Mintage | VG-8 | F-12 | VF-20 | XF-40 | MS-60 | MS-63 | Prf-63 |
|-----|------|---------|------|------|-------|-------|-------|-------|--------|
| 344a | 1999 March | — | — | — | — | — | — | — | 9.50 |

**Composition:** Nickel. **Reverse:** Owl, polar bear.

| KM# | Date | Mintage | VG-8 | F-12 | VF-20 | XF-40 | MS-60 | MS-63 | Prf-63 |
|-----|------|---------|------|------|-------|-------|-------|-------|--------|
| 345 | 1999 April | — | — | — | — | — | 0.50 | 1.00 | — |

**Weight:** 5.8319 g. **Composition:** 0.9250 Silver., 0.1734 oz. ASW. **Reverse:** Owl, polar bear.

| KM# | Date | Mintage | VG-8 | F-12 | VF-20 | XF-40 | MS-60 | MS-63 | Prf-63 |
|-----|------|---------|------|------|-------|-------|-------|-------|--------|
| 345a | 1999 April | — | — | — | — | — | — | — | 9.50 |

**Composition:** Nickel. **Reverse:** Voyageurs in canoe.

| KM# | Date | Mintage | VG-8 | F-12 | VF-20 | XF-40 | MS-60 | MS-63 | Prf-63 |
|-----|------|---------|------|------|-------|-------|-------|-------|--------|
| 346 | 1999 May | — | — | — | — | — | 0.50 | 1.00 | — |

**Weight:** 5.8319 g. **Composition:** 0.9250 Silver., 0.1734 oz. ASW. **Reverse:** Voyageurs in canoe.

| KM# | Date | Mintage | VG-8 | F-12 | VF-20 | XF-40 | MS-60 | MS-63 | Prf-63 |
|-----|------|---------|------|------|-------|-------|-------|-------|--------|
| 346a | 1999 May | — | — | — | — | — | — | — | 9.50 |

**Composition:** Nickel. **Reverse:** 19th-century locomotive.

| KM# | Date | Mintage | VG-8 | F-12 | VF-20 | XF-40 | MS-60 | MS-63 | Prf-63 |
|-----|------|---------|------|------|-------|-------|-------|-------|--------|
| 347 | 1999 June | — | — | — | — | — | 0.50 | 1.00 | — |

**Weight:** 5.8319 g. **Composition:** 0.9250 Silver., 0.1734 oz. ASW. **Reverse:** 19th-century locomotive.

| KM# | Date | Mintage | VG-8 | F-12 | VF-20 | XF-40 | MS-60 | MS-63 | Prf-63 |
|-----|------|---------|------|------|-------|-------|-------|-------|--------|
| 347a | 1999 June | — | — | — | — | — | — | — | 9.50 |

**Composition:** Nickel. **Reverse:** 6 stylized portraits.

| KM# | Date | Mintage | VG-8 | F-12 | VF-20 | XF-40 | MS-60 | MS-63 | Prf-63 |
|-----|------|---------|------|------|-------|-------|-------|-------|--------|
| 348 | 1999 July | — | — | — | — | — | 0.50 | 1.00 | — |

**Weight:** 5.8319 g. **Composition:** 0.9250 Silver., 0.1734 oz. ASW. **Reverse:** 6 stylized portraits.

| KM# | Date | Mintage | VG-8 | F-12 | VF-20 | XF-40 | MS-60 | MS-63 | Prf-63 |
|-----|------|---------|------|------|-------|-------|-------|-------|--------|
| 348a | 1999 July | — | — | — | — | — | — | — | 9.50 |

**Composition:** Nickel. **Reverse:** Hay harvesting.

| KM# | Date | Mintage | VG-8 | F-12 | VF-20 | XF-40 | MS-60 | MS-63 | Prf-63 |
|-----|------|---------|------|------|-------|-------|-------|-------|--------|
| 349 | 1999 August | — | — | — | — | — | 0.50 | 1.00 | — |

**Weight:** 5.8319 g. **Composition:** 0.9250 Silver., 0.1734 oz. ASW. **Reverse:** Hay harvesting.

| KM# | Date | Mintage | VG-8 | F-12 | VF-20 | XF-40 | MS-60 | MS-63 | Prf-63 |
|-----|------|---------|------|------|-------|-------|-------|-------|--------|
| 349a | 1999 August | — | — | — | — | — | — | — | 9.50 |

**Composition:** Nickel. **Reverse:** Childlike artwork.

| KM# | Date | Mintage | VG-8 | F-12 | VF-20 | XF-40 | MS-60 | MS-63 | Prf-63 |
|-----|------|---------|------|------|-------|-------|-------|-------|--------|
| 350 | 1999 September | — | — | — | — | — | 0.50 | 1.00 | — |

**Weight:** 5.8319 g. **Composition:** 0.9250 Silver., 0.1734 oz. ASW. **Reverse:** Childlike artwork.

| KM# | Date | Mintage | VG-8 | F-12 | VF-20 | XF-40 | MS-60 | MS-63 | Prf-63 |
|-----|------|---------|------|------|-------|-------|-------|-------|--------|
| 350a | 1999 September | — | — | — | — | — | — | — | 9.50 |

**Composition:** Nickel. **Reverse:** Aboriginal artwork.

| KM# | Date | Mintage | VG-8 | F-12 | VF-20 | XF-40 | MS-60 | MS-63 | Prf-63 |
|-----|------|---------|------|------|-------|-------|-------|-------|--------|
| 351 | 1999 October | — | — | — | — | — | 0.50 | 1.00 | — |

**Weight:** 5.8319 g. **Composition:** 0.9250 Silver., 0.1734 oz. ASW. **Reverse:** Aboriginal artwork

| KM# | Date | Mintage | VG-8 | F-12 | VF-20 | XF-40 | MS-60 | MS-63 | Prf-63 |
|-----|------|---------|------|------|-------|-------|-------|-------|--------|
| 351a | 1999 October | — | — | — | — | — | — | — | 9.50 |

**Composition:** Nickel. **Reverse:** Bush plane with landing skis

| KM# | Date | Mintage | VG-8 | F-12 | VF-20 | XF-40 | MS-60 | MS-63 | Prf-63 |
|-----|------|---------|------|------|-------|-------|-------|-------|--------|
| 352 | 1999 November | — | — | — | — | — | 0.50 | 1.00 | — |

**Weight:** 5.8319 g. **Composition:** 0.9250 Silver., 0.1734 oz. ASW. **Reverse:** Bush plane with landing skis.

| KM# | Date | Mintage | VG-8 | F-12 | VF-20 | XF-40 | MS-60 | MS-63 | Prf-63 |
|-----|------|---------|------|------|-------|-------|-------|-------|--------|
| 352a | 1999 November | — | — | — | — | — | — | — | 10.00 |

**Composition:** Nickel. **Reverse:** Eclectic geometric design.

| KM# | Date | Mintage | VG-8 | F-12 | VF-20 | XF-40 | MS-60 | MS-63 | Prf-63 |
|-----|------|---------|------|------|-------|-------|-------|-------|--------|
| 353 | 1999 December | — | — | — | — | — | 0.50 | 1.00 | — |

**Weight:** 5.8319 g. **Composition:** 0.9250 Silver., 0.1734 oz. ASW. **Reverse:** Eclectic geometric design.

| KM# | Date | Mintage | VG-8 | F-12 | VF-20 | XF-40 | MS-60 | MS-63 | Prf-63 |
|-----|------|---------|------|------|-------|-------|-------|-------|--------|
| 353a | 1999 December | — | — | — | — | — | — | — | 9.50 |

# 50 CENTS

**Weight:** 11.6638 g. **Composition:** 0.8000 Silver., .3000 oz. ASW.

| KM# | Date | Mintage | VG-8 | F-12 | VF-20 | XF-40 | MS-60 | MS-63 | Prf-63 |
|-----|------|---------|------|------|-------|-------|-------|-------|--------|
| 69 | 1967 Confederation centennial | 4,211,392 | — | — | — | 3.00 | 4.00 | 5.00 | — |

**Composition:** Nickel.

| KM# | Date | Mintage | VG-8 | F-12 | VF-20 | XF-40 | MS-60 | MS-63 | Prf-63 |
|-----|------|---------|------|------|-------|-------|-------|-------|--------|
| 208 | 1992 Confederation 125 | 445,000 | — | — | — | 0.50 | 1.00 | 1.50 | — |
| | 1992 Confederation 125 | 147,061 | — | — | — | — | — | — | 8.50 |

**Weight:** 11.6638 g. **Composition:** 0.9250 Silver., .3461 oz. ASW. **Obverse:** Atlantic puffin

| KM# | Date | Mintage | VG-8 | F-12 | VF-20 | XF-40 | MS-60 | MS-63 | Prf-63 |
|-----|------|---------|------|------|-------|-------|-------|-------|--------|
| 261 | 1995 | — | — | — | — | — | — | — | 13.50 |

**Weight:** 11.6638 g. **Composition:** 0.9250 Silver., .3461 oz. ASW.

| KM# | Date | Mintage | VG-8 | F-12 | VF-20 | XF-40 | MS-60 | MS-63 | Prf-63 |
|-----|------|---------|------|------|-------|-------|-------|-------|--------|
| 262 | 1995 Whooping crane | — | — | — | — | — | — | — | 13.50 |

**Weight:** 11.6638 g. **Composition:** 0.9250 Silver., .3461 oz. ASW. **Obverse:** Gray jays

| KM# | Date | Mintage | VG-8 | F-12 | VF-20 | XF-40 | MS-60 | MS-63 | Prf-63 |
|-----|------|---------|------|------|-------|-------|-------|-------|--------|
| 263 | 1995 | — | — | — | — | — | — | — | 13.50 |

**Weight:** 11.6638 g. **Composition:** 0.9250 Silver., .3461 oz. ASW.

| KM# | Date | Mintage | VG-8 | F-12 | VF-20 | XF-40 | MS-60 | MS-63 | Prf-63 |
|-----|------|---------|------|------|-------|-------|-------|-------|--------|
| 264 | 1995 White-tailed ptarmigans | — | — | — | — | — | — | — | 13.50 |

**Weight:** 11.6638 g. **Composition:** 0.9250 Silver., .3461 oz. ASW. **Obverse:** Moose calf

| KM# | Date | Mintage | VG-8 | F-12 | VF-20 | XF-40 | MS-60 | MS-63 | Prf-63 |
|-----|------|---------|------|------|-------|-------|-------|-------|--------|
| 283 | 1996 | — | — | — | — | — | — | — | 14.00 |

**Weight:** 11.6638 g. **Composition:** 0.9250 Silver., .3461 oz. ASW.

| KM# | Date | Mintage | VG-8 | F-12 | VF-20 | XF-40 | MS-60 | MS-63 | Prf-63 |
|-----|------|---------|------|------|-------|-------|-------|-------|--------|
| 284 | 1996 Wood ducklings | — | — | — | — | — | — | — | 15.00 |

**Weight:** 11.6638 g. **Composition:** 0.9250 Silver., .3461 oz. ASW. **Obverse:** Cougar kittens

| KM# | Date | Mintage | VG-8 | F-12 | VF-20 | XF-40 | MS-60 | MS-63 | Prf-63 |
|-----|------|---------|------|------|-------|-------|-------|-------|--------|
| 285 | 1996 | — | — | — | — | — | — | — | 15.00 |

**Weight:** 11.6638 g. **Composition:** 0.9250 Silver., .3461 oz. ASW.

| KM# | Date | Mintage | VG-8 | F-12 | VF-20 | XF-40 | MS-60 | MS-63 | Prf-63 |
|-----|------|---------|------|------|-------|-------|-------|-------|--------|
| 286 | 1996 Black bear cubs | — | — | — | — | — | — | — | 15.00 |

**Weight:** 11.6638 g. **Composition:** 0.9250 Silver., .3461 oz. ASW. **Obverse:** Duck tolling retriever

| KM# | Date | Mintage | VG-8 | F-12 | VF-20 | XF-40 | MS-60 | MS-63 | Prf-63 |
|-----|------|---------|------|------|-------|-------|-------|-------|--------|
| 292 | 1997 | — | — | — | — | — | — | — | 15.00 |

**Weight:** 11.6638 g. **Composition:** 0.9250 Silver., .3461 oz. ASW.

| KM# | Date | Mintage | VG-8 | F-12 | VF-20 | XF-40 | MS-60 | MS-63 | Prf-63 |
|-----|------|---------|------|------|-------|-------|-------|-------|--------|
| 293 | 1997 Labrador retriever | — | — | — | — | — | — | — | 16.00 |

**Weight:** 11.6638 g. **Composition:** 0.9250 Silver., .3461 oz. ASW. **Obverse:** Newfoundland

| KM# | Date | Mintage | VG-8 | F-12 | VF-20 | XF-40 | MS-60 | MS-63 | Prf-63 |
|-----|------|---------|------|------|-------|-------|-------|-------|--------|
| 294 | 1997 | — | — | — | — | — | — | — | 15.00 |

**Weight:** 11.6638 g. **Composition:** 0.9250 Silver., .3461 oz. ASW.

| KM# | Date | Mintage | VG-8 | F-12 | VF-20 | XF-40 | MS-60 | MS-63 | Prf-63 |
|-----|------|---------|------|------|-------|-------|-------|-------|--------|
| 295 | 1997 Eskimo dog | — | — | — | — | — | — | — | 13.00 |

**Weight:** 11.6638 g. **Composition:** 0.9250 Silver., .3461 oz. ASW.

| KM# | Date | Mintage | VG-8 | F-12 | VF-20 | XF-40 | MS-60 | MS-63 | Prf-63 |
|-----|------|---------|------|------|-------|-------|-------|-------|--------|
| 313 | in matte sets only 90th Anniversary Royal Canadian Mint | 25,000 | — | — | — | — | — | — | 32.25 |
| | in proof sets only 90th Anniversary Royal Canadian Mint | 25,000 | — | — | — | — | — | — | 32.25 |

**Weight:** 11.6638 g. **Composition:** 0.9250 Silver., .3461 oz. ASW.

| KM# | Date | Mintage | VG-8 | F-12 | VF-20 | XF-40 | MS-60 | MS-63 | Prf-63 |
|-----|------|---------|------|------|-------|-------|-------|-------|--------|
| 314 | 110 years Canadian speed and figure skating | — | — | — | — | — | — | — | 13.50 |

**Weight:** 11.6638 g. **Composition:** 0.9250 Silver., .3461 oz. ASW. **Obverse:** 100 years Canadian ski racing and jumping

| KM# | Date | Mintage | VG-8 | F-12 | VF-20 | XF-40 | MS-60 | MS-63 | Prf-63 |
|-----|------|---------|------|------|-------|-------|-------|-------|--------|
| 315 | | — | — | — | — | — | — | — | 13.50 |

**Weight:** 11.6638 g. **Composition:** 0.9250 Silver., .3461 oz. ASW.

| KM# | Date | Mintage | VG-8 | F-12 | VF-20 | XF-40 | MS-60 | MS-63 | Prf-63 |
|-----|------|---------|------|------|-------|-------|-------|-------|--------|
| 318 | 1998 Killer whales | — | — | — | — | — | — | — | 14.00 |

**Weight:** 11.6638 g. **Composition:** 0.9250 Silver., .3461 oz. ASW.

| KM# | Date | Mintage | VG-8 | F-12 | VF-20 | XF-40 | MS-60 | MS-63 | Prf-63 |
|-----|------|---------|------|------|-------|-------|-------|-------|--------|
| 319 | 1998 Humpback whale | — | — | — | — | — | — | — | 14.00 |

**Weight:** 11.6638 g. **Composition:** 0.9250 Silver., .3461 oz. ASW.

| KM# | Date | Mintage | VG-8 | F-12 | VF-20 | XF-40 | MS-60 | MS-63 | Prf-63 |
|-----|------|---------|------|------|-------|-------|-------|-------|--------|
| 320 | 1998 Beluga whale | — | — | — | — | — | — | — | 14.00 |

**Weight:** 11.6638 g. **Composition:** 0.9250 Silver., .3461 oz. ASW. **Obverse:** Blue whale

| KM# | Date | Mintage | VG-8 | F-12 | VF-20 | XF-40 | MS-60 | MS-63 | Prf-63 |
|-----|------|---------|------|------|-------|-------|-------|-------|--------|
| 321 | 1998 | — | — | — | — | — | — | — | 14.00 |

**Weight:** 11.6638 g. **Composition:** 0.9250 Silver., .3461 oz. ASW.

| KM# | Date | Mintage | VG-8 | F-12 | VF-20 | XF-40 | MS-60 | MS-63 | Prf-63 |
|-----|------|---------|------|------|-------|-------|-------|-------|--------|
| 327 | 110 years Canadian soccer | — | — | — | — | — | — | — | 13.50 |

**Weight:** 11.6638 g. **Composition:** 0.9250 Silver., .3461 oz. ASW. **Obverse:** 20 years Canadian auto racing

| KM# | Date | Mintage | VG-8 | F-12 | VF-20 | XF-40 | MS-60 | MS-63 | Prf-63 |
|-----|------|---------|------|------|-------|-------|-------|-------|--------|
| 328 | | — | — | — | — | — | — | — | 13.50 |

**Weight:** 11.6638 g. **Composition:** 0.9250 Silver., .3461 oz. ASW.

| KM# | Date | Mintage | VG-8 | F-12 | VF-20 | XF-40 | MS-60 | MS-63 | Prf-63 |
|-----|------|---------|------|------|-------|-------|-------|-------|--------|
| 333 | 1999 1904 Canadian open | — | — | — | — | — | — | — | 13.50 |

**Weight:** 11.6638 g. **Composition:** 0.9250 Silver., .3461 oz. ASW.

| KM# | Date | Mintage | VG-8 | F-12 | VF-20 | XF-40 | MS-60 | MS-63 | Prf-63 |
|-----|------|---------|------|------|-------|-------|-------|-------|--------|
| 334 | 1999 First U.S.-Canadian yacht race | — | — | — | — | — | — | — | 13.50 |

**Composition:** 0.9250 Silver. **Reverse:** 4 hockey players

| KM# | Date | Mintage | VG-8 | F-12 | VF-20 | XF-40 | MS-60 | MS-63 | Prf-63 |
|-----|------|---------|------|------|-------|-------|-------|-------|--------|
| 385 | Ice hockey | — | — | — | — | — | — | — | 13.50 |

**Composition:** 0.9250 Silver. **Reverse:** Motion study of a curler

| KM# | Date | Mintage | VG-8 | F-12 | VF-20 | XF-40 | MS-60 | MS-63 | Prf-63 |
|-----|------|---------|------|------|-------|-------|-------|-------|--------|
| 386 | Curling | — | — | — | — | — | — | — | 13.50 |

**Composition:** 0.9250 Silver.

| KM# | Date | Mintage | VG-8 | F-12 | VF-20 | XF-40 | MS-60 | MS-63 | Prf-63 |
|-----|------|---------|------|------|-------|-------|-------|-------|--------|
| 389 | 2000 Great horned owl | — | — | — | — | — | — | — | 13.50 |

**Composition:** 0.9250 Silver.

| KM# | Date | Mintage | VG-8 | F-12 | VF-20 | XF-40 | MS-60 | MS-63 | Prf-63 |
|-----|------|---------|------|------|-------|-------|-------|-------|--------|
| 390 | 2000 Red-tail hawk | — | — | — | — | — | — | — | 13.50 |

**Composition:** 0.9250 Silver.

| KM# | Date | Mintage | VG-8 | F-12 | VF-20 | XF-40 | MS-60 | MS-63 | Prf-63 |
|-----|------|---------|------|------|-------|-------|-------|-------|--------|
| 391 | 2000 Osprey | — | — | — | — | — | — | — | 13.50 |

**Composition:** 0.9250 Silver.

| KM# | Date | Mintage | VG-8 | F-12 | VF-20 | XF-40 | MS-60 | MS-63 | Prf-63 |
|-----|------|---------|------|------|-------|-------|-------|-------|--------|
| 392 | 2000 | — | — | — | — | — | — | — | 13.50 |

**Composition:** 0.9250 Silver. **Reverse:** Steeplechase

| KM# | Date | Mintage | VG-8 | F-12 | VF-20 | XF-40 | MS-60 | MS-63 | Prf-63 |
|-----|------|---------|------|------|-------|-------|-------|-------|--------|
| 393 | 2000 Canadian sports | — | — | — | — | — | — | — | 13.50 |

**Composition:** 0.9250 Silver. **Reverse:** Bowling

| KM# | Date | Mintage | VG-8 | F-12 | VF-20 | XF-40 | MS-60 | MS-63 | Prf-63 |
|-----|------|---------|------|------|-------|-------|-------|-------|--------|
| 394 | 2000 Canada sports | — | — | — | — | — | — | — | 13.50 |

# Canadian cats

## Cougar

**Weight:** 11.6638 g. **Composition:** 0.9250 Silver., .3461 oz. ASW.

| KM# | Date | Mintage | VG-8 | F-12 | VF-20 | XF-40 | MS-60 | MS-63 | Prf-63 |
|-----|------|---------|------|------|-------|-------|-------|-------|--------|
| 337 | 1999 Cougar | — | — | — | — | — | — | — | 13.50 |

## Cymric

**Weight:** 11.6638 g. **Composition:** 0.9250 Silver., .3461 oz. ASW.

| KM# | Date | Mintage | VG-8 | F-12 | VF-20 | XF-40 | MS-60 | MS-63 | Prf-63 |
|-----|------|---------|------|------|-------|-------|-------|-------|--------|
| 335 | 1999 Cymric | — | — | — | — | — | — | — | 14.00 |

## Lynx

**Weight:** 11.6638 g. **Composition:** 0.9250 Silver., .3461 oz. ASW.

| KM# | Date | Mintage | VG-8 | F-12 | VF-20 | XF-40 | MS-60 | MS-63 | Prf-63 |
|-----|------|---------|------|------|-------|-------|-------|-------|--------|
| 338 | 1999 Lynx | — | — | — | — | — | — | — | 13.50 |

## Tonkinese

**Weight:** 11.6638 g. **Composition:** 0.9250 Silver., .3461 oz. ASW.

| KM# | Date | Mintage | VG-8 | F-12 | VF-20 | XF-40 | MS-60 | MS-63 | Prf-63 |
|-----|------|---------|------|------|-------|-------|-------|-------|--------|
| 336 | 1999 Tonkinese | — | — | — | — | — | — | — | 14.00 |

# DOLLAR

**Weight:** 23.3276 g. **Composition:** 0.8000 Silver., 0.6000 oz. ASW.

| KM# | Date | Mintage | F-12 | VF-20 | XF-40 | AU-50 | MS-60 | MS-63 |
|-----|------|---------|------|-------|-------|-------|-------|-------|
| 30 | 1935 Silver Jubilee | 428,707 | 11.50 | 17.50 | 28.00 | 32.00 | 36.50 | 75.00 |

**Weight:** 23.3276 g. **Composition:** 0.8000 Silver., 0.6000 oz. ASW.

| KM# | Date | Mintage | F-12 | VF-20 | XF-40 | AU-50 | MS-60 | MS-63 |
|-----|------|---------|------|-------|-------|-------|-------|-------|
| 38 | 1939 Royal visit | 1,363,816 | 5.00 | 6.00 | 7.00 | 8.50 | 11.50 | 25.00 |
|  | 1939 specimen Royal visit | — | — | — | — | — | — | 650 |
|  | 1939 Royal visit | — | — | — | — | — | — | — |

**Weight:** 23.3276 g. **Composition:** 0.8000 Silver., 0.6000 oz. ASW.

| KM# | Date | Mintage | F-12 | VF-20 | XF-40 | AU-50 | MS-60 | MS-63 |
|-----|------|---------|------|-------|-------|-------|-------|-------|
| 47 | 1949 Newfoundland | 672,218 | 9.00 | 11.00 | 16.50 | 21.50 | 25.00 | 30.00 |
|  | 1949 Specimen Newfoundland | — | — | — | — | — | — | 1,000 |

**Weight:** 23.3276 g. **Composition:** 0.8000 Silver., 0.6000 oz. ASW.

| KM# | Date | Mintage | F-12 | VF-20 | XF-40 | AU-50 | MS-60 | MS-63 |
|-----|------|---------|------|-------|-------|-------|-------|-------|
| 55 | 1958 British Columbia | 3,039,630 |  | 4.25 | 4.50 | 5.00 | 9.00 | 12.00 |

**Weight:** 23.3276 g. **Composition:** 0.8000 Silver., 0.6000 oz. ASW.

| KM# | Date | Mintage | F-12 | VF-20 | XF-40 | AU-50 | MS-60 | MS-63 |
|-----|------|---------|------|-------|-------|-------|-------|-------|
| 58 | 1964 Charlottetown | 7,296,832 | — | — | — | BV | 4.50 | 7.00 |

**Weight:** 23.3276 g. **Composition:** 0.8000 Silver., 0.6000 oz. ASW. **Reverse:** Goose.

| KM# | Date | Mintage | MS-63 | P/L | Spec. |
|-----|------|---------|-------|-----|-------|
| 70 | 1967 | 6,767,496 | 7.50 | 9.00 | — |

**Composition:** Nickel. **Diameter:** 32 mm.

| KM# | Date | Mintage | MS-63 | P/L | Spec. |
|-----|------|---------|-------|-----|-------|
| 78 | 1970 Manitoba | 4,140,058 | 2.00 | — | — |
|  | 1970 Manitoba | 645,869 | — | 2.50 | — |

**Composition:** Nickel. **Diameter:** 32 mm.

| KM# | Date | Mintage | MS-63 | P/L | Spec. |
|-----|------|---------|-------|-----|-------|
| 79 | 1971 British Columbia | 4,260,781 | 2.00 | 2.25 | — |
|  | 1971 (c)2.50 British Columbia | 468,729 | — | 2.25 | — |

**Weight:** 23.3276 g. **Composition:** 0.5000 Silver., 0.3750 oz. ASW. **Diameter:** 36 mm.

| KM# | Date | Mintage | MS-63 | P/L | Spec. |
|---|---|---|---|---|---|
| 80 | 1971 British Columbia | 585,674 | — | — | 5.50 |

**Composition:** Nickel. **Diameter:** 32 mm.

| KM# | Date | Mintage | MS-63 | P/L | Spec. |
|---|---|---|---|---|---|
| 82 | 1973 Prince Edward Island | 3,196,452 | 2.00 | — | — |
| | 1973 (c) Prince Edward Island | 466,881 | — | 2.50 | — |

**Weight:** 23.3276 g. **Composition:** 0.5000 Silver., 0.3750 oz. ASW. **Diameter:** 36 mm. **Obverse:** Mountie

| KM# | Date | Mintage | MS-63 | P/L | Spec. |
|---|---|---|---|---|---|
| 83 | 1973 | 1,031,271 | — | — | 5.00 |

**Obverse:** Mountie with metal crest on case.

| KM# | Date | Mintage | MS-63 | P/L | Spec. |
|---|---|---|---|---|---|
| 83v | 1973 | Inc. above | — | — | 11.50 |

**Composition:** Nickel. **Diameter:** 32 mm.

| KM# | Date | Mintage | MS-63 | P/L | Spec. |
|---|---|---|---|---|---|
| 88 | 1974 Winnipeg | 2,799,363 | 2.00 | — | — |
| | 1974 (c) Winnipeg | 363,786 | — | 2.50 | — |

**Composition:** 0.5000 Silver. **Diameter:** 36 mm.

| KM# | Date | Mintage | MS-63 | P/L | Spec. |
|-----|------|---------|-------|-----|-------|
| 88a | 1974 Winnipeg | 728,947 | — | — | 5.00 |

**Weight:** 23.3276 g. **Composition:** 0.5000 Silver., 0.3750 oz. ASW. **Diameter:** 36 mm.

| KM# | Date | Mintage | MS-63 | P/L | Spec. |
|-----|------|---------|-------|-----|-------|
| 97 | 1975 Calgary | 930,956 | — | — | 5.00 |

**Weight:** 23.3276 g. **Composition:** 0.5000 Silver., 0.3750 oz. ASW. **Diameter:** 36 mm.

| KM# | Date | Mintage | MS-63 | P/L | Spec. |
|-----|------|---------|-------|-----|-------|
| 106 | 1976 Parliament Library | 578,708 | — | — | 5.50 |

**Diameter:** 36 mm.

| KM# | Date | Mintage | MS-63 | P/L | Spec. |
|-----|------|---------|-------|-----|-------|
| 118 | 1977 Silver Jubilee | 744,848 | — | — | 5.00 |

**Weight:** 23.3276 g. **Composition:** 0.5000 Silver., 0.3750 oz. ASW. **Diameter:** 36 mm.

| KM# | Date | Mintage | MS-63 | P/L | Spec. |
|-----|------|---------|-------|-----|-------|
| 121 | 1978 XI Games | 709,602 | — | — | 5.00 |

**Weight:** 23.3276 g. **Composition:** 0.5000 Silver., 0.3750 oz. ASW. **Diameter:** 36 mm.

| KM# | Date | Mintage | MS-63 | P/L | Spec. |
|-----|------|---------|-------|-----|-------|
| 124 | 1979 Griffon | 826,695 | — | — | 8.00 |

**Weight:** 23.3276 g. **Composition:** 0.5000 Silver., 0.3750 oz. ASW. **Diameter:** 36 mm.

| KM# | Date | Mintage | MS-63 | P/L | Spec. |
|-----|------|---------|-------|-----|-------|
| 128 | 1980 Arctic Territories | 539,617 | — | — | 16.50 |

**Weight:** 23.3276 g. **Composition:** 0.5000 Silver., 0.3750 oz. ASW. **Diameter:** 36 mm.

| KM# | Date | Mintage | MS-63 | P/L | (Proof) |
|-----|------|---------|-------|-----|---------|
| 130 | 1981 Railroad | 699,494 | 10.75 | — | 12.50 |

**Weight:** 23.3276 g. **Composition:** 0.5000 Silver., 0.3750 oz. ASW. **Diameter:** 36 mm.

| KM# | Date | Mintage | MS-63 | P/L | (Proof) |
|-----|------|---------|-------|-----|---------|
| 133 | 1982 Regina | 144,930 | 10.00 | — | — |
|     | 1982 Regina | 758,958 | — | — | 5.00 |

**Composition:** Nickel. **Diameter:** 32 mm.

| KM# | Date | Mintage | MS-63 | P/L | (Proof) |
|-----|------|---------|-------|-----|---------|
| 134 | 1982 Constitution | 9,709,422 | 3.00 | — | 6.00 |

**Weight:** 23.3276 g. **Composition:** 0.5000 Silver., 0.3750 oz. ASW. **Diameter:** 36 mm.

| KM# | Date | Mintage | MS-63 | P/L | (Proof) |
|-----|------|---------|-------|-----|---------|
| 138 | 1983 Edmonton University Games | 159,450 | 6.00 | — | — |
| | 1983 Edmonton University Games | 506,847 | — | — | 6.50 |

**Weight:** 23.3276 g. **Composition:** 0.5000 Silver., 0.3750 oz. ASW. **Diameter:** 36 mm.

| KM# | Date | Mintage | MS-63 | P/L | (Proof) |
|-----|------|---------|-------|-----|---------|
| 140 | 1984 Toronto Sesquicentennial | 133,610 | 14.75 | — | — |
| | 1984 Toronto Sesquicentennial | 732,542 | — | — | 5.00 |

**Composition:** Nickel. **Diameter:** 32 mm.

| KM# | Date | Mintage | MS-63 | P/L | (Proof) |
|-----|------|---------|-------|-----|---------|
| 141 | 1984 Cartier | 7,009,323 | 2.25 | — | — |
| | 1984 Cartier | 87,760 | — | — | 6.50 |

**Weight:** 23.3276 g. **Composition:** 0.5000 Silver., 0.3750 oz. ASW. **Diameter:** 36 mm. **Obverse:** Moose

| KM# | Date | Mintage | MS-63 | P/L | (Proof) |
|-----|------|---------|-------|-----|---------|
| 143 | 1985 National parks | 163,314 | 10.00 | — | — |
| | 1985 National parks | 733,354 | — | — | 6.00 |

**Weight:** 23.3276 g. **Composition:** 0.5000 Silver., 0.3750 oz. ASW. **Diameter:** 36 mm.

| KM# | Date | Mintage | MS-63 | P/L | (Proof) |
|-----|------|---------|-------|-----|---------|
| 149 | 1986 Vancouver | 125,949 | 15.75 | — | — |
| | 1986 Vancouver | 680,004 | — | — | 6.25 |

**Weight:** 23.3276 g. **Composition:** 0.5000 Silver., 0.3750 oz. ASW. **Diameter:** 36 mm.

| KM# | Date | Mintage | MS-63 | P/L | (Proof) |
|-----|------|---------|-------|-----|---------|
| 154 | 1987 John Davis | 118,722 | 10.00 | — | — |
| | 1987 John Davis | 602,374 | — | — | 9.00 |

**Weight:** 23.3276 g. **Composition:** 0.5000 Silver., 0.3750 oz. ASW. **Diameter:** 36 mm.

| KM# | Date | Mintage | MS-63 | P/L | (Proof) |
|-----|------|---------|-------|-----|---------|
| 161 | 1988 Ironworks | 106,872 | 24.50 | — | — |
| | 1988 Ironworks | 255,013 | — | — | 18.00 |

**Weight:** 23.3276 g. **Composition:** 0.5000 Silver., 0.3750 oz. ASW. **Diameter:** 36 mm.

| KM# | Date | Mintage | MS-63 | P/L | (Proof) |
|-----|------|---------|-------|-----|---------|
| 168 | 1989 MacKenzie River | 99,774 | 21.50 | — | — |
| | 1989 MacKenzie River | 244,062 | — | — | 18.00 |

**Weight:** 23.3276 g. **Composition:** 0.5000 Silver., 0.3750 oz. ASW. **Diameter:** 36 mm.

| KM# | Date | Mintage | MS-63 | P/L | (Proof) |
|-----|------|---------|-------|-----|---------|
| 170 | 1990 Henry Kelsey | 99,455 | 10.75 | — | — |
| | 1990 Henry Kelsey | 254,959 | — | — | 12.50 |

**Weight:** 23.3276 g. **Composition:** 0.5000 Silver., 0.3750 oz. ASW. **Diameter:** 36 mm.

| KM# | Date | Mintage | MS-63 | P/L | (Proof) |
|-----|------|---------|-------|-----|---------|
| 179 | 1991 S.S. Frontenac | 73,843 | 11.00 | — | — |
| | 1991 S.S. Frontenac | 195,424 | — | — | 23.50 |

**Composition:** Aureate. **Diameter:** 32 mm. **Previous Catalog#:** 186.2

| KM# | Date | Mintage | MS-63 | P/L | (Proof) |
|-----|------|---------|-------|-----|---------|
| 209 | Loon | 4,242,085 | 2.00 | — | 10.50 |

**Weight:** 11.6200 g. **Composition:** 0.9250 Silver., 0.3456 oz. ASW. **Diameter:** 36 mm.

| KM# | Date | Mintage | MS-63 | P/L | (Proof) |
|-----|------|---------|-------|-----|---------|
| 210 | 1992 Stagecoach service | 78,160 | 10.75 | — | — |
|     | 1992 Stagecoach service | 187,612 | — | — | 12.50 |

**Composition:** Aureate.

| KM# | Date | Mintage | MS-63 | P/L | (Proof) |
|-----|------|---------|-------|-----|---------|
| 218 | Parliament | 23,915,000 | 2.25 | — | — |
|     | Parliament | 24,227 | — | — | 11.50 |

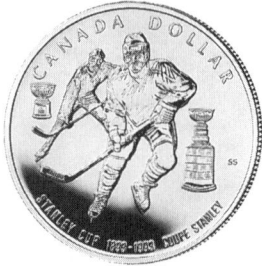

**Weight:** 11.6200 g. **Composition:** 0.9250 Silver., 0.3456 oz. ASW. **Diameter:** 36 mm.

| KM# | Date | Mintage | MS-63 | P/L | (Proof) |
|-----|------|---------|-------|-----|---------|
| 235 | 1993 Stanley Cup hockey | 88,150 | 9.50 | — | — |
|     | 1993 Stanley Cup hockey | 294,314 | — | — | 12.50 |

**Composition:** Aureate. **Diameter:** 26 mm.

| KM# | Date | Mintage | MS-63 | P/L | (Proof) |
|-----|------|---------|-------|-----|---------|
| 235a | 1993 Stanley Cup hockey | 54,524 | — | — | 12.50 |

**Composition:** Aureate. **Diameter:** 26 mm.

| KM# | Date | Mintage | MS-63 | P/L | (Proof) |
|-----|------|---------|-------|-----|---------|
| 248 | 1994 War Memorial | 15,000,000 | 2.25 | — | — |
|     | 1994 War Memorial | 54,524 | — | — | 12.50 |

**Weight:** 11.6200 g. **Composition:** 0.9250 Silver., 0.3456 oz. ASW. **Diameter:** 36 mm.

| KM# | Date | Mintage | MS-63 | P/L | (Proof) |
|-----|------|---------|-------|-------|---------|
| 251 | 1994 Last RCMP sled-dog patrol | 61,561 | 19.00 | — | — |
|     | 1994 Last RCMP sled-dog patrol | 170,374 | — | — | 24.50 |

**Weight:** 11.6200 g. **Composition:** 0.9250 Silver., 0.3456 oz. ASW.

| KM# | Date | Mintage | MS-63 | P/L | (Proof) |
|-----|------|---------|-------|-----|---------|
| 258 | 1995 Peacekeeping monument in Ottawa | — | 2.25 | — | — |
|  | 1995 Peacekeeping monument in Ottawa | 43,293 | — | — | 11.25 |

**Composition:** Aureate. **Diameter:** 26 mm.

| KM# | Date | Mintage | MS-63 | P/L | (Proof) |
|-----|------|---------|-------|-----|---------|
| 258a | 1995 Peacekeeping monument in Ottawa | 43,293 | — | — | 12.50 |

**Weight:** 11.6200 g. **Composition:** 0.9250 Silver., 0.3456 oz. ASW. **Diameter:** 36 mm.

| KM# | Date | Mintage | MS-63 | P/L | (Proof) |
|-----|------|---------|-------|-----|---------|
| 259 | 1995 Hudson Bay Co. | 61,819 | 10.75 | — | — |
|  | 1995 Hudson Bay Co. | 166,259 | — | — | 12.50 |

**Weight:** 11.6200 g. **Composition:** 0.9250 Silver., 0.3456 oz. ASW. **Diameter:** 36 mm.

| KM# | Date | Mintage | MS-63 | P/L | (Proof) |
|-----|------|---------|-------|-----|---------|
| 274 | 1996 McIntosh apple | 58,834 | 13.25 | — | — |
|  | 1996 McIntosh apple | 133,779 | — | — | 18.25 |

**Weight:** 11.6200 g. **Composition:** 0.9250 Silver., .3456 oz. ASW. **Diameter:** 36 mm.

| KM# | Date | Mintage | MS-63 | P/L | (Proof) |
|-----|------|---------|-------|-----|---------|
| 282 | 25th anniversary hockey victory | 155,252 | 10.75 | — | — |
|  | 25th anniversary hockey victory | 184,965 | — | — | 19.00 |

**Composition:** Aureate. **Diameter:** 26 mm.

| KM# | Date | Mintage | MS-63 | P/L | (Proof) |
|-----|------|---------|-------|-----|---------|
| 291 | 1997 Loon dollar 10th anniversary | — | 10.00 | — | — |

**Weight:** 11.6200 g. **Composition:** 0.9250 Silver., 0.3456 oz. ASW. **Diameter:** 36 mm.

| KM# | Date | Mintage | MS-63 | P/L | (Proof) |
|---|---|---|---|---|---|
| 296 | 1997 Loon dollar 10th anniversary | 24,995 | — | — | 65.00 |

 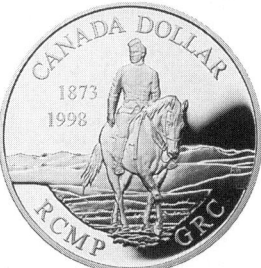

**Weight:** 11.6200 g. **Composition:** 0.9250 Silver., 0.3456 oz. ASW. **Diameter:** 36 mm. **Notes:** Individually cased prooflikes, proofs or specimens are from broken-up prooflike or specimen sets.

| KM# | Date | Mintage | MS-63 | P/L | (Proof) |
|---|---|---|---|---|---|
| 306 | 1998 120th anniversary Royal<br>Canadian Mounted Police | 79,777 | — | 14.50 | — |
| | 1998 120th anniversary Royal<br>Canadian Mounted Police | 120,172 | — | — | 20.00 |

**Weight:** 11.6200 g. **Composition:** 0.9250 Silver., 0.3456 oz. ASW. **Diameter:** 36 mm.

| KM# | Date | Mintage | MS-63 | P/L | (Proof) |
|---|---|---|---|---|---|
| 355 | 1999 International Year of Old<br>Persons | 25,000 | — | — | 33.50 |

**Weight:** 11.6200 g. **Composition:** 0.9250 Silver., .3456 oz. ASW. **Diameter:** 36 mm.

| KM# | Date | Mintage | MS-63 | P/L | (Proof) |
|---|---|---|---|---|---|
| 356 | Discovery of Queen Charlotte Isle | — | — | 13.50 | 21.00 |

**Composition:** 0.9250 Silver. **Reverse:** Human and space shuttle

| KM# | Date | Mintage | VG-8 | F-12 | VF-20 | XF-40 | MS-60 | MS-63 | Prf-63 |
|---|---|---|---|---|---|---|---|---|---|
| 401 | 2000 Voyage of Discovery | — | — | — | — | — | — | — | — |

# 2 DOLLARS

**Center Composition:** Aluminum-bronze **Ring Composition:** Nickel **Diameter:** 28 mm **Reverse:** Polar bear
**Notes:** The Type III design has two lines outlining the star.

| KM# | Date | Mintage | MS-63 | P/L | (Proof) |
|---|---|---|---|---|---|
| 270 | 1996 | 375,483,000 | 3.25 | 7.50 | 12.50 |
| | 1997 | 16,942,000 | 3.25 | — | — |
| | 1998 | 4,926,000 | 3.25 | — | — |
| | 1998W in mint sets only | — | — | — | 5.00 |

**Center Weight:** 5.7456 g. **Center Composition:** Gold, 0.1847 oz. AGW. **Ring Weight:** 5.0958 g. **Ring Composition:** Silver, 0.1638 oz. ASW. **Diameter:** 32 mm. **Reverse:** Polar bear

| KM# | Date | Mintage | MS-63 | P/L | (Proof) |
|---|---|---|---|---|---|
| 270a | 1996 | 5,000 | — | — | 265 |

**Center Weight:** 25.0000 g. **Center Composition:** 0.9250 Gold Plated Silver **Ring Composition:** Silver, 0.7434 oz. ASW. **Reverse:** Polar bear

| KM# | Date | Mintage | MS-63 | P/L | (Proof) |
|---|---|---|---|---|---|
| 270b | 1996 | 15,000,000 | — | — | 80.00 |
| | 1998 | — | — | — | 80.00 |

**Center Weight:** 8.8300 g. **Center Composition:** 0.9250 Gold Plated Silver **Ring Composition:** 0.9250 Silver, 0.2626 oz. ASW. **Reverse:** Polar bear

| KM# | Date | Mintage | MS-63 | P/L | (Proof) |
|---|---|---|---|---|---|
| 270c | 1997 | — | — | — | 23.50 |
| | 1998O in proof sets only | — | — | — | 20.00 |

**Center Composition:** Aluminum-bronze **Ring Composition:** Nickel

| KM# | Date | Mintage | MS-63 | P/L | (Proof) |
|---|---|---|---|---|---|
| 357 | 1999 Nunavut | — | 3.50 | — | — |

**Center Composition:** 0.9250 Silver **Ring Composition:** 0.9250 Silver **Notes:** Gold plated.

| KM# | Date | Mintage | VG-8 | F-12 | VF-20 | XF-40 | MS-60 | MS-63 | Prf-63 |
|---|---|---|---|---|---|---|---|---|---|
| 357a | 1999 Nunavut | — | — | — | — | — | — | — | — |

**Center Composition:** 0.9167 Gold **Ring Composition:** 0.1708 Gold

| KM# | Date | Mintage | VG-8 | F-12 | VF-20 | XF-40 | MS-60 | MS-63 | Prf-63 |
|---|---|---|---|---|---|---|---|---|---|
| 357b | 1999 Nunavut | (10,000) | — | — | — | — | — | — | — |

**Reverse:** Polar bear and 2 cubs

| KM# | Date | Mintage | VG-8 | F-12 | VF-20 | XF-40 | MS-60 | MS-63 | Prf-63 |
|---|---|---|---|---|---|---|---|---|---|
| 399 | 2000 Knowledge | — | — | — | — | — | — | 3.50 | — |

**Center Composition:** 0.9250 Silver **Ring Composition:** 0.9250 Silver **Reverse:** Polar bear and 2 cubs **Notes:** Gold plated

| KM# | Date | Mintage | VG-8 | F-12 | VF-20 | XF-40 | MS-60 | MS-63 | Prf-63 |
|---|---|---|---|---|---|---|---|---|---|
| 399a | 2000 Knowledge | (40,000) | — | — | — | — | — | — | — |

**Center Composition:** 0.9167 Gold **Ring Composition:** 0.1708 Gold

| KM# | Date | Mintage | VG-8 | F-12 | VF-20 | XF-40 | MS-60 | MS-63 | Prf-63 |
|---|---|---|---|---|---|---|---|---|---|
| 399b | 2000 | — | — | — | — | — | — | — | — |

# 5 DOLLARS

**Weight:** 24.3000 g. **Composition:** 0.9250 Silver., 0.7227 oz. ASW. **Diameter:** 38 mm. **Reverse:** Sailboat "Kingston" **Notes:** Series I.

| KM# | Date | Mintage | MS-63 | (Proof) |
|-----|------|---------|-------|---------|
| 84 | 1973 1976 Montreal Olympics | — | 5.00 | — |
| | 1973 1976 Montreal Olympics | 165,203 | — | 6.25 |

**Composition:** 0.9250 Silver., 0.7227 oz. ASW. **Reverse:** North American map. **Notes:** Series I.

| KM# | Date | Mintage | MS-63 | (Proof) |
|-----|------|---------|-------|---------|
| 85 | 1973 1976 Montreal Olympics | — | 5.00 | — |
| | 1973 1976 Montreal Olympics | 165,203 | — | 6.25 |

**Weight:** 24.3000 g. **Composition:** 0.9250 Silver., 0.7227 oz. ASW. **Diameter:** 39 mm. **Reverse:** Olympic rings. **Notes:** Series II.

| KM# | Date | Mintage | MS-63 | (Proof) |
|-----|------|---------|-------|---------|
| 89 | 1974 1976 Montreal Olympics | — | 5.00 | — |
| | 1974 1976 Montreal Olympics | 97,431 | — | 6.25 |

**Weight:** 24.3000 g. **Composition:** 0.9250 Silver., 0.7227 oz. ASW. **Obverse:** Athlete with torch. **Notes:** Series II.

| KM# | Date | Mintage | MS-63 | (Proof) |
|-----|------|---------|-------|---------|
| 90 | 1974 1976 Montreal Olympics | — | 5.00 | — |
| | 1974 1976 Montreal Olympics | 97,431 | — | 6.25 |

**Weight:** 24.3000 g. **Composition:** 0.9250 Silver., 0.7227 oz. ASW. **Diameter:** 39 mm. **Reverse:** Rowing. **Notes:** Series III.

| KM# | Date | Mintage | MS-63 | (Proof) |
|-----|------|---------|-------|---------|
| 91 | 1974 1976 Montreal Olympics | — | 5.00 | — |
| | 1974 1976 Montreal Olympics | 104,684 | — | 6.25 |

**Weight:** 24.3000 g. **Composition:** 0.9250 Silver., 0.7227 oz. ASW. **Reverse:** Canoeing. **Notes:** Series III.

| KM# | Date | Mintage | MS-63 | (Proof) |
|-----|------|---------|-------|---------|
| 92 | 1974 1976 Montreal Olympics | — | 5.00 | — |
| | 1974 1976 Montreal Olympics | 104,684 | — | 6.25 |

**Weight:** 24.3000 g. **Composition:** 0.9250 Silver., 0.7227 oz. ASW. **Diameter:** 36 mm. **Reverse:** Swimmer.
**Notes:** Series V.

| KM# | Date | Mintage | MS-63 | (Proof) |
|---|---|---|---|---|
| 100 | 1975 1976 Montreal Olympics | — | 5.00 | — |
| | 1975 1976 Montreal Olympics | 89,155 | — | 6.25 |

**Weight:** 24.3000 g. **Composition:** 0.9250 Silver., 0.7227 oz. ASW. **Reverse:** Diver. **Notes:** Series V.

| KM# | Date | Mintage | MS-63 | (Proof) |
|---|---|---|---|---|
| 101 | 1975 1976 Montreal Olympics | — | 5.00 | — |
| | 1975 1976 Montreal Olympics | 89,155 | — | 6.25 |

**Weight:** 24.3000 g. **Composition:** 0.9250 Silver., 0.7227 oz. ASW. **Diameter:** 36 mm. **Reverse:** Marathon.
**Notes:** Series IV.

| KM# | Date | Mintage | MS-63 | (Proof) |
|---|---|---|---|---|
| 98 | 1975 1976 Montreal Olympics | — | 5.00 | — |
| | 1975 1976 Montreal Olympics | 89,155 | — | 6.25 |

**Weight:** 24.3000 g. **Composition:** 0.9250 Silver., 0.7227 oz. ASW. **Reverse:** Women's javelin **Notes:** Series IV.

| KM# | Date | Mintage | MS-63 | (Proof) |
|-----|------|---------|-------|---------|
| 99 | 1975 1976 Montreal Olympics | — | 5.00 | — |
|    | 1975 1976 Montreal Olympics | 89,155 | — | 6.25 |

**Weight:** 24.3000 g. **Composition:** 0.9250 Silver., 0.7227 oz. ASW. **Diameter:** 38 mm. **Reverse:** Fencing. **Notes:** Series VI.

| KM# | Date | Mintage | MS-63 | (Proof) |
|-----|------|---------|-------|---------|
| 107 | 1976 1976 Montreal Olympics | — | 5.00 | — |
|     | 1976 1976 Montreal Olympics | 82,302 | — | 6.50 |

**Weight:** 24.3000 g. **Composition:** 0.9250 Silver., 0.7227 oz. ASW. **Obv. Legend:** Boxing. **Notes:** Series VI.

| KM# | Date | Mintage | MS-63 | (Proof) |
|-----|------|---------|-------|---------|
| 108 | 1976 1976 Montreal Olympics | — | 5.00 | — |
|     | 1976 1976 Montreal Olympics | 82,302 | — | 6.50 |

**Weight:** 24.3000 g. **Composition:** 0.9250 Silver., 0.7227 oz. ASW. **Diameter:** 38 mm. **Reverse:** Olympic village. **Notes:** Series VII.

| KM# | Date | Mintage | MS-63 | (Proof) |
|-----|------|---------|-------|---------|
| 109 | 1976 1976 Montreal Olympics | — | 5.00 | — |
|     | 1976 1976 Montreal Olympics | 76,908 | — | 6.50 |

**Weight:** 24.3000 g. **Composition:** 0.9250 Silver., 0.7227 oz. ASW. **Reverse:** Olympic flame. **Notes:** Series VII.

| KM# | Date | Mintage | MS-63 | (Proof) |
|-----|------|---------|-------|---------|
| 110 | 1976 1976 Montreal Olympics | — | 5.00 | — |
|     | 1976 1976 Montreal Olympics | 79,102 | — | 6.50 |

**Weight:** 31.3900 g. **Composition:** 0.9999 Silver., 1.0091 oz. ASW.

| KM# | Date | Mintage | MS-63 | (Proof) |
|-----|------|---------|-------|---------|
| 316 | 1998 in proof sets only Dr. Norman Bethune | 61,000 | — | 35.00 |

**Composition:** Copper-zinc-nickel. **Reverse:** Viking ship under sail **Notes:** Sold in sets with Norway 20 kroner, KM#465.

| KM# | Date | Mintage | VG-8 | F-12 | VF-20 | XF-40 | MS-60 | MS-63 | Prf-63 |
|-----|------|---------|------|------|-------|-------|-------|-------|--------|
| 398 | 1999 | — | — | — | — | — | — | — | — |

# 10 DOLLARS

**Weight:** 48.6000 g. **Composition:** 0.9250 Silver., 1.4454 oz. ASW. **Diameter:** 43 mm. **Reverse:** World map. **Notes:** Series I.

| KM# | Date | Mintage | MS-63 | (Proof) |
|-----|------|---------|-------|---------|
| 86.1 | 1973 1976 Montreal Olympics | 103,426 | 10.00 | — |
|      | 1973 1976 Montreal Olympics | 165,203 | — | 11.50 |

**Weight:** 48.6000 g. **Composition:** 0.9250 Silver., 1.4454 oz. ASW. **Reverse:** Montreal skyline. **Notes:** Series I.

| KM# | Date | Mintage | MS-63 | (Proof) |
|-----|------|---------|-------|---------|
| 87 | 1973 1976 Montreal Olympics | — | 10.00 | — |
| | 1973 1976 Montreal Olympics | 165,203 | — | 11.50 |

**Weight:** 48.6000 g. **Composition:** 0.9250 Silver., 1.4454 oz. ASW. **Reverse:** World map **Notes:** Series I.

| KM# | Date | Mintage | MS-63 | (Proof) |
|-----|------|---------|-------|---------|
| 86.2 | 1974 Error: mule 1976 Montreal Olympics | 320 | 235 | — |

**Weight:** 48.6000 g. **Composition:** 0.9250 Silver., 1.4454 oz. ASW. **Diameter:** 44 mm. **Reverse:** Head of Zeus. **Notes:** Series II.

| KM# | Date | Mintage | MS-63 | (Proof) |
|-----|------|---------|-------|---------|
| 93 | 1974 1976 Montreal Olympics | — | 10.00 | — |
| | 1974 1976 Montreal Olympics | 104,684 | — | 11.50 |

**Weight:** 48.6000 g. **Composition:** 0.9250 Silver., 1.4454 oz. ASW. **Reverse:** Temple of Zeus. **Notes:** Series II.

| KM# | Date | Mintage | MS-63 | (Proof) |
|-----|------|---------|-------|---------|
| 94 | 1974 1976 Montreal Olympics | — | 10.00 | — |
| | 1974 1976 Montreal Olympics | 104,684 | — | 11.50 |

**Weight:** 48.6000 g. **Composition:** 0.9250 Silver., 1.4454 oz. ASW. **Diameter:** 44 mm. **Reverse:** Cycling. **Notes:** Series III.

| KM# | Date | Mintage | MS-63 | (Proof) |
|-----|------|---------|-------|---------|
| 95 | 1974 1976 Montreal Olympics | — | 10.00 | — |
|  | 1974 1976 Montreal Olympics | 97,431 | — | 11.50 |

**Weight:** 48.6000 g. **Composition:** 0.9250 Silver., 1.4454 oz. ASW. **Reverse:** Lacrosse. **Notes:** Series III.

| KM# | Date | Mintage | MS-63 | (Proof) |
|-----|------|---------|-------|---------|
| 96 | 1974 1976 Montreal Olympics | — | 10.00 | — |
|  | 1974 1976 Montreal Olympics | 97,431 | — | 11.50 |

**Weight:** 48.6000 g. **Composition:** 0.9250 Silver., 1.4454 oz. ASW. **Reverse:** Men's hurdles. **Notes:** Series IV.

| KM# | Date | Mintage | MS-63 | (Proof) |
|-----|------|---------|-------|---------|
| 102 | 1975 1976 Montreal Olympics | — | 10.00 | — |
|  | 1975 1976 Montreal Olympics | 82,302 | — | 11.50 |

**Weight:** 48.6000 g. **Composition:** 0.9250 Silver., 1.4454 oz. ASW. **Reverse:** Women's shot put **Notes:** Series IV.

| KM# | Date | Mintage | MS-63 | (Proof) |
|---|---|---|---|---|
| 103 | 1975 1976 Montreal Olympics | — | 10.00 | — |
| | 1975 1976 Montreal Olympics | 82,302 | — | 11.50 |

**Weight:** 48.6000 g. **Composition:** 0.9250 Silver., 1.4454 oz. ASW. **Diameter:** 44 mm. **Reverse:** Sailing. **Notes:** Series V.

| KM# | Date | Mintage | MS-63 | (Proof) |
|---|---|---|---|---|
| 104 | 1975 1976 Montreal Olympics | — | 10.00 | — |
| | 1975 1976 Montreal Olympics | 89,155 | — | 11.50 |

**Weight:** 48.6000 g. **Composition:** 0.9250 Silver., 1.4454 oz. ASW. **Reverse:** Canoeing. **Notes:** Series V.

| KM# | Date | Mintage | MS-63 | (Proof) |
|---|---|---|---|---|
| 105 | 1975 1976 Montreal Olympics | — | 10.00 | — |
| | 1975 1976 Montreal Olympics | 89,155 | — | 11.50 |

**Weight:** 48.6000 g. **Composition:** 0.9250 Silver., 1.4454 oz. ASW. **Diameter:** 43 mm. **Reverse:** Football. **Notes:** Series VI.

| KM# | Date | Mintage | MS-63 | (Proof) |
|-----|------|---------|-------|---------|
| 111 | 1976 1976 Montreal Olympics | — | 10.00 | — |
|     | 1976 1976 Montreal Olympics | 76,908 | — | 12.00 |

**Weight:** 48.6000 g. **Composition:** 0.9250 Silver., 1.4454 oz. ASW. **Reverse:** Field hockey. **Notes:** Series VI.

| KM# | Date | Mintage | MS-63 | (Proof) |
|-----|------|---------|-------|---------|
| 112 | 1976 1976 Montreal Olympics | — | 10.00 | — |
|     | 1976 1976 Montreal Olympics | 76,908 | — | 12.00 |

**Weight:** 48.6000 g. **Composition:** 0.9250 Silver., 1.4454 oz. ASW. **Diameter:** 45 mm. **Reverse:** Olympic Stadium. **Notes:** Series VII.

| KM# | Date | Mintage | MS-63 | (Proof) |
|-----|------|---------|-------|---------|
| 113 | 1976 1976 Montreal Olympics | — | 10.00 | — |
|     | 1976 1976 Montreal Olympics | 79,102 | — | 12.00 |

**Weight:** 48.6000 g. **Composition:** 0.9250 Silver., 1.4454 oz. ASW. **Reverse:** Olympic Velodrome. **Notes:** Series VII.

| KM# | Date | Mintage | MS-63 | (Proof) |
|-----|------|---------|-------|---------|
| 114 | 1976 1976 Montreal Olympics | — | 10.25 | — |
|     | 1976 1976 Montreal Olympics | 79,102 | — | 12.00 |

# 15 DOLLARS

**Weight:** 33.6300 g. **Composition:** 0.9250 Silver., 1.0000 oz. ASW. **Diameter:** 39 mm. **Reverse:** Coaching track.

| KM# | Date | Mintage | MS-63 | (Proof) |
|-----|------|---------|-------|---------|
| 215 | 1992 1992 Olympics | 275,000 | — | 28.00 |

**Weight:** 33.6300 g. **Composition:** 0.9250 Silver., 1.0000 oz. ASW. **Reverse:** High jump, rings, speed skating.

| KM# | Date | Mintage | MS-63 | (Proof) |
|-----|------|---------|-------|---------|
| 216 | 1992 1992 Olympics | 275,000 | — | 28.00 |

**Center Weight:** 0.3700 g. **Center Composition:** 0.9999 Gold, 0.0118 oz. AGW. **Ring Weight:** 33.6300 g.
**Ring Composition:** 0.9250 Silver, 1.0000 oz. ASW. **Diameter:** 32 mm.

| KM# | Date | Mintage | MS-63 | (Proof) |
|-----|------|---------|-------|---------|
| 304 | 1998 Year of the Tiger | 68,888 | — | 165 |

**Center Weight:** 0.3700 g. **Center Composition:** 0.9999 Gold, 0.0118 oz. AGW. **Ring Weight:** 33.6300 g.
**Ring Composition:** 0.9250 Silver, 1.0000 oz. ASW.

| KM# | Date | Mintage | MS-63 | (Proof) |
|-----|------|---------|-------|---------|
| 331 | 1999 Year of the Rabbitt | — | | 50.00 |

**Weight:** 33.6300 g. **Composition:** 0.9250 Silver., 1 oz. ASW. **Center Weight:** 0.3700 g. **Center Composition:**
0.9999 Gold, 0.0118 oz. AGW. ASW.

| KM# | Date | Mintage | VG-8 | F-12 | VF-20 | XF-40 | MS-60 | MS-63 | Prf-63 |
|-----|------|---------|------|------|-------|-------|-------|-------|--------|
| 387 | 2000 | — | — | — | — | — | — | — | — |

# 20 DOLLARS

**Weight:** 18.2733 g. **Composition:** 0.9000 Gold., 0.5288 oz. AGW.

| KM# | Date | Mintage | VG-8 | F-12 | VF-20 | XF-40 | MS-60 | MS-63 | Prf-63 |
|-----|------|---------|------|------|-------|-------|-------|-------|--------|
| 71 | 1967 Centennial | (337,688) | — | — | — | — | — | — | — |

**Weight:** 33.6300 g. **Composition:** 0.9250 Silver., 1.0000 oz. ASW. **Diameter:** 32 mm. **Reverse:** Downhill
skier. **Edge:** Lettered.

| KM# | Date | Mintage | MS-63 | (Proof) |
|-----|------|---------|-------|---------|
| 145 | 1985 1988 Calgary Olympics | 406,360 | — | 21.50 |
| | 1985 Plain edge 1988 Calgary Olympics | Inc. above | — | 175 |

**Weight:** 33.6300 g. **Composition:** 0.9250 Silver., 1.0000 oz. ASW. **Reverse:** Speed skater. **Edge:** Lettered.

| KM# | Date | Mintage | MS-63 | (Proof) |
|---|---|---|---|---|
| 146 | 1985 1988 Calgary Olympics | 354,222 | — | 21.50 |
| | 1985 Plain edge 1988 Calgary Olympics | Inc. above | — | 175 |

**Weight:** 33.6300 g. **Composition:** 0.9250 Silver., 1.0000 oz. ASW. **Diameter:** 32 mm. **Reverse:** Biathlon. **Edge:** Lettered.

| KM# | Date | Mintage | MS-63 | (Proof) |
|---|---|---|---|---|
| 147 | 1986 1988 Calgary Olympics | 308,086 | — | 21.50 |
| | 1986 Plain edge 1988 Calgary Olympics | Inc. above | — | 175 |

**Weight:** 33.6300 g. **Composition:** 0.9250 Silver., 1.0000 oz. ASW. **Reverse:** Hockey. **Edge:** Lettered.

| KM# | Date | Mintage | MS-63 | (Proof) |
|---|---|---|---|---|
| 148 | 1986 1988 Calgary Olympics | 396,602 | — | 21.50 |
| | 1986 Plain edge 1988 Calgary Olympics | Inc. above | — | 175 |

**Weight:** 33.6300 g. **Composition:** 0.9250 Silver., 1.0000 oz. ASW. **Diameter:** 32 mm. **Reverse:** Cross-country skier.

| KM# | Date | Mintage | MS-63 | (Proof) |
|---|---|---|---|---|
| 150 | 1986 1988 Calgary Olympics | 303,199 | — | 21.50 |

**Weight:** 33.6300 g. **Composition:** 0.9250 Silver., 1.0000 oz. ASW. **Reverse:** Free-style skier. **Edge:** Lettered.

| KM# | Date | Mintage | MS-63 | (Proof) |
|---|---|---|---|---|
| 151 | 1986 1988 Calgary Olympics | 294,322 | — | 21.50 |
| | 1986 Plain edge 1988 Calgary Olympics | Inc. above | — | 175 |

**Weight:** 34.1070 g. **Composition:** 0.9250 Silver., 1.0000 oz. ASW. **Diameter:** 32 mm. **Reverse:** Figure skater.

| KM# | Date | Mintage | MS-63 | (Proof) |
|---|---|---|---|---|
| 155 | 1987 1988 Calgary Olympics | 334,875 | — | 21.50 |

**Weight:** 34.1070 g. **Composition:** 0.9250 Silver., 1.0000 oz. ASW. **Reverse:** Curling.

| KM# | Date | Mintage | MS-63 | (Proof) |
|---|---|---|---|---|
| 156 | 1987 1988 Calgary Olympics | 286,457 | — | 21.50 |

**Weight:** 34.1070 g. **Composition:** 0.9250 Silver., 1.0000 oz. ASW. **Diameter:** 32 mm. **Reverse:** Ski jumper.

| KM# | Date | Mintage | MS-63 | (Proof) |
|---|---|---|---|---|
| 159 | 1987 1988 Calgary Olympics | 290,954 | — | 21.50 |

**Weight:** 34.1070 g. **Composition:** 0.9250 Silver., 1.0000 oz. ASW. **Reverse:** Bobsled.

| KM# | Date | Mintage | MS-63 | (Proof) |
|---|---|---|---|---|
| 160 | 1987 1988 Calgary Olympics | 274,326 | — | 21.50 |

**Weight:** 31.1030 g. **Composition:** 0.9250 Silver., 0.9743 oz. ASW. **Cameo Composition:** Gold, 0.0257 oz. ASW. **Diameter:** 32 mm. **Reverse:** Lancaster/Fauquier.

| KM# | Date | Mintage | MS-63 | (Proof) |
|-----|------|---------|-------|---------|
| 172 | 1990 Aviation | 43,596 | — | 165 |

**Weight:** 31.1030 g. **Composition:** 0.9250 Silver., 0.9743 oz. ASW. **Cameo Composition:** Gold, 0.0257 oz. ASW. **Reverse:** Anson and Harvard.

| KM# | Date | Mintage | MS-63 | (Proof) |
|-----|------|---------|-------|---------|
| 173 | 1990 Aviation | 41,844 | — | 50.00 |

**Weight:** 31.1030 g. **Composition:** 0.9250 Silver., 0.9743 oz. ASW. **Cameo Composition:** Gold, 0.0257 oz. ASW. **Diameter:** 32 mm. **Reverse:** Silver Dart.

| KM# | Date | Mintage | MS-63 | (Proof) |
|-----|------|---------|-------|---------|
| 196 | 1991 Aviation | 28,791 | — | 45.00 |

**Weight:** 31.1030 g. **Composition:** 0.9250 Silver., 0.9742 oz. ASW. **Cameo Composition:** Gold, 0.0257 oz. ASW. **Reverse:** de Haviland Beaver.

| KM# | Date | Mintage | MS-63 | (Proof) |
|-----|------|---------|-------|---------|
| 197 | 1991 Aviation | 29,399 | — | 45.00 |

**Weight:** 31.1030 g. **Composition:** 0.9250 Silver., 0.9743 oz. ASW. **Cameo Composition:** Gold, 0.0257 oz. ASW. **Diameter:** 32 mm. **Reverse:** Curtiss JN-4 Canick ("Jenny").

| KM# | Date | Mintage | MS-63 | (Proof) |
|-----|------|---------|-------|---------|
| 224 | 1992 Aviation | 33,105 | — | 45.00 |

**Weight:** 31.1030 g. **Composition:** 0.9250 Silver., 0.9743 oz. ASW. **Cameo Composition:** Gold, 0.0257 oz. ASW. **Reverse:** de Haviland Gypsy Moth.

| KM# | Date | Mintage | MS-63 | (Proof) |
|-----|------|---------|-------|---------|
| 225 | 1992 Aviation | 32,537 | — | 45.00 |

**Weight:** 31.1030 g. **Composition:** 0.9250 Silver., 0.0257 oz. ASW. **Cameo Composition:** Gold, 0.0257 oz. ASW. **Diameter:** 32 mm. **Reverse:** Fairchild 71C float plane.

| KM# | Date | Mintage | MS-63 | (Proof) |
|-----|------|---------|-------|---------|
| 236 | 1993 Aviation | 32,199 | — | 45.00 |

**Weight:** 31.1030 g. **Composition:** 0.9250 Silver., 0.9743 oz. ASW. **Cameo Composition:** Gold, 0.0257 oz. ASW. **Reverse:** Lockheed 14.

| KM# | Date | Mintage | MS-63 | (Proof) |
|-----|------|---------|-------|---------|
| 237 | 1993 Aviation | 32,550 | — | 45.00 |

**Weight:** 31.1030 g. **Composition:** 0.9250 Silver., 0.9743 oz. ASW. **Cameo Composition:** Gold, 0.0257 oz. ASW. **Diameter:** 32 mm. **Reverse:** Curtiss HS-2L seaplane.

| KM# | Date | Mintage | MS-63 | (Proof) |
|-----|------|---------|-------|---------|
| 246 | 1994 Aviation | 31,242 | — | 45.00 |

**Weight:** 31.1030 g. **Composition:** 0.9250 Silver., 0.9743 oz. ASW. **Cameo Composition:** Gold, 0.0257 oz. ASW. **Reverse:** Vickers Vedette.

| KM# | Date | Mintage | MS-63 | (Proof) |
|-----|------|---------|-------|---------|
| 247 | 1994 Aviation | 30,880 | — | 45.00 |

**Weight:** 31.1030 g. **Composition:** 0.9250 Silver., 0.9743 oz. ASW. **Cameo Composition:** Gold, 0.0257 oz. ASW. **Diameter:** 32 mm. **Reverse:** C-FEA1 Fleet Cannuck.

| KM# | Date | Mintage | MS-63 | (Proof) |
|-----|------|---------|-------|---------|
| 271 | 1995 Aviation | 17,438 | — | 45.00 |

**Weight:** 31.1030 g. **Composition:** 0.9250 Silver., 0.9743 oz. ASW. **Cameo Composition:** Gold, 0.0257 oz. ASW. **Reverse:** DHC-1 Chipmunk.

| KM# | Date | Mintage | MS-63 | (Proof) |
|-----|------|---------|-------|---------|
| 272 | 1995 Aviation | 17,722 | — | 45.00 |

**Weight:** 31.1030 g. **Composition:** 0.9250 Silver., 0.9743 oz. ASW. **Cameo Composition:** Gold, 0.0257 oz. ASW. **Diameter:** 32 mm. **Reverse:** CF-100 Cannuck.

| KM# | Date | Mintage | MS-63 | (Proof) |
|-----|------|---------|-------|---------|
| 276 | 1996 Aviation | 18,508 | — | 45.00 |

**Weight:** 31.1030 g. **Composition:** 0.9250 Silver., 0.9743 oz. ASW. **Cameo Composition:** Gold, 0.0257 oz. ASW. **Obv. Legend:** CF-105 Arrow.

| KM# | Date | Mintage | MS-63 | (Proof) |
|-----|------|---------|-------|---------|
| 277 | 1996 Aviation | 27,163 | — | 50.00 |

**Weight:** 31.1030 g. **Composition:** 0.9250 Silver., 0.9743 oz. ASW. **Cameo Composition:** Gold, 0.0257 oz. ASW. **Diameter:** 32 mm. **Reverse:** Canadair F-86 Sabre.

| KM# | Date | Mintage | MS-63 | (Proof) |
|-----|------|---------|-------|---------|
| 297 | 1997 Aviation | 14,389 | — | 45.00 |

**Weight:** 31.1030 g. **Composition:** 0.9250 Silver., 0.9743 oz. ASW. **Cameo Composition:** Gold, 0.0257 oz. ASW. **Reverse:** Canadair CT-114 Tutor.

| KM# | Date | Mintage | MS-63 | (Proof) |
|-----|------|---------|-------|---------|
| 298 | 1997 Aviation | 15,669 | — | 45.00 |

**Weight:** 31.1030 g. **Composition:** 0.9250 Silver., 0.9743 oz. ASW. **Cameo Composition:** Gold, 0.0257 oz. ASW. **Diameter:** 32 mm. **Reverse:** CP-107 Argus.

| KM# | Date | Mintage | MS-63 | (Proof) |
|-----|------|---------|-------|---------|
| 329 | 1998 Aviation | 50,000,000 | — | 42.00 |

**Weight:** 31.1030 g. **Composition:** 0.9250 Silver., 0.9743 oz. ASW. **Cameo Composition:** Gold, 0.0257 oz. ASW. **Reverse:** CP-215 Waterbomber.

| KM# | Date | Mintage | MS-63 | (Proof) |
|-----|------|---------|-------|---------|
| 330 | 1998 Aviation | 50,000,000 | — | 42.00 |

**Weight:** 31.1030 g. **Composition:** 0.9250 Silver., 0.9743 oz. ASW. **Cameo Composition:** Gold, 0.0257 oz. ASW. **Diameter:** 32 mm. **Reverse:** DHC-6 Twin Otter.

| KM# | Date | Mintage | MS-63 | (Proof) |
|-----|------|---------|-------|---------|
| 339 | 1999 Aviation | 50,000,000 | — | 40.00 |

**Weight:** 31.1030 g. **Composition:** 0.9250 Silver., 0.9743 oz. ASW. **Cameo Composition:** Gold, 0.0257 oz. ASW. **Reverse:** DHC-8 Dash 8.

| KM# | Date | Mintage | MS-63 | (Proof) |
|-----|------|---------|-------|---------|
| 340 | 1999 Aviation | 50,000,000 | — | 40.00 |

**Composition:** 0.9250 Silver. **Reverse:** Locomotive below multicolored cameo

| KM# | Date | Mintage | VG-8 | F-12 | VF-20 | XF-40 | MS-60 | MS-63 | Prf-63 |
|-----|------|---------|------|------|-------|-------|-------|-------|--------|
| 395 | 2000 First Canadian locomotive | — | — | — | — | — | — | — | — |

**Composition:** 0.9250 Silver. **Reverse:** Car below multicolored cameo

| KM# | Date | Mintage | VG-8 | F-12 | VF-20 | XF-40 | MS-60 | MS-63 | Prf-63 |
|-----|------|---------|------|------|-------|-------|-------|-------|--------|
| 396 | 2000 First Canadian self-propelled car | — | — | — | — | — | — | — | — |

**Composition:** 0.9250 Silver. **Reverse:** Boat below multicolored cameo

| KM# | Date | Mintage | VG-8 | F-12 | VF-20 | XF-40 | MS-60 | MS-63 | Prf-63 |
|-----|------|---------|------|------|-------|-------|-------|-------|--------|
| 397 | 2000 Bluenose sailboat | — | — | — | — | — | — | — | — |

# 100 DOLLARS

**Weight:** 13.3375 g. **Composition:** 0.5830 Gold., 0.2500 oz. AGW. **Diameter:** 27 mm. **Obverse:** Beaded borders.

| KM# | Date | Mintage | MS-63 | (Proof) |
|-----|------|---------|-------|---------|
| 115 | 1976 1976 Montreal Olympics | 650,000 | 85.00 | — |

**Weight:** 16.9655 g. **Composition:** 0.9170 Gold., 0.5000 oz. AGW. **Diameter:** 25 mm. **Obverse:** Plain borders.

| KM# | Date | Mintage | MS-63 | (Proof) |
|-----|------|---------|-------|---------|
| 116 | 1976 1976 Montreal Olympics | 337,342 | — | 165 |

**Weight:** 16.9655 g. **Composition:** 0.9170 Gold., 0.5000 oz. AGW.

| KM# | Date | Mintage | MS-63 | (Proof) |
|-----|------|---------|-------|---------|
| 119 | 1977 Queen's silver jubilee. | 180,396 | — | 170 |

**Weight:** 16.9655 g. **Composition:** 0.9170 Gold., 0.5000 oz. AGW.

| KM# | Date | Mintage | MS-63 | (Proof) |
|-----|------|---------|-------|---------|
| 122 | 1978 Canadian unification. | 200,000 | — | 170 |

**Weight:** 16.9655 g. **Composition:** 0.9170 Gold., 0.5000 oz. AGW.

| KM# | Date | Mintage | MS-63 | (Proof) |
|-----|------|---------|-------|---------|
| 126 | 1979 International Year of the Child | 250,000 | — | 165 |

**Weight:** 16.9655 g. **Composition:** 0.9170 Gold., 0.5000 oz. AGW.

| KM# | Date | Mintage | MS-63 | (Proof) |
|-----|------|---------|-------|---------|
| 129 | 1980 Arctic Territories. | 300,000 | — | 170 |

**Weight:** 16.9655 g. **Composition:** 0.9170 Gold., 0.5000 oz. AGW.

| KM# | Date | Mintage | MS-63 | (Proof) |
|-----|------|---------|-------|---------|
| 131 | 1981 National anthem. | 102,000 | — | 175 |

**Weight:** 16.9655 g. **Composition:** 0.9170 Gold., 0.5000 oz. AGW.

| KM# | Date | Mintage | MS-63 | (Proof) |
|-----|------|---------|-------|---------|
| 137 | 1982 New Constitution New constitution. | 121,708 | — | 170 |

**Weight:** 16.9655 g. **Composition:** 0.9170 Gold., 0.5000 oz. AGW.

| KM# | Date | Mintage | MS-63 | (Proof) |
|-----|------|---------|-------|---------|
| 139 | 1983 400th anniversary of St. John's, Newfoundland | 83,128 | — | 170 |

**Weight:** 16.9655 g. **Composition:** 0.9170 Gold., 0.5000 oz. AGW.

| KM# | Date | Mintage | MS-63 | (Proof) |
|-----|------|---------|-------|---------|
| 142 | 1984 Jacques Cartier | 67,662 | — | 175 |

**Weight:** 16.9655 g. **Composition:** 0.9170 Gold., 0.5000 oz. AGW. **Reverse:** Big-horn sheep.

| KM# | Date | Mintage | MS-63 | (Proof) |
|-----|------|---------|-------|---------|
| 144 | 1985 National parks | 61,332 | — | 180 |

**Weight:** 16.9655 g. **Composition:** 0.9170 Gold., 0.5000 oz. AGW.

| KM# | Date | Mintage | MS-63 | (Proof) |
|-----|------|---------|-------|---------|
| 152 | 1986 Peace | 76,409 | — | 170 |

**Weight:** 13.3375 g. **Composition:** 0.5830 Gold., 0.2500 oz. AGW. **Reverse:** Torch and logo.

| KM# | Date | Mintage | MS-63 | (Proof) |
|-----|------|---------|-------|---------|
| 158 | 1987 lettered edge 1988 Calgary Olympics | 142,750 | — | 90.00 |
|     | 1987 plain edge 1988 Calgary Olympics | Inc. above | — | 350 |

**Weight:** 13.3375 g. **Composition:** 0.5830 Gold., 0.2500 oz. AGW.

| KM# | Date | Mintage | MS-63 | (Proof) |
|-----|------|---------|-------|---------|
| 162 | 1988 Whales | 52,594 | — | 110 |

**Weight:** 13.3375 g. **Composition:** 0.5830 Gold., 0.2500 oz. AGW.

| KM# | Date | Mintage | MS-63 | (Proof) |
|-----|------|---------|-------|---------|
| 169 | 1989 Sainte-Marie | 59,657 | — | 100.00 |

**Weight:** 13.3375 g. **Composition:** 0.5830 Gold., 0.2500 oz. AGW.

| KM# | Date | Mintage | MS-63 | (Proof) |
|-----|------|---------|-------|---------|
| 171 | 1990 International Literacy Year | 49,940 | — | 110 |

**Weight:** 13.3375 g. **Composition:** 0.5830 Gold., 0.2500 oz. AGW.

| KM# | Date | Mintage | MS-63 | (Proof) |
|-----|------|---------|-------|---------|
| 180 | 1991 S.S. Empress of India | 33,966 | — | 115 |

**Weight:** 13.3375 g. **Composition:** 0.5830 Gold., 0.2500 oz. AGW.

| KM# | Date | Mintage | MS-63 | (Proof) |
|---|---|---|---|---|
| 211 | 1992 Montreal. | 28,162 | — | 120 |

**Weight:** 13.3375 g. **Composition:** 0.5830 Gold., 0.2500 oz. AGW.

| KM# | Date | Mintage | MS-63 | (Proof) |
|---|---|---|---|---|
| 245 | 1993 Antique automobiles | 25,971 | — | 130 |

**Weight:** 13.3375 g. **Composition:** 0.5830 Gold., 0.2500 oz. AGW.

| KM# | Date | Mintage | MS-63 | (Proof) |
|---|---|---|---|---|
| 249 | 1994 World War II home front | 16,201 | — | 150 |

**Weight:** 13.3375 g. **Composition:** 0.5830 Gold., 0.2500 oz. AGW.

| KM# | Date | Mintage | MS-63 | (Proof) |
|---|---|---|---|---|
| 260 | 1995 Louisbourg | 16,916 | — | 150 |

**Weight:** 13.3375 g. **Composition:** 0.5830 Gold., 0.2500 oz. AGW.

| KM# | Date | Mintage | MS-63 | (Proof) |
|---|---|---|---|---|
| 273 | 1996 Klondike gold rush | 17,973 | — | 155 |

**Weight:** 13.3375 g. **Composition:** 0.5830 Gold., 0.2500 oz. AGW.

| KM# | Date | Mintage | MS-63 | (Proof) |
|-----|------|---------|-------|---------|
| 287 | 1997 Alexander Graham Bell | 25,000 | — | 175 |

**Weight:** 13.3375 g. **Composition:** 0.5830 Gold., 0.2500 oz. AGW.

| KM# | Date | Mintage | MS-63 | (Proof) |
|-----|------|---------|-------|---------|
| 307 | 1998 Discovery of insulin | 25,000 | — | 185 |

**Weight:** 13.3375 g. **Composition:** 0.5830 Gold., 0.2500 oz. AGW.

| KM# | Date | Mintage | MS-63 | (Proof) |
|-----|------|---------|-------|---------|
| 341 | 1999 50th anniversary Newfoundland unity with Canada | 15,000 | — | 185 |

**Weight:** 13.3375 g. **Composition:** 0.5830 Gold., .25 oz. AGW.

| KM# | Date | Mintage | VG-8 | F-12 | VF-20 | XF-40 | MS-60 | MS-63 | Prf-63 |
|-----|------|---------|------|------|-------|-------|-------|-------|--------|
| 402 | 2000 McClure's Arctic expedition | (15,000) | — | — | — | — | — | — | — |

# 150 DOLLARS

**Weight:** 13.6100 g. **Composition:** 0.7500 Gold., .3282 oz. AGW.

| KM# | Date | Mintage | VG-8 | F-12 | VF-20 | XF-40 | MS-60 | MS-63 | Prf-63 |
|-----|------|---------|------|------|-------|-------|-------|-------|--------|
| 388 | 2000 Year of the Dragon | (8,888) | — | — | — | — | — | — | — |

# 175 DOLLARS

**Weight:** 16.9700 g. **Composition:** 0.9170 Gold., 0.5000 oz. AGW. **Reverse:** Passing the torch.

| KM# | Date | Mintage | MS-63 | (Proof) |
|-----|------|---------|-------|---------|
| 217 | 1992 1992 Olympics | 22,092 | — | 320 |

# 200 DOLLARS

**Weight:** 17.1060 g. **Composition:** 0.9170 Gold., 0.5042 oz. AGW. **Diameter:** 29 mm.

| KM# | Date | Mintage | MS-63 | (Proof) |
|-----|------|---------|-------|---------|
| 178 | 1990 Canadian flag silver jubilee | 20,980 | — | 195 |

**Weight:** 17.1060 g. **Composition:** 0.9170 Gold., 0.5042 oz. AGW. **Diameter:** 29 mm.

| KM# | Date | Mintage | MS-63 | (Proof) |
|-----|------|---------|-------|---------|
| 202 | 1991 Hockey | 10,215 | — | 225 |

**Weight:** 17.1060 g. **Composition:** 0.9170 Gold., 0.5042 oz. AGW. **Diameter:** 29 mm.

| KM# | Date | Mintage | MS-63 | (Proof) |
|-----|------|---------|-------|---------|
| 230 | 1992 Niagara Falls | 9,465 | — | 245 |

**Weight:** 17.1350 g. **Composition:** 0.9170 Gold., 0.5500 oz. AGW. **Diameter:** 29 mm.

| KM# | Date | Mintage | MS-63 | (Proof) |
|-----|------|---------|-------|---------|
| 244 | 1993 Mounted police | 10,807 | — | 210 |

**Weight:** 17.1350 g. **Composition:** 0.9170 Gold., 0.5500 oz. AGW. **Diameter:** 29 mm.

| KM# | Date | Mintage | MS-63 | (Proof) |
|-----|------|---------|-------|---------|
| 250 | 1994 Novel: Anne of Green Gables | 8,017 | — | 220 |

**Weight:** 17.1350 g. **Composition:** 0.9170 Gold., 0.5500 oz. AGW. **Diameter:** 29 mm.

| KM# | Date | Mintage | MS-63 | (Proof) |
|-----|------|---------|-------|---------|
| 265 | 1995 Maple-syrup production | 7,621 | — | 235 |

**Weight:** 17.1350 g. **Composition:** 0.9170 Gold., 0.5500 oz. AGW. **Diameter:** 29 mm.

| KM# | Date | Mintage | MS-63 | (Proof) |
|-----|------|---------|-------|---------|
| 275 | 1996 Transcontinental Canadian Railway | 7,508 | — | 260 |

**Weight:** 17.1350 g. **Composition:** 0.9170 Gold., 0.5500 oz. AGW. **Diameter:** 29 mm.

| KM# | Date | Mintage | MS-63 | (Proof) |
|-----|------|---------|-------|---------|
| 288 | 1997 Haida mask | 10,020 | — | 350 |

**Weight:** 17.1350 g. **Composition:** 0.9170 Gold., 0.5500 oz. AGW.

| KM# | Date | Mintage | MS-63 | (Proof) |
|-----|------|---------|-------|---------|
| 317 | 1998 Legendary white buffalo | 25,000,000 | — | 275 |

**Weight:** 17.1350 g. **Composition:** 0.9170 Gold., 0.5500 oz. AGW. **Diameter:** 29 mm.

| KM# | Date | | | | | Mintage | MS-63 | (Proof) |
|---|---|---|---|---|---|---|---|---|
| 358 | 1999 Mikmaq butterfly | | | | | 25,000,000 | — | 275 |

**Weight:** 17.1350 g. **Composition:** 0.9170 Gold., .55 oz. AGW. **Reverse:** Inuit mother with infant

| KM# | Date | Mintage | VG-8 | F-12 | VF-20 | XF-40 | MS-60 | MS-63 | Prf-63 |
|---|---|---|---|---|---|---|---|---|---|
| 403 | 2000 Motherhood | (10,000) | — | — | — | — | — | — | — |

# 350 DOLLARS

**Weight:** 38.0500 g. **Composition:** 0.9999 Gold., 1.2233 oz. AGW.

| KM# | Date | Mintage | MS-63 | (Proof) |
|---|---|---|---|---|
| 308 | 1998 Flowers of Canada's coat of arms | 1,998 | — | 750 |

**Weight:** 38.0500 g. **Composition:** 0.9999 Gold., 1.2233 oz. AGW. **Notes:** Stack's A.G. Carter Jr. Sale 12-89 Gem BU realized $82,500.

| KM# | Date | Mintage | MS-63 | (Proof) |
|---|---|---|---|---|
| 370 | 1999 Lady's slipper | 1,999 | — | 675 |

**Weight:** 38.0500 g. **Composition:** 0.9999 Gold., 1.2233 oz. AGW. **Reverse:** Pacific dogwood flower

| KM# | Date | Mintage | VG-8 | F-12 | VF-20 | XF-40 | MS-60 | MS-63 | Prf-63 |
|---|---|---|---|---|---|---|---|---|---|
| 404 | 2000 | (2,000) | — | — | — | — | — | — | — |

# BULLION COINAGE

## SILVER 5 DOLLARS

**Weight:** 31.1000 g. **Composition:** 0.9999 Silver, 1.0000 oz. ASW. **Obverse:** Elizabeth II effigy **Reverse:** Maple leaf. **Obv. Designer:** Machin.

| KM# | Date | Mintage | MS-63 | (Proof) |
|-----|------|---------|-------|---------|
| 163 | 1988 | 1,155,931 | 8.00 | — |
|     | 1989 | 3,288,235 | 7.25 | — |
|     | 1989 | 43,965 | — | 28.50 |

**Weight:** 31.1000 g. **Composition:** 0.9999 Silver, 1.0000 oz. ASW. **Obverse:** New Elizabeth II effigy. **Reverse:** Maple leaf. **Obv. Designer:** de Pedery-Hunt.

| KM# | Date | Mintage | MS-63 | (Proof) |
|-----|------|---------|-------|---------|
| 187 | 1990 | 1,708,800 | 8.00 | — |
|     | 1991 | 644,300 | 10.00 | — |
|     | 1992 | 343,800 | 9.50 | — |
|     | 1993 | 889,946 | 7.50 | — |
|     | 1994 | 1,133,900 | 7.75 | — |
|     | 1995 | 326,244 | 7.75 | — |
|     | 1996 | 250,445 | 9.50 | — |
|     | 1997 | 100,970 | 10.00 | — |
|     | 1998 | — | 8.50 | — |
|     | 1998 Maple leaf w/oval "20 Years ANS" privy mark | — | — | 35.00 |
|     | 1999 | — | 7.50 | — |
|     | 2000 | — | 8.50 | — |

**Weight:** 31.1000 g. **Composition:** 0.9999 Silver, 1 oz. ASW. **Reverse:** Maple leaf with fireworks privy mark

| KM# | Date | Mintage | MS-63 | (Proof) |
|-----|------|---------|-------|---------|
| 363 | 1999/2000 | — | 8.50 | — |

# SILVER 50 DOLLARS

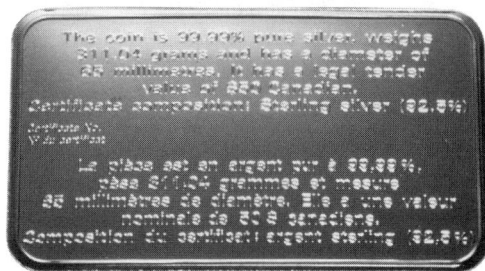

**Weight:** 311.0350 g. **Composition:** 0.9999 Silver, 10.0000 oz. ASW.

| KM# | Date | Mintage | MS-63 | (Proof) |
|-----|------|---------|-------|---------|
| 326 | 1998 | 25,000,000 | — | 145 |

# GOLD DOLLAR

**Weight:** 1.5551 g. **Composition:** 0.9999 Gold, 0.05 oz. AGW. **Reverse:** Maple leaf hologram

| KM# | Date | Mintage | MS-63 | (Proof) |
|-----|------|---------|-------|---------|
| 365 | 1999 | — | — | — |

**Weight:** 1.5551 g. **Composition:** 0.9999 Gold, 0.05 oz. AGW.

| KM# | Date | Mintage | MS-63 | (Proof) |
|-----|------|---------|-------|---------|
| 238 | 1993 | 37,080 | BV +37% | — |
| | 1994 | 78,860 | BV +37% | — |
| | 1995 | 85,920 | BV +37% | — |
| | 1996 | 56,520 | BV +37% | — |
| | 1997 | 59,720 | BV +37% | — |
| | 1998 | 44,260 | BV +37% | — |
| | 1999 Maple leaf with oval "20 Years ANS" privy mark | — | BV +46% | — |
| | 2000 Maple leaf with oval "2000" privy mark | — | — | — |

# GOLD 2 DOLLARS

**Weight:** 2.0735 g. **Composition:** 0.9999 Gold, 0.0666 oz. AGW. **Reverse:** Maple leaf

| KM# | Date | Mintage | MS-63 | (Proof) |
|-----|------|---------|-------|---------|
| 256 | 1994 | 5,493 | 55.00 | — |

# GOLD 5 DOLLARS

**Weight:** 3.1200 g. **Composition:** 0.9999 Gold, .1000 oz. AGW. **Obverse:** Elizabeth II effigy. **Reverse:** Maple leaf. **Obv. Designer:** Machin.

| KM# | Date | Mintage | MS-63 | (Proof) |
|-----|------|---------|-------|---------|
| 135 | 1982 | 246,000 | BV +14% | — |
| | 1983 | 304,000 | BV +14% | — |
| | 1984 | 262,000 | BV +14% | — |
| | 1985 | 398,000 | BV +14% | — |
| | 1986 | 529,516 | BV +14% | — |
| | 1987 | 459,000 | BV +14% | — |
| | 1988 | 506,500 | BV +14% | — |
| | 1989 | 539,000 | BV +14% | — |
| | 1989 | 16,992 | — | 75.00 |

**Weight:** 3.1200 g. **Composition:** 0.9999 Gold, 0.1000 oz. AGW. **Obverse:** Elizabeth II effigy. **Reverse:** Maple leaf. **Obv. Designer:** dePedery-Hunt.

| KM# | Date | Mintage | MS-63 | (Proof) |
|-----|------|---------|-------|---------|
| 188 | 1990 | 476,000 | BV +14% | — |
| | 1991 | 322,000 | BV +14% | — |
| | 1992 | 384,000 | BV +14% | — |
| | 1993 | 248,630 | BV +14% | — |
| | 1994 | 313,150 | BV +14% | — |
| | 1995 | 294,890 | BV +14% | — |
| | 1996 | 179,220 | BV +14% | — |
| | 1997 | 188,540 | BV +14% | — |
| | 1998 | 301,940 | BV +14% | — |
| | 1999 Maple leaf with oval "20 Years ANS" privy mark | — | BV +19% | — |
| | 2000 | — | BV +19% | — |

**Weight:** 3.1200 g. **Composition:** 0.9999 Gold, 0.1000 oz. AGW. **Reverse:** Maple leaf hologram

| KM# | Date | Mintage | MS-63 | (Proof) |
|-----|------|---------|-------|---------|
| 366 | 1999 | — | — | — |

# GOLD 10 DOLLARS

**Weight:** 7.7850 g. **Composition:** 0.9999 Gold, 0.2500 oz. AGW. **Obverse:** Elizabeth II effigy. **Reverse:** Maple leaf. **Obv. Designer:** Machin.

| KM# | Date | Mintage | MS-63 | (Proof) |
|-----|------|---------|-------|---------|
| 136 | 1982 | 184,000 | BV +10% | — |
| | 1983 | 308,800 | BV +10% | — |
| | 1984 | 242,400 | BV +10% | — |
| | 1985 | 620,000 | BV +10% | — |
| | 1986 | 915,200 | BV +10% | — |
| | 1987 | 376,000 | BV +10% | — |
| | 1988 | 436,000 | BV +10% | — |
| | 1989 | 328,800 | BV +10% | — |

| KM# | Date | Mintage | MS-63 | (Proof) |
|-----|------|---------|-------|---------|
|     | 1989 | 6,998   | —     | 175     |

**Weight:** 7.7850 g. **Composition:** 0.9999 Gold, 0.2500 oz. AGW. **Obverse:** Elizabeth II effigy. **Reverse:** Maple leaf. **Obv. Designer:** dePedery-Hunt.

| KM# | Date | Mintage | MS-63 | (Proof) |
|-----|------|---------|-------|---------|
| 189 | 1990 | 253,600 | BV +10% | — |
|     | 1991 | 166,400 | BV +10% | — |
|     | 1992 | 179,600 | BV +10% | — |
|     | 1993 | 158,452 | BV +10% | — |
|     | 1994 | 148,792 | BV +10% | — |
|     | 1995 | 127,596 | BV +10% | — |
|     | 1996 | 89,148  | BV +10% | — |
|     | 1997 | 98,104  | BV +10% | — |
|     | 1998 | 85,472  | BV +10% | — |
|     | 1999 Maple leaf with oval "20 Years ANS" privy mark | — | BV +15% | — |
|     | 2000 Maple leaf with oval "2000" privy mark | — | BV +15% | — |

**Weight:** 7.7850 g. **Composition:** 0.9999 Gold, 0.2500 oz. AGW. **Reverse:** Maple leaf hologram.

| KM# | Date | Mintage | MS-63 | (Proof) |
|-----|------|---------|-------|---------|
| 367 | 1999 | — | — | — |

# GOLD 20 DOLLARS

**Weight:** 15.5515 g. **Composition:** 0.9999 Gold, 0.5000 oz. AGW. **Diameter:** 32 mm. **Obverse:** Elizabeth II effigy. **Obv. Designer:** Machin.

| KM# | Date | Mintage | MS-63 | (Proof) |
|-----|------|---------|-------|---------|
| 153 | 1986 | 529,200 | BV +7% | — |
|     | 1987 | 332,800 | BV +7% | — |
|     | 1988 | 538,400 | BV +7% | — |
|     | 1989 | 259,200 | BV +7% | — |
|     | 1989 | 6,998   | —      | 275 |

**Weight:** 15.5515 g. **Composition:** 0.9999 Gold, 0.5000 oz. AGW. **Obverse:** Elizabeth II effigy. **Reverse:** Maple leaf. **Obv. Designer:** dePedery-Hunt.

| KM# | Date | Mintage | MS-63 | (Proof) |
|-----|------|---------|-------|---------|
| 190 | 1990 | 174,400 | BV +7% | — |
|     | 1991 | 96,200  | BV +7% | — |
|     | 1992 | 108,000 | BV +7% | — |
|     | 1993 | 99,492  | BV +7% | — |
|     | 1994 | 104,766 | BV +7% | — |
|     | 1995 | 103,162 | BV +7% | — |
|     | 1996 | 66,246  | BV +7% | — |
|     | 1997 | 63,354  | BV +7% | — |
|     | 1998 | 65,366  | BV +7% | — |
|     | 1999 Maple leaf with oval "20 Years ANS" privy mark | — | BV +12% | — |
|     | 2000 | — | BV +12% | — |

**Weight:** 15.5515 g. **Composition:** 0.9999 Gold, 0.5000 oz. AGW. **Reverse:** Maple leaf hologram.

| KM# | Date | Mintage | MS-63 | (Proof) |
|-----|------|---------|-------|---------|
| 368 | 1999 | — | — | — |

# GOLD 50 DOLLARS

**Weight:** 31.1030 g. **Composition:** 0.9990 Gold, 1.0000 oz. AGW. **Reverse:** Maple leaf flanked by .9999.

| KM# | Date | Mintage | MS-63 | (Proof) |
|-----|------|---------|-------|---------|
| 125.1 | 1979 | 1,000,000 | BV +4% | — |
| | 1980 | 1,251,500 | BV +4% | — |
| | 1981 | 863,000 | BV +4% | — |
| | 1982 | 883,000 | BV +4% | — |

**Weight:** 31.1030 g. **Composition:** 0.9999 Gold, 1.0000 oz. AGW. **Reverse:** Maple leaf flanked by .9999.

| KM# | Date | Mintage | MS-63 | (Proof) |
|-----|------|---------|-------|---------|
| 125.2 | 1983 | 843,000 | BV +4% | — |
| | 1984 | 1,067,500 | BV +4% | — |
| | 1985 | 1,908,000 | BV +4% | — |
| | 1986 | 779,115 | BV +4% | — |
| | 1987 | 978,000 | BV +4% | — |
| | 1988 | 826,500 | BV +4% | — |
| | 1989 | 856,000 | BV +4% | — |
| | 1989 | 17,781 | — | 425 |

**Weight:** 31.1030 g. **Composition:** 0.9999 Gold, 1.000 oz. AGW. **Obverse:** Elizabeth II effigy. **Reverse:** Maple leaf flanked by .9999. **Obv. Designer:** dePedery-Hunt.

| KM# | Date | Mintage | MS-63 | (Proof) |
|-----|------|---------|-------|---------|
| 191 | 1990 | 815,000 | BV +4% | — |
| | 1991 | 290,000 | BV +4% | — |
| | 1992 | 368,900 | BV +4% | — |
| | 1993 | 321,413 | BV +4% | — |
| | 1994 | 180,357 | BV +4% | — |
| | 1995 | 208,729 | BV +4% | — |
| | 1996 | 143,682 | BV +4% | — |
| | 1997 | 478,211 | BV +4% | — |
| | 1998 | 593,704 | BV +4% | — |
| | 1999 Maple leaf with oval "20 Years ANS" privy mark | — | BV +7% | — |
| | 2000 Maple leaf with oval | — | BV +7% | — |

**Weight:** 31.1030 g. **Composition:** 0.9999 Gold, 1.0000 oz. AGW. **Reverse:** Maple leaf hologram.

| KM# | Date | Mintage | MS-63 | (Proof) |
|-----|------|---------|-------|---------|
| 369 | 1999 | — | — | — |

**Weight:** 31.1030 g. **Composition:** 0.9999 Gold, 1.0000 oz. AGW. **Reverse:** Maple leaf with fireworks privy mark.

| KM# | Date | Mintage | MS-63 | (Proof) |
|-----|------|---------|-------|---------|
| 364 | 1999/2000 | — | — | — |

# PLATINUM DOLLAR

**Weight:** 1.5552 g. **Composition:** 0.9995 Platinum, 0.0500 oz. APW. **Reverse:** Maple leaf.

| KM# | Date | Mintage | MS-63 | (Proof) |
|-----|------|---------|-------|---------|
| 239 | 1993 | 2,120 | BV +35% | — |
|     | 1994 | 4,260 | BV +35% | — |
|     | 1995 | 460 | BV +35% | — |
|     | 1996 | 1,640 | BV +35% | — |
|     | 1997 | 1,340 | BV +35% | — |
|     | 1998 | 2,000 | BV +35% | — |
|     | 1999 | 2,000 | BV +35% | — |

# PLATINUM 2 DOLLARS

**Weight:** 2.0735 g. **Composition:** 0.9995 Platinum, 0.0666 oz. APW. **Reverse:** Maple leaf.

| KM# | Date | Mintage | MS-63 | (Proof) |
|-----|------|---------|-------|---------|
| 257 | 1994 | 1,470 | 325 | — |

# PLATINUM 5 DOLLARS

**Weight:** 3.1203 g. **Composition:** 0.9995 Platinum, 0.1000 oz. APW. **Obverse:** Elizabeth II effigy. **Obv. Designer:** Machin.

| KM# | Date | Mintage | MS-63 | (Proof) |
|---|---|---|---|---|
| 164 | 1988 | 74,000 | BV +18% | — |
| | 1989 | 18,000 | BV +18% | — |
| | 1989 | 11,999 | — | 90.00 |

**Weight:** 3.1203 g. **Composition:** 0.9995 Platinum, 0.1000 oz. APW. **Obverse:** Elizabeth II effigy. **Obv. Designer:** dePedery-Hunt.

| KM# | Date | Mintage | MS-63 | (Proof) |
|---|---|---|---|---|
| 192 | 1990 | 9,000 | BV +18% | — |
| | 1991 | 13,000 | BV +18% | — |
| | 1992 | 16,000 | BV +18% | — |
| | 1993 | 14,020 | BV +18% | — |
| | 1994 | 19,190 | BV +18% | — |
| | 1995 | 8,940 | BV +18% | — |
| | 1996 | 8,820 | BV +18% | — |
| | 1997 | 7,050 | BV +18% | — |
| | 1998 | 5,710 | BV +18% | — |
| | 1999 | 2,000 | BV +18% | — |

# PLATINUM 10 DOLLARS

**Weight:** 7.7857 g. **Composition:** 0.9995 Platinum, 0.2500 oz. APW. **Obverse:** Elizabeth II effigy. **Reverse:** Maple leaf. **Obv. Designer:** Machin.

| KM# | Date | Mintage | MS-63 | (Proof) |
|---|---|---|---|---|
| 165 | 1988 | 93,600 | BV +13% | — |
| | 1989 | 3,200 | BV +13% | — |
| | 1989 | 1,999 | — | 175 |

**Weight:** 7.7857 g. **Composition:** 0.9995 Platinum, 0.2500 oz. APW. **Obverse:** Elizabeth II effigy. **Reverse:** Maple leaf. **Obv. Designer:** dePedery-Hunt.

| KM# | Date | Mintage | MS-63 | (Proof) |
|---|---|---|---|---|
| 193 | 1990 | 1,600 | BV +13% | — |
| | 1991 | 7,200 | BV +13% | — |
| | 1992 | 11,600 | BV +13% | — |
| | 1993 | 8,048 | BV +13% | — |
| | 1994 | 9,456 | BV +13% | — |
| | 1995 | 6,524 | BV +13% | — |
| | 1996 | 6,160 | BV +13% | — |
| | 1997 | 4,552 | BV +13% | — |
| | 1998 | 3,816 | BV +13% | — |
| | 1999 | 2,000 | BV +13% | — |

# PLATINUM 20 DOLLARS

**Weight:** 15.5519 g. **Composition:** 0.9995 Platinum, 0.5000 oz. APW. **Obverse:** Elizabeth II effigy. **Reverse:** Maple leaf. **Obv. Designer:** Machin.

| KM# | Date | Mintage | MS-63 | (Proof) |
|-----|------|---------|-------|---------|
| 166 | 1988 | 23,600 | BV +9% | — |
|     | 1989 | 4,800 | BV +9% | — |
|     | 1989 | 1,999 | — | 350 |

**Weight:** 15.5519 g. **Composition:** 0.9995 Platinum, 0.5000 oz. APW. **Obverse:** Elizabeth II effigy. **Reverse:** Maple leaf. **Obv. Designer:** dePedery-Hunt.

| KM# | Date | Mintage | MS-63 | (Proof) |
|-----|------|---------|-------|---------|
| 194 | 1990 | 2,600 | BV +9% | — |
|     | 1991 | 5,600 | BV +9% | — |
|     | 1992 | 12,800 | BV +9% | — |
|     | 1993 | 6,022 | BV +9% | — |
|     | 1994 | 6,710 | BV +9% | — |
|     | 1995 | 6,308 | BV +9% | — |
|     | 1996 | 5,490 | BV +9% | — |
|     | 1997 | 3,990 | BV +9% | — |
|     | 1998 | 5,486 | BV +9% | — |
|     | 1999 | 500 | 325 | — |

# PLATINUM 30 DOLLARS

**Weight:** 3.1100 g. **Composition:** 0.9990 Platinum, 0.1000 oz. APW. **Reverse:** Polar bear swimming.

| KM# | Date | Mintage | MS-63 | (Proof) |
|-----|------|---------|-------|---------|
| 174 | 1990 | 2,629 | — | 70.00 |

**Weight:** 3.1100 g. **Composition:** 0.9990 Platinum, 0.1000 oz. APW. **Reverse:** Snowy owl.

| KM# | Date | Mintage | MS-63 | (Proof) |
|-----|------|---------|-------|---------|
| 198 | 1991 | 3,500 | — | 85.00 |

**Weight:** 3.1100 g. **Composition:** 0.9990 Platinum, 0.1000 oz. APW. **Reverse:** Cougar head and shoulders.

| KM# | Date | Mintage | MS-63 | (Proof) |
|-----|------|---------|-------|---------|
| 226 | 1992 | 3,500 | — | 85.00 |

**Weight:** 3.1100 g. **Composition:** 0.9990 Platinum, 0.1000 oz. APW. **Reverse:** Arctic fox.

| KM# | Date | Mintage | MS-63 | (Proof) |
|-----|------|---------|-------|---------|
| 240 | 1993 | 3,500 | — | 100.00 |

**Weight:** 3.1100 g. **Composition:** 0.9990 Platinum, 0.1000 oz. APW. **Reverse:** Sea otter. **Notes:** 1,500 sets only.

| KM# | Date | Mintage | MS-63 | (Proof) |
|-----|------|---------|-------|---------|
| 252 | 1994 | 1,500 | — | 110 |

**Weight:** 3.1100 g. **Composition:** 0.9990 Platinum, 0.1000 oz. APW. **Reverse:** Canadian lynx.

| KM# | Date | Mintage | MS-63 | (Proof) |
|-----|------|---------|-------|---------|
| 266 | 1995 | 620 | — | 100.00 |

**Weight:** 3.1100 g. **Composition:** 0.9990 Platinum, 0.1000 oz. APW. **Reverse:** Falcon portrait.

| KM# | Date | Mintage | MS-63 | (Proof) |
|-----|------|---------|-------|---------|
| 278 | 1996 | 489 | — | 100.00 |

**Weight:** 3.1320 g. **Composition:** 0.9995 Platinum, 0.1006 oz. APW. **Reverse:** Bison head.

| KM# | Date | Mintage | MS-63 | (Proof) |
|-----|------|---------|-------|---------|
| 300 | 1997 | 5,000 | — | 100.00 |

**Weight:** 3.1100 g. **Composition:** 0.9990 Platinum, 0.1 oz. APW. **Reverse:** Gray Wolf

| KM# | Date | Mintage | MS-63 | (Proof) |
|-----|------|---------|-------|---------|
| 322 | 1998 | 2,000 | — | 100.00 |

**Weight:** 3.1320 g. **Composition:** 0.9995 Platinum, 0.1006 oz. APW. **Reverse:** Musk ox.

| KM# | Date | Mintage | MS-63 | (Proof) |
|-----|------|---------|-------|---------|
| 359 | 1999 | 1,500 | — | 100.00 |

**Weight:** 3.1320 g. **Composition:** 0.9995 Platinum, .1006 oz. APW. **Reverse:** Pronghorn antelope head

| KM# | Date | Mintage | MS-63 | (Proof) |
|-----|------|---------|-------|---------|
| 405 | 2000 | — | — | 100.00 |

# PLATINUM 50 DOLLARS

**Weight:** 31.1030 g. **Composition:** 0.9995 Platinum, 1.0000 oz. APW. **Obverse:** Elizabeth II effigy. **Reverse:** Maple leaf. **Obv. Designer:** Machin.

| KM# | Date | Mintage | MS-63 | (Proof) |
|-----|------|---------|-------|---------|
| 167 | 1988 | 37,500 | BV +4% | — |
| | 1989 | 10,000 | BV +4% | — |
| | 1989 | 5,965 | — | 700 |

**Weight:** 31.1030 g. **Composition:** 0.9995 Platinum, 1.0000 oz. APW. **Obverse:** Elizabeth II effigy. **Reverse:** Maple leaf. **Obv. Designer:** dePedery-Hunt.

| KM# | Date | Mintage | MS-63 | (Proof) |
|-----|------|---------|-------|---------|
| 195 | 1990 | 15,100 | BV +4% | — |
| | 1991 | 31,900 | BV +4% | — |
| | 1992 | 40,500 | BV +4% | — |
| | 1993 | 17,666 | BV +4% | — |
| | 1994 | 36,245 | BV +4% | — |
| | 1995 | 25,829 | BV +4% | — |
| | 1996 | 62,273 | BV +4% | — |
| | 1997 | 25,480 | BV +4% | — |
| | 1998 | 10,403 | BV +4% | — |
| | 1999 | 1,300 | 480 | — |

# PLATINUM 75 DOLLARS

**Weight:** 7.7760 g. **Composition:** 0.9990 Platinum, 0.2500 oz. APW. **Reverse:** Polar bear resting.

| KM# | Date | Mintage | MS-63 | (Proof) |
|-----|------|---------|-------|---------|
| 175 | 1990 | 2,629 | — | 155 |

**Weight:** 7.7760 g. **Composition:** 0.9990 Platinum, 0.2500 oz. APW. **Reverse:** Snowy owls perched on branch.

| KM# | Date | Mintage | MS-63 | (Proof) |
|-----|------|---------|-------|---------|
| 199 | 1991 | 3,500 | — | 175 |

**Weight:** 7.7760 g. **Composition:** 0.9990 Platinum, 0.2500 oz. APW. **Obv. Legend:** Cougar prowling.

| KM# | Date | Mintage | MS-63 | (Proof) |
|-----|------|---------|-------|---------|
| 227 | 1992 | 3,500 | — | 175 |

**Weight:** 7.7760 g. **Composition:** 0.9990 Platinum, 0.2500 oz. APW. **Reverse:** 2 Arctic foxes.

| KM# | Date | Mintage | MS-63 | (Proof) |
|-----|------|---------|-------|---------|
| 241 | 1993 | 3,500 | — | 195 |

**Weight:** 7.7760 g. **Composition:** 0.9990 Platinum, 0.2500 oz. APW. **Reverse:** Sea otter eating urchin.

| KM# | Date | Mintage | MS-63 | (Proof) |
|-----|------|---------|-------|---------|
| 253 | 1994 | 1,500 | — | 215 |

**Weight:** 7.7760 g. **Composition:** 0.9990 Platinum, 0.2500 oz. APW. **Reverse:** 2 lynx kittens.

| KM# | Date | Mintage | MS-63 | (Proof) |
|-----|------|---------|-------|---------|
| 267 | 1995 | 1,500 | — | 195 |

**Weight:** 7.7760 g. **Composition:** 0.9990 Platinum, 0.2500 oz. APW. **Reverse:** Peregrine falcon, diving falcon.

| KM# | Date | Mintage | MS-63 | (Proof) |
|-----|------|---------|-------|---------|
| 279 | 1996 | 1,500 | — | 195 |

**Weight:** 7.7760 g. **Composition:** 0.9990 Platinum, 0.2500 oz. APW. **Reverse:** Two bison calves.

| KM# | Date | Mintage | MS-63 | (Proof) |
|-----|------|---------|-------|---------|
| 301 | 1997 | 1,500 | — | 195 |

**Weight:** 7.7760 g. **Composition:** 0.9990 Platinum, 0.2500 oz. APW. **Reverse:** Gray wolf.

| KM# | Date | Mintage | MS-63 | (Proof) |
|-----|------|---------|-------|---------|
| 323 | 1998 | 1,000 | — | 195 |

**Weight:** 7.7760 g. **Composition:** 0.9990 Platinum, 0.2500 oz. APW. **Obv. Legend:** Musk ox.

| KM# | Date | Mintage | MS-63 | (Proof) |
|-----|------|---------|-------|---------|
| 360 | 1999 | 500 | — | 195 |

**Weight:** 7.7760 g. **Composition:** 0.9990 Platinum, .25 oz. APW. **Reverse:** Standing pronghorn antelope

| KM# | Date | Mintage | MS-63 | (Proof) |
|-----|------|---------|-------|---------|
| 406 | 2000 | — | — | 195 |

# PLATINUM 150 DOLLARS

**Weight:** 15.5520 g. **Composition:** 0.9990 Platinum, 0.5000 oz. APW. **Reverse:** Polar bear walking.

| KM# | Date | Mintage | MS-63 | (Proof) |
|-----|------|---------|-------|---------|
| 176 | 1990 | 2,629 | — | 310 |

**Weight:** 15.5520 g. **Composition:** 0.9990 Platinum, 0.5000 oz. APW. **Reverse:** Snowy owl flying.

| KM# | Date | Mintage | MS-63 | (Proof) |
|-----|------|---------|-------|---------|
| 200 | 1991 | 3,500 | — | 335 |

**Weight:** 15.5520 g. **Composition:** 0.9990 Platinum, 0.5000 oz. APW. **Reverse:** Cougar mother and cub.

| KM# | Date | Mintage | MS-63 | (Proof) |
|-----|------|---------|-------|---------|
| 228 | 1992 | 3,500 | — | 335 |

**Weight:** 15.5520 g. **Composition:** 0.9990 Platinum, 0.5000 oz. APW. **Reverse:** Arctic fox by lake.

| KM# | Date | Mintage | MS-63 | (Proof) |
|-----|------|---------|-------|---------|
| 242 | 1993 | 3,500 | — | 370 |

**Weight:** 15.5520 g. **Composition:** 0.9990 Platinum, 0.5000 oz. APW. **Reverse:** Sea otter mother carrying pup.

| KM# | Date | Mintage | MS-63 | (Proof) |
|-----|------|---------|-------|---------|
| 254 | 1994 | — | — | 400 |

**Weight:** 15.5520 g. **Composition:** 0.9990 Platinum, 0.5000 oz. APW. **Reverse:** Prowling lynx.

| KM# | Date | Mintage | MS-63 | (Proof) |
|-----|------|---------|-------|---------|
| 268 | 1995 | 226 | — | 365 |

**Weight:** 15.5520 g. **Composition:** 0.9990 Platinum, 0.5000 oz. APW. **Reverse:** Peregrine falcon - falcon on branch.

| KM# | Date | Mintage | MS-63 | (Proof) |
|-----|------|---------|-------|---------|
| 280 | 1996 | 100 | — | 365 |

**Weight:** 15.5520 g. **Composition:** 0.9990 Platinum, 0.5000 oz. APW. **Reverse:** Bison bull.

| KM# | Date | Mintage | MS-63 | (Proof) |
|-----|------|---------|-------|---------|
| 302 | 1997 | 4,000 | — | 365 |

**Weight:** 15.5520 g. **Composition:** 0.9990 Platinum, 0.5000 oz. APW. **Reverse:** 2 gray wolf cubs.

| KM# | Date | Mintage | MS-63 | (Proof) |
|-----|------|---------|-------|---------|
| 324 | 1998 | 2,000 | — | 365 |

**Weight:** 15.5520 g. **Composition:** 0.9990 Platinum, 0.5000 oz. APW. **Reverse:** Musk ox.

| KM# | Date | Mintage | MS-63 | (Proof) |
|-----|------|---------|-------|---------|
| 361 | 1999 | 500 | — | 370 |

**Weight:** 15.5520 g. **Composition:** 0.9990 Platinum, .5 oz. APW. **Reverse:** 2 pronghorn antelope

| KM# | Date | Mintage | MS-63 | (Proof) |
|-----|------|---------|-------|---------|
| 407 | 2000 | — | — | 375 |

# PLATINUM 300 DOLLARS

**Weight:** 31.1035 g. **Composition:** 0.9990 Platinum, 1.0000 oz. APW. **Reverse:** Polar bear mother and cub

| KM# | Date | Mintage | MS-63 | (Proof) |
|-----|------|---------|-------|---------|
| 177 | 1990 | 2,629 | — | 675 |

**Weight:** 31.1035 g. **Composition:** 0.9990 Platinum, 1.0000 oz. APW. **Reverse:** Snowy owl with chicks

| KM# | Date | Mintage | MS-63 | (Proof) |
|-----|------|---------|-------|---------|
| 201 | 1991 | 3,500 | — | 710 |

**Weight:** 31.1035 g. **Composition:** 0.9990 Platinum, 1.0000 oz. APW. **Reverse:** Cougar resting in tree

| KM# | Date | Mintage | MS-63 | (Proof) |
|-----|------|---------|-------|---------|
| 229 | 1992 | 3,500 | — | 710 |

**Weight:** 31.1035 g. **Composition:** 0.9990 Platinum, 1.0000 oz. APW. **Reverse:** Mother fox and 3 kits

| KM# | Date | Mintage | MS-63 | (Proof) |
|-----|------|---------|-------|---------|
| 243 | 1993 | 3,500 | — | 740 |

**Weight:** 31.1035 g. **Composition:** 0.9990 Platinum, 1.0000 oz. APW. **Reverse:** 2 otters swimming

| KM# | Date | Mintage | MS-63 | (Proof) |
|-----|------|---------|-------|---------|
| 255 | 1994 | — | — | 800 |

**Weight:** 31.1035 g. **Composition:** 0.9990 Platinum, 1.0000 oz. APW. **Reverse:** Female lynx and 3 kittens

| KM# | Date | Mintage | MS-63 | (Proof) |
|-----|------|---------|-------|---------|
| 269 | 1995 | 1,500 | — | 725 |

**Weight:** 31.1035 g. **Composition:** 0.9990 Platinum, 1.0000 oz. APW. **Reverse:** Peregrine falcon feeding nestlings

| KM# | Date | Mintage | MS-63 | (Proof) |
|-----|------|---------|-------|---------|
| 281 | 1996 | 1,500 | — | 725 |

**Weight:** 31.1035 g. **Composition:** 0.9990 Platinum, 1.0000 oz. APW. **Reverse:** Bison family

| KM# | Date | Mintage | MS-63 | (Proof) |
|-----|------|---------|-------|---------|
| 303 | 1997 | 1,500 | — | 725 |

**Weight:** 31.1035 g. **Composition:** 0.9990 Platinum, 1.0000 oz. APW. **Reverse:** Gray wolf and 2 cubs

| KM# | Date | Mintage | MS-63 | (Proof) |
|-----|------|---------|-------|---------|
| 325 | 1998 | — | — | 725 |

**Weight:** 31.1035 g. **Composition:** 0.9990 Platinum, 1.0000 oz. APW. **Reverse:** Musk ox **Notes:** Some authorities list these as proof sets. However, the Canadian Mint does not. The coins are double struck with higher than usual pressure, but are considered to have the same quality as proof issue from the Royal Mint, London. A 1903H double set has been reported on display in Bombay, India. *Estimated.

| KM# | Date | Mintage | MS-63 | (Proof) |
|-----|------|---------|-------|---------|
| 362 | 1999 | 500 | — | 735 |

**Weight:** 31.1035 g. **Composition:** 0.9990 Platinum, 1 oz. APW. **Reverse:** 4 pronghorn antelope

| KM# | Date | Mintage | MS-63 | (Proof) |
|-----|------|---------|-------|---------|
| 408 | 2000 | 600 | — | 750 |

# Custom Proof-Like Sets (CPL)

| KM# | Date | Mintage | Identification | Issue Price | Mkt. Value |
|---|---|---|---|---|---|
| CPL1 | 1971 (7) | 33,517 | KM59.1 (2pcs.), 60.1, 62b-75.1, 77.1 | 6.50 | 5.25 |
| CPL2 | 1971 (7) | 38,198 | KM59.1 (2pcs.), 60.1, 62b, 75.1-77.1 | 6.50 | 5.25 |
| CPL3 | 1973 (7) | 35,676 | KM59.1 (2pcs.), 60.1, 75.1, 77.1, 81.1 | 6.50 | 5.25 |
| CPL4 | 1973 (7) | Inc. above | KM59.1 (2pcs.), 60.1, 75.1, 77.1, 81.1 | 6.50 | 140 |
| CPL5 | 1974 (7) | 44,296 | KM59.1 (2pcs.), 60.1, 62b-75.1, 88 | 8.00 | 5.25 |
| CPL6 | 1975 (7) | 36,851 | KM59.1 (2pcs.), 60.1, 62b-75.1, 76.2, | 8.00 | 5.25 |
| CPL7 | 1976 (7) | 28,162 | KM59.1 (2pcs.), 60.1, 62b-75.1, 76.2, | 8.00 | 6.00 |
| CPL8 | 1977 (7) | 44,198 | KM59.1 (2pcs.), 60.1, 62b-75.2, 77.1, | 8.15 | 6.00 |
| CPL9 | 1978 (7) | 41,000 | KM59.1 (2pcs.), 60.1, 62b-75.3, 77.1, | — | 6.00 |
| CPL10 | 1979 (7) | 31,174 | KM59.1 (2pcs.), 60.2, 74, 75.3, 77.2, 120 | 10.75 | 6.00 |
| CPL11 | 1980 (7) | 41,447 | KM60.2, 74, 75.3, 77.2, 120, 127 (2pcs.) | 10.75 | 6.75 |

# Mint Sets (MS)

Mint, or uncirculated, sets contain one uncirculated coin of each denomination from each mint produced for circulation that year. Values listed here are only for those sets sold by the U.S. Mint. Sets were not offered in years not listed. In years when the Mint did not offer the sets, some private companies compiled and marketed uncirculated sets. Mint sets from 1947 through 1958 contained two examples of each coin mounted in cardboard holders, which caused the coins to tarnish. Beginning in 1959, the sets have been packaged in sealed Pliofilm packets and include only one specimen of each coin struck for that year. Listings for 1965, 1966 and 1967 are for "special mint sets," which were of higher quality than regular mint sets and were prooflike. They were packaged in plastic cases. The 1970 large-date and small-date varieties are distinguished by the size of the date on the coin. The 1976 three-piece set contains the quarter, half dollar and dollar with the Bicentennial design. The 1971 and 1972 sets do not include a dollar coin; the 1979 set does not include an S-mint-marked dollar.

| KM# | Date | Mintage | Identification | Issue Price | Mkt. Value |
|---|---|---|---|---|---|
| MS1 | 1973 (4) | — | KM84-87, Olympic Commemoratives, Series I | 45.00 | 31.00 |
| MS2 | 1974 (4) | — | KM89-90, 93-94; Olympic Commemoratives, Series II | 48.00 | 31.00 |
| MS3 | 1974 (4) | — | KM91-92, 95-96; Olympic Commemoratives, Series III | 48.00 | 31.00 |
| MS4 | 1975 (4) | — | KM98-99, 102-103; Olympic Commemoratives, Series IV | 48.00 | 31.00 |
| MS5 | 1975 (4) | — | KM100-101, 104-105; Olympic Commemoratives, Series V | 60.00 | 31.00 |
| MS6 | 1976 (4) | — | KM107-108, 111-112; Olympic Commemoratives, Series VI | 60.00 | 31.00 |
| MS7 | 1976 (4) | — | KM109-110, 113-114; Olympic Commemoratives, Series VII | 60.00 | 31.00 |

# Olympic Commemoratives (OCP)

| KM# | Date | Mintage | Identification | Issue Price | Mkt. Value |
|---|---|---|---|---|---|
| OCP1 | 1973 (4) | — | KM84-87, Series I | 78.50 | 40.00 |
| OCP2 | 1974 (4) | — | KM89, 90, 93, 94, Series II | 88.50 | 40.00 |
| OCP3 | 1974 (4) | — | KM91, 92, 95, 96, SeriesIII | 88.50 | 40.00 |
| OCP4 | 1975 (4) | — | KM98, 99, 102, 103, SeriesIV | 88.50 | 40.00 |
| OCP5 | 1975 (4) | — | KM100, 101, 104, 105, Series V | 88.50 | 40.00 |
| OCP6 | 1976 (4) | — | KM107, 108, 111, 112, Series VI | 88.50 | 42.00 |
| OCP7 | 1976 (4) | — | KM109, 110, 113, 114, Series VII | 88.50 | 42.00 |

# Proof Sets (PS)

Proof coins are produced through a special process involving specially selected, highly polished planchets and dies. They usually receive two strikings from the coin press at increased pressure. The result is a coin with mirrorlike surfaces and, in recent years, a cameo effect on its raised design surfaces. Proof sets have been sold off and on by the U.S. Mint since 1858. Listings here are for sets from what is commonly called the modern era, since 1936. Values for earlier proofs are included in regular date listings. Sets were not offered in years not listed. Since 1968, proof coins have been produced at the San Francisco Mint; before that they were produced at the Philadelphia Mint. In 1942 the five-cent coin was struck in two compositions. Some proof sets for that year contain only one type (five-coin set); others contain both types. Two types of packaging were used in 1955 -- a box and a flat, plastic holder. The 1960 large-date and small-date sets are distinguished by the size of the date on the cent. Some 1968 sets are missing the mint mark on the dime, the result of an error in the preparation of an obverse die. The 1970 large-date and small-date sets are distinguished by the size of the date on the cent. Some 1970 sets are missing the mint mark on the dime, the result of an error in the preparation of an obverse die. Some 1971 sets are missing the mint mark on the five-cent piece, the result of an error in the preparation of an obverse die. The 1976 three-piece set contains the quarter, half dollar and dollar with the Bicentennial designs. The 1979 and 1981 Type II sets have clearer mint marks than the Type I sets for those years. Some 1983 sets are missing the mint mark on the dime, the result of an error in the preparation of an obverse die. Prestige sets contain the five regular-issue coins plus a commemorative silver dollar from that year.

| KM# | Date | Mintage | Identification | Issue Price | Mkt. Value |
|---|---|---|---|---|---|
| PS1 | 1981 (7) | 199,000 | KM60.2, 74, 75.3, 77.2, 120, 127, 130 | 36.00 | 16.50 |
| PS2 | 1982 (7) | 180,908 | KM60.2a, 74, 75.3, 77.2, 120, 132, 133 | 36.00 | 9.50 |
| PS3 | 1983 (7) | 166,779 | KM60.2a, 74, 75.3, 77.2, 120, 132, 138 | 36.00 | 12.50 |
| PS4 | 1984 (7) | 161,602 | KM60.2a, 74, 75.3, 77.2, 120, 132, 140 | 30.00 | 13.50 |
| PS5 | 1985 (7) | 157,037 | KM60.2a, 74, 75.3, 77.2, 120, 132, 143 | 30.00 | 14.00 |
| PS6 | 1986 (7) | 175,745 | KM60.2a, 74, 75.3, 77.2, 120, 132, 149 | 30.00 | 14.00 |
| PS7 | 1986 (7) | 179,004 | KM60.2a, 74, 75.3, 77.2, 120, 132, 154 | 34.00 | 15.50 |
| PS8 | 1988 (7) | 175,259 | KM60.2a, 74, 75.3, 77.2, 132, 157, 161 | 37.50 | 22.50 |

| KM# | Date | Mintage | Identification | Issue Price | Mkt. Value |
|---|---|---|---|---|---|
| PS9 | 1989 (7) | 170,928 | KM60.2a, 74, 75.3, 77.2, 132, 157, 168 | 40.00 | 22.50 |
| PS10 | 1989 (4) | 6,823 | KM125.2, 135-136, 153 | 1,190 | 1,000 |
| PS11 | 1989 (4) | 1,995 | KM164-167 | 1,700 | 1,325 |
| PS12 | 1989 (3) | 2,550 | KM125.2, 163, 167 | 1,530 | 1,225 |
| PS13 | 1989 (3) | 9,979 | KM135, 163-164 | 165 | 155 |
| PS14 | 1990 (7) | 158,068 | KM170, 181-186 | 41.00 | 22.50 |
| PS15 | 1990 (4) | 2,629 | KM174-177 | 1,720 | 1,175 |
| PS16 | 1991 (7) | 14,629 | KM179, 181-186 | — | 55.00 |
| PS17 | 1991 (4) | 873 | KM198-201 | 1,760 | 1,275 |
| PS18 | 1992 (13) | 84,397 | KM203a, 212a-214a, 218, 220a-223a, | — | 95.00 |
| PS19 | 1992 (7) | 147,061 | KM204-210 | 42.75 | 26.50 |
| PS20 | 1992 (4) | 3,500 | KM226-229 | 1,680 | 1,275 |
| PS21 | 1993 (7) | 143,065 | KM181-186, 235 | 42.75 | 22.00 |
| PS22 | 1993 (4) | 3,500 | KM240-243 | 1,329 | 1,300 |
| PS23 | 1994 (7) | 47,303 | KM181-186, 248 | 47.50 | 40.00 |
| PS24 | 1994 (7) | 99,121 | KM181-186, 251 | 43.00 | 32.50 |
| PS25 | 1994 (4) | 1,500 | KM252-255 | 915 | 1,450 |
| PS26 | 1995 (7) | Inc. above | KM181-186, 259 | 37.45 | 28.50 |
| PS27 | 1995 (7) | 50,000 | KM181-185, 258, 259 | 49.45 | 50.00 |
| PS28 | 1995 (4) | Inc. above | KM261-264 | 42.00 | 42.00 |
| PS29 | 1995 (4) | 682 | KM266-269 | 1,555 | 1,400 |
| PS30 | 1995 (2) | Inc. above | KM261-262 | 22.00 | 21.00 |
| PS31 | 1995 (2) | Inc. above | KM263-264 | 22.00 | 21.00 |
| PS32 | 1996 (4) | 423 | KM278-281 | 1,555 | 1,400 |
| PS33 | 1996 (7) | Inc. above | KM181a, 182b-185b, 186, 274 | 49.00 | 45.00 |
| PS34 | 1996 (4) | Inc. above | KM283-286 | 44.45 | 50.00 |
| PS35 | 1997 (8) | Inc. above | KM182b-184b, 209, 270c, 282, 289, | 60.00 | 50.00 |
| PS36 | 1997 (4) | Inc. above | KM292-295 | 44.45 | 50.00 |
| PS37 | 1997 (4) | Inc. above | KM300-303 | 1,530 | 1,400 |
| PS38 | 1998 (8) | Inc. above | KM182b-184b, 186, 270b, 289, 290a, | 59.45 | 60.00 |
| PS39 | ND (1998)(5) | 25,000 | KM309-313 | 73.50 | 73.50 |
| PS40 | ND(1998)(2) | 61,000 | KM316 w/China Y-727 | 72.50 | 70.00 |
| PS41 | 1998 (4) | Inc. above | KM318-321 | 44.45 | 45.00 |
| PS42 | 1998 (4) | 1,000 | KM322-325 | 1,552 | 1,400 |
| PS43 | ND(1998)(5) | 25,000 | KM310-313, 332 | 73.50 | 73.50 |
| PS44 | 1998 (8) | Inc. above | KM182b-184b, 186, 270b, 289, 290a, | 59.45 | 60.00 |
| PS45 | 1999 (4) | Inc. above | KM335-338 | 39.95 | 40.00 |
| PS46 | 1999 (12) | Inc. above | KM342a-353a | 99.45 | 100.00 |
| PS47 | 1999 (4) | Inc. above | KM359-362 | 1,425 | 1,450 |
| PS48 | 2000 (12) | — | KM373a-348a | 101 | 115 |
| PS49 | 2000 (4) | — | KM389-392 | 44.00 | 54.00 |
| PS50 | 2000 (4) | 600 | KM405-408 | 1,416 | 1,420 |

# Proof-Like Dollars

| KM# | Date | Mintage | Identification | Issue Price | Mkt. Value |
|---|---|---|---|---|---|
| D3 | 1953 (1) | 1,200 | KM54, Canoe w/shoulder fold | — | 275 |
| D4 | 1954 (1) | 5,300 | KM54, Canoe | 1.25 | 150 |
| D5 | 1955 (1) | 7,950 | KM54, Canoe | 1.25 | 125 |
| D5a | 1955 (1) | Inc. above | KM54, Arnprior | 1.25 | 185 |
| D6 | 1956 (1) | 10,212 | KM54, Canoe | 1.25 | 65.00 |
| D7 | 1957 (1) | 16,241 | KM54, Canoe | 1.25 | 28.00 |
| D8 | 1958 (1) | 33,237 | KM55, British Columbia | 1.25 | 26.00 |
| D9 | 1959 (1) | 45,160 | KM54, Canoe | 1.25 | 14.50 |
| D10 | 1960 (1) | 82,728 | KM54, Canoe | 1.25 | 9.50 |
| D11 | 1961 (1) | 120,928 | KM54, Canoe | 1.25 | 9.00 |
| D12 | 1962 (1) | 248,901 | KM54, Canoe | 1.25 | 7.50 |
| D13 | 1963 (1) | 963,525 | KM54, Canoe | 1.25 | 6.50 |
| D14 | 1964 (1) | 2,862,441 | KM58, Charlottetown | 1.25 | 6.50 |
| D15 | 1965 (1) | 2,904,352 | KM64, Canoe | — | 6.50 |
| D16 | 1966 (1) | 672,514 | KM64, Canoe | — | 6.50 |
| D17 | 1967 (1) | 1,036,176 | KM70, Confederation | — | 8.50 |

# Proof-Like Sets (PL)

| KM# | Date | Mintage | Identification | Issue Price | Mkt. Value |
|---|---|---|---|---|---|
| PL1 | 1953 (6) | 1,200 | KM49 w/o straps, 50-54 | 2.20 | 1,250 |
| PL2 | 1953 (6) | Inc. above | KM49-54 | 2.20 | 760 |
| PL3 | 1954 (6) | 3,000 | KM49-54 | 2.50 | 205 |
| PL4 | 1954 (6) | Inc. above | KM49 w/o straps, 50-54 | 2.50 | 475 |
| PL5 | 1955 (6) | 6,300 | KM49, 50a, 51-54 | 2.50 | 145 |
| PL6 | 1955 (6) | Inc. above | KM49, 50a, 51-54, Arnprior | 2.50 | 225 |
| PL7 | 1956 (6) | 6,500 | KM49, 50a, 51-54 | 2.50 | 80.00 |
| PL8 | 1957 (6) | 11,862 | KM49, 50a, 51-54 | 2.50 | 50.00 |
| PL9 | 1958 (6) | 18,259 | KM49, 50a, 51-53, 55 | 2.50 | 40.00 |
| PL10 | 1959 (6) | 31,577 | KM49, 50a, 51, 52, 54, 56 | 2.50 | 18.00 |
| PL11 | 1960 (6) | 64,097 | KM49, 50a, 51, 52, 54, 56 | 3.00 | 13.50 |
| PL12 | 1961 (6) | 98,373 | KM49, 50a, 51, 52, 54, 56 | 3.00 | 12.00 |
| PL13 | 1962 (6) | 200,950 | KM49, 50a, 51, 52, 54, 56 | 3.00 | 9.00 |

| KM# | Date | Mintage | Identification | Issue Price | Mkt. Value |
|-----|------|---------|----------------|-------------|------------|
| PL14 | 1963 (6) | 673,006 | KM49, 51, 52, 54, 56, 57 | 3.00 | 7.50 |
| PL15 | 1964 (6) | 1,653,162 | KM49, 51, 52, 56-58 | 3.00 | 7.50 |
| PL16 | 1965 (6) | 2,904,352 | KM59.1-60.1, 61-63, 64.1 | 4.00 | 7.50 |
| PL17 | 1966 (6) | 672,514 | KM59.1-60.1, 61-63, 64.1 | 4.00 | 7.50 |
| PL18 | 1967 (6) | 961,887 | KM65-70 (pliofilm flat pack) | 4.00 | 12.00 |
| PL18A | 1967 (6) | 70,583 | KM65-70 and Silver Medal (red box) | 12.00 | 16.50 |
| PL18B | 1967 (7) | 337,688 | KM65-71 (black box) | 40.00 | 250 |
| PL19 | 1968 (6) | 521,641 | KM59.1-60.1, 62b, 72a, 75.1-76.1 | 4.00 | 2.25 |
| PL20 | 1969 (6) | 326,203 | KM59.1-60.1, 62b, 75.1-77.1 | 4.00 | 2.25 |
| PL21 | 1970 (6) | 349,120 | KM59.1-60.1, 62b, 75.1, 77.1, 78 | 4.00 | 3.00 |
| PL22 | 1971 (6) | 253,311 | KM59.1-60.1, 62b, 75.1, 77.1, 79 | 4.00 | 2.25 |
| PL23 | 1972 (6) | 224,275 | KM59.1-60.1, 62b-77.1 | 4.00 | 2.25 |
| PL24 | 1973 (6) | 243,695 | KM59.1-60.1, 62b-75.1 obv. 120 | 4.00 | 2.25 |
| PL25 | 1973 (6) | Inc. above | KM59.1-60.1, 62b-75.1 obv. 132 bead | 4.00 | 125 |
| PL26 | 1974 (6) | 213,589 | KM59.1-60.1, 62b-75.1, 77.1, 88 | 5.00 | 2.25 |
| PL27.1 | 1975 (6) | 197,372 | KM59.1, 60.1, 62b-75.1, 76.2, 77.1 | 5.00 | 2.25 |
| PL27.2 | 1975 (6) | Inc. above | KM59.1, 60.1, 62b-75.1, 76.3, 77.1 | 5.00 | — |
| PL28 | 1976 (6) | 171,737 | KM59.1, 60.1, 62b-75.1, 76.2, 77.1 | 5.15 | 2.75 |
| PL29 | 1977 (6) | 225,307 | KM59.1, 60.1, 62b, 75.2, 77.1, 117.1 | 5.15 | 2.50 |
| PL30 | 1978 (6) | 260,000 | KM59.1-60.1, 62b, 75.3, 77.1, 120 | 5.25 | 2.25 |
| PL31 | 1979 (6) | 187,624 | KM59.2-60.2, 74, 75.3, 77.2, 120 | 6.25 | 2.75 |
| PL32 | 1980 (6) | 410,842 | KM60.2, 74, 75.3, 77.2, 120, 127 | 6.50 | 4.25 |
| PL33 | 1981 (6) | 186,250 | KM60.2, 74, 75.3, 77.2, 120, 123 | 5.00 | 3.25 |
| PL34 | 1982 (6) | 203,287 | KM60.2, 74, 75.3, 77.2, 120, 123 | 6.00 | 2.50 |
| PL36 | 1983 (6) | 190,838 | KM60.2a, 74, 75.3, 77.2, 120, 132 | 5.00 | 6.00 |
| PL37 | 1984 (6) | 181,249 | KM60.2a, 74, 75.3, 77.2, 120, 132 | 5.25 | 5.00 |
| PL38 | 1985 (6) | 173,924 | KM60.2a, 74, 75.3, 77.2, 120, 132 | 5.25 | 6.00 |
| PL39 | 1986 (6) | 167,338 | KM60.2a, 74, 75.3, 77.2, 120, 132 | 5.25 | 7.50 |
| PL40 | 1987 (6) | 212,136 | KM60.2a, 74, 75.3, 77.2, 120, 132 | 5.25 | 5.00 |
| PL41 | 1988 (6) | 182,048 | KM60.2a, 74, 75.3, 77.2, 132, 157 | 6.05 | 6.50 |
| PL42 | 1989 (6) | 173,622 | KM60.2a, 74, 75.3, 77.2, 132, 157 | 6.60 | 8.50 |
| PL43 | 1990 (6) | 170,791 | KM181-186 | 7.40 | 8.50 |
| PL44 | 1991 (6) | 147,814 | KM181-186 | 7.40 | 25.00 |
| PL45 | 1992 (6) | 217,597 | KM204-209 | 8.25 | 12.50 |
| PL46 | 1993 (6) | 171,680 | KM181-186 | 8.25 | 5.50 |
| PL47 | 1994 (6) | 141,676 | KM181-185, 258 | 8.50 | 6.50 |
| PL48 | 1994 (6) | 18,794 | KM181-185, 258 (Oh Canada holder) | — | 12.00 |
| PL49 | 1995 (6) | 143,892 | KM181-186 | 6.95 | 6.50 |
| PL50 | 1995 (6) | 50,927 | KM181-186 (Oh Canada holder) | 14.65 | 15.00 |
| PL51 | 1995 (6) | 36,443 | KM181-186 (Baby Gift holder) | — | 13.50 |
| PL52 | 1996 (6) | 116,736 | KM181-186 | — | 12.50 |
| PL53 | 1996 (6) | 29,747 | KM181-186 (Baby Gift holder) | — | 15.00 |
| PL54 | 1996 (6) | Inc. above | KM181a-185a, 186 | 8.95 | 10.00 |
| PL55 | 1996 (6) | Inc. above | KM181a-185a, 186 (Oh Canada holder) | 14.65 | 15.00 |
| PL56 | 1996 (6) | Inc. above | KM181a-185a, 186 (Baby Gift holder) | — | 15.00 |
| PL57 | 1997 (7) | Inc. above | KM182a-184a, 209, 270, 289-290 | 10.45 | 9.50 |
| PL58 | 1997 (7) | Inc. above | KM182a-184a, 270, 289-291 (Oh Canada holder) | 16.45 | 16.50 |
| PL59 | 1997 (7) | Inc. above | KM182a-184a, 209, 270, 289-290 (Baby Gift holder) | 18.50 | 17.50 |
| PL60 | 1998 (7) | Inc. above | KM182-184, 186, 270, 289-290 | 10.45 | 12.00 |
| PL61 | 1998 (7) | Inc. above | KM182-184, 186, 270, 289-290 (Oh Canada holder) | 16.45 | 16.50 |
| PL62 | 1998 (7) | Inc. above | KM182-184, 186, 270, 289-290 (Tiny | 16.45 | 16.50 |
| PL63 | 2000 (12) | — | KM373-384 | 16.95 | 17.00 |

# SPECIMEN SETS (SS)

| KM# | Date | Mintage | Identification | Issue Price | Mkt. Value |
|-----|------|---------|----------------|-------------|------------|
| SS1 | 1858 (4) | Inc. above | KM1-4, Reeded edge | — | 6,000 |
| SS2 | 1858 (4) | Inc. above | KM1-4, Plain edge | — | 6,000 |
| SS3 | 1858 (8) | Inc. above | KM1-4; Double Set | — | 12,500 |
| SS4 | 1858 (8) | Inc. above | KM1 (overdate), 2-4; Double Set | — | 14,000 |
| SS5 | 1870 (4) | 100 | KM2, 3, 5, 6 (reeded edges) | — | 12,500 |
| SS6 | 1870 (8) | Inc. above | KM2, 3, 5, 6; Double Set (plain edges) | — | 25,000 |
| SS7 | 1872 (4) | Inc. above | KM2, 3, 5, 6 | — | 12,500 |
| SS8 | 1875 (3) | Inc. above | KM2 (Large date), 3, 5 | — | 20,000 |
| SS9 | 1880 (3) | Inc. above | KM2, 3, 5 (Narrow 0) | — | 7,000 |
| SS10 | 1881 (5) | Inc. above | KM7, 2, 3, 5, 6 | — | 12,000 |
| SS11 | 1892 (2) | Inc. above | KM3, 5 | — | 10,000 |
| SS12 | 1902 (5) | 100 | KM8-12 | — | 10,000 |
| SS13 | 1902 (3) | Inc. above | KM9 (Large H), 10, 11 | — | 6,500 |
| SS14 | 1903 (3) | Inc. above | KM10, 12, 13 | — | 7,000 |
| SS15 | 1908 (5) | 1,000 | KM8, 10-13 | — | 2,200 |
| SS16 | 1911 (5) | 1,000 | KM15-19 | — | 5,500 |
| SS17 | 1911/12 | 5 | KM15-20, 26-27 | — | 52,250 |
| SS18 | 1921 (5) | Inc. above | KM22-25, 28 | — | 80,000 |
| SS19 | 1922 (2) | Inc. above | KM28, 29 | — | 800 |
| SS20 | 1923 (2) | Inc. above | KM28, 29 | — | 800 |
| SS21 | 1924 (2) | Inc. above | KM28, 29 | — | 800 |
| SS22 | 1925 (2) | Inc. above | KM28, 29 | — | 1,800 |
| SS23 | 1926 (2) | Inc. above | KM28, 29 (Near 6) | — | 1,800 |
| SS24 | 1927 (3) | Inc. above | KM24a, 28, 29 | — | 3,200 |

| KM# | Date | Mintage | Identification | Issue Price | Mkt. Value |
|---|---|---|---|---|---|
| SS25 | 1928 (4) | Inc. above | KM23a, 24a, 28, 29 | — | 2,800 |
| SS26 | 1929 (5) | Inc. above | KM23a,-25a, 28, 29 | — | 10,000 |
| SS27 | 1930 (4) | Inc. above | KM23a, 24a. 28, 29 | — | 6,500 |
| SS28 | 1931 (5) | Inc. above | KM23a-25a, 28, 29 | — | 8,500 |
| SS29 | 1932 (5) | Inc. above | KM23a-25a, 28, 29 | — | 10,000 |
| SS30 | 1934 (5) | Inc. above | KM23-25, 28, 29 | — | 8,500 |
| SS31 | 1936 (5) | Inc. above | KM23-25, 28, 29 | — | 8,500 |
| SS32 | 1936 (6) | Inc. above | KM23a(dot), 24a(dot), 25a, 28(dot), 29, | — | — |
| SS33 | 1937 (6) | 1,025 | KM32-37, Matte Finish | — | 750 |
| SS34 | 1937 (4) | Inc. above | KM32-35, Mirror Fields | — | 500 |
| SS35 | 1937 (6) | 75 | KM32-37, Mirror Fields | — | 1,550 |
| SS36 | 1938 (6) | Inc. above | KM32-37 | — | 25,000 |
| SS-A36 | 1939 (6) | Inc. above | KM32-35, 38, Matte Finish | — | — |
| SS-B36 | 1939 (6) | Inc. above | KM32-35, 38, Mirror Fields | — | — |
| SS-C36 | 1942 (2) | Inc. above | KM32, 33 | — | 300 |
| SS-D36 | 1943 (2) | Inc. above | KM32, 40 | — | 300 |
| SS-A37 | 1944 (2) | Inc. above | KM32, 40a | — | 300 |
| SS37 | 1944 (5) | 3 | KM32, 34-37, 40a | — | 11,300 |
| SS-A38 | 1945 (2) | Inc. above | KM32, 40a | — | 300 |
| SS38 | 1945 (6) | 6 | KM32, 34-37, 40a | — | 6,500 |
| SS39 | 1946 (6) | 15 | KM32, 34-37, 39a | — | 4,000 |
| SS40 | 1947 (6) | Inc. above | KM32, 34-36(7 curved), 37(7 pointed), | — | 8,500 |
| SS41 | 1947 (6) | Inc. above | KM32, 34-36(7 curved), 37(blunt 7), 39a | — | 6,200 |
| SS42 | 1947 (6) | Inc. above | KM32, 34-36(7 curved right), 37, 39a | — | 4,250 |
| SS43 | 1948 (6) | 30 | KM41-46 | — | 7,500 |
| SS44 | 1949 (6) | 20 | KM41-45, 47 | — | 3,200 |
| SS44A | 1949 (2) | Inc. above | KM47 | — | 1,550 |
| SS45 | 1950 (6) | 12 | KM41-46 | — | 2,300 |
| SS46 | 1950 (6) | Inc. above | KM41-45, 46 (Arnprior) | — | 4,500 |
| SS47 | 1951 (7) | 12 | KM41, 48, 42a, 43-46 (w/water lines) | — | 2,725 |
| SS48 | 1952 (6) | 2,317 | KM41, 42a, 43-46 (water lines) | — | 3,175 |
| SS48A | 1952 (6) | Inc. above | KM41, 42a, 43-46 (w/o water lines) | — | — |
| SS49 | 1953 (6) | 28 | KM49 w/o straps, 50-54 | — | 1,850 |
| SS50 | 1953 (6) | Inc. above | KM49 w/ straps, 50-54 | — | 1,250 |
| SS51 | 1964 (6) | Inc. above | KM49, 51, 52, 56-58 | — | 450 |
| SS52 | 1965 (6) | Inc. above | KM59.1-60.1, 61-63, 64.1 | — | 450 |
| SS56 | 1971 (7) | 66,860 | KM59.1-60.1, 62b-75.1, 77.1, 79 (2pcs.); Double Dollar Prestige Sets | 12.00 | 9.50 |
| SS57 | 1972 (7) | 36,349 | KM59.1,-60.1, 62b-75.1, 76.1 (2pcs.), 77; Double Dollar Prestige Sets | 12.00 | 14.50 |
| SS58 | 1973 (7) | 119,819 | KM59.1-60.1, 75.1, 77.1, 81.1, 82, 83; Double Dollar Prestige Sets | 12.00 | 10.00 |
| SS59 | 1973 (7) | Inc. above | KM59.1-60.1, 75.1, 77.1, 81.2, 82, 83; Double Dollar Prestige Sets | — | 125 |
| SS60 | 1974 (7) | 85,230 | KM59.1-60.1, 62b-75.1, 77.1, 88, 88a; Double Dollar Prestige Sets | 15.00 | 10.00 |
| SS61 | 1975 (7) | 97,263 | KM59.1-60.1, 62b-75.1, 76.2, 77.1, 97; Double Dollar Prestige Sets | 15.00 | 10.00 |
| SS62 | 1976 (7) | 87,744 | KM59.1-60.1, 62b-75.1, 76.2, 77.1, 106; Double Dollar Prestige Sets | 16.00 | 10.00 |
| SS63 | 1977 (7) | 142,577 | KM59.1-60.1, 62b, 75.2, 77.1, 117.1, 118; Double Dollar Prestige Sets | 16.50 | 10.00 |
| SS64 | 1978 (7) | 147,000 | KM59.1-60.1, 62b, 75.3, 77.1, 120, 121; Double Dollar Prestige Sets | 16.50 | 10.00 |
| SS65 | 1979 (7) | 155,698 | KM59.2-60.2, 74, 75.3, 77.2, 120, 124; Double Dollar Prestige Sets | 18.50 | 11.50 |
| SS66 | 1980 (7) | 162,875 | KM60.2, 74-75.3, 77.2, 120, 127, 128; Double Dollar Prestige Sets | 30.50 | 22.50 |
| SS67 | 1981 (6) | 71,300 | KM60.2, 74, 75.3, 77.2, 120, 127; Regular Specimen Sets Resumed | 10.00 | 6.00 |
| SS68 | 1982 (6) | 62,298 | KM60.2a, 74, 75.3, 77.2, 120, 132; Regular Specimen Sets Resumed | 11.50 | 6.00 |
| SS69 | 1983 (6) | 60,329 | KM60.2a, 74, 75.3, 77.2, 120, 132; Regular Specimen Sets Resumed | 12.75 | 6.00 |
| SS70 | 1984 (6) | 60,400 | KM60.2a, 74, 75.3, 77.2, 120, 132; Regular Specimen Sets Resumed | 10.00 | 6.00 |
| SS71 | 1985 (6) | 61,553 | KM60.2a, 74, 75.3, 77.2, 120, 132; Regular Specimen Sets Resumed | 10.00 | 6.50 |
| SS72 | 1986 (6) | 67,152 | KM60.2a, 74, 75.3, 77.2, 120, 132; Regular Specimen Sets Resumed | 10.00 | 6.50 |
| SS72A | 1987 (6) | 75,194 | KM60.2a, 74, 75.3, 77.2, 120, 132; Regular Specimen Sets Resumed | 11.00 | 7.00 |
| SS73 | 1988 (6) | 70,205 | KM60.2a, 74, 75.3, 77.2, 132, 157; Regular Specimen Sets Resumed | 12.30 | 8.00 |
| SS74 | 1989 (6) | 75,306 | KM60.2a, 74, 75.3, 77.2, 132, 157; Regular Specimen Sets Resumed | 14.50 | 14.50 |
| SS75 | 1990 (6) | 76,611 | KM181-186; Regular Specimen Sets Resumed | 15.50 | 14.50 |
| SS76 | 1991 (6) | 68,552 | KM181-186; Regular Specimen Sets Resumed | 15.50 | 32.50 |
| SS77 | 1992 (6) | 78,328 | KM204-209; Regular Specimen Sets Resumed | 16.25 | 21.50 |
| SS78 | 1993 (6) | 77,351 | KM181-186; Regular Specimen Sets Resumed | 16.25 | 16.50 |
| SS79 | 1994 (6) | 77,349 | KM181-186; Regular Specimen Sets Resumed | 16.50 | 19.50 |
| SS80 | 1995 (6) | Inc. above | KM181-186; Regular Specimen Sets Resumed | 13.95 | 19.50 |
| SS82 | 1996 (6) | Inc. above | KM181a-185a, 186; Regular Specimen Sets Resumed | 18.95 | 20.00 |
| SS83 | 1997 (7) | Inc. above | KM182a-184a, 270, 289-291; Regular Specimen Sets Resumed | 19.95 | 22.50 |
| SS84 | 1998 (7) | Inc. above | KM182-184, 186, 270, 289, 290; Regular Specimen Sets Resumed | 19.95 | 20.00 |
| SS85 | 1998 (7) | Inc. above | KM182-184, 186, 270, 289a, 290; Regular Specimen Sets Resumed | 19.95 | 20.00 |

# V.I.P. SPECIMEN SETS (VS)

| KM# | Date | Mintage | Identification | Issue Price | Mkt. Value |
|---|---|---|---|---|---|
| VS1 | 1969 | 4 known | — | — | 1,700 |
| VS2 | 1970 | 100 | KM59.1-60.1, 74.1-75.1, 77.1, 78 | — | 350 |
| VS3 | 1971 | 69 | KM59.1-60.1, 74.1-75.1, 77.1, 79(2pcs) | — | 375 |
| VS4 | 1972 | 25 | KM59.1-60.1, 74.1-75.1, 76.1, (2pcs), | — | 435 |
| VS5 | 1973 | 26 | KM59.1-60.1, 75.1, 77.1, 81.1, 82, 83 | — | 435 |
| VS6 | 1974 | 72 | KM59.1-60.1, 74.1-75.1, 77.1, 88, 88a | — | 375 |
| VS7 | 1975 | 94 | KM59.1-60.1, 74.1-75.1, 76.2, 77.1, 97 | — | 375 |
| VS8 | 1976 | Inc. above | KM59.1-60.1, 74.1-75.1, 76.2, 77.1, 106 | — | 375 |

## NEW BRUNSWICK

# DECIMAL COINAGE

## HALF CENT

**Composition:** Bronze.

| KM# | Date | Mintage | VG-8 | F-12 | VF-20 | XF-40 | MS-60 | MS-63 | Prf-63 |
|---|---|---|---|---|---|---|---|---|---|
| 5 | 1861 | 222,800 | 60.00 | 90.00 | 125 | 175 | 375 | 800 | — |
| | 1861 | — | — | — | — | — | — | 2,200 | — |

## CENT

**Composition:** Bronze.

| KM# | Date | Mintage | VG-8 | F-12 | VF-20 | XF-40 | MS-60 | MS-63 | Prf-63 |
|---|---|---|---|---|---|---|---|---|---|
| 6 | 1861 | 1,000,000 | 2.00 | 4.00 | 8.00 | 13.00 | 90.00 | 250 | — |
| | 1861 | — | — | — | — | — | — | 450 | — |
| | 1864 short 6 | 1,000,000 | 2.00 | 4.00 | 8.00 | 13.00 | 90.00 | 245 | — |
| | 1864 long 6 | Inc. above | 2.00 | 4.00 | 8.00 | 13.00 | 90.00 | 245 | — |

## 5 CENTS

**Weight:** 1.1620 g. **Composition:** 0.9250 Silver., .0346 oz. ASW.

| KM# | Date | Mintage | VG-8 | F-12 | VF-20 | XF-40 | MS-60 | MS-63 | Prf-63 |
|---|---|---|---|---|---|---|---|---|---|
| 7 | 1862 | 100,000 | 35.00 | 65.00 | 125 | 250 | 1,225 | 3,200 | — |
| | 1864 small 6 | 100,000 | 35.00 | 65.00 | 125 | 250 | 1,225 | 3,200 | — |
| | 1864 large 6 | Inc. above | 35.00 | 65.00 | 125 | 250 | 1,225 | 3,200 | — |

## 10 CENTS

**Weight:** 2.3240 g. **Composition:** 0.9250 Silver., .0691 oz. ASW.

| KM# | Date | Mintage | VG-8 | F-12 | VF-20 | XF-40 | MS-60 | MS-63 | Prf-63 |
|---|---|---|---|---|---|---|---|---|---|
| 8 | 1862 | 150,000 | 35.00 | 65.00 | 125 | 250 | 975 | 2,450 | — |
| | 1862 recut 2 | Inc. above | 40.00 | 85.00 | 200 | 400 | 1,500 | 3,250 | — |
| | 1862 | — | — | — | — | — | — | 2,850 | — |
| | 1864 | 100,000 | 35.00 | 65.00 | 125 | 250 | 1,150 | 2,750 | — |

# 20 Cents

**Weight:** 4.6480 g. **Composition:** 0.9250 Silver., .1382 oz. ASW.

| KM# | Date | Mintage | VG-8 | F-12 | VF-20 | XF-40 | MS-60 | MS-63 | Prf-63 |
|-----|------|---------|------|------|-------|-------|-------|-------|--------|
| 9 | 1862 | 150,000 | 13.00 | 20.00 | 55.00 | 125 | 750 | 2,350 | — |
| | 1862 | — | — | — | — | — | — | 2,850 | — |
| | 1864 | 150,000 | 13.00 | 20.00 | 55.00 | 125 | 750 | 2,500 | — |

# STERLING COINAGE

## Halfpenny Token

**Composition:** Copper.

| KM# | Date | Mintage | VG-8 | F-12 | VF-20 | XF-40 | MS-60 | MS-63 | Prf-63 |
|-----|------|---------|------|------|-------|-------|-------|-------|--------|
| 1 | 1843 | 480,000 | 3.00 | 6.00 | 11.50 | 30.00 | 110 | 265 | — |
| | 1843 | — | — | — | — | — | — | 750 | — |

**Composition:** Copper.

| KM# | Date | Mintage | VG-8 | F-12 | VF-20 | XF-40 | MS-60 | MS-63 | Prf-63 |
|-----|------|---------|------|------|-------|-------|-------|-------|--------|
| 3 | 1854 | 864,000 | 3.00 | 6.00 | 11.50 | 30.00 | 100.00 | 265 | — |

**Composition:** Bronze.

| KM# | Date | Mintage | VG-8 | F-12 | VF-20 | XF-40 | MS-60 | MS-63 | Prf-63 |
|-----|------|---------|------|------|-------|-------|-------|-------|--------|
| 3a | 1854 | — | — | — | — | — | — | 400 | — |

# 1 PENNY TOKEN

**Composition:** Copper.

| KM# | Date | Mintage | VG-8 | F-12 | VF-20 | XF-40 | MS-60 | MS-63 | Prf-63 |
|-----|------|---------|------|------|-------|-------|-------|-------|--------|
| 2 | 1843 | 480,000 | 3.75 | 7.50 | 15.00 | 37.50 | 165 | 325 | — |
| | 1843 | — | — | — | — | — | — | 800 | — |

# TOKENS
## 1 PENNY TOKEN

**Composition:** Copper.

| KM# | Date | Mintage | VG-8 | F-12 | VF-20 | XF-40 | MS-60 | MS-63 | Prf-63 |
|-----|------|---------|------|------|-------|-------|-------|-------|--------|
| 4 | 1854 | 432,000 | 3.75 | 7.50 | 15.00 | 40.00 | 175 | 350 | — |

## NEWFOUNDLAND

# CIRCULATION COINAGE
## CENT

**Composition:** Bronze.

| KM# | Date | Mintage | VG-8 | F-12 | VF-20 | XF-40 | MS-60 | MS-63 | Prf-63 |
|-----|------|---------|------|------|-------|-------|-------|-------|--------|
| 1 | 1865 | 240,000 | 2.00 | 3.00 | 6.00 | 14.50 | 120 | 550 | — |
| | 1872H | 200,000 | 2.50 | 4.00 | 7.00 | 15.00 | 60.00 | 160 | — |
| | 1872H | — | — | — | — | — | — | 800 | — |
| | 1873 | 200,025 | 2.50 | 4.50 | 13.00 | 30.00 | 225 | 1,100 | — |
| | 1873 | — | — | · — | — | — | — | 800 | — |
| | 1876H | 200,000 | 2.50 | 4.00 | 7.00 | 25.00 | 160 | 450 | — |

| KM# | Date | Mintage | VG-8 | F-12 | VF-20 | XF-40 | MS-60 | MS-63 | Prf-63 |
|---|---|---|---|---|---|---|---|---|---|
| | 1876H | — | — | — | — | — | — | 600 | — |
| | 1880 round O, even date | 400,000 | 2.00 | 3.00 | 6.00 | 14.50 | 90.00 | 300 | — |
| | 1880 round O, low O | Inc. above | 2.25 | 4.00 | 9.00 | 30.00 | 150 | 550 | — |
| | 1880 oval 0 | Inc. above | 85.00 | 130 | 180 | 325 | 700 | 1,400 | — |
| | 1885 | 40,000 | 16.50 | 27.00 | 55.00 | 92.00 | 400 | 1,250 | — |
| | 1888 | 50,000 | 15.00 | 25.00 | 40.00 | 90.00 | 450 | 1,970 | — |
| | 1890 | 200,000 | 2.00 | 3.00 | 5.50 | 14.50 | 140 | 450 | — |
| | 1894 | 200,000 | 2.25 | 3.50 | 6.00 | 15.00 | 140 | 475 | — |
| | 1896 | 200,000 | 2.00 | 3.00 | 5.50 | 14.50 | 120 | 350 | — |

**Composition:** Bronze.

| KM# | Date | Mintage | VG-8 | F-12 | VF-20 | XF-40 | MS-60 | MS-63 | Prf-63 |
|---|---|---|---|---|---|---|---|---|---|
| 9 | 1904H | 100,000 | 6.00 | 10.00 | 20.00 | 35.00 | 275 | 650 | — |
| | 1907 | 200,000 | 1.50 | 2.50 | 4.00 | 12.00 | 110 | 375 | — |
| | 1909 | 200,000 | 1.50 | 2.50 | 4.00 | 10.50 | 90.00 | 150 | — |
| | 1909 | — | — | — | — | — | — | 400 | — |

**Composition:** Bronze.

| KM# | Date | Mintage | VG-8 | F-12 | VF-20 | XF-40 | MS-60 | MS-63 | Prf-63 |
|---|---|---|---|---|---|---|---|---|---|
| 16 | 1913 | 400,000 | 0.75 | 1.50 | 2.00 | 4.00 | 40.00 | 75.00 | — |
| | 1917C | 702,350 | 0.75 | 1.50 | 2.00 | 4.00 | 65.00 | 185 | — |
| | 1919C | 300,000 | 0.80 | 1.60 | 2.25 | 5.00 | 100.00 | 275 | — |
| | 1919C | — | — | — | — | — | — | 220 | — |
| | 1920C | 302,184 | 0.75 | 1.50 | 3.50 | 12.00 | 145 | 650 | — |
| | 1929 | 300,000 | 0.75 | 1.50 | 2.00 | 4.00 | 55.00 | 100.00 | — |
| | 1929 | — | — | — | — | — | — | 185 | — |
| | 1936 | 300,000 | 0.75 | 1.25 | 1.75 | 3.00 | 28.00 | 75.00 | — |
| | 1936 | — | — | — | — | — | — | 250 | — |

**Composition:** Bronze.

| KM# | Date | Mintage | VG-8 | F-12 | VF-20 | XF-40 | MS-60 | MS-63 | Prf-63 |
|---|---|---|---|---|---|---|---|---|---|
| 18 | 1938 | 500,000 | 0.50 | 0.75 | 1.50 | 2.50 | 16.00 | 40.00 | — |
| | 1938 | — | — | — | — | — | — | 125 | — |
| | 1940 | 300,000 | 1.25 | 2.00 | 3.00 | 7.00 | 35.00 | 175 | — |
| | 1940 re-engraved date | — | 16.00 | 27.50 | 40.00 | 60.00 | 185 | 400 | — |
| | 1941C | 827,662 | 0.35 | 0.45 | 0.70 | 1.50 | 13.50 | 120 | — |
| | 1941C re-engraved date | — | 12.00 | 20.00 | 30.00 | 50.00 | 155 | 400 | — |
| | 1942 | 1,996,889 | 0.35 | 0.45 | 0.70 | 1.50 | 13.50 | 70.00 | — |
| | 1943C | 1,239,732 | 0.35 | 0.45 | 0.70 | 1.50 | 13.50 | 70.00 | — |
| | 1944C | 1,328,776 | 1.00 | 2.00 | 3.00 | 4.50 | 60.00 | 335 | — |
| | 1947C | 313,772 | 0.75 | 1.50 | 2.25 | 4.50 | 40.00 | 200 | — |

# 5 CENTS

**Weight:** 1.1782 g. **Composition:** 0.9250 Silver., .0350 oz. ASW.

| KM# | Date | Mintage | VG-8 | F-12 | VF-20 | XF-40 | MS-60 | MS-63 | Prf-63 |
|---|---|---|---|---|---|---|---|---|---|
| 2 | 1865 | 80,000 | 20.00 | 32.50 | 60.00 | 125 | 775 | 1,500 | — |
| | 1870 | 40,000 | 35.00 | 50.00 | 90.00 | 175 | 1,100 | 2,000 | — |
| | 1870 | — | — | — | — | — | — | 3,900 | — |
| | 1872H | 40,000 | 22.00 | 32.00 | 60.00 | 140 | 600 | 1,400 | — |

| KM# | Date | Mintage | VG-8 | F-12 | VF-20 | XF-40 | MS-60 | MS-63 | Prf-63 |
|---|---|---|---|---|---|---|---|---|---|
| | 1873 | 44,260 | 45.00 | 75.00 | 145 | 300 | 1,750 | 2,850 | — |
| | 1873H | Inc. above | 650 | 1,000 | 1,875 | 3,300 | 8,200 | 12,500 | — |
| | 1876H | 20,000 | 65.00 | 90.00 | 175 | 275 | 1,100 | 2,750 | — |
| | 1880 | 40,000 | 22.00 | 40.00 | 80.00 | 150 | 1,000 | 1,850 | — |
| | 1881 | 40,000 | 15.00 | 30.00 | 45.00 | 120 | 900 | 1,850 | — |
| | 1882H | 60,000 | 15.00 | 27.00 | 40.00 | 100.00 | 800 | 1,500 | — |
| | 1882H | — | — | — | — | — | — | 2,800 | — |
| | 1885 | 16,000 | 90.00 | 130 | 225 | 400 | 1,650 | 4,500 | — |
| | 1888 | 40,000 | 20.00 | 30.00 | 60.00 | 140 | 850 | 2,450 | — |
| | 1890 | 160,000 | 6.00 | 12.00 | 30.00 | 70.00 | 600 | 1,500 | — |
| | 1890 | — | — | — | — | — | — | 2,100 | — |
| | 1894 | 160,000 | 6.50 | 12.50 | 30.00 | 75.00 | 600 | 1,500 | — |
| | 1896 | 400,000 | 4.00 | 8.00 | 20.00 | 45.00 | 575 | 1,350 | — |

**Weight:** 1.1782 g. **Composition:** 0.9250 Silver., .0350 oz. ASW.

| KM# | Date | Mintage | VG-8 | F-12 | VF-20 | XF-40 | MS-60 | MS-63 | Prf-63 |
|---|---|---|---|---|---|---|---|---|---|
| 7 | 1903 | 100,000 | 3.00 | 6.00 | 18.00 | 45.00 | 425 | 1,200 | — |
| | 1904H | 100,000 | 2.00 | 5.00 | 14.00 | 35.00 | 160 | 275 | — |
| | 1908 | 400,000 | 1.75 | 3.50 | 11.50 | 25.00 | 160 | 400 | — |

**Weight:** 1.1782 g. **Composition:** 0.9250 Silver., .0350 oz. ASW.

| KM# | Date | Mintage | VG-8 | F-12 | VF-20 | XF-40 | MS-60 | MS-63 | Prf-63 |
|---|---|---|---|---|---|---|---|---|---|
| 13 | 1912 | 300,000 | 1.00 | 2.00 | 5.00 | 20.00 | 125 | 275 | — |
| | 1917C | 300,319 | 1.00 | 2.00 | 4.00 | 14.00 | 200 | 450 | — |
| | 1919C | 100,844 | 2.00 | 3.00 | 10.00 | 30.00 | 750 | 1,250 | — |
| | 1929 | 300,000 | 1.00 | 1.75 | 3.25 | 12.00 | 165 | 350 | — |
| | 1929 | — | — | — | — | — | — | 750 | — |

**Weight:** 1.1782 g. **Composition:** 0.9250 Silver., .0350 oz. ASW.

| KM# | Date | Mintage | VG-8 | F-12 | VF-20 | XF-40 | MS-60 | MS-63 | Prf-63 |
|---|---|---|---|---|---|---|---|---|---|
| 19 | 1938 | 100,000 | 0.80 | 0.90 | 1.50 | 4.00 | 65.00 | 150 | — |
| | 1938 | — | — | — | — | — | — | 350 | — |
| | 1940C | 200,000 | 0.80 | 0.90 | 1.50 | 4.00 | 60.00 | 200 | — |
| | 1941C | 621,641 | 0.60 | 0.90 | 1.50 | 2.50 | 15.00 | 30.00 | — |
| | 1942C | 298,348 | 0.85 | 0.90 | 2.00 | 2.50 | 15.00 | 30.00 | — |
| | 1943C | 351,666 | 0.55 | 0.85 | 1.25 | 2.50 | 15.00 | 27.50 | — |

**Weight:** 1.1664 g. **Composition:** 0.8000 Silver., .0300 oz. ASW.

| KM# | Date | Mintage | VG-8 | F-12 | VF-20 | XF-40 | MS-60 | MS-63 | Prf-63 |
|---|---|---|---|---|---|---|---|---|---|
| 19a | 1944C | 286,504 | 1.00 | 1.50 | 2.50 | 3.50 | 25.00 | 50.00 | — |
| | 1945C | 203,828 | 0.55 | 0.85 | 1.25 | 2.50 | 13.00 | 26.00 | — |
| | 1945C | — | — | — | — | — | — | 250 | — |
| | 1946C | 2,041 | 200 | 225 | 285 | 375 | 1,100 | 1,750 | — |
| | 1946C | — | — | — | — | — | — | 4,000 | — |
| | 1947C | 38,400 | 2.00 | 3.00 | 5.00 | 10.00 | 60.00 | 225 | — |
| | 1947C | — | — | — | — | — | — | 400 | — |

# 10 CENTS

**Weight:** 2.3564 g. **Composition:** 0.9250 Silver., .0701 oz. ASW.

| KM# | Date | Mintage | VG-8 | F-12 | VF-20 | XF-40 | MS-60 | MS-63 | Prf-63 |
|---|---|---|---|---|---|---|---|---|---|
| 3 | 1865 | 80,000 | 13.50 | 22.00 | 55.00 | 160 | 1,100 | 2,250 | — |

| KM# | Date | Mintage | VG-8 | F-12 | VF-20 | XF-40 | MS-60 | MS-63 | Prf-63 |
|---|---|---|---|---|---|---|---|---|---|
| | 1865 plain edge | — | — | — | — | — | — | 5,500 | — |
| | 1870 | 30,000 | 120 | 190 | 335 | 725 | 2,350 | 5,000 | — |
| | 1872H | 40,000 | 13.50 | 20.00 | 50.00 | 135 | 800 | 1,700 | — |
| | 1873 flat 3 | 23,614 | 15.00 | 35.00 | 90.00 | 345 | 1,675 | 2,900 | — |
| | 1873 round 3 | Inc. above | 15.00 | 35.00 | 90.00 | 345 | 1,675 | 2,900 | — |
| | 1876H | 10,000 | 20.00 | 35.00 | 80.00 | 225 | 1,400 | 2,500 | — |
| | 1880/70 | 10,000 | 22.00 | 45.00 | 100.00 | 275 | 1,800 | 2,950 | — |
| | 1882H | 20,000 | 15.00 | 30.00 | 80.00 | 310 | 2,185 | 3,410 | — |
| | 1882H | — | — | — | — | — | — | 3,400 | — |
| | 1885 | 8,000 | 60.00 | 110 | 200 | 475 | 2,100 | 4,250 | — |
| | 1888 | 30,000 | 11.50 | 27.50 | 70.00 | 345 | 2,185 | 2,500 | — |
| | 1890 | 100,000 | 5.50 | 11.50 | 20.00 | 75.00 | 700 | 1,550 | — |
| | 1890 | — | — | — | — | — | — | 3,200 | — |
| | 1894 | 100,000 | 5.50 | 11.50 | 20.00 | 75.00 | 700 | 1,550 | — |
| | 1894 | — | — | — | — | — | — | 1,750 | — |
| | 1896 | 230,000 | 5.00 | 10.00 | 20.00 | 75.00 | 600 | 1,500 | — |

**Weight:** 2.3564 g. **Composition:** 0.9250 Silver., .0701 oz. ASW.

| KM# | Date | Mintage | VG-8 | F-12 | VF-20 | XF-40 | MS-60 | MS-63 | Prf-63 |
|---|---|---|---|---|---|---|---|---|---|
| 8 | 1903 | 100,000 | 5.00 | 10.00 | 35.00 | 110 | 850 | 2,000 | — |
| | 1904H | 100,000 | 2.50 | 6.50 | 20.00 | 55.00 | 175 | 250 | — |

**Weight:** 2.3564 g. **Composition:** 0.9250 Silver., .0701 oz. ASW.

| KM# | Date | Mintage | VG-8 | F-12 | VF-20 | XF-40 | MS-60 | MS-63 | Prf-63 |
|---|---|---|---|---|---|---|---|---|---|
| 20 | 1938 | 100,000 | 0.75 | 1.50 | 2.75 | 7.00 | 80.00 | 225 | — |
| | 1938 | — | — | — | — | — | — | 500 | — |
| | 1940 | 100,000 | 0.65 | 1.20 | 2.50 | 6.00 | 80.00 | 225 | — |
| | 1941C | 483,630 | 0.60 | 1.40 | 2.20 | 3.50 | 27.00 | 85.00 | — |
| | 1942C | 293,736 | 0.60 | 1.50 | 2.20 | 3.50 | 27.00 | 90.00 | — |
| | 1943C | 104,706 | 0.60 | 1.50 | 2.40 | 3.50 | 45.00 | 165 | — |
| | 1944C | 151,471 | 1.00 | 1.50 | 2.50 | 6.00 | 80.00 | 250 | — |

**Weight:** 2.3328 g. **Composition:** 0.8000 Silver., .0600 oz. ASW.

| KM# | Date | Mintage | VG-8 | F-12 | VF-20 | XF-40 | MS-60 | MS-63 | Prf-63 |
|---|---|---|---|---|---|---|---|---|---|
| 20a | 1945C | 175,833 | 0.65 | 1.25 | 2.00 | 4.00 | 27.00 | 185 | — |
| | 1946C | 38,400 | 2.50 | 3.50 | 7.00 | 15.00 | 60.00 | 150 | — |
| | 1947C | 61,988 | 1.25 | 2.50 | 4.00 | 8.00 | 45.00 | 140 | — |

# 20 CENTS

**Weight:** 4.7127 g. **Composition:** 0.9250 Silver., .1401 oz. ASW.

| KM# | Date | Mintage | VG-8 | F-12 | VF-20 | XF-40 | MS-60 | MS-63 | Prf-63 |
|---|---|---|---|---|---|---|---|---|---|
| 4 | 1865 | 100,000 | 11.00 | 16.00 | 45.00 | 125 | 950 | 2,000 | — |
| | 1865 plain edge | — | — | — | — | — | — | 4,500 | — |
| | 1870 | 50,000 | 12.00 | 20.00 | 60.00 | 140 | 1,250 | 2,500 | — |
| | 1872H | 90,000 | 7.00 | 14.00 | 30.00 | 90.00 | 750 | 1,800 | — |
| | 1873 | 45,797 | 9.00 | 18.00 | 60.00 | 160 | 1,500 | 3,000 | — |
| | 1876H | 50,000 | 10.00 | 16.00 | 50.00 | 175 | 1,350 | 2,700 | — |
| | 1880/70 | 30,000 | 15.00 | 25.00 | 65.00 | 160 | 1,350 | 3,000 | — |
| | 1881 | 60,000 | 5.00 | 12.00 | 35.00 | 90.00 | 900 | 1,900 | — |
| | 1882H | 100,000 | 5.00 | 12.00 | 27.50 | 80.00 | 900 | 1,900 | — |
| | 1882H | — | — | — | — | — | — | 3,700 | — |
| | 1885 | 40,000 | 8.00 | 12.50 | 40.00 | 120 | 1,300 | 2,600 | — |
| | 1888 | 75,000 | 5.00 | 10.00 | 32.00 | 100.00 | 900 | 2,200 | — |

| KM# | Date | Mintage | VG-8 | F-12 | VF-20 | XF-40 | MS-60 | MS-63 | Prf-63 |
|---|---|---|---|---|---|---|---|---|---|
| | 1890 | 100,000 | 4.00 | 7.00 | 22.00 | 70.00 | 625 | 1,600 | — |
| | 1890 | — | — | — | — | — | — | 2,750 | — |
| | 1894 | 100,000 | 4.00 | 7.00 | 22.00 | 60.00 | 650 | 1,700 | — |
| | 1896 small 96 | 125,000 | 3.00 | 6.00 | 20.00 | 70.00 | 700 | 1,800 | — |
| | 1896 large 96 | Inc. above | 4.00 | 10.00 | 22.00 | 90.00 | 725 | 1,900 | — |
| | 1899 small 99 | 125,000 | 15.00 | 30.00 | 55.00 | 175 | 1,000 | 2,200 | — |
| | 1899 large 99 | Inc. above | 3.25 | 6.50 | 18.00 | 65.00 | 700 | 1,900 | — |
| | 1900 | 125,000 | 3.00 | 5.00 | 15.00 | 55.00 | 700 | 1,900 | — |

**Weight:** 4.7127 g. **Composition:** 0.9250 Silver., .1401 oz. ASW.

| KM# | Date | Mintage | VG-8 | F-12 | VF-20 | XF-40 | MS-60 | MS-63 | Prf-63 |
|---|---|---|---|---|---|---|---|---|---|
| 10 | 1904H | 75,000 | 6.00 | 16.00 | 50.00 | 175 | 2,000 | 4,250 | — |
| | 1904H | — | — | — | — | — | — | 4,550 | — |

**Weight:** 4.7127 g. **Composition:** 0.9250 Silver., .1401 oz. ASW.

| KM# | Date | Mintage | VG-8 | F-12 | VF-20 | XF-40 | MS-60 | MS-63 | Prf-63 |
|---|---|---|---|---|---|---|---|---|---|
| 15 | 1912 | 350,000 | 2.00 | 3.00 | 8.00 | 30.00 | 275 | 650 | — |

# 25 CENTS

**Weight:** 5.8319 g. **Composition:** 0.9250 Silver., .1734 oz. ASW.

| KM# | Date | Mintage | VG-8 | F-12 | VF-20 | XF-40 | MS-60 | MS-63 | Prf-63 |
|---|---|---|---|---|---|---|---|---|---|
| 17 | 1917C | 464,779 | 1.50 | 2.00 | 4.00 | 8.00 | 120 | 250 | — |
| | 1919C | 163,939 | 1.50 | 2.25 | 4.25 | 12.00 | 220 | 700 | — |

# 50 CENTS

**Weight:** 11.7818 g. **Composition:** 0.9250 Silver., .3504 oz. ASW.

| KM# | Date | Mintage | VG-8 | F-12 | VF-20 | XF-40 | MS-60 | MS-63 | Prf-63 |
|---|---|---|---|---|---|---|---|---|---|
| 6 | 1870 | 50,000 | 12.00 | 15.00 | 55.00 | 300 | 1,400 | 3,600 | — |
| | 1870 plain edge | — | — | — | — | — | — | 6,500 | — |
| | 1872H | 48,000 | 10.00 | 15.00 | 50.00 | 250 | 1,250 | 3,600 | — |
| | 1873 | 37,675 | 30.00 | 65.00 | 200 | 700 | 4,350 | 6,000 | — |
| | 1874 | 80,000 | 20.00 | 32.00 | 100.00 | 425 | 2,500 | 5,000 | — |
| | 1876H | 28,000 | 20.00 | 32.00 | 100.00 | 375 | 2,250 | 5,250 | — |

| KM# | Date | Mintage | VG-8 | F-12 | VF-20 | XF-40 | MS-60 | MS-63 | Prf-63 |
|-----|------|---------|------|------|-------|-------|-------|-------|--------|
|     | 1880 | 24,000 | 20.00 | 32.00 | 100.00 | 400 | 2,250 | 5,250 | — |
|     | 1881 | 50,000 | 11.50 | 22.00 | 85.00 | 300 | 2,250 | 5,250 | — |
|     | 1882H | 100,000 | 9.00 | 14.00 | 55.00 | 250 | 1,600 | 3,600 | — |
|     | 1882H | — | — | — | — | — | — | 5,500 | — |
|     | 1885 | 40,000 | 14.00 | 25.00 | 80.00 | 325 | 2,250 | 5,500 | — |
|     | 1888 | 20,000 | 18.00 | 38.00 | 100.00 | 400 | 2,200 | 5,200 | — |
|     | 1894 | 40,000 | 5.00 | 13.00 | 50.00 | 200 | 2,000 | 3,800 | — |
|     | 1896 | 60,000 | 5.00 | 10.00 | 35.00 | 150 | 1,400 | 3,600 | — |
|     | 1898 | 76,607 | 5.00 | 10.00 | 35.00 | 150 | 1,700 | 3,600 | — |
|     | 1899 wide 9's | 150,000 | 5.00 | 10.00 | 30.00 | 125 | 1,500 | 3,600 | — |
|     | 1899 narrow 9's | Inc. above | 5.00 | 10.00 | 30.00 | 125 | 1,500 | 3,600 | — |
|     | 1900 | 150,000 | 5.00 | 10.00 | 30.00 | 125 | 1,500 | 3,600 | — |

**Weight:** 11.7800 g. **Composition:** 0.9250 Silver., .3504 oz. ASW.

| KM# | Date | Mintage | VG-8 | F-12 | VF-20 | XF-40 | MS-60 | MS-63 | Prf-63 |
|-----|------|---------|------|------|-------|-------|-------|-------|--------|
| 11 | 1904H | 140,000 | 3.25 | 5.00 | 13.00 | 35.00 | 225 | 650 | — |
|    | 1907 | 100,000 | 3.00 | 5.00 | 13.00 | 45.00 | 250 | 800 | — |
|    | 1908 | 160,000 | 3.25 | 4.50 | 12.50 | 32.50 | 175 | 600 | — |
|    | 1909 | 200,000 | 3.25 | 4.50 | 12.50 | 35.00 | 200 | 600 | — |

**Weight:** 11.7800 g. **Composition:** 0.9250 Silver., .3504 oz. ASW.

| KM# | Date | Mintage | VG-8 | F-12 | VF-20 | XF-40 | MS-60 | MS-63 | Prf-63 |
|-----|------|---------|------|------|-------|-------|-------|-------|--------|
| 12 | 1911 | 200,000 | 2.75 | 3.25 | 6.00 | 20.00 | 175 | 450 | — |
|    | 1917C | 375,560 | 2.75 | 3.25 | 6.00 | 16.50 | 125 | 285 | — |
|    | 1918C | 294,824 | 2.75 | 3.25 | 6.00 | 16.50 | 125 | 285 | — |
|    | 1919C | 306,267 | 2.75 | 3.25 | 6.00 | 16.50 | 125 | 380 | — |

# 2 DOLLARS

**Weight:** 3.3284 g. **Composition:** 0.9170 Gold., .0981 oz. AGW.

| KM# | Date | Mintage | F-12 | VF-20 | XF-40 | AU-50 | MS-60 | MS-63 |
|-----|------|---------|------|-------|-------|-------|-------|-------|
| 5 | 1865 | 10,000 | 125 | 150 | 210 | 350 | 1,050 | 4,950 |
|   | 1865 plain edge, about 10 known, specimen | 10,000 | — | — | — | — | — | 9,000 |
|   | 1870 | 10,000 | 150 | 180 | 225 | 410 | 1,050 | 5,850 |
|   | 1870 plain edge; about 5 pcs. known; specimen | — | — | — | — | — | — | 10,500 |
|   | 1872 | 6,050 | 150 | 275 | 300 | 590 | 2,100 | 8,650 |
|   | 1872 about 10 pcs. known; specimen | — | — | — | — | — | — | 12,500 |
|   | 1880 | 2,500 | 775 | 950 | 1,150 | 2,300 | 4,650 | 14,250 |
|   | 1880/70 specimen; Bowers and Merena Norweb sale 11-96, specimen 64 realized $70,400 | — | — | — | — | — | — | — |
|   | 1881 | 10,000 | 110 | 145 | 180 | 300 | 1,100 | 4,750 |
|   | 1881 specimen | — | — | — | — | — | — | — |
|   | 1882H | 25,000 | 105 | 140 | 175 | 200 | 375 | 1,300 |
|   | 1882H specimen | — | — | — | — | — | — | 4,250 |

| KM# | Date | Mintage | F-12 | VF-20 | XF-40 | AU-50 | MS-60 | MS-63 |
|---|---|---|---|---|---|---|---|---|
| | 1885 | 10,000 | 110 | 145 | 180 | 300 | 475 | 1,900 |
| | 1885 specimen; Bowers and Merena Norweb sale 11-96, specimen 66 realized $44,000 | — | — | — | — | — | — | — |
| | 1888 | 25,000 | 105 | 140 | 175 | 200 | 365 | 1,550 |
| | 1888 | — | — | — | — | — | — | — |

## NOVA SCOTIA

# DECIMAL COINAGE

## HALF CENT

**Composition:** Bronze.

| KM# | Date | Mintage | VG-8 | F-12 | VF-20 | XF-40 | MS-60 | MS-63 | Prf-63 |
|---|---|---|---|---|---|---|---|---|---|
| 7 | 1861 | 400,000 | 3.00 | 5.00 | 8.00 | 12.00 | 60.00 | 165 | — |
| | 1864 | 400,000 | 3.00 | 5.00 | 8.00 | 12.00 | 55.00 | 165 | — |
| | 1864 | — | — | — | — | — | — | 300 | — |

## CENT

**Composition:** Bronze. **Notes:** The Royal Mint report records mintage of 1 million for 1862, which is considered incorrect.

| KM# | Date | Mintage | VG-8 | F-12 | VF-20 | XF-40 | MS-60 | MS-63 | Prf-63 |
|---|---|---|---|---|---|---|---|---|---|
| 8 | 1861 | 800,000 | 2.00 | 3.00 | 5.00 | 10.00 | 70.00 | 215 | — |
| | 1862 | Est. 1,000,000— | 15.00 | 22.50 | 45.00 | 95.00 | 385 | 1,300 | — |
| | 1864 | 800,000 | 2.00 | 3.00 | 5.00 | 10.00 | 70.00 | 215 | — |

# STERLING COINAGE

## HALFPENNY TOKEN

**Composition:** Copper.

| KM# | Date | Mintage | VG-8 | F-12 | VF-20 | XF-40 | MS-60 | MS-63 | Prf-63 |
|---|---|---|---|---|---|---|---|---|---|
| 1a | 1382 1382(error) | — | 500 | 700 | 1,650 | — | — | — | — |
| | 1832/1382 | — | 6.00 | 15.00 | 50.00 | 100.00 | — | — | — |
| | 1832 (imitation) | — | 3.00 | 6.00 | 18.00 | 40.00 | 50.00 | 100.00 | — |

**Composition:** Copper.

| KM# | Date | Mintage | VG-8 | F-12 | VF-20 | XF-40 | MS-60 | MS-63 | Prf-63 |
|-----|------|---------|------|------|-------|-------|-------|-------|--------|
| 1 | 1823 | 400,000 | 3.00 | 5.00 | 8.00 | 20.00 | 75.00 | 150 | — |
| | 1823 without hyphen | Inc. above | 5.00 | 10.00 | 20.00 | 35.00 | 170 | 350 | — |
| | 1824 | 118,636 | 3.00 | 5.00 | 12.50 | 25.00 | 150 | 225 | — |
| | 1832 | 800,000 | 3.00 | 5.00 | 7.50 | 15.00 | 60.00 | 150 | — |

**Composition:** Copper.

| KM# | Date | Mintage | VG-8 | F-12 | VF-20 | XF-40 | MS-60 | MS-63 | Prf-63 |
|-----|------|---------|------|------|-------|-------|-------|-------|--------|
| 3 | 1840 small 0 | 300,000 | 3.50 | 5.00 | 10.00 | 22.00 | 115 | 165 | — |
| | 1840 medium 0 | Inc. above | 2.50 | 4.00 | 7.50 | 15.00 | 95.00 | 125 | — |
| | 1840 large 0 | Inc. above | 4.00 | 6.00 | 12.50 | 27.50 | 125 | 185 | — |
| | 1843 | 300,000 | 3.00 | 5.00 | 12.00 | 25.00 | 85.00 | 160 | — |

**Composition:** Copper.

| KM# | Date | Mintage | VG-8 | F-12 | VF-20 | XF-40 | MS-60 | MS-63 | Prf-63 |
|-----|------|---------|------|------|-------|-------|-------|-------|--------|
| 5 | 1856 without LCW | 720,000 | 2.00 | 4.00 | 7.50 | 15.00 | 70.00 | 175 | — |
| | 1856 without LCW | — | — | — | — | — | — | 600 | — |
| | 1856 without LCW, inverted A for V in PROVINCE | — | — | — | — | — | — | 600 | — |

**Composition:** Bronze.

| KM# | Date | Mintage | VG-8 | F-12 | VF-20 | XF-40 | MS-60 | MS-63 | Prf-63 |
|-----|------|---------|------|------|-------|-------|-------|-------|--------|
| 5a | 1856 with LCW | — | — | — | — | — | — | 600 | — |

# 1 PENNY TOKEN

**Composition:** Copper.

| KM# | Date | Mintage | VG-8 | F-12 | VF-20 | XF-40 | MS-60 | MS-63 | Prf-63 |
|-----|------|---------|------|------|-------|-------|-------|-------|--------|
| 2 | 1824 | 217,776 | 3.00 | 6.00 | 10.00 | 25.00 | 100.00 | 250 | — |
| | 1832 | 200,000 | 3.00 | 6.00 | 10.00 | 22.50 | 80.00 | 230 | — |

**Composition:** Copper.

| KM# | Date | Mintage | VG-8 | F-12 | VF-20 | XF-40 | MS-60 | MS-63 | Prf-63 |
|-----|------|---------|------|------|-------|-------|-------|-------|--------|
| 2a | 1832 (imitation) | — | 3.75 | 7.50 | 22.50 | 42.50 | — | — | — |

**Composition:** Copper. **Diameter:** 32 mm.

| KM# | Date | Mintage | VG-8 | F-12 | VF-20 | XF-40 | MS-60 | MS-63 | Prf-63 |
|---|---|---|---|---|---|---|---|---|---|
| 4 | 1840 | 150,000 | 2.50 | 5.00 | 7.50 | 20.00 | 100.00 | 175 | — |
|  | 1843/0 | 150,000 | 12.00 | 20.00 | 40.00 | 80.00 | 150 | — | — |
|  | 1843 | Inc. above | 3.00 | 6.00 | 10.00 | 22.50 | 110 | 200 | — |

**Composition:** Copper.

| KM# | Date | Mintage | VG-8 | F-12 | VF-20 | XF-40 | MS-60 | MS-63 | Prf-63 |
|---|---|---|---|---|---|---|---|---|---|
| 6 | 1856 w/o LCW | 360,000 | 2.50 | 5.00 | 8.50 | 19.00 | 110 | 135 | — |
|  | 1856 w/LCW | Inc. above | 2.50 | 5.00 | 7.00 | 15.00 | 85.00 | 115 | — |

**Composition:** Bronze.

| KM# | Date | Mintage | VG-8 | F-12 | VF-20 | XF-40 | MS-60 | MS-63 | Prf-63 |
|---|---|---|---|---|---|---|---|---|---|
| 6a | 1856 | — | — | — | — | — | — | 400 | — |

## PRINCE EDWARD ISLAND

# DECIMAL COINAGE

## CENT

**Composition:** Bronze.

| KM# | Date | Mintage | VG-8 | F-12 | VF-20 | XF-40 | MS-60 | MS-63 | Prf-63 |
|---|---|---|---|---|---|---|---|---|---|
| 4 | 1871 | 2,000,000 | 1.75 | 2.50 | 4.50 | 10.50 | 75.00 | 185 | — |
|  | 1871 | — | — | — | — | — | — | 2,000 | — |

# Mexico

## COLONIAL COB COINAGE
### RULERS
Philip V, 1700-1724, 1724-1746
Luis I, 1724

### MINT MARKS
Mo, MXo - Mexico City Mint

### ASSAYERS INITIALS

| Letter | Date | Name |
|---|---|---|
| L | 1678-1703 | Martin Lopez |
| J | 1708-1723 | Jose E. de Leon |
| D | 1724-1727 | ? |
| R | 1729-1730 | Nicolas de Roxas |
| G | 1730 | — |
| F | 1730-1733 | Felipe Rivas de Angulo |
| F | 1733-1784 | Francisco de la Pena |
| M | 1733-1763 | Manuel de la Pena |

## 1/2 REAL

**.931 SILVER, 1.69 g**
**Philip V**
Obv: Legend around crowned PHILIPVS monogram.
Rev: Legend around cross, lions and castles.

| KM# | Date | Good | VG | Fine | VF |
|---|---|---|---|---|---|
| 24 | 1701 L | 30.00 | 40.00 | 55.00 | 90.00 |
| | 1702 L | 25.00 | 35.00 | 50.00 | 65.00 |
| | 1703 L | 25.00 | 35.00 | 50.00 | 65.00 |
| | 1704 L | 30.00 | 42.50 | 65.00 | 85.00 |
| | 1705 L | 30.00 | 42.50 | 65.00 | 85.00 |
| | 1706 L | 30.00 | 42.50 | 65.00 | 85.00 |
| | 1707 L | 30.00 | 42.50 | 65.00 | 85.00 |
| | 1708 J | 35.00 | 50.00 | 70.00 | 110.00 |
| | 1709 J | 30.00 | 42.50 | 65.00 | 85.00 |
| | 1710 J | 30.00 | 42.50 | 65.00 | 85.00 |
| | 1711 J | 30.00 | 42.50 | 65.00 | 85.00 |
| | 1712 J | 30.00 | 42.50 | 65.00 | 85.00 |
| | 1714 J | 30.00 | 42.50 | 65.00 | 85.00 |
| | 1715 J | 30.00 | 42.50 | 65.00 | 85.00 |
| | 1716 J | 30.00 | 42.50 | 65.00 | 85.00 |
| | 1717 J | 30.00 | 42.50 | 65.00 | 85.00 |
| | 1718 J | 30.00 | 42.50 | 65.00 | 85.00 |
| | 1719 J | 30.00 | 42.50 | 65.00 | 85.00 |
| | 1720 J | 30.00 | 42.50 | 65.00 | 85.00 |
| | 1721 J | 30.00 | 42.50 | 65.00 | 85.00 |
| | 1722 J | 42.50 | 55.00 | 80.00 | 125.00 |
| | 1723 J | 42.50 | 55.00 | 80.00 | 125.00 |
| | 1724 J | 50.00 | 65.00 | 85.00 | 140.00 |
| | 1724 D | 50.00 | 65.00 | 85.00 | 140.00 |
| | 1725 D | 50.00 | 65.00 | 85.00 | 140.00 |
| | 1726 D | 35.00 | 50.00 | 70.00 | 110.00 |
| | 1727 D | 35.00 | 50.00 | 70.00 | 110.00 |
| | 1728 D | 35.00 | 50.00 | 70.00 | 110.00 |

**.916 SILVER, 1.69 g**

| | | | | | |
|---|---|---|---|---|---|
| 24a | 1729 D | 35.00 | 50.00 | 70.00 | 110.00 |
| | 1730 G | 35.00 | 50.00 | 70.00 | 110.00 |
| | 1730 D | 35.00 | 50.00 | 70.00 | 110.00 |
| | 1731 F | 35.00 | 50.00 | 70.00 | 110.00 |
| | 1732 F | 35.00 | 50.00 | 70.00 | 110.00 |
| | 1733 F | 35.00 | 50.00 | 70.00 | 110.00 |
| | Date off flan | 15.00 | 20.00 | 25.00 | 30.00 |

**.931 SILVER, 1.69 g**
**Luis I**
Obv: Legend around crowned LVDOVICVS
monogram. Rev: Legend around cross,
lions and castles.

| KM# | Date | Good | VG | Fine | VF |
|---|---|---|---|---|---|
| 25 | 1724 D | 225.00 | 350.00 | 500.00 | 600.00 |
| | 1725 D | 225.00 | 350.00 | 500.00 | 600.00 |
| | 1726 D | 250.00 | 370.00 | 550.00 | 650.00 |
| | Date off flan | 100.00 | 200.00 | 250.00 | 300.00 |

## REAL

### ROYAL STRIKES

**Philip V**

Full struck sample specimens referred to as "Royal"
strikes are seldom encountered and are considered rare.

### CIRCULATION STRIKES

**.931 SILVER, 3.38 g**
Obv. leg: PHILIPVS V DEI G and date
around crowned arms.

| | | | | | |
|---|---|---|---|---|---|
| 30 | 1701 L | 45.00 | 60.00 | 70.00 | 115.00 |
| | 1702 L | 45.00 | 60.00 | 70.00 | 115.00 |
| | 1703 L | 45.00 | 60.00 | 70.00 | 115.00 |
| | 1704 L | 45.00 | 60.00 | 70.00 | 115.00 |
| | 1705 L | 45.00 | 60.00 | 70.00 | 115.00 |
| | 1706 L | 45.00 | 60.00 | 70.00 | 115.00 |
| | 1707 L | 45.00 | 60.00 | 70.00 | 115.00 |
| | 1708 J | 45.00 | 60.00 | 70.00 | 115.00 |
| | 1709 J | 45.00 | 60.00 | 70.00 | 115.00 |
| | 1710 J | 45.00 | 60.00 | 70.00 | 115.00 |
| | 1711 J | 45.00 | 60.00 | 70.00 | 115.00 |
| | 1712 J | 45.00 | 60.00 | 70.00 | 115.00 |
| | 1713 J | 35.00 | 45.00 | 57.50 | 85.00 |
| | 1714 J | 35.00 | 45.00 | 57.50 | 85.00 |
| | 1715 J | 45.00 | 60.00 | 70.00 | 100.00 |
| | 1716 J | 45.00 | 60.00 | 70.00 | 100.00 |
| | 1717 J | 45.00 | 60.00 | 70.00 | 100.00 |
| | 1718 J | 45.00 | 60.00 | 70.00 | 100.00 |
| | 1719 J | 45.00 | 60.00 | 70.00 | 100.00 |
| | 1720 J | 45.00 | 60.00 | 70.00 | 100.00 |
| | 1721 J | 45.00 | 60.00 | 70.00 | 100.00 |
| | 1722 J | 45.00 | 60.00 | 70.00 | 100.00 |
| | 1723 J | 45.00 | 60.00 | 70.00 | 100.00 |
| | 1724 J | 45.00 | 60.00 | 70.00 | 100.00 |
| | 1726 D | 45.00 | 60.00 | 70.00 | 100.00 |
| | 1727 D | 45.00 | 60.00 | 70.00 | 100.00 |
| | 1728 D | 45.00 | 60.00 | 70.00 | 100.00 |
| | 1729 F | 45.00 | 60.00 | 70.00 | 100.00 |

**.916 SILVER**

| | | | | | |
|---|---|---|---|---|---|
| 30a | 1729 R | 45.00 | 60.00 | 70.00 | 100.00 |
| | 1730 R | 45.00 | 60.00 | 70.00 | 100.00 |
| | 1730 F | 45.00 | 60.00 | 70.00 | 100.00 |
| | 1730 G | 45.00 | 60.00 | 70.00 | 100.00 |
| | 1731 F | 45.00 | 60.00 | 70.00 | 100.00 |
| | Date off flan | 10.00 | 15.00 | 20.00 | 30.00 |

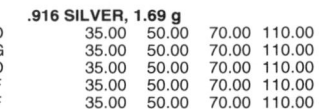

## 2 REALES

### ROYAL STRIKES

#### Philip V

Fully struck sample specimens referred to as "Royal" strikes are seldom encountered and are considered rare.

### CIRCULATION STRIKES

**.931 SILVER, 6.77 g**
Obv. leg: PHILIPVS V DEI G and date
around crowned arms.

| KM# | Date | Good | VG | Fine | VF |
|---|---|---|---|---|---|
| 35 | 1701 L | 25.00 | 40.00 | 50.00 | 75.00 |
| | 1702 L | 25.00 | 40.00 | 50.00 | 75.00 |
| | 1703 L | 25.00 | 40.00 | 50.00 | 75.00 |
| | 1704 L | 35.00 | 75.00 | 150.00 | 250.00 |
| | 1705 L | 25.00 | 40.00 | 50.00 | 75.00 |
| | 1706 L | 25.00 | 40.00 | 50.00 | 75.00 |
| | 1707 L | 35.00 | 75.00 | 150.00 | 250.00 |
| | 1708 J | 25.00 | 40.00 | 50.00 | 75.00 |
| | 1710 J | 25.00 | 40.00 | 50.00 | 75.00 |
| | 1711 J | 25.00 | 40.00 | 50.00 | 75.00 |
| | 1712 J | 25.00 | 40.00 | 50.00 | 75.00 |
| | 1713 J | 25.00 | 40.00 | 50.00 | 75.00 |
| | 1714 J | 25.00 | 40.00 | 50.00 | 80.00 |
| | 1715 J | 25.00 | 40.00 | 50.00 | 80.00 |
| | 1716 J | 25.00 | 40.00 | 50.00 | 75.00 |
| | 1717 J | 25.00 | 40.00 | 50.00 | 75.00 |
| | 1718 J | 25.00 | 40.00 | 50.00 | 75.00 |
| | 1719 J | 25.00 | 40.00 | 50.00 | 75.00 |
| | 1720 J | 25.00 | 40.00 | 50.00 | 75.00 |
| | 1721 J | 25.00 | 40.00 | 60.00 | 100.00 |
| | 1722 J | 25.00 | 40.00 | 50.00 | 75.00 |
| | 1723 J | 25.00 | 40.00 | 50.00 | 75.00 |
| | 1724 J | 36.00 | 50.00 | 60.00 | 100.00 |
| | 1725 D | 36.00 | 57.50 | 75.00 | 125.00 |
| | 1725 R | 36.00 | 40.00 | 50.00 | 100.00 |
| | 1726 D | 36.00 | 57.50 | 75.00 | 125.00 |
| | 1727 D | 36.00 | 57.50 | 75.00 | 125.00 |
| | 1728 D | 28.00 | 37.50 | 75.00 | 125.00 |
| | **.916 SILVER** | | | | |
| 35a | 1729 R | 28.00 | 37.50 | 75.00 | 125.00 |
| | 1730 R | 28.00 | 37.50 | 75.00 | 125.00 |
| | 1731 MF | 25.00 | 30.00 | 60.00 | 100.00 |
| | 1731/0 J | 25.00 | 30.00 | 60.00 | 100.00 |
| | 1733 F | 25.00 | 40.00 | 80.00 | 150.00 |
| | Date off flan | 10.00 | 20.00 | 35.00 | 50.00 |

## 4 REALES

### ROYAL STRIKES

#### Philip V

Fully struck examples on round planchets, referred to as "Royal" strikes are seldom encountered and are considered rare.

### CIRCULATION STRIKES

**.931 SILVER, 13.54 g**
Obv. leg: PHILIPVS V DEI G and date
around crowned arms.

| KM# | Date | Good | VG | Fine | VF |
|---|---|---|---|---|---|
| 40 | 1701 L | 80.00 | 125.00 | 225.00 | 375.00 |
| | 1702 L | 80.00 | 125.00 | 225.00 | 375.00 |
| | 1703 L | 45.00 | 90.00 | 150.00 | 250.00 |
| | 1704 L | 80.00 | 125.00 | 225.00 | 375.00 |
| | 1705 L | 65.00 | 100.00 | 200.00 | 300.00 |
| | 1706 L | 65.00 | 100.00 | 200.00 | 300.00 |
| | 1707 L | 65.00 | 100.00 | 200.00 | 300.00 |
| | 1708 J | 30.00 | 70.00 | 120.00 | 200.00 |
| | 1709 J | 65.00 | 100.00 | 200.00 | 300.00 |
| | 1710 J | 50.00 | 90.00 | 175.00 | 250.00 |
| | 1711 J | 50.00 | 90.00 | 175.00 | 250.00 |
| | 1712 J | 80.00 | 125.00 | 225.00 | 375.00 |
| | 1713 J | 80.00 | 125.00 | 225.00 | 375.00 |
| | 1714 J | 65.00 | 100.00 | 200.00 | 300.00 |
| | 1715 J | 80.00 | 125.00 | 225.00 | 375.00 |
| | 1716 J | 65.00 | 100.00 | 200.00 | 300.00 |
| | 1717 J | 80.00 | 125.00 | 225.00 | 375.00 |
| | 1718 J | 80.00 | 125.00 | 225.00 | 375.00 |
| | 1719 J | 65.00 | 100.00 | 200.00 | 300.00 |
| | 1720 J | 65.00 | 100.00 | 200.00 | 300.00 |
| | 1721 J | 65.00 | 100.00 | 200.00 | 300.00 |
| | 1722 J | 90.00 | 150.00 | 300.00 | 500.00 |
| | 1723 J | 90.00 | 150.00 | 300.00 | 500.00 |
| | 1725 D | 90.00 | 150.00 | 300.00 | 500.00 |
| | 1726 D | 90.00 | 150.00 | 300.00 | 500.00 |
| | 1727 D | 90.00 | 150.00 | 300.00 | 500.00 |
| | 1728 D | 80.00 | 125.00 | 225.00 | 375.00 |
| | **.916 SILVER, 13.54 g** | | | | |
| 40a | 1729 D | 80.00 | 125.00 | 250.00 | 400.00 |
| | 1730 R | 80.00 | 125.00 | 250.00 | 400.00 |
| | 1730 G | 80.00 | 125.00 | 250.00 | 400.00 |
| | 1731 F | 80.00 | 125.00 | 250.00 | 400.00 |
| | 1732/1 F | 75.00 | 100.00 | 220.00 | 350.00 |
| | 1732 F | 65.00 | 90.00 | 185.00 | 300.00 |
| | 1733 F | 65.00 | 90.00 | 185.00 | 300.00 |
| | 1734 F | 65.00 | 90.00 | 185.00 | 300.00 |
| | Date off flan | 40.00 | 50.00 | 70.00 | 100.00 |
| | (Klippe) | | | | |

**Similar to KM#40a.**

| 41 | 1733 MF | 200.00 | 250.00 | 300.00 | 400.00 |
|---|---|---|---|---|---|
| | 1734 MF | 250.00 | 300.00 | 400.00 | 500.00 |
| | 1734/3 MF | 225.00 | 250.00 | 300.00 | 400.00 |
| | 1740/30 MF | 250.00 | 275.00 | 350.00 | 450.00 |
| | 1742/32 MF | — | — | — | — |
| | 1743/33 MF | — | — | — | — |

**.931 SILVER, 13.54 g**
Luis I
Obv. leg: LVDOVICUS I DEI G
around crowned arms.

| KM# | Date | Good | VG | Fine | VF |
|-----|------|------|-----|------|-----|
| 42 | 1724 D | 650.00 | 1000. | 1500. | 2500. |
|  | 1725 D | 750.00 | 1200. | 2000. | 3000. |
|  | Date off flan | 225.00 | 350.00 | 500.00 | 850.00 |

## 8 REALES
### ROYAL STRIKES

**Philip V**

Fully struck examples on round planchets, referred to as "Royal" strikes are seldom encountered and are considered rare.

### CIRCULATION STRIKES

**.931 SILVER, 27.07 g**
**Obv. leg: PHILIPVS V DEI G and date**
**around crowned arms.**

| KM# | Date | Good | VG | Fine | VF |
|-----|------|------|-----|------|-----|
| 47 | 1701 L | 100.00 | 175.00 | 275.00 | 400.00 |
|  | 1702 L | 125.00 | 200.00 | 300.00 | 450.00 |
|  | 1703 L | 125.00 | 200.00 | 300.00 | 450.00 |
|  | 1704 L | 150.00 | 250.00 | 400.00 | 600.00 |
|  | 1706 L | 150.00 | 250.00 | 400.00 | 600.00 |
|  | 1707 L | 150.00 | 250.00 | 400.00 | 600.00 |
|  | 1707 J | 150.00 | 250.00 | 400.00 | 600.00 |
|  | 1708 J | 125.00 | 200.00 | 300.00 | 450.00 |
|  | 1709 J | 100.00 | 175.00 | 275.00 | 400.00 |
|  | 1710 J | 150.00 | 250.00 | 400.00 | 600.00 |
|  | 1711 J | 100.00 | 175.00 | 275.00 | 400.00 |
|  | 1712 J | 125.00 | 200.00 | 300.00 | 450.00 |

| KM# | Date | Good | VG | Fine | VF |
|-----|------|------|------|------|------|
| 47 | 1713 J | 60.00 | 100.00 | 165.00 | 250.00 |
|  | 1714 J | 60.00 | 100.00 | 165.00 | 250.00 |
|  | 1715 J | 100.00 | 175.00 | 275.00 | 400.00 |
|  | 1716 J | 100.00 | 175.00 | 275.00 | 400.00 |
|  | 1717 J | 100.00 | 175.00 | 275.00 | 400.00 |
|  | 1718 J | 100.00 | 175.00 | 275.00 | 400.00 |
|  | 1719 J | 100.00 | 175.00 | 275.00 | 400.00 |
|  | 1720 J | 100.00 | 175.00 | 275.00 | 400.00 |
|  | 1721 J | 125.00 | 200.00 | 300.00 | 450.00 |
|  | 1722 J | 100.00 | 175.00 | 275.00 | 400.00 |
|  | 1723 J | 125.00 | 200.00 | 300.00 | 450.00 |
|  | 1724 D | 125.00 | 200.00 | 300.00 | 450.00 |
|  | 1725 D | 180.00 | 350.00 | 500.00 | 900.00 |
|  | 1726 D | 180.00 | 350.00 | 500.00 | 900.00 |
|  | 1727 D | 180.00 | 350.00 | 500.00 | 900.00 |
|  | 1728 D | 200.00 | 400.00 | 600.00 | 1000. |
|  | Date off flan | 25.00 | 50.00 | 85.00 | 125.00 |

**.916 SILVER**

| KM# | Date | Good | VG | Fine | VF |
|-----|------|------|------|------|------|
| 47a | 1729 R | 75.00 | 150.00 | 250.00 | 375.00 |
|  | 1730 R | 75.00 | 150.00 | 250.00 | 375.00 |
|  | 1730 G | 100.00 | 175.00 | 275.00 | 400.00 |
|  | 1730 F | 75.00 | 150.00 | 250.00 | 375.00 |
|  | 1731/0 F | 250.00 | 450.00 | 650.00 | 1200. |
|  | 1731 F | 75.00 | 150.00 | 250.00 | 375.00 |
|  | 1732 F | 75.00 | 150.00 | 250.00 | 375.00 |
|  | 1733 F | 75.00 | 150.00 | 250.00 | 400.00 |
|  | Date off flan | 25.00 | 50.00 | 85.00 | 125.00 |

**(Klippe)**

**Similar to KM#47a.**

| KM# | Date | Good | VG | Fine | VF |
|-----|------|------|------|------|------|
| 48 | 1733 F | 150.00 | 250.00 | 375.00 | 600.00 |
|  | 1733 MF | 100.00 | 150.00 | 250.00 | 375.00 |
|  | 1734/3 MF | 100.00 | 175.00 | 275.00 | 400.00 |
|  | 1734 MF | 100.00 | 175.00 | 275.00 | 400.00 |
|  | Date off flan | 25.00 | 50.00 | 85.00 | 125.00 |

## 2 ESCUDOS

**6.7700 g, .917 GOLD, .1996 oz AGW**
**Mint mark: MXo**
**Obv. leg: CAROLVS II DEI G and date**
**around crowned arms.**
**Rev: Legend around cross.**

| KM# | Date | VG | Fine | VF | XF |
|---|---|---|---|---|---|
| 52 | 1701 L | 1400. | 1800. | 2200. | 2500. |
| | Date off flan | 800.00 | 1000. | 1200. | 1500. |

### ROYAL STRIKES

**Philip V**

Fully struck examples on round planchets, referred to as "Royal" strikes are seldom encountered and are considered rare.

### CIRCULATION STRIKES

**Obv. leg: PHILIPVS V DEI G and date**
**around crowned arms.**

| | | VG | Fine | VF | XF |
|---|---|---|---|---|---|
| 53.1 | 1704 L | 1200. | 1700. | 2000. | 2400. |
| | 1705 L | 1200. | 1700. | 2000. | 2400. |
| | 1707 L | 1200. | 1700. | 2000. | 2400. |
| | 1708 J | 1200. | 1700. | 2000. | 2400. |
| | 1709 J | 1200. | 1700. | 2000. | 2400. |
| | 1710 J | 1200. | 1700. | 2000. | 2400. |
| | 1711 J | 1200. | 1700. | 2000. | 2400. |
| | 1712 J | 1200. | 1700. | 2000. | 2400. |
| | 1713 J | 1200. | 1700. | 2000. | 2400. |
| | Date off flan | 800.00 | 1000. | 1200. | 1500. |

**Mint mark: Mo**

| | | VG | Fine | VF | XF |
|---|---|---|---|---|---|
| 53.2 | 1714 J | 1200. | 1700. | 2000. | 2400. |
| | 1717 J | — | — | Rare | — |
| | 1722 J | — | — | Rare | — |
| | 1723 J | — | — | Rare | — |
| | 1729 R | — | — | Rare | — |
| | 1731 F | — | — | Rare | — |
| | Date off flan | 800.00 | 1000. | 1200. | 1500. |

**Luis I**

| | | | | | |
|---|---|---|---|---|---|
| A54 | ND D | — | — | Rare | — |

---

**.931 SILVER, 27.07 g**
**Luis I**
**Obv. leg: LVDOVICVS I DEI G.**

| KM# | Date | Good | VG | Fine | VF |
|---|---|---|---|---|---|
| 49 | 1724 D | 1500. | 2000. | 2500. | 3000. |
| | 1725 D | 1500. | 2000. | 2500. | 3000. |
| | Date off flan | 400.00 | 600.00 | 1000. | 1500. |

## ESCUDO

### ROYAL STRIKES

**Philip V**

Fully struck examples on round planchets referred to as "Royal" strikes are seldom encountered and are considered rare.

### CIRCULATION STRIKES

**3.3800 g, .917 GOLD, .0997 oz AGW**
**Mint mark: MXo**
**Obv. leg: PHILIPVS V DEI G and date**
**around crowned arms.**

| KM# | Date | VG | Fine | VF | XF |
|---|---|---|---|---|---|
| 51.1 | 1702 L | 1100. | 1400. | 1700. | 2000. |
| | 1703 L | 1100. | 1400. | 1700. | 2000. |
| | 1704 L | 1100. | 1400. | 1700. | 2000. |
| | 1706 M | 1100. | 1400. | 1700. | 2000. |
| | 1707 L | 1100. | 1400. | 1700. | 2000. |
| | 1708 L | 1100. | 1400. | 1700. | 2000. |
| | 1709 J | 1100. | 1400. | 1700. | 2000. |
| | 1710 J | 1100. | 1400. | 1700. | 2000. |
| | 1711 J | 1100. | 1400. | 1700. | 2000. |
| | 1712 J | 1100. | 1400. | 1700. | 2000. |
| | Date off flan | 700.00 | 850.00 | 1000. | 1200. |

**Mint mark: Mo**

| KM# | Date | VG | Fine | VF | XF |
|---|---|---|---|---|---|
| 51.2 | 1713 J | 1100. | 1400. | 1700. | 2000. |
| | 1714 J | 1100. | 1400. | 1700. | 2000. |
| | Date off flan | 700.00 | 850.00 | 1000. | 1200. |

# 4 ESCUDOS
## ROYAL STRIKES

**Philip V**

Fully struck examples on round planchets, referred to as "Royal" strikes are seldom encountered and are considered rare.

## CIRCULATION STRIKES

**13.5400 g, .917 GOLD, .3992 oz AGW**
**Mint mark: MXo**
Obv. leg: PHILIPVS V DEI G and date
around crowned arms.
Rev: Legend around cross.

| KM# | Date | VG | Fine | VF | XF |
|---|---|---|---|---|---|
| 55.1 | 1701 L | 3000. | 3750. | 4500. | 5000. |
| | 1702 L | 3000. | 3750. | 4500. | 5000. |
| | 1703 L | 3000. | 3750. | 4500. | 5000. |
| | 1704 L | 3000. | 3750. | 4500. | 5000. |
| | 1705 L | 3000. | 3750. | 4500. | 5000. |
| | 1706 L | 3000. | 3750. | 4500. | 5000. |
| | 1707 L | 3000. | 3750. | 4500. | 5000. |
| | 1708 J | 3000. | 3750. | 4500. | 5000. |
| | 1709 J | 3000. | 3750. | 4500. | 5000. |
| | 1710 J | 3000. | 3750. | 4500. | 5000. |
| | 1711 J | 3000. | 3750. | 4500. | 5000. |
| | 1712 J | 3000. | 3750. | 4500. | 5000. |
| | 1713 J | 3000. | 3750. | 4500. | 5000. |
| | Date off flan | 2000. | 2500. | 3000. | 3500. |

**Mint mark: Mo**

| | | | | | |
|---|---|---|---|---|---|
| 55.2 | 1714 J | 3000. | 3750. | 4500. | 5000. |
| | 1720 J | — | — | Rare | — |
| | Date off flan | 2000. | 2500. | 3000. | 3500. |

# 8 ESCUDOS
## ROYAL STRIKES

**Philip V**

Fully struck examples on round planchets, referred to as "Royal" strikes are seldom encountered and are considered rare.

## CIRCULATION STRIKES

**27.0700 g, .917 GOLD, .7980 oz AGW**
**Mint mark: MXo**
Obv. leg: PHILIPVS V DEI G and date
around crowned arms.
Rev: Legend around cross.

| KM# | Date | VG | Fine | VF | XF |
|---|---|---|---|---|---|
| 57.1 | 1701 L | 4000. | 4750. | 5500. | 6000. |
| | 1702 L | 4000. | 4750. | 5500. | 6000. |
| | 1703 L | 4000. | 4750. | 5500. | 6000. |
| | 1704 L | 4000. | 4750. | 5500. | 6000. |
| | 1705 L | 4000. | 4750. | 5500. | 6000. |
| | 1706 L | 4000. | 4750. | 5500. | 6000. |
| | 1707 L | 4000. | 4750. | 5500. | 6000. |
| | 1708 J | 4000. | 4750. | 5500. | 6000. |
| | 1709 J | 4000. | 4750. | 5500. | 6000. |
| | 1710 J | 4000. | 4750. | 5500. | 6000. |
| | 1711 J | 4000. | 4750. | 5500. | 6000. |
| | 1712 J | 4000. | 4750. | 5500. | 6000. |
| | 1713 J | 4000. | 4750. | 5500. | 6000. |
| | Date off flan | 2500. | 3000. | 3500. | 4000. |

## ROYAL STRIKES

Fully struck examples on round planchets, referred to as "Royal" strikes are seldom encountered and are considered rare.

## CIRCULATION STRIKES

**Mint mark: Mo**

| KM# | Date | VG | Fine | VF | XF |
|---|---|---|---|---|---|
| 57.2 | 1714 J | 4500. | 5500. | 6500. | 8000. |
| | 1714 J date on rev. | | | | |
| | | 5000. | 6000. | 7000. | 9000. |
| | 1715 J | — | — | Rare | — |
| | 1717 J | — | — | Rare | — |
| | 1718 J | — | — | Rare | — |
| | 1720 J | — | — | Rare | — |
| | 1723 J | — | — | Rare | — |
| | 1728 D | — | — | Rare | — |
| | 1729 R | — | — | Rare | — |
| | 1730 R | — | — | Rare | — |
| | 1730 F | — | — | Rare | — |
| | 1731 F | — | — | Rare | — |
| | 1732 F | — | — | Rare | — |
| | Date off flan | 2500. | 3000. | 3500. | 4000. |

**Obv. leg: LVDOVICVS I DEI G and date around crowned arms.**
**Rev: Legend around cross.**

| | | | | | |
|---|---|---|---|---|---|
| 58 | 1725 D | — | — | Rare | — |
| | Date off flan | — | — | Rare | — |

# COLONIAL MILLED COINAGE

## RULERS

Philip V, 1700-1746
Ferdinand VI, 1746-1759
Charles III, 1760-1788
Charles IV, 1788-1808
Ferdinand VII, 1808-1821

## MINT MARKS

Mo - Mexico City Mint

## ASSAYERS INITIALS

| Letter | Date | Name |
|---|---|---|
| F | 1733-1784 | Francisco de la Pena |
| M | 1733-1763 | Manuel de la Pena |
| M | 1754-1770 | Manuel Assorin |
| F | 1762-1770 | Francisco de Rivera |
| M | 1770-1777 | Manuel de Rivera |
| F | 1777-1803 | Francisco Arance Cobos |
| M | 1784-1801 | Mariano Rodriguez |
| T | 1801-1810 | Tomas Butron Miranda |
| H | 1803-1814 | Henrique Buenaventura Azorin |
| J | 1809-1833 | Joaquin Davila Madrid |
| J | 1812-1833 | Jose Garcia Ansaldo |

## MONETARY SYSTEM

16 Pilones = 1 Real
8 Tlaco = 1 Real
16 Reales = 1 Escudo

## 1/8 (PILON)
(1/16 Real)

**COPPER**
**Obv: Crowned F VII monogram.**
**Rev: Castles and lions in wreath.**

| KM# | Date | VG | Fine | VF | XF |
|---|---|---|---|---|---|
| 59 | 1814 | 10.00 | 20.00 | 45.00 | 120.00 |
| | 1815 | 10.00 | 20.00 | 45.00 | 120.00 |

## 1/4 (TLACO)
(1/8 Real)

**COPPER**
**Obv. leg: FERDIN. VII. . around crowned F.VII.**

| KM# | Date | VG | Fine | VF | XF |
|---|---|---|---|---|---|
| 63 | 1814 | 12.00 | 25.00 | 50.00 | 150.00 |
| | 1815 | 12.00 | 25.00 | 50.00 | 150.00 |
| | 1816 | 12.00 | 25.00 | 50.00 | 150.00 |

## 2/4 (2 TLACO)
(1/4 Real)

**COPPER**
**Obv. leg: FERDIN. VII. . around crowned F.VII.**

| KM# | Date | VG | Fine | VF | XF |
|---|---|---|---|---|---|
| 64 | 1814 | 12.00 | 25.00 | 50.00 | 150.00 |
| | 1815/4 | 15.00 | 30.00 | 60.00 | 165.00 |
| | 1815 | 12.00 | 25.00 | 50.00 | 150.00 |
| | 1816 | 12.00 | 25.00 | 50.00 | 150.00 |
| | 1821 | 20.00 | 40.00 | 75.00 | 200.00 |

## 1/4 REAL

**.8450 g, .903 SILVER, .0245 oz ASW**
**Obv: Castle. Rev: Lion.**

| KM# | Date | VG | Fine | VF | XF |
|---|---|---|---|---|---|
| 62 | 1796 | 15.00 | 30.00 | 55.00 | 90.00 |
| | 1797 | 15.00 | 30.00 | 55.00 | 90.00 |
| | 1798 | 12.50 | 22.00 | 50.00 | 75.00 |
| | 1799/8 | 12.50 | 22.00 | 50.00 | 75.00 |
| | 1799 | 10.00 | 20.00 | 40.00 | 70.00 |
| | 1800 | 10.00 | 25.00 | 55.00 | 90.00 |
| | 1801 | 10.00 | 20.00 | 40.00 | 70.00 |
| | 1802 | 10.00 | 20.00 | 40.00 | 70.00 |
| | 1803 | 10.00 | 20.00 | 40.00 | 70.00 |
| | 1804 | 10.00 | 20.00 | 40.00 | 75.00 |
| | 1805/4 | 12.50 | 25.00 | 55.00 | 85.00 |
| | 1805 | 10.00 | 22.00 | 50.00 | 75.00 |
| | 1806 | 10.00 | 22.00 | 50.00 | 80.00 |
| | 1807/797 | 15.00 | 30.00 | 55.00 | 85.00 |
| | 1807 | 12.50 | 25.00 | 50.00 | 80.00 |
| | 1808 | 12.50 | 25.00 | 50.00 | 80.00 |
| | 1809/8 | 12.50 | 25.00 | 50.00 | 80.00 |
| | 1809 | 12.50 | 25.00 | 50.00 | 80.00 |
| | 1810 | 12.50 | 25.00 | 50.00 | 75.00 |
| | 1811 | 12.50 | 25.00 | 50.00 | 75.00 |
| | 1812 | 12.50 | 25.00 | 50.00 | 75.00 |
| | 1813 | 10.00 | 20.00 | 40.00 | 70.00 |
| | 1815 | 12.50 | 22.00 | 50.00 | 75.00 |
| | 1816 | 10.00 | 20.00 | 40.00 | 70.00 |

**NOTE:** Earlier dates (1796-1800) exist for this type.

# 1/2 REAL

**1.6900 g, .917 SILVER, .0498 oz ASW**
**Obv. leg: PHILIP.V.D.G. HISPAN.ET IND. REX.**

| KM# | Date | VG | Fine | VF | XF |
|-----|------|-----|------|-----|-----|
| 65 | 1732 | — | — | Rare | — |
| | 1732 F | 500.00 | 800.00 | 1200. | 2000. |
| | 1733 F(MX) | 375.00 | 600.00 | 1000. | 1500. |
| | 1733 MF(MX) | | | | |
| | | 400.00 | 600.00 | 1000. | 1500. |
| | 1733 F | 200.00 | 325.00 | 550.00 | 800.00 |
| | 1733 MF | 300.00 | 400.00 | 600.00 | 800.00 |
| | 1734/3 MF | 12.00 | 25.00 | 45.00 | 85.00 |
| | 1734 MF | 12.00 | 25.00 | 45.00 | 85.00 |
| | 1735/4 MF | 10.00 | 20.00 | 45.00 | 85.00 |
| | 1735 MF | 10.00 | 20.00 | 45.00 | 85.00 |
| | 1736/5 MF | 10.00 | 20.00 | 45.00 | 85.00 |
| | 1736 MF | 10.00 | 20.00 | 45.00 | 85.00 |
| | 1737/6 MF | 10.00 | 20.00 | 45.00 | 85.00 |
| | 1737 MF | 10.00 | 20.00 | 45.00 | 85.00 |
| | 1738/7 MF | 10.00 | 20.00 | 45.00 | 85.00 |
| | 1738 MF | 10.00 | 20.00 | 45.00 | 85.00 |
| | 1739 MF | 10.00 | 20.00 | 45.00 | 85.00 |
| | 1740/30MF | 8.00 | 18.00 | 40.00 | 75.00 |
| | 1740/39MF | 8.00 | 18.00 | 40.00 | 75.00 |
| | 1740 MF | 8.00 | 18.00 | 40.00 | 75.00 |
| | 1741/39MF | 8.00 | 18.00 | 40.00 | 75.00 |
| | 1741/0MF | 8.00 | 18.00 | 40.00 | 75.00 |
| | 1741 MF | 8.00 | 18.00 | 40.00 | 75.00 |

**Obv. leg:.PHS.V.D.G. HISP.ET IND.R.**

| KM# | Date | VG | Fine | VF | XF |
|-----|------|-----|------|-----|-----|
| 66 | 1742 M | 8.00 | 18.00 | 40.00 | 75.00 |
| | 1743 M | 8.00 | 18.00 | 40.00 | 75.00 |
| | 1744/3 M | 8.00 | 18.00 | 40.00 | 75.00 |
| | 1744 M | 8.00 | 18.00 | 40.00 | 75.00 |
| | 1745 M | 8.00 | 18.00 | 40.00 | 75.00 |
| | 1746 M | 8.00 | 18.00 | 40.00 | 75.00 |
| | 1747 M | 8.00 | 18.00 | 40.00 | 75.00 |

**Obv. leg: FRD.VI.D.G.HISP.ET IND.R.**

| KM# | Date | VG | Fine | VF | XF |
|-----|------|-----|------|-----|-----|
| 67 | 1747/6 M | — | — | — | — |
| | 1747 M | 8.00 | 18.00 | 40.00 | 75.00 |
| | 1748/7 M | 8.00 | 18.00 | 40.00 | 75.00 |
| | 1748 M | 8.00 | 18.00 | 40.00 | 75.00 |
| | 1749 M | 8.00 | 18.00 | 40.00 | 75.00 |
| | 1750 M | 8.00 | 18.00 | 40.00 | 75.00 |
| | 1751 M | 10.00 | 20.00 | 45.00 | 85.00 |
| | 1752 M | 8.00 | 18.00 | 40.00 | 75.00 |
| | 1753 M | 8.00 | 18.00 | 40.00 | 75.00 |
| | 1754 M | 12.00 | 25.00 | 55.00 | 100.00 |
| | 1755/6 M | 12.00 | 25.00 | 55.00 | 100.00 |
| | 1755 M | 8.00 | 18.00 | 40.00 | 75.00 |
| | 1756/5 M | 8.00 | 18.00 | 40.00 | 75.00 |
| | 1756 M | 8.00 | 18.00 | 40.00 | 75.00 |
| | 1757/6 M | 8.00 | 18.00 | 40.00 | 75.00 |
| | 1757 M | 8.00 | 18.00 | 40.00 | 75.00 |
| | 1758/7 M | 8.00 | 18.00 | 40.00 | 75.00 |
| | 1758 M | 8.00 | 18.00 | 40.00 | 75.00 |
| | 1759 M | 8.00 | 18.00 | 40.00 | 75.00 |
| | 1760 M | 10.00 | 20.00 | 45.00 | 85.00 |

**Obv. leg: CAR.III.D.G.HISP.ET IND.R.**

| KM# | Date | VG | Fine | VF | XF |
|-----|------|-----|------|-----|-----|
| 68 | 1760 M | 8.00 | 18.00 | 40.00 | 75.00 |
| | 1761 M | 8.00 | 18.00 | 40.00 | 75.00 |
| | 1762 M | 8.00 | 18.00 | 40.00 | 75.00 |
| | 1763/2 M | 8.00 | 18.00 | 40.00 | 75.00 |
| | 1763 M | 8.00 | 18.00 | 40.00 | 75.00 |
| | 1764 M | 8.00 | 18.00 | 40.00 | 75.00 |
| | 1765 M | 8.00 | 18.00 | 40.00 | 75.00 |
| | 1766 M | 8.00 | 18.00 | 40.00 | 75.00 |
| | 1767 M | 10.00 | 20.00 | 45.00 | 85.00 |
| | 1768/6 M | 10.00 | 20.00 | 42.00 | 80.00 |
| | 1768 M | 8.00 | 18.00 | 40.00 | 75.00 |
| | 1769 M | 10.00 | 20.00 | 42.00 | 80.00 |
| | 1770 M | 10.00 | 20.00 | 42.00 | 80.00 |
| | 1770 F | 15.00 | 30.00 | 60.00 | 100.00 |
| | 1771 F | 10.00 | 20.00 | 42.00 | 80.00 |

**1.6900 g, .903 SILVER, .0490 oz ASW**
**Obv. leg: CAROLUS.III.DEI.GRATIA.**
**Rev: Inverted FM and mint mark.**

| KM# | Date | VG | Fine | VF | XF |
|-----|------|-----|------|-----|-----|
| 69.1 | 1772 FM | 5.00 | 12.00 | 27.00 | 65.00 |
| | 1773 FM | 4.50 | 10.00 | 25.00 | 55.00 |

**Rev: Normal initials and mint mark.**

| KM# | Date | VG | Fine | VF | XF |
|-----|------|-----|------|-----|-----|
| 69.2 | 1772 FM | 9.00 | 18.00 | 35.00 | 80.00 |
| | 1773 FM | 4.50 | 10.00 | 25.00 | 60.00 |
| | 1773 FM CAROLS (error) | | | | |
| | | 300.00 | — | — | — |
| | 1774 FM | 4.50 | 10.00 | 25.00 | 55.00 |
| | 1775 FM | 4.50 | 10.00 | 25.00 | 55.00 |
| | 1776 FM | 4.50 | 10.00 | 25.00 | 55.00 |
| | 1777/6 FM | 10.00 | 18.00 | 35.00 | 75.00 |
| | 1777 FM | 7.00 | 15.00 | 30.00 | 65.00 |
| | 1778 FF | 4.50 | 10.00 | 25.00 | 55.00 |
| | 1779 FF | 4.50 | 10.00 | 25.00 | 55.00 |
| | 1780/79 FF | 6.00 | 12.50 | 30.00 | 75.00 |
| | 1780/g FF | 4.50 | 10.00 | 25.00 | 55.00 |
| | 1780 FF | 4.50 | 10.00 | 25.00 | 55.00 |
| | 1781 FF | 4.50 | 10.00 | 25.00 | 55.00 |
| | 1782/1 FF | 6.00 | 12.50 | 30.00 | 75.00 |
| | 1782 FF | 4.50 | 10.00 | 25.00 | 55.00 |
| | 1783 FF | 4.50 | 10.00 | 25.00 | 55.00 |
| | 1783 FM | 125.00 | 300.00 | 450.00 | — |
| | 1784 FF | 4.50 | 10.00 | 25.00 | 55.00 |
| | 1784 FM | 7.00 | 15.00 | 35.00 | 80.00 |
| | 1785 FM | 5.00 | 12.00 | 27.00 | 60.00 |
| | 1786 FM | 4.50 | 10.00 | 25.00 | 55.00 |
| | 1787 FM | 4.50 | 10.00 | 25.00 | 55.00 |
| | 1788 FM | 4.50 | 10.00 | 25.00 | 55.00 |
| | 1789 FM | 8.00 | 16.00 | 40.00 | 100.00 |

**Obv. leg: .CAROLUS.IV. . ., armored bust**
**of Charles III.**

| KM# | Date | VG | Fine | VF | XF |
|-----|------|-----|------|-----|-----|
| 70 | 1789 FM | 12.00 | 25.00 | 50.00 | 100.00 |
| | 1790 FM | 12.00 | 25.00 | 50.00 | 100.00 |

**Obv: Armored bust of Charles III, leg: .CAROLUS.IIII.**

| KM# | Date | VG | Fine | VF | XF |
|-----|------|-----|------|-----|-----|
| 71 | 1790 FM | 12.00 | 25.00 | 50.00 | 100.00 |

## 1/2 REAL

**Obv: Armored bust of Charles IIII.**
**Rev: Pillars and arms.**

| KM# | Date | VG | Fine | VF | XF |
|-----|------|-----|------|-----|-----|
| 72 | 1792 FM | 6.00 | 12.00 | 25.00 | 50.00 |
| | 1793 FM | 6.00 | 12.00 | 25.00 | 50.00 |
| | 1794/3 FM | 7.50 | 15.00 | 30.00 | 75.00 |
| | 1794 FM | 5.00 | 10.00 | 22.00 | 45.00 |
| | 1795 FM | 4.00 | 10.00 | 22.00 | 45.00 |
| | 1796 FM | 4.00 | 10.00 | 22.00 | 45.00 |
| | 1797 FM | 4.00 | 10.00 | 22.00 | 45.00 |
| | 1798/7 FM | 5.00 | 11.50 | 25.00 | 50.00 |
| | 1798 FM | 4.00 | 10.00 | 22.00 | 45.00 |
| | 1799 FM | 4.00 | 10.00 | 22.00 | 45.00 |
| | 1800/799 FM | 5.00 | 11.50 | 25.00 | 50.00 |
| | 1800 FM | 4.00 | 10.00 | 22.00 | 45.00 |
| | 1800 FT | — | — | — | — |
| | 1801 FM | 7.50 | 15.00 | 30.00 | 80.00 |
| | 1801 FT | 4.00 | 10.00 | 22.00 | 45.00 |
| | 1802 FT | 4.00 | 10.00 | 22.00 | 45.00 |
| | 1803 FT | 5.00 | 11.50 | 25.00 | 50.00 |
| | 1804 TH | 4.00 | 10.00 | 22.00 | 45.00 |
| | 1805 TH | 4.00 | 10.00 | 22.00 | 45.00 |
| | 1806 TH | 4.00 | 10.00 | 22.00 | 45.00 |
| | 1807/6 TH | 5.00 | 11.50 | 25.00 | 50.00 |
| | 1807 TH | 4.00 | 10.00 | 22.00 | 45.00 |
| | 1808/7 TH | 5.00 | 11.50 | 25.00 | 50.00 |
| | 1808 TH | 4.00 | 10.00 | 22.00 | 45.00 |

**Obv: Armored bust of Ferdinand VII.**

| | Date | VG | Fine | VF | XF |
|-----|------|-----|------|-----|-----|
| 73 | 1808 TH | 3.50 | 8.00 | 20.00 | 35.00 |
| | 1809 TH | 3.50 | 8.00 | 20.00 | 35.00 |
| | 1810 TH | 5.00 | 10.00 | 22.00 | 45.00 |
| | 1810 HJ | 3.50 | 8.00 | 20.00 | 35.00 |
| | 1811 HJ | 3.50 | 8.00 | 20.00 | 35.00 |
| | 1812 HJ | 3.50 | 8.00 | 20.00 | 35.00 |
| | 1812 JJ | 12.00 | 25.00 | 45.00 | 100.00 |
| | 1813 TH | 3.50 | 8.00 | 20.00 | 35.00 |
| | 1813 JJ | 6.00 | 12.00 | 25.00 | 75.00 |
| | 1813 HJ | 7.50 | 15.00 | 35.00 | 90.00 |
| | 1814 JJ | 5.00 | 10.00 | 22.00 | 45.00 |

**Obv: Draped bust of Ferdinand VII.**

| | Date | VG | Fine | VF | XF |
|-----|------|-----|------|-----|-----|
| 74 | 1814 JJ | 3.50 | 8.00 | 22.00 | 45.00 |
| | 1815 JJ | 3.50 | 8.00 | 20.00 | 40.00 |
| | 1816 JJ | 3.50 | 8.00 | 20.00 | 40.00 |
| | 1817/6 JJ | — | — | — | — |
| | 1817 JJ | 3.50 | 8.00 | 22.00 | 45.00 |
| | 1818/7 JJ | 3.50 | 8.00 | 25.00 | 50.00 |
| | 1818 JJ | 3.50 | 8.00 | 25.00 | 50.00 |
| | 1819 JJ | 3.50 | 8.00 | 20.00 | 40.00 |
| | 1820 JJ | 3.50 | 8.00 | 25.00 | 50.00 |
| | 1821 JJ | 3.50 | 8.00 | 20.00 | 40.00 |

## REAL

**3.3800 g, .917 SILVER, .0996 oz ASW**
**Obv. leg: PHILIP.V.D.G.HISPAN.ET IND.REX.**

| KM# | Date | VG | Fine | VF | XF |
|-----|------|-----|------|-----|-----|
| 75.1 | 1732 | — | — | Rare | — |
| | 1732 F | 125.00 | 225.00 | 350.00 | 550.00 |
| | 1733 F(MX) | 150.00 | 350.00 | 425.00 | 750.00 |
| | 1733/2 MF(MX) | | | | |
| | | 150.00 | 350.00 | 425.00 | 750.00 |
| | 1733 MF(MX) | | | | |
| | | 150.00 | 350.00 | 425.00 | 750.00 |
| | 1733 F | — | — | Rare | — |
| | 1733 MF | 100.00 | 200.00 | 300.00 | 500.00 |
| | 1734/3 MF | 15.00 | 30.00 | 65.00 | 150.00 |
| | 1734 MF | 12.00 | 25.00 | 60.00 | 140.00 |
| | 1735 MF | 12.00 | 25.00 | 60.00 | 140.00 |
| | 1736 MF | 12.00 | 25.00 | 60.00 | 140.00 |
| | 1737 MF | 12.00 | 25.00 | 60.00 | 140.00 |
| | 1738 MF | 12.00 | 25.00 | 60.00 | 140.00 |
| | 1739 MF | 12.00 | 25.00 | 60.00 | 140.00 |
| | 1740 MF | 12.00 | 25.00 | 60.00 | 140.00 |
| | 1741 MF | 12.00 | 25.00 | 60.00 | 140.00 |

**Obv. leg: PHS.V.D.G.HISP.ET.IND.R.**

| | Date | VG | Fine | VF | XF |
|-----|------|-----|------|-----|-----|
| 75.2 | 1742 M | 10.00 | 20.00 | 50.00 | 120.00 |
| | 1743 M | 10.00 | 20.00 | 50.00 | 120.00 |
| | 1744/3 M | 10.00 | 20.00 | 50.00 | 120.00 |
| | 1744 M | 10.00 | 20.00 | 50.00 | 120.00 |
| | 1745 M | 8.00 | 18.00 | 50.00 | 120.00 |
| | 1746/5 M | 12.00 | 25.00 | 75.00 | 200.00 |
| | 1746 M | 10.00 | 20.00 | 55.00 | 125.00 |
| | 1747 M | 10.00 | 20.00 | 55.00 | 125.00 |

**Obv. leg: .FRD.VI.D.G.HISP.ET IND.R.**

| | Date | VG | Fine | VF | XF |
|-----|------|-----|------|-----|-----|
| 76 | 1747 M | 10.00 | 20.00 | 50.00 | 100.00 |
| | 1748/7 M | 10.00 | 20.00 | 50.00 | 100.00 |
| | 1748 M | 10.00 | 20.00 | 50.00 | 100.00 |
| | 1749/8 M | 10.00 | 20.00 | 50.00 | 100.00 |
| | 1749 M | 10.00 | 20.00 | 50.00 | 100.00 |
| | 1750/49 M | 10.00 | 20.00 | 50.00 | 100.00 |
| | 1750 M | 10.00 | 20.00 | 50.00 | 100.00 |
| | 1751 M | 10.00 | 20.00 | 55.00 | 110.00 |
| | 1752 M | 10.00 | 20.00 | 50.00 | 100.00 |
| | 1753 M | 10.00 | 20.00 | 50.00 | 100.00 |
| | 1754 M | 10.00 | 20.00 | 55.00 | 110.00 |
| | 1755/4 M | 10.00 | 20.00 | 50.00 | 100.00 |
| | 1755 M | 10.00 | 20.00 | 50.00 | 100.00 |
| | 1756 M | 10.00 | 20.00 | 55.00 | 110.00 |
| | 1757 M | 10.00 | 20.00 | 55.00 | 110.00 |
| | 1758/5 M | 10.00 | 20.00 | 50.00 | 100.00 |
| | 1758 M | 10.00 | 20.00 | 50.00 | 100.00 |
| | 1759 M | 10.00 | 20.00 | 55.00 | 110.00 |
| | 1760 M | 10.00 | 20.00 | 55.00 | 110.00 |

**Obv. leg: CAR.III.D.G.HISP.ET IND.R.**

| KM# | Date | VG | Fine | VF | XF |
|---|---|---|---|---|---|
| 77 | 1760 M | 20.00 | 40.00 | 90.00 | 250.00 |
| | 1761/O M | 10.00 | 20.00 | 55.00 | 125.00 |
| | 1761 M | 10.00 | 20.00 | 50.00 | 100.00 |
| | 1761/2 M | 10.00 | 20.00 | 50.00 | 100.00 |
| | 1762 M | 10.00 | 20.00 | 50.00 | 100.00 |
| | 1763/2 M | 12.00 | 25.00 | 60.00 | 120.00 |
| | 1763 M | 10.00 | 20.00 | 50.00 | 100.00 |
| | 1764 M | 10.00 | 20.00 | 55.00 | 110.00 |
| | 1765 M | 10.00 | 20.00 | 55.00 | 110.00 |
| | 1766 M | 10.00 | 20.00 | 50.00 | 100.00 |
| | 1767 M | 10.00 | 20.00 | 55.00 | 110.00 |
| | 1768 M | 10.00 | 20.00 | 50.00 | 100.00 |
| | 1769 M | 10.00 | 20.00 | 50.00 | 100.00 |
| | 1770/69M | 10.00 | 20.00 | 55.00 | 125.00 |
| | 1770 M | 10.00 | 20.00 | 55.00 | 125.00 |
| | 1770 F | 20.00 | 40.00 | 90.00 | 250.00 |
| | 1771 F | 20.00 | 40.00 | 90.00 | 250.00 |

**3.3800 g, .903 SILVER, .0981 oz ASW**
**Obv. leg: CAROLUS.III.DEI.GRATIA.**
**Rev: Inverted FM and mint mark.**

| | | | | | |
|---|---|---|---|---|---|
| 78.1 | 1772 FM | 5.00 | 10.00 | 25.00 | 60.00 |
| | 1773 FM | 5.00 | 10.00 | 25.00 | 60.00 |

**Rev: Normal initials and mint mark.**

| | | | | | |
|---|---|---|---|---|---|
| 78.2 | 1773 FM | 6.50 | 12.50 | 32.00 | 90.00 |
| | 1774 FM | 5.00 | 10.00 | 25.00 | 60.00 |
| | 1775/4 FM | 6.00 | 12.00 | 28.00 | 75.00 |
| | 1775 FM | 5.00 | 10.00 | 25.00 | 60.00 |
| | 1776 FM | 5.00 | 10.00 | 25.00 | 60.00 |
| | 1777 FM | 5.00 | 10.00 | 25.00 | 60.00 |
| | 1778 FF | 5.00 | 10.00 | 25.00 | 60.00 |
| | 1779 FF | 5.00 | 10.00 | 25.00 | 60.00 |
| | 1780 FF | 5.00 | 10.00 | 25.00 | 60.00 |
| | 1780 F F/M | 5.00 | 10.00 | 25.00 | 60.00 |
| | 1781 FF | 5.00 | 10.00 | 25.00 | 60.00 |
| | 1782 FF | 5.00 | 10.00 | 25.00 | 60.00 |
| | 1783 FF | 5.00 | 10.00 | 25.00 | 60.00 |
| | 1784 FF | 5.00 | 10.00 | 25.00 | 60.00 |
| | 1785 FM | 5.00 | 10.00 | 25.00 | 60.00 |
| | 1785 FF | 5.00 | 10.00 | 25.00 | 60.00 |
| | 1786 FM | 5.00 | 10.00 | 25.00 | 60.00 |
| | 1787 FM | 12.00 | 25.00 | 50.00 | 100.00 |
| | 1787 FF | 15.00 | 30.00 | 60.00 | 125.00 |
| | 1788 FM | 5.00 | 10.00 | 25.00 | 60.00 |
| | 1788 FF | 50.00 | 100.00 | 200.00 | — |
| | 1789 FM | 6.00 | 12.00 | 28.00 | 75.00 |

**Obv. leg: CAROLUS.IV. . ., armored bust**
**of Charles III.**

| | | | | | |
|---|---|---|---|---|---|
| 79 | 1789 FM | 15.00 | 30.00 | 60.00 | 150.00 |
| | 1790 FM | 15.00 | 30.00 | 60.00 | 150.00 |

**Obv. leg: CAROLUS.IIII, armored bust of Charles III.**

| | | | | | |
|---|---|---|---|---|---|
| 80 | 1790 FM | 17.00 | 35.00 | 70.00 | 165.00 |

**3.3800 g, .903 SILVER, .0981 oz ASW**
**Obv: Armored bust of Charles IIII.**

| KM# | Date | VG | Fine | VF | XF |
|---|---|---|---|---|---|
| 81 | 1792 FM | 10.00 | 20.00 | 35.00 | 90.00 |
| | 1793 FM | 15.00 | 30.00 | 60.00 | 150.00 |
| | 1794 FM | 25.00 | 50.00 | 100.00 | 250.00 |
| | 1795 FM | 15.00 | 30.00 | 60.00 | 150.00 |
| | 1796 FM | 5.00 | 10.00 | 25.00 | 65.00 |
| | 1797/6 FM | 8.00 | 15.00 | 28.00 | 80.00 |
| | 1797 FM | 5.00 | 10.00 | 25.00 | 60.00 |
| | 1798/7 FM | 5.00 | 10.00 | 25.00 | 65.00 |
| | 1798 FM | 5.00 | 10.00 | 25.00 | 60.00 |
| | 1799 FM | 5.00 | 10.00 | 25.00 | 60.00 |
| | 1800 FM | 5.00 | 10.00 | 25.00 | 60.00 |
| | 1801 FM | 8.00 | 15.00 | 28.00 | 80.00 |
| | 1801 FT | 5.00 | 10.00 | 25.00 | 60.00 |
| | 1802 FM | 5.00 | 10.00 | 25.00 | 60.00 |
| | 1802 FT | 5.00 | 10.00 | 25.00 | 60.00 |
| | 1803 FT | 5.00 | 10.00 | 25.00 | 60.00 |
| | 1804 TH | 5.00 | 10.00 | 25.00 | 60.00 |
| | 1805 TH | 5.00 | 10.00 | 25.00 | 60.00 |
| | 1806 TH | 5.00 | 10.00 | 25.00 | 60.00 |
| | 1807/6 TH | 5.00 | 10.00 | 25.00 | 65.00 |
| | 1807 TH | 5.00 | 10.00 | 25.00 | 60.00 |
| | 1808/7 TH | 5.00 | 10.00 | 25.00 | 65.00 |
| | 1808 TH | 5.00 | 10.00 | 25.00 | 60.00 |

**Obv: Armored bust of Ferdinand VII.**

| | | | | | |
|---|---|---|---|---|---|
| 82 | 1809 TH | 8.00 | 15.00 | 28.00 | 90.00 |
| | 1810/09 TH | 8.00 | 15.00 | 28.00 | 90.00 |
| | 1810 TH | 8.00 | 15.00 | 28.00 | 90.00 |
| | 1810 HJ | 10.00 | 20.00 | 40.00 | 120.00 |
| | 1811 HJ | 8.00 | 15.00 | 28.00 | 90.00 |
| | 1811 TH | 25.00 | 35.00 | 60.00 | 250.00 |
| | 1812 HJ | 4.00 | 9.00 | 28.00 | 80.00 |
| | 1812 JJ | 10.00 | 20.00 | 40.00 | 120.00 |
| | 1813 HJ | 10.00 | 20.00 | 40.00 | 120.00 |
| | 1813 JJ | 50.00 | 100.00 | 150.00 | 250.00 |
| | 1814 HJ | 50.00 | 100.00 | 175.00 | 300.00 |
| | 1814 JJ | 50.00 | 100.00 | 175.00 | 300.00 |

**Obv: Draped bust of Ferdinand VII.**

| | | | | | |
|---|---|---|---|---|---|
| 83 | 1814 JJ | 25.00 | 50.00 | 100.00 | 350.00 |
| | 1815 JJ | 10.00 | 20.00 | 40.00 | 120.00 |
| | 1815 HJ | 15.00 | 30.00 | 60.00 | 150.00 |
| | 1816 JJ | 5.00 | 10.00 | 25.00 | 70.00 |
| | 1817 JJ | 5.00 | 10.00 | 25.00 | 70.00 |
| | 1818 JJ | 30.00 | 60.00 | 125.00 | 500.00 |
| | 1819 JJ | 5.00 | 10.00 | 25.00 | 70.00 |
| | 1820 JJ | 5.00 | 10.00 | 25.00 | 70.00 |
| | 1821/0 JJ | 8.00 | 15.00 | 30.00 | 110.00 |
| | 1821 JJ | 5.00 | 10.00 | 25.00 | 50.00 |

# 2 REALES

**6.7700 g, .917 SILVER, .1996 oz ASW**
**Obv. leg: PHILIP.V.D.G.HISPAN.ET IND. REX.**

| KM# | Date | VG | Fine | VF | XF |
|---|---|---|---|---|---|
| 84 | 1732 | — | — | Rare | — |
| | 1732 F | 800.00 | 1300. | 1750. | 2750. |
| | 1733 F(MX) | 600.00 | 900.00 | 1500. | 2500. |
| | 1733 F | 600.00 | 800.00 | 1350. | 2250. |
| | 1733 MF(MX) | | | | |
| | | 350.00 | 600.00 | 1000. | 1650. |
| | 1733 MF | 600.00 | 900.00 | 1500. | 2500. |
| | 1734/3 MF | 20.00 | 40.00 | 85.00 | 170.00 |
| | 1734 MF | 20.00 | 40.00 | 85.00 | 170.00 |
| | 1735/3 MF | 15.00 | 30.00 | 75.00 | 150.00 |
| | 1735/4 MF | 15.00 | 30.00 | 75.00 | 150.00 |
| | 1735 MF | 15.00 | 30.00 | 75.00 | 150.00 |
| | 1736/3 MF | 18.00 | 35.00 | 80.00 | 160.00 |
| | 1736/4 MF | 18.00 | 35.00 | 80.00 | 160.00 |
| | 1736/5 MF | 18.00 | 35.00 | 80.00 | 160.00 |
| | 1736 MF | 18.00 | 35.00 | 80.00 | 160.00 |
| | 1737/3 MF | 18.00 | 35.00 | 80.00 | 160.00 |
| | 1737 MF | 18.00 | 35.00 | 80.00 | 160.00 |
| | 1738/7 MF | 18.00 | 35.00 | 80.00 | 160.00 |
| | 1738 MF | 18.00 | 35.00 | 80.00 | 160.00 |
| | 1739 MF | 18.00 | 35.00 | 80.00 | 160.00 |
| | 1740/30 MF | 18.00 | 35.00 | 80.00 | 160.00 |
| | 1740 MF | 18.00 | 35.00 | 80.00 | 160.00 |
| | 1741 MF | 18.00 | 35.00 | 80.00 | 160.00 |

**Obv. leg: PHS.V.D.G.HISP.ET IND.R.**

| KM# | Date | VG | Fine | VF | XF |
|---|---|---|---|---|---|
| 85 | 1742 M | 15.00 | 30.00 | 75.00 | 125.00 |
| | 1743/2 M | 15.00 | 30.00 | 75.00 | 125.00 |
| | 1743 M | 15.00 | 30.00 | 75.00 | 125.00 |
| | 1744/2 M | 15.00 | 30.00 | 75.00 | 125.00 |
| | 1744/3 M | 15.00 | 30.00 | 75.00 | 125.00 |
| | 1744 M | 15.00 | 30.00 | 75.00 | 125.00 |
| | 1745/4 M | 15.00 | 30.00 | 75.00 | 125.00 |
| | 1745 M | 15.00 | 30.00 | 75.00 | 125.00 |
| | 1745 M HIP | 300.00 | 500.00 | — | — |
| | 1746/5 M | 15.00 | 30.00 | 75.00 | 125.00 |
| | 1746 M | 15.00 | 30.00 | 75.00 | 125.00 |
| | 1747 M | 15.00 | 30.00 | 75.00 | 125.00 |
| | 1749 M | 250.00 | 450.00 | 650.00 | 1000. |
| | 1750 M | 250.00 | 450.00 | 650.00 | 1000. |

**Obv. leg: FRD.VI.D.G.HISP.ET IND.R.**

| KM# | Date | VG | Fine | VF | XF |
|---|---|---|---|---|---|
| 86 | 1747 M | 16.00 | 32.00 | 78.00 | 135.00 |

| KM# | Date | VG | Fine | VF | XF |
|---|---|---|---|---|---|
| 86 | 1748/7 M | 16.00 | 32.00 | 78.00 | 135.00 |
| | 1748 M | 15.00 | 30.00 | 75.00 | 125.00 |
| | 1749 M | 15.00 | 30.00 | 75.00 | 125.00 |
| | 1750 M | 15.00 | 30.00 | 75.00 | 125.00 |
| | 1751/41 M | 18.00 | 35.00 | 80.00 | 150.00 |
| | 1751 M | 15.00 | 30.00 | 75.00 | 125.00 |
| | 1752 M | 15.00 | 30.00 | 75.00 | 125.00 |
| | 1753/2 M | 18.00 | 35.00 | 80.00 | 150.00 |
| | 1753 M | 18.00 | 35.00 | 80.00 | 150.00 |
| | 1754 M | 18.00 | 35.00 | 80.00 | 150.00 |
| | 1755 M | 18.00 | 35.00 | 80.00 | 150.00 |
| | 1756 M | 18.00 | 35.00 | 80.00 | 150.00 |
| | 1757/6 M | 15.00 | 30.00 | 75.00 | 125.00 |
| | 1757 M | 15.00 | 30.00 | 75.00 | 125.00 |
| | 1758 M | 15.00 | 30.00 | 75.00 | 125.00 |
| | 1759/8 M | 15.00 | 30.00 | 75.00 | 125.00 |
| | 1759 M | 20.00 | 40.00 | 90.00 | 175.00 |
| | 1760 M | 20.00 | 40.00 | 90.00 | 175.00 |

**Obv. leg: CAR.III.D.G.HISP.ET IND.R.**

| KM# | Date | VG | Fine | VF | XF |
|---|---|---|---|---|---|
| 87 | 1760 M | 15.00 | 30.00 | 75.00 | 125.00 |
| | 1761 M | 15.00 | 30.00 | 75.00 | 125.00 |
| | 1762 M | 15.00 | 30.00 | 75.00 | 125.00 |
| | 1763/2 M | 15.00 | 30.00 | 75.00 | 125.00 |
| | 1763 M | 15.00 | 30.00 | 75.00 | 125.00 |
| | 1764 M | 15.00 | 30.00 | 75.00 | 125.00 |
| | 1765 M | 15.00 | 30.00 | 75.00 | 125.00 |
| | 1766 M | 18.00 | 35.00 | 80.00 | 160.00 |
| | 1767 M | 15.00 | 30.00 | 75.00 | 125.00 |
| | 1768/6 M | 15.00 | 30.00 | 75.00 | 125.00 |
| | 1768 M | 15.00 | 30.00 | 75.00 | 125.00 |
| | 1769 M | 15.00 | 30.00 | 75.00 | 125.00 |
| | 1770 M | 350.00 | 550.00 | — | — |
| | 1770 F | — | — | Rare | — |
| | 1771 F | 15.00 | 30.00 | 75.00 | 125.00 |

**6.7700 g, .903 SILVER, .1965 oz ASW**
**Obv. leg: CAROLUS.III.DEI.GRATIA.**
**Rev: Inverted FM and mint mark.**

| KM# | Date | VG | Fine | VF | XF |
|---|---|---|---|---|---|
| 88.1 | 1772 FM | 7.00 | 15.00 | 30.00 | 100.00 |
| | 1773 FM | 7.00 | 15.00 | 30.00 | 100.00 |

**Rev: Normal initials and mint mark.**

| KM# | Date | VG | Fine | VF | XF |
|---|---|---|---|---|---|
| 88.2 | 1773 FM | 7.00 | 15.00 | 30.00 | 100.00 |
| | 1774 FM | 7.00 | 15.00 | 30.00 | 100.00 |
| | 1775 FM | 7.00 | 15.00 | 30.00 | 100.00 |
| | 1776 FM | 7.00 | 15.00 | 30.00 | 100.00 |
| | 1777 FM | 7.00 | 15.00 | 30.00 | 100.00 |
| | 1778 FF | 7.00 | 15.00 | 30.00 | 100.00 |
| | 1778 F/FM | 7.00 | 15.00 | 30.00 | 100.00 |
| | 1779 FF | 7.00 | 15.00 | 30.00 | 100.00 |
| | 1780 FF | 7.00 | 15.00 | 30.00 | 100.00 |
| | 1781 FF | 7.00 | 15.00 | 30.00 | 100.00 |
| | 1782 FF | 7.00 | 15.00 | 30.00 | 100.00 |
| | 1783 FF | 7.00 | 15.00 | 30.00 | 100.00 |
| | 1784 FF | 7.00 | 15.00 | 30.00 | 100.00 |
| | 1784 FF DEI GRTIA (error) | | | | |
| | | 100.00 | 150.00 | 250.00 | 600.00 |
| | 1784 FM | 70.00 | 120.00 | 225.00 | 575.00 |

| KM# | Date | VG | Fine | VF | XF |
|---|---|---|---|---|---|
| 88.2 | 1785 FM | 7.00 | 15.00 | 30.00 | 100.00 |
| | 1786 FM | 7.00 | 15.00 | 30.00 | 100.00 |
| | 1786 FF | 200.00 | 350.00 | 550.00 | 950.00 |
| | 1787 FM | 7.00 | 15.00 | 30.00 | 100.00 |
| | 1788 FM | 7.00 | 15.00 | 30.00 | 100.00 |
| | 1789 FM | 12.00 | 25.00 | 50.00 | 150.00 |

**Obv. leg: CAROLUS.IV. . ., armored bust of Charles III.**

| 89 | 1789 FM | 15.00 | 30.00 | 75.00 | 200.00 |
|---|---|---|---|---|---|
| | 1790 FM | 15.00 | 30.00 | 75.00 | 200.00 |

**Obv. leg: CAROLUS.IIII. . ., armored bust of Charles III.**

| 90 | 1790 FM | 17.00 | 35.00 | 80.00 | 200.00 |
|---|---|---|---|---|---|

**6.7700 g, .903 SILVER, .1965 oz ASW**
**Obv: Armored bust of Carolus IIII.**

| 91 | 1792 FM | 15.00 | 30.00 | 60.00 | 200.00 |
|---|---|---|---|---|---|
| | 1793 FM | 15.00 | 30.00 | 60.00 | 200.00 |
| | 1794/3 FM | 50.00 | 100.00 | 200.00 | 450.00 |
| | 1794 FM | 40.00 | 75.00 | 150.00 | 400.00 |
| | 1795 FM | 7.00 | 15.00 | 30.00 | 85.00 |
| | 1796 FM | 7.00 | 15.00 | 30.00 | 85.00 |
| | 1797 FM | 7.00 | 15.00 | 30.00 | 85.00 |
| | 1798 FM | 7.00 | 15.00 | 30.00 | 85.00 |
| | 1799/8 FM | 7.00 | 15.00 | 32.00 | 90.00 |
| | 1799 FM | 7.00 | 15.00 | 30.00 | 85.00 |
| | 1800 FM | 7.00 | 15.00 | 30.00 | 85.00 |
| | 1801 FT | 7.00 | 15.00 | 30.00 | 85.00 |
| | 1801 FM | 20.00 | 40.00 | 75.00 | 250.00 |
| | 1802 FT | 7.00 | 15.00 | 30.00 | 85.00 |
| | 1803 FT | 7.00 | 15.00 | 30.00 | 85.00 |
| | 1804 TH | 7.00 | 15.00 | 30.00 | 85.00 |
| | 1805 TH | 7.00 | 15.00 | 30.00 | 85.00 |
| | 1806/5 TH | 7.00 | 15.00 | 32.00 | 90.00 |
| | 1806 TH | 7.00 | 15.00 | 30.00 | 85.00 |
| | 1807/5 TH | 7.00 | 15.00 | 32.00 | 90.00 |
| | 1807/6 TH | 15.00 | 30.00 | 60.00 | 200.00 |
| | 1807 TH | 7.00 | 15.00 | 30.00 | 85.00 |
| | 1808/7 TH | 7.00 | 15.00 | 32.00 | 90.00 |
| | 1808 TH | 7.00 | 15.00 | 30.00 | 85.00 |

**Obv: Armored bust of Ferdinand VII.**

| KM# | Date | VG | Fine | VF | XF |
|---|---|---|---|---|---|
| 92 | 1809 TH | 15.00 | 30.00 | 75.00 | 200.00 |
| | 1810 TH | 15.00 | 30.00 | 75.00 | 200.00 |
| | 1810 HJ | 15.00 | 30.00 | 75.00 | 200.00 |
| | 1811 HJ | 15.00 | 30.00 | 75.00 | 200.00 |
| | 1811/0 HJ/TH | 40.00 | 80.00 | 150.00 | 300.00 |
| | 1811 HJ/TH | 40.00 | 80.00 | 150.00 | 300.00 |
| | 1811 TH | 150.00 | 250.00 | 350.00 | 750.00 |

**Obv: Draped bust of Ferdinand VII.**

| 93 | 1812 HJ | 40.00 | 100.00 | 200.00 | 500.00 |
|---|---|---|---|---|---|
| | 1812 TH | 60.00 | 125.00 | 250.00 | 550.00 |
| | 1812 JJ | 10.00 | 20.00 | 60.00 | 200.00 |
| | 1813 HJ | 40.00 | 100.00 | 200.00 | 500.00 |
| | 1813 JJ | 20.00 | 60.00 | 125.00 | 350.00 |
| | 1813 TH | 15.00 | 30.00 | 100.00 | 400.00 |
| | 1814/3 JJ | 15.00 | 30.00 | 100.00 | 400.00 |
| | 1814 JJ | 15.00 | 30.00 | 100.00 | 400.00 |
| | 1815 JJ | 6.00 | 12.00 | 28.00 | 85.00 |
| | 1816 JJ | 6.00 | 12.00 | 28.00 | 85.00 |
| | 1817 JJ | 6.00 | 12.00 | 28.00 | 85.00 |
| | 1818 JJ | 6.00 | 12.00 | 28.00 | 85.00 |
| | 1819 JJ | 6.00 | 12.00 | 28.00 | 85.00 |
| | 1820 JJ | 175.00 | — | — | — |
| | 1821/0 JJ | 7.00 | 15.00 | 30.00 | 90.00 |
| | 1821 JJ | 6.00 | 12.00 | 28.00 | 85.00 |

# 4 REALES

**13.5400 g, .917 SILVER, .3992 oz ASW**
**Obv. leg: PHILLIP.V.D.G.HISPAN.ET IND.REX.**

| 94 | 1732 | — | — | Rare Specimen | |
|---|---|---|---|---|---|
| | 1732 F | 2000. | 3000. | 5000. | 10,000. |
| | 1733 F | 1500. | 2000. | 4000. | 6500. |
| | 1733 MF | 1200. | 1800. | 2500. | 4500. |
| | 1733 MF(MX) | 1500. | 2200. | 3250. | 5500. |
| | 1733 F(MX) | 1500. | 2500. | 3500. | 6000. |
| | 1734/3 MF | 150.00 | 300.00 | 600.00 | 1200. |
| | 1734 MF | 150.00 | 300.00 | 600.00 | 1200. |
| | 1735 MF | 100.00 | 175.00 | 300.00 | 600.00 |
| | 1736 MF | 100.00 | 175.00 | 300.00 | 600.00 |
| | 1737 MF | 100.00 | 175.00 | 300.00 | 600.00 |
| | 1738/7 MF | 100.00 | 175.00 | 300.00 | 600.00 |
| | 1738 MF | 100.00 | 175.00 | 300.00 | 600.00 |
| | 1739 MF | 100.00 | 175.00 | 300.00 | 600.00 |

| KM# | Date | VG | Fine | VF | XF |
|---|---|---|---|---|---|
| 94 | 1740/30 MF | 100.00 | 200.00 | 325.00 | 625.00 |
| | 1740 MF | 100.00 | 175.00 | 300.00 | 600.00 |
| | 1741 MF | 100.00 | 175.00 | 300.00 | 600.00 |
| | 1742/1 MF | 100.00 | 175.00 | 300.00 | 600.00 |
| | 1742 MF | 100.00 | 175.00 | 300.00 | 600.00 |
| | 1743 MF | 100.00 | 175.00 | 300.00 | 600.00 |
| | 1744/3 MF | 100.00 | 200.00 | 325.00 | 625.00 |
| | 1744 MF | 100.00 | 175.00 | 300.00 | 600.00 |
| | 1745 MF | 100.00 | 175.00 | 300.00 | 600.00 |
| | 1746 MP | 100.00 | 175.00 | 300.00 | 600.00 |
| | 1747 MF | 150.00 | 275.00 | 400.00 | 650.00 |

**13.5400 g, .903 SILVER, .3931 oz ASW**
**Obv. leg: CAROLUS.III.DEI.GRATIA.**
**Rev: Inverted FM and mint mark.**

| KM# | Date | VG | Fine | VF | XF |
|---|---|---|---|---|---|
| 97.1 | 1772 FM | 90.00 | 125.00 | 250.00 | 500.00 |
| | 1773 FM | 100.00 | 175.00 | 300.00 | 650.00 |

**Obv. leg: FERDND.VI.D.G.HISPAN.ET IND.REX.**

| 95 | 1747 MF | 100.00 | 150.00 | 300.00 | 550.00 |
|---|---|---|---|---|---|
| | 1748/7 MF | 100.00 | 150.00 | 300.00 | 550.00 |
| | 1748 MF | 100.00 | 125.00 | 250.00 | 500.00 |
| | 1749 MF | 150.00 | 225.00 | 350.00 | 650.00 |
| | 1750/40 MF | 100.00 | 125.00 | 250.00 | 500.00 |
| | 1750 MF | 100.00 | 125.00 | 250.00 | 500.00 |
| | 1751 MF | 100.00 | 125.00 | 250.00 | 500.00 |
| | 1752 MF | 100.00 | 125.00 | 250.00 | 500.00 |
| | 1753 MF | 100.00 | 125.00 | 300.00 | 550.00 |
| | 1754 MM | 250.00 | 375.00 | 500.00 | 850.00 |
| | 1754 MF | 250.00 | 375.00 | 500.00 | 850.00 |
| | 1755 MM | 100.00 | 125.00 | 250.00 | 500.00 |
| | 1756 MM | 100.00 | 150.00 | 300.00 | 550.00 |
| | 1757 MM | 100.00 | 150.00 | 300.00 | 550.00 |
| | 1758 MM | 100.00 | 125.00 | 250.00 | 500.00 |
| | 1759 MM | 100.00 | 125.00 | 250.00 | 500.00 |
| | 1760/59 MM | 100.00 | 175.00 | 350.00 | 600.00 |
| | 1760 MM | 100.00 | 175.00 | 350.00 | 600.00 |

**Rev: Normal initials and mint mark.**

| 97.2 | 1773 MF | 200.00 | 300.00 | 400.00 | 800.00 |
|---|---|---|---|---|---|
| | 1774 FM | 50.00 | 100.00 | 200.00 | 500.00 |
| | 1775 FM | 50.00 | 100.00 | 200.00 | 500.00 |
| | 1776 FM | 50.00 | 100.00 | 200.00 | 500.00 |
| | 1777 FM | 50.00 | 100.00 | 200.00 | 500.00 |
| | 1778 FM | 50.00 | 100.00 | 200.00 | 500.00 |
| | 1779 FF | 50.00 | 100.00 | 200.00 | 500.00 |
| | 1780 FF | 50.00 | 100.00 | 200.00 | 500.00 |
| | 1781 FF | 250.00 | 350.00 | 500.00 | 1000. |
| | 1782 FF | 50.00 | 100.00 | 200.00 | 500.00 |
| | 1783 FF | 50.00 | 100.00 | 200.00 | 500.00 |
| | 1784 FF | 50.00 | 100.00 | 200.00 | 500.00 |
| | 1784 FM | 100.00 | 200.00 | 350.00 | 600.00 |
| | 1785 FM | 100.00 | 200.00 | 350.00 | 600.00 |
| | 1786 FM | 50.00 | 100.00 | 200.00 | 500.00 |
| | 1787 FM | 50.00 | 100.00 | 200.00 | 500.00 |
| | 1788 FM | 50.00 | 100.00 | 200.00 | 500.00 |
| | 1789 FM | 50.00 | 100.00 | 200.00 | 500.00 |

**Obv. leg: CAROLVS.III.D.G.HISPAN.ET IND.REX.**

| 96 | 1760 MM | 100.00 | 150.00 | 250.00 | 900.00 |
|---|---|---|---|---|---|
| | 1761 MM | 100.00 | 150.00 | 250.00 | 900.00 |
| | 1761 MM cross between H and I | | | | |
| | | 100.00 | 150.00 | 250.00 | 900.00 |
| | 1762 MM | 75.00 | 125.00 | 250.00 | 500.00 |
| | 1762 MF | 100.00 | 150.00 | 300.00 | 600.00 |
| | 1763/1 MM | 100.00 | 150.00 | 300.00 | 600.00 |
| | 1763/2 MF | 100.00 | 150.00 | 300.00 | 600.00 |
| | 1763 MM | 100.00 | 150.00 | 300.00 | 600.00 |
| | 1763 MF | 100.00 | 200.00 | 350.00 | 800.00 |
| | 1764 MM | 400.00 | 600.00 | 1000. | 2000. |
| | 1764 MF | 350.00 | 500.00 | 1000. | 2000. |
| | 1765 MF | 350.00 | 500.00 | 1000. | 2000. |
| | 1766 MF | 250.00 | 350.00 | 550.00 | 1250. |
| | 1767 MF | 100.00 | 150.00 | 300.00 | 600.00 |
| | 1768 MF | 75.00 | 125.00 | 250.00 | 500.00 |
| | 1769 MF | 75.00 | 125.00 | 250.00 | 500.00 |
| | 1770 MF | 75.00 | 125.00 | 250.00 | 500.00 |
| | 1771 MF | 125.00 | 200.00 | 325.00 | 700.00 |
| | 1771 FM | 150.00 | 275.00 | 450.00 | 900.00 |

**Obv. leg: CAROLUS.IV. . .., armored bust**
**of Charles III.**

| 98 | 1789 FM | 65.00 | 125.00 | 250.00 | 550.00 |
|---|---|---|---|---|---|
| | 1790 FM | 50.00 | 100.00 | 200.00 | 500.00 |

Obv. leg: CAROLUS.IIII. . ., armored bust
of Charles III.

| KM# | Date | VG | Fine | VF | XF |
|-----|------|-----|------|-----|-----|
| 99 | 1790 FM | 65.00 | 125.00 | 250.00 | 550.00 |

**13.5400 g, .903 SILVER, .3931 oz ASW**
**Obv: Armored bust of Charles IIII.**
**Rev: Pillars, arms.**

| | | | | | |
|-----|------|-----|------|-----|-----|
| 100 | 1792 FM | 35.00 | 65.00 | 150.00 | 400.00 |
| | 1793 FM | 75.00 | 125.00 | 200.00 | 500.00 |
| | 1794/3 FM | 35.00 | 65.00 | 150.00 | 400.00 |
| | 1794 FM | 35.00 | 65.00 | 150.00 | 400.00 |
| | 1795 FM | 35.00 | 65.00 | 150.00 | 400.00 |
| | 1796 FM | 150.00 | 250.00 | 400.00 | 800.00 |
| | 1797 FM | 60.00 | 120.00 | 200.00 | 500.00 |
| | 1798/7 FM | 35.00 | 65.00 | 150.00 | 400.00 |
| | 1798 FM | 35.00 | 65.00 | 150.00 | 400.00 |
| | 1799 FM | 35.00 | 65.00 | 150.00 | 400.00 |
| | 1800 FM | 35.00 | 65.00 | 150.00 | 400.00 |
| | 1801 FM | 35.00 | 65.00 | 150.00 | 400.00 |
| | 1801 FT | 60.00 | 120.00 | 200.00 | 500.00 |
| | 1802 FT | 200.00 | 300.00 | 500.00 | 1000. |
| | 1803 FT | 75.00 | 135.00 | 225.00 | 550.00 |
| | 1803 TH | 350.00 | 450.00 | 650.00 | 1250. |
| | 1804 TH | 40.00 | 75.00 | 175.00 | 450.00 |
| | 1805 TH | 35.00 | 65.00 | 150.00 | 400.00 |
| | 1806 TH | 35.00 | 65.00 | 150.00 | 400.00 |
| | 1807 TH | 35.00 | 65.00 | 150.00 | 400.00 |
| | 1808/7 TH | 40.00 | 75.00 | 175.00 | 450.00 |
| | 1808 TH | 40.00 | 75.00 | 175.00 | 450.00 |

**Obv: Armored bust of Ferdinand VII.**

| KM# | Date | VG | Fine | VF | XF |
|-----|------|-----|------|-----|-----|
| 101 | 1809 HJ | 75.00 | 135.00 | 250.00 | 800.00 |
| | 1810 TH | 75.00 | 135.00 | 250.00 | 800.00 |
| | 1810 HJ | 75.00 | 135.00 | 250.00 | 800.00 |
| | 1811 HJ | 75.00 | 135.00 | 250.00 | 800.00 |
| | 1812 HJ | 500.00 | 750.00 | 1000. | 2000. |

**Obv: Draped bust of Ferdinand VII.**

| | | | | | |
|-----|------|-----|------|-----|-----|
| 102 | 1816 JJ | 150.00 | 200.00 | 325.00 | 700.00 |
| | 1817 JJ | 250.00 | 400.00 | 500.00 | 1000. |
| | 1818/7 JJ | 250.00 | 400.00 | 500.00 | 1000. |
| | 1818 JJ | 250.00 | 400.00 | 500.00 | 1000. |
| | 1819 JJ | 175.00 | 250.00 | 325.00 | 700.00 |
| | 1820 JJ | 175.00 | 250.00 | 325.00 | 700.00 |
| | 1821 JJ | 75.00 | 135.00 | 250.00 | 650.00 |

# 8 REALES

**27.0700 g, .917 SILVER, .7982 oz ASW**
**Obv. leg: PHILIP.V.D.G.HISPAN.ET IND.REX.**

| KM# | Date | VG | Fine | VF | XF |
|---|---|---|---|---|---|
| 103 | 1732 F | 2750. | 4750. | 8000. | *Rare |
| | 1733/2 F(MX) | 3000. | 5250. | 9000. | *Rare |
| | 1733 F | 2000. | 3000. | 5000. | *Rare |
| | 1733 F(MX) | — | — | *Rare | — |
| | 1733 MF(MX) | — | — | *Rare | — |
| | 1733 MF | 700.00 | 1500. | 2500. | 4250. |
| | 1734/3 MF | 100.00 | 150.00 | 275.00 | 575.00 |
| | 1734 MF | 100.00 | 150.00 | 250.00 | 500.00 |
| | 1735 MF | 100.00 | 150.00 | 250.00 | 500.00 |
| | 1736/5 MF | 100.00 | 150.00 | 275.00 | 575.00 |
| | 1736 MF | 100.00 | 150.00 | 250.00 | 500.00 |
| | 1737 MF | 65.00 | 100.00 | 200.00 | 475.00 |
| | 1738/6 MF | 65.00 | 100.00 | 200.00 | 475.00 |
| | 1738/7 MF | 65.00 | 100.00 | 200.00 | 475.00 |
| | 1738 MF | 65.00 | 100.00 | 200.00 | 475.00 |
| | 1739/6 MF | 65.00 | 100.00 | 200.00 | 475.00 |
| | 1739/8 MF | 65.00 | 100.00 | 200.00 | 475.00 |
| | 1739 MF | 65.00 | 100.00 | 200.00 | 475.00 |
| | 1740/30 MF | 100.00 | 150.00 | 275.00 | 575.00 |
| | 1740/39 MF | 100.00 | 150.00 | 275.00 | 575.00 |
| | 1740 MF | 65.00 | 100.00 | 200.00 | 475.00 |
| | 1741/31 MF | 65.00 | 100.00 | 200.00 | 475.00 |
| | 1741 MF | 65.00 | 100.00 | 200.00 | 475.00 |
| | 1742/32 MF | 75.00 | 125.00 | 250.00 | 500.00 |
| | 1742/1 MF | 65.00 | 100.00 | 200.00 | 475.00 |
| | 1742 MF | 65.00 | 100.00 | 200.00 | 475.00 |
| | 1743/2 MF | 65.00 | 100.00 | 200.00 | 475.00 |
| | 1743 MF | 65.00 | 100.00 | 200.00 | 475.00 |
| | 1744/34 MF | 65.00 | 100.00 | 200.00 | 475.00 |
| | 1744/3 MF | 65.00 | 100.00 | 200.00 | 475.00 |
| | 1744 MF | 65.00 | 100.00 | 200.00 | 475.00 |
| | 1745 MF | 65.00 | 100.00 | 200.00 | 475.00 |
| | 1746/5 MF | 100.00 | 150.00 | 275.00 | 575.00 |
| | 1746 MF | 65.00 | 100.00 | 200.00 | 475.00 |
| | 1747 MF | 65.00 | 100.00 | 200.00 | 475.00 |

**\*NOTE:** Ponterio AMAT sale 3-91 AU 1732 F realized $28,000., XF 1733/2 F (MX) realized $27,000., XF 1733 F realized $11,500., XF 1733 MF (MX) realized $35,000.
**\*NOTE:** Bonhams Patterson sale 7-96 XF 1732 F realized $13,825., gVF 1733 F (MX) $11,710., gVF 1733 MF (MX) realized $21,145.
**NOTE:** Ponterio CICF sale 4-01 choice EF 1732 F realized $18,000.

**Obv. leg: FERDND.VI.D.G.HISPAN.ET IND.REX**
**Rev: W/Royal crown on left pillar.**

| KM# | Date | VG | Fine | VF | XF |
|---|---|---|---|---|---|
| 104.1 | 1747 MF | 55.00 | 100.00 | 175.00 | 300.00 |
| | 1748/7 MF | 60.00 | 120.00 | 250.00 | 450.00 |
| | 1748 MF | 50.00 | 75.00 | 125.00 | 250.00 |
| | 1749 MF | 50.00 | 75.00 | 125.00 | 250.00 |
| | 1750 MF | 50.00 | 75.00 | 125.00 | 250.00 |
| | 1751/0 MF | 55.00 | 100.00 | 165.00 | 275.00 |
| | 1751 MF | 50.00 | 75.00 | 125.00 | 250.00 |
| | 1752/1 MF | 55.00 | 100.00 | 165.00 | 275.00 |
| | 1752 MF | 50.00 | 75.00 | 125.00 | 250.00 |
| | 1753/2 MF | 55.00 | 100.00 | 165.00 | 275.00 |
| | 1753 MF | 50.00 | 75.00 | 125.00 | 250.00 |
| | 1754/3 MF | 55.00 | 100.00 | 185.00 | 325.00 |
| | 1754 MF | 50.00 | 75.00 | 125.00 | 250.00 |
| | 1754 MM/MF | | | | |
| | | 300.00 | 700.00 | 1500. | 3500. |
| | 1754 MM | 300.00 | 700.00 | 1500. | 3500. |

**Rev: Imperial crown.**

| KM# | Date | VG | Fine | VF | XF |
|---|---|---|---|---|---|
| 104.2 | 1754 MM | 75.00 | 125.00 | 250.00 | 475.00 |
| | 1754 MM | 150.00 | 285.00 | 550.00 | 950.00 |
| | 1755/4 MM | 55.00 | 100.00 | 185.00 | 325.00 |
| | 1755 MM | 50.00 | 75.00 | 125.00 | 250.00 |
| | 1756/5 MM | 55.00 | 100.00 | 165.00 | 275.00 |
| | 1756 MM | 50.00 | 75.00 | 125.00 | 250.00 |
| | 1757/6 MM | 55.00 | 100.00 | 185.00 | 325.00 |
| | 1757 MM | 50.00 | 75.00 | 125.00 | 250.00 |
| | 1758 MM | 50.00 | 75.00 | 125.00 | 250.00 |
| | 1759 MM | 50.00 | 75.00 | 125.00 | 250.00 |
| | 1760/59 MM | 55.00 | 100.00 | 165.00 | 275.00 |
| | 1760 MM | 50.00 | 75.00 | 125.00 | 250.00 |

**Obv. leg: CAROLUS.III.D.G.HISPAN.ET IND.REX.**

| | | | | | |
|---|---|---|---|---|---|
| 105 | 1760/59 MM CAROLUS.III/Ferdin.Vi | | | | |
| | | 450.00 | 700.00 | — | — |
| | 1760 MM  CAROLUS.III/FERDIN. VI. recut | | | | |
| | die | 60.00 | 100.00 | 150.00 | 325.00 |

| KM# | Date | VG | Fine | VF | XF |
|---|---|---|---|---|---|
| 105 | 1760 MM | 60.00 | 100.00 | 150.00 | 300.00 |
| | 1761/50 MM* | | | | |
| | | 65.00 | 110.00 | 165.00 | 325.00 |
| | 1761/51 MM* | | | | |
| | | 65.00 | 110.00 | 165.00 | 325.00 |
| | 1761/0 MM** | | | | |
| | | 65.00 | 110.00 | 165.00 | 325.00 |
| | 1761 MM** | | | | |
| | | 60.00 | 100.00 | 150.00 | 275.00 |
| | 1761 MM* | | | | |
| | | 65.00 | 110.00 | 165.00 | 325.00 |
| | 1762/1 MM** | | | | |
| | | 70.00 | 120.00 | 175.00 | 450.00 |
| | 1762/1 MM | 70.00 | 120.00 | 175.00 | 450.00 |
| | 1762 MM** | | | | |
| | | 60.00 | 100.00 | 150.00 | 275.00 |
| | 1762 MM* | | | | |
| | | 50.00 | 75.00 | 125.00 | 250.00 |
| | 1762 MF | 500.00 | 750.00 | 1250. | 2300. |
| | 1763/53 MF | 50.00 | 75.00 | 125.00 | 250.00 |
| | 1763/1 MF | 50.00 | 75.00 | 125.00 | 250.00 |
| | 1763/2 MM | 300.00 | 450.00 | 750.00 | 1350. |
| | 1763/2 MF | 50.00 | 75.00 | 125.00 | 250.00 |
| | 1763/72 MF | 50.00 | 75.00 | 125.00 | 250.00 |
| | 1763 MM | 450.00 | 650.00 | 1150. | 2250. |
| | 1763 MF | 50.00 | 75.00 | 125.00 | 250.00 |
| | 1764/54 MF | 50.00 | 75.00 | 125.00 | 250.00 |
| | 1764/54 MF CAR/CRA | | | | |
| | | 50.00 | 75.00 | 125.00 | 250.00 |
| | 1764/1 MF | 50.00 | 75.00 | 125.00 | 250.00 |
| | 1764/3 MF | 50.00 | 75.00 | 125.00 | 250.00 |
| | 1764 MF | 50.00 | 75.00 | 125.00 | 250.00 |
| | 1765 MF | 50.00 | 75.00 | 125.00 | 250.00 |
| | 1766/5 MF | 75.00 | 150.00 | 225.00 | 575.00 |
| | 1766 MF | 50.00 | 75.00 | 125.00 | 250.00 |
| | 1767/17 MF | 50.00 | 75.00 | 125.00 | 250.00 |
| | 1767/6 MF | 50.00 | 75.00 | 125.00 | 250.00 |
| | 1767 MF | 50.00 | 75.00 | 125.00 | 250.00 |
| | 1768/6 MF | 50.00 | 75.00 | 125.00 | 250.00 |
| | 1768/7 MF | 85.00 | 165.00 | 250.00 | 600.00 |
| | 1768 MF | 50.00 | 75.00 | 125.00 | 250.00 |
| | 1769 MF | 50.00 | 75.00 | 125.00 | 250.00 |
| | 1770/60 MF | 100.00 | 185.00 | 300.00 | 650.00 |
| | 1770/60 FM | 100.00 | 185.00 | 300.00 | 650.00 |
| | 1770/69 FM | 100.00 | 185.00 | 300.00 | 650.00 |
| | 1770 MF | 50.00 | 75.00 | 125.00 | 250.00 |
| | 1770 FM/F | 50.00 | 75.00 | 125.00 | 250.00 |
| | 1770 FM | 50.00 | 75.00 | 125.00 | 250.00 |
| | 1771/0 FM | 50.00 | 75.00 | 125.00 | 250.00 |
| | 1771 FM | 50.00 | 75.00 | 125.00 | 250.00 |
| | 1772 FM | — | — | Rare | — |

*NOTE: Tip of cross between I and S in legend.
**NOTE: Tip of cross between H and I in legend.

27.0700 g, .903 SILVER, .7859 oz ASW
MF (error) inverted

FM (normal)

Obv. leg: CAROLUS.III.DEI.GRATIA.
Rev: Inverted initials and mint mark.

| KM# | Date | VG | Fine | VF | XF |
|---|---|---|---|---|---|
| 106.1 | 1772 FM | 25.00 | 50.00 | 120.00 | 250.00 |
| | 1772 MF | 150.00 | 350.00 | 750.00 | 1250. |
| | 1773 FM | 25.00 | 50.00 | 100.00 | 175.00 |

Rev: Normal initials and mint mark.

| | Date | VG | Fine | VF | XF |
|---|---|---|---|---|---|
| 106.2 | 1773 FM | 25.00 | 50.00 | 80.00 | 160.00 |
| | 1774 FM | 25.00 | 45.00 | 75.00 | 150.00 |
| | 1775 FM | 25.00 | 45.00 | 75.00 | 150.00 |
| | 1776 FM | 25.00 | 45.00 | 75.00 | 150.00 |
| | 1777/6 FM | 35.00 | 65.00 | 120.00 | 300.00 |
| | 1777 FM | 25.00 | 45.00 | 75.00 | 150.00 |
| | 1777 FF | 35.00 | 50.00 | 100.00 | 250.00 |
| | 1778 FM | — | — | *Rare | — |
| | 1778/7FF | 25.00 | 45.00 | 75.00 | 150.00 |
| | 1778 FF | 25.00 | 45.00 | 75.00 | 150.00 |
| | 1779 FF | 25.00 | 45.00 | 75.00 | 150.00 |
| | 1780 FF | 25.00 | 45.00 | 75.00 | 150.00 |
| | 1781 FF | 25.00 | 45.00 | 75.00 | 150.00 |
| | 1782 FF | 25.00 | 45.00 | 75.00 | 150.00 |
| | 1783 FF | 25.00 | 45.00 | 75.00 | 150.00 |
| | 1783 FM | 4000. | 6000. | 9000. | — |
| | 1784 FF | 150.00 | 300.00 | 500.00 | 1250. |
| | 1784 FM | 25.00 | 45.00 | 75.00 | 150.00 |
| | 1785 FM | 25.00 | 45.00 | 75.00 | 150.00 |
| | 1786/5 FM | 25.00 | 45.00 | 75.00 | 150.00 |
| | 1786 FM | 25.00 | 45.00 | 75.00 | 150.00 |
| | 1787/6 FM | 100.00 | 250.00 | 450.00 | 1200. |
| | 1787 FM | 25.00 | 45.00 | 75.00 | 150.00 |
| | 1788 FM | 25.00 | 45.00 | 75.00 | 150.00 |
| | 1789 FM | 50.00 | 100.00 | 150.00 | 225.00 |

*NOTE: Superior Casterline sale 5-89 VF realized $17,600.

**Obv. leg: CAROLUS.IV. . ., armored bust of Charles III.**

| KM# | Date | VG | Fine | VF | XF |
|---|---|---|---|---|---|
| 107 | 1789 FM | 40.00 | 65.00 | 120.00 | 250.00 |
| | 1790 FM | 30.00 | 50.00 | 100.00 | 200.00 |

**Obv. leg: CAROLUS.IIII. . ., armored bust of Charles III.**

| 108 | 1790 FM | 30.00 | 50.00 | 100.00 | 200.00 |
|---|---|---|---|---|---|

**Obv: Armored bust of Charles IIII.**

| KM# | Date | VG | Fine | VF | XF |
|---|---|---|---|---|---|
| 109 | 1791 FM | 20.00 | 35.00 | 50.00 | 100.00 |
| | 1792 FM | 20.00 | 35.00 | 50.00 | 100.00 |
| | 1793 FM | 20.00 | 35.00 | 50.00 | 100.00 |
| | 1794 FM | 20.00 | 35.00 | 50.00 | 100.00 |
| | 1795/4 FM | 20.00 | 35.00 | 50.00 | 100.00 |
| | 1795 FM | 20.00 | 35.00 | 50.00 | 100.00 |
| | 1796 FM | 20.00 | 35.00 | 50.00 | 100.00 |
| | 1797 FM | 20.00 | 35.00 | 50.00 | 100.00 |
| | 1798 FM | 20.00 | 35.00 | 50.00 | 100.00 |
| | 1799 FM | 20.00 | 35.00 | 50.00 | 100.00 |
| | 1800/700 FM | 20.00 | 35.00 | 50.00 | 100.00 |
| | 1800 FM | 20.00 | 35.00 | 50.00 | 100.00 |
| | 1801/791 FM | 35.00 | 60.00 | 100.00 | 250.00 |
| | 1801/0 FM | 35.00 | 60.00 | 100.00 | 250.00 |
| | 1801/0 FT/FM | 20.00 | 35.00 | 50.00 | 100.00 |
| | 1801 FM | 20.00 | 40.00 | 100.00 | 250.00 |
| | 1801 FT/M | 35.00 | 60.00 | 100.00 | 250.00 |
| | 1801 FT | 20.00 | 35.00 | 50.00 | 100.00 |
| | 1802/1 FT | 35.00 | 60.00 | 100.00 | 250.00 |
| | 1802 FT | 20.00 | 35.00 | 50.00 | 100.00 |
| | 1802 FT/FM | 20.00 | 35.00 | 50.00 | 100.00 |
| | 1803 FT | 20.00 | 35.00 | 50.00 | 110.00 |
| | 1803 FM | 600.00 | 900.00 | — | — |
| | 1803 FT/FM | 20.00 | 35.00 | 50.00 | 100.00 |
| | 1803 TH | 75.00 | 150.00 | 250.00 | 500.00 |
| | 1804/3 TH | 35.00 | 60.00 | 100.00 | 250.00 |
| | 1804 TH short crosslet | 20.00 | 35.00 | 50.00 | 100.00 |
| | 1804 TH long crosslet | 20.00 | 35.00 | 50.00 | 100.00 |
| | 1805/4 TH | 40.00 | 80.00 | 125.00 | 275.00 |
| | 1805 TH narrow date | 20.00 | 35.00 | 50.00 | 100.00 |
| | 1805 TH wide date | 20.00 | 35.00 | 50.00 | 100.00 |
| | 1806 TH | 20.00 | 35.00 | 50.00 | 100.00 |
| | 1807/6 TH | 150.00 | 250.00 | 350.00 | 700.00 |
| | 1807 TH | 20.00 | 35.00 | 50.00 | 100.00 |
| | 1870 TH(error 1807) | 150.00 | 250.00 | 350.00 | 700.00 |
| | 1808/7 TH | 20.00 | 35.00 | 50.00 | 100.00 |
| | 1808 TH | 20.00 | 35.00 | 50.00 | 100.00 |

**Obv: Armored bust of Ferdinand VII.**

| KM# | Date | VG | Fine | VF | XF |
|-----|------|-----|------|-----|-----|
| 110 | 1808 TH | 25.00 | 40.00 | 75.00 | 145.00 |
| | 1809/8 TH | 25.00 | 40.00 | 75.00 | 145.00 |
| | 1809 HJ | 25.00 | 40.00 | 75.00 | 145.00 |
| | 1809 HJ/TH | 20.00 | 35.00 | 55.00 | 120.00 |
| | 1809 TH/JH | 20.00 | 35.00 | 55.00 | 120.00 |
| | 1809 TH | 20.00 | 35.00 | 55.00 | 120.00 |
| | 1810/09 HJ | 25.00 | 40.00 | 75.00 | 145.00 |
| | 1810 HJ | 25.00 | 40.00 | 75.00 | 145.00 |
| | 1810 HJ/TH | 25.00 | 40.00 | 75.00 | 145.00 |
| | 1810 TH | 75.00 | 150.00 | 300.00 | 600.00 |
| | 1811/0 HJ | 20.00 | 35.00 | 55.00 | 120.00 |
| | 1811 HJ | 20.00 | 35.00 | 55.00 | 120.00 |
| | 1811 HJ/TH | 20.00 | 35.00 | 50.00 | 100.00 |

**Obv: Draped bust of Ferdinand VII.**

| KM# | Date | VG | Fine | VF | XF |
|-----|------|-----|------|-----|-----|
| 111 | 1811 HJ | 20.00 | 40.00 | 60.00 | 125.00 |
| | 1812 HJ | 50.00 | 75.00 | 125.00 | 250.00 |
| | 1812 JJ/HJ | 20.00 | 35.00 | 50.00 | 100.00 |
| | 1812 JJ | 20.00 | 35.00 | 50.00 | 100.00 |
| | 1813 HJ | 50.00 | 75.00 | 125.00 | 250.00 |
| | 1813 JJ | 20.00 | 35.00 | 50.00 | 100.00 |
| | 1814/3 HJ | 1200. | 2500. | 5000. | — |
| | 1814/3 JJ/HJ | 20.00 | 35.00 | 50.00 | 100.00 |
| | 1814/3 JJ | 20.00 | 35.00 | 50.00 | 100.00 |
| | 1814 JJ | 20.00 | 35.00 | 50.00 | 100.00 |
| | 1814 HJ | 500.00 | 800.00 | 1500. | 3000. |
| | 1815/4 JJ | 20.00 | 35.00 | 50.00 | 100.00 |
| | 1815 JJ | 20.00 | 35.00 | 50.00 | 100.00 |
| | 1816/5 JJ | 20.00 | 35.00 | 50.00 | 90.00 |
| | 1816 JJ | 20.00 | 35.00 | 50.00 | 90.00 |
| | 1817 JJ | 20.00 | 35.00 | 50.00 | 90.00 |
| | 1818 JJ | 20.00 | 35.00 | 50.00 | 90.00 |
| | 1819 JJ | 20.00 | 35.00 | 50.00 | 90.00 |
| | 1820 JJ | 20.00 | 35.00 | 50.00 | 90.00 |
| | 1821 JJ | 20.00 | 35.00 | 50.00 | 90.00 |

## 1/2 ESCUDO

**1.6900 g, .875 GOLD, .0475 oz AGW**
**Obv. leg: FERD.VII.D.G.HISP.ET IND.**

| | | | | | |
|-----|------|-----|------|-----|-----|
| 112 | 1814 JJ | 200.00 | 300.00 | 400.00 | 550.00 |
| | 1815/4 JJ | 150.00 | 200.00 | 250.00 | 400.00 |
| | 1815 JJ | 150.00 | 200.00 | 250.00 | 400.00 |
| | 1816 JJ | 100.00 | 150.00 | 225.00 | 375.00 |
| | 1817 JJ | 150.00 | 200.00 | 250.00 | 400.00 |
| | 1818 JJ | 150.00 | 200.00 | 250.00 | 400.00 |
| | 1819 JJ | 150.00 | 200.00 | 250.00 | 400.00 |
| | 1820 JJ | 200.00 | 300.00 | 400.00 | 550.00 |

## ESCUDO

**3.3800 g, .917 GOLD, .0996 oz AGW**
**Obv. leg: PHILIP.V.D.G.HISPAN.ET IND.REX**

| KM# | Date | VG | Fine | VF | XF |
|-----|------|-----|------|-----|-----|
| 113 | 1732 F | 1000. | 2000. | 3000. | 4000. |
| | 1733/2 F | 1000. | 2000. | 3000. | 4000. |
| | 1733 F | 1000. | 2000. | 3000. | 4000. |
| | 1734/3 MF | 150.00 | 250.00 | 400.00 | 850.00 |
| | 1734 MF | 150.00 | 250.00 | 400.00 | 850.00 |
| | 1735/4 MF | 150.00 | 250.00 | 400.00 | 850.00 |
| | 1735 MF | 150.00 | 250.00 | 400.00 | 850.00 |
| | 1736/5 MF | 150.00 | 250.00 | 400.00 | 850.00 |
| | 1736 MF | 150.00 | 250.00 | 400.00 | 850.00 |
| | 1737 MF | 200.00 | 300.00 | 600.00 | 1200. |
| | 1738/7 MF | 200.00 | 300.00 | 600.00 | 1200. |
| | 1738 MF | 200.00 | 300.00 | 600.00 | 1200. |
| | 1739 MF | 200.00 | 300.00 | 600.00 | 1200. |
| | 1740 MF | 200.00 | 300.00 | 600.00 | 1200. |
| | 1741 MF | 200.00 | 300.00 | 600.00 | 1200. |
| | 1742 MF | 200.00 | 300.00 | 600.00 | 1200. |
| | 1743/2 MF | 150.00 | 275.00 | 450.00 | 800.00 |
| | 1743 MF | 150.00 | 250.00 | 400.00 | 700.00 |
| | 1744 MF | 150.00 | 250.00 | 400.00 | 700.00 |
| | 1745 MF | 150.00 | 250.00 | 400.00 | 700.00 |
| | 1746 MF | 150.00 | 250.00 | 400.00 | 700.00 |
| | 1747 MF | — | — | Rare | — |

**Obv. leg: FERD.VI.D.G.HISPAN.**
**ET IND.REX., long bust.**

| | | | | | |
|-----|------|-----|------|-----|-----|
| 114 | 1747 MF | 1650. | 3000. | 5000. | 7500. |

**Obv: Short bust.**

| | | | | | |
|-----|------|-----|------|-----|-----|
| 115.1 | 1748 MF | 250.00 | 350.00 | 550.00 | 950.00 |
| | 1749 MF | 300.00 | 450.00 | 700.00 | 1150. |
| | 1750 MF | 150.00 | 250.00 | 400.00 | 800.00 |
| | 1751 MF | 150.00 | 250.00 | 400.00 | 800.00 |

**Rev: W/o 1 S by arms.**

| | | | | | |
|-----|------|-----|------|-----|-----|
| 115.2 | 1752 MF | 125.00 | 225.00 | 375.00 | 750.00 |
| | 1753/2 MF | 150.00 | 250.00 | 400.00 | 800.00 |
| | 1753 MF | 150.00 | 250.00 | 400.00 | 800.00 |
| | 1754 MF | 150.00 | 250.00 | 400.00 | 800.00 |
| | 1755 MM | 150.00 | 250.00 | 400.00 | 800.00 |
| | 1756 MF | 150.00 | 250.00 | 400.00 | 800.00 |
| | 1756 MM | 150.00 | 250.00 | 400.00 | 800.00 |

**Obv: Armored bust.**

| KM# | Date | VG | Fine | VF | XF |
|---|---|---|---|---|---|
| A116 | 1757 MM | 150.00 | 250.00 | 400.00 | 800.00 |
| | 1758 MM | 150.00 | 250.00 | 400.00 | 800.00 |
| | 1759 MM | 150.00 | 250.00 | 400.00 | 800.00 |

**Obv. leg: CAROLVS.III.D.G.HISPAN.ET IND.REX**
**Rev. leg: NOMINA MAGNA SEQUOR**

| KM# | Date | VG | Fine | VF | XF |
|---|---|---|---|---|---|
| 116 | 1760 MM | 400.00 | 800.00 | 1500. | 2500. |
| | 1761/0 MM | 400.00 | 800.00 | 1500. | 2500. |
| | 1761 MM | 400.00 | 800.00 | 1500. | 2500. |

**Obv. leg: CAR.III.D.G.HISP.ET IND.R., large bust.**
**Rev. leg: IN.UTROQ. FELIX.**

| KM# | Date | VG | Fine | VF | XF |
|---|---|---|---|---|---|
| 117 | 1762 MF | 250.00 | 375.00 | 600.00 | 1000. |
| | 1762 MM | 250.00 | 375.00 | 600.00 | 1000. |
| | 1763 MF | 250.00 | 375.00 | 600.00 | 1000. |
| | 1763 MM | 275.00 | 425.00 | 700.00 | 1100. |
| | 1764 MM | 250.00 | 375.00 | 600.00 | 1000. |
| | 1765 MF | 250.00 | 375.00 | 600.00 | 1000. |
| | 1766 MF | 250.00 | 375.00 | 600.00 | 1000. |
| | 1767 MF | 250.00 | 375.00 | 600.00 | 1000. |
| | 1768 MF | 250.00 | 375.00 | 600.00 | 1000. |
| | 1769 MF | 250.00 | 375.00 | 600.00 | 1000. |
| | 1770 MF | 250.00 | 375.00 | 600.00 | 1000. |
| | 1771 MF | 250.00 | 375.00 | 600.00 | 1000. |

**3.3800 g, .901 GOLD, .0979 oz AGW**
**Obv. leg: CAROL.III.D.G. HISPAN.ET IND.R.**
**Rev. leg: . . .FELIX.A.D.; initials and**
**mint mark upright.**

| KM# | Date | VG | Fine | VF | XF |
|---|---|---|---|---|---|
| 118.1 | 1772 FM | 125.00 | 175.00 | 285.00 | 525.00 |
| | 1773 FM | 125.00 | 175.00 | 285.00 | 525.00 |

**Rev: Initials and mint mark inverted.**

| | | | | | |
|---|---|---|---|---|---|
| 118.2 | 1772 FM | 125.00 | 175.00 | 285.00 | 525.00 |
| | 1773 FM | 125.00 | 175.00 | 285.00 | 525.00 |
| | 1774 FM | 125.00 | 175.00 | 285.00 | 525.00 |
| | 1775 FM | 125.00 | 175.00 | 285.00 | 525.00 |
| | 1776 FM | 125.00 | 175.00 | 285.00 | 525.00 |

**3.3800 g, .875 GOLD, .0950 oz AGW**

| | | | | | |
|---|---|---|---|---|---|
| 118.2a | 1777 FM | 125.00 | 175.00 | 285.00 | 525.00 |
| | 1778 FF | 125.00 | 175.00 | 285.00 | 525.00 |
| | 1779 FF | 125.00 | 175.00 | 285.00 | 525.00 |
| | 1780 FF | 125.00 | 175.00 | 285.00 | 525.00 |
| | 1781 FF | 125.00 | 175.00 | 285.00 | 525.00 |
| | 1782 FF | 125.00 | 175.00 | 285.00 | 525.00 |
| | 1783/2 FF | 125.00 | 175.00 | 285.00 | 525.00 |
| | 1783 FF | 125.00 | 175.00 | 285.00 | 525.00 |
| | 1784 FF | 125.00 | 175.00 | 285.00 | 525.00 |
| | 1784 FM | 125.00 | 175.00 | 285.00 | 525.00 |
| | 1785 FM | 125.00 | 175.00 | 285.00 | 525.00 |

| KM# | Date | VG | Fine | VF | XF |
|---|---|---|---|---|---|
| 118.2a | 1786 FM | 125.00 | 175.00 | 285.00 | 525.00 |
| | 1787 FM | 125.00 | 175.00 | 285.00 | 525.00 |
| | 1788 FM | 125.00 | 175.00 | 285.00 | 525.00 |

**Rev: Initial letters and mint mark upright.**

| | | | | | |
|---|---|---|---|---|---|
| 118.1a | 1787 FM | 125.00 | 175.00 | 285.00 | 525.00 |
| | 1788 FM | 125.00 | 175.00 | 285.00 | 525.00 |

**Obv: Bust of Charles III, leg: CAROLUS.IV.D.G. . .**

| | | | | | |
|---|---|---|---|---|---|
| 119 | 1789 FM | 300.00 | 550.00 | 1000. | 2000. |
| | 1790 FM | 300.00 | 550.00 | 1000. | 2000. |

**3.3800 g, .875 GOLD, .0950 oz AGW**
**Obv: Armored bust of Charles IV.**

| | | | | | |
|---|---|---|---|---|---|
| 120 | 1792 MF | 125.00 | 165.00 | 235.00 | 345.00 |
| | 1793 FM | 125.00 | 165.00 | 235.00 | 345.00 |
| | 1794 FM | 125.00 | 165.00 | 235.00 | 345.00 |
| | 1795 FM | 125.00 | 165.00 | 235.00 | 345.00 |
| | 1796 FM | 125.00 | 165.00 | 235.00 | 345.00 |
| | 1797 FM | 125.00 | 165.00 | 235.00 | 345.00 |
| | 1798 FM | 125.00 | 165.00 | 235.00 | 345.00 |
| | 1799 FM | 125.00 | 165.00 | 235.00 | 345.00 |
| | 1800 FM | 125.00 | 165.00 | 235.00 | 345.00 |
| | 1801 FT | 125.00 | 165.00 | 235.00 | 345.00 |
| | 1801 FM | 125.00 | 165.00 | 235.00 | 345.00 |
| | 1802 FT | 125.00 | 165.00 | 235.00 | 345.00 |
| | 1803 FT | 125.00 | 165.00 | 235.00 | 345.00 |
| | 1804/3 TH | 125.00 | 165.00 | 235.00 | 345.00 |
| | 1804 TH | 125.00 | 165.00 | 235.00 | 345.00 |
| | 1805 TH | 125.00 | 165.00 | 235.00 | 345.00 |
| | 1806 TH | 125.00 | 165.00 | 235.00 | 345.00 |
| | 1807 TH | 125.00 | 165.00 | 235.00 | 345.00 |
| | 1808 TH | 125.00 | 165.00 | 235.00 | 345.00 |

**Obv: Armored bust of Ferdinand VII.**

| | | | | | |
|---|---|---|---|---|---|
| 121 | 1809 HJ | 125.00 | 165.00 | 235.00 | 400.00 |
| | 1810 HJ | 125.00 | 165.00 | 235.00 | 400.00 |
| | 1811 HJ | 125.00 | 165.00 | 235.00 | 400.00 |
| | 1812 HJ | 150.00 | 250.00 | 300.00 | 500.00 |

**Obv: Undraped bust of Ferdinand VII.**

| | | | | | |
|---|---|---|---|---|---|
| 122 | 1814 HJ | 150.00 | 250.00 | 300.00 | 500.00 |
| | 1815 JJ | 150.00 | 250.00 | 300.00 | 500.00 |
| | 1815 HJ | 150.00 | 250.00 | 300.00 | 500.00 |
| | 1816 JJ | 175.00 | 275.00 | 325.00 | 550.00 |
| | 1817 JJ | 150.00 | 250.00 | 300.00 | 500.00 |
| | 1818 JJ | 150.00 | 250.00 | 300.00 | 500.00 |
| | 1819 JJ | 150.00 | 250.00 | 300.00 | 500.00 |
| | 1820 JJ | 150.00 | 250.00 | 300.00 | 500.00 |

# 2 ESCUDOS

6.7700 g, .917 GOLD, .1996 oz AGW
Obv. leg: PHILIP.V.D.G.HISPAN.ET IND.REX.
Rev. leg: INITIUM SAPIENTIAE TIMOR DOMINI.

| KM# | Date | VG | Fine | VF | XF |
|---|---|---|---|---|---|
| 124 | 1732 F | 1000. | 1500. | 2000. | 3000. |
| | 1733 F | 750.00 | 1000. | 1500. | 2500. |
| | 1734 MF | 400.00 | 500.00 | 900.00 | 1400. |
| | 1735 MF | 400.00 | 500.00 | 900.00 | 1400. |
| | 1736/5 MF | 400.00 | 500.00 | 900.00 | 1400. |
| | 1736 MF | 400.00 | 500.00 | 900.00 | 1400. |
| | 1737 MF | 400.00 | 500.00 | 900.00 | 1400. |
| | 1738/7 MF | 400.00 | 500.00 | 900.00 | 1400. |
| | 1738 MF | 400.00 | 500.00 | 900.00 | 1400. |
| | 1739 MF | 400.00 | 500.00 | 900.00 | 1400. |
| | 1740 MF | 400.00 | 500.00 | 900.00 | 1400. |
| | 1741 MF | 400.00 | 500.00 | 900.00 | 1400. |
| | 1742 MF | 400.00 | 500.00 | 900.00 | 1400. |
| | 1743 MF | 400.00 | 500.00 | 900.00 | 1400. |
| | 1744/3 MF | 400.00 | 500.00 | 900.00 | 1400. |
| | 1744 MF | 400.00 | 500.00 | 900.00 | 1400. |
| | 1745 MF | 400.00 | 500.00 | 900.00 | 1400. |
| | 1746 MF | 400.00 | 500.00 | 900.00 | 1400. |
| | 1747 MF | 400.00 | 500.00 | 900.00 | 1400. |

Obv. leg: FERD.VI.D.G. . ., large bust.
Rev. leg: INITIUM. . .

| KM# | Date | VG | Fine | VF | XF |
|---|---|---|---|---|---|
| 125 | 1747 MF | 3000. | 5500. | 9000. | 15,000. |

Obv. leg: FERD.VI.D.G. . ., small young bust.
Rev. leg: NOMINA MAGNA SEQUOR.

| KM# | Date | VG | Fine | VF | XF |
|---|---|---|---|---|---|
| 126.1 | 1748 MF | 450.00 | 800.00 | 1600. | 3150. |
| | 1749/8 MF | 450.00 | 800.00 | 1600. | 3150. |
| | 1749 MF | 600.00 | 900.00 | 1850. | 3750. |
| | 1750 MF | 400.00 | 750.00 | 1500. | 3000. |
| | 1751 MF | 400.00 | 750.00 | 1500. | 3000. |

Rev: W/o 2 S by arms.

| 126.2 | 1752 MF | 400.00 | 750.00 | 1500. | 3000. |
|---|---|---|---|---|---|
| | 1753 MF | 400.00 | 750.00 | 1500. | 3000. |
| | 1754 MF | 600.00 | 900.00 | 1850. | 3750. |
| | 1755 MM | 400.00 | 750.00 | 1500. | 3000. |
| | 1756 MM | 600.00 | 900.00 | 1850. | 3750. |
| | 1756 MF | 450.00 | 800.00 | 1600. | 3150. |

Obv. leg: FERDND.VI.D.G. . ., armored bust.

| KM# | Date | VG | Fine | VF | XF |
|---|---|---|---|---|---|
| 127 | 1757 MM | 450.00 | 800.00 | 1600. | 3150. |
| | 1758 MM | 450.00 | 800.00 | 1600. | 3150. |
| | 1759 MM | 450.00 | 800.00 | 1600. | 3150. |

Obv. leg: CAROLVS.III.D.G. . ., young bust.

| 128 | 1760 MM | 550.00 | 1000. | 2000. | 4000. |
|---|---|---|---|---|---|
| | 1761 MM | 550.00 | 1000. | 2000. | 4000. |

Obv. leg: CAROLUS.III.D.G. . ., large young bust.
Rev. leg: IN.UTROQ.FELIX.AUSPICE.DEO

| 129 | 1762 MF | 650.00 | 1250. | 2500. | 4500. |
|---|---|---|---|---|---|
| | 1763 MF | 650.00 | 1250. | 2500. | 4500. |
| | 1764 MF | 650.00 | 1250. | 2500. | 4500. |
| | 1764 MM | 650.00 | 1250. | 2500. | 4500. |
| | 1765 MF | 650.00 | 1250. | 2500. | 4500. |
| | 1766 MF | 650.00 | 1250. | 2500. | 4500. |
| | 1767 MF | 650.00 | 1250. | 2500. | 4500. |
| | 1768 MF | 650.00 | 1250. | 2500. | 4500. |
| | 1769 MF | 650.00 | 1250. | 2500. | 4500. |
| | 1770 MF | 650.00 | 1250. | 2500. | 4500. |
| | 1771 MF | 650.00 | 1250. | 2650. | 4750. |
| | 1771 MF | 650.00 | 1250. | 2500. | 4500. |

6.7700 g, .901 GOLD, .1961 oz AGW
Obv. leg: CAROLUS.III.D.G. . ., older bust.
Rev: Initials and mint mark upright.

| 130.1 | 1772 FM | 250.00 | 450.00 | 600.00 | 1000. |
|---|---|---|---|---|---|
| | 1773 FM | 250.00 | 450.00 | 600.00 | 1000. |

Rev: Initials and mint mark inverted.

| 130.2 | 1773 FM | 250.00 | 450.00 | 600.00 | 1000. |
|---|---|---|---|---|---|
| | 1774 FM | 250.00 | 450.00 | 600.00 | 1000. |
| | 1775 FM | 250.00 | 450.00 | 600.00 | 1000. |
| | 1776 FM | 250.00 | 450.00 | 600.00 | 1000. |

6.7700 g, .875 GOLD, .1904 oz AGW

| 130.2a | 1777 FM | 200.00 | 350.00 | 500.00 | 900.00 |
|---|---|---|---|---|---|
| | 1778 FF | 200.00 | 350.00 | 500.00 | 900.00 |
| | 1779 FF | 200.00 | 350.00 | 500.00 | 900.00 |
| | 1780 FF | 200.00 | 350.00 | 500.00 | 900.00 |
| | 1781 FF/FM | 200.00 | 350.00 | 500.00 | 900.00 |
| | 1781 FF | 200.00 | 350.00 | 500.00 | 900.00 |
| | 1782 FF | 200.00 | 350.00 | 500.00 | 900.00 |
| | 1783 FF | 200.00 | 350.00 | 500.00 | 900.00 |
| | 1784 FF | 200.00 | 350.00 | 500.00 | 900.00 |
| | 1784 FM | 500.00 | 750.00 | 1000. | 1500. |
| | 1785 FM | 200.00 | 350.00 | 500.00 | 900.00 |
| | 1786 FM | 200.00 | 350.00 | 500.00 | 900.00 |
| | 1787 FM | 200.00 | 350.00 | 500.00 | 900.00 |
| | 1788 FM | 200.00 | 350.00 | 500.00 | 900.00 |

Rev: Initials and mint mark upright.

| KM# | Date | VG | Fine | VF | XF |
|-----|------|------|------|------|------|
| 130.1a | 1788 FM | 200.00 | 350.00 | 500.00 | 900.00 |

**Obv. leg: CAROL.IV.D.G. . ., bust of Charles III.**

| KM# | Date | VG | Fine | VF | XF |
|-----|------|------|------|------|------|
| 131 | 1789 FM | 650.00 | 1200. | 2000. | 3500. |
|  | 1790 FM | 650.00 | 1200. | 2000. | 3500. |

**6.7700 g, .875 GOLD, .1904 oz AGW**
**Obv: Armored bust of Charles IV.**

| KM# | Date | VG | Fine | VF | XF |
|-----|------|------|------|------|------|
| 132 | 1791 FM | 300.00 | 400.00 | 650.00 | 1000. |
|  | 1792 FM | 125.00 | 250.00 | 375.00 | 600.00 |
|  | 1793 FM | 125.00 | 250.00 | 375.00 | 600.00 |
|  | 1794 FM | 125.00 | 250.00 | 375.00 | 600.00 |
|  | 1795 FM | 125.00 | 250.00 | 375.00 | 600.00 |
|  | 1796 FM | 125.00 | 250.00 | 375.00 | 600.00 |
|  | 1797 FM | 125.00 | 250.00 | 425.00 | 750.00 |
|  | 1798 FM | 125.00 | 250.00 | 375.00 | 600.00 |
|  | 1799 FM | 125.00 | 250.00 | 375.00 | 600.00 |
|  | 1800 FM | 125.00 | 250.00 | 375.00 | 600.00 |
|  | 1801 FM | 125.00 | 250.00 | 375.00 | 600.00 |
|  | 1802 FT | 125.00 | 250.00 | 375.00 | 600.00 |
|  | 1803 FT | 125.00 | 250.00 | 375.00 | 600.00 |
|  | 1804 TH | 125.00 | 250.00 | 375.00 | 600.00 |
|  | 1805 TH | 125.00 | 250.00 | 375.00 | 600.00 |
|  | 1806 TH | 125.00 | 250.00 | 375.00 | 600.00 |
|  | 1807 TH | 125.00 | 250.00 | 375.00 | 600.00 |
|  | 1808 TH | 125.00 | 250.00 | 375.00 | 600.00 |

**Obv: Undraped bust of Ferdinand VII.**

| KM# | Date | VG | Fine | VF | XF |
|-----|------|------|------|------|------|
| 134 | 1814 HJ | 250.00 | 425.00 | 700.00 | 1200. |
|  | 1814 JJ | 250.00 | 425.00 | 700.00 | 1200. |
|  | 1815 JJ | 250.00 | 425.00 | 700.00 | 1200. |
|  | 1816 JJ | 250.00 | 425.00 | 700.00 | 1200. |
|  | 1817 JJ | 250.00 | 425.00 | 700.00 | 1200. |
|  | 1818 JJ | 250.00 | 425.00 | 700.00 | 1200. |
|  | 1819 JJ | 250.00 | 425.00 | 700.00 | 1200. |
|  | 1820 JJ | 250.00 | 425.00 | 700.00 | 1200. |

## 4 ESCUDOS

**13.5400 g, .917 GOLD, .3992 oz AGW**
**Obv. leg: PHILIP.V.D.G.HISPAN.ET IND.REX.**
**Rev. leg: INITIUM SAPIENTIAE TIMOR DOMINI.**

| KM# | Date | VG | Fine | VF | XF |
|-----|------|------|------|------|------|
| 135 | 1732 | — | — | Rare | — |
|  | 1732 F | — | — | Rare | — |
|  | 1733 F | — | — | Rare | — |
|  | 1734/3 F | 1000. | 1650. | 3000. | 5000. |
|  | 1734 MF | 850.00 | 1500. | 2750. | 4750. |
|  | 1735 MF | 850.00 | 1500. | 2750. | 4750. |

| KM# | Date | VG | Fine | VF | XF |
|-----|------|------|------|------|------|
| 135 | 1736 MF | 850.00 | 1500. | 2750. | 4750. |
|  | 1737 MF | 750.00 | 1350. | 2500. | 4500. |
|  | 1738/7 MF | 750.00 | 1350. | 2500. | 4500. |
|  | 1738 MF | 750.00 | 1350. | 2500. | 4500. |
|  | 1739 MF | 750.00 | 1350. | 2500. | 4500. |
|  | 1740/30 MF | 750.00 | 1350. | 2500. | 4500. |
|  | 1740 MF | 750.00 | 1350. | 2500. | 4500. |
|  | 1741 MF | 750.00 | 1350. | 2500. | 4500. |
|  | 1742 MF | 750.00 | 1350. | 2500. | 4500. |
|  | 1743 MF | 750.00 | 1350. | 2500. | 4500. |
|  | 1744 MD | 750.00 | 1350. | 2500. | 4500. |
|  | 1745 MF | 750.00 | 1350. | 2500. | 4500. |
|  | 1746 MF | 750.00 | 1350. | 2500. | 4500. |
|  | 1747 MF | 750.00 | 1350. | 2500. | 4500. |

**Obv. leg: FERDND.VI.D.G. . ., large bust.**

| KM# | Date | VG | Fine | VF | XF |
|-----|------|------|------|------|------|
| 136 | 1747 MF | 7500. | 13,500. | 20,000. | 30,000. |

**Obv. leg: FERDND.VI.D.G. . ., small bust.**
**Rev. leg: NOMINA MAGNA. . ., 4S divided by arms.**

| KM# | Date | VG | Fine | VF | XF |
|-----|------|------|------|------|------|
| 137 | 1748 MF | 1500. | 3000. | 5000. | 8000. |
|  | 1749 MF | 1500. | 3000. | 5000. | 8000. |
|  | 1750 MF | 1500. | 3000. | 5000. | 8000. |
|  | 1751 MF | 1500. | 3000. | 5000. | 8000. |

**Rev: W/o value.**

| KM# | Date | VG | Fine | VF | XF |
|-----|------|------|------|------|------|
| 138 | 1752 MF | 1000. | 2000. | 3500. | 6000. |
|  | 1753 MF | 1000. | 2000. | 3500. | 6000. |
|  | 1754 MF | 1000. | 2000. | 3500. | 6000. |
|  | 1755 MM | 1000. | 2000. | 3500. | 6000. |
|  | 1756 MM | 1000. | 2000. | 3500. | 6000. |

**Obv. leg: FERDND.VI.D.G. . ., large full bust.**

| KM# | Date | VG | Fine | VF | XF |
|-----|------|-----|------|-----|-----|
| 139 | 1757 MM | 1250. | 2500. | 4000. | 6500. |
|     | 1758 MM | 1250. | 2500. | 4000. | 6500. |
|     | 1759 MM | 1250. | 2500. | 4000. | 6500. |

**Obv. leg: CAROLVS.III.D.G. . ., young bust.**
**Rev. leg: NOMINA MAGNA SEQUOR**

| KM# | Date | VG | Fine | VF | XF |
|-----|------|-----|------|-----|-----|
| 140 | 1760 MM | 3500. | 6500. | 10,000. | 20,000. |
|     | 1761 MM | 3500. | 6500. | 10,000. | 20,000. |

**Obv. leg: CAROLUS.III.D.G. . ., large young bust.**
**Rev. leg: IN.UTROQ.FELIX.AUSPICE.DEO.**

| KM# | Date | VG | Fine | VF | XF |
|-----|------|-----|------|-----|-----|
| 141 | 1762 MF | 2500. | 4500. | 7500. | 15,000. |
|     | 1763 MF | 2500. | 4500. | 7500. | 15,000. |
|     | 1764 MF | 2500. | 4500. | 7500. | 15,000. |
|     | 1765 MF | 2500. | 4500. | 7500. | 15,000. |
|     | 1766 MF | 2500. | 4500. | 7500. | 15,000. |
|     | 1767 MF | 2500. | 4500. | 7500. | 15,000. |
|     | 1768 MF | 2500. | 4500. | 7500. | 15,000. |
|     | 1769 MF | 2500. | 4500. | 7500. | 15,000. |
|     | 1770 MF | 2500. | 4500. | 7500. | 15,000. |
|     | 1771 MF | 2500. | 4500. | 7500. | 15,000. |

**13.5400 g, .901 GOLD, .3922 oz AGW**
**Obv. leg: CAROL.III.D.G. . .**
**Rev: Initials and mint mark upright.**

| KM# | Date | VG | Fine | VF | XF |
|-----|------|-----|------|-----|-----|
| 142.1 | 1772 FM | 400.00 | 650.00 | 1000. | 2000. |
|       | 1773 FM | 400.00 | 650.00 | 1000. | 2000. |

**Rev: Initials and mint mark inverted.**

| KM# | Date | VG | Fine | VF | XF |
|-----|------|-----|------|-----|-----|
| 142.2 | 1773 FM | 400.00 | 600.00 | 900.00 | 1850. |
|       | 1774 FM | 400.00 | 600.00 | 900.00 | 1850. |
|       | 1775 FM | 400.00 | 600.00 | 900.00 | 1850. |
|       | 1776 FM | 400.00 | 600.00 | 900.00 | 1850. |

**13.5400 g, .875 GOLD, .3809 oz AGW**

| KM# | Date | VG | Fine | VF | XF |
|-----|------|-----|------|-----|-----|
| 142.2a | 1777 FM | 400.00 | 600.00 | 900.00 | 1850. |
|        | 1778 FF | 400.00 | 600.00 | 900.00 | 1850. |
|        | 1779 FF | 400.00 | 600.00 | 900.00 | 1850. |
|        | 1780 FF | 400.00 | 600.00 | 900.00 | 1850. |
|        | 1781 FF | 400.00 | 600.00 | 900.00 | 1850. |
|        | 1782 FF | 400.00 | 600.00 | 900.00 | 1850. |
|        | 1783 FF | 400.00 | 600.00 | 900.00 | 1850. |
|        | 1784 FF | 400.00 | 600.00 | 900.00 | 1850. |
|        | 1784 FM | 400.00 | 600.00 | 900.00 | 1850. |
|        | 1785 FM | 400.00 | 600.00 | 900.00 | 1850. |

| KM# | Date | VG | Fine | VF | XF |
|-----|------|-----|------|-----|-----|
| 142.2a | 1786 FM | 400.00 | 600.00 | 900.00 | 1850. |
|        | 1787 FM | 400.00 | 600.00 | 900.00 | 1850. |
|        | 1788 FM | 400.00 | 600.00 | 900.00 | 1850. |
|        | 1789 FM | 400.00 | 600.00 | 900.00 | 1850. |

**Rev: Initials and mint mark upright.**

| KM# | Date | VG | Fine | VF | XF |
|-----|------|-----|------|-----|-----|
| 142.1a | 1788 FM | 400.00 | 650.00 | 1000. | 2000. |

**Obv. leg: CAROL.IV.D.G. . ., bust of Charles III.**

| KM# | Date | VG | Fine | VF | XF |
|-----|------|-----|------|-----|-----|
| 143.1 | 1789 FM | 500.00 | 700.00 | 1100. | 2150. |
|       | 1790 FM | 500.00 | 700.00 | 1100. | 2150. |

**Obv. leg: CAROL. IIII D.G. . ., bust of Charles III.**

| KM# | Date | VG | Fine | VF | XF |
|-----|------|-----|------|-----|-----|
| 143.2 | 1790 FM | 600.00 | 1000. | 1800. | 3000. |

**Obv: Armored bust of Charles IIII.**

| KM# | Date | VG | Fine | VF | XF |
|-----|------|-----|------|-----|-----|
| 144 | 1792 FM | 300.00 | 500.00 | 750.00 | 1600. |
|     | 1793 FM | 300.00 | 500.00 | 750.00 | 1600. |
|     | 1794/3 FM | 300.00 | 500.00 | 750.00 | 1600. |
|     | 1794 FM | 300.00 | 500.00 | 750.00 | 1600. |
|     | 1795 FM | 300.00 | 500.00 | 750.00 | 1600. |
|     | 1796 FM | 300.00 | 500.00 | 750.00 | 1600. |
|     | 1797 FM | 300.00 | 500.00 | 750.00 | 1600. |
|     | 1798/7 FM | 300.00 | 500.00 | 750.00 | 1600. |
|     | 1798 FM | 300.00 | 500.00 | 750.00 | 1600. |
|     | 1799 FM | 300.00 | 500.00 | 750.00 | 1600. |
|     | 1800 FM | 300.00 | 500.00 | 750.00 | 1600. |
|     | 1801 FM | 300.00 | 500.00 | 750.00 | 1600. |
|     | 1801 FT | 300.00 | 500.00 | 750.00 | 1600. |
|     | 1802 FT | 300.00 | 500.00 | 750.00 | 1600. |
|     | 1803 FT | 300.00 | 500.00 | 750.00 | 1600. |
|     | 1804/3 TH | 300.00 | 500.00 | 750.00 | 1600. |
|     | 1804 TH | 300.00 | 500.00 | 750.00 | 1600. |
|     | 1805 TH | 300.00 | 500.00 | 750.00 | 1600. |
|     | 1806/5 TH | 300.00 | 500.00 | 750.00 | 1600. |
|     | 1806 TH | 300.00 | 500.00 | 750.00 | 1600. |
|     | 1807 TH | 300.00 | 500.00 | 750.00 | 1600. |
|     | 1808/0 TH | 300.00 | 500.00 | 750.00 | 1600. |
|     | 1808 TH | 300.00 | 500.00 | 750.00 | 1600. |

**Obv: Armored bust of Ferdinand VII.**

| KM# | Date | VG | Fine | VF | XF |
|-----|------|-----|------|-----|-----|
| 145 | 1810 HJ | 450.00 | 600.00 | 950.00 | 1800. |
|     | 1811 HJ | 350.00 | 500.00 | 850.00 | 1700. |
|     | 1812 HJ | 350.00 | 500.00 | 850.00 | 1700. |

Obv: Undraped bust of Ferdinand VII.

| KM# | Date | VG | Fine | VF | XF |
|-----|------|-----|------|-----|-----|
| 146 | 1814 HJ | 400.00 | 700.00 | 1200. | 2700. |
| | 1815 HJ | 400.00 | 700.00 | 1200. | 2700. |
| | 1815 JJ | 400.00 | 700.00 | 1200. | 2700. |
| | 1816 JJ | 400.00 | 700.00 | 1200. | 2700. |
| | 1817 JJ | 400.00 | 700.00 | 1200. | 2700. |
| | 1818 JJ | 400.00 | 700.00 | 1200. | 2700. |
| | 1819 JJ | 400.00 | 700.00 | 1200. | 2700. |
| | 1820 JJ | 400.00 | 700.00 | 1200. | 2700. |

## 8 ESCUDOS

27.0700 g, .917 GOLD, .7981 oz AGW
Obv. leg: PHILIP.V.D.G.HISPAN.ET IND.REX.
Rev. leg: INITIUM SAPIENTIAE TIMOR DOMINI.

| KM# | Date | VG | Fine | VF | XF |
|-----|------|-----|------|-----|-----|
| 148 | 1732 | — | — | Rare | — |
| | 1732 F | — | — | Rare | — |
| | 1733 F | — | — | Rare | — |
| | 1734 MF | 1000. | 1650. | 2750. | 4850. |
| | 1735 MF | 1000. | 1500. | 2500. | 4500. |
| | 1736 MF | 1000. | 1500. | 2500. | 4500. |
| | 1737 MF | 1000. | 1500. | 2500. | 4500. |
| | 1738/7 MF | 1000. | 1500. | 2500. | 4500. |
| | 1738 MF | 1000. | 1500. | 2500. | 4500. |
| | 1739 MF | 1000. | 1500. | 2500. | 4500. |
| | 1740 MF | 1000. | 1500. | 2500. | 4500. |
| | 1741 MF | 1000. | 1500. | 2500. | 4500. |
| | 1742 MF | 1000. | 1500. | 2500. | 4500. |
| | 1743 MF | 1000. | 1500. | 2500. | 4500. |
| | 1744 MF | 1000. | 1500. | 2500. | 4500. |
| | 1745 MF | 1000. | 1500. | 2500. | 4500. |
| | 1746 MF | 1000. | 1500. | 2500. | 4500. |
| | 1747 MF | 1000. | 1500. | 2500. | 4500. |

Obv. leg: FERDND.VI.D.G. . ., young bust.

| KM# | Date | VG | Fine | VF | XF |
|-----|------|-----|------|-----|-----|
| 149 | 1747 MF | 9000. | 15,000. | 22,000. | 35,000. |

Obv. leg: FERDND.VI.D.G. . ., small bust.
Rev. leg: NOMINA MAGNA SEQUOR

| | | | | | |
|-----|------|-----|------|-----|-----|
| 150 | 1748 MF | 1200. | 2000. | 3500. | 6000. |
| | 1749/8 MF | 1200. | 2000. | 3500. | 6000. |
| | 1749 MF | 1200. | 2000. | 3500. | 6000. |
| | 1750 MF | 1200. | 2000. | 3500. | 6000. |
| | 1751 MF | 1200. | 2000. | 3500. | 6000. |

Obv. leg: FERDND.VI.D.G. . ., large bust.
Rev: W/o 8 S divided by arms.

| | | | | | |
|-----|------|-----|------|-----|-----|
| 151 | 1752 MF | 1200. | 2000. | 3500. | 6000. |
| | 1753 MF | 1200. | 2000. | 3500. | 6000. |
| | 1754 MF | 1200. | 2000. | 3500. | 6000. |
| | 1755 MM | 1200. | 2000. | 3500. | 6000. |
| | 1756 MM | 1200. | 2000. | 3500. | 6000. |

Obv. leg: FERDND.VI.D.G. . ., medium, full bust.

| | | | | | |
|-----|------|-----|------|-----|-----|
| 152 | 1757 MM | 1200. | 2000. | 3500. | 6000. |
| | 1758 MM | 1200. | 2000. | 3500. | 6000. |
| | 1759 MM | 1200. | 2000. | 3500. | 6000. |

Obv. leg: CAROLVS.III.D.G. . ., young bust.
w/Order of the Golden Fleece at date.

| KM# | Date | VG | Fine | VF | XF |
|------|------|------|------|------|------|
| 153 | 1760 MM | 1750. | 3000. | 5000. | 9000. |
| | 1761 MM | 2000. | 3500. | 5500. | 10,000. |

Obv. leg: CAROLVS.III.D.G. . ., young bust.
w/Order of the Golden Fleece on chest.

| | | | | | |
|------|------|------|------|------|------|
| 154 | 1761 MM | 1750. | 3000. | 5250. | 9500. |

Obv. leg: CAROLVS.III.D.G. . ., large bust.
Rev. leg: IN.UTROQ.FELIX.AUSPICE.

| | | | | | |
|------|------|------|------|------|------|
| 155 | 1762 MF | 1600. | 2750. | 4500. | 8500. |
| | 1762 MM | 1600. | 2750. | 4500. | 8500. |
| | 1763 MF | 1600. | 2750. | 4500. | 8500. |
| | 1763 MM | 1600. | 2750. | 4500. | 8500. |
| | 1764 MF | 1750. | 3000. | 5000. | 9000. |
| | 1764 MM | 1750. | 3000. | 5000. | 9000. |
| | 1765/4 MF | 1750. | 3000. | 5000. | 9000. |
| | 1765 MF | 1750. | 3000. | 5000. | 9000. |
| | 1765 MM | 1500. | 2500. | 4000. | 7500. |
| | 1766 MF | 1500. | 2500. | 4000. | 7500. |
| | 1767 MF | 1500. | 2500. | 4000. | 7500. |
| | 1768 MF | 1500. | 2500. | 4000. | 7500. |
| | 1769 MF | 1500. | 2500. | 4000. | 7500. |
| | 1770 MF | 1500. | 2500. | 4000. | 7500. |
| | 1771 MF | 1750. | 3000. | 5000. | 9000. |

27.0700 g, .901 GOLD, .7841 oz AGW
Obv. leg: CAROL.III.D.G. . ., mature bust.
Rev. leg: . . . AUSPICE.DEO.; initials and
mint mark upright.

| KM# | Date | VG | Fine | VF | XF |
|------|------|------|------|------|------|
| 156.1 | 1772 FM | 500.00 | 750.00 | 1250. | 2000. |
| | 1773 FM | 550.00 | 850.00 | 1350. | 2250. |

Rev: Initials and mint mark inverted.

| 156.2 | 1773 FM | 500.00 | 700.00 | 1100. | 1650. |
|------|------|------|------|------|------|
| | 1774 FM | 500.00 | 700.00 | 1100. | 1650. |
| | 1775 FM | 500.00 | 700.00 | 1100. | 1650. |
| | 1776 FM | 500.00 | 700.00 | 1100. | 1650. |

27.0700 g, .875 GOLD, .7616 oz AGW

| 156.2a | 1777/6 FM | 500.00 | 700.00 | 1100. | 1650. |
|------|------|------|------|------|------|
| | 1777 FM | 500.00 | 700.00 | 1100. | 1650. |
| | 1778 FF | 500.00 | 700.00 | 1100. | 1650. |
| | 1779 FF | 500.00 | 700.00 | 1100. | 1650. |
| | 1780 FF | 500.00 | 700.00 | 1100. | 1650. |
| | 1781 FF | 500.00 | 700.00 | 1100. | 1650. |
| | 1782 FF | 500.00 | 700.00 | 1100. | 1650. |
| | 1783 FF | 500.00 | 700.00 | 1100. | 1650. |
| | 1784 FF | 500.00 | 700.00 | 1100. | 1650. |
| | 1784 FM | 500.00 | 700.00 | 1100. | 1650. |
| | 1785 FM | 500.00 | 700.00 | 1100. | 1650. |
| | 1786 FM | 500.00 | 700.00 | 1100. | 1650. |
| | 1787 FM | 500.00 | 700.00 | 1100. | 1650. |
| | 1788 FM | 500.00 | 700.00 | 1100. | 1650. |

Rev: Initials and mint mark upright.

| 156.1a | 1788 FM | 600.00 | 900.00 | 1500. | 2500. |
|------|------|------|------|------|------|

Obv. leg: CAROL.IV.D.G. . ., bust of Charles III.
Rev: IN UTROQ. . . A.D., arms, Order chain.

| 157 | 1789 FM | 500.00 | 700.00 | 1150. | 2000. |
|------|------|------|------|------|------|
| | 1790 FM | 500.00 | 700.00 | 1150. | 2000. |

**Obv: Armored bust of Ferdinand VII.**

| KM# | Date | VG | Fine | VF | XF |
|---|---|---|---|---|---|
| 160 | 1808 TH | 400.00 | 500.00 | 750.00 | 1250. |
| | 1809 HJ | 400.00 | 500.00 | 750.00 | 1350. |
| | 1810 HJ | 375.00 | 475.00 | 700.00 | 1200. |
| | 1811/0 HJ | 425.00 | 525.00 | 800.00 | 1350. |
| | 1811 HJ | 425.00 | 525.00 | 800.00 | 1350. |
| | 1811 JJ | 375.00 | 475.00 | 700.00 | 1200. |
| | 1812 JJ | 375.00 | 475.00 | 700.00 | 1200. |

**Obv. leg: CAROL.IIII.D.G. . ., bust of Charles III.**

| KM# | Date | VG | Fine | VF | XF |
|---|---|---|---|---|---|
| 158 | 1790 FM | 500.00 | 700.00 | 1150. | 2000. |

**Obv: Armored bust of Charles IIII.**
**Rev. leg: IN UTROQ. FELIX., arms, Order chain.**

| 159 | 1791 FM | 350.00 | 450.00 | 625.00 | 1000. |
|---|---|---|---|---|---|
| | 1792 FM | 350.00 | 450.00 | 625.00 | 1000. |
| | 1793 FM | 350.00 | 450.00 | 625.00 | 1000. |
| | 1794 FM | 350.00 | 450.00 | 625.00 | 1000. |
| | 1795 FM | 350.00 | 450.00 | 625.00 | 1000. |
| | 1796/5 FM | 400.00 | 500.00 | 700.00 | 1150. |
| | 1796 FM | 350.00 | 450.00 | 625.00 | 1000. |
| | 1797 FM | 350.00 | 450.00 | 625.00 | 1000. |
| | 1798 FM | 350.00 | 450.00 | 625.00 | 1000. |
| | 1799 FM | 350.00 | 450.00 | 625.00 | 1000. |
| | 1800 FM | 350.00 | 450.00 | 625.00 | 1000. |
| | 1801/0 FT | 400.00 | 500.00 | 700.00 | 1150. |
| | 1801 FM | 350.00 | 450.00 | 625.00 | 1000. |
| | 1801 FT | 350.00 | 450.00 | 625.00 | 1000. |
| | 1802 FT | 350.00 | 450.00 | 625.00 | 1000. |
| | 1803 FT | 350.00 | 450.00 | 625.00 | 1000. |
| | 1804/3 TH | 400.00 | 500.00 | 700.00 | 1150. |
| | 1804 TH | 350.00 | 450.00 | 625.00 | 1000. |
| | 1805 TH | 350.00 | 450.00 | 625.00 | 1000. |
| | 1806 TH | 350.00 | 450.00 | 625.00 | 1000. |
| | 1807/6 TH | 400.00 | 500.00 | 700.00 | 1150. |
| | 1807 TH | 350.00 | 450.00 | 625.00 | 1000. |
| | 1808 TH | 450.00 | 600.00 | 800.00 | 1250. |

**Obv: Undraped bust of Ferdinand VII.**

| 161 | 1814 JJ | 360.00 | 465.00 | 650.00 | 1000. |
|---|---|---|---|---|---|
| | 1815/4 JJ | 400.00 | 500.00 | 700.00 | 1150. |
| | 1815/4 HJ | 400.00 | 500.00 | 700.00 | 1150. |
| | 1815 JJ | 360.00 | 465.00 | 650.00 | 1000. |
| | 1815 HJ | 360.00 | 465.00 | 650.00 | 1000. |
| | 1816/5 JJ | 400.00 | 500.00 | 700.00 | 1150. |
| | 1816 JJ | 360.00 | 465.00 | 650.00 | 1000. |
| | 1817 JJ | 400.00 | 500.00 | 700.00 | 1150. |
| | 1818/7 JJ | 360.00 | 465.00 | 675.00 | 1100. |
| | 1818 JJ | 360.00 | 465.00 | 675.00 | 1100. |
| | 1819 JJ | 360.00 | 465.00 | 675.00 | 1100. |
| | 1820 JJ | 360.00 | 465.00 | 675.00 | 1100. |
| | 1821 JJ | 400.00 | 500.00 | 750.00 | 1300. |

# PROCLAMATION MEDALLIC ISSUES (Q)

The 'Q' used in the following listings refer to *Standard Catalog of Mexican Coins, Paper Money, Stocks, Bonds and Medals*, Krause Publications, Inc., copyright 1981.

## Chiapa
### REAL

**SILVER**
**Obv. leg: FERNANDO VII REY DE ESPANA Y DE SUS INDIAS, crowned arms between pillars, IR below.
INDIAS. Rev: Legend in 5 lines within wreath,
PROCLA/MADO/ENCIUD/R.DECHIAPPA/1808.**

| KM# | Date | | Fine | VF | XF | Unc |
|---|---|---|---|---|---|---|
| Q8 | 1808 | | 22.50 | 35.00 | 50.00 | — |

## 2 REALES

**SILVER**
**Obv. leg: FERNANDO VII REY DE ESPANA Y DE SUS INDIAS.**

| Q10 | 1808 | | 50.00 | 70.00 | 100.00 | — |
|---|---|---|---|---|---|---|

## Mexico City
### 1/2 REAL

**SILVER, 1.60 g**
Obv. leg: A CARLOS IV REY DE ESPANA
Y DE LAS YNDIAS. Rev. leg:
PROCLAMADO EN MEXICO ANO DE 1789.

| | | | | | |
|---|---|---|---|---|---|
| Q22 | 1789 | 20.00 | 28.50 | 40.00 | — |

**BRONZE, 18mm**

| | | | | | |
|---|---|---|---|---|---|
| Q22a | 1789 | 22.50 | 35.00 | 50.00 | — |

**SILVER, 17mm**
Obv: Crowned arms in double-lined circle.

| | | | | | |
|---|---|---|---|---|---|
| Q23 | 1789 | 20.00 | 28.50 | 40.00 | — |

**BRONZE**

| | | | | | |
|---|---|---|---|---|---|
| Q23a | 1789 | 22.50 | 35.00 | 50.00 | — |

### REAL

**SILVER**

| | | | | | |
|---|---|---|---|---|---|
| Q24 | 1789 | 20.00 | 28.50 | 40.00 | — |

**BRONZE, 21mm**

| | | | | | |
|---|---|---|---|---|---|
| Q24a | 1789 | 22.50 | 35.00 | 50.00 | — |

**SILVER**
Obv: Crowned arms in double-lined circle.

| | | | | | |
|---|---|---|---|---|---|
| Q-A24 | 1789 | 20.00 | 28.50 | 40.00 | — |

**COPPER**

| | | | | | |
|---|---|---|---|---|---|
| Q-A24a | 1789 | 22.50 | 35.00 | 50.00 | — |

### 2 REALES

**SILVER, 6.70 g**

| | | | | | |
|---|---|---|---|---|---|
| Q25 | 1789 | 35.00 | 50.00 | 75.00 | — |

**BRONZE**

| | | | | | |
|---|---|---|---|---|---|
| Q25a | 1789 | 30.00 | 45.00 | 60.00 | — |

### 4 REALES

**SILVER, 13.60 g**

| | | | | | |
|---|---|---|---|---|---|
| Q27 | 1789 | 100.00 | 150.00 | 225.00 | — |

| KM# | Date | BRONZE Fine | VF | XF | Unc |
|---|---|---|---|---|---|
| Q27a | 1789 | 70.00 | 100.00 | 150.00 | — |

### 8 REALES

**SILVER, 27.00 g**

| | | | | | |
|---|---|---|---|---|---|
| Q28 | 1789 | 200.00 | 275.00 | 400.00 | — |

**BRONZE**

| | | | | | |
|---|---|---|---|---|---|
| Q28a | 1789 | 70.00 | 100.00 | 150.00 | — |

## Queretaro
### 2 REALES

**SILVER**
Obv. leg: FERNANDO VII REY DE ESPANA.

| | | | | | |
|---|---|---|---|---|---|
| Q64 | 1808 | 35.00 | 50.00 | 75.00 | — |

### 4 REALES

**SILVER**

| | | | | | |
|---|---|---|---|---|---|
| Q-A66 | 1808 | 140.00 | 200.00 | 300.00 | — |

## 8 REALES

| | | SILVER | | | |
|---|---|---|---|---|---|
| KM# | Date | Fine | VF | XF | Unc |
| Q68 | 1808 | 300.00 | 425.00 | 600.00 | — |

# WAR OF INDEPENDENCE

## ROYALIST ISSUES
### (1810-1821)
## Provisional Mints
### RULER
Ferdinand VII, 1808-1821

### MINT MARKS
CA - Chihuahua
D - Durango
GA - Guadalajara
GO - Guanajuato
ZS - Zacatecas

### MONETARY SYSTEM
16 Reales = 1 Escudo

### CHIHUAHUA

The Chihuahua Mint was established by a decree of October 8, 1810 as a temporary mint. Their first coins were cast 8 reales using Mexico City coins as patterns and obliterating/changing the mint mark and moneyer initials. Two c/m were placed on the obverse - on the left, a T designating its having been received by the Royal Treasurer and on the right crowned pillars of Hercules with pomegranate beneath; the symbol of the comptroller.

In 1814 standard dies were available and from 1814 to 1822 standard 8 reales were struck. Only the one denomination was made at this mint.

### MINT MARK: CA

## 8 REALES

**CAST SILVER**
**Obv: Imaginary bust of Ferdinand VII;**
**leg: FERDIN.VII.DEI.GRATIA.**
**c/m: 'T' at left and pomegranate**
**pillars at right.**

| KM# | Date | Good | VG | Fine | VF |
|---|---|---|---|---|---|
| 123 | 1810 RP | — | — | Rare | — |
| | 1811 RP | 45.00 | 60.00 | 100.00 | 150.00 |
| | 1812 RP | 30.00 | 40.00 | 60.00 | 90.00 |
| | 1813/2 RP | 32.50 | 45.00 | 70.00 | 100.00 |
| | 1813 RP | 30.00 | 40.00 | 60.00 | 90.00 |

**27.0700 g, .903 SILVER, .7860 oz ASW**
**Obv: Draped bust of Ferdinand VII.**
**Rev: Similar to KM#123.**

| KM# | Date | VG | Fine | VF | XF |
|---|---|---|---|---|---|
| 111.1 | 1813 RP | — | Reported, not confirmed | | |
| | 1814 RP | — | Reported, not confirmed | | |
| | 1815 RP | 200.00 | 275.00 | 350.00 | 500.00 |
| | 1816 RP | 80.00 | 125.00 | 150.00 | 275.00 |
| | 1817 RP | 100.00 | 150.00 | 185.00 | 275.00 |
| | 1818 RP | 100.00 | 150.00 | 185.00 | 275.00 |
| | 1819 RP | 125.00 | 175.00 | 250.00 | 350.00 |
| | 1820 RP | 200.00 | 275.00 | 350.00 | 500.00 |
| | 1821 RP | 200.00 | 275.00 | 350.00 | 500.00 |
| | 1822 RP | 400.00 | 600.00 | 800.00 | 1100. |

**NOTE:** KM#111.1 is normally found counterstamped over earlier cast 8 Reales, KM#123.

## DURANGO

The Durango mint was authorized as a temporary mint on the same day as the Chihuahua Mint, October 8, 1810. The mint opened in 1811 and made coins of 6 denominations between 1811 and 1822.

**MINT MARK: D**

### 1/8 REAL

**COPPER**
**Obv: Crown above double F7 monogram.**
**Rev: EN DURANGO, value, date.**

| KM# | Date | VG | Fine | VF | XF |
|-----|------|-----|------|-----|-----|
| 60 | 1812 | 32.50 | 75.00 | 125.00 | 250.00 |
| | 1813 | — | — | Rare | — |
| | 1814 | — | — | Rare | — |

**Rev: Spray added above date.**

| | | | | | |
|-----|------|-----|------|-----|-----|
| 61 | 1814 | 15.00 | 30.00 | 50.00 | 90.00 |
| | 1815 | 18.00 | 35.00 | 60.00 | 100.00 |
| | 1816 | 18.00 | 35.00 | 60.00 | 100.00 |
| | 1817 | 15.00 | 30.00 | 50.00 | 90.00 |
| | 1818 | 15.00 | 30.00 | 50.00 | 90.00 |
| | 1818 OCTAVO DD REAL (error) | | | | |
| | | 45.00 | 80.00 | — | — |

### 1/2 REAL

**1.6900 g, .903 SILVER, .0491 oz ASW**
**Obv: Draped bust of Ferdinand VII.**

| | | | | | |
|------|---------|--------|--------|--------|-------|
| 74.1 | 1813 RM | 250.00 | 450.00 | 750.00 | 1800. |
| | 1814 MZ | 250.00 | 450.00 | 750.00 | 1850. |
| | 1816 MZ | 250.00 | 450.00 | 750.00 | 1850. |

### REAL

**3.3800 g, .903 SILVER, .0981 oz ASW**
**Obv: Draped bust of Ferdinand VII.**

| | | | | | |
|------|---------|--------|--------|--------|-------|
| 83.1 | 1813 RM | 250.00 | 450.00 | 650.00 | 1650. |
| | 1814 MZ | 250.00 | 450.00 | 650.00 | 1650. |
| | 1815 MZ | 250.00 | 450.00 | 650.00 | 1650. |

### 2 REALES

**6.7700 g, .903 SILVER, .1966 oz ASW**
**Obv: Armored bust of Ferdinand VII.**

| | | | | | |
|------|---------|--------|--------|--------|-------|
| 92.2 | 1811 RM | 250.00 | 400.00 | 650.00 | 1650. |
| | 1812 RM | — | — | Rare | — |

**Obv: Draped bust of Ferdinand VII.**

| | | | | | |
|------|---------|--------|--------|--------|-------|
| 93.1 | 1812 MZ | 250.00 | 400.00 | 650.00 | 1650. |
| | 1812 RM | 1200. | 2000. | — | — |
| | 1813 MZ | 300.00 | 600.00 | 1000. | 2750. |
| | 1813 RM | 300.00 | 600.00 | 1000. | 2750. |
| | 1814 MZ | 300.00 | 600.00 | 1000. | 2750. |
| | 1815 MZ | 300.00 | 600.00 | 1000. | 2750. |
| | 1816 MZ | 300.00 | 600.00 | 1000. | 2750. |
| | 1817 MZ | 300.00 | 600.00 | 1000. | 2750. |

## 4 REALES

**13.5400 g, .903 SILVER, .3931 oz ASW**
**Obv: Draped bust of Ferdinand VII.**

| KM# | Date | VG | Fine | VF | XF |
|-------|---------|--------|--------|-------|-------|
| 102.1 | 1814 MZ | 550.00 | 1000. | 1650. | 4500. |
| | 1816 MZ | 450.00 | 900.00 | 1400. | 4000. |
| | 1817 MZ | 450.00 | 900.00 | 1400. | 4000. |

## 8 REALES

**27.0700 g, .903 SILVER, .7860 oz ASW**
**Obv: Armored bust of Ferdinand VII.**

| | | | | | |
|-------|---------|--------|--------|-------|-------|
| 110.1 | 1811 RM | 600.00 | 1000. | 1750. | 5000. |
| | 1812 RM | 350.00 | 650.00 | 1000. | 3500. |
| | 1813 MZ | 350.00 | 650.00 | 1000. | 3500. |
| | 1814 MZ | 350.00 | 650.00 | 1000. | 3500. |

**Obv: Draped bust of Ferdinand VII.**

| | | | | | |
|-------|----------|--------|--------|--------|-------|
| 111.2 | 1812 MZ | 350.00 | 500.00 | 800.00 | 1750. |
| | 1812 RM | 125.00 | 175.00 | 275.00 | 800.00 |
| | 1813 RM | 150.00 | 200.00 | 325.00 | 850.00 |
| | 1813 MZ | 125.00 | 175.00 | 275.00 | 750.00 |
| | 1814 MZ | 150.00 | 225.00 | 275.00 | 750.00 |
| | 1815 MZ | 75.00 | 125.00 | 225.00 | 600.00 |
| | 1816 MZ | 50.00 | 75.00 | 125.00 | 325.00 |
| | 1817 MZ | 30.00 | 50.00 | 90.00 | 250.00 |
| | 1818 MZ | 50.00 | 75.00 | 125.00 | 350.00 |
| | 1818 RM | 50.00 | 75.00 | 125.00 | 325.00 |
| | 1818 CG/RM | | | | |
| | | 100.00 | 125.00 | 150.00 | 350.00 |
| | 1818 CG | 50.00 | 75.00 | 125.00 | 325.00 |
| | 1819 CG/RM | 50.00 | 100.00 | 150.00 | 300.00 |
| | 1819 CG | 30.00 | 60.00 | 100.00 | 250.00 |
| | 1820 CG | 30.00 | 60.00 | 100.00 | 250.00 |
| | 1821 CG | 30.00 | 40.00 | 80.00 | 225.00 |
| | 1822 CG | 30.00 | 50.00 | 90.00 | 240.00 |

**NOTE:** Occasionally these are found struck over Guadalajara 8 reales and are very rare in general, specimens dated prior to 1816 are rather weakly struck.

## GUADALAJARA

The Guadalajara Mint made its first coins in 1812 and the mint operated until April 30, 1815. It was to reopen in 1818 and continue operations until 1822. It was the only Royalist mint to strike gold coins, both 4 and 8 escudos. In addition to these it struck the standard 5 denominations in silver.

## 1/2 REAL

**1.6900 g, .903 SILVER, .0491 oz ASW**
**Obv: Draped bust of Ferdinand VII.**

| KM#<br>74.2 | Date | VG | Fine | VF | XF |
|------|------|-----|------|-----|------|
| | 1812 MR | — | — | Rare | — |
| | 1814 MR | 40.00 | 100.00 | 200.00 | 300.00 |
| | 1815 MR | 200.00 | 350.00 | 500.00 | 1000. |

## REAL

**3.3800 g, .903 SILVER, .0981 oz ASW**
**Obv: Draped bust of Ferdinand VII.**

| 83.2 | 1814 MR | 125.00 | 175.00 | 325.00 | 600.00 |
|------|---------|--------|--------|--------|--------|
| | 1815 MR | 300.00 | 500.00 | — | — |

## 2 REALES

**6.7700 g, .903 SILVER, .1966 oz ASW**
**Obv: Draped bust of Ferdinand VII.**

| 93.2 | 1812 MR | 300.00 | 500.00 | 800.00 | 2500. |
|------|---------|--------|--------|--------|-------|
| | 1814 MR | 75.00 | 125.00 | 250.00 | 600.00 |
| | 1815/4 MR | 425.00 | 725.00 | 1100. | 3600. |
| | 1815 MR | 400.00 | 700.00 | 1000. | 3500. |
| | 1821 FS | 200.00 | 250.00 | 350.00 | 900.00 |

## 4 REALES

**13.5400 g, .903 SILVER, .3931 oz ASW**
**Obv: Draped bust of Ferdinand VII.**

| 102.2 | 1814 MR | 40.00 | 65.00 | 150.00 | 250.00 |
|-------|---------|-------|-------|--------|--------|
| | 1815 MR | 80.00 | 150.00 | 300.00 | 500.00 |

**Obv: Large bust.**

| 102.3 | 1814 MR | 50.00 | 100.00 | 200.00 | 400.00 |
|-------|---------|-------|--------|--------|--------|

**Obv: Large bust w/berries in laurel.**

| KM#<br>102.4 | Date | VG | Fine | VF | XF |
|------|------|-----|------|-----|------|
| | 1814 MR | — | — | Rare | — |

## 8 REALES

**27.0700 g, .903 SILVER, .7860 oz ASW**
**Obv: Draped bust of Ferdinand VII.**

| 111.3 | 1812 MR | 2000. | 3500. | 5000. | 7000. |
|-------|---------|-------|-------|-------|-------|
| | 1813/2 MR | 60.00 | 100.00 | 150.00 | 400.00 |
| | 1813 MR | 60.00 | 100.00 | 150.00 | 400.00 |
| | 1814 MR | 20.00 | 35.00 | 60.00 | 180.00 |
| | 1815 MR | 150.00 | 200.00 | 350.00 | 750.00 |
| | 1818 FS | 30.00 | 50.00 | 75.00 | 200.00 |
| | 1821/18 FS | 30.00 | 50.00 | 75.00 | 200.00 |
| | 1821 FS | 25.00 | 35.00 | 60.00 | 165.00 |
| | 1822/1 FS | 30.00 | 50.00 | 75.00 | 200.00 |
| | 1822 FS | 30.00 | 50.00 | 75.00 | 200.00 |

**NOTE:** Die varieties exist. Early dates are also encountered struck over other types.

## 4 ESCUDOS

**13.5400 g, .875 GOLD, .3809 oz ASW**
**Obv: Uniformed bust of Ferdinand VII.**

| 147 | 1812 MR | — | — | Rare | — |
|-----|---------|---|---|------|---|

## 8 ESCUDOS

**27.0700 g, .875 GOLD, .7616 oz AGW**
**Obv: Large uniformed bust of Ferdinand VII.**

| KM# | Date | VG | Fine | VF | XF |
|-----|------|-----|------|-----|-----|
| 162 | 1812 MR | — | Reported, not confirmed | | |
| | 1813 MR | 5250. | 8250. | 12,500. | 21,000. |

**Obv: Small uniformed bust of Ferdinand VII.**

| 163 | 1813 MR | 10,000. | 16,000. | 30,000. | 45,000. |

**NOTE:** Spink America Gerber sale 6-96 VF or better realized $46,200.

**Obv: Undraped bust of Ferdinand VII.**

| 161.1 | 1821 FS | 1500. | 2500. | 4500. | 7500. |

**Obv: Draped bust of Ferdinand VII.**

| KM# | Date | VG | Fine | VF | XF |
|-----|------|-----|------|-----|-----|
| 164 | 1821 FS | 7000. | 9500. | 14,000. | 23,000. |

## GUANAJUATO

The Guanajuato Mint was authorized December 24, 1812 and started production shortly thereafter; closing for unknown reasons on May 15, 1813. The mint was reopened in April, 1821 by the insurgents, who struck coins of the old royal Spanish design to pay their army, even after independence, well into 1822. Only the 2 and 8 reales coins were made.

**MINT MARK: Go**

### 2 REALES

**6.7700 g, .903 SILVER, .1966 oz ASW**
**Obv: Draped bust of Ferdinand VII.**

| 93.3 | 1821 JM | 35.00 | 65.00 | 100.00 | 185.00 |
|------|---------|-------|-------|--------|--------|
| | 1822 JM | 30.00 | 50.00 | 75.00 | 145.00 |

### 8 REALES

**27.0700 g, .903 SILVER, .7860 oz ASW**
**Obv: Draped bust of Ferdinand VII.**

| 111.4 | 1812 JJ | 1250. | 2500. | — | — |
|-------|---------|-------|-------|--------|--------|
| | 1813 JJ | 125.00 | 175.00 | 275.00 | 600.00 |
| | 1821 JM | 25.00 | 50.00 | 75.00 | 200.00 |
| | 1822/0 JM | 40.00 | 100.00 | 150.00 | 300.00 |
| | 1822 JM | 20.00 | 35.00 | 60.00 | 185.00 |

## NUEVA VISCAYA

(Later became Durango State)

This 8 reales, intended for the province of Nueva Viscaya, was minted in the newly-opened Durango Mint during February and March of 1811, before the regular coinage of Durango was started.

## 8 REALES

**.903 SILVER**
**Obv. leg: MON.PROV. DE NUEV.VIZCAYA,**
**arms of Durango. Rev: Royal arms.**

| KM# | Date | Good | VG | Fine | VF |
|-----|------|------|-----|------|-----|
| 181 | 1811 RM | 1000. | 2250. | 2850. | 5500. |

**NOTE:** Several varieties exist.

## OAXACA

The city of Oaxaca was in the midst of a coin shortage when it became apparent the city would be taken by the Insurgents. Royalist forces under Lt. Gen. Saravia had coins made. They were cast in a blacksmith shop. 1/2, 1 and 8 reales were made only briefly in 1812 before the Royalists surrendered the city.

### 1/2 REAL

**.903 SILVER**
**Obv: Cross separating castle, lion, F,7O.**
**Rev. leg: OAXACA around shield.**

| | | | | | |
|-----|------|------|-----|------|-----|
| 166 | 1812 | 1000. | 1500. | 2500. | 3500. |

### REAL

**.903 SILVER**

| | | | | | |
|-----|------|------|-----|------|-----|
| 167 | 1812 | 350.00 | 650.00 | 1200. | 2500. |

## 8 REALES

**.903 SILVER**

| KM# | Date | Good | VG | Fine | VF |
|-----|------|------|-----|------|-----|
| 168 | 1812 c/m:A | 1300. | 1900. | 3300. | 5000. |
| | 1812 c/m:B | 1300. | 1900. | 3300. | 5000. |
| | 1812 c/m:C | 1300. | 1900. | 3300. | 5000. |
| | 1812 c/m:D | 1300. | 1900. | 3300. | 5000. |
| | 1812 c/m:K | 1300. | 1900. | 3300. | 5000. |
| | 1812 c/m:L | 1300. | 1900. | 3300. | 5000. |
| | 1812 c/m:Mo | 1300. | 1900. | 3300. | 5000. |
| | 1812 c/m:N | 1300. | 1900. | 3300. | 5000. |
| | 1812 c/m:O | 1300. | 1900. | 3300. | 5000. |
| | 1812 c/m:R | 1300. | 1900. | 3300. | 5000. |
| | 1812 c/m:V | 1300. | 1900. | 3300. | 5000. |
| | 1812 c/m:Z | 1300. | 1900. | 3300. | 5000. |

**NOTE:** The above issue usually has a second c/m: O between crowned pillars.

## REAL DEL CATORCE

(City in San Luis Potosi)

Real del Catorce is an important mining center in the Province of San Luis Potosi. In 1811 an 8 reales coin was struck under very primitive conditions while the city was still in Royalist hands. Few survive.

### 8 REALES

**.903 SILVER**
Obv. leg: EL R.D. CATORC. POR FERNA. VII.
Rev. leg: MONEDA. PROVISIONAL.VALE.8R.

| KM# | Date | VG | Fine | VF | XF |
|-----|------|-----|------|-----|-----|
| 169 | 1811 | | 4500. | 9000. 16,000. 65,000. | |

**NOTE:** Spink America Gerber Sale 6-96 VF or XF
realized $63,800.

## SAN FERNANDO DE BEXAR

Struck by Jose Antonio de la Garza, the 'jolas' are the
only known coins issued under Spanish rule in the continental United States of America.

### 1/2 REAL
(Jola)

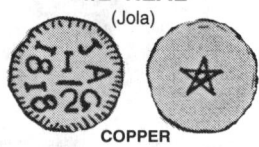

**COPPER**

| KM# | Date | Mintage | Good | VG | Fine | VF |
|-----|------|---------|------|-----|------|-----|
| Tn1 (170) | 1818 | 8,000 | 350.00 | 650.00 | 1250. | 2500. |

| | | | | | | |
|-----|------|---------|------|-----|------|-----|
| Tn2 (171) | 1818 | Inc. Ab. | 500.00 | 750.00 | 1500. | 3000. |

**NOTE:** Bowers and Merena ANA Millennium sale 8-00,
EF-40 realized $12,650.

## SAN LUIS POTOSI

### Sierra De Pinos
Villa

### 1/4 REAL

**COPPER**

| KM# | Date | Good | VG | Fine | VF |
|-----|------|------|-----|------|-----|
| A172 | 1814 | 75.00 | 125.00 | 200.00 | 300.00 |

**SILVER**

| | | | | | |
|-----|------|------|-----|------|-----|
| A172a | 1814 | | — | Rare | — |

## SOMBRERETE

(Under Royalist Vargas)

The Sombrerete Mint opened on October 8, 1810 in an
area that boasted some of the richest mines in Mexico.
The mint operated only until July 16, 1811, only to
reopen in 1812 and finally close for good at the end of the
year. Mines, Administrator Fernando Vargas, was also in
charge of the coining, all coins bear his name.

### 1/2 REAL

**.903 SILVER**
Obv. leg: FERDIN.VII.SOMBRERETE. . .,
around crowned globes.
Rev. leg: VARGAS above lys in oval, sprays.

| KM# | Date | Good | VG | Fine | VF |
|-----|------|------|-----|------|-----|
| 172 | 1811 | 45.00 | 70.00 | 150.00 | 250.00 |
| | 1812 | 50.00 | 90.00 | 175.00 | 275.00 |

### REAL

**.903 SILVER**
Obv. leg: FERDIN.VII.SOMBRERETE. . .,
around crowned globes.
Rev. leg: VARGAS above lys in oval, sprays.

| | | | | | |
|-----|------|------|-----|------|-----|
| 173 | 1811 | 45.00 | 70.00 | 150.00 | 250.00 |
| | 1812 | 50.00 | 90.00 | 175.00 | 275.00 |

### 2 REALES

**.903 SILVER**
Obv: R.CAXA.DE.SOMBRERETE, royal arms.
Rev. c/m: VARGAS, 1811, S between crowned pillars.

| | | | | | |
|-----|------|------|-----|------|-----|
| 174 | 1811 SE | 100.00 | 250.00 | 450.00 | 700.00 |

### 4 REALES

**.903 SILVER**
Obv. leg: R.CAXA.DE.SOMBRERETE, royal arms.
Rev. leg: Small VARGAS/1811.

| | | | | | |
|-----|------|------|-----|------|-----|
| 175.1 | 1811 | 75.00 | 150.00 | 300.00 | 650.00 |

Rev: Large VARGAS/1812.

| | | | | | |
|-----|------|------|-----|------|-----|
| 175.2 | 1812 | 50.00 | 100.00 | 200.00 | 450.00 |

## 8 REALES

.903 SILVER
Obv. leg: R.CAXA. DE SOMBRERETE.
Rev. c/m: VARGAS, date, S between crowned pillars.

| KM# | Date | Good | VG | Fine | VF |
|---|---|---|---|---|---|
| 176 | 1810 | 1000. | 1750. | 2750. | 4000. |
| | 1811 | 225.00 | 325.00 | 450.00 | 600.00 |

Obv. leg: R.CAXA. DE SOMBRETE, crowned arms.
Rev. leg: VARGAS/date/3

| 177 | 1811 | 125.00 | 185.00 | 245.00 | 500.00 |
|---|---|---|---|---|---|
| | 1812 | 125.00 | 175.00 | 225.00 | 475.00 |

## VALLADOLID MICHOACAN
### (Now Morelia)

Valladolid, capitol of Michoacan province, was a strate-
gically important center for military thrusts into the adjoin-
ing provinces. The Royalists made every effort to retain
the position. In 1813, with the advance of the insurgent
forces, it became apparent that to maintain the position
would be very difficult. During 1813 it was necessary to
make coins in the city due to lack of traffic with other
areas. These were made only briefly before the city fell
and were also used by the insurgents with appropriate
countermarks.

## 8 REALES

.903 SILVER
Obv: Royal arms in wreath, value at sides.
Rev: PROVISIONAL/DE VALLADOLID.

| KM# | Date | Good | VG | Fine | VF |
|---|---|---|---|---|---|
| 178 | 1813 | — | — | Rare | — |

Obv: Bust, leg: FERDIN. VII.
Rev: Arms, pillars, P.D.V. in legend.

| 179 | 1813 | — | — | *Rare | — |

*NOTE: Spink America Gerber sale 6-96 good realized
$23,100.

## ZACATECAS

The city of Zacatecas, in a rich mining region has
provided silver for the world since the mid-1500's. On
November 14, 1810 a mint began production for the
Royalist cause. Zacatecas was the most prolific during
the War of Independence. Four of the 5 "standard"
silver denominations were made here, 4 Reales were
not. The first, a local type showing mountains of silver on
the coins were made only in 1810 and 1811. Some
1811's were made by the Insurgents who took the city on
April 15, 1811, later retaken by the Royalists on May 21,
1811. Zacatecas struck the standard Ferdinand VII bust
type until 1922.

### MINT MARKS: Z, ZS, Zs
## 1/2 REAL

.903 SILVER
Obv: Local arms w/flowers and castles.

| 180 | 1810 | 75.00 | 125.00 | 200.00 | 400.00 |
|---|---|---|---|---|---|
| 1181 | (error 1811) | | | | |
| | | 30.00 | 50.00 | 90.00 | 175.00 |

Obv: Royal arms.
Rev. leg: MONEDA PROVISIONAL DE
ZACATECAS., mountain.

| 181 | 1811 | 30.00 | 50.00 | 90.00 | 175.00 |
|---|---|---|---|---|---|

Obv: Provincial bust FERDIN. VII.
Rev. leg: MONEDA PROVISIONAL DE ZACATECAS.

| 182 | 1811 | 30.00 | 40.00 | 65.00 | 135.00 |
|---|---|---|---|---|---|
| | 1812 | 25.00 | 35.00 | 60.00 | 120.00 |

1.6900 g, .903 SILVER, .0491 oz ASW
Obv: Armored bust of Ferdinand VII.

| 73.1 | 1813 FP | 25.00 | 45.00 | 85.00 | 175.00 |
|---|---|---|---|---|---|
| | 1813 AG | 20.00 | 40.00 | 60.00 | 100.00 |
| | 1814 AG | 15.00 | 30.00 | 60.00 | 100.00 |
| | 1815 AG | 12.50 | 25.00 | 40.00 | 60.00 |
| | 1816 AG | 10.00 | 15.00 | 25.00 | 50.00 |
| | 1817 AG | 10.00 | 15.00 | 25.00 | 50.00 |
| | 1818 AG | 10.00 | 15.00 | 25.00 | 50.00 |
| | 1819 AG | 10.00 | 15.00 | 25.00 | 50.00 |

Obv: Draped bust Ferdinand VII.

| KM# | Date | VG | Fine | VF | XF |
|-----|------|-----|------|-----|-----|
| 74.3 | 1819 AG | 8.00 | 12.00 | 25.00 | 50.00 |
| | 1820 AG | 8.00 | 12.00 | 25.00 | 50.00 |
| | 1820 RG | 5.00 | 10.00 | 20.00 | 45.00 |
| | 1821 AG | 150.00 | 250.00 | 450.00 | 850.00 |
| | 1821 RG | 5.00 | 10.00 | 20.00 | 45.00 |

## REAL

 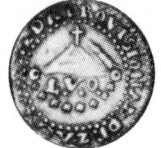

**.903 SILVER**
**Obv: Local arms w/flowers and castles.**

| KM# | Date | Good | VG | Fine | VF |
|-----|------|------|-----|------|-----|
| 183 | 1810 | 100.00 | 150.00 | 300.00 | 500.00 |
| | 1181 (error 1811) | | | | |
| | | 20.00 | 40.00 | 80.00 | 175.00 |

**Obv: Royal arms.**
**Rev. leg: MONEDA PROVISIONAL DE ZACATECAS., mountain.**

| | | | | | |
|-----|------|------|-----|------|-----|
| 184 | 1811 | 15.00 | 30.00 | 60.00 | 135.00 |

**Obv: Provincial bust, leg: FERDIN. VII.**
**Rev. leg: MONEDA PROVISIONAL DE ZACATECAS, arms, pillars.**

| | | | | | |
|-----|------|------|-----|------|-----|
| 185 | 1811 | 50.00 | 85.00 | 120.00 | 200.00 |
| | 1812 | 40.00 | 70.00 | 100.00 | 175.00 |

**3.3800 g, .903 SILVER, .0981 oz ASW**
**Obv: Armored bust of Ferdinand VII.**

| KM# | Date | Good | VG | Fine | VF |
|-----|------|------|-----|------|-----|
| 82.1 | 1813 FP | 50.00 | 100.00 | 150.00 | 250.00 |
| | 1814 FP | 20.00 | 35.00 | 50.00 | 85.00 |
| | 1814 AG | 20.00 | 35.00 | 50.00 | 85.00 |
| | 1815 AG | 20.00 | 35.00 | 50.00 | 85.00 |
| | 1816 AG | 10.00 | 20.00 | 30.00 | 65.00 |
| | 1817 AG | 6.50 | 12.50 | 20.00 | 45.00 |
| | 1818 AG | 6.50 | 12.50 | 20.00 | 45.00 |
| | 1819 AG | 5.00 | 9.00 | 15.00 | 35.00 |
| | 1820 AG | 4.00 | 7.50 | 12.50 | 30.00 |

**Obv: Draped bust of Ferdinand VII.**

| KM# | Date | VG | Fine | VF | XF |
|-----|------|-----|------|-----|-----|
| 83.3 | 1820 AG | 5.00 | 10.00 | 20.00 | 60.00 |
| | 1820 RG | 5.00 | 10.00 | 20.00 | 60.00 |
| | 1821 AG | 15.00 | 30.00 | 45.00 | 90.00 |
| | 1821 AZ | 10.00 | 20.00 | 40.00 | 85.00 |
| | 1821 RG | 6.00 | 12.00 | 25.00 | 65.00 |
| | 1822 AZ | 6.00 | 12.00 | 25.00 | 65.00 |
| | 1822 RG | 15.00 | 30.00 | 45.00 | 90.00 |

## 2 REALES

**.903 SILVER**
**Obv: Local arms w/flowers and castles.**

| KM# | Date | Good | VG | Fine | VF |
|-----|------|------|-----|------|-----|
| 186 | 1810 | — | — | Rare | — |
| | 1181 (error 1811) | | | | |
| | | 25.00 | 40.00 | 70.00 | 120.00 |

**Obv: Royal arms.**
**Rev. leg: MONEDA PROVISIONAL DE ZACATECAS., mountain above L.V.O.**

| | | | | | |
|-----|------|------|-----|------|-----|
| 187 | 1811 | 15.00 | 30.00 | 60.00 | 100.00 |

**Rev. leg: MONEDA PROVISIONAL DE ZACATECAS, crowned arms, pillars.**

| KM# | Date | Good | VG | Fine | VF |
|-----|------|------|-----|------|-----|
| 188 | 1811 | 35.00 | 65.00 | 135.00 | 225.00 |
| | 1812 | 30.00 | 60.00 | 125.00 | 200.00 |

**6.7700 g, .903 SILVER, .1966 oz ASW**
**Obv: Large armored bust of Ferdinand VII.**

| | | | | | |
|-----|------|------|-----|------|-----|
| 92.1 | 1813 FP | 35.00 | 50.00 | 75.00 | 125.00 |
| | 1814 FP | 35.00 | 50.00 | 75.00 | 125.00 |
| | 1814 AG | 35.00 | 50.00 | 75.00 | 125.00 |
| | 1815 AG | 6.50 | 12.50 | 25.00 | 55.00 |
| | 1816 AG | 6.50 | 12.50 | 25.00 | 55.00 |
| | 1817 AG | 6.50 | 12.50 | 25.00 | 55.00 |
| | 1818 AG | 6.50 | 12.50 | 25.00 | 55.00 |

**Obv: Small armored bust of Ferdinand VII.**

| KM# | Date | VG | Fine | VF | XF |
|-----|------|-----|------|-----|-----|
| A92 | 1819 AG | 45.00 | 100.00 | 200.00 | 400.00 |

**Obv: Draped bust of Ferdinand VII.**

| KM# | Date | VG | Fine | VF | XF |
|-----|------|-----|------|-----|-----|
| 93.4 | 1818 AG | 6.50 | 12.50 | 25.00 | 50.00 |
| | 1819 AG | 10.00 | 20.00 | 40.00 | 85.00 |
| | 1820 AG | 10.00 | 20.00 | 40.00 | 85.00 |
| | 1820 RG | 10.00 | 20.00 | 40.00 | 85.00 |
| | 1821 AG | 10.00 | 20.00 | 40.00 | 85.00 |
| | 1821 AZ/RG | 10.00 | 20.00 | 40.00 | 85.00 |
| | 1821 AZ | 10.00 | 20.00 | 40.00 | 85.00 |
| | 1821 RG | 10.00 | 20.00 | 40.00 | 85.00 |
| | 1822 AG | 10.00 | 20.00 | 40.00 | 85.00 |
| | 1822 AZ | 15.00 | 30.00 | 60.00 | 125.00 |
| | 1822 RG | 10.00 | 20.00 | 40.00 | 85.00 |

## 8 REALES

**.903 SILVER**
**Obv: Local arm w/flowers and castles.**
**Rev: Similar to KM#190.**

| KM# | Date | Good | VG | Fine | VF |
|-----|------|------|-----|------|-----|
| 189 | 1810 | 300.00 | 500.00 | 750.00 | 1250. |
| | 1181 (error 1811) | | | | |
| | | 100.00 | 150.00 | 225.00 | 350.00 |

**NOTE:** Also exists with incomplete date.

**Obv. leg: FERDIN.VII.DEI. . ., royal arms.**
**Rev. leg: MONEDA PROVISIONAL DE ZACATECAS, mountain above L.V.O.**

| KM# | Date | Good | VG | Fine | VF |
|-----|------|------|-----|------|-----|
| 190 | 1811 | 65.00 | 100.00 | 135.00 | 220.00 |

**Obv: Armored bust of Ferdinand VII.**
**Rev. leg: MONEDA PROVISIONAL DE ZACATECAS, crowned arms, pillars.**

| KM# | Date | Good | VG | Fine | VF |
|-----|------|------|-----|------|-----|
| 191 | 1811 | 45.00 | 75.00 | 145.00 | 275.00 |
| | 1812 | 50.00 | 85.00 | 160.00 | 300.00 |

**Obv: Draped bust of Ferdinand VII.**
**Rev. leg: MONEDA PROVISIONAL DE ZACATECAS, crowned arms, pillars.**

| | | | | | |
|-----|------|------|-----|------|-----|
| 192 | 1812 | | 75.00 | 150.00 | 275.00 | 450.00 |

**27.0700 g, .903 SILVER, .7860 oz ASW**
**Obv: Draped bust of Ferdinand VII.**

| KM# | Date | VG | Fine | VF | XF |
|---|---|---|---|---|---|
| 111.5 | 1813 AG | 125.00 | 200.00 | 250.00 | 350.00 |
| | 1813 FP | 75.00 | 125.00 | 175.00 | 275.00 |
| | 1814 AG | 100.00 | 150.00 | 200.00 | 300.00 |
| | 1814 AG D over horizontal D in IND | | | | |
| | | 125.00 | 175.00 | 225.00 | 325.00 |
| | 1814 AG/FP | 100.00 | 150.00 | 200.00 | 300.00 |
| | 1814 FP | 150.00 | 250.00 | 350.00 | 450.00 |
| | 1815 AG | 50.00 | 100.00 | 150.00 | 250.00 |
| | 1816 AG | 35.00 | 50.00 | 65.00 | 125.00 |
| | 1817 AG | 35.00 | 50.00 | 65.00 | 125.00 |
| | 1818 AG | 30.00 | 40.00 | 50.00 | 100.00 |
| | 1819 AG | 30.00 | 40.00 | 50.00 | 100.00 |
| | 1820 AG 18/11 error | | | | |
| | | 100.00 | 200.00 | 300.00 | 400.00 |
| | 1820 AG | 30.00 | 40.00 | 50.00 | 100.00 |
| | 1820 RG | 30.00 | 40.00 | 50.00 | 100.00 |
| | 1821/81 RG | 75.00 | 150.00 | 225.00 | 300.00 |
| | 1821 RG | 15.00 | 25.00 | 35.00 | 65.00 |
| | 1821 AZ | 50.00 | 100.00 | 150.00 | 200.00 |
| | 1822 RG | 40.00 | 60.00 | 100.00 | 175.00 |

**Rev: Crown with lower rear arc.**

| KM# | Date | VG | Fine | VF | XF |
|---|---|---|---|---|---|
| 111.6 | 1821 RG | 160.00 | 320.00 | 550.00 | 750.00 |

# COUNTERMARKED COINAGE
## Crown and Flag
(Refer to Multiple Countermarks)
## LCM - La Comandancia Militar
NOTE: This countermark exists in 15 various sizes.
## 2 REALES

**.903 SILVER**
**c/m: LCM on Mexico KM#92.**

| KM# | Date | Year | Good | VG | Fine | VF |
|---|---|---|---|---|---|---|
| 193.1 | ND | (1809 TH) | 85.00 | 165.00 | 250.00 | 400.00 |

**c/m: LCM on Zacatecas KM#187.**

| | | | | | | |
|---|---|---|---|---|---|---|
| 193.2 | ND | (1811) | 85.00 | 165.00 | 250.00 | 400.00 |

# 8 REALES

**CAST SILVER**
**c/m: LCM on Chihuahua KM#123.**

| KM# | Date | VG | Fine | VF | XF |
|---|---|---|---|---|---|
| 194.1 | ND (1811 RP) | 100.00 | 200.00 | 300.00 | 450.00 |
| | ND (1812 RP) | 100.00 | 200.00 | 300.00 | 450.00 |

**.903 SILVER**
**c/m: LCM on Chihuahua KM#111.1 struck**
**over KM#123.**

| | | | | | |
|---|---|---|---|---|---|
| 194.2 | ND (1815 RP) | 200.00 | 275.00 | 400.00 | 550.00 |
| | ND (1817 RP) | 125.00 | 175.00 | 225.00 | 300.00 |
| | ND (1820 RP) | 125.00 | 175.00 | 225.00 | 300.00 |
| | ND (1821 RP) | 125.00 | 175.00 | 225.00 | 300.00 |

**c/m: LCM on Durango KM#111.2.**

| KM# | Date | Good | VG | Fine | VF |
|-----|------|------|-----|------|-----|
| 194.3 | ND (1812 RM) | 70.00 | 125.00 | 190.00 | 250.00 |
| | ND (1821 CG) | 70.00 | 125.00 | 190.00 | 250.00 |

**c/m: LCM on Guadalajara KM#111.3.**

| | | | | | |
|-----|------|------|-----|------|-----|
| 194.4 | ND (1813 MR) | 150.00 | 225.00 | 300.00 | 475.00 |
| | ND (1820 FS) | — | — | Rare | — |

**c/m: LCM on Guanajuato KM#111.4.**

| | | | | | |
|-----|------|------|-----|------|-----|
| 194.5 | ND (1813 JM) | 225.00 | 350.00 | 475.00 | 650.00 |

**c/m: LCM on Nueva Vizcaya KM#165.**

| | | | | | |
|-----|------|------|-----|------|-----|
| 194.6 | ND (1811 RM) | — | — | Rare | — |

**c/m: LCM on Mexico KM#111.**

| | | | | | |
|-----|------|------|-----|------|-----|
| 194.7 | ND (1811 HJ) | 125.00 | 225.00 | 350.00 | 600.00 |
| | ND (1812 JJ) | 110.00 | 135.00 | 190.00 | 325.00 |
| | ND (1817 JJ) | 50.00 | 65.00 | 85.00 | 125.00 |
| | ND (1818 JJ) | 50.00 | 65.00 | 85.00 | 125.00 |
| | ND (1820 JJ) | — | — | — | — |

**c/m: LCM on Sombrerete KM#176.**

| | | | | | |
|-----|------|------|-----|------|-----|
| 194.8 | ND (1811) | — | — | Rare | — |
| | ND (1812) | — | — | Rare | — |

**c/m: LCM on Zacatecas KM#190.**

| | | | | | |
|-----|------|------|-----|------|-----|
| 194.9 | ND (1811) | 225.00 | 350.00 | 450.00 | — |

**c/m: LCM on Zacatecas KM#111.5.**

| | | | | | |
|-----|------|------|-----|------|-----|
| 194.10 | ND (1813 FP) | — | — | — | — |
| | ND (1814 AG) | — | — | — | — |
| | ND (1822 RG) | — | — | — | — |

# LCV - Las Cajas de Veracruz
(The Royal Treasury
of the City of Veracruz)

## 7 REALES
**SILVER**
**c/m: LCV and 7 on underweight 8 Reales.**

| KM# | Date | Year | Good | VG | Fine | VF |
|-----|------|------|------|-----|------|-----|
| 195 | ND | (-) | — | — | Rare | — |

## 7-1/4 REALES
**SILVER**
**c/m: LCV and 7-1/4 on underweight 8 Reales.**

| | | | | | | |
|-----|------|------|------|-----|------|-----|
| 196 | ND | (-) | — | — | Rare | — |

## 7-1/2 REALES
**SILVER**
**c/m: LCV and 7-1/2 on underweight 8 Reales.**

| | | | | | | |
|-----|------|------|------|-----|------|-----|
| 197 | ND | (-) | — | — | Rare | — |

## 7-3/4 REALES

**SILVER**
**c/m: LCV and 7-3/4 on underweight 8 Reales.**

| | | | | | | |
|-----|------|------|------|-----|------|-----|
| 198 | ND | (-) | 300.00 | 375.00 | 450.00 | 600.00 |

## 8 REALES
**CAST SILVER**
**c/m: LCV on Chihuahua KM#123.**

| | | | | | | |
|-----|------|------|------|-----|------|-----|
| A198 | ND (1811 RP) | | 150.00 | 250.00 | 400.00 | 500.00 |

**SILVER**
**c/m: LCV on Zacatecas KM#191.**

| KM# | Date | Year | Good | VG | Fine | VF |
|-----|------|------|------|-----|------|-----|
| 199 | ND | (1811) | 175.00 | 225.00 | 275.00 | 350.00 |
| | ND | (1812) | 175.00 | 225.00 | 275.00 | 350.00 |

## MS (Monogram) - Manuel Salcedo

## 8 REALES

SILVER
c/m: MS monogram on Mexico KM#110.

| KM# | Date | | Good | VG | Fine | VF |
|-----|------|---|------|-----|------|-----|
| 200 | ND | (1809 TH) | 150.00 | 250.00 | 400.00 | 500.00 |
| | ND | (1810 HJ) | 150.00 | 250.00 | 400.00 | 500.00 |
| | ND | (1811 HJ) | 150.00 | 250.00 | 400.00 | 500.00 |

## MVA - Monclova

## 8 REALES

SILVER
c/m: MVA/1811 on Chihuahua KM#111.1; struck over cast Mexico KM#110.

| | | | | | | |
|-----|------|---|------|-----|------|-----|
| 201 | ND | 1809 | 250.00 | 450.00 | 700.00 | 1000. |
| | ND | (1816 RP) | 250.00 | 450.00 | 700.00 | 1000. |
| | ND | (1821 RP) | 250.00 | 450.00 | 700.00 | 1000. |

c/m: MVA/1812 on Chihuahua KM#111.1; struck over cast Mexico KM#109.

| | | | | | | |
|-----|------|---|------|-----|------|-----|
| 202.1 | 1812 | (1810) | 125.00 | 175.00 | 250.00 | 350.00 |

c/m: MVA/1812 on cast Mexico KM#109.

| KM# | Date | | Good | VG | Fine | VF |
|-----|------|---|------|-----|------|-----|
| 202.2 | 1812 | (1798 FM) | 100.00 | 150.00 | 250.00 | 350.00 |
| | 1812 | (1802 FT) | 100.00 | 150.00 | 250.00 | 350.00 |

c/m: MVA/1812 on cast Mexico KM#110.

| | | | | | | |
|-----|------|---|------|-----|------|-----|
| 202.3 | 1812 | (1809 HJ) | 100.00 | 150.00 | 250.00 | 350.00 |
| | 1812 | (1809 TH) | 100.00 | 150.00 | 250.00 | 350.00 |
| | 1812 | (1810 HJ) | 100.00 | 150.00 | 250.00 | 350.00 |

c/m: MVA/1812 on Zacatecas KM#189.

| | | | | | | |
|-----|------|---|------|-----|------|-----|
| 202.5 | 1812 | (1813) | 300.00 | 350.00 | 450.00 | 550.00 |

## PDV - Provisional de Valladolid
## VTIL - (Util = useful)
(Refer to Multiple countermarks)

## INSURGENT COINAGE
### Supreme National Congress of America
#### 1/2 REAL

STRUCK COPPER
Obv. leg: FERDIN. VII DEI GRATIA, eagle on bridge.
Rev. leg: S.P.CONG.NAT.IND.
GUV.T., value, bow, quiver, etc.

| KM# | Date | Good | VG | Fine | VF |
|-----|------|------|-----|------|-----|
| 203 | 1811 | 27.50 | 45.00 | 60.00 | 100.00 |

## REAL

STRUCK SILVER
Similar to 1/2 Real, KM#203.

| | | | | | |
|-----|------|------|-----|------|-----|
| 204 | 1811 | | 45.00 | 75.00 | 125.00 | 200.00 |

## 2 REALES

**STRUCK SILVER**

| KM# | Date | Good | VG | Fine | VF |
|-----|------|------|-----|------|------|
| 205 | 1812 | 225.00 | 325.00 | 475.00 | 750.00 |

## 8 REALES

**CAST SILVER**

| KM# | Date | Good | VG | Fine | VF |
|-----|------|------|-----|------|------|
| 206 | 1811 | 150.00 | 250.00 | 350.00 | 500.00 |
| | 1812 | 150.00 | 250.00 | 350.00 | 500.00 |

**STRUCK SILVER**

| KM# | Date | Good | VG | Fine | VF |
|-----|------|------|-----|------|------|
| 207 | 1811 | — | — | — | — |
| | 1812 | 300.00 | 600.00 | 1000. | 1500. |

**STRUCK COPPER**
Obv. leg: FERDIN.VII. . . ., eagle on bridge.
Rev. leg: PROVICIONAL POR LA SUPREMA JUNTA
DE AMERICA, bow, sword and quiver.

| KM# | Date | Good | VG | Fine | VF |
|-----|------|------|-----|------|------|
| 208 | 1811 | 100.00 | 150.00 | 225.00 | 450.00 |
| | 1812 | 100.00 | 150.00 | 225.00 | 450.00 |

## National Congress
### 1/2 REAL

**STRUCK COPPER**

---

Obv. leg: VICE FERD. VII DEI GRATIA ET,
eagle on bridge.
Rev. leg: S. P. CONG. NAT. IND.
GUV. T., value, bow, quiver, etc.

| KM# | Date | Good | VG | Fine | VF |
|-----|------|------|-----|------|------|
| 209 | 1811 | 45.00 | 85.00 | 150.00 | 200.00 |
| | 1812 | 27.50 | 60.00 | 100.00 | 150.00 |
| | 1813 | 27.50 | 60.00 | 100.00 | 150.00 |
| | 1814 | 45.00 | 85.00 | 150.00 | 200.00 |

**.903 SILVER**

| KM# | Date | Good | VG | Fine | VF |
|-----|------|------|-----|------|------|
| 210 | 1812 | 27.50 | 60.00 | 100.00 | 150.00 |
| | 1813 | 45.00 | 90.00 | 175.00 | 275.00 |

**NOTE:** 1812 exists with the date reading inwards and outwards.

## REAL

**.903 SILVER**

| KM# | Date | Good | VG | Fine | VF |
|-----|------|------|-----|------|------|
| 211 | 1812 | 22.50 | 45.00 | 80.00 | 125.00 |
| | 1813 | 22.50 | 45.00 | 80.00 | 125.00 |

**NOTE:** 1812 exists with the date reading either inward or outward.

## 2 REALES

**STRUCK COPPER**

| KM# | Date | Good | VG | Fine | VF |
|-----|------|------|-----|------|------|
| 212 | 1812 | 100.00 | 150.00 | 200.00 | 275.00 |
| | 1813 | 23.50 | 50.00 | 75.00 | 120.00 |
| | 1814 | 32.50 | 75.00 | 110.00 | 165.00 |

**STRUCK SILVER**

| KM# | Date | Good | VG | Fine | VF |
|-----|------|------|-----|------|------|
| A213 | 1813 | 950.00 | 1750. | 3000. | 4850. |

**.903 SILVER**

| KM# | Date | Good | VG | Fine | VF |
|-----|------|------|-----|------|------|
| 213 | 1813 | 75.00 | 155.00 | 265.00 | 375.00 |

**NOTE:** These dies were believed to be intended for the striking of 2 Escudos.

## 4 REALES

**.903 SILVER**
**Mint: Mexico City**

| KM# | Date | Good | VG | Fine | VF |
|-----|------|------|------|------|------|
| 214 | 1813 | 600.00 | 1200. | 2450. | 4400. |

## 8 REALES

**.903 SILVER**
**Mint: Mexico City**
**Obv: Small crowned eagle.**

| | | | | | |
|-----|------|------|------|------|------|
| 215.1 | 1812 | 600.00 | 1150. | 2350. | 4250. |

**Obv: Large crowned eagle.**

| | | | | | |
|-----|------|------|------|------|------|
| 215.2 | 1813 | 600.00 | 1150. | 2350. | 4250. |

## American Congress
### REAL

**.903 SILVER**
**Obv: Eagle on cactus,**
**leg: CONGRESO AMERICANO.**
**Rev: F.7 on spread mantle,**
**leg: DEPOSIT D.L.AUCTORI J.**

| | | | | | |
|-----|------|------|------|------|------|
| 216 | ND(1813) | 35.00 | 75.00 | 120.00 | 200.00 |

**Obv: Eagle on cactus, leg: CONGR.AMER.**
**Rev: F.7 on spread mantle,**
**leg: DEPOS.D.L.AUT.D.**

| KM# | Date | Good | VG | Fine | VF |
|-----|------|------|------|------|------|
| 217 | ND(1813) | 35.00 | 75.00 | 120.00 | 200.00 |

## NUEVA GALICIA

### (Later became Jalisco State)

In early colonial times, Nueva Galicia was an extensive province which substantially combined later provinces of Zacatecas and Jalisco. These are states of Mexico today although the name was revived during the War of Independence. The only issue was 2 reales of rather enigmatic origin. No decrees or other authorization to strike this coin has yet been located or reported.

## 2 REALES

**.903 SILVER**
**Obv. leg: PROVYCIONAL. . ., N.G. in center, date.**
**Rev:. . .a.juniana82R. . . in center.**

| KM# | Date | Good | VG | Fine | VF |
|-----|------|------|------|------|------|
| 218 | 1813 | 1000. | 2500. | 4500. | — |

## OAXACA

Oaxaca was the hub of Insurgent activity in the south where coinage started in July 1811 and continued until October 1814. The Oaxaca issues represent episodic strikings, usually under dire circumstances by various individuals. Coins were commonly made of copper due to urgency and were intended to be redeemed at face value in gold or silver once silver was available to the Insurgents. Some were later made in silver, but most appear to be of more recent origin, to statisfy collectors.

## SUD

### (Under General Morelos)

### 1/2 REAL

**COPPER**
**Obv: Bow, arrow, SUD.**
**Rev: Morelos monogram Mo, date.**

| KM# | Date | Good | VG | Fine | VF |
|-----|------|------|------|------|------|
| 219 | 1811 | 6.75 | 11.50 | 20.00 | 35.00 |
| | 1812 | 6.75 | 11.50 | 20.00 | 35.00 |
| | 1813 | 5.50 | 9.00 | 17.50 | 30.00 |
| | 1814 | 9.00 | 16.50 | 25.00 | 40.00 |

**NOTE:** Uniface strikes exist of #219.

**SILVER**

| | | | | | |
|-----|------|------|------|------|------|
| 220.1 | 1811 | — | — | — | — |
| | 1812 | — | — | — | — |
| | 1813 | — | — | — | — |

**SILVER, cast**

| KM# | Date | Good | VG | Fine | VF |
|-----|------|------|-----|------|-----|
| 220.2 | 1811 | — | — | — | — |
| | 1812 | — | — | — | — |
| | 1813 | 25.00 | 50.00 | 100.00 | 150.00 |

**NOTE:** Use caution as most silver specimens examined appear questionable and may be considered spurious.

**SILVER**
**Obv. leg: PROVICIONAL DE OAXACA, bow, arrow.**
**Rev. leg: AMERICA MORELOS, lion.**

| | | | | | |
|-----|------|------|-----|------|-----|
| 221 | 1812 | 35.00 | 60.00 | 100.00 | 150.00 |
| | 1813 | 35.00 | 60.00 | 100.00 | 150.00 |

**COPPER**

| | | | | | |
|-----|------|------|-----|------|-----|
| 221a | 1812 | 27.50 | 42.50 | 70.00 | 100.00 |
| | 1813 | 20.00 | 35.00 | 60.00 | 85.00 |

**Obv: Similar to KM#220.**
**Rev: Similar to KM#221 but w/1/2 at left of lion.**

| | | | | | |
|-----|------|------|-----|------|-----|
| A222 | 1813 | 27.50 | 42.50 | 70.00 | 100.00 |

## REAL

**COPPER**

| KM# | Date | Good | VG | Fine | VF |
|-----|------|------|-----|------|-----|
| 222 | 1811 | 4.75 | 9.00 | 18.00 | 38.00 |
| | 1812 | 3.75 | 7.00 | 14.00 | 30.00 |
| | 1813 | 3.75 | 7.00 | 14.00 | 30.00 |

**SILVER**

| | | | | | |
|-----|------|------|-----|------|-----|
| 222a | 1812 | — | — | — | — |
| | 1813 | — | — | — | — |

**SILVER, cast**

| | | | | | |
|-----|------|------|-----|------|-----|
| 223 | 1812 | — | — | — | — |
| | 1813 | 27.50 | 60.00 | 115.00 | 160.00 |

**NOTE:** See note below 1/2 Real, KM#220.2

**COPPER**
**Obv: Bow, arrow/SUD.**
**Rev. leg: AMERICA MORELOS, lion.**

| | | | | | |
|-----|------|------|-----|------|-----|
| 224 | 1813 | 27.50 | 42.50 | 75.00 | 110.00 |

**SILVER**

| | | | | | |
|-----|------|------|------|------|------|
| 225 | 1813 | — | — | Rare | — |

## 2 REALES

**COPPER**

| KM# | Date | Good | VG | Fine | VF |
|-----|------|------|-----|------|-----|
| 226.1 | 1811 | 12.50 | 25.00 | 55.00 | 100.00 |
| | 1811 inverted 2 | | | | |
| | | 15.00 | 30.00 | 60.00 | 120.00 |
| | 1812 | 2.50 | 4.00 | 6.50 | 12.00 |
| | 1813 | 3.00 | 5.00 | 8.00 | 15.00 |
| | 1814 | 13.50 | 28.00 | 65.00 | 120.00 |

**SILVER**

| | | | | | |
|-----|------|------|------|------|------|
| 226.1a | 1812 | 175.00 | 300.00 | 500.00 | 750.00 |

**Obv: 3 large stars added.**

| KM# | Date | Good | VG | Fine | VF |
|-----|------|------|-----|------|-----|
| 226.2 | 1814 | 10.00 | 20.00 | 40.00 | 60.00 |

**Obv. leg: SUD-OXA, bow, arrow.**
**Rev: Morelos monogram, value, date.**

| | | | | | |
|-----|------|------|-----|------|-----|
| 227 | 1813 | 60.00 | 100.00 | 200.00 | 300.00 |
| | 1814 | 60.00 | 100.00 | 200.00 | 300.00 |

**Obv. leg: SUD. OAXACA**

| | | | | | |
|-----|------|------|-----|------|-----|
| 228 | 1814 | 60.00 | 100.00 | 200.00 | 325.00 |

**SILVER, cast**

| | | | | | |
|-----|------|------|-----|------|-----|
| 229 | 1812 | 60.00 | 100.00 | 150.00 | 225.00 |
| | 1812 filled D in SUD | | | | |
| | | 60.00 | 100.00 | 150.00 | 225.00 |

**NOTE:** See note below 1/2 Real, KM#220.2.

## 4 REALES

**SILVER, cast**

| KM# | Date | Good | VG | Fine | VF |
|-----|------|------|-----|------|-----|
| 230 | 1811 | — | — | — | — |
| | 1812 | — | — | — | — |

**NOTE:** All known examples are modern fabrications.

**Obv. leg: SUD-OXA, bow, arrow.**
**Rev: Morelos monogram.**

| | | | | | |
|-----|------|------|-----|------|-----|
| *231 | 1813 | 125.00 | 250.00 | 400.00 | 800.00 |

## COPPER
**Obv. leg: SUD-OXA, bow, arrow.**
**Rev: Morelos monogram.**

| KM# | Date | Good | VG | Fine | VF |
|---|---|---|---|---|---|
| 232 | 1814 | 100.00 | 150.00 | 200.00 | 400.00 |

## 8 REALES

## COPPER
**Plain fields.**

| KM# | Date | Good | VG | Fine | VF |
|---|---|---|---|---|---|
| 233.1 | 1812 | 15.00 | 30.00 | 60.00 | 90.00 |
| **SILVER** | | | | | |
| 233.1a | 1812 | 100.00 | 150.00 | 250.00 | 450.00 |

**Ornate flowery fields.**

| KM# | Date | Good | VG | Fine | VF |
|---|---|---|---|---|---|
| 234 | 1811 | 75.00 | 125.00 | 150.00 | 225.00 |
| | 1812 | 4.00 | 6.00 | 10.00 | 20.00 |
| | 1813 | 4.00 | 6.00 | 10.00 | 20.00 |
| | 1814 | 10.00 | 15.00 | 25.00 | 50.00 |

**SILVER**
**Floreate fields.**

| KM# | Date | Good | VG | Fine | VF |
|---|---|---|---|---|---|
| 234a | 1811 | — | — | 2500. | 4000. |
| | 1812 | — | — | 1200. | 2000. |

## COPPER

| | | | | | |
|---|---|---|---|---|---|
| 233.2 | 1812 | 6.00 | 8.00 | 12.00 | 15.00 |
| | 1813 | 6.00 | 8.00 | 12.00 | 15.00 |
| | 1814 | 10.00 | 12.00 | 15.00 | 20.00 |
| **SILVER** | | | | | |
| 233.2a | 1812 | — | — | 1200. | 2000. |

## COPPER
**Similar to KM#233.4 but lines below bow slant left.**

| | | | | | |
|---|---|---|---|---|---|
| 233.3 | 1813 | 10.00 | 17.50 | 30.00 | 50.00 |

**SILVER, cast**

| | | | | | |
|---|---|---|---|---|---|
| 235 | 1811 | — | — | — | — |
| | 1812 | 75.00 | 125.00 | 200.00 | 350.00 |
| | 1813 | 60.00 | 100.00 | 175.00 | 300.00 |
| | 1814 | — | — | — | — |

**NOTE:** Most silver specimens available in today's market are considered spurious.

**.903 SILVER, struck**
**Obv: PROV. D. OAXACA, M monogram.**
**Rev: Lion shield w/or w/o bow above.**

| | | | | | |
|---|---|---|---|---|---|
| 236 | 1812 | — | — | Rare | — |

**Obv: W/o leg.**

| | | | | | |
|---|---|---|---|---|---|
| 237 | 1813 | — | — | Rare | — |

**Obv: Bow/M/SUD. .**
**Rev: PROV. DE, . . ., arms.**

| | | | | | |
|---|---|---|---|---|---|
| 238 | 1813 | — | — | Rare | — |

**SILVER, cast**
**Similar to 4 Reales, KM#231.**

| | | | | | |
|---|---|---|---|---|---|
| 239 | 1814 | — | — | Rare | — |

**Obv: Lines below bow slant right.**

| | | | | | |
|---|---|---|---|---|---|
| 233.4 | 1813 | 10.00 | 17.50 | 30.00 | 50.00 |
| **SILVER** | | | | | |
| **Obv: 8 dots below bow, plain fields.** | | | | | |
| 233.5a | 1812 | — | — | 1200. | 2000. |

| KM# | Date | Good | VG | Fine | VF |
|-----|------|------|-----|------|-----|
| 243 | 1813 | 37.50 | 70.00 | 125.00 | 200.00 |

### REAL

**COPPER**
**Similar to 1/2 Real, KM#243.**

| | | | | | |
|-----|------|------|-----|------|-----|
| 244 | 1813 | 13.50 | 25.00 | 50.00 | 80.00 |

### 2 REALES

**COPPER**
**Similar to 1/2 Real, KM#243.**

| KM# | Date | Good | VG | Fine | VF |
|-----|------|------|-----|------|-----|
| 245 | 1813 | 9.00 | 22.50 | 35.00 | 50.00 |

**COPPER**

| KM# | Date | Good | VG | Fine | VF |
|-----|------|------|-----|------|-----|
| 240 | 1814 | 35.00 | 70.00 | 150.00 | 250.00 |

**OAXACA spelled out.**

| | | | | | |
|-----|------|------|-----|------|-----|
| 241 | 1814 | 100.00 | 200.00 | 350.00 | 550.00 |

| | | | | | |
|-----|------|------|-----|------|-----|
| 246 | 1814 | 22.50 | 50.00 | 100.00 | 175.00 |

**SILVER, cast**

| | | | | | |
|-----|------|------|-----|------|-----|
| 247 | 1814 | — | — | Rare | — |

**NOTE:** See note below 1/2 Real, KM#220.2.

### 8 REALES

## Huautla
### 8 REALES

**COPPER**
**Obv. leg: MONEDA PROVI.CIONAL PS.ES.**
**around bow, arrow/SUD.**
**Rev. leg: FABRICADO EN HUAUTLA.**

| KM# | Date | Good | VG | Fine | VF |
|-----|------|------|-----|------|-----|
| 242 | 1812 | 1000. | 1500. | 2000. | — |

## Tierra Caliente
(Hot Country)
**Under General Morelos**
### 1/2 REAL

**COPPER**
**Obv: Bow, T.C., SUD.**
**Rev: Morelos monogram, value, date.**

**COPPER**

| KM# | Date | Good | VG | Fine | VF |
|-----|------|------|-----|------|-----|
| 248 | 1813 | 9.00 | 20.00 | 40.00 | 75.00 |

**SILVER, cast**

| | | | | | |
|-----|------|------|-----|------|-----|
| 249 | 1813 | — | — | — | — |

**NOTE:** See note below 1/2 Real, KM#220.2.

## PUEBLA

The coins of Puebla emanated from Zacatlan, the head-quarters of the hit-and-run Insurgent leader Osorno. The mint opened in April 1812 and operated through 1813.

## Zacatlan
(Struck by General Osorno)
### 1/2 REAL

**COPPER**
Obv: Osorno monogram, ZACATLAN, date.
Rev: Crossed arrows, wreath, value.

| KM# | Date | Good | VG | Fine | VF |
|-----|------|------|-----|------|-----|
| 250 | 1813 | — | — | Rare | — |

### REAL

**COPPER**

| | | | | | |
|-----|------|------|-----|------|-----|
| 251 | 1813 | 100.00 | 150.00 | 225.00 | 450.00 |

**COPPER**

| | | | | | |
|-----|------|------|-----|------|-----|
| 252 | 1813 | 125.00 | 175.00 | 275.00 | 500.00 |

## VERACRUZ

In Zongolica, in the province of Veracruz, 2 priests and a lawyer decided to raise an army to fight for independence. Due to isolation from other Insurgent forces, they decided to make their own coins. Records show that they intended to mint coins of 1/2, 1, 2, 4, and 8 reales, but specimens are extant of only the three higher denominations.

## Zongolica
### 2 REALES

**.903 SILVER**
Obv. leg: VIVA FERNANDO VII Y AMERICA, bow and arrow.
Rev. leg: ZONGOLICA, value, crossed palm branch, sword, date.

| KM# | Date | Good | VG | Fine | VF |
|-----|------|------|-----|------|-----|
| 253 | 1812 | 85.00 | 175.00 | 300.00 | 500.00 |

### 4 REALES
**.903 SILVER**
Similar to 2 Reales, KM#253.

| | | | | | |
|-----|------|------|-----|------|-----|
| 254 | 1812 | 600.00 | 800.00 | 1200. | 2000. |

## 8 REALES

**.903 SILVER**

| KM# | Date | Good | VG | Fine | VF |
|-----|------|------|-----|------|-----|
| 255 | 1812 | — | — | *Rare | — |

**\*NOTE:** Spink America Gerber sale 6-96 VF to XF realized $57,200.

# COUNTERMARKED COINAGE
## Congress of Chilpanzingo

**Type A: Hand holding bow and arrow between quiver w/arrows, sword and bow.**

**Type B: Crowned eagle on bridge.**
### 1/2 REAL
**SILVER**
c/m: Type A on cast Mexico City KM#72.

| KM# | Date | Year | Good | VG | Fine | VF |
|-----|------|------|------|-----|------|-----|
| 256.1 | ND | (1812) | 42.50 | 70.00 | 90.00 | 120.00 |

c/m: Type A on Zacatecas KM#181.

| | | | | | | |
|-----|------|------|------|-----|------|-----|
| 256.2 | ND | (1811) | 50.00 | 75.00 | 100.00 | 125.00 |

### REAL
**CAST SILVER**
c/m: Type A on cast Mexico City KM#81.

| | | | | | | |
|-----|------|------|------|-----|------|-----|
| A257 | ND | (1803) | 18.50 | 30.00 | 50.00 | 80.00 |

## 2 REALES

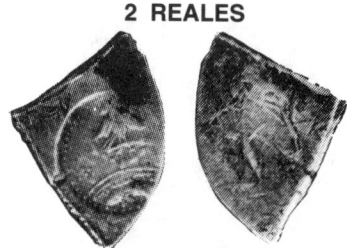

**SILVER**
**c/m: Type B on 1/4 cut of 8 Reales.**

| KM# | Date | Year | Good | VG | Fine | VF |
|---|---|---|---|---|---|---|
| 257.1 | ND | — | — | — | Unique | — |

**c/m: Type B on Zacatecas KM#186.**

| | | | | | | |
|---|---|---|---|---|---|---|
| 257.2 | ND | (1811) | — | — | Unique | — |

## 8 REALES

**SILVER**
**c/m: Type A on cast Mexico City KM#109.**

| KM# | Date | Year | Good | VG | Fine | VF |
|---|---|---|---|---|---|---|
| 258.1 | ND | (1805 TH) | 45.00 | 65.00 | 85.00 | 125.00 |

**c/m: Type A on cast Mexico City KM#110.**

| | | | | | | |
|---|---|---|---|---|---|---|
| 258.2 | ND | (1810 HJ) | 50.00 | 75.00 | 100.00 | 150.00 |

**c/m: Type A on cast Mexico City KM#111.**

| | | | | | | |
|---|---|---|---|---|---|---|
| 258.3 | ND | (1811 HJ) | 45.00 | 65.00 | 85.00 | 125.00 |
| | ND | (1812 HJ) | 100.00 | 125.00 | 175.00 | 275.00 |

**c/m: Type B on Chihuahua KM#111.1.**

| | | | | | | |
|---|---|---|---|---|---|---|
| 259.1 | ND | (1816 RP) | 200.00 | 250.00 | 300.00 | 350.00 |

**c/m: Type B on cast Mexico City KM#111.**

| | | | | | | |
|---|---|---|---|---|---|---|
| 259.2 | ND | (1811 HJ) | 130.00 | 140.00 | 150.00 | 175.00 |

**c/m: Type B on Valladolid KM#178.**

| KM# | Date | Year | Good | VG | Fine | VF |
|---|---|---|---|---|---|---|
| 259.3 | ND | (1813) | 1000. | 2000. | 3000. | 5000. |

**c/m: Type B on Zacatecas KM#190.**

| | | | | | | |
|---|---|---|---|---|---|---|
| 259.4 | ND | (1810) | 400.00 | 500.00 | 600.00 | 750.00 |

# Ensaie
## 8 REALES

**SILVER**
**c/m: Eagle over ENSAIE on Mexico City KM#110.**

| | | | | | | |
|---|---|---|---|---|---|---|
| 260.1 | ND | (1811 HJ) | 150.00 | 200.00 | 275.00 | 350.00 |

**c/m: Eagle over ENSAIE crude sling below
on Zacatecas KM#189.**

| | | | | | | |
|---|---|---|---|---|---|---|
| 260.2 | ND | (1811) | 200.00 | 400.00 | 600.00 | 800.00 |

**c/m: Eagle over ENSAIE, crude sling below
on Zacatecas KM#190.**

| | | | | | | |
|---|---|---|---|---|---|---|
| 260.3 | ND | (1810) | — | — | — | — |
| | ND | (1811) | 100.00 | 150.00 | 200.00 | 300.00 |

**c/m: Eagle over ENSAIE, crude sling below
on Zacatecas KM#191.**

| | | | | | | |
|---|---|---|---|---|---|---|
| 260.4 | ND | (1810) | 500.00 | 700.00 | 900.00 | 1200. |
| | ND | (1811) | 250.00 | 300.00 | 375.00 | 500.00 |
| | ND | (1812) | 200.00 | 250.00 | 285.00 | 400.00 |

## Jose Maria Liceaga

J.M.L. with banner on cross, crossed olive branches.
(J.M.L./V., D.s, S.M.,S.Y.S.L., Ve, A.P.,
s.r.a., Sea, P.G.,S.,S.M.,E.)

### 1/2 REAL

SILVER
c/m: JML/SM on cast Mexico City 1/2 Real.

| KM# | Date | Year | Good | VG | Fine | VF |
|-----|------|------|------|-----|------|-----|
| A260 | ND | — | 100.00 | 150.00 | 200.00 | 275.00 |

### 2 REALES

SILVER
c/m: J.M.L./Ve on 1/4 cut of 8 Reales.

| KM# | Date | Good | VG | Fine | VF |
|-----|------|------|-----|------|-----|
| 261.1 | ND | — | 175.00 | 225.00 | 300.00 | — |

c/m: J.M.L./V. on Zacatecas KM#186-187.
261.2   ND     (1811) 200.00 225.00 250.00 300.00

c/m: J.M.L./DS on Zacatecas KM#186-187.
261.3   ND     (1811) 200.00 235.00 275.00 325.00

c/m: J.M.L./S.M. on Zacatecas KM#186-187.
261.4   ND     (1811) 200.00 235.00 275.00 325.00

c/m: J.M.L./S.Y. on Zacatecas KM#186-187.
261.5   ND     (1811) 200.00 235.00 275.00 325.00

### 8 REALES

SILVER
c/m: J.M.L./D.S. on Zacatecas KM#189-190.
262.1   ND     (1811) 250.00 325.00 425.00 550.00

c/m: J.M.L./E on Zacatecas KM#189-190.

| KM# | Date | Year | Good | VG | Fine | VF |
|-----|------|------|------|------|------|-----|
| 262.2 | ND | (1811) | 225.00 | 300.00 | 400.00 | 550.00 |

c/m: J.M.L./P.G. on Durango KM#111.2.
262.3   ND (1813 RM) 200.00 275.00 375.00 525.00

c/m: J.M.L./S.F. on Zacatecas KM#189-190.
262.4   ND     (1811) 200.00 275.00 375.00 525.00

c/m: J.M.L./S.M. on Zacatecas KM#189-190.
262.5   ND     (1811) 200.00 275.00 375.00 525.00

c/m: J.M.L./V.E. on Zacatecas KM#189-190.
262.6   ND     (1811) 200.00 275.00 375.00 525.00

## Don Jose Maria De Linares

## 8 REALES

**SILVER**
**c/m: LINA/RES* on Mexico City KM#110.**

| KM# | Date | Good | VG | Fine | VF |
|---|---|---|---|---|---|
| 263.1 | ND (1808 TH) | 250.00 | 300.00 | 375.00 | 500.00 |

**c/m: LINA/RES * on Zacatecas KM#189-190.**

| | | | | | |
|---|---|---|---|---|---|
| 263.2 | ND (1811) | 300.00 | 375.00 | 450.00 | 575.00 |

**c/m: LINA/RES* on Zacatecas, KM#191-192.**

| | | | | | |
|---|---|---|---|---|---|
| 263.3 | ND (1812) | 250.00 | 300.00 | 375.00 | 500.00 |

## L.V.S. - Labor Vincit Semper

**NOTE:** Some authorities believe L.V.S. is for 'La Villa de Sombrerete'.

### 8 REALES

**CAST SILVER**
**c/m: L.V.S. on Chihuahua KM#123.**

| | | | | | |
|---|---|---|---|---|---|
| 264.1 | ND (1811 RP) | 275.00 | 350.00 | 450.00 | 550.00 |
| | ND (1812 RP) | 200.00 | 250.00 | 300.00 | 375.00 |

**c/m: L.V.S. on Chihuahua KM#111.1 overstruck on KM#123.**

| KM# | Date Year | Good | VG | Fine | VF |
|---|---|---|---|---|---|
| 264.2 | ND (1816 RP) | 250.00 | 300.00 | 325.00 | 375.00 |
| | ND (1817 RP) | 250.00 | 300.00 | 325.00 | 375.00 |
| | ND (1818 RP) | 250.00 | 300.00 | 325.00 | 375.00 |
| | ND (1819 RP) | 400.00 | 450.00 | 500.00 | 600.00 |
| | ND (1820 RP) | 450.00 | 500.00 | 550.00 | 650.00 |

**c/m: L.V.S. on Guadalajara KM#111.3.**

| | | | | | |
|---|---|---|---|---|---|
| 264.3 | ND (1817) | 185.00 | 220.00 | 250.00 | 310.00 |

**c/m: L.V.S. on Nueva Vizcaya KM#165.**

| | | | | | |
|---|---|---|---|---|---|
| 264.4 | ND (1811 RM) | 1150. | 3150. | 5250. | 8250. |

**c/m: L.V.S. on Sombrerete KM#177.**

| | | | | | |
|---|---|---|---|---|---|
| 264.5 | ND (1811) | 300.00 | 350.00 | 450.00 | 550.00 |
| | ND (1812) | 300.00 | 350.00 | 450.00 | 550.00 |

**c/m: L.V.S. on Zacatecas KM#189-190.**

| | | | | | |
|---|---|---|---|---|---|
| 264.6 | ND (1811) | 350.00 | 400.00 | 450.00 | 550.00 |

**c/m: L.V.S. on Zacatecas KM#192.**

| | | | | | |
|---|---|---|---|---|---|
| 264.7 | ND (1813) | 350.00 | 400.00 | 450.00 | 550.00 |

## Morelos
### Morelos monogram

**Type A: Stars above and below monogram in circle.**

**Type B: Dots above and below monogram in oval.**

**Type C: Monogram in rectangle.**
**NOTE:** Many specimens of Type C available in today's market are considered spurious.

### 2 REALES

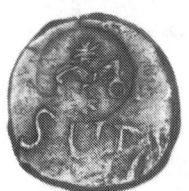 

**COPPER**
**c/m: Type A on Oaxaca Sud, KM#226.1.**

| | | | | | |
|---|---|---|---|---|---|
| A265 | 1812 | — | — | — | — | — |

# 8 REALES

**SILVER**
**c/m: Type A on cast Mexico City KM#109.**

| KM# | Date | Year | Good | VG | Fine | VF |
|-----|------|------|------|-----|------|-----|
| 265.1 | ND | (1797 FM) | 45.00 | 50.00 | 60.00 | 85.00 |
| | ND | (1798 FM) | 45.00 | 50.00 | 60.00 | 85.00 |
| | ND | (1800 FM) | 45.00 | 50.00 | 60.00 | 85.00 |
| | ND | (1807 TH) | 45.00 | 50.00 | 60.00 | 85.00 |

**c/m: Type A on Mexico City KM#110.**

| | | | | | | |
|-----|------|------|------|-----|------|-----|
| 265.2 | ND | (1809 TH) | 55.00 | 65.00 | 85.00 | 120.00 |
| | ND | (1811 HJ) | 55.00 | 65.00 | 85.00 | 120.00 |

**c/m: Type A on Mexico City KM#111.**

| | | | | | | |
|-----|------|------|------|-----|------|-----|
| 265.3 | ND | (1812 JJ) | 50.00 | 60.00 | 75.00 | 110.00 |

**COPPER**
**c/m: Type A on Oaxaca Sud KM#233.2.**

| | | | | | | |
|-----|------|------|------|-----|------|-----|
| 265.4 | ND | (1812) | 12.50 | 17.50 | 25.00 | 40.00 |
| | ND | (1813) | 12.50 | 17.50 | 25.00 | 40.00 |
| | ND | (1814) | 12.50 | 17.50 | 25.00 | 40.00 |

**CAST SILVER**
**c/m: Type A on Supreme National Congress KM#206.**

| KM# | Date | Year | Good | VG | Fine | VF |
|-----|------|------|------|-----|------|-----|
| 265.5 | ND | (1811) | 200.00 | 250.00 | 375.00 | 600.00 |

**SILVER**
**c/m: Type A on Zacatecas KM#189-190.**

| | | | | | | |
|-----|------|------|------|-----|------|-----|
| 265.6 | ND | (1811) | 200.00 | 250.00 | 375.00 | 600.00 |

**c/m: Type A on Zacatecas KM#191.**

| | | | | | | |
|-----|------|------|------|-----|------|-----|
| 265.7 | ND | (1811) | 200.00 | 250.00 | 375.00 | 600.00 |

**c/m: Type B on Guatemala 8 Reales, C#67.**

| | | | | | | |
|-----|------|------|------|-----|------|-----|
| 266.1 | ND | (1810 M) | — | — | Rare | — |

**c/m: Type B on Mexico City KM#110.**

| | | | | | | |
|-----|------|------|------|-----|------|-----|
| 266.2 | ND | (1809 TH) | 45.00 | 55.00 | 65.00 | 90.00 |

**c/m: Type C on Zacatecas KM#189-190.**

| | | | | | | |
|-----|------|------|------|-----|------|-----|
| 267 | ND | (1811) | 300.00 | 350.00 | 425.00 | 650.00 |

# Norte
**Issued by the Supreme National Congress and the Army of the North.**

**c/m: Eagle on cactus; star to left; NORTE below.**

## 1/2 REAL

**SILVER**
**c/m: On Zacatecas KM#180.**

| | | | | | | |
|-----|------|------|------|-----|------|-----|
| 268 | ND | (1811) | 250.00 | 300.00 | 375.00 | 450.00 |

## 2 REALES

**SILVER**
**c/m: On Zacatecas KM#187.**

| KM# | Date | Year | Good | VG | Fine | VF |
|-----|------|------|------|-----|------|-----|
| 269 | ND | (1811) | 225.00 | 275.00 | 325.00 | 400.00 |

**c/m: On Zacatecas KM#188.**

| | | | | | | |
|-----|------|------|------|-----|------|-----|
| A269 | ND | (1812) | — | — | — | — |

## 4 REALES

**SILVER**
**c/m: On Sombrerete KM#175.**

| KM# | Date | Year | Good | VG | Fine | VF |
|---|---|---|---|---|---|---|
| B269 | ND | (1812) | 100.00 | 150.00 | 200.00 | 275.00 |

## 8 REALES

**SILVER**
**c/m: On Chihuahua KM#111.1.**

| 270.1 | ND | (1813 RP) | 250.00 | 350.00 | 450.00 | 550.00 |
|---|---|---|---|---|---|---|

**c/m: On Guanajuato KM#111.4.**

| 270.2 | ND | (1813 JM) | 400.00 | 550.00 | 700.00 | 800.00 |
|---|---|---|---|---|---|---|

**c/m: On Zacatecas KM#189-190.**

| 270.3 | ND | (1811) | 300.00 | 400.00 | 500.00 | 650.00 |
|---|---|---|---|---|---|---|

**c/m: On Zacatecas KM#191.**

| KM# | Date | Year | Good | VG | Fine | VF |
|---|---|---|---|---|---|---|
| 270.4 | ND | (1811) | 200.00 | 300.00 | 400.00 | 550.00 |
|  | ND | (1812) | 200.00 | 300.00 | 400.00 | 550.00 |

## Osorno

**c/m: Osorno monogram.**
**(Jose Francisco Osorno)**

## 1/2 REAL

**SILVER**
**c/m: On Mexico City KM#72.**

| 271.1 | ND | (1798 FM) | 65.00 | 100.00 | 150.00 | 200.00 |
|---|---|---|---|---|---|---|
|  | ND | (1802 FT) | 65.00 | 100.00 | 150.00 | 200.00 |
|  | ND | (1806) | 65.00 | 100.00 | 150.00 | 200.00 |

**c/m: On Mexico City KM#73.**

| 271.2 | ND | (1809) | 65.00 | 100.00 | 150.00 | 200.00 |
|---|---|---|---|---|---|---|

## REAL

**SILVER**
**c/m: On Mexico City KM#81.**

| 272.1 | ND | (1803 FT) | 65.00 | 100.00 | 150.00 | 200.00 |
|---|---|---|---|---|---|---|

**c/m: On Potosi Real.**

| 272.2 | ND | — | 75.00 | 115.00 | 175.00 | 250.00 |
|---|---|---|---|---|---|---|

**c/m: On Guatemala Real, KM#54.**

| 272.3 | ND | (1804) | 75.00 | 115.00 | 175.00 | 250.00 |
|---|---|---|---|---|---|---|

## 2 REALES

**SILVER**
**c/m: On Mexico City KM#88.2.**

| A272.1 |  | (1788 FM) | 75.00 | 125.00 | 175.00 | 250.00 |
|---|---|---|---|---|---|---|

**c/m: On Mexico City KM#91.**

| KM# | Date | Good | VG | Fine | VF |
|---|---|---|---|---|---|
| A272.2 | (1808 TH) | 75.00 | 125.00 | 175.00 | 250.00 |

**c/m: On cast Mexico City KM#92.**

| A272.3 (A272.1) | ND (1809 TH) | 75.00 | 125.00 | 175.00 | 250.00 |

**c/m: On Zacatlan KM#252.**

| A272.4 (A272.2) | ND (1813) | 150.00 | 200.00 | 300.00 | 400.00 |

## 4 REALES

**SILVER**
**c/m: On Mexico City KM#97.2.**

| 273.1 | ND (1782 FF) | 85.00 | 150.00 | 200.00 | 275.00 |

**c/m: On Mexico City KM#100.**

| 273.2 | ND (1799 FM) | 85.00 | 150.00 | 200.00 | 275.00 |

## 8 REALES

**SILVER**
**c/m: On Lima 8 Reales, C#101.**

| 274.1 | ND (1811 JP) | 200.00 | 225.00 | 250.00 | 300.00 |

**c/m: On Mexico City KM#110.**

| KM# | Date | Year | Good | VG | Fine | VF |
|---|---|---|---|---|---|---|
| 274.2 | ND | (1809 TH) | 125.00 | 150.00 | 225.00 | 300.00 |
| | ND | (1810 HJ) | 125.00 | 150.00 | 225.00 | 300.00 |
| | ND | (1811 HJ) | 125.00 | 150.00 | 225.00 | 300.00 |

## S.J.N.G. - Suprema Junta National Gubernativa
(Refer to Multiple countermarks)

## VILLA/GRAN

(Julian Villagran)

## 2 REALES

**CAST SILVER**
**c/m: On cast Mexico City KM#91.**

| 298 | ND (1799 FM) | 150.00 | 200.00 | 250.00 | 350.00 |
| | ND (1802 FT) | 150.00 | 200.00 | 250.00 | 350.00 |

## 8 REALES

**CAST SILVER**
**c/m: VILLA/GRAN on cast Mexico City KM#109.**

| KM# | Date | Year | Good | VG | Fine | VF |
|---|---|---|---|---|---|---|
| 275 | ND | (1796 FM) | 200.00 | 250.00 | 300.00 | 400.00 |
| | ND | (1806 TH) | 200.00 | 250.00 | 300.00 | 400.00 |

## UNCLASSIFIED COUNTERMARKS
### General Vicente Guerrero

The countermark of an eagle facing left within a pearled oval has been attributed by some authors as that of General Vicente Guerrero, a leader of the insurgents in the south, 1816-1821.

### 1/2 REAL

**SILVER**
**c/m: Eagle on Mexico City 1/2 Real.**

| 276 | ND | — | 40.00 | 60.00 | 80.00 | 175.00 |

## REAL

**SILVER**
**c/m: Eagle on Mexico City KM#78.**

| KM# | Date | Good | VG | Fine | VF |
|-----|------|------|-----|------|-----|
| 277 | ND (1772 FM) | 35.00 | 50.00 | 75.00 | 165.00 |

### 2 REALES

**SILVER**
**c/m: Eagle on Mexico City KM#88.**

| 278.1 | ND (1784 FM) | 40.00 | 60.00 | 100.00 | 225.00 |
| | (1798) | 40.00 | 60.00 | 100.00 | 220.00 |

**c/m: Eagle on Mexico City KM#91.**

| 278.2 | ND (1807 PJ) | 30.00 | 50.00 | 80.00 | 200.00 |

### 8 REALES

**SILVER**
**c/m: Eagle on Zacatecas KM#191.**

| KM# | Date | Year | Good | VG | Fine | VF |
|-----|------|------|------|-----|------|-----|
| 279 | ND | (1811) | 100.00 | 150.00 | 200.00 | 350.00 |

## ZMY

### 8 REALES

**SILVER**
**c/m: ZMY on Zacatecas KM#191.**

| 286 | ND | (1812) | 100.00 | 150.00 | 210.00 | 275.00 |

# MULTIPLE COUNTERMARKS

Many combinations of Royalist and Insurgent counter-marks are usually found on the cast copies produced by Chihuahua and Mexico City and on the other crude provisional issues of this period. Struck Mexico City coins were used to make molds for casting necessity issues and countermarked afterwards to show issuing authority. Some were marked again by either both or separate opposing friendly forces to authorize circulation in their areas of occupation. Some countermarks are only obtainable with companion markings.

## Chilpanzingo
## Crown and Flag
### 8 REALES

**SILVER**
**c/m: Chilpanzingo Type B and**
**crown and flag on Zacatecas KM#189-190.**

| KM# | Date | | Good | VG | Fine | VF |
|-----|------|---|------|-----|------|-----|
| 280 | ND | (1811) | — | — | — | — |

## Chilpanzingo/ENSAIE
### 8 REALES

**SILVER**
**c/m: Chilpanzingo Type B and ENSAIE on**
**Zacatecas KM#189.**

| KM# | Date | Year | Good | VG | Fine | VF |
|-----|------|------|------|-----|------|-----|
| A297 | ND | — | 175.00 | 250.00 | 350.00 | — |

## Chilpanzingo/LVA
### 8 REALES

**SILVER**
**c/m: Chilpanzingo Type A and LVA on**
**Mexico City KM#109.**

| 297 | ND (1805 TH) | 45.00 | 75.00 | 145.00 | 250.00 |

## Chilpanzingo/LVS
### 8 REALES

SILVER
c/m: Chilpanzingo Type A and
script LVS on cast Mexico City KM#110.

| KM# | Date | Year | Good | VG | Fine | VF |
|-----|------|------|------|-----|------|-----|
| 281 | ND (1809 HJ) | | 45.00 | 65.00 | 135.00 | 250.00 |

## Chilpanzingo/Morelos
### 8 REALES

SILVER
c/m: Chilpanzingo Type A and Morelos
monogram Type A on cast Mexico City KM#109.

| KM# | Date | Year | Good | VG | Fine | VF |
|-----|------|------|------|-----|------|-----|
| 284 | ND (1806 TH) | | 35.00 | 50.00 | 100.00 | 200.00 |
| | ND (1807 TH) | | 35.00 | 50.00 | 100.00 | 200.00 |

c/m: Chilpanzingo Type A and Morelos monogram
Type A on struck Mexico City KM#110.

| | | | | | | |
|-----|------|------|------|-----|------|-----|
| 285.1 | ND (1809 TH) | | 45.00 | 65.00 | 135.00 | 250.00 |

c/m: Chilpanzingo Type A and Morelos monogram
Type A on cast Mexico City KM#110.

| KM# | Date | Good | VG | Fine | VF |
|-----|------|------|-----|------|-----|
| 285.2 | ND (1810 HJ) | 35.00 | 45.00 | 60.00 | 140.00 |
| | ND (1811 HJ) | 35.00 | 45.00 | 60.00 | 140.00 |

c/m: Chilpanzingo Type A and Morelos monogram
Type A on cast Mexico City KM#111.

| | | | | | |
|-----|------|------|-----|------|-----|
| 285.3 | ND (1811 HJ) | 75.00 | 120.00 | 175.00 | 275.00 |

## Chilpanzingo/Morelos/LVS
### 8 REALES

SILVER
c/m: Chilpanzingo Type A, Morelos Type A and
LVS monogram on cast Mexico City KM#110.

| KM# | Date | Year | Good | VG | Fine | VF |
|-----|------|------|------|-----|------|-----|
| 286 | ND (1809 HJ) | | 50.00 | 75.00 | 125.00 | 275.00 |

## Chilpanzingo/P.D.V.
### 8 REALES

SILVER
c/m: Chilpanzingo Type B and P.D.V. (Provisional
De Valladolid) on Valladolid KM#178.

| | | | | | | |
|-----|------|------|------|-----|------|-----|
| 287 | ND | (1813) | — | — | — | — |

## Chilpanzingo/S.J.N.G.
### 8 REALES

SILVER
c/m: Chilpanzingo Type B and S.J.N.G.
(Suprema Junta Nacional Gubernativa)
on Zacatecas KM#189-190.

| KM# | Date | Year | Good | VG | Fine | VF |
|------|------|--------|------|------|------|------|
| 288 | ND | (1811) | — | — | — | — |

## C.M.S./S.C.M.
### 2 REALES

SILVER
c/m: C.M.S. (Comandancia Militar Suriana) and
eagle w/S.C.M. (Soberano Congreso Mexicano)
on Mexico City 2 Reales.

| | | | | | | |
|------|------|------|------|------|------|------|
| 289 | ND | | — | — | — | — |

## ENSAIE/J.M.L.
### 8 REALES

SILVER
c/m: ENSAIE and J.M.L. on Zacatecas, KM#190.

| KM# | Date | Year | Good | VG | Fine | VF |
|------|------|--------|--------|--------|--------|--------|
| A290 | ND | (1811) | 100.00 | 175.00 | 275.00 | 350.00 |

## ENSAIE/VTIL
### 8 REALES

SILVER
c/m: ENSAIE and VTIL on Zacatecas KM#189-190.

| KM# | Date | | Good | VG | Fine | VF |
|------|------|--------|--------|--------|--------|--------|
| 290 | ND | (1811) | 100.00 | 175.00 | 275.00 | 350.00 |

## J.M.L./VTIL
### 2 REALES

SILVER
c/m: J.M.L./D.S. and VTIL on Zacatecas, KM#186.

| | | | | | | |
|------|------|--------|--------|--------|--------|--------|
| A286 | ND | (1811) | 75.00 | 125.00 | 175.00 | 250.00 |

c/m: J.M.L./V.E. and VTIL on Zacatecas KM#186.

| | | | | | | |
|------|------|--------|--------|--------|--------|--------|
| B286 | ND | (1810) | 75.00 | 125.00 | 175.00 | 250.00 |
| | ND | (1811) | 75.00 | 125.00 | 175.00 | 250.00 |

### 8 REALES

SILVER
c/m: J.M.L./D.S. and VTIL on Mexico City KM#110.

| KM# | Date | Year | Good | VG | Fine | VF |
|------|------|---------|--------|--------|--------|--------|
| 291 | ND | 1810 HJ | 85.00 | 150.00 | 250.00 | 400.00 |

## L.C.M./Morelos
### 8 REALES

**SILVER**
c/m: LCM and Morelos monogram
Type A on cast Mexico City KM#109.

| KM# | Date | Year | Good | VG | Fine | VF |
|---|---|---|---|---|---|---|
| 282 | ND | (1792 FM) | — | — | — | — |

## Morelos/Morelos
### 8 REALES

**SILVER**
c/m: Morelos Type A and C on cast
Mexico City KM#109.

| 283 | ND | (1806 TH) | — | — | — | — |

## LCM/MVA-1812
### 8 REALES

**SILVER**
c/m: LCM and MVA/1812 on Chihuahua KM#123.

| 292 | 1812 | (1810 RP) | — | — | — | — |

c/m: LCM and MVA 1812 on Chihuahua KM#110.

| KM# | Date | Year | Good | VG | Fine | VF |
|---|---|---|---|---|---|---|
| A293 | 1812 | (1810 HJ) | — | — | — | — |

c/m: LCM and MVA 1812 on Chihuahua KM#111.1.

| 293 | 1812 | (1817) | 200.00 | 300.00 | 550.00 | 850.00 |
| | 1812 | (1818) | 200.00 | 300.00 | 550.00 | 850.00 |

**NOTE:** KM293 represents questionable issues - as the host date is later than the c/m date. However, there is no documentation existing to indicate for how long or even when these c/m's were applied.

## L.V.S./MVA-1812
### 8 REALES

**SILVER**
c/m: Script LVA and Morelos monogram Type A
on cast Mexico City KM#110.

| KM# | Date | Year | Good | VG | Fine | VF |
|---|---|---|---|---|---|---|
| 294 | ND | (HJ) | 45.00 | 75.00 | 135.00 | 250.00 |

**SILVER**
c/m: L.V.S. and MVA/1812 on Chihuahua KM#111.1.

| A295 | 1812 | (1817) | 400.00 | 650.00 | 1000. | 1500. |

**NOTE:** KM#295 represents a questionable issue - as the host date is later than the c/m date. However, there is no documentation existing to indicate for how long or even when these c/m's were applied.

## M.d.S./S.C.M.
### 2 REALES

**SILVER**
c/m: M.d.S. (Militar del Sur) and eagle
w/S.C.M. (Soberano Congreso Mexicano)
on Mexico City 2 Reales.

| 295 | ND | | — | 250.00 | 450.00 | 650.00 | — |

## OSORNO/VILLAGRAN
### 8 REALES

**SILVER**
c/m: Osorno monogram and VILLA/GRAN on cast
Mexico City KM#110.

| KM# | Date | Year | Good | VG | Fine | VF |
|-----|------|------|------|-----|------|-----|
| 296 | ND | (1809 TH) | — | — | — | — |

## S.J.N.G./VTIL
### 8 REALES

**SILVER**
c/m: S.J.N.G. and VTIL on Zacatecas KM#191.

| | | | | | |
|-----|------|------|------|------|------|
| 298 | ND | — | 35.00 | 50.00 | 75.00 | 200.00 |

# EMPIRE OF ITURBIDE
### RULERS
Augustin I Iturbide, 1822-1823

### MINT MARKS
Mo - Mexico City

### ASSAYERS INITIALS
JA - Jose Garcia Ansaldo, 1812-1833
JM - Joaquin Davila Madrid,
    1809-1833

### 1/8 REAL

**COPPER**
Mint: Nueva Viscaya

| KM# | Date | Mintage | Good | VG | Fine | VF |
|-----|------|---------|------|-----|------|-----|
| 299 | 1821 | — | 22.50 | 50.00 | 85.00 | 150.00 |
| | 1822 | — | 6.00 | 12.50 | 27.50 | 55.00 |
| | 1823 | — | 6.00 | 12.50 | 25.00 | 45.00 |

## 1/4 REAL

**COPPER**
Mint: Nueva Viscaya

| KM# | Date | Mintage | Good | VG | Fine | VF |
|-----|------|---------|------|-----|------|-----|
| 300 | 1822 | — | 150.00 | 275.00 | 400.00 | 550.00 |

### 1/2 REAL

**.903 SILVER**
Mint mark: Mo

| KM# | Date | Mintage | Fine | VF | XF | Unc |
|-----|------|---------|------|-----|-----|------|
| 301 | 1822 JM | — | 20.00 | 40.00 | 80.00 | 300.00 |
| | 1823 JM | — | 15.00 | 30.00 | 60.00 | 250.00 |

### REAL

**.903 SILVER**
Mint mark: Mo

| | | | | | | |
|-----|------|------|------|------|------|------|
| 302 | 1822 JM | — | 175.00 | 350.00 | 550.00 | 900.00 |

### 2 REALES

**.903 SILVER**
Mint mark: Mo

| | | | | | | |
|-----|------|------|------|------|------|------|
| 303 | 1822 JM | — | 50.00 | 100.00 | 350.00 | 1000. |
| | 1823 JM | — | 40.00 | 80.00 | 250.00 | 850.00 |

### 8 REALES

**.903 SILVER**
**Mint mark: Mo**

| KM# | Date | Mintage | Fine | VF | XF | Unc |
|---|---|---|---|---|---|---|
| 304 | 1822 JM | — | 75.00 | 150.00 | 300.00 | 950.00 |

**Obv: Bust similar to 8 Escudos, KM#313.**
**Rev: Similar to KM#304.**

| | | | | | | |
|---|---|---|---|---|---|---|
| 305 | 1822 JM | — | — | — | Rare | — |

**Type I. Obv: Leg. divided. Rev: 8 R.J.M. at upper left of eagle.**

| | | | | | | |
|---|---|---|---|---|---|---|
| 306.1 | 1822 JM | — | 90.00 | 170.00 | 450.00 | 1300. |

**Rev: Cross on crown.**

| | | | | | | |
|---|---|---|---|---|---|---|
| 306.2 | 1822 JM | — | 650.00 | 1000. | — | — |

**Type II. Obv: Similar to KM#306.**
**Rev: Similar to KM#310.**

| | | | | | | |
|---|---|---|---|---|---|---|
| 307 | 1822 JM | — | 150.00 | 350.00 | 650.00 | 2250. |

**Type III. Obv: Continuous leg. w/long smooth truncation. Rev: Similar to KM#306.**

| | | | | | | |
|---|---|---|---|---|---|---|
| 308 | 1822 JM | — | 175.00 | 500.00 | 950.00 | 2250. |

**NOTE:** Variety with long, straight truncation is valued at $5,000. in uncirculated condition.

**Type IV. Obv: Similar to KM#308.**
**Rev: Similar to KM#310.**

| KM# | Date | Mintage | Fine | VF | XF | Unc |
|---|---|---|---|---|---|---|
| 309 | 1822 JM | — | 50.00 | 120.00 | 250.00 | 850.00 |

**Type V. Obv. continuous leg. w/short irregular truncation. Rev: 8 R.J.M. below eagle.**

| | | | | | | |
|---|---|---|---|---|---|---|
| 310 | 1822 JM | — | 50.00 | 120.00 | 225.00 | 900.00 |
| | 1823 JM | — | 50.00 | 120.00 | 225.00 | 900.00 |

**Type VI. Obv: Bust w/long truncation.**
**Rev: Similar to KM#310.**

| | | | | | | |
|---|---|---|---|---|---|---|
| 311 | 1822 JM | — | — | — | Rare | — |

# 4 SCUDOS

**.875 GOLD**
**Mint mark: Mo**

| KM# | Date | Mintage | Fine | VF | XF | Unc |
|---|---|---|---|---|---|---|
| 312 | 1823 JM | — | 1000. | 1750. | 2850. | 5500. |

## 8 SCUDOS

**.875 GOLD**
Mint mark: Mo
Obv. leg: AUGUSTINUS.

| KM# | Date | Mintage | Fine | VF | XF | Unc |
|---|---|---|---|---|---|---|
| 313.1 | 1822 JM | — | 1200. | 2000. | 3750. | — |

**NOTE:** Superior Casterline sale 5-89 choice AU realized $11,000.

**Obv. leg: AUGSTINUS (error).**

| | | | | | | |
|---|---|---|---|---|---|---|
| 313.2 | 1822 JM | — | 1250. | 2250. | 4200. | — |

| | | | | | | |
|---|---|---|---|---|---|---|
| 314 | 1823 JM | — | 1000. | 1800. | 3250. | 6000. |

## REPUBLIC

### MINT MARKS

A, AS - Alamos
CE - Real de Catorce
CA,CH - Chihuahua
C, Cn, Gn(error) - Culiacan
D, Do - Durango
EoMo - Estado de Mexico
Ga - Guadalajara
GC - Guadalupe y Calvo
G, Go - Guanajuato
H, Ho - Hermosillo
M, Mo - Mexico City
O, OA - Oaxaca
SLP, PI, P, I/P - San Luis Potosi
Z, Zs - Zacatecas

### ASSAYERS INITIALS

#### ALAMOS MINT

| Initials | Years | Mintmaster |
|---|---|---|
| PG | 1862-1868 | Pascual Gaxiola |
| DL, L | 1866-1879 | Domingo Larraguibel |
| AM | 1872-1874 | Antonio Moreno |
| ML, L | 1878-1895 | Manuel Larraguibel |

#### REAL DE CATORCE MINT

| | | |
|---|---|---|
| ML | 1863 | Mariano Leon |

#### CHIHUAHUA MINT

| | | |
|---|---|---|
| MR | 1831-1834 | Mariano Cristobal Ramirez |
| AM | 1833-1839 | Jose Antonio Mucharraz |
| MJ | 1832 | Jose Mariano Jimenez |
| RG | 1839-1856 | Rodrigo Garcia |
| JC | 1856-1865 | Joaquin Campa |
| BA | 1858 | Bruno Arriada |
| FP | 1866 | Francisco Potts |
| JG | 1866-1868 | Jose Maria Gomez del Campo |
| MM, M | 1868-1895 | Manuel Merino |
| AV | 1873-1880 | Antonio Valero |
| EA | 1877 | Eduardo Avila |
| JM | 1877 | Jacobo Mucharraz |
| GR | 1877 | Guadalupe Rocha |
| MG | 1880-1882 | Manuel Gameros |

#### CULIACAN MINT

| | | |
|---|---|---|
| CE | 1846-1870 | Clemente Espinosa de los Monteros |
| C | 1870 | ??? |
| PV | 1860-1861 | Pablo Viruega |
| MP, P | 1871-1876 | Manuel Onofre Parodi |
| GP | 1876 | Celso Gaxiola & Manuel Onofre Parodi |
| CG, G | 1876-1878 | Celso Gaxiola |
| JD, D | 1878-1882 | Juan Dominguez |
| AM, M | 1882-1899 | Antonio Moreno |
| F | 1870 | Fernando Ferrari |
| JQ, Q | 1899-1903 | Jesus S. Quiroz |
| FV, V | 1903 | Francisco Valdez |
| MH, H | 1904 | Merced Hernandez |
| RP, P | 1904-1905 | Ramon Ponce de Leon |

#### DURANGO MINT

| | | |
|---|---|---|
| RL | 1825-1832 | ??? |
| RM | 1830-1848 | Ramon Mascarenas |
| OMC | 1840 | Octavio Martinez de Castro |
| CM | 1848-1876 | Clemente Moron |
| JMR | 1849-1852, | Jose Maria Ramirez |
| CP, P | 1853-1864, 1867-1873 | Carlos Leon de la Pena |
| LT | 1864-1865 | ??? |
| JMP, P | 1877 | Carlos Miguel de la Palma |
| PE, E | 1878 | Pedro Espejo |
| TB, B | 1878-1880 | Trinidad Barrera |
| JP | 1880-1894 | J. Miguel Palma |
| MC, C | 1882-1890 | Manuel M. Canseco or Melchor Calderon |
| JB | 1885 | Jacobo Blanco |
| ND, D | 1892-1895 | Norberto Dominguez |

### ESTADO DE MEXICO MINT

| Initials | Years | Mintmaster |
|---|---|---|
| L | 1828-1830 | Luis Valazquez de la Cadena |
| F | 1828-1830 | Francisco Parodi |

### GUADALAJARA MINT

| FS | 1818-1835 | Francisco Suarez |
|---|---|---|
| JM | 1830-1832 | ??? |
| JG | 1836-1839 | Juan de Dios Guzman |
|  | 1842-1867 |  |
| MC | 1839-1846 | Manuel Cueras |
| JM | 1867-1869 | Jesus P. Manzano |
| IC, C | 1869-1877 | Ignacio Canizo y Soto |
| MC | 1874-1875 | Manuel Contreras |
| JA, A | 1877-1881 | Julio Arancivia |
| FS, S | 1880-1882 | Fernando Sayago |
| TB, B | 1883-1884 | Trinidad Barrera |
| AH, H | 1884-1885 | Antonio Hernandez y Prado |
| JS, S | 1885-1895 | Jose S. Schiafino |

### GUADALUPE Y CALVO MINT

| MP | 1844-1852 | Manuel Onofre Parodi |
|---|---|---|

### GUANAJUATO MINT

| JJ | 1825-1826 | Jose Mariano Jimenez |
|---|---|---|
| MJ, MR, JM, PG, |  |  |
| PJ, PF |  | ??? |
| PM | 1841-1848, | Patrick Murphy |
|  | 1853-1861 |  |
| YF | 1862-1868 | Yldefonso Flores |
| YE | 1862-1863 | Ynocencio Espinoza |
| FR | 1870-1878 | Faustino Ramirez |
| SB, RR | ??? |  |
| RS | 1891-1900 | Rosendo Sandoval |

### HERMOSILLO MINT

| PP | 1835-1836 | Pedro Peimbert |
|---|---|---|
| FM | 1871-1876 | Florencio Monteverde |
| MP | 1866 | Manuel Onofre Parodi |
| PR | 1866-1875 | Pablo Rubio |
| R | 1874-1875 | Pablo Rubio |
| GR | 1877 | Guadalupe Rocha |
| AF, F | 1876-1877 | Alejandro Fourcade |
| JA, A | 1877-1883 | Jesus Acosta |
| FM, M | 1883-1886 | Fernando Mendez |
| FG, G | 1886-1895 | Fausto Gaxiola |

### MEXICO CITY MINT

Because of the great number of assayers for this mint (Mexico City is a much larger mint than any of the others) there is much confusion as to which initial stands for which assayer at any one time. Therefore we feel that it would be of no value to list the assayers.

### OAXACA MINT

| AE | 1859-1891 | Agustin Endner |
|---|---|---|
| E | 1889-1890 | Agustin Endner |
| FR | 1861-1864 | Francisco de la Rosa |
| EN | 1890 | Eduardo Navarro Luna |
| N | 1890 | Eduardo Navarro Luna |

### POTOSI MINT

| JS | 1827-1842 | Juan Sanabria |
|---|---|---|
| AM | 1838,1843- |  |
|  | 1849 | Jose Antonio Mucharraz |
| PS | 1842-1843,1848-1849, |  |
|  | 1857-1861,1867- |  |
|  | 1870 | Pompaso Sanabria |
| S | 1869-1870 | Pomposo Sanabria |
| MC | 1849-1859 | Mariano Catano |
| RO | 1859-1865 | Romualdo Obregon |
| MH, H | 1870-1885 | Manuel Herrera Razo |
| O | 1870-1873 | Juan R. Ochoa |
| CA, G | 1867-1870 | Carlos Aguirre Gomez |
| BE, E | 1879-1881 | Blas Escontria |
| LC, C | 1885-1886 | Luis Cuevas |
| MR, R | 1886-1893 | Mariano Reyes |

### ZACATECAS MINT

| A | 1825-1829 | Adalco |
|---|---|---|
| Z | 1825-1826 | Mariano Zaldivar |
| V | 1824-1831 | Jose Mariano Vela |
| O | 1829-1867 | Manuel Ochoa |

| Initials | Years | Mintmaster |
|---|---|---|
| M | 1831-1867 | Manuel Miner |
| VL | 1860-1866 | Vicente Larranaga |
| JS | 1867-1868, |  |
|  | 1876-1886 | J.S. de Santa Ana |
| YH | 1868-1874 | Ygnacio Hierro |
| JA | 1874-1876 | Juan H. Acuna |
| FZ | 1886-1905 | Francisco de P. Zarate |
| FM | 1904-1905 | Francisco Mateos |

# PROFILE EAGLE COINAGE

The first coins of the Republic were of the distinctive Profile Eagle style, sometimes called the "Hooked Neck Eagle." They were struck first in Mexico City in 1823 in denominations of eight reales and eight escudos. In 1824 they were produced at the Durango and Guanajuato mints in addition to Mexico City. Denominations included the one half, one, two and eight reales. No gold escudos of this design was struck in 1824. In 1825, only the eight reales was struck briefly at the Guanajuato mint.

## 1/2 REAL

**1.6900 g, .903 SILVER, .0490 oz ASW**
**Mint mark: Mo**
Obv: Full breast Profile eagle.
Rev: Cap and rays.

| KM# | Date | Mintage | Fine | VF | XF | Unc |
|---|---|---|---|---|---|---|
| 369 | 1824 JM | — | 45.00 | 75.00 | 150.00 | 600.00 |

**NOTE:** Die varieties exist.

## REAL

**3.3800 g, .903 SILVER, .081 oz ASW**
**Mint mark: Do**
Obv: Thin Profile eagle.
Rev: Reversed S.

| | | | | | | |
|---|---|---|---|---|---|---|
| 371.1 | 1824 RL | — | 3750. | 7500. | 10,000. | 15,000. |

**Rev: Regular S.**

| | | | | | |
|---|---|---|---|---|---|
| 371.2 | 1824 RL | 3 known | — | — | Rare | — |

# 2 REALES

**6.7600 g, .903 SILVER, .1962 oz ASW**
**Mint mark: Do**
**Obv: Thin Profile eagle.**
**Rev: Cap and rays.**

| KM# | Date | Mintage | Fine | VF | XF | Unc |
|-----|------|---------|------|-----|-----|-----|
| 373.1 | 1824 RL | — | 50.00 | 125.00 | 850.00 | 2200. |

**NOTE:** Die varieties exist.

**Type I Reverse**
**Mint mark: D**
**Rev: Dot before 2 R in legend.**

| 373.2 | 1824 RL | — | 100.00 | 200.00 | 1000. | 3000. |
|-----|------|---------|------|-----|-----|-----|

**Type II Reverse**
**Rev: No dot before 2 R in legend.**

| 373.3 | 1824 RL | — | 100.00 | 200.00 | 1000. | 3000. |
|-----|------|---------|------|-----|-----|-----|

**Mint mark: Mo**
**Obv: Medium Profile eagle.**

| 373.4 | 1824 JM | — | 30.00 | 70.00 | 450.00 | 2000. |
|-----|------|---------|------|-----|-----|-----|

**NOTE:** Die varieties exist. No coins are known with visible feather details on the eagle's breast.

# 8 REALES

Typical Defiant
Snake Obverse

Typical Submissive
Snake Obverse

Typical Folded
Snake Obverse

**NOTE:** Legible Libertads on the Cap are common on Durango eight reales.

**Med. Libertad      Small Libertad      Large Libertad**
**Cap Reverse        Cap Reverse         Cap Reverse**

**NOTE:** The three styles of obverses and the three styles of reverses were combined in to make six distinct varieties of coins.

**27.0700 g, .903 SILVER, .7859 oz ASW**
**Mint mark: Do**
**Obv: Thin Profile eagle, defiant snake.**
**Rev: Medium Libertad.**

| KM# | Date | Mintage | Fine | VF | XF | Unc |
|---|---|---|---|---|---|---|
| 376.1 | 1824 RL | — | 500.00 | 1200. | 4500. | 7000. |

**NOTE:** Five die varieties are known. All are rare.

**Obv: Thin Profile eagle, defiant snake.**
**Rev: Small Libertad.**

| | | | | | | |
|---|---|---|---|---|---|---|
| 376.2 | 1824 RL | — | 300.00 | 400.00 | 1600. | 3500. |

**NOTE:** Ten die varieties are known. Some are rare.

**Obv: Thin Profile eagle, submissive snake.**
**Rev: Small Libertad.**

| | | | | | | |
|---|---|---|---|---|---|---|
| 376.3 | 1824 RL | — | 200.00 | 350.00 | 1250. | 2750. |

**NOTE:** Six die varieties are known. Some are rare.

**Obv: Thin Profile eagle, submissive snake.**
**Rev: Large Libertad.**

| | | | | | | |
|---|---|---|---|---|---|---|
| 376.4 | 1824 RL | — | 200.00 | 350.00 | 1250. | 2750. |

**NOTE:** Eleven die varieties known. Some are rare.

**Obv: Thin Profile eagle, folded snake.**
**Rev: Small Libertad.**

| | | | | | | |
|---|---|---|---|---|---|---|
| 376.5 | 1824 RL | — | 200.00 | 350.00 | 1200. | 2500. |

**NOTE:** Only one die varieity is known.

**Obv: Thin Profile eagle, folded snake.**
**Rev: Large Libertad.**

| | | | | | | |
|---|---|---|---|---|---|---|
| 376.6 | 1824 RL | — | 200.00 | 400.00 | 1500. | 3000. |

**NOTE:** Eleven die varieties known. Some are rare.

**Mint mark: Go**
**Obv: Full breast Profile eagle.**
**Rev: Cap and rays.**

| | | | | | | |
|---|---|---|---|---|---|---|
| A376.1 | 1824 JM | — | 250.00 | 400.00 | 1100. | 3500. |
| | 1825/4 JJ | — | 600.00 | 1200. | 2750. | 7000. |
| | 1825 JJ | — | 500.00 | 750.00 | 1400. | 5500. |

**1825/4 JJ overdate**
**NOTE:** This coin exists w/o the results of the warped obverse die shown above, but most examples include it.

**NOTE:** Other easily identified die varieties are the 1824 w/the missing superscript "s" for granos and the 1825 w/a dash under the "I" of MEXICANA resulting from a die chip, but these die varieties are not rare.
**NOTE:** Guanajuato eight reales are characterized by flat strikes on large, thin planchets. Visible feather details on the eagle's breast and legible Libertads on the cap are the exception.

Tight snake loop at eagle's beak.

Open snake loop at eagle's beak.

The Standard or Republic Edge

The Colonial or Circle & Rectangle

The standard Flat-Topped Three

**Mint mark: Mo**
**Edge: Standard or Republic.**

**Obv: Full breast Profile eagle.**

| KM# | Date | Mintage | Fine | VF | XF | Unc |
|---|---|---|---|---|---|---|
| A376.2 | 1823 JM | — | 150.00 | 300.00 | 800.00 | 4500. |
| | 1824 JM | — | 125.00 | 250.00 | 700.00 | 4000. |

**Edge: Colonial or Circle and Rectangle.**

| | | | | | | |
|---|---|---|---|---|---|---|
| A376.3 | 1823 JM | — | — | — | Rare | — |

The Round-Topped Three

**Edge: Standard or Republic.**
**Rev: Round topped three.**

| | | | | | | |
|---|---|---|---|---|---|---|
| A376.4 | 1823 JM | — | 2000. | 4000. | 6000. | 8000. |

**NOTE:** Many die varieties exist. Illustration of one of the die differences is the size of the snake loop at the eagle's beak. This difference is not apparent except on the 1824 Mo eight reales.

**Obv: REPULICA (error).**

| | | | | | | |
|---|---|---|---|---|---|---|
| A376.5 | 1824 JM | — | 6000. | 9000. | 11,000. | — |

**NOTE:** Legible Libertads on the cap are not as prevalent on the Mexico City eight reales as on the Durango eight reales. They are much more numerous than on the Guanajuato eight reales.

## 8 ESCUDOS

Type I Obverse/Reverse

**NOTE:** The cap on the reverse of the curved tail Type I points to the "A" of LIBERTAD.

**27.0700 g, .675 GOLD, .7616 oz AGW**
**Mint mark: Mo**
**Obv: Snakes tail curved.**
**Rev: Cap points to "A" of LIBERTAD.**

| KM# | Date | Mintage | Fine | VF | XF | Unc |
|---|---|---|---|---|---|---|
| 382.1 | 1823 JM | — | 6000. | 9000. | 12,500. | 20,000. |

Type II Obverse/Reverse

**NOTE:** The cap on the reverse of the looped tail Type II points to the "T" of LIBERTAD.

**Obv: Snakes tail looped.**
**Rev: Cap points to "T" of LIBERTAD.**

| | | | | | | |
|---|---|---|---|---|---|---|
| 382.2 | 1823 JM | — | 5000. | 8000. | 12,000. | 18,000. |

**NOTE:** The quality of the strikes of Type I coins is almost always superior to that of the Type II. Details of the eagle feathers, cactus and lettering on the open book are better on most Type I coins but the Type II coins are scarcer. Type I coins outnumber Type II coins by about two to one.

## State and Federal Issues
### 1/16 REAL
(Medio Octavo)

**COPPER**
**Mint: Jalisco**
**Obv. leg: DEPARTAMENTO DE JALISCO**

| KM# | Date | Mintage | Good | VG | Fine | VF |
|-----|------|---------|------|-----|------|-----|
| 316 | 1860 | — | 3.00 | 5.00 | 10.00 | 50.00 |

**Obv. leg: ESTADO LIBRE DE JALISCO**

| KM# | Date | Mintage | Good | VG | Fine | VF |
|-----|------|---------|------|-----|------|-----|
| 317 | 1861 | — | 2.50 | 4.00 | 8.50 | 42.50 |

**Mint: Mexico City**
**Obv. leg: REPUBLICA MEXICANA**

| KM# | Date | Mintage | VG | Fine | VF | XF |
|-----|------|---------|-----|------|-----|-----|
| 315 | 1831 | — | 10.00 | 20.00 | 50.00 | 100.00 |
| | 1832/1 | — | 12.00 | 22.00 | 55.00 | 125.00 |
| | 1832 | — | 10.00 | 20.00 | 50.00 | 100.00 |
| | 1833 | — | 10.00 | 20.00 | 50.00 | 100.00 |

**BRASS**

| | | | | | | |
|-----|------|---------|-----|------|-----|-----|
| 315a | 1832 | — | 13.50 | 22.50 | 60.00 | 150.00 |
| | 1833 | — | 10.00 | 17.50 | 50.00 | 100.00 |
| | 1835 | — | 400.00 | 800.00 | 1250. | 2500. |

# 1/8 REAL
## (Octavo Real)
### COPPER
**Mint: Chihuahua**
**Obv. leg: ESTADO SOBERANO DE CHIHUAHUA**

| KM# | Date | Mintage | Good | VG | Fine | VF |
|-----|------|---------|------|-----|------|-----|
| 318 | 1833 | — | 350.00 | 750.00 | — | — |
| | 1834 | — | 350.00 | 750.00 | — | — |
| | 1835/3 | — | 350.00 | 750.00 | — | — |

**Obv. leg: ESTADO DE CHIHUAHUA**

| | | | | | | |
|-----|------|---------|------|-----|------|-----|
| 319 | 1855 | — | 3.50 | 5.00 | 18.00 | 60.00 |

**Mint: Durango**
**Rev. leg: LIBERTAD**

| | | | | | | |
|-----|------|---------|------|-----|------|-----|
| 320 | 1824 | — | 5.00 | 10.00 | 35.00 | 100.00 |
| | 1828 | — | 150.00 | 250.00 | 400.00 | 1000. |

**NOTE:** These pieces were frequently struck over 1/8 Real, dated 1821-23 of Nueva Vizcaya. All known examples with these host dates are collectable contemporary counterfeits.

**Rev. leg: OCTo.DE.R.DE DO., date.**

| | | | | | | |
|-----|------|---------|------|-----|------|-----|
| 321 | 1828 | — | 6.00 | 15.00 | 35.00 | 100.00 |

**Obv. leg: ESTADO DE DURANGO**

| | | | | | | |
|-----|------|---------|------|-----|------|-----|
| 322 | 1833 | — | — | — | Rare | — |

**Obv. leg: REPUBLICA MEXICANA**

| KM# | Date | | Good | VG | Fine | VF |
|-----|------|-----|------|-----|------|-----|
| 323 | 1842/33 | — | 13.50 | 20.00 | 40.00 | 115.00 |
| | 1842 | — | 8.50 | 15.00 | 32.50 | 100.00 |

**Obv. leg: REPUBLICA MEXICANA**
**Rev. leg: DEPARTAMENTO DE DURANGO**

| | | | | | | |
|-----|------|-----|------|-----|------|-----|
| 324 | 1845 | — | 22.50 | 50.00 | 100.00 | 250.00 |
| | 1846 | — | — | — | Rare | — |
| | 1847 | — | 3.50 | 5.00 | 9.00 | 32.50 |

**Obv. leg: REPUBLICA MEXICANA**
**Rev. leg: ESTADO DE DURANGO**

| | | | | | | |
|-----|------|-----|------|-----|------|-----|
| 325 | 1851 | — | 3.50 | 6.50 | 10.00 | 30.00 |
| | 1852/1 | — | 3.50 | 6.50 | 10.00 | 30.00 |
| | 1852 | — | 3.00 | 5.00 | 8.00 | 30.00 |
| | 1854 | — | 6.00 | 10.00 | 17.50 | 65.00 |

**Mint: Guanajuato**
**Obv. leg: ESTADO LIBRE DE GUANAJUATO**

| | | | | | | |
|-----|------|-----|------|-----|------|-----|
| 326 | 1829 | — | 3.00 | 5.00 | 10.00 | 25.00 |
| | 1829 error w/GUANJUATO | | | | | |
| | | — | 4.00 | 6.50 | 12.50 | 27.50 |
| | 1830 | — | 7.50 | 12.00 | 20.00 | 75.00 |

**BRASS, 29mm**

| | | | | | | |
|-----|------|-----|------|-----|------|-----|
| 327 | 1856 | — | 7.50 | 12.00 | 20.00 | 75.00 |

**25mm**

| KM# | Date | Mintage | Good | VG | Fine | VF |
|-----|------|---------|------|-----|------|-----|
| 328 | 1856 | — | 3.50 | 6.00 | 10.00 | 30.00 |
|     | 1857 | — | 3.50 | 6.00 | 10.00 | 30.00 |

**COPPER**

| KM# | Date | Mintage | Good | VG | Fine | VF |
|-----|------|---------|------|-----|------|-----|
| 328a | 1857 | — | 8.50 | 20.00 | 35.00 | 60.00 |

**Mint: Jalisco**
**Obv. leg: ESTADO LIBRE DE JALISCO**

| KM# | Date | Mintage | Good | VG | Fine | VF |
|-----|------|---------|------|-----|------|-----|
| 329 | 1828 | — | 3.00 | 5.00 | 8.00 | 22.50 |
|     | 1831 | — | 100.00 | 200.00 | 300.00 | 400.00 |
|     | 1832/28 | — | 3.50 | 5.50 | 9.00 | 25.00 |
|     | 1832 | — | 3.50 | 5.50 | 9.00 | 25.00 |
|     | 1833 | — | 3.50 | 5.50 | 9.00 | 25.00 |
|     | 1834 | — | 50.00 | 100.00 | 175.00 | 300.00 |

| KM# | Date | Mintage | Good | VG | Fine | VF |
|-----|------|---------|------|-----|------|-----|
| 330 | 1856 | — | 4.00 | 7.00 | 10.00 | 25.00 |
|     | 1857 | — | 4.00 | 7.00 | 10.00 | 25.00 |
|     | 1858 | — | 4.00 | 7.00 | 10.00 | 25.00 |
|     | 1861 | — | 100.00 | 200.00 | 300.00 | 400.00 |
|     | 1862/1 | — | 4.00 | 7.00 | 10.00 | 25.00 |
|     | 1862 | — | 4.00 | 7.00 | 10.00 | 25.00 |

**Obv. leg: DEPARTAMENTO DE JALISCO**

| KM# | Date | Mintage | Good | VG | Fine | VF |
|-----|------|---------|------|-----|------|-----|
| 331 | 1858 | — | 3.25 | 6.00 | 9.00 | 22.50 |
|     | 1859 | — | 2.75 | 5.50 | 8.00 | 20.00 |
|     | 1860/59 | — | 3.25 | 6.00 | 9.00 | 22.50 |
|     | 1860 | — | 3.25 | 6.00 | 9.00 | 22.50 |
|     | 1862 | — | 4.50 | 9.00 | 22.50 | 50.00 |

**Mint: Mexico City**
**27mm**
**Obv. leg: REPUBLICA MEXICANA**

| KM# | Date | Mintage | VG | Fine | VF | XF |
|-----|------|---------|-----|------|-----|-----|
| 332 | 1829 | — | 450.00 | 900.00 | 1500. | 2500. |

**21mm**
**Obv. leg: REPUBLICA MEXICANA**

| KM# | Date | Mintage | Good | VG | Fine | VF |
|-----|------|---------|------|-----|------|-----|
| 333 | 1829 | — | 7.50 | 12.00 | 25.00 | 55.00 |
|     | 1830 | — | 1.00 | 2.00 | 6.00 | 20.00 |
|     | 1831 | — | 1.50 | 3.50 | 7.00 | 25.00 |
|     | 1832 | — | 1.50 | 3.50 | 7.00 | 25.00 |
|     | 1833/2 | — | 1.50 | 3.50 | 7.00 | 25.00 |
|     | 1833 | — | 1.50 | 2.75 | 6.00 | 20.00 |
|     | 1834 | — | 1.50 | 2.75 | 6.00 | 20.00 |
|     | 1835/4 | — | 1.75 | 3.50 | 7.00 | 25.00 |
|     | 1835 | — | 1.50 | 2.75 | 6.00 | 20.00 |

**Obv. leg: LIBERTAD**

| KM# | Date | Mintage | Good | VG | Fine | VF |
|-----|------|---------|------|-----|------|-----|
| 334 | 1841 | — | 6.00 | 15.00 | 30.00 | 75.00 |
|     | 1842 | — | 2.50 | 5.00 | 10.00 | 30.00 |
|     | 1850 | — | 12.50 | 20.00 | 30.00 | 80.00 |
|     | 1861 | — | 5.00 | 12.00 | 25.00 | 70.00 |

**Mint: Occidente**
**Obv. leg: ESTADO DE OCCIDENTE**

| KM# | Date | Mintage | Good | VG | Fine | VF |
|-----|------|---------|------|-----|------|-----|
| 335 | 1828 reverse S | — | 13.50 | 28.50 | 45.00 | 100.00 |
|     | 1829 | — | 13.50 | 28.50 | 45.00 | 100.00 |

**Mint: Potosi**
**Obv. leg: ESTADO LIBRE DE SAN LUIS POTOSI**

| KM# | Date | Mintage | Good | VG | Fine | VF |
|-----|------|---------|------|-----|------|-----|
| 336 | 1829 | — | 6.00 | 9.00 | 15.00 | 50.00 |
|     | 1830 | — | 8.00 | 12.00 | 20.00 | 60.00 |
|     | 1831 | — | 5.00 | 8.00 | 12.00 | 40.00 |
|     | 1859 | — | 5.00 | 8.00 | 12.00 | 40.00 |
|     | 1865/1 | — | — | Reported, not confirmed | | |

**Mint: Sonora**
**Obv. leg: ESTO LIBE Y SOBO DE SONORA, 28mm.**

| KM# | Date | Mintage | Good | VG | Fine | VF |
|-----|------|---------|------|-----|------|-----|
| 337 | 1859 | — | — | Rare | — | — |

**Mint: Zacatecas**
**Obv. leg: ESTo LIBe FEDo DE ZACATECAS**

| KM# | Date Mintage | Good | VG | Fine | VF |
|---|---|---|---|---|---|
| 338 | 1825 — | 3.00 | 5.50 | 12.00 | 25.00 |
| | 1827 — | 3.00 | 5.50 | 12.00 | 25.00 |
| | 1827 inverted A for V in OCTAVO | | | | |
| | — | 12.00 | 20.00 | 40.00 | 100.00 |
| | 1827 OCTAVA (error) | | | | |
| | — | 15.00 | 25.00 | 50.00 | 120.00 |
| | 1827 Inverted 1 | | | | |
| | — | 12.00 | 20.00 | 40.00 | 100.00 |
| | 1829 — | — | — | Rare | — |
| | 1830 — | 2.75 | 5.00 | 8.00 | 20.00 |
| | 1831 — | 4.50 | 6.75 | 13.50 | 27.50 |
| | 1832 — | 2.75 | 5.00 | 8.00 | 20.00 |
| | 1833 — | 2.75 | 5.00 | 8.00 | 20.00 |
| | 1835 — | 3.50 | 6.00 | 10.00 | 25.00 |
| | 1846 — | 3.50 | 6.00 | 10.00 | 25.00 |
| | 1851 — | 125.00 | 175.00 | 250.00 | 350.00 |
| | 1852 — | 3.50 | 6.00 | 10.00 | 25.00 |
| | 1858 — | 2.75 | 5.00 | 8.00 | 20.00 |
| | 1859 — | 2.75 | 5.00 | 8.00 | 20.00 |
| | 1862 — | 2.75 | 5.00 | 8.00 | 20.00 |
| | 1863 reversed 6 in date | | | | |
| | — | 2.75 | 5.00 | 8.00 | 20.00 |

**Obv. leg: DEPARTAMENTO DE ZACATECAS**

| | | | | | |
|---|---|---|---|---|---|
| 339 | 1836 — | 4.00 | 8.00 | 15.00 | 40.00 |
| | 1845 — | 6.00 | 10.00 | 20.00 | 50.00 |
| | 1846 — | 5.00 | 9.00 | 18.50 | 45.00 |

## 1/4 REAL
### (Un Quarto/Una Quartilla)
### (Copper/Brass Series)

**COPPER**
**Mint: Chihuahua**
**Obv. leg: ESTADO SOBERANO DE CHIHUAHUA**

| KM# | Date Mintage | Good | VG | Fine | VF |
|---|---|---|---|---|---|
| 340 | 1833 — | 8.00 | 12.00 | 45.00 | 85.00 |
| | 1834 — | 6.00 | 10.00 | 25.00 | 55.00 |
| | 1835 — | 5.00 | 8.00 | 12.00 | 50.00 |

**Obv. leg: ESTADO LIBRE DE CHIHUAHUA**

| | | | | | |
|---|---|---|---|---|---|
| 341 | 1846 — | 3.50 | 6.00 | 12.00 | 50.00 |

**NOTE:** Varieties with or without fraction bar.

**Obv. leg: ESTADO DE CHIHUAHUA**

| KM# | Date | Mintage | Good | VG | Fine | VF |
|---|---|---|---|---|---|---|
| 342 | 1855 | — | 2.50 | 5.00 | 11.50 | 50.00 |
| | 1856 | — | 2.50 | 5.00 | 11.50 | 50.00 |

**Obv. leg: DEPARTAMENTO DE CHIHUAHUA**

| | | | | | |
|---|---|---|---|---|---|
| 343 | 1855 | — | 3.00 | 5.00 | 10.00 | 50.00 |
| | 1855 DE (reversed D) | | | | |
| | — | 3.00 | 5.00 | 10.00 | 50.00 |

**Obv. leg: E. CHIHA LIBERTAD**

| | | | | | |
|---|---|---|---|---|---|
| 344 | 1860 — | 2.00 | 4.00 | 8.00 | 25.00 |
| | 1861 — | 2.00 | 4.00 | 8.00 | 25.00 |
| | 1865/1 — | 2.50 | 5.50 | 10.00 | 30.00 |
| | 1865 — | 10.00 | 20.00 | 35.00 | 95.00 |
| | 1866/5 — | 10.00 | 20.00 | 35.00 | 95.00 |
| | 1866 coin rotation | | | | |
| | — | 2.00 | 4.00 | 8.00 | 25.00 |
| | 1866 medal rotation | | | | |
| | — | 2.00 | 4.00 | 8.00 | 25.00 |

**Mint: Durango**
**Obv. leg: REPUBLICA MEXICANA**

| | | | | | |
|---|---|---|---|---|---|
| 345 | 1845 | — | — | — | Rare | — |

**Obv. leg: REPUBLICA MEXICANA**
**Rev: DURANGO, date, value.**

| | | | | | |
|---|---|---|---|---|---|
| 346 | 1858 | — | — | — | Rare | — |

**Obv. leg: ESTADO DE DURANGO**
**Rev. leg: CONSTITUCION**

| KM# | Date | Mintage | Good | VG | Fine | VF |
|-----|------|---------|------|-----|------|-----|
| 347 | 1858 | — | 3.00 | 6.50 | 13.50 | 50.00 |

**NOTE:** Variety exists in brass.

**Obv. leg: DEPARTAMENTO DE DURANGO**
**Rev. leg: LIBERTAD EN EL ORDEN.**

| | | | | | | |
|-----|------|---|------|------|-------|-------|
| 348 | 1860 | — | 2.00 | 5.00 | 13.50 | 38.50 |
| | 1866 | — | 2.00 | 5.00 | 13.50 | 38.50 |

**Obv. leg: ESTADO DE DURANGO**
**Rev. leg: INDEPENDENCIA Y LIBERTAD**

| | | | | | | |
|-----|------|---|------|------|-------|-------|
| 349 | 1866 | — | 2.75 | 6.00 | 15.00 | 45.00 |

**Rev. leg: SUFRAGIO LIBRE**

| | | | | | | |
|-----|------|---|------|------|-------|-------|
| 350 | 1872 | — | 2.00 | 4.00 | 10.00 | 22.50 |

**NOTE:** Variety exists in brass.

 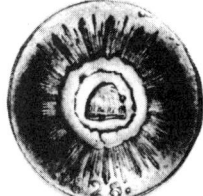

**Mint: Guanajuato**
**Obv. leg: ESTADO LIBRE DE GUANAJUATO**

| | | | | | | |
|-----|------|---|------|------|-------|-------|
| 351 | 1828 | — | 3.75 | 7.00 | 11.00 | 40.00 |
| | 1828 error w/GUANJUATO | | | | | |
| | | — | 3.75 | 7.00 | 11.00 | 40.00 |
| | 1829 | — | 4.50 | 9.00 | 13.50 | 40.00 |

**Obv. leg: EST. LIB. DE GUANAXUATO**
**Rev. leg: OMNIA VINCIT LABOR**

| KM# | Date | Mintage | Good | VG | Fine | VF |
|-----|------|---------|-------|-------|-------|--------|
| 352 | 1856 | — | 12.00 | 25.00 | 50.00 | 100.00 |
| | 1857 | — | 6.00 | 9.00 | 15.00 | 45.00 |

**BRASS**

| | | | | | | |
|------|------|---|------|------|-------|-------|
| 352a | 1856 | — | 3.25 | 6.75 | 11.00 | 27.50 |
| | 1857 | — | 3.25 | 6.75 | 11.00 | 27.50 |

**COPPER**
**Mint: Jalisco**
**Obv. leg: ESTADO LIBRE DE JALISCO**

| | | | | | | |
|-----|--------|---|------|------|-------|-------|
| 353 | 1828 | — | 3.25 | 6.00 | 12.00 | 35.00 |
| | 1829/8 | — | 2.50 | 5.00 | 8.00 | 35.00 |
| | 1829 | — | 2.50 | 5.00 | 8.00 | 35.00 |
| | 1830/20 | — | 2.50 | 5.00 | 8.00 | 30.00 |
| | 1830/29 | — | 2.50 | 5.00 | 8.00 | 30.00 |
| | 1830 | — | 2.50 | 5.00 | 8.00 | 30.00 |
| | 1831 | — | — | — | Rare | — |
| | 1832/20 | — | 2.50 | 5.00 | 8.00 | 30.00 |
| | 1832/28 | — | 2.50 | 5.00 | 8.00 | 30.00 |
| | 1832 | — | 2.50 | 5.00 | 8.00 | 30.00 |
| | 1833/2 | — | 2.50 | 5.00 | 8.00 | 30.00 |
| | 1834 | — | 2.50 | 5.00 | 8.00 | 30.00 |
| | 1835/3 | — | 2.50 | 5.00 | 8.00 | 30.00 |
| | 1835 | — | 2.50 | 5.00 | 8.00 | 30.00 |
| | 1836 | — | — | — | Rare | — |

**Obv. leg: DEPARTAMENTO DE JALISCO**

| | | | | | | |
|-----|------|---|---|---|------|---|
| 354 | 1836 | — | — | — | Rare | — |

**Obv. leg: ESTADO LIBRE DE JALISCO**

| KM# | Date | Mintage | Good | VG | Fine | VF |
|-----|------|---------|------|------|------|------|
| 355 | 1858 | — | 3.00 | 5.00 | 8.00 | 20.00 |
|     | 1861 | — | 3.00 | 5.00 | 10.00 | 25.00 |
|     | 1862 | — | 3.00 | 5.00 | 8.00 | 20.00 |

**Obv. leg: DEPARTAMENTO DE JALISCO**

| KM# | Date | Mintage | Good | VG | Fine | VF |
|-----|------|---------|------|------|------|------|
| 356 | 1858 | — | 3.00 | 5.00 | 8.00 | 20.00 |
|     | 1859/8 | — | 3.00 | 5.00 | 8.00 | 20.00 |
|     | 1859 | — | 3.00 | 5.00 | 8.00 | 20.00 |
|     | 1860 | — | 3.00 | 5.00 | 8.00 | 20.00 |

| KM# | Date | Mintage | Good | VG | Fine | VF |
|-----|------|---------|------|------|------|------|
| 359 | 1828 | — | 2.50 | 4.00 | 6.75 | 15.00 |
|     | 1829 | — | 2.50 | 4.00 | 6.75 | 15.00 |
|     | 1830 | — | 2.50 | 4.00 | 6.75 | 15.00 |
|     | 1832 | — | 2.50 | 4.00 | 6.75 | 15.00 |
|     | 1859 large LIBRE | | | | | |
|     |      | — | 2.50 | 4.00 | 6.75 | 15.00 |
|     | 1859 small LIBRE | | | | | |
|     |      | — | 2.50 | 4.00 | 6.75 | 15.00 |
|     | 1860 | — | 2.50 | 4.00 | 6.75 | 15.00 |

**Mint: Mexico City**
**Obv. leg: REPUBLICA MEXICANA.**

**Rev. leg: REPUBLICA MEXICANA**

| KM# | Date | Mintage | VG | Fine | VF | XF |
|-----|------|---------|------|------|------|------|
| 357 | 1829 | — | 8.00 | 25.00 | 60.00 | 150.00 |

| KM# | Date | Mintage | Good | VG | Fine | VF |
|-----|------|---------|------|------|------|------|
| 360 | 1862 | 1,367 | 2.50 | 4.00 | 6.75 | 13.50 |
|     | 1862 LIBR | | | | | |
|     | Inc. Ab. | | 2.50 | 4.00 | 6.75 | 13.50 |

**Milled edge**
**Obv. leg: ESTADO LIBRE Y SOBERANO DE S.L. POTOSI**
**Rev. leg: LIBERTAD Y REFORMA**

| | | | | | | |
|-----|------|---------|------|------|------|------|
| 361 | 1867 | 3.177 | 2.50 | 3.75 | 7.00 | 18.50 |
|     | 1867 AFG I.A. | | 2.50 | 3.75 | 7.00 | 18.50 |

**Reduced size.**

| | | | | | | |
|-----|------|---------|------|------|------|------|
| 358 | 1829 | — | 12.00 | 25.00 | 50.00 | 150.00 |
|     | 1830 | — | 1.50 | 2.75 | 5.00 | 10.00 |
|     | 1831 | — | 1.50 | 2.75 | 5.00 | 10.00 |
|     | 1832 | — | 5.50 | 10.00 | 20.00 | 35.00 |
|     | 1833 | — | 1.50 | 2.75 | 5.00 | 10.00 |
|     | 1834/3 | — | 1.75 | 3.00 | 6.00 | 12.00 |
|     | 1834 | — | 1.50 | 2.75 | 5.00 | 10.00 |
|     | 1835 | — | 1.50 | 2.75 | 5.00 | 10.00 |
|     | 1836/5 | — | 1.75 | 3.00 | 6.00 | 12.00 |
|     | 1836 | — | 1.50 | 2.75 | 5.00 | 10.00 |
|     | 1837 | — | 6.50 | 13.50 | 22.50 | 45.00 |

**Plain edge**

| | | | | | | |
|-----|------|---------|------|------|------|------|
| 362 | 1867 Inc. Ab. | | 2.50 | 3.75 | 7.00 | 18.50 |
|     | 1867 AFG I.A. | | 2.50 | 3.75 | 7.00 | 18.50 |

**BRASS**
**c/m: JM**

| | | | | | | |
|-----|------|---------|------|------|------|------|
| 358a.1 | 1831 | — | 8.00 | 15.00 | 35.00 | 75.00 |

**W/o countermark**

| | | | | | | |
|-----|------|---------|------|------|------|------|
| 358a.2 | 1831 | — | — | — | — | — |

**Mint: Sinaloa**
**Obv. leg: ESTADO LIBRE Y SOBERANO DE SINALOA**

| | | | | | | |
|-----|------|---------|------|------|------|------|
| 363 | 1847 | — | 3.50 | 5.50 | 9.00 | 20.00 |
|     | 1848 | — | 3.50 | 5.50 | 9.00 | 20.00 |
|     | 1859 | — | 3.00 | 4.50 | 6.00 | 13.50 |
|     | 1861 | — | 1.50 | 3.00 | 4.00 | 9.00 |
|     | 1862 | — | 1.50 | 3.00 | 4.00 | 9.00 |
|     | 1863 | — | 2.50 | 4.00 | 5.00 | 10.00 |
|     | 1864/3 | — | 2.50 | 4.00 | 5.00 | 10.00 |
|     | 1864 | — | 1.50 | 3.00 | 4.00 | 9.00 |
|     | 1865 | — | 3.00 | 5.50 | 7.00 | 15.00 |
|     | 1866/5 | 7.401 | 2.50 | 3.50 | 5.00 | 10.00 |
|     | 1866 Inc. Ab. | | 1.50 | 3.00 | 4.00 | 9.00 |

**COPPER**
**Mint: Potosi**
**Obv. leg: ESTADO LIBRE DE SAN LUIS POTOSI**
**Rev. leg: MEXICO LIBRE**

**BRASS**

| | | | | | | |
|-----|------|---------|------|------|------|------|
| 363a | 1847 | — | 5.00 | 10.00 | 20.00 | 50.00 |

**COPPER**
**Mint: Sonora**
**Obv. leg: EST.D.SONORA UNA CUART**

| KM# | Date | Mintage | Good | VG | Fine | VF |
|-----|------|---------|------|------|------|------|
| 364 | 1831 | — | — | — | Rare | — |
| | 1832 | — | 3.00 | 5.00 | 13.50 | 50.00 |
| | 1833/2 | — | 2.00 | 4.00 | 11.00 | 37.50 |
| | 1833 | — | 2.00 | 4.00 | 11.00 | 37.50 |
| | 1834 | — | 2.00 | 4.00 | 11.00 | 37.50 |
| | 1835/3 | — | 2.00 | 4.00 | 11.00 | 37.50 |
| | 1835 | — | 2.00 | 4.00 | 11.00 | 37.50 |
| | 1836 | — | 2.00 | 4.00 | 11.00 | 37.50 |

**COPPER**
**Obv. leg: DEPARTAMENTO DE ZACATECAS**

| KM# | Date | Mintage | Good | VG | Fine | VF |
|-----|------|---------|------|------|------|------|
| 367 | 1836 | — | 4.00 | 8.50 | 13.50 | 25.00 |
| | 1845 | — | — | — | Rare | — |
| | 1846 | — | 3.50 | 6.75 | 9.00 | 20.00 |

**SILVER SERIES**

**0.8450 g, .903 SILVER, .0245 oz ASW**
**Mint mark: CA**

| KM# | Date | Mintage | VG | Fine | VF | XF |
|-----|------|---------|------|------|------|------|
| 368 | 1843 RG | — | 75.00 | 125.00 | 300.00 | 500.00 |

**Mint mark: C**

| KM# | Date | Mintage | VG | Fine | VF | XF |
|-----|------|---------|------|------|------|------|
| 368.1 | 1855 LR | — | 50.00 | 100.00 | 200.00 | 400.00 |

**Mint mark: Do**

| KM# | Date | Mintage | VG | Fine | VF | XF |
|-----|------|---------|------|------|------|------|
| 368.2 | 1842 LR | — | 12.00 | 20.00 | 40.00 | 125.00 |
| | 1843 LR | — | 20.00 | 25.00 | 60.00 | 150.00 |

**Obv. leg: ESTO.LIBE.Y SOBO.DE SONORA**

| KM# | Date | Mintage | Good | VG | Fine | VF |
|-----|------|---------|------|------|------|------|
| 365 | 1859 | — | 2.00 | 5.00 | 8.00 | 20.00 |
| | 1861/59 | — | 3.00 | 6.50 | 11.00 | 25.00 |
| | 1861 | — | 2.00 | 5.00 | 8.00 | 20.00 |
| | 1862 | — | 2.00 | 5.00 | 8.00 | 20.00 |
| | 1863/2 | — | 6.00 | 15.00 | 30.00 | 50.00 |

**Mint mark: Ga**

| KM# | Date | Mintage | VG | Fine | VF | XF |
|-----|------|---------|------|------|------|------|
| 368.3 | 1842 JG | — | 2.50 | 5.50 | 8.00 | 20.00 |
| | 1843/2 JG | — | — | — | — | — |
| | 1843 JG | — | 6.00 | 9.00 | 12.50 | 30.00 |
| | 1843 MC | — | 4.00 | 6.50 | 9.00 | 25.00 |
| | 1844 MC | — | 4.00 | 6.50 | 9.00 | 25.00 |
| | 1844 LR | — | 2.50 | 5.00 | 7.50 | 15.00 |
| | 1845 LR | — | 2.50 | 4.50 | 7.50 | 15.00 |
| | 1846 LR | — | 5.00 | 8.00 | 10.00 | 25.00 |
| | 1847 LR | — | 4.00 | 6.50 | 9.00 | 25.00 |
| | 1848 LR | — | — | — | Rare | — |
| | 1850 LR | — | — | — | Rare | — |
| | 1851 LR | — | 6.00 | 10.00 | 20.00 | 50.00 |
| | 1852 LR | — | 50.00 | 100.00 | 135.00 | 200.00 |
| | 1854/3 LR | — | 50.00 | 100.00 | 135.00 | 200.00 |
| | 1854 LR | — | 5.00 | 10.00 | 12.50 | 30.00 |
| | 1855 LR | — | 5.00 | 8.00 | 10.00 | 30.00 |
| | 1857 LR | — | 6.50 | 10.00 | 15.00 | 27.50 |
| | 1862 LR | — | 5.50 | 10.00 | 15.00 | 30.00 |

**BRASS**
**Mint: Zacatecas**
**Obv. leg: ESTO LIBE FEDO DE ZACATECAS**

| KM# | Date | Mintage | Good | VG | Fine | VF |
|-----|------|---------|------|------|------|------|
| 366 | 1824 | — | — | — | Rare | — |
| | 1825 | — | 2.50 | 5.00 | 8.00 | 20.00 |
| | 1826 | — | 100.00 | 150.00 | 200.00 | 300.00 |
| | 1827/17 | — | 2.50 | 5.00 | 8.00 | 20.00 |
| | 1829 | — | 2.50 | 5.00 | 8.00 | 20.00 |
| | 1830 | — | 2.50 | 5.00 | 8.00 | 20.00 |
| | 1831 | — | 50.00 | 100.00 | 125.00 | 250.00 |
| | 1832 | — | 2.50 | 5.00 | 8.00 | 20.00 |
| | 1833 | — | 2.50 | 5.00 | 8.00 | 20.00 |
| | 1834 | — | — | — | Rare | — |
| | 1835 | — | 2.50 | 5.00 | 8.00 | 20.00 |
| | 1846 | — | 2.50 | 5.00 | 8.00 | 20.00 |
| | 1847 | — | 2.50 | 5.00 | 8.00 | 20.00 |
| | 1852 | — | 2.50 | 5.00 | 8.00 | 20.00 |
| | 1853 | — | 2.50 | 5.00 | 8.00 | 20.00 |
| | 1855 | — | 4.50 | 10.00 | 20.00 | 65.00 |
| | 1858 | — | 2.50 | 5.00 | 8.00 | 20.00 |
| | 1859 | — | 2.50 | 5.00 | 8.00 | 20.00 |
| | 1860 | — | 100.00 | 150.00 | 200.00 | 300.00 |
| | 1862/57 | — | 2.50 | 5.00 | 8.00 | 20.00 |
| | 1862/59/7 | — | 10.00 | 20.00 | 40.00 | 80.00 |
| | 1862 | — | 2.50 | 5.00 | 8.00 | 20.00 |
| | 1863/2 | — | 2.50 | 5.00 | 8.00 | 20.00 |
| | 1863 | — | 2.50 | 5.00 | 8.00 | 20.00 |
| | 1864/58 | — | 4.00 | 10.00 | 25.00 | 60.00 |

**Mint mark: GC**

| KM# | Date | Mintage | VG | Fine | VF | XF |
|-----|------|---------|------|------|------|------|
| 368.4 | 1844 LR | — | 50.00 | 75.00 | 125.00 | 200.00 |

**Mint mark: Go**

| KM# | Date | Mintage | VG | Fine | VF | XF |
|-----|------|---------|------|------|------|------|
| 368.5 | 1842 PM | — | 4.00 | 6.00 | 10.00 | 20.00 |
| | 1842 LR | — | 2.00 | 4.00 | 8.00 | 15.00 |
| | 1843/2 LR | — | 4.00 | 6.00 | 10.00 | 20.00 |
| | 1843 LR | — | 2.00 | 4.00 | 8.00 | 15.00 |
| | 1844/3 LR | — | — | — | — | — |
| | 1844 LR | — | 2.00 | 4.00 | 8.00 | 15.00 |
| | 1845 LR | — | 8.00 | 15.00 | 30.00 | 60.00 |
| | 1846/5 LR | — | — | — | — | — |
| | 1846 LR | — | 4.00 | 6.00 | 10.00 | 20.00 |
| | 1847 LR | — | 2.00 | 4.00 | 8.00 | 15.00 |
| | 1848/7 LR | — | 2.00 | 4.00 | 8.00 | 15.00 |
| | 1848 LR | — | 2.00 | 4.00 | 8.00 | 15.00 |

| KM# | Date Mintage | VG | Fine | VF | XF |
|---|---|---|---|---|---|
| 368.5 | 1849/7 LR | — | 8.00 | 15.00 | 30.00 | 60.00 |
| | 1849 LR | — | 2.00 | 4.00 | 8.00 | 15.00 |
| | 1850 LR | — | 2.00 | 4.00 | 8.00 | 15.00 |
| | 1851 LR | — | 2.00 | 4.00 | 8.00 | 15.00 |
| | 1852 LR | — | 2.00 | 4.00 | 8.00 | 15.00 |
| | 1853 LR | — | 2.00 | 4.00 | 8.00 | 15.00 |
| | 1855 LR | — | 4.00 | 8.00 | 15.00 | 30.00 |
| | 1856/4 LR | — | — | — | — | — |
| | 1856 LR | — | 5.00 | 10.00 | 20.00 | 35.00 |
| | 1862/1 LR | — | 3.00 | 5.00 | 10.00 | 20.00 |
| | 1862 LR | — | 2.00 | 4.00 | 8.00 | 15.00 |
| | 1863 LR | — | 2.00 | 4.00 | 8.00 | 15.00 |

**Mint mark: Mo**

| KM# | Date Mintage | VG | Fine | VF | XF |
|---|---|---|---|---|---|
| 368.6 | 1842 LR | — | 2.00 | 4.00 | 8.00 | 15.00 |
| | 1843 LR | — | 2.00 | 4.00 | 8.00 | 15.00 |
| | 1844/3 LR | — | 8.00 | 12.00 | 20.00 | 40.00 |
| | 1844 LR | — | 4.00 | 6.00 | 10.00 | 20.00 |
| | 1845 LR | — | 4.00 | 6.00 | 10.00 | 20.00 |
| | 1846 LR | — | 2.00 | 4.00 | 8.00 | 15.00 |
| | 1850 LR | — | 5.00 | 10.00 | 20.00 | 35.00 |
| | 1858 LR | — | 4.00 | 8.00 | 15.00 | 30.00 |
| | 1859 LR | — | 4.00 | 6.00 | 10.00 | 20.00 |
| | 1860 LR | — | 4.00 | 6.00 | 10.00 | 20.00 |
| | 1861 LR | — | 4.00 | 6.00 | 10.00 | 20.00 |
| | 1862 LR | — | 4.00 | 6.00 | 10.00 | 20.00 |
| | 1863/53 LR | — | — | — | — | — |
| | 1863 LR | — | 4.00 | 6.00 | 10.00 | 20.00 |

**Mint mark: S.L.Pi**

| KM# | Date Mintage | VG | Fine | VF | XF |
|---|---|---|---|---|---|
| 368.7 | 1842 | — | 2.00 | 4.00 | 8.00 | 15.00 |
| | 1843/2 | — | 4.00 | 6.00 | 10.00 | 20.00 |
| | 1843 | — | 2.00 | 4.00 | 8.00 | 15.00 |
| | 1844 | — | 2.00 | 4.00 | 8.00 | 15.00 |
| | 1845/3 | — | 4.00 | 6.00 | 10.00 | 25.00 |
| | 1845/4 | — | 4.00 | 6.00 | 10.00 | 25.00 |
| | 1845 | — | 2.00 | 4.00 | 8.00 | 15.00 |
| | 1847/5 | — | 4.00 | 6.00 | 10.00 | 20.00 |
| | 1847 | — | 2.00 | 4.00 | 8.00 | 15.00 |
| | 1851/47 | — | 4.00 | 8.00 | 15.00 | 30.00 |
| | 1854 | — | 125.00 | 200.00 | 275.00 | 400.00 |
| | 1856 | — | 4.00 | 8.00 | 15.00 | 30.00 |
| | 1857 | — | 5.00 | 10.00 | 20.00 | 35.00 |
| | 1862/57 | — | 10.00 | 20.00 | 40.00 | 85.00 |

**Mint mark: Zs**

| KM# | Date Mintage | VG | Fine | VF | XF |
|---|---|---|---|---|---|
| 368.8 | 1842/1 LR | — | 4.00 | 8.00 | 15.00 | 30.00 |
| | 1842 LR | — | 4.00 | 6.00 | 10.00 | 20.00 |

## 1/2 REAL

**Mint mark: A**

| KM# | Date Mintage | Fine | VF | XF | Unc |
|---|---|---|---|---|---|
| 370 | 1862 PG | — | — | Rare | — |

**Mint mark: Ca**
**Obv: Facing eagle.**

| KM# | Date Mintage | Fine | VF | XF | Unc |
|---|---|---|---|---|---|
| 370.1 | 1844 RG | — | 75.00 | 125.00 | 175.00 | 275.00 |
| | 1845 RG | — | 75.00 | 125.00 | 150.00 | 250.00 |

**Mint mark: C, Co**

| KM# | Date Mintage | Fine | VF | XF | Unc |
|---|---|---|---|---|---|
| 370.2 | 1846 CE | — | 30.00 | 50.00 | 75.00 | 150.00 |
| | 1848/7 CE | — | 15.00 | 25.00 | 45.00 | 90.00 |
| | 1849/8 CE | — | 15.00 | 25.00 | 45.00 | 90.00 |
| | 1849 CE | — | — | — | — | — |
| | 1852 CE | — | 12.50 | 20.00 | 40.00 | 80.00 |
| | 1853/1 CE | — | 12.50 | 20.00 | 40.00 | 80.00 |
| | 1854 CE | — | 20.00 | 35.00 | 50.00 | 100.00 |
| | 1856 CE | — | 12.50 | 20.00 | 40.00 | 80.00 |
| | 1857/6 CE | — | 20.00 | 35.00 | 50.00 | 100.00 |
| | 1857 CE | — | 15.00 | 25.00 | 45.00 | 90.00 |
| | 1858 CE (error 1 for 1/2) | | | | | |
| | | — | 12.50 | 20.00 | 40.00 | 80.00 |
| | 1860/59 PV | — | 20.00 | 35.00 | 50.00 | 100.00 |
| | 1860 PV | — | 12.50 | 20.00 | 40.00 | 80.00 |
| | 1861 PV | — | 12.50 | 20.00 | 40.00 | 80.00 |
| | 1863 CE (error 1 for 1/2) | | | | | |
| | | — | 15.00 | 25.00 | 45.00 | 90.00 |
| | 1867 CE | — | 12.50 | 20.00 | 40.00 | 80.00 |

| KM# | Date Mintage | Fine | VF | XF | Unc |
|---|---|---|---|---|---|
| 370.2 | 1869 CE 6/5 (error 1 for 1/2) | | | | | |
| | | — | 12.50 | 20.00 | 40.00 | 80.00 |

**Mint mark: D, Do**

| KM# | Date Mintage | Fine | VF | XF | Unc |
|---|---|---|---|---|---|
| 370.3 | 1832 RM | — | 125.00 | 225.00 | 350.00 | 600.00 |
| | 1832 RM/L | — | — | — | — | — |
| | 1833/2 RM/L | | | | | |
| | | — | 75.00 | 100.00 | 150.00 | 225.00 |
| | 1833/1 RM/L | | | | | |
| | | — | 12.50 | 20.00 | 40.00 | 80.00 |
| | 1833 RM | — | 25.00 | 40.00 | 75.00 | 150.00 |
| | 1834/1 RM | — | 25.00 | 40.00 | 75.00 | 150.00 |
| | 1834 RM | — | 12.50 | 20.00 | 40.00 | 80.00 |
| | 1837/1 RM | — | 12.50 | 20.00 | 40.00 | 80.00 |
| | 1837/4 RM | — | 12.50 | 20.00 | 40.00 | 80.00 |
| | 1837/6 RM | — | 12.50 | 20.00 | 40.00 | 80.00 |
| | 1841/33 RM | — | 15.00 | 25.00 | 50.00 | 100.00 |
| | 1842/32 RM | — | 12.50 | 20.00 | 40.00 | 80.00 |
| | 1842 RM | — | 12.50 | 20.00 | 40.00 | 80.00 |
| | 1842 RM 8R (error) | | | | | |
| | | — | 12.50 | 20.00 | 40.00 | 80.00 |
| | 1842 RM 1/2/8R | | | | | |
| | | — | 12.50 | 20.00 | 40.00 | 80.00 |
| | 1843/33 RM | — | 15.00 | 25.00 | 50.00 | 100.00 |
| | 1843 RM | — | 15.00 | 25.00 | 50.00 | 100.00 |
| | 1845/31 RM | — | 12.50 | 20.00 | 40.00 | 80.00 |
| | 1845/34 RM | — | 12.50 | 20.00 | 40.00 | 80.00 |
| | 1845/35 RM | — | 12.50 | 20.00 | 40.00 | 80.00 |
| | 1845 RM | — | 15.00 | 25.00 | 50.00 | 100.00 |
| | 1846 RM | — | 30.00 | 50.00 | 80.00 | 200.00 |
| | 1848/5 RM | — | 35.00 | 55.00 | 110.00 | 250.00 |
| | 1848/36 RM | — | 25.00 | 40.00 | 75.00 | 200.00 |
| | 1849 JMR | — | 25.00 | 40.00 | 75.00 | 200.00 |
| | 1850 RM | — | — | — | Rare | — |
| | 1850 JMR | — | 25.00 | 40.00 | 75.00 | 200.00 |
| | 1851 JMR | — | 20.00 | 35.00 | 50.00 | 100.00 |
| | 1852/1 JMR | — | 65.00 | 125.00 | 250.00 | 600.00 |
| | 1852 JMR | — | 30.00 | 50.00 | 80.00 | 200.00 |
| | 1853 CP | — | 12.50 | 20.00 | 40.00 | 80.00 |
| | 1854 CP | — | 25.00 | 40.00 | 75.00 | 200.00 |
| | 1855 CP | — | 25.00 | 40.00 | 60.00 | 150.00 |
| | 1856/5 CP | — | 20.00 | 35.00 | 50.00 | 100.00 |
| | 1857 CP | — | 20.00 | 35.00 | 50.00 | 100.00 |
| | 1858/7 CP | — | 20.00 | 35.00 | 50.00 | 100.00 |
| | 1859 CP | — | 20.00 | 35.00 | 50.00 | 100.00 |
| | 1860/59 CP | — | 40.00 | 65.00 | 135.00 | 300.00 |
| | 1861 CP | — | 125.00 | 200.00 | 300.00 | 600.00 |
| | 1862 CP | — | 25.00 | 40.00 | 60.00 | 125.00 |
| | 1864 LT | — | 50.00 | 100.00 | 200.00 | 450.00 |
| | 1869 CP | — | 40.00 | 65.00 | 125.00 | 275.00 |

**Mint mark: EoMo**

| KM# | Date Mintage | Fine | VF | XF | Unc |
|---|---|---|---|---|---|
| 370.4 | 1829 LF | — | 175.00 | 300.00 | 500.00 | 1400. |

**Mint mark: Ga**

| KM# | Date Mintage | Fine | VF | XF | Unc |
|---|---|---|---|---|---|
| 370.5 | 1825 FS | — | 25.00 | 40.00 | 75.00 | 150.00 |
| | 1826 FS | — | 10.00 | 15.00 | 35.00 | 80.00 |
| | 1828/7 FS | — | 12.50 | 20.00 | 40.00 | 90.00 |
| | 1829 FS | — | 7.50 | 15.00 | 30.00 | 70.00 |
| | 1830/29 FS | — | 40.00 | 60.00 | 100.00 | 200.00 |
| | 1831 LP | — | — | — | Rare | — |
| | 1832 FS | — | 10.00 | 20.00 | 35.00 | 80.00 |
| | 1834/3 FS | — | 65.00 | 100.00 | 175.00 | 250.00 |
| | 1834 FS | — | 10.00 | 20.00 | 35.00 | 80.00 |
| | 1835/4/3 FS/LP | | | | | |
| | | — | 15.00 | 25.00 | 40.00 | 90.00 |
| | 1837/6 JG | — | 50.00 | 100.00 | 150.00 | 250.00 |
| | 1838/7 JG | — | 15.00 | 25.00 | 40.00 | 90.00 |
| | 1839/8 JG/FS | | | | | |
| | | — | 35.00 | 75.00 | 150.00 | 250.00 |
| | 1839 MC | — | 10.00 | 20.00 | 35.00 | 80.00 |
| | 1840/39 MC/JG | | | | | |
| | | — | — | — | — | — |
| | 1840 MC | — | 15.00 | 25.00 | 40.00 | 90.00 |
| | 1841 MC | — | 20.00 | 35.00 | 50.00 | 100.00 |
| | 1842/1 JG | — | 15.00 | 25.00 | 40.00 | 90.00 |
| | 1842 JG | — | 10.00 | 20.00 | 35.00 | 80.00 |
| | 1843/2 JG | — | 15.00 | 30.00 | 50.00 | 100.00 |
| | 1843 JG | — | 10.00 | 20.00 | 35.00 | 80.00 |
| | 1843 MC/JG | — | 10.00 | 20.00 | 35.00 | 80.00 |
| | 1843 MC | — | 10.00 | 20.00 | 35.00 | 80.00 |
| | 1844 MC | — | 10.00 | 20.00 | 35.00 | 80.00 |
| | 1845 MC | — | 10.00 | 20.00 | 35.00 | 80.00 |
| | 1845 JG | — | 10.00 | 20.00 | 35.00 | 80.00 |
| | 1846 MC | — | 10.00 | 20.00 | 35.00 | 80.00 |

| KM# | Date | Mintage | Fine | VF | XF | Unc |
|---|---|---|---|---|---|---|
| 370.5 | 1846 JG | — | 10.00 | 20.00 | 35.00 | 80.00 |
| | 1847 JG | — | 10.00 | 20.00 | 35.00 | 80.00 |
| | 1848/7 JG | — | 10.00 | 20.00 | 35.00 | 80.00 |
| | 1849 JG | — | 10.00 | 20.00 | 35.00 | 80.00 |
| | 1850/49 JG | — | — | — | — | — |
| | 1850 JG | — | 10.00 | 20.00 | 35.00 | 80.00 |
| | 1851/0 JG | — | 10.00 | 20.00 | 35.00 | 80.00 |
| | 1852 JG | — | 10.00 | 20.00 | 35.00 | 80.00 |
| | 1853 JG | — | 10.00 | 20.00 | 35.00 | 80.00 |
| | 1854 JG | — | 10.00 | 20.00 | 35.00 | 80.00 |
| | 1855/4 JG | — | 10.00 | 20.00 | 35.00 | 80.00 |
| | 1855 JG | — | 10.00 | 20.00 | 35.00 | 80.00 |
| | 1856 JG | — | 10.00 | 20.00 | 35.00 | 80.00 |
| | 1857 JG | — | 10.00 | 20.00 | 35.00 | 80.00 |
| | 1858/7 JG | — | 10.00 | 20.00 | 35.00 | 80.00 |
| | 1858 JG | — | 10.00 | 20.00 | 35.00 | 80.00 |
| | 1859/7 JG | — | 10.00 | 20.00 | 35.00 | 80.00 |
| | 1860/59 JG | — | 10.00 | 20.00 | 35.00 | 80.00 |
| | 1861 JG | — | 5.00 | 12.50 | 25.00 | 60.00 |
| | 1862/1 JG | — | 15.00 | 25.00 | 40.00 | 90.00 |

**Mint mark: GC**

| KM# | Date | Mintage | Fine | VF | XF | Unc |
|---|---|---|---|---|---|---|
| 370.6 | 1844 MP | — | 50.00 | 100.00 | 150.00 | 350.00 |
| | 1845 MP | — | 25.00 | 50.00 | 100.00 | 200.00 |
| | 1846 MP | — | 25.00 | 50.00 | 100.00 | 200.00 |
| | 1847 MP | — | 25.00 | 50.00 | 100.00 | 300.00 |
| | 1848 MP | — | 20.00 | 40.00 | 75.00 | 150.00 |
| | 1849 MP | — | 25.00 | 50.00 | 100.00 | 200.00 |
| | 1850 MP | — | 30.00 | 60.00 | 125.00 | 250.00 |
| | 1851 MP | — | 25.00 | 50.00 | 100.00 | 200.00 |

**Mint mark: Go**

| KM# | Date | Mintage | Fine | VF | XF | Unc |
|---|---|---|---|---|---|---|
| 370.7 | 1826 MJ | — | 125.00 | 250.00 | 400.00 | 1000. |
| | 1827/6 MJ | — | 7.50 | 15.00 | 30.00 | 75.00 |
| | 1828/7 MJ | — | 7.50 | 15.00 | 30.00 | 75.00 |
| | 1828 MJ denomination 2/1 | | | | | |
| | | — | — | — | — | — |
| | 1828 JG | — | — | — | — | — |
| | 1828 MR | — | 50.00 | 100.00 | 150.00 | 250.00 |
| | 1829/8 MJ | — | 5.00 | 10.00 | 25.00 | 50.00 |
| | 1829 MJ | — | 5.00 | 10.00 | 25.00 | 50.00 |
| | 1829 MJ reversed N in MEXICANA | | | | | |
| | | — | 5.00 | 10.00 | 25.00 | 50.00 |
| | 1830 MJ | — | 5.00 | 10.00 | 25.00 | 50.00 |
| | 1831/29 MJ | — | 15.00 | 30.00 | 60.00 | 150.00 |
| | 1831 MJ | — | 10.00 | 20.00 | 40.00 | 80.00 |
| | 1832/1 MJ | — | 7.50 | 15.00 | 30.00 | 75.00 |
| | 1832 MJ | — | 7.50 | 15.00 | 30.00 | 75.00 |
| | 1833 MJ round top 3 | | | | | |
| | | — | 10.00 | 20.00 | 40.00 | 80.00 |
| | 1833 MJ flat top 3 | | | | | |
| | | — | 10.00 | 20.00 | 40.00 | 80.00 |
| | 1834 PJ | — | 5.00 | 10.00 | 25.00 | 50.00 |
| | 1835 PJ | — | 5.00 | 10.00 | 25.00 | 50.00 |
| | 1836/5 PJ | — | 7.50 | 15.00 | 30.00 | 75.00 |
| | 1836 PJ | — | 5.00 | 10.00 | 25.00 | 50.00 |
| | 1837 PJ | — | 5.00 | 10.00 | 25.00 | 50.00 |
| | 1838/7 PJ | — | 5.00 | 10.00 | 25.00 | 50.00 |
| | 1839 PJ | — | 5.00 | 10.00 | 25.00 | 50.00 |
| | 1839 PJ (error: REPUBLIGA) | | | | | |
| | | — | 10.00 | 25.00 | 50.00 | |
| | 1840/39 PJ | — | 7.50 | 10.00 | 25.00 | 75.00 |
| | 1840 PJ straight J | | | | | |
| | | — | 5.00 | 10.00 | 25.00 | 50.00 |
| | 1840 PJ curved J | | | | | |
| | | — | 5.00 | 10.00 | 25.00 | 50.00 |
| | 1841/31 PJ | — | 5.00 | 10.00 | 25.00 | 50.00 |
| | 1841 PJ | — | 5.00 | 10.00 | 25.00 | 50.00 |
| | 1842/1 PJ | — | 5.00 | 10.00 | 25.00 | 50.00 |
| | 1842/1 PM | — | 5.00 | 10.00 | 25.00 | 50.00 |
| | 1842 PM/J | — | 5.00 | 10.00 | 25.00 | 50.00 |
| | 1842 PJ | — | 5.00 | 10.00 | 25.00 | 50.00 |
| | 1842 PM | — | 5.00 | 10.00 | 25.00 | 50.00 |
| | 1843/33 PM 1/2 over 8 | | | | | |
| | | — | 5.00 | 10.00 | 25.00 | 50.00 |
| | 1843 PM convex wings | | | | | |
| | | — | 5.00 | 10.00 | 25.00 | 50.00 |
| | 1843 PM concave wings | | | | | |
| | | — | 5.00 | 10.00 | 25.00 | 50.00 |
| | 1844/3 PM | — | 5.00 | 10.00 | 25.00 | 50.00 |
| | 1844 PM | — | 10.00 | 20.00 | 40.00 | 90.00 |
| | 1845/4 PM | — | 5.00 | 10.00 | 25.00 | 50.00 |
| | 1845 PM | — | 5.00 | 10.00 | 25.00 | 50.00 |
| | 1846/4 PM | — | 5.00 | 10.00 | 25.00 | 50.00 |
| | 1846/5 PM | — | 5.00 | 10.00 | 25.00 | 50.00 |

| KM# | Date | Mintage | Fine | VF | XF | Unc |
|---|---|---|---|---|---|---|
| 370.7 | 1846 PM | — | 5.00 | 10.00 | 25.00 | 50.00 |
| | 1847/6 PM | — | 7.50 | 15.00 | 30.00 | 60.00 |
| | 1847 PM | — | 7.50 | 15.00 | 30.00 | 60.00 |
| | 1848/35 PM | — | 5.00 | 10.00 | 25.00 | 50.00 |
| | 1848 PM | — | 5.00 | 10.00 | 25.00 | 50.00 |
| | 1848 PF/M | — | 5.00 | 10.00 | 25.00 | 50.00 |
| | 1849/39 PF | — | 5.00 | 10.00 | 25.00 | 50.00 |
| | 1849 PF | — | 5.00 | 10.00 | 25.00 | 50.00 |
| | 1849 PF (error: MEXCANA) | | | | | |
| | | — | 5.00 | 10.00 | 25.00 | 50.00 |
| | 1850 PF | — | 5.00 | 10.00 | 25.00 | 50.00 |
| | 1851 PF | — | 5.00 | 10.00 | 25.00 | 50.00 |
| | 1852/1 PF | — | 5.00 | 10.00 | 25.00 | 50.00 |
| | 1852 PF | — | 2.50 | 7.50 | 17.50 | 40.00 |
| | 1853 PF/R | — | 5.00 | 10.00 | 25.00 | 50.00 |
| | 1853 PF | — | 5.00 | 10.00 | 25.00 | 50.00 |
| | 1854 PF | — | 5.00 | 10.00 | 25.00 | 50.00 |
| | 1855 PF | — | 5.00 | 10.00 | 25.00 | 50.00 |
| | 1856/4 PF | — | 5.00 | 10.00 | 25.00 | 50.00 |
| | 1856/5 PF | — | 5.00 | 10.00 | 25.00 | 50.00 |
| | 1856 PF | — | 5.00 | 10.00 | 25.00 | 50.00 |
| | 1857/6 PF | — | 5.00 | 10.00 | 25.00 | 50.00 |
| | 1857 PF | — | 5.00 | 10.00 | 25.00 | 50.00 |
| | 1858/7 PF | — | 7.50 | 15.00 | 30.00 | 60.00 |
| | 1858 PF | — | 5.00 | 10.00 | 25.00 | 50.00 |
| | 1859 PF | — | 5.00 | 10.00 | 25.00 | 50.00 |
| | 1860 PF small 1/2 | | | | | |
| | | — | 5.00 | 10.00 | 25.00 | 50.00 |
| | 1860 PF large 1/2 | | | | | |
| | | — | 5.00 | 10.00 | 25.00 | 50.00 |
| | 1860/59 PF | — | 5.00 | 10.00 | 25.00 | 50.00 |
| | 1861 PF small 1/2 | | | | | |
| | | — | 5.00 | 10.00 | 25.00 | 50.00 |
| | 1861 PF large 1/2 | | | | | |
| | | — | 5.00 | 10.00 | 25.00 | 50.00 |
| | 1862/1 YE | — | 5.00 | 10.00 | 25.00 | 50.00 |
| | 1862 YE | — | 2.50 | 7.50 | 17.50 | 40.00 |
| | 1862 YF | — | 5.00 | 10.00 | 25.00 | 50.00 |
| | 1867 YF | — | 2.50 | 7.50 | 17.50 | 40.00 |
| | 1868 YF | — | 2.50 | 7.50 | 17.50 | 40.00 |

**NOTE:** Varieties exist.

**Mint mark: Ho**

| KM# | Date | Mintage | Fine | VF | XF | Unc |
|---|---|---|---|---|---|---|
| 370.8 | 1839 PP | — | — | — | Unique | — |
| | 1862 FM | — | 500.00 | 650.00 | 1000. | — |
| | 1867 PR/FM 6/inverted 6, & 7/1 | | | | | |
| | | — | 100.00 | 175.00 | 250.00 | 500.00 |

**Mint mark: Mo**

| KM# | Date | Mintage | Fine | VF | XF | Unc |
|---|---|---|---|---|---|---|
| 370.9 | 1825 JM short top 5 | | | | | |
| | | — | 10.00 | 20.00 | 40.00 | 80.00 |
| | 1825 JM long top 5 | | | | | |
| | | — | 10.00 | 20.00 | 40.00 | 80.00 |
| | 1826/5 JM | — | 10.00 | 20.00 | 40.00 | 80.00 |
| | 1826 JM | — | 5.00 | 10.00 | 20.00 | 60.00 |
| | 1827/6 JM | — | 5.00 | 10.00 | 20.00 | 60.00 |
| | 1827 JM | — | 5.00 | 10.00 | 20.00 | 60.00 |
| | 1828/7 JM | — | 7.50 | 15.00 | 25.00 | 85.00 |
| | 1828 JM | — | 10.00 | 20.00 | 40.00 | 90.00 |
| | 1829 JM | — | 7.50 | 15.00 | 25.00 | 75.00 |
| | 1830 JM | — | 5.00 | 10.00 | 20.00 | 60.00 |
| | 1831 JM | — | 5.00 | 10.00 | 20.00 | 60.00 |
| | 1832 JM | — | 7.50 | 12.50 | 27.50 | 60.00 |
| | 1833 MJ | — | 7.50 | 12.50 | 27.50 | 60.00 |
| | 1834 ML | — | 5.00 | 10.00 | 20.00 | 60.00 |
| | 1835 ML | — | 5.00 | 10.00 | 20.00 | 60.00 |
| | 1836/5 ML/MF | | | | | |
| | | — | 7.50 | 15.00 | 25.00 | 65.00 |
| | 1836 ML | — | 7.50 | 15.00 | 25.00 | 65.00 |
| | 1838 ML | — | 5.00 | 10.00 | 20.00 | 60.00 |
| | 1839/8 ML | — | 5.00 | 10.00 | 25.00 | 65.00 |
| | 1839 ML | — | 5.00 | 10.00 | 20.00 | 50.00 |
| | 1840 ML | — | 5.00 | 10.00 | 20.00 | 50.00 |
| | 1841 ML | — | 5.00 | 10.00 | 20.00 | 50.00 |
| | 1842 ML | — | 5.00 | 10.00 | 20.00 | 50.00 |
| | 1842 MM | — | 5.00 | 10.00 | 20.00 | 50.00 |
| | 1843 MM | — | 10.00 | 20.00 | 40.00 | 80.00 |
| | 1844 MF | — | 5.00 | 10.00 | 20.00 | 50.00 |
| | 1845/4 MF | — | 5.00 | 10.00 | 25.00 | 60.00 |
| | 1845 MF | — | 5.00 | 10.00 | 20.00 | 50.00 |
| | 1846 MF | — | 5.00 | 10.00 | 20.00 | 50.00 |
| | 1847 RC | — | 10.00 | 20.00 | 40.00 | 80.00 |
| | 1847 RC R/M | — | 10.00 | 20.00 | 40.00 | 80.00 |
| | 1848/7 GC/RC | | | | | |
| | | — | 5.00 | 10.00 | 20.00 | 50.00 |

| KM# | Date Mintage | Fine | VF | XF | Unc |
|---|---|---|---|---|---|
| 370.9 | 1849 GC — | 5.00 | 10.00 | 20.00 | 50.00 |
| | 1850 GC — | 5.00 | 10.00 | 20.00 | 50.00 |
| | 1851 GC — | 5.00 | 10.00 | 20.00 | 50.00 |
| | 1852 GC — | 5.00 | 10.00 | 20.00 | 50.00 |
| | 1853 GC — | 5.00 | 10.00 | 20.00 | 50.00 |
| | 1854 GC — | 5.00 | 10.00 | 20.00 | 50.00 |
| | 1855 GC — | 5.00 | 10.00 | 20.00 | 50.00 |
| | 1855 GF/GC — | 7.50 | 12.50 | 25.00 | 65.00 |
| | 1856/5 GF — | 7.50 | 12.50 | 25.00 | 65.00 |
| | 1857 GF — | 5.00 | 10.00 | 20.00 | 50.00 |
| | 1858 FH — | 3.00 | 5.00 | 12.50 | 40.00 |
| | 1858 FH F/G | | | | |
| | — | 5.00 | 10.00 | 20.00 | 50.00 |
| | 1858/9 FH — | 5.00 | 10.00 | 20.00 | 50.00 |
| | 1859 FH — | 3.00 | 6.00 | 15.00 | 50.00 |
| | 1860 FH/GC | | | | |
| | — | 5.00 | 10.00 | 20.00 | 50.00 |
| | 1860/59 FH — | 7.50 | 12.50 | 25.00 | 65.00 |
| | 1860 FH — | 3.00 | 6.00 | 15.00 | 50.00 |
| | 1860 TH — | 5.00 | 10.00 | 20.00 | 50.00 |
| | 1861 CH — | 3.00 | 6.00 | 15.00 | 45.00 |
| | 1862/52 CH — | 5.00 | 10.00 | 20.00 | 50.00 |
| | 1862 CH — | 3.00 | 6.00 | 15.00 | 45.00 |
| | 1863/55 TH/GC | | | | |
| | — | 5.00 | 10.00 | 20.00 | 50.00 |
| | 1863 CH/GC — | 5.00 | 10.00 | 20.00 | 50.00 |
| | 1863 CH — | 3.00 | 6.00 | 15.00 | 45.00 |

**Mint mark: Pi**

| KM# | Date Mintage | Fine | VF | XF | Unc |
|---|---|---|---|---|---|
| 370.10 | 1831 JS — | 7.50 | 12.50 | 25.00 | 65.00 |
| | 1841/36 JS — | 20.00 | 40.00 | 75.00 | 125.00 |
| | 1842/1 PS — | 20.00 | 40.00 | 75.00 | 125.00 |
| | 1842/1 PS P/J | | | | |
| | — | 60.00 | 80.00 | 150.00 | 300.00 |
| | 1842 PS/JS — | 50.00 | 75.00 | 125.00 | 250.00 |
| | 1842 JS — | 20.00 | 40.00 | 75.00 | 125.00 |
| | 1843/2 PS — | 17.50 | 25.00 | 40.00 | 80.00 |
| | 1843 PS — | 15.00 | 25.00 | 35.00 | 70.00 |
| | 1843 AM — | 10.00 | 15.00 | 25.00 | 60.00 |
| | 1844 AM — | 10.00 | 15.00 | 30.00 | 65.00 |
| | 1845 AM — | 250.00 | 375.00 | 500.00 | 1500. |
| | 1846/5 AM — | 40.00 | 75.00 | 125.00 | 200.00 |
| | 1847/6 AM — | 15.00 | 25.00 | 40.00 | 80.00 |
| | 1848 AM — | 15.00 | 25.00 | 40.00 | 80.00 |
| | 1849 MC/AM — | 15.00 | 25.00 | 40.00 | 80.00 |
| | 1849 MC — | 12.50 | 20.00 | 35.00 | 70.00 |
| | 1850/49 MC — | — | — | — | — |
| | 1850PI MC — | 10.00 | 15.00 | 25.00 | 60.00 |
| | 1850P MC — | — | — | — | — |
| | 1851 MC — | 10.00 | 15.00 | 25.00 | 60.00 |
| | 1852 MC — | 10.00 | 20.00 | 30.00 | 65.00 |
| | 1853 MC — | 7.50 | 12.50 | 20.00 | 60.00 |
| | 1854 MC — | 7.50 | 12.50 | 20.00 | 60.00 |
| | 1855 MC — | 15.00 | 20.00 | 35.00 | 70.00 |
| | 1856 MC — | 15.00 | 25.00 | 50.00 | 100.00 |
| | 1856 P (no I) — | — | — | — | — |
| | 1857 MC — | 7.50 | 12.50 | 20.00 | 60.00 |
| | 1857 PS — | 10.00 | 15.00 | 30.00 | 65.00 |
| | 1858 MC — | 12.50 | 20.00 | 35.00 | 70.00 |
| | 1858 PS — | 12.50 | 20.00 | 35.00 | 70.00 |
| | 1859 MC — | — | | Rare | — |
| | 1860/59 PS — | 12.50 | 20.00 | 35.00 | 70.00 |
| | 1861 RO — | 10.00 | 15.00 | 30.00 | 60.00 |
| | 1862/1 RO — | 15.00 | 25.00 | 50.00 | 125.00 |
| | 1862 RO — | 15.00 | 25.00 | 50.00 | 125.00 |
| | 1863/2 RO — | 15.00 | 25.00 | 45.00 | 100.00 |

**Mint·mark: Z, Zs**

| KM# | Date Mintage | Fine | VF | XF | Unc |
|---|---|---|---|---|---|
| 370.11 | 1826 AZ — | 5.00 | 10.00 | 20.00 | 60.00 |
| | 1826 AO — | 5.00 | 10.00 | 20.00 | 60.00 |
| | 1827 AO — | 5.00 | 10.00 | 20.00 | 60.00 |
| | 1828/7 AO — | 5.00 | 10.00 | 20.00 | 60.00 |
| | 1829 AO — | 5.00 | 10.00 | 20.00 | 60.00 |
| | 1830 OV — | 5.00 | 10.00 | 20.00 | 60.00 |
| | 1831 OV — | 25.00 | 50.00 | 75.00 | 150.00 |
| | 1831 OM — | 5.00 | 10.00 | 20.00 | 60.00 |
| | 1832 OM — | 5.00 | 10.00 | 20.00 | 60.00 |
| | 1833 OM — | 5.00 | 10.00 | 20.00 | 60.00 |
| | 1834 OM — | 5.00 | 10.00 | 20.00 | 60.00 |
| | 1835/4 OM — | 5.00 | 10.00 | 20.00 | 60.00 |
| | 1835 OM — | 5.00 | 10.00 | 20.00 | 60.00 |
| | 1836 OM — | 5.00 | 10.00 | 20.00 | 60.00 |
| | 1837 OM — | 10.00 | 20.00 | 40.00 | 80.00 |
| | 1838 OM — | 5.00 | 10.00 | 20.00 | 60.00 |
| | 1839 OM — | 7.50 | 15.00 | 30.00 | 65.00 |

| KM# | Date Mintage | Fine | VF | XF | Unc |
|---|---|---|---|---|---|
| 370.11 | 1840 OM — | 10.00 | 25.00 | 45.00 | 90.00 |
| | 1841 OM — | 10.00 | 25.00 | 45.00 | 90.00 |
| | 1842/1 OM — | 5.00 | 10.00 | 20.00 | 60.00 |
| | 1842 OM — | 5.00 | 10.00 | 20.00 | 60.00 |
| | 1843 OM — | 40.00 | 75.00 | 115.00 | 250.00 |
| | 1844 OM — | 5.00 | 10.00 | 20.00 | 60.00 |
| | 1845 OM — | 5.00 | 10.00 | 20.00 | 60.00 |
| | 1846 OM — | 7.50 | 15.00 | 30.00 | 65.00 |
| | 1847 OM — | 5.00 | 10.00 | 20.00 | 50.00 |
| | 1848 OM — | 5.00 | 10.00 | 20.00 | 50.00 |
| | 1849 OM — | 5.00 | 10.00 | 20.00 | 50.00 |
| | 1850 OM — | 5.00 | 10.00 | 20.00 | 50.00 |
| | 1851 OM — | 5.00 | 10.00 | 20.00 | 50.00 |
| | 1852 OM — | 5.00 | 10.00 | 20.00 | 50.00 |
| | 1853 OM — | 5.00 | 10.00 | 20.00 | 50.00 |
| | 1854/3 OM — | 5.00 | 10.00 | 20.00 | 50.00 |
| | 1854 OM — | 5.00 | 10.00 | 20.00 | 50.00 |
| | 1855/3 OM — | 7.50 | 15.00 | 30.00 | 65.00 |
| | 1855 OM — | 5.00 | 10.00 | 20.00 | 50.00 |
| | 1856 OM — | 5.00 | 10.00 | 20.00 | 50.00 |
| | 1857 MO — | 5.00 | 10.00 | 20.00 | 50.00 |
| | 1858 MO — | 5.00 | 10.00 | 20.00 | 50.00 |
| | 1859 MO — | 6.00 | 8.50 | 17.50 | 35.00 |
| | 1859 VL — | 6.00 | 8.50 | 17.50 | 40.00 |
| | 1860/50 VL inverted A for V | | | | |
| | — | 5.00 | 10.00 | 20.00 | 50.00 |
| | 1860/59 VL inverted A for V | | | | |
| | — | 5.00 | 10.00 | 20.00 | 50.00 |
| | 1860 MO — | 5.00 | 10.00 | 20.00 | 50.00 |
| | 1860 VL — | 5.00 | 10.00 | 20.00 | 50.00 |
| | 1861/0 VL inverted A for V | | | | |
| | — | 7.50 | 15.00 | 30.00 | 65.00 |
| | 1861 VL inverted A for V | | | | |
| | — | 5.00 | 10.00 | 20.00 | 50.00 |
| | 1862 VL inverted A for V | | | | |
| | — | 5.00 | 10.00 | 20.00 | 50.00 |
| | 1863/1 VL inverted A for V | | | | |
| | — | 7.50 | 15.00 | 30.00 | 65.00 |
| | 1863 VL inverted A for V | | | | |
| | — | 5.00 | 10.00 | 20.00 | 50.00 |
| | 1869 YH — | 5.00 | 10.00 | 20.00 | 50.00 |

# REAL

**Mint mark: Ca**

| KM# | Date Mintage | Fine | VF | XF | Unc |
|---|---|---|---|---|---|
| 372 | 1844 RG — | 500.00 | 1000. | 1500. | 2750. |
| | 1845 RG — | 500.00 | 1000. | 1500. | 2750. |
| | 1855 RG — | 100.00 | 150.00 | 225.00 | 450.00 |

**Mint mark: C**

| KM# | Date Mintage | Fine | VF | XF | Unc |
|---|---|---|---|---|---|
| 372.1 | 1846 CE — | 12.50 | 25.00 | 40.00 | 110.00 |
| | 1848 CE — | 12.50 | 25.00 | 40.00 | 110.00 |
| | 1850 CE — | 12.50 | 25.00 | 40.00 | 110.00 |
| | 1851/0 CE — | 12.50 | 25.00 | 40.00 | 110.00 |
| | 1852/1 CE — | 7.50 | 15.00 | 30.00 | 100.00 |
| | 1853/2 CE — | 7.50 | 15.00 | 30.00 | 100.00 |
| | 1854 CE — | 7.50 | 15.00 | 30.00 | 100.00 |
| | 1856 CE — | 40.00 | 65.00 | 100.00 | 225.00 |
| | 1857/4 CE — | 10.00 | 20.00 | 35.00 | 100.00 |
| | 1857/6 CE — | 10.00 | 20.00 | 35.00 | 100.00 |
| | 1858 CE — | 5.00 | 7.50 | 15.00 | 100.00 |
| | 1859 CE — | — | — | — | — |
| | 1860/9 PV — | 7.50 | 15.00 | 30.00 | 100.00 |
| | 1860 PV — | 5.00 | 7.50 | 15.00 | 100.00 |
| | 1861 PV — | 5.00 | 7.50 | 15.00 | 100.00 |
| | 1863 CE | | | | |
| | 3 known — | — | 1650. | 2250. |
| | 1869 CE — | 5.00 | 7.50 | 15.00 | 100.00 |

**Mint mark: Do**

| KM# | Date Mintage | Fine | VF | XF | Unc |
|---|---|---|---|---|---|
| 372.2 | 1832/1 RM — | 5.00 | 10.00 | 20.00 | 90.00 |
| | 1832 RM/RL — | 10.00 | 15.00 | 30.00 | 100.00 |
| | 1832 RM — | 5.00 | 10.00 | 20.00 | 100.00 |
| | 1834/24 RM/RL | | | | |
| | — | 15.00 | 25.00 | 50.00 | 150.00 |
| | 1834/3 RM/RL | | | | |
| | — | 15.00 | 25.00 | 50.00 | 150.00 |

| KM# | Date | Mintage | Fine | VF | XF | Unc |
|---|---|---|---|---|---|---|
| 372.2 | 1834 RM | — | 10.00 | 20.00 | 40.00 | 110.00 |
| | 1836/4 RM | — | 5.00 | 7.50 | 15.00 | 100.00 |
| | 1836 RM | — | 5.00 | 7.50 | 15.00 | 100.00 |
| | 1837 RM 3/2 | — | 12.50 | 20.00 | 40.00 | 110.00 |
| | 1837 RM | — | 12.50 | 20.00 | 40.00 | 110.00 |
| | 1841 RM | — | 7.50 | 15.00 | 30.00 | 100.00 |
| | 1842/32 RM | — | 10.00 | 20.00 | 40.00 | 110.00 |
| | 1842 RM | — | 7.50 | 15.00 | 30.00 | 100.00 |
| | 1843 RM | — | 5.00 | 7.50 | 15.00 | 100.00 |
| | 1844/34 RM | — | 15.00 | 25.00 | 45.00 | 125.00 |
| | 1845 RM | — | 5.00 | 7.50 | 15.00 | 100.00 |
| | 1846 RM | — | 7.50 | 15.00 | 30.00 | 100.00 |
| | 1847 RM | — | 10.00 | 15.00 | 35.00 | 100.00 |
| | 1848/31 RM | — | 10.00 | 15.00 | 35.00 | 100.00 |
| | 1848/33 RM | — | 10.00 | 15.00 | 35.00 | 100.00 |
| | 1848/5 RM | — | 10.00 | 15.00 | 35.00 | 100.00 |
| | 1848 RM | — | 7.50 | 12.50 | 20.00 | 100.00 |
| | 1849/8 CM | — | 10.00 | 15.00 | 30.00 | 100.00 |
| | 1850 JMR | — | 15.00 | 25.00 | 45.00 | 125.00 |
| | 1851 JMR | — | 15.00 | 25.00 | 45.00 | 120.00 |
| | 1852 JMR | — | 15.00 | 25.00 | 45.00 | 120.00 |
| | 1853 CP | — | 12.50 | 20.00 | 35.00 | 100.00 |
| | 1854/1 CP | — | 10.00 | 15.00 | 25.00 | 100.00 |
| | 1854 CP | — | 7.50 | 12.50 | 20.00 | 100.00 |
| | 1855 CP | — | 10.00 | 15.00 | 25.00 | 100.00 |
| | 1856 CP | — | 12.50 | 20.00 | 35.00 | 100.00 |
| | 1857 CP | — | 12.50 | 20.00 | 35.00 | 100.00 |
| | 1858 CP | — | 12.50 | 20.00 | 35.00 | 100.00 |
| | 1859 CP | — | 7.50 | 12.50 | 20.00 | 100.00 |
| | 1860/59 CP | — | 10.00 | 15.00 | 25.00 | 100.00 |
| | 1861 CP | — | 15.00 | 25.00 | 40.00 | 110.00 |
| | 1862/1 CP | — | 225.00 | 300.00 | 450.00 | 1250. |
| | 1864 LT | — | 15.00 | 25.00 | 40.00 | 110.00 |

**Mint mark: EoMo**

| KM# | Date | Mintage | Fine | VF | XF | Unc |
|---|---|---|---|---|---|---|
| 372.3 | 1828 LF | — | 200.00 | 300.00 | 450.00 | 1500. |

**Mint mark: Ga**

| KM# | Date | Mintage | Fine | VF | XF | Unc |
|---|---|---|---|---|---|---|
| 372.4 | 1826 FS | — | 15.00 | 30.00 | 50.00 | 125.00 |
| | 1828/7 FS | — | 15.00 | 30.00 | 50.00 | 125.00 |
| | 1829/8/7 FS | — | — | — | — | — |
| | 1829 FS | — | 15.00 | 30.00 | 50.00 | 125.00 |
| | 1830 FS | — | 250.00 | 350.00 | 500.00 | — |
| | 1831 LP | — | 15.00 | 30.00 | 50.00 | 125.00 |
| | 1831 LP/FS | — | 300.00 | 450.00 | 600.00 | — |
| | 1832 FS | — | 250.00 | 350.00 | 500.00 | — |
| | 1833/2 G FS | — | 100.00 | 150.00 | 275.00 | 550.00 |
| | 1833 FS | — | 75.00 | 125.00 | 225.00 | 500.00 |
| | 1834/3 FS | — | 75.00 | 125.00 | 225.00 | 500.00 |
| | 1835 FS | — | — | — | — | — |
| | 1837/6 JG/FS | | | | | |
| | | — | 12.50 | 20.00 | 35.00 | 100.00 |
| | 1838/7 JG/FS | | | | | |
| | | — | 12.50 | 20.00 | 35.00 | 100.00 |
| | 1839 JG | — | 250.00 | 350.00 | 500.00 | — |
| | 1840 JG | — | 12.50 | 20.00 | 35.00 | 100.00 |
| | 1840 MC | — | 7.50 | 12.50 | 25.00 | 70.00 |
| | 1841 MC | — | 50.00 | 75.00 | 125.00 | 250.00 |
| | 1842/0 JG/MC | | | | | |
| | | — | 10.00 | 15.00 | 30.00 | 100.00 |
| | 1842 JG | — | 7.50 | 12.50 | 20.00 | 100.00 |
| | 1843 JG | — | 150.00 | 200.00 | 300.00 | 750.00 |
| | 1843 MC | — | 5.00 | 7.50 | 15.00 | 100.00 |
| | 1844 MC | — | 7.50 | 12.50 | 20.00 | 100.00 |
| | 1845 MC | — | 10.00 | 15.00 | 25.00 | 100.00 |
| | 1845 JG | — | 5.00 | 7.50 | 20.00 | 100.00 |
| | 1846 JG | — | 12.50 | 20.00 | 35.00 | 100.00 |
| | 1847/6 JG | — | 10.00 | 15.00 | 25.00 | 100.00 |
| | 1847 JG | — | 10.00 | 15.00 | 25.00 | 100.00 |
| | 1848 JG | — | 400.00 | 550.00 | 700.00 | — |
| | 1849 JG | — | 7.50 | 12.50 | 20.00 | 100.00 |
| | 1850 JG | — | 175.00 | 275.00 | 400.00 | — |
| | 1851 JG | — | 10.00 | 15.00 | 25.00 | 100.00 |
| | 1852 JG | — | 10.00 | 15.00 | 25.00 | 100.00 |
| | 1853/2 JG | — | 10.00 | 15.00 | 25.00 | 100.00 |
| | 1854 JG | — | 10.00 | 15.00 | 25.00 | 100.00 |
| | 1855 JG | — | 15.00 | 25.00 | 40.00 | 100.00 |
| | 1856 JG | — | 7.50 | 12.50 | 20.00 | 100.00 |
| | 1857/6 JG | — | 12.50 | 20.00 | 35.00 | 100.00 |
| | 1858/7 JG | — | 15.00 | 25.00 | 40.00 | 110.00 |
| | 1859/8 JG | — | 25.00 | 50.00 | 75.00 | 150.00 |
| | 1860/59 JG | — | 30.00 | 60.00 | 90.00 | 225.00 |
| | 1861/0 JG | — | 20.00 | 30.00 | 50.00 | 125.00 |
| | 1861 JG | — | 25.00 | 50.00 | 100.00 | 250.00 |
| | 1862 JG | — | 7.50 | 12.50 | 20.00 | 100.00 |

**Mint mark: GC**

| KM# | Date | Mintage | Fine | VF | XF | Unc |
|---|---|---|---|---|---|---|
| 372.5 | 1844 MP | — | 40.00 | 60.00 | 100.00 | 250.00 |
| | 1845 MP | — | 40.00 | 60.00 | 100.00 | 250.00 |
| | 1846 MP | — | 40.00 | 60.00 | 100.00 | 250.00 |
| | 1847 MP | — | 40.00 | 60.00 | 100.00 | 250.00 |
| | 1848 MP | — | 40.00 | 60.00 | 100.00 | 250.00 |
| | 1849/7 MP | — | 40.00 | 60.00 | 100.00 | 250.00 |
| | 1849/8 MP | — | 40.00 | 60.00 | 100.00 | 250.00 |
| | 1849 MP | — | 40.00 | 60.00 | 100.00 | 250.00 |
| | 1850 MP | — | 40.00 | 60.00 | 100.00 | 250.00 |
| | 1851 MP | — | 40.00 | 60.00 | 100.00 | 250.00 |

**Mint mark: Go**

| KM# | Date | Mintage | Fine | VF | XF | Unc |
|---|---|---|---|---|---|---|
| 372.6 | 1826/5 JJ | — | 5.00 | 7.50 | 15.00 | 85.00 |
| | 1826 MJ | — | 4.00 | 6.00 | 15.00 | 85.00 |
| | 1827 MJ | — | 4.00 | 6.00 | 15.00 | 65.00 |
| | 1827 JM | — | 10.00 | 15.00 | 25.00 | 75.00 |
| | 1828/7 MR | — | 4.00 | 6.00 | 15.00 | 85.00 |
| | 1828 MJ, straight J, small 8 | | | | | |
| | | — | 4.00 | 6.00 | 15.00 | 85.00 |
| | 1828Go MJ, full J, large 8 | | | | | |
| | | — | 4.00 | 6.00 | 15.00 | 85.00 |
| | 1828G MJ, full J, large 8 | | | | | |
| | | — | 4.00 | 6.00 | 15.00 | 85.00 |
| | 1828/6 MR/JJ | — | 4.00 | 6.00 | 15.00 | 85.00 |
| | 1828 MR | — | 4.00 | 6.00 | 15.00 | 85.00 |
| | 1829/8 MG small eagle | | | | | |
| | | — | 4.00 | 6.00 | 15.00 | 85.00 |
| | 1829 MJ small eagle | | | | | |
| | | — | 4.00 | 6.00 | 15.00 | 85.00 |
| | 1829 MJ large eagle | | | | | |
| | | — | 4.00 | 6.00 | 15.00 | 85.00 |
| | 1830 MJ small initials | | | | | |
| | | — | 4.00 | 6.00 | 15.00 | 85.00 |
| | 1830 MJ medium initials | | | | | |
| | | — | 4.00 | 6.00 | 15.00 | 85.00 |
| | 1830 MJ large initials | | | | | |
| | | — | 4.00 | 6.00 | 15.00 | 85.00 |
| | 1830 MJ reversed N in MEXICANA | | | | | |
| | | — | 4.00 | 6.00 | 15.00 | 85.00 |
| | 1830 MJ 3/2 | — | 4.00 | 6.00 | 15.00 | 85.00 |
| | 1831/0 MJ reversed N in MEXICANA | | | | | |
| | | — | 4.00 | 6.00 | 15.00 | 85.00 |
| | 1831 MJ | — | 4.00 | 6.00 | 15.00 | 85.00 |
| | 1832/1 MJ | — | 15.00 | 30.00 | 50.00 | 125.00 |
| | 1832 MJ | — | 15.00 | 30.00 | 50.00 | 125.00 |
| | 1833 MJ top of 3 round | | | | | |
| | | — | 4.00 | 6.00 | 15.00 | 85.00 |
| | 1833 MJ top of 3 flat | | | | | |
| | | — | 4.00 | 6.00 | 15.00 | 85.00 |
| | 1834 PJ | — | 4.00 | 6.00 | 15.00 | 85.00 |
| | 1835 PJ | — | 7.50 | 12.50 | 20.00 | 85.00 |
| | 1836 PJ | — | 4.00 | 6.00 | 15.00 | 85.00 |
| | 1837 PJ | — | 15.00 | 30.00 | 50.00 | 125.00 |
| | 1838/7 PJ | — | 10.00 | 20.00 | 35.00 | 85.00 |
| | 1839 PJ | — | 4.00 | 6.00 | 15.00 | 85.00 |
| | 1840/39 PJ | — | 4.00 | 6.00 | 15.00 | 85.00 |
| | 1840 PJ | — | 4.00 | 6.00 | 15.00 | 85.00 |
| | 1841/31 PJ | — | 10.00 | 20.00 | 35.00 | 85.00 |
| | 1841 PJ | — | 4.00 | 6.00 | 15.00 | 85.00 |
| | 1842 PJ | — | 4.00 | 6.00 | 15.00 | 85.00 |
| | 1842 PM | — | 4.00 | 6.00 | 15.00 | 85.00 |
| | 1843 PM convex wings | | | | | |
| | | — | 4.00 | 6.00 | 15.00 | 85.00 |
| | 1843 PM concave wings | | | | | |
| | | — | 4.00 | 6.00 | 15.00 | 85.00 |
| | 1844 PM | — | 4.00 | 6.00 | 15.00 | 85.00 |
| | 1845/4 PM | — | 4.00 | 6.00 | 15.00 | 85.00 |
| | 1845 PM | — | 4.00 | 6.00 | 15.00 | 85.00 |
| | 1846/5 PM | — | 7.50 | 12.50 | 20.00 | 85.00 |
| | 1846 PM | — | 4.00 | 6.00 | 15.00 | 85.00 |
| | 1847/6 PM | — | 4.00 | 6.00 | 15.00 | 85.00 |
| | 1847 PM | — | 4.00 | 6.00 | 15.00 | 85.00 |
| | 1848 PM | — | 4.00 | 6.00 | 15.00 | 85.00 |
| | 1849 PF | — | 10.00 | 20.00 | 35.00 | 85.00 |
| | 1850 PF | — | 4.00 | 6.00 | 15.00 | 85.00 |
| | 1851 PF | — | 10.00 | 20.00 | 35.00 | 100.00 |
| | 1853/2 PF | — | 7.50 | 12.50 | 20.00 | 75.00 |
| | 1853 PF | — | 4.00 | 6.00 | 15.00 | 75.00 |
| | 1853 PF/M 5/4 | | | | | |
| | | — | 7.50 | 12.50 | 20.00 | 75.00 |
| | 1854/3 PF | — | 4.00 | 6.00 | 15.00 | 75.00 |
| | 1854 PF large eagle | | | | | |
| | | — | 4.00 | 6.00 | 15.00 | 75.00 |

| KM# | Date Mintage | Fine | VF | XF | Unc |
|---|---|---|---|---|---|
| 372.6 | 1854 PF small eagle | | | | |
| | — | 4.00 | 6.00 | 15.00 | 75.00 |
| | 1855/3 PF — | 4.00 | 6.00 | 15.00 | 75.00 |
| | 1855/4 PF — | 4.00 | 6.00 | 15.00 | 75.00 |
| | 1855 PF — | 4.00 | 6.00 | 15.00 | 75.00 |
| | 1856/5 PF — | 4.00 | 6.00 | 15.00 | 75.00 |
| | 1856 PF — | 4.00 | 6.00 | 15.00 | 75.00 |
| | 1857/6 PF — | 4.00 | 6.00 | 15.00 | 75.00 |
| | 1857 PF — | 4.00 | 6.00 | 15.00 | 75.00 |
| | 1858 PF — | 4.00 | 6.00 | 15.00 | 75.00 |
| | 1859 PF — | 4.00 | 6.00 | 15.00 | 75.00 |
| | 1860/50 PF — | 4.00 | 6.00 | 15.00 | 75.00 |
| | 1860 PF — | 4.00 | 6.00 | 15.00 | 75.00 |
| | 1861 PF — | 4.00 | 6.00 | 15.00 | 75.00 |
| | 1862 YE — | 4.00 | 6.00 | 15.00 | 75.00 |
| | 1862/1 YF — | 7.50 | 12.50 | 20.00 | 75.00 |
| | 1862 YF — | 4.00 | 6.00 | 15.00 | 75.00 |
| | 1867 YF — | 4.00 | 6.00 | 15.00 | 75.00 |
| | 1868/7 YF — | 4.00 | 6.00 | 15.00 | 75.00 |

**Mint mark: Ho**

| KM# | Date Mintage | Fine | VF | XF | Unc |
|---|---|---|---|---|---|
| 372.7 | 1867 small 7/1 PR | | | | |
| | — | 50.00 | 65.00 | 100.00 | 250.00 |
| | 1867 large 7/small 7 PR | | | | |
| | — | 50.00 | 65.00 | 100.00 | 250.00 |
| | 1868 PR — | 50.00 | 65.00 | 100.00 | 250.00 |

**Mint mark: Mo**

| KM# | Date Mintage | Fine | VF | XF | Unc |
|---|---|---|---|---|---|
| 372.8 | 1825 JM — | 10.00 | 20.00 | 40.00 | 110.00 |
| | 1826 JM — | 7.50 | 15.00 | 30.00 | 100.00 |
| | 1827/6 JM — | 7.50 | 15.00 | 30.00 | 75.00 |
| | 1827 JM — | 5.00 | 10.00 | 20.00 | 70.00 |
| | 1828 JM — | 7.50 | 15.00 | 30.00 | 100.00 |
| | 1830/29 JM — | 5.00 | 10.00 | 20.00 | 100.00 |
| | 1830 JM — | 5.00 | 12.50 | 25.00 | 100.00 |
| | 1831 JM — | 100.00 | 200.00 | 300.00 | 750.00 |
| | 1832 JM — | 5.00 | 10.00 | 20.00 | 100.00 |
| | 1833/2 MJ — | 5.00 | 10.00 | 20.00 | 100.00 |
| | 1850 GC — | 5.00 | 10.00 | 20.00 | 100.00 |
| | 1852 GC — | 275.00 | 425.00 | 575.00 | — |
| | 1854 GC — | 10.00 | 20.00 | 40.00 | 100.00 |
| | 1855 GF — | 5.00 | 10.00 | 20.00 | 80.00 |
| | 1856 GF — | 5.00 | 10.00 | 20.00 | 80.00 |
| | 1857 GF — | 5.00 | 10.00 | 20.00 | 80.00 |
| | 1858 FH — | 5.00 | 10.00 | 20.00 | 80.00 |
| | 1859 FH — | 5.00 | 10.00 | 20.00 | 80.00 |
| | 1861 CH — | 5.00 | 10.00 | 20.00 | 80.00 |
| | 1862 CH — | 5.00 | 10.00 | 20.00 | 80.00 |
| | 1863/2 CH — | 7.50 | 12.50 | 25.00 | 80.00 |

**Mint mark: Pi**

| KM# | Date Mintage | Fine | VF | XF | Unc |
|---|---|---|---|---|---|
| 372.9 | 1831 JS — | 5.00 | 10.00 | 20.00 | 125.00 |
| | 1837 JS — | 750.00 | 850.00 | 1000. | — |
| | 1838/7 JS — | 250.00 | 300.00 | 375.00 | — |
| | 1838 JS — | 20.00 | 35.00 | 60.00 | 125.00 |
| | 1840/39 JS — | 7.50 | 15.00 | 30.00 | 125.00 |
| | 1840 JS — | 7.50 | 15.00 | 30.00 | 125.00 |
| | 1841 JS — | 7.50 | 15.00 | 30.00 | 125.00 |
| | 1842 JS — | 15.00 | 30.00 | 55.00 | 150.00 |
| | 1842 PS — | 5.00 | 10.00 | 20.00 | 125.00 |
| | 1843 PS — | 12.50 | 20.00 | 35.00 | 125.00 |
| | 1843 AM — | 40.00 | 60.00 | 80.00 | 150.00 |
| | 1844 AM — | 40.00 | 60.00 | 80.00 | 150.00 |
| | 1845 AM — | 7.50 | 15.00 | 30.00 | 125.00 |
| | 1846/5 AM — | 7.50 | 15.00 | 30.00 | 125.00 |
| | 1847/6 AM — | 7.50 | 15.00 | 30.00 | 125.00 |
| | 1847 AM — | 7.50 | 15.00 | 30.00 | 125.00 |
| | 1848/7 AM — | 7.50 | 15.00 | 30.00 | 125.00 |
| | 1849 PS — | 7.50 | 15.00 | 30.00 | 125.00 |
| | 1849/8 SP — | 60.00 | 100.00 | 150.00 | — |
| | 1849 SP — | 15.00 | 25.00 | 40.00 | 125.00 |
| | 1850 MC — | 5.00 | 10.00 | 20.00 | 125.00 |
| | 1851/0 MC — | 7.50 | 15.00 | 30.00 | 125.00 |
| | 1851 MC — | 7.50 | 15.00 | 30.00 | 125.00 |
| | 1852/1/0 MC | | | | |
| | — | 10.00 | 20.00 | 35.00 | 125.00 |
| | 1852 MC — | 7.50 | 15.00 | 30.00 | 125.00 |
| | 1853/1 MC — | 12.50 | 20.00 | 35.00 | 125.00 |
| | 1853 MC — | 10.00 | 20.00 | 35.00 | 125.00 |
| | 1854/2 MC — | 30.00 | 60.00 | 100.00 | — |
| | 1854/3 MC — | 20.00 | 40.00 | 60.00 | 150.00 |
| | 1855/4 MC — | 20.00 | 40.00 | 60.00 | 150.00 |
| | 1855 MC — | 15.00 | 25.00 | 45.00 | 125.00 |
| | 1856 MC — | 15.00 | 25.00 | 45.00 | 125.00 |
| | 1857 PS — | 20.00 | 35.00 | 55.00 | 135.00 |

| KM# | Date Mintage | Fine | VF | XF | Unc |
|---|---|---|---|---|---|
| 372.9 | 1857 MC — | 20.00 | 40.00 | 60.00 | 150.00 |
| | 1858 MC — | 12.50 | 20.00 | 35.00 | 125.00 |
| | 1859 PS — | 10.00 | 15.00 | 30.00 | 125.00 |
| | 1860/59 PS — | 10.00 | 15.00 | 30.00 | 125.00 |
| | 1861 PS — | 7.50 | 12.50 | 20.00 | 125.00 |
| | 1861 RO — | 12.50 | 20.00 | 35.00 | 125.00 |
| | 1862/1 RO — | 12.50 | 20.00 | 35.00 | 90.00 |
| | 1862 RO — | 7.50 | 12.50 | 20.00 | 125.00 |

**Mint mark: Zs**

| KM# | Date Mintage | Fine | VF | XF | Unc |
|---|---|---|---|---|---|
| 372.10 | 1826 AZ — | 5.00 | 12.50 | 35.00 | 120.00 |
| | 1826 AO — | 5.00 | 12.50 | 35.00 | 120.00 |
| | 1827 AO — | 5.00 | 12.50 | 35.00 | 120.00 |
| | 1828/7 AO — | 5.00 | 12.50 | 35.00 | 120.00 |
| | 1828 AO — | 5.00 | 12.50 | 35.00 | 120.00 |
| | 1828 AO inverted V for A | | | | |
| | 1829 AO — | 5.00 | 12.50 | 35.00 | 120.00 |
| | 1830 ZsOV — | 5.00 | 12.50 | 35.00 | 120.00 |
| | 1830 ZOV — | 5.00 | 12.50 | 35.00 | 120.00 |
| | 1831 OV — | 5.00 | 12.50 | 35.00 | 120.00 |
| | 1831 OM — | 5.00 | 12.50 | 30.00 | 120.00 |
| | 1832 OM — | 5.00 | 12.50 | 30.00 | 120.00 |
| | 1833/2 OM — | 5.00 | 12.50 | 30.00 | 120.00 |
| | 1833/2 OM/V | | | | |
| | — | 5.00 | 12.50 | 30.00 | 120.00 |
| | 1833 OM — | 5.00 | 12.50 | 30.00 | 120.00 |
| | 1834/3 OM — | 5.00 | 12.50 | 30.00 | 120.00 |
| | 1834 OM — | 5.00 | 12.50 | 30.00 | 120.00 |
| | 1835/4 OM — | 20.00 | 35.00 | 60.00 | 150.00 |
| | 1835 OM — | 4.00 | 8.00 | 20.00 | 65.00 |
| | 1836/5 OM — | 4.00 | 8.00 | 20.00 | 85.00 |
| | 1836 OM — | 4.00 | 8.00 | 20.00 | 85.00 |
| | 1837 OM — | 4.00 | 8.00 | 20.00 | 85.00 |
| | 1838 OM — | 4.00 | 8.00 | 20.00 | 85.00 |
| | 1839 OM — | 4.00 | 8.00 | 20.00 | 85.00 |
| | 1040 OM — | 4.00 | 0.00 | 20.00 | 85.00 |
| | 1841 OM — | 20.00 | 40.00 | 60.00 | 150.00 |
| | 1842/1 OM — | 4.00 | 8.00 | 20.00 | 85.00 |
| | 1842 OM — | 4.00 | 8.00 | 20.00 | 85.00 |
| | 1843 OM — | 4.00 | 8.00 | 20.00 | 85.00 |
| | 1844 OM — | 4.00 | 8.00 | 20.00 | 85.00 |
| | 1845/4 OM — | 5.00 | 12.50 | 30.00 | 100.00 |
| | 1845 OM — | 4.00 | 8.00 | 20.00 | 85.00 |
| | 1846 OM old font and obv. | | | | |
| | — | 4.00 | 8.00 | 20.00 | 85.00 |
| | 1846 OM new font and obv. | | | | |
| | — | 4.00 | 8.00 | 20.00 | 85.00 |
| | 1847 OM — | 4.00 | 8.00 | 20.00 | 85.00 |
| | 1848 OM — | 4.00 | 8.00 | 20.00 | 85.00 |
| | 1849 OM — | 10.00 | 25.00 | 50.00 | 125.00 |
| | 1850 OM — | 4.00 | 6.00 | 15.00 | 85.00 |
| | 1851 OM — | 4.00 | 6.00 | 15.00 | 85.00 |
| | 1852 OM — | 4.00 | 6.00 | 15.00 | 85.00 |
| | 1853 OM — | 4.00 | 6.00 | 15.00 | 85.00 |
| | 1854/2 OM — | 4.00 | 6.00 | 15.00 | 85.00 |
| | 1854/3 OM — | 4.00 | 6.00 | 15.00 | 85.00 |
| | 1854 OM — | 4.00 | 6.00 | 15.00 | 85.00 |
| | 1855/4 OM — | 4.00 | 6.00 | 15.00 | 85.00 |
| | 1855 OM — | 4.00 | 6.00 | 15.00 | 85.00 |
| | 1855 MO — | 4.00 | 6.00 | 15.00 | 85.00 |
| | 1856 MO — | 4.00 | 6.00 | 15.00 | 85.00 |
| | 1856 MO/OM — | 4.00 | 6.00 | 15.00 | 85.00 |
| | 1857 MO — | 4.00 | 6.00 | 15.00 | 85.00 |
| | 1858 MO — | 4.00 | 6.00 | 15.00 | 85.00 |
| | 1859 MO — | 4.00 | 6.00 | 15.00 | 75.00 |
| | 1860 VL — | 4.00 | 6.00 | 15.00 | 75.00 |
| | 1860 VL inverted A for V | | | | |
| | — | 4.00 | 6.00 | 15.00 | 75.00 |
| | 1861 VL — | 4.00 | 6.00 | 15.00 | 75.00 |
| | 1861 VL inverted A for V | | | | |
| | — | 4.00 | 6.00 | 15.00 | 75.00 |
| | 1862 VL — | 5.00 | 12.50 | 30.00 | 100.00 |
| | 1868 JS — | 25.00 | 45.00 | 90.00 | 175.00 |
| | 1869 YH — | 4.00 | 8.00 | 20.00 | 75.00 |

# 2 REALES

**Mint mark: A**
**Obv: Facing eagle, reeded edge.**

| KM# | Date | Mintage | Fine | VF | XF | Unc |
|---|---|---|---|---|---|---|
| 374 | 1872 AM | .015 | 40.00 | 100.00 | 200.00 | 500.00 |

**Mint mark: Ce**

| KM# | Date | Mintage | Fine | VF | XF | Unc |
|---|---|---|---|---|---|---|
| 374.1 | 1863 ML | — | 125.00 | 200.00 | 325.00 | 675.00 |

**Mint mark: Ca**

| KM# | Date | Mintage | Fine | VF | XF | Unc |
|---|---|---|---|---|---|---|
| 374.2 | 1832 MR | — | 30.00 | 60.00 | 100.00 | 200.00 |
| | 1833 MR | — | 30.00 | 60.00 | 125.00 | 500.00 |
| | 1834 MR | — | 35.00 | 75.00 | 125.00 | 500.00 |
| | 1834 AM | — | 35.00 | 75.00 | 125.00 | 500.00 |
| | 1835 AM | — | 35.00 | 75.00 | 125.00 | 500.00 |
| | 1836 AM | — | 20.00 | 40.00 | 80.00 | 200.00 |
| | 1844 RG | — | — | — | Unique | — |
| | 1845 RG | — | 20.00 | 40.00 | 80.00 | 200.00 |
| | 1855 RG | — | 20.00 | 40.00 | 80.00 | 200.00 |

**Mint mark: C**

| KM# | Date | Mintage | Fine | VF | XF | Unc |
|---|---|---|---|---|---|---|
| 374.3 | 1846/1146 CE | | | | | |
| | | — | 25.00 | 50.00 | 100.00 | 225.00 |
| | 1847 CE | — | 12.50 | 20.00 | 40.00 | 200.00 |
| | 1848 CE | — | 12.50 | 20.00 | 40.00 | 200.00 |
| | 1850 CE | — | 25.00 | 50.00 | 75.00 | 200.00 |
| | 1851 CE | — | 12.50 | 20.00 | 40.00 | 200.00 |
| | 1852/1 CE | — | 12.50 | 20.00 | 40.00 | 200.00 |
| | 1853/2 CE | — | 12.50 | 20.00 | 40.00 | 200.00 |
| | 1854 CE | — | 15.00 | 30.00 | 50.00 | 200.00 |
| | 1856 CE | — | 20.00 | 35.00 | 70.00 | 200.00 |
| | 1857 CE | — | 12.50 | 20.00 | 40.00 | 200.00 |
| | 1860 PV | — | 12.50 | 20.00 | 40.00 | 200.00 |
| | 1861 PV | — | 12.50 | 20.00 | 40.00 | 200.00 |
| | 1869 CE | — | 12.50 | 20.00 | 40.00 | 200.00 |

**Mint mark: Do**

| KM# | Date | Mintage | Fine | VF | XF | Unc |
|---|---|---|---|---|---|---|
| 374.4 | 1826 RL | — | 20.00 | 40.00 | 60.00 | 200.00 |
| | 1832 RM style of pre-1832 | | | | | |
| | | — | 20.00 | 40.00 | 60.00 | 200.00 |
| | 1832 RM style of post-1832 | | | | | |
| | | — | 20.00 | 40.00 | 60.00 | 200.00 |
| | 1834/2 RM | — | 20.00 | 40.00 | 60.00 | 200.00 |
| | 1834/3 RM | — | 20.00 | 40.00 | 60.00 | 200.00 |
| | 1835/4 RM/RL | | | | | |
| | | — | 200.00 | 300.00 | 500.00 | — |
| | 1841/31 RM | — | 50.00 | 75.00 | 125.00 | 250.00 |
| | 1841 RM | — | 50.00 | 75.00 | 125.00 | 250.00 |
| | 1842/32 RM | — | 12.50 | 20.00 | 40.00 | 200.00 |
| | 1843 RM/RL | — | 12.50 | 20.00 | 40.00 | 200.00 |
| | 1844 RM | — | 35.00 | 50.00 | 80.00 | 200.00 |
| | 1845/34 RM/RL | | | | | |
| | | — | 12.50 | 20.00 | 40.00 | 200.00 |
| | 1846/36 RM | — | 100.00 | 150.00 | 200.00 | 350.00 |
| | 1848/36 RM | — | 12.50 | 20.00 | 40.00 | 200.00 |
| | 1848/37 RM | — | 12.50 | 20.00 | 40.00 | 200.00 |
| | 1848/7 RM | — | 12.50 | 20.00 | 40.00 | 200.00 |
| | 1848 RM | — | 12.50 | 20.00 | 40.00 | 200.00 |
| | 1849 CM/RM | — | 12.50 | 20.00 | 40.00 | 200.00 |
| | 1849 CM | — | 12.50 | 20.00 | 40.00 | 200.00 |
| | 1851 JMR/RL | | | | | |
| | | — | 12.50 | 20.00 | 40.00 | 200.00 |
| | 1852 JMR | — | 12.50 | 20.00 | 40.00 | 200.00 |
| | 1854 CP/CR | — | 30.00 | 40.00 | 80.00 | 200.00 |
| | 1855 CP | — | 250.00 | 350.00 | 500.00 | — |
| | 1856 CP | — | 100.00 | 150.00 | 250.00 | 500.00 |
| | 1858 CP | — | 12.50 | 20.00 | 40.00 | 200.00 |
| | 1859/8 CP | — | 12.50 | 20.00 | 40.00 | 200.00 |
| | 1861 CP | — | 12.50 | 20.00 | 40.00 | 200.00 |

**Mint mark: EoMo**

| KM# | Date | Mintage | Fine | VF | XF | Unc |
|---|---|---|---|---|---|---|
| 374.5 | 1828 LF | — | 325.00 | 525.00 | 900.00 | 2500. |

**Mint mark: Ga**

| KM# | Date | Mintage | Fine | VF | XF | Unc |
|---|---|---|---|---|---|---|
| 374.6 | 1825 FS | — | 20.00 | 40.00 | 80.00 | 200.00 |
| | 1826 FS | — | 20.00 | 40.00 | 80.00 | 200.00 |
| | 1828/7 FS | — | 100.00 | 150.00 | 225.00 | 400.00 |
| | 1829 FS | — | — | — | Rare | — |
| | 1832/0 FS/LP | | | | | |
| | | — | 100.00 | 150.00 | 225.00 | 350.00 |
| | 1832 FS | — | 12.50 | 20.00 | 40.00 | 200.00 |
| | 1833/2 FS/LP | | | | | |
| | | — | 12.50 | 20.00 | 40.00 | 200.00 |
| | 1834/27 FS | — | — | — | Rare | — |
| | 1834 FS | — | 12.50 | 20.00 | 40.00 | 200.00 |
| | 1835 FS | — | 2100. | — | — | — |
| | 1837 JG | — | 12.50 | 20.00 | 40.00 | 200.00 |
| | 1838 JG | — | 12.50 | 20.00 | 40.00 | 200.00 |
| | 1840/30 MC | — | 12.50 | 20.00 | 40.00 | 200.00 |
| | 1841 MC | — | 12.50 | 20.00 | 40.00 | 200.00 |
| | 1842/32 JG/MC | | | | | |
| | | — | 35.00 | 50.00 | 100.00 | 200.00 |
| | 1842 JG | — | 20.00 | 40.00 | 80.00 | 200.00 |
| | 1843 JG | — | 12.50 | 20.00 | 40.00 | 200.00 |
| | 1843 MC/JG | — | 12.50 | 20.00 | 40.00 | 200.00 |
| | 1844 MC | — | 12.50 | 20.00 | 40.00 | 200.00 |
| | 1845/3 MC/JG | | | | | |
| | | — | 12.50 | 20.00 | 40.00 | 200.00 |
| | 1845/4 MC/JG | | | | | |
| | | — | 12.50 | 20.00 | 40.00 | 200.00 |
| | 1845 JG | — | 12.50 | 20.00 | 40.00 | 200.00 |
| | 1846 JG | — | 12.50 | 20.00 | 40.00 | 200.00 |
| | 1847/6 JG | — | 25.00 | 40.00 | 80.00 | 200.00 |
| | 1848/7 JG | — | 12.50 | 20.00 | 40.00 | 200.00 |
| | 1849 JG | — | 12.50 | 20.00 | 40.00 | 200.00 |
| | 1850/40 JG | — | 12.50 | 20.00 | 40.00 | 200.00 |
| | 1851 JG | — | 250.00 | 350.00 | 500.00 | — |
| | 1852 JG | — | 12.50 | 20.00 | 40.00 | 200.00 |
| | 1853/1 JG | — | 12.50 | 20.00 | 40.00 | 200.00 |
| | 1854/3 JG | — | 250.00 | 350.00 | 500.00 | — |
| | 1855 JG | — | 35.00 | 50.00 | 80.00 | 200.00 |
| | 1856 JG | — | 12.50 | 20.00 | 40.00 | 200.00 |
| | 1857 JG | — | 250.00 | 350.00 | 500.00 | — |
| | 1859/8 JG | — | 12.50 | 20.00 | 40.00 | 200.00 |
| | 1859 JG | — | 12.50 | 20.00 | 40.00 | 200.00 |
| | 1862/1 JG | — | 12.50 | 20.00 | 40.00 | 200.00 |

**Mint mark: GC**

| KM# | Date | Mintage | Fine | VF | XF | Unc |
|---|---|---|---|---|---|---|
| 374.7 | 1844 MP | — | 40.00 | 60.00 | 125.00 | 275.00 |
| | 1845 MP | — | 40.00 | 60.00 | 125.00 | 275.00 |
| | 1846 MP | — | 50.00 | 100.00 | 150.00 | 300.00 |
| | 1847 MP | — | 35.00 | 50.00 | 100.00 | 250.00 |
| | 1848 MP | — | 50.00 | 100.00 | 150.00 | 300.00 |
| | 1849 MP | — | 50.00 | 100.00 | 150.00 | 300.00 |
| | 1850 MP | — | 125.00 | 250.00 | — | — |
| | 1851/0 MP | — | 50.00 | 100.00 | 150.00 | 300.00 |
| | 1851 MP | — | 50.00 | 100.00 | 150.00 | 300.00 |

**Mint mark: Go**

| KM# | Date | Mintage | Fine | VF | XF | Unc |
|---|---|---|---|---|---|---|
| 374.8 | 1825 JJ | — | 7.50 | 15.00 | 30.00 | 150.00 |
| | 1826/5 JJ | — | 7.50 | 15.00 | 30.00 | 150.00 |
| | 1826 JJ | — | 7.50 | 10.00 | 25.00 | 150.00 |
| | 1826 MJ | — | 7.50 | 10.00 | 25.00 | 150.00 |
| | 1827/6 MJ | — | 7.50 | 10.00 | 25.00 | 150.00 |
| | 1827 MJ | — | 7.50 | 10.00 | 25.00 | 150.00 |
| | 1828/7 MR | — | 7.50 | 15.00 | 30.00 | 150.00 |
| | 1828 MJ | — | 7.50 | 10.00 | 20.00 | 150.00 |
| | 1828 JM | — | 7.50 | 10.00 | 20.00 | 150.00 |
| | 1829 MJ | — | 7.50 | 10.00 | 20.00 | 150.00 |
| | 1831 MJ | — | 7.50 | 10.00 | 20.00 | 150.00 |
| | 1832 MJ | — | 7.50 | 10.00 | 20.00 | 150.00 |
| | 1833 MJ | — | 7.50 | 10.00 | 20.00 | 150.00 |
| | 1834 PJ | — | 7.50 | 10.00 | 20.00 | 150.00 |
| | 1835/4 PJ | — | 7.50 | 15.00 | 30.00 | 150.00 |
| | 1835 PJ | — | 7.50 | 10.00 | 20.00 | 150.00 |
| | 1836 PJ | — | 7.50 | 10.00 | 20.00 | 150.00 |
| | 1837/6 PJ | — | 7.50 | 10.00 | 20.00 | 150.00 |
| | 1837 PJ | — | 7.50 | 10.00 | 20.00 | 150.00 |
| | 1838/7 PJ | — | 7.50 | 10.00 | 20.00 | 150.00 |
| | 1838 PJ | — | 7.50 | 10.00 | 20.00 | 150.00 |
| | 1839/8 PJ | — | 7.50 | 15.00 | 30.00 | 150.00 |
| | 1839 PJ | — | 7.50 | 10.00 | 20.00 | 150.00 |
| | 1840 PJ | — | 7.50 | 10.00 | 20.00 | 150.00 |
| | 1841 PJ | — | 7.50 | 10.00 | 20.00 | 150.00 |
| | 1842 PJ | — | 7.50 | 10.00 | 20.00 | 150.00 |
| | 1842 PM/PJ | — | 7.50 | 10.00 | 20.00 | 150.00 |
| | 1842 PM | — | 7.50 | 10.00 | 20.00 | 150.00 |
| | 1843/2 PM concave wings, thin rays, sm. letters | | | | | |
| | | — | 7.50 | 10.00 | 20.00 | 150.00 |

| KM# | Date | Mintage | Fine | VF | XF | Unc |
|---|---|---|---|---|---|---|
| 374.8 | 1843 PM convex wings, thick rays, lg. letters | | | | | |
| | | — | 7.50 | 10.00 | 20.00 | 150.00 |
| | 1844 PM | — | 7.50 | 10.00 | 20.00 | 150.00 |
| | 1845/4 PM | — | 7.50 | 10.00 | 20.00 | 150.00 |
| | 1845 PM | — | 7.50 | 10.00 | 20.00 | 150.00 |
| | 1846/5 PM | — | 10.00 | 15.00 | 35.00 | 150.00 |
| | 1846 PM | — | 7.50 | 10.00 | 20.00 | 150.00 |
| | 1847 PM | — | 7.50 | 10.00 | 20.00 | 150.00 |
| | 1848/7 PM | — | 7.50 | 15.00 | 30.00 | 150.00 |
| | 1848 PM | — | 7.50 | 10.00 | 20.00 | 150.00 |
| | 1848 PF | — | 100.00 | 150.00 | 250.00 | 500.00 |
| | 1849/8 PF/PM | | | | | |
| | | — | 7.50 | 10.00 | 20.00 | 150.00 |
| | 1849 PF | — | 7.50 | 10.00 | 20.00 | 150.00 |
| | 1850/40 PF | — | 7.50 | 10.00 | 20.00 | 150.00 |
| | 1850 PF | — | 7.50 | 10.00 | 20.00 | 150.00 |
| | 1851 PF | — | 7.50 | 10.00 | 20.00 | 150.00 |
| | 1852/1 PF | — | 7.50 | 10.00 | 20.00 | 150.00 |
| | 1852 PF | — | 7.50 | 10.00 | 20.00 | 150.00 |
| | 1853 PF | — | 7.50 | 10.00 | 20.00 | 150.00 |
| | 1854/3 PF | — | 7.50 | 10.00 | 20.00 | 150.00 |
| | 1854 PF old font and obv. | | | | | |
| | | — | 7.50 | 10.00 | 20.00 | 150.00 |
| | 1854 PF new font and obv. | | | | | |
| | | — | 7.50 | 10.00 | 20.00 | 150.00 |
| | 1855 PF | — | 7.50 | 10.00 | 20.00 | 150.00 |
| | 1855 PF star in G of mint mark | | | | | |
| | | — | 7.50 | 10.00 | 20.00 | 150.00 |
| | 1856/5 PF | — | 10.00 | 15.00 | 35.00 | 150.00 |
| | 1856 PF | — | 10.00 | 15.00 | 25.00 | 150.00 |
| | 1857/6 PF | — | 7.50 | 10.00 | 20.00 | 150.00 |
| | 1857 PF | — | 7.50 | 10.00 | 20.00 | 150.00 |
| | 1858/7 PF | — | 7.50 | 10.00 | 20.00 | 150.00 |
| | 1858 PF | — | 7.50 | 10.00 | 20.00 | 150.00 |
| | 1859/7 PF | — | 7.50 | 10.00 | 20.00 | 150.00 |
| | 1859 PF | — | 7.50 | 10.00 | 20.00 | 150.00 |
| | 1860/7 PF | — | 7.50 | 10.00 | 20.00 | 150.00 |
| | 1860/50 PF | — | 7.50 | 10.00 | 20.00 | 150.00 |
| | 1860/59 PF | — | 7.50 | 10.00 | 20.00 | 150.00 |
| | 1860 PF | — | 7.50 | 10.00 | 20.00 | 150.00 |
| | 1861/51 PF | — | 7.50 | 10.00 | 20.00 | 150.00 |
| | 1861/57 PF | — | 7.50 | 10.00 | 20.00 | 150.00 |
| | 1861/0 PF | — | 7.50 | 10.00 | 20.00 | 150.00 |
| | 1861 PF | — | 7.50 | 10.00 | 20.00 | 150.00 |
| | 1862/1 YE | — | 7.50 | 10.00 | 20.00 | 125.00 |
| | 1862 YE | — | 7.50 | 10.00 | 20.00 | 125.00 |
| | 1862/57 YF | — | 7.50 | 10.00 | 20.00 | 125.00 |
| | 1862/57 YF F/E | | | | | |
| | | — | 7.50 | 10.00 | 20.00 | 125.00 |
| | 1862 YE/PF | — | 7.50 | 10.00 | 20.00 | 125.00 |
| | 1862 YF | — | 7.50 | 10.00 | 20.00 | 125.00 |
| | 1863/52 YF | — | 7.50 | 10.00 | 20.00 | 125.00 |
| | 1863 YF | — | 7.50 | 10.00 | 20.00 | 125.00 |
| | 1863/52 YF/PE | | | | | |
| | | — | 7.50 | 10.00 | 20.00 | 125.00 |
| | 1867/57 YF | — | 7.50 | 10.00 | 20.00 | 125.00 |
| | 1868/57 YF | — | 10.00 | 15.00 | 25.00 | 125.00 |

NOTE: Varieties exist.

### Mint mark: Ho

| KM# | Date | Mintage | Fine | VF | XF | Unc |
|---|---|---|---|---|---|---|
| 374.9 | 1861 FM | — | 200.00 | 300.00 | 400.00 | 650.00 |
| | 1862/52 Ho FM/C. CE | | | | | |
| | | — | 250.00 | 350.00 | 500.00 | — |
| | 1867/1 PR/FM | | | | | |
| | | — | 75.00 | 150.00 | 250.00 | 500.00 |

### Mint mark: Mo

| KM# | Date | Mintage | Fine | VF | XF | Unc |
|---|---|---|---|---|---|---|
| 374.10 | 1825 JM | — | 10.00 | 15.00 | 30.00 | 175.00 |
| | 1826 JM | — | 10.00 | 15.00 | 30.00 | 175.00 |
| | 1827 JM | — | 10.00 | 15.00 | 30.00 | 175.00 |
| | 1828 JM | — | 10.00 | 15.00 | 30.00 | 175.00 |
| | 1829/8 JM | — | 10.00 | 15.00 | 30.00 | 175.00 |
| | 1829 JM | — | 10.00 | 15.00 | 30.00 | 175.00 |
| | 1830 JM | — | 40.00 | 60.00 | 125.00 | 250.00 |
| | 1831 JM | — | 10.00 | 15.00 | 30.00 | 175.00 |
| | 1832 JM | — | 100.00 | 200.00 | 400.00 | — |
| | 1833/2 MJ/JM | | | | | |
| | | — | 10.00 | 15.00 | 30.00 | 175.00 |
| | 1834 ML | — | 50.00 | 100.00 | 200.00 | 400.00 |
| | 1836 ML | — | Reported, not confirmed | | | |
| | 1836 MF | — | 10.00 | 15.00 | 30.00 | 175.00 |
| | 1837 ML | — | 10.00 | 15.00 | 30.00 | 175.00 |
| | 1840/7 ML | — | 150.00 | 225.00 | 350.00 | — |
| | 1840 ML | — | 150.00 | 225.00 | 350.00 | — |
| | 1841 ML | — | 10.00 | 15.00 | 30.00 | 175.00 |

| KM# | Date | Mintage | Fine | VF | XF | Unc |
|---|---|---|---|---|---|---|
| 374.10 | 1842 ML | — | — | — | Rare | — |
| | 1847 RC narrow date | | | | | |
| | | — | 10.00 | 15.00 | 30.00 | 175.00 |
| | 1847 RC wide date | | | | | |
| | | — | 10.00 | 15.00 | 30.00 | 175.00 |
| | 1848 GC | — | 10.00 | 15.00 | 30.00 | 175.00 |
| | 1849 GC | — | 10.00 | 15.00 | 30.00 | 175.00 |
| | 1850 GC | — | 10.00 | 15.00 | 30.00 | 175.00 |
| | 1851 GC | — | 40.00 | 60.00 | 125.00 | 250.00 |
| | 1852 GC | — | 10.00 | 15.00 | 30.00 | 175.00 |
| | 1853 GC | — | 10.00 | 15.00 | 30.00 | 175.00 |
| | 1854/44 GC | — | 10.00 | 15.00 | 30.00 | 175.00 |
| | 1855 GC | — | 10.00 | 15.00 | 30.00 | 175.00 |
| | 1855 GF/GC | — | 10.00 | 15.00 | 30.00 | 175.00 |
| | 1855 GF | — | 10.00 | 15.00 | 30.00 | 175.00 |
| | 1856/5 GF/GC | | | | | |
| | | — | 10.00 | 15.00 | 30.00 | 175.00 |
| | 1857 GF | — | 10.00 | 15.00 | 30.00 | 175.00 |
| | 1858 FH | — | 7.50 | 12.50 | 25.00 | 150.00 |
| | 1858 FH/GF | — | 7.50 | 12.50 | 25.00 | 150.00 |
| | 1859 FH | — | 7.50 | 12.50 | 25.00 | 150.00 |
| | 1860 FH | — | 7.50 | 12.50 | 25.00 | 150.00 |
| | 1860 TH | — | 7.50 | 12.50 | 25.00 | 150.00 |
| | 1861 TH | — | — | Reported, not confirmed | | |
| | 1861 CH | — | 7.50 | 12.50 | 25.00 | 150.00 |
| | 1862 CH | — | 7.50 | 12.50 | 25.00 | 150.00 |
| | 1863 CH | — | 7.50 | 12.50 | 25.00 | 150.00 |
| | 1863 TH | — | 7.50 | 12.50 | 25.00 | 150.00 |
| | 1867 CH | — | 7.50 | 12.50 | 25.00 | 150.00 |
| | 1868 CH | — | 10.00 | 15.00 | 30.00 | 150.00 |
| | 1868 PH | — | 7.50 | 12.50 | 25.00 | 150.00 |

NOTE: Varieties exist.

### Mint mark: Pi

| KM# | Date | Mintage | Fine | VF | XF | Unc |
|---|---|---|---|---|---|---|
| 374.11 | 1829 JS | — | 10.00 | 15.00 | 30.00 | 200.00 |
| | 1830/20 JS | — | 20.00 | 30.00 | 60.00 | 200.00 |
| | 1837 JS | — | 10.00 | 15.00 | 30.00 | 200.00 |
| | 1841 JS | — | 10.00 | 15.00 | 30.00 | 200.00 |
| | 1842/1 JS | — | 10.00 | 15.00 | 30.00 | 200.00 |
| | 1842 JS | — | 10.00 | 15.00 | 30.00 | 200.00 |
| | 1842 PS | — | 20.00 | 35.00 | 60.00 | 200.00 |
| | 1843 PS | — | 12.50 | 20.00 | 40.00 | 200.00 |
| | 1843 AM | — | 10.00 | 15.00 | 30.00 | 200.00 |
| | 1844 AM | — | 10.00 | 15.00 | 30.00 | 200.00 |
| | 1845 AM | — | 10.00 | 15.00 | 30.00 | 200.00 |
| | 1846 AM | — | 10.00 | 15.00 | 30.00 | 200.00 |
| | 1849 MC | — | 10.00 | 15.00 | 30.00 | 200.00 |
| | 1850 MC | — | 10.00 | 15.00 | 30.00 | 200.00 |
| | 1856 MC | — | 40.00 | 60.00 | 125.00 | 250.00 |
| | 1857 MC | — | — | — | — | — |
| | 1858 MC | — | 12.50 | 20.00 | 40.00 | 200.00 |
| | 1859 MC | — | 50.00 | 70.00 | 100.00 | 200.00 |
| | 1861 PS | — | 10.00 | 15.00 | 30.00 | 200.00 |
| | 1862 RO | — | 12.50 | 20.00 | 40.00 | 200.00 |
| | 1863 RO | — | 100.00 | 250.00 | 350.00 | 500.00 |
| | 1868 PS | — | 10.00 | 15.00 | 30.00 | 200.00 |
| | 1869/8 PS | — | 10.00 | 15.00 | 30.00 | 200.00 |
| | 1869 PS | — | 10.00 | 15.00 | 30.00 | 200.00 |

### Mint mark: Zs

| KM# | Date | Mintage | Fine | VF | XF | Unc |
|---|---|---|---|---|---|---|
| 374.12 | 1825 AZ | — | 10.00 | 15.00 | 30.00 | 150.00 |
| | 1826 AV (A is inverted V) | | | | | |
| | | — | 7.50 | 10.00 | 25.00 | 150.00 |
| | 1826 AZ (A is inverted V) | | | | | |
| | | — | 7.50 | 10.00 | 25.00 | 150.00 |
| | 1826 AO | — | 10.00 | 15.00 | 30.00 | 150.00 |
| | 1827 AO (A is inverted V) | | | | | |
| | | — | 6.00 | 8.00 | 12.00 | 150.00 |
| | 1827 AO | — | 6.00 | 8.00 | 12.00 | 150.00 |
| | 1828/7 AO | — | 15.00 | 30.00 | 60.00 | 175.00 |
| | 1828 AO | — | 7.50 | 10.00 | 25.00 | 100.00 |
| | 1828 AO (A is inverted V) | | | | | |
| | | — | 7.50 | 10.00 | 25.00 | 150.00 |
| | 1829 AO | — | 7.50 | 10.00 | 25.00 | 150.00 |
| | 1829 OV | — | 7.50 | 10.00 | 25.00 | 150.00 |
| | 1830 OV | — | 7.50 | 10.00 | 25.00 | 150.00 |
| | 1831 OV | — | 7.50 | 10.00 | 25.00 | 150.00 |
| | 1831 OM/OV | — | 7.50 | 10.00 | 25.00 | 150.00 |
| | 1831 OM | — | 7.50 | 10.00 | 25.00 | 150.00 |
| | 1832/1 OM | — | 15.00 | 30.00 | 60.00 | 150.00 |
| | 1832 OM | — | 7.50 | 10.00 | 25.00 | 150.00 |
| | 1833/27 OM | — | 7.50 | 10.00 | 25.00 | 150.00 |
| | 1833/2 OM | — | 7.50 | 10.00 | 25.00 | 150.00 |
| | 1833 OM | — | 7.50 | 10.00 | 25.00 | 150.00 |
| | 1834 OM | — | 40.00 | 60.00 | 125.00 | 200.00 |

| KM# | Date | Mintage | Fine | VF | XF | Unc |
|-----|------|---------|------|-----|-----|-----|
| 374.12 | 1835 OM | — | 7.50 | 10.00 | 25.00 | 150.00 |
| | 1836 OM | — | 7.50 | 10.00 | 25.00 | 150.00 |
| | 1837 OM | — | 7.50 | 10.00 | 25.00 | 150.00 |
| | 1838 OM | — | 15.00 | 30.00 | 60.00 | 150.00 |
| | 1839 OM | — | 7.50 | 10.00 | 20.00 | 150.00 |
| | 1840 OM | — | 7.50 | 10.00 | 20.00 | 150.00 |
| | 1841/0 OM | — | 7.50 | 10.00 | 20.00 | 150.00 |
| | 1841 OM | — | 7.50 | 10.00 | 20.00 | 150.00 |
| | 1842 OM narrow date | | | | | |
| | | — | 7.50 | 10.00 | 20.00 | 150.00 |
| | 1842 OM wide date | | | | | |
| | | — | 7.50 | 10.00 | 20.00 | 150.00 |
| | 1843 OM | — | 7.50 | 10.00 | 20.00 | 150.00 |
| | 1844 OM | — | 7.50 | 10.00 | 20.00 | 150.00 |
| | 1845 OM small letters and leaves | | | | | |
| | | — | 7.50 | 10.00 | 20.00 | 150.00 |
| | 1845 OM large letters and leaves | | | | | |
| | | — | 7.50 | 10.00 | 20.00 | 150.00 |
| | 1846 OM | — | 7.50 | 10.00 | 20.00 | 150.00 |
| | 1847 OM | — | 7.50 | 10.00 | 20.00 | 150.00 |
| | 1848 OM | — | 7.50 | 10.00 | 20.00 | 150.00 |
| | 1849 OM | — | 7.50 | 10.00 | 20.00 | 150.00 |
| | 1850 OM | — | 7.50 | 10.00 | 20.00 | 150.00 |
| | 1851 OM | — | 7.50 | 10.00 | 20.00 | 150.00 |
| | 1852 OM | — | 7.50 | 10.00 | 20.00 | 150.00 |
| | 1853 OM | — | 7.50 | 10.00 | 20.00 | 150.00 |
| | 1854/3 OM | — | 7.50 | 10.00 | 20.00 | 150.00 |
| | 1854 OM | — | 7.50 | 10.00 | 20.00 | 150.00 |
| | 1855/4 OM | — | 7.50 | 10.00 | 20.00 | 150.00 |
| | 1855 OM | — | 7.50 | 10.00 | 20.00 | 150.00 |
| | 1855 MO | — | 7.50 | 10.00 | 20.00 | 150.00 |
| | 1856/5 MO | — | 7.50 | 10.00 | 20.00 | 150.00 |
| | 1856 MO | — | 7.50 | 10.00 | 20.00 | 150.00 |
| | 1857 MO | — | 7.50 | 10.00 | 20.00 | 150.00 |
| | 1858 MO | — | 7.50 | 10.00 | 20.00 | 150.00 |
| | 1859 MO | — | 7.50 | 10.00 | 20.00 | 150.00 |
| | 1860/59 MO | — | 7.50 | 10.00 | 20.00 | 150.00 |
| | 1860 MO | — | 7.50 | 10.00 | 20.00 | 100.00 |
| | 1860 VL | — | 7.50 | 10.00 | 20.00 | 150.00 |
| | 1861 VL | — | 7.50 | 10.00 | 20.00 | 150.00 |
| | 1862 VL | — | 7.50 | 10.00 | 20.00 | 100.00 |
| | 1863 MO | — | 12.50 | 20.00 | 40.00 | 150.00 |
| | 1863 VL | — | 7.50 | 10.00 | 20.00 | 150.00 |
| | 1864 MO | — | 7.50 | 10.00 | 20.00 | 150.00 |
| | 1864 VL | — | 7.50 | 10.00 | 20.00 | 150.00 |
| | 1865 MO | — | 7.50 | 10.00 | 20.00 | 150.00 |
| | 1867 JS | — | 7.50 | 10.00 | 20.00 | 150.00 |
| | 1868 JS | — | 10.00 | 15.00 | 35.00 | 150.00 |
| | 1868 YH | — | 7.50 | 10.00 | 20.00 | 150.00 |
| | 1869 YH | — | 7.50 | 10.00 | 20.00 | 150.00 |
| | 1870 YH | — | 7.50 | 10.00 | 20.00 | 150.00 |

NOTE: Varieties exist.

# 4 REALES

**13.5400 g, .903 SILVER, .3925 oz ASW**
**Mint mark: Ce**
**Obv: Facing eagle.**

| KM# | Date | Mintage | Fine | VF | XF | Unc |
|-----|------|---------|------|-----|-----|-----|
| 375 | 1863 ML large C | | | | | |
| | | — | 200.00 | 500.00 | 850.00 | 4000. |
| | 1863 ML small C | | | | | |
| | | — | 350.00 | 650.00 | 1250. | 4750. |

**Mint mark: C**

| KM# | Date | Mintage | Fine | VF | XF | Unc |
|-----|------|---------|------|-----|-----|-----|
| 375.1 | 1846 CE | — | 400.00 | 550.00 | 900.00 | — |
| | 1850 CE | — | 75.00 | 125.00 | 250.00 | 650.00 |
| | 1852 CE | — | 200.00 | 300.00 | 500.00 | 1250. |
| | 1857 CE | — | — | — | Rare | — |
| | 1858 CE | — | 100.00 | 200.00 | 350.00 | 1000. |
| | 1860 PV | — | 25.00 | 50.00 | 125.00 | 650.00 |

**Mint mark: Ga**

| KM# | Date | Mintage | Fine | VF | XF | Unc |
|-----|------|---------|------|-----|-----|-----|
| 375.2 | 1842/1 JG | — | — | Reported, not confirmed | | |
| | 1842 JG | — | — | Reported, not confirmed | | |
| | 1843 MC | — | 20.00 | 40.00 | 80.00 | 450.00 |
| | 1844/3 MC | — | 30.00 | 60.00 | 125.00 | 450.00 |
| | 1844 MC | — | 20.00 | 40.00 | 80.00 | 450.00 |
| | 1845 MC | — | 20.00 | 40.00 | 80.00 | 450.00 |
| | 1845 JG | — | 20.00 | 40.00 | 80.00 | 450.00 |
| | 1846 JG | — | 20.00 | 40.00 | 80.00 | 450.00 |
| | 1847 JG | — | 40.00 | 80.00 | 150.00 | 450.00 |
| | 1848/7 JG | — | 40.00 | 80.00 | 150.00 | 450.00 |
| | 1849 JG | — | 40.00 | 80.00 | 150.00 | 450.00 |
| | 1850 JG | — | 65.00 | 125.00 | 250.00 | 600.00 |
| | 1852 JG | — | — | — | Rare | — |
| | 1854 JG | — | — | — | Rare | — |
| | 1855 JG | — | 100.00 | 200.00 | 400.00 | 1250. |
| | 1856 JG | — | — | — | Rare | — |
| | 1857/6 JG | — | 65.00 | 125.00 | 250.00 | 650.00 |
| | 1858 JG | — | 125.00 | 250.00 | 450.00 | 1250. |
| | 1859/8 JG | — | 125.00 | 250.00 | 450.00 | 1250. |
| | 1860 JG | — | 850.00 | 1450. | — | — |
| | 1863/2 JG | — | 150.00 | 300.00 | 1250. | 6000. |
| | 1863 JG | — | 150.00 | 300.00 | 1250. | 6000. |

**Mint mark: GC**

| KM# | Date | Mintage | Fine | VF | XF | Unc |
|-----|------|---------|------|-----|-----|-----|
| 375.3 | 1844 MP | — | 1000. | 2000. | 3000. | — |
| | 1845 MP | — | 3000. | 4000. | 5000. | 9000. |
| | 1846 MP | — | 1700. | 2800. | — | — |
| | 1847 MP | — | 1500. | 2500. | — | — |
| | 1849 MP | — | 2000. | 3000. | — | — |
| | 1850 MP | — | 500.00 | 1000. | — | — |

**Mint mark: Go**

| KM# | Date | Mintage | Fine | VF | XF | Unc |
|-----|------|---------|------|-----|-----|-----|
| 375.4 | 1835 PJ | — | 12.50 | 25.00 | 60.00 | 400.00 |
| | 1836/5 PJ | — | 15.00 | 30.00 | 75.00 | 400.00 |
| | 1836 PJ | — | 15.00 | 30.00 | 75.00 | 400.00 |
| | 1837 PJ | — | 12.50 | 25.00 | 60.00 | 400.00 |
| | 1838/7 PJ | — | 15.00 | 30.00 | 75.00 | 400.00 |
| | 1838 PJ | — | 12.50 | 30.00 | 75.00 | 400.00 |
| | 1839 PJ | — | 12.50 | 25.00 | 60.00 | 400.00 |
| | 1840/30 PJ | — | 20.00 | 50.00 | 100.00 | 400.00 |
| | 1841/31 PJ | — | 150.00 | 250.00 | 450.00 | 1250. |
| | 1842 PJ | — | — | — | Rare | — |
| | 1842 PM | — | 15.00 | 30.00 | 75.00 | 400.00 |
| | 1843/2 PM eagle w/convex wings, thick rays | | | | | |
| | | — | 12.50 | 25.00 | 60.00 | 400.00 |
| | 1843 PM eagle w/concave wings, thin rays | | | | | |
| | | — | 12.50 | 25.00 | 60.00 | 400.00 |
| | 1844/3 PM | — | 15.00 | 30.00 | 75.00 | 400.00 |
| | 1844 PM | — | 20.00 | 50.00 | 100.00 | 400.00 |
| | 1845 PM | — | 20.00 | 50.00 | 100.00 | 400.00 |
| | 1846/5 PM | — | 15.00 | 30.00 | 75.00 | 400.00 |
| | 1846 PM | — | 15.00 | 30.00 | 75.00 | 400.00 |
| | 1847/6 PM | — | 15.00 | 30.00 | 75.00 | 400.00 |
| | 1847 PM | — | 15.00 | 30.00 | 75.00 | 400.00 |
| | 1848/7 PM | — | 20.00 | 50.00 | 100.00 | 400.00 |
| | 1848 PM | — | 20.00 | 50.00 | 100.00 | 400.00 |
| | 1849 PF | — | 20.00 | 50.00 | 100.00 | 400.00 |
| | 1850 PF | — | 12.50 | 25.00 | 60.00 | 400.00 |
| | 1851 PF | — | 12.50 | 25.00 | 60.00 | 400.00 |
| | 1852 PF | — | 15.00 | 30.00 | 75.00 | 400.00 |
| | 1852 PF 5/4 | — | 20.00 | 50.00 | 100.00 | 350.00 |
| | 1853 PF | — | 15.00 | 30.00 | 75.00 | 400.00 |
| | 1854 PF large eagle | | | | | |
| | | — | 15.00 | 30.00 | 75.00 | 400.00 |
| | 1854 PF small eagle | | | | | |
| | | — | 15.00 | 30.00 | 75.00 | 400.00 |
| | 1855/4 PF | — | 15.00 | 30.00 | 75.00 | 400.00 |
| | 1855 PF | — | 12.50 | 25.00 | 60.00 | 400.00 |
| | 1856 PF | — | 12.50 | 25.00 | 60.00 | 400.00 |
| | 1857 PF | — | 20.00 | 50.00 | 100.00 | 400.00 |
| | 1858 PF | — | 20.00 | 50.00 | 100.00 | 400.00 |
| | 1859 PF | — | 20.00 | 50.00 | 100.00 | 400.00 |
| | 1860/59 PF | — | 15.00 | 30.00 | 75.00 | 400.00 |
| | 1860 PF | — | 15.00 | 30.00 | 75.00 | 400.00 |
| | 1861/51 PF | — | 15.00 | 30.00 | 75.00 | 400.00 |
| | 1861 PF | — | 20.00 | 50.00 | 100.00 | 400.00 |
| | 1862/1 YE | — | 15.00 | 30.00 | 75.00 | 400.00 |
| | 1862/1 YF | — | 15.00 | 30.00 | 75.00 | 400.00 |
| | 1862 YE/PF | — | 15.00 | 30.00 | 75.00 | 400.00 |
| | 1862 YE | — | 15.00 | 30.00 | 75.00 | 400.00 |
| | 1862 YF | — | 15.00 | 30.00 | 75.00 | 400.00 |
| | 1863/53 YF | — | 15.00 | 30.00 | 75.00 | 400.00 |

| KM# | Date Mintage | Fine | VF | XF | Unc |
|---|---|---|---|---|---|
| 375.4 | 1863 YF/PF — | 15.00 | 30.00 | 75.00 | 400.00 |
| | 1863 YF — | 15.00 | 30.00 | 75.00 | 400.00 |
| | 1867/57 YF/PF | | | | |
| | — | 15.00 | 30.00 | 75.00 | 400.00 |
| | 1868/58 YF/PF | | | | |
| | — | 15.00 | 30.00 | 75.00 | 400.00 |
| | 1868 YF/Y — | 15.00 | 30.00 | 75.00 | 350.00 |
| | 1870 FR — | 15.00 | 30.00 | 75.00 | 400.00 |

**NOTE:** Varieties exist. Some 1862 dates appear to be 1869 because of weak dies.

**Mint mark: Ho**

| KM# | Date Mintage | Fine | VF | XF | Unc |
|---|---|---|---|---|---|
| 375.5 | 1861 FM — | 200.00 | 350.00 | 500.00 | 1850. |
| | 1867/1 PR/FM | | | | |
| | — | 150.00 | 275.00 | 400.00 | 1750. |

**Mint mark: Mo**

| KM# | Date Mintage | Fine | VF | XF | Unc |
|---|---|---|---|---|---|
| 375.6 | 1827/6 JM — | 200.00 | 400.00 | — | — |
| | 1850 GC — | — | — | Rare | — |
| | 1852 GC — | — | — | Rare | — |
| | 1854 GC — | — | — | Rare | — |
| | 1855 GF/GC — | 50.00 | 100.00 | 200.00 | 1250. |
| | 1855 GF — | 100.00 | 200.00 | 350.00 | 1500. |
| | 1856 GF/GC — | 20.00 | 50.00 | 150.00 | 1000. |
| | 1856 GF — | — | — | Rare | — |
| | 1859 FH — | 20.00 | 50.00 | 150.00 | 1000. |
| | 1861 CH — | 15.00 | 35.00 | 125.00 | 1000. |
| | 1862 CH — | 20.00 | 50.00 | 150.00 | 1000. |
| | 1863/2 CH — | 20.00 | 50.00 | 150.00 | 1000. |
| | 1863 CH — | 75.00 | 150.00 | 300.00 | 1500. |
| | 1867 CH — | 20.00 | 50.00 | 150.00 | 1000. |
| | 1868 CH/PH — | 30.00 | 75.00 | 200.00 | 1250. |
| | 1868 CH — | 20.00 | 50.00 | 150.00 | 1000. |
| | 1868 PH — | 30.00 | 75.00 | 200.00 | 1250. |

**Mint mark: O**

| KM# | Date Mintage | Fine | VF | XF | Unc |
|---|---|---|---|---|---|
| 375.7 | 1861 FR ornamental edge | | | | |
| | — | 225.00 | 450.00 | 750.00 | 2750. |
| | 1861 FR herringbone edge | | | | |
| | — | 300.00 | 550.00 | 850.00 | 2850. |
| | 1861 FR obliquely reeded edge | | | | |
| | — | 200.00 | 400.00 | 700.00 | — |

**Mint mark: Pi**

| KM# | Date Mintage | Fine | VF | XF | Unc |
|---|---|---|---|---|---|
| 375.8 | 1837 JS — | 200.00 | 350.00 | — | — |
| | 1838 JS — | 150.00 | 250.00 | 400.00 | 850.00 |
| | 1842 PS — | 50.00 | 100.00 | 200.00 | 550.00 |
| | 1843/2 PS — | 50.00 | 100.00 | 200.00 | 550.00 |
| | 1843/2 PS 3 cut from 8 punch | | | | |
| | — | 50.00 | 100.00 | 200.00 | 550.00 |
| | 1843 AM — | 30.00 | 75.00 | 150.00 | 550.00 |
| | 1843 PS — | 50.00 | 100.00 | 200.00 | 550.00 |
| | 1844 AM — | 30.00 | 75.00 | 150.00 | 550.00 |
| | 1845/4 AM — | 20.00 | 50.00 | 100.00 | 550.00 |
| | 1845 AM — | 20.00 | 50.00 | 100.00 | 550.00 |
| | 1846 AM — | 20.00 | 50.00 | 100.00 | 550.00 |
| | 1847 AM — | 75.00 | 150.00 | 250.00 | 650.00 |
| | 1848 AM — | — | — | Rare | — |
| | 1849 MC/AM — | 20.00 | 50.00 | 100.00 | 550.00 |
| | 1849 MC — | 20.00 | 50.00 | 100.00 | 550.00 |
| | 1849 PS — | 20.00 | 50.00 | 100.00 | 550.00 |
| | 1850 MC — | 20.00 | 50.00 | 100.00 | 550.00 |
| | 1851 MC — | 20.00 | 50.00 | 100.00 | 550.00 |
| | 1852 MC — | 20.00 | 50.00 | 100.00 | 550.00 |
| | 1853 MC — | 20.00 | 50.00 | 100.00 | 550.00 |
| | 1854 MC — | 100.00 | 200.00 | 400.00 | 1100. |
| | 1855 MC — | 175.00 | 300.00 | 500.00 | 1500. |
| | 1856 MC — | 250.00 | 400.00 | 700.00 | — |
| | 1857 MC — | — | — | Rare | — |
| | 1857 PS — | — | — | Rare | — |
| | 1858 MC — | 100.00 | 200.00 | 400.00 | 1000. |
| | 1859 MC — | 2000. | 3000. | — | — |
| | 1860 PS — | 300.00 | 450.00 | 700.00 | — |
| | 1861 PS — | 30.00 | 75.00 | 150.00 | 550.00 |
| | 1861 RO/PS — | 30.00 | 75.00 | 150.00 | 550.00 |
| | 1861 RO — | 50.00 | 100.00 | 200.00 | 550.00 |
| | 1862 RO — | 30.00 | 75.00 | 150.00 | 550.00 |
| | 1863 RO — | 30.00 | 75.00 | 150.00 | 550.00 |
| | 1864 RO — | 1600. | 2600. | — | — |
| | 1868 PS — | 30.00 | 75.00 | 150.00 | 550.00 |
| | 1869/8 PS — | 30.00 | 75.00 | 150.00 | 550.00 |
| | 1869 PS — | 30.00 | 75.00 | 150.00 | 550.00 |

**Mint mark: Zs**

| KM# | Date Mintage | Fine | VF | XF | Unc |
|---|---|---|---|---|---|
| 375.9 | 1830 OM — | 20.00 | 50.00 | 100.00 | 400.00 |
| | 1831 OM — | 15.00 | 30.00 | 75.00 | 400.00 |

| KM# | Date Mintage | Fine | VF | XF | Unc |
|---|---|---|---|---|---|
| 375.9 | 1832/1 OM — | 20.00 | 50.00 | 100.00 | 400.00 |
| | 1832 OM — | 20.00 | 50.00 | 100.00 | 400.00 |
| | 1833/2 OM — | 20.00 | 50.00 | 100.00 | 400.00 |
| | 1833/27 OM — | 15.00 | 30.00 | 75.00 | 400.00 |
| | 1833 OM — | 15.00 | 30.00 | 75.00 | 400.00 |
| | 1834/3 OM — | 20.00 | 50.00 | 100.00 | 400.00 |
| | 1834 OM — | 15.00 | 30.00 | 75.00 | 400.00 |
| | 1835 OM — | 15.00 | 30.00 | 75.00 | 400.00 |
| | 1836 OM — | 15.00 | 30.00 | 75.00 | 400.00 |
| | 1837/5 OM — | 20.00 | 50.00 | 100.00 | 400.00 |
| | 1837/6 OM — | 20.00 | 50.00 | 100.00 | 400.00 |
| | 1837 OM — | 20.00 | 50.00 | 100.00 | 400.00 |
| | 1838/7 OM — | 15.00 | 30.00 | 75.00 | 400.00 |
| | 1839 OM — | 250.00 | 375.00 | 500.00 | — |
| | 1840 OM — | — | — | Rare | — |
| | 1841 OM — | 15.00 | 30.00 | 75.00 | 400.00 |
| | 1842 OM small letters | | | | |
| | — | 75.00 | 150.00 | 300.00 | 850.00 |
| | 1842 OM large letters | | | | |
| | — | 15.00 | 30.00 | 75.00 | 400.00 |
| | 1843 OM — | 15.00 | 30.00 | 75.00 | 400.00 |
| | 1844 OM — | 20.00 | 50.00 | 100.00 | 400.00 |
| | 1845 OM — | 20.00 | 50.00 | 100.00 | 400.00 |
| | 1846/5 OM — | 25.00 | 60.00 | 125.00 | 400.00 |
| | 1846 OM — | 20.00 | 50.00 | 100.00 | 400.00 |
| | 1847 OM — | 15.00 | 30.00 | 75.00 | 400.00 |
| | 1848/6 OM — | 50.00 | 75.00 | 125.00 | 400.00 |
| | 1848 OM — | 20.00 | 50.00 | 100.00 | 400.00 |
| | 1849 OM — | 20.00 | 50.00 | 100.00 | 400.00 |
| | 1850 OM — | 20.00 | 50.00 | 100.00 | 400.00 |
| | 1851 OM — | 15.00 | 30.00 | 75.00 | 400.00 |
| | 1852 OM — | 15.00 | 30.00 | 75.00 | 400.00 |
| | 1853 OM — | 20.00 | 50.00 | 100.00 | 400.00 |
| | 1854/3 OM — | 30.00 | 75.00 | 150.00 | 400.00 |
| | 1855/4 OM — | 20.00 | 50.00 | 100.00 | 400.00 |
| | 1855 OM — | 15.00 | 30.00 | 75.00 | 400.00 |
| | 1856 OM — | 15.00 | 30.00 | 75.00 | 400.00 |
| | 1856 MO — | 20.00 | 50.00 | 100.00 | 400.00 |
| | 1857/5 MO — | 20.00 | 50.00 | 100.00 | 400.00 |
| | 1857 O/M — | 20.00 | 50.00 | 100.00 | 400.00 |
| | 1857 MO — | 15.00 | 30.00 | 75.00 | 400.00 |
| | 1858 MO — | 20.00 | 50.00 | 100.00 | 400.00 |
| | 1859 MO — | 15.00 | 30.00 | 75.00 | 400.00 |
| | 1860/59 MO — | 20.00 | 50.00 | 100.00 | 400.00 |
| | 1860 MO — | 15.00 | 30.00 | 75.00 | 400.00 |
| | 1860 VL — | 20.00 | 50.00 | 100.00 | 400.00 |
| | 1861/0 VL — | 20.00 | 50.00 | 100.00 | 400.00 |
| | 1861 VL — | 15.00 | 30.00 | 75.00 | 400.00 |
| | 1861 VL 6/5 — | 20.00 | 50.00 | 100.00 | 350.00 |
| | 1862/1 VL — | 20.00 | 50.00 | 100.00 | 400.00 |
| | 1862 VL — | 20.00 | 50.00 | 100.00 | 400.00 |
| | 1863 VL — | 20.00 | 50.00 | 100.00 | 400.00 |
| | 1863 MO — | 20.00 | 50.00 | 100.00 | 400.00 |
| | 1864 VL — | 15.00 | 30.00 | 75.00 | 400.00 |
| | 1868 JS — | 20.00 | 50.00 | 100.00 | 400.00 |
| | 1868 YH — | 15.00 | 30.00 | 75.00 | 400.00 |
| | 1869 YH — | 15.00 | 30.00 | 75.00 | 400.00 |
| | 1870 YH — | 15.00 | 30.00 | 75.00 | 400.00 |

## 8 REALES

## Mint mark: A, As

| KM# | Date | Mintage | Fine | VF | XF | Unc |
|---|---|---|---|---|---|---|
| 377 | 1864 PG | — | 750.00 | 1250. | 2000. | — |
| | 1865/4 PG | — | — | — | Rare | — |
| | 1865 PG | — | 500.00 | 750.00 | 1000. | — |
| | 1866/5 PG | — | — | — | Rare | — |
| | 1866 PG | — | 1250. | 2250. | — | — |
| | 1866 DL | — | — | — | Rare | — |
| | 1867 DL | — | 1150. | 2150. | — | — |
| | 1868 DL | — | 50.00 | 90.00 | 150.00 | 300.00 |
| | 1869/8 DL | — | 50.00 | 90.00 | 150.00 | — |
| | 1869 DL | — | 50.00 | 80.00 | 120.00 | 300.00 |
| | 1870 DL | — | 30.00 | 60.00 | 120.00 | 300.00 |
| | 1871 DL | — | 20.00 | 35.00 | 75.00 | 200.00 |
| | 1872 AM/DL | — | 25.00 | 50.00 | 100.00 | 300.00 |
| | 1872 AM | — | 25.00 | 50.00 | 100.00 | 250.00 |
| | 1873 AM | .509 | 15.00 | 25.00 | 50.00 | 150.00 |
| | 1874/3 DL | — | 25.00 | 50.00 | 100.00 | 250.00 |
| | 1874 DL | — | 15.00 | 25.00 | 50.00 | 150.00 |
| | 1875A DL 7/7 | — | 40.00 | 80.00 | 120.00 | 300.00 |
| | 1875A DL | — | 15.00 | 25.00 | 50.00 | 150.00 |
| | 1875AsDL | — | 30.00 | 60.00 | 110.00 | 250.00 |
| | 1876 DL | — | 15.00 | 25.00 | 50.00 | 150.00 |
| | 1877 DL | .515 | 15.00 | 25.00 | 50.00 | 150.00 |
| | 1878 DL | .513 | 15.00 | 25.00 | 50.00 | 150.00 |
| | 1879 DL | — | 20.00 | 35.00 | 75.00 | 175.00 |
| | 1879 ML | — | 30.00 | 60.00 | 125.00 | 350.00 |
| | 1880 ML | — | 12.00 | 15.00 | 30.00 | 140.00 |
| | 1881 ML | .966 | 12.00 | 15.00 | 30.00 | 140.00 |
| | 1882 ML | .480 | 12.00 | 15.00 | 30.00 | 140.00 |
| | 1883 ML | .464 | 12.00 | 15.00 | 30.00 | 140.00 |
| | 1884 ML | — | 12.00 | 15.00 | 30.00 | 140.00 |
| | 1885 ML | .280 | 12.00 | 15.00 | 30.00 | 140.00 |
| | 1886 ML | .857 | 12.00 | 15.00 | 25.00 | 110.00 |
| | 1886/0 As/Cn ML/JD | I.A. | 15.00 | 20.00 | 35.00 | 160.00 |
| | 1887 ML | .650 | 12.00 | 15.00 | 25.00 | 110.00 |
| | 1888/7 ML | .508 | 30.00 | 60.00 | 100.00 | 400.00 |
| | 1888 ML | I.A. | 12.00 | 15.00 | 25.00 | 110.00 |
| | 1889 ML | .427 | 12.00 | 15.00 | 25.00 | 110.00 |
| | 1890 ML | .450 | 12.00 | 15.00 | 25.00 | 110.00 |
| | 1891 ML | .533 | 12.00 | 15.00 | 25.00 | 110.00 |
| | 1892/0 ML | — | 20.00 | 30.00 | 60.00 | 160.00 |
| | 1892 ML | .465 | 12.00 | 15.00 | 25.00 | 110.00 |
| | 1893 ML | .734 | 12.00 | 12.00 | 22.00 | 85.00 |
| | 1894 ML | .725 | 10.00 | 12.00 | 22.00 | 85.00 |
| | 1895 ML | .477 | 10.00 | 12.00 | 22.00 | 85.00 |

NOTE: Varieties exist.

## Mint mark: Ce

| KM# | Date | Mintage | Fine | VF | XF | Unc |
|---|---|---|---|---|---|---|
| 377.1 | 1863 ML | — | 425.00 | 700.00 | 1350. | 3000. |
| | 1863 CeML/PiMC | — | 425.00 | 750.00 | 1500. | 3250. |

## Mint mark: Ca

| KM# | Date | Mintage | Fine | VF | XF | Unc |
|---|---|---|---|---|---|---|
| 377.2 | 1831 MR | — | 1000. | 1750. | 2250. | 3250. |
| | 1832 MR | — | 125.00 | 200.00 | 300.00 | 600.00 |
| | 1833 MR | — | 250.00 | 550.00 | 1000. | — |
| | 1834 MR | — | 300.00 | 600.00 | 1150. | — |
| | 1834 AM | — | 350.00 | 500.00 | 700.00 | — |
| | 1835 AM | — | 150.00 | 250.00 | 475.00 | 900.00 |
| | 1836 AM | — | 100.00 | 200.00 | 300.00 | 600.00 |
| | 1837 AM | — | 550.00 | 1150. | — | — |
| | 1838 AM | — | 100.00 | 200.00 | 300.00 | 600.00 |
| | 1839 RG | — | 750.00 | 1250. | 2500. | — |

| KM# | Date | Mintage | Fine | VF | XF | Unc |
|---|---|---|---|---|---|---|
| 377.2 | 1840 RG 1 dot after date | | | | | |
| | | — | 300.00 | 500.00 | 800.00 | 1500. |
| | 1840 RG 3 dots after date | | | | | |
| | | — | 300.00 | 500.00 | 800.00 | 1500. |
| | 1841 RG | — | 50.00 | 100.00 | 150.00 | 300.00 |
| | 1842 RG | — | 25.00 | 40.00 | 75.00 | 150.00 |
| | 1843 RG | — | 40.00 | 80.00 | 125.00 | 250.00 |
| | 1844/1 RG | — | 35.00 | 70.00 | 100.00 | 200.00 |
| | 1844 RG | — | 25.00 | 40.00 | 75.00 | 160.00 |
| | 1845 RG | — | 25.00 | 40.00 | 75.00 | 160.00 |
| | 1846 RG | — | 30.00 | 60.00 | 100.00 | 250.00 |
| | 1847 RG | — | 40.00 | 80.00 | 125.00 | 250.00 |
| | 1848 RG | — | 35.00 | 70.00 | 125.00 | 250.00 |
| | 1849 RG | — | 30.00 | 60.00 | 100.00 | 200.00 |
| | 1850/40 RG | — | 40.00 | 80.00 | 125.00 | 250.00 |
| | 1850 RG | — | 30.00 | 60.00 | 100.00 | 200.00 |
| | 1851/41 RG | — | 100.00 | 200.00 | 300.00 | 500.00 |
| | 1851 RG | — | 150.00 | 250.00 | 400.00 | 750.00 |
| | 1852/42 RG | — | 150.00 | 250.00 | 400.00 | 750.00 |
| | 1852 RG | — | 150.00 | 250.00 | 400.00 | 750.00 |
| | 1853/43 RG | — | 150.00 | 250.00 | 400.00 | 750.00 |
| | 1853 RG | — | 150.00 | 250.00 | 350.00 | 700.00 |
| | 1854/44 RG | — | 100.00 | 200.00 | 300.00 | 500.00 |
| | 1854 RG | — | 50.00 | 100.00 | 150.00 | 300.00 |
| | 1855/45 RG | — | 100.00 | 200.00 | 350.00 | 650.00 |
| | 1855 RG | — | 50.00 | 100.00 | 150.00 | 300.00 |
| | 1856/45 RG | — | 275.00 | 450.00 | 750.00 | 1250. |
| | 1856/5 JC | — | 400.00 | 700.00 | 1500. | 3500. |
| | 1857 JC/RG | — | 40.00 | 80.00 | 125.00 | 250.00 |
| | 1857 JC | — | 50.00 | 100.00 | 150.00 | 250.00 |
| | 1858 JC | — | 35.00 | 70.00 | 125.00 | 250.00 |
| | 1858 BA | — | 2000. | 3500. | — | — |
| | 1859 JC | — | 40.00 | 80.00 | 125.00 | 250.00 |
| | 1860 JC | — | 20.00 | 40.00 | 90.00 | 175.00 |
| | 1861 JC | — | 15.00 | 25.00 | 55.00 | 125.00 |
| | 1862 JC | — | 15.00 | 25.00 | 55.00 | 125.00 |
| | 1863 JC | — | 20.00 | 35.00 | 75.00 | 150.00 |
| | 1864 JC | — | 20.00 | 35.00 | 75.00 | 150.00 |
| | 1865 JC | — | 100.00 | 200.00 | 350.00 | 600.00 |
| | 1865 FP | — | 1350. | 2150. | 3250. | — |
| | 1866 JC | — | 750.00 | 1150. | 2250. | — |
| | 1866 FP | — | 1000. | 2000. | 3250. | 5000. |
| | 1866 JG | — | 850.00 | 1650. | 2750. | 4250. |
| | 1867 JG | — | 100.00 | 200.00 | 350.00 | 600.00 |
| | 1868 JG | — | 75.00 | 150.00 | 250.00 | 400.00 |
| | 1868 MM | — | 65.00 | 125.00 | 200.00 | 350.00 |
| | 1869 MM | — | 20.00 | 35.00 | 65.00 | 135.00 |
| | 1870 MM | — | 20.00 | 35.00 | 65.00 | 135.00 |
| | 1871/0 MM | — | 15.00 | 25.00 | 55.00 | 125.00 |
| | 1871 MM | — | 15.00 | 25.00 | 55.00 | 125.00 |
| | 1871 MM first M/inverted M | | | | | |
| | | — | 20.00 | 35.00 | 65.00 | 135.00 |
| | 1873 MM | — | 20.00 | 35.00 | 65.00 | 135.00 |
| | 1873 MM/T | | | | | |
| | | — | 15.00 | 25.00 | 55.00 | 125.00 |
| | 1874 MM | — | 12.00 | 15.00 | 30.00 | 100.00 |
| | 1875 MM | — | 12.00 | 15.00 | 30.00 | 100.00 |
| | 1876 MM | — | 12.00 | 15.00 | 30.00 | 100.00 |
| | 1877 EA | .472 | 20.00 | 40.00 | 85.00 | 200.00 |
| | 1877 GR | I.A. | 25.00 | 45.00 | 65.00 | 150.00 |
| | 1877 JM | I.A. | 12.00 | 15.00 | 30.00 | 100.00 |
| | 1877 AV | I.A. | 100.00 | 200.00 | 350.00 | 750.00 |
| | 1878 AV | .439 | 12.00 | 15.00 | 25.00 | 80.00 |
| | 1879 AV | — | 12.00 | 15.00 | 25.00 | 80.00 |
| | 1880 AV | — | 200.00 | 350.00 | 600.00 | 1250. |
| | 1880 PM | — | 500.00 | 800.00 | 1250. | 2500. |
| | 1880 MG normal initials | | | | | |
| | | — | 12.00 | 15.00 | 25.00 | 100.00 |
| | 1880 MG tall initials | | | | | |
| | | — | 12.00 | 15.00 | 25.00 | 100.00 |
| | 1880 MM | — | 12.00 | 15.00 | 25.00 | 100.00 |
| | 1881 MG | 1.085 | 10.00 | 12.00 | 20.00 | 65.00 |
| | 1882 MG | .779 | 10.00 | 12.00 | 20.00 | 65.00 |
| | 1882 MM | I.A. | 10.00 | 12.00 | 20.00 | 65.00 |
| | 1882 MM M sideways | | | | | |
| | | Inc. Ab. | 20.00 | 45.00 | 100.00 | 175.00 |
| | 1883 sideways M MM | | | | | |
| | | .818 | — | — | — | — |
| | 1883/2 MM/G | — | 12.00 | 15.00 | 30.00 | 80.00 |
| | 1883 MM | I.A. | 10.00 | 12.00 | 20.00 | 65.00 |
| | 1884/3 MM | — | 12.00 | 15.00 | 30.00 | 90.00 |
| | 1884 MM | — | 10.00 | 12.00 | 20.00 | 65.00 |
| | 1885/4 MM | | | | | |
| | | 1.345 | 15.00 | 25.00 | 55.00 | 125.00 |

| KM# | Date | Mintage | Fine | VF | XF | Unc |
|---|---|---|---|---|---|---|
| 377.2 | 1885/6 MM | I.A. | 15.00 | 25.00 | 55.00 | 125.00 |
| | 1885 MM | I.A. | 10.00 | 12.00 | 20.00 | 65.00 |
| | 1886 MM | 2.483 | 10.00 | 12.00 | 20.00 | 65.00 |
| | 1887 MM | 2.625 | 10.00 | 12.00 | 20.00 | 65.00 |
| | 1888/7 MM | | | | | |
| | | 2.434 | 15.00 | 25.00 | 65.00 | 135.00 |
| | 1888 MM | I.A. | 10.00 | 12.00 | 20.00 | 65.00 |
| | 1889 MM | 2.681 | 10.00 | 12.00 | 20.00 | 65.00 |
| | 1890/89 MM | — | 15.00 | 25.00 | 55.00 | 125.00 |
| | 1890 MM | 2.137 | 10.00 | 12.00 | 20.00 | 65.00 |
| | 1891/0 MM | | | | | |
| | | 2.268 | 15.00 | 25.00 | 55.00 | 135.00 |
| | 1891 MM | I.A. | 10.00 | 12.00 | 20.00 | 80.00 |
| | 1892 MM | 2.527 | 10.00 | 12.00 | 20.00 | 65.00 |
| | 1893 MM | 2.632 | 10.00 | 12.00 | 20.00 | 65.00 |
| | 1894 MM | 2.642 | 10.00 | 12.00 | 20.00 | 65.00 |
| | 1895 MM | 1.112 | 10.00 | 12.00 | 20.00 | 65.00 |
| | 1895 MM | 1.112 | 10.00 | 12.00 | 20.00 | 65.00 |

NOTE: Varieties exist.

**Mint mark: C, Cn**

| KM# | Date | Mintage | Fine | VF | XF | Unc |
|---|---|---|---|---|---|---|
| 377.3 | 1846 CE | — | 150.00 | 300.00 | 800.00 | 1500. |
| | 1846 CE dot after G | | | | | |
| | | — | 175.00 | 385.00 | 900.00 | 1650. |
| | 1846 CE no dot after G | | | | | |
| | | — | 125.00 | 265.00 | 750.00 | 1450. |
| | 1847 CE | — | 400.00 | 700.00 | 1500. | — |
| | 1848 CE | — | 125.00 | 250.00 | 450.00 | 1000. |
| | 1849 CE | — | 75.00 | 125.00 | 200.00 | 400.00 |
| | 1850 CE | — | 75.00 | 125.00 | 200.00 | 400.00 |
| | 1851 CE | — | 125.00 | 250.00 | 450.00 | 1000. |
| | 1852/1 CE | — | 100.00 | 150.00 | 250.00 | 500.00 |
| | 1852 CE | — | 100.00 | 200.00 | 300.00 | 600.00 |
| | 1853/0 CE | — | 200.00 | 350.00 | 700.00 | 1300. |
| | 1853/2/0 | — | 200.00 | 400.00 | 750.00 | 1400. |
| | 1853 CE thick rays | | | | | |
| | | — | 100.00 | 175.00 | 300.00 | 600.00 |
| | 1853 CE (error:) MEXIGANA | | | | | |
| | | — | 200.00 | 350.00 | 650.00 | — |
| | 1854 CE | — | 750.00 | 1250. | — | — |
| | 1854 CE large eagle & hat | | | | | |
| | | — | 175.00 | 350.00 | 750.00 | 1200. |
| | 1855/6 CE | — | 40.00 | 60.00 | 100.00 | 200.00 |
| | 1855 CE | — | 25.00 | 40.00 | 75.00 | 150.00 |
| | 1856 CE | — | 50.00 | 100.00 | 175.00 | 350.00 |
| | 1857 CE | — | 20.00 | 35.00 | 75.00 | 150.00 |
| | 1858 CE | — | 30.00 | 40.00 | 75.00 | 150.00 |
| | 1859 CE | — | 20.00 | 35.00 | 75.00 | 150.00 |
| | 1860/9 PV/CV | | | | | |
| | | — | 50.00 | 70.00 | 100.00 | 200.00 |
| | 1860/9 PV/E | — | 50.00 | 70.00 | 100.00 | 200.00 |
| | 1860 CE | — | 25.00 | 40.00 | 75.00 | 150.00 |
| | 1860 PV | — | 40.00 | 60.00 | 90.00 | 175.00 |
| | 1861/0 CE | — | 50.00 | 80.00 | 120.00 | 250.00 |
| | 1861 PV/CE | — | 75.00 | 125.00 | 200.00 | 350.00 |
| | 1861 CE | — | 20.00 | 35.00 | 60.00 | 150.00 |
| | 1862 CE | — | 20.00 | 35.00 | 60.00 | 150.00 |
| | 1863/2 CE | — | 30.00 | 50.00 | 75.00 | 200.00 |
| | 1863 CE | — | 20.00 | 30.00 | 60.00 | 150.00 |
| | 1864 CE | — | 30.00 | 60.00 | 100.00 | 300.00 |
| | 1865 CE | — | 125.00 | 200.00 | 325.00 | 650.00 |
| | 1866 CE | — | 400.00 | 750.00 | 1250. | 2250. |
| | 1867 CE | — | 125.00 | 200.00 | 350.00 | 700.00 |
| | 1868/7 CE | — | 30.00 | 40.00 | 75.00 | 150.00 |
| | 1868/8 | — | 50.00 | 100.00 | 150.00 | 300.00 |
| | 1868 CE | — | 30.00 | 40.00 | 75.00 | 150.00 |
| | 1869 CE | — | 30.00 | 40.00 | 75.00 | 175.00 |
| | 1870 CE | — | 50.00 | 100.00 | 150.00 | 350.00 |
| | 1873 MP | — | 50.00 | 100.00 | 150.00 | 300.00 |
| | 1874/3 MP | — | 30.00 | 40.00 | 75.00 | 150.00 |
| | 1874C MP | — | 20.00 | 30.00 | 45.00 | 100.00 |
| | 1874CN MP | — | 125.00 | 200.00 | 300.00 | 600.00 |
| | 1875 MP | — | 12.00 | 15.00 | 22.00 | 80.00 |
| | 1876 GP | — | 12.00 | 15.00 | 30.00 | 90.00 |
| | 1876 CG | — | 12.00 | 15.00 | 22.00 | 80.00 |
| | 1877 CG | .339 | 12.00 | 15.00 | 22.00 | 80.00 |
| | 1877 Gn CG (error) | | | | | |
| | | — | 65.00 | 125.00 | 200.00 | 400.00 |
| | 1877 JA | I.A. | 35.00 | 75.00 | 125.00 | 250.00 |
| | 1878/7 CG | .483 | 35.00 | 75.00 | 125.00 | 250.00 |
| | 1878 CG | I.A. | 15.00 | 25.00 | 35.00 | 125.00 |
| | 1878 JD/CG | — | 25.00 | 35.00 | 50.00 | 150.00 |
| | 1878 JD | I.A. | 15.00 | 20.00 | 30.00 | 125.00 |

| KM# | Date | Mintage | Fine | VF | XF | Unc |
|---|---|---|---|---|---|---|
| 377.3 | 1878 JD D/retrograde D | | | | | |
| | | I.A. | 20.00 | 30.00 | 40.00 | 150.00 |
| | 1879 JD | — | 12.00 | 15.00 | 30.00 | 135.00 |
| | 1880/70 JD | — | 15.00 | 20.00 | 30.00 | 90.00 |
| | 1880 JD | — | 12.00 | 15.00 | 22.00 | 120.00 |
| | 1881/0 JD | | | | | |
| | | 1.032 | 15.00 | 20.00 | 30.00 | 90.00 |
| | 1881C JD | I.A. | 12.00 | 15.00 | 22.00 | 80.00 |
| | 1881CnJD | I.A. | 40.00 | 60.00 | 90.00 | 150.00 |
| | 1882 JD | .397 | 12.00 | 15.00 | 22.00 | 80.00 |
| | 1882 AM | I.A. | 12.00 | 15.00 | 22.00 | 80.00 |
| | 1883 AM | .333 | 12.00 | 15.00 | 22.00 | 125.00 |
| | 1884 AM | — | 12.00 | 15.00 | 22.00 | 80.00 |
| | 1885/6 AM | .227 | 20.00 | 30.00 | 45.00 | 110.00 |
| | 1885C AM | I.A. | 35.00 | 70.00 | 150.00 | 350.00 |
| | 1885CnAM | I.A. | 12.00 | 15.00 | 22.00 | 80.00 |
| | 1885GnAM (error) | | | | | |
| | | Inc. Ab. | 25.00 | 50.00 | 100.00 | 275.00 |
| | 1886 AM | .571 | 12.00 | 15.00 | 22.00 | 80.00 |
| | 1887 AM | .732 | 12.00 | 15.00 | 22.00 | 80.00 |
| | 1888 AM | .768 | 12.00 | 15.00 | 22.00 | 80.00 |
| | 1889 AM | 1.075 | 12.00 | 15.00 | 22.00 | 80.00 |
| | 1890 AM | .874 | 10.00 | 12.00 | 20.00 | 65.00 |
| | 1891 AM | .777 | 10.00 | 12.00 | 20.00 | 65.00 |
| | 1892 AM | .681 | 10.00 | 12.00 | 20.00 | 65.00 |
| | 1893 AM | 1.144 | 10.00 | 12.00 | 20.00 | 65.00 |
| | 1894 AM | 2.118 | 10.00 | 12.00 | 20.00 | 65.00 |
| | 1895 AM | 1.834 | 10.00 | 12.00 | 20.00 | 65.00 |
| | 1896 AM | 2.134 | 10.00 | 12.00 | 20.00 | 65.00 |
| | 1897 AM | 1.580 | 10.00 | 12.00 | 20.00 | 65.00 |

NOTE: Varieties exist.

**Mint mark: Do**

| KM# | Date | Mintage | Fine | VF | XF | Unc |
|---|---|---|---|---|---|---|
| 377.4 | 1825 RL | — | 30.00 | 65.00 | 150.00 | 375.00 |
| | 1826 RL | — | 40.00 | 85.00 | 200.00 | 475.00 |
| | 1827/6 RL | — | 35.00 | 60.00 | 85.00 | 200.00 |
| | 1827/8 RL | — | 150.00 | 275.00 | 500.00 | — |
| | 1827 RL | — | 30.00 | 50.00 | 90.00 | 200.00 |
| | 1828/7 RL | — | 35.00 | 60.00 | 90.00 | 200.00 |
| | 1828 RL | — | 25.00 | 50.00 | 80.00 | 175.00 |
| | 1829 RL | — | 25.00 | 50.00 | 80.00 | 175.00 |
| | 1830 RM B on eagles claw | | | | | |
| | | — | 25.00 | 50.00 | 90.00 | 200.00 |
| | 1831 RM B on eagles claw | | | | | |
| | | — | 20.00 | 30.00 | 60.00 | 150.00 |
| | 1832 RM Mexican dies, B on eagles claw | | | | | |
| | | — | 35.00 | 60.00 | 120.00 | 300.00 |
| | 1832/1 RM/RL French dies | | | | | |
| | | — | 25.00 | 35.00 | 75.00 | 165.00 |
| | 1833/2 RM/RL | | | | | |
| | | — | 20.00 | 35.00 | 75.00 | 165.00 |
| | 1833 RM | — | 15.00 | 30.00 | 60.00 | 150.00 |
| | 1834/3/2 RM/RL | | | | | |
| | | — | 20.00 | 35.00 | 75.00 | 165.00 |
| | 1834 RM | — | 15.00 | 25.00 | 50.00 | 150.00 |
| | 1835/4 RM/RL | | | | | |
| | | — | 20.00 | 35.00 | 65.00 | 150.00 |

| KM# | Date Mintage | Fine | VF | XF | Unc |
|---|---|---|---|---|---|
| 377.4 | 1835 RM — | 20.00 | 35.00 | 65.00 | 150.00 |
| | 1836/1 RM — | 20.00 | 30.00 | 65.00 | 150.00 |
| | 1836/4 RM — | 20.00 | 35.00 | 65.00 | 150.00 |
| | 1836/5/4 RM/RL | | | | |
| | — | 75.00 | 150.00 | 250.00 | 500.00 |
| | 1836 RM — | 20.00 | 30.00 | 55.00 | 150.00 |
| | 1836 RM M on snake | | | | |
| | — | 20.00 | 30.00 | 55.00 | 150.00 |
| | 1837/1 RM — | 20.00 | 30.00 | 55.00 | 150.00 |
| | 1837 RM — | 20.00 | 30.00 | 55.00 | 150.00 |
| | 1838/1 RM — | 20.00 | 30.00 | 60.00 | 165.00 |
| | 1838/7 RM — | 20.00 | 30.00 | 60.00 | 165.00 |
| | 1838 RM — | 20.00 | 30.00 | 55.00 | 150.00 |
| | 1839/1 RM/RL | | | | |
| | — | 20.00 | 30.00 | 55.00 | 150.00 |
| | 1839/1 RM — | 20.00 | 30.00 | 55.00 | 150.00 |
| | 1839 RM — | 20.00 | 30.00 | 55.00 | 150.00 |
| | 1840/38/31 RM | | | | |
| | — | 20.00 | 30.00 | 55.00 | 150.00 |
| | 1840/39 RM — | 20.00 | 30.00 | 55.00 | 150.00 |
| | 1840 RM — | 20.00 | 30.00 | 55.00 | 150.00 |
| | 1841/31 RM — | 65.00 | 125.00 | 275.00 | 450.00 |
| | 1841/39 RM/L— | 25.00 | 50.00 | 85.00 | 200.00 |
| | 1841/39 RM — | 25.00 | 50.00 | 85.00 | 200.00 |
| | 1842/31 RM B below cactus | | | | |
| | — | 125.00 | 250.00 | 400.00 | 750.00 |
| | 1842/31 RM — | 40.00 | 80.00 | 125.00 | 250.00 |
| | 1842/32 RM — | 40.00 | 80.00 | 125.00 | 300.00 |
| | 1842 RM eagle of 1832-41 | | | | |
| | — | 20.00 | 30.00 | 55.00 | 150.00 |
| | 1842 RM pre 1832 eagle resumed | | | | |
| | — | 20.00 | 30.00 | 55.00 | 150.00 |
| | 1842 RM — | 40.00 | 80.00 | 125.00 | 250.00 |
| | 1843/33 RM — | 50.00 | 90.00 | 150.00 | 250.00 |
| | 1843 RM — | 50.00 | 90.00 | 150.00 | 250.00 |
| | 1844/34 RM — | 100.00 | 200.00 | 300.00 | 500.00 |
| | 1844/35 RM — | 100.00 | 200.00 | 300.00 | 500.00 |
| | 1844/43 RM — | 60.00 | 120.00 | 220.00 | 425.00 |
| | 1845/31 RM — | 100.00 | 200.00 | 300.00 | 500.00 |
| | 1845/34 RM — | 35.00 | 75.00 | 125.00 | 250.00 |
| | 1845/35 RM — | 35.00 | 75.00 | 125.00 | 250.00 |
| | 1845 RM — | 20.00 | 30.00 | 55.00 | 150.00 |
| | 1846/31 RM — | 20.00 | 30.00 | 55.00 | 150.00 |
| | 1846/36 RM — | 20.00 | 30.00 | 55.00 | 150.00 |
| | 1846 RM — | 20.00 | 30.00 | 55.00 | 150.00 |
| | 1847 RM — | 25.00 | 50.00 | 80.00 | 185.00 |
| | 1848/7 RM — | 125.00 | 250.00 | 400.00 | 750.00 |
| | 1848/7 CM/RM | | | | |
| | — | 100.00 | 200.00 | 350.00 | 700.00 |
| | 1848 CM/RM— | 100.00 | 200.00 | 350.00 | 700.00 |
| | 1848 RM — | 100.00 | 200.00 | 300.00 | 600.00 |
| | 1848 CM — | 50.00 | 100.00 | 200.00 | 400.00 |
| | 1849/39 CM — | 100.00 | 200.00 | 350.00 | 700.00 |
| | 1849 CM — | 65.00 | 125.00 | 250.00 | 550.00 |
| | 1849 JMR/CM oval 0 | | | | |
| | — | 200.00 | 325.00 | 450.00 | 800.00 |
| | 1849 DoJMR oval O | | | | |
| | — | 200.00 | 400.00 | 600.00 | 1000. |
| | 1849 DoJMR round O | | | | |
| | — | 200.00 | 400.00 | 600.00 | 1000. |
| | 1850 JMR — | 100.00 | 150.00 | 250.00 | 500.00 |
| | 1851/0 JMR — | 65.00 | 125.00 | 225.00 | 475.00 |
| | 1851 JMR — | 100.00 | 150.00 | 250.00 | 500.00 |
| | 1852 CP/JMR | | | | |
| | — | 450.00 | 800.00 | 1500. | — |
| | 1852 CP — | 750.00 | 1200. | 2250. | — |
| | 1852 JMR — | 175.00 | 250.00 | 375.00 | 650.00 |
| | 1853 CP/JMR | | | | |
| | — | 125.00 | 235.00 | 350.00 | 600.00 |
| | 1853 CP — | 200.00 | 350.00 | 600.00 | 1200. |
| | 1854 CP — | 25.00 | 35.00 | 65.00 | 300.00 |
| | 1855 CP eagle type of 1854 | | | | |
| | — | 50.00 | 100.00 | 175.00 | 350.00 |
| | 1855 CP eagle type of 1856 | | | | |
| | — | 50.00 | 100.00 | 175.00 | 350.00 |
| | 1856 CP — | 50.00 | 100.00 | 175.00 | 350.00 |
| | 1857 CP — | 35.00 | 65.00 | 125.00 | 250.00 |
| | 1858/7 CP — | 25.00 | 35.00 | 70.00 | 165.00 |
| | 1858 CP — | 20.00 | 30.00 | 60.00 | 165.00 |
| | 1859 CP — | 20.00 | 30.00 | 60.00 | 165.00 |
| | 1860/59 CP — | 30.00 | 50.00 | 100.00 | 200.00 |
| | 1860 CP — | 20.00 | 30.00 | 60.00 | 165.00 |
| | 1861/0 CP — | 20.00 | 30.00 | 60.00 | 165.00 |
| | 1861 CP — | 20.00 | 30.00 | 50.00 | 125.00 |

| KM# | Date Mintage | Fine | VF | XF | Unc |
|---|---|---|---|---|---|
| 377.4 | 1862/1 CP — | 25.00 | 35.00 | 60.00 | 125.00 |
| | 1862 CP — | 20.00 | 30.00 | 60.00 | 175.00 |
| | 1863/1 CP — | 30.00 | 60.00 | 90.00 | 200.00 |
| | 1863/2 CP — | 25.00 | 50.00 | 75.00 | 175.00 |
| | 1863/53 CP — | 30.00 | 60.00 | 90.00 | 200.00 |
| | 1863 CP — | 25.00 | 50.00 | 75.00 | 175.00 |
| | 1864 CP — | 100.00 | 150.00 | 250.00 | 500.00 |
| | 1864 LT — | 25.00 | 40.00 | 80.00 | 175.00 |
| | 1864 LT/T — | 25.00 | 40.00 | 80.00 | 175.00 |
| | 1864 LT/CP — | 50.00 | 100.00 | 175.00 | 350.00 |
| | 1865 LT — | — | — | Rare | — |
| | 1866/4 CM — | 2750. | 5500. | — | — |
| | 1866 CM — | 1750. | 3250. | 5500. | 8000. |
| | 1867 CM — | 3500. | — | — | — |
| | 1867/6 CP — | 200.00 | 400.00 | 600.00 | 1200. |
| | 1867 CP — | 175.00 | 300.00 | 500.00 | 1000. |
| | 1867 CP/CM — | 125.00 | 250.00 | 400.00 | 900.00 |
| | 1867 CP/LT — | 200.00 | 400.00 | 650.00 | 1250. |
| | 1868 CP — | 25.00 | 40.00 | 80.00 | 175.00 |
| | 1869 CP — | 20.00 | 30.00 | 50.00 | 135.00 |
| | 1870/69 CP — | 20.00 | 30.00 | 50.00 | 125.00 |
| | 1870/9 CP — | 20.00 | 30.00 | 50.00 | 125.00 |
| | 1870 CP — | 20.00 | 30.00 | 50.00 | 125.00 |
| | 1873 CP — | 125.00 | 225.00 | 325.00 | 600.00 |
| | 1873 CM — | 30.00 | 50.00 | 100.00 | 200.00 |
| | 1874/3 CM — | 12.00 | 15.00 | 22.00 | 100.00 |
| | 1874 CM — | 10.00 | 15.00 | 22.00 | 75.00 |
| | 1874 JH — | 1150. | 1750. | 2750. | — |
| | 1875 CM — | 10.00 | 15.00 | 22.00 | 80.00 |
| | 1875 JH — | 80.00 | 150.00 | 250.00 | 450.00 |
| | 1876 CM — | 10.00 | 15.00 | 22.00 | 80.00 |
| | 1877 CM .431 | 1450. | 2500. | — | — |
| | 1877 CP I.A. | 10.00 | 15.00 | 22.00 | 80.00 |
| | 1877 JMP I.A. | 750.00 | 1250. | 2000. | — |
| | 1878 PE .409 | 15.00 | 25.00 | 40.00 | 100.00 |
| | 1878 TB I.A. | 10.00 | 15.00 | 25.00 | 90.00 |
| | 1879 TB — | 10.00 | 15.00 | 22.00 | 80.00 |
| | 1880/70 TB — | 60.00 | 100.00 | 175.00 | 350.00 |
| | 1880/70 TB/JP | | | | |
| | — | 150.00 | 250.00 | 375.00 | 650.00 |
| | 1880/70 JP — | 15.00 | 25.00 | 40.00 | 100.00 |
| | 1880 TB — | 150.00 | 250.00 | 375.00 | 650.00 |
| | 1880 JP — | 10.00 | 15.00 | 22.00 | 80.00 |
| | 1881 JP .928 | 10.00 | 15.00 | 25.00 | 90.00 |
| | 1882 JP .414 | 10.00 | 15.00 | 22.00 | 80.00 |
| | 1882 MC/JP | | | | |
| | Inc. Ab. | 30.00 | 60.00 | 100.00 | 200.00 |
| | 1882 MC I.A. | 25.00 | 50.00 | 75.00 | 150.00 |
| | 1883/73 MC | | | | |
| | .452 | 15.00 | 25.00 | 40.00 | 90.00 |
| | 1883 MC I.A. | 10.00 | 15.00 | 22.00 | 80.00 |
| | 1884/3 MC — | 15.00 | 25.00 | 40.00 | 90.00 |
| | 1884 MC — | 10.00 | 15.00 | 22.00 | 80.00 |
| | 1885 MC .547 | 10.00 | 12.00 | 20.00 | 70.00 |
| | 1885 JB I.A. | 25.00 | 35.00 | 50.00 | 125.00 |
| | 1886/5 MC — | 15.00 | 25.00 | 40.00 | 100.00 |
| | 1886/3 MC — | 15.00 | 25.00 | 40.00 | 100.00 |
| | 1886 MC I.A. | 10.00 | 12.00 | 20.00 | 70.00 |
| | 1887 MC 1.004 | 10.00 | 12.00 | 20.00 | 70.00 |
| | 1888/7 MC — | 65.00 | 125.00 | 250.00 | 450.00 |
| | 1888 MC .996 | 10.00 | 12.00 | 20.00 | 70.00 |
| | 1889 MC .874 | 10.00 | 12.00 | 20.00 | 70.00 |
| | 1890 MC 1.119 | 10.00 | 12.00 | 20.00 | 70.00 |
| | 1890 JP I.A. | 10.00 | 12.00 | 20.00 | 70.00 |
| | 1891 JP 1.487 | 10.00 | 12.00 | 20.00 | 70.00 |
| | 1892 JP 1.597 | 10.00 | 12.00 | 20.00 | 70.00 |
| | 1892 ND I.A. | 25.00 | 50.00 | 100.00 | 200.00 |
| | 1893 ND 1.617 | 10.00 | 12.00 | 20.00 | 70.00 |
| | 1894 ND 1.537 | 10.00 | 12.00 | 20.00 | 70.00 |
| | 1895/3 ND .761 | 15.00 | 25.00 | 40.00 | 100.00 |
| | 1895 ND I.A. | 10.00 | 12.00 | 20.00 | 70.00 |
| | 1895 ND/P — | 15.00 | 25.00 | 40.00 | 100.00 |

**NOTE:** Varieties exist.

**Mint mark: EoMo**

| KM# | Date | Mintage | Fine | VF | XF | Unc |
|---|---|---|---|---|---|---|
| 377.5 | 1828 LF/LP | — | 350.00 | 850.00 | 2150. | — |
| | 1828 LF | — | 350.00 | 850.00 | 2150. | 5500. |
| | 1829 LF | — | 300.00 | 750.00 | 1850. | 4500. |
| | 1830/20 LF | — | 1250. | 2750. | 4250. | — |
| | 1830 LF | — | 1000. | 2000. | 3250. | 6000. |

**Mint mark: Ga**

| KM# | Date | Mintage | Fine | VF | XF | Unc |
|---|---|---|---|---|---|---|
| 377.6 | 1825 FS | — | 150.00 | 275.00 | 475.00 | 1000. |
| | 1826/5 FS | — | 125.00 | 250.00 | 450.00 | 1000. |
| | 1826 FS | — | 125.00 | 250.00 | 450.00 | 1000. |
| | 1827/87 FS | — | 125.00 | 250.00 | 450.00 | 1000. |
| | 1827 FS | — | 125.00 | 250.00 | 450.00 | 1000. |
| | 1287 FS (error) | 8500. | 9500. | — | — | — |
| | 1828 FS | — | 200.00 | 375.00 | 550.00 | 1200. |
| | 1829/8 FS | — | 200.00 | 375.00 | 550.00 | 1200. |
| | 1829 FS | — | 175.00 | 325.00 | 475.00 | 950.00 |
| | 1830/29 FS | — | 100.00 | 175.00 | 300.00 | 600.00 |
| | 1830 FS | — | 100.00 | 175.00 | 300.00 | 600.00 |
| | 1830 LP/FS | — | 800.00 | 1450. | — | — |
| | 1831 LP | — | 200.00 | 400.00 | 600.00 | 1200. |
| | 1831 FS/LP | — | 300.00 | 500.00 | 750.00 | 1500. |
| | 1831 FS | — | 125.00 | 275.00 | 400.00 | — |
| | 1832/1 FS | — | 50.00 | 100.00 | 175.00 | 300.00 |
| | 1832/1 FS/LP | — | 50.00 | 100.00 | 175.00 | 300.00 |
| | 1832 FS/LP | — | 75.00 | 150.00 | 285.00 | 550.00 |
| | 1832 FS | — | 25.00 | 50.00 | 100.00 | 225.00 |
| | 1833/2/1 FS/LP | — | 45.00 | 75.00 | 125.00 | 250.00 |
| | 1833/2 FS | — | 25.00 | 50.00 | 100.00 | 225.00 |
| | 1834/2 FS | — | 60.00 | 125.00 | 200.00 | 350.00 |
| | 1834/3 FS | — | 60.00 | 125.00 | 200.00 | 350.00 |
| | 1834/0 FS | — | 60.00 | 125.00 | 200.00 | 350.00 |
| | 1834 FS | — | 50.00 | 100.00 | 150.00 | 300.00 |
| | 1835 FS | — | 25.00 | 50.00 | 100.00 | 225.00 |
| | 1836/5 FS | — | 175.00 | 350.00 | — | — |
| | 1836/1 JG/FS | — | 40.00 | 80.00 | 125.00 | 250.00 |
| | 1836 FS | — | 275.00 | 450.00 | 750.00 | — |
| | 1836 JG/FS | — | 25.00 | 50.00 | 100.00 | 250.00 |
| | 1836 JG | — | 25.00 | 50.00 | 100.00 | 250.00 |
| | 1837/6 JG/FS | — | 50.00 | 100.00 | 175.00 | 300.00 |
| | 1837/6 JG | — | 45.00 | 90.00 | 160.00 | 285.00 |
| | 1837 JG | — | 40.00 | 80.00 | 125.00 | 250.00 |
| | 1838/7 JG | — | 100.00 | 175.00 | 300.00 | 550.00 |
| | 1838 JG | — | 100.00 | 150.00 | 275.00 | 500.00 |
| | 1839 MC | — | 100.00 | 200.00 | 350.00 | 600.00 |

| KM# | Date | Mintage | Fine | VF | XF | Unc |
|---|---|---|---|---|---|---|
| 377.6 | 1839 MC/JG | — | 100.00 | 200.00 | 300.00 | 550.00 |
| | 1839 JG | — | 60.00 | 125.00 | 200.00 | 350.00 |
| | 1840/30 MC | — | 50.00 | 75.00 | 150.00 | 275.00 |
| | 1840 MC | — | 30.00 | 60.00 | 125.00 | 250.00 |
| | 1841 MC | — | 30.00 | 60.00 | 125.00 | 250.00 |
| | 1842/1 JG/MG | — | 100.00 | 150.00 | 250.00 | 450.00 |
| | 1842/1 JG/MC | — | 100.00 | 150.00 | 250.00 | 450.00 |
| | 1842 JG | — | 25.00 | 50.00 | 100.00 | 225.00 |
| | 1842 JG/MG | — | 25.00 | 50.00 | 100.00 | 225.00 |
| | 1843/2 MC/JG | — | 25.00 | 50.00 | 100.00 | 225.00 |
| | 1843 MC/JG | — | 25.00 | 50.00 | 100.00 | 225.00 |
| | 1843 JG | — | 400.00 | 600.00 | 900.00 | 1650. |
| | 1843 MC | — | 50.00 | 100.00 | 150.00 | 300.00 |
| | 1844 MC | — | 50.00 | 100.00 | 150.00 | 300.00 |
| | 1845 MC | — | 75.00 | 150.00 | 300.00 | 700.00 |
| | 1845 JG | — | 500.00 | 850.00 | 1250. | 1850. |
| | 1846 JG | — | 40.00 | 80.00 | 150.00 | 300.00 |
| | 1847 JG | — | 100.00 | 150.00 | 225.00 | 400.00 |
| | 1848/7 JG | — | 55.00 | 85.00 | 125.00 | 250.00 |
| | 1848 JG | — | 50.00 | 75.00 | 100.00 | 225.00 |
| | 1849 JG | — | 90.00 | 125.00 | 175.00 | 325.00 |
| | 1849/39 JG | — | 250.00 | 500.00 | — | — |
| | 1850 JG | — | 50.00 | 100.00 | 150.00 | 300.00 |
| | 1851 JG | — | 125.00 | 200.00 | 350.00 | 650.00 |
| | 1852 JG | — | 100.00 | 150.00 | 250.00 | 450.00 |
| | 1853/2 JG | — | 125.00 | 175.00 | 250.00 | 475.00 |
| | 1853 JG | — | 90.00 | 125.00 | 175.00 | 300.00 |
| | 1854/3 JG | — | 65.00 | 90.00 | 125.00 | 250.00 |
| | 1854 JG | — | 50.00 | 75.00 | 110.00 | 225.00 |
| | 1855/4 JG | — | 50.00 | 100.00 | 150.00 | 275.00 |
| | 1855 JG | — | 25.00 | 50.00 | 100.00 | 225.00 |
| | 1856/4 JG | — | 60.00 | 125.00 | 175.00 | 300.00 |
| | 1856/5 56 | — | 60.00 | 125.00 | 175.00 | 300.00 |
| | 1856 JG | — | 50.00 | 100.00 | 150.00 | 275.00 |
| | 1857 JG | — | 50.00 | 100.00 | 225.00 | 450.00 |
| | 1858 JG | — | 100.00 | 150.00 | 300.00 | 500.00 |
| | 1859/7 JG | — | 25.00 | 50.00 | 110.00 | 225.00 |
| | 1859/8 JG | — | 25.00 | 50.00 | 110.00 | 225.00 |
| | 1859 JG | — | 20.00 | 40.00 | 80.00 | 175.00 |
| | 1860 JG w/o dot | — | 350.00 | 750.00 | 1200. | 2250. |
| | 1860 JG dot in loop of snakes tail (base alloy) | — | 2000. | 3250. | 4500. | — |
| | 1861 JG | — | 2200. | 5750. | — | — |
| | 1862 JG | — | 850.00 | 1350. | 2750. | 4500. |
| | 1863/52 JG | — | — | — | — | — |
| | 1863/59 JG | — | 45.00 | 50.00 | 85.00 | 145.00 |
| | 1863/2 JG | — | 30.00 | 50.00 | 90.00 | 175.00 |
| | 1863/4 JG | — | 45.00 | 75.00 | 150.00 | 250.00 |
| | 1863 JG | — | 25.00 | 45.00 | 75.00 | 150.00 |
| | 1863 FV | — | — | — | Rare | — |
| | 1867 JM | — | — | — | Rare | — |
| | 1868/7 JM | — | 50.00 | 75.00 | 125.00 | 200.00 |
| | 1868 JM | — | 50.00 | 75.00 | 125.00 | 200.00 |
| | 1869 JM | — | 50.00 | 75.00 | 125.00 | 200.00 |
| | 1869 IC | — | 75.00 | 125.00 | 200.00 | 375.00 |
| | 1870/60 IC | — | 60.00 | 90.00 | 150.00 | 275.00 |
| | 1870 IC | — | 60.00 | 90.00 | 150.00 | 275.00 |
| | 1873 IC | — | 15.00 | 25.00 | 50.00 | 125.00 |
| | 1874 IC | — | 10.00 | 15.00 | 22.00 | 90.00 |
| | 1874 MC | — | 25.00 | 50.00 | 100.00 | 200.00 |
| | 1875 IC | — | 15.00 | 30.00 | 60.00 | 125.00 |
| | 1875 MC | — | 10.00 | 15.00 | 22.00 | 90.00 |
| | 1876 IC | .559 | 15.00 | 30.00 | 50.00 | 100.00 |
| | 1876 MC | I.A. | 125.00 | 175.00 | 250.00 | 375.00 |
| | 1877 IC | .928 | 10.00 | 15.00 | 22.00 | 90.00 |
| | 1877/6 JA | — | 10.00 | 15.00 | 22.00 | 90.00 |
| | 1877 JA | I.A. | 10.00 | 15.00 | 22.00 | 90.00 |
| | 1878 JA | .764 | 10.00 | 15.00 | 22.00 | 90.00 |
| | 1879 JA | — | 10.00 | 15.00 | 22.00 | 90.00 |
| | 1880/70 FS | — | 15.00 | 25.00 | 50.00 | 125.00 |
| | 1880 JA | — | 10.00 | 15.00 | 22.00 | 90.00 |
| | 1880 FS | — | 10.00 | 15.00 | 22.00 | 90.00 |
| | 1881 FS | 1.300 | 10.00 | 15.00 | 22.00 | 90.00 |
| | 1882/1 FS | .537 | 15.00 | 25.00 | 50.00 | 125.00 |
| | 1882 FS | I.A. | 10.00 | 15.00 | 22.00 | 90.00 |
| | 1882 TB/FS | I.A. | 50.00 | 100.00 | 175.00 | 300.00 |
| | 1882 TB | I.A. | 50.00 | 100.00 | 175.00 | 300.00 |
| | 1883 TB | .561 | 15.00 | 25.00 | 40.00 | 125.00 |
| | 1884 TB | — | 10.00 | 12.00 | 20.00 | 85.00 |
| | 1884 AH | — | 10.00 | 12.00 | 20.00 | 85.00 |

| KM# | Date | Mintage | Fine | VF | XF | Unc |
|---|---|---|---|---|---|---|
| | 1885 AH | .443 | 10.00 | 12.00 | 20.00 | 90.00 |
| | 1885 JS | I.A. | 30.00 | 60.00 | 100.00 | 200.00 |
| | 1886 JS/H | — | 10.00 | 12.00 | 20.00 | 85.00 |
| | 1886 JS | 1.039 | 10.00 | 12.00 | 20.00 | 85.00 |
| | 1887 JS | .878 | 10.00 | 12.00 | 20.00 | 85.00 |
| | 1888 JS | 1.159 | 10.00 | 12.00 | 20.00 | 85.00 |
| | 1889 JS | 1.583 | 10.00 | 12.00 | 20.00 | 85.00 |
| | 1890 JS | 1.658 | 10.00 | 12.00 | 20.00 | 85.00 |
| | 1891 JS | 1.507 | 10.00 | 12.00 | 20.00 | 85.00 |
| | 1892/1 JS | | | | | |
| | | 1.627 | 15.00 | 25.00 | 50.00 | 125.00 |
| | 1892 JS | I.A. | 10.00 | 12.00 | 20.00 | 80.00 |
| | 1893 JS | 1.952 | 10.00 | 12.00 | 20.00 | 80.00 |
| | 1894 JS | 2.046 | 10.00 | 12.00 | 20.00 | 80.00 |
| | 1895/3 JS | — | 12.00 | 20.00 | 35.00 | 100.00 |
| | 1895 JS | 1.146 | 10.00 | 12.00 | 20.00 | 65.00 |

**NOTE:** Varieties exist. The 1830 LP/FS is currently only known with a Philippine countermark.

**Mint mark: GC**

| KM# | Date | Mintage | Fine | VF | XF | Unc |
|---|---|---|---|---|---|---|
| 377.7 | 1844 MP | — | 350.00 | 500.00 | 1000. | 2000. |
| | 1844 MP (error) reversed S in Ds, Gs | | | | | |
| | | — | 400.00 | 600.00 | 1200. | 2250. |
| | 1845 MP eagle's tail square | | | | | |
| | | — | 125.00 | 200.00 | 325.00 | 700.00 |
| | 1845 MP eagle's tail round | | | | | |
| | | — | 175.00 | 350.00 | 650.00 | 1200. |
| | 1846 MP eagle's tail square | | | | | |
| | | — | 175.00 | 350.00 | 750.00 | 1650. |
| | 1846 MP eagle's tail round | | | | | |
| | | — | 125.00 | 200.00 | 350.00 | 750.00 |
| | 1847 MP | — | 150.00 | 250.00 | 400.00 | 800.00 |
| | 1848 MP | — | 175.00 | 300.00 | 500.00 | 900.00 |
| | 1849 MP | — | 175.00 | 300.00 | 525.00 | 1000. |
| | 1850 MP | — | 175.00 | 300.00 | 575.00 | 1100. |
| | 1851 MP | — | 300.00 | 500.00 | 900.00 | 1600. |
| | 1852 MP | — | 350.00 | 600.00 | 1250. | 2500. |

**Mint mark: Go**

| KM# | Date | Mintage | Fine | VF | XF | Unc |
|---|---|---|---|---|---|---|
| 377.8 | 1825 JJ | — | 40.00 | 70.00 | 150.00 | 300.00 |
| | 1825 JJ error mint mark G | | | | | |
| | | — | 1250. | 1650. | — | — |
| | 1826 JJ straight J's | | | | | |
| | | — | 40.00 | 80.00 | 175.00 | 350.00 |
| | 1826 JJ full J's | | | | | |
| | | — | 30.00 | 60.00 | 125.00 | 250.00 |
| | 1826 MJ | — | 250.00 | 450.00 | 850.00 | — |
| | 1827 MJ | — | 40.00 | 75.00 | 125.00 | 250.00 |
| | 1827 MJ/JJ | — | 40.00 | 75.00 | 125.00 | 250.00 |
| | 1827 MR | — | 100.00 | 200.00 | 350.00 | 600.00 |
| | 1828 MJ error mint mark Goo | | | | | |
| | | — | — | — | — | — |
| | 1828 MJ | — | 30.00 | 60.00 | 125.00 | 250.00 |
| | 1828/7 MR | — | 150.00 | 300.00 | 600.00 | 1200. |
| | 1828 MR | — | 150.00 | 300.00 | 600.00 | 1200. |
| | 1829 MJ | — | 20.00 | 35.00 | 55.00 | 165.00 |
| | 1830 MJ oblong beading and narrow J | | | | | |
| | | — | 20.00 | 30.00 | 55.00 | 165.00 |
| | 1830 MJ regular beading and wide J | | | | | |
| | | — | 20.00 | 30.00 | 55.00 | 165.00 |
| | 1831 MJ colon after date | | | | | |
| | | — | 12.00 | 20.00 | 40.00 | 150.00 |
| | 1831 MJ 2 stars after date | | | | | |
| | | — | 12.00 | 20.00 | 40.00 | 150.00 |
| | 1832 MJ | — | 12.00 | 20.00 | 40.00 | 150.00 |
| | 1832 MJ 1 of date over inverted 1 | | | | | |
| | | — | 20.00 | 35.00 | 65.00 | 175.00 |
| | 1833 MJ/1 | — | 20.00 | 35.00 | 65.00 | 175.00 |

| KM# | Date | Mintage | Fine | VF | XF | Unc |
|---|---|---|---|---|---|---|
| 377.8 | 1833 MJ | — | 12.00 | 20.00 | 40.00 | 150.00 |
| | 1833 JM | — | 400.00 | 750.00 | 1250. | 2500. |
| | 1834 PJ | — | 12.00 | 20.00 | 40.00 | 150.00 |
| | 1835 PJ star on cap | | | | | |
| | | — | 12.00 | 20.00 | 40.00 | 150.00 |
| | 1835 PJ dot on cap | | | | | |
| | | — | 12.00 | 20.00 | 40.00 | 150.00 |
| | 1836 PJ | — | 12.00 | 20.00 | 40.00 | 150.00 |
| | 1837 PJ | — | 12.00 | 20.00 | 40.00 | 150.00 |
| | 1838 PJ | — | 12.00 | 20.00 | 40.00 | 150.00 |
| | 1839 PJ/JJ | — | 12.00 | 20.00 | 40.00 | 150.00 |
| | 1839 PJ | — | 12.00 | 20.00 | 40.00 | 150.00 |
| | 1840/30 PJ | — | 20.00 | 30.00 | 50.00 | 150.00 |
| | 1840 PJ | — | 12.00 | 20.00 | 35.00 | 125.00 |
| | 1841/31 PJ | — | 12.00 | 20.00 | 35.00 | 125.00 |
| | 1841 PJ | — | 12.00 | 20.00 | 35.00 | 125.00 |
| | 1842/1 PM | — | 20.00 | 30.00 | 50.00 | 125.00 |
| | 1842/31 PM/PJ | | | | | |
| | | — | 25.00 | 35.00 | 60.00 | 150.00 |
| | 1842 PJ | — | 20.00 | 30.00 | 50.00 | 125.00 |
| | 1842 PM/PJ | — | 12.00 | 20.00 | 35.00 | 125.00 |
| | 1842 PM | — | 12.00 | 20.00 | 35.00 | 125.00 |
| | 1843 PM dot after date | | | | | |
| | | — | 12.00 | 20.00 | 35.00 | 125.00 |
| | 1843 PM triangle of dots after date | | | | | |
| | | — | 12.00 | 20.00 | 35.00 | 125.00 |
| | 1844 PM | — | 12.00 | 20.00 | 35.00 | 125.00 |
| | 1845 PM | — | 12.00 | 20.00 | 35.00 | 125.00 |
| | 1846/5 PM eagle type of 1845 | | | | | |
| | | — | 20.00 | 30.00 | 50.00 | 150.00 |
| | 1846 PM early type of 1847 | | | | | |
| | | — | 15.00 | 25.00 | 40.00 | 135.00 |
| | 1847 PM narrow date | | | | | |
| | | — | 12.00 | 20.00 | 35.00 | 125.00 |
| | 1847 PM wide date | | | | | |
| | | — | 12.00 | 20.00 | 35.00 | 125.00 |
| | 1848/7 PM | — | 20.00 | 35.00 | 65.00 | 150.00 |
| | 1848 PM | — | 20.00 | 35.00 | 65.00 | 150.00 |
| | 1848 PF | — | 12.00 | 20.00 | 35.00 | 125.00 |
| | 1849 PF | — | 12.00 | 20.00 | 35.00 | 125.00 |
| | 1850 PF | — | 12.00 | 20.00 | 35.00 | 125.00 |
| | 1851/0 PF | — | 20.00 | 30.00 | 50.00 | 150.00 |
| | 1851 PF | — | 12.00 | 20.00 | 35.00 | 125.00 |
| | 1852/1 PF | — | 20.00 | 30.00 | 50.00 | 150.00 |
| | 1852 PF | — | 12.00 | 20.00 | 35.00 | 125.00 |
| | 1853/2 PF | — | 20.00 | 30.00 | 50.00 | 150.00 |
| | 1853 PF | — | 12.00 | 20.00 | 35.00 | 125.00 |
| | 1854 PF | — | 12.00 | 20.00 | 35.00 | 125.00 |
| | 1855 PF large letters | | | | | |
| | | — | 12.00 | 20.00 | 35.00 | 125.00 |
| | 1855 PF small letters | | | | | |
| | | — | 12.00 | 20.00 | 35.00 | 125.00 |
| | 1856/5 PF | — | 20.00 | 30.00 | 50.00 | 150.00 |
| | 1856 PF | — | 12.00 | 20.00 | 35.00 | 125.00 |
| | 1857/5 PF | — | 20.00 | 30.00 | 50.00 | 150.00 |
| | 1857/6 PF | — | 20.00 | 35.00 | 70.00 | 200.00 |
| | 1857 PF | — | 12.00 | 15.00 | 20.00 | 75.00 |
| | 1858/7 PI | — | 12.00 | 20.00 | 35.00 | 125.00 |
| | 1858 PF | — | 12.00 | 20.00 | 35.00 | 125.00 |
| | 1859/7 PF | — | 12.00 | 20.00 | 35.00 | 125.00 |
| | 1859/8 PF | — | 20.00 | 30.00 | 50.00 | 150.00 |
| | 1859 PF | — | 12.00 | 20.00 | 35.00 | 125.00 |
| | 1860/50 PF | — | 20.00 | 30.00 | 50.00 | 150.00 |
| | 1860/59 PF | — | 12.00 | 18.00 | 25.00 | 85.00 |
| | 1860 PF | — | 12.00 | 15.00 | 20.00 | 75.00 |
| | 1861/51 PF | — | 15.00 | 20.00 | 30.00 | 100.00 |
| | 1861/0 PF | — | 12.00 | 15.00 | 20.00 | 75.00 |
| | 1861 PF | — | 12.00 | 15.00 | 20.00 | 75.00 |
| | 1862 6/5 YE | — | 12.00 | 15.00 | 20.00 | 75.00 |
| | 1862 YE/PF | — | 12.00 | 15.00 | 20.00 | 75.00 |
| | 1862 YE | — | 12.00 | 15.00 | 20.00 | 75.00 |
| | 1862 YF | — | 12.00 | 15.00 | 20.00 | 75.00 |
| | 1862 YF/PF | — | 12.00 | 15.00 | 20.00 | 75.00 |
| | 1863/53 YF | — | 12.00 | 18.00 | 25.00 | 85.00 |
| | 1863/54 YF | — | 15.00 | 20.00 | 30.00 | 100.00 |
| | 1863 YE | — | — | — | Rare | — |
| | 1863 YF | — | 12.00 | 15.00 | 20.00 | 75.00 |
| | 1867/57 YF | — | 15.00 | 20.00 | 30.00 | 100.00 |
| | 1867 YF | — | 12.00 | 15.00 | 20.00 | 75.00 |
| | 1868/58 YF | — | 15.00 | 20.00 | 30.00 | 100.00 |
| | 1868/7 YF | — | 15.00 | 20.00 | 30.00 | 100.00 |
| | 1868 YF | — | 12.00 | 15.00 | 20.00 | 75.00 |
| | 1870/60 FR | — | 20.00 | 30.00 | 50.00 | 150.00 |
| | 1870 YF | — | 1800. | 3000. | 5000. | 7500. |

| KM# | Date | Mintage | Fine | VF | XF | Unc |
|---|---|---|---|---|---|---|
| 377.8 | 1870 FR/YF | — | 20.00 | 35.00 | 70.00 | 200.00 |
| | 1870 FR | — | 12.00 | 15.00 | 20.00 | 75.00 |
| | 1873 FR | — | 12.00 | 15.00 | 20.00 | 75.00 |
| | 1874/3 FR | — | 15.00 | 20.00 | 30.00 | 85.00 |
| | 1874 FR | — | 15.00 | 25.00 | 35.00 | 100.00 |
| | 1875/3 FR | — | 15.00 | 20.00 | 30.00 | 85.00 |
| | 1875/6 FR | — | 15.00 | 20.00 | 30.00 | 85.00 |
| | 1875 FR small circle w/dot on eagle | | | | | |
| | | — | 12.00 | 15.00 | 20.00 | 75.00 |
| | 1876/5 FR | — | 15.00 | 20.00 | 30.00 | 85.00 |
| | 1876 FR | — | 12.00 | 15.00 | 20.00 | 60.00 |
| | 1877 FR | 2.477 | 12.00 | 15.00 | 20.00 | 60.00 |
| | 1878/7 FR | | | | | |
| | | 2.273 | 15.00 | 20.00 | 30.00 | 75.00 |
| | 1878/7 SM | — | 15.00 | 20.00 | 30.00 | 75.00 |
| | 1878 FR | I.A. | 12.00 | 15.00 | 20.00 | 65.00 |
| | 1878 SM,S/F | — | 15.00 | 20.00 | 25.00 | 70.00 |
| | 1878 SM | — | 12.00 | 15.00 | 20.00 | 65.00 |
| | 1879/7 SM | — | 15.00 | 20.00 | 30.00 | 75.00 |
| | 1879/8 SM | — | 15.00 | 20.00 | 30.00 | 75.00 |
| | 1879/8 SM/FR | | | | | |
| | | — | 15.00 | 20.00 | 30.00 | 75.00 |
| | 1879 SM | — | 12.00 | 15.00 | 20.00 | 65.00 |
| | 1879 SM/FR | — | 15.00 | 20.00 | 30.00 | 75.00 |
| | 1880/70 SB | — | 15.00 | 20.00 | 30.00 | 75.00 |
| | 1880 SB/SM | — | 12.00 | 15.00 | 20.00 | 65.00 |
| | 1880 SB | — | 12.00 | 15.00 | 20.00 | 65.00 |
| | 1881/71 SB | — | | | | |
| | | 3.974 | 15.00 | 20.00 | 30.00 | 75.00 |
| | 1881/0 SB | I.A. | 15.00 | 20.00 | 30.00 | 75.00 |
| | 1881 SB | I.A. | 12.00 | 15.00 | 20.00 | 65.00 |
| | 1882 SB | 2.015 | 12.00 | 15.00 | 20.00 | 75.00 |
| | 1883 SB | 2.100 | 35.00 | 75.00 | 125.00 | 250.00 |
| | 1883 BR | I.A. | 12.00 | 15.00 | 20.00 | 65.00 |
| | 1883 BR/SR | — | 12.00 | 15.00 | 20.00 | 65.00 |
| | 1883 BR/SB | | | | | |
| | | Inc. Ab. | 12.00 | 15.00 | 20.00 | 65.00 |
| | 1884/73 BR | — | 20.00 | 30.00 | 40.00 | 100.00 |
| | 1884/74 BR | — | 20.00 | 30.00 | 40.00 | 100.00 |
| | 1884/3 BR | — | 20.00 | 30.00 | 60.00 | 150.00 |
| | 1884 BR | — | 12.00 | 15.00 | 20.00 | 65.00 |
| | 1884/74 RR | — | 50.00 | 100.00 | 175.00 | 350.00 |
| | 1884 RR | — | 25.00 | 50.00 | 100.00 | 250.00 |
| | 1885/75 RR | | | | | |
| | | 2.363 | 15.00 | 20.00 | 30.00 | 75.00 |
| | 1885 RR | I.A. | 12.00 | 15.00 | 20.00 | 65.00 |
| | 1886/75 RR | | | | | |
| | | 4.127 | 15.00 | 20.00 | 25.00 | 70.00 |
| | 1886/76 RR | | | | | |
| | | Inc. Ab. | 12.00 | 15.00 | 20.00 | 65.00 |
| | 1886/5 RR/BR | | | | | |
| | | Inc. Ab. | 12.00 | 15.00 | 20.00 | 65.00 |
| | 1886 RR | I.A. | 12.00 | 15.00 | 20.00 | 65.00 |
| | 1887 RR | 4.205 | 10.00 | 15.00 | 20.00 | 65.00 |
| | 1888 RR | 3.985 | 10.00 | 15.00 | 20.00 | 65.00 |
| | 1889 RR | 3.646 | 10.00 | 15.00 | 20.00 | 65.00 |
| | 1890 RR | 3.615 | 10.00 | 15.00 | 20.00 | 65.00 |
| | 1891 RS/R | — | 10.00 | 15.00 | 20.00 | 65.00 |
| | 1891 RS | 3.197 | 10.00 | 15.00 | 20.00 | 65.00 |
| | 1891 RR | — | | Contemporary counterfeit | | |
| | 1892/0 RS | — | 10.00 | 15.00 | 20.00 | 65.00 |
| | 1892 RS | 3.672 | 10.00 | 15.00 | 20.00 | 65.00 |
| | 1893 RS | 3.854 | 10.00 | 15.00 | 20.00 | 65.00 |
| | 1894 RS | 4.127 | 10.00 | 15.00 | 20.00 | 65.00 |
| | 1895/1 RS | | | | | |
| | | 3.768 | 15.00 | 20.00 | 25.00 | 75.00 |
| | 1895/3 RS | I.A. | 15.00 | 20.00 | 25.00 | 75.00 |
| | 1895 RS | I.A. | 10.00 | 15.00 | 20.00 | 65.00 |
| | 1896/1 Go/As RS/ML | | | | | |
| | | 5.229 | 15.00 | 20.00 | 25.00 | 75.00 |
| | 1896/1 RS | I.A. | 12.00 | 15.00 | 20.00 | 65.00 |
| | 1896 Go/Ga RS | | | | | |
| | | Inc. Ab. | — | — | — | — |
| | 1896 RS | I.A. | 10.00 | 12.00 | 18.00 | 60.00 |
| | 1897 RS | 4.344 | 10.00 | 12.00 | 18.00 | 60.00 |

**NOTE:** Varieties exist.

**Mint mark: Ho**

| KM# | Date | Mintage | Fine | VF | XF | Unc |
|---|---|---|---|---|---|---|
| 377.9 | 1835 PP | — | — | — | Rare | — |
| | 1836 PP | — | — | — | Rare | — |
| | 1839 PR | — | — | — | Unique | — |
| | 1861 FM reeded edge | | | | | |
| | | — | 4500. | 7500. | | |
| | 1862 FM plain edge, snakes tail left, long ray over *8R | | | | | |
| | | — | — | — | Rare | — |
| | 1862 FM plain edge, snakes tail left | | | | | |
| | | — | 1550. | 2700. | — | — |
| | 1862 FM reeded edge, snakes tail right | | | | | |
| | | — | 1650. | 2750. | — | — |
| | 1863 FM | — | 150.00 | 300.00 | 800.00 | — |
| | 1864 FM | — | 850.00 | 1650. | 2750. | — |
| | 1864 PR/FM | — | 1200. | 2200. | — | — |
| | 1864 PR | — | 650.00 | 1250. | 2150. | 3350. |
| | 1865 FM | — | 250.00 | 500.00 | 950.00 | 1850. |
| | 1866 FM | — | 1150. | 2150. | 3500. | 5500. |
| | 1866 MP | — | 950.00 | 1750. | 3000. | 4650. |
| | 1867 FM | — | 100.00 | 175.00 | 275.00 | 500.00 |
| | 1868 PR | — | 20.00 | 35.00 | 65.00 | 175.00 |
| | 1869 PR | — | 40.00 | 60.00 | 125.00 | 250.00 |
| | 1870 PR | — | 100.00 | 175.00 | 275.00 | 550.00 |
| | 1871/0 PR | — | 50.00 | 75.00 | 125.00 | 250.00 |
| | 1871 PR | — | 30.00 | 50.00 | 90.00 | 200.00 |
| | 1872/1 PR | — | 35.00 | 60.00 | 90.00 | 200.00 |
| | 1872 PR | — | 30.00 | 50.00 | 75.00 | 175.00 |
| | 1873 PR | .351 | 30.00 | 50.00 | 85.00 | 150.00 |
| | 1874 PR | — | 15.00 | 20.00 | 40.00 | 125.00 |
| | 1875 PR | — | 15.00 | 20.00 | 40.00 | 125.00 |
| | 1876 AF | — | 15.00 | 20.00 | 40.00 | 125.00 |
| | 1877 AF | .410 | 20.00 | 30.00 | 50.00 | 150.00 |
| | 1877 GR | I.A. | 100.00 | 150.00 | 225.00 | 400.00 |
| | 1877 JA | I.A. | 25.00 | 50.00 | 85.00 | 175.00 |
| | 1878 JA | .451 | 15.00 | 20.00 | 40.00 | 120.00 |
| | 1879 JA | — | 15.00 | 20.00 | 40.00 | 120.00 |
| | 1880 JA | — | 15.00 | 20.00 | 40.00 | 120.00 |
| | 1881 JA | .586 | 15.00 | 20.00 | 40.00 | 120.00 |
| | 1882 HoJA O above H | | | | | |
| | | .240 | 25.00 | 40.00 | 65.00 | 125.00 |
| | 1882 HoJA O after H | | | | | |
| | | I.A. | 25.00 | 40.00 | 65.00 | 125.00 |
| | 1883/2 JA | .204 | 200.00 | 350.00 | 500.00 | 1000. |
| | 1883/2 FM/JA | | | | | |
| | | I.A. | 25.00 | 40.00 | 75.00 | 150.00 |
| | 1883 FM/JA | — | 27.00 | 45.00 | 85.00 | 165.00 |
| | 1883 FM | I.A. | 20.00 | 30.00 | 60.00 | 125.00 |
| | 1883 JA | I.A. | 275.00 | 450.00 | 800.00 | 1500. |
| | 1884/3 FM | — | 20.00 | 25.00 | 50.00 | 125.00 |
| | 1884 FM | — | 15.00 | 20.00 | 40.00 | 120.00 |
| | 1885 FM | .132 | 15.00 | 20.00 | 40.00 | 125.00 |
| | 1886 FM | .225 | 20.00 | 30.00 | 45.00 | 125.00 |
| | 1886 FG | I.A. | 20.00 | 30.00 | 45.00 | 125.00 |
| | 1887/6 FG | — | 20.00 | 35.00 | 65.00 | 150.00 |
| | 1887 FG | .150 | 20.00 | 35.00 | 65.00 | 150.00 |
| | 1888 FG | .364 | 12.00 | 18.00 | 25.00 | 100.00 |
| | 1889 FG | .490 | 12.00 | 18.00 | 25.00 | 100.00 |
| | 1890 FG | .565 | 12.00 | 18.00 | 25.00 | 100.00 |
| | 1891 FG | .738 | 12.00 | 18.00 | 25.00 | 100.00 |
| | 1892 FG | .643 | 12.00 | 18.00 | 25.00 | 100.00 |
| | 1893 FG | .518 | 12.00 | 18.00 | 25.00 | 100.00 |
| | 1894 FG | .504 | 12.00 | 18.00 | 25.00 | 100.00 |
| | 1895 FG | .320 | 12.00 | 18.00 | 25.00 | 100.00 |

**NOTE:** Varieties exist.

**Mint mark: Mo**

| KM# | Date Mintage | Fine | VF | XF | Unc |
|---|---|---|---|---|---|
| 377.10 | 1824 JM round tail | | | | |
| | — | 75.00 | 125.00 | 250.00 | 500.00 |
| | 1824 JM square tail | | | | |
| | — | 75.00 | 125.00 | 250.00 | 500.00 |
| | 1825 JM — | 25.00 | 40.00 | 75.00 | 200.00 |
| | 1826/5 JM — | 25.00 | 40.00 | 75.00 | 200.00 |
| | 1826 JM — | 20.00 | 30.00 | 55.00 | 165.00 |
| | 1827 JM medal alignment | | | | |
| | — | 25.00 | 35.00 | 60.00 | 175.00 |
| | 1827 JM coin alignment | | | | |
| | — | 25.00 | 35.00 | 60.00 | 175.00 |
| | 1828 JM — | 30.00 | 60.00 | 100.00 | 250.00 |
| | 1829 JM — | 20.00 | 30.00 | 90.00 | 220.00 |
| | 1830/20 JM — | 35.00 | 65.00 | 150.00 | 300.00 |
| | 1830 JM — | 30.00 | 50.00 | 90.00 | 220.00 |
| | 1831 JM — | 30.00 | 50.00 | 100.00 | 240.00 |
| | 1832/1 JM — | 25.00 | 40.00 | 65.00 | 180.00 |
| | 1832 JM — | 20.00 | 30.00 | 55.00 | 165.00 |
| | 1833 MJ — | 25.00 | 40.00 | 80.00 | 200.00 |
| | 1833 ML — | 450.00 | 650.00 | 950.00 | 2000. |
| | 1834/3 ML — | 25.00 | 35.00 | 60.00 | 175.00 |
| | 1834 ML — | 20.00 | 30.00 | 55.00 | 165.00 |
| | 1835 ML narrow date | | | | |
| | — | 20.00 | 30.00 | 55.00 | 165.00 |
| | 1835 ML wide date | | | | |
| | — | 20.00 | 30.00 | 55.00 | 165.00 |

## 8 REALES

| | | | | | |
|---|---|---|---|---|---|
| 1836 ML | — | 50.00 | 100.00 | 150.00 | 325.00 |
| 1836 ML/MF | — | 50.00 | 100.00 | 150.00 | 325.00 |
| 1836 MF | — | 30.00 | 50.00 | 90.00 | 220.00 |
| 1836 MF/ML | — | 35.00 | 60.00 | 100.00 | 240.00 |
| 1837/6 ML | — | 30.00 | 50.00 | 80.00 | 200.00 |
| 1837/6 MM | — | 30.00 | 50.00 | 80.00 | 200.00 |
| 1837/6 MM/ML | | | | | |
| | — | 30.00 | 50.00 | 80.00 | 200.00 |
| 1837/6 MM/MF | | | | | |
| | — | 30.00 | 50.00 | 80.00 | 200.00 |
| 1837 ML | — | 30.00 | 50.00 | 80.00 | 200.00 |
| 1837 MM | — | 75.00 | 125.00 | 175.00 | 325.00 |
| 1838 MM | — | 30.00 | 50.00 | 80.00 | 200.00 |
| 1838 ML | — | 20.00 | 35.00 | 60.00 | 180.00 |
| 1838 ML/MM | — | 20.00 | 35.00 | 60.00 | 180.00 |
| 1839 ML narrow date | | | | | |
| | — | 15.00 | 25.00 | 50.00 | 165.00 |
| 1839 ML wide date | | | | | |
| | — | 15.00 | 25.00 | 50.00 | 165.00 |
| 1840 ML | — | 15.00 | 25.00 | 50.00 | 165.00 |
| 1841 ML | — | 15.00 | 25.00 | 45.00 | 150.00 |
| 1842 ML | — | 15.00 | 25.00 | 45.00 | 150.00 |
| 1842 MM | — | 15.00 | 25.00 | 45.00 | 150.00 |
| 1843 MM | — | 15.00 | 25.00 | 45.00 | 150.00 |
| 1844 MF/MM | — | — | — | — | — |
| 1844 MF | — | 15.00 | 25.00 | 45.00 | 150.00 |
| 1845/4 MF | — | 15.00 | 25.00 | 45.00 | 150.00 |
| 1845 MF | — | 15.00 | 25.00 | 45.00 | 150.00 |
| 1846/5 MF | — | 15.00 | 25.00 | 50.00 | 165.00 |
| 1846 MF | — | 15.00 | 25.00 | 50.00 | 165.00 |
| 1847/6 MF | — | 2000. | 3550. | — | — |
| 1847 MF | — | 1650. | 3000. | 5000. | 7500. |
| 1847 RC | — | 20.00 | 30.00 | 55.00 | 165.00 |
| 1847 RC/MF | — | 15.00 | 25.00 | 45.00 | 150.00 |
| 1848 GC | — | 15.00 | 25.00 | 45.00 | 150.00 |
| 1849/8 GC | — | 20.00 | 35.00 | 60.00 | 180.00 |
| 1849 GC | — | 15.00 | 25.00 | 45.00 | 150.00 |
| 1850/40 GC | — | 25.00 | 50.00 | 100.00 | 240.00 |

| KM# | Date Mintage | Fine | VF | XF | Unc |
|---|---|---|---|---|---|
| 377.10 | 1850/49 GC — | 25.00 | 50.00 | 100.00 | 240.00 |
| | 1850 GC — | 20.00 | 40.00 | 75.00 | 200.00 |
| | 1851 GC — | 20.00 | 40.00 | 60.00 | 175.00 |
| | 1852 GC — | 20.00 | 40.00 | 75.00 | 200.00 |
| | 1853 GC — | 15.00 | 25.00 | 50.00 | 160.00 |
| | 1854 GC — | 12.00 | 15.00 | 30.00 | 125.00 |
| | 1855 GC — | 20.00 | 35.00 | 65.00 | 180.00 |
| | 1855 GF — | 12.00 | 15.00 | 30.00 | 125.00 |
| | 1855 GF/GC — | 12.00 | 15.00 | 30.00 | 125.00 |
| | 1856/4 GF — | 15.00 | 25.00 | 45.00 | 145.00 |
| | 1856/5 GF — | 15.00 | 25.00 | 45.00 | 145.00 |
| | 1856 GF — | 12.00 | 15.00 | 30.00 | 125.00 |
| | 1857 GF — | 10.00 | 15.00 | 30.00 | 125.00 |
| | 1858/7 FH/GF | | | | |
| | — | 10.00 | 15.00 | 30.00 | 125.00 |
| | 1858 FH narrow date | | | | |
| | — | 10.00 | 15.00 | 30.00 | 125.00 |
| | 1858 FH wide date | | | | |
| | — | 10.00 | 15.00 | 30.00 | 125.00 |
| | 1859 FH — | 10.00 | 15.00 | 30.00 | 125.00 |
| | 1859/8 FH — | 25.00 | 50.00 | 100.00 | 240.00 |
| | 1860/59 FH — | 15.00 | 20.00 | 30.00 | 125.00 |
| | 1860 FH — | 10.00 | 15.00 | 30.00 | 125.00 |
| | 1860 TH — | 12.00 | 18.00 | 40.00 | 145.00 |
| | 1861 TH — | 12.00 | 18.00 | 40.00 | 145.00 |
| | 1861 CH — | 10.00 | 15.00 | 20.00 | 75.00 |
| | 1862 CH — | 10.00 | 15.00 | 20.00 | 75.00 |
| | 1863 CH — | 10.00 | 15.00 | 20.00 | 75.00 |
| | 1863 CH/TH — | 10.00 | 15.00 | 20.00 | 75.00 |
| | 1863 TH — | 10.00 | 15.00 | 20.00 | 75.00 |
| | 1867 CH — | 10.00 | 15.00 | 20.00 | 65.00 |
| | 1867 CH/TH — | 20.00 | 45.00 | 70.00 | 185.00 |
| | 1868 CH — | 10.00 | 15.00 | 20.00 | 65.00 |
| | 1868 CH/PH — | 10.00 | 15.00 | 20.00 | 65.00 |
| | 1868 PH narrow date | | | | |
| | — | 10.00 | 15.00 | 20.00 | 65.00 |
| | 1868 PH wide date | | | | |
| | — | 10.00 | 15.00 | 20.00 | 65.00 |
| | 1869 CH — | 10.00 | 15.00 | 20.00 | 65.00 |
| | 1873 MH — | 10.00 | 15.00 | 20.00 | 65.00 |
| | 1873 MH/HH — | 12.00 | 18.00 | 25.00 | 75.00 |
| | 1874/69 MH — | 20.00 | 45.00 | 70.00 | 185.00 |
| | 1874 MH — | 12.00 | 18.00 | 25.00 | 75.00 |
| | 1874 BH/MH — | 12.00 | 18.00 | 25.00 | 75.00 |
| | 1874 BH — | 12.00 | 18.00 | 25.00 | 85.00 |
| | 1875 BH — | 10.00 | 15.00 | 20.00 | 65.00 |
| | 1876/4 BH — | 12.00 | 18.00 | 25.00 | 75.00 |
| | 1876/5 BH — | 12.00 | 18.00 | 25.00 | 75.00 |
| | 1876 BH — | 10.00 | 15.00 | 20.00 | 65.00 |
| | 1877 MH .898 | 10.00 | 15.00 | 20.00 | 65.00 |
| | 1877 MH/BH | | | | |
| | Inc. Ab. | 12.00 | 18.00 | 25.00 | 75.00 |
| | 1878 MH 2.154 | 10.00 | 15.00 | 20.00 | 65.00 |
| | 1879/8 MH — | 10.00 | 15.00 | 20.00 | 75.00 |
| | 1879 MH — | 10.00 | 15.00 | 20.00 | 65.00 |
| | 1880/79 MH — | 15.00 | 20.00 | 30.00 | 75.00 |
| | 1880 MH — | 10.00 | 15.00 | 20.00 | 75.00 |
| | 1881 MH 5.712 | 10.00 | 15.00 | 20.00 | 65.00 |
| | 1882/1 MH | | | | |
| | 2.746 | 12.00 | 15.00 | 20.00 | 75.00 |
| | 1882 MH I.A. | 10.00 | 15.00 | 20.00 | 65.00 |
| | 1883/2 MH | | | | |
| | 2.726 | 12.00 | 18.00 | 25.00 | 85.00 |
| | 1883 MH narrow date | | | | |
| | I.A. | 10.00 | 15.00 | 20.00 | 65.00 |
| | 1883 MH wide date | | | | |
| | — | 10.00 | 15.00 | 20.00 | 65.00 |
| | 1884/3 MH — | 15.00 | 20.00 | 30.00 | 75.00 |
| | 1884 MH — | 10.00 | 15.00 | 20.00 | 65.00 |
| | 1885 MH 3.649 | 10.00 | 15.00 | 20.00 | 65.00 |
| | 1886 MH 7.558 | 10.00 | 12.00 | 18.00 | 60.00 |
| | 1887 MH 7.681 | 10.00 | 12.00 | 18.00 | 60.00 |
| | 1888 MH narrow date | | | | |
| | 7.179 | 10.00 | 12.00 | 18.00 | 60.00 |
| | 1888 MH wide date | | | | |
| | — | 10.00 | 12.00 | 18.00 | 60.00 |
| | 1889 MH 7.332 | 10.00 | 15.00 | 20.00 | 65.00 |
| | 1890 MH narrow date | | | | |
| | 7.412 | 10.00 | 12.00 | 18.00 | 60.00 |
| | 1890 MH wide date | | | | |
| | — | 10.00 | 12.00 | 18.00 | 60.00 |
| | 1890 AM I.A. | 10.00 | 12.00 | 18.00 | 60.00 |
| | 1891 AM 8.076 | 10.00 | 12.00 | 18.00 | 60.00 |
| | 1892 AM 9.392 | 10.00 | 12.00 | 18.00 | 60.00 |

| KM# | Date | Mintage | Fine | VF | XF | Unc |
|-----|------|---------|------|-----|-----|-----|
| 377.10 | 1893 AM | 10.773 | 10.00 | 12.00 | 18.00 | 55.00 |
| | 1894 AM | 12.394 | 10.00 | 12.00 | 18.00 | 45.00 |
| | 1895 AM | 10.474 | 10.00 | 12.00 | 18.00 | 45.00 |
| | 1895 AB | I.A. | 10.00 | 12.00 | 18.00 | 60.00 |
| | 1896 AB | 9.327 | 10.00 | 12.00 | 18.00 | 60.00 |
| | 1896 AM | I.A. | 10.00 | 12.00 | 18.00 | 60.00 |
| | 1897 AM | 8.621 | 10.00 | 12.00 | 18.00 | 60.00 |

NOTE: Varieties exist. 1874 CP is a die struck counterfeit.

### Mint mark: O, Oa

| KM# | Date | Mintage | Fine | VF | XF | Unc |
|-----|------|---------|------|-----|-----|-----|
| 377.11 | 1858O AE | — | 2500. | 4000. | — | — |
| | 1858OaAE | — | — | — | Unique | — |
| | 1859 AE A in O of mm | | | | | |
| | | — | 500.00 | 900.00 | 1750. | — |
| | 1860 AE A in O of mm | | | | | |
| | | — | 200.00 | 450.00 | 800.00 | — |
| | 1861 O FR | — | 125.00 | 250.00 | 550.00 | 1350. |
| | 1861OaFR | — | 150.00 | 350.00 | 700.00 | — |
| | 1862O FR | — | 40.00 | 80.00 | 200.00 | 375.00 |
| | 1862OaFR | — | 65.00 | 125.00 | 250.00 | 450.00 |
| | 1863O FR | — | 30.00 | 60.00 | 100.00 | 250.00 |
| | 1863O AE | — | 30.00 | 60.00 | 100.00 | 250.00 |
| | 1863OaAE A in O of mm | | | | | |
| | | — | 100.00 | 150.00 | 250.00 | 450.00 |
| | 1863OaAE A above O in mm | | | | | |
| | | — | 1000. | 1750. | 2750. | — |
| | 1864 FR | — | 25.00 | 50.00 | 75.00 | 200.00 |
| | 1865 AE | — | 1850. | 3000. | — | — |
| | 1867 AE | — | 40.00 | 80.00 | 150.00 | 400.00 |
| | 1868 AE | — | 40.00 | 80.00 | 150.00 | 400.00 |
| | 1869 AE | — | 30.00 | 60.00 | 100.00 | 250.00 |
| | 1873 AE | — | 200.00 | 300.00 | 550.00 | 1350. |
| | 1874 AE | .142 | 15.00 | 30.00 | 50.00 | 200.00 |
| | 1875/4 AE | .131 | 25.00 | 50.00 | 75.00 | 200.00 |
| | 1875 AE | I.A. | 15.00 | 30.00 | 40.00 | 135.00 |
| | 1876 AE | .140 | 20.00 | 35.00 | 55.00 | 200.00 |
| | 1877 AE | .139 | 20.00 | 30.00 | 50.00 | 200.00 |
| | 1878 AE | .125 | 20.00 | 30.00 | 50.00 | 200.00 |
| | 1879 AE | .153 | 20.00 | 30.00 | 50.00 | 200.00 |
| | 1880 AE | .143 | 15.00 | 30.00 | 45.00 | 150.00 |
| | 1881 AE | .134 | 20.00 | 35.00 | 60.00 | 150.00 |
| | 1882 AE | .100 | 20.00 | 35.00 | 60.00 | 150.00 |
| | 1883 AE | .122 | 15.00 | 30.00 | 45.00 | 150.00 |
| | 1884 AE | .142 | 15.00 | 30.00 | 50.00 | 150.00 |
| | 1885 AE | .158 | 15.00 | 30.00 | 40.00 | 135.00 |
| | 1886 AE | .120 | 15.00 | 30.00 | 45.00 | 150.00 |
| | 1887/6 AE | .115 | 25.00 | 50.00 | 80.00 | 200.00 |
| | 1887 AE | I.A. | 15.00 | 25.00 | 40.00 | 135.00 |
| | 1888 AE | .145 | 15.00 | 25.00 | 40.00 | 135.00 |
| | 1889 AE | .150 | 20.00 | 30.00 | 60.00 | 175.00 |
| | 1890 AE | .181 | 20.00 | 30.00 | 60.00 | 175.00 |
| | 1891 EN | .160 | 15.00 | 25.00 | 40.00 | 135.00 |
| | 1892 EN | .120 | 15.00 | 25.00 | 40.00 | 135.00 |
| | 1893 EN | .066 | 45.00 | 75.00 | 125.00 | 300.00 |

NOTE: Varieties exist.

### Mint mark: Pi

| KM# | Date | Mintage | Fine | VF | XF | Unc |
|-----|------|---------|------|-----|-----|-----|
| 377.12 | 1827 JS | — | 3800. | — | — | — |
| | 1827 SA | — | 6000. | 9000. | — | — |
| | 1828/7 JS | — | 275.00 | 425.00 | 650.00 | 1250. |
| | 1828 JS | — | 225.00 | 375.00 | 550.00 | 1100. |
| | 1829 JS | — | 35.00 | 65.00 | 125.00 | 250.00 |
| | 1830 JS | — | 30.00 | 50.00 | 100.00 | 200.00 |
| | 1831/0 JS | — | 35.00 | 75.00 | 200.00 | 350.00 |
| | 1831 JS | — | 25.00 | 35.00 | 75.00 | 200.00 |
| | 1832/22 JS | — | 25.00 | 35.00 | 65.00 | 165.00 |
| | 1832 JS 8/0 | — | 40.00 | 80.00 | 175.00 | 300.00 |
| | 1832 JS | — | 25.00 | 35.00 | 65.00 | 165.00 |
| | 1833/2 JS | — | 30.00 | 45.00 | 80.00 | 250.00 |
| | 1833 JS narrow date | | | | | |
| | | — | 20.00 | 30.00 | 50.00 | 150.00 |
| | 1833 JS wide date | | | | | |
| | | — | 20.00 | 30.00 | 50.00 | 150.00 |
| | 1834/3 JS | — | 35.00 | 65.00 | 125.00 | 300.00 |
| | 1834 JS | — | 15.00 | 25.00 | 50.00 | 150.00 |
| | 1835/4 JS | — | 60.00 | 125.00 | 250.00 | 500.00 |
| | 1835 JS denomination 8R | | | | | |
| | | — | 20.00 | 30.00 | 65.00 | 175.00 |
| | 1835 JS denomination 8Rs | | | | | |
| | | — | 15.00 | 25.00 | 50.00 | 150.00 |
| | 1836 JS | — | 20.00 | 30.00 | 55.00 | 150.00 |
| | 1837 JS | — | 30.00 | 50.00 | 85.00 | 200.00 |
| | 1838 JS | — | 20.00 | 30.00 | 55.00 | 150.00 |
| | 1839 JS | — | 20.00 | 40.00 | 70.00 | 150.00 |
| | 1840 JS | — | 20.00 | 30.00 | 60.00 | 150.00 |
| | 1841PiJS | — | 25.00 | 40.00 | 85.00 | 200.00 |
| | 1841iPJS (error) | | | | | |
| | | — | 200.00 | 350.00 | 550.00 | — |
| | 1842/1 JS | — | 40.00 | 65.00 | 125.00 | 300.00 |
| | 1842/1 PS/JS | | | | | |
| | | — | 35.00 | 55.00 | 90.00 | 200.00 |
| | 1842 JS eagle type of 1843 | | | | | |
| | | — | 30.00 | 50.00 | 80.00 | 175.00 |
| | 1842 PS | — | 30.00 | 50.00 | 80.00 | 175.00 |
| | 1842 PS/JS eagle type of 1841 | | | | | |
| | | — | 30.00 | 50.00 | 80.00 | 175.00 |
| | 1843/2 PS round top 3 | | | | | |
| | | — | 50.00 | 75.00 | 150.00 | 300.00 |
| | 1843 PS flat top 3 | | | | | |
| | | — | 60.00 | 100.00 | 200.00 | 475.00 |
| | 1843 AM round top 3 | | | | | |
| | | — | 20.00 | 30.00 | 55.00 | 150.00 |
| | 1843 AM flat top 3 | | | | | |
| | | — | 20.00 | 30.00 | 55.00 | 150.00 |
| | 1844 AM | — | 20.00 | 30.00 | 55.00 | 150.00 |
| | 1845/4 AM | — | 35.00 | 55.00 | 120.00 | 250.00 |
| | 1845 AM | — | 25.00 | 50.00 | 100.00 | 225.00 |
| | 1846/5 AM | — | 40.00 | 65.00 | 125.00 | 300.00 |
| | 1846 AM | — | 15.00 | 25.00 | 50.00 | 150.00 |
| | 1847 AM | — | 30.00 | 50.00 | 85.00 | 175.00 |
| | 1848/7 AM | — | 30.00 | 60.00 | 100.00 | 200.00 |
| | 1848 AM | — | 30.00 | 50.00 | 85.00 | 175.00 |
| | 1849/8 PS/AM | | | | | |
| | | — | 950.00 | 1750. | — | — |
| | 1849 PS | — | 950.00 | 1750. | — | — |
| | 1849 MC/PS | — | 60.00 | 125.00 | 250.00 | 500.00 |
| | 1849 AM | — | 1850. | 3250. | 5000. | — |
| | 1849 MC | — | 60.00 | 125.00 | 250.00 | 500.00 |
| | 1850 MC | — | 40.00 | 80.00 | 150.00 | 300.00 |
| | 1851 MC | — | 75.00 | 150.00 | 275.00 | 550.00 |
| | 1852 MC | — | 75.00 | 125.00 | 200.00 | 400.00 |
| | 1853 MC | — | 150.00 | 275.00 | 400.00 | 850.00 |

| KM# | Date | Mintage | Fine | VF | XF | Unc |
|---|---|---|---|---|---|---|
| 377.12 | 1854 MC | — | 100.00 | 150.00 | 250.00 | 500.00 |
| | 1855 MC | — | 100.00 | 150.00 | 250.00 | 500.00 |
| | 1856 MC | — | 65.00 | 100.00 | 200.00 | 400.00 |
| | 1857 MC | — | 400.00 | 700.00 | 1250. | — |
| | 1857 PS/MC | — | 150.00 | 250.00 | 450.00 | 1000. |
| | 1857 PS | — | 125.00 | 200.00 | 350.00 | 650.00 |
| | 1858 MC/PS | — | 250.00 | 400.00 | 650.00 | 1200. |
| | 1858 MC | — | 250.00 | 400.00 | 650.00 | 1200. |
| | 1858 PS | — | 650.00 | 1150. | 1750. | — |
| | 1859/8 MC/PS | | | | | |
| | | — | 3650. | 5750. | — | — |
| | 1859 MC/PS | — | 900.00 | 1750. | — | — |
| | 1859 MC | — | 2000. | 3500. | 5000. | — |
| | 1859 PS/MC | — | 800.00 | 1500. | 2500. | — |
| | 1860 FC | — | — | — | Rare | — |
| | 1860 FE | — | — | — | Rare | — |
| | 1860 MC | — | 1750. | 2750. | 6000. | — |
| | 1860 PS/FE | — | 500.00 | 1000. | — | — |
| | 1860 PS | — | 400.00 | 600.00 | 900.00 | 1750. |
| | 1860 RO | — | — | — | *Rare | — |
| | 1861 PS | — | 30.00 | 60.00 | 90.00 | 175.00 |
| | 1861 RO | — | 25.00 | 35.00 | 55.00 | 125.00 |
| | 1862/1 RO | — | 20.00 | 25.00 | 50.00 | 125.00 |
| | 1862 RO | — | 15.00 | 20.00 | 40.00 | 100.00 |
| | 1862 RO oval O in RO | | | | | |
| | | — | 15.00 | 20.00 | 40.00 | 100.00 |
| | 1862 RO round O in RO, 6 is inverted 9 | | | | | |
| | | — | 20.00 | 30.00 | 50.00 | 125.00 |
| | 1863/2 RO | — | 25.00 | 35.00 | 65.00 | 150.00 |
| | 1863 RO | — | 15.00 | 20.00 | 40.00 | 125.00 |
| | 1863 6/inverted 6 | | | | | |
| | | — | 25.00 | 35.00 | 55.00 | 125.00 |
| | 1863 FC | — | 2750. | 4750. | — | — |
| | 1864 RO | — | — | — | Rare | — |
| | 1867 CA | — | 300.00 | 500.00 | — | — |
| | 1867 LR | — | 250.00 | 400.00 | 650.00 | — |
| | 1867 PS/CA | — | 850.00 | — | — | — |
| | 1867 PS | — | 30.00 | 60.00 | 125.00 | 275.00 |
| | 1868/7 PS | — | 30.00 | 60.00 | 125.00 | 250.00 |
| | 1868 PS | — | 20.00 | 30.00 | 50.00 | 125.00 |
| | 1869/8 PS | — | 20.00 | 25.00 | 45.00 | 125.00 |
| | 1869 PS | — | 15.00 | 20.00 | 40.00 | 125.00 |
| | 1870/69 PS | — | 750.00 | 1450. | 3500. | — |
| | 1870 PS | — | 650.00 | 1250. | 2500. | — |
| | 1873 MH | — | 18.00 | 25.00 | 45.00 | 100.00 |
| | 1874/3 MH | — | 25.00 | 50.00 | 120.00 | 250.00 |
| | 1874 MH | — | 10.00 | 12.00 | 22.00 | 120.00 |
| | 1875 MH | — | 10.00 | 12.00 | 22.00 | 100.00 |
| | 1876/5 MH | — | 18.00 | 25.00 | 45.00 | 150.00 |
| | 1876 MH | — | 10.00 | 12.00 | 22.00 | 100.00 |
| | 1877/6 MH | — | 165.00 | 325.00 | 550.00 | — |
| | 1877 MH | 1.018 | 10.00 | 12.00 | 22.00 | 120.00 |
| | 1878 MH | 1.046 | 15.00 | 30.00 | 100.00 | 225.00 |
| | 1879/8 MH | — | 15.00 | 20.00 | 30.00 | 125.00 |
| | 1879 MH | — | 10.00 | 12.00 | 22.00 | 100.00 |
| | 1879 BE | — | 25.00 | 50.00 | 75.00 | 150.00 |
| | 1879 MR | — | 30.00 | 50.00 | 100.00 | 200.00 |
| | 1880 MR | — | 250.00 | 375.00 | 750.00 | — |
| | 1880 MH/R | — | 10.00 | 12.00 | 22.00 | 100.00 |
| | 1880 MH | — | 10.00 | 12.00 | 22.00 | 100.00 |
| | 1881 MH/R | — | 10.00 | 12.00 | 22.00 | 100.00 |
| | 1881 MH | 2.100 | 10.00 | 12.00 | 22.00 | 100.00 |
| | 1882/1 MH | | | | | |
| | | 1.602 | 15.00 | 20.00 | 30.00 | 125.00 |
| | 1882 MH | I.A. | 10.00 | 12.00 | 22.00 | 100.00 |
| | 1883/2 MH | — | 15.00 | 20.00 | 30.00 | 125.00 |
| | 1883 MH | 1.545 | 10.00 | 12.00 | 22.00 | 100.00 |
| | 1884/3 MH | — | 15.00 | 20.00 | 30.00 | 125.00 |
| | 1884 MH/MM | | | | | |
| | | — | 12.00 | 15.00 | 22.00 | 90.00 |
| | 1884 MH | — | 10.00 | 12.00 | 20.00 | 80.00 |
| | 1885/4 MH | | | | | |
| | | 1.736 | 15.00 | 20.00 | 30.00 | 125.00 |
| | 1885/8 MH | I.A. | 15.00 | 20.00 | 30.00 | 125.00 |
| | 1885 MH | I.A. | 10.00 | 12.00 | 20.00 | 80.00 |
| | 1885 LC | I.A. | 12.00 | 18.00 | 25.00 | 100.00 |
| | 1886 LC | 3.347 | 10.00 | 12.00 | 20.00 | 80.00 |
| | 1886 MR | I.A. | 10.00 | 12.00 | 20.00 | 80.00 |
| | 1887 MR | 2.922 | 10.00 | 12.00 | 20.00 | 80.00 |
| | 1888/7 MR | — | 15.00 | 20.00 | 30.00 | 125.00 |
| | 1888 MR | 2.438 | 10.00 | 12.00 | 20.00 | 70.00 |
| | 1889 MR | 2.103 | 10.00 | 12.00 | 20.00 | 80.00 |
| | 1890 MR | 1.562 | 10.00 | 12.00 | 20.00 | 70.00 |
| | 1891 MR | 1.184 | 10.00 | 12.00 | 20.00 | 70.00 |

| KM# | Date | Mintage | Fine | VF | XF | Unc |
|---|---|---|---|---|---|---|
| 377.12 | 1892 MR | 1.336 | 10.00 | 12.00 | 20.00 | 70.00 |
| | 1893 MR | .530 | 10.00 | 12.00 | 20.00 | 80.00 |

NOTE: Varieties exist.

**Mint mark: Zs**

| KM# | Date | Mintage | Fine | VF | XF | Unc |
|---|---|---|---|---|---|---|
| 377.13 | 1825 AZ | — | 25.00 | 35.00 | 65.00 | 175.00 |
| | 1826/5 AZ | — | 25.00 | 45.00 | 85.00 | 200.00 |
| | 1826 AZ | — | 100.00 | 200.00 | 400.00 | 800.00 |
| | 1826 AV | — | 175.00 | 350.00 | 600.00 | 1500. |
| | 1826/5 AO/AZ | | | | | |
| | | — | 300.00 | 600.00 | 1000. | 2000. |
| | 1826 AO | — | 200.00 | 350.00 | 750.00 | 2000. |
| | 1827 AO/AZ | — | 35.00 | 50.00 | 125.00 | 250.00 |
| | 1827 AO | — | 25.00 | 45.00 | 85.00 | 200.00 |
| | 1828 AO | — | 15.00 | 20.00 | 45.00 | 165.00 |
| | 1829 AO | — | 15.00 | 20.00 | 45.00 | 165.00 |
| | 1829 OV | — | 50.00 | 90.00 | 150.00 | 300.00 |
| | 1830 OV | — | 15.00 | 20.00 | 45.00 | 165.00 |
| | 1831 OV | — | 25.00 | 50.00 | 90.00 | 200.00 |
| | 1831 OM | — | 15.00 | 25.00 | 55.00 | 165.00 |
| | 1832/1 OM | — | 20.00 | 25.00 | 45.00 | 165.00 |
| | 1832 OM | — | 15.00 | 20.00 | 40.00 | 150.00 |
| | 1833/2 OM | — | 20.00 | 30.00 | 45.00 | 165.00 |
| | 1833 OM/MM | | | | | |
| | | — | 15.00 | 25.00 | 40.00 | 150.00 |
| | 1833 OM | — | 15.00 | 20.00 | 35.00 | 150.00 |
| | 1834 OM | — | 15.00 | 20.00 | 35.00 | 150.00 |
| | 1835 OM | — | 15.00 | 20.00 | 40.00 | 150.00 |
| | 1836/4 OM | — | 20.00 | 30.00 | 50.00 | 165.00 |
| | 1836/5 OM | — | 20.00 | 30.00 | 50.00 | 165.00 |
| | 1836 OM | — | 15.00 | 20.00 | 35.00 | 150.00 |
| | 1837 OM | — | 15.00 | 20.00 | 35.00 | 150.00 |
| | 1838/7 OM | — | 20.00 | 30.00 | 45.00 | 165.00 |
| | 1838 OM | — | 15.00 | 20.00 | 35.00 | 150.00 |
| | 1839 OM | — | 15.00 | 20.00 | 35.00 | 150.00 |
| | 1840 OM | — | 15.00 | 20.00 | 35.00 | 150.00 |
| | 1841 OM | — | 15.00 | 20.00 | 35.00 | 150.00 |
| | 1842 OM eagle type of 1841 | | | | | |
| | | — | 15.00 | 20.00 | 35.00 | 150.00 |
| | 1842 OM eagle type of 1843 | | | | | |
| | | — | 15.00 | 20.00 | 35.00 | 150.00 |
| | 1843 OM | — | 15.00 | 20.00 | 35.00 | 150.00 |
| | 1844 OM | — | 15.00 | 20.00 | 35.00 | 150.00 |
| | 1845 OM | — | 15.00 | 20.00 | 35.00 | 150.00 |
| | 1846 OM | — | 15.00 | 20.00 | 35.00 | 150.00 |
| | 1847 OM | — | 15.00 | 20.00 | 35.00 | 150.00 |
| | 1848/7 OM | — | 20.00 | 30.00 | 45.00 | 165.00 |
| | 1848 OM | — | 15.00 | 20.00 | 35.00 | 150.00 |
| | 1849 OM | — | 15.00 | 20.00 | 35.00 | 80.00 |
| | 1850 OM | — | 15.00 | 20.00 | 35.00 | 150.00 |
| | 1851 OM | — | 15.00 | 20.00 | 35.00 | 150.00 |
| | 1852 OM | — | 15.00 | 20.00 | 35.00 | 150.00 |
| | 1853 OM | — | 30.00 | 45.00 | 75.00 | 200.00 |
| | 1854/3 OM | — | 20.00 | 30.00 | 60.00 | 175.00 |
| | 1854 OM | — | 15.00 | 25.00 | 45.00 | 165.00 |
| | 1855 OM | — | 20.00 | 30.00 | 60.00 | 175.00 |
| | 1855 MO | — | 30.00 | 60.00 | 90.00 | 200.00 |
| | 1856/5 MO | — | 20.00 | 30.00 | 45.00 | 165.00 |
| | 1856 MO | — | 15.00 | 20.00 | 35.00 | 150.00 |
| | 1857/5 MO | — | 20.00 | 30.00 | 45.00 | 165.00 |
| | 1857 MO | — | 15.00 | 20.00 | 35.00 | 150.00 |
| | 1858/7 MO | — | 15.00 | 20.00 | 35.00 | 150.00 |
| | 1858 MO | — | 15.00 | 20.00 | 35.00 | 150.00 |
| | 1859/8 MO | — | 15.00 | 20.00 | 35.00 | 150.00 |
| | 1859 MO | — | 15.00 | 20.00 | 35.00 | 150.00 |
| | 1859 VL/MO | — | 25.00 | 50.00 | 75.00 | 175.00 |

| KM# | Date | Mintage | Fine | VF | XF | Unc |
|---|---|---|---|---|---|---|
| 377.13 | 1859 VL | — | 20.00 | 40.00 | 60.00 | 165.00 |
| | 1860/50 MO | — | 10.00 | 12.00 | 20.00 | 80.00 |
| | 1860/59 MO | — | 10.00 | 12.00 | 20.00 | 80.00 |
| | 1860 MO | — | 10.00 | 12.00 | 20.00 | 80.00 |
| | 1860 VL/MO | — | 10.00 | 12.00 | 20.00 | 80.00 |
| | 1860 VL | — | 10.00 | 12.00 | 20.00 | 80.00 |
| | 1861/0 VL/MO | | | | | |
| | | — | 10.00 | 12.00 | 20.00 | 80.00 |
| | 1861/0 VL | — | 10.00 | 12.00 | 20.00 | 80.00 |
| | 1861 VL | — | 10.00 | 12.00 | 20.00 | 80.00 |
| | 1862/1 VL | — | 15.00 | 20.00 | 35.00 | 100.00 |
| | 1862 VL | — | 10.00 | 12.00 | 20.00 | 80.00 |
| | 1863 VL | — | 10.00 | 12.00 | 20.00 | 80.00 |
| | 1863 MO | — | 10.00 | 12.00 | 20.00 | 80.00 |
| | 1864/3 VL | — | 15.00 | 20.00 | 35.00 | 100.00 |
| | 1864 VL | — | 10.00 | 12.00 | 20.00 | 80.00 |
| | 1864 MO | — | 15.00 | 20.00 | 35.00 | 100.00 |
| | 1865/4 MO | — | 200.00 | 450.00 | 800.00 | 1550. |
| | 1865 MO | — | 150.00 | 300.00 | 600.00 | 1250. |
| | 1866 VL | — | Contemporary counterfeit | | | |
| | 1867 JS | — | — | — | Rare | — |
| | 1868 JS | — | 10.00 | 12.00 | 20.00 | 80.00 |
| | 1868 YH | — | 10.00 | 12.00 | 20.00 | 80.00 |
| | 1869 YH | — | 10.00 | 12.00 | 20.00 | 80.00 |
| | 1870 YH | — | — | — | Rare | — |
| | 1873 YH | — | 10.00 | 12.00 | 20.00 | 80.00 |
| | 1874 YH | — | 10.00 | 12.00 | 20.00 | 80.00 |
| | 1874 JA/YA | — | 10.00 | 12.00 | 20.00 | 80.00 |
| | 1874 JA | — | 10.00 | 12.00 | 20.00 | 80.00 |
| | 1875 JA | — | 10.00 | 12.00 | 20.00 | 80.00 |
| | 1876 JA | — | 10.00 | 12.00 | 20.00 | 80.00 |
| | 1876 JS | — | 10.00 | 12.00 | 20.00 | 80.00 |
| | 1877 JS | 2.700 | 10.00 | 12.00 | 20.00 | 80.00 |
| | 1878 JS | 2.310 | 10.00 | 12.00 | 20.00 | 80.00 |
| | 1879/8 JS | — | 15.00 | 20.00 | 35.00 | 100.00 |
| | 1879 JS | — | 10.00 | 12.00 | 20.00 | 80.00 |
| | 1880 JS | — | 10.00 | 12.00 | 20.00 | 80.00 |
| | 1881 JS | 5.592 | 10.00 | 12.00 | 20.00 | 80.00 |
| | 1882/1 JS | 2.485 | 15.00 | 20.00 | 35.00 | 100.00 |
| | 1882 JS straight J | Inc. Ab. | 10.00 | 12.00 | 20.00 | 65.00 |
| | 1882 JS full J | Inc. Ab. | 10.00 | 12.00 | 20.00 | 65.00 |
| | 1883/2 JS | 2.563 | 15.00 | 20.00 | 35.00 | 100.00 |
| | 1883 JS | I.A. | 10.00 | 12.00 | 20.00 | 80.00 |
| | 1884 JS | — | 10.00 | 12.00 | 20.00 | 80.00 |
| | 1885 JS | 2.252 | 10.00 | 12.00 | 20.00 | 65.00 |
| | 1886/5 JS | 5.303 | 15.00 | 20.00 | 35.00 | 100.00 |
| | 1886/8 JS | I.A. | 15.00 | 20.00 | 35.00 | 100.00 |
| | 1886 JS | I.A. | 10.00 | 12.00 | 20.00 | 65.00 |
| | 1886 FZ | I.A. | 10.00 | 12.00 | 20.00 | 65.00 |
| | 1887ZsFZ | 4.733 | 10.00 | 12.00 | 20.00 | 65.00 |
| | 1887Z FZ | I.A. | 20.00 | 30.00 | 50.00 | 100.00 |
| | 1888/7 FZ | 5.132 | 12.00 | 15.00 | 25.00 | 80.00 |
| | 1888 FZ | I.A. | 10.00 | 12.00 | 20.00 | 65.00 |
| | 1889 FZ | 4.344 | 10.00 | 12.00 | 20.00 | 65.00 |
| | 1890 FZ | 3.887 | 10.00 | 12.00 | 20.00 | 65.00 |
| | 1891 FZ | 4.114 | 10.00 | 12.00 | 20.00 | 65.00 |
| | 1892/1 FZ | 4.238 | 12.00 | 15.00 | 25.00 | 80.00 |
| | 1892 FZ narrow date | I.A. | 10.00 | 12.00 | 20.00 | 65.00 |
| | 1892 FZ wide date | — | 10.00 | 12.00 | 20.00 | 65.00 |
| | 1893 FZ | 3.872 | 10.00 | 12.00 | 20.00 | 65.00 |
| | 1894 FZ | 3.081 | 10.00 | 12.00 | 20.00 | 65.00 |
| | 1895 FZ | 4.718 | 10.00 | 12.00 | 20.00 | 65.00 |
| | 1896 FZ | 4.226 | 10.00 | 12.00 | 20.00 | 55.00 |
| | 1897 FZ | 4.877 | 10.00 | 12.00 | 20.00 | 55.00 |

NOTE: Varieties exist.

## 1/2 ESCUDO

**1.6900 g, .875 GOLD, .0475 oz AGW**

**Mint mark: C**
**Obv: Facing eagle.**

| KM# | Date | Mintage | VG | Fine | VF | XF |
|---|---|---|---|---|---|---|
| 378 | 1848 CE | — | 35.00 | 50.00 | 75.00 | 150.00 |
| | 1853 CE | — | 35.00 | 50.00 | 75.00 | 150.00 |
| | 1854 CE | — | 50.00 | 100.00 | 150.00 | 250.00 |
| | 1856 CE | — | 50.00 | 100.00 | 150.00 | 250.00 |
| | 1857 CE | — | 50.00 | 100.00 | 150.00 | 250.00 |
| | 1859 CE | — | 35.00 | 50.00 | 75.00 | 150.00 |
| | 1860 CE | — | 35.00 | 50.00 | 75.00 | 150.00 |
| | 1862 CE | — | 35.00 | 50.00 | 75.00 | 125.00 |
| | 1863 CE | — | 35.00 | 50.00 | 75.00 | 125.00 |
| | 1866 CE | — | 35.00 | 50.00 | 75.00 | 125.00 |
| | 1867 CE | — | 35.00 | 50.00 | 75.00 | 125.00 |
| | 1870 CE | — | 75.00 | 150.00 | 275.00 | 450.00 |

**Mint mark: Do**

| KM# | Date | Mintage | VG | Fine | VF | XF |
|---|---|---|---|---|---|---|
| 378.1 | 1833 RM/RL | — | 35.00 | 50.00 | 75.00 | 150.00 |
| | 1834/1 RM | — | 35.00 | 50.00 | 75.00 | 150.00 |
| | 1834/3 RM | — | 35.00 | 50.00 | 75.00 | 150.00 |
| | 1835/2 RM | — | 35.00 | 50.00 | 75.00 | 150.00 |
| | 1835/3 RM | — | 35.00 | 50.00 | 75.00 | 150.00 |
| | 1835/4 RM | — | 35.00 | 50.00 | 75.00 | 150.00 |
| | 1836/4 RM | — | 35.00 | 50.00 | 75.00 | 150.00 |
| | 1837 RM | — | 35.00 | 50.00 | 75.00 | 150.00 |
| | 1838 RM | — | 40.00 | 60.00 | 100.00 | 175.00 |
| | 1843 RM | — | 40.00 | 60.00 | 100.00 | 175.00 |
| | 1844/33 RM | — | 40.00 | 60.00 | 100.00 | 175.00 |
| | 1844/33 RM/RL | — | 65.00 | 125.00 | 275.00 | 450.00 |
| | 1845 CM | — | 40.00 | 60.00 | 100.00 | 175.00 |
| | 1846 RM | — | 40.00 | 60.00 | 100.00 | 175.00 |
| | 1848 RM | — | 40.00 | 60.00 | 100.00 | 175.00 |
| | 1850/33 JMR | — | 40.00 | 60.00 | 100.00 | 175.00 |
| | 1851 JMR | — | 40.00 | 60.00 | 100.00 | 200.00 |
| | 1852 JMR | — | 40.00 | 60.00 | 100.00 | 175.00 |
| | 1853/33 CP | — | 75.00 | 150.00 | 300.00 | 500.00 |
| | 1853 CP | — | 35.00 | 50.00 | 75.00 | 150.00 |
| | 1854 CP | — | 35.00 | 50.00 | 75.00 | 150.00 |
| | 1855 CP | — | 35.00 | 50.00 | 75.00 | 150.00 |
| | 1859 CP | — | 35.00 | 50.00 | 75.00 | 150.00 |
| | 1861 CP | — | 35.00 | 50.00 | 75.00 | 150.00 |
| | 1862 CP | — | 35.00 | 50.00 | 75.00 | 150.00 |
| | 1864 LT | — | 75.00 | 125.00 | 250.00 | 400.00 |

**Mint mark: Ga**

| KM# | Date | Mintage | VG | Fine | VF | XF |
|---|---|---|---|---|---|---|
| 378.2 | 1825 FS | — | 40.00 | 60.00 | 100.00 | 175.00 |
| | 1829 FS | — | 40.00 | 60.00 | 100.00 | 175.00 |
| | 1831 FS | — | 40.00 | 60.00 | 100.00 | 175.00 |
| | 1834 FS | — | 40.00 | 60.00 | 100.00 | 175.00 |
| | 1835 FS | — | 40.00 | 60.00 | 100.00 | 175.00 |
| | 1837 JG | — | 40.00 | 60.00 | 100.00 | 175.00 |
| | 1838 JG | — | 40.00 | 60.00 | 100.00 | 175.00 |
| | 1839 JG | — | — | — | — | — |
| | 1842 JG | — | — | — | — | — |
| | 1847 JG | — | 40.00 | 60.00 | 100.00 | 175.00 |
| | 1850 JG | — | 35.00 | 50.00 | 75.00 | 150.00 |
| | 1852 JG | — | 35.00 | 50.00 | 75.00 | 150.00 |
| | 1859 JG | — | 40.00 | 60.00 | 100.00 | 175.00 |
| | 1861 JG | — | 35.00 | 50.00 | 75.00 | 150.00 |

**Mint mark: GC**

| KM# | Date | Mintage | VG | Fine | VF | XF |
|---|---|---|---|---|---|---|
| 378.3 | 1846 MP | — | 50.00 | 75.00 | 100.00 | 175.00 |
| | 1847 MP | — | 50.00 | 75.00 | 100.00 | 175.00 |
| | 1848/7 MP | — | 50.00 | 75.00 | 100.00 | 200.00 |
| | 1850 MP | — | 50.00 | 75.00 | 100.00 | 175.00 |
| | 1851 MP | — | 50.00 | 75.00 | 100.00 | 175.00 |

**Mint mark: Go**

| KM# | Date | Mintage | VG | Fine | VF | XF |
|---|---|---|---|---|---|---|
| 378.4 | 1845 PM | — | 30.00 | 40.00 | 65.00 | 125.00 |
| | 1849 PF | — | 30.00 | 40.00 | 65.00 | 125.00 |
| | 1851/41 PF | — | 30.00 | 40.00 | 65.00 | 125.00 |
| | 1851 PF | — | 30.00 | 40.00 | 65.00 | 125.00 |
| | 1852 PF | — | 30.00 | 40.00 | 65.00 | 125.00 |
| | 1853 PF | — | 30.00 | 40.00 | 65.00 | 125.00 |
| | 1855 PF | — | 30.00 | 50.00 | 80.00 | 150.00 |
| | 1857 PF | — | 30.00 | 40.00 | 65.00 | 125.00 |
| | 1858/7 PF | — | 30.00 | 40.00 | 65.00 | 125.00 |
| | 1859 PF | — | 30.00 | 40.00 | 65.00 | 125.00 |
| | 1860 PF | — | 30.00 | 40.00 | 65.00 | 125.00 |
| | 1861 PF | — | 30.00 | 40.00 | 65.00 | 125.00 |
| | 1862/1 YE | — | 30.00 | 40.00 | 65.00 | 125.00 |
| | 1863 PF | — | 30.00 | 50.00 | 80.00 | 150.00 |
| | 1863 YF | — | 30.00 | 40.00 | 65.00 | 125.00 |

**Mint mark: Mo**

| KM# | Date | Mintage | VG | Fine | VF | XF |
|---|---|---|---|---|---|---|
| 378.5 | 1825/1 JM | — | 50.00 | 75.00 | 125.00 | 200.00 |

| KM# | Date Mintage | VG | Fine | VF | XF |
|---|---|---|---|---|---|
| 378.5 | 1825/4 JM — | 50.00 | 75.00 | 125.00 | 200.00 |
| | 1825 JM — | 30.00 | 40.00 | 80.00 | 150.00 |
| | 1827/6 JM — | 50.00 | 75.00 | 125.00 | 200.00 |
| | 1827 JM — | 30.00 | 40.00 | 80.00 | 150.00 |
| | 1829 JM — | 30.00 | 40.00 | 80.00 | 150.00 |
| | 1831/0 JM — | 50.00 | 75.00 | 125.00 | 200.00 |
| | 1831 JM — | 30.00 | 40.00 | 60.00 | 125.00 |
| | 1832 JM — | 30.00 | 40.00 | 60.00 | 125.00 |
| | 1833 MJ olive & oak branches reversed | | | | |
| | — | 30.00 | 50.00 | 90.00 | 175.00 |
| | 1834 ML — | 30.00 | 40.00 | 60.00 | 125.00 |
| | 1835 ML — | 30.00 | 40.00 | 80.00 | 150.00 |
| | 1838 ML — | 30.00 | 50.00 | 90.00 | 175.00 |
| | 1839 ML — | 30.00 | 50.00 | 90.00 | 175.00 |
| | 1840 ML — | 30.00 | 40.00 | 60.00 | 125.00 |
| | 1841 ML — | 30.00 | 40.00 | 60.00 | 125.00 |
| | 1842 ML — | 30.00 | 40.00 | 80.00 | 150.00 |
| | 1842 MM — | 30.00 | 40.00 | 80.00 | 150.00 |
| | 1843 MM — | 30.00 | 40.00 | 60.00 | 125.00 |
| | 1844 MF — | 30.00 | 40.00 | 60.00 | 125.00 |
| | 1845 MF — | 30.00 | 40.00 | 60.00 | 125.00 |
| | 1846/5 MF — | 30.00 | 40.00 | 60.00 | 125.00 |
| | 1846 MF — | 30.00 | 40.00 | 60.00 | 125.00 |
| | 1848 GC — | 30.00 | 40.00 | 60.00 | 125.00 |
| | 1850 GC — | 30.00 | 40.00 | 60.00 | 125.00 |
| | 1851 GC — | 30.00 | 40.00 | 60.00 | 125.00 |
| | 1852 GC — | 30.00 | 40.00 | 60.00 | 125.00 |
| | 1853 GC — | 30.00 | 40.00 | 60.00 | 125.00 |
| | 1854 GC — | 30.00 | 40.00 | 60.00 | 125.00 |
| | 1855 GF — | 30.00 | 40.00 | 60.00 | 125.00 |
| | 1856/4 GF — | 30.00 | 40.00 | 60.00 | 125.00 |
| | 1857 GF — | 30.00 | 40.00 | 60.00 | 125.00 |
| | 1858/7 FH/GF | | | | |
| | — | 35.00 | 50.00 | 75.00 | 150.00 |
| | 1858 FH — | 30.00 | 40.00 | 60.00 | 125.00 |
| | 1859 FH — | 30.00 | 40.00 | 60.00 | 125.00 |
| | 1860/59 FH — | 30.00 | 40.00 | 60.00 | 125.00 |
| | 1861 CH/FH — | 30.00 | 40.00 | 80.00 | 150.00 |
| | 1862 CH — | 30.00 | 40.00 | 60.00 | 125.00 |
| | 1863/57 CH/GF | | | | |
| | — | 30.00 | 40.00 | 60.00 | 125.00 |
| | 1868/58 PH — | 30.00 | 40.00 | 80.00 | 150.00 |
| | 1869/59 CH — | 30.00 | 40.00 | 80.00 | 150.00 |
| | **Mint mark: Zs** | | | | |
| 378.6 | 1860 VL — | 35.00 | 50.00 | 75.00 | 150.00 |
| | 1862/1 VL — | 35.00 | 50.00 | 75.00 | 150.00 |
| | 1862 VL — | 30.00 | 40.00 | 65.00 | 125.00 |

## ESCUDO

**3.3800 g, .875 GOLD, .0950 oz AGW**
**Mint mark: C**
**Obv: Facing eagle.**

| KM# | Date Mintage | VG | Fine | VF | XF |
|---|---|---|---|---|---|
| 379 | 1846 CE — | 75.00 | 100.00 | 200.00 | 350.00 |
| | 1847 CE — | 50.00 | 75.00 | 125.00 | 175.00 |
| | 1848 CE — | 50.00 | 75.00 | 125.00 | 175.00 |
| | 1849/8 CE — | 60.00 | 100.00 | 150.00 | 225.00 |
| | 1850 CE — | 50.00 | 75.00 | 125.00 | 175.00 |
| | 1851 CE — | 60.00 | 100.00 | 150.00 | 225.00 |
| | 1853/1 CE — | 60.00 | 100.00 | 150.00 | 225.00 |
| | 1854 CE — | 50.00 | 75.00 | 125.00 | 175.00 |
| | 1856/5/4 CE — | 60.00 | 100.00 | 150.00 | 225.00 |
| | 1856 CE — | 50.00 | 75.00 | 125.00 | 175.00 |
| | 1857/1 CE — | 60.00 | 100.00 | 150.00 | 225.00 |
| | 1857 CE — | 50.00 | 75.00 | 125.00 | 175.00 |
| | 1861 PV — | 50.00 | 75.00 | 125.00 | 175.00 |
| | 1862 CE — | 50.00 | 75.00 | 125.00 | 175.00 |
| | 1863 CE — | 50.00 | 75.00 | 125.00 | 175.00 |
| | 1866 CE — | 50.00 | 75.00 | 125.00 | 175.00 |
| | 1870 CE — | 50.00 | 75.00 | 125.00 | 175.00 |
| | **Mint mark: Do** | | | | |
| 379.1 | 1833/2 RM/RL | | | | |
| | — | 75.00 | 125.00 | 200.00 | 300.00 |
| | 1834 RM — | 60.00 | 100.00 | 150.00 | 200.00 |
| | 1835 RM — | — | — | — | — |

| KM# | Date Mintage | VG | Fine | VF | XF |
|---|---|---|---|---|---|
| 379.1 | 1836 RM/RL — | 60.00 | 100.00 | 150.00 | 200.00 |
| | 1838 RM — | 60.00 | 100.00 | 150.00 | 200.00 |
| | 1846/38 RM — | 75.00 | 125.00 | 200.00 | 300.00 |
| | 1850 JMR — | 75.00 | 125.00 | 175.00 | 225.00 |
| | 1851/31 JMR | | | | |
| | — | 75.00 | 125.00 | 200.00 | 300.00 |
| | 1851 JMR — | 75.00 | 125.00 | 175.00 | 225.00 |
| | 1853 CP — | 75.00 | 125.00 | 175.00 | 225.00 |
| | 1854/34 CP — | 75.00 | 125.00 | 175.00 | 225.00 |
| | 1854/44 CP/RP | | | | |
| | — | 75.00 | 125.00 | 175.00 | 225.00 |
| | 1855 CP — | 75.00 | 125.00 | 175.00 | 225.00 |
| | 1859 CP — | 75.00 | 125.00 | 175.00 | 225.00 |
| | 1861 CP — | 75.00 | 125.00 | 175.00 | 225.00 |
| | 1864 LT/CP — | 75.00 | 125.00 | 175.00 | 225.00 |
| | **Mint mark: Ga** | | | | |
| 379.2 | 1825 FS — | 60.00 | 90.00 | 125.00 | 200.00 |
| | 1826 FS — | 60.00 | 90.00 | 125.00 | 200.00 |
| | 1829 FS — | — | — | — | — |
| | 1831 FS — | 60.00 | 90.00 | 125.00 | 200.00 |
| | 1834 FS — | 60.00 | 90.00 | 125.00 | 200.00 |
| | 1835 JG — | 60.00 | 90.00 | 125.00 | 200.00 |
| | 1842 JG/MC — | 60.00 | 90.00 | 125.00 | 200.00 |
| | 1843 MC — | 60.00 | 90.00 | 125.00 | 200.00 |
| | 1847 JG — | 60.00 | 90.00 | 125.00 | 200.00 |
| | 1848/7 JG — | 60.00 | 90.00 | 125.00 | 200.00 |
| | 1849 JG — | 60.00 | 90.00 | 125.00 | 200.00 |
| | 1850/40 JG — | 65.00 | 125.00 | 225.00 | 325.00 |
| | 1850 JG — | 60.00 | 90.00 | 125.00 | 200.00 |
| | 1852/1 JG — | 60.00 | 90.00 | 125.00 | 200.00 |
| | 1856 JG — | 60.00 | 90.00 | 125.00 | 200.00 |
| | 1857 JG — | 60.00 | 90.00 | 125.00 | 200.00 |
| | 1859/7 JG — | 60.00 | 90.00 | 125.00 | 200.00 |
| | 1860/59 JG — | 65.00 | 100.00 | 175.00 | 275.00 |
| | 1860 JG — | 60.00 | 90.00 | 125.00 | 200.00 |
| | **Mint mark: GC** | | | | |
| 379.3 | 1844 MP — | 75.00 | 100.00 | 175.00 | 250.00 |
| | 1845 MP — | 75.00 | 100.00 | 175.00 | 250.00 |
| | 1846 MP — | 75.00 | 100.00 | 175.00 | 250.00 |
| | 1847 MP — | 75.00 | 100.00 | 175.00 | 250.00 |
| | 1848 MP — | 75.00 | 100.00 | 175.00 | 250.00 |
| | 1849 MP — | 75.00 | 100.00 | 175.00 | 250.00 |
| | 1850 MP — | 75.00 | 100.00 | 175.00 | 250.00 |
| | 1851 MP — | 75.00 | 100.00 | 175.00 | 250.00 |
| | **Mint mark: Go** | | | | |
| 379.4 | 1845 PM — | 60.00 | 75.00 | 125.00 | 200.00 |
| | 1849 PF — | 60.00 | 75.00 | 125.00 | 200.00 |
| | 1851 PF — | 60.00 | 75.00 | 125.00 | 200.00 |
| | 1853 PF — | 60.00 | 75.00 | 125.00 | 200.00 |
| | 1860 PF — | 75.00 | 125.00 | 200.00 | 300.00 |
| | 1862 YE — | 60.00 | 75.00 | 125.00 | 200.00 |
| | **Mint mark: Mo** | | | | |
| 379.5 | 1825 JM — | 50.00 | 70.00 | 100.00 | 150.00 |
| | 1827/6 JM — | 50.00 | 70.00 | 100.00 | 150.00 |
| | 1827 JM — | 50.00 | 70.00 | 100.00 | 150.00 |
| | 1830/29 JM — | 50.00 | 70.00 | 100.00 | 150.00 |
| | 1831 JM — | 50.00 | 70.00 | 100.00 | 150.00 |
| | 1832 JM — | 50.00 | 70.00 | 125.00 | 175.00 |
| | 1833 MJ — | 50.00 | 70.00 | 100.00 | 150.00 |
| | 1834 ML — | 50.00 | 70.00 | 125.00 | 175.00 |
| | 1841 ML — | 50.00 | 70.00 | 125.00 | 175.00 |
| | 1843 MM — | 50.00 | 70.00 | 100.00 | 150.00 |
| | 1845 MF — | 50.00 | 70.00 | 100.00 | 150.00 |
| | 1846/5 MF — | 50.00 | 70.00 | 125.00 | 175.00 |
| | 1848 GC — | 50.00 | 70.00 | 125.00 | 175.00 |
| | 1850 GC — | 50.00 | 70.00 | 125.00 | 175.00 |
| | 1856/4 GF — | 50.00 | 70.00 | 100.00 | 150.00 |
| | 1856/5 GF — | 50.00 | 70.00 | 100.00 | 150.00 |
| | 1856 GF — | 50.00 | 70.00 | 100.00 | 150.00 |
| | 1858 FH — | 50.00 | 70.00 | 125.00 | 175.00 |
| | 1859 FH — | 50.00 | 70.00 | 100.00 | 150.00 |
| | 1860 TH — | 50.00 | 70.00 | 125.00 | 175.00 |
| | 1861 CH — | 50.00 | 70.00 | 100.00 | 150.00 |
| | 1862 CH — | 50.00 | 70.00 | 125.00 | 175.00 |
| | 1863 TH — | 50.00 | 70.00 | 100.00 | 150.00 |
| | 1869 CH — | 50.00 | 70.00 | 100.00 | 150.00 |
| | **Mint mark: Zs** | | | | |
| 379.6 | 1853 OM — | 100.00 | 125.00 | 200.00 | 300.00 |
| | 1860/59 VL V is inverted A | | | | |
| | — | 100.00 | 150.00 | 200.00 | 350.00 |
| | 1860 VL — | 75.00 | 100.00 | 150.00 | 200.00 |
| | 1862 VL — | 75.00 | 100.00 | 150.00 | 200.00 |

## 2 ESCUDOS

**6.7700 g, .875 GOLD, .1904 oz AGW**
**Mint mark: C**
**Obv: Facing eagle.**

| KM# | Date Mintage | VG | Fine | VF | XF |
|---|---|---|---|---|---|
| 380 | 1846 CE | — 100.00 | 150.00 | 225.00 | 325.00 |
| | 1847 CE | — 100.00 | 150.00 | 225.00 | 325.00 |
| | 1848 CE | — 100.00 | 150.00 | 225.00 | 325.00 |
| | 1852 CE | — 100.00 | 150.00 | 225.00 | 325.00 |
| | 1854 CE | — 100.00 | 175.00 | 250.00 | 375.00 |
| | 1856/4 CE | — 100.00 | 175.00 | 250.00 | 375.00 |
| | 1857 CE | — 100.00 | 150.00 | 225.00 | 325.00 |

**Mint mark: Do**

| | | | | | |
|---|---|---|---|---|---|
| 380.1 | 1833 RM | — 300.00 | 450.00 | 700.00 | 1200. |
| | 1837/4 RM | — — | — | — | — |
| | 1837 RM | — — | — | — | — |
| | 1844 RM | — 275.00 | 400.00 | 600.00 | 1000. |

**Mint mark: EoMo**

| | | | | | |
|---|---|---|---|---|---|
| 380.2 | 1828 LF | — 700.00 | 1000. | 1750. | 2500. |

**Mint mark: Ga**

| | | | | | |
|---|---|---|---|---|---|
| 380.3 | 1835 FS | — 100.00 | 150.00 | 225.00 | 325.00 |
| | 1836/5 JG | — 100.00 | 150.00 | 225.00 | 300.00 |
| | 1839/5 JG | — — | — | — | — |
| | 1839 JG | — 100.00 | 150.00 | 200.00 | 285.00 |
| | 1840 MC | — 100.00 | 150.00 | 200.00 | 285.00 |
| | 1841 MC | — 100.00 | 150.00 | 250.00 | 400.00 |
| | 1847/6 JG | — 100.00 | 150.00 | 225.00 | 300.00 |
| | 1848// JG | — 100.00 | 150.00 | 225.00 | 300.00 |
| | 1850/40 JG | — 100.00 | 150.00 | 200.00 | 285.00 |
| | 1851 JG | — 100.00 | 150.00 | 200.00 | 285.00 |
| | 1852 JG | — 100.00 | 150.00 | 225.00 | 325.00 |
| | 1853 JG | — 100.00 | 150.00 | 200.00 | 285.00 |
| | 1854/2 JG | — — | — | — | — |
| | 1858 JG | — 100.00 | 150.00 | 200.00 | 285.00 |
| | 1859/8 JG | — 100.00 | 150.00 | 225.00 | 300.00 |
| | 1859 JG | — 100.00 | 150.00 | 200.00 | 285.00 |
| | 1860/50 JG | — 100.00 | 150.00 | 225.00 | 300.00 |
| | 1860 JG | — 100.00 | 150.00 | 225.00 | 300.00 |
| | 1861/59 JG | — 100.00 | 150.00 | 200.00 | 285.00 |
| | 1861/0 JG | — 100.00 | 150.00 | 200.00 | 285.00 |
| | 1863/1 JG | — 100.00 | 150.00 | 200.00 | 285.00 |
| | 1870 IC | — 100.00 | 150.00 | 200.00 | 285.00 |

**Mint mark: GC**

| | | | | | |
|---|---|---|---|---|---|
| 380.4 | 1844 MP | — 150.00 | 200.00 | 275.00 | 400.00 |
| | 1845 MP | — 750.00 | 1250. | 2000. | 3000. |
| | 1846 MP | — 750.00 | 1250. | 2000. | 3000. |
| | 1847 MP | — 125.00 | 175.00 | 350.00 | 500.00 |
| | 1848 MP | — 150.00 | 200.00 | 350.00 | 450.00 |
| | 1849 MP | — 150.00 | 200.00 | 300.00 | 400.00 |
| | 1850 MP | — 150.00 | 200.00 | 300.00 | 400.00 |

**Mint mark: Go**

| | | | | | |
|---|---|---|---|---|---|
| 380.5 | 1845 PM | — 100.00 | 150.00 | 250.00 | 400.00 |
| | 1849 PF | — 100.00 | 150.00 | 250.00 | 400.00 |
| | 1853 PF | — 100.00 | 150.00 | 250.00 | 400.00 |
| | 1856 PF | — 100.00 | 150.00 | 250.00 | 400.00 |
| | 1859 PF | — 100.00 | 150.00 | 250.00 | 400.00 |
| | 1860/59 PF | — 100.00 | 150.00 | 250.00 | 400.00 |
| | 1860 PF | — 100.00 | 150.00 | 250.00 | 400.00 |
| | 1862 YE | — 100.00 | 150.00 | 250.00 | 400.00 |

**Mint mark: Ho**

| | | | | | |
|---|---|---|---|---|---|
| 380.6 | 1861 FM | — 500.00 | 1000. | 1500. | 2000. |

**Mint mark: Mo**

| | | | | | |
|---|---|---|---|---|---|
| 380.7 | 1825 JM | — 100.00 | 150.00 | 200.00 | 285.00 |
| | 1827/6 JM | — 100.00 | 150.00 | 200.00 | 285.00 |
| | 1827 JM | — 100.00 | 150.00 | 200.00 | 285.00 |
| | 1830/29 JM | — 100.00 | 150.00 | 200.00 | 285.00 |
| | 1831 JM | — 100.00 | 150.00 | 200.00 | 285.00 |
| | 1833 ML | — 100.00 | 150.00 | 200.00 | 285.00 |
| | 1841 ML | — 100.00 | 150.00 | 200.00 | 285.00 |

| KM# | Date Mintage | VG | Fine | VF | XF |
|---|---|---|---|---|---|
| 380.7 | 1844 MF | — 100.00 | 150.00 | 200.00 | 285.00 |
| | 1845 MF | — 100.00 | 150.00 | 200.00 | 285.00 |
| | 1846 MF | — 125.00 | 200.00 | 400.00 | 600.00 |
| | 1848 GC | — 100.00 | 150.00 | 200.00 | 285.00 |
| | 1850 GC | — 100.00 | 150.00 | 200.00 | 285.00 |
| | 1856/5 GF | — 100.00 | 150.00 | 200.00 | 285.00 |
| | 1856 GF | — 100.00 | 150.00 | 200.00 | 285.00 |
| | 1858 FH | — 100.00 | 150.00 | 200.00 | 285.00 |
| | 1859 FH | — 100.00 | 150.00 | 200.00 | 285.00 |
| | 1861 TH | — 100.00 | 150.00 | 200.00 | 285.00 |
| | 1861 CH | — 100.00 | 150.00 | 200.00 | 300.00 |
| | 1862 CH | — 100.00 | 150.00 | 200.00 | 300.00 |
| | 1863 TH | — 100.00 | 150.00 | 200.00 | 300.00 |
| | 1868 PH | — 100.00 | 150.00 | 200.00 | 300.00 |
| | 1869 CH | — 100.00 | 150.00 | 200.00 | 300.00 |

**Mint mark: Zs**

| | | | | | |
|---|---|---|---|---|---|
| 380.8 | 1860 VL | — 150.00 | 300.00 | 600.00 | 1200. |
| | 1862 VL | — 250.00 | 500.00 | 800.00 | 1200. |
| | 1864 MO | — 150.00 | 300.00 | 600.00 | 1200. |

## 4 ESCUDOS

**13.5400 g, .875 GOLD, .3809 oz AGW**
**Mint mark: C**
**Facing eagle**

| | | | | | |
|---|---|---|---|---|---|
| 381 | 1846 CE | — 1200. | 1700. | — | — |
| | 1847 CE | — 400.00 | 650.00 | 850.00 | 1350. |
| | 1848 CE | — 600.00 | 900.00 | 1250. | 1850. |

**Mint mark: Do**

| | | | | | |
|---|---|---|---|---|---|
| 381.1 | 1832 RM/LR | — | — | — | Rare | — |
| | 1832 RM | — 600.00 | 900.00 | 1250. | 1850. |
| | 1833 RM/RL | — | — | — | Rare | — |
| | 1852 JMR | — | — | — | Rare | — |

**Mint mark: Ga**

| | | | | | |
|---|---|---|---|---|---|
| 381.2 | 1844 MC | — 500.00 | 750.00 | 1000. | 1600. |
| | 1844 JG | — 400.00 | 650.00 | 850.00 | 1350. |

**Mint mark: GC**

| | | | | | |
|---|---|---|---|---|---|
| 381.3 | 1844 MP | — 400.00 | 650.00 | 850.00 | 1350. |
| | 1845 MP | — 350.00 | 500.00 | 700.00 | 1000. |
| | 1846 MP | — 400.00 | 650.00 | 850.00 | 1350. |
| | 1848 MP | — 400.00 | 650.00 | 850.00 | 1350. |
| | 1850 MP | — 500.00 | 750.00 | 1000. | 1600. |

**Mint mark: Go**

| | | | | | |
|---|---|---|---|---|---|
| 381.4 | 1829/8 MJ | — 200.00 | 300.00 | 450.00 | 850.00 |
| | 1829 JM | — 200.00 | 300.00 | 450.00 | 850.00 |
| | 1829 MJ | — 200.00 | 300.00 | 450.00 | 850.00 |
| | 1831 MJ | — 200.00 | 300.00 | 450.00 | 850.00 |
| | 1832 MJ | — 200.00 | 300.00 | 450.00 | 850.00 |
| | 1833 MJ | — 200.00 | 300.00 | 500.00 | 900.00 |
| | 1834 PJ | — 250.00 | 450.00 | 650.00 | 1000. |
| | 1835 PJ | — 250.00 | 450.00 | 650.00 | 1000. |
| | 1836 PJ | — 200.00 | 300.00 | 500.00 | 900.00 |
| | 1837 PJ | — 200.00 | 300.00 | 500.00 | 900.00 |
| | 1838 PJ | — 200.00 | 300.00 | 500.00 | 900.00 |
| | 1839 PJ | — 250.00 | 450.00 | 650.00 | 1000. |
| | 1840 PJ | — 200.00 | 300.00 | 500.00 | 900.00 |
| | 1841 PJ | — 250.00 | 450.00 | 650.00 | 1000. |
| | 1845 PM | — 200.00 | 300.00 | 500.00 | 900.00 |
| | 1847/5 YE | — 250.00 | 450.00 | 650.00 | 1000. |
| | 1847 PM | — 250.00 | 450.00 | 650.00 | 1000. |
| | 1849 PF | — 250.00 | 450.00 | 650.00 | 1000. |
| | 1851 PF | — 250.00 | 450.00 | 650.00 | 1000. |
| | 1852 PF | — 200.00 | 300.00 | 500.00 | 900.00 |
| | 1855 PF | — 200.00 | 300.00 | 500.00 | 900.00 |
| | 1857/5 PF | — 200.00 | 300.00 | 500.00 | 900.00 |
| | 1858/7 PF | — 200.00 | 300.00 | 500.00 | 900.00 |
| | 1858 PF | — 200.00 | 300.00 | 500.00 | 900.00 |
| | 1859/7 PF | — 250.00 | 450.00 | 650.00 | 1000. |

MEXICO  533

| KM# | Date | Mintage | VG | Fine | VF | XF |
|---|---|---|---|---|---|---|
| 381.4 | 1860 PF | — | 275.00 | 475.00 | 750.00 | 1200. |
| | 1862 YE | — | 200.00 | 300.00 | 500.00 | 900.00 |
| | 1863 YF | — | 200.00 | 300.00 | 500.00 | 900.00 |

**Mint mark: Ho**

| KM# | Date | Mintage | VG | Fine | VF | XF |
|---|---|---|---|---|---|---|
| 381.5 | 1861 FM | — | 1000. | 1500. | 2500. | 3750. |

**Mint mark: Mo**

| KM# | Date | Mintage | VG | Fine | VF | XF |
|---|---|---|---|---|---|---|
| 381.6 | 1825 JM | — | 200.00 | 300.00 | 525.00 | 950.00 |
| | 1827/6 JM | — | 200.00 | 300.00 | 500.00 | 900.00 |
| | 1829 JM | — | 200.00 | 350.00 | 650.00 | 1000. |
| | 1831 JM | — | 200.00 | 350.00 | 650.00 | 1000. |
| | 1832 JM | — | 275.00 | 475.00 | 750.00 | 1200. |
| | 1844 MF | — | 200.00 | 350.00 | 650.00 | 1000. |
| | 1850 GC | — | 200.00 | 350.00 | 650.00 | 1000. |
| | 1856 GF | — | 200.00 | 300.00 | 500.00 | 900.00 |
| | 1857/6 GF | — | 200.00 | 300.00 | 500.00 | 900.00 |
| | 1857 GF | — | 200.00 | 300.00 | 500.00 | 900.00 |
| | 1858 FH | — | 200.00 | 350.00 | 650.00 | 1000. |
| | 1859/8 FH | — | 200.00 | 350.00 | 650.00 | 1000. |
| | 1861 CH | — | 400.00 | 800.00 | 1200. | 1750. |
| | 1863 CH | — | 200.00 | 350.00 | 650.00 | 1000. |
| | 1868 PH | — | 200.00 | 300.00 | 500.00 | 900.00 |
| | 1869 CH | — | 200.00 | 300.00 | 500.00 | 900.00 |

**Mint mark: O, Oa**

| KM# | Date | Mintage | VG | Fine | VF | XF |
|---|---|---|---|---|---|---|
| 381.7 | 1861 FR | — | 1500. | 2500. | 4000. | 6500. |

**Mint mark: Zs**

| KM# | Date | Mintage | VG | Fine | VF | XF |
|---|---|---|---|---|---|---|
| 381.8 | 1862 VL | — | 750.00 | 1250. | 2250. | 3750. |

# 8 ESCUDOS

**Mint mark: A**
**Obv: Facing eagle.**

| KM# | Date | Mintage | Fine | VF | XF | Unc |
|---|---|---|---|---|---|---|
| 383 | 1864 PG | — | 650.00 | 1250. | 2250. | — |
| | 1866 DL | — | — | — | 7500. | — |
| | 1868/7 DL | — | 1500. | 2250. | 3250. | — |
| | 1869 DL | — | 650.00 | 1250. | 2250. | — |
| | 1870 DL | — | 1500. | 2250. | 3250. | — |
| | 1872 AM | — | — | — | Rare | — |

**Mint mark: Ca**

| KM# | Date | Mintage | Fine | VF | XF | Unc |
|---|---|---|---|---|---|---|
| 383.1 | 1841 RG | — | 400.00 | 750.00 | 1250. | 1750. |
| | 1842 RG | — | 350.00 | 500.00 | 1000. | 1500. |
| | 1843 RG | — | 350.00 | 500.00 | 1000. | 1500. |
| | 1844 RG | — | 350.00 | 500.00 | 1000. | 1500. |
| | 1845 RG | — | 350.00 | 500.00 | 1000. | 1500. |
| | 1846 RG | — | 500.00 | 1250. | 1500. | 2000. |
| | 1847 RG | — | 1000. | 2500. | — | — |
| | 1848 RG | — | 350.00 | 500.00 | 1000. | 1500. |
| | 1849 RG | — | 350.00 | 500.00 | 1000. | 1500. |
| | 1850/40 RG | — | 350.00 | 500.00 | 1000. | 1500. |
| | 1851/41 RG | — | 350.00 | 500.00 | 1000. | 1500. |
| | 1852/42 RG | — | 350.00 | 500.00 | 1000. | 1500. |
| | 1853/43 RG | — | 350.00 | 500.00 | 1000. | 1500. |
| | 1854/44 RG | — | 350.00 | 500.00 | 1000. | 1500. |
| | 1855/43 RG | — | 400.00 | 650.00 | 1250. | 1750. |
| | 1856/46 RG | — | 325.00 | 475.00 | 750.00 | 1250. |
| | 1857 JC/RG | — | 325.00 | 475.00 | 750.00 | 1250. |
| | 1858 JC | — | 325.00 | 475.00 | 750.00 | 1250. |
| | 1858 BA/RG | — | 325.00 | 475.00 | 750.00 | 1250. |
| | 1859 JC/RG | — | 325.00 | 475.00 | 750.00 | 1250. |
| | 1860 JC/RG | — | 350.00 | 500.00 | 1000. | 1500. |
| | 1861 JC | — | 350.00 | 475.00 | 750.00 | 1250. |
| | 1862 JC | — | 350.00 | 475.00 | 750.00 | 1250. |
| | 1863 JC | — | 500.00 | 1000. | 1750. | 2250. |
| | 1864 JC | — | 400.00 | 750.00 | 1250. | 1750. |
| | 1865 JC | — | 750.00 | 1500. | 2500. | 3500. |

| KM# | Date | Mintage | Fine | VF | XF | Unc |
|---|---|---|---|---|---|---|
| 383.1 | 1866 JC | — | 350.00 | 500.00 | 1000. | 1500. |
| | 1866 FP | — | 600.00 | 1250. | 2000. | 2500. |
| | 1866 JG | — | 350.00 | 500.00 | 1000. | 1500. |
| | 1867 JG | — | 350.00 | 475.00 | 750.00 | 1250. |
| | 1868 JG concave wings | | | | | |
| | | — | 350.00 | 475.00 | 750.00 | 1250. |
| | 1869 MM regular eagle | | | | | |
| | | — | 350.00 | 475.00 | 750.00 | 1250. |
| | 1870/60 MM | — | 350.00 | 475.00 | 750.00 | 1250. |
| | 1871/61 MM | — | 350.00 | 475.00 | 750.00 | 1250. |

**Mint mark: C**

| KM# | Date | Mintage | Fine | VF | XF | Unc |
|---|---|---|---|---|---|---|
| 383.2 | 1846 CE | — | 350.00 | 500.00 | 1000. | 1750. |
| | 1847 CE | — | 350.00 | 500.00 | 800.00 | 1250. |
| | 1848 CE | — | 350.00 | 500.00 | 1000. | 1750. |
| | 1849 CE | — | 325.00 | 450.00 | 700.00 | 1250. |
| | 1850 CE | — | 325.00 | 450.00 | 700.00 | 1250. |
| | 1851 CE | — | 350.00 | 500.00 | 800.00 | 1250. |
| | 1852 CE | — | 350.00 | 500.00 | 800.00 | 1250. |
| | 1853/1 CE | — | 325.00 | 450.00 | 700.00 | 1250. |
| | 1854 CE | — | 325.00 | 450.00 | 700.00 | 1250. |
| | 1855/4 CE | — | 350.00 | 500.00 | 1000. | 1750. |
| | 1855 CE | — | 350.00 | 500.00 | 800.00 | 1250. |
| | 1856 CE | — | 325.00 | 450.00 | 700.00 | 1250. |
| | 1857 CE | — | 325.00 | 450.00 | 700.00 | 1250. |
| | 1857 CE w/o periods after C's | | | | | |
| | | — | — | — | — | — |
| | 1858 CE | — | 325.00 | 450.00 | 700.00 | 1250. |
| | 1859 CE | — | 325.00 | 450.00 | 700.00 | 1250. |
| | 1860/58 CE | — | 350.00 | 500.00 | 800.00 | 1250. |
| | 1860 CE | — | 350.00 | 500.00 | 800.00 | 1250. |
| | 1860 PV | — | 325.00 | 450.00 | 700.00 | 1250. |
| | 1861 PV | — | 350.00 | 500.00 | 800.00 | 1250. |
| | 1861 CE | — | 350.00 | 500.00 | 800.00 | 1250. |
| | 1862 CE | — | 350.00 | 500.00 | 800.00 | 1250. |
| | 1863 CE | — | 350.00 | 500.00 | 800.00 | 1250. |
| | 1864 CE | — | 325.00 | 450.00 | 700.00 | 1250. |
| | 1865 CE | — | 350.00 | 500.00 | 800.00 | 1250. |
| | 1866/5 CE | — | 325.00 | 450.00 | 700.00 | 1250. |
| | 1866 CE | — | 325.00 | 450.00 | 700.00 | 1250. |
| | 1867 CB (error) | | | | | |
| | | — | 325.00 | 450.00 | 700.00 | 1250. |
| | 1867 CE/CB | — | 325.00 | 450.00 | 700.00 | 1250. |
| | 1868 CB (error) | | | | | |
| | | — | 350.00 | 500.00 | 800.00 | 1250. |
| | 1869 CE | — | 350.00 | 500.00 | 800.00 | 1250. |
| | 1870 CE | — | 350.00 | 500.00 | 800.00 | 1250. |

**Mint mark: Do**

| KM# | Date | Mintage | Fine | VF | XF | Unc |
|---|---|---|---|---|---|---|
| 383.3 | 1832 RM | — | 850.00 | 1750. | 2000. | 3000. |
| | 1833 RM/RL | — | 350.00 | 500.00 | 800.00 | 1250. |

| KM# | Date | Mintage | Fine | VF | XF | Unc |
|---|---|---|---|---|---|---|
| 383.3 | 1834 RM | — | 350.00 | 500.00 | 800.00 | 1250. |
| | 1835 RM | — | 350.00 | 500.00 | 800.00 | 1250. |
| | 1836 RM/RL | — | 350.00 | 500.00 | 800.00 | 1250. |
| | 1836 RM M on snake | | | | | |
| | | — | 350.00 | 500.00 | 800.00 | 1250. |
| | 1837 RM | — | 350.00 | 500.00 | 800.00 | 1250. |
| | 1838/6 RM | — | 350.00 | 500.00 | 800.00 | 1250. |
| | 1838 RM | — | 350.00 | 500.00 | 800.00 | 1250. |
| | 1839 RM | — | 325.00 | 450.00 | 700.00 | 1250. |
| | 1840/30 RM/RL | | | | | |
| | | — | 400.00 | 600.00 | 1000. | 1750. |
| | 1841/30 RM | — | 550.00 | 750.00 | 1250. | 2000. |
| | 1841/31 RM | — | 350.00 | 500.00 | 800.00 | 1250. |
| | 1841/34 RM | — | 350.00 | 500.00 | 800.00 | 1250. |
| | 1841 RM/RL | — | 350.00 | 500.00 | 800.00 | 1250. |
| | 1842/32 RM | — | 350.00 | 500.00 | 800.00 | 1250. |
| | 1843/33 RM | — | 550.00 | 750.00 | 1250. | 2000. |
| | 1843/1 RM | — | 350.00 | 500.00 | 800.00 | 1250. |
| | 1843 RM | — | 350.00 | 500.00 | 800.00 | 1250. |
| | 1844/34 RM/RL | | | | | |
| | | — | 500.00 | 1000. | 1500. | 2500. |
| | 1844 RM | — | 450.00 | 800.00 | 1250. | 2000. |
| | 1845/36 RM | — | 400.00 | 600.00 | 1000. | 1750. |
| | 1845 RM | — | 400.00 | 600.00 | 1000. | 1750. |
| | 1846 RM | — | 350.00 | 500.00 | 800.00 | 1250. |
| | 1847/37 RM | — | 350.00 | 500.00 | 800.00 | 1250. |
| | 1848/37 RM | — | — | — | — | — |
| | 1848/38 CM | — | 350.00 | 500.00 | 800.00 | 1250. |
| | 1849/39 CM | — | 350.00 | 500.00 | 800.00 | 1250. |
| | 1849 JMR | — | 400.00 | 750.00 | 1250. | 2000. |
| | 1850 JMR | — | 400.00 | 750.00 | 1250. | 2000. |
| | 1851 JMR | — | 400.00 | 750.00 | 1250. | 2000. |
| | 1852/1 JMR | — | 450.00 | 800.00 | 1250. | 2000. |
| | 1852 CP | — | 450.00 | 800.00 | 1250. | 2000. |
| | 1853 CP | — | 450.00 | 800.00 | 1250. | 2000. |
| | 1854 CP | — | 400.00 | 600.00 | 1000. | 1750. |
| | 1855/4 CP | — | 350.00 | 500.00 | 800.00 | 1250. |
| | 1855 CP | — | 350.00 | 500.00 | 800.00 | 1250. |
| | 1856 CP | — | 400.00 | 600.00 | 1000. | 1750. |
| | 1857 CP French style eagle, 1832-57 | | | | | |
| | | — | 350.00 | 500.00 | 800.00 | 1250. |
| | 1857 CP Mexican style eagle | | | | | |
| | | — | 350.00 | 500.00 | 800.00 | 1250. |
| | 1858 CP | — | 350.00 | 500.00 | 800.00 | 1250. |
| | 1859 CP | — | 350.00 | 500.00 | 800.00 | 1250. |
| | 1860/59 CP | — | 450.00 | 700.00 | 1250. | 2200. |
| | 1861/0 CP | — | 400.00 | 600.00 | 1000. | 1750. |
| | 1862/52 CP | — | 350.00 | 500.00 | 800.00 | 1250. |
| | 1862/1 CP | — | 350.00 | 500.00 | 800.00 | 1250. |
| | 1862 CP | — | 350.00 | 500.00 | 800.00 | 1250. |
| | 1863/53 CP | — | 350.00 | 500.00 | 800.00 | 1250. |
| | 1864 LT | — | 350.00 | 500.00 | 800.00 | 1250. |
| | 1865/4 LT | — | 500.00 | 1000. | 1650. | 2750. |
| | 1866/4 CM | — | 1250. | 2000. | 2500. | — |
| | 1866 CM | — | 400.00 | 600.00 | 1000. | 1750. |
| | 1867/56 CP | — | 400.00 | 600.00 | 1000. | 1750. |
| | 1867/4 CP | — | 350.00 | 500.00 | 800.00 | 1250. |
| | 1868/4 CP/LT | | | | | |
| | | — | — | — | — | — |
| | 1869 CP | — | 500.00 | 1250. | 1750. | 2750. |
| | 1870 CP | — | 400.00 | 600.00 | 1000. | 1750. |

**Mint mark: EoMo**

| KM# | Date | Mintage | Fine | VF | XF | Unc |
|---|---|---|---|---|---|---|
| 383.4 | 1828 LF | — | 3500. | 5500. | 8500. | — |
| | 1829 LF | — | 3500. | 5500. | 8500. | — |

**Mint mark: Ga**

| KM# | Date | Mintage | Fine | VF | XF | Unc |
|---|---|---|---|---|---|---|
| 383.5 | 1825 FS | — | 500.00 | 1000. | 1250. | 1750. |
| | 1826 FS | — | 500.00 | 1000. | 1250. | 1750. |
| | 1830 FS | — | 500.00 | 1000. | 1250. | 1750. |
| | 1836 FS | — | 750.00 | 1500. | 2000. | 3000. |
| | 1836 JG | — | 1000. | 2500. | 3500. | — |
| | 1837 JG | — | 1000. | 2500. | 3500. | — |
| | 1840 MC | — | 750.00 | 1500. | 2000. | 3000. |
| | 1841/31 MC | — | 1000. | 2500. | — | — |
| | 1841 MC | — | 850.00 | 1650. | 2250. | — |
| | 1842 JG | — | — | — | — | — |
| | 1843 MC | — | — | — | — | — |
| | 1845 MC | — | 400.00 | 850.00 | 1100. | 1650. |
| | 1847 JG | — | 2250. | — | — | — |
| | 1849 JG | — | 500.00 | 1000. | 1250. | 1750. |
| | 1850 JG | — | 400.00 | 850.00 | 1100. | 1650. |
| | 1851 JG | — | 400.00 | 850.00 | 1100. | 1650. |
| | 1852/1 JG | — | 500.00 | 1000. | 1250. | 1750. |
| | 1855 JG | — | 1000. | 2500. | 3500. | — |

| KM# | Date | Mintage | Fine | VF | XF | Unc |
|---|---|---|---|---|---|---|
| 383.5 | 1856 JG | — | 400.00 | 850.00 | 1100. | 1650. |
| | 1857 JG | — | 400.00 | 850.00 | 1100. | 1650. |
| | 1861/0 JG | — | 500.00 | 1000. | 1250. | 1750. |
| | 1861 JG | — | 400.00 | 700.00 | 1200. | 1750. |
| | 1863/1 JG | — | 500.00 | 1000. | 1250. | 1750. |
| | 1866 JG | — | 400.00 | 850.00 | 1100. | 1650. |

**Mint mark: GC**

| KM# | Date | Mintage | Fine | VF | XF | Unc |
|---|---|---|---|---|---|---|
| 383.6 | 1844 MP | — | 550.00 | 750.00 | 1250. | 2000. |
| | 1845 MP eagle's tail square | | | | | |
| | | — | 550.00 | 750.00 | 1250. | 2000. |
| | 1845 MP eagle's tail round | | | | | |
| | | — | 550.00 | 750.00 | 1250. | 2000. |
| | 1846 MP eagle's tail square | | | | | |
| | | — | 450.00 | 650.00 | 1000. | 1750. |
| | 1846 MP eagle's tail round | | | | | |
| | | — | 450.00 | 650.00 | 1000. | 1750. |
| | 1847 MP | — | 450.00 | 650.00 | 1000. | 1750. |
| | 1848 MP | — | 550.00 | 750.00 | 1250. | 2000. |
| | 1849 MP | — | 550.00 | 750.00 | 1250. | 2000. |
| | 1850 MP | — | 450.00 | 650.00 | 1000. | 1750. |
| | 1851 MP | — | 450.00 | 650.00 | 1000. | 1750. |
| | 1852 MP | — | 550.00 | 750.00 | 1250. | 2000. |

**Mint mark: Go**

| KM# | Date | Mintage | Fine | VF | XF | Unc |
|---|---|---|---|---|---|---|
| 383.7 | 1828 MJ | — | 700.00 | 1750. | 2250. | 3000. |
| | 1829 MJ | — | 600.00 | 1500. | 2000. | 2750. |
| | 1830 MJ | — | 350.00 | 500.00 | 750.00 | 1000. |
| | 1831 MJ | — | 600.00 | 1500. | 2000. | 2750. |
| | 1832 MJ | — | 500.00 | 1250. | 1750. | 2500. |
| | 1833 MJ | — | 350.00 | 500.00 | 700.00 | 1000. |
| | 1834 PJ | — | 350.00 | 500.00 | 700.00 | 1000. |
| | 1835 PJ | — | 350.00 | 500.00 | 700.00 | 1000. |
| | 1836 PJ | — | 400.00 | 650.00 | 900.00 | 1250. |
| | 1837 PJ | — | 400.00 | 650.00 | 900.00 | 1250. |
| | 1838/7 PJ | — | 350.00 | 500.00 | 700.00 | 1000. |
| | 1838 PJ | — | 350.00 | 500.00 | 800.00 | 1200. |
| | 1839/8 PJ | — | 350.00 | 500.00 | 700.00 | 1000. |
| | 1839 PJ regular eagle | | | | | |
| | | — | 350.00 | 500.00 | 800.00 | 1200. |
| | 1840 PJ concave wings | | | | | |
| | | — | 350.00 | 500.00 | 700.00 | 1000. |
| | 1841 PJ | — | 350.00 | 500.00 | 700.00 | 1000. |
| | 1842 PJ | — | 325.00 | 400.00 | 500.00 | 900.00 |
| | 1842 PM | — | 350.00 | 500.00 | 700.00 | 1000. |
| | 1843 PM small eagle | | | | | |
| | | — | 350.00 | 500.00 | 700.00 | 1000. |
| | 1844/3 PM | — | 400.00 | 650.00 | 900.00 | 1250. |
| | 1844 PM | — | 350.00 | 500.00 | 700.00 | 1000. |
| | 1845 PM | — | 350.00 | 500.00 | 700.00 | 1000. |
| | 1846/5 PM | — | 350.00 | 500.00 | 800.00 | 1200. |

| KM# | Date | Mintage | Fine | VF | XF | Unc |
|-----|------|---------|------|-----|-----|-----|
| 383.7 | 1846 PM | — | 350.00 | 500.00 | 700.00 | 1000. |
| | 1847 PM | — | 400.00 | 650.00 | 900.00 | 1250. |
| | 1848/7 PM | — | 350.00 | 500.00 | 700.00 | 1000. |
| | 1848 PM | — | 350.00 | 500.00 | 700.00 | 1000. |
| | 1848 PF | — | 350.00 | 500.00 | 700.00 | 1000. |
| | 1849 PF | — | 325.00 | 400.00 | 500.00 | 900.00 |
| | 1850 PF | — | 325.00 | 400.00 | 500.00 | 900.00 |
| | 1851 PF | — | 375.00 | 500.00 | 700.00 | 1000. |
| | 1852 PF | — | 375.00 | 500.00 | 700.00 | 1000. |
| | 1853 PF | — | 325.00 | 400.00 | 500.00 | 900.00 |
| | 1854 PF eagle of 1853 | | | | | |
| | | — | 350.00 | 500.00 | 700.00 | 1000. |
| | 1854 PF eagle of 1855 | | | | | |
| | | — | 350.00 | 500.00 | 700.00 | 1000. |
| | 1855/4 PF | — | 400.00 | 650.00 | 900.00 | 1250. |
| | 1855 PF | — | 350.00 | 500.00 | 700.00 | 1000. |
| | 1856 PF | — | 350.00 | 500.00 | 700.00 | 1000. |
| | 1857 PF | — | 350.00 | 500.00 | 700.00 | 1000. |
| | 1858 PF | — | 350.00 | 500.00 | 700.00 | 1000. |
| | 1859 PF | — | 325.00 | 400.00 | 500.00 | 800.00 |
| | 1860/50 PF | — | 325.00 | 400.00 | 500.00 | 900.00 |
| | 1860/59 PF | — | 400.00 | 650.00 | 900.00 | 1250. |
| | 1860 PF | — | 375.00 | 500.00 | 700.00 | 1100. |
| | 1861/0 PF | — | 325.00 | 400.00 | 500.00 | 800.00 |
| | 1861 PF | — | 325.00 | 400.00 | 500.00 | 800.00 |
| | 1862/1 YE | — | 350.00 | 500.00 | 700.00 | 1000. |
| | 1862 YE | — | 350.00 | 500.00 | 700.00 | 1000. |
| | 1862 YF | — | — | — | — | — |
| | 1863/53 YF | — | 350.00 | 500.00 | 700.00 | 1000. |
| | 1863 PF | — | 350.00 | 500.00 | 700.00 | 1000. |
| | 1867/57 YF/PF | | | | | |
| | | — | 350.00 | 500.00 | 700.00 | 1000. |
| | 1867 YF | — | 350.00 | 500.00 | 700.00 | 1000. |
| | 1868/58 YF | — | 350.00 | 500.00 | 700.00 | 1000. |
| | 1870 FR | — | 325.00 | 400.00 | 500.00 | 900.00 |

### Mint mark: Ho

| KM# | Date | Mintage | Fine | VF | XF | Unc |
|-----|------|---------|------|-----|-----|-----|
| 383.8 | 1863 FM | — | 400.00 | 650.00 | 1000. | 2000. |
| | 1864 FM | — | 600.00 | 1250. | 1750. | 2750. |
| | 1864 PR/FM | — | 400.00 | 650.00 | 1000. | 2000. |
| | 1865 FM/PR | — | 500.00 | 800.00 | 1250. | 2500. |
| | 1867/57 PR | — | 400.00 | 650.00 | 1000. | 2000. |
| | 1868 PR | — | 500.00 | 800.00 | 1250. | 2500. |
| | 1868 PR/FM | — | 500.00 | 800.00 | 1250. | 2500. |
| | 1869 PR/FM | — | 400.00 | 650.00 | 1000. | 2000. |
| | 1869 PR | — | 400.00 | 650.00 | 1000. | 2000. |
| | 1870 PR | — | 400.00 | 650.00 | 1000. | 2000. |
| | 1871/0 PR | — | 500.00 | 800.00 | 1250. | 2500. |
| | 1871 PR | — | 500.00 | 800.00 | 1250. | 2500. |
| | 1872/1 PR | — | 600.00 | 1250. | 1750. | 2750. |
| | 1873 PR | — | 400.00 | 650.00 | 1000. | 2000. |

Large book.

### Small book.
### Mint mark: Mo

| KM# | Date | Mintage | Fine | VF | XF | Unc |
|-----|------|---------|------|-----|-----|-----|
| 383.9 | 1824 JM lg. book reverse | | | | | |
| | | — | 500.00 | 1000. | 1250. | 2000. |
| | 1825 JM sm. book reverse | | | | | |
| | | — | 325.00 | 400.00 | 500.00 | 1000. |
| | 1826/5 JM | — | 700.00 | 1750. | 2250. | 3000. |
| | 1827 JM | — | 350.00 | 500.00 | 700.00 | 1000. |
| | 1828 JM | — | 350.00 | 500.00 | 700.00 | 1000. |
| | 1829 JM | — | 350.00 | 500.00 | 700.00 | 1000. |
| | 1830 JM | — | 350.00 | 500.00 | 700.00 | 1000. |
| | 1831 JM | — | 350.00 | 500.00 | 700.00 | 1000. |
| | 1832/1 JM | — | 350.00 | 500.00 | 700.00 | 1000. |
| | 1832 JM | — | 350.00 | 500.00 | 700.00 | 1000. |
| | 1833 MJ | — | 400.00 | 750.00 | 1000. | 1500. |
| | 1833 ML | — | 325.00 | 400.00 | 500.00 | 900.00 |
| | 1834 ML | — | 400.00 | 750.00 | 1000. | 1500. |
| | 1835/4 ML | — | 500.00 | 1000. | 1250. | 2000. |
| | 1836 ML | — | 325.00 | 400.00 | 500.00 | 900.00 |
| | 1836 MF | — | 500.00 | 700.00 | 1200. | 2000. |
| | 1837/6 ML | — | 325.00 | 400.00 | 500.00 | 900.00 |
| | 1838 ML | — | 325.00 | 400.00 | 500.00 | 900.00 |
| | 1839 ML | — | 325.00 | 400.00 | 500.00 | 900.00 |
| | 1840 ML | — | 325.00 | 400.00 | 500.00 | 900.00 |
| | 1841 ML | — | 325.00 | 400.00 | 500.00 | 900.00 |
| | 1842/1 ML | — | — | — | — | — |
| | 1842 ML | — | 325.00 | 400.00 | 500.00 | 900.00 |
| | 1842 MM | — | — | — | — | — |
| | 1843 MM | — | 325.00 | 400.00 | 500.00 | 900.00 |
| | 1844 MF | — | 325.00 | 400.00 | 500.00 | 900.00 |
| | 1845 MF | — | 325.00 | 400.00 | 500.00 | 900.00 |
| | 1846 MF | — | 500.00 | 1000. | 1250. | 2000. |
| | 1847 MF | — | 950.00 | 2250. | — | — |
| | 1847 RC | — | 325.00 | 500.00 | 800.00 | 1250. |
| | 1848 GC | — | 325.00 | 400.00 | 500.00 | 900.00 |
| | 1849 GC | — | 325.00 | 400.00 | 500.00 | 900.00 |
| | 1850 GC | — | 325.00 | 400.00 | 500.00 | 900.00 |
| | 1851 GC | — | 325.00 | 400.00 | 500.00 | 900.00 |
| | 1852 GC | — | 325.00 | 400.00 | 500.00 | 900.00 |
| | 1853 GC | — | 325.00 | 400.00 | 500.00 | 900.00 |
| | 1854/44 GC | — | 325.00 | 400.00 | 500.00 | 900.00 |
| | 1854/3 GC | — | 325.00 | 400.00 | 500.00 | 900.00 |
| | 1855 GF | — | 325.00 | 400.00 | 500.00 | 900.00 |
| | 1856/5 GF | — | 325.00 | 400.00 | 500.00 | 900.00 |
| | 1856 GF | — | 325.00 | 400.00 | 500.00 | 900.00 |
| | 1857 GF | — | 325.00 | 400.00 | 500.00 | 900.00 |
| | 1858 FH | — | 325.00 | 400.00 | 500.00 | 900.00 |
| | 1859 FH | — | 400.00 | 750.00 | 1000. | 1500. |
| | 1860 FH | — | 325.00 | 400.00 | 500.00 | 900.00 |
| | 1860 TH | — | 325.00 | 400.00 | 500.00 | 900.00 |
| | 1861/51 CH | — | 325.00 | 400.00 | 500.00 | 900.00 |
| | 1862 CH | — | 325.00 | 400.00 | 500.00 | 900.00 |
| | 1863/53 CH | — | 325.00 | 400.00 | 500.00 | 900.00 |
| | 1863/53 TH | — | 325.00 | 400.00 | 500.00 | 900.00 |
| | 1867 CH | — | 325.00 | 400.00 | 500.00 | 900.00 |
| | 1868 CH | — | 325.00 | 400.00 | 500.00 | 900.00 |
| | 1868 PH | — | 325.00 | 400.00 | 500.00 | 900.00 |
| | 1869 CH | — | 325.00 | 400.00 | 500.00 | 900.00 |

**NOTE:** Formerly reported 1825/3 JM is merely a reworked 5.

## 5 CENTAVOS

**1.3537 g, .903 SILVER, .0393 oz ASW**
**Mint mark: G**

| KM# | Date | Mintage | Fine | VF | XF | Unc |
|-----|------|---------|------|-----|-----|-----|
| 385 | 1864 | .090 | 17.50 | 35.00 | 75.00 | 320.00 |
| | 1865 | — | 20.00 | 30.00 | 55.00 | 285.00 |
| | 1866 | — | 75.00 | 150.00 | 300.00 | 1800. |

**Mint mark: M**

| | | | | | | |
|-----|------|---------|------|-----|-----|-----|
| 385.1 | 1864 | — | 12.50 | 20.00 | 55.00 | 285.00 |
| | 1866/4 | — | 25.00 | 40.00 | 75.00 | 385.00 |
| | 1866 | — | 20.00 | 35.00 | 65.00 | 375.00 |

**Mint mark: P**

| | | | | | | |
|-----|------|---------|------|-----|-----|-----|
| 385.2 | 1864 | — | 100.00 | 215.00 | 950.00 | 2300. |

**Mint mark: Z**

| | | | | | | |
|-----|------|---------|------|-----|-----|-----|
| 385.3 | 1865 | — | 25.00 | 45.00 | 150.00 | 425.00 |

**Mint mark: O**

| KM# | Date | Mintage | Fine | VF | XF | Unc |
|-----|------|---------|------|-----|-----|-----|
| 383.10 | 1858 AE | — | 2000. | 3000. | 4000. | 6000. |
| | 1859 AE | — | 1000. | 2500. | 3750. | 5500. |
| | 1860 AE | — | 1000. | 2500. | 3750. | 5500. |
| | 1861 FR | — | 450.00 | 850.00 | 1250. | 2750. |
| | 1862 FR | — | 450.00 | 850.00 | 1250. | 2750. |
| | 1863 FR | — | 450.00 | 850.00 | 1250. | 2750. |
| | 1864 FR | — | 450.00 | 850.00 | 1250. | 2750. |
| | 1867 AE | — | 450.00 | 850.00 | 1250. | 2750. |
| | 1868 AE | — | 450.00 | 850.00 | 1250. | 2750. |
| | 1869 AE | — | 450.00 | 850.00 | 1250. | 2750. |

**Mint mark: Zs**

| | | | | | | |
|-----|------|---------|------|-----|-----|-----|
| 383.11 | 1858 MO | — | 400.00 | 750.00 | 1000. | 2000. |
| | 1859 MO | — | 325.00 | 400.00 | 500.00 | 900.00 |
| | 1860/59 VL/MO | | | | | |
| | | — | 2000. | 3000. | 4000. | — |
| | 1860/9 MO | — | 400.00 | 750.00 | 1000. | 2000. |
| | 1860 MO | — | 375.00 | 500.00 | 700.00 | 1000. |
| | 1861/0 VL | — | 375.00 | 500.00 | 700.00 | 1000. |
| | 1861 VL | — | 375.00 | 500.00 | 700.00 | 1000. |
| | 1862 VL | — | 375.00 | 500.00 | 700.00 | 1100. |
| | 1863 VL | — | 375.00 | 525.00 | 750.00 | 1150. |
| | 1863 MO | — | 375.00 | 500.00 | 700.00 | 1000. |
| | 1864 MO | — | 750.00 | 1000. | 1500. | 3000. |
| | 1865 MO | — | 375.00 | 500.00 | 700.00 | 1000. |
| | 1865 MP | — | | Contemporary counterfeit | | |
| | 1868 JS | — | 400.00 | 600.00 | 800.00 | 1250. |
| | 1868 YH | — | 400.00 | 600.00 | 800.00 | 1250. |
| | 1869 YH | — | 400.00 | 600.00 | 800.00 | 1250. |
| | 1870 YH | — | 400.00 | 600.00 | 800.00 | 1250. |
| | 1871 YH | — | 400.00 | 600.00 | 800.00 | 1250. |

# EMPIRE OF MAXIMILIAN

**RULER**
Maximilian, Emperor, 1864-1867

**MINT MARKS**
Refer To Republic Coinage

**MONETARY SYSTEM**
100 Centavos = 1 Peso (8 Reales)

## CENTAVO

## 10 CENTAVOS

**2.7073 g, .903 SILVER, .0786 oz ASW**
**Mint mark: G**

| | | | | | | |
|-----|------|---------|------|-----|-----|-----|
| 386 | 1864 | .045 | 20.00 | 45.00 | 90.00 | 325.00 |
| | 1865 | — | 30.00 | 60.00 | 110.00 | 375.00 |

**Mint mark: M**

| | | | | | | |
|-----|------|---------|------|-----|-----|-----|
| 386.1 | 1864 | — | 15.00 | 25.00 | 55.00 | 285.00 |
| | 1866/4 | — | 25.00 | 35.00 | 70.00 | 320.00 |
| | 1866/5 | — | 25.00 | 40.00 | 85.00 | 375.00 |
| | 1866 | — | 20.00 | 35.00 | 75.00 | 375.00 |

**Mint mark: P**

| | | | | | | |
|-----|------|---------|------|-----|-----|-----|
| 386.2 | 1864 | — | 70.00 | 150.00 | 300.00 | 600.00 |

**Mint mark: Z**

| | | | | | | |
|-----|------|---------|------|-----|-----|-----|
| 386.3 | 1865 | — | 25.00 | 55.00 | 165.00 | 475.00 |

## 50 CENTAVOS

**COPPER**
**Mint mark: M**

| | | | | | | |
|-----|------|---------|------|-----|-----|-----|
| 384 | 1864 | — | 40.00 | 75.00 | 225.00 | 1100. |

**13.5365 g, .903 SILVER, .3929 oz ASW**
**Mint mark: Mo**

| | | | | | | |
|-----|------|---------|------|-----|-----|-----|
| 387 | 1866 | .031 | 40.00 | 95.00 | 200.00 | 600.00 |

# PESO

**27.0700 g, .903 SILVER, .7857 oz ASW**
**Mint mark: Go**

| KM# | Date | Mintage | Fine | VF | XF | Unc |
|-----|------|---------|------|-----|-----|-----|
| 388 | 1866 | — | 300.00 | 500.00 | 800.00 | 2150. |

**Mint mark: Mo**

| KM# | Date | Mintage | Fine | VF | XF | Unc |
|-----|------|---------|------|-----|-----|-----|
| 388.1 | 1866 | 2.148 | 30.00 | 45.00 | 125.00 | 375.00 |
| | 1867 | 1.238 | 40.00 | 65.00 | 175.00 | 425.00 |

**Mint mark: Pi**

| KM# | Date | Mintage | Fine | VF | XF | Unc |
|-----|------|---------|------|-----|-----|-----|
| 388.2 | 1866 | — | 45.00 | 90.00 | 275.00 | 725.00 |

# 20 PESOS

**33.8400 g, .875 GOLD, .9520 oz AGW**
**Mint mark: Mo**

| KM# | Date | Mintage | Fine | VF | XF | Unc |
|-----|------|---------|------|-----|-----|-----|
| 389 | 1866 | 8,274 | 500.00 | 900.00 | 1350. | 2500. |

# GOLD PESO FANTASIES

Modern gold 'Peso' fantasies of Maximilian exist. Five varieties exist, some dated 1865. One has an eagle in a plain field above a wreath on the reverse. On the second type a numeral '1' appears to either side of the eagle, and the metallic content is designated below: LEY-ORO-K22.

# TRIAL STRIKES (TS)

| KM# | Date | Mintage | Identification | Mkt.Val. |
|-----|------|---------|---------------|----------|
| TS1 | 1866 Mo | — | 20 Pesos, Copper | — |

# REPUBLIC
# DECIMAL COINAGE

100 Centavos = 1 Peso

# UN (1) CENTAVO

**COPPER**
**Mint mark: Mo**
**Obv: Seated Liberty.**

| KM# | Date | Mintage | Fine | VF | XF | Unc |
|-----|------|---------|------|-----|-----|-----|
| 390 | 1863 round top 3, reeded edge | | | | | |
| | | — | 15.00 | 30.00 | 75.00 | 500.00 |
| | 1863 round top 3, plain edge | | | | | |
| | | — | 15.00 | 30.00 | 75.00 | 500.00 |
| | 1863 flat top 3, reeded edge | | | | | |
| | | — | 12.00 | 28.00 | 70.00 | 500.00 |

**Mint mark: SLP**

| KM# | Date | Mintage | Fine | VF | XF | Unc |
|-----|------|---------|------|-----|-----|-----|
| 390.1 | 1863 | 1.025 | 15.00 | 30.00 | 60.00 | 300.00 |

**Mint mark: As**
**Obv: Standing eagle.**

| KM# | Date | Mintage | Fine | VF | XF | Unc |
|-----|------|---------|------|-----|-----|-----|
| 391 | 1875 | — | — | — | Rare | — |
| | 1876 | .050 | 100.00 | 200.00 | 300.00 | 650.00 |
| | 1880 | — | 25.00 | 50.00 | 100.00 | 400.00 |
| | 1881 | — | 30.00 | 60.00 | 125.00 | 250.00 |

**Mint mark: Cn**

| KM# | Date | Mintage | Fine | VF | XF | Unc |
|-----|------|---------|------|-----|-----|-----|
| 391.1 | 1874 | .266 | 12.50 | 17.50 | 35.00 | 150.00 |
| | 1875/4 | .153 | 15.00 | 20.00 | 45.00 | 150.00 |
| | 1875 | Inc. Ab. | 10.00 | 15.00 | 25.00 | 150.00 |
| | 1876 | .154 | 5.00 | 8.00 | 15.00 | 150.00 |
| | 1877/6 | .993 | 7.50 | 11.50 | 17.50 | 175.00 |
| | 1877 | Inc. Ab. | 6.00 | 9.00 | 15.00 | 150.00 |
| | 1880 | .142 | 7.50 | 10.00 | 12.50 | 150.00 |
| | 1881 | .167 | 7.50 | 10.00 | 25.00 | 175.00 |
| | 1897 large N in mm. | | | | | |
| | | .300 | 2.50 | 5.00 | 12.00 | 50.00 |
| | 1897 small N in mm. | | | | | |
| | | Inc. Ab. | 2.50 | 5.00 | 9.00 | 45.00 |

**Mint mark: Do**

| KM# | Date | Mintage | Fine | VF | XF | Unc |
|-----|------|---------|------|-----|-----|-----|
| 391.2 | 1879 | .110 | 10.00 | 17.50 | 35.00 | 150.00 |
| | 1880 | .069 | 40.00 | 90.00 | 175.00 | 500.00 |
| | 1891 | — | 8.00 | 11.00 | 30.00 | 150.00 |
| | 1891 Do/Mo | — | 8.00 | 11.00 | 30.00 | 150.00 |

**Mint mark: Ga**

| KM# | Date | Mintage | Fine | VF | XF | Unc |
|-----|------|---------|------|-----|-----|-----|
| 391.3 | 1872 | .263 | 15.00 | 30.00 | 60.00 | 200.00 |
| | 1873 | .333 | 6.00 | 9.00 | 25.00 | 150.00 |
| | 1874 | .076 | 15.00 | 25.00 | 50.00 | 175.00 |
| | 1875 | — | 10.00 | 15.00 | 30.00 | 150.00 |
| | 1876 | .303 | 3.00 | 6.00 | 17.50 | 150.00 |
| | 1877 | .108 | 4.00 | 6.00 | 20.00 | 150.00 |
| | 1878 | .543 | 4.00 | 6.00 | 15.00 | 150.00 |
| | 1881/71 | .975 | 7.00 | 9.00 | 20.00 | 175.00 |
| | 1881 | Inc. Ab. | 7.00 | 9.00 | 20.00 | 175.00 |
| | 1889 Ga/Mo | — | 3.50 | 5.00 | 25.00 | 125.00 |
| | 1890 | — | 4.00 | 7.50 | 20.00 | 100.00 |

**Mint mark: Go**

| KM# | Date | Mintage | Fine | VF | XF | Unc |
|-----|------|---------|------|-----|-----|-----|
| 391.4 | 1874 | — | 20.00 | 40.00 | 80.00 | 250.00 |
| | 1875 | .190 | 11.50 | 20.00 | 60.00 | 200.00 |
| | 1876 | — | 125.00 | 200.00 | 350.00 | 750.00 |
| | 1877 | — | — | — | Rare | — |
| | 1878 | .576 | 8.00 | 11.00 | 30.00 | 175.00 |
| | 1880 | .890 | 6.00 | 10.00 | 25.00 | 175.00 |

**Mint mark: Ho**

| KM# | Date | Mintage | Fine | VF | XF | Unc |
|-----|------|---------|------|----|----|-----|
| 391.5 | 1875 | 3,500 | 450.00 | — | — | — |
| | 1070 | 0,500 | 00.00 | 100.00 | 000.00 | 000.00 |
| | 1880 short H, round O | | | | | |
| | | .102 | 7.50 | 15.00 | 35.00 | 150.00 |
| | 1880 tall H, oval O | | | | | |
| | | Inc. Ab. | 7.50 | 15.00 | 35.00 | 150.00 |
| | 1881 | .459 | 5.00 | 10.00 | 25.00 | 150.00 |

**Mint mark: Mo**

| KM# | Date | Mintage | Fine | VF | XF | Unc |
|-----|------|---------|------|----|----|-----|
| 391.6 | 1869 | 1.874 | 7.50 | 25.00 | 60.00 | 200.00 |
| | 1870/69 | 1.200 | 10.00 | 25.00 | 60.00 | 225.00 |
| | 1870 | Inc. Ab. | 8.00 | 20.00 | 50.00 | 200.00 |
| | 1871 | .918 | 8.00 | 15.00 | 40.00 | 200.00 |
| | 1872/1 | 1.625 | 6.50 | 10.00 | 30.00 | 200.00 |
| | 1872 | Inc. Ab. | 6.00 | 9.00 | 25.00 | 200.00 |
| | 1873 | 1.605 | 4.00 | 7.50 | 20.00 | 200.00 |
| | 1874/3 | 1.700 | 5.00 | 7.00 | 15.00 | 100.00 |
| | 1874 | Inc. Ab. | 3.00 | 5.50 | 15.00 | 100.00 |
| | 1874. | Inc. Ab. | 5.00 | 10.00 | 25.00 | 200.00 |
| | 1875 | 1.495 | 6.00 | 8.00 | 30.00 | 100.00 |
| | 1876 | 1.600 | 3.00 | 5.50 | 12.50 | 100.00 |
| | 1877 | 1.270 | 3.00 | 5.50 | 13.50 | 100.00 |
| | 1878/5 | 1.900 | 7.50 | 11.00 | 22.50 | 125.00 |
| | 1878/6 | Inc. Ab. | 7.50 | 11.00 | 22.50 | 125.00 |
| | 1878/7 | Inc. Ab. | 7.50 | 11.00 | 20.00 | 125.00 |
| | 1878 | Inc. Ab. | 6.00 | 9.00 | 13.50 | 100.00 |
| | 1879/8 | 1.505 | 4.50 | 6.50 | 13.50 | 100.00 |
| | 1879 | Inc. Ab. | 3.00 | 5.50 | 12.50 | 75.00 |
| | 1880/70 | 1.130 | 5.50 | 7.50 | 15.00 | 100.00 |
| | 1880/72 | I.A. | 20.00 | 50.00 | 100.00 | 250.00 |
| | 1880/79 | I.A. | 15.00 | 35.00 | 75.00 | 175.00 |
| | 1880 | Inc. Ab. | 4.25 | 6.00 | 12.50 | 75.00 |
| | 1881 | 1.060 | 4.50 | 7.00 | 15.00 | 75.00 |
| | 1886 | 12.687 | 1.50 | 2.00 | 10.00 | 40.00 |
| | 1887 | 7.292 | 1.50 | 2.00 | 10.00 | 35.00 |
| | 1888/78 | 9.984 | 2.50 | 3.00 | 10.00 | 30.00 |
| | 1888/7 | Inc. Ab. | 2.50 | 3.00 | 10.00 | 30.00 |
| | 1888 | Inc. Ab. | 1.50 | 2.00 | 10.00 | 30.00 |
| | 1889 | 19.970 | 2.00 | 3.00 | 10.00 | 30.00 |
| | 1890/89 | | | | | |
| | | 18.726 | 2.50 | 3.00 | 12.00 | 40.00 |
| | 1890/990 | I.A. | 2.50 | 3.00 | 12.00 | 40.00 |
| | 1890 | Inc. Ab. | 1.50 | 2.00 | 10.00 | 30.00 |
| | 1891 | 14.544 | 1.50 | 2.00 | 10.00 | 30.00 |
| | 1892 | 12.908 | 1.50 | 2.00 | 10.00 | 30.00 |
| | 1893/2 | 5.078 | 2.50 | 3.00 | 12.00 | 35.00 |
| | 1893 | Inc. Ab. | 1.50 | 2.00 | 10.00 | 30.00 |
| | 1894/3 | 1.896 | 3.00 | 6.00 | 15.00 | 50.00 |
| | 1894 | Inc. Ab. | 2.00 | 3.00 | 12.00 | 35.00 |
| | 1895/3 | 3.453 | 3.00 | 4.50 | 12.50 | 35.00 |
| | 1895/85 | I.A. | 3.00 | 6.00 | 15.00 | 50.00 |
| | 1895 | Inc. Ab. | 2.00 | 3.00 | 10.00 | 30.00 |
| | 1896 | 3.075 | 2.00 | 3.00 | 10.00 | 30.00 |
| | 1897 | 4.150 | 1.50 | 2.00 | 10.00 | 30.00 |

**NOTE:** Varieties exist.

**Mint mark: Oa**

| KM# | Date | Mintage | Fine | VF | XF | Unc |
|-----|------|---------|------|----|----|-----|
| 391.7 | 1872 | .016 | 300.00 | 500.00 | 1200. | — |
| | 1873 | .011 | 350.00 | 600.00 | — | — |
| | 1874 | 4,835 | 450.00 | — | — | — |
| | 1875 | 2,860 | 500.00 | — | — | — |

**Mint mark: Pi**

| KM# | Date | Mintage | Fine | VF | XF | Unc |
|-----|------|---------|------|----|----|-----|
| 391.8 | 1871 | — | — | — | Rare | — |
| | 1877 | .249 | — | — | Rare | — |
| | 1878 | .751 | 12.50 | 25.00 | 50.00 | 200.00 |
| | 1891 Pi/Mo | — | 10.00 | 17.50 | 35.00 | 150.00 |
| | 1891 | — | 8.00 | 15.00 | 30.00 | 150.00 |

**Mint mark: Zs**

| KM# | Date | Mintage | Fine | VF | XF | Unc |
|-----|------|---------|------|----|----|-----|
| 391.9 | 1872 | .055 | 22.50 | 30.00 | 100.00 | 300.00 |
| | 1873 | 1.460 | 4.00 | 8.00 | 25.00 | 150.00 |
| | 1874/3 | .685 | 5.50 | 11.00 | 30.00 | 250.00 |
| | 1874 | Inc. Ab. | 4.00 | 8.00 | 25.00 | 200.00 |
| | 1875/4 | .200 | 8.50 | 17.00 | 45.00 | 250.00 |
| | 1875 | Inc. Ab. | 7.00 | 14.00 | 35.00 | 200.00 |
| | 1876 | — | 5.00 | 10.00 | 25.00 | 200.00 |
| | 1877 | — | 50.00 | 125.00 | 300.00 | 750.00 |
| | 1878 | — | 4.50 | 9.00 | 25.00 | 200.00 |
| | 1880 | .100 | 5.00 | 10.00 | 30.00 | 200.00 |
| | 1881 | 1.200 | 4.25 | 8.00 | 25.00 | 150.00 |

**COPPER-NICKEL**
**Mint: Mexico City**

| KM# | Date | Mintage | Fine | VF | XF | Unc |
|-----|------|---------|------|----|----|-----|
| 392 | 1882 | 99.955 | 7.50 | 12.50 | 17.50 | 35.00 |
| | 1883 | Inc. Ab. | .50 | .75 | 1.00 | 1.50 |

**COPPER**
**Obv: Restyled eagle.**

| | | | | | | |
|-----|------|---------|------|----|----|-----|
| 393 | 1898 | 1.529 | 4.00 | 6.00 | 15.00 | 50.00 |

**NOTE:** Varieties exist.

**Mint mark: C, Cn**
**Reduced size.**

| | | | | | | |
|-----|------|---------|------|----|----|-----|
| 394 | 1901 | .220 | 15.00 | 22.50 | 35.00 | 65.00 |
| | 1902 | .320 | 15.00 | 22.50 | 50.00 | 90.00 |
| | 1903 | .536 | 7.50 | 12.50 | 20.00 | 50.00 |
| | 1904/3 | .148 | 35.00 | 50.00 | 75.00 | 125.00 |
| | 1905 | .110 | 100.00 | 150.00 | 300.00 | 550.00 |

**NOTE:** Varieties exist.

**Mint mark: M,Mo**

| | | | | | | |
|-----|------|---------|------|----|----|-----|
| 394.1 | 1899 | .051 | 150.00 | 175.00 | 300.00 | 800.00 |
| | 1900 wide date | | | | | |
| | | 4.010 | 2.50 | 4.00 | 8.00 | 28.00 |
| | 1900 narrow date | | | | | |
| | | Inc. Ab. | 2.50 | 4.00 | 8.00 | 28.00 |
| | 1901 | 1.494 | 3.00 | 8.00 | 17.50 | 50.00 |
| | 1902/899 | | | | | |
| | | 2.090 | 30.00 | 60.00 | 100.00 | 175.00 |
| | 1902 | Inc. Ab. | 2.25 | 4.00 | 10.00 | 40.00 |
| | 1903 | 8.400 | 1.50 | 3.00 | 7.00 | 25.00 |
| | 1904/3 | 10.250 | 5.00 | 10.00 | 20.00 | 55.00 |
| | 1904 | Inc. Ab. | 1.50 | 3.00 | 7.00 | 25.00 |
| | 1905 | 3.643 | 2.25 | 4.00 | 10.00 | 40.00 |

**NOTE:** Varieties exist.

# 2 CENTAVOS

**COPPER-NICKEL**
**Mint: Mexico City**

| | | | | | | |
|-----|------|---------|------|----|----|-----|
| 395 | 1882 | 50.023 | 2.00 | 3.00 | 7.50 | 15.00 |
| | 1883/2 | Inc. Ab. | 2.00 | 3.00 | 7.50 | 15.00 |
| | 1883 | Inc. Ab. | .50 | .75 | 1.00 | 2.50 |

# 5 CENTAVOS

**1.3530 g, .903 SILVER, .0392 oz ASW**
**Mint mark: Ca**
**Obv: Facing eagle. Rev: Denomination in wreath.**

| KM# | Date | Mintage | Fine | VF | XF | Unc |
|---|---|---|---|---|---|---|
| 396 | 1868 | — | 40.00 | 65.00 | 125.00 | 450.00 |
| | 1869 | *.030 | 25.00 | 40.00 | 100.00 | 400.00 |
| | 1870/69 | — | 35.00 | 55.00 | 120.00 | 425.00 |
| | 1870 | .035 | 30.00 | 50.00 | 100.00 | 400.00 |

**Mint mark: SLP**

| KM# | Date | Mintage | Fine | VF | XF | Unc |
|---|---|---|---|---|---|---|
| 396.1 | 1863 | — | 75.00 | 125.00 | 350.00 | 1200. |

**Mint mark: Mo**
**Rev: Cap and rays.**

| KM# | Date | Mintage | Fine | VF | XF | Unc |
|---|---|---|---|---|---|---|
| 397 | 1867/3 | — | 25.00 | 50.00 | 125.00 | 425.00 |
| | 1867 | — | 20.00 | 40.00 | 100.00 | 400.00 |
| | 1868/7 | — | 25.00 | 50.00 | 150.00 | 500.00 |
| | 1868 | — | 20.00 | 40.00 | 100.00 | 400.00 |

**NOTE:** Varieties exist.

**Mint mark: P**

| KM# | Date | Mintage | Fine | VF | XF | Unc |
|---|---|---|---|---|---|---|
| 397.1 | 1868/7 | .034 | 25.00 | 50.00 | 125.00 | 450.00 |
| | 1868 | Inc. Ab. | 20.00 | 45.00 | 100.00 | 400.00 |
| | 1869 | .014 | 200.00 | 300.00 | 600.00 | — |

**Mint mark: As**
**Obv: Standing eagle.**

| KM# | Date | Mintage | Fine | VF | XF | Unc |
|---|---|---|---|---|---|---|
| 398 | 1874 DL | — | 10.00 | 20.00 | 40.00 | 150.00 |
| | 1875 DL | — | 10.00 | 20.00 | 40.00 | 150.00 |
| | 1876 L | — | 22.00 | 45.00 | 70.00 | 160.00 |
| | 1878 L mule, gold peso obverse | | | | | |
| | | — | 250.00 | 350.00 | 650.00 | — |
| | 1879 L mule, gold peso obverse | | | | | |
| | | — | 40.00 | 65.00 | 120.00 | 275.00 |
| | 1880 L mule, gold peso obverse | | | | | |
| | | .012 | 55.00 | 85.00 | 165.00 | 325.00 |
| | 1886 L | .043 | 12.00 | 25.00 | 50.00 | 165.00 |
| | 1886 L mule, gold peso obverse | | | | | |
| | | Inc. Ab. | 55.00 | 85.00 | 165.00 | 300.00 |
| | 1887 L | .020 | 25.00 | 50.00 | 75.00 | 165.00 |
| | 1888 L | .032 | 12.00 | 25.00 | 50.00 | 125.00 |
| | 1889 L | .016 | 25.00 | 50.00 | 100.00 | 200.00 |
| | 1890 L | .030 | 25.00 | 50.00 | 85.00 | 175.00 |
| | 1891 L | 8,000 | 65.00 | 125.00 | 200.00 | 400.00 |
| | 1892 L | .013 | 20.00 | 40.00 | 60.00 | 125.00 |
| | 1893 L | .024 | 10.00 | 20.00 | 45.00 | 90.00 |
| | 1895 L | .020 | 10.00 | 20.00 | 45.00 | 90.00 |

**Mint mark: CH, Ca**

| KM# | Date | Mintage | Fine | VF | XF | Unc |
|---|---|---|---|---|---|---|
| 398.1 | 1871 M | .014 | 20.00 | 40.00 | 100.00 | 250.00 |
| | 1873 M crude date | | | | | |
| | | — | 100.00 | 150.00 | 250.00 | 500.00 |
| | 1874 M crude date | | | | | |
| | | — | 25.00 | 50.00 | 75.00 | 150.00 |
| | 1886 M | .025 | 7.50 | 15.00 | 30.00 | 100.00 |
| | 1887 M | .037 | 7.50 | 15.00 | 30.00 | 100.00 |
| | 1887 Ca/MoM | | | | | |
| | | Inc. Ab. | 10.00 | 20.00 | 40.00 | 125.00 |
| | 1888 M | .145 | 1.50 | 3.00 | 6.00 | 25.00 |
| | 1889 M | .044 | 5.00 | 10.00 | 20.00 | 50.00 |
| | 1890 M | .102 | 1.50 | 3.00 | 6.00 | 25.00 |
| | 1891 M | .164 | 1.50 | 3.00 | 6.00 | 25.00 |
| | 1892 M | .085 | 1.50 | 3.00 | 6.00 | 25.00 |
| | 1892 M 9/inverted 9 | | | | | |

| KM# | Date | Mintage | Fine | VF | XF | Unc |
|---|---|---|---|---|---|---|
| 398.1 | | Inc. Ab. | 2.00 | 4.00 | 7.50 | 30.00 |
| | 1893 M | .133 | 1.50 | 3.00 | 6.00 | 25.00 |
| | 1894 M | .108 | 1.50 | 3.00 | 6.00 | 25.00 |
| | 1895 M | .074 | 2.00 | 4.00 | 7.50 | 30.00 |

**Mint mark: Cn**

| KM# | Date | Mintage | Fine | VF | XF | Unc |
|---|---|---|---|---|---|---|
| 398.2 | 1871 P | — | 125.00 | 200.00 | 350.00 | — |
| | 1873 P | 4,992 | 50.00 | 100.00 | 200.00 | 400.00 |
| | 1874 P | — | 25.00 | 50.00 | 100.00 | 200.00 |
| | 1875 P | — | — | — | Rare | — |
| | 1876 P | — | 25.00 | 50.00 | 100.00 | 200.00 |
| | 1886 M | .010 | 25.00 | 50.00 | 100.00 | 200.00 |
| | 1887 M | .010 | 25.00 | 50.00 | 100.00 | 200.00 |
| | 1888 M | .119 | 1.50 | 3.00 | 6.00 | 30.00 |
| | 1889 M | .066 | 4.00 | 7.50 | 15.00 | 50.00 |
| | 1890/9 M | — | 2.00 | 4.00 | 8.00 | 40.00 |
| | 1890 M | .180 | 1.50 | 3.00 | 6.00 | 25.00 |
| | 1890 D (error) | | | | | |
| | | Inc. Ab. | 125.00 | 175.00 | 250.00 | — |
| | 1891 M | .087 | 2.00 | 4.00 | 7.50 | 25.00 |
| | 1894 M | .024 | 4.00 | 7.50 | 15.00 | 40.00 |
| | 1896 M | .016 | 7.50 | 12.50 | 25.00 | 75.00 |
| | 1897 M | .223 | 1.50 | 2.50 | 5.00 | 20.00 |

**Mint mark: Do**

| KM# | Date | Mintage | Fine | VF | XF | Unc |
|---|---|---|---|---|---|---|
| 398.3 | 1874 M | — | 100.00 | 150.00 | 225.00 | 500.00 |
| | 1877 P | 4,795 | 75.00 | 125.00 | 225.00 | 450.00 |
| | 1878/7 F/P | | | | | |
| | | 4,300 | 200.00 | 300.00 | 450.00 | — |
| | 1879 B | — | 125.00 | 200.00 | 350.00 | — |
| | 1880 B | — | — | — | Rare | — |
| | 1881 P | 3,020 | 300.00 | 500.00 | 800.00 | — |
| | 1887 C | .042 | 5.00 | 8.00 | 17.50 | 60.00 |
| | 1888/9 C | .091 | 6.00 | 10.00 | 20.00 | 70.00 |
| | 1888 C | Inc. Ab. | 4.00 | 7.50 | 15.00 | 55.00 |
| | 1889 C | .049 | 3.50 | 6.00 | 12.50 | 50.00 |
| | 1890 C | .136 | 4.00 | 7.50 | 15.00 | 55.00 |
| | 1890 P | Inc. Ab. | 5.00 | 8.00 | 17.50 | 60.00 |
| | 1891/0 P | .048 | 3.50 | 6.00 | 12.50 | 50.00 |
| | 1891 P | Inc. Ab. | 3.00 | 5.00 | 10.00 | 45.00 |
| | 1894 D | .038 | 3.50 | 6.00 | 12.50 | 50.00 |

**Mint mark: Ga**

| KM# | Date | Mintage | Fine | VF | XF | Unc |
|---|---|---|---|---|---|---|
| 398.4 | 1877 A | — | 15.00 | 30.00 | 60.00 | 150.00 |
| | 1881 S | .156 | 4.00 | 7.50 | 15.00 | 60.00 |
| | 1886 S | .087 | 2.00 | 4.00 | 7.50 | 25.00 |
| | 1888 S lg.G | | | | | |
| | | .262 | 2.00 | 4.00 | 10.00 | 30.00 |
| | 1888 S sm.g | | | | | |
| | | Inc. Ab. | 2.00 | 4.00 | 10.00 | 30.00 |
| | 1889 S | .178 | 1.50 | 3.00 | 7.50 | 25.00 |
| | 1890 S | .068 | 4.00 | 7.50 | 12.50 | 35.00 |
| | 1891 S | .050 | 4.00 | 6.50 | 10.00 | 35.00 |
| | 1892 S | .078 | 2.00 | 4.00 | 7.50 | 25.00 |
| | 1893 S | .044 | 4.00 | 7.50 | 15.00 | 45.00 |

**Mint mark: Go**

| KM# | Date | Mintage | Fine | VF | XF | Unc |
|---|---|---|---|---|---|---|
| 398.5 | 1869 S | .080 | 15.00 | 30.00 | 75.00 | 175.00 |
| | 1871 S | .100 | 5.00 | 10.00 | 25.00 | 75.00 |
| | 1872 S | .030 | 30.00 | 60.00 | 125.00 | 250.00 |
| | 1873 S | .040 | 30.00 | 60.00 | 125.00 | 250.00 |
| | 1874 S | — | 7.00 | 12.00 | 25.00 | 75.00 |
| | 1875 S | — | 8.00 | 15.00 | 30.00 | 75.00 |
| | 1876 S | — | 8.00 | 15.00 | 30.00 | 75.00 |
| | 1877 S | — | 7.00 | 12.00 | 20.00 | 75.00 |
| | 1878/7 S | .020 | 8.00 | 15.00 | 25.00 | 75.00 |
| | 1879 S | — | 8.00 | 15.00 | 25.00 | 75.00 |
| | 1880 S | .055 | 15.00 | 30.00 | 60.00 | 200.00 |
| | 1881/0 S | .160 | 5.00 | 8.00 | 17.50 | 60.00 |
| | 1881 S | Inc. Ab. | 4.00 | 6.00 | 12.00 | 45.00 |
| | 1886 R | .230 | 1.50 | 3.00 | 6.00 | 30.00 |
| | 1887 R/S | — | 1.50 | 3.00 | 6.00 | 30.00 |
| | 1887 R | .230 | 1.50 | 2.50 | 5.00 | 30.00 |
| | 1888 R | .320 | 1.50 | 2.50 | 5.00 | 20.00 |
| | 1889 R | .060 | 4.00 | 6.00 | 12.00 | 45.00 |
| | 1890/5 R/S | — | 1.50 | 3.00 | 6.00 | 30.00 |
| | 1890 R | .250 | 1.50 | 2.50 | 5.00 | 20.00 |
| | 1891/0 R | .168 | 1.80 | 3.00 | 6.00 | 30.00 |
| | 1891 R | Inc. Ab. | 1.50 | 2.50 | 5.00 | 20.00 |
| | 1892 R | .138 | 1.50 | 3.00 | 6.00 | 25.00 |
| | 1893 R | .200 | 1.25 | 2.50 | 5.00 | 20.00 |
| | 1894 R | .200 | 1.25 | 2.50 | 5.00 | 20.00 |
| | 1896 R | .525 | 1.25 | 2.00 | 4.00 | 15.00 |
| | 1896 R/S | — | 1.50 | 3.00 | 6.00 | 25.00 |
| | 1897 R | .596 | 1.50 | 2.00 | 4.00 | 15.00 |

### Mint mark: Ho

| KM# | Date | Mintage | Fine | VF | XF | Unc |
|-----|------|---------|------|-----|-----|-----|
| 398.6 | 1874/69 R | — | 125.00 | 225.00 | 350.00 | — |
| | 1874 R | — | 100.00 | 200.00 | 325.00 | — |
| | 1878/7 A | .022 | — | — | Rare | — |
| | 1878 A | Inc. Ab. | 20.00 | 40.00 | 80.00 | 175.00 |
| | 1878 A mule, gold peso obverse | | | | | |
| | | Inc. Ab. | 40.00 | 80.00 | 150.00 | 300.00 |
| | 1880 A | .043 | 7.50 | 15.00 | 30.00 | 75.00 |
| | 1886 G | .044 | 5.00 | 10.00 | 20.00 | 75.00 |
| | 1887 G | .020 | 5.00 | 10.00 | 20.00 | 75.00 |
| | 1888 G | .012 | 7.50 | 15.00 | 30.00 | 85.00 |
| | 1889 G | .067 | 3.00 | 6.00 | 12.50 | 40.00 |
| | 1890 G | .050 | 3.00 | 6.00 | 12.50 | 40.00 |
| | 1891 G | .046 | 3.00 | 6.00 | 12.50 | 40.00 |
| | 1893 G | .084 | 2.50 | 5.00 | 10.00 | 30.00 |
| | 1894 G | .068 | 2.00 | 4.00 | 10.00 | 30.00 |

### Mint mark: Mo

| KM# | Date | Mintage | Fine | VF | XF | Unc |
|-----|------|---------|------|-----|-----|-----|
| 398.7 | 1869/8 C | .040 | 8.00 | 15.00 | 40.00 | 120.00 |
| | 1870 C | .140 | 4.00 | 7.00 | 20.00 | 60.00 |
| | 1871 C | .103 | 9.00 | 20.00 | 40.00 | 100.00 |
| | 1871 M Inc. Ab. | | 7.50 | 12.50 | 25.00 | 60.00 |
| | 1872 M | .266 | 5.00 | 8.00 | 20.00 | 55.00 |
| | 1873 M | .020 | 40.00 | 60.00 | 100.00 | 225.00 |
| | 1874/69 M | — | 7.50 | 15.00 | 30.00 | 75.00 |
| | 1874 M | — | 4.00 | 7.00 | 17.50 | 50.00 |
| | 1874/3 B | — | 5.00 | 8.00 | 22.50 | 55.00 |
| | 1874 B | — | 5.00 | 8.00 | 22.50 | 55.00 |
| | 1875 B | — | 4.00 | 7.00 | 15.00 | 50.00 |
| | 1875 B/M | — | 6.00 | 9.00 | 17.50 | 60.00 |
| | 1876/5 B | — | 4.00 | 7.00 | 15.00 | 50.00 |
| | 1876 B | — | 4.00 | 7.00 | 12.50 | 50.00 |
| | 1877/6 M | .080 | 4.00 | 7.00 | 15.00 | 60.00 |
| | 1877 M Inc. Ab. | | 4.00 | 7.00 | 12.50 | 60.00 |
| | 1878/7 M | .100 | 4.00 | 7.00 | 15.00 | 55.00 |
| | 1878 M Inc. Ab. | | 2.50 | 5.00 | 12.50 | 45.00 |
| | 1879/8 M | — | 8.00 | 12.50 | 22.50 | 55.00 |
| | 1879 M | — | 4.50 | 7.00 | 15.00 | 50.00 |
| | 1879 M 9/inverted 9 | | | | | |
| | | — | 10.00 | 15.00 | 25.00 | 75.00 |
| | 1880/76 M/B | | | | | |
| | | — | 5.00 | 7.50 | 15.00 | 50.00 |
| | 1880/76 M | — | 5.00 | 7.50 | 15.00 | 50.00 |
| | 1880 M | — | 4.00 | 6.00 | 12.00 | 40.00 |
| | 1881/0 M | .180 | 4.00 | 6.00 | 10.00 | 35.00 |
| | 1881 M Inc. Ab. | | 3.00 | 4.50 | 9.00 | 35.00 |
| | 1886/0 M | .398 | 2.00 | 2.75 | 7.50 | 25.00 |
| | 1886/1 M | I.A. | 2.00 | 2.75 | 7.50 | 25.00 |
| | 1886 M Inc. Ab. | | 1.75 | 2.25 | 6.00 | 20.00 |
| | 1887 m | .720 | 1.75 | 2.00 | 5.00 | 20.00 |
| | 1887 M/m | I.A. | 1.75 | 2.00 | 6.00 | 20.00 |
| | 1888/7 M | 1.360 | 2.25 | 2.50 | 6.00 | 20.00 |
| | 1888 M Inc. Ab. | | 1.75 | 2.00 | 5.00 | 20.00 |
| | 1889/8 M | 1.242 | 2.25 | 2.50 | 6.00 | 20.00 |
| | 1889 M Inc. Ab. | | 1.75 | 2.00 | 5.00 | 20.00 |
| | 1890/00 M | | | | | |
| | | 1.694 | 1.75 | 2.75 | 6.00 | 20.00 |
| | 1890 M Inc. Ab. | | 1.50 | 2.00 | 5.00 | 20.00 |
| | 1891 M | 1.030 | 1.75 | 2.00 | 5.00 | 20.00 |
| | 1892 M | 1.400 | 1.75 | 2.00 | 5.00 | 20.00 |
| | 1892 M 9/inverted 9 | | | | | |
| | | Inc. Ab. | 2.00 | 2.75 | 7.50 | 20.00 |
| | 1893 M | .220 | 1.75 | 2.00 | 5.00 | 15.00 |
| | 1894 M | .320 | 1.75 | 2.00 | 5.00 | 15.00 |
| | 1895 M | .078 | 3.00 | 5.00 | 8.00 | 25.00 |
| | 1896 B | .080 | 1.75 | 2.00 | 5.00 | 20.00 |
| | 1897 M | .160 | 1.75 | 2.00 | 5.00 | 15.00 |

**NOTE:** Varieties exist.

### Mint mark: Oa

| KM# | Date | Mintage | Fine | VF | XF | Unc |
|-----|------|---------|------|-----|-----|-----|
| 398.8 | 1890 E | .048 | — | — | Rare | — |
| | 1890 N Inc. Ab. | | 65.00 | 125.00 | 200.00 | 350.00 |

### Mint mark: Pi

| KM# | Date | Mintage | Fine | VF | XF | Unc |
|-----|------|---------|------|-----|-----|-----|
| 398.9 | 1869 S | — | 300.00 | 400.00 | 500.00 | — |
| | 1870 G/MoC | | | | | |
| | | .020 | — | — | Rare | — |
| | 1870 O Inc. Ab. | | 200.00 | 300.00 | 400.00 | — |
| | 1871 O | 5,400 | — | — | Rare | — |
| | 1872 O | — | 75.00 | 100.00 | 175.00 | 400.00 |
| | 1873 | 5,000 | — | — | Rare | — |
| | 1874 H | — | 30.00 | 50.00 | 100.00 | 225.00 |
| | 1875 H | — | 7.50 | 12.50 | 30.00 | 75.00 |
| | 1876 H | — | 10.00 | 20.00 | 45.00 | 100.00 |
| | 1877 H | — | 7.50 | 12.50 | 20.00 | 60.00 |

| KM# | Date | Mintage | Fine | VF | XF | Unc |
|-----|------|---------|------|-----|-----|-----|
| 398.9 | 1878/7 H | — | — | — | Rare | — |
| | 1878 H | — | 60.00 | 90.00 | 150.00 | 300.00 |
| | 1880 H | 6,200 | — | — | Rare | — |
| | 1881 H | 4,500 | — | — | Rare | — |
| | 1886 R | .033 | 12.50 | 25.00 | 50.00 | 125.00 |
| | 1887/0 R | .169 | 4.00 | 7.50 | 15.00 | 45.00 |
| | 1887 R Inc. Ab. | | 3.00 | 5.00 | 10.00 | 32.00 |
| | 1888 R | .210 | 2.00 | 4.00 | 9.00 | 30.00 |
| | 1889/7 R | .197 | 2.50 | 5.00 | 10.00 | 32.00 |
| | 1889 R Inc. Ab. | | 2.00 | 4.00 | 9.00 | 30.00 |
| | 1890 R | .221 | 2.00 | 3.00 | 6.00 | 25.00 |
| | 1891/89 R/B | | | | | |
| | | .176 | 2.00 | 4.00 | 8.00 | 25.00 |
| | 1891 R Inc. Ab. | | 2.00 | 3.00 | 6.00 | 20.00 |
| | 1891/0 R/B | — | 2.00 | 4.00 | 8.00 | 25.00 |
| | 1892/89 R | .182 | 2.00 | 4.00 | 8.00 | 25.00 |
| | 1892/0 R | I.A. | 2.00 | 4.00 | 8.00 | 25.00 |
| | 1892 R Inc. Ab. | | 2.00 | 3.00 | 6.00 | 20.00 |
| | 1893 R | .041 | 5.00 | 10.00 | 20.00 | 60.00 |

**NOTE:** Varieties exist.

### Mint mark: Zs

| KM# | Date | Mintage | Fine | VF | XF | Unc |
|-----|------|---------|------|-----|-----|-----|
| 398.10 | 1870 H | .040 | 12.50 | 25.00 | 50.00 | 125.00 |
| | 1871 H | .040 | 12.50 | 25.00 | 50.00 | 125.00 |
| | 1872 H | .040 | 12.50 | 25.00 | 50.00 | 125.00 |
| | 1873/2 H | .020 | 35.00 | 65.00 | 125.00 | 275.00 |
| | 1873 H Inc. Ab. | | 25.00 | 50.00 | 100.00 | 250.00 |
| | 1874 H | — | 7.50 | 12.50 | 25.00 | 75.00 |
| | 1874 A | — | 40.00 | 75.00 | 150.00 | 300.00 |
| | 1875 A | — | 7.50 | 12.50 | 25.00 | 75.00 |
| | 1876 A | — | 50.00 | 75.00 | 100.00 | 200.00 |
| | 1876/5 S | — | 15.00 | 30.00 | 60.00 | 150.00 |
| | 1876 S | — | 12.50 | 25.00 | 50.00 | 125.00 |
| | 1877 S | — | 3.00 | 6.00 | 12.00 | 40.00 |
| | 1878 S | .060 | 3.00 | 6.00 | 12.00 | 40.00 |
| | 1879/8 S | — | 3.00 | 6.00 | 15.00 | 50.00 |
| | 1879 S | — | 3.00 | 6.00 | 12.00 | 40.00 |
| | 1880/79 S | .130 | 6.00 | 10.00 | 20.00 | 60.00 |
| | 1880 S Inc. Ab. | | 5.00 | 8.00 | 16.00 | 45.00 |
| | 1881 S | .210 | 2.50 | 5.00 | 10.00 | 35.00 |
| | 1886/4 S | .360 | 6.00 | 10.00 | 20.00 | 60.00 |
| | 1886 3 Inc. Ab. | | 2.00 | 3.00 | 6.00 | 20.00 |
| | 1886 Z Inc. Ab. | | 5.00 | 10.00 | 25.00 | 65.00 |
| | 1887 Z | .400 | 2.00 | 3.00 | 6.00 | 25.00 |
| | 1888/7 Z | .500 | 2.00 | 3.00 | 6.00 | 25.00 |
| | 1888 Z Inc. Ab. | | 2.00 | 3.00 | 6.00 | 25.00 |
| | 1889 Z | .520 | 2.00 | 3.00 | 6.00 | 25.00 |
| | 1889 Z 9/inverted 9 | | | | | |
| | | Inc. Ab. | 2.00 | 3.00 | 6.00 | 25.00 |
| | 1889 ZsZ/MoM | | | | | |
| | | Inc. Ab. | 2.00 | 3.00 | 6.00 | 25.00 |
| | 1890 Z | .580 | 1.75 | 2.50 | 5.00 | 20.00 |
| | 1890 ZsZ/MoM | | | | | |
| | | Inc. Ab. | 2.00 | 3.00 | 6.00 | 25.00 |
| | 1890 ZsZ 9/8 | | | | | |
| | | — | 2.00 | 3.00 | 6.00 | 25.00 |
| | 1890 ZsZ 0/9 Z/M | | | | | |
| | | — | 2.00 | 3.00 | 6.00 | 25.00 |
| | 1891 Z | .420 | 1.75 | 2.50 | 5.00 | 20.00 |
| | 1892 Z | .346 | 1.75 | 2.50 | 5.00 | 20.00 |
| | 1893 Z | .258 | 1.75 | 2.50 | 5.00 | 20.00 |
| | 1894 Z | .228 | 1.75 | 2.50 | 5.00 | 20.00 |
| | 1894 ZoZ (error) | | | | | |
| | | Inc. Ab. | 2.00 | 4.00 | 8.00 | 30.00 |
| 398.10 | 1895 Z | .260 | 1.75 | 2.50 | 5.00 | 20.00 |
| | 1895 Z | .260 | 1.75 | 2.50 | 5.00 | 20.00 |
| | 1895/4 ZsZ | — | 2.00 | 3.00 | 6.00 | 25.00 |
| | 1896 Z | .200 | 1.75 | 2.50 | 5.00 | 20.00 |
| | 1896 6/inverted 6 | | | | | |
| | | Inc. Ab. | 2.00 | 3.00 | 6.00 | 25.00 |
| | 1897/6 Z | .200 | 2.00 | 3.00 | 6.00 | 25.00 |
| | 1897 Z Inc. Ab. | | 1.75 | 2.50 | 5.00 | 20.00 |

**COPPER-NICKEL**
**Mint: Mexico City**

| KM# | Date | Mintage | Fine | VF | XF | Unc |
|-----|------|---------|------|-----|-----|-----|
| 399 | 1882 | Inc. Ab. | .50 | 1.00 | 2.50 | 7.50 |
| | 1883 | Inc. Ab. | 25.00 | 50.00 | 80.00 | 250.00 |

**.903 SILVER**
**Mint mark: Cn**
**Obv: Restyled eagle.**

| KM# | Date | Mintage | Fine | VF | XF | Unc |
|---|---|---|---|---|---|---|
| 400 | 1898 M | .044 | 1.75 | 4.00 | 8.00 | 20.00 |
| | 1899 M | .111 | 5.50 | 8.50 | 20.00 | 50.00 |
| | 1899 Q Inc. Ab. | | 1.75 | 2.50 | 4.50 | 15.00 |
| | 1900/800 Q | | | | | |
| | | .239 | 3.50 | 5.00 | 12.50 | 30.00 |
| | 1900 Q round Q, single tail | | | | | |
| | | Inc. Ab. | 1.75 | 3.00 | 6.00 | 16.50 |
| | 1900 Q narrow C, oval Q | | | | | |
| | | Inc. Ab. | 1.75 | 3.00 | 6.00 | 16.50 |
| | 1900 Q wide C, oval Q | | | | | |
| | | Inc. Ab. | 1.75 | 3.00 | 6.00 | 16.50 |
| | 1901 Q | .148 | 1.75 | 2.50 | 4.50 | 15.00 |
| | 1902 Q narrow C, heavy serifs | | | | | |
| | | .262 | 1.75 | 3.00 | 6.00 | 16.50 |
| | 1902 Q wide C, light serifs | | | | | |
| | | Inc. Ab. | 1.75 | 3.00 | 6.00 | 16.50 |
| | 1903/1 Q | .331 | 2.00 | 3.00 | 6.00 | 16.50 |
| | 1903 Q Inc. Ab. | | 1.75 | 2.50 | 4.50 | 15.00 |
| | 1903/1898 V | | | | | |
| | | Inc. Ab. | 3.50 | 4.50 | 9.00 | 22.50 |
| | 1903 V Inc. Ab. | | 1.75 | 2.50 | 4.50 | 15.00 |
| | 1904 H | .352 | 1.75 | 2.50 | 5.00 | 16.50 |
| | 1904 H 0/9 | — | 1.75 | 2.50 | 5.00 | 16.50 |
| | 1904 H/C | — | 1.75 | 2.50 | 5.00 | 16.50 |

**NOTE:** Varieties exist.

**Mint mark: Go**

| KM# | Date | Mintage | Fine | VF | XF | Unc |
|---|---|---|---|---|---|---|
| 400.1 | 1898 R mule, gold peso obverse | | | | | |
| | | .180 | 7.50 | 15.00 | 30.00 | 75.00 |
| | 1899 R | .260 | 1.75 | 2.50 | 4.50 | 15.00 |
| | 1900 R | .200 | 1.75 | 2.50 | 4.50 | 15.00 |

**NOTE:** Varieties exist.

**Mint mark: Mo**

| KM# | Date | Mintage | Fine | VF | XF | Unc |
|---|---|---|---|---|---|---|
| 400.2 | 1898 M | .080 | 2.00 | 4.00 | 7.00 | 25.00 |
| | 1899 M | .168 | 1.75 | 2.50 | 4.50 | 15.00 |
| | 1900/800 M | | | | | |
| | | .300 | 4.50 | 6.50 | 10.00 | 30.00 |
| | 1900 M Inc. Ab. | | 1.75 | 2.50 | 4.50 | 15.00 |
| | 1901 M | .100 | 1.75 | 2.50 | 4.50 | 15.00 |
| | 1902 M | .144 | 1.25 | 2.00 | 3.75 | 12.00 |
| | 1902/1 MoM | — | 1.75 | 3.00 | 6.00 | 16.50 |
| | 1903 M | .500 | 1.25 | 2.00 | 3.75 | 12.00 |
| | 1904/804 M | | | | | |
| | | 1.090 | 1.75 | 3.00 | 6.00 | 16.50 |
| | 1904/94 M I.A. | | 1.75 | 3.00 | 6.00 | 16.50 |
| | 1904 M Inc. Ab. | | 1.75 | 3.00 | 6.00 | 15.00 |
| | 1905 M | .344 | 1.75 | 3.75 | 7.50 | 18.50 |

**Mint mark: Zs**

| KM# | Date | Mintage | Fine | VF | XF | Unc |
|---|---|---|---|---|---|---|
| 400.3 | 1898 Z | .100 | 1.75 | 2.25 | 4.50 | 12.50 |
| | 1899 Z | .050 | 2.00 | 3.00 | 7.00 | 20.00 |
| | 1900 Z | .055 | 1.75 | 2.50 | 5.00 | 16.50 |
| | 1901 Z | .040 | 1.75 | 2.50 | 5.00 | 16.50 |
| | 1902/1 Z | .034 | 2.00 | 4.50 | 9.00 | 22.50 |
| | 1902 Z Inc. Ab. | | 1.75 | 3.75 | 7.50 | 18.50 |
| | 1903 Z | .217 | 1.25 | 2.00 | 5.00 | 12.50 |
| | 1904 Z | .191 | 1.75 | 2.50 | 5.00 | 12.50 |
| | 1904 M Inc. Ab. | | 1.75 | 2.50 | 6.00 | 16.50 |
| | 1905 M | .046 | 2.00 | 4.50 | 9.00 | 22.50 |

# 10 CENTAVOS

**2.7070 g, .903 SILVER, .0785 oz ASW**
**Mint mark: Ca**

**Obv: Eagle. Rev: Value within wreath.**

| KM# | Date | Mintage | Fine | VF | XF | Unc |
|---|---|---|---|---|---|---|
| 401 | 1868/7 | — | 30.00 | 60.00 | 150.00 | 550.00 |
| | 1868 | — | 30.00 | 60.00 | 150.00 | 550.00 |
| | 1869 | .015 | 25.00 | 50.00 | 125.00 | 600.00 |
| | 1870 | .017 | 22.50 | 45.00 | 100.00 | 550.00 |

**Mint mark: SLP**

| KM# | Date | Mintage | Fine | VF | XF | Unc |
|---|---|---|---|---|---|---|
| 401.2 | 1863 | — | 75.00 | 150.00 | 275.00 | 900.00 |

**Mint mark: Mo**

| KM# | Date | Mintage | Fine | VF | XF | Unc |
|---|---|---|---|---|---|---|
| 402 | 1867/3 | — | 50.00 | 100.00 | 200.00 | 550.00 |
| | 1867 | — | 20.00 | 50.00 | 150.00 | 450.00 |
| | 1868/7 | — | 20.00 | 50.00 | 175.00 | 500.00 |
| | 1868 | — | 20.00 | 55.00 | 175.00 | 500.00 |

**Mint mark: P**

| KM# | Date | Mintage | Fine | VF | XF | Unc |
|---|---|---|---|---|---|---|
| 402.1 | 1868/7 | .038 | 45.00 | 90.00 | 175.00 | 650.00 |
| | 1868 | Inc. Ab. | 20.00 | 40.00 | 100.00 | 550.00 |
| | 1869/7 | 4,900 | 55.00 | 125.00 | 250.00 | 800.00 |

**Mint mark: As**

| KM# | Date | Mintage | Fine | VF | XF | Unc |
|---|---|---|---|---|---|---|
| 403 | 1874 DL | — | 20.00 | 40.00 | 80.00 | 175.00 |
| | 1875 L | — | 5.00 | 10.00 | 25.00 | 90.00 |
| | 1876 L | — | 10.00 | 18.00 | 40.00 | 110.00 |
| | 1878/7 L | — | 10.00 | 18.00 | 45.00 | 120.00 |
| | 1878 L | — | 5.00 | 10.00 | 30.00 | 100.00 |
| | 1879 L | — | 10.00 | 18.00 | 40.00 | 110.00 |
| | 1880 L | .013 | 10.00 | 18.00 | 40.00 | 110.00 |
| | 1882 L | .022 | 10.00 | 18.00 | 40.00 | 110.00 |
| | 1883 L | 8,520 | 25.00 | 50.00 | 100.00 | 225.00 |
| | 1884 L | — | 7.50 | 12.50 | 35.00 | 100.00 |
| | 1885 L | .015 | 7.50 | 12.50 | 35.00 | 100.00 |
| | 1886 L | .045 | 7.50 | 12.50 | 35.00 | 100.00 |
| | 1887 L | .015 | 7.50 | 12.50 | 35.00 | 100.00 |
| | 1888 L | .038 | 7.50 | 12.50 | 35.00 | 100.00 |
| | 1889 L | .020 | 7.50 | 12.50 | 35.00 | 100.00 |
| | 1890 L | .040 | 7.50 | 12.50 | 35.00 | 100.00 |
| | 1891 L | .038 | 7.50 | 12.50 | 35.00 | 100.00 |
| | 1892 L | .057 | 5.00 | 10.00 | 25.00 | 90.00 |
| | 1893 L | .070 | 10.00 | 18.00 | 40.00 | 110.00 |

**NOTE:** Varieties exist. An 1891 As L over 1889 HoG
exists which was evidently produced at the Alamos Mint
using dies sent from the Hermosillo Mint.

**2.7070 g, .903 SILVER, .0785 oz ASW**
**Mint mark: CH, Ca**

| KM# | Date | Mintage | Fine | VF | XF | Unc |
|---|---|---|---|---|---|---|
| 403.1 | 1871 M | 8,150 | 15.00 | 30.00 | 60.00 | 150.00 |
| | 1873 M crude date | | | | | |
| | | — | 35.00 | 75.00 | 125.00 | 175.00 |
| | 1874 M | — | 10.00 | 17.50 | 35.00 | 100.00 |
| | 1880/70 G | | | | | |
| | | 7,620 | 20.00 | 40.00 | 80.00 | 175.00 |
| | 1880 G/g | I.A. | 15.00 | 25.00 | 50.00 | 125.00 |
| | 1881 | 340 pcs. | — | — | Rare | — |
| | 1883 M | 9,000 | 10.00 | 20.00 | 40.00 | 125.00 |
| | 1884/73 | — | 5.00 | 30.00 | 60.00 | 150.00 |
| | 1884 M | — | 10.00 | 20.00 | 40.00 | 125.00 |
| | 1886 M | .045 | 7.50 | 12.50 | 30.00 | 100.00 |
| | 1887/3 M/G | | | | | |
| | | .096 | 5.00 | 10.00 | 20.00 | 75.00 |
| | 1887 M/G | — | 2.00 | 4.00 | 8.00 | 75.00 |
| | 1887 M Inc. Ab. | | 2.00 | 4.00 | 8.00 | 75.00 |
| | 1888 M/G | — | 2.00 | 4.00 | 8.00 | 75.00 |
| | 1888 M | .299 | 1.50 | 2.50 | 5.00 | 75.00 |
| | 1888 Ca/Mo | | | | | |
| | | Inc. Ab. | 1.50 | 2.50 | 5.00 | 75.00 |
| | 1889/8 M | .115 | 2.00 | 4.00 | 8.00 | 75.00 |
| | 1889 M small 89 (5 Centavo font) | | | | | |
| | | Inc. Ab. | 2.00 | 4.00 | 8.00 | 75.00 |
| | 1890/80 M | .140 | 2.00 | 4.00 | 8.00 | 75.00 |

| KM# | Date | Mintage | Fine | VF | XF | Unc |
|---|---|---|---|---|---|---|
| 403.1 | 1890/89 M I.A. | | 2.00 | 4.00 | 8.00 | 75.00 |
| | 1890 M Inc. Ab. | | 1.50 | 3.00 | 7.00 | 75.00 |
| | 1891 M | .103 | 1.50 | 3.00 | 7.00 | 75.00 |
| | 1892 M | .169 | 1.50 | 3.00 | 7.00 | 75.00 |
| | 1892 M 9/inverted 9 | | | | | |
| | Inc. Ab. | | 2.00 | 4.00 | 8.00 | 75.00 |
| | 1893 M | .246 | 1.50 | 3.00 | 7.00 | 75.00 |
| | 1894 M | .163 | 1.50 | 3.00 | 7.00 | 75.00 |
| | 1895 M | .127 | 1.50 | 3.00 | 7.00 | 75.00 |

NOTE: Varieties exist.

### Mint mark: Cn

| KM# | Date | Mintage | Fine | VF | XF | Unc |
|---|---|---|---|---|---|---|
| 403.2 | 1871 P | — | — | — | Rare | — |
| | 1873 P | 8,732 | 20.00 | 50.00 | 100.00 | 225.00 |
| | 1881 D | 9,440 | 75.00 | 175.00 | 325.00 | 500.00 |
| | 1882 D | .012 | 75.00 | 125.00 | 200.00 | 400.00 |
| | 1885 M mule gold 2-1/2 Peso obv. | | | | | |
| | | .018 | 25.00 | 50.00 | 100.00 | 200.00 |
| | 1886 M mule, gold 2-1/2 Peso obv. | | | | | |
| | | .013 | 50.00 | 100.00 | 150.00 | 300.00 |
| | 1887 M | .011 | 20.00 | 40.00 | 75.00 | 175.00 |
| | 1888 M | .056 | 5.00 | 10.00 | 25.00 | 125.00 |
| | 1889 M | .042 | 5.00 | 10.00 | 20.00 | 75.00 |
| | 1890 M | .132 | 2.00 | 4.00 | 7.50 | 75.00 |
| | 1891 M | .084 | 5.00 | 10.00 | 20.00 | 75.00 |
| | 1892/1 M | .037 | 4.00 | 8.00 | 15.00 | 75.00 |
| | 1892 M Inc. Ab. | | 2.50 | 5.00 | 10.00 | 75.00 |
| | 1894 M | .043 | 2.50 | 5.00 | 10.00 | 75.00 |
| | 1895 M | .023 | 2.50 | 5.00 | 10.00 | 60.00 |
| | 1896 M | .121 | 1.50 | 2.50 | 5.00 | 50.00 |

### Mint mark: Do

| KM# | Date | Mintage | Fine | VF | XF | Unc |
|---|---|---|---|---|---|---|
| 403.3 | 1878 E | 2,500 | 100.00 | 175.00 | 300.00 | 600.00 |
| | 1879 B | — | — | — | Rare | — |
| | 1880/70 B | — | — | — | Rare | — |
| | 1880/79 B | — | — | — | Rare | — |
| | 1884 C | — | 30.00 | 60.00 | 100.00 | 225.00 |
| | 1886 C | .013 | 75.00 | 150.00 | 300.00 | 500.00 |
| | 1887 C | .081 | 4.00 | 8.00 | 15.00 | 100.00 |
| | 1888 C | .031 | 6.00 | 12.00 | 30.00 | 100.00 |
| | 1889 C | .055 | 4.00 | 8.00 | 15.00 | 100.00 |
| | 1890 C | .050 | 4.00 | 8.00 | 15.00 | 100.00 |
| | 1891 P | .139 | 2.00 | 4.00 | 8.00 | 80.00 |
| | 1892 P | .212 | 2.00 | 4.00 | 8.00 | 80.00 |
| | 1892 D Inc. Ab. | | 2.00 | 4.00 | 8.00 | 80.00 |
| | 1893 D | .258 | 2.00 | 4.00 | 8.00 | 80.00 |
| | 1893 D/C I.A. | | 2.50 | 5.00 | 10.00 | 80.00 |
| | 1894 D | .184 | 1.50 | 3.00 | 6.00 | 80.00 |
| | 1894 D/C I.A. | | 2.00 | 4.00 | 8.00 | 80.00 |
| | 1895 D | .142 | 1.50 | 3.00 | 6.00 | 80.00 |

### Mint mark: Ga

| KM# | Date | Mintage | Fine | VF | XF | Unc |
|---|---|---|---|---|---|---|
| 403.4 | 1871 C | 4,734 | 75.00 | 125.00 | 200.00 | 500.00 |
| | 1873/1 C | .025 | 10.00 | 15.00 | 35.00 | 150.00 |
| | 1873 C Inc.Ab. | | 10.00 | 15.00 | 35.00 | 150.00 |
| | 1874 C | — | 10.00 | 15.00 | 35.00 | 150.00 |
| | 1877 A | — | 10.00 | 15.00 | 30.00 | 150.00 |
| | 1881 S | .115 | 5.00 | 10.00 | 25.00 | 150.00 |
| | 1883 B | .090 | 4.00 | 8.00 | 15.00 | 90.00 |
| | 1884 B | — | 5.00 | 10.00 | 20.00 | 90.00 |
| | 1884 B/S | — | 6.00 | 12.50 | 25.00 | 90.00 |
| | 1884 H | — | 3.00 | 5.00 | 10.00 | 90.00 |
| | 1885 H | .093 | 3.00 | 5.00 | 10.00 | 90.00 |
| | 1886 S | .151 | 2.50 | 4.00 | 9.00 | 90.00 |
| | 1887 S | .162 | 1.50 | 3.00 | 6.00 | 90.00 |
| | 1888 S | .225 | 1.50 | 3.00 | 6.00 | 90.00 |
| | 1888 GaS/HoG | | | | | |
| | Inc. Ab. | | 1.50 | 3.00 | 6.00 | 90.00 |
| | 1889 S | .310 | 1.50 | 3.00 | 6.00 | 40.00 |
| | 1890 S | .303 | 1.50 | 3.00 | 6.00 | 40.00 |
| | 1891 S | .199 | 5.00 | 10.00 | 20.00 | 45.00 |
| | 1892 S | .329 | 1.50 | 3.00 | 6.00 | 40.00 |
| | 1893 S | .225 | 1.50 | 3.00 | 6.00 | 40.00 |
| | 1894 S | .243 | 3.00 | 6.00 | 12.00 | 40.00 |
| | 1895 S | .080 | 1.50 | 3.00 | 6.00 | 40.00 |

NOTE: Varieties exist.

### Mint mark: Go

| KM# | Date | Mintage | Fine | VF | XF | Unc |
|---|---|---|---|---|---|---|
| 403.5 | 1869 S | 7,000 | 20.00 | 40.00 | 80.00 | 200.00 |
| | 1871/0 S | .060 | 15.00 | 25.00 | 50.00 | 125.00 |
| | 1872 S | .060 | 15.00 | 25.00 | 50.00 | 125.00 |
| | 1873 S | .050 | 15.00 | 25.00 | 50.00 | 125.00 |
| | 1874 S | — | 15.00 | 25.00 | 50.00 | 125.00 |
| | 1875 S | — | 250.00 | 350.00 | 500.00 | 800.00 |
| | 1876 S | — | 10.00 | 20.00 | 40.00 | 100.00 |
| 403.5 | 1877 S | — | 80.00 | 120.00 | 200.00 | 400.00 |
| | 1878/7 S | .010 | 10.00 | 20.00 | 45.00 | 110.00 |
| | 1878 O Inc. Ab. | | 7.50 | 10.00 | 20.00 | 70.00 |
| | 1879 S | — | 7.50 | 12.00 | 20.00 | 75.00 |
| | 1880 S | — | 100.00 | 200.00 | 300.00 | 450.00 |
| | 1881/71 S | .100 | 3.00 | 5.00 | 10.00 | 75.00 |
| | 1881/0 S I.A. | | 3.50 | 5.00 | 10.00 | 75.00 |
| | 1881 S Inc. Ab. | | 3.00 | 5.00 | 10.00 | 75.00 |
| | 1882/1 S | .040 | 3.00 | 6.00 | 12.00 | 75.00 |
| | 1883 B | — | 3.00 | 5.00 | 10.00 | 75.00 |
| | 1884 B | — | 1.50 | 3.00 | 6.00 | 75.00 |
| | 1884 S | — | 6.00 | 12.50 | 25.00 | 90.00 |
| | 1885 R | .100 | 1.50 | 3.00 | 6.00 | 75.00 |
| | 1886 R | .095 | 3.00 | 5.00 | 10.00 | 75.00 |
| | 1887 R | .330 | 2.50 | 5.00 | 10.00 | 75.00 |
| | 1888 R | .270 | 1.50 | 3.00 | 6.00 | 75.00 |
| | 1889 R | .205 | 2.00 | 4.00 | 8.00 | 75.00 |
| | 1889 GoR/HoG | | | | | |
| | Inc. Ab. | | 3.00 | 5.00 | 10.00 | 75.00 |
| | 1890 R | .270 | 1.50 | 3.00 | 6.00 | 35.00 |
| | 1890 GoR/Cn M | | | | | |
| | Inc. Ab. | | 1.50 | 3.00 | 6.00 | 35.00 |
| | 1891 R | .523 | 1.50 | 3.00 | 6.00 | 35.00 |
| | 1891 R/G | — | 1.50 | 3.00 | 6.00 | 35.00 |
| | 1891 GoR/HoG | | | | | |
| | Inc. Ab. | | 1.50 | 3.00 | 6.00 | 35.00 |
| | 1892 R | .440 | 1.50 | 3.00 | 6.00 | 35.00 |
| | 1893/1 R | .389 | 3.00 | 5.00 | 10.00 | 35.00 |
| | 1893 R Inc. Ab. | | 1.50 | 3.00 | 6.00 | 35.00 |
| | 1894 R | .400 | 1.50 | 2.50 | 5.00 | 35.00 |
| | 1895 R | .355 | 1.50 | 2.50 | 5.00 | 35.00 |
| | 1896 R | .190 | 1.50 | 2.50 | 5.00 | 35.00 |
| | 1897 R | .205 | 1.50 | 2.50 | 5.00 | 35.00 |

NOTE: Varieties exist.

### Mint mark: Ho

| KM# | Date | Mintage | Fine | VF | XF | Unc |
|---|---|---|---|---|---|---|
| 403.6 | 1874 R | — | 30.00 | 60.00 | 100.00 | 200.00 |
| | 1876 F | 3,140 | 200.00 | 300.00 | 450.00 | 750.00 |
| | 1878 A | — | 5.00 | 10.00 | 15.00 | 85.00 |
| | 1879 A | — | 25.00 | 50.00 | 90.00 | 175.00 |
| | 1880 A | — | 3.00 | 6.00 | 12.50 | 85.00 |
| | 1881 A | .028 | 4.00 | 7.00 | 15.00 | 85.00 |
| | 1882/1 A | .025 | 5.00 | 10.00 | 20.00 | 85.00 |
| | 1882/1 a I.A. | | 6.00 | 12.50 | 25.00 | 85.00 |
| | 1882 A Inc. Ab. | | 4.00 | 7.00 | 15.00 | 85.00 |
| | 1883 | 7,000 | 65.00 | 100.00 | 200.00 | 400.00 |
| | 1884 A | — | 35.00 | 75.00 | 150.00 | 300.00 |
| | 1884/3 M | — | 10.00 | 20.00 | 40.00 | 90.00 |
| | 1884 M | — | 7.50 | 15.00 | 30.00 | 85.00 |
| | 1885 M | .021 | 12.50 | 25.00 | 50.00 | 100.00 |
| | 1886 M | .010 | — | — | Rare | — |
| | 1886 M Inc. Ab. | | 7.50 | 12.50 | 25.00 | 85.00 |
| | 1887 G | — | 25.00 | 50.00 | 75.00 | 150.00 |
| | 1888 G | .025 | 6.00 | 12.50 | 25.00 | 85.00 |
| | 1889 G | .042 | 3.00 | 6.00 | 10.00 | 85.00 |
| | 1890 G | .048 | 3.00 | 6.00 | 10.00 | 85.00 |
| | 1891/80 G | .136 | 3.00 | 6.00 | 10.00 | 85.00 |
| | 1891/0 G I.A. | | 3.00 | 6.00 | 10.00 | 85.00 |
| | 1891 G Inc. Ab. | | 3.00 | 6.00 | 10.00 | 85.00 |
| | 1892 G | .067 | 3.00 | 6.00 | 10.00 | 85.00 |
| | 1893 G | .067 | 3.00 | 6.00 | 10.00 | 85.00 |

### Mint mark: Mo

| KM# | Date | Mintage | Fine | VF | XF | Unc |
|---|---|---|---|---|---|---|
| 403.7 | 1869/8 C | .030 | 10.00 | 20.00 | 40.00 | 100.00 |
| | 1869 C Inc. Ab. | | 8.00 | 17.50 | 35.00 | 90.00 |
| | 1870 C | .110 | 3.00 | 7.50 | 15.00 | 50.00 |
| | 1871 C | .084 | 50.00 | 75.00 | 125.00 | 250.00 |
| | 1871 M Inc. Ab. | | 12.00 | 17.50 | 45.00 | 125.00 |
| | 1872/69 M | .198 | 10.00 | 20.00 | 35.00 | 100.00 |
| | 1872 M Inc. Ab. | | 3.00 | 7.50 | 15.00 | 65.00 |
| | 1873 M | .040 | 10.00 | 15.00 | 30.00 | 75.00 |
| | 1874 M | — | 5.00 | 10.00 | 20.00 | 65.00 |
| | 1874 M/C | — | 5.00 | 10.00 | 20.00 | 65.00 |
| | 1874/64 B | — | 5.00 | 10.00 | 20.00 | 65.00 |
| | 1874 B/M | — | 20.00 | 40.00 | 60.00 | 125.00 |
| | 1874 B | — | 5.00 | 10.00 | 15.00 | 65.00 |
| | 1875 B | — | 20.00 | 40.00 | 60.00 | 125.00 |
| | 1876/5 B | — | 3.00 | 5.00 | 9.00 | 65.00 |
| | 1876/5 B/M | — | 3.00 | 5.00 | 9.00 | 65.00 |
| | 1877/6 M | — | 3.00 | 5.00 | 9.00 | 65.00 |
| | 1877/6 M/B | — | 3.00 | 5.00 | 9.00 | 65.00 |
| | 1877 M | — | 3.00 | 5.00 | 9.00 | 65.00 |
| | 1878/7 M | .100 | 3.00 | 5.00 | 9.00 | 65.00 |
| | 1878 M Inc. Ab. | | 3.00 | 5.00 | 9.00 | 65.00 |
| | 1879/69 M | — | 3.00 | 5.00 | 9.00 | 65.00 |

| KM# | Date | Mintage | Fine | VF | XF | Unc |
|---|---|---|---|---|---|---|
| 403.7 | 1879 M/C | — | 3.00 | 5.00 | 9.00 | 65.00 |
| | 1880/79 M | — | 3.00 | 5.00 | 9.00 | 65.00 |
| | 1881/0 M | .510 | 3.00 | 5.00 | 9.00 | 35.00 |
| | 1881 M Inc. Ab. | | 3.00 | 5.00 | 9.00 | 35.00 |
| | 1882/1 M | .550 | 3.00 | 5.00 | 9.00 | 35.00 |
| | 1882 M Inc. Ab. | | 3.00 | 5.00 | 9.00 | 35.00 |
| | 1883/2 M | .250 | 3.00 | 5.00 | 9.00 | 35.00 |
| | 1884 M | — | 3.00 | 5.00 | 9.00 | 35.00 |
| | 1885 M | .470 | 3.00 | 5.00 | 9.00 | 35.00 |
| | 1886 M | .603 | 3.00 | 5.00 | 9.00 | 35.00 |
| | 1887/6 M | — | 3.00 | 5.00 | 9.00 | 35.00 |
| | 1887 M | .580 | 3.00 | 5.00 | 9.00 | 35.00 |
| | 1888/7 MoM | | | | | |
| | | .710 | 3.00 | 5.00 | 9.00 | 35.00 |
| | 1888 MoM I.A. | | 3.00 | 5.00 | 9.00 | 35.00 |
| | 1888 MOM I.A. | | 3.00 | 5.00 | 9.00 | 35.00 |
| | 1889/8 M | .622 | 3.00 | 5.00 | 9.00 | 35.00 |
| | 1889 M Inc. Ab. | | 3.00 | 5.00 | 9.00 | 35.00 |
| | 1890/89 M | .815 | 3.00 | 5.00 | 9.00 | 35.00 |
| | 1890 M Inc. Ab. | | 3.00 | 5.00 | 9.00 | 35.00 |
| | 1891 M | .859 | 1.50 | 2.50 | 7.00 | 25.00 |
| | 1892 M | 1.030 | 1.50 | 2.50 | 7.00 | 25.00 |
| | 1893 M | .310 | 1.50 | 2.50 | 7.00 | 25.00 |
| | 1893 M/C I.A. | | 1.50 | 2.50 | 7.00 | 25.00 |
| | 1893 Mo/Ho M/G | | | | | |
| | | — | 1.50 | 2.50 | 7.00 | 25.00 |
| | 1894/3 M | — | 5.00 | 10.00 | 20.00 | 60.00 |
| | 1894 M | .350 | 5.00 | 10.00 | 20.00 | 60.00 |
| | 1895 M | .320 | 1.50 | 2.50 | 7.00 | 25.00 |
| | 1896 B/G | .340 | 1.50 | 2.50 | 7.00 | 25.00 |
| | 1896 M Inc. Ab. | 35.00 | 70.00 | 100.00 | 150.00 | |
| | 1897 M | .170 | 1.50 | 2.50 | 5.00 | 20.00 |

**NOTE:** Varieties exist.

**Mint mark: Oa**

| KM# | Date | Mintage | Fine | VF | XF | Unc |
|---|---|---|---|---|---|---|
| 403.8 | 1889 E | .021 | 200.00 | 400.00 | 600.00 | — |
| | 1890 E | .031 | 100.00 | 150.00 | 250.00 | 500.00 |
| | 1890 N Inc. Ab. | — | — | Rare | — | |

**Mint mark: Pi**

| KM# | Date | Mintage | Fine | VF | XF | Unc |
|---|---|---|---|---|---|---|
| 403.9 | 1869/8 S | 4,000 | — | — | Rare | — |
| | 1870/69 O | .018 | — | — | Rare | — |
| | 1870 G Inc. Ab. | 125.00 | 200.00 | 325.00 | 600.00 | |
| | 1871 O | .021 | 50.00 | 100.00 | 150.00 | 300.00 |
| | 1872 O | .016 | 150.00 | 225.00 | 350.00 | 650.00 |
| | 1873 O | 4,750 | — | — | Rare | — |
| | 1874 H | — | 25.00 | 50.00 | 100.00 | 200.00 |
| | 1875 H | — | 75.00 | 125.00 | 200.00 | 400.00 |
| | 1876 H | — | 75.00 | 125.00 | 200.00 | 400.00 |
| | 1877 H | — | 75.00 | 125.00 | 200.00 | 400.00 |
| | 1878 H | — | 250.00 | 500.00 | 750.00 | — |
| | 1879 H | — | — | — | — | — |
| | 1880 H | — | 150.00 | 250.00 | 350.00 | — |
| | 1881 H | 7,600 | 250.00 | 350.00 | 500.00 | — |
| | 1882 H | 4,000 | — | — | Rare | — |
| | 1883 H | — | 125.00 | 200.00 | 300.00 | 500.00 |
| | 1884 H | — | 25.00 | 50.00 | 100.00 | 200.00 |
| | 1885 H | .051 | 25.00 | 50.00 | 100.00 | 200.00 |
| | 1885 C Inc. Ab. | — | — | Rare | — | |
| | 1886 C | .052 | 15.00 | 30.00 | 60.00 | 150.00 |
| | 1886 R Inc. Ab. | 5.00 | 10.00 | 20.00 | 65.00 | |
| | 1887 R | .118 | 2.50 | 5.00 | 10.00 | 50.00 |
| | 1888 R | .136 | 2.50 | 5.00 | 10.00 | 50.00 |
| | 1889/8 R/G | — | 7.50 | 12.50 | 20.00 | 60.00 |
| | 1889/7 R | .131 | 7.50 | 12.50 | 20.00 | 60.00 |
| | 1890 R | .204 | 1.50 | 3.00 | 7.50 | 40.00 |
| | 1891/89 R | .163 | 2.50 | 5.00 | 10.00 | 40.00 |
| | 1891 R Inc. Ab. | 1.50 | 3.50 | 6.00 | 30.00 | |
| | 1892/0 R | .200 | 2.00 | 4.00 | 8.00 | 40.00 |
| | 1892 R Inc. Ab. | 1.50 | 2.50 | 5.00 | 40.00 | |
| | 1892 R/G | — | 2.00 | 4.00 | 8.00 | 40.00 |
| | 1893 R | .048 | 7.50 | 10.00 | 17.50 | 60.00 |
| | 1893 R/G | — | 1.50 | 10.00 | 17.50 | 60.00 |

**NOTE:** Varieties exist.

**Mint mark: Zs**

| KM# | Date | Mintage | Fine | VF | XF | Unc |
|---|---|---|---|---|---|---|
| 403.10 | 1870 H | .020 | 100.00 | 150.00 | 200.00 | 400.00 |
| | 1871/0 H | .010 | — | — | — | — |
| | 1871 H Inc. Ab. | — | — | — | — | |
| | 1872 H | .010 | 150.00 | 200.00 | 275.00 | 500.00 |
| | 1873 H | .010 | 250.00 | 350.00 | 600.00 | — |
| | 1874/3 H | — | 50.00 | 75.00 | 150.00 | 300.00 |
| | 1874 A | — | 200.00 | 300.00 | 500.00 | — |
| | 1875 A | — | 5.00 | 10.00 | 25.00 | 100.00 |
| | 1876 A | — | 5.00 | 10.00 | 25.00 | 100.00 |

| KM# | Date | Mintage | Fine | VF | XF | Unc |
|---|---|---|---|---|---|---|
| 403.10 | 1876 S | — | 100.00 | 200.00 | 300.00 | 500.00 |
| | 1877 S small S | | | | | |
| | | — | 7.50 | 12.50 | 25.00 | 100.00 |
| | 1877 S regular S | | | | | |
| | | — | 7.50 | 12.50 | 25.00 | 100.00 |
| | 1878/7 S | .030 | 5.00 | 10.00 | 20.00 | 80.00 |
| | 1878 S Inc. Ab. | 5.00 | 10.00 | 20.00 | 80.00 | |
| | 1879 S | — | 5.00 | 10.00 | 20.00 | 80.00 |
| | 1880 S | — | 5.00 | 10.00 | 20.00 | 80.00 |
| | 1881/0 S | .120 | 3.00 | 6.00 | 12.50 | 50.00 |
| | 1881 S Inc. Ab. | 3.00 | 6.00 | 12.50 | 50.00 | |
| | 1882/1 S | .064 | 12.50 | 25.00 | 50.00 | 125.00 |
| | 1882 S Inc. Ab. | 12.50 | 25.00 | 50.00 | 125.00 | |
| | 1883/73 S | .102 | 2.00 | 4.00 | 8.00 | 50.00 |
| | 1883 S Inc. Ab. | 2.00 | 4.00 | 8.00 | 50.00 | |
| | 1884/3 S | — | 2.00 | 4.00 | 8.00 | 50.00 |
| | 1884 S | — | 2.00 | 4.00 | 8.00 | 50.00 |
| | 1885 S | .297 | 1.50 | 2.50 | 5.00 | 50.00 |
| | 1885 S small S in mint mark | | | | | |
| | Inc. Ab. | 2.50 | 4.00 | 8.00 | 50.00 | |
| | 1885 Z w/o assayers initial (error) | | | | | |
| | Inc. Ab. | 3.50 | 7.50 | 15.00 | 65.00 | |
| | 1886 S | .274 | 1.50 | 2.50 | 5.00 | 30.00 |
| | 1886 Z | I.A. | 12.50 | 25.00 | 50.00 | 125.00 |
| | 1887 ZsZ | .233 | 1.50 | 2.50 | 5.00 | 30.00 |
| | 1887 Z Z (error) | | | | | |
| | Inc. Ab. | 3.50 | 7.50 | 15.00 | 50.00 | |
| | 1888 ZsZ | .270 | 1.50 | 2.50 | 5.00 | 30.00 |
| | 1888 Z Z (error) | | | | | |
| | Inc. Ab. | 3.50 | 7.50 | 15.00 | 40.00 | |
| | 1889/7 Z/S | | | | | |
| | | .240 | 4.00 | 8.00 | 12.50 | 40.00 |
| | 1889 Z/S I.A. | 1.50 | 4.00 | 8.00 | 30.00 | |
| | 1889 Z/G | — | 1.50 | 4.00 | 8.00 | 30.00 |
| | 1889 Z Inc. Ab. | 1.50 | 2.50 | 5.00 | 30.00 | |
| | 1890 ZsZ | .410 | 1.50 | 2.50 | 5.00 | 30.00 |
| | 1890 Z Z (error) | | | | | |
| | Inc. Ab. | 3.75 | 7.50 | 15.00 | 40.00 | |
| | 1891 Z | 1.105 | 1.50 | 2.50 | 5.00 | 30.00 |
| | 1891 ZsZ double s | | | | | |
| | Inc. Ab. | 2.00 | 4.00 | 7.00 | 30.00 | |
| | 1892 Z | 1.102 | 1.50 | 2.50 | 5.00 | 30.00 |
| | 1892 Z/G | — | 2.00 | 4.00 | 7.00 | 30.00 |
| | 1893/2 Z | — | 2.00 | 4.00 | 8.00 | 40.00 |
| | 1893 Z | 1.011 | 1.50 | 2.50 | 5.00 | 25.00 |
| | 1894 Z | .892 | 1.50 | 2.50 | 5.00 | 30.00 |
| | 1895 Z | .920 | 1.50 | 2.50 | 5.00 | 30.00 |
| | 1895 Z 9/5 | — | 2.00 | 4.00 | 7.00 | 30.00 |
| | 1896/5 ZsZ | .700 | 1.50 | 2.50 | 5.00 | 30.00 |
| | 1896 ZsZ I.A. | 1.50 | 2.50 | 5.00 | 30.00 | |
| | 1896 Z Z (error) | | | | | |
| | Inc. Ab. | 3.75 | 7.50 | 15.00 | 40.00 | |
| | 1896/5 Z/G | — | 1.50 | 2.50 | 5.00 | 30.00 |
| | 1896 Z/G | — | 1.50 | 2.50 | 5.00 | 30.00 |
| | 1897/6 ZsZ | .900 | 2.00 | 5.00 | 10.00 | 30.00 |
| | 1897/6 Z Z (error) | | | | | |
| | Inc. Ab. | 3.75 | 7.50 | 15.00 | 40.00 | |
| | 1897 Z Inc. Ab. | 1.50 | 2.50 | 5.00 | 30.00 | |

**NOTE:** Varieties exist.

**Mint mark: Cn**
**Obv: Restyled eagle.**

| KM# | Date | Mintage | Fine | VF | XF | Unc |
|---|---|---|---|---|---|---|
| 404 | 1898 M | 9,870 | 50.00 | 100.00 | 150.00 | 300.00 |
| | 1899 Q round Q, single tail | | | | | |
| | | .080 | 5.00 | 7.50 | 15.00 | 40.00 |
| | 1899 Q oval Q, double tail | | | | | |
| | Inc. Ab. | 5.00 | 7.50 | 15.00 | 40.00 | |
| | 1900 Q | .160 | 1.50 | 2.50 | 5.00 | 20.00 |
| | 1901 Q | .235 | 1.50 | 2.50 | 5.00 | 20.00 |
| | 1902 Q | .186 | 1.50 | 2.50 | 5.00 | 20.00 |
| | 1903 Q | .256 | 1.50 | 2.50 | 6.00 | 20.00 |
| | 1903 V Inc. Ab. | 1.50 | 2.50 | 5.00 | 15.00 | |
| | 1904 H | .307 | 1.50 | 2.50 | 5.00 | 15.00 |

**NOTE:** Varieties exist.

**Mint mark: Go**

| KM# | Date | Mintage | Fine | VF | XF | Unc |
|---|---|---|---|---|---|---|
| 404.1 | 1898 R | .435 | 1.50 | 2.50 | 5.00 | 20.00 |

| KM# | Date | Mintage | Fine | VF | XF | Unc |
|---|---|---|---|---|---|---|
| 404.1 | 1899 R | .270 | 1.50 | 2.50 | 5.00 | 25.00 |
|  | 1900 R | .130 | 7.50 | 12.50 | 25.00 | 60.00 |

**Mint mark: Mo**

| KM# | Date | Mintage | Fine | VF | XF | Unc |
|---|---|---|---|---|---|---|
| 404.2 | 1898 M | .130 | 1.50 | 2.50 | 5.00 | 20.00 |
|  | 1899 M | .190 | 1.50 | 2.50 | 5.00 | 20.00 |
|  | 1900 M | .311 | 1.50 | 2.50 | 5.00 | 20.00 |
|  | 1901 M | .080 | 2.50 | 3.50 | 7.00 | 22.50 |
|  | 1902 M | .181 | 1.50 | 2.50 | 5.00 | 20.00 |
|  | 1903 M | .581 | 1.50 | 2.50 | 5.00 | 20.00 |
|  | 1904 M | 1.266 | 1.25 | 2.00 | 4.50 | 18.00 |
|  | 1904 MM (error) |  |  |  |  |  |
|  |  | Inc. Ab. | 2.50 | 5.00 | 10.00 | 25.00 |
|  | 1905 M | .266 | 2.00 | 3.75 | 7.50 | 20.00 |

**Mint mark: Zs**

| KM# | Date | Mintage | Fine | VF | XF | Unc |
|---|---|---|---|---|---|---|
| 404.3 | 1898 Z | .240 | 1.50 | 2.50 | 7.50 | 20.00 |
|  | 1899 Z | .105 | 1.50 | 3.00 | 10.00 | 22.00 |
|  | 1900 Z | .219 | 7.50 | 10.00 | 20.00 | 45.00 |
|  | 1901 Z | .070 | 2.50 | 5.00 | 10.00 | 25.00 |
|  | 1902 Z | .120 | 2.50 | 5.00 | 10.00 | 25.00 |
|  | 1903 Z | .228 | 1.50 | 3.00 | 10.00 | 20.00 |
|  | 1904 Z | .368 | 1.50 | 3.00 | 10.00 | 20.00 |
|  | 1904 M Inc. Ab. |  | 1.50 | 3.00 | 10.00 | 25.00 |
|  | 1905 M | .066 | 7.50 | 15.00 | 30.00 | 60.00 |

## 20 CENTAVOS

**5.4150 g, .903 SILVER, .1572 oz ASW**
**Mint mark: Cn**
**Obv: Restyled eagle.**

| KM# | Date | Mintage | Fine | VF | XF | Unc |
|---|---|---|---|---|---|---|
| 405 | 1898 M | .114 | 5.00 | 12.50 | 35.00 | 140.00 |
|  | 1899 M | .044 | 12.00 | 20.00 | 45.00 | 225.00 |
|  | 1899 Q Inc. Ab. |  | 20.00 | 35.00 | 100.00 | 250.00 |
|  | 1900 Q | .068 | 6.50 | 12.50 | 35.00 | 140.00 |
|  | 1901 Q | .185 | 5.00 | 10.00 | 30.00 | 120.00 |
|  | 1902/802 Q |  |  |  |  |  |
|  |  | .098 | 6.00 | 10.00 | 30.00 | 120.00 |
|  | 1902 Q Inc. Ab. |  | 4.00 | 9.00 | 30.00 | 120.00 |
|  | 1903 Q | .093 | 4.00 | 9.00 | 30.00 | 120.00 |
|  | 1904/3 H | .258 | — | — | — | — |
|  | 1904 H Inc. Ab. |  | 5.00 | 10.00 | 30.00 | 120.00 |

**Mint mark: Go**

| KM# | Date | Mintage | Fine | VF | XF | Unc |
|---|---|---|---|---|---|---|
| 405.1 | 1898 R | .135 | 4.00 | 8.00 | 20.00 | 100.00 |
|  | 1899 R | .215 | 4.00 | 8.00 | 20.00 | 100.00 |
|  | 1900/800 R |  |  |  |  |  |
|  |  | .038 | 10.00 | 20.00 | 50.00 | 150.00 |

**Mint mark: Mo**

| KM# | Date | Mintage | Fine | VF | XF | Unc |
|---|---|---|---|---|---|---|
| 405.2 | 1898 M | .150 | 4.00 | 8.00 | 20.00 | 90.00 |
|  | 1899 M | .425 | 4.00 | 8.00 | 20.00 | 90.00 |
|  | 1900/800 M |  |  |  |  |  |
|  |  | .295 | 4.00 | 8.00 | 20.00 | 90.00 |
|  | 1901 M | .110 | 4.00 | 8.00 | 20.00 | 90.00 |
|  | 1902 M | .120 | 4.00 | 8.00 | 20.00 | 90.00 |
|  | 1903 M | .213 | 4.00 | 8.00 | 20.00 | 90.00 |
|  | 1904 M | .276 | 4.00 | 8.00 | 20.00 | 90.00 |
|  | 1905 M | .117 | 6.50 | 20.00 | 50.00 | 150.00 |

**NOTE:** Varieties exist.

**Mint mark: Zs**

| KM# | Date | Mintage | Fine | VF | XF | Unc |
|---|---|---|---|---|---|---|
| 405.3 | 1898 Z | .195 | 5.00 | 10.00 | 20.00 | 100.00 |
|  | 1899 Z | .210 | 5.00 | 10.00 | 20.00 | 100.00 |
|  | 1900/800 Z |  |  |  |  |  |
|  |  | .097 | 5.00 | 10.00 | 20.00 | 100.00 |
|  | 1901/O Z | .130 | 25.00 | 50.00 | 100.00 | 250.00 |
|  | 1901 Z Inc. Ab. |  | 5.00 | 10.00 | 20.00 | 100.00 |
|  | 1902 Z | .105 | 5.00 | 10.00 | 20.00 | 100.00 |
|  | 1903 Z | .143 | 5.00 | 10.00 | 20.00 | 100.00 |
|  | 1904 Z | .246 | 5.00 | 10.00 | 20.00 | 100.00 |
|  | 1904 M Inc. Ab. |  | 5.00 | 10.00 | 20.00 | 100.00 |
|  | 1905 M | .059 | 10.00 | 20.00 | 50.00 | 150.00 |

## 25 CENTAVOS

**6.7680 g, .903 SILVER, .1965 oz ASW**
**Mint mark: A, As**

| KM# | Date | Mintage | Fine | VF | XF | Unc |
|---|---|---|---|---|---|---|
| 406 | 1874 L | — | 20.00 | 40.00 | 90.00 | 200.00 |
|  | 1875 L | — | 15.00 | 30.00 | 70.00 | 200.00 |
|  | 1876 L | — | 30.00 | 50.00 | 100.00 | 200.00 |
|  | 1877 L | .011 | 200.00 | 300.00 | 500.00 | — |
|  | 1877. Inc. Ab. |  | 10.00 | 25.00 | 60.00 | 200.00 |
|  | 1878 L | .025 | 10.00 | 25.00 | 60.00 | 200.00 |
|  | 1879 L | — | 10.00 | 25.00 | 60.00 | 200.00 |
|  | 1880 L | — | 10.00 | 25.00 | 60.00 | 200.00 |
|  | 1880.L | — | 10.00 | 25.00 | 60.00 | 200.00 |
|  | 1881 L | 8,800 | 500.00 | 700.00 | — | — |
|  | 1882 L | 7,777 | 15.00 | 35.00 | 80.00 | 200.00 |
|  | 1883 L | .028 | 10.00 | 25.00 | 60.00 | 200.00 |
|  | 1884 L | — | 10.00 | 25.00 | 60.00 | 200.00 |
|  | 1885 L | — | 20.00 | 40.00 | 90.00 | 200.00 |
|  | 1886 L | .046 | 15.00 | 30.00 | 70.00 | 200.00 |
|  | 1887 L | .012 | 12.50 | 27.50 | 65.00 | 200.00 |
|  | 1888 L | .020 | 12.50 | 27.50 | 65.00 | 200.00 |
|  | 1889 L | .014 | 12.50 | 27.50 | 65.00 | 200.00 |
|  | 1890 L | .023 | 10.00 | 25.00 | 60.00 | 200.00 |

**Mint mark: CA, CH, Ca**

| KM# | Date | Mintage | Fine | VF | XF | Unc |
|---|---|---|---|---|---|---|
| 406.1 | 1871 M | .018 | 25.00 | 50.00 | 100.00 | 200.00 |
|  | 1872 M very crude date |  |  |  |  |  |
|  |  | .024 | 50.00 | 100.00 | 150.00 | 300.00 |
|  | 1883 M | .012 | 10.00 | 25.00 | 50.00 | 175.00 |
|  | 1885/3 M | .035 | 10.00 | 25.00 | 50.00 | 175.00 |
|  | 1885 M Inc.Ab. |  | 10.00 | 25.00 | 50.00 | 175.00 |
|  | 1886 M | .022 | 10.00 | 25.00 | 50.00 | 175.00 |
|  | 1887/6 M | .026 | 10.00 | 15.00 | 30.00 | 175.00 |
|  | 1887 M Inc. Ab. |  | 10.00 | 15.00 | 30.00 | 175.00 |
|  | 1888 M | .014 | 10.00 | 25.00 | 50.00 | 175.00 |
|  | 1889 M | .050 | 10.00 | 15.00 | 30.00 | 175.00 |

**Mint mark: Cn**

| KM# | Date | Mintage | Fine | VF | XF | Unc |
|---|---|---|---|---|---|---|
| 406.2 | 1871 P | — | 250.00 | 500.00 | 750.00 | — |
|  | 1872 P | 2,780 | 300.00 | 550.00 | 800.00 | — |
|  | 1873 P | .020 | 100.00 | 150.00 | 250.00 | 500.00 |
|  | 1874 P | — | 20.00 | 50.00 | 125.00 | 250.00 |
|  | 1875 P | — | 250.00 | 500.00 | 750.00 | — |
|  | 1876 P | — | — | — | Rare | — |
|  | 1878/7 D/S | — | 100.00 | 150.00 | 250.00 | 500.00 |
|  | 1878 Cn/Go D/S | 100.00 | 150.00 | 250.00 | 500.00 |  |
|  | 1878 D | — | 100.00 | 150.00 | 250.00 | 500.00 |
|  | 1879 D | — | 15.00 | 35.00 | 70.00 | 175.00 |
|  | 1880 D | — | 250.00 | 500.00 | 750.00 | — |
|  | 1881/0 D | .018 | 15.00 | 30.00 | 60.00 | 175.00 |
|  | 1882 D | — | 200.00 | 350.00 | 600.00 | — |
|  | 1882 M | — | — | — | Rare | — |
|  | 1883 M | .015 | 50.00 | 100.00 | 150.00 | 300.00 |
|  | 1884 M | — | 20.00 | 40.00 | 80.00 | 175.00 |
|  | 1885/4 M | .019 | 20.00 | 40.00 | 80.00 | 175.00 |
|  | 1886 M | .022 | 12.50 | 20.00 | 50.00 | 175.00 |
|  | 1887 M | .032 | 12.50 | 20.00 | 50.00 | 175.00 |
|  | 1888 M | .086 | 7.50 | 15.00 | 30.00 | 175.00 |
|  | 1888 M Cn/Me | — | — | — | — | — |
|  | 1889 M | .050 | 10.00 | 25.00 | 50.00 | 175.00 |
|  | 1890 M 9/8 | — | 7.50 | 17.50 | 40.00 | 175.00 |
|  | 1890 M | .091 | 7.50 | 17.50 | 40.00 | 175.00 |
|  | 1892/0 M | .016 | 20.00 | 40.00 | 80.00 | 200.00 |
|  | 1892 M Inc. Ab. |  | 20.00 | 40.00 | 80.00 | 200.00 |

**Mint mark: Do**

| KM# | Date | Mintage | Fine | VF | XF | Unc |
|---|---|---|---|---|---|---|
| 406.3 | 1873 P 892 pcs. | — | — | — | Rare | — |
|  | 1877 P | — | 25.00 | 50.00 | 100.00 | 200.00 |
|  | 1878/7 E | — | 250.00 | 500.00 | 750.00 | — |
|  | 1878 B | — | — | — | Rare | — |
|  | 1879 B | — | 50.00 | 75.00 | 125.00 | 250.00 |
|  | 1880 B | — | — | — | Rare | — |
|  | 1882 C | .017 | 25.00 | 50.00 | 100.00 | 225.00 |
|  | 1884/3 C | — | 25.00 | 50.00 | 100.00 | 200.00 |

| KM# | Date | Mintage | Fine | VF | XF | Unc |
|---|---|---|---|---|---|---|
| 406.3 | 1885 C | .015 | 20.00 | 40.00 | 80.00 | 200.00 |
| | 1885 C/S | — | 20.00 | 40.00 | 80.00 | 200.00 |
| | 1886 C | .033 | 15.00 | 30.00 | 60.00 | 200.00 |
| | 1887 C | .027 | 10.00 | 20.00 | 50.00 | 200.00 |
| | 1888 C | .025 | 10.00 | 20.00 | 50.00 | 200.00 |
| | 1889 C | .029 | 10.00 | 20.00 | 50.00 | 200.00 |
| | 1890 C | .068 | 7.50 | 15.00 | 40.00 | 200.00 |

**Mint mark: Ga**

| KM# | Date | Mintage | Fine | VF | XF | Unc |
|---|---|---|---|---|---|---|
| 406.4 | 1880 A | .038 | 25.00 | 50.00 | 100.00 | 200.00 |
| | 1881/0 S | .039 | 25.00 | 50.00 | 100.00 | 200.00 |
| | 1881 S Inc. Ab. | | 25.00 | 50.00 | 100.00 | 200.00 |
| | 1882 S | .018 | 25.00 | 50.00 | 100.00 | 200.00 |
| | 1883/2 B/S | — | 50.00 | 100.00 | 150.00 | 300.00 |
| | 1884 B | — | 20.00 | 40.00 | 80.00 | 150.00 |
| | 1889 S | .030 | 20.00 | 40.00 | 80.00 | 150.00 |

**Mint mark: Go**

| KM# | Date | Mintage | Fine | VF | XF | Unc |
|---|---|---|---|---|---|---|
| 406.5 | 1870 S | .128 | 10.00 | 20.00 | 50.00 | 125.00 |
| | 1871 S | .172 | 10.00 | 20.00 | 50.00 | 125.00 |
| | 1872/1 S | .178 | 10.00 | 20.00 | 50.00 | 125.00 |
| | 1872 S Inc. Ab. | | 10.00 | 20.00 | 50.00 | 125.00 |
| | 1873 S | .120 | 10.00 | 20.00 | 50.00 | 125.00 |
| | 1874 S | — | 15.00 | 30.00 | 60.00 | 150.00 |
| | 1875/4 S | — | 15.00 | 30.00 | 60.00 | 150.00 |
| | 1875 S | — | 10.00 | 20.00 | 50.00 | 125.00 |
| | 1876 S | — | 20.00 | 40.00 | 80.00 | 175.00 |
| | 1877 S | .124 | 10.00 | 20.00 | 50.00 | 125.00 |
| | 1878 S | .146 | 10.00 | 20.00 | 50.00 | 125.00 |
| | 1879 S | — | 10.00 | 20.00 | 50.00 | 125.00 |
| | 1880 S | — | 20.00 | 40.00 | 80.00 | 175.00 |
| | 1881 S | .408 | 7.50 | 17.50 | 45.00 | 125.00 |
| | 1882 S | .204 | 7.50 | 17.50 | 45.00 | 125.00 |
| | 1883 B | .168 | 7.50 | 17.50 | 45.00 | 125.00 |
| | 1884/69 B | — | 7.50 | 17.50 | 45.00 | 125.00 |
| | 1884/3 B | — | 7.50 | 17.50 | 45.00 | 125.00 |
| | 1884/3 B/R | — | 7.50 | 17.50 | 45.00 | 125.00 |
| | 1884 B | — | 7.50 | 17.50 | 45.00 | 125.00 |
| | 1885/65 R | .300 | 7.50 | 17.50 | 45.00 | 125.00 |
| | 1885/69 R I.A. | | 7.50 | 17.50 | 45.00 | 125.00 |
| | 1885 R Inc. Ab. | | 7.50 | 17.50 | 45.00 | 125.00 |
| | 1886/66 R | .322 | 7.50 | 17.50 | 45.00 | 125.00 |
| | 1886/69 R/S Inc. Ab. | | 7.50 | 17.50 | 45.00 | 125.00 |
| | 1886/5/69R Inc. Ab. | | 7.50 | 15.00 | 45.00 | 125.00 |
| | 1886 R Inc. Ab. | | 7.50 | 15.00 | 45.00 | 125.00 |
| | 1887 R | .254 | 7.50 | 15.00 | 45.00 | 125.00 |
| | 1887 Go/Cn R/D Inc. Ab. | | 7.50 | 15.00 | 45.00 | 125.00 |
| | 1888 R | .312 | 7.50 | 15.00 | 45.00 | 125.00 |
| | 1889/8 R | .304 | 7.50 | 15.00 | 45.00 | 125.00 |
| | 1889/8 Go/Cn R/D Inc. Ab. | | 7.50 | 15.00 | 45.00 | 125.00 |
| | 1889 R Inc. Ab. | | 7.50 | 15.00 | 45.00 | 125.00 |
| | 1890 R | .236 | 7.50 | 15.00 | 45.00 | 125.00 |

**NOTE:** Varieties exist.

**Mint mark: Ho**

| KM# | Date | Mintage | Fine | VF | XF | Unc |
|---|---|---|---|---|---|---|
| 406.6 | 1874 R | .023 | 10.00 | 20.00 | 40.00 | 125.00 |
| | 1874/64 R I.A. | | 10.00 | 20.00 | 40.00 | 125.00 |
| | 1874/69 R | — | 10.00 | 20.00 | 40.00 | 125.00 |
| | 1875 R | — | — | — | Rare | — |
| | 1876/4 F/R | .034 | 10.00 | 20.00 | 50.00 | 150.00 |
| | 1876 F/R I.A. | | 10.00 | 25.00 | 60.00 | 150.00 |
| | 1876 F Inc. Ab. | | 10.00 | 25.00 | 55.00 | 135.00 |
| | 1877 F | — | 10.00 | 20.00 | 50.00 | 125.00 |
| | 1878 A | .023 | 10.00 | 20.00 | 50.00 | 125.00 |
| | 1879 A | — | 10.00 | 20.00 | 50.00 | 125.00 |
| | 1880 A | — | 15.00 | 30.00 | 60.00 | 125.00 |
| | 1881 A | .019 | 15.00 | 30.00 | 60.00 | 125.00 |
| | 1882 A | 8,120 | 20.00 | 40.00 | 80.00 | 150.00 |
| | 1883 M | 2,000 | 100.00 | 200.00 | 300.00 | 600.00 |
| | 1884 M | — | 12.50 | 25.00 | 50.00 | 150.00 |
| | 1885 M | — | 10.00 | 20.00 | 50.00 | 125.00 |
| | 1886 G | 6,400 | 30.00 | 60.00 | 125.00 | 250.00 |
| | 1887 G | .012 | 10.00 | 20.00 | 40.00 | 125.00 |
| | 1888 G | .020 | 10.00 | 20.00 | 40.00 | 125.00 |
| | 1889 G | .028 | 10.00 | 20.00 | 40.00 | 125.00 |
| | 1890/80 G | .018 | 25.00 | 50.00 | 100.00 | 125.00 |
| | 1890 G Inc. Ab. | | 25.00 | 50.00 | 100.00 | 125.00 |

**NOTE:** Varieties exist.

**Mint mark: Mo**

| KM# | Date | Mintage | Fine | VF | XF | Unc |
|---|---|---|---|---|---|---|
| 406.7 | 1869 C | .076 | 10.00 | 25.00 | 50.00 | 125.00 |
| | 1870/69 C | — | 6.00 | 12.00 | 30.00 | 125.00 |
| | 1870/9 C | .136 | 6.00 | 12.00 | 30.00 | 125.00 |
| | 1870 C Inc. Ab. | | 6.00 | 12.00 | 30.00 | 125.00 |
| | 1871 M | .138 | 6.00 | 12.00 | 30.00 | 125.00 |
| | 1872 M | .220 | 6.00 | 12.00 | 30.00 | 125.00 |
| | 1873/1 M | .048 | 10.00 | 25.00 | 50.00 | 125.00 |
| | 1873 M Inc. Ab. | | 10.00 | 25.00 | 50.00 | 125.00 |
| | 1874/69 B/M | — | 10.00 | 25.00 | 50.00 | 125.00 |
| | 1874/3 M | — | 10.00 | 25.00 | 50.00 | 125.00 |
| | 1874/3 B | — | 10.00 | 25.00 | 50.00 | 125.00 |
| | 1874/3 B/M | — | 10.00 | 25.00 | 50.00 | 125.00 |
| | 1874 M | — | 6.00 | 12.00 | 30.00 | 125.00 |
| | 1874 B/M | — | 10.00 | 25.00 | 50.00 | 125.00 |
| | 1875 B | — | 6.00 | 12.00 | 30.00 | 125.00 |
| | 1876/5 B | — | 7.50 | 15.00 | 40.00 | 125.00 |
| | 1876 B | — | 6.00 | 12.00 | 30.00 | 125.00 |
| | 1877 M | .056 | 10.00 | 25.00 | 50.00 | 125.00 |
| | 1878/1 M | .120 | 10.00 | 25.00 | 50.00 | 125.00 |
| | 1878/7 M I.A. | | 10.00 | 25.00 | 50.00 | 125.00 |
| | 1878 M Inc. Ab. | | 6.00 | 12.00 | 30.00 | 125.00 |
| | 1879 M | — | 10.00 | 20.00 | 40.00 | 125.00 |
| | 1880 M | — | 7.50 | 15.00 | 35.00 | 125.00 |
| | 1881/0 M | .300 | 10.00 | 25.00 | 50.00 | 125.00 |
| | 1881 M Inc. Ab. | | 10.00 | 25.00 | 50.00 | 125.00 |
| | 1882 M | .212 | 7.50 | 15.00 | 35.00 | 125.00 |
| | 1883 M | .108 | 7.50 | 15.00 | 35.00 | 125.00 |
| | 1884/3 M | — | 10.00 | 25.00 | 50.00 | 125.00 |
| | 1884 M | — | 10.00 | 20.00 | 40.00 | 125.00 |
| | 1885 M | .216 | 10.00 | 20.00 | 40.00 | 125.00 |
| | 1886/5 M | .436 | 7.50 | 15.00 | 35.00 | 125.00 |
| | 1886 M Inc. Ab. | | 7.50 | 15.00 | 35.00 | 125.00 |
| | 1887 M | .376 | 7.50 | 15.00 | 35.00 | 125.00 |
| | 1888 M | .192 | 7.50 | 15.00 | 35.00 | 125.00 |
| | 1889 M | .132 | 7.50 | 15.00 | 35.00 | 125.00 |
| | 1890 M | .060 | 10.00 | 20.00 | 40.00 | 125.00 |

**NOTE:** Varieties exist.

**Mint mark: Pi**

| KM# | Date | Mintage | Fine | VF | XF | Unc |
|---|---|---|---|---|---|---|
| 406.8 | 1869 S | — | 25.00 | 75.00 | 150.00 | 300.00 |
| | 1870 G | .050 | 10.00 | 30.00 | 75.00 | 150.00 |
| | 1870 O Inc. Ab. | | 15.00 | 35.00 | 85.00 | 175.00 |
| | 1871 O | .030 | 10.00 | 30.00 | 75.00 | 150.00 |
| | 1872 O | .046 | 10.00 | 30.00 | 75.00 | 150.00 |
| | 1873 O | .013 | 15.00 | 40.00 | 90.00 | 175.00 |
| | 1874 H | — | 15.00 | 40.00 | 90.00 | 200.00 |
| | 1875 H | — | 10.00 | 20.00 | 60.00 | 150.00 |
| | 1876/5 H | — | 15.00 | 30.00 | 80.00 | 175.00 |
| | 1876 H | — | 10.00 | 25.00 | 65.00 | 150.00 |
| | 1877 H | .019 | 10.00 | 25.00 | 65.00 | 150.00 |
| | 1878 H | — | 15.00 | 30.00 | 60.00 | 150.00 |
| | 1879/8 H | — | 10.00 | 25.00 | 60.00 | 150.00 |
| | 1879 H | — | 10.00 | 25.00 | 60.00 | 150.00 |
| | 1879 E | — | 100.00 | 200.00 | 300.00 | 600.00 |
| | 1880 H | — | 20.00 | 40.00 | 100.00 | 200.00 |
| | 1880 H/M | — | 20.00 | 40.00 | 100.00 | 200.00 |
| | 1881 H | .050 | 20.00 | 40.00 | 80.00 | 175.00 |
| | 1881 E Inc. Ab. | | — | — | Rare | — |
| | 1882 H | .020 | 10.00 | 20.00 | 60.00 | 150.00 |
| | 1883 H | .017 | 10.00 | 25.00 | 65.00 | 150.00 |
| | 1884 H | — | 10.00 | 25.00 | 65.00 | 150.00 |
| | 1885/4 H | — | 10.00 | 20.00 | 60.00 | 150.00 |
| | 1885 H | .043 | 10.00 | 20.00 | 60.00 | 150.00 |
| | 1886 C | .078 | 10.00 | 25.00 | 65.00 | 150.00 |
| | 1886 R Inc. Ab. | | 7.50 | 20.00 | 50.00 | 150.00 |
| | 1886 R 6/inverted 6 Inc. Ab. | | 7.50 | 20.00 | 50.00 | 150.00 |
| | 1887 Pi/ZsR | .092 | 7.50 | 20.00 | 50.00 | 150.00 |
| | 1887 Pi/ZsB Inc. Ab. | 100.00 | 150.00 | 300.00 | 500.00 |
| | 1887 R | — | 7.50 | 20.00 | 50.00 | 150.00 |
| | 1888 R | .106 | 7.50 | 20.00 | 50.00 | 150.00 |
| | 1888 Pi/ZsR Inc. Ab. | | 10.00 | 20.00 | 50.00 | 150.00 |
| | 1888 R/B I.A. | | 10.00 | 20.00 | 50.00 | 150.00 |
| | 1889 R | .115 | 7.50 | 15.00 | 40.00 | 150.00 |
| | 1889 Pi/ZsR Inc. Ab. | | 10.00 | 20.00 | 50.00 | 150.00 |
| | 1889 R/B I.A. | | 10.00 | 20.00 | 50.00 | 150.00 |
| | 1890 R | .064 | 10.00 | 20.00 | 50.00 | 150.00 |
| | 1890 Pi/ZsR/B Inc. Ab. | | 7.50 | 15.00 | 40.00 | 150.00 |
| | 1890 R/B I.A. | | 10.00 | 20.00 | 50.00 | 150.00 |

NOTE: Varieties exist.

### Mint mark: Zs

| KM# | Date | Mintage | Fine | VF | XF | Unc |
|---|---|---|---|---|---|---|
| 406.9 | 1870 H | .152 | 6.00 | 15.00 | 50.00 | 125.00 |
| | 1871 H | .250 | 6.00 | 15.00 | 60.00 | 125.00 |
| | 1872 H | .260 | 6.00 | 15.00 | 50.00 | 125.00 |
| | 1872 H Zs/Cu— | — | — | — | — | — |
| | 1873 H | .132 | 6.00 | 15.00 | 50.00 | 125.00 |
| | 1874 H | — | 10.00 | 20.00 | 60.00 | 125.00 |
| | 1874 A | — | 10.00 | 20.00 | 60.00 | 125.00 |
| | 1875 A | — | 7.00 | 20.00 | 60.00 | 125.00 |
| | 1876 A | — | 6.00 | 15.00 | 50.00 | 125.00 |
| | 1876 S | — | 6.00 | 15.00 | 50.00 | 125.00 |
| | 1877 S | .350 | 6.00 | 15.00 | 50.00 | 125.00 |
| | 1878 S | .252 | 6.00 | 15.00 | 50.00 | 125.00 |
| | 1878/1 S | — | 7.00 | 20.00 | 60.00 | 125.00 |
| | 1878/7 S | — | 7.00 | 20.00 | 60.00 | 125.00 |
| | 1879 S | — | 6.00 | 15.00 | 50.00 | 125.00 |
| | 1880 S | — | 6.00 | 15.00 | 50.00 | 125.00 |
| | 1881/0 S | .570 | 6.00 | 15.00 | 50.00 | 125.00 |
| | 1881 S Inc. Ab. | | 6.00 | 15.00 | 50.00 | 125.00 |
| | 1882/1 S | .300 | 10.00 | 17.50 | 55.00 | 125.00 |
| | 1882 S Inc. Ab. | | 6.00 | 15.00 | 50.00 | 125.00 |
| | 1883/2 S | .193 | 10.00 | 17.50 | 55.00 | 125.00 |
| | 1883 S Inc. Ab. | | 6.00 | 15.00 | 50.00 | 125.00 |
| | 1884/3 S | — | 10.00 | 17.50 | 55.00 | 125.00 |
| | 1884 S | — | 6.00 | 15.00 | 50.00 | 125.00 |
| | 1885 S | .309 | 6.00 | 15.00 | 50.00 | 125.00 |
| | 1886/2 S | — | 10.00 | 17.50 | 55.00 | 125.00 |
| | 1886/5 S | .613 | 6.00 | 15.00 | 50.00 | 125.00 |
| | 1886 S Inc. Ab. | | 6.00 | 15.00 | 50.00 | 125.00 |
| | 1886 Z Inc. Ab. | | 6.00 | 15.00 | 55.00 | 125.00 |
| | 1887 Z | .389 | 6.00 | 15.00 | 50.00 | 125.00 |
| | 1888 Z | .408 | 6.00 | 15.00 | 50.00 | 125.00 |
| | 1889 Z | .400 | 6.00 | 15.00 | 50.00 | 125.00 |
| | 1890 Z | .269 | 6.00 | 15.00 | 50.00 | 125.00 |

NOTE: Varieties exist.

## 50 CENTAVOS

### 13.5360 g, .903 SILVER, .3930 oz ASW
### Mint mark: A, As
### Rev: Balance scale.

| KM# | Date | Mintage | Fine | VF | XF | Unc |
|---|---|---|---|---|---|---|
| 407 | 1875 L | — | 12.00 | 25.00 | 70.00 | 400.00 |
| | 1876/5 L | — | 25.00 | 50.00 | 120.00 | 450.00 |
| | 1876 L | — | 12.00 | 25.00 | 70.00 | 400.00 |
| | 1876.L | — | — | — | — | — |
| | 1877 L | .026 | 15.00 | 30.00 | 85.00 | 450.00 |
| | 1878 L | — | 12.00 | 25.00 | 70.00 | 400.00 |
| | 1879 L | — | 25.00 | 50.00 | 120.00 | 450.00 |
| | 1880 L | .057 | 12.00 | 25.00 | 70.00 | 400.00 |
| | 1881 L | .018 | 15.00 | 30.00 | 80.00 | 450.00 |
| | 1884 L | 6,286 | 65.00 | 120.00 | 250.00 | 650.00 |
| | 1885 As/HoL | | | | | |
| | | .021 | 15.00 | 35.00 | 90.00 | 450.00 |
| | 1888 L | — | 4000. | 5000. | 6000. | — |

### Mint mark: Ca, CHa

| KM# | Date | Mintage | Fine | VF | XF | Unc |
|---|---|---|---|---|---|---|
| 407.1 | 1883/9 M | — | 30.00 | 60.00 | 125.00 | 500.00 |
| | 1883 M | .012 | 30.00 | 60.00 | 125.00 | 500.00 |
| | 1884 M | — | 25.00 | 50.00 | 125.00 | 500.00 |
| | 1885 M | .013 | 15.00 | 35.00 | 90.00 | 400.00 |
| | 1886 M | .018 | 20.00 | 40.00 | 100.00 | 450.00 |
| | 1887 M | .026 | 25.00 | 65.00 | 150.00 | 500.00 |

### Mint mark: Cn

| KM# | Date | Mintage | Fine | VF | XF | Unc |
|---|---|---|---|---|---|---|
| 407.2 | 1871 P | — | 400.00 | 550.00 | 750.00 | 1500. |
| | 1873 P | — | 400.00 | 550.00 | 750.00 | 1500. |
| | 1874 P | — | 200.00 | 300.00 | 500.00 | 1000. |
| | 1875/4 P | — | 20.00 | 40.00 | 75.00 | 450.00 |
| | 1875 P | — | 12.00 | 25.00 | 50.00 | 450.00 |
| | 1876 P | — | 15.00 | 30.00 | 60.00 | 450.00 |
| | 1877/6 G | — | 15.00 | 30.00 | 60.00 | 450.00 |
| | 1877 G | — | 12.00 | 25.00 | 50.00 | 450.00 |

| KM# | Date | Mintage | Fine | VF | XF | Unc |
|---|---|---|---|---|---|---|
| 407.2 | 1878 G | .018 | 20.00 | 40.00 | 75.00 | 450.00 |
| | 1878 D Cn/Mo | | | | | |
| | Inc. Ab. | | 30.00 | 60.00 | 100.00 | 450.00 |
| | 1878 D Inc. Ab. | | 15.00 | 35.00 | 75.00 | 450.00 |
| | 1879 D | — | 12.00 | 25.00 | 50.00 | 450.00 |
| | 1879 D/G | — | 12.00 | 25.00 | 50.00 | 450.00 |
| | 1880/8 D | — | 15.00 | 30.00 | 60.00 | 450.00 |
| | 1880 D | — | 15.00 | 30.00 | 60.00 | 450.00 |
| | 1881/0 D | .188 | 15.00 | 30.00 | 60.00 | 450.00 |
| | 1881 D Inc. Ab. | | 15.00 | 30.00 | 60.00 | 450.00 |
| | 1881 G Inc. Ab. | 125.00 | 175.00 | 275.00 | 550.00 |
| | 1882 D | — | 175.00 | 225.00 | 325.00 | 1000. |
| | 1882 G | — | 100.00 | 250.00 | 300.00 | 1000. |
| | 1883 D | .019 | 25.00 | 50.00 | 100.00 | 500.00 |
| | 1885/3 CN/Pi M/H | | | | | |
| | | 9,254 | 30.00 | 60.00 | 100.00 | 500.00 |
| | 1885 CN | — | 30.00 | 60.00 | 100.00 | 500.00 |
| | 1886 M/G | 7,030 | 50.00 | 100.00 | 150.00 | 800.00 |
| | 1886 M Inc. Ab. | | 40.00 | 80.00 | 150.00 | 800.00 |
| | 1887 M | .076 | 20.00 | 40.00 | 100.00 | 450.00 |
| | 1888 M | — | 4000. | 5000. | 6000. | — |
| | 1892 M | 8,200 | 40.00 | 80.00 | 150.00 | 800.00 |

### Mint mark: Do

| KM# | Date | Mintage | Fine | VF | XF | Unc |
|---|---|---|---|---|---|---|
| 407.3 | 1871 P 591 pcs. | | — | — | Rare | — |
| | 1873 P | 4,010 | 150.00 | 250.00 | 500.00 | 1250. |
| | 1873 M/P | I.A. | 150.00 | 250.00 | 500.00 | 1250. |
| | 1874 M | — | 20.00 | 40.00 | 175.00 | 750.00 |
| | 1875 M | — | 20.00 | 40.00 | 80.00 | 350.00 |
| | 1875 H | — | 150.00 | 250.00 | 450.00 | 1000. |
| | 1876/5 M | — | 35.00 | 70.00 | 150.00 | 500.00 |
| | 1876 M | — | 35.00 | 70.00 | 150.00 | 500.00 |
| | 1877 P | 2,000 | 30.00 | 45.00 | 150.00 | 1250. |
| | 1878 B | — | — | — | Rare | — |
| | 1879 B | — | — | — | Rare | — |
| | 1880 P | — | 30.00 | 60.00 | 125.00 | 500.00 |
| | 1881 P | .010 | 40.00 | 80.00 | 150.00 | 550.00 |
| | 1882 C | 8,957 | 30.00 | 75.00 | 200.00 | 800.00 |
| | 1884/2 C | — | 20.00 | 50.00 | 125.00 | 600.00 |
| | 1884 C | — | — | — | — | — |
| | 1885 B | — | 15.00 | 40.00 | 100.00 | 500.00 |
| | 1885 B/P | — | 15.00 | 40.00 | 100.00 | 500.00 |
| | 1886 C | .016 | 15.00 | 40.00 | 100.00 | 500.00 |
| | 1887 Do/MoC | | | | | |
| | | .028 | 15.00 | 40.00 | 100.00 | 500.00 |
| | 1887 C | — | 15.00 | 40.00 | 100.00 | 500.00 |

### Mint mark: Go

| KM# | Date | Mintage | Fine | VF | XF | Unc |
|---|---|---|---|---|---|---|
| 407.4 | 1869 S | — | 15.00 | 35.00 | 75.00 | 550.00 |
| | 1870 S | .166 | 12.00 | 25.00 | 50.00 | 450.00 |
| | 1871 S | .148 | 12.00 | 25.00 | 50.00 | 450.00 |
| | 1872/1 S | .144 | 15.00 | 30.00 | 60.00 | 500.00 |
| | 1872 S Inc. Ab. | | 12.00 | 25.00 | 50.00 | 450.00 |
| | 1873 S | .050 | 12.00 | 25.00 | 50.00 | 450.00 |
| | 1874 S | — | 12.00 | 25.00 | 50.00 | 450.00 |
| | 1875 S | — | 15.00 | 35.00 | 75.00 | 450.00 |
| | 1876/5 S | — | 12.00 | 25.00 | 50.00 | 450.00 |
| | 1877 S | .076 | 12.00 | 25.00 | 60.00 | 450.00 |
| | 1878 S | .037 | 15.00 | 30.00 | 75.00 | 550.00 |
| | 1879/8 S | — | 15.00 | 30.00 | 60.00 | 500.00 |
| | 1879 S | — | 12.00 | 25.00 | 50.00 | 450.00 |
| | 1880 S | — | 12.00 | 25.00 | 50.00 | 450.00 |
| | 1881/79 S | .032 | 15.00 | 30.00 | 60.00 | 500.00 |
| | 1881 S Inc. Ab. | | 12.00 | 25.00 | 50.00 | 450.00 |
| | 1882 S | .018 | 12.00 | 25.00 | 50.00 | 450.00 |
| | 1883/2 B/S | — | 15.00 | 30.00 | 60.00 | 500.00 |
| | 1883 B | — | 12.00 | 25.00 | 50.00 | 450.00 |
| | 1883 S | — | — | — | Rare | — |
| | 1884 B/S | — | 15.00 | 30.00 | 60.00 | 500.00 |
| | 1885/4 R/B | — | 15.00 | 30.00 | 60.00 | 500.00 |
| | 1885 R | .053 | 12.00 | 25.00 | 50.00 | 450.00 |
| | 1886/5 R/B | | | | | |
| | | .059 | 15.00 | 30.00 | 60.00 | 500.00 |
| | 1886/5 R/S | | | | | |
| | Inc. Ab. | | 20.00 | 40.00 | 75.00 | 500.00 |
| | 1886 R Inc. Ab. | | 20.00 | 40.00 | 50.00 | 450.00 |
| | 1887 R | .018 | 20.00 | 40.00 | 75.00 | 550.00 |
| | 1888 R 1 known | — | — | — | Rare | — |

NOTE: Varieties exist.

### 13.5360 g, .903 SILVER, .3930 oz ASW
### Mint mark: Ho

| KM# | Date | Mintage | Fine | VF | XF | Unc |
|---|---|---|---|---|---|---|
| 407.5 | 1874 R | — | 20.00 | 40.00 | 100.00 | 600.00 |
| | 1875/4 R | — | 20.00 | 50.00 | 125.00 | 600.00 |
| | 1875 R | — | 20.00 | 50.00 | 125.00 | 600.00 |

| KM# | Date | Mintage | Fine | VF | XF | Unc |
|---|---|---|---|---|---|---|
| 407.5 | 1876/5 F/R | — | 15.00 | 35.00 | 100.00 | 550.00 |
| | 1876 F | — | 15.00 | 35.00 | 100.00 | 550.00 |
| | 1877 F | — | 50.00 | 75.00 | 150.00 | 650.00 |
| | 1880/70 A | — | 15.00 | 35.00 | 100.00 | 550.00 |
| | 1880 A | — | 15.00 | 35.00 | 100.00 | 550.00 |
| | 1881 A | .013 | 15.00 | 35.00 | 100.00 | 550.00 |
| | 1882 A | — | 75.00 | 150.00 | 250.00 | 750.00 |
| | 1888 G | — | 2000. | 3000. | 4000. | — |
| | 1894 G | .059 | 15.00 | 30.00 | 100.00 | 450.00 |
| | 1895 G | 8,000 | 250.00 | 350.00 | 500.00 | 1250. |

NOTE: Varieties exist.

### Mint mark: Mo

| KM# | Date | Mintage | Fine | VF | XF | Unc |
|---|---|---|---|---|---|---|
| 407.6 | 1869 C | .046 | 15.00 | 35.00 | 95.00 | 600.00 |
| | 1870 C | .052 | 15.00 | 30.00 | 90.00 | 550.00 |
| | 1871 C | .014 | 40.00 | 75.00 | 150.00 | 650.00 |
| | 1871 M/C | I.A. | 35.00 | 75.00 | 150.00 | 600.00 |
| | 1872/1 M | .060 | 35.00 | 75.00 | 150.00 | 550.00 |
| | 1872 M Inc. Ab. | | 35.00 | 75.00 | 150.00 | 550.00 |
| | 1873 M | 6,000 | 35.00 | 75.00 | 150.00 | 600.00 |
| | 1874/3 M | — | 200.00 | 400.00 | 600.00 | 1250. |
| | 1874/2 B | — | 15.00 | 30.00 | 75.00 | 500.00 |
| | 1874/2 B/M | — | 15.00 | 30.00 | 75.00 | 500.00 |
| | 1874/3 B/M | — | 15.00 | 30.00 | 75.00 | 500.00 |
| | 1874 B | — | 15.00 | 30.00 | 75.00 | 500.00 |
| | 1875 B | — | 15.00 | 30.00 | 75.00 | 550.00 |
| | 1876/5 B | — | 15.00 | 30.00 | 75.00 | 500.00 |
| | 1876 B | — | 12.00 | 25.00 | 75.00 | 500.00 |
| | 1877/2 M | — | 20.00 | 40.00 | 100.00 | 550.00 |
| | 1877 M | — | 15.00 | 30.00 | 90.00 | 500.00 |
| | 1878/7 M | 8,000 | 25.00 | 50.00 | 125.00 | 600.00 |
| | 1878 M Inc. Ab. | | 15.00 | 35.00 | 100.00 | 550.00 |
| | 1879 M | — | 25.00 | 50.00 | 125.00 | 550.00 |
| | 1880 M | — | 100.00 | 150.00 | 250.00 | 750.00 |
| | 1881 M | .016 | 25.00 | 50.00 | 125.00 | 600.00 |
| | 1881/0 M | — | 30.00 | 50.00 | 125.00 | 600.00 |
| | 1882/1 M | 2,000 | 30.00 | 60.00 | 150.00 | 750.00 |
| | 1883/2 M | 4,000 | 150.00 | 225.00 | 350.00 | 1000. |
| | 1884 M | — | 150.00 | 225.00 | 350.00 | 1000. |
| | 1885 M | .012 | 30.00 | 60.00 | 150.00 | 600.00 |
| | 1886/5 M | .066 | 15.00 | 35.00 | 90.00 | 475.00 |
| | 1886 M Inc. Ab. | | 12.00 | 25.00 | 75.00 | 450.00 |
| | 1887/6 M | .088 | 15.00 | 35.00 | 90.00 | 475.00 |
| | 1887 M Inc. Ab. | | 15.00 | 35.00 | 75.00 | 475.00 |
| | 1888 M | — | 3000. | 4000. | 5000. | — |

### Mint mark: Pi

| KM# | Date | Mintage | Fine | VF | XF | Unc |
|---|---|---|---|---|---|---|
| 407.7 | 1870/780 G | .050 | 25.00 | 45.00 | 110.00 | 500.00 |
| | 1870 G Inc. Ab. | | 20.00 | 40.00 | 100.00 | 450.00 |
| | 1870 O Inc. Ab. | | 20.00 | 40.00 | 100.00 | 450.00 |
| | 1871 O | — | 15.00 | 30.00 | 80.00 | 400.00 |
| | 1871 O/G | .064 | 15.00 | 30.00 | 80.00 | 400.00 |
| | 1872 O | .052 | 15.00 | 30.00 | 80.00 | 400.00 |
| | 1872 O/G | I.A. | 15.00 | 30.00 | 80.00 | 400.00 |
| | 1873 O | .032 | 20.00 | 40.00 | 100.00 | 450.00 |
| | 1873 H Inc. Ab. | | 25.00 | 50.00 | 125.00 | 550.00 |
| | 1874 H/O | — | 15.00 | 30.00 | 80.00 | 400.00 |
| | 1875/3 H | — | 15.00 | 30.00 | 80.00 | 400.00 |
| | 1875 H | — | 15.00 | 30.00 | 80.00 | 400.00 |
| | 1876 H | — | 30.00 | 60.00 | 150.00 | 700.00 |
| | 1877 H | .034 | 20.00 | 40.00 | 100.00 | 450.00 |
| | 1878 H | 9,700 | 20.00 | 40.00 | 100.00 | 450.00 |
| | 1879/7 H | — | 15.00 | 35.00 | 90.00 | 450.00 |
| | 1879 H | — | 15.00 | 35.00 | 90.00 | 400.00 |
| | 1880 H | — | 20.00 | 40.00 | 100.00 | 450.00 |
| | 1881 H | .028 | 20.00 | 40.00 | 100.00 | 450.00 |
| | 1882 H | .022 | 15.00 | 30.00 | 80.00 | 400.00 |
| | 1883 H 8/8 | .029 | 50.00 | 100.00 | 200.00 | 750.00 |
| | 1883 H Inc. Ab. | | 15.00 | 30.00 | 80.00 | 400.00 |
| | 1884 H | — | 50.00 | 100.00 | 175.00 | 600.00 |
| | 1885/3 H | — | 20.00 | 40.00 | 100.00 | 450.00 |
| | 1885/0 H | .045 | 20.00 | 40.00 | 100.00 | 450.00 |
| | 1885/4 H | I.A. | 20.00 | 40.00 | 100.00 | 450.00 |
| | 1885 H Inc. Ab. | | 25.00 | 50.00 | 125.00 | 450.00 |
| | 1885 C Inc. Ab. | | 15.00 | 30.00 | 80.00 | 400.00 |
| | 1886/1 R | .092 | 50.00 | 100.00 | 175.00 | 600.00 |
| | 1886/1 C | — | 25.00 | 40.00 | 100.00 | 450.00 |
| | 1886 C Inc. Ab. | | 15.00 | 30.00 | 80.00 | 400.00 |
| | 1886 R Inc. Ab. | | 15.00 | 30.00 | 80.00 | 400.00 |
| | 1887 R | .032 | 15.00 | 30.00 | 90.00 | 450.00 |
| | 1888 R | — | Contemporary counterfeits | | | |

### Mint mark: Zs

| KM# | Date | Mintage | Fine | VF | XF | Unc |
|---|---|---|---|---|---|---|
| 407.8 | 1870 H | .086 | 12.00 | 25.00 | 60.00 | 450.00 |
| | 1871 H | .146 | 12.00 | 25.00 | 50.00 | 400.00 |
| | 1872 H | .132 | 12.00 | 25.00 | 50.00 | 400.00 |
| | 1873 H | .056 | 12.00 | 25.00 | 50.00 | 400.00 |
| | 1874 H | — | 12.00 | 25.00 | 50.00 | 400.00 |
| | 1874 A | — | — | — | Rare | — |
| | 1875 A | — | 12.00 | 25.00 | 50.00 | 400.00 |
| | 1876/5 A | — | 15.00 | 30.00 | 60.00 | 450.00 |
| | 1876 A | — | 12.00 | 25.00 | 50.00 | 400.00 |
| | 1876 S | — | 100.00 | 200.00 | 350.00 | 750.00 |
| | 1877 S | .100 | 12.00 | 25.00 | 50.00 | 400.00 |
| | 1878/7 S | .254 | 15.00 | 30.00 | 60.00 | 450.00 |
| | 1878 S Inc. Ab. | | 15.00 | 30.00 | 60.00 | 400.00 |
| | 1879 S | — | 12.00 | 25.00 | 50.00 | 400.00 |
| | 1880 S | — | 12.00 | 25.00 | 50.00 | 400.00 |
| | 1881 S | .201 | 12.00 | 25.00 | 50.00 | 400.00 |
| | 1882/1 S | 2,000 | 50.00 | 100.00 | 250.00 | 650.00 |
| | 1882 S Inc. Ab. | | 50.00 | 100.00 | 250.00 | 650.00 |
| | 1883 Zs/Za S | .031 | 30.00 | 60.00 | 100.00 | 450.00 |
| | 1883 S Inc. Ab. | | 25.00 | 50.00 | 100.00 | 450.00 |
| | 1884/3 S | — | 15.00 | 30.00 | 60.00 | 450.00 |
| | 1884 S | — | 12.00 | 25.00 | 50.00 | 400.00 |
| | 1885/4 S | 2,000 | 25.00 | 50.00 | 125.00 | 450.00 |
| | 1885 S Inc. Ab. | | 25.00 | 50.00 | 125.00 | 450.00 |
| | 1886 Z | 2,000 | 150.00 | 275.00 | 400.00 | 1000. |
| | 1887 Z | .063 | 30.00 | 60.00 | 125.00 | 450.00 |

NOTE: Varieties exist.

## PESO

**27.0730 g, .903 SILVER, .7860 oz ASW**
**Mint mark: CH**
**Rev: Balance scale.**

| KM# | Date | Mintage | Fine | VF | XF | Unc |
|---|---|---|---|---|---|---|
| 408 | 1872 P/M | .747 | 750.00 | 1500. | 3500. | — |
| | 1872 P Inc. Ab. | | 350.00 | 700.00 | 1500. | — |
| | 1872/1 M | I.A. | 25.00 | 40.00 | 75.00 | 400.00 |
| | 1872 M Inc. Ab. | | 17.50 | 25.00 | 50.00 | 250.00 |
| | 1873 M | .320 | 20.00 | 30.00 | 60.00 | 265.00 |
| | 1873 M/P | I.A. | 25.00 | 40.00 | 75.00 | 350.00 |

### Mint mark: Cn

| KM# | Date | Mintage | Fine | VF | XF | Unc |
|---|---|---|---|---|---|---|
| 408.1 | 1870 E | — | 40.00 | 80.00 | 150.00 | 500.00 |
| | 1871/11 P | .478 | 25.00 | 45.00 | 90.00 | 350.00 |
| | 1871 P Inc. Ab. | | 20.00 | 40.00 | 75.00 | 300.00 |
| | 1872/1 P | — | 20.00 | 40.00 | 75.00 | 300.00 |
| | 1872 P | .209 | 20.00 | 40.00 | 75.00 | 300.00 |
| | 1873 P narrow date | .527 | 20.00 | 40.00 | 75.00 | 300.00 |
| | 1873 P wide date Inc. Ab. | | 20.00 | 40.00 | 75.00 | 300.00 |

### Mint mark: Do

| KM# | Date | Mintage | Fine | VF | XF | Unc |
|---|---|---|---|---|---|---|
| 408.2 | 1870 P | — | 50.00 | 100.00 | 175.00 | 450.00 |
| | 1871 P | .427 | 25.00 | 50.00 | 75.00 | 300.00 |
| | 1872 P | .296 | 20.00 | 40.00 | 75.00 | 350.00 |
| | 1872 PT | I.A. | 100.00 | 175.00 | 250.00 | 675.00 |
| | 1873 P | .203 | 25.00 | 45.00 | 85.00 | 350.00 |

### Mint mark: Ga

| KM# | Date | Mintage | Fine | VF | XF | Unc |
|---|---|---|---|---|---|---|
| 408.3 | 1870 C | — | 650.00 | 850.00 | — | — |
| | 1871 C | .829 | 25.00 | 65.00 | 135.00 | 600.00 |
| | 1872 C | .485 | 40.00 | 90.00 | 175.00 | 650.00 |
| | 1873/2 C | .277 | 40.00 | 90.00 | 175.00 | 700.00 |
| | 1873 C Inc. Ab. | | 25.00 | 65.00 | 135.00 | 600.00 |

### Mint mark: Go

| KM# | Date | Mintage | Fine | VF | XF | Unc |
|---|---|---|---|---|---|---|
| 408.4 | 1871/0 S | 3.946 | 30.00 | 50.00 | 90.00 | 350.00 |

| KM# | Date | Mintage | Fine | VF | XF | Unc |
|---|---|---|---|---|---|---|
| 408.4 | 1871/3 S | I.A. | 20.00 | 35.00 | 70.00 | 275.00 |
| | 1871 S | Inc. Ab. | 12.00 | 20.00 | 40.00 | 220.00 |
| | 1872 S | 4.067 | 12.00 | 20.00 | 40.00 | 250.00 |
| | 1873/2 S | 1.560 | 15.00 | 25.00 | 50.00 | 250.00 |
| | 1873 S | Inc. Ab. | 12.00 | 20.00 | 45.00 | 250.00 |
| | 1873/Go/Mo/S/M | | | | | |
| | | Inc. Ab. | 12.00 | 20.00 | 45.00 | 250.00 |

**Mint mark: Mo**

| KM# | Date | Mintage | Fine | VF | XF | Unc |
|---|---|---|---|---|---|---|
| 408.5 | 1869 C | — | 35.00 | 65.00 | 135.00 | 450.00 |
| | 1870/69 C | | | | | |
| | | 5.115 | 15.00 | 25.00 | 55.00 | 275.00 |
| | 1870 C | Inc. Ab. | 12.00 | 20.00 | 40.00 | 250.00 |
| | 1870 M/C | I.A. | 18.00 | 30.00 | 60.00 | 275.00 |
| | 1870 M | Inc. Ab. | 18.00 | 30.00 | 60.00 | 275.00 |
| | 1871/0 M | | | | | |
| | | 6.974 | 15.00 | 25.00 | 55.00 | 275.00 |
| | 1871 M | Inc. Ab. | 12.00 | 20.00 | 40.00 | 250.00 |
| | 1872/1 M | — | 15.00 | 25.00 | 50.00 | 275.00 |
| | 1872/1 M/C | | | | | |
| | | 4.801 | 15.00 | 25.00 | 50.00 | 275.00 |
| | 1872 M | Inc. Ab. | 12.00 | 20.00 | 40.00 | 250.00 |
| | 1873 M | 1.765 | 12.00 | 20.00 | 40.00 | 250.00 |

**NOTE:** The 1869 C with large LEY on the scroll is a pattern.

**Mint mark: Oa**

| KM# | Date | Mintage | Fine | VF | XF | Unc |
|---|---|---|---|---|---|---|
| 408.6 | 1869 E | — | 275.00 | 400.00 | 600.00 | 2000. |
| | 1870 OAE small A | | | | | |
| | | Inc. Ab. | 15.00 | 30.00 | 75.00 | 400.00 |
| | 1870 OA E large A | | | | | |
| | | Inc. Ab. | 100.00 | 150.00 | 300.00 | 900.00 |
| | 1871/69 E | .140 | 30.00 | 50.00 | 125.00 | 550.00 |
| | 1871 OaE small A | | | | | |
| | | Inc. Ab. | 15.00 | 30.00 | 60.00 | 300.00 |
| | 1871 OA E large A | | | | | |
| | | Inc. Ab. | 15.00 | 30.00 | 75.00 | 400.00 |
| | 1872 OaE small A | | | | | |
| | | .180 | 15.00 | 30.00 | 75.00 | 400.00 |
| | 1872 OA E large A | | | | | |
| | | Inc. Ab. | 50.00 | 100.00 | 200.00 | 450.00 |
| | 1873 E | .105 | 15.00 | 30.00 | 75.00 | 350.00 |

**Mint mark: Pi**

| KM# | Date | Mintage | Fine | VF | XF | Unc |
|---|---|---|---|---|---|---|
| 408.7 | 1870 S | 1.967 | 200.00 | 350.00 | 500.00 | 1000. |
| | 1870 S/A | I.A. | 200.00 | 350.00 | 500.00 | 1000. |
| | 1870 G | Inc. Ab. | 25.00 | 50.00 | 125.00 | 450.00 |
| | 1870 H | Inc. Ab. | | Contemporary counterfeit | | |
| | 1870 O/G | I.A. | 25.00 | 35.00 | 125.00 | 450.00 |
| | 1870 O | Inc. Ab. | 20.00 | 30.00 | 100.00 | 350.00 |
| | 1871/69 O | | | | | |
| | | 2.103 | 75.00 | 150.00 | 250.00 | 500.00 |
| | 1871 O/G | I.A. | 15.00 | 30.00 | 60.00 | 300.00 |
| | 1871 O | — | 15.00 | 30.00 | 60.00 | 300.00 |
| | 1872 O | 1.873 | 15.00 | 30.00 | 60.00 | 300.00 |
| | 1873 O | .893 | 15.00 | 30.00 | 60.00 | 300.00 |
| | 1873 H | Inc. Ab. | 15.00 | 30.00 | 60.00 | 300.00 |

**NOTE:** Varieties exist.

**Mint mark: Zs**

| KM# | Date | Mintage | Fine | VF | XF | Unc |
|---|---|---|---|---|---|---|
| 408.8 | 1870 H | 4.519 | 12.00 | 20.00 | 40.00 | 220.00 |
| | 1871 H | 4.459 | 12.00 | 20.00 | 40.00 | 220.00 |
| | 1872 H | 4.039 | 12.00 | 20.00 | 40.00 | 220.00 |
| | 1873/1 H | Inc. Ab. | 12.00 | 20.00 | 40.00 | 220.00 |
| | 1873 H | 1.782 | 12.00 | 20.00 | 40.00 | 220.00 |

**NOTE:** Varieties exist.

**Mint mark: Cn**
**Liberty cap**

| KM# | Date | Mintage | Fine | VF | XF | Unc |
|---|---|---|---|---|---|---|
| 409 | 1898 AM | 1.720 | 10.00 | 15.00 | 30.00 | 65.00 |
| | 1898 Cn/MoAM | | | | | |
| | | I.A. | 15.00 | 30.00 | 90.00 | 150.00 |
| | 1899 AM | 1.722 | 25.00 | 50.00 | 90.00 | 175.00 |
| | 1899 JQ | I.A. | 10.00 | 15.00 | 50.00 | 125.00 |
| | 1900 JQ | 1.804 | 10.00 | 15.00 | 30.00 | 85.00 |
| | 1901 JQ | 1.473 | 10.00 | 15.00 | 30.00 | 85.00 |
| | 1902 JQ | 1.194 | 10.00 | 15.00 | 45.00 | 125.00 |
| | 1903 JQ | 1.514 | 10.00 | 15.00 | 35.00 | 90.00 |
| | 1903 FV | I.A. | 25.00 | 50.00 | 100.00 | 225.00 |
| | 1904 MH | 1.554 | 10.00 | 15.00 | 30.00 | 85.00 |
| | 1904 RP | I.A. | 50.00 | 100.00 | 150.00 | 350.00 |
| | 1905 RP | .598 | 25.00 | 50.00 | 100.00 | 250.00 |

**Mint mark: Go**

| KM# | Date | Mintage | Fine | VF | XF | Unc |
|---|---|---|---|---|---|---|
| 409.1 | 1898 RS | 4.256 | 10.00 | 15.00 | 35.00 | 75.00 |
| | 1898 Go/MoRS | | | | | |
| | | Inc. Ab. | 20.00 | 30.00 | 60.00 | 125.00 |
| | 1899 RS | 3.207 | 10.00 | 15.00 | 30.00 | 75.00 |
| | 1900 RS | 1.489 | 25.00 | 50.00 | 100.00 | 250.00 |

**NOTE:** Varieties exist.

**Mint mark: Mo**

| KM# | Date | Mintage | Fine | VF | XF | Unc |
|---|---|---|---|---|---|---|
| 409.2 | 1898 AM original strike - rev. w/139 Beads | | | | | |
| | | 10.156 | 9.00 | 11.50 | 18.50 | 60.00 |
| | 1898 AM restrike (1949) - rev. w/134 Beads | | | | | |
| | | 10.250 | 9.00 | 11.50 | 16.50 | 40.00 |
| | 1899 AM | 7.930 | 10.00 | 12.50 | 20.00 | 70.00 |
| | 1900 AM | 8.226 | 10.00 | 12.50 | 20.00 | 70.00 |
| | 1901 AM | 14.505 | 9.00 | 11.50 | 20.00 | 70.00 |
| | 1902/1 AM | | | | | |
| | | 16.224 | 150.00 | 300.00 | 500.00 | 950.00 |
| | 1902 AM | I.A. | 9.00 | 11.50 | 20.00 | 70.00 |
| | 1903 AM | | | | | |
| | | 22.396 | 9.00 | 11.50 | 20.00 | 70.00 |
| | 1903 MA (error) | | | | | |
| | | Inc. Ab. | 1500. | 2500. | 3500. | 7500. |
| | 1904 AM | 14.935 | 9.00 | 11.50 | 20.00 | 70.00 |
| | 1905 AM | 3.557 | 15.00 | 25.00 | 55.00 | 125.00 |
| | 1908 AM | 7.575 | 10.00 | 12.50 | 20.00 | 60.00 |
| | 1908 GV | I.A. | 10.00 | 12.50 | 18.50 | 40.00 |
| | 1909 GV | 2.924 | 10.00 | 12.50 | 18.50 | 40.00 |

**NOTE:** Varieties exist.

**Mint mark: Zs**

| KM# | Date | Mintage | Fine | VF | XF | Unc |
|---|---|---|---|---|---|---|
| 409.3 | 1898 FZ | 5.714 | 10.00 | 12.50 | 20.00 | 60.00 |
| | 1899 FZ | 5.618 | 10.00 | 12.50 | 20.00 | 65.00 |
| | 1900 FZ | 5.357 | 10.00 | 12.50 | 20.00 | 65.00 |
| | 1901 AZ | 5.706 | 4000. | 6500. | 10,000. | — |
| | 1901 FZ | I.A. | 10.00 | 12.50 | 20.00 | 55.00 |
| | 1902 FZ | 7.134 | 10.00 | 12.50 | 20.00 | 55.00 |
| | 1903/2 FZ | | | | | |
| | | 3.080 | 12.50 | 15.00 | 50.00 | 125.00 |
| | 1903 FZ | I.A. | 10.00 | 12.50 | 20.00 | 65.00 |
| | 1904 FZ | 2.423 | 10.00 | 15.00 | 25.00 | 85.00 |
| | 1904 FM | I.A. | 10.00 | 15.00 | 25.00 | 75.00 |
| | 1905 FM | .995 | 20.00 | 40.00 | 60.00 | 150.00 |

**NOTE:** Varieties exist.

**1.6920 g, .875 GOLD, .0476 oz AGW**
**Mint mark: As**

| KM# | Date | Mintage | Fine | VF | XF | Unc |
|---|---|---|---|---|---|---|
| 410 | 1888 L | — | — | — | Rare | — |
| | 1888 AsL/MoM | | | | | |
| | | — | — | — | Rare | — |

**Mint mark: Ca**

| KM# | Date | Mintage | Fine | VF | XF | Unc |
|---|---|---|---|---|---|---|
| 410.1 | 1888 Ca/MoM | | | | | |
| | | 104 pcs. | — | — | Rare | — |

**Mint mark: Cn**

| KM# | Date | Mintage | Fine | VF | XF | Unc |
|---|---|---|---|---|---|---|
| 410.2 | 1873 P | 1,221 | 75.00 | 100.00 | 150.00 | 250.00 |
| | 1875 P | — | 85.00 | 125.00 | 150.00 | 250.00 |
| | 1878 G | | | | | |
| | | 248 pcs. | 100.00 | 175.00 | 225.00 | 475.00 |
| | 1879 D | — | 100.00 | 150.00 | 175.00 | 285.00 |

| KM# | Date | Mintage | Fine | VF | XF | Unc |
|---|---|---|---|---|---|---|
| 410.2 | 1881/0 D | | | | | |
| | | 338 pcs. | 100.00 | 150.00 | 175.00 | 285.00 |
| | 1882 D | | | | | |
| | | 340 pcs. | 100.00 | 150.00 | 175.00 | 285.00 |
| | 1883 D | — | 100.00 | 150.00 | 175.00 | 285.00 |
| | 1884 M | — | 100.00 | 150.00 | 175.00 | 285.00 |
| | 1886/4 M | | | | | |
| | | 277 pcs. | 100.00 | 150.00 | 225.00 | 450.00 |
| | 1888/7 M | 2,586 | 100.00 | 175.00 | 225.00 | 450.00 |
| | 1888 M | Inc. Ab. | 65.00 | 100.00 | 150.00 | 265.00 |
| | 1889 M | — | — | — | Rare | — |
| | 1891/89 M | | | | | |
| | | 969 pcs. | 75.00 | 100.00 | 150.00 | 265.00 |
| | 1892 M | | | | | |
| | | 780 pcs. | 75.00 | 100.00 | 150.00 | 265.00 |
| | 1893 M | | | | | |
| | | 498 pcs. | 85.00 | 125.00 | 150.00 | 265.00 |
| | 1894 M | | | | | |
| | | 493 pcs. | 80.00 | 125.00 | 150.00 | 265.00 |
| | 1895 M | 1,143 | 65.00 | 100.00 | 150.00 | 250.00 |
| | 1896/5 M | 1,028 | 65.00 | 100.00 | 150.00 | 250.00 |
| | 1897 M | | | | | |
| | | 785 pcs. | 65.00 | 100.00 | 150.00 | 250.00 |
| | 1898 M | 3,521 | 65.00 | 100.00 | 150.00 | 225.00 |
| | 1898 Cn/MoM | | | | | |
| | | Inc. Ab. | 65.00 | 100.00 | 150.00 | 250.00 |
| | 1899 Q | 2,000 | 65.00 | 100.00 | 150.00 | 225.00 |
| | 1901/0 Q | 2,350 | 65.00 | 100.00 | 150.00 | 225.00 |
| | 1902 Q | 2,480 | 65.00 | 100.00 | 150.00 | 225.00 |
| | 1902 Cn/MoQ/C | | | | | |
| | | Inc. Ab. | 65.00 | 100.00 | 150.00 | 225.00 |
| | 1904 H | 3,614 | 65.00 | 100.00 | 150.00 | 225.00 |
| | 1904 Cn/Mo/ H | | | | | |
| | | Inc. Ab. | 65.00 | 100.00 | 150.00 | 250.00 |
| | 1905 P | 1,000 | — | Reported, not confirmed | | |

**Mint mark: Go**

| KM# | Date | Mintage | Fine | VF | XF | Unc |
|---|---|---|---|---|---|---|
| 410.3 | 1870 S | — | 100.00 | 125.00 | 150.00 | 265.00 |
| | 1871 S | | | | | |
| | | 500 pcs. | 100.00 | 175.00 | 225.00 | 475.00 |
| | 1888 R | | | | | |
| | | 210 pcs. | 125.00 | 200.00 | 250.00 | 550.00 |
| | 1890 R | 1,916 | 75.00 | 100.00 | 150.00 | 265.00 |
| | 1892 R | | | | | |
| | | 533 pcs. | 100.00 | 150.00 | 175.00 | 350.00 |
| | 1894 R | | | | | |
| | | 180 pcs. | 150.00 | 200.00 | 250.00 | 550.00 |
| | 1895 R | | | | | |
| | | 676 pcs. | 100.00 | 150.00 | 175.00 | 325.00 |
| | 1896/5 R | 4,671 | 65.00 | 100.00 | 150.00 | 250.00 |
| | 1897/6 R | 4,280 | 65.00 | 100.00 | 150.00 | 250.00 |
| | 1897 R | Inc. Ab. | 65.00 | 100.00 | 150.00 | 250.00 |
| | 1898 R regular obv. | | | | | |
| | | 5,193 | 65.00 | 100.00 | 150.00 | 250.00 |
| | 1898 R mule, 5 Centavos obv., normal rev. | | | | | |
| | | Inc. Ab. | 75.00 | 100.00 | 150.00 | 250.00 |
| | 1899 R | 2,748 | 65.00 | 100.00 | 150.00 | 250.00 |
| | 1900/800 R | | | | | |
| | | 864 pcs. | 75.00 | 125.00 | 150.00 | 285.00 |

**Mint mark: Ho**

| KM# | Date | Mintage | Fine | VF | XF | Unc |
|---|---|---|---|---|---|---|
| 410.4 | 1875 R | 310 pcs. | — | — | Rare | — |
| | 1876 F | — | — | — | Rare | — |
| | 1888 G/MoM | — | — | — | Rare | — |

**Mint mark: Mo**

| KM# | Date | Mintage | Fine | VF | XF | Unc |
|---|---|---|---|---|---|---|
| 410.5 | 1870 C | 2,540 | 40.00 | 60.00 | 90.00 | 185.00 |
| | 1871 M/C | | | | | |
| | | 1,000 | 50.00 | 100.00 | 150.00 | 250.00 |
| | 1872 M/C | | | | | |
| | | 3,000 | 40.00 | 60.00 | 90.00 | 185.00 |
| | 1873/1 M | | | | | |
| | | 2,900 | 40.00 | 60.00 | 90.00 | 185.00 |
| | 1873 M | Inc. Ab. | 40.00 | 60.00 | 90.00 | 185.00 |
| | 1874 M | — | 40.00 | 60.00 | 90.00 | 185.00 |
| | 1875 B/M | — | 40.00 | 60.00 | 90.00 | 185.00 |
| | 1876/5 B/M | — | 40.00 | 60.00 | 90.00 | 185.00 |
| | 1877 M | — | 40.00 | 60.00 | 90.00 | 185.00 |
| | 1878 M | 2,000 | 40.00 | 60.00 | 90.00 | 185.00 |
| | 1879 M | — | 40.00 | 60.00 | 90.00 | 185.00 |
| | 1880/70 M | — | 40.00 | 60.00 | 90.00 | 185.00 |
| | 1881/71 M | | | | | |
| | | 1,000 | 40.00 | 60.00 | 90.00 | 185.00 |
| | 1882/72 M | — | 40.00 | 60.00 | 90.00 | 185.00 |
| | | — | 40.00 | 60.00 | 90.00 | 185.00 |

| KM# | Date | Mintage | Fine | VF | XF | Unc |
|---|---|---|---|---|---|---|
| 410.5 | 1883/72 M | | | | | |
| | | 1,000 | 40.00 | 60.00 | 90.00 | 185.00 |
| | 1884 M | — | 40.00 | 60.00 | 90.00 | 185.00 |
| | 1885/71 M | — | 40.00 | 60.00 | 90.00 | 185.00 |
| | 1885 M | — | 40.00 | 60.00 | 90.00 | 185.00 |
| | 1886 M | 1,700 | 40.00 | 60.00 | 90.00 | 185.00 |
| | 1887 M | 2,200 | 40.00 | 60.00 | 90.00 | 185.00 |
| | 1888 M | 1,000 | 40.00 | 60.00 | 90.00 | 185.00 |
| | 1889 M | | | | | |
| | | 500 pcs. | 100.00 | 150.00 | 200.00 | 285.00 |
| | 1890 M | | | | | |
| | | 570 pcs. | 100.00 | 150.00 | 200.00 | 285.00 |
| | 1891 M | | | | | |
| | | 746 pcs. | 100.00 | 150.00 | 200.00 | 285.00 |
| | 1892/0 M | | | | | |
| | | 2,895 | 40.00 | 60.00 | 90.00 | 185.00 |
| | 1893 M | 5,917 | 40.00 | 60.00 | 90.00 | 185.00 |
| | 1894/3M | — | 40.00 | 60.00 | 90.00 | 185.00 |
| | 1894 M | 6,244 | 40.00 | 60.00 | 90.00 | 185.00 |
| | 1895 M | 8,994 | 40.00 | 60.00 | 90.00 | 185.00 |
| | 1895 B | Inc. Ab. | 40.00 | 60.00 | 90.00 | 185.00 |
| | 1896 B | 7,166 | 40.00 | 60.00 | 90.00 | 185.00 |
| | 1896 M | Inc. Ab. | 40.00 | 60.00 | 90.00 | 185.00 |
| | 1897 M | 5,131 | 40.00 | 60.00 | 90.00 | 185.00 |
| | 1898/7 M | 5,368 | 40.00 | 60.00 | 90.00 | 185.00 |
| | 1899 M | 9,515 | 40.00 | 60.00 | 90.00 | 185.00 |
| | 1900/800 M | | | | | |
| | | 9,301 | 40.00 | 60.00 | 90.00 | 185.00 |
| | 1900/880 M | | | | | |
| | | Inc. Ab. | 40.00 | 60.00 | 90.00 | 185.00 |
| | 1900/890 M | | | | | |
| | | Inc. Ab. | 40.00 | 60.00 | 90.00 | 185.00 |
| | 1900 M | Inc. Ab. | 40.00 | 60.00 | 90.00 | 185.00 |
| | 1901/801 M large date | | | | | |
| | | 8,293 | 40.00 | 60.00 | 90.00 | 185.00 |
| | 1901 M small date | | | | | |
| | | Inc. Ab. | 40.00 | 60.00 | 90.00 | 185.00 |
| | 1902 M large date | | | | | |
| | | .011 | 40.00 | 60.00 | 90.00 | 185.00 |
| | 1902 M small date | | | | | |
| | | Inc. Ab. | 40.00 | 60.00 | 90.00 | 185.00 |
| | 1903 M large date | | | | | |
| | | .010 | 40.00 | 60.00 | 90.00 | 185.00 |
| | 1903 M small date | | | | | |
| | | Inc. Ab. | 50.00 | 80.00 | 120.00 | 200.00 |
| | 1904 M | 9,845 | 40.00 | 60.00 | 90.00 | 185.00 |
| | 1905 M | 3,429 | 40.00 | 60.00 | 90.00 | 185.00 |

**Mint mark: Zs**

| KM# | Date | Mintage | Fine | VF | XF | Unc |
|---|---|---|---|---|---|---|
| 410.6 | 1872 H | 2,024 | 125.00 | 150.00 | 175.00 | 275.00 |
| | 1875/3 A | — | 125.00 | 150.00 | 200.00 | 325.00 |
| | 1878 S | — | 125.00 | 150.00 | 175.00 | 275.00 |
| | 1888 Z | 280 pcs. | 175.00 | 225.00 | 325.00 | 700.00 |
| | 1889 Z | 492 pcs. | 150.00 | 175.00 | 225.00 | 450.00 |
| | 1890 Z | 738 pcs. | 150.00 | 175.00 | 225.00 | 450.00 |

# 2-1/2 PESOS

**4.2300 g, .875 GOLD, .1190 oz AGW**
**Mint mark: As**

| KM# | Date | Mintage | Fine | VF | XF | Unc |
|---|---|---|---|---|---|---|
| 411 | 1888 As/MoL | — | — | — | Rare | — |

**Mint mark: Cn**

| KM# | Date | Mintage | Fine | VF | XF | Unc |
|---|---|---|---|---|---|---|
| 411.1 | 1893 M | 141 pcs. | 1500. | 2000. | 2500. | 3500. |

**Mint mark: Do**

| KM# | Date | Mintage | Fine | VF | XF | Unc |
|---|---|---|---|---|---|---|
| 411.2 | 1888 C | — | — | — | Rare | — |

**Mint mark: Go**

| KM# | Date | Mintage | Fine | VF | XF | Unc |
|---|---|---|---|---|---|---|
| 411.3 | 1871 S | 600 pcs. | 1250. | 2000. | 2500. | 3250. |
| | 1888 Go/MoR | | | | | |
| | | 110 pcs. | 1750. | 2250. | 2750. | 3500. |

**Mint mark: Ho**

| KM# | Date | Mintage | Fine | VF | XF | Unc |
|---|---|---|---|---|---|---|
| 411.4 | 1874 R | — | — | — | Rare | — |
| | 1888 G | — | — | — | Rare | — |

### Mint mark: Mo

| KM# | Date | Mintage | Fine | VF | XF | Unc |
|---|---|---|---|---|---|---|
| 411.5 | 1870 C | | | | | |
| | | 820 pcs. | 150.00 | 250.00 | 350.00 | 750.00 |
| | 1872 M/C | | | | | |
| | | 800 pcs. | 150.00 | 250.00 | 350.00 | 750.00 |
| | 1873/2 M | — | 200.00 | 350.00 | 750.00 | 1350. |
| | 1874 M | — | 200.00 | 350.00 | 750.00 | 1350. |
| | 1874 B/M | — | 200.00 | 350.00 | 750.00 | 1350. |
| | 1875 B | — | 200.00 | 350.00 | 750.00 | 1350. |
| | 1876 B | — | 250.00 | 500.00 | 1000. | 1600. |
| | 1877 M | — | 200.00 | 350.00 | 750.00 | 1350. |
| | 1878 M | | | | | |
| | | 400 pcs. | 200.00 | 350.00 | 750.00 | 1350. |
| | 1879 M | — | 200.00 | 350.00 | 750.00 | 1350. |
| | 1880/79 M | — | 200.00 | 350.00 | 750.00 | 1350. |
| | 1881 M | | | | | |
| | | 400 pcs. | 200.00 | 350.00 | 750.00 | 1350. |
| | 1882 M | — | 200.00 | 350.00 | 750.00 | 1350. |
| | 1883/73 M | | | | | |
| | | 400 pcs. | 200.00 | 350.00 | 750.00 | 1350. |
| | 1884 M | — | 250.00 | 500.00 | 1000. | 1600. |
| | 1885 M | — | 200.00 | 350.00 | 750.00 | 1350. |
| | 1886 M | | | | | |
| | | 400 pcs. | 200.00 | 350.00 | 750.00 | 1350. |
| | 1887 M | | | | | |
| | | 400 pcs. | 200.00 | 350.00 | 750.00 | 1350. |
| | 1888 M | | | | | |
| | | 540 pcs. | 200.00 | 350.00 | 750.00 | 1350. |
| | 1889 M | | | | | |
| | | 240 pcs. | 150.00 | 300.00 | 525.00 | 950.00 |
| | 1890 M | | | | | |
| | | 420 pcs. | 200.00 | 350.00 | 750.00 | 1350. |
| | 1891 M | | | | | |
| | | 188 pcs. | 200.00 | 350.00 | 750.00 | 1350. |
| | 1892 M | | | | | |
| | | 240 pcs. | 200.00 | 350.00 | 750.00 | 1350. |

### Mint mark: Zs

| KM# | Date | Mintage | Fine | VF | XF | Unc |
|---|---|---|---|---|---|---|
| 411.6 | 1872 H | 1,300 | 200.00 | 350.00 | 500.00 | 1200. |
| | 1873 H | — | 175.00 | 325.00 | 450.00 | 850.00 |
| | 1875/3 A | — | 200.00 | 350.00 | 750.00 | 1350. |
| | 1877 S | — | 200.00 | 350.00 | 750.00 | 1350. |
| | 1878 S | 300 pcs. | 200.00 | 350.00 | 750.00 | 1350. |
| | 1888 Zs/MoS | | | | | |
| | | 80 pcs. | 300.00 | 500.00 | 1000. | 1800. |
| | 1889 Zs/MoZ | | | | | |
| | | 184 pcs. | 250.00 | 450.00 | 950.00 | 1600. |
| | 1890 Z | 326 pcs. | 200.00 | 350.00 | 750.00 | 1350. |

## CINCO (5) PESOS

**8.4600 g, .875 GOLD, .2380 oz AGW**
**Mint mark: As**

| KM# | Date | Mintage | Fine | VF | XF | Unc |
|---|---|---|---|---|---|---|
| 412 | 1875 L | — | — | — | — | — |
| | 1878 L | 383 pcs. | 900.00 | 1700. | 3000. | 4500. |

**Mint mark: Ca**

| KM# | Date | Mintage | Fine | VF | XF | Unc |
|---|---|---|---|---|---|---|
| 412.1 | 1888 M | | | | | |
| | | 120 pcs. | — | — | Rare | — |

**8.4600 g, .875 GOLD, .2380 oz AGW**
**Mint mark: Cn**

| KM# | Date | Mintage | Fine | VF | XF | Unc |
|---|---|---|---|---|---|---|
| 412.2 | 1873 P | — | 300.00 | 600.00 | 1000. | 1500. |
| | 1874 P | — | — | — | — | — |
| | 1875 P | — | 300.00 | 500.00 | 700.00 | 1250. |
| | 1876 P | — | 300.00 | 500.00 | 700.00 | 1250. |
| | 1877 G | — | 300.00 | 500.00 | 700.00 | 1250. |
| | 1882 | 174 pcs. | — | — | Rare | — |
| | 1888 M | — | 500.00 | 1000. | 1350. | 2000. |
| | 1890 M | | | | | |
| | | 435 pcs. | 250.00 | 500.00 | 750.00 | 1250. |
| | 1891 M | 1,390 | 250.00 | 400.00 | 500.00 | 1000. |
| | 1894 M | | | | | |
| | | 484 pcs. | 250.00 | 500.00 | 750.00 | 1600. |

| KM# | Date | Mintage | Fine | VF | XF | Unc |
|---|---|---|---|---|---|---|
| 412.2 | 1895 M | | | | | |
| | | 142 pcs. | 500.00 | 750.00 | 1500. | 2500. |
| | 1900 Q | 1,536 | 150.00 | 300.00 | 400.00 | 900.00 |
| | 1903 Q | 1,000 | 150.00 | 300.00 | 400.00 | 750.00 |

**Mintmark: Do**

| KM# | Date | Mintage | Fine | VF | XF | Unc |
|---|---|---|---|---|---|---|
| 412.3 | 1873/2 P | — | 700.00 | 1250. | 1800. | 3000. |
| | 1877 P | — | 700.00 | 1250. | 1800. | 3000. |
| | 1878 E | — | 700.00 | 1250. | 1800. | 3000. |
| | 1879/7 B | — | 700.00 | 1250. | 1800. | 3000. |
| | 1879 B | — | 700.00 | 1250. | 1800. | 3000. |

**Mint mark: Go**

| KM# | Date | Mintage | Fine | VF | XF | Unc |
|---|---|---|---|---|---|---|
| 412.4 | 1871 S | 1,600 | 400.00 | 800.00 | 1250. | 2500. |
| | 1887 R | | | | | |
| | | 140 pcs. | 600.00 | 1200. | 1500. | 2750. |
| | 1888 R | 65 pcs. | — | — | Rare | — |
| | 1893 R | 16 pcs. | — | — | Rare | — |

**Mint mark: Ho**

| KM# | Date | Mintage | Fine | VF | XF | Unc |
|---|---|---|---|---|---|---|
| 412.5 | 1874 R | — | 1750. | 2500. | 3000. | 4500. |
| | 1877 R | | | | | |
| | | 990 pcs. | 750.00 | 1250. | 2000. | 3000. |
| | 1877 A | Inc. Ab. | 650.00 | 1100. | 1750. | 2750. |
| | 1888 G | — | — | — | Rare | — |

**Mint mark: Mo**

| KM# | Date | Mintage | Fine | VF | XF | Unc |
|---|---|---|---|---|---|---|
| 412.6 | 1870 C | | | | | |
| | | 550 pcs. | 200.00 | 400.00 | 550.00 | 900.00 |
| | 1871/69 M | | | | | |
| | | 1,600 | 150.00 | 300.00 | 400.00 | 650.00 |
| | 1871 M | Inc. Ab. | 150.00 | 300.00 | 400.00 | 650.00 |
| | 1872 M | 1,600 | 150.00 | 300.00 | 400.00 | 650.00 |
| | 1873/2 M | — | 200.00 | 400.00 | 550.00 | 850.00 |
| | 1874 M | — | 200.00 | 400.00 | 550.00 | 850.00 |
| | 1875/3 B/M | — | 200.00 | 400.00 | 550.00 | 950.00 |
| | 1875 B | — | 200.00 | 400.00 | 550.00 | 950.00 |
| | 1876/5 B/M | — | 200.00 | 400.00 | 550.00 | 1000. |
| | 1877 M | — | 250.00 | 450.00 | 750.00 | 1250. |
| | 1878/7 M | | | | | |
| | | 400 pcs. | 200.00 | 400.00 | 550.00 | 1250. |
| | 1878 M | Inc. Ab. | 200.00 | 400.00 | 550.00 | 1250. |
| | 1879/8 M | — | 200.00 | 400.00 | 550.00 | 1250. |
| | 1880 M | — | 200.00 | 400.00 | 550.00 | 1250. |
| | 1881 M | — | 200.00 | 400.00 | 550.00 | 1250. |
| | 1882 M | | | | | |
| | | 200 pcs. | 250.00 | 450.00 | 750.00 | 1250. |
| | 1883 M | | | | | |
| | | 200 pcs. | 250.00 | 450.00 | 750.00 | 1250. |
| | 1884 M | — | 250.00 | 450.00 | 750.00 | 1250. |
| | 1886 M | | | | | |
| | | 200 pcs. | 250.00 | 450.00 | 750.00 | 1250. |
| | 1887 M | | | | | |
| | | 200 pcs. | 250.00 | 450.00 | 750.00 | 1250. |
| | 1888 M | | | | | |
| | | 250 pcs. | 200.00 | 400.00 | 550.00 | 1250. |
| | 1889 M | | | | | |
| | | 190 pcs. | 250.00 | 450.00 | 750.00 | 1250. |
| | 1890 M | | | | | |
| | | 149 pcs. | 250.00 | 450.00 | 750.00 | 1250. |
| | 1891 M | | | | | |
| | | 156 pcs. | 250.00 | 450.00 | 750.00 | 1250. |
| | 1892 M | | | | | |
| | | 214 pcs. | 250.00 | 450.00 | 750.00 | 1250. |
| | 1893 M | 1,058 | 200.00 | 400.00 | 500.00 | 800.00 |
| | 1897 M | | | | | |
| | | 370 pcs. | 200.00 | 400.00 | 550.00 | 1000. |
| | 1898 M | | | | | |
| | | 376 pcs. | 200.00 | 400.00 | 550.00 | 1000. |
| | 1900 M | 1,014 | 150.00 | 300.00 | 400.00 | 650.00 |
| | 1901 M | 1,071 | 150.00 | 300.00 | 400.00 | 650.00 |
| | 1902 M | 1,478 | 150.00 | 300.00 | 400.00 | 650.00 |
| | 1903 M | 1,162 | 150.00 | 300.00 | 400.00 | 650.00 |
| | 1904 M | 1,415 | 150.00 | 300.00 | 400.00 | 650.00 |
| | 1905 M | | | | | |
| | | 563 pcs. | 200.00 | 400.00 | 550.00 | 1500. |

**Mint mark: Zs**

| KM# | Date | Mintage | Fine | VF | XF | Unc |
|---|---|---|---|---|---|---|
| | 1874 A | — | 250.00 | 500.00 | 750.00 | 1500. |
| | 1875 A | — | 200.00 | 400.00 | 500.00 | 1000. |
| | 1877 S/A | — | 200.00 | 400.00 | 550.00 | 1000. |
| | 1878/7 S/A | — | 200.00 | 400.00 | 550.00 | 1000. |
| | 1883 S | — | 150.00 | 300.00 | 450.00 | 700.00 |
| | 1888 Z | 70 pcs. | 1000. | 1500. | 2000. | 3000. |
| | 1889 Z | | | | | |
| | | 373 pcs. | 200.00 | 300.00 | 500.00 | 850.00 |
| | 1892 Z | 1,229 | 150.00 | 300.00 | 450.00 | 700.00 |

# DIEZ (10) PESOS

**16.9200 g, .875 GOLD, .4760 oz AGW**
**Mint mark: As**
**Rev: Balance scale.**

| KM# | Date | Mintage | Fine | VF | XF | Unc |
|---|---|---|---|---|---|---|
| 413 | 1874 DL | — | — | — | Rare | — |
| | 1875 L | 642 pcs. | 600.00 | 1250. | 2500. | 3500. |
| | 1878 L | 977 pcs. | 500.00 | 1000. | 2000. | 3000. |
| | 1879 L | 1,078 | 500.00 | 1000. | 2000. | 3000. |
| | 1880 L | 2,629 | 500.00 | 1000. | 2000. | 3000. |
| | 1881 L | 2,574 | 500.00 | 1000. | 2000. | 3000. |
| | 1882 L | 3,403 | 500.00 | 1000. | 2000. | 3000. |
| | 1883 L | 3,597 | 500.00 | 1000. | 2000. | 3000. |
| | 1884 L | — | — | — | Rare | — |
| | 1885 L | 4,562 | 500.00 | 1000. | 2000. | 3000. |
| | 1886 L | 4,643 | 500.00 | 1000. | 2000. | 3000. |
| | 1887 L | 3,667 | 500.00 | 1000. | 2000. | 3000. |
| | 1888 L | 4,521 | 500.00 | 1000. | 2000. | 3000. |
| | 1889 L | 5,615 | 500.00 | 1000. | 2000. | 3000. |
| | 1890 L | 4,920 | 500.00 | 1000. | 2000. | 3000. |
| | 1891 L | 568 pcs. | 500.00 | 1000. | 2000. | 3000. |
| | 1892 L | — | — | — | — | — |
| | 1893 L | 817 pcs. | 500.00 | 1000. | 2000. | 3000. |
| | 1894/3 L | 1,658 | — | — | — | — |
| | 1894 L | Inc. Ab. | 500.00 | 1000. | 2000. | 3000. |
| | 1895 L | 1,237 | 500.00 | 1000. | 2000. | 3000. |

**Mint mark: Ca**

| KM# | Date | Mintage | Fine | VF | XF | Unc |
|---|---|---|---|---|---|---|
| 413.1 | 1888 M | 175 pcs. | | | 7500. | — |

**16.9200 g, .875 GOLD, .4760 oz AGW**
**Mint mark: Cn**

| KM# | Date | Mintage | Fine | VF | XF | Unc |
|---|---|---|---|---|---|---|
| 413.2 | 1881 D | — | 400.00 | 600.00 | 1000. | 1750. |
| | 1882 D | 874 pcs. | 400.00 | 600.00 | 1000. | 1750. |
| | 1882 E | Inc. Ab. | 400.00 | 600.00 | 1000. | 1750. |
| | 1883 D | 221 pcs. | — | — | — | — |
| | 1883 M | Inc. Ab. | 400.00 | 600.00 | 1000. | 1750. |
| | 1884 D | — | 400.00 | 600.00 | 1000. | 1750. |
| | 1884 M | — | 400.00 | 600.00 | 1000. | 1750. |
| | 1885 M | 1,235 | 400.00 | 600.00 | 1000. | 1750. |
| | 1886 M | 981 pcs. | 400.00 | 600.00 | 1000. | 1750. |
| | 1887 M | 2,289 | 400.00 | 600.00 | 1000. | 1750. |
| | 1888 M | 767 pcs. | 400.00 | 600.00 | 1000. | 1750. |
| | 1889 M | 859 pcs. | 400.00 | 600.00 | 1000. | 1750. |
| | 1890 M | 1,427 | 400.00 | 600.00 | 1000. | 1750. |
| | 1891 M | 670 pcs. | 400.00 | 600.00 | 1000. | 1750. |
| | 1892 M | 379 pcs. | 400.00 | 600.00 | 1000. | 1750. |
| | 1893 M | 1,806 | 400.00 | 600.00 | 1000. | 1750. |
| | 1895 M | 179 pcs. | 500.00 | 1000. | 1500. | 2500. |
| | 1903 Q | 774 pcs. | 400.00 | 600.00 | 1000. | 1750. |

**Mint mark: Do**

| KM# | Date | Mintage | Fine | VF | XF | Unc |
|---|---|---|---|---|---|---|
| 413.3 | 1872 P | 1,755 | 350.00 | 500.00 | 800.00 | 1250. |
| | 1873/2 P | 1,091 | 350.00 | 550.00 | 900.00 | 1450. |
| | 1873/2 M/P | Inc. Ab. | 350.00 | 550.00 | 900.00 | 1450. |
| | 1874 M | — | 350.00 | 550.00 | 900.00 | 1450. |
| | 1875 M | — | 350.00 | 550.00 | 900.00 | 1450. |
| | 1876 M | — | 450.00 | 750.00 | 1250. | 2000. |
| | 1877 P | — | 350.00 | 550.00 | 900.00 | 1450. |
| | 1878 E | 582 pcs. | 350.00 | 550.00 | 900.00 | 1450. |
| | 1879/8 B | — | 350.00 | 550.00 | 900.00 | 1450. |
| | 1879 B | — | 350.00 | 550.00 | 900.00 | 1450. |
| | 1880 P | 2,030 | 350.00 | 550.00 | 900.00 | 1450. |
| | 1881/79 P | 2,617 | 350.00 | 550.00 | 900.00 | 1450. |
| | 1882 P | 1,528 | — | — | Rare | — |
| | 1882 C | Inc. Ab. | 350.00 | 550.00 | 900.00 | 1450. |
| | 1883 C | 793 pcs. | 450.00 | 750.00 | 1250. | 2000. |
| | 1884 C | 108 pcs. | 450.00 | 750.00 | 1250. | 2000. |

**Mint mark: Ga**

| KM# | Date | Mintage | Fine | VF | XF | Unc |
|---|---|---|---|---|---|---|
| 413.4 | 1870 C | 490 pcs. | 500.00 | 800.00 | 1000. | 1550. |
| | 1871 C | 1,910 | 400.00 | 800.00 | 1500. | 2250. |
| | 1872 C | 780 pcs. | 500.00 | 1000. | 2000. | 2500. |
| | 1873 C | 422 pcs. | 500.00 | 1000. | 2000. | 3000. |
| | 1874/3 C | 477 pcs. | 500.00 | 1000. | 2000. | 3000. |
| | 1875 C | 710 pcs. | 500.00 | 1000. | 2000. | 3000. |
| | 1878 A | 183 pcs. | 600.00 | 1200. | 2500. | 3500. |
| | 1879 A | 200 pcs. | 600.00 | 1200. | 2500. | 3500. |
| | 1880 S | 404 pcs. | 500.00 | 1000. | 2000. | 3000. |
| | 1881 S | 239 pcs. | 600.00 | 1200. | 2500. | 3500. |
| | 1891 S | 196 pcs. | 600.00 | 1200. | 2500. | 3500. |

**Mint mark: Go**

| KM# | Date | Mintage | Fine | VF | XF | Unc |
|---|---|---|---|---|---|---|
| 413.5 | 1872 S | 1,400 | 2000. | 4000. | 6500. | 10,000. |
| | 1887 H | 80 pcs. | — | — | *Rare | — |
| | 1888 R | 68 pcs. | — | — | Rare | — |

**\*NOTE:** Stack's Rio Grande Sale 6-93, P/L AU realized, $12,650.

**Mint mark: Ho**

| KM# | Date | Mintage | Fine | VF | XF | Unc |
|---|---|---|---|---|---|---|
| 413.6 | 1874 R | — | — | — | Rare | — |
| | 1876 F | 357 pcs. | — | — | Rare | — |
| | 1878 A | 814 pcs. | 1750. | 3000. | 3500. | 5500. |
| | 1879 A | — | 1000. | 2000. | 2500. | 4000. |
| | 1880 A | — | 1000. | 2000. | 2500. | 4000. |
| | 1881 A | — | — | — | Rare | — |

**Mint mark: Mo**

| KM# | Date | Mintage | Fine | VF | XF | Unc |
|---|---|---|---|---|---|---|
| 413.7 | 1870 C | 480 pcs. | 500.00 | 900.00 | 1200. | 2000. |
| | 1872/1 M/C | 2,100 | 350.00 | 550.00 | 900.00 | 1350. |
| | 1873 M | — | 400.00 | 600.00 | 950.00 | 1450. |
| | 1874/3 M | — | 400.00 | 600.00 | 950.00 | 1450. |
| | 1875 B/M | — | 400.00 | 600.00 | 950.00 | 1450. |
| | 1876 B | — | — | — | Rare | — |
| | 1878 M | 300 pcs. | 400.00 | 600.00 | 950.00 | 1450. |
| | 1879 M | — | — | — | — | — |
| | 1881 M | 100 pcs. | 500.00 | 1000. | 1600. | 2500. |
| | 1882 M | — | 400.00 | 600.00 | 950.00 | 1450. |
| | 1883 M | 100 pcs. | 600.00 | 1000. | 1600. | 2500. |
| | 1884 M | — | 600.00 | 1000. | 1600. | 2500. |
| | 1885 M | — | 400.00 | 600.00 | 950.00 | 1450. |
| | 1886 M | 100 pcs. | 600.00 | 1000. | 1600. | 2500. |
| | 1887 M | 100 pcs. | 600.00 | 1000. | 1625. | 2750. |
| | 1888 M | 144 pcs. | 450.00 | 750.00 | 1200. | 2000. |
| | 1889 M | 88 pcs. | 600.00 | 1000. | 1600. | 2500. |
| | 1890 M | 137 pcs. | 600.00 | 1000. | 1600. | 2500. |
| | 1891 M | 133 pcs. | 600.00 | 1000. | 1600. | 2500. |
| | 1892 M | 45 pcs. | 600.00 | 1000. | 1600. | 2500. |
| | 1893 M | 1,361 | 350.00 | 550.00 | 900.00 | 1350. |
| | 1897 M | 239 pcs. | 400.00 | 600.00 | 950.00 | 1450. |
| | 1898/7 M | 244 pcs. | 425.00 | 625.00 | 1000. | 1750. |

| KM# | Date | Mintage | Fine | VF | XF | Unc |
|---|---|---|---|---|---|---|
| 413.7 | 1900 M | | | | | |
| | | 733 pcs. | 400.00 | 600.00 | 950.00 | 1450. |
| | 1901 M | | | | | |
| | | 562 pcs. | 350.00 | 500.00 | 800.00 | 1250. |
| | 1902 M | | | | | |
| | | 719 pcs. | 350.00 | 500.00 | 800.00 | 1250. |
| | 1903 M | | | | | |
| | | 713 pcs. | 350.00 | 500.00 | 800.00 | 1250. |
| | 1904 M | | | | | |
| | | 694 pcs. | 350.00 | 500.00 | 800.00 | 1250. |
| | 1905 M | | | | | |
| | | 401 pcs. | 400.00 | 600.00 | 950.00 | 1500. |

**Mint mark: Oa**

| KM# | Date | Mintage | Fine | VF | XF | Unc |
|---|---|---|---|---|---|---|
| 413.8 | 1870 E | 4,614 | 400.00 | 600.00 | 900.00 | 1350. |
| | 1871 E | 2,705 | 400.00 | 600.00 | 900.00 | 1350. |
| | 1872 E | 5,897 | 400.00 | 600.00 | 900.00 | 1350. |
| | 1873 E | 3,537 | 400.00 | 600.00 | 950.00 | 1500. |
| | 1874 E | 2,205 | 400.00 | 600.00 | 1200. | 1800. |
| | 1875 E | | | | | |
| | | 312 pcs. | 450.00 | 750.00 | 1400. | 2250. |
| | 1876 E | | | | | |
| | | 766 pcs. | 450.00 | 750.00 | 1400. | 2250. |
| | 1877 E | | | | | |
| | | 463 pcs. | 450.00 | 750.00 | 1400. | 2250. |
| | 1878 E | | | | | |
| | | 229 pcs. | 450.00 | 750.00 | 1400. | 2250. |
| | 1879 E | | | | | |
| | | 210 pcs. | 450.00 | 750.00 | 1400. | 2250. |
| | 1880 E | | | | | |
| | | 238 pcs. | 450.00 | 750.00 | 1400. | 2250. |
| | 1881 E | | | | | |
| | | 961 pcs. | 400.00 | 600.00 | 1200. | 2000. |
| | 1882 E | | | | | |
| | | 170 pcs. | 600.00 | 1000. | 1500. | 2500. |
| | 1883 E | | | | | |
| | | 111 pcs. | 600.00 | 1000. | 1500. | 2500. |
| | 1884 E | | | | | |
| | | 325 pcs. | 450.00 | 750.00 | 1400. | 2250. |
| | 1885 E | | | | | |
| | | 370 pcs. | 450.00 | 750.00 | 1400. | 2250. |
| | 1886 E | | | | | |
| | | 400 pcs. | 450.00 | 750.00 | 1400. | 2250. |
| | 1887 E | — | 700.00 | 1250. | 2250. | 4000. |
| | 1888 E | — | — | — | — | — |

**Mint mark: Zs**

| KM# | Date | Mintage | Fine | VF | XF | Unc |
|---|---|---|---|---|---|---|
| 413.9 | 1871 H | 2,000 | 350.00 | 500.00 | 800.00 | 1250. |
| | 1872 H | 3,092 | 300.00 | 500.00 | 750.00 | 1150. |
| | 1873 H | | | | | |
| | | 936 pcs. | 400.00 | 600.00 | 950.00 | 1450. |
| | 1874 H | — | 400.00 | 600.00 | 950.00 | 1450. |
| | 1875/3 A | — | 400.00 | 600.00 | 1000. | 1750. |
| | 1876/5 S | — | 400.00 | 600.00 | 1000. | 1750. |
| | 1877 S/H | | | | | |
| | | 506 pcs. | 400.00 | 600.00 | 1000. | 1750. |
| | 1878 S | | | | | |
| | | 711 pcs. | 400.00 | 600.00 | 1000. | 1750. |
| | 1879/8 S | — | 450.00 | 750.00 | 1400. | 2250. |
| | 1879 S | — | 450.00 | 750.00 | 1400. | 2250. |
| | 1880 S | 2,089 | 350.00 | 550.00 | 950.00 | 1450. |
| | 1881 S | | | | | |
| | | 736 pcs. | 400.00 | 600.00 | 1000. | 1750. |
| | 1882 S | 1,599 | 350.00 | 550.00 | 950.00 | 1450. |
| | 1883/2 S | | | | | |
| | | 256 pcs. | 400.00 | 600.00 | 1000. | 1750. |
| | 1884/3 S | — | 350.00 | 550.00 | 950.00 | 1600. |
| | 1884 S | — | 350.00 | 550.00 | 950.00 | 1600. |
| | 1885 S | 1,588 | 350.00 | 550.00 | 950.00 | 1450. |
| | 1886 S | 5,364 | 350.00 | 550.00 | 950.00 | 1450. |
| | 1887 Z | 2,330 | 350.00 | 550.00 | 950.00 | 1450. |
| | 1888 Z | 4,810 | 350.00 | 550.00 | 950.00 | 1450. |
| | 1889 Z | 6,154 | 300.00 | 500.00 | 750.00 | 1250. |
| | 1890 Z | 1,321 | 350.00 | 550.00 | 950.00 | 1450. |
| | 1891 Z | 1,930 | 350.00 | 550.00 | 950.00 | 1450. |
| | 1892 Z | 1,882 | 350.00 | 550.00 | 950.00 | 1450. |
| | 1893 Z | 2,899 | 350.00 | 550.00 | 950.00 | 1450. |
| | 1894 Z | 2,501 | 350.00 | 550.00 | 950.00 | 1450. |
| | 1895 Z | 1,217 | 350.00 | 550.00 | 950.00 | 1450. |

# VEINTE (20) PESOS

**33.8400 g, .875 GOLD, .9520 oz AGW**
**Mint mark: As**
**Rev: Balance scale.**

| KM# | Date | Mintage | Fine | VF | XF | Unc |
|---|---|---|---|---|---|---|
| 414 | 1876 L | 276 pcs. | — | — | Rare | — |
| | 1877 L | 166 pcs. | — | — | Rare | — |
| | 1878 L | — | — | — | — | — |
| | 1888 L | — | — | — | Rare | — |

**Mint mark: CH, Ca**

| KM# | Date | Mintage | Fine | VF | XF | Unc |
|---|---|---|---|---|---|---|
| 414.1 | 1872 M | | | | | |
| | | 995 pcs. | 500.00 | 700.00 | 1000. | 2500. |
| | 1873 M | | | | | |
| | | 950 pcs. | 500.00 | 700.00 | 1000. | 2500. |
| | 1874 M | 1,116 | 450.00 | 675.00 | 950.00 | 2500. |
| | 1875 M | | | | | |
| | | 750 pcs. | 500.00 | 700.00 | 1000. | 2500. |
| | 1876 M | | | | | |
| | | 600 pcs. | 500.00 | 800.00 | 1250. | 2750. |
| | 1877 | 55 pcs. | — | — | Rare | — |
| | 1882 M | 1,758 | 450.00 | 675.00 | 950.00 | 2500. |
| | 1883 M | | | | | |
| | | 161 pcs. | 600.00 | 1000. | 1500. | 3000. |
| | 1884 M | | | | | |
| | | 496 pcs. | 500.00 | 700.00 | 1000. | 2500. |
| | 1885 M | | | | | |
| | | 122 pcs. | 600.00 | 1000. | 1500. | 3000. |
| | 1887 M | | | | | |
| | | 550 pcs. | 500.00 | 700.00 | 1000. | 2500. |
| | 1888 M | | | | | |
| | | 351 pcs. | 500.00 | 700.00 | 1000. | 2500. |
| | 1889 M | | | | | |
| | | 464 pcs. | 500.00 | 700.00 | 1000. | 2500. |
| | 1890 M | 1,209 | 450.00 | 675.00 | 950.00 | 2500. |
| | 1891 M | 2,004 | 425.00 | 650.00 | 900.00 | 2250. |
| | 1893 M | | | | | |
| | | 418 pcs. | 500.00 | 700.00 | 950.00 | 2500. |
| | 1895 M | | | | | |
| | | 133 pcs. | 600.00 | 1000. | 1500. | 3000. |

**Mint mark: Cn**

| KM# | Date | Mintage | Fine | VF | XF | Unc |
|---|---|---|---|---|---|---|
| 414.2 | 1870 E | 3,749 | 450.00 | 675.00 | 950.00 | 2000. |
| | 1871 P | 3,046 | 450.00 | 675.00 | 950.00 | 2000. |
| | 1872 P | 972 pcs. | 450.00 | 675.00 | 950.00 | 2000. |
| | 1873 P | 1,317 | 450.00 | 675.00 | 950.00 | 2000. |
| | 1874 P | — | 450.00 | 675.00 | 950.00 | 2000. |
| | 1875 P | — | 600.00 | 1200. | 1800. | 2500. |
| | 1876 P | — | 450.00 | 675.00 | 950.00 | 2000. |
| | 1876 G | — | 450.00 | 675.00 | 950.00 | 2000. |
| | 1877 G | | | | | |
| | | 167 pcs. | 600.00 | 1000. | 1500. | 3000. |
| | 1878 | 842 pcs. | — | — | Rare | — |
| | 1881/0 D | 2,039 | — | — | — | — |
| | 1881 D- Inc. Ab. | 450.00 | 675.00 | 950.00 | 2000. |
| | 1882/1 D | | | | | |
| | | 736 pcs. | 450.00 | 675.00 | 950.00 | 2000. |
| | 1883 M | 1,836 | 450.00 | 675.00 | 950.00 | 2000. |
| | 1884 M | — | 450.00 | 675.00 | 950.00 | 2000. |
| | 1885 M | | | | | |
| | | 544 pcs. | 450.00 | 675.00 | 950.00 | 2000. |
| | 1886 M | | | | | |
| | | 882 pcs. | 450.00 | 675.00 | 950.00 | 2000. |

| KM# | Date | Mintage | Fine | VF | XF | Unc |
|---|---|---|---|---|---|---|
| 414.2 | 1887 M | | | | | |
| | | 837 pcs. | 450.00 | 675.00 | 950.00 | 2000. |
| | 1888 M | | | | | |
| | | 473 pcs. | 450.00 | 675.00 | 950.00 | 2000. |
| | 1889 M | 1,376 | 450.00 | 675.00 | 950.00 | 2000. |
| | 1890 M | — | 450.00 | 675.00 | 950.00 | 2000. |
| | 1891 M | | | | | |
| | | 237 pcs. | 500.00 | 900.00 | 1200. | 2250. |
| | 1892 M | | | | | |
| | | 526 pcs. | 450.00 | 675.00 | 950.00 | 2000. |
| | 1893 M | 2,062 | 450.00 | 675.00 | 950.00 | 2000. |
| | 1894 M | 4,516 | 450.00 | 675.00 | 950.00 | 2000. |
| | 1895 M | 3,193 | 450.00 | 675.00 | 950.00 | 2000. |
| | 1896 M | 4,072 | 450.00 | 675.00 | 950.00 | 2000. |
| | 1897/6 M | | | | | |
| | | 959 pcs. | 450.00 | 675.00 | 950.00 | 2000. |
| | 1897 M Inc. Ab. | | 450.00 | 675.00 | 950.00 | 2000. |
| | 1898 M | 1,660 | 450.00 | 675.00 | 950.00 | 2000. |
| | 1899 M | 1,243 | 450.00 | 675.00 | 950.00 | 2000. |
| | 1899 Q Inc. Ab. | | 500.00 | 900.00 | 1200. | 2250. |
| | 1900 Q | 1,558 | 450.00 | 675.00 | 950.00 | 2000. |
| | 1901/0 Q | 1,496 | — | — | — | — |
| | 1901 Q Inc. Ab. | | 450.00 | 675.00 | 950.00 | 2000. |
| | 1902 Q | 1,059 | 450.00 | 675.00 | 950.00 | 2000. |
| | 1903 Q | 1,121 | 450.00 | 675.00 | 950.00 | 2000. |
| | 1904 H | 4,646 | 450.00 | 675.00 | 950.00 | 2000. |
| | 1905 P | 1,738 | 500.00 | 900.00 | 1200. | 2250. |

**Mint mark: Do**

| KM# | Date | Mintage | Fine | VF | XF | Unc |
|---|---|---|---|---|---|---|
| 414.3 | 1870 P | | | | | |
| | | 416 pcs. | 1000. | 1500. | 2000. | 2500. |
| | 1871/0 P | 1,073 | 1000. | 1750. | 2250. | 2750. |
| | 1871 P Inc. Ab. | | 1000. | 1500. | 2000. | 2500. |
| | 1872/1 PT | — | 1500. | 3000. | 4500. | 7000. |
| | 1876 M | — | 1000. | 1500. | 2000. | 2500. |
| | 1877 P | 94 pcs. | 1500. | 2250. | 2750. | 3250. |
| | 1878 | 258 pcs. | — | — | Rare | — |

**Mint mark: Go**

| KM# | Date | Mintage | Fine | VF | XF | Unc |
|---|---|---|---|---|---|---|
| 414.4 | 1870 S | 3,250 | 425.00 | 650.00 | 900.00 | 1500. |
| | 1871 S | .020 | 425.00 | 650.00 | 900.00 | 1500. |
| | 1872 S | .018 | 425.00 | 650.00 | 900.00 | 1500. |
| | 1873 S | 7,000 | 425.00 | 650.00 | 900.00 | 1500. |
| | 1874 S | — | 425.00 | 650.00 | 900.00 | 1500. |
| | 1875 S | — | 425.00 | 650.00 | 900.00 | 1500. |
| | 1876 S | — | 425.00 | 650.00 | 900.00 | 1500. |
| | 1876 M/S | — | — | — | — | — |
| | 1877 M/S | .015 | — | — | Rare | — |
| | 1877 R Inc. Ab. | | 425.00 | 650.00 | 900.00 | 1500. |
| | 1877 S Inc. Ab. | — | — | Rare | — | |
| | 1878/7 M/S | | | | | |
| | | .013 | 650.00 | 1250. | 2000. | 2800. |
| | 1878 M Inc. Ab. | | 650.00 | 1250. | 2000. | 2800. |
| | 1878 S Inc. Ab. | | 425.00 | 650.00 | 900.00 | 1500. |
| | 1879 S | 8,202 | 500.00 | 800.00 | 1200. | 2300. |
| | 1880 S | 7,375 | 425.00 | 650.00 | 900.00 | 1500. |
| | 1881 S | 4,909 | 425.00 | 650.00 | 900.00 | 1500. |
| | 1882 S | 4,020 | 425.00 | 650.00 | 900.00 | 1500. |
| | 1883/2 B | 3,705 | 500.00 | 750.00 | 1150. | 2250. |
| | 1883 B Inc. Ab. | | 425.00 | 650.00 | 900.00 | 1500. |
| | 1884 B | 1,798 | 425.00 | 650.00 | 900.00 | 1500. |
| | 1885 R | 2,660 | 425.00 | 650.00 | 900.00 | 1500. |
| | 1886 R | 1,090 | 550.00 | 800.00 | 1250. | 2500. |
| | 1887 R | 1,009 | 550.00 | 800.00 | 1250. | 2500. |
| | 1888 R | 1,011 | 550.00 | 800.00 | 1250. | 2500. |
| | 1889 R | | | | | |
| | | 956 pcs. | 550.00 | 800.00 | 1250. | 2500. |
| | 1890 R | | | | | |
| | | 879 pcs. | 550.00 | 800.00 | 1250. | 2500. |
| | 1891 R | | | | | |
| | | 818 pcs. | 550.00 | 800.00 | 1250. | 2500. |
| | 1892 R | | | | | |
| | | 730 pcs. | 550.00 | 800.00 | 1250. | 2500. |
| | 1893 R | 3,343 | 425.00 | 650.00 | 1000. | 2000. |
| | 1894/3 R | 6,734 | 425.00 | 650.00 | 900.00 | 1500. |
| | 1894 R | I.A. | 425.00 | 650.00 | 900.00 | 1500. |
| | 1895/3 R | 7,118 | 425.00 | 650.00 | 900.00 | 1500. |
| | 1895 R | I.A. | 425.00 | 650.00 | 900.00 | 1500. |

| KM# | Date | Mintage | Fine | VF | XF | Unc |
|---|---|---|---|---|---|---|
| 414.4 | 1896 R | 9,219 | 425.00 | 650.00 | 900.00 | 1500. |
| | 1897/6 R | 6,781 | 425.00 | 650.00 | 900.00 | 1500. |
| | 1897 R | I.A. | 425.00 | 650.00 | 900.00 | 1500. |
| | 1898 R | 7,710 | 425.00 | 650.00 | 900.00 | 1500. |
| | 1899 R | 8,527 | 425.00 | 650.00 | 900.00 | 1500. |
| | 1900 R | 4,512 | 550.00 | 800.00 | 1250. | 2350. |

**Mint mark: Ho**

| KM# | Date | Mintage | Fine | VF | XF | Unc |
|---|---|---|---|---|---|---|
| 414.5 | 1874 R | — | — | — | Rare | — |
| | 1875 R | — | — | — | Rare | — |
| | 1876 F | — | — | — | Rare | — |
| | 1888 G | — | — | — | Rare | — |

**33.8400 g, .875 GOLD, .9520 oz AGW**
**Mint mark: Mo**

| KM# | Date | Mintage | Fine | VF | XF | Unc |
|---|---|---|---|---|---|---|
| 414.6 | 1870 C | .014 | 400.00 | 600.00 | 850.00 | 1450. |
| | 1871 M | .021 | 400.00 | 600.00 | 850.00 | 1450. |
| | 1872/1 M | .011 | 400.00 | 600.00 | 850.00 | 1600. |
| | 1872 M | I.A. | 400.00 | 600.00 | 850.00 | 1450. |
| | 1873 M | 5,600 | 400.00 | 600.00 | 850.00 | 1450. |
| | 1874/2 M | — | 400.00 | 600.00 | 850.00 | 1450. |
| | 1874/2 B | — | 450.00 | 700.00 | 1000. | 1600. |
| | 1875 B | — | 425.00 | 650.00 | 900.00 | 1500. |
| | 1876 B | — | 425.00 | 650.00 | 900.00 | 1500. |
| | 1876 M | — | — | Reported, not confirmed | | |
| | 1877 M | 2,000 | 450.00 | 700.00 | 1100. | 2000. |
| | 1878 M | 7,000 | 425.00 | 650.00 | 900.00 | 1500. |
| | 1879 M | — | 425.00 | 650.00 | 900.00 | 1750. |
| | 1880 M | — | 425.00 | 650.00 | 900.00 | 1750. |
| | 1881/0 M | .011 | 425.00 | 600.00 | 850.00 | 1450. |
| | 1881 M | I.A. | 425.00 | 600.00 | 850.00 | 1450. |
| | 1882/1 M | 5,800 | 425.00 | 600.00 | 850.00 | 1450. |
| | 1882 M | I.A. | 425.00 | 600.00 | 850.00 | 1450. |
| | 1883/1 M | 4,000 | 425.00 | 600.00 | 850.00 | 1450. |
| | 1883 M | I.A. | 425.00 | 600.00 | 850.00 | 1450. |
| | 1884/3 M | — | 425.00 | 650.00 | 900.00 | 1500. |
| | 1884 M | — | 425.00 | 650.00 | 900.00 | 1500. |
| | 1885 M | 6,000 | 425.00 | 650.00 | 900.00 | 1750. |
| | 1886 M | .010 | 400.00 | 600.00 | 850.00 | 1450. |
| | 1887 M | .012 | 600.00 | 800.00 | 1500. | 2500. |
| | 1888 M | 7,300 | 400.00 | 600.00 | 850.00 | 1450. |
| | 1889 M | 6,477 | 400.00 | 600.00 | 900.00 | 1650. |
| | 1890 M | 7,852 | 400.00 | 600.00 | 850.00 | 1500. |
| | 1891/0 M | 8,725 | 400.00 | 600.00 | 850.00 | 1500. |
| | 1891 M | I.A. | 400.00 | 600.00 | 850.00 | 1500. |
| | 1892 M | .011 | 400.00 | 600.00 | 850.00 | 1450. |
| | 1893 M | .015 | 400.00 | 600.00 | 850.00 | 1450. |
| | 1894 M | .014 | 400.00 | 600.00 | 850.00 | 1450. |
| | 1895 M | .013 | 400.00 | 600.00 | 850.00 | 1450. |
| | 1896 B | .014 | 400.00 | 600.00 | 850.00 | 1450. |
| | 1897/6 M | .012 | 400.00 | 600.00 | 850.00 | 1450. |
| | 1897 M | I.A. | 400.00 | 600.00 | 850.00 | 1450. |
| | 1898 M | .020 | 400.00 | 600.00 | 850.00 | 1450. |
| | 1899 M | .023 | 400.00 | 600.00 | 850.00 | 1450. |
| | 1900 M | .021 | 400.00 | 600.00 | 850.00 | 1450. |
| | 1901 M | .029 | 400.00 | 600.00 | 850.00 | 1450. |
| | 1902 M | .038 | 400.00 | 600.00 | 850.00 | 1450. |
| | 1903/2 M | .031 | 400.00 | 600.00 | 850.00 | 1450. |
| | 1903 M | I.A. | 400.00 | 600.00 | 850.00 | 1450. |
| | 1904 M | .052 | 400.00 | 600.00 | 850.00 | 1450. |
| | 1905 M | 9,757 | 400.00 | 600.00 | 850.00 | 1450. |

**Mint mark: Oa**

| KM# | Date | Mintage | Fine | VF | XF | Unc |
|---|---|---|---|---|---|---|
| 414.7 | 1870 E | 1,131 | 750.00 | 1500. | 2500. | 5000. |
| | 1871 E | 1,591 | 750.00 | 1500. | 2500. | 5000. |
| | 1872 E | | | | | |
| | | 255 pcs. | 1000. | 1750. | 3000. | 7000. |
| | 1888 E | | | | | |
| | | 170 pcs. | 2000. | 3000. | 5000. | — |

**Mint mark: Zs**

| KM# | Date | Mintage | Fine | VF | XF | Unc |
|---|---|---|---|---|---|---|
| 414.8 | 1871 H | 1,000 | 3500. | 6500. | 7000. | 9000. |
| | 1875 A | — | 4000. | 6000. | 7500. | 9500. |
| | 1878 S | | | | | |
| | | 441 pcs. | 4000. | 6000. | 7500. | 9500. |
| | 1888 Z | 50 pcs. | — | — | Rare | — |
| | 1889 Z | | | | | |
| | | 640 pcs. | 3500. | 5500. | 7000. | 9000. |

# United States of Mexico

## CENTAVO

### Zapata Issue
Reduced size, 16mm.

| KM# | Date | Mintage | Fine | VF | XF | Unc |
|-----|------|---------|------|-----|-----|-----|
| 416 | 1915 | .179 | 16.00 | 27.50 | 50.00 | 75.50 |

### BRONZE, 20mm

| KM# | Date | Mintage | Fine | VF | XF | Unc |
|-----|------|---------|------|-----|-----|-----|
| 415 | 1905 narrow date | | | | | |
| | | 6.040 | 3.25 | 5.75 | 12.50 | 95.00 |
| | 1905 wide date | | | | | |
| | | — | 3.25 | 5.75 | 12.50 | 95.00 |
| | 1906 narrow date | | | | | |
| | | *67.505 | .50 | .75 | 1.25 | 14.00 |
| | 1906 wide date | | | | | |
| | | Inc. Ab. | .65 | 1.25 | 2.25 | 22.00 |
| | 1910 narrow date | | | | | |
| | | 8.700 | 1.50 | 2.50 | 6.50 | 90.00 |
| | 1910 wide date | | | | | |
| | | — | 1.50 | 2.50 | 6.50 | 90.00 |
| | 1911 narrow date | | | | | |
| | | 16.450 | .60 | 1.00 | 2.75 | 22.50 |
| | 1911 wide date | | | | | |
| | | Inc Ab. | .75 | 1.25 | 5.00 | 32.00 |
| | 1912 | 12.650 | .75 | 1.25 | 3.00 | 32.00 |
| | 1913 | 12.850 | .65 | 1.00 | 2.75 | 33.00 |
| | 1914 narrow date | | | | | |
| | | 17.350 | .60 | .85 | 2.50 | 14.50 |
| | 1914 wide date | | | | | |
| | | Inc Ab. | .60 | .85 | 2.50 | 14.50 |
| | 1915 | 2.277 | 9.00 | 21.50 | 65.00 | 250.00 |
| | 1916 | .500 | 30.00 | 65.00 | 165.00 | 1200. |
| | 1920 | 1.433 | 15.00 | 30.00 | 65.00 | 400.00 |
| | 1921 | 3.470 | 4.25 | 13.50 | 42.50 | 275.00 |
| | 1922 | 1.880 | 8.00 | 15.00 | 45.00 | 300.00 |
| | 1923 | 4.800 | .50 | .75 | 1.75 | 11.50 |
| | 1924/3 | 2.000 | 50.00 | 140.00 | 250.00 | 500.00 |
| | 1924 | Inc. Ab. | 4.00 | 10.00 | 20.00 | 225.00 |
| | 1925 | 1.550 | 3.75 | 9.25 | 20.00 | 215.00 |
| | 1926 | 5.000 | .90 | 1.75 | 3.50 | 26.00 |
| | 1927/6 | 6.000 | 25.00 | 40.00 | 60.00 | 140.00 |
| | 1927 | Inc. Ab. | .60 | 1.25 | 4.50 | 36.00 |
| | 1928 | 5.000 | .60 | .80 | 3.25 | 16.50 |
| | 1929 | 4.500 | .60 | .80 | 1.75 | 18.00 |
| | 1930 | 7.000 | .75 | 1.00 | 2.25 | 19.00 |
| | 1933 | 10.000 | .25 | .35 | 1.75 | 16.50 |
| | 1934 | 7.500 | .40 | .95 | 3.25 | 35.00 |
| | 1935 | 12.400 | .15 | .25 | .40 | 11.50 |
| | 1936 | 20.100 | .15 | .20 | .30 | 8.00 |
| | 1937 | 20.000 | .15 | .25 | .35 | 3.50 |
| | 1938 | 10.000 | .10 | .15 | .30 | 2.25 |
| | 1939 | 30.000 | .10 | .20 | .30 | 1.25 |
| | 1940 | 10.000 | .20 | .30 | .60 | 6.50 |
| | 1941 | 15.800 | .15 | .25 | .35 | 2.25 |
| | 1942 | 30.400 | .15 | .20 | .30 | 1.25 |
| | 1943 | 4.310 | .30 | .50 | .75 | 9.00 |
| | 1944 | 5.645 | .15 | .25 | .50 | 7.00 |
| | 1945 | 26.375 | .10 | .15 | .25 | 1.00 |
| | 1946 | 42.135 | — | .15 | .20 | .60 |
| | 1947 | 13.445 | — | .10 | .15 | .80 |
| | 1948 | 20.040 | — | .15 | .30 | 1.10 |
| | 1949 | 6.235 | .10 | .15 | .30 | 1.75 |

*NOTE: 50,000,000 pcs. were struck at the Birmingham Mint.
NOTE: Varieties exist. Wide and narrow dates exist for 1911 and 1914.

### BRASS, 16mm

| KM# | Date | Mintage | Fine | VF | XF | Unc |
|-----|------|---------|------|-----|-----|-----|
| 417 | 1950 | 12.815 | .15 | .30 | 1.75 | 2.00 |
| | 1951 | 25.740 | .15 | .25 | .65 | 1.10 |
| | 1952 | 24.610 | .10 | .25 | .40 | .75 |
| | 1953 | 21.160 | .10 | .25 | .40 | .85 |
| | 1954 | 25.675 | .10 | .15 | .85 | 1.20 |
| | 1955 | 9.820 | .15 | .25 | .85 | 1.50 |
| | 1956 | 11.285 | .15 | .25 | .80 | 1.45 |
| | 1957 | 9.805 | .15 | .25 | .85 | 1.35 |
| | 1958 | 12.155 | .10 | .25 | .45 | .80 |
| | 1959 | 11.875 | .10 | .25 | .75 | 1.25 |
| | 1960 | 10.360 | .10 | .15 | .40 | .65 |
| | 1961 | 6.385 | .10 | .15 | .45 | .85 |
| | 1962 | 4.850 | .10 | .15 | .55 | .90 |
| | 1963 | 7.775 | .10 | .15 | .25 | .45 |
| | 1964 | 4.280 | .10 | .15 | .20 | .35 |
| | 1965 | 2.255 | .10 | .15 | .25 | .40 |
| | 1966 | 1.760 | .10 | .25 | .60 | .75 |
| | 1967 | 1.290 | .10 | .15 | .40 | .70 |
| | 1968 | 1.000 | .10 | .20 | .85 | 1.25 |
| | 1969 | 1.000 | .10 | .15 | .75 | 1.25 |

### Reduced size, 13mm.

| KM# | Date | Mintage | Fine | VF | XF | Unc |
|-----|------|---------|------|-----|-----|-----|
| 418 | 1970 | 1.000 | .20 | .40 | 1.30 | 1.80 |
| | 1972 | 1.000 | .20 | .45 | 2.50 | 3.25 |
| | 1972/2 | — | .50 | 1.25 | 3.25 | 5.00 |
| | 1973 | 1.000 | 1.65 | 2.75 | 8.00 | 9.75 |

## 2 CENTAVOS

### BRONZE, 25mm

| KM# | Date | Mintage | Fine | VF | XF | Unc |
|-----|------|---------|------|-----|-----|-----|
| 419 | 1905 | .050 | 125.00 | 275.00 | 425.00 | 1200. |
| | 1906/inverted 6 | | | | | |
| | | 9.998 | 25.00 | 50.00 | 110.00 | 375.00 |
| | 1906 wide date | | | | | |
| | | I.A. | 4.00 | 10.00 | 21.50 | 80.00 |
| | 1906 narrow date | | | | | |
| | | *I.A. | 6.50 | 12.50 | 25.00 | 85.00 |
| | 1920 | 1.325 | 6.50 | 21.50 | 60.00 | 350.00 |
| | 1921 | 4.275 | 2.50 | 4.75 | 10.00 | 90.00 |
| | 1922 | — | 225.00 | 550.00 | 1350. | 4000. |
| | 1924 | .750 | 8.50 | 20.00 | 50.00 | 450.00 |

| KM# | Date | Mintage | Fine | VF | XF | Unc |
|---|---|---|---|---|---|---|
| 419 | 1925 | 3.660 | 2.50 | 3.50 | 9.00 | 40.00 |
| | 1926 | 4.750 | 1.00 | 2.25 | 5.50 | 35.00 |
| | 1927 | 7.250 | .60 | 1.00 | 4.50 | 22.75 |
| | 1928 | 3.250 | .75 | 1.50 | 3.75 | 25.00 |
| | 1929 | .250 | 45.00 | 120.00 | 500.00 | 1000. |
| | 1935 | 1.250 | 4.25 | 9.25 | 22.50 | 200.00 |
| | 1939 | 5.000 | .60 | .90 | 2.25 | 20.00 |
| | 1941 | 3.550 | .45 | .60 | 1.25 | 18.00 |

**\*NOTE:** 5,000,000 pcs. were struck at the Birmingham Mint.

**Zapata Issue**
**Reduced size, 20mm.**

| | | | | | | |
|---|---|---|---|---|---|---|
| 420 | 1915 | .487 | 6.50 | 9.00 | 13.50 | 65.00 |

# 5 CENTAVOS

### NICKEL

| KM# | Date | Mintage | Fine | VF | XF | Unc |
|---|---|---|---|---|---|---|
| 421 | 1905 | 1.420 | 6.00 | 9.50 | 22.50 | 290.00 |
| | 1906/5 | 10.615 | 12.00 | 23.50 | 60.00 | 375.00 |
| | 1906 | *Inc. Ab. | .75 | 1.20 | 3.25 | 50.00 |
| | 1907 | 4.000 | 1.25 | 3.50 | 10.00 | 350.00 |
| | 1909 | 2.052 | 3.25 | 9.50 | 42.50 | 360.00 |
| | 1910 | 6.181 | 1.15 | 3.20 | 5.50 | 77.00 |
| | 1911 narrow date | | | | | |
| | | 4.487 | .75 | 3.00 | 5.00 | 85.00 |
| | 1911 wide date | | | | | |
| | Inc. Ab. | | 2.50 | 4.25 | 9.00 | 110.00 |
| | 1912 small mint mark | | | | | |
| | | .420 | 97.50 | 120.00 | 210.00 | 725.00 |
| | 1912 large mint mark | | | | | |
| | Inc. Ab. | | 60.00 | 85.00 | 160.00 | 575.00 |
| | 1913 | 2.035 | 1.65 | 3.75 | 9.00 | 100.00 |
| | 1914 | 2.000 | .75 | 1.75 | 3.50 | 60.00 |

**NOTE:** 5,000,000 pcs. appear to have been struck at the Birmingham Mint in 1914 and all of 1909-1911. The Mexican Mint report does not mention receiving the 1914 dated coins.

**NOTE:** Varieties exist. Wide and narrow dates exist for 1913.

### BRONZE

| KM# | Date | Mintage | Fine | VF | XF | Unc |
|---|---|---|---|---|---|---|
| 422 | 1914 | 2.500 | 10.00 | 21.50 | 45.00 | 225.00 |
| | 1915 | 11.424 | 2.50 | 4.50 | 14.50 | 125.00 |
| | 1916 | 2.860 | 13.50 | 32.00 | 170.00 | 690.00 |
| | 1917 | .800 | 60.00 | 150.00 | 320.00 | 820.00 |
| | 1918 | 1.332 | 28.00 | 70.00 | 175.00 | 625.00 |
| | 1919 | .400 | 100.00 | 190.00 | 335.00 | 925.00 |
| | 1920 | 5.920 | 3.00 | 7.50 | 40.00 | 285.00 |
| | 1921 | 2.080 | 9.00 | 21.50 | 70.00 | 275.00 |
| | 1924 | .780 | 35.00 | 80.00 | 235.00 | 625.00 |
| | 1925 | 4.040 | 4.75 | 10.00 | 42.50 | 225.00 |
| | 1926 | 3.160 | 5.50 | 11.00 | 43.50 | 300.00 |
| | 1927 | 3.600 | 3.25 | 6.75 | 27.50 | 220.00 |

| KM# | Date | Mintage | Fine | VF | XF | Unc |
|---|---|---|---|---|---|---|
| 422 | 1928 large date | | | | | |
| | | 1.740 | 10.00 | 17.50 | 68.00 | 250.00 |
| | 1928 small date | | | | | |
| | Inc. Ab. | 25.00 | 45.00 | 90.00 | 385.00 |
| | 1929 | 2.400 | 4.75 | 10.00 | 40.00 | 180.00 |
| | 1930 large oval 0 in date | | | | | |
| | | 2.600 | 4.00 | 7.50 | 27.50 | 210.00 |
| | 1930 small square 0 in date | | | | | |
| | Inc. Ab. | 50.00 | 115.00 | 220.00 | 565.00 |
| | 1931 | — | 475.00 | 675.00 | 1000. | 3250. |
| | 1933 | 8.000 | 1.25 | 2.00 | 3.25 | 25.00 |
| | 1934 | 10.000 | 1.00 | 1.50 | 2.50 | 22.50 |
| | 1935 | 21.980 | .75 | 1.20 | 2.25 | 20.00 |

### COPPER-NICKEL

| KM# | Date | Mintage | Fine | VF | XF | Unc |
|---|---|---|---|---|---|---|
| 423 | 1936 | 46.700 | .65 | 1.25 | 6.50 | 9.00 |
| | 1937 | 49.060 | .50 | 1.00 | 6.00 | 9.00 |
| | 1938 | 3.340 | 5.00 | 12.50 | 65.00 | 250.00 |
| | 1940 | 22.800 | .75 | 1.50 | 8.00 | 12.00 |
| | 1942 | 7.100 | 1.50 | 3.20 | 35.00 | 45.00 |

### BRONZE
**'Josefa' Ortiz de Dominguez**

| KM# | Date | Mintage | Fine | VF | XF | Unc |
|---|---|---|---|---|---|---|
| 424 | 1942 | .900 | 20.00 | 60.00 | 375.00 | 500.00 |
| | 1943 | 54.660 | .40 | .65 | 3.00 | 4.00 |
| | 1944 | 53.463 | .25 | .35 | .75 | 1.00 |
| | 1945 | 44.262 | .25 | .35 | .90 | 1.65 |
| | 1946 | 49.054 | .50 | .75 | 2.00 | 2.75 |
| | 1951 | 50.758 | .60 | .85 | 3.00 | 4.75 |
| | 1952 | 17.674 | 1.25 | 2.25 | 9.25 | 11.50 |
| | 1953 | 31.568 | 1.10 | 1.75 | 7.00 | 10.00 |
| | 1954 | 58.680 | .40 | .75 | 2.75 | 4.00 |
| | 1955 | 31.114 | 1.85 | 2.50 | 10.00 | 14.00 |

### COPPER-NICKEL
**'White Josefa'**

| | | | | | | |
|---|---|---|---|---|---|---|
| 425 | 1950 | 5.700 | .75 | 1.50 | 6.25 | 8.00 |

**NOTE:** 5,600,000 pieces struck at Connecticut melted.

### BRASS

| KM# | Date | Mintage | Fine | VF | XF | Unc |
|---|---|---|---|---|---|---|
| 426 | 1954 dot | — | 9.00 | 32.00 | 325.00 | 375.00 |
| | 1954 w/o dot | — | 12.00 | 25.00 | 250.00 | 290.00 |
| | 1955 | 12.136 | .75 | 1.50 | 9.00 | 12.50 |
| | 1956 | 60.216 | .20 | .30 | .90 | 1.50 |
| | 1957 | 55.288 | .15 | .20 | .90 | 1.50 |
| | 1958 | 104.624 | .15 | .20 | .60 | 1.00 |
| | 1959 | 106.000 | .15 | .25 | .90 | 1.50 |

| KM# | Date | Mintage | VF | XF | Unc | BU |
|---|---|---|---|---|---|---|
| 426 | 1960 | 99.144 | .10 | .15 | .50 | .75 |
| | 1961 | 61.136 | .10 | .15 | .40 | .70 |
| | 1962 | 47.232 | .10 | .15 | .30 | .55 |
| | 1963 | 156.680 | — | .15 | .20 | .35 |
| | 1964 | 71.168 | — | .15 | .20 | .40 |
| | 1965 | 155.720 | — | .15 | .25 | .35 |
| | 1966 | 124.944 | — | .15 | .40 | .65 |
| | 1967 | 118.816 | — | .15 | .25 | .40 |
| | 1968 | 189.588 | — | .15 | .50 | .75 |
| | 1969 | 210.492 | — | .15 | .55 | .80 |

### COPPER-NICKEL

| 426a | 1960 | — 300.00 | 450.00 | — | — |
|---|---|---|---|---|---|
| | 1962 | 19 pcs. 300.00 | 450.00 | — | — |
| | 1965 | — 300.00 | 450.00 | — | — |

### BRONZE

| KM# | Date | Mintage | VF | XF | Unc | BU |
|---|---|---|---|---|---|---|
| 430 | 1919 | 1.232 | 20.00 | 47.50 | 440.00 | 525.00 |
| | 1920 | 6.612 | 12.50 | 38.50 | 400.00 | 475.00 |
| | 1921 | 2.255 | 30.00 | 65.00 | 625.00 | 800.00 |
| | 1935 | 5.970 | 12.00 | 23.50 | 125.00 | 175.00 |

### BRASS
**Reduced size, 18mm.**

| 427 | 1970 | 163.368 | .10 | .15 | .35 | .45 |
|---|---|---|---|---|---|---|
| | 1971 | 198.844 | .10 | .15 | .25 | .30 |
| | 1972 | 225.000 | .10 | .15 | .25 | .30 |
| | 1973 flat top 3 | | | | | |
| | | 595.070 | .10 | .15 | .25 | .40 |
| | 1973 round top 3 | | | | | |
| | | Inc. Ab. | .10 | .15 | .20 | .30 |
| | 1974 | 401.584 | .10 | .15 | .30 | .40 |
| | 1975 | 342.308 | .10 | .15 | .25 | .35 |
| | 1976 | 367.524 | .10 | .15 | .40 | .60 |

**NOTE:** Due to some minor alloy variations this type is often encountered with a bronze color toning.

### 1.6600 g, .720 SILVER, .0384 oz ASW

| 431 | 1925/15 | 5.350 | 18.00 | 35.00 | 110.00 | 125.00 |
|---|---|---|---|---|---|---|
| | 1925/3 | Inc. Ab. | 18.00 | 35.00 | 115.00 | 130.00 |
| | 1925 | Inc. Ab. | 2.00 | 4.00 | 35.00 | 47.50 |
| | 1926/16 | 2.650 | 25.00 | 55.00 | 160.00 | 175.00 |
| | 1926 | Inc. Ab. | 3.50 | 6.00 | 62.50 | 80.00 |
| | 1927 | 2.810 | 2.25 | 3.00 | 17.50 | 21.50 |
| | 1928 | 5.270 | 1.75 | 2.25 | 12.00 | 14.25 |
| | 1930 | 2.000 | 3.75 | 5.00 | 18.75 | 22.50 |
| | 1933 | 5.000 | 1.50 | 3.00 | 10.00 | 12.50 |
| | 1934 | 8.000 | 1.75 | 2.25 | 8.00 | 9.50 |
| | 1935 | 3.500 | 2.75 | 4.00 | 11.00 | 13.50 |

## 10 CENTAVOS

### 2.5000 g, .800 SILVER, .0643 oz ASW

| 428 | 1905 | 3.920 | 5.25 | 7.00 | 35.00 | 50.00 |
|---|---|---|---|---|---|---|
| | 1906 | 8.410 | 4.75 | 6.25 | 25.00 | 35.00 |
| | 1907/6 | 5.950 | 45.00 | 115.00 | 275.00 | 350.00 |
| | 1907 | Inc. Ab. | 5.50 | 7.75 | 35.00 | 42.50 |
| | 1909 | 2.620 | 8.00 | 12.50 | 70.00 | 90.00 |
| | 1910/00 | 3.450 | 10.00 | 32.00 | 75.00 | 100.00 |
| | 1910 | Inc. Ab. | 8.00 | 12.50 | 25.00 | 30.00 |
| | 1911 narrow date | | | | | |
| | | 2.550 | 10.00 | 15.00 | 88.00 | 125.00 |
| | 1911 wide date | | | | | |
| | | Inc. Ab. | 6.00 | 8.50 | 42.50 | 60.00 |
| | 1912 | 1.350 | 9.00 | 16.00 | 120.00 | 135.00 |
| | 1912 low 2 | I.A. | 8.00 | 15.00 | 110.00 | 130.00 |
| | 1913/2 | 1.990 | 7.50 | 14.00 | 35.00 | 65.00 |
| | 1913 | Inc. Ab. | 6.00 | 8.50 | 30.00 | 40.00 |
| | 1914 | 3.110 | 4.50 | 5.75 | 13.50 | 20.00 |

**NOTE:** Wide and narrow dates exist for 1914.

### COPPER-NICKEL

| 432 | 1936 | 33.030 | .65 | 2.25 | 8.25 | 10.00 |
|---|---|---|---|---|---|---|
| | 1937 | 3.000 | 2.75 | 42.50 | 200.00 | 250.00 |
| | 1938 | 3.650 | 1.75 | 5.50 | 60.00 | 75.00 |
| | 1939 | 6.920 | 1.00 | 3.50 | 30.00 | 40.00 |
| | 1940 | 12.300 | .40 | 1.00 | 5.00 | 6.50 |
| | 1942 | 14.380 | .60 | 1.50 | 7.00 | 8.50 |
| | 1945 | 9.558 | .40 | .70 | 3.50 | 4.00 |
| | 1946 | 46.230 | .25 | .45 | 2.25 | 3.10 |

### 1.8125 g, .800 SILVER, .0466 oz ASW
**Reduced size, 15mm.**

| 429 | 1919 | 8.360 | 8.00 | 15.00 | 90.00 | 110.00 |
|---|---|---|---|---|---|---|

### BRONZE
**Benito Juarez**

| 433 | 1955 | 1.818 | .60 | 3.00 | 22.00 | 30.00 |
|---|---|---|---|---|---|---|
| | 1956 | 5.255 | .50 | 3.00 | 22.00 | 35.00 |
| | 1957 | 11.925 | .20 | .40 | 5.50 | 8.00 |
| | 1959 | 26.140 | .20 | .35 | .65 | 1.25 |
| | 1966 | 5.873 | .15 | .25 | .65 | 1.50 |
| | 1967 | 32.318 | .10 | .15 | .30 | .40 |

**COPPER-NICKEL**
**Variety I**
**Rev: 5 full rows of kernels, sharp stem, wide date.**

| KM# | Date | Mintage | VF | XF | Unc | BU |
|-----|------|---------|-----|-----|-----|-----|
| 434.1 | 1974 | 6.000 | — | .35 | .85 | 1.00 |
| | 1975 | 5.550 | .10 | .35 | .85 | 1.75 |
| | 1976 | 7.680 | .10 | .20 | .30 | .40 |
| | 1977 | 144.650 | 1.25 | 2.25 | 3.50 | 4.50 |
| | 1978 | 271.870 | — | 1.00 | 1.50 | 2.25 |
| | 1979 | 375.660 | — | .50 | 1.00 | 1.75 |
| | 1980/79 | 21.290 | 2.45 | 3.75 | 6.00 | 7.00 |
| | 1980 | I.A. | 1.50 | 2.00 | 4.50 | 5.00 |

**BRONZE**

| KM# | Date | Mintage | VF | XF | Unc | BU |
|-----|------|---------|-----|-----|-----|-----|
| 437 | 1920 | 4.835 | 40.00 | 110.00 | 600.00 | 700.00 |
| | 1935 | 20.000 | 5.50 | 8.50 | 85.00 | 125.00 |

**Variety II**
**Rev: 5 full, plus 1 partial row at left, blunt stem,**
**narrow date.**

| 434.2 | 1974 | Inc. Ab. | — | .10 | .25 | .35 |
|-----|------|---------|-----|-----|-----|-----|
| | 1977 | Inc. Ab. | — | .10 | .30 | .35 |
| | 1978 | Inc. Ab. | — | .10 | .30 | .40 |
| | 1979 | Inc. Ab. | .15 | .50 | 1.00 | 2.00 |
| | 1980 | Inc. Ab. | — | .10 | .30 | .35 |

**Variety III**
**Rev: 5 full, plus 1 partial row, blunt**
**stem and wide date.**

| 434.3 | 1980/79 | — | — | — | — | — |
|-----|------|---------|-----|-----|-----|-----|

**Variety III**
**Rev: 5 full, plus 1 partial row,**
**sharp stem and narrow date.**

| 434.4 | 1979 | — | — | — | — | — |
|-----|------|---------|-----|-----|-----|-----|

# 20 CENTAVOS

**3.3333 g, .720 SILVER, .0772 oz ASW**

| 438 | 1920 | 3.710 | 4.75 | 10.00 | 165.00 | 215.00 |
|-----|------|---------|-----|-----|-----|-----|
| | 1921 | 6.160 | 4.50 | 10.00 | 100.00 | 145.00 |
| | 1925 | 1.450 | 8.00 | 17.00 | 125.00 | 150.00 |
| | 1926/5 | 1.465 | 18.00 | 45.00 | 325.00 | 375.00 |
| | 1926 | Inc. Ab. | 4.50 | 6.25 | 80.00 | 110.00 |
| | 1927 | 1.405 | 3.75 | 6.25 | 80.00 | 115.00 |
| | 1928 | 3.630 | 2.50 | 4.50 | 14.50 | 19.50 |
| | 1930 | 1.000 | 3.50 | 6.25 | 22.00 | 30.00 |
| | 1933 | 2.500 | 2.25 | 2.75 | 10.00 | 11.50 |
| | 1934 | 2.500 | 2.25 | 3.00 | 11.00 | 12.50 |
| | 1935 | 2.460 | 2.25 | 2.75 | 10.00 | 11.50 |
| | 1937 | 10.000 | 2.25 | 2.50 | 4.75 | 5.50 |
| | 1939 | 8.800 | 1.75 | 2.00 | 4.00 | 5.00 |
| | 1940 | 3.000 | 1.75 | 2.00 | 3.50 | 5.00 |
| | 1941 | 5.740 | 1.50 | 2.00 | 3.00 | 3.50 |
| | 1942 | 12.460 | 1.50 | 2.00 | 3.25 | 3.80 |
| | 1943 | 3.955 | 2.00 | 2.50 | 3.50 | 4.25 |

**5.0000 g, .800 SILVER, .1286 oz ASW**

| 435 | 1905 | 2.565 | 9.00 | 15.00 | 150.00 | 175.00 |
|-----|------|---------|-----|-----|-----|-----|
| | 1906 | 6.860 | 7.25 | 14.50 | 60.00 | 80.00 |
| | 1907 straight 7 | | | | | |
| | | 4.000 | 8.50 | 17.50 | 65.00 | 95.00 |
| | 1907 curved 7 | | | | | |
| | | 5.435 | 7.50 | 13.50 | 70.00 | 90.00 |
| | 1908 | .350 | 85.00 | 200.00 | 1500. | — |
| | 1910 | 1.135 | 9.50 | 15.00 | 80.00 | 95.00 |
| | 1911 | 1.150 | 14.00 | 32.00 | 125.00 | 150.00 |
| | 1912 | .625 | 25.00 | 70.00 | 335.00 | 375.00 |
| | 1913 | 1.000 | 14.50 | 30.00 | 95.00 | 115.00 |
| | 1914 | 1.500 | 10.00 | 21.50 | 62.50 | 75.00 |

**BRONZE**

| 439 | 1943 | 46.350 | .75 | 2.75 | 18.00 | 25.00 |
|-----|------|---------|-----|-----|-----|-----|
| | 1944 | 83.650 | .40 | .65 | 8.00 | 10.00 |
| | 1945 | 26.801 | 1.10 | 3.50 | 9.50 | 12.00 |
| | 1946 | 25.695 | .90 | 2.00 | 6.00 | 8.25 |
| | 1951 | 11.385 | 2.50 | 5.50 | 80.00 | 100.00 |
| | 1952 | 6.560 | 2.50 | 4.50 | 25.00 | 32.50 |
| | 1953 | 26.948 | .35 | .75 | 7.25 | 11.00 |
| | 1954 | 40.108 | .35 | .80 | 8.00 | 11.50 |
| | 1955 | 16.950 | 2.50 | 6.00 | 60.00 | 75.00 |

**3.6250 g, .800 SILVER, .0932 oz ASW**
**Reduced size, 19mm.**

| 436 | 1919 | 4.155 | 25.00 | 50.00 | 195.00 | 245.00 |
|-----|------|---------|-----|-----|-----|-----|

| KM# | Date | Mintage | VF | XF | Unc | BU |
|---|---|---|---|---|---|---|
| 440 | 1955 | | | | | |
| | | Inc. KM439 | .65 | 1.50 | 13.50 | 18.50 |
| | 1956 | 22.431 | .30 | .35 | 3.00 | 5.00 |
| | 1957 | 13.455 | .45 | 1.25 | 9.00 | 12.00 |
| | 1959 | 6.017 | 4.00 | 7.50 | 65.00 | 95.00 |
| | 1960 | 39.756 | .15 | .25 | .85 | 1.25 |
| | 1963 | 14.869 | .25 | .35 | .90 | 1.25 |
| | 1964 | 28.654 | .25 | .40 | .90 | 1.25 |
| | 1965 | 74.162 | .20 | .40 | .85 | 1.20 |
| | 1966 | 43.745 | .15 | .25 | .90 | 1.30 |
| | 1967 | 46.487 | .20 | .55 | 1.20 | 1.50 |
| | 1968 | 15.477 | .30 | .55 | 1.35 | 1.65 |
| | 1969 | 63.647 | .20 | .40 | 1.00 | 1.50 |
| | 1970 | 76.287 | .15 | .20 | .90 | 1.30 |
| | 1971 | 49.892 | .30 | .50 | 1.40 | 1.75 |

| 441 | 1971 | | | | | |
|---|---|---|---|---|---|---|
| | | Inc. KM440 | .20 | .35 | 1.75 | 2.35 |
| | 1973 | 78.398 | .25 | .35 | .95 | 1.50 |
| | 1974 | 34.200 | .20 | .35 | 1.25 | 1.75 |

**COPPER-NICKEL**
**Francisco Madero**

| 442 | 1974 | 112.000 | .10 | .15 | .25 | .30 |
|---|---|---|---|---|---|---|
| | 1975 | 611.000 | .10 | .15 | .30 | .35 |
| | 1976 | 394.000 | .10 | .15 | .35 | .45 |
| | 1977 | 394.350 | .10 | .15 | .40 | .45 |
| | 1978 | 527.950 | .10 | .15 | .25 | .30 |
| | 1979 | 524.615 | .10 | .15 | .30 | .40 |
| | 1979 Doubled die obv. large/small letters | | | | | |
| | | — | 1.25 | 2.00 | 4.00 | 8.00 |
| | 1980 | 326.500 | .15 | .25 | .40 | .60 |
| | 1981 open 8 | | | | | |
| | | 106.205 | .30 | .50 | 1.00 | 2.00 |
| | 1981 closed 8, high date | | | | | |
| | | 248.500 | .30 | .50 | 1.00 | 2.00 |
| | 1981 closed 8, low date | | | | | |
| | | — | 1.00 | 1.50 | 3.50 | 4.25 |
| | 1981/1982 | — | 30.00 | 75.00 | 160.00 | 190.00 |
| | 1982 | 286.855 | .40 | .60 | .90 | 1.10 |
| | 1983 round top 3 | | | | | |
| | | 100.930 | .25 | .40 | 1.75 | 2.25 |
| | 1983 flat top 3 | | | | | |
| | | Inc. Ab. | .25 | .50 | 1.25 | 1.75 |
| | 1983 | 998 pcs. | — | — | Proof | 15.00 |

**NOTE:** The 1981/1982 overdate is often mistaken as 1982/1981.

**BRONZE**
**Olmec Culture**

| 491 | 1983 | 260.000 | .20 | .25 | .90 | 1.10 |
|---|---|---|---|---|---|---|
| | 1983 | 53 pcs. | — | — | Proof | 165.00 |
| | 1984 | 180.320 | .20 | .25 | 1.50 | 1.70 |

# 25 CENTAVOS

**3.3330 g, .300 SILVER, .0321 oz ASW**

| KM# | Date | Mintage | VF | XF | Unc | BU |
|---|---|---|---|---|---|---|
| 443 | 1950 | 77.060 | .50 | .75 | 1.75 | 2.25 |
| | 1951 | 41.172 | .50 | .75 | 1.60 | 2.00 |
| | 1952 | 29.264 | .75 | 1.10 | 1.80 | 2.50 |
| | 1953 | 38.144 | .60 | .70 | 1.50 | 2.00 |

**COPPER-NICKEL**
**Francisco Madero**

| 444 | 1964 | 20.686 | — | .15 | .25 | .40 |
|---|---|---|---|---|---|---|
| | 1966 closed beak | | | | | |
| | | .180 | .65 | 1.00 | 2.50 | 3.00 |
| | 1966 open beak | | | | | |
| | | Inc. Ab. | 1.75 | 3.50 | 10.00 | 14.00 |

# 50 CENTAVOS

**12.5000 g, .800 SILVER, .3215 oz ASW**

| 445 | 1905 | 2.446 | 12.50 | 20.00 | 150.00 | 225.00 |
|---|---|---|---|---|---|---|
| | 1906 open 9 | | | | | |
| | | 16.966 | 5.00 | 10.00 | 30.00 | 50.00 |
| | 1906 closed 9 | | | | | |
| | | Inc Ab. | 4.50 | 8.50 | 27.50 | 40.00 |
| | 1907 straight 7 | | | | | |
| | | 18.920 | 4.50 | 7.25 | 25.00 | 28.50 |
| | 1907 curved 7 | | | | | |
| | | 14.841 | 5.25 | 8.00 | 25.00 | 28.50 |
| | 1908 | .488 | 65.00 | 150.00 | 525.00 | 625.00 |
| | 1912 | 3.736 | 10.00 | 12.50 | 45.00 | 60.00 |
| | 1913/07 | 10.510 | 30.00 | 70.00 | 225.00 | 275.00 |
| | 1913/2 | Inc. Ab. | 18.00 | 22.50 | 65.00 | 85.00 |
| | 1913 | Inc. Ab. | 5.50 | 8.50 | 25.00 | 30.00 |
| | 1914 | 7.710 | 6.75 | 13.50 | 30.00 | 40.00 |
| | 1916 narrow date | | | | | |
| | | .480 | 50.00 | 75.00 | 200.00 | 290.00 |
| | 1916 wide date | | | | | |
| | | Inc Ab. | 50.00 | 75.00 | 200.00 | 290.00 |
| | 1917 | 37.112 | 5.50 | 8.50 | 20.00 | 22.50 |
| | 1918 | 1.320 | 60.00 | 110.00 | 250.00 | 335.00 |

**9.0625 g, .800 SILVER, .2331 oz ASW**
**Reduced size, 27mm.**

| KM# | Date | Mintage | VF | XF | Unc | BU |
|---|---|---|---|---|---|---|
| 446 | 1918/7 | 2.760 | 525.00 | 625.00 | 1250. | — |
|  | 1918 | Inc. Ab. | 15.00 | 50.00 | 325.00 | 400.00 |
|  | 1919 | 29.670 | 7.00 | 16.50 | 100.00 | 125.00 |

**8.3333 g, .720 SILVER, .1929 oz ASW**

| 447 | 1919 | 10.200 | 8.00 | 18.50 | 87.50 | 110.00 |
|---|---|---|---|---|---|---|
|  | 1920 | 27.166 | 6.00 | 8.50 | 65.00 | 80.00 |
|  | 1921 | 21.864 | 6.50 | 9.00 | 80.00 | 95.00 |
|  | 1925 | 3.280 | 14.00 | 30.00 | 130.00 | 160.00 |
|  | 1937 | 20.000 | 3.75 | 5.00 | 7.50 | 8.50 |
|  | 1938 | .100 | 40.00 | 75.00 | 225.00 | 300.00 |
|  | 1939 | 10.440 | 5.25 | 7.25 | 14.00 | 16.50 |
|  | 1942 | .800 | 5.50 | 7.50 | 15.00 | 17.00 |
|  | 1943 | 41.512 | 2.75 | 4.00 | 5.50 | 6.50 |
|  | 1944 | 55.806 | 3.00 | 3.75 | 5.50 | 6.50 |
|  | 1945 | 56.766 | 3.00 | 3.75 | 6.00 | 6.50 |

**7.9730 g, .420 SILVER, .1076 oz ASW**

| 448 | 1935 | 70.800 | 2.20 | 2.75 | 5.00 | 6.00 |
|---|---|---|---|---|---|---|

**6.6600 g, .300 SILVER, .0642 oz ASW**
**Cuauhtemoc**

| 449 | 1950 | 13.570 | 1.50 | 1.80 | 3.00 | 4.00 |
|---|---|---|---|---|---|---|
|  | 1951 | 3.650 | 2.00 | 2.50 | 3.75 | 5.00 |

**BRONZE**

| 450 | 1955 | 3.502 | 1.20 | 2.20 | 27.50 | 35.00 |
|---|---|---|---|---|---|---|
|  | 1956 | 34.643 | .65 | 1.00 | 3.25 | 4.50 |
|  | 1957 | 9.675 | 1.00 | 2.00 | 6.50 | 7.50 |
|  | 1959 | 4.540 | .35 | .50 | 1.50 | 2.00 |

**COPPER-NICKEL**

| KM# | Date | Mintage | VF | XF | Unc | BU |
|---|---|---|---|---|---|---|
| 451 | 1964 | 43.806 | .15 | .20 | .45 | .65 |
|  | 1965 | 14.326 | .20 | .25 | .45 | .65 |
|  | 1966 | 1.726 | .20 | .40 | 1.30 | 1.75 |
|  | 1967 | 55.144 | .20 | .30 | .65 | 1.00 |
|  | 1968 | 80.438 | .15 | .30 | .65 | .80 |
|  | 1969 | 87.640 | .20 | .35 | .80 | 1.15 |

**Obv: Stylized eagle.**

| 452 | 1970 | 76.236 | .15 | .20 | .90 | 1.25 |
|---|---|---|---|---|---|---|
|  | 1971 | 125.288 | .15 | .20 | .90 | 1.30 |
|  | 1972 | 16.000 | 1.25 | 2.00 | 3.00 | 4.75 |
|  | 1975 Dots |  |  |  |  |  |
|  |  | 177.958 | .60 | 1.25 | 3.50 | 6.00 |
|  | 1975 No dots |  |  |  |  |  |
|  |  | Inc. Ab. | .15 | .20 | .50 | .75 |
|  | 1976 Dots |  |  |  |  |  |
|  |  | 37,480 | .75 | 1.25 | 5.00 | 6.00 |
|  | 1976 No dots |  |  |  |  |  |
|  |  | Inc. Ab. | .15 | .20 | .50 | .75 |
|  | 1977 | 12.410 | 6.50 | 10.00 | 32.50 | 42.50 |
|  | 1978 | 85.400 | .15 | .25 | .50 | .75 |
|  | 1979 round 2nd 9 in date |  |  |  |  |  |
|  |  | 229.000 | .15 | .25 | .50 | .65 |
|  | 1979 square 9's in date |  |  |  |  |  |
|  |  | Inc. Ab. | .20 | .40 | 1.60 | 2.10 |
|  | 1980 narrow date, square 9 |  |  |  |  |  |
|  |  | 89.978 | .45 | .75 | 1.00 | 2.00 |
|  | 1980 wide date, round 9 |  |  |  |  |  |
|  |  | 178.188 | .20 | .25 | 1.00 | 1.15 |
|  | 1981 rectangular 9, narrow date |  |  |  |  |  |
|  |  | 142.212 | .50 | .75 | 1.75 | 2.50 |
|  | 1981 round 9, wide date |  |  |  |  |  |
|  |  | Inc. Ab. | .30 | .50 | 1.25 | 1.75 |
|  | 1982 | 45.474 | .20 | .40 | 1.50 | 2.40 |
|  | 1983 | 90.318 | .50 | .75 | 2.25 | 2.85 |
|  | 1983 | 998 pcs. | — | — | Proof | 15.00 |

**NOTE:** Coins dated 1975 and 1976 exist with and without dots in centers of three circles on plumage on reverse. Edge varieties exist.

**STAINLESS STEEL**
**Palenque Culture**

| 492 | 1983 | 99.540 | — | .30 | 1.50 | 2.50 |
|---|---|---|---|---|---|---|
|  | 1983 | 53 pcs. | — | — | Proof | 165.00 |

## UN (1) PESO

**27.0700 g, .903 SILVER, .7859 oz ASW**
**'Caballito'**

| KM# | Date | Mintage | VF | XF | Unc | BU |
|-----|------|---------|-----|-----|-----|-----|
| 453 | 1910 | 3.814 | 30.00 | 45.00 | 155.00 | 250.00 |
| | 1911 long lower left ray on rev. | | | | | |
| | | 1.227 | 45.00 | 75.00 | 200.00 | 275.00 |
| | 1911 short lower left ray on rev. | | | | | |
| | | Inc. Ab. | 135.00 | 225.00 | 600.00 | 800.00 |
| | 1912 | .322 | 95.00 | 200.00 | 350.00 | 500.00 |
| | 1913/2 | 2.880 | 45.00 | 75.00 | 265.00 | 400.00 |
| | 1913 | Inc. Ab. | 45.00 | 70.00 | 170.00 | 250.00 |
| | 1914 | .120 | 600.00 | 950.00 | 3000. | — |

**NOTE:** 1913 coins exist with even and unevenly spaced date.

**18.1300 g, .800 SILVER, .4663 oz ASW**

| KM# | Date | Mintage | VF | XF | Unc | BU |
|-----|------|---------|-----|-----|-----|-----|
| 454 | 1918 | 3.050 | 30.00 | 115.00 | 1350. | 2100. |
| | 1919 | 6.151 | 18.00 | 45.00 | 900.00 | 1600. |

**16.6600 g, .720 SILVER, .3856 oz ASW**

| KM# | Date | Mintage | VF | XF | Unc | BU |
|-----|------|---------|-----|-----|-----|-----|
| 455 | 1920/10 | 8.830 | 50.00 | 90.00 | 320.00 | — |
| | 1920 | Inc. Ab. | 6.50 | 18.00 | 150.00 | 200.00 |
| | 1921 | 5.480 | 8.00 | 20.00 | 160.00 | 200.00 |
| | 1922 | 33.620 | 3.25 | 5.00 | 20.00 | 26.00 |
| | 1923 | 35.280 | 3.25 | 5.00 | 20.00 | 28.00 |
| | 1924 | 33.060 | 3.25 | 5.00 | 20.00 | 26.00 |
| | 1925 | 9.160 | 4.50 | 9.50 | 60.00 | 80.00 |
| | 1926 | 28.840 | 3.25 | 5.00 | 20.00 | 25.00 |
| | 1927 | 5.060 | 5.00 | 10.00 | 55.00 | 80.00 |
| | 1932 open 9 | | | | | |
| | | 50.770 | 2.75 | 4.00 | 5.00 | 7.00 |

| KM# | Date | Mintage | VF | XF | Unc | BU |
|-----|------|---------|-----|-----|-----|-----|
| 455 | 1932 closed 9 | | | | | |
| | | Inc Ab. | 2.75 | 4.00 | 5.00 | 7.00 |
| | 1933/2 | 43.920 | 15.00 | 25.00 | 80.00 | — |
| | 1933 | Inc. Ab. | 2.75 | 4.00 | 5.00 | 7.00 |
| | 1934 | 22.070 | 3.25 | 4.50 | 9.00 | 10.50 |
| | 1935 | 8.050 | 4.50 | 6.00 | 11.50 | 13.50 |
| | 1938 | 30.000 | 2.75 | 4.00 | 6.00 | 7.50 |
| | 1940 | 20.000 | 2.75 | 3.50 | 5.00 | 6.50 |
| | 1943 | 47.662 | 2.75 | 3.25 | 4.50 | 6.00 |
| | 1944 | 39.522 | 2.75 | 3.50 | 4.50 | 6.00 |
| | 1945 | 37.300 | 2.75 | 3.50 | 4.50 | 6.00 |

**14.0000 g, .500 SILVER, .2250 oz ASW**
**Jose Morelos y Pavon**

| KM# | Date | Mintage | VF | XF | Unc | BU |
|-----|------|---------|-----|-----|-----|-----|
| 456 | 1947 | 61.460 | 1.75 | 2.50 | 4.50 | 5.50 |
| | 1948 | 22.915 | 2.25 | 3.50 | 5.50 | 6.50 |
| | 1949 | *4.000 | — | 1200. | 1600. | 2500. |
| | 1949 | — | — | — | Proof | 5000. |

**\*NOTE:** Not released for circulation.

**13.3300 g, .300 SILVER, .1285 oz ASW**
**Jose Morelos y Pavon**

| KM# | Date | Mintage | VF | XF | Unc | BU |
|-----|------|---------|-----|-----|-----|-----|
| 457 | 1950 | 3.287 | 2.50 | 4.00 | 7.00 | 8.50 |

**16.0000 g, .100 SILVER, .0514 oz ASW**
**100th Anniversary of Constitution**

| KM# | Date | Mintage | VF | XF | Unc | BU |
|-----|------|---------|-----|-----|-----|-----|
| 458 | 1957 | .500 | 3.50 | 5.00 | 13.50 | 18.00 |

**Jose Morelos y Pavon**

| KM# | Date | Mintage | VF | XF | Unc | BU |
|---|---|---|---|---|---|---|
| 459 | 1957 | 28.273 | .65 | 1.00 | 2.25 | 3.00 |
| | 1958 | 41.899 | .65 | .85 | 1.85 | 2.50 |
| | 1959 | 27.369 | 1.25 | 2.00 | 5.50 | 7.00 |
| | 1960 | 26.259 | .65 | 1.10 | 3.25 | 3.50 |
| | 1961 | 52.601 | .50 | .90 | 2.25 | 3.00 |
| | 1962 | 61.094 | .50 | .90 | 2.10 | 2.75 |
| | 1963 | 26.394 | BV | .80 | 2.00 | 2.40 |
| | 1964 | 15.615 | BV | .75 | 2.00 | 2.40 |
| | 1965 | 5.004 | BV | .60 | 1.85 | 2.00 |
| | 1966 | 30.998 | BV | .60 | 1.85 | 2.00 |
| | 1967 | 9.308 | BV | .60 | 2.75 | 3.50 |

### COPPER-NICKEL
### Jose Morelos y Pavon

| KM# | Date | Mintage | VF | XF | Unc | BU |
|---|---|---|---|---|---|---|
| 460 | 1970 narrow date | | | | | |
| | | 102.715 | .25 | .35 | .75 | .90 |
| | 1970 wide date | | | | | |
| | | Inc. Ab. | 1.25 | 2.50 | 8.00 | 10.00 |
| | 1971 | 426.222 | .20 | .25 | .50 | .65 |
| | 1972 | 120.000 | .20 | .25 | .40 | .65 |
| | 1974 | 63.700 | .20 | .25 | .65 | .90 |

| | | | | | | |
|---|---|---|---|---|---|---|
| | 1975 tall narrow date | | | | | |
| | | 205.979 | .25 | .45 | 1.00 | 1.35 |

| | | | | | | |
|---|---|---|---|---|---|---|
| | 1975 short wide date | | | | | |
| | | Inc. Ab. | .30 | .40 | .75 | 1.00 |
| | 1976 | 94.489 | .15 | .20 | .50 | .75 |
| | 1977 thick date | | | | | |
| | | 94.364 | .25 | .45 | 1.00 | 1.25 |
| | 1977 thin date | | | | | |
| | | Inc. Ab. | 1.00 | 2.00 | 6.50 | 13.50 |
| | 1978 closed 8 | | | | | |
| | | 208.300 | .20 | .30 | .65 | 1.15 |
| | 1978 open 8 | | | | | |
| | | 55.140 | .75 | 1.50 | 11.00 | 16.50 |
| | 1979 thin date | | | | | |
| | | 117.884 | .20 | .30 | 1.00 | 1.50 |
| | 1979 thick date | | | | | |
| | | Inc. Ab. | .40 | .60 | 1.25 | 1.75 |
| | 1980 closed 8 | | | | | |
| | | 318.800 | .25 | .35 | 1.00 | 1.20 |
| | 1980 open 8 | | | | | |
| | | 23.865 | .75 | 1.50 | 9.00 | 12.75 |
| | 1981 closed 8 | | | | | |
| | | 413.349 | .20 | .30 | .85 | 1.00 |
| | 1981 open 8 | | | | | |
| | | 58.616 | .50 | 1.25 | 7.00 | 8.50 |
| | 1982 | 235.000 | .25 | .75 | 2.25 | 2.50 |
| | 1983 wide date | | | | | |
| | | 100.000 | .50 | 1.10 | 3.00 | 3.50 |
| | 1983 narrow date | | | | | |
| | | Inc. Ab. | .30 | .45 | 3.25 | 3.75 |
| | 1983 | 1,051 | — | — | Proof | 15.00 |

### STAINLESS STEEL
### Jose Morelos y Pavon

| KM# | Date | Mintage | VF | XF | Unc | BU |
|---|---|---|---|---|---|---|
| 496 | 1984 | 722.802 | .10 | .25 | .65 | .85 |
| | 1985 | 985.000 | .10 | .25 | .50 | .75 |
| | 1986 | 740.000 | .10 | .25 | .50 | .75 |
| | 1987 | 250.000 | — | .25 | .50 | .80 |
| | 1987 | 2 known | — | — | Proof | 1250. |

## DOS (2) PESOS

### 1.6666 g, .900 GOLD, .0482 oz AGW

| KM# | Date | Mintage | Fine | VF | XF | Unc |
|---|---|---|---|---|---|---|
| 461 | 1919 | 1.670 | — | BV | 25.00 | 32.00 |
| | 1920 | 4.282 | — | BV | 25.00 | 32.00 |
| | 1944 | .010 | 27.50 | 35.00 | 50.00 | 80.00 |
| | 1945 | *.140 | — | — | | BV + 20% |
| | 1946 | .168 | 30.00 | 45.00 | 55.00 | 80.00 |
| | 1947 | .025 | 27.50 | 35.00 | 50.00 | 65.00 |
| | 1948 | .045 | — | no specimens known | | |

**\*NOTE:** During 1951-1972 a total of 4,590,493 pieces were restruck, most likely dated 1945. In 1996 matte restrikes were produced.

### 26.6667 g, .900 SILVER, .7717 oz ASW
### Centennial of Independence

| KM# | Date | Mintage | VF | XF | Unc | BU |
|---|---|---|---|---|---|---|
| 462 | 1921 | 1.278 | 30.00 | 55.00 | 285.00 | 425.00 |

## DOS Y MEDIO (2-1/2) PESOS

### 2.0833 g, .900 GOLD, .0602 oz AGW

| KM# | Date | Mintage | Fine | VF | XF | Unc |
|---|---|---|---|---|---|---|
| 463 | 1918 | 1.704 | — | BV | 28.00 | 45.00 |
| | 1919 | .984 | — | BV | 28.00 | 45.00 |
| | 1920/10 | .607 | — | BV | 55.00 | 100.00 |
| | 1920 | Inc. Ab. | — | BV | 28.00 | 45.00 |
| | 1944 | .020 | — | BV | 28.00 | 45.00 |
| | 1945 | *.180 | — | — | | BV + 18% |
| | 1946 | .163 | — | BV | 28.00 | 45.00 |
| | 1947 | .024 | 200.00 | 265.00 | 325.00 | 400.00 |
| | 1948 | .063 | BV | 35.00 | 40.00 | 65.00 |

**\*NOTE:** During 1951-1972 a total of 5,025,087 pieces were restruck, most likely dated 1945. In 1996 matte restrikes were produced.

## CINCO (5) PESOS

### 4.1666 g, .900 GOLD, .1205 oz AGW

| KM# | Date | Mintage | Fine | VF | XF | Unc |
|-----|------|---------|------|-----|-----|-----|
| 464 | 1905 | .018 | 100.00 | 150.00 | 200.00 | 400.00 |
| | 1906 | 4.638 | — | BV | 50.00 | 70.00 |
| | 1907 | 1.088 | — | BV | 50.00 | 70.00 |
| | 1910 | .100 | BV | 55.00 | 70.00 | 120.00 |
| | 1918/7 | .609 | BV | 55.00 | 70.00 | 120.00 |
| | 1918 | Inc. Ab. | — | BV | 50.00 | 70.00 |
| | 1919 | .506 | — | BV | 50.00 | 70.00 |
| | 1920 | 2.385 | — | BV | 50.00 | 70.00 |
| | 1955 | *.048 | — | — | | BV + 11% |

**\*NOTE:** During 1955-1972 a total of 1,767,645 pieces were restruck, most likely dated 1955. In 1996 matte restrikes were produced.

### 30.0000 g, .900 SILVER, .8681 oz ASW
#### Cuauhtemoc

| KM# | Date | Mintage | VF | XF | Unc | BU |
|-----|------|---------|-----|-----|-----|-----|
| 465 | 1947 | 5.110 | BV | 6.25 | 8.75 | 10.00 |
| | 1948 | 26.740 | BV | 6.00 | 8.00 | 9.00 |

### 27.7800 g, .720 SILVER, .6431 oz ASW
#### Opening of Southern Railroad

| KM# | Date | Mintage | VF | XF | Unc | BU |
|-----|------|---------|-----|-----|-----|-----|
| 466 | 1950 | .200 | 22.50 | 27.50 | 35.00 | 45.00 |

**NOTE:** It is recorded that 100,000 pieces were melted to be used for the 1968 Mexican Olympic 25 Pesos.

#### Miguel Hidalgo y Costilla

| | | | | | | |
|-----|------|---------|-----|-----|-----|-----|
| 467 | 1951 | 4.958 | BV | 5.75 | 7.00 | 10.00 |
| | 1952 | 9.595 | BV | 5.50 | 6.75 | 9.00 |
| | 1953 | 20.376 | BV | 5.25 | 6.75 | 9.00 |
| | 1954 | .030 | 27.50 | 45.00 | 70.00 | 85.00 |

#### Bicentennial of Hidalgo's Birth

| | | | | | | |
|-----|------|---------|-----|-----|-----|-----|
| 468 | 1953 | 1.000 | BV | 5.50 | 7.50 | 10.00 |

| KM# | Date | Mintage | VF | XF | Unc | BU |
|---|---|---|---|---|---|---|
| 472 | 1973 | 19.405 | 1.25 | 2.10 | 5.00 | 7.50 |
| | 1974 | 34.500 | .50 | .80 | 1.75 | 2.25 |
| | 1976 small date | | | | | |
| | | 26.121 | .75 | 1.45 | 3.50 | 4.25 |
| | 1976 large date | | | | | |
| | | 121.550 | .35 | .50 | 1.50 | 1.75 |
| | 1977 | 102.000 | .50 | .75 | 1.50 | 2.00 |
| | 1978 | 25.700 | 1.00 | 1.50 | 5.25 | 6.75 |

**18.0500 g, .720 SILVER, .4178 oz ASW**
**Reduced size, 36mm.**

| KM# | Date | Mintage | VF | XF | Unc | BU |
|---|---|---|---|---|---|---|
| 469 | 1955 | 4.271 | 3.25 | 4.00 | 4.75 | 7.00 |
| | 1956 | 4.596 | 3.25 | 4.00 | 4.75 | 7.00 |
| | 1957 | 3.464 | 3.25 | 4.00 | 4.75 | 7.00 |

**Quetzalcoatl**

| 485 | 1980 | 266.900 | .25 | .50 | 1.75 | 2.25 |
|---|---|---|---|---|---|---|
| | 1981 | 30.500 | .45 | .65 | 2.75 | 3.25 |
| | 1982 | 20.000 | 1.50 | 2.35 | 4.25 | 5.25 |
| | 1982 | 1,051 | — | — | Proof | 18.00 |
| | 1983 | 7 known | — | — | Proof | 1150. |
| | 1984 | 16.300 | 1.25 | 2.00 | 4.75 | 6.00 |
| | 1985 | 76.900 | 2.25 | 4.00 | 4.50 | 5.25 |

**100th Anniversary of Constitution**

| 470 | 1957 | .200 | 5.50 | 7.50 | 13.50 | 15.50 |
|---|---|---|---|---|---|---|

**BRASS**
**Circulation Coinage**

| 502 | 1985 | 30.000 | — | .15 | .35 | .50 |
|---|---|---|---|---|---|---|
| | 1987 | 81.900 | 8.00 | 9.50 | 12.50 | 15.00 |
| | 1988 | 76.600 | — | .10 | .25 | .35 |
| | 1988 | 2 known | — | — | Proof | 600.00 |

## DIEZ (10) PESOS

**Centennial of Carranza's Birth**

| 471 | 1959 | 1.000 | BV | 4.50 | 6.50 | 9.50 |
|---|---|---|---|---|---|---|

**8.3333 g, .900 GOLD, .2411 oz AGW**
**Miguel Hidalgo**

| KM# | Date | Mintage | Fine | VF | XF | Unc |
|---|---|---|---|---|---|---|
| 473 | 1905 | .039 | 110.00 | 125.00 | 155.00 | 200.00 |
| | 1906 | 2.949 | — | BV | 100.00 | 150.00 |
| | 1907 | 1.589 | — | BV | 100.00 | 150.00 |
| | 1908 | .890 | — | BV | 100.00 | 150.00 |
| | 1910 | .451 | — | BV | 100.00 | 150.00 |
| | 1916 | .026 | 110.00 | 120.00 | 150.00 | 275.00 |
| | 1917 | 1.967 | — | BV | 100.00 | 150.00 |
| | 1919 | .266 | — | BV | 100.00 | 150.00 |
| | 1920 | .012 | 150.00 | 250.00 | 400.00 | 650.00 |
| | 1959 | *.050 | — | — | | BV + 7% |

**Small date          Large date**
**COPPER-NICKEL**
**Vicente Guerrero**

| 472 | 1971 | 28.457 | .50 | .95 | 2.50 | 3.25 |
|---|---|---|---|---|---|---|
| | 1972 | 75.000 | .60 | 1.25 | 2.00 | 2.50 |

**\*NOTE:** During 1961-1972 a total of 954,983 pieces were restruck, most likely dated 1959. In 1996 matte restrikes were produced.

**150th Anniversary - War of Independence**

| KM# | Date | Mintage | VF | XF | Unc | BU |
|-----|------|---------|-----|------|------|-------|
| 476 | 1960 | 1.000 | BV | 6.00 | 9.00 | 12.00 |

**28.8800 g, .900 SILVER, .8357 oz ASW**
**Miguel Hidalgo**

| KM# | Date | Mintage | VF | XF | Unc | BU |
|-----|------|---------|-----|------|------|-------|
| 474 | 1955 | .585 | BV | 6.00 | 8.75 | 11.50 |
|     | 1956 | 3.535 | BV | 5.50 | 8.50 | 12.00 |

**COPPER-NICKEL**
**Miguel Hidalgo**
**Thin flan, 1.6mm.**

| KM# | Date | Mintage | VF | XF | Unc | BU |
|-------|------|---------|------|------|-------|--------|
| 477.1 | 1974 | 3.900 | .50 | 1.00 | 3.50 | 4.25 |
|       | 1974 | — | — | — | Proof | 625.00 |
|       | 1975 | 1.000 | 2.25 | 3.25 | 7.75 | 15.00 |
|       | 1976 | 74.500 | .25 | .75 | 1.75 | 2.25 |
|       | 1977 | 79.620 | .50 | 1.00 | 2.00 | 3.00 |

**Thick flan, 2.3mm.**

| KM# | Date | Mintage | VF | XF | Unc | BU |
|-------|------|---------|------|------|-------|--------|
| 477.2 | 1978 | 124.850 | .50 | .75 | 2.50 | 2.75 |
|       | 1979 | 57.200 | .50 | .75 | 2.25 | 2.50 |
|       | 1980 | 55.200 | .50 | .75 | 2.50 | 3.75 |
|       | 1981 | 222.768 | .40 | .60 | 2.25 | 2.60 |
|       | 1982 | 151.770 | .50 | .80 | 2.50 | 3.50 |
|       | 1982 | 1,051 | — | — | Proof | 18.00 |
|       | 1983 | 3 known | — | — | Proof | 1600. |
|       | 1985 | 58.000 | 1.25 | 1.75 | 5.75 | 7.50 |

**STAINLESS STEEL**
**Miguel Hidalgo**

| KM# | Date | Mintage | VF | XF | Unc | BU |
|-----|------|---------|-----|-----|-------|--------|
| 512 | 1985 | 257.000 | — | .15 | .50 | .75 |
|     | 1986 | 392.000 | — | .15 | .50 | 1.50 |
|     | 1987 | 305.000 | — | .15 | .35 | .50 |
|     | 1988 | 500.300 | — | .15 | .25 | .35 |
|     | 1989 | — | .20 | .25 | .75 | 1.50 |
|     | 1990 | — | — | .25 | .75 | 1.25 |
|     | 1990 | 2 known | — | — | Proof | 500.00 |

**NOTE:** Date varieties exist.

**100th Anniversary of Constitution**

| KM# | Date | Mintage | VF | XF | Unc | BU |
|-----|------|---------|-------|-------|-------|-------|
| 475 | 1957 | .100 | 12.50 | 22.50 | 40.00 | 48.00 |

## VEINTE (20) PESOS

**16.6666 g, .900 GOLD, .4823 oz AGW**

| KM# | Date | Mintage | Fine | VF | XF | Unc |
|-----|------|---------|------|-----|-----|-----|
| 478 | 1917 | .852 | — | BV | 170.00 | 200.00 |
| | 1918 | 2.831 | — | BV | 170.00 | 200.00 |
| | 1919 | 1.094 | — | BV | 170.00 | 200.00 |
| | 1920/10 | .462 | — | BV | 175.00 | 210.00 |
| | 1920 | Inc. Ab. | — | BV | 170.00 | 200.00 |
| | 1921/11 | .922 | — | BV | 175.00 | 210.00 |
| | 1921 | Inc. Ab. | — | BV | 170.00 | 200.00 |
| | 1959 | *.013 | — | — | | BV + 4% |

**\*NOTE:** During 1960-1971 a total of 1,158,414 pieces were restruck, most likely dated 1959. In 1996 matte restrikes were produced.

**COPPER-NICKEL**

| KM# | Date | Mintage | VF | XF | Unc | BU |
|-----|------|---------|-----|-----|------|------|
| 486 | 1980 | 84.900 | .50 | .85 | 2.50 | 3.40 |
| | 1981 | 250.573 | .60 | .80 | 2.50 | 3.50 |
| | 1982 | 236.892 | 1.00 | 1.75 | 2.75 | 3.85 |
| | 1982 | 1,051 | — | — | Proof | 18.00 |
| | 1983 | 3 known | — | — | Proof | — |
| | 1984 | 55.000 | 1.00 | 1.50 | 3.75 | 7.50 |

**BRASS**
**Guadalupe Victoria, First President**

| KM# | Date | Mintage | VF | XF | Unc | BU |
|-----|------|---------|-----|-----|------|------|
| 508 | 1985 wide date | | | | | |
| | | 25.000 | .10 | .20 | 1.00 | 1.25 |
| | 1985 narrow date | | | | | |
| | | Inc. Ab. | .10 | .25 | 1.50 | 2.00 |
| | 1986 | 10.000 | 1.00 | 1.75 | 5.00 | 6.00 |
| | 1988 | 355.200 | .10 | .20 | .50 | 1.00 |
| | 1989 | — | .15 | .30 | 1.50 | 2.00 |
| | 1990 | — | .15 | .30 | 1.50 | 2.50 |
| | 1990 | 3 known | — | — | Proof | 475.00 |

## VEINTICINCO (25) PESOS

**22.5000 g, .720 SILVER, .5209 oz ASW**
**Summer Olympics - Mexico City**
**Type I, rings aligned.**

| KM# | Date | Mintage | VF | XF | Unc | BU |
|-----|------|---------|-----|-----|------|------|
| 479.1 | 1968 | 27.182 | BV | 4.00 | 4.75 | 6.00 |

**Type II, center ring low.**

| | | | | | | |
|-----|------|---------|-----|-----|------|------|
| 479.2 | 1968 | Inc. Ab. | 4.00 | 5.00 | 9.00 | 10.50 |

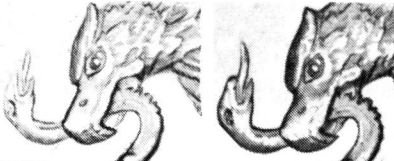

**Normal tongue    Long curved tongue**
**Type III, center rings low.**
**Snake with long curved tongue.**

| | | | | | | |
|-----|------|---------|-----|-----|------|------|
| 479.3 | 1968 | Inc. Ab. | 4.25 | 5.25 | 9.50 | 11.00 |

**Benito Juarez**

| | | | | | | |
|-----|------|---------|-----|-----|------|------|
| 480 | 1972 | 2.000 | BV | 4.00 | 5.50 | 6.50 |

**7.7760 g, .720 SILVER, .1800 oz ASW, 24mm**
**1986 World Cup Soccer Games**

| KM# | Date | Mintage | VF | XF | Unc | BU |
|-----|------|---------|----|----|-----|-----|
| 497 | 1985 | .354 | — | — | — | 7.50 |

**8.4060 g, .925 SILVER, .2450 oz ASW**
**Rev: W/o fineness statement.**

| | | | | | | |
|-----|------|------|----|----|-------|------|
| 497a | 1986 | — | — | — | Proof | 9.00 |

**1986 World Cup Soccer Games**

| | | | | | |
|-----|------|------|----|-------|------|
| 503 | 1985 | .277 | — | — | Proof | 9.00 |

**1986 World Cup Soccer Games**

| | | | | | |
|-----|------|------|----|-------|------|
| 514 | 1985 | .234 | — | — | Proof | 9.00 |

**1986 World Cup Soccer Games**

| | | | | | |
|-----|------|------|----|-------|------|
| 519 | 1986 | — | — | — | Proof | 9.00 |

**7.7758 g, .999 SILVER, .2500 oz ASW**
**Eagle Warrior**

| KM# | Date | Mintage | VF | XF | Unc |
|-----|------|---------|----|----|-----|
| 554 | 1992 | .050 | — | — | 6.50 |
| | 1992 | 3,000 | — | Proof | 10.50 |

# 50 PESOS

**41.6666 g, .900 GOLD, 1.2057 oz AGW**
**Centennial of Independence**

| KM# | Date | Mintage | Fine | VF | XF | Unc |
|-----|------|---------|------|----|----|-----|
| 481 | 1921 | .180 | — | — | BV | 475.00 |
| | 1922 | .463 | — | — | BV | 420.00 |
| | 1923 | .432 | — | — | BV | 420.00 |
| | 1924 | .439 | — | — | BV | 420.00 |
| | 1925 | .716 | — | — | BV | 420.00 |
| | 1926 | .600 | — | — | BV | 420.00 |
| | 1927 | .606 | — | — | BV | 420.00 |
| | 1928 | .538 | — | — | BV | 420.00 |
| | 1929 | .458 | — | — | BV | 420.00 |
| | 1930 | .372 | — | — | BV | 420.00 |
| | 1931 | .137 | — | — | BV | 440.00 |
| | 1944 | .593 | — | — | BV | 420.00 |
| | 1945 | 1.012 | — | — | BV | 420.00 |
| | 1946 | 1.588 | — | — | BV | 420.00 |
| | 1947 | .309 | — | — | | BV + 3% |
| | 1947 | — | — | — | —Specimen | 6500. |

**NOTE:** During 1949-1972 a total of 3,975,654 pieces were restruck, most likely dated 1947. In 1996 matte restrikes were produced.

**COPPER-NICKEL**
**Coyolxauhqui**

| KM# | Date | Mintage | VF | XF | Unc | BU |
|-----|------|---------|------|------|-------|--------|
| 490 | 1982 | 222.890 | 1.00 | 2.50 | 5.00 | 6.25 |
| | 1983 | 45.000 | 1.50 | 3.00 | 6.00 | 6.50 |
| | 1983 | 1,051 | — | — | Proof | 22.00 |
| | 1984 | 73.537 | 1.00 | 1.35 | 3.50 | 4.00 |
| | 1984 | 4 known | — | — | Proof | 750.00 |

**NOTE:** Doubled die examples of 1982 and 1983 dates exist.

### Benito Juarez

| KM# | Date | Mintage | VF | XF | Unc | BU |
|---|---|---|---|---|---|---|
| 495 | 1984 | 94.216 | .65 | 1.25 | 2.75 | 3.50 |
| | 1985 | 296.000 | .25 | .45 | 1.50 | 2.25 |
| | 1986 | 50.000 | 5.00 | 7.00 | 11.00 | 12.50 |
| | 1987 | 210.000 | .25 | .45 | 1.00 | 1.25 |
| | 1988 | 80.200 | 6.25 | 9.00 | 12.50 | 14.50 |

### STAINLESS STEEL

| | | | | | | |
|---|---|---|---|---|---|---|
| 495a | 1988 | 353.300 | — | .20 | .75 | 1.50 |
| | 1990 | — | — | .30 | 1.00 | 2.00 |
| | 1992 | — | — | .25 | 1.00 | 2.75 |

### 1986 World Cup Soccer Games

| KM# | Date | Mintage | VF | XF | Unc | BU |
|---|---|---|---|---|---|---|
| 523 | 1986 | .190 | — | — | Proof | 13.50 |

**15.5520 g, .720 SILVER, .3601 oz ASW**
**1986 World Cup Soccer Games**

| | | | | | | |
|---|---|---|---|---|---|---|
| 498 | 1985 | .347 | — | — | — | 8.50 |

**16.8310 g, .925 SILVER, .5000 oz ASW**
**Rev: W/o fineness statement.**

| | | | | | | |
|---|---|---|---|---|---|---|
| 498a | 1986 | .010 | — | — | Proof | 13.50 |

**15.5500 g, .999 SILVER, .5000 oz ASW**
**50th Anniversary - Nationalization of Oil Industry**

| | | | | | | |
|---|---|---|---|---|---|---|
| 532 | ND(1988) | .030 | — | — | 12.00 | 15.00 |

**15.5517 g, .999 SILVER, .5000 oz ASW**
**Eagle Warrior**

| KM# | Date | Mintage | VF | XF | Unc |
|---|---|---|---|---|---|
| 555 | 1992 | .050 | — | — | 8.50 |
| | 1992 | 3,000 | — | Proof | 18.50 |

### 1986 World Cup Soccer Games

| | | | | | | |
|---|---|---|---|---|---|---|
| 504 | 1985 | .347 | — | — | Proof | 13.50 |

# CIEN (100) PESOS

### 1986 World Cup Soccer Games

| | | | | | | |
|---|---|---|---|---|---|---|
| 515 | 1985 | .234 | — | — | Proof | 13.50 |

**Low 7's          High 7's**
**27.7700 g, .720 SILVER, .6429 oz ASW**
**Jose Morelos y Pavon**

| KM# | Date | Mintage | VF | XF | Unc | BU |
|-----|------|---------|-----|-----|-----|-----|
| 483.1 | 1977 low 7's, sloping shoulder | | | | | |
| | | 5.225 | BV | 4.00 | 6.00 | 10.00 |
| | 1977 high 7's, sloping shoulder | | | | | |
| | | Inc. Ab. | BV | 4.00 | 6.00 | 10.50 |

| 483.2 | 1977 date in line, higher right shoulder | | | | | |
|-----|------|---------|-----|-----|-----|-----|
| (484) | | Inc. KM483 | BV | 4.00 | 5.00 | 6.50 |
| | 1978 | 9.879 | BV | 4.00 | 6.50 | 8.50 |
| | 1979 | .784 | BV | 4.00 | 6.50 | 8.50 |
| | 1979 | — | — | — | Proof | 550.00 |

**ALUMINUM-BRONZE**
**Venustiano Carranza**

| 493 | 1984 | 227.809 | .45 | .60 | 2.75 | 4.00 |
|-----|------|---------|-----|-----|-----|-----|
| | 1985 | 377.423 | .30 | .50 | 2.00 | 3.00 |
| | 1986 | 43.000 | 1.00 | 2.50 | 4.75 | 7.50 |
| | 1987 | 165.000 | .60 | 1.25 | 2.50 | 3.50 |
| | 1988 | 433.100 | .30 | .50 | 2.00 | 2.75 |
| | 1989 | — | .35 | .65 | 2.00 | 2.75 |
| | 1990 | — | .15 | .40 | 1.50 | 2.50 |
| | 1990 | 1 known | — | — | Proof | 650.00 |
| | 1991 | — | .15 | .25 | 1.00 | 2.50 |
| | 1992 | — | .30 | .75 | 1.75 | 3.00 |

**31.1030 g, .720 SILVER, .7201 oz ASW**
**1986 World Cup Soccer Games**

| KM# | Date | Mintage | VF | XF | Unc | BU |
|-----|------|---------|-----|-----|-----|-----|
| 499 | 1985 | .302 | — | — | — | 12.50 |

**32.6250 g, .925 SILVER, 1.0000 oz ASW**
**Rev: W/o fineness statement.**

| 499a | 1985 | 9,006 | — | — | Proof | 18.50 |
|-----|------|---------|-----|-----|-----|-----|

**1986 World Cup Soccer Games**
**Rev: W/o fineness statement.**

| 505 | 1985 | 9,006 | — | — | Proof | 18.50 |
|-----|------|---------|-----|-----|-----|-----|

**1986 World Cup Soccer Games**
**Rev: W/o fineness statement.**

| 521 | 1986 | .208 | — | — | Proof | 18.50 |
|-----|------|---------|-----|-----|-----|-----|

**1986 World Cup Soccer Games**
**Rev: W/o fineness statement.**

| KM# | Date | Mintage | VF | XF | Unc | BU |
|-----|------|---------|----|----|-----|----|
| 524 | 1986 | .190 | — | — | Proof | 18.50 |

**World Wildlife Fund - Monarch Butterflies**

| 537 | 1987 | *.030 | — | — | Proof | 40.00 |
|-----|------|-------|----|----|-------|-------|

**31.1030 g, .999 SILVER, 1.0000 oz ASW**
**50th Anniversary - Nationalization of Oil Industry**

| 533 | 1988 | .010 | — | — | 28.00 | 35.00 |
|-----|------|------|----|----|-------|-------|

**33.6250 g, .925 SILVER, 1.0000 oz ASW**
**Save the Children**

| 539 | 1991 | .030 | — | — | Proof | 35.00 |
|-----|------|------|----|----|-------|-------|

**27.0000 g, .925 SILVER, .8029 oz ASW**
**Ibero - American Series - Pillars**

| KM# | Date | Mintage | VF | XF | Unc | BU |
|-----|------|---------|----|----|-----|----|
| 540 | 1991 | .050 | — | — | Proof | 45.00 |
|  | 1992 | .075 | — | — | Proof | 42.00 |

**31.1035 g, .999 SILVER, 1.0000 oz ASW**
**Eagle Warrior**

| KM# | Date | Mintage | VF | XF | Unc |
|-----|------|---------|----|----|-----|
| 556 | 1992 | .205 | — | — | 11.50 |
|  | 1992 | 4,000 | — | Proof | 36.00 |

**Xochipilli - The God of Joy, Music and Dance**

| 562 | 1992 | 4,000 | — | — | Proof | 36.00 |
|-----|------|-------|----|----|-------|-------|

### Brasero Efigie - The God of Rain

| KM# | Date | Mintage | VF | XF | Unc |
|-----|------|---------|-----|-------|-------|
| 563 | 1992 | 4,000 | — | Proof | 36.00 |

### Huehueteotl - The God of Fire

| 564 | 1992 | 4,000 | — | Proof | 36.00 |

### Save the Harbor Porpoise

| KM# | Date | Mintage | VF | XF | Unc | BU |
|-----|------|---------|-----|-----|-------|-------|
| 566 | 1992 | — | — | — | Proof | 40.00 |

## 200 PESOS

### COPPER-NICKEL
### 175th Anniversary of Independence

| 509 | 1985 | 75.000 | — | .25 | 3.25 | 4.75 |

### 75th Anniversary of 1910 Revolution

| KM# | Date | Mintage | VF | XF | Unc | BU |
|-----|------|---------|-----|-----|-------|-------|
| 510 | 1985 | 98.590 | — | .25 | 3.25 | 4.25 |

### 1986 World Cup Soccer Games

| 525 | 1986 | 50.000 | — | 1.00 | 3.50 | 4.50 |

**62.2060 g, .999 SILVER, 2.0000 oz ASW**
### 1986 World Cup Soccer Games

| 526 | 1986 | .050 | — | — | 40.00 | 50.00 |

## 250 PESOS

**8.6400 g, .900 GOLD, .2500 oz AGW**
### 1986 World Cup Soccer Games

| 500.1 | 1985 | .100 | — | — | — | 100.00 |
|       | 1986 | — | — | — | — | 100.00 |

**Rev: W/o fineness statement.**

| KM# | Date | Mintage | VF | XF | Unc | BU |
|-----|------|---------|----|----|-----|-----|
| 500.2 | 1985 | 4,506 | — | — | Proof | 110.00 |
| | 1986 | — | — | — | Proof | 135.00 |

**1986 World Cup Soccer Games**

| 506.1 | 1985 | .088 | — | — | — | 110.00 |
|-----|------|---------|----|----|-----|-----|

**Rev: W/o fineness statement.**

| 506.2 | 1985 | *.080 | — | — | Proof | 115.00 |
|-----|------|---------|----|----|-----|-----|

**33.4500 g, .925 SILVER, 1.0000 oz ASW**
**75th Anniversary of 1910 Revolution**

| KM# | Date | Mintage | VF | XF | Unc | BU |
|-----|------|---------|----|----|-----|-----|
| 511 | 1985 | .040 | — | — | Proof | 32.50 |

**7.7758 g, .999 GOLD, .2500 oz AGW**
**Native Culture - Sculpture of Jaguar Head**

| KM# | Date | Mintage | VF | XF | Unc |
|-----|------|---------|----|----|-----|
| 558 | 1992 | .010 | — | — | 145.00 |
| | 1992 | 2,000 | — | Proof | 275.00 |

## 500 PESOS

**COPPER-NICKEL**
**Francisco Madero**

| 529 | 1986 | 20.000 | — | 1.00 | 2.50 | 3.00 |
|-----|------|---------|----|----|-----|-----|
| | 1987 | 180.000 | — | .75 | 2.00 | 2.50 |
| | 1988 | 230.000 | — | .50 | 2.00 | 2.50 |
| | 1988 | 2 known | — | — | Proof | 650.00 |
| | 1989 | — | — | .75 | 2.00 | 3.00 |
| | 1992 | — | — | 1.00 | 2.25 | 3.50 |

**17.2800 g, .900 GOLD, .5000 oz AGW**
**50th Anniversary - Nationalization of Oil Industry**
**Rev: Monument.**
**Similar to 5000 Pesos, KM#531.**

| 534 | 1988 | — | — | — | — | 225.00 |
|-----|------|---------|----|----|-----|-----|

**17.2800 g, .900 GOLD, .5000 oz AGW**
**1986 World Cup Soccer Games**
**Obv: Eagle facing left w/snake in beak.**

| KM# | Date | Mintage | VF | XF | Unc | BU |
|-----|------|---------|----|----|-----|-----|
| 501.1 | 1985 | .102 | — | — | — | 210.00 |
| | 1986 | — | — | — | — | 210.00 |

**Rev: W/o fineness statement.**

| 501.2 | 1985 | 5,506 | — | — | Proof | 225.00 |
|-----|------|---------|----|----|-----|-----|
| | 1986 | — | — | — | Proof | 225.00 |

**15.5517 g, .999 GOLD, .5000 oz AGW**
**Native Culture - Sculpture of Jaguar Head**

| KM# | Date | Mintage | VF | XF | Unc |
|-----|------|---------|----|----|-----|
| 559 | 1992 | .010 | — | — | 200.00 |
| | 1992 | 2,000 | — | Proof | 400.00 |

## 1000 PESOS

**1986 World Cup Soccer Games**

| 507.1 | 1985 | — | — | — | — | 225.00 |
|-----|------|---------|----|----|-----|-----|

**Rev: W/o fineness statement.**

| 507.2 | 1985 | — | — | — | Proof | 225.00 |
|-----|------|---------|----|----|-----|-----|

**17.2800 g, .900 GOLD, .5000 oz AGW**

### 175th Anniversary of Independence

| KM# | Date | Mintage | VF | XF | Unc | BU |
|-----|------|---------|-----|-----|-------|-------|
| 513 | 1985 | — | — | — | Proof | 325.00 |

**31.1030 g, .999 GOLD, 1.0000 oz AGW**
**1986 World Cup Soccer Games**

| | | | | | | |
|-----|------|---------|-----|-----|-----|-------|
| 527 | 1986 | — | — | — | — | 550.00 |

**34.5590 g, .900 GOLD, 1.0000 oz AGW**
**50th Anniversary - Nationalization of Oil Industry**
**Similar to 5000 Pesos, KM#531.**
**Rev: Portrait of Cardenas.**

| | | | | | | |
|-----|------|---------|-----|-----|-------|-------|
| 535 | 1988 | — | — | — | Proof | 440.00 |

### ALUMINUM-BRONZE
### Juana de Asbaje

| KM# | Date | Mintage | VF | XF | Unc | BU |
|-----|------|---------|-----|-----|-------|--------|
| 536 | 1988 | 229.300 | .85 | 1.25 | 3.75 | 4.25 |
| | 1989 | — | .85 | 1.25 | 3.45 | 4.25 |
| | 1990 | — | .85 | 1.25 | 2.25 | 4.25 |
| | 1990 | 2 known | — | — | Proof | 550.00 |
| | 1991 | — | 1.00 | 1.50 | 2.50 | 4.25 |
| | 1992 | — | 1.00 | 1.50 | 2.25 | 3.50 |

**31.1035 g, .999 GOLD, 1.0000 oz AGW**
**Native Culture - Sculpture of Jaguar Head**

| KM# | Date | Mintage | VF | XF | Unc |
|-----|------|---------|-----|-------|--------|
| 560 | 1992 | .018 | — | — | 400.00 |
| | 1992 | 2,000 | — | Proof | 600.00 |

## 2000 PESOS

**62.2000 g, .999 GOLD, 2.0000 oz AGW**
**1986 World Cup Soccer Games**

| KM# | Date | Mintage | VF | XF | Unc | BU |
|-----|------|---------|-----|-----|-----|--------|
| 528 | 1986 | — | — | — | — | 900.00 |

## 5000 PESOS

### COPPER-NICKEL
**50th Anniversary - Nationalization of Oil Industry**

| | | | | | | |
|-----|---------|--------|-----|------|------|-------|
| 531 | ND(1988) | | | | | |
| | | 50.000 | — | 4.75 | 7.75 | 10.00 |

## 10000 PESOS

**155.5175 g, .999 SILVER, 5.0000 oz ASW**
**Illustration reduced. Actual size: 65mm.**
**Native Warriors Taking Female Captive**

| KM# | Date | Mintage | VF | XF | Unc |
|-----|------|---------|-----|-------|-------|
| 557 | 1992 | .052 | — | — | 46.00 |
| | 1992 | 3,005 | — | Proof | 80.00 |

# MONETARY REFORM

1 New Peso = 1000 Old Pesos

## 5 CENTAVOS

### STAINLESS STEEL

| KM# | Date | Mintage | VF | XF | Unc |
|---|---|---|---|---|---|
| 546 | 1992 | — | — | .15 | .25 |
| | 1993 | — | — | .15 | .25 |
| | 1994 | — | — | .15 | .25 |
| | 1995 | — | — | .15 | .25 |
| | 1996 | — | — | .15 | .25 |
| | 1997 | — | — | .15 | .25 |
| | 1998 | — | — | .15 | .25 |
| | 1999 | — | — | .15 | .25 |

## 10 CENTAVOS

### STAINLESS STEEL

| | | | | | |
|---|---|---|---|---|---|
| 547 | 1992 | — | — | .20 | .30 |
| | 1993 | — | — | .20 | .30 |
| | 1994 | — | — | .20 | .30 |
| | 1995 | — | — | .20 | .30 |
| | 1995 | — | — | Proof | .60 |
| | 1996 | — | — | .20 | .30 |
| | 1997 | — | — | .20 | .30 |
| | 1998 | — | — | .20 | .30 |
| | 1999 | — | — | .20 | .30 |
| | 2000 | — | — | .20 | .30 |

## 20 CENTAVOS

### ALUMINUM-BRONZE

| | | | | | |
|---|---|---|---|---|---|
| 548 | 1992 | — | — | .25 | .35 |
| | 1993 | — | — | .25 | .35 |
| | 1994 | — | — | .25 | .35 |
| | 1995 | — | — | .25 | .35 |
| | 1995 | — | — | Proof | .75 |
| | 1996 | — | — | .25 | .35 |
| | 1998 | — | — | .25 | .35 |
| | 1999 | — | — | .25 | .35 |
| | 2000 | — | — | .25 | .35 |

## 50 CENTAVOS

### ALUMINUM-BRONZE

| | | | | | |
|---|---|---|---|---|---|
| 549 | 1992 | — | — | .45 | .85 |
| | 1993 | — | — | .45 | .75 |
| | 1994 | — | — | .45 | .75 |
| | 1995 | — | — | .45 | .75 |
| | 1995 | — | — | Proof | .90 |
| | 1996 | — | — | .45 | .75 |
| | 1997 | — | — | .45 | .75 |

# NEW PESO

### STAINLESS STEEL ring, ALUMINUM-BRONZE center

| KM# | Date | Mintage | VF | XF | Unc |
|---|---|---|---|---|---|
| 550 | 1992 | — | — | .60 | 1.25 |
| | 1993 | — | — | .60 | 1.25 |
| | 1994 | — | — | .60 | 1.25 |
| | 1995 | — | — | .60 | 1.25 |
| | 1995 | — | — | Proof | 2.50 |

### 7.7601 g, .999 SILVER, .2498 oz ASW
### Bajorrelieve Del El Tajin

| | | | | | |
|---|---|---|---|---|---|
| 567 | 1993 | .100 | — | — | 6.50 |
| | 1993 | 3,000 | — | Proof | 10.50 |

### Chaac Mool

| | | | | | |
|---|---|---|---|---|---|
| 572 | 1994 | .030 | — | Matte | 6.50 |
| | 1994 | 2,000 | — | Proof | 10.50 |

# PESO

### 7.775 g, .999 SILVER, .2500 oz ASW
### Senor De Las Limas
### Similar to 5 Pesos, KM#595.

| KM# | Date | Mintage | VF | XF | Unc |
|---|---|---|---|---|---|
| 593 | 1996 | .010 | — | — | 4.00 |
| | 1996 | — | — | Proof | 25.00 |
| | 1998 | — | — | Matte | 3.25 |

**STAINLESS STEEL ring,**
**ALUMINUM-BRONZE center**
**Similar to KM#550, but denom. w/o N.**

| KM# | Date | Mintage | VF | XF | Unc | BU |
|-----|------|---------|----|----|-----|-----|
| 603 | 1996 | | — | — | — | 1.25 |
| | 1997 | | | | | 1.25 |
| | 1998 | | — | | — | 1.25 |
| | 1999 | | — | — | — | 1.25 |
| | 2000 | | — | — | — | 1.25 |

**7.7759 g, .999 SILVER, .2500 oz ASW**
**Disco De La Muerte**
**Obv: Mexican eagle.**

| | | | | | | |
|-----|------|---------|----|----|-----|-----|
| 617 | 1997 | | — | — | — | 4.00 |
| | 1997 | | — | — | Proof | 10.50 |
| | 1998 | | — | — | Matte | 10.50 |
| | 2000 | | — | — | — | 1.25 |

## 2 NEW PESOS

**STAINLESS STEEL ring,**
**ALUMINUM-BRONZE center**

| 551 | 1992 | | — | — | 1.50 | 2.50 |
|-----|------|---------|----|----|-----|-----|
| | 1993 | | — | — | 1.00 | 2.35 |
| | 1994 | | — | — | 1.00 | 2.35 |
| | 1995 | | — | — | 1.00 | 2.35 |
| | 1995 | | — | — | Proof | 4.50 |

**15.5516 g, .999 SILVER, .4995 oz ASW**
**Bajorrelieve Del El Tajin**

| 568 | 1993 | .100 | — | — | 6.50 |
|-----|------|---------|----|----|-----|
| | 1993 | 3,000 | — | Proof | 10.50 |

**Chaac Mool**

| KM# | Date | Mintage | VF | XF | Unc |
|-----|------|---------|----|----|-----|
| 573 | 1994 | .030 | — | Matte | 6.50 |
| | 1994 | 2,000 | — | Proof | 10.50 |

## 2 PESOS

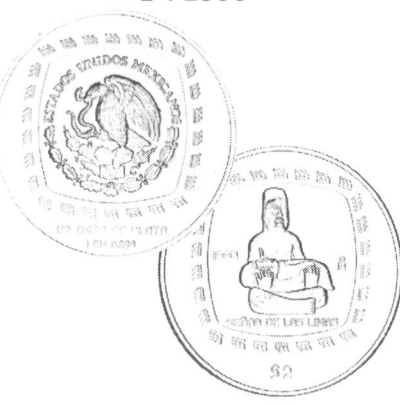

**15.5517 g, .999 SILVER, .5000 oz ASW**
**Senor De Las Limas**
**Similar to 5 Pesos, KM#595.**

| 594 | 1996 | .010 | — | — | 6.00 |
|-----|------|---------|----|----|-----|
| | 1996 | | — | Proof | 18.50 |
| | 1998 | | — | Matte | 8.50 |

**STAINLESS STEEL ring,**
**ALUMINUM-BRONZE center**
**Similar to KM#551, but denom. w/o N.**

| 604 | 1996 | | — | — | — | 2.50 |
|-----|------|---------|----|----|-----|-----|
| | 1997 | | — | — | — | 2.50 |
| | 1998 | | — | — | — | 2.50 |
| | 1999 | | — | — | — | 2.50 |
| | 2000 | | — | — | — | 2.50 |

## 5 NEW PESOS

**STAINLESS STEEL ring,**
**ALUMINUM-BRONZE center**

| 552 | 1992 | | — | — | 2.00 | 4.00 |
|-----|------|---------|----|----|-----|-----|
| | 1993 | | — | — | 2.00 | 4.00 |
| | 1994 | | — | — | 2.00 | 4.00 |
| | 1995 | | — | — | Proof | 25.00 |

**31.1035 g, .999 SILVER, .9991 oz ASW**
**Bajorrelieve Del El Tajin**

| 569 | 1993 | .100 | — | — | 12.00 |
|-----|------|---------|----|----|-----|
| | 1993 | 2,200 | — | Proof | 36.00 |

**Palma Con Cecodrilo**
Obv: National emblem.
Rev: Aerial view of crocodile.

| KM# | Date | Mintage | VF | XF | Unc |
|-----|------|---------|----|----|----|
| 582 | 1993 | — | — | — | 12.00 |
| | 1993 | 2,655 | — | Proof | 36.00 |

**Anciano Con Brasero**
Rev: Kneeling figure sculpture.

| 583 | 1993 | — | — | — | 12.00 |
|-----|------|---------|----|----|----|
| | 1993 | 2,655 | — | Proof | 36.00 |

**Carita Sonriente**
Rev: Sculptured head.

| 584 | 1993 | — | — | — | 12.00 |
|-----|------|---------|----|----|----|
| | 1993 | 3,000 | — | Proof | 36.00 |

**Chaac Mool**

| KM# | Date | Mintage | VF | XF | Unc |
|-----|------|---------|----|----|----|
| 574 | 1994 | .050 | — | Matte | 12.00 |
| | 1994 | 2,200 | — | Proof | 36.00 |

**Tomb of Palenque Memorial Stone**

| 575 | 1994 | — | — | — | 12.00 |
|-----|------|---------|----|----|----|
| | 1994 | 2,200 | — | Proof | 36.00 |

**Mascaron Del Dios Chaac**
Rev: Elaborately carved wall segment
w/hook or loop.

| 577 | 1994 | — | — | — | 12.00 |
|-----|------|---------|----|----|----|
| | 1994 | 2,200 | — | Proof | 36.00 |

**Dintel 26**
Rev: 2 seated figures wall carving.

| KM# | Date | Mintage | VF | XF | Unc |
|-----|------|---------|-----|-----|-----|
| 578 | 1994 | — | — | | 12.00 |
| | 1994 | 2,200 | — | Proof | 36.00 |

**27.0000 g, .925 SILVER, .8030 oz ASW**
**Environmental Protection - Pacific Ridley Sea Turtle**

| | | | | | |
|-----|------|------|-----|-----|-----|
| 588 | 1994 | .020 | — | Proof | 37.50 |

# 5 PESOS

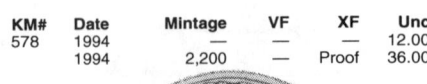

**El Luchador**

| KM# | Date | Mintage | VF | XF | Unc |
|-----|------|---------|-----|-----|-----|
| 597 | 1996 | .030 | — | — | 13.50 |
| | 1996 | — | — | Proof | 36.00 |
| | 1998 | — | — | Matte | 10.00 |

**Hacha Ceremonial**

| | | | | | |
|-----|------|------|-----|-----|-----|
| 598 | 1996 | .030 | — | Proof | 36.00 |
| | 1998 | — | — | Matte | 10.00 |

**31.1035 g, .999 SILVER, 1.0000 oz ASW**
**Senor De Las Limas**

| | | | | | |
|-----|------|------|-----|-----|-----|
| 595 | 1996 | .030 | — | — | 12.00 |
| | 1996 | .030 | — | Proof | 36.00 |
| | 1998 | — | — | Matte | 16.25 |

**STAINLESS STEEL ring,**
**w/ALUMINUM BRONZE center**
**Similar to KM#552, but denom. w/o N.**

| | | | | | |
|-----|------|------|-----|-----|-----|
| 605 | 1996 | — | — | — | 5.50 |
| | 1997 | — | — | — | 5.50 |
| | 1998 | — | — | — | 5.50 |
| | 1999 | — | — | — | 5.50 |
| | 2000 | — | — | — | 5.50 |

**Hombre Jaguar**

| | | | | | |
|-----|------|------|-----|-----|-----|
| 596 | 1996 | .030 | — | — | 13.50 |
| | 1996 | — | — | Proof | 36.00 |
| | 1998 | — | — | Matte | 10.00 |

**31.1035 g, .999 SILVER, 1.0000 oz ASW**
**Teohituacan - Disco de la Muerte**
**Obv: Eagle and snake.**

| KM# | Date | Mintage | VF | XF | Unc |
|-----|------|---------|-----|-----|-----|
| 619 | 1997 | *.030 | — | Proof | 36.00 |
| (617) | 1998 | — | — | — | 13.50 |

**Teohituacan - Mascara**
**Obv: Eagle and snake.**

| | | | | | |
|-----|------|---------|-----|-----|-----|
| 620 | 1997 | *.030 | — | Proof | 36.00 |
| (618) | 1998 | — | — | — | 13.50 |

**Teohituacan - Vasija**
**Obv: Eagle and snake.**

| | | | | | |
|-----|------|---------|-----|-----|-----|
| 621 | 1997 | — | — | — | 9.00 |
| (619) | 1997 | *.030 | — | Proof | 36.00 |
| | 1998 | — | — | Matte | 13.50 |

**Teohituacan - Jugador of Pelota**
**Obv: Eagle and snake.**

| | | | | | |
|-----|------|---------|-----|-----|-----|
| 622 | 1997 | — | — | — | 9.00 |
| (620) | 1997 | *.030 | — | Proof | 36.50 |
| | 1998 | — | — | Matte | 10.00 |

**31.1035 g, .999 SILVER, 1.0000 oz ASW**
**World Wildlife Fund - 2 Lobo**
**Obv: Mexican eagle.**

| KM# | Date | Mintage | VF | XF | Unc |
|-----|------|---------|-----|-----|-----|
| 627 | 1998 | *.015 | — | Proof | 45.00 |

**27.0000 g, .925 SILVER, .8030 oz ASW**
**Jarabe Tapatio - 2 Dancers**
**Obv: Mexican emblem within circle of arms.**

| | | | | | |
|-----|------|---------|-----|-----|-----|
| 629 | 1997 | .020 | — | Proof | 30.00 |

# 10 NEW PESOS

**ALUMINUM-BRONZE ring w/**
**11.1400 g, .925 SILVER, .1666 oz ASW center**

| | | | | | |
|-----|------|---------|-----|-----|-----|
| 553 | 1992 | — | — | — | 7.50 |
| | 1993 | — | — | — | 7.50 |
| | 1994 | — | — | — | 7.50 |
| | 1995 | — | — | — | 7.50 |

Illustration reduced. Actual size: 64.9mm.
Pyramid del Castillo

| KM# | Date | Mintage | VF | XF | Unc |
|-----|------|---------|-----|-------|-------|
| 576 | 1994 | .020 | — | Matte | 46.50 |
|     | 1994 | 1,000 | — | Proof | 80.00 |

## 10 PESOS

155.5175 g, .999 SILVER, 4.9956 oz ASW
Illustration reduced. Actual size: 64.9mm.
Piramide Del El Tajin

| KM# | Date | Mintage | VF | XF | Unc |
|-----|------|---------|-----|-------|-------|
| 570 | 1993 | .050 | — | — | 46.00 |
|     | 1993 | 3,000 | — | Proof | 78.00 |

1555.5175 g, .999 SILVER, 5.0000 oz ASW
Illustration reduced. Actual size: 65mm.
Cabeza Olmeca

| | Date | Mintage | VF | XF | Unc |
|-----|------|---------|-----|-------|-------|
| 599 | 1996 | .010 | — | Proof | 80.00 |
|     | 1998 | — | — | — | 46.00 |

### Octavio Paz

| KM# | Date | Mintage | VF | XF | Unc |
|---|---|---|---|---|---|
| 638 | 2000 | — | — | — | 15.00 |

## 25 NEW PESOS

**7.7758 g, .999 GOLD, .2500 oz AGW**
**Hacha Ceremonial**
**Similar to 100 New Pesos, KM#587.**

| 585 | 1993 | .016 | — | — | 145.00 |
|---|---|---|---|---|---|
|  | 1993 | 800 pcs. | — | Proof | 275.00 |

**Personaje de Jaina**
**Rev: Seated figure.**

| 579 | 1994 | 2,000 | — | — | 165.00 |
|---|---|---|---|---|---|
|  | 1994 | 500 pcs. | — | Proof | 325.00 |

## 25 PESOS

**7.7758 g, .999 GOLD, .2500 oz AGW**
**Sacerdote**
**Similar to 100 Pesos, KM#602.**

| 600 | 1996 | .010 | — | — | 225.00 |
|---|---|---|---|---|---|
|  | 1996 | — | — | Proof | 275.00 |

**NOTE:** KM#622 previously listed here does not exist and has been removed.

**Serpiente Emplumada**
**Similar to 100 Pesos, KM#626.**
**Obv: Mexican eagle.**

| 624 | 1997 | — | — | — | 200.00 |
|---|---|---|---|---|---|
|  | 1997 | .010 | — | Proof | 275.00 |

## 50 NEW PESOS

**COPPER-NICKEL ZINC center in BRASS ring**
**Obv: National emblem. Rev: Aztec design.**

| KM# | Date | Mintage | VF | XF | Unc |
|---|---|---|---|---|---|
| 616 | 1997 | — | — | — | 7.50 |
|  | 1998 | — | — | — | 7.50 |
|  | 1999 | — | — | — | 7.50 |

**1,555.5175 g, .999 SILVER, 5.0000 oz ASW**
**Illustration reduced. Actual size: 65mm.**
**Piramide Del Sol**
**Obv: Mexican eagle.**

| 623 | 1997 | — | — | — | 50.00 |
|---|---|---|---|---|---|
|  | 1997 | .010 | — | Proof | 95.00 |
|  | 1998 | — | — | Matte | 46.00 |

## 20 NEW PESOS

**ALUMINUM-BRONZE ring w/**
**16.9000 g, .925 SILVER, .2499 oz ASW center**

| 561 | 1993 | — | — | — | 12.00 |
|---|---|---|---|---|---|
|  | 1994 | — | — | — | 12.00 |
|  | 1995 | — | — | — | 12.00 |

## 20 PESOS

**6.2210 g, .999 GOLD, .1998 oz AGW**
**UNICEF**
**Rev: Child playing with lasso.**

| 641 | 1999 | — | — | — | 170.00 |
|---|---|---|---|---|---|

**COPPER-NICKEL center in BRASS ring**
**Xiutecuhtli**
**Rev: Aztec w/torch.**

| 637 | 2000 | — | — | — | 15.00 |
|---|---|---|---|---|---|

**34.0000 g, .925 SILVER, .5051 oz ASW center**
**in BRASS ring**
**Nino Heroes**

| 571 | 1993 | — | — | — | 28.00 |
|---|---|---|---|---|---|
|  | 1994 | — | — | — | 28.00 |
|  | 1995 | — | — | — | 28.00 |

**15.5517 g, .999 GOLD, .5000 oz AGW**
**Hacha Ceremonial**
**Similar to 100 New Pesos, KM#587.**

| 586 | 1993 | .016 | — | — | 275.00 |
|---|---|---|---|---|---|
|  | 1993 | 500 pcs. | — | Proof | 425.00 |

**Personaje de Jaina**
**Rev: Seated figure.**

| 580 | 1994 | 1,000 | — | — | 300.00 |
|---|---|---|---|---|---|
|  | 1994 | 500 pcs. | — | Proof | 525.00 |

## 50 PESOS

**15.5517 g, .999 GOLD, .5000 oz AGW**
**Sacerdote**
Similar to 100 Pesos, KM#602.

| KM# | Date | Mintage | VF | XF | Unc |
|---|---|---|---|---|---|
| 601 | 1996 | .010 | — | — | 425.00 |
| | 1996 | — | — | Proof | 475.00 |

**15.5517 g, .999 GOLD, .5000 oz AGW**
**Serpiente Emplumada**
Similar to 100 Pesos, KM#626.
Obv: Mexican eagle.

| KM# | Date | Mintage | VF | XF | Unc |
|---|---|---|---|---|---|
| 625 | 1997 | — | — | — | 350.00 |
| | 1997 | .010 | — | Proof | 475.00 |

## 100 NEW PESOS

**31.1035 g, .999 GOLD, 1.0000 oz AGW**
**Hacha Ceremonial**

| | | | | | |
|---|---|---|---|---|---|
| 587 | 1993 | 7,158 | — | — | 525.00 |
| | 1993 | 500 pcs. | — | Proof | 675.00 |

**Personaje de Jaina**

| | | | | | |
|---|---|---|---|---|---|
| 581 | 1994 | 1,000 | — | — | 575.00 |
| | 1994 | 500 pcs. | — | Proof | 800.00 |

## 100 PESOS

**31.1035 g, .999 GOLD, 1.0000 oz AGW**
**Sacerdote**

| | | | | | |
|---|---|---|---|---|---|
| 602 | 1996 | .010 | — | — | 600.00 |
| | 1996 | — | — | Proof | 600.00 |

**Teohituacan - Serpiente Emplumada**
**Obv: Eagle and snake.**

| KM# | Date | Mintage | VF | XF | Unc |
|---|---|---|---|---|---|
| 626 | 1997 | — | — | — | 600.00 |
| (624) | 1997 | *.010 | — | Proof | 670.00 |

# SILVER BULLION ISSUES

## 1/20 ONZA TROY de PLATA

(1/20 Troy Ounce of Silver)

**1.5551 g, .999 SILVER, .0500 oz ASW**

| KM# | Date | Mintage | VF | XF | Unc | BU |
|---|---|---|---|---|---|---|
| 542 | 1991 | .054 | — | — | — | 2.45 |
| | 1992 | .296 | — | — | — | 2.45 |
| | 1992 | 5,000 | — | — | Proof | 10.00 |
| | 1993 | .100 | — | — | — | 2.45 |
| | 1993 | — | — | — | Proof | 10.00 |
| | 1994 | .090 | — | — | — | 2.45 |
| | 1994 | .050 | — | — | Proof | 10.00 |
| | 1995 | .010 | — | — | — | 2.45 |
| | 1995 | 2,000 | — | — | Proof | 10.00 |

**Obv: Mexican eagle. Rev: Winged Victory.**

| | | | | | | |
|---|---|---|---|---|---|---|
| 609 | 1996 | — | — | — | — | 2.45 |
| | 1996 | — | — | — | Proof | 10.00 |
| | 1997 | — | — | — | — | 2.45 |
| | 1997 | — | — | — | Proof | 10.00 |
| | 1998 | — | — | — | — | 2.45 |
| | 1998 | — | — | — | Proof | 10.00 |
| | 1999 | — | — | — | — | 2.45 |
| | 1999 | — | — | — | Proof | 10.00 |
| | 2000 | — | — | — | — | 2.45 |
| | 2000 | — | — | — | Proof | 10.00 |

## 1/10 ONZA TROY de PLATA

(1/10 Troy Ounce of Silver)

**3.1103 g, .999 SILVER, .1000 oz ASW**

| | | | | | | |
|---|---|---|---|---|---|---|
| 543 | 1991 | .054 | — | — | — | 2.55 |
| | 1992 | .300 | — | — | — | 2.55 |
| | 1992 | 5,000 | — | — | Proof | 12.00 |
| | 1993 | .100 | — | — | — | 2.55 |
| | 1993 | — | — | — | Proof | 12.00 |
| | 1994 | .090 | — | — | — | 2.55 |
| | 1994 | .050 | — | — | Proof | 12.00 |
| | 1995 | .010 | — | — | — | 2.55 |
| | 1995 | 2,000 | — | — | Proof | 12.00 |

**Obv: Mexican eagle. Rev: Winged Victory.**

| KM# | Date | Mintage | VF | XF | Unc | BU |
|---|---|---|---|---|---|---|
| 610 | 1996 | — | — | — | — | 2.55 |
| | 1996 | — | — | — | Proof | 12.00 |
| | 1997 | — | — | — | — | 2.55 |
| | 1997 | — | — | — | Proof | 12.00 |
| | 1998 | — | — | — | — | 2.55 |
| | 1998 | — | — | — | Proof | 12.00 |
| | 1999 | — | — | — | — | 2.55 |
| | 1999 | — | — | — | Proof | 12.00 |
| | 2000 | — | — | — | — | 2.55 |
| | 2000 | — | — | — | Proof | 12.00 |

| KM# | Date | Mintage | VF | XF | Unc | BU |
|---|---|---|---|---|---|---|
| 545 | 1991 | .051 | — | — | — | 6.00 |
| | 1992 | .119 | — | — | — | 6.00 |
| | 1992 | 5,000 | — | — | Proof | 17.50 |
| | 1993 | .072 | — | — | — | 6.00 |
| | 1993 | — | — | — | Proof | 17.50 |
| | 1994 | .090 | — | — | — | 6.00 |
| | 1994 | .050 | — | — | Proof | 17.50 |
| | 1995 | .015 | — | — | — | 6.00 |
| | 1995 | 2,000 | — | — | Proof | 17.50 |

## 1/4 ONZA TROY de PLATA
(1/4 Troy Ounce of Silver)

**7.7758 g, .999 SILVER, .2500 oz ASW**

| KM# | Date | Mintage | VF | XF | Unc | BU |
|---|---|---|---|---|---|---|
| 544 | 1991 | .050 | — | — | — | 4.50 |
| | 1992 | .104 | — | — | — | 4.50 |
| | 1992 | 5,000 | — | — | Proof | 15.00 |
| | 1993 | .087 | — | — | — | 4.50 |
| | 1993 | — | — | — | Proof | 15.00 |
| | 1994 | .090 | — | — | — | 4.50 |
| | 1994 | .050 | — | — | Proof | 15.00 |
| | 1995 | .015 | — | — | — | 4.50 |
| | 1995 | 2,000 | — | — | Proof | 15.00 |

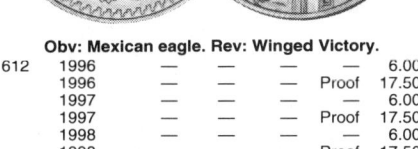

**Obv: Mexican eagle. Rev: Winged Victory.**

| KM# | Date | Mintage | VF | XF | Unc | BU |
|---|---|---|---|---|---|---|
| 612 | 1996 | — | — | — | — | 6.00 |
| | 1996 | — | — | — | Proof | 17.50 |
| | 1997 | — | — | — | — | 6.00 |
| | 1997 | — | — | — | Proof | 17.50 |
| | 1998 | — | — | — | — | 6.00 |
| | 1998 | — | — | — | Proof | 17.50 |

## ONZA TROY de PLATA
(Troy Ounce of Silver)

**Obv: Mexican eagle. Rev: Winged Victory.**

| KM# | Date | Mintage | VF | XF | Unc | BU |
|---|---|---|---|---|---|---|
| 611 | 1996 | — | — | — | — | 4.50 |
| | 1996 | — | — | — | Proof | 15.00 |
| | 1997 | — | — | — | — | 4.50 |
| | 1997 | — | — | — | Proof | 15.00 |
| | 1998 | — | — | — | — | 4.50 |
| | 1998 | — | — | — | Proof | 15.00 |
| | 1999 | — | — | — | — | 4.50 |
| | 1999 | — | — | — | Proof | 15.00 |
| | 2000 | — | — | — | — | 4.50 |
| | 2000 | — | — | — | Proof | 15.00 |

**33.6250 g, .925 SILVER, 1.0000 oz ASW**
**Obv: Mint mark above coin press.**

| KM# | Date | Mintage | VF | XF | Unc | BU |
|---|---|---|---|---|---|---|
| M49a | 1949 | 1.000 | 10.00 | 12.50 | 17.50 | 27.50 |

## 1/2 ONZA TROY de PLATA
(1/2 Troy Ounce of Silver)

**15.5517 g, .999 SILVER, .5000 oz ASW**

**Type 1. Obv: Wide spacing between DE MONEDA**
**Rev: Mint mark below balance scale.**

| KM# | Date | Mintage | VF | XF | Unc | BU |
|---|---|---|---|---|---|---|
| M49b.1 | 1978 | .280 | — | BV | 6.75 | 14.00 |

**Type 2. Obv: Close spacing between DE MONEDA**

| KM# | Date | Mintage | VF | XF | Unc | BU |
|---|---|---|---|---|---|---|
| M49b.2 | 1978 | Inc. Ab. | — | BV | 6.75 | 12.00 |

| KM# | Date | Mintage | VF | XF | Unc | BU |
|---|---|---|---|---|---|---|
| 613 | 1997 | — | — | — | — | 13.50 |
|  | 1997 | — | — | — | Proof | 32.50 |
|  | 1998 | — | — | — | — | 16.50 |
|  | 1998 | — | — | — | Proof | 35.00 |
|  | 1999 | — | — | — | — | 14.50 |
|  | 1999 | — | — | — | Proof | 35.00 |

# LIBERTAD SERIES

**Type 3. Rev: Left scale pan points to U in UNA.**

| M49b.3 | 1979 | 4.508 | — | BV | 6.75 | 13.50 |
|---|---|---|---|---|---|---|

**Type 4. Rev: Left scale pan points between U and N of UNA.**

| M49b.4 | 1979 | Inc. Ab. | — | BV | 6.75 | 13.50 |
|---|---|---|---|---|---|---|

**31.1000 g, .999 SILVER, 1.0000 oz ASW**

**Libertad**

| KM# | Date | Mintage | VF | XF | Unc | BU |
|---|---|---|---|---|---|---|
| 494.1 | 1982 | 1.050 | — | — | BV | 12.00 |
|  | 1983 | 1.002 | — | — | BV | 12.00 |
|  | 1983 | 998 pcs. | — | — | Proof | 185.00 |
|  | 1984 | 1.014 | — | — | BV | 12.00 |
|  | 1985 | 2.017 | — | — | BV | 12.00 |
|  | 1986 | 1.699 | — | — | BV | 12.50 |
|  | 1986 | .030 | — | — | Proof | 22.00 |
|  | 1987 | .500 | — | — | BV | 36.50 |
|  | 1987 | .012 | — | — | Proof | 45.00 |
|  | 1988 | 1.501 | — | BV | BV | 34.00 |
|  | 1988 | — | — | — | Proof | R,NC |
|  | 1989 | 1.397 | — | — | BV | 23.00 |
|  | 1989 | .010 | — | — | Proof | 40.00 |

**Reeded edge.**

| 494.2 | 1988 | .010 | — | — | Proof | 60.00 |
|---|---|---|---|---|---|---|
|  | 1990 | 1.200 | — | — | BV | 12.50 |
|  | 1990 | .010 | — | — | Proof | 22.00 |
|  | 1991 | 1.651 | — | — | BV | 15.00 |

**Mule. Obv: KM#494.3. Rev: KM#494.2.**

| 494.5 | 1991 | .010 | — | — | Proof | 32.00 |
|---|---|---|---|---|---|---|

**Type 5.**

| M49b.5 | 1980 | 6.104 | — | BV | 6.75 | 11.00 |
|---|---|---|---|---|---|---|
|  | 1980/70 | I.A. | — | BV | 6.75 | 14.50 |

**Obv: Mexican eagle. Rev: Winged Victory.**

| 613 | 1996 | — | — | — | — | 11.50 |
|---|---|---|---|---|---|---|
|  | 1996 | — | — | — | Proof | 34.00 |

**Obv: Eight dots below eagle's left talons. Rev: Revised design and lettering.**

| 494.3 | 1991 | Inc. Ab. | — | — | BV | 20.00 |
|---|---|---|---|---|---|---|
|  | 1992 | 2.458 | — | — | BV | 12.50 |
|  | 1992 | .010 | — | — | Proof | 32.00 |

## 5 ONZAS TROY de PLATA

**Obv: Seven dots below eagle's left talons,
dull claws on right talon, thick letters.**

| KM# | Date | Mintage | VF | XF | Unc | BU |
|-----|------|---------|-----|-----|-----|-----|
| 494.4 | 1993 | 1.000 | — | — | BV | 12.50 |
| | 1993 | — | — | — | Proof | 34.00 |
| | 1994 | .400 | — | — | BV | 12.50 |
| | 1994 | .010 | — | — | Proof | 34.00 |
| | 1995 | .500 | — | — | BV | 12.50 |
| | 1995 | 2,000 | — | — | Proof | 35.00 |

**Obv: Modern Mexican eagle within
circle of obsolete versions.**

| 639 | 2000 | — | — | — | — | 10.00 |
|-----|------|---|---|---|---|-------|
| | 2000 | — | — | — | Proof | 35.00 |

## 2 ONZAS TROY de PLATA

**155.5175 g, .999 SILVER, 5.0000 oz ASW
Obv: Mexican eagle. Rev: Winged Victory.
Illustration reduced. Actual size: 65mm.**

| KM# | Date | Mintage | VF | XF | Unc | BU |
|-----|------|---------|-----|-----|-----|-----|
| 615 | 1996 | — | — | — | — | 48.50 |
| | 1996 | — | — | — | Proof | 75.00 |
| | 1997 | — | — | — | — | 48.50 |
| | 1997 | — | — | — | Proof | 75.00 |
| | 1998 | — | — | — | — | 48.50 |
| | 1998 | — | — | — | Proof | 75.00 |

# GOLD BULLION ISSUES
## 1/20 ONZA ORO PURO
(1/20 Ounce of Pure Gold)

**1.7500 g, .900 GOLD, .0500 oz AGW
Obv: Winged Victory. Rev: Calendar stone.**

| 530 | 1987 | — | — | — | BV + 30% |
|-----|------|---|---|---|----------|
| | 1988 | — | — | — | BV + 30% |

**1.5551 g, .999 GOLD, .500 oz AGW
Obv: Winged Victory.
Rev: Eagle and snake.**

| 589 | 1991 | .010 | — | — | BV + 30% |
|-----|------|------|---|---|----------|
| | 1992 | — | — | — | BV + 30% |
| | 1993 | — | — | — | BV + 30% |
| | 1994 | — | — | — | BV + 30% |

**Rev: Teocuitlatl and an Indian working.**

| 642 | 2000 | — | — | — | Proof | 50.00 |
|-----|------|---|---|---|-------|-------|

## 1/15 ONZA ORO PURO
(1/15 Ounce of Pure Gold)

 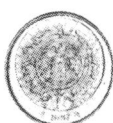

**Obv: Winged Victory above legend.**

| 628 | 1987 | — | — | — | BV + 25% |
|-----|------|---|---|---|----------|

**62.2070 g, .999 SILVER, 2.0000 oz ASW
Obv: Mexican eagle. Rev: Winged Victory.**

| 614 | 1996 | — | — | — | — | 22.00 |
|-----|------|---|---|---|---|-------|
| | 1996 | — | — | — | Proof | 42.50 |
| | 1997 | — | — | — | — | 20.00 |
| | 1997 | — | — | — | Proof | 42.50 |
| | 1998 | — | — | — | — | 27.50 |
| | 1998 | — | — | — | Proof | 42.50 |
| | 1999 | — | — | — | — | 22.50 |
| | 1999 | — | — | — | Proof | 42.50 |
| | 2000 | — | — | — | — | 22.50 |
| | 2000 | — | — | — | Proof | 42.50 |

## 1/10 ONZA ORO PURO
(1/10 Ounce of Pure Gold)

**3.1103 g, .999 GOLD, .1000 oz AGW**

| KM# | Date | Mintage | VF | XF | Unc | BU |
|-----|------|---------|-----|-----|-----|-----|
| 541 | 1991 | .010 | — | — | BV + 20% | |
| | 1992 | .051 | — | — | BV + 20% | |
| | 1993 | .010 | — | — | BV + 20% | |

## 1/4 ONZA ORO PURO
(1/4 Ounce of Pure Gold)

**8.6396 g, .900 GOLD, .2500 oz AGW**
**Similar to KM#488.**

| | | | | | | |
|-----|------|---------|-----|-----|-----|-----|
| 487 | 1981 | .313 | — | — | BV + 11% | |
| | 1994 | 2,500 | — | — | BV + 11% | |

**7.7758 g, .999 GOLD, .2500 oz AGW**
**Obv: Winged Victory above legend.**
**Rev: Eagle and snake.**

| | | | | | | |
|-----|------|---------|-----|-----|-----|-----|
| 590 | 1991 | .010 | — | — | BV + 11% | |
| | 1992 | .028 | — | — | BV + 11% | |
| | 1993 | 2,500 | — | — | BV + 11% | |

## 1/2 ONZA ORO PURO
(1/2 Ounce of Pure Gold)

**17.2792 g, .900 GOLD, .5000 oz AGW**

| | | | | | | |
|-----|------|---------|-----|-----|-----|-----|
| 488 | 1981 | .193 | — | — | BV + 8% | |
| | 1989 | 704 pcs. | — | — | Proof 500.00 | |
| | 1994 | 2,500 | — | — | BV + 8% | |

**15.5517 g, .999 GOLD, .5000 oz AGW**
**Obv: Winged Victory above legend.**
**Rev: Eagle and snake.**

| | | | | | | |
|-----|------|---------|-----|-----|-----|-----|
| 591 | 1991 | .010 | — | — | BV + 8% | |
| | 1992 | .025 | — | — | BV + 8% | |
| | 1993 | 2,500 | — | — | BV + 8% | |

## ONZA ORO PURO
(1 Ounce of Pure Gold)

**34.5585 g, .900 GOLD, 1.0000 oz AGW**
**Similar to KM#488.**

| | | | | | | |
|-----|------|---------|-----|-----|-----|-----|
| 489 | 1981 | .596 | — | — | BV + 3% | |
| | 1985 | — | — | — | BV + 3% | |
| | 1988 | — | — | — | BV + 3% | |
| | 1994 | 1,000 | — | — | BV + 3% | |

**31.1035 g, .999 GOLD, 1.0000 oz AGW**
**Obv: Winged Victory above legend.**
**Rev: Eagle and snake.**

| | | | | | | |
|-----|------|---------|-----|-----|-----|-----|
| 592 | 1991 | .109 | — | — | BV + 3% | |
| | 1992 | .046 | — | — | BV + 3% | |
| | 1993 | .010 | — | — | BV + 3% | |

## (50 PESOS)

**41.6666 g, .900 GOLD, 1.2057 oz AGW**

| KM# | Date | Mintage | VF | XF | Unc | BU |
|-----|------|---------|-----|-----|-----|-----|
| 482 | 1943 | .089 | — | — | BV | 525.00 |

# PLATINUM BULLION ISSUES
## 1/4 ONZA
(1/4 ounce)

**7.7775 g, .999 PLATINUM, .2500 oz APW**

| | | | | | | |
|-----|------|---------|-----|-----|-----|-----|
| 538 | 1989 | 704 pcs. | — | — | Proof 300.00 | |

# MEDALLIC ISSUES (M)
## (10 PESOS)

**8.3333 g, .900 GOLD, .2411 oz AGW**
**200th Anniversary - Birth of Hidalgo**

| | | | | | | |
|------|------|---|---|---|-----|--------|
| M91a | 1953 | — | — | — | BV | 110.00 |

**Centennial of Constitution**

| | | | | | | |
|-------|------|-------|---|---|-----|--------|
| M123a | 1957 | *.073 | — | — | BV | 110.00 |

**\*NOTE: Mintage includes #M122a.**

## (20 PESOS)

**16.6666 g, .900 GOLD, .4823 oz AGW**
**200th Anniversary - Birth of Hidalgo**

| | | | | | | |
|------|------|---|---|---|-----|--------|
| M92a | 1953 | — | — | — | BV | 200.00 |

## (50 PESOS)

**41.6666 g, .900 GOLD, 1.2057 oz AGW**
**Centennial of Constitution**

| KM# | Date | Mintage | VF | XF | Unc | BU |
|-----|------|---------|----|----|----|----|
| M122a | 1957 | | | | | |
| | Inc. M123a | | — | — | BV | 520.00 |

## MINT SETS (MS)

| KM# | Date | Mintage | Identification | Issue Price | Mkt. Val. |
|-----|------|---------|----------------|-------------|-----------|
| MS1 | 1977(16) | 500 | — | — | 500.00 |
| MSA2 | 1977(9) | — | 434.1,434.2,442,452, 460 thick date, 460 thin date,472,477.1,484,Type 2 for 3 ring binder | — | 85.00 |
| MS2 | 1978(9) | 500 | KM434.1,434.2,442,452, 460 open 8, 460 closed 8, 472,477,484,Type 1 flat pack | — | 150.00 |
| MS3 | 1978(9) | — | KM434.1,434.2,442,452, 460 open 8, 460 closed 8, 472,477.2,484,Type 2 for 3 ring binder | — | 65.00 |
| MS4 | 1979(8) | — | KM434.2,442,452 square 9, 452 round 9, 460(2), 472, 477.2,484, Type 1 flat pack | 11.00 | 8.00 |
| MS5 | 1979(8) | — | KM434.1,434.2,442,452 square 9, 452 round 9, 460,477,484, Type 2 for 3 ring binder | 11.00 | 9.00 |
| MS6 | 1980(9) | — | KM434.2, 442, 452 square 9, 452 round 9, 460 open 8, 460 closed 8, 477.2, 485-486 | 4.20 | 11.00 |
| MS7 | 1981(9) | — | KM442 open 8, 442 closed 8, 452 rectangular 9, 452 round 9, 460 open 8, 460 closed 8, 477.2, 485,486 | — | 15.00 |

| KM# | Date | Mintage | Identification | Issue Price | Mkt. Val. |
|-----|------|---------|----------------|-------------|-----------|
| MS8 | 1982(7) | — | KM442,452,460,477,485, 486,490 | — | 14.00 |
| MS9 | 1983(11) | — | KM442(2), 452(2), 460(2), 490(1), 491(2), 492(2) | — | 12.50 |
| MS10 | 1983(9) | — | KM442(2),452(2),460(2), 490(1),491(2),492(2) for 3 ring binder | — | 12.50 |
| MS11 | 1984(8) | — | KM485-486,490-491,493, 495(2),496 | — | 17.50 |
| MS12 | 1985(12) | — | KM477.2,485,493(2), 495(2),496,502,508,509, 510,512 | — | 16.00 |
| MS13 | 1986(7) | — | KM493,495,496,508,512, 525,529 | — | 18.00 |
| MS14 | 1985/1986(7) | — | KM493,495-496,502,508 509,512 | — | 18.50 |
| MS15 | 1987(9) | — | KM493,495(2),496,502(2), 512, 529(2) | — | 35.00 |
| MS16 | 1988(8) | — | KM493,495a,502,508,512, 529,531,536 | — | 20.00 |
| MS17 | 1996(6) | — | KM546-549,603-604 | 12.00 | 15.00 |

**NOTE:** The 1978 and 1979 sets were issued in 2 varieties of plastic holders, one of which has holes for insertion in an official 3 ring binder which was sold for $3.30.

**NOTE:** In 1989 The Banco de Mexico began preparing mint sets in hard plastic case by year with coins dated from 1970 thru 1999. The 2000 set is in a soft case.

## PROOF SETS (PS)

| KM# | Date | Mintage | Identification | Issue Price | Mkt. Val. |
|-----|------|---------|----------------|-------------|-----------|
| PS1 | 1982/1983(8) | 998 | KM442,452,460,485, 477.2,486,490,494.1 | 495.00 | 275.00 |
| PS2 | 1982/1983(8) | *2 | KM460,477.2,485,486, 490,491,492,PnB169 (in white box with Mo. in gold) | — | — |
| PS3 | 1982/1983(7) | *23 | KM460,477.2,485,486, 490,491,492(in white box with Mo in gold) | — | 500.00 |
| PS4 | 1982/1983(7) | *17 | KM460,477.2,485,486, 490,491,492 (in white box) | — | 500.00 |
| PS5 | 1982/1983(7) | *8 | KM460,477.2,485,486, 490,491,492 (in white box) | — | 500.00 |
| PS6 | 1983(7) | 3 | KM460,477.2,485,486, 490,491,492 | — | — |
| PS7 | 1985/1986(12) | — | KM497a-499a,503-505, 514-515,519,521, 523-524 | — | 250.00 |
| PS8 | 1985(4) | — | KM500.2-501.2,506.2, 507.2 | — | 700.00 |
| PS9 | 1985(3) | — | KM499a,514,515 (in blue box) | — | 60.00 |
| PS10 | 1985(3) | — | KM503-505 (in blue box) | — | 60.00 |
| PS11 | 1985(2) | — | KM511,513 | — | 350.00 |
| PS12 | 1989(3) | 704 | KM488,494,538, Rainbow | 730.00 | 850.00 |
| PS13 | 1992(5) | 5,000 | KM494.3,542-545 | — | 87.50 |
| PS14 | 1993(5) | 5,000 | KM494.4,542-545 | — | 87.50 |
| PS15 | 1994(5) | 5,000 | KM494.4,542-545 | — | 85.00 |
| PS16 | 1995(8) | — | KM546-550,552,553, 555 | 45.00 | 45.00 |

**\*NOTE:** KM#PS2, PS3, PS4 and PS5 are commonly referred to as pattern proof sets.

# Bibliography

Boyd, Julian P. (Editor). *The Papers of Thomas Jefferson.* Vol. 7. New Jersey: Princeton University Press, 1953.

Bowers, Q. David. *The History of United States Coinage as Illustrated by the Garrett Collection.* Los Angeles: Bowers & Ruddy Galleries, 1979.

Breen, Walter. *Walter Breen's Complete Encyclopedia of U.S. and Colonial Coins.* New York: F.C.I. Press, Doubleday, 1988.

Bressett, Ken, and Kosoff, A. *Official A.N.A. Grading Standards for United States Coins,* Fourth Edition. Colorado Springs, Colo.: American Numismatic Association, 1991.

Brown, Martin R., and Dunn, John W. *A Guide to the Grading of United States Coins.* Fourth and Fifth Editions. Racine, Wis.: Whitman Publishing Co., 1964 and 1969.

Bullowa, David M. *Numismatic Notes and Monographs No. 83: The Commemorative Coinage of the United States 1892-1938.* New York, N.Y.: American Numismatic Society, 1938.

Evans, George G. *Illustrated History of the United States Mint.* Revised Edition. Philadelphia: George G. Evans, 1892.

Fitzpatrick, John C. (Editor). *The Writings of George Washington.* Vol. 28. Washington: U.S. Government Printing Office, 1938.

Heath, Dr. George. *The Numismatist,* September 1888 and February 1892.

Hepburn, A. Barton. *A History of Currency in the United States.* Revised Edition. New York: Sentry Press, 1967.

Krueger, Kurt R. "Grading: Bestial Pandemonium Unleashed." *The Numismatist,* January 1976. Colorado Springs, Colo.: American Numismatic Association, 1975.

Ruddy, James F. *Photograde.* Wolfeboro, N.H.: Bowers and Merena Galleries Inc., 1983.

Sheldon, William H. *Early American Cents.* New York: Harper & Row. 1949.

Syrett, Harold C. *The Papers of Alexander Hamilton.* Vol. 7. New York: Columbia University Press, 1963.

Taxay, Don. *The U.S. Mint and Coinage: An Illustrated History From 1776 to the Present.* Second Edition. New York: Arco Publishing Co., 1969.

U.S. Congress. Senate. *International Monetary Conference.* 1878. Senate Ex. Doc., 58. 45th Congress, Third Session. Washington, 1879.

U.S. Congress. Senate. *Coinage Laws of the United States 1792 to 1894 with an Appendix of Statistics Relating to Coins and Currency.* Fourth Edition. Washington, D.C.: Government Printing Office, 1894.

Van Allen, Leroy C., and Mallis, A. George. *Comprehensive Catalog and Encyclopedia of U.S. Morgan and Peace Silver Dollars.* New York: F.C.I. Press, 1976.

Willem, John M. *The United States Trade Dollar: America's Only Unwanted, Unhonored Coin.* New York: By the author, 1959; reprint edition, Racine, Wis.: Western Publishing Co., 1965.

Yeoman, R.S. *A Guidebook of United States Coins.* 45th Edition. Racine, Wis.: Western Publishing Co., 1991.

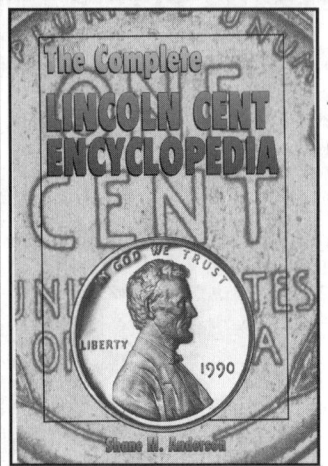
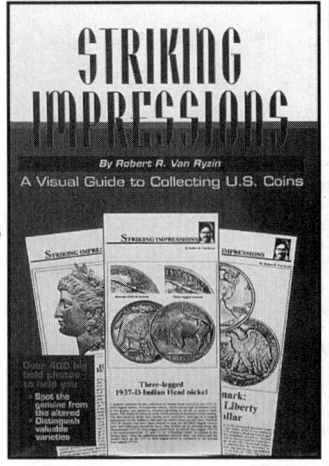